The Complete History of GAELIC GAMES

FULL GAA RECORDS FROM 1887 TO 2017 INCLUSIVE

CONTENTS

Réamhfhocal ón Uachtaráin
Teachtaireacht ón Ard Stiúrthóir
Championship Statistics

HURLING

RÉAMHFHOCAL ÓN UACHTARÁN

Táim brea sásta an teachtaireacht a scríobh ag cur fáilte roimh an eagrán is déanaí seo den foilseacháin iontach seo.

It is a great pleasure to be associated with this most important publication and extremely valued member of the GAA library.

We are, as a people, a nation of story tellers — inspired by the places we come from and the people who make us who we are.

Our history is important to us. Our heroes are important to us and passing on memory and record of deeds and feats is important to us.

Every goal and point that brought our Association from its first final to its most recent is painstakingly and loving collated and chronicled here.

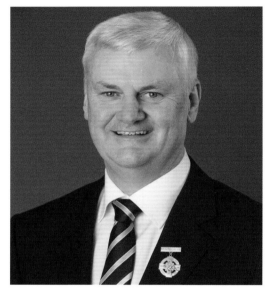

Wherever and whenever GAA people meet, the talk inevitably turns to great games and great players and great moments.

This book facilitates that sort of rich debate — settles arguments too, no doubt, and ultimately helps keep the memory of past glory alive for future generations.

As I travel the country in this role I am repeatedly struck by the store of knowledge that our supporters can summon when discussing Gaelic games. It is never something confined to their own county. Rather, their love of the Games goes beyond borders and boundaries when they talk and discuss and debate.

I want to acknowledge the countless hours that clearly were needed from the hands of many

to enable this publication to exist and extend the thanks of the Association to DBA for their commitment to ensuring that this impeccable record is kept up to date.

I look forward to taking my own trips down memory lane and leafing through this book, checking facts and statistics and reliving great days gone by.

Rath Dé ar an obair.

Aogán Ó Fearghail

Aogán Ó Fearghail

TEACHTAIREACHT ÓN ARD STIÚRTHÓIR

Is pribhléíd agus ónoir mór dom an teachtaireacht seo a scríobh don foilseacháin oll tabhachtach seo.

I know that there are many people who still refer to this guide as 'the Raymond Smith Book' as it was that late, great chronicler of Gaelic games who did such sterling work in the area of GAA records and statistics.

I am delighted that in 2017 we have a thorough, up to date record of the GAA playing archives and I have no doubt that Raymond would approve.

In welcoming its arrival, I also want to pay tribute to the heroic efforts of so many of our volunteers and supporters who, out of their love of our Games, have chosen to keep their own records on GAA events in their particular county – work that has made compilations such as this that much easier.

We are indebted to these individuals who have taken it upon themselves to ensure that facts and figures and records are preserved for posterity. There has never been more analysis of Gaelic games and in turn it has made books such as this ever more valuable.

I also am aware that for Gaelic games correspondents this book is akin to a bible and the pages are well worn from the checking and rechecking of deeds of the past as our heroes of today are measured up against the legends who have gone before them.

Records matter. They offer a map on where we have come from, they help explain why some counties can play with a swagger and an air of confidence that a positive history has bestowed

on them. Equally it can explain why others can seem to carry an invisible burden – weighed down by gaps and famines in their record of success and achievement.

No doubt people will look through these pages and see records that are there to be broken and it is that constant evolution of striving to make progress which has driven our Association and is something no doubt that will continue.

We owe a debt of gratitude to the team in DBA for ensuring that this book continues to exist and thank all who contributed for their efforts.

Bain taitneamh as.

Páraic Ó Dufaigh

Hurling Final Marksmen

70 minute finals

Eddie Keher
(Kilkenny)
2-7 v Galway
1975

Pat Moylan
(Cork)
0-10 v Wexford
1976

Ned Buggy
(Wexford)
1-4 v Cork
1977

Charlie McCarthy
(Cork)
0-7 v Kilkenny
1978

Liam O'Brien
(Kilkenny)
1-7 v Galway
1979

Eamonn Cregan
(Limerick)
2-7 v Galway
1980

Pat Delaney
(Offaly)
0-5 v Galway
1981

Christy Heffernan
(Kilkenny)
2-3 v Cork
1982

Billy Fitzpatrick
(Kilkenny)
0-10 v Cork
1983

John Fenton
(Cork)
0-7 v Offaly
1984

Seánie O'Leary
(Cork)
2-1 v Offaly

PJ Molloy
(Galway)
1-6 v Offaly
1985

John Fenton
(Cork)
1-4 v Galway
1986

Kevin Hennessy
(Cork)
2-1 v Galway

Ger Fennelly
(Kilkenny)
0-7 v Galway
1987

Nicky English
(Tipperary)
0-6 v Galway
1988

Nicky English
(Tipperary)
2-12 v Antrim
1989

Joe Cooney
(Galway)
1-7 v Cork
1990

DJ Carey
(Kilkenny)
0-9 v Tipperary
1991

Michael Cleary
(Tipperary)
1-6 v Kilkenny

DJ Carey
(Kilkenny)
1-4 v Cork
1992

PJ Delaney
(Kilkenny)
1-4 v Galway
1993

Damien Quigley
(Limerick)
2-2 v Offaly
1994

Johnny Dooley
(Offaly)
0-5 v Clare
1995

Tom Dempsey
(Wexford)
1-3 v Limerick
1996

James O'Connor
(Clare)
0-7 v Tipperary
1997

Brian Whelahan
(Offaly)
1-6 v Kilkenny
1998

Henry Shefflin
(Kilkenny)
0-5 v Cork
1999

DJ Carey
(Kilkenny)
2-4 v Offaly
2000

Eugene Cloonan
(Galway)
1-5 v Tipperary
2001

Henry Shefflin
(Kilkenny)
1-7 v Clare
2002

Martin Comerford
(Kilkenny)
1-4 v Cork
2003

Joe Deane
(Cork)
0-5 v Kilkenny
2004

Henry Shefflin
(Kilkenny)
0-5 v Cork

Ben O'Connor
(Cork)
1-7 v Galway
2005

Henry Shefflin
(Kilkenny)
0-8 v Cork
2006

Eddie Brennan
(Kilkenny)
1-5 v Limerick
2007

Eoin Kelly
(Waterford)
1-9 v Kilkenny
2008

Eoin Kelly
(Tipperary)
0-13 v Kilkenny
2009

Richie Power
(Kilkenny)
1-9 v Tipperary
2010

Eoin Kelly
(Tipperary)
0-8 v Kilkenny
2011

Henry Shefflin
(Kilkenny)
0-12 v Galway
2012

Joe Canning
(Galway)
1-9 v Kilkenny

Colin Ryan
(Clare)
0-12 v Cork
2013

Shane O'Donnell
(Clare)
3-3 v Cork*

TJ Reid
(Kilkenny)
1-8 v Tipperary
2014

Séamus Callanan
(Tipperary)
2-5 v Kilkenny*

Joe Canning
(Galway)
1-8 v Kilkenny
2015

Séamus Callanan
(Tipperary)
0-13 v Kilkenny
2016

Pauric Mahony
(Waterford)
0-11 v Galway
2017

*Replay

Football Final Marksmen

Jimmy Keaveney (Dublin) 0-6 v Kerry
1975

Jimmy Keaveney (Dublin) 1-2 v Kerry
1976

Jimmy Keaveney (Dublin) 2-6 v Armagh
1977

Eoin Liston (Kerry) 3-2 v Dublin
1978

Mikey Sheehy (Kerry) 2-6 v Dublin
1979

Mikey Sheehy (Kerry) 1-6 v Roscommon
1980

Mikey Sheehy (Kerry) 0-4 v Offaly
1981

Matt Connor (Offaly) 0-4 v Kerry

Matt Connor (Offaly) 0-7 v Kerry
1982

Barney Rock (Dublin) 1-6 v Galway
1983

Barney Rock (Dublin) 1-5 v Kerry
1984

Joe McNally (Dublin) 2-0 v Kerry
1985

Pat Spillane (Kerry) 1-4 v Tyrone
1986

Brian Stafford (Meath) 0-7 v Cork
1987

Mikey Sheehy (Kerry) 1-4 v Tyrone

Brian Stafford (Meath) 0-8 v Cork
1988

Michael Fitzmaurice (Mayo) 0-7 v Cork
1989

Brian Stafford (Meath) 0-6 v Cork
1990

Bernard Flynn (Meath) 0-6 v Down
1991

Manus Boyle (Donegal) 0-9 v Dublin
1992

Enda Gormley (Derry) 0-6 v Cork
1993

Larry Tompkins (Cork) 0-8 v Meath

Mickey Linden (Down) 0-4 v Dublin
1994

Peter Canavan (Tyrone) 0-11 v Dublin
1995

Trevor Giles (Meath) 1-4 v Mayo
1996

Maurice Fitzgerald (Kerry) 0-9 v Mayo
1997

Pádraic Joyce (Galway) 1-2 v Kildare
1998

Philip Clifford (Cork) 0-5 v Meath
1999

Charlie Redmond (Dublin) 0-4 v Down

Pádraic Joyce (Galway) 0-6 v Kerry
2000

Pádraic Joyce (Galway) 0-10 v Meath
2001

Dara Ó Cinnéide (Kerry) 0-5 v Armagh
2002

Peter Canavan (Tyrone) 0-5 v Armagh
2003

Dara Ó Cinnéide (Kerry) 0-8 v Mayo
2004

Colm Cooper (Kerry) 0-5 v Tyrone
2005

Oisín McConville (Armagh) 1-2 v Kerry

Colm Cooper (Kerry) 1-5 v Mayo

Kevin O'Neill (Mayo) 2-0 v Kerry
2006

Colm Cooper (Kerry) 1-5 v Cork
2007

Colm Cooper (Kerry) 0-6 v Tyrone
2008

Colm Cooper (Kerry) 0-6 v Cork
2009

Daniel Goulding (Cork) 0-9 v Down
2010

Bernard Brogan (Dublin) 0-6 v Kerry
2011

Colm Cooper (Kerry) 1-3 v Dublin

Michael Murphy (Donegal) 1-4 v Mayo
2012

Bernard Brogan (Dublin) 2-3 v Mayo
2013

Paul Geaney (Kerry) 1-2 v Donegal
2014

James O'Donoghue (Kerry) 0-3 v Dublin
2015

Dean Rock (Dublin) 0-9 v Mayo*
2016

Dean Rock (Dublin) 0-7 v Mayo
2017

Colm McFadden (Donegal) 1-4 v Mayo

Kieran Donaghy (Kerry) 1-2 v Donegal

Cillian O'Connor (Mayo) 0-9 v Dublin*

Cillian O'Connor (Mayo) 0-7 v Dublin

*Replay

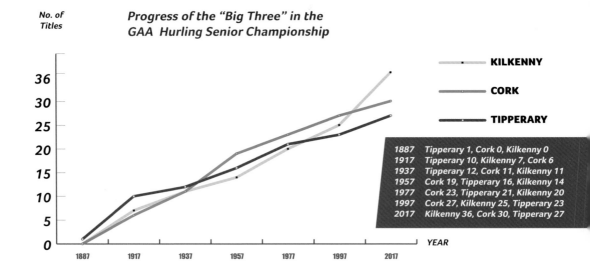

No. of Titles

Progress of the "Big Three" in the GAA Hurling Senior Championship

KILKENNY

CORK

TIPPERARY

1887	Tipperary 1, Cork 0, Kilkenny 0
1917	Tipperary 10, Kilkenny 7, Cork 6
1937	Tipperary 12, Cork 11, Kilkenny 11
1957	Cork 19, Tipperary 16, Kilkenny 14
1977	Cork 23, Tipperary 21, Kilkenny 20
1997	Cork 27, Kilkenny 25, Tipperary 23
2017	Kilkenny 36, Cork 30, Tipperary 27

YEAR

Senior Hurling Championship Final (Success Rate)	% win	Won	Lost
KERRY	100%	1	0
TIPPERARY	68%	27	13
CORK	61%	30	19
KILKENNY	58%	36	26
OFFALY	57%	4	3
CLARE	50%	4	4
LIMERICK	47%	7	8
WEXFORD	35%	6	11
WATERFORD	33%	2	4
LAOIS	33%	1	2
DUBLIN	30%	6	14
LONDON	25%	1	3
GALWAY	17%	5	19
ANTRIM	0%	0	2

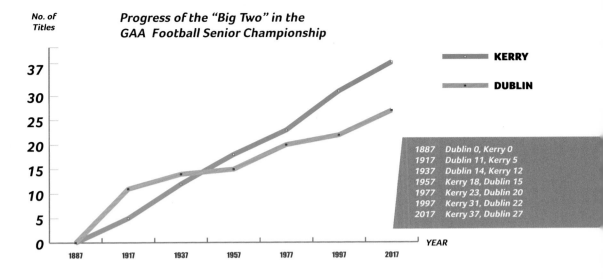

Progress of the "Big Two" in the GAA Football Senior Championship

No. of Titles

KERRY
DUBLIN

Year	Results
1887	Dublin 0, Kerry 0
1917	Dublin 11, Kerry 5
1937	Dublin 14, Kerry 12
1957	Kerry 18, Dublin 15
1977	Kerry 23, Dublin 20
1997	Kerry 31, Dublin 22
2017	Kerry 37, Dublin 27

Senior Football Championship Final (Success Rate)	% win	Won	Lost
LIMERICK	100%	2	0
DOWN	83%	5	1
TIPPERARY	80%	4	1
DUBLIN	68%	27	13
DONEGAL	67%	2	1
KERRY	63%	37	22
WEXFORD	63%	5	3
TYRONE	60%	3	2
LOUTH	50%	3	3
OFFALY	50%	3	3
DERRY	50%	1	1
CAVAN	45%	5	6
KILDARE	44%	4	5
MEATH	44%	7	9
GALWAY	41%	9	13
ROSCOMMON	40%	2	3
CORK	30%	7	16
ARMAGH	25%	1	3
MAYO	19%	3	13
LONDON	0%	0	5
ANTRIM	0%	0	2
LAOIS	0%	0	2
CLARE	0%	0	1
MONAGHAN	0%	0	1
WATERFORD	0%	0	1

Senior Hurling Championship
TOP SCORERS

565

HENRY SHEFFLIN, KILKENNY
(27-484)

441	Eddie Keher, Kilkenny	(35-336)
431	Eoin Kelly, Tipperary	(21-368)
417	Joe Canning, Galway	(25-342)
324	Patrick Horgan, Cork	(12-288)
307	Christy Ring, Cork	(33-208)
297	DJ Carey, Kilkenny	(34-195)
273	Nickey Rackard, Wexford	(59-96)
	Séamus Callanan, Tipperary	(27-192)
259	Joe Deane, Cork	(10-229)

APPEARANCES

73

BRENDAN CUMMINS,
TIPPERARY

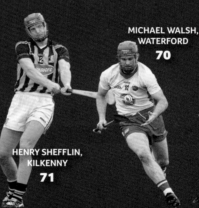

HENRY SHEFFLIN,
KILKENNY
71

MICHAEL WALSH,
WATERFORD
70

JJ DELANEY,
KILKENNY
66

TONY BROWNE,
WATERFORD
65

CHRISTY RING,
CORK
65

EOIN KELLY,
TIPPERARY
63

BEN O'CONNOR,
CORK
62

LAR CORBETT,
TIPPERARY
60

DAVY FITZGERALD,
CLARE
60

Senior Football Championship
TOP SCORERS

310	Cillian O'Connor, Mayo	(20-250)
292	Mikey Sheehy, Kerry	(29-205)
284	John Doyle, Kildare	(8-260)
265	Pádraic Joyce, Galway	(12-229)
259	Bernard Brogan, Dublin	(21-196)
253	Paddy Bradley, Derry	(17-202)
241	Maurice Fitzgerald, Kerry	(12-205)
233	Brian Stafford, Meath	(9-206)
230	Oisín McConville, Armagh	(11-197)

352

**COLM COOPER, KERRY
(23-283)**

APPEARANCES

**MARC Ó SÉ,
KERRY
88**

**TOMÁS Ó SÉ,
KERRY
88**

**SEÁN CAVANAGH,
TYRONE
89**

**STEPHEN CLUXTON,
DUBLIN**

91

**COLM COOPER,
KERRY
85**

**DARRAGH Ó SÉ,
KERRY
81**

**TOM O'SULLIVAN,
KERRY
76**

**CONOR GORMLEY,
TYRONE
75**

**BRIAN DOOHER,
TYRONE
73**

**ANDY MORAN,
MAYO
72**

Kilkenny has the shortest reign as All-Ireland champions. On 30 June 1907 they beat Cork 7-7 to 2-9 in the 1905 final – two weeks later they were defeated by Dublin in the 1906 Leinster hurling final.

July 1907

0-00
0-00

The only scoreless draw in GAA history occurred in the 1895 Munster football championship between Cork and Kerry in Limerick. With five minutes to go the teams were scoreless when the ball burst and a replacement could not be found. The referee declared the match a draw.

When Kilkenny met Wexford in the 1890 Leinster football championship, in Waterford, the referee, Dan Fraher, discovered that he had no football. Nor had anyone else in the grounds. Someone was dispatched to the town to purchase one. It was seven o'clock before the match finished – by then many of the Wexford supporters had missed the steamer back to New Ross.

When Wexford played in the 1914 All-Ireland football final, their trainer was Jem Roche, who had fought Tommy Burns for the world heavyweight boxing title in Dublin seven years earlier. The fight was one of the shortest on record, lasting just 88 seconds.

In 1924 Naas drew with Caragh in a seven-a-side match organised in connection with a local carnival. The medals sat in the carnival secretary's drawer until he noticed that the match had not been replayed. The replay took place in 1959, 35 years after the original game, between teams made up of the sons of those who had played in the original match.

Winner 1924

The most one-sided senior competitive match on record was between Wexford and Kildare in the Croke Cup hurling competition in 1897. Wexford won by 14-15 to 1-1. The most one-sided championship match was Offaly's win over Louth by 10-23 to nil in the 1910 Leinster hurling championship.

In the history of the GAA, five All-Ireland finals have not taken place: the 1888 football and hurling finals, the 1910 football final, the 1911 hurling final and the 1925 football final.

Virtual Winner

After the 1895 All-Ireland football final, in which Tipperary beat Meath by four points to three, the referee noticed that he had made an error in the score and that the match should have been a draw. Sportingly, Meath did not contest the result and Tipperary remained champions. In recognition of this Meath were awarded 'Virtual All-Ireland' medals for 1895.

At the first All-Ireland hurling final, held at Birr in 1888, tree branches were used as goalposts. The Tipperary team turned up so late that the Galway team had begun to eat a meal at a nearby hotel – only for the fact that so many had travelled by train to watch the game, it would have been cancelled.

Meath were once Leinster football champions for 20 minutes. At 1.45pm on 22 October 1911 they were awarded the title because their opponents Kilkenny had failed to show. At 2.15pm Kilkenny turned up, the title was taken from Meath and the match was played. Kilkenny won 2-4 to 1-1.

HURLING

ROLL OF HONOUR

SENIOR

Kilkenny *(36)* 1904, 1905, 1907, 1909, 1911, 1912, 1913, 1922, 1932, 1933, 1935, 1939, 1947, 1957, 1963, 1967, 1969, 1972, 1974, 1975, 1979, 1982, 1983, 1992, 1993, 2000, 2002, 2003, 2006, 2007, 2008, 2009, 2011, 2012, 2014, 2015.

Cork *(30)* 1890, 1892, 1893, 1894, 1902, 1903, 1919, 1926, 1928, 1929, 1931, 1941, 1942, 1943, 1944, 1946, 1952, 1953, 1954, 1966, 1970, 1976, 1977, 1978, 1984, 1986, 1990, 1999, 2004, 2005.

Tipperary *(27)* 1887, 1895, 1896, 1898, 1899, 1900, 1906, 1908, 1916, 1925, 1930, 1937, 1945, 1949, 1950, 1951, 1958, 1961, 1962, 1964, 1965, 1971, 1989, 1991, 2001, 2010, 2016.

Limerick *(7)* 1897, 1918, 1921, 1934, 1936, 1940, 1973.

Dublin *(6)* 1889, 1917, 1920, 1924, 1927, 1938.

Wexford *(6)* 1910, 1955, 1956, 1960, 1968, 1996.

Galway *(5)* 1923, 1980, 1987, 1988, 2017.

Offaly *(4)* 1981, 1985, 1994, 1998.

Clare *(4)* 1914, 1995, 1997, 2013.

Waterford *(2)* 1948, 1959.

Kerry *(1)* 1891.

London *(1)* 1901.

Laois *(1)* 1915.

MINOR

Kilkenny *(21)* 1931, 1935, 1936, 1950, 1960, 1961, 1962, 1972, 1973, 1975, 1977, 1981, 1988, 1990, 1991, 1993, 2002, 2003, 2008, 2010, 2014.

Tipperary *(20)* 1930, 1932, 1933, 1934, 1947, 1949, 1952, 1953, 1955, 1956, 1957, 1959, 1976, 1980, 1982, 1996, 2006, 2007, 2012, 2016.

Cork *(18)* 1928, 1937, 1938, 1939, 1941, 1951, 1964, 1967, 1969, 1970, 1971, 1974, 1978, 1979, 1985, 1995, 1998, 2001.

Galway *(11)* 1983, 1992, 1994, 1999, 2000, 2004, 2005, 2009, 2011, 2015, 2017.

Dublin *(4)* 1945, 1946, 1954, 1965.

Wexford *(3)* 1963, 1966, 1968.

Limerick *(3)* 1940, 1958, 1984.

Offaly *(3)* 1986, 1987, 1989.

Waterford *(3)* 1929, 1948, 2013.

Clare *(1)* 1997.

U21

Cork   *(11)*   1966, 1968, 1969, 1970, 1971, 1973, 1976, 1982, 1988, 1997, 1998.

Kilkenny   *(11)*   1974, 1975, 1977, 1984, 1990, 1994, 1999, 2003, 2004, 2006, 2008.

Galway   *(10)*   1972, 1978, 1983, 1986, 1991, 1993, 1996, 2005, 2007, 2011.

Tipperary   *(9)*   1964, 1967, 1979, 1980, 1981, 1985, 1989, 1995, 2010.

Limerick   *(6)*   1987, 2000, 2001, 2002, 2015, 2017.

Clare   *(4)*   2009, 2012, 2013, 2014.

Waterford   *(2)*   1992, 2016.

Wexford   *(1)*   1965.

JUNIOR

Cork   *(11)*   1912, 1916, 1925, 1940, 1947, 1950, 1955, 1958, 1983, 1987, 1994.

Tipperary   *(9)*   1913, 1915, 1924, 1926, 1930, 1933, 1953, 1989, 1991.

Kilkenny   *(9)*   1928, 1946, 1951, 1956, 1984, 1986, 1988, 1990, 1995.

Meath   *(6)*   1927, 1948, 1970, 1998, 1999, 2004.

London   *(5)*   1938, 1949, 1959, 1960, 1963.

Limerick   *(4)*   1935, 1941, 1954, 1957.

Dublin   *(3)*   1932, 1937, 1952.

Warwickshire   *(3)*   1968, 1969, 1973.

Armagh   *(3)*   1978, 1979, 2000.

Roscommon   *(3)*   1965, 1974, 2001.

Mayo   *(3)*   1980, 1981, 2003.

Offaly   *(2)*   1923, 1929.

Waterford   *(2)*   1931, 1934.

Kildare   *(2)*   1962, 1966.

Wicklow   *(2)*   1967, 1971.

Kerry   *(2)*   1961, 1972.

Louth   *(2)*   1976, 1977.

Derry   *(2)*   1975, 1982.

Wexford   *(2)*   1985, 1992.

Clare   *(2)*   1914, 1993.

Galway   *(2)*   1939, 1996.

Westmeath   *(1)*   1936.

Down   *(1)*   1964.

Monaghan   *(1)*   1997.

Antrim   *(1)*   2002.

INTERMEDIATE

Cork	**(8)**	1965, 1997, 2001, 2003, 2004, 2006, 2009, 2014.
Tipperary	**(7)**	1963, 1966, 1971, 1972, 2000, 2012, 2013.
Kilkenny	**(5)**	1973, 2008, 2010, 2016, 2017.
Wexford	**(4)**	1961, 1964, 2005, 2007.
Galway	**(3)**	1999, 2002, 2015.
London	**(2)**	1967, 1968.
Carlow	**(1)**	1962.
Kildare	**(1)**	1969.
Antrim	**(1)**	1970.
Limerick	**(1)**	1998.
Clare	**(1)**	2011.

SENIOR 'B'

London (5)	1985, 1987, 1988, 1990, 1995.
Antrim (3)	1978, 1981, 1982.
Kerry (3)	1976, 1983, 1986.
Kildare (3)	1974, 1980, 1989.
Westmeath (3)	1975, 1984, 1991.
Laois (2)	1977, 1979.
Carlow (1)	1992.
Meath (1)	1993.
Roscommon (1)	1994.
Derry (1)	1996.
Wicklow (1)	2003.

SENIOR CHAMPIONSHIP RESULTS 1887-2017

1887
01/08/1888, Final, Birr
Tipperary (Thurles)   1-1   nil   Galway (Meelick)
Open draw. Counties represented by county champions. Actual score Tipperary, 1 goal, 1 point and 1 forfeit point.

1888
Championship unfinished owing to U.S.A. invasion by GAA athletes.

1889
03/11/1889, Final, Inchicore
Dublin (Kickhams)   5-1   1-6   Clare (Tulla)

1890
16/11/1890, Final, Clonturk Park
Cork (Aghabullogue)   N/A   N/A   Wexford (Castlebridge)
Final unfinished. Cork (Aghabullogue) awarded title. When play terminated (following Cork's withdrawal on the grounds of alleged excessively rough play by the opposition), Wexford (Castlebridge) were leading by 2-2 to 1-6 (a goal at this time exceeded any number of points).

1891
28/02/1892, Final, Clonturk Park
Kerry (Ballyduff)   2-3   1-5   Wexford (Crossabeg)
(After 30 minutes extra-time. Scores at end of normal time Kerry 1-1; Wexford 1-1.)

1892
26/03/1893, Final, Clonturk Park
Cork   N/A   N/A   Dublin
Final unfinished. When play terminated Cork were leading Dublin by 2-4 to 1-1. Cork awarded title as Dublin left the pitch with ten minutes remaining. County champions permitted to select players from other clubs within county.

1893
24/06/1894, Final, Phoenix Park
Cork (Blackrock)   6-8   0-2   Kilkenny (Confederation)

1894
24/03/1895, Final, Clonturk Park
Cork (Blackrock)   5-20   2-0   Dublin (Rapparees)

1895
15/03/1896, Final, Jones's Road
Tipperary (Tubberadora) 6-8   0-10   Kilkenny (Tullaroan)

1896
27/03/1898, Final, Jones's Road
Tipperary (Tubberadora) 8-14   0-4   Dublin (Commercials)
Goal made equal to three points from 1896

1897

30/10/1898, Semi-Final, Jones's Road
Kilkenny 3-4   0-4   Galway
20/11/1898, Final, Tipperary
Limerick (Kilfinane)   3-4   2-4   Kilkenny (Tullaroan)

1898

17/12/1899, Semi-Final, Athenry
Tipperary 3-14   1-3   Galway
25/03/1900, Final, Jones's Road
Tipperary (Tubberadora)   7-13   3-10 Kilkenny (Three Castles)

1899

No Semi-Final
24/03/1901, Final, Jones's Road
Tipperary (Moycarkey) 3-12   1-4   Wexford (Blackwater)
Unfinished. Tipperary awarded title.

1900

29/06/1902, Semi-Final, Carrick-on-Suir
Tipperary 1-11   1-8   Kilkenny
20/07/1902, Semi-Final, Terenure
Galway 3-17   0-1   Antrim
(Note: This was actually the half-time score. The game was so one-sided that reporters present did not bother to record the exact final score given later in some records as 3-44 to 0-1, as Antrim failed to raise a flag in the second half.)
21/09/1902, Home Final, Terenure
Tipperary 6-13   1-5 Galway
26/10/1902, Final, Jones's Road
Tipperary (Two-Mile-Borris) 2-5   0-6   London (Desmonds)

1901

12/04/1903, Semi-Final, Jones's Road
Wexford 4-9   1-2   Antrim
17/05/1903, Semi-Final, Limerick
Cork 7- 12   1 -3   Galway
14/06/1903, Home Final, Carrick-on-Suir
Cork 2-8   0-6   Wexford
02/08/1903, Final, Jones's Road
London (Selection)   1-5   0-4   Cork (Redmonds)

1902

20/03/1904, Semi-Final, Tipperary
Cork 10-13   0-0   Galway
05/06/1904, Semi-Final, Drogheda
Dublin 6-19   0-6   Derry
03/07/1904, Home Final, Tipperary
Cork 1-7   1-7   Dublin
17/07/1904, Home Final, Tipperary, Replay
Cork 2-6   0-1   Dublin
11/09/1904, Final, Cork
Cork (Dungourney) 3-13   0-0   London (Brian Boru)

1903

07/05/1905, Semi-Final, Limerick
Cork w.o. from Galway
18/06/1905, Semi-Final, Jones's Road
Kilkenny 6-29   3-2   Antrim
16/07/1905, Home Final, Dungarvan

Cork (Blackrock)   8-9   0-8   Kilkenny (Threecastles)
12/11/1905, Final, Jones's Road
Cork 3-16   1-1   London (Hibernians)

1904

06/05/1906, Semi-Final, Jones's Road
Cork 4-18   2-3   Antrim
13/05/1906, Semi-Final, Athlone
Kilkenny 2-8   1-7   Galway
24/06/1906, Final, Carrick-on-Suir
Kilkenny (Tullaroan)   1-9   1-8   Cork (St. Finbarr's)

1905

05/08/1906, Quarter-Final, Jones's Road
Kilkenny 2-21   0-5   Lancashire
05/08/1906, Quarter-Final, Belfast
Antrim 3-13   3-11   Glasgow
02/09/1906, Semi-Final, Limerick
Cork 5-13   0-4   Galway
30/09/1906, Semi-Final, Jones's Road
Dublin 5-8   1-9   Antrim
(Kilkenny qualified for All-Ireland final by beating Dublin in the Leinster final on October 21).
14/04/1907, Final, Tipperary
Cork 5-10   3-13   Kilkenny
(Objection and counter-objection. Replay ordered).
30/06/1907, Final, Dungarvan, Replay
Kilkenny (Erin's Own) 7-7   2-9   Cork (St. Finbarr's)

1906

19/05/1907, Quarter-Final, Belfast
Kilkenny 7-21   1-3   Antrim
04/08/1907, Semi-Final, Wexford
Dublin 4-10   2-2   London
(Note: Two different versions of Dublin's score appear in old newspaper files).
08/09/1907, Semi-Final , Limerick
Tipperary 7-14   0-2   Galway
27/10/1907, Final, Kilkenny
Tipperary (Thurles) 3-16   3-8   Dublin (Faughs)

1907

15/03/1908, Semi-Final, Dundalk
Dublin 5-10   2-5   Antrim
10/05/1908, Semi-Final, Limerick
Cork 2-8   1-7   Galway
(Unfinished. Cork awarded game). (Kilkenny qualified for the All-Ireland final by beating Dublin in the Leinster final on May 24, 1908.)
21/06/1908, Final, Dungarvan
Kilkenny (Mooncoin) 3-12   4-8   Cork (Dungourney)

1908

14/02/1909, Semi-Final, Limerick
Tipperary 5-15   1-0   Galway
21/02/1909, Semi-Final, Jones's Road
Dublin 4-12   0-3   Cavan
25/04/1909, Final, Jones's Road
Tipperary 2-5   1-8   Dublin
27/06/1909, Final, Athy, Replay
Tipperary (Thurles) 3-15   1-5   Dublin (Kickhams)

1909

17/10/1909, Semi-Final, Limerick
Tipperary 6-7   5-7   Galway
14/11/1909, Semi-Final, Jones's Road
Kilkenny 3-17   0-3   Derry
12/12/1909, Final, Cork
Kilkenny (Mooncoin) 4-6   0-12   Tipperary (Thurles)

1910

31/07/1910, Quarter-Final, Belfast
Glasgow 1-13   0-7   Antrim
04/09/1910, Quarter-Final, Waterford
Kilkenny 5-11   0-3   London
(Note: Kilkenny, as reigning All-Ireland champions, nominated to represent Leinster in Quarter-Final.)
21/08/1910, Semi-Final, Tuam
Cork 7-3   1-0   Galway
02/10/1910, Semi-Final, Jones's Road
Dublin 6-6   5-1   Glasgow
(Note: Cork nominated to represent Munster in All-Ireland Semi-Final but then beaten in Munster final by Limerick, who contested All-Ireland final.)
(Wexford qualified for the All-Ireland final by beating Dublin in the Leinster final on October 23. Dublin had defeated Kilkenny in the Leinster Semi-final)
20/11/1910, Final, Jones's Road
Wexford (Castlebridge) 7-0   6-2   Limerick (Castleconnell)

1911

26/11/1911, Semi-Final, Jones's Road
Kilkenny 5-5   1-1   Antrim
03/12/1911, Semi-Final, Portlaoise
Limerick 8-1   2-0   Galway
(Limerick, Munster champions, refused to replay the final match which was postponed on February 18, 1912 in Cork owing to state of pitch. The final fixture was made for May 12, 1912.)
28/7/1912, Final, Dungarvan
Kilkenny 3-3   2-1   Tipperary
(Substitute contest, Tipperary nominated by Munster Council)

1912

25/08/1912, Semi-Final, Jones's Road
Limerick 11-3   2-0   Antrim
29/09/1912, Semi-Final, Jones's Road
Kilkenny 8-3   2-2   Galway
(Cork defeated Limerick in Munster championship on September 1 and Tipperary in Munster final on October 27 to qualify for All-Ireland final.)
17/11/1912, Final, Jones's Road
Kilkenny (Tullaroan) 2-1   1-3   Cork (Blackrock)

1913

21/06/1913, Quarter-Final, Glasgow
Kilkenny 10-6   5-2   Glasgow
04/08/1913, Semi-Final, Liverpool
Kilkenny 4-4   1-4   Lancashire
19/10/1913, Semi-Final, Jones's Road
Tipperary 10-0   0-1   Roscommon
02/11/1913, Final, Croke Park
Kilkenny (Mooncoin) 2-4   1-2   Tipperary (Toomevara)
(15-aside). (Note: Ulster did not compete, their champions entered the Junior Championship).

1914

06/09/1914, Semi-Final, Portlaoise
Cork 6-6   0-0   Galway
18/10/1914, Final, Croke Park
Clare (Quin) 5-1   1-0   Laois (Kilcotton)
(Note: Cork nominated to represent Munster in All-Ireland Semi-Final but they subsequently lost the Munster final to Clare.)

1915

08/08/1915, Semi-Final, Gort
Clare 2-1   1-1   Galway
24/10/1915, Final, Croke Park
Laois (Ballygeehan) 6-2   4-1   Cork (Redmonds)
(Note: Clare nominated to represent Munster in All-Ireland Semi-Final but subsequently lost to Cork in the Munster final.)

1916

22/10/1916, Semi-Final, Athlone
Tipperary 8-1   0-0   Galway
(Unfinished. Galway did not resume for second-half.)
21/01/1917, Final, Croke Park
Tipperary (Boherlahan) 5-4   3-2   Kilkenny (Tullaroan)

1917

No Semi-Final
28/10/1917, Final, Croke Park
Dublin (Collegians) 5-4   4-2   Tipperary (Boherlahan)

1918

26/01/1919, Final, Croke Park
Limerick (Newcastle West) 9-5   1-3   Wexford (Selection)

1919

31/08/1919, Semi-Final, Limerick
Cork 3-8   0-2   Galway
21/09/2019, Final, Croke Park
Cork (Selection) 6-4   2-4   Dublin (Collegians)

1920

24/10/1920, Semi-Final, Croke Park
Dublin 6-3   1-4   Galway
14/05/1922, Final, Croke Park
Dublin (Faughs) 4-9   4-3   Cork (Selection)

1921

25/06/1922, Semi-Final, Limerick
Limerick 6-0   2-2   Galway
04/03/1923, Final, Croke Park
Limerick 8-5   3-2   Dublin

1922

26/08/1923, Semi-Final, Galway
Tipperary 3-2   1-3   Galway
09/09/1923, Final, Croke Park
Kilkenny 4-2   2-6   Tipperary

1923
27/04/1924, Semi-Final, Croke Park
Limerick 7-4   0-1   Donegal
18/05/1924, Semi-Final, Croke Park
Galway 5-4   2-0   Kilkenny
14/09/1924, Final, Croke Park
Galway 7-3   4-5   Limerick

1924
09/11/1924, Semi-Final, Croke Park
Dublin 8-4   3-1   Antrim
23/11/1924, Semi-Final, Croke Park
Galway 3-1   2-3   Tipperary
14/12/1924, Final, Croke Park
Dublin 5-3   2-6   Galway

1925
26/07/1925, Semi-Final, Croke Park
Tipperary 12-9   2-3   Antrim
09/08/1925, Semi-Final, Croke Park
Galway 9-4   6-0   Kilkenny
06/09/1925, Final, Croke Park
Tipperary 5-6   1-5   Galway

1926
29/08/1926, Semi-Final, Croke Park
Kilkenny 6-2   5-1   Galway
24/10/1926, Final, Croke Park
Cork 4-6   2-0   Kilkenny

1927
21/08/1927, Semi-Final, Thurles
Cork 5-6   0-2   Galway
04/09/1927, Final, Croke Park
Dublin 4-8   1-3   Cork

1928
26/08/1928, Semi-Final, Kilkenny
Cork 5-3   0-2   Dublin
09/09/1928, Final, Croke Park
Cork 6-12   1-0   Galway

1929
11/08/1929, Semi-Final, Birr
Galway 7-7   7-1   Kilkenny
01/09/1929, Final, Croke Park
Cork 4-9   1-3   Galway

1930
17/08/1930, Semi-Final, Birr
Tipperary 6-8   2-4   Galway
07/09/1930, Final, Croke Park
Tipperary 2-7   1-3   Dublin

1931
16/08/1931, Semi-Final, Croke Park
Kilkenny 7-2   3-1   Galway
06/09/1931, Final, Croke Park
Cork 1-6   1-6   Kilkenny
11/10/1931, Replay, Croke Park
Cork 2-5   2-5   Kilkenny
01/11/1931, 2nd Replay, Croke Park
Cork 5-8   3-4   Kilkenny

1932
14/08/1932, Semi-Final, Limerick
Clare 9-4   4-14   Galway
04/09/1932, Final, Croke Park
Kilkenny 3-3   2-3   Clare

1933
13/08/1933, Semi-Final, Birr
Kilkenny 5-10   3-8   Galway
03/09/1933, Final, Croke Park
Kilkenny 1-7   0-6   Limerick

1934
05/08/1934, Semi-Final, Roscrea
Limerick 4-4   2-4   Galway
02/09/1934, Final, Croke Park
Limerick 2-7   3-4   Dublin
30/09/1934, Final Croke Park, Replay
Limerick 5-2   2-6   Dublin

1935
04/08/1935, Semi-Final, Birr
Kilkenny 6-10   1-8   Galway
01/09/1935, Final, Croke Park
Kilkenny 2-5   2-4   Limerick

1936
16/08/1936, Semi-Final, Roscrea
Limerick 4-9   2-4   Galway
(Match unfinished. Limerick awarded game.)
06/09/1936, Final, Croke Park
Limerick 5-6   1-5   Kilkenny

1937
08/08/1937, Semi-Final, Birr
Kilkenny 0-8   0-6   Galway
05/09/1937, Final, Killarney
Tipperary 3-11   0-3   Kilkenny

1938
07/08/1938, Semi-Final, Ennis
Waterford 4-8   3-1   Galway
04/09/1938, Final, Croke Park
Dublin 2-5   1-6   Waterford

1939
06/08/1939, Semi-Final, Roscrea
Kilkenny 1-16   3-1   Galway
03/09/1939, Final, Croke Park
Kilkenny 2-7   3-3   Cork

1940
11/08/1940, Semi-Final, Ennis
Limerick 3-6   0-5   Galway
01/09/1940, Final, Croke Park
Limerick 3-7   1-7   Kilkenny

1941
14/09/1941, Semi-Final, Roscrea
Dublin   2-4   2-2   Galway
28/09/1941, Final, Croke Park
Cork (nominated) 5-11 0-6   Dublin

1942
26/07/1942, Semi-Final, Limerick
Cork   6-8   2-4   Galway
06/09/1942, Final, Croke Park
Cork   2-14   3-4   Dublin

1943
04/07/1943, Quarter-Final, Corrigan Park, Belfast
Antrim   7-0   6-2   Galway
01/08/1943, Semi-Final, Corrigan Park, Belfast
Antrim   3-3   1-6   Kilkenny
05/09/1943, Final, Croke Park
Cork   5-16   0-4   Antrim

1944
13/08/1944, Semi-Final, Ennis
Cork   1-10   3-3   Galway
13/08/1944, Semi-Final, Corrigan Park, Belfast
Dublin   6-12   3-1   Antrim
03/09/1944, Final, Croke Park
Cork   2-13   1-2   Dublin

1945
29/07/1945, Semi-Final, Birr
Kilkenny 5-3   2-11   Galway
05/08/1945, Semi-Final, Croke Park
Tipperary 5-9   1-6   Antrim
02/09/1945, Final, Croke Park
Tipperary 5-6   3-6   Kilkenny

1946
28/07/1946, Semi-Final, Birr
Cork   2-10   0-3   Galway
04/08/1946, Semi-Final, Croke Park
Kilkenny 7-11   0-7   Antrim
01/09/1946, Final, Croke Park
Cork   7-5   3-8   Kilkenny

1947
27/07/1947, Semi-Final, Birr
Kilkenny 2-9   1-11   Galway
03/08/1947, Semi-Final, Croke Park
Cork   7-10   0-5   Antrim
07/09/1947, Final, Croke Park
Kilkenny 0-14   2-7   Cork

1948
01/08/1948, Semi-Final, Croke Park
Dublin   8-13   2-6   Antrim
15/08/1948, Semi-Final, Croke Park
Waterford 3-7   1-6   Galway
05/09/1948, Final, Croke Park
Waterford 6-7   4-2   Dublin

1949
31/07/1949, Semi-Final, Croke Park
Tipperary 6-18   1-4   Antrim
07/08/1949, Semi-Final, Croke Park
Laois   4-6   3-5   Galway
04/09/1949, Final, Croke Park
Tipperary 3-11   0-3   Laois

1950
13/08/1950, Semi-Final, Tuam
Tipperary 4-7   2-6   Galway
03/09/1950, Final, Croke Park
Tipperary 1-9   1-8   Kilkenny

1951
29/07/1951, Semi-Final, Croke Park
Wexford   3-11   2-9   Galway
02/09/1951, Final, Croke Park
Tipperary 7-7   3-9   Wexford

1952
27/07/1952, Semi-Final, Limerick
Cork   1-5   0-6   Galway
07/09/1952, Final, Croke Park
Cork   2-14   0-7   Dublin

1953
16/08/1953, Semi-Final, Croke Park
Galway   3-5   1-10   Kilkenny
06/09/1953, Final, Croke Park
Cork   3-3   0-8   Galway

1954
08/08/1954, Semi-Final, Croke Park
Wexford   12-17   2-3   Antrim
08/08/1954, Semi-Final, Croke Park
Cork   4-13   2-1   Galway
05/09/1954, Final, Croke Park
Cork   1-9   1-6   Wexford

1955
07/08/1955, Semi-Final, Croke Park
Wexford   2-12   2-3   Limerick
04/09/1955, Final, Croke Park
Wexford   3-13   2-8   Galway

1956
29/07/1956, Semi-Final, Croke Park
Wexford   5-13   1-8   Galway
23/09/1956, Final, Croke Park
Wexford   2-14   2-8   Cork

1957
28/07/1957, Semi-Final, Croke Park
Waterford 4-12   0-11   Galway
01/09/1957, Final, Croke Park
Kilkenny 4-10   3-12   Waterford

1958
10/08/1958, Semi-Final, Croke Park
Tipperary 1-13   1-8   Kilkenny
07/09/1958, Final, Croke Park
Tipperary 4-9   2-5   Galway
(Note: After the 1958 Final Galway made their debut in the Munster championship where they remained until 1969. Accordingly, the Semi-Final sequence was suspended until 1969 when London returned to the championship.)

1959
06/09/1959, Final, Croke Park
Waterford 1-17   5-5   Kilkenny
04/10/1959, Replay, Croke Park
Waterford 3-12   1-10   Kilkenny

1960
04/09/1960, Final, Croke Park
Wexford   2-15   0-11   Tipperary

1961
03/09/1961, Final, Croke Park
Tipperary 0-16   1-12   Dublin

1962
02/09/1962, Final, Croke Park
Tipperary 3- 10   2-11   Wexford

1963
01/09/1963, Final, Croke Park
Kilkenny   4-17   6-8   Waterford

1964
06/09/1964, Final, Croke Park
Tipperary 5-13   2-8   Kilkenny

1965
05/09/1965, Final, Croke Park
Tipperary 2-16   0-10   Wexford

1966
04/09/1966, Final, Croke Park
Cork   3-9   1-10   Kilkenny

1967
03/09/1967, Final   Croke Park
Kilkenny   3-8   2-7   Tipperary

1968
01/09/1968, Final, Croke Park
Wexford   5-8   3-12   Tipperary

1969
17/08/1969, Semi-Final, Croke Park
Kilkenny   3-22   1-10   London
07/09/1969, Final Croke Park
Kilkenny   2-15   2-9   Cork

1970
16/08/1970, Semi-Final, Croke Park
Cork   4-20   2-9   London
16/08/1970, Semi-Final, Athlone
Wexford   3-17   5-9   Galway
06/09/1970, Final, Croke Park
Cork   6-21   5-10   Wexford
(Note: First 80-minute Final)

1971
25/07/1971, Quarter-Final, Castlebar
Galway   7-24   1-8   Antrim
15/08/1971, Semi-Final, Croke Park
Kilkenny   2-23   2-8   London
15/08/1971, Semi-Final, Birr
Tipperary 3-26   6-8   Galway
05/09/1971, Final, Croke Park
Tipperary 5-17   5-14   Kilkenny

1972
23/07/1972, Quarter-Final, Ballycastle
Galway   7-16   4-7   Antrim
06/08/1972, Semi-Final, Croke Park
Kilkenny   5-28   3-7   Galway
06/08/1972, Semi-Final, Cork
Cork   7-20   1-12   London
03/09/1972, Final, Croke Park
Kilkenny   3-24   5-11   Cork

1973
29/07/1973, Quarter-Final, Ballinasloe
London   4-7   3-5   Galway
05/08/1973, Semi-Final, Ennis
Limerick   1-15   0-7   London
02/09/1973, Final, Croke Park
Limerick   1-21   1-14   Kilkenny

1974
07/07/1974, Preliminary Round, Athlone
Galway   3-19   4-10   Kildare
21/07/1974 Quarter-Final, Athlone
Galway   3-13   0-6   London
04/08/1974, Semi-Final, Birr
Kilkenny   2-32   3-17   Galway
01/09/1974, Final, Croke Park
Kilkenny   3-19   1-13   Limerick
(Note: The All-Ireland 'B' Champions were allowed into the All-Ireland series in 1974.)

1975
06/07/1975, Quarter-Final, Athlone
Galway   6-14   1-8   Westmeath
17/08/1975, Semi-Final, Croke Park
Galway   4-15   2-19   Cork
07/09/1975, Final, Croke Park
Kilkenny   2-22   2-10   Galway
(Note: The 70-minute Final was introduced in 1975)

1976
18/07/1976, Quarter-Final, Limerick
Galway   3-12   3-9   Kerry
15/08/1976, Semi-Final, Páirc Uí Chaoimh
Wexford   5-14   2-23   Galway
22/08/1976, Semi-Final, Páirc Uí Chaoimh, Replay
Wexford   3-14   2-14   Galway
05/09/1976, Final, Croke Park
Cork   2-21   4-11   Wexford

1977
17/07/1977, Quarter-Final, Birr
Galway   *2-12*   *0-8*   **Laois**
07/08/1977, Semi-Final, Croke Park
Cork   *3-14*   *1-15*   **Galway**
04/09/1977, Final, Croke Park
Cork   *1-17*   *3-8*   **Wexford**

1978
23/07/1978, Quarter-Final, Croke Park
Galway   *4-19*   *3-10*   **Antrim**
06/08/1978, Semi-Final, Croke Park
Kilkenny   *4-20*   *4-13*   **Galway**
03/09/1978, Final, Croke Park
Cork   *1-15*   *2-8*   **Kilkenny**

1979
01/07/1979, Quarter-Final, Birr
Galway   *1-23*   *3-10*   **Laois**
05/08/1979, Semi-Final, Croke Park
Galway   *2-14*   *1-13*   **Cork**
02/09/1979, Final, Croke Park
Kilkenny   *2-12*   *1-8*   **Galway**

1980
20/07/1980, Quarter-Final, Croke Park
Galway   *5-15*   *1-11*   **Kildare**
03/08/1980, Semi-Final, Croke Park
Galway   *4-9*   *3-10*   **Offaly**
07/09/1980, Final, Croke Park
Galway   *2-15*   *3-9*   **Limerick**

1981
19/07/1981, Quarter-Final, Croke Park
Galway   *6-23*   *3-11*   **Antrim**
02/08/1981, Semi-Final, Croke Park
Galway   *1-8*   *0-11*   **Limerick**
16/08/1981, Semi-Final, Croke Park, Replay
Galway   *4-16*   *2-17*   **Limerick**
06/09/1981, Final, Croke Park
Offaly   *2-12*   *0-15*   **Galway**

1982
18/07/1982, Quarter-Final, Croke Park
Galway   *6-19*   *3-12*   **Antrim**
08/08/1982, Semi-Final, Croke Park
Kilkenny   *2-20*   *2-10*   **Galway**
05/09/1982, Final, Croke Park
Kilkenny   *3-18*   *1-13*   **Cork**

1983
10/07/1983, Preliminary Round, O'Toole Park
Antrim   *3-13*   *2-10*   **Kerry**
24/07/1983, Quarter-Final, Mullingar
Galway   *3-22*   *2-5*   **Antrim**
07/08/1983, Semi-Final, Croke Park
Cork   *5-14*   *1-16*   **Galway**
04/09/1983, Final, Croke Park
Kilkenny   *2-14*   *2-12*   **Cork**

1984
22/07/1984, Quarter-Final, Birr
Galway   *2-17*   *2-8*   **Westmeath**
05/08/1984, Semi-Final, Thurles
Offaly   *4-15*   *1-10*   **Galway**
05/08/1984, Semi-Final, Croke Park
Cork   *3-26*   *2-5*   **Antrim**
02/09/1984, Final, Thurles
Cork   *3-16*   *1-12*   **Offaly**

1985
21/07/1985, Quarter-Final, Casement Park
Antrim   *3-12*   *1-15*   **London**
04/08/1985, Semi-Final, Croke Park
Galway   *4-12*   *5-5*   **Cork**
04/08/1985, Semi-Final, Armagh
Offaly   *3-17*   *0-12*   **Antrim**
01/09/1985, Final, Croke Park
Offaly   *2-11*   *1-12*   **Galway**

1986
19/07/1986, Quarter-Final, Ennis
Galway   *4-24*   *1-3*   **Kerry**
10/08/1986, Semi-Final, Thurles
Galway   *4-12*   *0-13*   **Kilkenny**
10/08/1986, Semi-Final, Croke Park
Cork   *7-11*   *1-24*   **Antrim**
07/09/1986, Final, Croke Park
Cork   *4-13*   *2-15*   **Galway**

1987
19/07/1987, Quarter-Final, Casement Park
Antrim   *3-14*   *1-15*   **London**
09/08/1987, Semi-Final, Croke Park
Galway   *3-20*   *2-17*   **Tipperary**
16/08/1987, Semi-Final, Dundalk
Kilkenny   *2-18*   *2-11*   **Antrim**
06/09/1987, Final, Croke Park
Galway   *1-12*   *0-9*   **Kilkenny**

1988
16/07/1988, Quarter-Final, Athenry
Galway   *4-30*   *2-8*   **London**
07/08/1988, Semi-Final, Croke Park
Tipperary   *3-15*   *2-10*   **Antrim**
07/08/1988, Semi-Final, Croke Park
Galway   *3-18*   *3-11*   **Offaly**
04/09/1988, Final, Croke Park
Galway   *1-15*   *0-14*   **Tipperary**

1989
23/07/1989, Quarter-Final, Dundalk
Antrim   *4-14*   *0-7*   **Kildare**
06/08/1989, Semi-Final, Croke Park
Antrim   *4-15*   *1-15*   **Offaly**
06/08/1989, Semi-Final, Croke Park
Tipperary   *1-17*   *2-11*   **Galway**
03/09/1989, Final, Croke Park
Tipperary   *4-24*   *3-9*   **Antrim**

1990

22/07/1990, Quarter-Final, Ballinasloe
Galway 1-23 2-11 *London*
05/08/1990, Semi-Final, Croke Park
Cork 2-20 1-13 *Antrim*
05/08/1990, Semi-Final, Croke Park
Galway 1-16 2-7 *Offaly*
02/09/1990, Final, Croke Park
Cork 5-15 2-21 *Galway*

1991

21/07/1991, Quarter-Final, Dundalk
Antrim 5-11 1-5 *Westmeath*
04/08/1991, Semi-Final, Croke Park
Tipperary 3-13 1-9 *Galway*
04/08/1991, Semi-Final, Croke Park
Kilkenny 2-18 1-19 *Antrim*
01/09/1991, Final, Croke Park
Tipperary 1-16 0-15 *Kilkenny*

1992

26/07/1992, Quarter-Final, Carlow
Galway 4-19 3-9 *Carlow*
09/08/1992, Semi-Final, Croke Park
Cork 2-17 1-11 *Down*
09/08/1992, Semi-Final, Croke Park
Kilkenny 2-13 1-12 *Galway*
06/09/1992, Final, Croke Park
Kilkenny 3-10 1-12 *Cork*

1993

25/07/1993, Quarter-Final, Castleblayney
Antrim 3-27 4-10 *Meath*
08/08/1993, Semi-Final, Croke Park
Galway 1-16 1-14 *Tipperary*
08/08/1993, Semi-Final, Croke Park
Kilkenny 4-18 1-9 *Antrim*
05/09/1993, Final, Croke Park
Kilkenny 2-17 1-15 *Galway*

1994

17/07/1994, Quarter-Final, Athleague
Galway 2-21 2-6 *Roscommon*
07/08/1994, Semi-Final, Croke Park
Limerick 2-23 0-11 *Antrim*
07/08/1994, Semi-Final, Croke Park
Offaly 2-13 1-10 *Galway*
04/09/1994, Final, Croke Park
Offaly 3-16 2-13 *Limerick*

1995

23/07/1995, Quarter-Final, Ruislip
Down 0-16 0-9 *London*
06/08/1995, Semi-Final, Croke Park
Clare 3-12 1-13 *Galway*
06/08/1995, Semi-Final, Croke Park
Offaly 2-19 2-8 *Down*
03/09/1995, Final, Croke Park
Clare 1-13 2-8 *Offaly*

1996

16/06/1996, Preliminary Round, Gaelic Park (New York)
New York 1-16 0-14 *London*
07/07/1996, Preliminary Round, Gaelic Park (New York)
New York 4-16 0-13 *Derry*
20/07/1996, Quarter-Final, Athenry
Galway 4-22 0-8 *New York*
04/08/1996, Semi-Final, Croke Park
Limerick 1-17 0-13 *Antrim*
04/08/1996, Semi-Final, Croke Park
Wexford 2-13 3-7 *Galway*
01/09/1996, Final, Croke Park
Wexford 1-13 0-14 *Limerick*

(Note: Beaten Munster and Leinster finalists allowed back into championship at Quarter-Final stage from 1997.)

1997

26/07/1997, Quarter-Final, Clones
Tipperary 3-24 3-8 *Down*
27/07/1997, Quarter-Final, Thurles
Kilkenny 4-15 3-16 *Galway*
10/08/1997, Semi-Final, Croke Park
Clare 1-17 1-13 *Kilkenny*
17/08/1997, Semi-Final, Croke Park
Tipperary 2-16 0-15 *Wexford*
14/09/1997, Final, Croke Park
Clare 0-20 2-13 *Tipperary*

1998

26/07/1998, Quarter-Final, Croke Park
Waterford 1-20 1-10 *Galway*
26/07/1998, Quarter-Final, Croke Park
Offaly 2-18 2-9 *Antrim*
09/08/1998, Semi-Final, Croke Park
Offaly 1-13 1-13 *Clare*
16/08/1998, Semi-Final, Croke Park
Kilkenny 1-11 1-10 *Waterford*
22/08/1998, Semi-Final, Croke Park, Replay
Clare 1-16 2-10 *Offaly*
(Note: Referee played short time, refixture ordered.)
29/08/1998, Semi-Final, Thurles, Refixture
Offaly 0-16 0-13 *Clare*
13/09/1998, Final, Croke Park
Offaly 2-16 1-13 *Kilkenny*

1999

25/07/1999, Quarter-Final, Croke Park
Offaly 4-22 0-12 *Antrim*
25/07/1999, Quarter-Final, Croke Park
Clare 3-15 2-18 *Galway*
02/08/1999, Quarter-Final, Croke Park, Replay
Clare 3-18 2-14 *Galway*
08/08/1999, Semi-Final, Croke Park
Cork 0-19 0-16 *Offaly*
15/08/1999, Semi-Final, Croke Park
Kilkenny 2-14 1-13 *Clare*
12/09/1999, Final, Croke Park
Cork 0-13 0-12 *Kilkenny*

2000

23/07/2000, Quarter-Final, Croke Park
Galway *1-14* *0-15* **Tipperary**
23/07/2000, Quarter-Final, Croke Park
Offaly *2-23* *2-17* **Derry**
06/08/2000, Semi-Final, Croke Park
Offaly *0-19* *0-15* **Cork**
13/08/2000, Semi-Final, Croke Park
Kilkenny *2-19* *0-17* **Galway**
10/09/2000, Final, Croke Park
Kilkenny *5-15* *1-14* **Offaly**

2001

29/07/2001, Quarter-Final, Croke Park
Wexford *4-10* *2-15* **Limerick**
29/07/2001, Quarter-Final, Croke Park
Galway *4-23* *1-11* **Derry**
12/08/2001, Semi-Final, Croke Park
Tipperary *1-16* *3-10* **Wexford**
18/08/2001, Semi-Final, Croke Park , Replay
Tipperary *3-12* *0-10* **Wexford**
19/08/2001, Semi-Final, Croke Park
Galway *2-15* *1-13* **Kilkenny**
09/09/2001, Final, Croke Park
Tipperary *2-18* *2-15* **Galway**

2002

28/07/2002, Quarter-Final, Croke Park
Tipperary *1-25* *2-12* **Antrim**
28/07/2002, Quarter-Final, Croke Park
Clare *1-15* *0-17* **Galway**
11/08/2002, Semi-Final, Croke Park
Clare *1-16* *1-13* **Waterford**
18/08/2002, Semi-Final, Croke Park
Kilkenny *1-20* *1-16* **Tipperary**
08/09/2002, Final, Croke Park
Kilkenny *2-20* *0-19* **Clare**

2003

27/07/2003, Quarter-Final, Croke Park
Tipperary *2-16* *2-11* **Offaly**
27/07/2003, Quarter-Final, Croke Park
Wexford *2-15* *2-12* **Antrim**
10/08/2003, Semi-Final, Croke Park
Cork *2-20* *3-17* **Wexford**
16/08/2003, Semi-Final, Croke Park, Replay
Cork *3-17* *2-7* **Wexford**
17/08/2003, Semi-Final, Croke Park
Kilkenny *3-18* *0-15* **Tipperary**
14/09/2003, Final, Croke Park
Kilkenny *1-14* *1-11* **Cork**

2004

25/07/2004, Quarter-Final, Croke Park
Cork *2-26* *0-10* **Antrim**
25/07/2004, Quarter-Final, Croke Park
Kilkenny *1-13* *1-13* **Clare**
31/07/2004, Quarter-Final Thurles, Replay
Kilkenny *1-11* *0-9* **Clare**
08/08/2004, Semi-Final, Croke Park
Kilkenny *3-12* *0-18* **Waterford**
15/08/2004, Semi-Final, Croke Park

Cork *1-27* *0-12* **Wexford**
12/09/2004, Final, Croke Park
Cork *0-17* *0-9* **Kilkenny**

2005

24/07/2005, Quarter-Final, Croke Park
Cork *1-18* *1-13* **Waterford**
24/07/2005, Quarter-Final, Croke Park
Clare *1-20* *0-12* **Wexford**
31/07/2005, Quarter-Final, Croke Park
Galway *2-20* *2-18* **Tipperary**
31/07/2005, Quarter-Final, Croke Park
Kilkenny *0-18* *0-13* **Limerick**
14/08/2005, Semi-Final, Croke Park
Cork *0-16* *0-15* **Clare**
21/08/2005, Semi-Final, Croke Park
Galway *5-18* *4-18* **Kilkenny**
11/09/2005, Final Croke Park
Cork *1-21* *1-16* **Galway**

2006

22/07/2006, Quarter-Final, Thurles
Cork *0-19* *0-18* **Limerick**
22/07/2006, Quarter-Final, Thurles
Kilkenny *2-22* *3-14* **Galway**
23/07/2006, Quarter-Final, Croke Park
Clare *1-27* *1-15* **Wexford**
23/07/2006, Quarter-Final, Croke Park
Waterford *1-22* *3-14* **Tipperary**
06/08/2006, Semi-Final, Croke Park
Cork *1-16* *1-15* **Waterford**
13/08/2006, Semi-Final, Croke Park
Kilkenny *2-21* *1-16* **Clare**
03/09/2006, Final, Croke Park
Kilkenny *1-16* *1-13* **Cork**

2007

28/07/2007, Quarter-Final, Croke Park
Kilkenny *3-22* *1-18* **Galway**
28/07/2007, Quarter-Final, Croke Park
Wexford *3-10* *1-14* **Tipperary**
29/07/2007, Quarter-Final, Croke Park
Limerick *1-23* *1-16* **Clare**
29/07/2007, Quarter-Final, Croke Park
Waterford *3-16* *3-16* **Cork**
05/08/2007, Quarter-Final, Croke Park, Replay
Waterford *2-17* *0-20* **Cork**
05/08/2007, Semi-Final, Croke Park
Kilkenny *0-23* *1-10* **Wexford**
12/08/2007, Semi-Final, Croke Park
Limerick *5-11* *2-15* **Waterford**
02/09/2007, Final, Croke Park
Kilkenny *2-19* *1-15* **Limerick**

2008

27/07/2008, Quarter-Final, Thurles
Cork *2-19* *2-17* **Clare**
27/07/2008, Quarter-Final, Thurles
Waterford *2-19* *3-15* **Wexford**
10/08/2008, Semi-Final, Croke Park
Kilkenny *1-23* *0-17* **Cork**
17/08/2008, Semi-Final, Croke Park

Waterford 1-20   1-18   Tipperary
07/09/2008, Final, Croke Park
Kilkenny 3-30   1-13   Waterford

2009
26/07/2009, Quarter-Final, Thurles
Waterford 1-16   0-18   Galway
26/07/2009, Quarter-Final, Thurles
Limerick 2-18   1-17   Dublin
09/08/2009, Semi-Final, Croke Park
Kilkenny 2-23   3-15   Waterford
16/08/2009, Semi-Final, Croke Park
Tipperary 6-19   2-7   Limerick
06/09/2009, Final, Croke Park
Kilkenny 2-22   0-23   Tipperary

2010
25/07/2010, Quarter-Final, Croke Park
Cork   1-25   0-19   Antrim
25/07/2010, Quarter-Final, Croke Park
Tipperary 3-17   3-16   Galway
08/08/2010, Semi-Final, Croke Park
Kilkenny 3-22   0-19   Cork
15/08/2010, Semi-Final, Croke Park
Tipperary 3-19   1-18   Waterford
05/09/2010, Final, Croke Park
Tipperary 4-17   1-18   Kilkenny

2011
24/07/2011, Quarter-Final, Thurles
Dublin   3-13   0-18   Limerick
24/07/2011, Quarter-Final, Thurles
Waterford 2-23   2-13   Galway
07/08/2011, Semi-Final, Croke Park
Kilkenny 2-19   1-16   Waterford
14/08/2011, Semi-Final, Croke Park
Tipperary 1-19   0-18   Dublin
04/09/2011, Final, Croke Park
Kilkenny 2-17   1-16   Tipperary

2012
29/07/2012, Quarter-Final, Thurles
Kilkenny 4-16   1-16   Limerick
29/07/2012, Quarter-Final, Thurles
Cork   1-19   0-19   Waterford
12/08/2012, Semi-Final, Croke Park
Galway   0-22   0-17   Cork
19/08/2012, Semi-Final, Croke Park
Kilkenny 4-24   1-15   Tipperary
09/09/2012, Final, Croke Park
Kilkenny 0-19   2-13   Galway
30/09/2012, Replay, Croke Park
Kilkenny 3-22   3-11   Galway

2013
28/07/2013, Quarter-Final, Thurles
Cork   0-19   0-14   Kilkenny
28/07/2013, Quarter-Final, Thurles
Clare   1-23   2-14   Galway
11/08/2013, Semi-Final, Croke Park
Cork   1-24   1-19   Dublin

18/08/2013, Semi-Final, Croke Park
Clare   1-22   0-18   Limerick
08/09/2013, Final, Croke Park
Clare   0-25   3-16   Cork
28/09/2013, Replay, Croke Park
Clare   5-16   3-16   Cork

2014
27/07/2014, Quarter-Final, Thurles
Tipperary 2-23   0-16   Dublin
27/07/2014, Quarter-Final, Thurles
Limerick 4-26   1-11   Wexford
10/08/2014, Semi-Final, Croke Park
Kilkenny 2-13   0-17   Limerick
17/08/2014, Semi-Final, Croke Park
Tipperary 2-18   1-11   Cork
07/09/2014, Final, Croke Park
Kilkenny 3-22   1-28   Tipperary
27/09/2014, Replay, Croke Park
Kilkenny 2-17   2-14   Tipperary

2015
26/7/2015, Quarter-Final: Thurles
Waterford 2-21   1-19   Dublin
26/7/2015, Quarter-Final: Thurles
Galway   2-28   0-22   Cork
9/8/2015, Semi-Final: Croke Park
Kilkenny 1-21   0-18   Waterford
16/8/2015, Semi-Final: Croke Park
Galway   0-26   3-16   Tipperary
6/9/2015, Final: Croke Park
Kilkenny 1-22   1-18   Galway

2016
24/7/2016, Quarter-Final: Thurles
Waterford 0-21   1-11   Wexford
24/7/2016, Quarter-Final: Thurles
Galway   2-17   0-17   Clare
7/8/2016, Semi-Final: Croke Park
Kilkenny 1-21   0-24   Waterford
13/8/2016, Replay: Thurles
Kilkenny 2-19   2-17   Waterford
14/8/2016, Semi-Final: Croke Park
Tipperary 2-19   2-18   Galway
4/9/2016, Final: Croke Park
Tipperary 2-29   2-20   Kilkenny

2017
22/7/2017, Quarter-Final: Páirc Uí Chaoimh
Tipperary 0-28   3-16   Clare
23/7/2017, Quarter-Final: Páirc Uí Chaoimh
Waterford 1-23   1-19   Wexford
6/8/2017, Semi-Final: Croke Park
Galway   0-22   1-18   Tipperary
13/8/2017, Semi-Final: Croke Park
Waterford 4-19   0-20   Cork
3/9/2017, Final: Croke Park
Galway   0-26   2-17   Waterford

ALL-IRELAND HURLING FINAL TEAMS

1887

Tipperary J.Stapleton (capt.), M.Maher, T.Maher, A.Maher, T.Burke, Martin McNamara, Ed.Murphy, Jer Dwyer, Tom Stapleton, Ned Bowe, Tom Healy, Dan Ryan, Jer. Ryan, Pat Leahy, Tim Dwyer, Jack Mockler, Jack Dunne, Tom Carroll, John Leamy, M.Carroll, P.Lambe.
Galway Patk.Larkin, John Mannion, Owen Griffin, John Saunders, Thos Foley, Ml.Conway, Ml.Kelly, John Mannion, Darby Mannion, Pat Haverty, James Haverty, Martin Griffin, Owen Griffin, John Cosgrave, A.Cosgrave, Ml. Cullen, Thos. Hanly, P.Madden, Ml. Kelly, Ml. Mannion, John Mannion.
Non-playing captain: Jas. Lynam.

1888

No final played owing to visit of a team of hurlers and athletes to the USA.

1889

Dublin N.O'Shea (capt.), Frank Coughlan, T.Butler, John Lambe, Dan Kerwick, J.D.O'Byrne, Thos.McKenna, W.J.Spain, James Harper, Chos.Hackett, Thos.Maher, J.Bishop, T.Belton, Polk.Ryan, J.Cahill, Ed.Gilligan, F.Palmer, S.Riordan, Patk.O'Shea, Patk.Riordan, Ml.Madigan.
Clare Thos.Coughlan, D.McKenna, Daniel McNamara, John McNamara, D.Quilney, Daniel Moroney, M.O'Dea, Wm.Moroney, Ml.Corry, Ed.Corry, Patk.O'Neill, T.O'Connell, Ml.Flynn, P.Vaughan, John McKenna, Martin Russell, Patk.McGrath, T.Donnellan, J.Moloney, J.King, M.Kinnery.
Non-playing captain: John Considine.

1890

Cork Dan Lane (capt.), J.Henchion, John Buckley, D.Lenihan, Dan Looney, Dan Drew, Tom O'Connor, Tom Twomey, M.Horgan, Pat Buckley, J.Reilly, Tim Kelleher, John Kelleher, P.O'Riordan, Dan O'Sullivan, Tom Good, D.Horgan, John Lenihan, Jer O'Sullivan, E.Reilly, Pad O'Riordan.
Wexford Nick Daly (capt.), E.Leacy, L.Leacy, T.Devereaux, O.Daly, J.Murphy, W.Neville, J.Murphy, P.McDonald, J.Rossiter, W.Furlong, J.O'Leary, W.Doran, G.Sinnott, P.Furlong, P.Devereaux, W.Fortune, G.Browne, M.Browne, J.Fogart, W.O'Leary.

1891

Kerry J.Mahony (capt.), M.Kelly, M.McCarthy, P.Carroll, P.Wynne, M.J.O'Sullivan, R.Kissane, F.Crowley, J.Crowley, J.O'Sullivan, T.Dunne, J.Murphy, M.Fitzmaurice, J.McDonnell, T.D.McCarthy, T.E.McCarthy, M.Riordan, P.Quane, J.Quane, P.Rourke, P.Kirby. Sub: J.Murphy (Dromartin) for T.Murphy.
Wexford N.Daly (capt.), J.Leary, E.Leacy, L.Leacy, M.Lacy, James Murphy, John Murphy, T.Murphy, N.Murphy, M.Browne, G.Browne, P.Quirke, P.Byrne, M.Kirwan, M.Redmond, P.Harpur, N.Moher, O.Daly, P.McDonnell, T.Devereaux, M.Harpur.

1892

Cork W.O'Callaghan (capt.), J.Kenneally, M Casserly, J.Keegan, J.Leaby, M.Sheehan, C.O'Callaghan, D.Halloran, T.Irwin, J.Conway, J.O'Connor, W.O'Connor, D.Scannell, J.Cashman, D.Coughlan, D.Drew, P.Buckley.
Dublin P.Egan (capt.), A.Carroll, J.Dooley, A.Maher, T.Meagher, C.Kennedy, W.Hinton, J.Kavanagh, T.Belton, R.Stakelum, M.Kennedy, E.Gilligan, J.Ryan, P.Whelan, D.Murphy, N.Murphy, D Healy.

1893

Cork John Murphy (capt.), Jer. Norbeg, D.Scannell, Ml.Murphy, D.Hayes, P.Coughlan, Jas. Young, S.Hegarty, Ml.Cronin, Patk.O'Keeffe, J.Cullinane, John O'Leary, Jas. Delea, J.O'Connor, John Cashman, W.J.O'Connell, Patk.Flaherty.
Kilkenny D.Whelan (capt.), J.Delaney, J.Grace, J.Lalor, P.Maher, E.Teehan, J.Walsh, M.Coogan, M.Berry, M.Morrissey, J.McCarthy, R.Grace, J.King, J.Doheny, P.Brennan, J.De Loughrey, P.Malone.

1894

Cork S.Hayes (capt.), D.Hayes, P.Coughlan, J.O'Leary, M.Murphy, J.Cashman, J.Kidney, J.Delea, M.Cronin, D.Coughlan, J.Kelleher, J.Norberg, S.Hegarty, J.Cullinane, J.O'Connor, J.Young, W.J.O'Connell.
Dublin John McCabe (capt.), John Greene, M.Brady, L.Byrne, M.Connor, J.Lawler, L.Lawler, Dan Gillis, S.Donovan, J.Quigley, D.Cregan, Ed. McCabe, M.Kelly, N.Harding, P.O'Toole, P Lawlor, J.O'Mullane.

1895

Tipperary M.Maher (capt.), E.Maher, Phil Byrne, W.Kerwick, John Maher, D.Walsh, John Walsh, Peter Maher, T.Flanagan, Jas.Flanagan, P.Riordon, Jas.Gleeson, Fergus Moriarty, John Connolly, J.Maher (F), E.Brennan, W.Devane.
Kilkenny M.Dalton, P.Maher, J.Lalor, E.Teehon, E.Dunne, P.Egan, P.Ryan, M.Coogan, M.Meagher, J.Walsh, W.Walsh, J.Dunne, P.Malone, J.Grace (capt.), J.Doheny, T.Grace, J.Doheny.

1896

Tipperary M.Maher (capt.), J.Maher (F), P.Byrne, W.Devane, M.Wall, E.Maher, E.Brennan, J.Walsh, T.Condon, J.Connolly, J.Flanagan, T.Ryan, P.Scanlon, T.Flanagan, E.D.Ryan, P.Doherty, D.Walsh.
Dublin P.Buckley (capt.), W.Carroll, P.Egan, J.Hill, D.Ryan, J.O'Dwyer, J.Donohue, M.Hackett, E.Hackett, J.Delaney, Joseph Ryan, D.Ryan, Jerry Ryan, John Eviston, T.O'Dwyer, P.Purcell, W.O'Connell.

1897

Limerick D.Grimes (capt.), J."Seán Óge" Hanly, M.Flynn, P.Flynn, M.Finn, P.O'Brien, T.Brazill, J.Condon, J.Catterall, J.Hynes, P.Butler, J.Flood, P.Mulcahy, M.Downes, J.Reidy, John Finn, P.Buskin.
Kilkenny J.Walsh (capt.), J.Doheny, P.Maher, M.Dalton, E.Teehan, M.Lawlor, John Lawlor, James Lawlor, John Grace, M.Malone, J.Walsh, M.Merry, J.Quinn, P.Fielding, P.Ryan, E.Dunne, P.Malone.

1898

Tipperary M.Maher (capt.), E.Maher, E.Brennan, J.Walsh, J.Connolly, T.Ryan, W.Devane, E.Ryan, P.Byrne, W.Dunne, T.Condon, J.O'Keeffe, J.Maher (N.), D.Walsh, J.Maher (F.), Dick O'Keeffe, John Ryan.
Kilkenny E.Hennessy (capt.}, J.Ryan, John Lalor, M.Dalton, T.Murphy, P.Maher, T.Grace, Jer. Doheny, P.Malone, M.Malone, P.Young, E.Teehan, Jas.Lawlor, John Lowlor, John Quinn, Martin Lawlor, Jas.Quinn.

1899

Tipperary T.Condon (capt.), Joe O'Keeffe, "Big Bill" Gleeson, J.Gleeson, R.O'Keeffe, Jas.O'Keeffe, D.Walsh, M.Maher, J.Walsh, J.Flanagan, J.Ryan, M.Wall, W.Dunne, P.Byrne, J.Maher, "Little Bill" Gleeson, T.Ryan.

Wexford Jas.Furlong (capt.), J.Corrigan, T.Byrne, John Shiel, Martin Murphy, T.Cullen, A.Dempsey, Con Dempsey, M.Byrne, M.Brien, D.Whelan (snr.), D.Whelan (jnr.), J.Shiel (jnr.), M.Coughlan, A.Delaney, M.Murphy, Jack Shiel.

1900
Tipperary E.Hayes, (capt.), P.Hayes, M.Ryan, M.Purcell, T.Allen, P.Maher, W.Maher, M.Maher, J.Walsh, T.Ryan, E.Maher, "Big Bill" Gleeson, "Little Bill" Gleeson, J.O'Keeffe, M.Wall, T.Semple, Jack Gleeson.
London D.Horgan (capt), M.Horgan, Jer. Connell, J.Lynch, Jer. Healy, T.Doody, Seán Óg Hanly, J.Grimes, D.Roche, J.Coughlan, J.Keogh, M.L.McMahon, J.O'Brien, P.McNamara, D.McNamara, J.Leary, M.Cofler.

Home Final
Tipperary E.Hayes (capt.), P.Hayes, M.Ryan, M.Purcell, T.Allen, W.Maher, J.Walsh, T.Ryan, E.Maher, "Big Bill" Gleeson, "Little Bill" Gleeson, M.Wall, J.O'Keeffe, P.Maher, J.Gleeson, T.Semple, M.Maher.
Galway J.Mitchel (capt.), M.Keighery, J.Coy, M.Cunningham, M.Stankard, J.Sylver, M.Holland, T.Leary, T.Connors, P.Taylor, M.Leary, T.Larkin, P.Burke, J.Larkin, W.Fallon, J.Quinn, D.Farrell.

1901
London J.Coughlan (capt.), P.King, J.King, P.Crowe, J.Fitzgerald, J.O'Brien, T.Barry, Jas. Barry, Jer. Connell, D.Horgan, M.Horgan, Séamus Lynch, Tim Doody, M.McMahon, E.Barrett, Jer.Kelleher, J.Crowley.
Cork P.Cantillon (capt.), J.Ronayne, J.Leonard, D.McGrath, J.Kelleher, T.Hallahan, J.O'Neill, D.O'Keeffe, T.Powell, M.O'Reilly, J.Barrett, W.Sheehan, P.Sullivan, J.O'Leary, D.Daly, C.Young, J.Delea.

'Home' Final
Cork P.Cantillon (capt.), J.Delea, D.McGrath, T.Irwin, J.Leonard, D.O'Keeffe, T.Powell, J.Kelleher, J.Ronayne, J.O'Neill, T.Hallinan, C.Young, P.Sullivan, J.O'Leary, D.Daly, W.Sheehan, M.O'Reilly.
Wexford J.Furlong (capt.), J.Corrigan, J.Murphy, M.O'Brien, Ml.O'Brien, M.Cummins, T.Dempsey, Con Dempsey, S.Donohue, T.Byrne, M.Byrne, P.Rath, O.Synnott, D.Crean, B.Murphy, J.Shiel, T.Cullen.

1902
Cork J.Kelleher (capt.), J.Ronayne, J.Desmond, J.O'Shea, W.Daly, J.Daly, T.Mahony, T.Lynch, P.Leaky, T.Coughlan, W.Parfrey, S.Riordan, J.Leahy, W.Fitzgibbon, D.McGrath, D.O'Keeffe, M.O'Shea.
London J.Nestor, J.Herbert, M.McMahon, J.Burke, T.Doody, P.Flanagan, T.Barry, J.Barry, T.Ryan, C.Sugrue, J.O'Leary, T.Donohue, T.Cummins, E.Barrett, P.D.Mehigan, J.Crowley, P.Clancy.

'Home' Final Replay
Cork J.Kelleher (capt.), J.Ronayne, J.Desmond, J.O'Shea, W.Doly, J.Daly, T.Mahony, M.O'Shea, P.Leahy, T.Coughlan, D.Coughlan, S.Riordan, W.Parfey, W.Fitzgibbon, D.McGrath, D.O'Keeffe, J.O'Leary. Sub: W.O'Neill.
Note: W.Moloney, C.Young, T.Lynch and P.Cantillon played in drawn game instead of M.O'Shea, D.Coughlan, S.Riordan and W.Fitzgibbon.

Dublin D.McCormack (capt.), J.O'Brien, J.Cleary, P.Mahony, A.Harty, M.Callaghan, J.Callaghan, J.Conway, C.Dillon, W.P.Allen, J.Quinlan, P.Flynn, J.Kennedy, J.Grace, W.Connolly, J.Delaney, T.Gleeson.
Note: P.Mulcahy, J.Gleeson and W.Scanlon played for Dublin in the drawn game instead of P.Mahony, P.Flynn and J.Delaney.

1903
Cork S.Riordan (capt.), T.Coughlan, J.Coughlan, D.Kidney, L.Flaherty, J.Kelleher, J.Desmond, J.O'Leary, W.Mackessy, A.Buckley, D.Buckley, W.Hennessy, W.O'Neill, P.O'Sullivan, M.O'Leary, D.O'Keeffe, D.McGrath.
London P.King (capt.), J.Nestor, C.Sugrue, W.Power, D.Roche, P.J.Crotly, I.Kelleher, D.Horgan, J.O'Brien, J.Barry, M.J.O'Halloran, Seán Óg Hanly, P.McMahon, J.Bleech, J.O'Farrell, T.Doody, M.Larkin.

'Home' Final
Cork S.Riordan (capt.), T.Coughlan, J.Coughlan, D.Kidney, L.Flaherty, J.Kelleher, J.Desmond, J.O'Leary, W.Mackessy, A.Buckley, D.Buckley, W.Hennessy, W.O'Neill, P.O'Sullivan, M.O'Leary, D.O'Keeffe, D.McGrath.
Kilkenny M.Dalton (capt.), Jas Lalor, T.Murphy, M.Shortall, D.Grace, P.Maher, J.Doheny, S.Walton, J.Hoyne, P.Saunders, J.Kerwick, J.Fielding, P.Fielding, E.Doyle, J.Synnott, J.Quinn, J.Rochford.

1904
Kilkenny J.Doheny (capt.), P.Maher, S.Walton, J.Hoyne, P.Saunders, J.Lawlor, R.Doyle, E.Doyle, P.Fielding, R.Walsh, J.Rochford, D.Grace, R.Brennan, D.Stapleton, P.Lanigan, J.Anthony, M.Lawlor. Sub: Jim Dunne for D Stapleton.
Cork D.Harrington (capt.), W.O'Neill, D.Sheehan, M.O'Leary, D.Linehan, W.Moloney, P.O'Sullivan, D.McCarthy, J.Kelleher, W.Hennessy, J.Desmond, J.Ronayne, T.Coughlan, S.Riordan, D.O'Keeffe, D.McGrath W.Sheehan.

1905
Kilkenny D.J.Stapleton (capt.), J.Hoyne, T.Kenny, D.Kennedy, J.Anthony, J.J.Brennan, R.Walsh, J.Glennon, M.Gargan, S.Walton, J.Kelly, P.Lanigan, E.Doyle, J.Lawlor, R.Doyle, J.Rochford, M.Lawlor.
Cork Jas.Kelleher (capt.), W.Hennessy, J.Ronayne, W.Mackessy, A.Buckley, D.McGrath, M.O'Leary, J.A.Beckett, W.Moloney, John Kelly, D.O'Leary, Chris Nolan, J.Harrington, D.McCarthy, P.O'Sullivan, W.O'Neill, "Sonny" Jim McCarthy. Sub: C.Young.

Note: The above teams took part in disputed final on 14/4/1907. The following teams contested the refixed final on 30/6/1907.

Refixed Final
Kilkenny D.J.Stapleton (capt.), J.Hoyne, T.Kenny, D.Kennedy, J.Anthony, J.J.Brennan, R.Walsh, E.Teehan, Dan Grace, S.Walton, J.Kelly, P.Lanigan, E.Doyle, M.Lawlor, J.Lawlor, R.Doyle, J.Rochford. Sub: Tom Murphy for D.Stapleton.
Cork J.Kelleher, W.Hennessy, J.Ronayne, W.Mackessy, A.Buckley, D.McGrath, M O'Leary, J.A.Beckett, W.Moloney, C.Young (capt.), John Kelly, D.O'Leary, Chris Nolan, P.D.Mehigan, ("Carbery"), D.Linehan, P.Leahy, W.O'Neill.

1906

Tipperary Tom Semple (capt.), J.Hayes, J.O'Brien, P.Burke, M.O'Brien, T.Kerwick, P.Brolan, H.Shelley, J.Mockler, T.Kenna, P.Riordan, T.Allen, P.Maher, J.Burke, J.Gleeson, J.O'Keeffe, T.Gleeson.

Dublin D.McCormack (capt.), A.C.Harty, P.Hogan, J.Cleary, J.O'Riordan, M.Murphy, J.Quinlan, J.O'Dwyer, P.Kennedy, W.Leonard, W.Murphy, T.Warner, B.O'Brien, M.O'Callaghan, J.Grace, M.Quinn, W.O'Callaghan.

1907

Kilkenny R."Drug" Walsh (capt.), R.Doyle, M.Doyle, E.Doyle, R.Doherty, J.Kelly, T.Kenny, M.Gargan, D.Stapleton, D.Kennedy, J.Keoghan, J.Rochford, D.Grace, P.Lanigan, J.Power, J.Anthony, S.Walton.

Cork Jim Kelleher (capt.), J.Roynane, J.Desmond, W.Hennessy, T.Mahony, P.Leahy, J.O'Shea, T.Lynch, G.Buckley, J.Kelleher, T.Coughlan, S.Riordan, W.Parfrey, W.Kidney, D.O'Keeffe, J.A.Beckett, W.O'Neill.

1908

REPLAY

Tipperary Tom Semple (capt.), T.Kerwick, J.Mockler, J.O'Brien, H.Shelley, A.Corew, J.Mooney, T.Kenna, P.Burke, P.Brolan, J.Moloughney, J.Burke, T.Gleeson, M.O'Dwyer, J.Fitzgerald, P.Fitzgerald, Martin O'Brien.

Note: Jack Gleeson, Joe O'Keeffe, Bob Mockler and William Harris played in drawn game for Tipperary. Michael O'Dwyer, John Fitzgerald, Pat Fitzgerald and Jimmy Burke came on for replay.

Dublin J.Grace, A.Fitzgerald, D.McCormack, W.Connolly, W.O'Callaghan, W.Leonard, R.O'Brien, J.O'Brien, J.Callaghan, D.Kelleher, P.Grace, J.Lynch, M.Quinn, T.Quane, J.McDonald, D.Doyle, J.Nolan. Sub: P.Neville for R.O'Brien.

Note: P.O'Meara, W.Dillane, J.Collison, H.Boland and R.White played in drawn game. P.Grace, D.McCormack, R.O'Brien, D.Doyle and J.Nolan came on for replay.

1909

Kilkenny R."Drug" Walsh (capt.), E.Doyle, M.Doyle, R.Doherty, J.Kelly, W.Hennebry, J.Delahunty, J.Dunphy, D.Kennedy, J.Keoghan, S.Walton, J.Rochford, M.Gargan, M.Shortall, J.Ryan, P.Lanigan, R.Doyle. Sub: R.Grace for R.Doherty.

Tipperary Tom Semple (capt.), J.O'Brien, T.Kerwick, P.P.Burke, J.Fitzgerald, J.Mockler, J.Moloughney, A.Carew, M.O'Brien, P.Fitzgerald, J.Mooney, R.Mockler, H.Shelly, T.Gleeson, J.Burke, P.Brolan J.Hackett. Sub: E.Hayes.

1910

Wexford R.Doyle (capt.), R.Fortune, M.Cummins, P.Mackey, M.Parker, J.Mythen, A.Kehoe, J.Shortall, Seán Kennedy, S.Donohue, P.Roche, D.Kavanagh, J.Fortune, W.McHugh, P.Corcoran, M.Neville, W.Devereux.

Limerick J.Mackey (capt.), J.Burke, M.Mangan, M.Fehilly, T.Mangan, C.Scanlon, M.Harrington, Egan Clancy, E.Treacy, T.O'Brien, T.Hayes, J.Madden, P.Flaherty, M.Danagher, J.Carroll, D.Conway, M.Sweeney.

1911

No Final: Kilkenny awarded walk-over from Limerick. The Kilkenny team that played Tipperary in lieu of final was the same team as played in 1912, so effectively comprised the 1911 All-Ireland champion side.

1912

Kilkenny S.Walton (capt.), J.T.Power, P.Grace, D.Kennedy, J.J.Brennan, P.Lanigan, J.Keoghan, R.Walsh, R.Grace, J.Rochford, E.Doyle, T.McCormack, R.Doyle, M.Doyle, M.Gargan, J.Kelly, R.Doherty.

Cork A.Fitzgerald, D.Barry, P.Mahony, W.Mackessy, B.Murphy (capt.), M.Dorney, D.Kennefick, C.Sheehan, J.Murphy, M.Kidney, J.Kelleher, M.Byrne, J.Kennedy, W.Walsh, P.O'Brien L.Flaherty, T.Nagle.

1913

Kilkenny R."Drug" Walsh (capt.), J.Power, J.Keoghan, J.Rochford, J.Lennon, D.Kennedy, R.Grace, M.Gargan, J.J.Brennan, P.Grace, R.Doherty, R.Doyle, S.Walton, M.Doyle, J.Kelly.

Tipperary P."Wedger" Meagher (capt.), J.O'Meara, F.McGrath, S.Hackett, R.Mockler, J.Raleigh, T.Gleeson, J.Harty, E.Gilmartin, E.Cawley, P.Brolan, H.Shelley, J.Murphy, W.Kelly, E.O'Keeffe. Sub: J.McKenna for W.Kelly.

1914

Clare A.Power (capt.), J.Power, M.Flanagan, E.Grace, T.McGrath, P.McInerney, J.Shalloo, W.Considine, B.Considine, M.Moloney, R.Doherty, J.Fox, J.Clancy, J.Guerin, S.Spellisey. Subs: J.Rogers for S.Spellisey, P.Moloney for J.Fox.

Laois Jack Carroll (capt.), R.O'Keeffe, Jim Carroll, W.Lenihan, J.Jones, T.Hyland, R.Reilly, T.Higgins, P.Goulding, J.Daly, E.P.McEvoy, F.Killeen, T.Jones, J.Hiney, T.Finlay.

1915

Laois J.Finlay (capt.), J.Walsh, T.Finlay, Jas.Carroll, John Carroll, Jos.Carroll, J.Daly, P.Campion, Joe Phelan, J.Hiney, John Phelan, E.McEvoy, R.O'Keeffe, J.Dunphy, P.Ryan.

Cork C.Sheehan (capt.), "Bowler" Walsh, L.Flaherty, W.Fitzgerald, Seán Hyde, J.Ramsell, M.Byrne, F.Buckley, J.Kennedy, T.O'Riordan, P.Halloran, T.Nagle, Seán Óg Murphy, J.Murphy, B.Murphy.

1916

Tipperary J.Leahy (capt.), T.Dwan, J.Doherty, W.Dwyer, T.Shanahan, J.Power, J.Fitzpatrick, J.Collison, P.Leahy, H.Shelly, J.Murphy, R.Walsh, D.Walsh, W.Dwyer, A.O'Donnell.

Kilkenny S.Walton (capt.), J.Kerwick, J.Walsh, T.Hanrahan, J.Ryan, D.Kennedy, J.Holohan, R.Grace, J.Whelan, P.Clohosey, J.Byrne, W.Finn, R.Tobin, M.Kennedy, P.Walsh.

1917

Dublin T.Daly, John Ryan (capt.), S.Hyde, S.O'Donovan, H.Burke, C.Stuart, J.Phelan, R.Mockler, T.Moore, J.Cleary, F.Burke, M.Neville, M.Hackett, M.Hayes, P.Kenefick. Sub: B.Considine came on shortly after start of match.

Tipperary J.Leahy (capt.), J.Power, W.Dwyer, J.Nagle, P.Leary, J.Doherty, R.Walsh, W.Dwyer, H.Shelly, M.Leahy, T.Shanahan, S.Hackett, J.O'Meara, J.Collison, J.Fitzpatrick.

1918

Limerick W.Hough (capt.), P.McInerney, D.Lanigan, R.McConkey, W.Gleeson, J.Keane, M.Rochford, D.Troy, T.McGrath, M.Murphy, P.Barry, W.Ryan, R.Ryan, J.Humpheries, P.Kennedy.

Wexford M.Cummins (capt:), M.Stafford, C.Hyland, D.Kavanagh, P.Roche, L.Leary, J.Fortune, R.Walsh, N.Leary, J.Synnott, J.Fogarty, M.Neville, M.Murphy, P.Fagan, R.Lambert.

1919

Cork J.Kennedy (capt.), E.Gray, J.O'Keeffe, S.Óg Murphy, P.Aherne, C.Lucy, J.J.Hassett, T.Nagle, P.O'Halloran, M.Murphy, F.Kelleher, D.Ring, C.Sheehan, R.Gorman, J.B.Murphy.
Dublin C.Stuart (capt.), R.Mockler, Seán Hyde, F.Burke, B.Considine, M.Murphy, M.Hayes, T.Moore, T.Daly, J.Ryan (Grocers), J.Cleary, J.Phelan, M.Neville, T Hayes, Dr.J.Ryan (U.C.D.).

1920

Dublin R.Mockler (capt.), M.Hayes, M.Neville, T.Moore, T.Hayes, Jas.Cleary, E.Tobin, R.Doherty, Jas.Walsh, T.Daly (goal), F.Burke, J.J.Callanan, Joseph Phelan, John Ryan (Grocers), J.Clune.
Cork R.O'Gorman (capt.), J.Kennedy, E.Gray, J.O'Keeffe, J.Hassett, C.Lucey, P.Halloron, P.("Balty") Aherne, Seán Óg Murphy, E.Coughlan, M.Murphy, F.Kelleher, C.Sheehan, Denis Ring, Dannix Ring.

1921

Limerick R.McConkey (capt.), M.Murphy (goal), W.Gleeson, J.Humphreys, D.Lanigan, D.Murnane, W.Houch, J.Keane, W.Ryan, G.Howard, P.McInerney, T.Mangan, M.Mullane, C.Ryan, T.McGrath.
Dublin R.Mockler (capt.), Martin Hayes, Tom Hayes, M.Neville, Tom Moore, Jas.Walsh, R.Doherty, J.Clune, F.Burke, J.J.Callanan, T.Daly (goal), E.Tobin, M.Darcy, J.Cleary, Jos.Bannon. Sub: J.Kennedy for T.Hayes.

1922

Kilkenny W.Dunphy (capt.), E.Dunphy, M.McDonald (goal), J.Holohan, J.Tobin, T.Carroll, R.Grace, W.Kenny, P.Glendon, P.Aylward, M.Lawlor, J.Roberts, P.Donohoe, M.Power, R.Tobin.
Tipperary J.Leahy, (capt.), J.Power, A.O'Donnell, P.Power, P.Browne, J.Cleary, M.Kennedy, S.Hackett, J.O'Meara, J.J.Hayes, P.Spillane, J.Fitzpatrick, T.Dwan, W.Dwan, J.Darcy.

1923

Galway M.Kenny (capt.), J.Mahony (goal), M.Derivan, I.Harney, J.Power, A.Kelly, B.Gibbs, E.Gilmartin, J.Morris, Martin King, T.Fleming, R.Morrissey, L.McGrath, M.Gill, J.Garvey.
Limerick P.McInerney (capt.), J.Hanley (goal), D.Murnane, W.Hough, D.Lanigan, W.Gleeson, Jas.Humphries, M.Neville, J.J.Kinnane, J.Keane, T.McGrath, M.Cross, R.McConkey, J.O'Grady, M.Fitzgibbon. Subs: S.Shanny for J.J.Kinnane, J.O'Shea for R.McConkey.

1924

Dublin T.Daly (goal), Joe Bannon, W Small, T.Kelly, M.Gill, Jas.Walsh, R.Mockler, P.Aylward, R.Doherty, M.Holland, D.O'Neill, G.Howard, Tom Barry, W.Banim, T.Finlay.
Note: Frank Wall, non-playing captain.
Galway M.Kenny (capt.), J.Mahony (goal), M.Derivan, I.Harney, J.Power, A.Kelly, B.Gibbs, E.Gilmartin, J Morris, M.King, T.Fleming, R.Morrissey, L.McGrath, J.Garvey, J Keogh.

1925

Tipperary Johnny Leahy (capt.), A.O'Donnell (goal), M.Mockler, M.D'Arcy, J.J.Hayes, M.Kennedy, S.Hackett, J.Power, P.Leahy, P.Cahill, T.Duffy, J.D'Arcy, W.Ryan, P.Power, P.O'Dwyer. Sub: S.Kenny for M.Mockler.
Galway A.Kelly (capt.), J.Mahony (goal), J.Stanford, J.Fallon, Mick Derivan, M.Broderick, P.J.Morrissey, I.Harney, M.King, P.O'Donnell, M.Connaire, M.Houlihan, Richard Morrissey, J.Shaughnessy, P.Rooney. Sub: P.Finn for J.Shaughnessy.

1926

Cork Seán Óg Murphy (capt.), J.Coughlan (goal), Mce. Murphy, E.O'Connell, D.B.Murphy, Ml.Murphy, J.O'Regan, J.Hurley, E.Coughlan, Wm.Higgins, P.Delea, J.Kearney, Matt Murphy, M.Ahearne, P.Ahearne.
Kilkenny R.Grace (capt.), R.Cantwell (goal), Wm.Meagher, P.O'Reilly, T.Carroll, E.Doyle, W.Barry, W.Dunphy, M.Power, L.Meagher, J.Carroll, M. Brennan.E.Dunphy, H.Meagher, J.Roberts.

1927

Dublin M.Gill (capt.), P.McInerney, W.Phelan, E.Tobin, J.Gleeson, T.O'Rourke, G.Howard, M.Power, E.Faky, T.Daly, T.Barry, J.Walsh, D.O'Neill, J.Bannon, M.Hayes.
Cork Seán Óg Murphy (capt.), E.O'Connell, D.B.Murphy, M.Murphy, J.Hurley, E.Coughlan, M.Leary, P.Ahearne, M.Ahearne, P.Delea, J.O'Regan, P.Daly, Maurice Murphy, W.Higgins, J.Burke (goal).

1928

Cork Seán Óg Murphy (capt.), E.O'Connell, J.Hurley, E.Coughlan, P.Ahearne, P.Delea, M.Ahearne, M.Leahy, M.Burke, M.Madden, D.B.Murphy, J.O'Regan, T.Barry, P.O'Grady, M.O'Connell.
Galway J.Power (capt.), M.Derivan, I.Harney, J.Mahony, P.Green, R.McCann, J.Shaughnessy, R.Morrissey, P.Gilligan, M.Broderick, F.Kealy, M.Cunningham, W.Curran, M.King, T.Mullins. Sub: J.Deely for Mick King.

1929

Cork D.Barry Murphy (capt.), J.Burke (goal), M.Madden, P.Collins, T.Barry, J.O'Regan, M.O'Connell, J.Kenneally, M.Ahearne, P.Ahearne, P.Delea, J.Hurley, E.Coughlan, P.O'Grady, E.O'Connell. Subs: D.McCarthy for P.Aherne.
Galway J.Mahony (goal), P.Clarke, T.Fleming, J.Shaughnessy, W.Keane, L.Geoghegan, F.Keely, M.Cunningham, I.Harney, C.Cooney, P.Corcoran, J.Derivan, R.Morrissey W.Derivan, J.Deely. Subs: M.Broderick for J.Shaughnessy, A.Furey for W.Derivan.

1930

Tipperary J.J.Callanan (capt.), J.O'Loughlin, J.Maher, M.Ryan, J.Harney, J.Lanigan, T.O'Meara (goal), M.Kennedy, P.McKenna, P.Purcell, P.Cahill, M.F.Cronin, T.Butler, T.Leahy, T.Treacy. Sub: J.Heeney.
Dublin Jas.Walsh (capt.), J.Dwyer (goal), T.O'Meara, E.Campion, M.Gill, C.Griffin, C.MacMahon, P.McInerney, M.Finn, T.Quinlan, T.Burke, Matt Power, E.Byrne, T.Teehan, J.Gleeson. Subs: H.Quirke, M.Daniels.

1931

2nd REPLAY
Cork J.Coughlan, M.Madden, E.O'Connell, P."Fox" Collins, D.Barry Murphy, J.Regan, T.Barry, J.Hurley, M.O'Connell, E.Coughlan (capt.), M.Aherne, P.O'Grady, P.Delea, P.Aherne, W.Clancy.
Note: The above team played in all three matches. George Garrett (Blackrock) come on as a sub in the first and second replay.
Kilkenny J.Dermody, P.Phelan, P.O'Reilly, D.Treacy, T.Carroll, P.Byrne, E.Doyle, E.Byrne, Tommy Leahy, J.Duggan, J.Leahy, M.Power, D.Dunne, M.Larkin, P.Walsh. Sub: Martin Murphy.
Note: Lory Meagher (capt.), Paddy Larkin and Billy Dalton played in the first and second games. Martin White and Dick Morrissey played in the first game. Jack Duggan came on as a sub in the first game for Dick Morrisssey. He played in second game. Paddy Walsh played in second game. Tommy Leahy came on as a sub in second game for Lory Meagher.

1932

Kilkenny   J.Dermody, P.Larkin, P.O'Reilly, J.Carroll, P.Phelan, P.Byrne, E.Doyle, E.Byrne, L.Meagher, J.Walsh (capt.), Mar.Power, Tom Leahy, J.Dunne, M.White, Matty Power.

Clare   Tom Daly, J.Higgins, P.McInerney, J.J.Doyle (capt.), J.Houlihan, J.Hogan, L.Blake, J.Gleeson, T.McInerney, M.Falvey, M.Connery, Michael O'Rourke, J.Mullane, T.Burnell, T.Considine.

1933

Kilkenny   E.Doyle (capt.), John Dunne, J.Dermody (goal), L.Meagher, P.Phelan, P.Larkin, M.White, P.O'Reilly, P.Byrne, J.Walsh, J.Fitzpatrick, E.Byrne, Tommy Leahy, Martin Power, Matty Power. Subs: J.Duggan for M.White, J.O'Connell for J.Dermody.

Limerick   M.Fitzgibbon {capt.), P Scanlan (goal), T.Ryan, J.Mackey, M.Mackey, M.Cross, T.McCarthy, P.Clohessy, D.Clohessy, E.Cregan, M.Ryan, P.Ryan, J.Roche, G.Howard, C.O'Brien. Sub: W.O'Donoghue.

1934

Replay

Limerick   T.Shinny (goal), E.Cregan, T.McCarthy, M Kennedy, M.Cross, P.Clohessy, G.Howard, T.Ryan (capt.), M.Ryan, J.Mackey, M.Mackey, J.Roche, J.O'Connell, D.Clohessy, J.Close.
Note: Paddy Scanlon and Bob McConkey played in drawn game. Tom Shinny and Jackie O'Connell came on for replay. M.Condon came on as sub in drawn game.

Dublin   C.Forde (goal), A.Murphy, J.Bannon, T.Teehan, J.Walsh, D.Canniffe, P.Roche, Ed.Wade, M.Daniels, S.Hegarty, T.Treacy, S.Muldowney, S.Feeney (capt.), D.O'Neill, J O'Connell. Subs: C.McMahon for A.Murphy, J.Culleton for C.Forde.
Note: C.Boland (capt.) played in drawn game. S.Feeney (capt.) came on for replay. F.McCormack and J.Culleton came on as subs in drawn game.

1935

Kilkenny   J.O'Connell (goal), P.Larkin, P.O'Reilly, P.Blanchfield, E.Byrne, P.Byrne, P.Phelan, L.Meagher (capt.), Tommy Leahy, J.Walsh, J.Duggan, M.White, J.Dunne, L.Byrne, Matty Power. Subs: L.Duggan for J.Dunne, J.Dunne for Duggan.

Limerick   P.Scanlan (goal), E.Cregan, T.McCarthy, M.Kennedy, M.Cross, P.Clohessy, G.Howard, T.Ryan (capt.), M.Ryan, J.Mackey, M.Mackey, J.Roche, J.O'Connell, P.McMahon, J.Close.

1936

Limerick   P.Scanlan (goal), T.McCarthy, P.O'Carroll, M.Kennedy, M.Cross, P.Clohessy, G.Howard, T.Ryan, M.Ryan, J.Mackey, M.Mackey (capt.), J.Roche, D.Clohessy, P.McMahon, J.Power.

Kilkenny   J.O'Connell (goal), P.Larkin (capt.), P.O'Reilly, P.Blanchfield, P.Byrne, L.Byrne, P.Phelan, L.Meagher, Tom Leahy, J.Walsh, M.White, J.Duggan, J.Dunne, L.Byrne, Matty Power. Sub: W.Burke for P.Blanchfield.

1937

Tipperary   T.Butler (goal), D.O'Gorman, G.Cornally, J.Lanigan (capt.), J.Ryan, J.Maher, W.Wall, J.Cooney, J.Gleeson, Jim Coffey, T.Treacy, T.Doyle, W.O'Donnell, D.Murphy, P."Sweeper" Ryan. Subs: D.Mackey for J.Gleeson, T.Kennedy for W.Wall.

Kilkenny   J.Duggan (capt.), J.O'Connell (goal), P.Larkin, P.Byrne, P.Blanchfield, E.Byrne, W.Burke, P.Phelan, T.Leahy, V.Madigan, J.Morrissey, P.Obbins, L.Duggan, M.White, Matty Power. Sub: L.Meagher for Tommy Leahy.

1938

Dublin   M.Daniels (capt.), C.Forde, T.Teehan, M.Butler, C.McMahon, M.Gill, P.Farrell, J.Byrne, H.Gray, R.Ryan, M.McDonnell, P.Doody, M.Brophy, M.Flynn, W.Loughnane. Sub: J.Gilmartin.

Waterford   M.Hickey (capt.), M.Curley, C.Ware J.Fanning, W.Walshe, J.Keane, J.Mountain, C.Moylon S.Feeney, W.Barron, T.Greaney, P.Sheehan, J.Halpin, L.Byrne, D.Goode.

1939

Kilkenny   J.O'Connell (goal), P.Grace, P.Larkin, P.Blanchfield, R.Hinks, W.Burke, P.Phelan, J.Walsh (capt.), J.Kelly, J.Langton, Ter.Leahy, J.Gargan, J.Mulcahy, J.O'Brien, J.Phelan. Sub: R.Brannagan for J.Gargan.

Cork   J.Buttimer, A.Lotty, Batt Thornhill, W.Murphy, W.Campbell, J.Quirke, J.Young, J.Lynch (capt.), J.Barrett, C.Buckley, R.Dinneen, W.Tabb, J.Ryng, T.O'Sullivan, M.Brennan.

1940

Limerick   P.Scanlan, J.McCarthy, M.Hickey, M.Kennedy, T.Cooke, P.Clohessy, P.Cregan, T.Ryan, J.Roche, J.Mackey, M.Mackey (capt.), R.Stokes, E.Chawke, P.McMahon, J.Power. Sub: A.Herbert for P.Clohessy.

Kilkenny   J.O'Connell, P.Grace, P.Larkin, P.Blanchfield, R.Hinks, W.Burke, P.Phelan, J.Walsh, J.Kelly, J.Langton (capt.), Terry Leahy, J.Gargan, J.Mulcahy, S.O'Brien, Jas.Phelan.

1941

Cork   J.Buttimer, W.Murphy, B.Thornhill, A.Lotty, W.Campbell, C.Cottrill, D.J.Buckley, S.Barrett, J.Lynch, C.Ring, C.Buckley (capt,), J.Young, J.Quirke, T.O'Sullivan, M Brennan. Subs: P.O'Donovan for J.Lynch, J.Ryng for M.Brennan.

Dublin   C.Forde, D.Nicholls, M.Connolly, C.McMahon, M.Gill (jnr.), P.Farrell, J.Byrne, H.Gray, F.White, M.McDonnell, E.Wade (capt.), G.Glenn, E.O'Boyle, P.McSweeney, C.Downes. Sub: D.Conway for C.Forde.

1942

Cork   E.Porter, W.Murphy, B.Thornhill, C.Murphy, A.Lotty, D.J.Buckley, J.Young, J.Lynch (capt.), P.O'Donovan, C.Ring, Seán Condon, M.Kennefick, C.Tobin, J.Quirke, D.Beckett. Sub: J.Buttimer for E.Porter.

Dublin   J.Donegan, C.O'Dwyer, M.Butler, P.McCormack, E.O'Brien, F.White, (capt.), Jim Byrne, E.Wade, H.Gray, M.Ryan, M.McDonnell, J.Roche, D.Devitt, P.Kennedy, J.Mullane. Subs: S.Skehal for J.Roche, M.Griffin for S.Skehal.

1943

Cork   T.Mulcahy, W.Murphy, B.Thornhill, C.Murphy, A.Lotly, D.J.Buckley, J.Young, J.Lynch, C.Cottrell, S.Condon, C.Ring, M.Kenefick (capt.), J.Quirke, T.O'Sullivan, M.Brennan. Subs: P.O'Donovan for S.Condon, B.Murphy for T.Sullivan.

Antrim   J.Hurl, J.Currie, K.Murphy, W.Graham, P.McGarry, J.Walsh (capt.), P.McKeown, J.Bateson, N.Campbell, D.McKillop, J.Butler, Joe Mullan, K.Armstrong, D.McAllister, S.Mulholland. Sub: S.McNeill for J.Walsh.

1944

Cork   T.Mulcahy, W.Murphy, B.Thornhill, D.J.Buckley, P.O'Donovan, C.Murphy, A.Lotly, J.Lynch, C.Cottrell, C.Ring, S.Condon (capt.), J.Young, J.Quirke, J.Morrison, J.Kelly. Sub: P.Healy for C.Murphy.

Dublin J.Donegan, J.O'Neill, M.Butler (capt.), P McCormack, F.White, C.Flanogan, J.Egan, M.Hassett, H.Gray, T.Leahy, E.Wade, J.Byrne, P.Maher, C.Downes, M.Ryan. Sub: M.Gill for J.Egan.

1945

Tipperary Jim Maher, J.Devitt, G.Cornally, F.Coffey, M.Murphy, John Maher (capt.), T.Purcell, H.Goldsboro, T.Wall, "Mutt" Ryan, T.Doyle, E.Gleeson, John Coffey, A.Brennan, P."Sweeper" Ryan.
Kilkenny J.Walsh, P.Grace, M.Kelly, P.Blanchfield (capt.), J.Heffernan, W.Burke, J.Meagher, D.Kennedy, T.Murphy, J.Gargan, J.Langton, T.Maher, T.Walton, S.O'Brien, J.Mulcahy. Subs: W.Walsh for W.Burke, J.Kelly for D.Kennedy.

1946

Cork T.Mulcahy, W.Murphy, C.Murphy, D.J.Buckley, P.O'Donovan A.Lotty, J.Young, J.Lynch, C.Cottrell, P.Healy, C.Ring (capt.), C.Murphy, M.O'Riordan, G.O'Riordan, J.Kelly.
Kilkenny Jim Donegan, P.Grace, M.Butler, W.Walsh, J.Kelly, S.Downey, J.Mulcahy (capt.), D.Kennedy, T.Leahy, J.Gargan, J.Langton, L.Reidy, T.Walton, S.O'Brien, P.O'Brien. Subs: T.Murphy, M.Kelly (Mooncoin).

1947

Kilkenny J.Donegan, P.Grace, P.("Diamond") Hayden, M.Marnell, J.Kelly, P.Prendergast, J.Mulcahy, D.Kennedy (capt.), J.Heffernan, T.Walton, Terry Leahy, J.Langton, Shem Downey, W.Cahill, L.Reidy. Sub: E.Kavanagh for P.Prendergast.
Cork T.Mulcahy, W.Murphy, C.Murphy, D.J.Buckley, P.Donovan, A.Lotty, J.Young, J.Lynch, C.Cottrell, S.Condon (capt.), C.Ring, C.Murphy, M.O'Riordan, G.O'Riordan, J.Kelly.

1948

Waterford J.Ware (capt.), A.Fleming, J.Cusack, J.Goode, M.Hickey, V.Baston M.Hayes, J.O'Connor, E.Carew, K.O'Connor, J.Keane, C.Moylan, W.Galvin, E.Daly, T.Curran.
Dublin K.Matthews, E.Dunphy, D.Walsh, S.Cronin, A.Herbert, J.Butler, P.Donnelly, M.Hassett, L.Donnelly, J.Kennedy, D.Cantwell, S.Óg O'Callaghan, M.Williams, J.Prior, F.Cummins (capt.).

1949

Tipperary A.Reddan, M.Byrne, A.Brennan, J.Doyle, P.Stakelum (capt.), F.Coffey, T.Doyle, S.Kenny, P.Shanahan, Tommy Ryan, Mick Ryan, J.Kennedy, J.Ryan, "Sonny" Maher, S.Bannon. Sub: P.Kenny for F.Coffey.
Laois T.Fitzpatrick, L.White, J.Bergin, P.McCormack, J.Murray, T.Byrne, P.Rustchitzko (capt.), J.Styles, W.Bohane, P.Hogan, H.Grey, P.O'Brien, P.Lalor, D.Forde, P.Kelly. Subs: W.Dargan for P.O'Brien, A.Dunne for P.Rustchitzko.

1950

Tipperary A.Reddan, M.Byrne, A.Brennan, J.Doyle, J.Finn, P.Stakelum, T.Doyle, S.Bannon, P.Shanahan, E.Ryan, Mick Ryan, S.Kenny (capt.), P.Kenny, "Sonny" Maher, J.Kennedy. Sub: Tommy Ryan for "Sonny" Maher.
Kilkenny R.Dowling, J.Hogan, P."Diamond" Hayden, M.Marnell, J.Kelly, P.Prendergast, W.Walsh, D.Kennedy, Shem Downey, J.Heffernan, M.Kenny (capt.), J.Langton, W.Costigan, J.Mulcahy, L.Reidy. Sub: T.Walton for Costigan.

1951

Tipperary A.Reddan, M.Byrne, A.Brennan, J.Doyle, J.Finn (capt.), P.Stakelum, T.Doyle, P.Shanahan, J.Hough, E.Ryan, Mick Ryan, Tim Ryan, P.Kenny, "Sonny" Maher, S.Bannon. Sub: S.Kenny for P.Kenny.

Wexford R.Brennan, M.Byrne, N.O'Donnell, M.O'Hanlon, S.Thorpe, R.Rackard, W.Rackard, E.Wheeler, J.Morrissey, Padge Kehoe, J.Cummins, T.Russell, T.Flood, N.Rackard (capt), Paddy Kehoe.

1952

Cork D.Creedon, G.O'Riordan, J.Lyons, A.O'Shaughnessy, M.Fouhy, V.Twomey, S.O'Brien, J.Twomey, G.Murphy, W.Griffin, W.J.Daly, C.Ring, L.Abernethy, L.Dowling, P.Barry (capt.). Subs: M.O'Riordan for Griffin, J.Lynam for Abernethy.
Dublin K.Matthews, S.Cronin, P.Ryan, J.O'Callaghan, D.Ferguson, J.Prior (capt.), T.Fahy, C.Murphy, N.Allen, G.Kelly, R.McCarthy, S.Kennedy, J.Finan, A.O'Brien, A.Herbert. Subs: M.Wilson for Finan, M.Williams for Kennedy.

1953

Cork D.Creedon, G.O'Riordan, J.Lyons, A.O'Shaughnessy, M.Fouhy, D.Hayes, V.Twomey, J.Twomey G.Murphy, W.J.Daly, J.Hartnett, C.Ring (capt.), T.O'Sullivan, L.Dowling, P.Barry.
Galway S.Duggan, C.Corless, W.O'Neill, J.Brophy, M.Burke (capt.), J.Molloy, E.Quinn, J.Salmon, W.Duffy, J Duggan, H.Gordon, J.Killeen, M.McInerney, J.Gallagher, P Nolan. Subs: M.J.Flaherty for Nolan, P.Duggan for J.Duggan.

1954

Cork D.Creedon, G.O'Riordan, J.Lyons, A.O'Shaughnessy, M.Fouhy, V.Twomey, D.Hayes, G.Murphy, M.Woore, W.J.Daly, J.Hartnett, C.Ring (Capt.), J.Clifford, E.Goulding, P.Barry. Sub: Tom O'Sullivan for Paddy Barry.
Wexford A.Foley, W.Rackard, N.O'Donnell, M.O'Hanlon, J.English, R.Rackard, E.Wheeler, J.Morrissey, S.Hearne, Paddy Kehoe, T.Flood, Padge Kehoe (capt.), T.Ryan, N.Rackard, R.Donovan. Subs: T.Bolger for O'Donnell, D.Aherne for Paddy Kehoe.

1955

Wexford A.Foley, R.Rackard, N.O'Donnell (capt.), M.O'Hanlon, J.English, W.Rackard, M.Morrissey, J.Morrissey, S.Hearne, Paddy Kehoe, E.Wheeler, Padge Kehoe, T.Ryan, N.Rackard, T.Flood. Subs: O.Gough for Wheeler, Wheeler for Gough, D.Aherne for Ryan.
Galway T.Boland, J.Fives, B.Power, W.O'Neill, M.Burke, J.Molloy, T.Kelly, J.Salmon, W.Duffy, J.Duggan (capt.), J.Young, P.Duggan, P.Egan, J.Burke, T.Sweeney. Subs: H.Gordon for Power, M.Elwood for Sweeney.

1956

Wexford A.Foley, R.Rackard, N.O'Donnell, M.Morrissey, J.English (capt.), W.Rackard, J.Morrissey, S.Hearne, E.Wheeler, Padge Kehoe, M.Codd, T.Flood, T.Ryan, N.Rackard, T.Dixon.
Cork M.Cashman, J.Brohan, J.Lyons, A.O'Shaughnessy (capt.), M.Fouhy, W.J.Daly, P.Philpott, E.Goulding, P.Dowling, M.Regan, J.Hartnett, P.Barry, C.O'Shea, T.Kelly, C.Ring. Subs: V.Twomey for O'Shaughnessy, G.Murphy for Hartnet.

1957

Kilkenny O.Walsh, T.Walsh, J.Walsh, J.Maher, P.Buggy, M.Walsh, J.McGovern, M.Brophy, J.Sutton, D.Heaslip, M.Kenny, M.Kelly (capt.), R.Rocket, W.Dwyer, S.Clohessy. Sub: W.Walsh for Sutton.
Waterford R.Roche, T.Cunningham, A.Flynn, J.Barron, M.O'Connor, M.Óg Morrissey, S.Power, J.O'Connor, P.Grimes (capt.), M.Flannelly, T.Cheasty, L.Guinan, F.Walsh, J.Kiely, D.Whelan.

1958
Tipperary J.O'Grady, M.Byrne, M.Maher, K.Carey, J.Finn, A.Wall (capt.), John Doyle, J.Hough, T.English, D.Nealon, T.Larkin, Jimmy Doyle, L.Keane, L.Devaney, L Connolly.
Galway M.Sweeney, F.Spillane, P.Burke, S.Cullinane (capt.), J.Duggan, J.Fives, F.Benson, J.Salmon, P.J.Lally, T.Sweeney, J.Young, T.Kelly, P.J.Lawless, W.O'Neill, T.Conway. Subs: E.Dervan for Spillane, M.Fox for Young.

1959
Replay
Waterford E.Power, J.Harney, A.Flynn, J.Barron, M.Lacey, M.Óg Morrissey, Jackie Condon, S.Power, P.Grimes, M.Flannelly, T.Cheasty, F.Walsh (capt.), L.Guinan, T.Cunningham, J.Kiely. Subs: M.O'Connor for Lacey, D.Whelan for Cunningham.
Note: D.Whelan and C.Ware (Waterford) who played in the drawn game were replaced by T.Cunningham and M.Flannelly who retained their places for the replay.
Kilkenny O.Walsh, T.Walsh, J.Maher, P.Buggy, T.Kelly, J.McGovern, P.Kelly, M.Walsh, D.Heaslip, M.Fleming, S.Clohosey (capt.), R.Carroll, W.Dwyer, T.O'Connell. Sub: E.Keher for McGovern, M.Kelly for M.Fleming.
Note: Mick Brophy played in drawn game. Tim Kelly came on for replay. Subs in drawn game: Tim Kelly for J.McGovern, John Sutton for Mick Fleming, Mick Fleming for John Sutton.

1960
Wexford P.Nolan, J.Mitchell, N.O'Donnell (capt.), T.Neville, J.English, W.Rackard, J.Nolan, E.Wheeler, J.Morrissey, J.O'Brien, Padge Keogh, S.Quaid, O.McGrath, J.Harding, T.Flood. Subs: Seán Power for Quaid, M.Morrissey for Power.
Tipperary T.Moloney, M.Hassett, M.Maher, K.Carey, M.Burns, A.Wall (capt.), John Doyle, T.English, Tom Ryan (Killenaule), Jimmy Doyle, L.Devaney, D.Nealon.L.Connolly, Tom Moloughney, S.McLoughlin. Subs: W.Moloughney for McLoughlin, N.Murphy for English.

1961
Tipperary D.O'Brien, M.Hassett (capt.), M.Maher, K.Carey, M.Burns, A.Wall, John Doyle, M.O'Gara, T.English, Jimmy Doyle, L.Devaney, D.Nealon, J.McKenna, W.Moloughney, T.Moloughney. Subs: T.Ryan (Killenaule) for McKenna, J.Hough for O'Gara, S.McLoughlin for Wall.
Dublin J.Grey, D.Ferguson, N.Drumgoole (capt.), L.Foley, L.Ferguson, C.Hayes, S.Lynch, D.Foley, F.Whelan, A.Boothman, M.Bohan, L.Shannon, B.Boothman, P.Croke, W.Jackson. Sub: E.Malone for Bohan.

1962
Tipperary D.O'Brien, John Doyle, M.Maher, K.Carey, M.O'Gara, A.Wall, M.Burns, T.English, L.Devaney, Jimmy Doyle (capt.), J.McKenna, T.Ryan (Killenaule), D.Nealon, T.Moloughney, S.McLoughlin. Subs: L.Connolly for O'Gara, T.Ryan (Toomevara) for Jimmy Doyle.
Wexford P.Nolan, T.Neville, N.O'Donnell, E.Colfer, J.English, W.Rackard (capt.), J.Nolan, P.Wilson, M.Lyng, J.O'Brien, Padge Kehoe, P.Lynch, O.McGrath, E.Wheeler, T.Flood.

1963
Kilkenny O.Walsh, P.Larkin, C.Whelan, M.Treacy, S.Cleere (capt.), T.Carroll, M.Coogan, P.Moran, S.Clohosey, D.Heaslip, J.McGovern, E.Keher, T.Walsh, W.Dwyer.T.Murphy. Sub: O.Gough for McGovern.
Waterford E.Power, T.Cunningham, A.Flynn, J.Byrne, L.Guinan, M.Óg Morrissey, J.Irish, M.Dempsey, Joe Condon (capt.), M.Flannelly, T.Cheasty, F.Walsh, S.Power, J.Barron.P.Grimes. Subs: P.Flynn for E.Power, J.Meaney for Condon, M.Walsh for Byrne.

1964
Tipperary J.O'Donoghue, John Doyle, M.Maher, K.Carey, M.Burns, A.Wall, M.Murphy (capt.), T.English.M.Roche, Jimmy Doyle, L.Kiely, M Keating, D.Nealon.J.McKenna, S.McLoughlin. Subs: M.Lonergan for Maher, L.Devaney for Kiely.
Kilkenny O.Walsh, C.Whelan, P.Dillon, P.Larkin, P.Henderson, T.Carroll, M.Coogan, P.Moran, S.Buckley (capt.), S.Cleere, J.Teehan, E.Keher, T.Walsh, T.Forrestal, T.Murphy. Subs: W.Murphy (Carrickshock) for Coogan, D.Heaslip for T.Murphy.

1965
Tipperary J.O'Donoghue, John Doyle, M.Maher, K.Carey, M.Burns, A.Wall, L.Gaynor, T.English, M.Roche, Jimmy Doyle (capt.), L.Kiely, L.Devaney, D.Nealon, J.McKenna, S.McLoughlin.
Wexford P.Nolan, W.O'Neill, D.Quigley, E.Colfer, V.Staples, T.Neville (capt.), W.Murphy, P.Wilson, M.Byrne, J.O'Brien, J.Nolan, R.Shannon, P.Quigley, M.Codd, J.Foley. Subs: E.Wheeler for J.Nolan, O.McGrath for P.Quigley.

1966
Cork P.Barry, P.Doolan, T.O'Donoghue, D.Murphy, A.Connolly, J.O'Sullivan, P.Fitzgerald, J.McCarthy, M.Waters, S.Barry, J.O'Halloran, G.McCarthy (capt.), C.McCarthy, C.Sheehan, J.Bennett.
Kilkenny O.Walsh, P.Henderson, J Lynch (capt.), J.Treacy, S.Cleere, T.Carroll, M.Coogan, P.Moran, J.Teehan, E.Keher, C.Dunne, S.Buckley, J.Dunphy, P.Dillon, T.Walsh. Subs: T.Murphy for P.Dillon, P.Carroll for T.Murphy.

1967
Kilkenny O.Walsh, T.Carroll, P.Dillon, J.Treacy (capt.), S.Cleere, P.Henderson, M.Coogan, P.Moran, J.Teehan, E.Keher, T.Walsh, C.Dunne, J.Bennett, J.Lynch, Martin Brennan. Subs: R.Blanchfield for E.Keher, J.Kinsella for J.Bennett, P.Carroll for T.Walsh.
Tipperary J.O'Donoghue, J.Doyle, K.Carey, N.O'Gorman, M.Burns, A.Wall, L.Gaynor, T.English, M.Roche (capt.), J.Flanagan, L.Devaney, Jimmy Doyle, M.Keating, S.McLoughlin. Subs: L.Kiely for S.McLoughlin, M.Lonergan for M.Burns, P.J.Ryan for T.English.

1968
Wexford P.Nolan, T.Neville, E.Kelly, E.Colfer, V.Staples, D.Quigley (capt.), W.Murphy, P.Wilson, D.Bernie, P.Lynch, T.Doran, C.Jacob, J.O'Brien, S.Whelan, J.Berry. Sub: J.Quigley for S.Whelan.
Tipperary J.O'Donoghue, J.Costigan.N.O'Gorman, J.Gleeson, M.Burns, M.Roche (capt.), L.Gaynor, P.J.Ryan, D.Nealon, M.Keating, J.Ryan, J.Doyle, L.Devaney, J.McKenna, S.McLoughlin. Sub: F.Loughnane for Jimmy Doyle.

1969
Kilkenny
O.Walsh, T.Carroll, P.Dillon, J.Treacy, W.Murphy (Rower-Inistioge), P.Henderson, M.Coogan, F.Cummins, M.Lawler, C.Dunne, P.Delaney, E.Keher (capt.), J.Millea, Martin Brennan, T.Murphy. Subs: P.Kavanagh for Dunne, P.Moran for Delaney, S.Buckley for Murphy.
Cork P.Barry, A.Maher, T.O'Donoghue, D.Murphy (capt.), D.Clifford, W.Walsh, G.McCarthy, D.Coughlan, R.Tuohy, T.Ryan, C.Cullinane, P.Hegarty, J.McCarthy, R.Cummins, Eddie O'Brien. Subs: J.O'Halloron for O'Brien, J.Murphy for Tuohy, S.Looney for Ryan.

1970

Cork P.Barry (capt.), A.Maher, P.McDonnell, J.Horgan, D.Clifford, P.Hegarty, C.Roche, G.McCarthy, S.Looney, T.Ryan, W.Walsh, C.Cullinane, C.McCarthy, R.Cummins, Eddie O'Brien. Subs: S.Murphy for Clifford.
Wexford P.Nolan, E.Colfer, M.Collins (capt.), T.Neville, M.Browne, D.Quigley, T.O'Connor, D.Bernie, M.Jacob, M.Quigley, P.Quigley, J.Quigley, M.Butler, T.Doran, J.Berry. Subs: T.Byrne for Butler, J.Russell for Neville.

1971

Tipperary P.O'Sullivan, L.King, J.Kelly, J.Gleeson, T.O'Connor (capt.), M.Roche, L.Gaynor, P.J.Ryan, S.Hogan, F.Loughnane, N.O'Dwyer, D.Ryan, J.Flanagan, R.Ryan, M.Keating. Subs: Jimmy Doyle for Hogan, P.Byrne for Flanagan.
Kilkenny O.Walsh, P.Larkin, P.Dillon, J.Tracey, W.Murphy (Rower-Inistioge), P.Henderson (capt.), M.Coogan, F.Cummins, P.Lalor, M.Murphy, P.Delaney, E.Keher, Mick Brennan, K.Purcell, E.Byrne. Subs: P.Moran for W.Murphy, P.Cullen for Brennan, T.Carroll for Larkin.

1972

Kilkenny N.Skehan (capt.), P.Larkin, P.Dillon, J.Treacy, P.Lawlor, P.Henderson, E.Morrissey, F.Cummins, L.O'Brien, M.Crotty, P.Delaney, J.Kinsella, E.Byrne, K.Purcell, E.Keher. Subs: M.Murphy for Byrne, M.Coogan for Larkin, P.Moran for Kinsella.
Cork P.Barry, A.Maher, P.McDonnell, B.Murphy, F.Norberg (capt.), S.Looney, C.Roche, J.McCarthy, D.Coughlan, G.McCarthy, M.Malone, P.Hegarty, C.McCarthy, R.Cummins, S.O'Leary. Subs: Ted O'Brien for Norberg, D.Collins for Hegarty.

1973

Limerick S.Horgan, W.Moore, P.Hartigan, J.O'Brien, P.Bennis, E.Cregan, S.Foley, R.Bennis, E.Grimes (capt.), B.Hartigan, M.Dowling, L.O'Donoghue, F.Nolan, E.Rea, J.McKenna. Subs: T.Ryan for B.Hartigan.
Kilkenny N.Skehan, P.Larkin, N.Orr, P.Cullen, P.Lawlor, P.Henderson, B.Cody, F.Cummins, L.O'Brien, C.Dunne, P.Deloney (capt.), P.Broderick, M.Crotty, J.Lynch, Mick Brennan. Subs: K.Purcell for Broderick, W.Harte for Cummins, J.Kinsella for Lynch.

1974

Kilkenny N.Skehan, P.Larkin, N.Orr (capt.), J.Treacy, P.Lawlor, P.Henderson, T.McCormack, L.O'Brien, F.Cummins, M.Crotty, P.Delaney, W.Fitzpatrick, Mick Brennan, K.Purcell, E.Keher.
Limerick S.Horgan, W.Moore, P.Hartigan, J.O'Brien, T.Ryan, E.Cregan, S.Foley (capt.}, B.Hartigan, E.Grimes, J.McKenna, R.Bennis, M.Ruth, L.O'Donoghue, E.Rea.F.Nolan. Subs: P.Bennis for Ryan, P.Kelly for B.Hartigan, P.Fitzmaurice for McKenna.

1975

Kilkenny N.Skehan, P.Larkin, N.Orr, B.Cody, P.Lawlor, P.Henderson, T.McCormack, L.O'Brien, F.Cummins, M.Crotty, P.Delaney, W.Fitzpatrick (capt.), Mick Brennan, K.Purcell, E.Keher.
Galway M.Conneely, N.McInerney, J.Clarke, P.Lally.J.McDonagh, S.Silke, I.Clarke, S.Murphy, John Connolly (capt.), G.Cooney, F.Burke, P.J.Molloy, M.Barrett, P.J.Qualter, P.Fahy. Subs: M.Connolly for Barrett, Ted Murphy for Lally, J.Grealish for Murphy.

1976

Cork M.Coleman, B.Murphy, P.McDonnell, M.Doherty, P.Barry, J.Crowley, D.Coughlan, G.McCarthy, P.Moylan, M.Malone, B.Cummins, J.Barry Murphy, C.McCarthy, R.Cummins (capt.), S.O'Leary. Subs: E.O'Donoghue for O'Leary, J.Horgan for Barry.
Wexford J.Nolan, T.O'Connor, W.Murphy, J.Prendergast, L.Bennett, M.Jacob, C.Doran, E.Buggy, W.Rowesome, J.Murphy, M.Quigley, J.Quigley, M.Butler, T.Doran (capt.), C.Keogh. Subs: D.Rowesome for Keogh, M.Casey for W.Rowesome.

1977

Cork M.Coleman, B.Murphy, M.Doherty (capt.), J.Horgan, D.McCurtain, J.Crowley, D.Coughlan, T.Cashman, T.Crowley, M.Malone, G.McCarthy, J.Barry Murphy, C.McCarthy, R.Cummins, S.O'Leary. Subs: P.Moylan for Malone, Tadgh Murphy for G.McCarthy.
Wexford J.Nolan, T.O'Connor, W.Murphy, J.Prendergast, L.Bennett.M.Jacob, C.Doran, D.Bernie, E.Buggy, C.Keogh, M.Quigley, M.Butler, J.Quigley, T.Doran (capt.), J.Murphy. Subs: J.Russell for Prendergast, M.Casey for J.Murphy, E.Walsh for Bernie.

1978

Cork M.Coleman, B.Murphy, M.O'Doherty, J.Horgan, D.McCurtain, J.Crowley, D.Coughlan, T.Cashman, P.Moylan, J.Barry Murphy, G.McCarthy, T.Crowley, C.McCarthy (capt.), R.Cummins, S.O'Leary. Subs: J.Allen for Cashman, E.O'Donoghue for O'Leary.
Kilkenny N.Skehan, P.Prendergast, P.Larkin, D.O'Hara, J.Hennessy, G.Henderson (capt.), R.Reid, F.Cummins, L.O'Brien, K.Fennelly, M.Crotty, W.Fitzpatrick, Mick Brennan, B.Cody, M.Ruth. Subs T.Malone for Fennelly, P.Henderson for O'Brien.

1979

Kilkenny N.Skehan, P.Larkin, P.Prendergast, J.Henderson, R.Reid, G.Henderson, N.Brennan.J.Hennessy, F.Cummins, G.Fennelly (capt.), W.Fitzpatrick, L.O'Brien, Mick Brennan, M.Crotty, M.Ruth. Subs: K.Fennelly for Crotty, D.O'Hara for Prendergast.
Galway S.Shinnors, N.McInerney, C.Hayes, A.Fenton, J.McDonagh (capt.), S.Silke, I.Clarke, John Connolly, S.Mahon.B.Forde, F.Burke, Joe Connolly, P.J.Molloy, N.Lane, F.Gantley. Subs: S.Linnane for Forde, M.Whelan for Burke.

1980

Galway M.Conneely, C.Hayes, N.McInerney, Jimmy Cooney, S.Linnane, S.Silke, S.Coen, M.Connolly, S.Mahon, F.Burke, Joe Connolly (capt.), P.J.Molloy, B.Forde, John Connolly, N.Lane. Subs: F.Gantley for M.Connolly, J.Ryan for Molloy.
Limerick T.Quaid, D.Murray, L.Enright, Dom Punch, L.O'Donoghue, M.Carroll, S.Foley (capt.), J.Carroll, David Punch, P.Fitzmaurice, J.Flanagan, W.Fitzmaurice.O.O'Connor, J.McKenna, E.Cregan. Subs: B.Carroll for Flanagan, P.Herbert for M.Carroll, E.Grimes for W.Fitzmaurice.

1981

Offaly D.Martin, T.Donoghue, E.Coughlan, P.Fleury, A.Fogarty, P.Delaney, G.Coughlan, J.Kelly, L.Currams, P.Kirwan, B.Bermingham, M.Corrigan, P.Carroll, P.Horan (capt.), J.Flaherty. Subs: B.Keeshan for O'Donoghue, D.Owens for Kirwan.
Galway M.Conneely, S.Coen, N.McInerney, Jimmy Cooney, S.Linnane, S.Silke (capt.), I.Clarke, M.Connolly, S.Mahon, F.Gantley, Joe Connolly, P.J.Molloy, B.Forde, John Connolly, N.Lane. Subs: F.Burke for Gantley, P.Ryan for Forde.

1982

Kilkenny   N.Skehan, J.Henderson, B.Cody (capt.), D.O'Hara, N.Brennan, G.Henderson, P.Prendergast, J.Hennessy, F.Cummins, R.Power, G.Fennelly, K.Brennan, W.Fitzpatrick, C.Heffernan, L.Fennelly.

Cork   G.Cunningham, B.Murphy, M.O'Doherty, J.Blake, J.Buckley, J.Crowley, D.MacCurtain, T.Cashman, T.Crowley A.O'Sullivan, P.Horgan, J.Barry Murphy (capt.), S.O'Leary, R.Cummins, E.O'Donoghue. Subs: B.Óg Murphy for Buckley, K.Hennessy for O'Sullivan, F.Collins for MacCurtain.

1983

Kilkenny   N.Skehan, J.Henderson, B.Cody, D.O'Hara, J.Hennessy, G.Henderson, P.Prendergast, F.Cummins, G.Fennelly, R.Power, K.Brennan, L.Fennelly (capt.), W.Fitzpatrick, C.Heffernan, H.Ryan. Sub: P.Lannon for Power.

Cork   G.Cunningham, B.Murphy, D.O'Grady, D.MacCurtain, P.Horgan, J.Crowley, T.Cashman, J.Buckley, J.Fenton, B.Óg Murphy, K.Hennessy, T.Crowley, T.Mulcahy, J.Barry Murphy (capt.), E.O'Donoghue. Subs: F.Collins for Fenton, A.O'Sullivan for Mulcahy, S.O'Leary for B.Óg Murphy.

1984

Cork   G.Cunningham, D.Mulcahy, D.O'Grady, J.Hodgins, T.Cashman, J.Crowley, D.MacCurtain, J.Fenton (capt.), P.Hartnett, K.Hennessy, T.Crowley, A.O'Sullivan, T.Mulcahy, J.Barry Murphy, S.O'Leary.

Offaly   D.Martin, L.Carroll, E.Coughlan, P.Fleury (capt.), A.Fogarty, P.Delaney, G.Coughlan, T.Conneely, J.Kelly, M.Corrigan, B.Bermingham, P.Carroll, D.Fogarty, P.Horan, Joe Dooley. Subs: P.Corrigan for Bermingham, P.Kirwan for Dooley.

1985

Offaly   J.Troy, A.Fogarty, E.Coughlan, P.Fleury (capt.), T.Conneely, P.Delaney, G.Coughlan, D.Owens, J.Kelly, P.Corrigan, B.Bermingham, M.Corrigan, P.Cleary, P.Horan, J.Dooley. Subs: D.Fogarty for Owens, B.Keeshan for Conneely.

Galway   P.Murphy, O.Kilkenny, C.Hayes, S.Linnane, P.Finnerty, A.Keady, A.Kilkenny, M.Connolly (capt.), S.Mahon, M.McGrath, B.Lynskey, Joe Cooney, B.Forde, N.Lane, P.J.Molloy. Subs: J.Murphy for McGrath, A Cunningham for Fcrde, M.Haverty for Connolly.

1986

Cork   G.Cunningham, D.Mulcahy, R.Brown, J.Crowley, P.Hartnett, T.Cashman (capt.), D.Walsh, J.Fenton, J.Cashman, T.McCarthy, T.Mulcahy, A.O'Sullivan, G.Fitzgerald, J.Barry Murphy, K.Hennessy. Sub: K.Kingston for Fenton.

Galway   J.Commins, S.Linnane, C.Hayes, O.Kilkenny, P.Finnerty, A.Keady, G.McInerney, S.Mahon, P.Piggott, A.Kilkenny, B.Lynskey, M.Naughton, A.Cunningham, Joe Cooney, N.Lane (capt.). Subs: P.J.Molloy for Piggott, M.Connolly for Mahon, P.Murphy for Cunnningham.

1987

Galway   J.Commins, S.Linnane, C.Hayes (capt.), O.Kilkenny, P.Finnerty, A.Keady, G.McInerney, S.Mahon, P.Malone, M.McGrath, J.Cooney, M.Naughton, E.Ryan, B.Lynskey, A.Cunningham. Subs.N.Lane for Naughton, P.J.Molloy for Cunningham, A.Kilkenny for McGrath.

Kilkenny   K.Fennelly, J.Hennessy, P.Prendergast (capt.), J.Henderson, L.Walsh, G.Henderson, S.Fennelly, G.Fennelly, L.Ryan, K.Brennan, C.Heffernan, R.Power, P.Walsh, L.Fennelly, H.Ryan. Subs: T.Lennon for P.Walsh, L.McCarthy for Power.

1988

Galway   J.Commins, S.Linnane C.Hayes (capt.), O.Kilkenny, P Finnerty, A.Keady, G.McInerney, M.Coleman, P.Malone, A.Cunningham, B.Lynskey, M.Naughton, M.McGrath, Joe Cooney, E.Ryan. Subs: N.Lane for Cunningham, A.Kilkenny for Naughton, G.Burke for Lynskey.

Tipperary   K.Hogan, P.Delaney, C.O'Donovan, J.Heffernan, B.Ryan, N.Sheehy, J.Kennedy, Colm Bonnar, D.Ryan, D.O'Connell, J.Leary, P.Fox, N.English (capt.), A.Ryan, J.Hayes. Sub: Cormac Bonnar for J.Hayes.

1989

Tipperary   K.Hogan, J.Heffernan, C.O'Donovan, N.Sheehy, Conal Bonnar, B.Ryan (Capt.}, J.Kennedy, Colm Bonnar, D.Carr, J.Leahy, D.Ryan, M.Cleary, P.Fox, Cormac Bonnar, N.English. Subs: J.Hayes for Cormac Bonnar, D.O'Connell for Leary, A.Ryan for Cleary.

Antrim   N.Patterson, G.O'Kane, T.Donnelly, D.Donnelly, J.McNaughton, D.McKinley, L.McKeegan, P.McKillen, D.McMullan, C.Barr (Capt.), A.McCarry, O.McFetridge, D.Armstrong, B.Donnelly, T.McNaughton. Subs: D.McNaughton for McMullan, D.McKillop for O'Kane, M.Sullivan for McKinley.

1990

Cork   G.Cunningham, J.Considine, D.Walsh, S.O'Gormon, S.McCarthy, J.Cashman, K.McGuckian, B.O'Sullivan, T.McCarthy, G.Fitzgerald, M.Foley, Tony O'Sullivan, T.McCarthy, T.Mulcahy (Capt.), K.Hennessy, J.Fitzgibbon. Subs: D.Quirke for McGuckian, C.Casey for B.O'Sullivan.

Galway   J.Commins, D.Fahy, S.Treacy, O.Kilkenny, P.Finnerty, T.Keady, G.McInerney, M.Coleman, P.Malone, A.Cunningham, Joe Cooney (Capt.), M.Naughton, M.McGrath, N.Lane, E.Ryan. Subs: T.Monaghan for Malone, B.Lynskey for Cunningham.

1991

Tipperary   K.Hogan, P.Delaney, N.Sheedy, M.Ryan, Colm Bonnar, B.Ryan, Conal Bonnar, D.Carr (Capt.), A.Ryan, M.Cleary, D.Ryan, J.Leahy, P.Fox, Cormac Bonnar, N.English. Subs: C.Stakelum for Cormac Bonnar, D.O'Connell for N.English.

Kilkenny   M.Walsh, W.Hennessy, J.Henderson, L.Simpson, L.Walsh, P.Dwyer, E.O'Connor, R.Power, M.Phelan, J.Power, C.Heffernan (Capt.), D.J.Carey, E.Morrissey, L.Fennelly, L.McCarthy. Subs: A.Ronan for McCarthy, L.Ryan for Power.

1992

Kilkenny   M.Walsh, E.O'Connor, P.Dwyer, L.Simpson, L.Walsh, P.O'Neill, W.O'Connor, M.Phelan, W.Hennessy, L.McCarthy, J.Power, D.J.Carey, E.Morrissey, L.Fennelly (Capt.), J.Brennan. Subs: C.Heffernan for Brennan, A.Ronan for Morrissey.

Cork   G.Cunningham, S.O'Gorman, D.Mulcahy, B.Corcoran, C.Casey, J.Cashman, D.Walsh, P.Buckley, S.McCarthy, Teddy McCarthy, T.Mulcahy, A.O'Sullivan, G.Fitzgerald (Capt.), J.Fitzgibbon, K.Hennessy. Subs: P.Hartnett for Walsh, G.Manley for Fitzgerald, M.Foley for Buckley.

1993

Kilkenny   M.Walsh, E.O'Connor (Capt.), P.Dwyer, L.Simpson, L.Keoghan, P.O'Neill, W.O'Connor, W.Hennessy, M.Phelan, L.McCarthy, J.Power, D.J.Carey, E.Morrissey, P.J.Delaney, A.Ronan. Subs: J.Brennan for Morrissey, T.Murphy for Phelan, C.Heffernan for Delaney.

Galway   R.Burke, P.Cooney, S.Treacy, M.Killilea, T.Helebert, G.McInerney, P.Kelly, M.Coleman, P.Malone, B.Keogh, J.McGrath, J.Cooney, M.McGrath (Capt.), J.Rabbitte, L.Burke. Subs: J.Campbell for J.McGrath, P.Finnerty for Keogh.

1994

Offaly   Jim Troy, S.McGuckian, K.Kinahan, M.Hanamy (Capt.), B.Whelahan, H.Rigney, K.Martin, J.Pilkington, D.Regan, Johnny Dooley, John Troy, Joe Dooley, B.Dooley, B.Kelly, D.Pilkington. Sub: P.O'Connor for Joe Dooley.
Limerick   J.Quaid, S.McDonagh, M.Nash, J.O'Connor, D.Clarke, G.Hegarty, D.Nash, C.Carey, M.Houlihan, F.Carroll, G.Kirby (Capt.), M.Galligan, T.J.Ryan, P.Heffernan, D.Quigley. Sub: L.O'Connor for Galligan.

1995

Clare   D.Fitzgerald, M.O'Halloran, B.Lohan, F.Lohan, L.Doyle, S.McMahon, A.Daly (Capt.), J.O'Connor, O.Baker, F.Tuohy, P.J.O'Connell, F.Hegarty, S.McNamara, C.Clancy, G.O'Loughlin. Subs: E.Taaffe for McNamara, C.Lyons for Clancy, A.Neville for Taaffe.
Offaly   D.Hughes, S.McGuckian, K.Kinahan, M.Hanamy, B.Whelahan, H.Rigney, K.Martin, J.Pilkington (Capt.), D.Regan, Johnny Dooley, John Troy, M.Duignan, B.Dooley, P.O'Connor, Joe Dooley. Subs: D.Pilkington for O'Connor, B.Kelly for Joe Dooley.

1996

Wexford   D.Fitzhenry, C.Kehoe, G.Cushe, J.O'Connor, R.Guiney, L.Dunne, L.O'Gorman, A.Fenlon, G.O'Connor, R.McCarthy, M.Storey (Capt.), L.Murphy, T.Dempsey, G.Laffan, E.Scallan. Subs: B.Byrne for Murphy, P.Finn for Guiney, P.Codd for Laffan.
Limerick   J.Quaid, S.McDonagh, M.Nash, D.Nash, D.Clarke, C.Carey (Capt.), M.Foley, M.Houlihan, S.O'Neill, F.Carroll, G.Kirby, B.Foley, O.O'Neill, D.Quigley, T.J.Ryan. Subs: P.Tobin for O.O'Neill, B.Tobin for Ryan, T.Herbert for B.Foley.

1997

Clare   D.Fitzgerald, M.O'Halloran, B.Lohan, F.Lohan, L.Doyle, S.McMahon, A.Daly (Capt.), O.Baker, C.Lynch, J.O'Connor, C.Clancy, P.J.O'Connell, N.Gilligan, G.O'Loughlin, F.Tuohy. Subs: F.Hegarty for Tuohy, D.Forde for O'Connell, B.Murphy for Hegarty.
Tipperary   B.Cummins, P.Shelly, N.Sheehy, M.Ryan, L.Sheedy, Colm Bonnar, Conal Bonnar, T.Dunne, C.Gleeson (Capt.), L.McGrath, D.Ryan, J.Leahy, M.Cleary, E.O'Neill, B.O'Meara. Subs: A.Ryan for McGrath, L.Cahill for Cleary.

1998

Offaly   S.Byrne, S.Whelahan, K.Kinahan, M.Hanamy, B.Whelahan, H.Rigney (Capt.), K.Martin, J.Pilkington, Johnny Dooley, M.Duignan, John Troy, G.Hannify, B.Dooley, J.Errity, Joe Dooley. Subs: P.Mulhaire for G.Hannify, D.Hannify for B.Dooley, J.Ryan for Johnny Dooley.
Kilkenny   J.Dermody, T.Hickey (Capt.), P.O'Neill, W.O'Connor, M.Kavanagh, C.Brennan, L.Keoghan, P.Larkin, P.Barry, D.J.Carey, A.Comerford, B.McEvoy, K.O'Shea, P.J.Delaney, C.Carter. Subs: N.Moloney for O'Shea, S.Ryan for Comerford, J.Costelloe for Kavanagh.

1999

Cork   D.Óg Cusack, F.Ryan, D.O'Sullivan, J.Browne, W.Sherlock, B.Corcoran, S.Óg Ó hAilpín, M.Landers (Capt.), M.O'Connell, T.McCarthy, F.McCormack, N.Ronan, S.McGrath, J.Deane, B.O'Connor. Subs: A.Browne for Ronan, K.Murray for Landers.
Kilkenny   J.McGarry, P.Larkin, C.Brennan, W.O'Connor, M.Kavanagh, P.O'Neill, P.Barry, A.Comerford, D.Byrne (Capt.), D.J.Carey, J.Power, B.McEvoy, K.O'Shea, H.Shefflin, C.Carter. Subs: P.J.Delaney for Power, N.Moloney for Carter.

2000

Kilkenny   J.McGarry, M.Kavanagh, N.Hickey, W.O'Connor (Capt.), P.Larkin, E.Kennedy, P.Barry, A.Comerford, B.McEvoy, D.Byrne, J.Power, J.Hoyne, C.Carter, D.J.Carey, H.Shefflin. Subs: C.Brennan for McEvoy, E.Brennan for C.Brennan.
Offaly   S.Byrne, S.Whelahan, K.Kinahan, N.Claffey, B.Whelahan, J.Errity, K.Martin, Johnny Dooley, G.Oakley, J.Pilkington, G.Hanniffy, B.Murphy, M.Duignan, J.Ryan, Joe Dooley. Subs: D.Franks for Claffey, J.Troy for Ryan, P.Mulhare for Murphy.

2001

Tipperary   B.Cummins, T.Costello, P.Maher, P.Ormonde, E.Corcoran, D.Kennedy, P.Kelly, T.Dunne (Capt.), E.Enright, M.O'Leary, J.Carroll, P.Corbett, E.Kelly, D.Ryan, E.O'Neill. Subs: D.Fahy for Costello, P.O'Brien for O'Neill, M.Ryan for P.Kelly, C.Gleeson for Kennedy.
Galway   M.Crimmins, G.Kennedy, M.Healy, O.Canning, D.Hardiman, L.Hodgins, C.Moore, D.Tierney, R.Murray, J.Rabbitte, M.Kerins, K.Broderick, A.Kerins, E.Cloonan, F.Healy. Subs: B.Higgins for Hardiman, O.Fahy for Rabbitte.

2002

Kilkenny   J.McGarry, M.Kavanagh, N.Hickey, P.Larkin, R.Mullally, P.Barry, J.J.Delaney, A.Comerford (Capt.), D.Lyng, J.Hoyne, H.Shefflin, J.Coogan, E.Brennan, M.Comerford, D.J.Carey. Subs: C.Carter for Coogan, B.McEvoy for Hoyne, J.Power for Brennan.
Clare   D.Fitzgerald, B.Quinn, B.Lohan, F.Lohan, D.Hoey, S.McMahon, G.Quinn, J.Reddan, C.Lynch, J.O'Connor, T.Griffin, A.Markham, T.Carmody, N.Gilligan, D.Forde. Subs: O.Baker for Reddan, G.Considine for Forde, A.Quinn for Markham, C.Plunkett for Baker.

2003

Kilkenny   J.McGarry, M.Kavanagh, N.Hickey, J.Ryall, S.Dowling, P.Barry, J.J.Delaney, D.Lyng, P.Mullally, H.Shefflin, J.Hoyne, T.Walsh, D.J.Carey (Capt.), M.Comerford, E.Brennan. Subs: C.Phelan for Walsh, A.Comerford for Ryall, R.Mullally for P.Mullally, J.Coogan for Brennan.
Cork   D.Óg Cusack, W.Sherlock, D.O'Sullivan, P.Mulcahy, T.Kenny, R.Curran, Seán Óg Ó hAilpín, J.Gardiner, M.O'Connell, B.O'Connor, N.McCarthy, T.McCarthy, Setanta Ó hAilpín, J.Deane, A.Browne. Subs: J.O'Connor for O'Connell, S.McGrath for B.O'Connor.

2004

Cork   D.Óg Cusack, W.Sherlock, D.O'Sullivan, B.Murphy, J.Gardiner, R.Curran, S.Óg Ó hAilpín, T.Kenny, J.O'Connor, B.O'Connor (Capt.), N.McCarthy, T.McCarthy, K.Murphy, B.Corcoran, J.Deane. Sub: J.Browne for B.Murphy.
Kilkenny   J.McGarry, M.Kavanagh, N.Hickey, J.Ryall, T.Walsh, P.Barry, J.J.Delaney, D.Lyng, K.Coogan, H.Shefflin, J.Hoyne, D.J.Carey, J.Fitzpatrick, M.Comerford, E.Brennan. Subs: C.Phelan for Fitzpatrick, S.Dowling for Coogan.

2005

Cork   D.Óg Cusack, B.Murphy, D.O'Sullivan, P.Mulcahy, J.Gardiner, R.Curran, S.Óg Ó hAilpín (Capt.), T.Kenny, J.O'Connor, K.Murphy (Sarsfields), N.McCarthy, T.McCarthy, B.O'Connor, B.Corcoran, J.Deane. Subs: N.Ronan for K.Murphy (Sarsfields), K.Murphy (Erin's Own) for N.McCarthy.
Galway   L.Donoghue, D.Joyce, T.Óg Regan, O.Canning, D.Hardiman, S.Kavanagh, D.Collins, F.Healy, D.Tierney, R.Murray, D.Forde, A.Kerins, G.Farragher, N.Healy, D.Hayes. Subs: K.Broderick for N.Healy, K.Hayes for Forde.

2006

Kilkenny   J.McGarry, M.Kavanagh, N.Hickey, J.Tyrrell, T.Walsh, J.Tennyson, J.Ryall, D.Lyng, J.Fitzpatrick, E.Brennan, M.Comerford, E.Larkin, R.Power, H.Shefflin, A.Fogarty. Subs: W.O'Dwyer for Larkin, R.Mullally for Lyng.

Cork   D.Óg Cusack, P.Mulcahy, D.O'Sullivan, B.Murphy, J.Gardiner, R.Curran, S.Óg Ó hAilpín, T.Kenny, J.O'Connor, T.McCarthy, N.McCarthy, N.Ronan, B.O'Connor, B.Corcoran, J.Deane. Subs: K.Murphy (Sarsfields) for Ronan, W.Sherlock for Mulcahy, C.Naughton for T.McCarthy, C.O'Connor for K.Murphy, C.Cusack for Kenny.

2007

Kilkenny   P.J.Ryan, M.Kavanagh, N.Hickey, J.Tyrrell, T.Walsh, B.Hogan, J.J.Delaney, D.Lyng, J.Fitzpatrick, W.O'Dwyer, M.Comerford, E.Larkin, E.Brennan, H.Shefflin, A.Fogarty. Subs: J.Tennyson for Hickey, R.Power for O'Dwyer, M.Fennelly for Shefflin.

Limerick   B.Murray, D.Reale, S.Lucey, S.Hickey, P.Lawlor, B.Geary, M.Foley, D.O'Grady, M.O'Brien, M.Fitzgerald, O.Moran, S.O'Connor, A.O'Shaughnessy, B.Begley, D.Ryan. Subs: N.Moran for M.O'Brien, J.O'Brien for O'Connor, P.Tobin for Fitzgerald, K.Tobin for Ryan, M.O'Riordan for Lawlor.

2008

Kilkenny   P.J.Ryan, M.Kavanagh, N.Hickey, J.Tyrrell, T.Walsh, B.Hogan, J.J.Delaney, J.Fitzpatrick, D.Lyng, H.Shefflin, M.Comerford, E.Larkin, E.Brennan, R.Power, A.Fogarty. Subs: T.J.Reid for Comerford, J.McGarry for Ryan.

Waterford   C.Hennessy, A.Kearney, D.Prendergast, E.Murphy, T.Browne, K.McGrath, K.Moran, M.Walsh, J.Nagle, D.Shanahan, S.Molumphy, S.Prendergast, E.McGrath, J.Mullane, E.Kelly. Subs: S.O'Sullivan for Nagle, J.Kennedy for S.Prendergast, P.Flynn for E.McGrath, T.Feeney for D.Prendergast, D.Bennett for Shanahan.

2009

Kilkenny   P.J.Ryan, M.Kavanagh, J.J.Delaney, J.Tyrrell, T Walsh, B.Hogan, J.Tennyson, D.Lyng, M.Rice, E.Brennan, E.Larkin, R.Power, R.Hogan, H.Shefflin, A.Fogarty. Subs: T.J.Reid for Fogarty, M.Fennelly for Lyng, M.Comerford for R.Hogan.

Tipperary   B.Cummins, P.Stapleton, P.Maher, P.Curran, D.Fanning, C.O'Mahony, J.Woodlock, S.McGrath, N.McGrath, J.O'Brien, S.Callanan, P.Kerwick, E.Kelly, L.Corbett. Subs: B.Dunne for O'Brien, W.Ryan for Kerwick, M.Webster for Woodlock.

2010

Tipperary   B.Cummins, P.Stapleton, P.Curran, M.Cahill, D.Fanning, C.O'Mahony, Pádraic Maher, B.Maher, S.McGrath, G.Ryan, L.Corbett, Patrick Maher, E.Kelly, N.McGrath, J.O'Brien. Subs: C.O'Brien for O'Mahony, S.Callanan for J.O'Brien, B.Dunne for McGrath, D.Young for Fanning, S.Hennessy for B.Maher.

Kilkenny   P.J.Ryan, J.Dalton, N.Hickey, J.Tyrrell, T.Walsh, J.Tennyson, J.J.Delaney, J.Fitzpatrick, M.Fennelly, T.J.Reid, H.Shefflin, E.Larkin, E.Brennan, R.Power, A.Fogarty. Subs: M.Rice for Shefflin, D.Lyng for Fitzpatrick, M.Comerford for Brennan, R.Hogan for Fogarty, J.Mulhall for Reid.

2011

Kilkenny   D.Herity, J.Tyrrell, N.Hickey, P.Murphy, T.Walsh, B.Hogan, J.J.Delaney, M.Fennelly, M.Rice, E.Brennan, R.Power, H.Shefflin, C.Fennelly, E.Larkin, R.Hogan. Subs: T.J.Reid for Brennan, J.Mulhall for R.Hogan.

Tipperary   B.Cummins, P.Stapleton, P.Curran, M.Cahill, J.O'Keeffe, C.O'Mahony, Pádraic Maher, G.Ryan, S.McGrath, S.Callanan, N.McGrath, Patrick Maher, E.Kelly, J.O'Brien, L.Corbett. Subs: B.Maher for O'Keeffe, B.Dunne for S.McGrath, P.Bourke for Callanan, D.Young for O'Mahony, J.O'Neill for O'Brien.

2012
Replay

Kilkenny   D.Herity, P.Murphy, J.J.Delaney, J.Tyrrell, T.Walsh, B.Hogan, K.Joyce, M.Fennelly, C.Buckley, E.Larkin, H.Shefflin, T.J.Reid, W.Walsh, R.Hogan, R.Power. Subs: C.Fennelly for W.Walsh, N.Hickey for Joyce, A.Fogarty for Reid.
Note: C.Fennelly, and A.Fogarty played in the drawn game instead of W.Walsh and C.Buckley. Sub in the drawn game – M.Ruth for C.Fennelly.

Galway   J.Skehill, F.Moore, K.Hynes, J.Coen, D.Collins, T.Óg Regan, N.Donohue, I.Tannian, A.Smith, N.Burke, D.Burke, J.Canning, J.Regan, C.Donnellan, D.Hayes. Subs: J.Cooney for Donohue, J.Glynn for J.Regan, F.Flannery for Skehill, C.Cooney for N.Burke, D.Glennon for Smith.
Note: Galway started with the same 15 as the drawn match. Subs in the drawn match – C.Cooney for Regan, J.Glynn for C.Cooney, J.Cooney for N.Burke, D.Glennon for Hayes.

2013
Replay

Clare   P.Kelly, D.O'Donovan, D.McInerney, C.Dillon, P.O'Connor, B.Bugler, Conor Ryan, C.Gslvin, P.Donnellan, J.Conlon, T.Kelly, Colin Ryan, P.Collins, S.O'Donnell, C.McGrath. Subs: C.McInerney for Galvin, N.O'Connell for Collins, D.Honan for O'Donnell, S.Morey for Kelly.
Note: D.Honan started instead of S.O'Donnell in drawn match. Subs in drawn match – C.McInerney for Honan, N.O'Connell for Galvin, F.Lynch for Conlon.

Cork   A.Nash, B.Murphy, S.O'Neill, C.O'Sullivan, C.Joyce, S.McDonnell, W.Egan, L.McLoughlin, D.Kearney, S.Harnedy, C.McCarthy, P.Cronin, L.O'Farrell, P.Horgan, C.Lehane. Subs: S.White for Egan, S.Moylan for O'Farrell, T.Kenny for Kearney, C.Naughton for McCarthy, K.Murphy for McDonnell.
Note: J.Coughlan started instead of C.McCarthy in the drawn match. Subs in the drawn match – S.Moylan for Coughlan, C.McCarthy for McLoughlin, C.Naughton for McCarthy, T.Kenny for Egan, S.White for Kearney.

2014
Replay

Kilkenny   E.Murphy, P.Murphy, J.J.Delaney, J.Tyrrell, P.Walsh, K.Joyce, C.Buckley, M.Fennelly, C.Fogarty, C.Fennelly, R.Hogan, E.Larkin, R.Power, T.J.Reid, J.Power. Subs: H.Shefflin for Hogan, L.Ryan for M.Fennelly.
Note: J.Holden, B.Hogan and W.Walsh started the drawn match instead of P.Walsh, K.Joyce and J.Power. Subs in the drawn match – A.Fogarty for Walsh, P.Walsh for Holden, H.Shefflin for C.Fennelly, J.Power for R.Hogan.

Tipperary   D.Gleeson, C.Barrett, J.Barry, P.Stapleton, B.Maher, Pádraic Maher, K.Bergin, S.McGrath, J.Woodlock, G.Ryan, N.McGrath, L.Corbett, J.O'Dwyer, S.Callanan, P.Maher. Subs: M.Cahill for S.McGrath, C.O'Mahony for Ryan, S.Bourke for Corbett, E.Kelly for N.McGrath, C.O'Brien for O'Dwyer.
Note: Tipperary started with the same 15 in the drawn match. Subs in the drawn match – M.Cahill for Ryan, E.Kelly for Woodlock, J.Forde for S.McGrath, J.O'Brien for Callanan.

2015

Kilkenny E.Murphy, P.Murphy, J.Holden, S.Prendergast, P.Walsh, K.Joyce, C.Buckley, M.Fennelly, C.Fogarty, W.Walsh, R.Hogan, T.J.Reid, G.Aylward, C.Fennelly, E.Larkin. Subs: R.Power for R.Hogan, J.Power for Aylward.
Galway C.Callanan, J.Coen, J.Hanbury, P.Mannion, A.Harte, I.Tannian, Daithí Burke, A.Smith, David Burke, C.Whelan, C.Donnellan, J.Glynn, J.Flynn, J.Canning, C.Mannion. Subs: D.Collins for Harte, C.Cooney for Smith, G.Lally for Donnellan, S.Moloney for Flynn.

2016

Tipperary D.Gleeson, C.Barrett, J.Barry, M.Cahill, S.Kennedy, R.Maher, Pádraic Maher, B.Maher, M.Breen, D.McCormack, Patrick Maher, N.McGrath, J.McGrath, S.Callanan, J.O'Dwyer. Subs: J.Forde for Breen, N.O'Meara for McCormack, D.Maher for Cahill, K.Bergin for N.McGrath, T.Hamill for Kennedy.
Kilkenny E.Murphy, S.Prendergast, J.Holden, P.Murphy, P.Walsh, K.Joyce, C.Buckley, T.J.Reid, C.Fogarty, W.Walsh, R.Hogan, E.Larkin, K.Kelly, C.Fennelly, L.Blanchfield. Subs: R.Lennon for Joyce, L.Ryan for Larkin.

2017

Galway C.Callanan, A.Tuohey, Daithí Burke, A.Harte, P.Mannion, G.McInerney, J.Hanbury, J.Coen, David Burke, J.Cooney, C.Mannion, J.Canning, C.Whelan, J.Glynn, C.Cooney. Subs: N.Burke for Glynn, J.Flynn for Mannion, S.Moloney for David Burke.
Waterford S.O'Keeffe, S.Fives, B.Coughlan, N.Connors, T.de Búrca, Philip Mahony, K.Bennett, D.Fives, J.Barron, K.Moran, M.Walsh, A.Gleeson, Pauric Mahony, J.Dillon, S.Bennett. Subs: M.Shanahan for S.Bennett, B.O'Halloran for Dillon, T.Ryan for Walsh, C.Dunford for Barron, P.Curran for K.Bennett.

CAPTAINS OF WINNING ALL-IRELAND SENIOR HURLING TEAMS

1887	J. Stapleton (Tipperary)
1888	No final
1889	N. O'Shea (Dublin)
1890	D. Lane (Cork)
1891	J. Mahony (Kerry)
1892	W. O'Callaghan (Cork)
1893	J. Murphy (Cork)
1894	S. Hayes (Cork)
1895	M. Maher (Tipperary)
1896	M. Maher (Tipperary)
1897	D. Grimes (Limerick)
1898	M. Maher (Tipperary)
1899	T. Condon (Tipperary)
1900	E. Hayes (Tipperary)
1901	J. Coughlan (London)
1902	J. Kelleher (Cork)
1903	S. Riordan (Cork)
1904	J. Doheny (Kilkenny)
1905	D. J. Stapleton (Kilkenny)
1906	T. Semple (Tipperary)
1907	R. "Drug" Walsh (Kilkenny)
1908	T. Semple (Tipperary)
1909	R. "Drug" Walsh (Kilkenny)
1910	R. Doyle (Wexford)
1911	No Final
1912	S. Walton (Kilkenny)
1913	R."Drug" Walsh (Kilkenny)
1914	A. Power (Clare)
1915	J. Finlay (Laois)
1916	J. Leahy (Tipperary)
1917	J. Ryan (Dublin)
1918	W. Hough (Limerick)
1919	J. Kennedy (Cork)
1920	R. Mockler (Dublin)
1921	R. McConkey (Limerick)
1922	W. Dunphy (Kilkenny)
1923	M. Kenny (Galway)
1924	F. Wall (Dublin)
1925	J. Leahy (Tipperary)
1926	S. Óg Murphy (Cork)
1927	M. Gill (Dublin)
1928	S. Óg Murphy (Cork)

Year	Player	Year	Player
1929	D. Barry-Murphy (Cork)	1974	N. Orr (Kilkenny)
1930	J. J. Callanan (Tipperary)	1975	W. Fitzpatrick (Kilkenny)
1931	E. Coughlan (Cork)	1976	R. Cummins (Cork)
1932	J. Walsh (Kilkenny)	1977	M. O'Doherty (Cork)
1933	E. Doyle (Kilkenny)	1978	C. McCarthy (Cork)
1934	T. Ryan (Limerick)	1979	K. Fennelly (Kilkenny)
1935	L. Meagher (Kilkenny)	1980	Joe Connolly (Galway)
1936	M. Mackey (Limerick)	1981	P. Horan (Offaly)
1937	J. Lanigan (Tipperary)	1982	B. Cody (Kilkenny)
1938	M. Daniels (Dublin)	1983	L. Fennelly (Kilkenny)
1939	J. Walsh (Kilkenny)	1984	J. Fenton (Cork)
1940	M. Mackey (Limerick)	1985	P. Fleury (Offaly)
1941	C. Buckley (Cork)	1986	T. Cashman (Cork)
1942	J. Lynch (Cork)	1987	C. Hayes (Galway)
1943	M. Kennefick (Cork)	1988	C. Hayes (Galway)
1944	S. Condon (Cork)	1989	B. Ryan (Tipperary)
1945	J. Maher (Tipperary)	1990	T. Mulcahy (Cork)
1946	C. Ring (Cork)	1991	D. Carr (Tipperary)
1947	D. Kennedy (Kilkenny)	1992	L. Fennelly (Kilkenny)
1948	J. Ware (Waterford)	1993	E. O'Connor (Kilkenny)
1949	P. Stakelum (Tipperary)	1994	M. Hanamy (Offaly)
1950	S. Kenny (Tipperary)	1995	A. Daly (Clare)
1951	J. Finn (Tipperary)	1996	M. Storey (Wexford)
1952	P. Barry (Cork)	1997	A. Daly (Clare)
1953	C. Ring (Cork)	1998	H. Rigney (Offaly)
1954	C. Ring (Cork)	1999	M. Landers (Cork)
1955	N. O'Donnell (Wexford)	2000	W. O'Connor (Kilkenny)
1956	J. English (Wexford)	2001	T. Dunne (Tipperary)
1957	M. Kelly (Kilkenny)	2002	A. Comerford (Kilkenny)
1958	A. Wall (Tipperary)	2003	D. J. Carey (Kilkenny)
1959	F. Walsh (Waterford)	2004	B. O'Connor (Cork)
1960	N. O'Donnell (Wexford)	2005	S. Óg Ó hAilpín (Cork)
1961	M. Hassett (Tipperary)	2006	J. Tyrrell (Kilkenny)
1962	Jimmy Doyle (Tipperary)	2007	H. Shefflin (Kilkenny)
1963	S. Cleere (Kilkenny)	2008	J. Fitzpatrick (Kilkenny)
1964	M. Murphy (Tipperary)	2009	M. Fennelly (Kilkenny)
1965	Jimmy Doyle (Tipperary)	2010	E. Kelly (Tipperary)
1966	G. McCarthy (Cork)	2011	B. Hogan (Kilkenny)
1967	J. Treacy (Kilkenny)	2012	E. Larkin (Kilkenny)
1968	D. Quigley (Wexford)	2013	P. Donnellan (Clare)
1969	E. Keher (Kilkenny)	2014	L. Ryan (Kilkenny)
1970	P. Barry (Cork)	2015	J. Holden (Kilkenny)
1971	T. O'Connor (Tipperary)	2016	B. Maher (Tipperary)
1972	N. Skehan (Kilkenny)	2017	D. Burke (Galway)
1973	E. Grimes (Limerick)		

SENIOR HURLING FINAL REFEREES

1887	P. White (Offaly)
1889	P. Tobin (Dublin)
1890	J. Sheehy (Limerick)
1891	P. Tobin (Dublin)
1892	D. Fraher (Waterford)
1893	J. J. Kenny (Dublin)
1894	J. J. Kenny (Dublin)
1895	J. J. Kenny (Dublin)
1896	D. Wood (Dublin)
1897	J. J. McCabe (Dublin)
1898	J. J. McCabe (Dublin)
1899	A. McKeogh (Dublin)
1900	J. McCarthy (Kilkenny)
1901	J. McCarthy (Kilkenny)
1902	L. J. O'Toole (Dublin)
1903	J. McCarthy (Kilkenny)
1904	M. F. Crowe (Limerick)
1905	M. F. Crowe (Limerick)
1906	T. Irwin (Cork)
1907	M. F. Crowe (Limerick)
1908	T. Irwin (Cork), Draw; J. McCarthy (Cork), Replay
1909	M. F. Crowe (Limerick)
1910	M. F. Crowe (Limerick)
1912	M. F. Crowe (Limerick)
1913	M. F. Crowe (Limerick)
1914	J. Lalor (Kilkenny)
1915	W. Walsh (Waterford)
1916	W. Walsh (Waterford)
1917	W. Walsh (Waterford)
1918	W. Walsh (Waterford)
1919	W. Walsh (Waterford)
1920	T. McGrath (Clare)
1921	W. Walsh (Waterford)
1922	P. Dunphy (Laois)
1923	P. Kennifick (Cork)
1924	P. O Caoimh (Cork)
1925	P. McCullagh (Wexford)
1926	P. McCullagh (Wexford)
1927	D. Lanigan (Limerick)
1928	John Roberts (Kilkenny)
1929	S. Robbins (Offaly)
1930	S. Jordan (Galway)
1931	S. Robbins (Offaly), First 2 games; W. Walsh (Waterford), 3rd game,
1932	S. Robbins (Offaly)
1933	S. Jordan (Galway)
1934	S. Jordan (Galway) Draw and Replay
1935	T. Daly (Clare)
1936	J. O'Regan (Cork)
1937	J. Flaherty (Offaly)
1938	I. Harney (Galway)
1939	J. Flaherty (Offaly)
1940	J. J. Callanan (Tipperary)
1941	W. O'Donnell (Tipperary)
1942	M. Hennessy (Clare)
1943	J. J. Stuart (Dublin)
1944	M. Hennessy (Clare)
1945	V. Baston (Waterford)
1946	J. Flaherty (Offaly)
1947	P. Purcell (Tipperary)
1948	C. Murphy (Cork)
1949	M. J. Flaherty (Galway)
1950	C. Murphy.(Cork)
1951	W. O'Donoghue (Limerick)
1952	W. O'Donoghue (Limerick)
1953	P. Connell (Offaly)
1954	J. Mulcahy (Kilkenny)
1955	R. Stakelum (Tipperary)
1956	T. O'Sullivan (Limerick)
1957	S. Gleeson (Limerick)
1958	Matt Spain (Offaly)
1959	G. Fitzgerald (Limerick), Draw and Replay
1960	J. Dowling (OfFaly)
1961	G. Fitzgerald (Limerick)
1962	J. Dowling (Offaly)
1963	J. Hatton (Wicklow)
1964	A. Higgins (Golway)
1965	M. Hayes (Clare)
1966	J. Hatton (Wicklow)
1967	M. Hayes (Clare)
1968	J. Dowling (Offaly)
1969	S. O'Connor (Limerick)
1970	J. Hatton (Wicklow)
1971	F. Murphy (Cork)
1972	M. Spain (Offaly)
1973	M. Slattery (Clare)
1974	J. Moloney (Tipperary)
1975	S. O'Connor (Limerick)
1976	P. Johnson (Kilkenny)
1977	S. O'Grady (Limerick)

1978	J. Rankins (Laois)
1979	G. Ryan (Tipperary)
1980	N. O'Donohue (Dublin)
1981	F. Murphy (Cork)
1982	N. O'Donoghue (Dublin)
1983	N. Duggan (Limerick)
1984	P. Long (Kilkenny)
1985	G. Ryan (Tipperary)
1986	J. F. Bailey (Dublin)
1987	T. Murray (Limerick)
1988	G. Kirwan (Offaly)
1989	P. Delaney (Laois)
1990	J. Moore (Waterford)
1991	Willie Horgan (Cork)
1992	D. Murphy (Wexford)
1993	T. Murray (Limerick)
1994	W. Barrett (Tipperary)
1995	D. Murphy (Wexford)
1996	P. Horan (Offaly)
1997	D. Murphy (Wexford)
1998	D. Murphy (Wexford)
1999	P. O'Connor (Limerick)
2000	W. Barrett (Tipperary)
2001	P. O'Connor (Limerick)
2002	A. MacSuibhne (Dublin)
2003	P. O'Connor (Limerick)
2004	A. Mac Suibhne (Dublin)
2005	S. Roche (Tipperary)
2006	B. Kelly (Westmeath)
2007	D. Kirwan (Cork)
2008	B. Kelly (Westmeath)
2009	D. Kirwan (Cork)
2010	M. Wadding (Waterford)
2011	B. Gavin (Offaly)
2012	B. Kelly (Westmeath), Draw; J. McGrath (Westmeath), Replay
2013	B. Gavin (Offaly), Draw; J. McGrath (Westmeath), Replay
2014	B. Kelly (Westmeath), Draw; B. Gavin (Offaly), Replay
2015	J. Owens (Wexford)
2016	B. Gavin (Offaly)
2017	F. Horgan (Tipperary)

MUNSTER SENIOR HURLING FINALS

Year	Team	Score	Score	Team
1887	Open Draw			
1888	Cork/Clare (unfinished due to American "Invasion")			
1889	Clare w.o. Kerry			
1890	Cork	2-0	0-1	Kerry
1891	Limerick	1-2	1-1	Kerry (objection)
Replay	Kerry	2-4	0-1	Limerick
1892	Cork	5-3	2-5	Kerry
1893	Cork	5-3	0-0	Limerick
1894	Cork	3-4	1-2	Tipperary
1895	Tipperary	7-8	0-2	Limerick
1896	Tipperary	1-3	1-3	Cork
	(unfinished, replay ordered)			
Replay	Tipperary	7-9	2-3	Cork
1897	Limerick	4-9	1-6	Cork
1898	Tipperary	3-0	2-3	Cork
	(unfinished owing to fading light)			
Replay	Tipperary	1-13	1-2	Cork
1899	Tipperary	5-16	0-8	Clare
1900	Tipperary	6-11	2-1	Kerry
1901	Cork	3-10	2-6	Clare
1902	Cork	2-9	1-5	Limerick
1903	Cork	5-16	1-1	Waterford
1904	Cork	3-10	3-4	Tipperary
1905	Cork	7-12	1-4	Limerick
1906	Tipperary	3-4	0-9	Cork
1907	Cork	1-6	1-4	Tipperary
1908	Tipperary, w.o., Kerry, scr.			
1909	Tipperary	2-10	2-6	Cork
1910	Limerick	5-1	4-2	Cork
1911	Limerick	5-3	4-3	Tipperary
1912	Cork	5-1	31	Tipperary
1913	Tipperary	8-1	5-3	Cork
1914	Clare	3-2	3-1	Cork
1915	Cork	8-2	2-1	Clare
1916	Tipperary	5-0	1-2	Cork
1917	Tipperary	3-4	3-4	Limerick
Replay	Tipperary	6-4	3-1	Limerick
1918	Limerick	11-3	1-2	Clare
1919	Cork	3-5	1-6	Limerick
1920	Cork	3-4	0-5	Limerick
1921	Limerick	5-2	1-2	Cork
1922	Tipperary	2-2	2-2	Limerick
Replay	Tipperary	4-2	1-4	Limerick
1923	Limerick	2-3	1-0	Tipperary

1924	Tipperary	3-1	2-2	Limerick
1925	Tipperary	6-6	1-2	Waterford
1926	Tipperary	1-2	0-0	Cork
	(first game abandoned)			
	Cork	4-1	3-4	Tipperary
Replay	Cork	3-6	2-4	Tipperary
1927	Cork	5-3	3-4	Clare
1928	Cork	2-2	2-2	Clare
Replay	Cork	6-4	2-2	Clare
1929	Cork	4-6	2-3	Waterford
1930	Tipperary	6-4	2-8	Clare
1931	Cork	1-9	4-0	Waterford
Replay	Cork	5-4	1-2	Waterford
1932	Clare	5-2	4-1	Cork
1933	Limerick	3-7	1-2	Waterford
	(unfinished Limerick awarded game)			
1934	Limerick	4-8	2-5	Waterford
1935	Limerick	5-5	1-4	Tipperary
1936	Limerick	8-5	4-6	Tipperary
1937	Tipperary	6-3	4-3	Limerick
1938	Waterford	3-5	2-5	Clare
1939	Cork	4-3	3-4	Limerick
1940	Limerick	4-3	3-6	Cork
Replay	Limerick	3-3	2-4	Cork
1941	Tipperary	5-4	2-5	Cork
	(played in October after All-Ireland Final)			
1942	Cork	4-15	4-1	Tipperary
1943	Cork	2-13	3-8	Waterford
1944	Limerick	4-13	6-7	Cork
Replay	Cork	4-6	3-6	Limerick
1945	Tipperary	4-3	2-6	Limerick
1946	Cork	3-8	1-3	Limerick
1947	Cork	2-6	2-3	Limerick
1948	Waterford	4-7	3-9	Cork
1949	Tipperary	1-16	2-10	Limerick
1950	Tipperary	2-17	3-11	Cork
1951	Tipperary	2-11	2-9	Cork
1952	Cork	1-11	2-6	Tipperary
1953	Cork	3-10	1-11	Tipperary
1954	Cork	2-8	1-8	Tipperary
1955	Limerick	2-16	2-6	Clare
1956	Cork	5-5	3-5	Limerick
1957	Waterford	1-11	1-6	Cork
1958	Tipperary	4-12	1-5	Waterford
1959	Waterford	3-9	2-9	Cork
1960	Tipperary	4-13	4-11	Cork
1961	Tipperary	3-6	0-7	Cork

1962	Tipperary	5-14	2-3	Waterford
1963	Waterford	0-11	0-8	Tipperary
1964	Tipperary	3-13	1-5	Cork
1965	Tipperary	4-11	0-5	Cork
1966	Cork	4-9	2-9	Waterford
1967	Tipperary	4-12	2-6	Clare
1968	Tipperary	2-13	1-7	Cork
1969	Cork	4-6	0-9	Tipperary
1970	Cork	3-10	3-8	Tipperary
	(First 80-minute Final)			
1971	Tipperary	4-16	3-18	Limerick
1972	Cork	6-18	2-8	Clare
1973	Limerick	6-7	2-18	Tipperary
1974	Limerick	6-14	3-9	Clare
1975	Cork	3-14	0-12	Limerick
	(70-minute Final introduced)			
1976	Cork	3-15	4-5	Limerick
1977	Cork	4-15	4-10	Clare
1978	Cork	0-13	0-11	Clare
1979	Cork	2-14	0-9	Limerick
1980	Limerick	2-14	2-10	Cork
1981	Limerick	3-12	2-9	Clare
1982	Cork	5-31	3-6	Waterford
1983	Cork	3-22	0-12	Waterford
1984	Cork	4-15	3-14	Tipperary
1985	Cork	4-17	4-11	Tipperary
1986	Cork	2-18	3-12	Clare
1987	Tipperary	1-18	1-18	Cork
Replay	Tipperary	4-22	1-22	Cork (aet)
1988	Tipperary	2-19	1-13	Cork
1989	Tipperary	0-26	2-8	Waterford
1990	Cork	4-16	2-14	Tipperary
1991	Tipperary	2-16	4-10	Cork
Replay	Tipperary	4-19	4-15	Cork
1992	Cork	1-22	3-11	Limerick
1993	Tipperary	3-27	2-12	Clare
1994	Limerick	0-25	2-10	Clare
1995	Clare	1-17	0-11	Limerick
1996	Limerick	0-19	1-16	Tipperary
Replay	Limerick	4-7	0-16	Tipperary
1997	Clare	1-18	0-18	Tipperary
1998	Clare	1-16	3-10	Waterford
Replay	Clare	2-16	0-10	Waterford
1999	Cork	1-15	0-14	Clare
2000	Cork	0-23	3-12	Tipperary
2001	Tipperary	2-16	1-17	Limerick

2002	Waterford	2-23	3-12	Tipperary
2003	Cork	3-16	3-12	Waterford
2004	Waterford	3-16	1-21	Cork
2005	Cork	1-21	1-16	Tipperary
2006	Cork	2-14	1-14	Tipperary
2007	Waterford	3-17	1-14	Limerick
2008	Tipperary	2-21	0-19	Clare
2009	Tipperary	4-14	2-16	Waterford
2010	Waterford	2-15	2-15	Cork
Replay	Waterford	1-16	1-13	Cork (aet)
2011	Tipperary	7-19	0-19	Waterford
2012	Tipperary	2-17	0-16	Waterford
2013	Limerick	0-24	0-15	Cork
2014	Cork	2-24	0-24	Limerick
2015	Tipperary	0-21	0-16	Waterford
2016	Tipperary	5-19	0-13	Waterford
2017	Cork	1-25	1-20	Clare

LEINSTER SENIOR HURLING FINALS

1887	Open Draw			
1888	Kilkenny	0-7	0-3	Dublin
1889	Dublin w.o. from Laois			
	(Louth only other county to compete)			
1890	Wexford	2-9	0-3	Laois
1891	Wexford w.o. from Laois			
1892	Dublin unopposed			
1893	Kilkenny w.o. from Dublin			
1894	Dublin unopposed			
1895	Kilkenny	1-5	0-5	Dublin
1896	Dublin	1-8	0-6	Kilkenny
	(replay ordered, objection)			
	Dublin	4-6	0-0	Kilkenny
1897	Kilkenny w.o. from Wexford			
1898	Kilkenny	4-12	3-2	Dublin
1899	Wexford	2-12	1-4	Dublin
1900	Kilkenny	4-11	4-10	Dublin
1901	Wexford	7-6	1-3	Offaly
1902	Dublin	0-8	1-4	Kilkenny
1903	Kilkenny	1-5	1-5	Dublin
	(Kilkenny awarded title; Dublin goal disputed)			
1904	Kilkenny	2-8	2-6	Dublin
1905	Kilkenny	2-8	2-2	Dublin
1906	Dublin	1-14	0-5	Kilkenny
1907	Kilkenny	4-14	1-9	Dublin
1908	Dublin w.o. Kilkenny *scr.*			
1909	Kilkenny	5-16	2-7	Laois
1910	Wexford	3-3	1-1	Dublin
1911	Kilkenny	4-6	3-1	Dublin
1912	Kilkenny	6-6	2-4	Laois
1913	Kilkenny	0-3	1-0	Dublin
Replay	Kilkenny	7-5	2-1	Dublin
1914	Laois	3-2	2-4	Kilkenny
1915	Laois	3-2	0-5	Dublin
1916	Kilkenny	11-3	2-2	Wexford
1917	Dublin	5-1	4-0	Kilkenny
1918	Wexford	2-3	1-2	Dublin
1919	Dublin	1-5	1-2	Kilkenny
1920	Dublin	4-5	2-2	Kilkenny
1921	Dublin	4-4	1-5	Kilkenny
1922	Kilkenny	3-4	1-2	Dublin
1923	Kilkenny	4-1	1-1	Dublin
1924	Dublin	4-4	3-1	Offaly
1925	Kilkenny awarded title on objection			
	(Dublin "won" at Croke Park 6-4 to 4-7)			

1926	Kilkenny	3-8	1-4	Offaly
1927	Dublin	7-7	4-6	Kilkenny
1928	Dublin	9-7	4-3	Offaly
1929	Kilkenny	N/A	N/A	Dublin

Declared void (both teams disqualified for being late on field after Kilkenny had beaten Dublin by 3-5 to 2-6 in the final)

1930	Dublin	4-7	2-2	Laois
1931	Kilkenny	4-7	4-2	Laois
1932	Kilkenny	4-6	3-5	Dublin
1933	Kilkenny	7-5	5-5	Dublin
1934	Dublin	2-8	4-2	Kilkenny
Replay	Dublin	3-5	2-2	Kilkenny
1935	Kilkenny	3-8	0-6	Laois
1936	Kilkenny	4-6	2-5	Laois
1937	Kilkenny	5-3	2-4	Westmeath
1938	Dublin	2-3	2-3	Kilkenny
Replay	Dublin	4-9	3-5	Kilkenny
1939	Kilkenny	2-12	4-3	Dublin
1940	Kilkenny	3-6	2-5	Dublin
1941	Dublin	2-8	1-8	Kilkenny
1942	Dublin	4-8	1-4	Kilkenny
1943	Kilkenny	3-9	2-6	Dublin
1944	Dublin	4-7	3-3	Wexford
1945	Kilkenny	5-12	3-4	Dublin
1946	Kilkenny	3-8	1-12	Dublin
1947	Kilkenny	7-10	3-6	Dublin
1948	Dublin	5-9	3-3	Laois
1949	Laois	3-8	3-6	Kilkenny
1950	Kilkenny	3-11	2-11	Wexford
1951	Wexford	3-12	4-3	Laois
1952	Dublin	7-2	3-6	Wexford
1953	Kilkenny	1-13	3-5	Wexford
1954	Wexford	8-5	1-4	Dublin
1955	Wexford	2-7	2-7	Kilkenny
Replay	Wexford	5-6	3-9	Kilkenny
1956	Wexford	4-8	3-10	Kilkenny
1957	Kilkenny	6-9	1-5	Wexford
1958	Kilkenny	5-12	4-9	Wexford
1959	Kilkenny	2-9	1-11	Dublin
1960	Wexford	3-10	2-11	Kilkenny
1961	Dublin	7-5	4-8	Wexford
1962	Wexford	3-9	2-10	Kilkenny
1963	Kilkenny	2-10	0-9	Dublin
1964	Kilkenny	4-11	1-8	Dublin
1965	Wexford	2-11	3-7	Kilkenny
1966	Kilkenny	1-15	2-6	Wexford

1967	Kilkenny	4-10	1-12	Wexford
1968	Wexford	3-13	4-9	Kilkenny
1969	Kilkenny	3-9	0-16	Offaly
1970	Wexford	4-16	3-14	Kilkenny

(First 80-minute final)

1971	Kilkenny	6-16	3-16	Wexford
1972	Kilkenny	6-13	6-13	Wexford
Replay	Kilkenny	3-16	1-14	Wexford
1973	Kilkenny	4-22	3-15	Wexford
1974	Kilkenny	6-13	2-24	Wexford
1975	Kilkenny	2-20	2-14	Wexford

(70-minute final introduced)

1976	Wexford	2-20	1-6	Kilkenny
1977	Wexford	3-17	3-14	Kilkenny
1978	Kilkenny	2-16	1-16	Wexford
1979	Kilkenny	2-21	2-17	Wexford
1980	Offaly	3-17	5-10	Kilkenny
1981	Offaly	3-12	2-13	Wexford
1982	Kilkenny	1-11	0-12	Offaly
1983	Kilkenny	1-17	0-13	Offaly
1984	Offaly	1-15	2-11	Wexford
1985	Offaly	5-15	0-17	Laois
1986	Kilkenny	4-10	1-11	Offaly
1987	Kilkenny	2-14	0-17	Offaly
1988	Offaly	3-12	1-14	Wexford
1989	Offaly	3-15	4-9	Kilkenny
1990	Offaly	1-19	2-11	Dublin
1991	Kilkenny	1-13	1-11	Dublin
1992	Kilkenny	3-16	2-9	Wexford
1993	Kilkenny	2-14	1-17	Wexford
Replay	Kilkenny	2-12	0-11	Wexford
1994	Offaly	1-18	0-14	Wexford
1995	Offaly	2-16	2-5	Kilkenny
1996	Wexford	2-23	2-15	Offaly
1997	Wexford	2-14	1-11	Kilkenny
1998	Kilkenny	3-10	1-11	Offaly
1999	Kilkenny	5-14	1-16	Offaly
2000	Kilkenny	2-21	1-13	Offaly
2001	Kilkenny	2-19	0-12	Wexford
2002	Kilkenny	0-19	0-17	Wexford
2003	Kilkenny	2-23	2-12	Wexford
2004	Wexford	2-12	1-11	Offaly
2005	Kilkenny	0-22	1-16	Wexford
2006	Kilkenny	1-23	2-12	Wexford
2007	Kilkenny	2-24	1-12	Wexford
2008	Kilkenny	5-21	0-17	Wexford

2009	Kilkenny	2-18	0-18	Dublin
2010	Kilkenny	1-19	1-12	Galway
2011	Kilkenny	4-17	1-15	Dublin
2012	Galway	2-21	2-11	Kilkenny
2013	Dublin	2-25	2-13	Galway
2014	Kilkenny	0-24	1-9	Dublin
2015	Kilkenny	1-25	2-15	Galway
2016	Kilkenny	1-26	0-22	Galway
2017	Galway	0-29	1-17	Wexford

ULSTER SENIOR HURLING FINALS

1900	Antrim unopposed			
1901	Antrim bt. Derry by 41 pts. to 12. *(Exact score not given.)*			
1902	Derry	2-7	2-5	Antrim
1903	Antrim	2-4	0-5	Donegal
1904	Antrim			
1905	No record			
1906	Donegal	5-21	0-1	Antrim
1907	Antrim	4-17	1-6	Derry
1908	Derry	2-8	0-2	Cavan
1909	Antrim beat Monaghan			
1910	Antrim beat Donegal			
1911	Antrim w.o. Monaghan scr.			
1912	Antrim beat Monaghan			
1913	Antrim	3-3	0-0	Monaghan
1914	Monaghan	2-0	2-0	Antrim
Replay	Monaghan	4-3	1-0	Antrim
1915	Monaghan	1-5	1-2	Antrim
1916	Antrim	3-1	1-1	Monaghan
1917 - 1922	Abandoned			
1923	Donegal	7-1	3-0	Antrim
1924	Antrim	5-3	4-0	Donegal
1925	Antrim	5-4	4-5	Donegal
1926	Antrim	4-3	3-1	Cavan
1927	Antrim	5-4	3-3	Cavan
1928	Antrim	4-5	1-1	Cavan
1929	Antrim declared champions. Donegal disqualified.			
1930	Antrim	10-4	2-0	Down
1931	Antrim	4-10	0-1	Derry
1932	Donegal	5-4	4-5	Antrim
1933	Antrim	1-7	2-1	Donegal
1934	Antrim	3-4	2-2	Donegal
1935	Antrim	7-9	0-3	Donegal
1936	Antrim	2-10	3-2	Cavan
1937	Antrim	6-7	3-2	Donegal
1938	Antrim	3-5	2-2	Donegal
1939	Antrim	9-8	4-2	Down
1940	Antrim	4-4	1-3	Down
1941	Down	5-3	2-5	Antrim
1942	Abandoned			
1943	Antrim	6-8	2-0	Down
1944	Antrim	5-7	6-4	Monaghan
Replay	Antrim	7-3	0-1	Monaghan
1945	Antrim	8-2	2-4	Donegal

1946	Antrim	6-3	2-1	Armagh
1947	Antrim unopposed			
1948	Antrim unopposed			
1949	Antrim unopposed			
1950 - 1988	No finals			
1989	Antrim	2-16	0-9	Down
1990	Antrim	4-11	2-11	Down
1991	Antrim	3-14	3-10	Down
1992	Down	2-16	0-11	Antrim
1993	Antrim	0-24	0-11	Down
1994	Antrim	1-19	1-13	Down
1995	Down	3-7	1-13	Antrim
Replay	Down	1-19	2-10	Antrim
1996	Antrim	1-20	2-12	Down
1997	Down	3-14	0-19	Antrim
1998	Antrim	1-19	2-13	Derry
1999	Antrim	2-19	1-9	Derry
2000	Derry	4-8	0-19	Antrim
2001	Derry	1-17	3-10	Down
2002	Antrim	3-16	1-18	Down
2003	Antrim	3-21	1-12	Derry
2004	Antrim	1-15	1-15	Down
Replay	Antrim	3-14	0-18	Down
2005	Antrim	2-22	1-18	Down
2006	Antrim	2-20	1-14	New York
2007	Antrim	2-24	0-4	Down
2008	Antrim	3-18	2-16	Down
2009	Antrim	3-20	4-15	Down
2010	Antrim	4-22	1-12	Down
2011	Antrim	2-20	2-12	Armagh
2012	Antrim	3-18	0-9	Derry
2013	Antrim	4-21	1-17	Down
2014	Antrim	2-17	2-16	Derry
2015	Antrim	1-15	1-14	Down
2016	Antrim	6-21	4-14	Armagh
2017	Antrim	5-22	1-12	Armagh

CONNACHT SENIOR HURLING FINALS

1913-1915	Galway represented Province in All-Ireland series			
1916-1922	No competition			
1923-1924	Galway represented Province in All-Ireland series			
1925	Galway	7-5	1-3	Roscommon
1926	Galway	7-8	2-3	Roscommon
1927-1928	Galway represented Province in All-Ireland series			
1929	Galway	10-4	1-1	Sligo
1930	Galway	5-7	3-2	Sligo
1931	Galway beat Roscommon by 37 points to 0-10 (exact score not given)			
1932	West & South Galway 2-4 1-0 East & North Galway			
1933	Galway represented Province in All-Ireland series *Special Final: Roscommon 3-5 2-1 Mayo*			
1934	Galway	7-4	1-2	Mayo
1935	Galway	4-2	1-2	Mayo
1936	Mayo	0-14	0-13	Galway
1937	Galway	5-7	3-2	Roscommon
1938	Galway	8-3	2-1	Roscommon
1939	Galway	7-6	1-3	Mayo
1940	Galway	6-5	1-4	Roscommon
1941	Galway represented Province in All-Ireland series			
1942-1945	No competition			
1946	Galway	6-6	3-6	Roscommon
1947	Galway	4-8	1-9	Roscommon
1948	Galway	4-8	0-0	Roscommon
1949	Galway	6-8	1-7	Roscommon
1950	Galway	6-6	5-4	Mayo
1951	Galway	6-12	4-4	Roscommon
1952	Roscommon	4-5	2-3	Galway
1953	Roscommon 2-5 3-1 Galway *Galway awarded title on an objection*			
1954	Galway beat Sligo			
1955	Galway	6-8	4-4	Roscommon
1956	Galway	3-9	3-7	Roscommon
1957	Galway	5-13	1-5	Roscommon
1958	Roscommon 4-6 3-5 Galway Note: *Galway competed in Munster 1959-1969*			
1959	Roscommon 3-5	0-6	Mayo	
1960	Roscommon 9-18	2-2	Mayo	
1961	Roscommon 5-15	5-1	Leitrim	
1962	Roscommon 7-5	4-1	Leitrim	
1963	Roscommon 2-14	2-1	Sligo	
1964	Roscommon 1-9	0-4	Mayo	

1965	Roscommon 1-6	0-5	Mayo
1966	Roscommon 6-6	1-4	Leitrim
1967	Mayo 5-8	0-8	Sligo
1968	Sligo		
1969	Leitrim		
1970	Leitrim		
1971	Roscommon		
1972	Roscommon 7-9	0-4	Mayo
1973	Sligo		
1974	Roscommon 5-6	0-6	Leitrim
1975	Leitrim 1-8	2-5	Mayo
	Leitrim beat Mayo (Replay)		
1976	Leitrim 2-13	2-1	Sligo
1977-1982	No competition		
1983-1996	Galway represented Province in All-Ireland series		
1997-2001	No competition		
2002	Mayo 4-11	0-9	Sligo
2003	Mayo 4-12	0-11	Leitrim
2004	Mayo 1-10	2-3	Sligo

CHRISTY RING CUP FINALS

2005	Westmeath	1-23	2-18	Down
2006	Antrim	5-13	1-7	Carlow
2007	Westmeath	2-15	0-13	Kildare
2008	Carlow	3-22	4-16	Westmeath (aet)
2009	Carlow	1-15	0-14	Down
2010	Westmeath	2-16	1-18	Kerry
2011	Kerry	2-21	2-8	Wicklow
2012	London	4-18	1-17	Wicklow
2013	Down	3-16	2-17	Kerry
2014	Kildare	4-18	2-22	Kerry
2015	Kerry	1-20	0-12	Derry
2016	Meath	2-17	1-20	Antrim
Replay	Meath	4-21	5-17	Antrim (aet)
2017	Carlow	5-23	4-15	Antrim

CHRISTY RING CUP FINAL TEAMS

2005
Westmeath M.Briody, M.Williams, C.Murtagh, C.Jordan, B.Murtagh, D.McCormack, B.Connaughton, R.Whelan, E.Loughlin, G.Gavin, J.Shaw, A.Mitchell, B.Kennedy, K.Cosgrove, J.Clarke. Subs: D.Curley for Connaughton, P.Greville for Williams.
Down Graham Clarke, L.Clarke, S.Murray, C.Coulter, Gabriel Clarke, G.Savage, S.Wilson, G.Adair, A.Savage, E.Clarke, P.Braniff, B.McGourty, M.Coulter, G.Johnson, S.Clarke.

2006
Antrim D.Quinn, B.McAuley, J.McKeague, J.Campbell, M.Molloy, K.McKeegan, C.Herron, C.Cunning, M.Scullion, J.Scullion, K.Kelly, M.Dallas, J.McIntosh, P.Richmond, B.McFall. Subs: D.McKillop for Scullion, P.McGill for Cunning, B.Delargy for Scullion, J.McKernan for Campbell.
Carlow F.Foley, E.Nolan, T.Doyle, A.Gaule, E.Coady, S.Kavanagh, L.Kenny, C.Hughes, D.Roberts, P.Coady, D.Murphy, A.Brennan, P.Kehoe, R.Foley, S.McMahon. Subs: D.Shaw for Kenny, M.Keating for Brennan, S.McMahon for Kehoe, J.Waters for Hughes.

2007
Westmeath M.Briody, N.Gavin, P.Greville, C.Jordan, P.Dowdall, D.McCormack, B.Connaughton, J.Shaw, P.Clarke, R.Whelan, B.Murtagh, A.Mitchell, B.Kennedy, D.McNicholas, D.Carty. Subs: E.Loughlin for Whelan, A.Price for Gavin, J.Clarke for P.Clarke, B.Smyth for Murtagh.
Kildare C.Cunningham, T.Finnerty, P.Reidy, R.Tynan, D.Harney, D.Kennedy, M.Moloney, C.Buggy, B.White, K.Divilly, T.Spain, P.O'Brien, B.Byrne, A.McAndrew, O.Lynch. Subs: J.Doran for Tynan, B.Coulston for Byrne, M.Dowd for Spain, D.Nolan for O'Brien, R.Hoban for Moloney.

2008
Carlow D.Miley, A.Gaule, D.Shaw, J.Rodgers, E.Coady, S.Kavanagh, R.Coady, D.Roberts, A.Brennan, R.Dunbarr, C.Hughes, M.Brennan, J.Coady, R.Foley, C.Doyle. Subs: J.Hickey for

A.Brennan, K.English for Dunbarr, D.Murphy for Foley, B.Lawler for J.Coady, S.Murphy for Roberts, J.Doran for R.Coady, R.Foley for Hughes, R.Dunbarr for Murphy.
Westmeath M.Briody, G.Gavin, P.Greville, A.Price, B.Connaughton, D.McCormack, P.Dowdall, L.Smyth, P.Clarke, A.Mitchell, B.Murtagh, E.Price, R.Jackson, D.McNicholas, J.Shaw. Subs: B.Smyth for Jackson, C.Jordan for Greville, N.Gavin for G.Gavin, P.Gilsenan for Jordan, P.Greville for Mitchell, C.Flanagan for L.Smyth.

2009

Carlow F.Foley, W.Hickey, S.Kavanagh, D.Shaw, E.Coady, J.Rodgers, D.Byrne, J.Hickey, D.Roberts, R.Dunbar, M.Brennan, C.Doyle, A Gaule, R.Foley, P.Kehoe. Subs: E.Byrne for Dunbar, J.Coady for Kehoe.
Down G.Clarke, F.Conway, S.Murray, S.Ennis, R.McGratton, K.Courtney, M.Ennis, A.Savage, C.Woods, C.O'Prey, P.Braniff, S.Wilson, J.Coyle, G.Johnston, O.Clarke. Subs A.Higgins for Clarke, M.Coulter for Coyle.

2010

Westmeath P.Burke, A.Price, J.Shaw, E.Price, R.Whelan, A.Mitchell, D.McCormack, J.Clarke, L.Smyth, S.Bardon, B.Murtagh, E.Loughlin, P.Greville, B.Leharte, P.Carthy. Subs: P.Dowdall for Price, C.Jordan for McCormack, A.Dowdall for Loughlin, A.Dermody for Bardon.
Kerry B.Rochford, C.Harris, T.Murnane, J.Fitzgerald, J.Godley, L.Boyle, A.Healy, M.Conway, J.Griffin, J.Egan, M.Boyle, D.O'Connell, J.Flaherty, B.O'Brien, S.Nolan. Subs: S.Brick for Flaherty, J.McCarthy for Fitzgerald.

2011

Kerry B.Rochford, P.O'Grady, J.Godley, E.Fitzgerald, C.Harris, J.Casey, A.Keane, D.Dineen, J.Griffin, M.Boyle, G.O'Brien, D.O'Connell, J.Egan, M.Conway, S.Nolan. Subs: J.Flaherty for Conway, L.Boyle for O'Brien, J.Fitzgerald for E.Fitzgerald, C.Harty for Nolan, A.Royle for Egan.
Wicklow W.O'Gorman, J.Connors, G.Keogh, B.Cuddihy, S.Kelly, L.Kennedy, G.Bermingham, E.Kearns, R.Keddy, A.O'Brien, E.Glynn, L.Glynn, T.Doyle, J.O'Neill, D.Hyland. Subs: J.Quirke for Doyle, E.O'Neill for Connors, W.Collins for Bermingham, J.Murphy for E.Glynn, E.Dunne for Kelly.

2012

London T.Williams, E.Walsh, B.Costello, G.Fennelly, L.Mackey, D.Maher, M.Walsh, C.Quinn, P.J.Rowe, P.Sloane, J.Egan, S.Egan, J.Maher, J.Finn, T.Dunne. Subs: B.Smyth for S.Egan, K.Walsh for Sloane, E.Cooney for Dunne, H.Vaughan for Smyth.
Wicklow J.Murphy, B.Cuddihy, G.Keogh, J.Connors, J.Henderson, S.Kelly, G.Bermingham, E.Kearns, R.Keddy, T.Doyle, W.O'Gorman, E.Dunne, E.Glynn, J.O'Neill, A.O'Brien. Subs: E.O'Neill for Connors, C.Moorehouse for Doyle, L.Kennedy for Dunne.

2013

Down S.Keith, M.Conlon, P.Hughes, B.Toner, F.Conway, C.Woods, M.Ennis, D.Hughes, C.Coulter, P.Braniff, K.McGarry, D.Toner, P.Sheehan, G.Johnson, J.Doyle. Subs: S.Nicholson for Conway, J.McCusker for Sheehan, M.Turley for D.Toner, M.Hughes for B.Toner.
Kerry B.Rochford, P.Costello, T.Murnane, R.Horgan, D.O'Connell, L.Boyle, D.Dineen, J.Griffin, D.Collins, C.Harty, W.O'Dwyer, P.Boyle, B.O'Leary, A.Boyle, S.Nolan. Subs: J.Egan for Costello, G.O'Brien for Harty, S.Maunsell for O'Brien.

2014

Kildare P.Dermody, J.Doran, F.Ó Muineacháin, N.Ó Muineacháin, D.Harney, M.Moloney, R.Hoban, E.O'Neill, M.Fitzgerald, R.Kelly, P.Divilly, B.Deay, G.Keegan, T.Murphy, R.McLoughney. Subs: P.Reidy for R.Kelly, J.O'Malley for Murphy.
Kerry T.Flynn, B.Murphy, T.Murnane, D.Fitzell, S.Weir, D.Dineen, T.Casey, D.O'Connell, C.Harty, M.Boyle, D.Collins, S.Nolan, P.Boyle, D.Butler, J.Egan. Subs: J.Griffin for Fitzell, B.O'Leary for M.Boyle, J.Leahy for T.Casey, J.Casey for Butler.

2015

Kerry S.Murphy, R.Horgan, P.Costelloe, B.Murphy, K.Carmody, D.Dineen, D.Collins, J.Griffin, P.Kelly, M.O'Leary, J.Egan, C.Harty, M.Boyle, S.Nolan, P.Boyle. Subs: J.O'Neill for P.Boyle, D.Butler for O'Leary, S.Weir for M.Boyle, J.Flaherty for Harty, D.Fitzell for Dineen.
Derry D.McDermott, M.Warnock, C.Quinn, S.McCullagh, L.Hinphey, C.McSorley, K.Hinphey, S.McGuigan, B.Quigley, P.Henry, P.Cleary, P.McCloskey, A.Grant, R.Convery, A.Kelly. Subs: N.Ferris for McCloskey, D.Flanagan for Quigley, J.O'Dwyer for Cleary, R.McCloskey for McSorley, M.Conway for Grant.

2016

Meath S.McCann, S.Geraghty, D.Donoghue, R.Sherlock, S.Brennan, D.Healy, K.Keoghan, S.Heavey, S.Morris, J.Toher, J.Keena, A.Gannon, G.McGowan, N.Heffernan, S.Clynch. Subs: K.Keena for Clynch, S.Whitty for McGowan, S.Quigley for Heffernan.
Antrim C.O'Connell, S.McCrory, T.McCloskey, M.Burke, O.McFadden, N.McAuley, C.McKinley, E.Campbell, E.McCloskey, N.McKenna, C.Carson, J.Connolly, C.Johnston, J.Dillon, C.Clarke. Subs: P.Burke for M.Burke, M.Dudley for Dillon, F.Donnelly for McFadden.

Replay

Meath S.McCann, S.Geraghty, R.Sherlock, D.Donoghue, S.Brennan, K.Keoghan, S.Whitty, S.Heavey, S.Morris, J.Keena, D.Healy, A.Gannon, G.McGowan, J.Toher, N.Heffernan. Subs: S.Clynch for Brennan, S.Quigley for Heavey, K.Keena for Heffernan, M.O'Grady for J.Keena, J.Keena for O'Grady.
Antrim E.Gillan, P.Burke, T.McCloskey, S.McCrory, O.McFadden, N.McAuley, F.Donnelly, E.Campbell, E.McCloskey, N.McKenna, C.Johnston, S.McAfee, N.Elliott, B.McCarry, C.Clarke. Subs: P.J.O'Connell for Elliott, D.McKernan for McCarry, J.Connolly for T.McCloskey, D.Hamill for McKenna, McKenna for Johnston, J.Dillon for O'Connell.

2017

Carlow J.Carroll, A.Corcoran, P.Doyle, G.Bennett, R.Coady, D.English, R.Kelly, J.Kavanagh, D.Byrne, J.M.Nolan, M.Kavanagh, J.Doyle, D.Murphy, E.Byrne, P.Coady. Subs: K.McDonald for J.Kavanagh, C.Nolan for P.Coady, S.Murphy for Byrne, J.Murphy for D.Murphy, S.Whelan for Doyle.
Antrim C.O'Connell, S.McCrory, J.Dillon, S.Rooney, C.Johnson, P.Burke, A.Graffin, C.McKinley, P.Shiels, N.McAuley, C.McCann, E.Campbell, C.Johnston, N.McManus, C.Clarke. Subs: N.McKenna for McAuley, D.McKernan for McCann, P.McGill for Shiels, M.Donnelly for Dillon, C.Cunning for Johnston.

CAPTAINS OF WINNING CHRISTY RING CUP TEAMS

2005	J.Shaw (Westmeath)
2006	K.McKeegan (Antrim)
2007	D.McCormack (Westmeath)
2008	E.Coady (Carlow)
2009	M.Brennan (Carlow)
2010	A.Mitchell (Westmeath)
2011	M.Boyle (Kerry)
2012	C.Quinn (London)
2013	P.Braniff (Down)
2014	N.Ó Muineacháin (Kildare)
2015	J.Griffin (Kerry)
2016	J.Toher (Meath)
2017	M.Kavanagh (Carlow)

CHRISTY RING CUP FINAL REFEREES

2005	D. Richardson (Limerick)
2006	J.McGrath (Westmeath)
2007	J.Sexton (Cork)
2008	N.Cosgrove (Tipperary)
2009	T.Ryan (Tipperary)
2010	T.Carroll (Offaly)
2011	G.Duffy (Antrim)
2012	D.Hughes (Carlow)
2013	C.Browne (Galway)
2014	S.Cleere (Kilkenny)
2015	J.Keane (Galway)
2016	J.O'Brien (Tipperary)
Replay	C.McAllister (Cork)
2017	M.Murtagh (Westmeath)

NICKEY RACKARD CUP FINALS

2005	London	5-8	1-5	Louth
2006	Derry	5-15	1-11	Donegal
2007	Roscommon	1-12	0-13	Armagh
2008	Sligo	3-19	3-10	Louth
2009	Meath	2-18	1-15	London
2010	Armagh	3-15	3-14	London
2011	London	2-20	0-11	Louth
2012	Armagh	3-20	1-15	Louth
2013	Donegal	3-20	3-16	Roscommon
2014	Tyrone	1-17	1-16	Fingal
2015	Roscommon	2-12	1-14	Armagh
2016	Mayo	2-16	1-15	Armagh
2017	Derry	3-23	2-15	Armagh

NICKEY RACKARD CUP FINAL TEAMS

2005
London J.J.Burke, E.Phelan, T.Simms, B.Forde, J.Dillon, F.McMahon, B.Foley, M.Harding, M.O'Meara, D.Smyth, J.Ryan, J.McGaughan, D.Bourke, B.Shorthall, K.McMullan. Subs: G.Fenton for O'Meara, E.Kinlon for Smyth, S.Quinn for Shorthall, P.Doyle for Phelan, P.Finnegan for McMullan.
Louth S.Smith, D.Black, A.Carter, S.Darcy, D.Mulholland, P.Dunne, R.Byrne, D.McCarthy, S.Callan, T.Hilliard, J.Carter, D.Byrne, G.Smith, D.Dunne, N.McEneaney. Subs: S.Conroy for Black, G.Collins for R.Byrne, S.Byrne for J.Carter, A.Mynes for McEneaney, N.Byrne for Darcy.

2006
Derry K.Stevenson, S.McCullagh, M.Conway, E.McKeever, C.Brunton, L.Hinphey, P.Sweeney, R.Kennedy, P.O'Kane, R.Convery, G.Biggs, D.McGrellis, S.McBride, K.Hinphey, J.O'Dwyer. Subs: R.McCloskey for Sweeney, P.Hearty for O'Dwyer, A.Rafferty for L.Hinphey, C.Quinn for Biggs, Biggs for McGrellis.
Donegal G.Grindle, M.McGrath, C.Dowds, J.Callaghan, J.Donnelly, A.Begley, J.McGee, M.McCann, E.Organ, K.Campbell, C.Breathnach, A.McDaid, D.Cullen, G.Dwyer, N.Campbell. Subs: C.McLaughlin for Callaghan, P.Tooher for Dwyer, J.Dolan for McDaid.

2007
Roscommon D.Connell, N.Cunniffe, C.Moran, M.Keaveney, A.Cunniffe, M.Kelly, L.Murray, M.Connaughton, T.Lennon, J.Moran, Gerry Fallon, T.Reddington, Cathal Kelly, Colm Kelly, S.Sweeney. Subs: Gary Fallon for Reddington, B.Kelly for Gerry Fallon.
Armagh J.Burke, T.McCann, E.McDonnell, P.Kirk, P.McArdle, P.McCormack, B.McCormack, B.McCann, C.Christie, R.Gaffney, C.McCann, G.Enright, D.Coulter, C.McAlinden, F.Bradley. Subs: C.Carville for C.McCann, K.McCreevy for Enright.

2008
Sligo C.Brennan, F.Coyne, W.Gill, R.Cox, D.Clarke, M.Burke, L.Reidy, J.Mullins, D.Colleary, M.Gilmartin, D.Burke, P.Seevers, L.Cadden, K.Raymond, J.Bannerton. Subs: C.Herity for Cadden, M.Shelley for Bannerton, C.O'Mahony for Gilmartin.

Louth   S.Smith, C.Kerrigan, T.Teefy, B.Hassett, D.Callan, A.Carter, J.Carter, T.Hilliard, S.Kerrigan, S.Fennell, R.Byrne, G.Smith, S.Conroy, S.Callan, D.Murphy. Subs: M.Kirwan for Teefy, D.Dunne for Smith, E.McCarthy for Kerrigan, C.Connolly for Fennell, P.Dunne for Conroy.

2009

Meath   S.Quinn, C.Burke, E.Fitzgerald, M.Foley, M.Horan, P.Fagan, D.Kirby, J.Boyle, P.Garvey, P.Durnin, N.Hackett, M.Cole, J.Keena, N.Horan, K.Fagan. Subs: G.O'Neill for Cole, R.Masse for Durnin.
London   P.Gannon, S.Fox, C.Burke, E.Phelan, K.Forde, N.Healy, K.Kennedy, K.Downes, F.McMahon, M.Mythen, C.O'Dwyer, T.Twomey, H.Vaughan, M.Finn, K.McMullan. Subs: E.Morrisey for Forde, F.Tierney for Twomey, N.Coady for McMahon.

2010

Armagh   J.Burke, B.Mallon, P.Gaffney, F.McMullan, B.McCormack, E.McDonnell, N.Curry, P.McArdle, B.Green, R.Gaffney, J.Corvan, K.McKernan, P.McCormack, G.Enright, P.Green. Subs: C.Carvill for McArdle, M.Lennon for McKernan.
London   J.J.Burke, C.Burke, M.Ryan, E.Phelan, M.Fitzsimons, C.Forde, K.Kennedy, N.Forde, J.Reddin, M.Mythen, R.O'Connell, A.Fitzgerald, D.Maher, M.Finn, T.Toomey. Subs: N.Coady for Phelan, B.Forde for C.Burke, P.Stevenson for Finn, F.Tierney for Fitzsimons, K.Walsh for Reddin.

2011

London   A.Ryan, T.Hogan, B.Costello, C.Burke, M.Walsh, C.Forde, G.Hill, E.Cooney, K.Bolger, R.O'Connell, S>Ryan, N.Forde, P.Sloane, M.Finn, H.Vaughan. Subs: K.Canty for Cooney, J.Maher for Vaughan, D.Maher for Hill, J.Mulcahy for Bolger, B.Hassett for Sloane.
Louth   E.McArdle, M.Wallace, C.Kerrigan, A.Wallace, D.Horan, R.Byrne, Donagh O'Sullivan, G.Smyth, D.Dunne, D.Kettle, S.Callan, D.Murphy, B.Corcoran, P.Brennan, Diarmuid O'Sullivan. Subs: W.Morrisey for Brennan, D.O'Hanrahan for Smyth, S.Fennell for Kettle, K.McNally for Diarmuid O'Sullivan, K.Walsh for Corcoran.

2012

Armagh   S.Doherty, P.Hughes, C.Clifford, C.McKee, K.McKernan, N.Curry, P.Gaffney, R.McGrattan, J.King, D.Carvill, C.Carvill, R.Gaffney, C.Corvan, P.McCormack, D.Coulter. Subs: F.Bradley for Coulter, J.Corvan for D.Carvill, M.Maguire for King, A.Carvill for C.Corvan.
Louth   J.Connolly, D.Rafferty, W.Morrisey, M.Wallace, D.O'Sullivan, R.Byrne, D.Horan, S.Callan, D.O'Hanrahan, B.Corcoran, S.Fennell, D.Murphy, K.McNally, D.Dunne, A.Wallace. Subs: G.Rellis for O'Hanrahan, G.Smyth for McNally, D.McArdle for M.Wallace, S.Maguire for Murphy.

2013

Donegal   P.Burns, B.Hannigan, J.McGhee, M.McGrath, C.McDermott, J.Donnelly, J.Boyle, R.McDermott, D.Cullen, L.Henderson, S.McVeigh, E.McDermott, C.Matthewson, P.Hannigan, S.Boyle. Subs: P.Sheridan for S.Boyle, J.Browne for McGhee, K.Campbell for E.McDermott.
Roscommon P.Dolan, S.Curley, R.O'Meara, I.Delaney, S.Melia, M.Kelly, N.Keenan, J.Lawlor, A.Murphy, Cormac Kelly, Gerry Fallon, C.Egan, R.Fallon, Gary Fallon, Cathal Kelly. Subs: N.Kilroy for Egan, D.Nolan for Murphy, C.Dolan for Keenan, E.Kenny for Cormac Kelly.

2014

Tyrone   J.Devlin, C.McNally, R.Devlin, M.O'Gorman, M.Grogan, S.Donnelly, A.Kelly, M.Winters, G.Fox, C.Grogan, T.Morgan, C.Cross, M.Mulgrew, D.Casey, G.Gilmore. Subs: M.Devlin for Winters, D.Marshall for Gilmore.
Fingal   H.Murray-Hession, P.Coyne, N.Ring, A.Morris, B.Kelly, D.Vaughan, I.Kennedy, D.Hattie, P.Sheridan, D.Kelly, A.Richardson, P.Daly, C.O'Flynn, S.Smyth, J.M.Sheridan. Subs: D.Butterly for Richardson, C.Foley for D.Kelly.

2015

Roscommon N.Fallon, I.Delaney, P.Kellehan, L.Kilcline, D.Leonard, M.Kelly, T.Seale, C.Dolan, J.Kilkenny, J.Moran, R.O'Meara, J.Fallon, C.Egan, K.Kilkenny, A.Murphy. Subs: C.Kelly for Dolan, J.Coyne for Seale, C.Kenny for Egan, E.Flanagan for Murphy, G.Fallon for J.Fallon.
Armagh   S.Doherty, S.Renaghan, C.Clifford, C.Devlin, S.Gaffney, N.Curry, K.McKernan, J.Corvan, D.Coulter, R.Gaffney, C.Carvill, D.Carvill, M.Moan, E.McGuinness, C.Corvan. Subs: C.Gorman for Moan, C.McKee for E.McGuinness, A.McGuinness for D.Carvill.

2016

Mayo   D.O'Brien, B.Hunt, G.McManus, E.Collins, C.Freeman, K.Higgins, A.Lyons, D.Kenny, C.Charlton, J.McManus, K.Feeney, S.Regan, S.Boland, P.O'Flynn, D.McTigue. Subs: P.Connell for Lyons, F.Boland for McTigue, C.Scahill for O'Flynn, K.McDermott for Hunt, G.Nolan for S.Boland,
Armagh   S.Doherty, C.Clifford, A.McGuinness, C.Devlin, J.Corvan, N.Curry, C.Toner, K.McKernan, S.Renaghan, R.Gaffney, C.Carvill, D.Carvill, D.Coulter, E.McGuinness, C.Corvan. Subs: J.King for Renaghan, P.McKearney for J.Corvan, O.Curry for Coulter.

2017

Derry   D.McDermott, P.Turner, S.Cassidy, D.McCloskey, P.Cleary, O.McCloskey, L.Óg Hinphey, C.McAllister, C.McKaigue, G.Bradley, M.McGrath, A.Grant, B.Rogers, B.Cassidy, C.Waldron. Subs: K.Hinphey for McAllister, N.Waldron for Turner, C.Doherty for C.Waldron, R.Convery for Grant, B.Óg McGilligan for Cleary.
Armagh   S.Doherty, C.Clifford, A.McGuinness, T.Nevin, J.Corvan, N.Curry, C.Devlin, P.Gaffney, O.Curry, D.Carvill, E.McGuinness, C.Corvan, D.McKenna, R.Gaffney, C.Carvill. Subs: F.Bradley for McKenna, D.Magee for A.McGuinness, D.Gaffney for E.McGuinness, D.Bridges for Devlin, C.Gorman for C.Corvan.

CAPTAINS OF WINNING NICKEY RACKARD CUP TEAMS

2005	F.McMahon (London)
2006	M.Conway (Derry)
2007	M.Connaughton (Roscommon)
2008	D.Burke (Sligo)
2009	N.Hackett (Meath)
2010	P.McCormack (Armagh)
2011	N.Forde (London)
2012	R.Gaffney (Armagh)
2013	J.Boyle (Donegal)
2014	D.Casey (Tyrone)
2015	M.Kelly (Roscommon)
2016	B.Hunt (Mayo)
2017	O.McCloskey (Derry)

NICKEY RACKARD CUP FINAL REFEREES

2005	T.Mahon (Fermanagh)
2006	D.Connolly (Kilkenny)
2007	J.Kelly (Wexford)
2008	S.Whelan (Wexford)
2009	O.Elliott (Antrim)
2010	D.Magee (Down)
2011	M.Haverty (Galway)
2012	P.O'Dwyer (Carlow)
2013	P.Murphy (Carlow)
2014	D.O'Driscoll (Limerick)
2015	J.O'Brien (Tipperary)
2016	J.Murphy (Limerick)
2017	S.Hynes (Galway)

LORY MEAGHER CUP FINALS

2009	Tyrone	5-11	3-16	Donegal
2010	Longford	1-20	1-12	Donegal
2011	Donegal	2-12	0-17	Tyrone
2012	Tyrone	2-24	3-20	Fermanagh (aet)
2013	Warwickshire	2-16	0-10	Longford
2014	Longford	3-18	3-16	Fermanagh
2015	Fermanagh	3-16	1-17	Sligo
2016	Louth	4-15	4-11	Sligo
2017	Warwickshire	0-17	0-11	Leitrim

LORY MEAGHER CUP FINAL TEAMS

2009
Tyrone   D.McCabe, S.P.Begley, D.Maguire, M.Kelly, T.McIntosh, S.Donnelly, C.Gallagher, J.Kelly, T.Hughes, D.Lavery, P.O'Connor, S.McKiver, C.Grogan, R.O'Neill, G.Fox.
Subs: P.McMahon for Fox, A.Kelly for O'Connor.
Donegal   R.Scanlon, M.McGrath, J.Boyle, W.Scanlon, J.Donnelly, C.Breathnach, C.McLaughlin, D.Cullen, S.Boyle, C.Matthewson, S.McVeigh, K.Campbell, L.Henderson, G.O'Dwyer, N.Campbell. Subs: M.McCann for O'Dwyer, P.Hannigan for Matthewson, M.McGee for McVeigh.

2010
Longford   P.Cullen, B.Stakem, S.Browne, C.Finnucane, C.Egan, S.Hannon, P.Donnellan, M.Coyle, E.Donnellan, S.Stakelum, N.Casey, D.Tanner, G.Ghee, J.O'Brien, J.Newman. Subs: F.Daly for Stakelum, J.Minnock for Casey, B.Stakelum for Newman, S.Lynam for R.Donnellan.
Donegal   P.O'Brien, C.Breathnach, P.Hannigan, J.McGhee, J.Donnelly, D.Cullen, B.Friel, E.McDermott, A.McDermott, S.Boyle, M.Patton, L.Henderson, K.Campbell, M.McCann, N.Campbell. Subs: J.Boyle for S.Boyle, S.McVeigh for Patton, M.McGhee for N.Campbell, E.Organ for McCann.

2011
Donegal   P.O'Brien, S.O'Connor, C.Breathnach, A.McDermott, J.Donnelly, C.Dowds, J.Boyle, S.McVeigh, P.Sheridan, E.Organ, S.Boyle, C.Matthewson, M.McCann, E.McDermott, N.Campbell. Subs: P.Hannigan for Organ, L.Henderson for McCann, M.McGhee for S.Boyle.
Tyrone   J.Devlin, Ryan O'Neill, D.Maguire, R.Winters, S.P.Begley, S.Donnelly, M.Grogan, C.Gallagher, M.O'Gorman, G.Fox, J.Kelly, A.Kelly, C.McErlean, Rory O'Neill, C.Grogan. Subs: P.O'Connor for McErlean, T.Hughes for O'Gorman, M.Winters for A.Kelly.

2012
Tyrone   Jason Kelly, M.Kelly, D.Maguire, R.Winters, M.O'Gorman, M.Grogan, S.McCrory, Justin Kelly, C.Gallagher, A.Kelly, S.McKiver, D.Casey, G.Gilmore, S.Óg Grogan, C.Grogan. Subs: J.Devlin for Jason Kelly, R.O'Neill for Gilmore, S.P.Begley for O'Gorman, S.Donnelly for McCrory, S.Hagan for Casey, Casey for McKiver, P.McHugh for Gallagher, P.O'Connor for Hagan.

Fermanagh D.McPhillips, D.Teague, E.Morrisey, F.Bannon, F.McBrien, M.Slevin, K.Kehoe, J.Duffy, R.Bogue, J.P.McGarry, D.McGarry, A.Breslin, S.Corrigan, S.Curran, P.McGoldrick. Subs: B.Smith for McGoldrick, S.Mulholland for McBrien, C.McGarry for Mulholland, McBrien for Kehoe, McGoldrick for C.McGarry.

2013

Warwickshire T.Goulding, B.Bermingham, L.Knocker, C.Brough, D.Kennedy, E.Gleeson, C.Mackey, M.Bermingham, A.Morrisey, C.Robbins, P.Duggan, C.Behan, S.Hennessy, A.O'Neill, E.Lyons. Subs: R.McEntee for O'Neill, S.Wallace for Kennedy, E.McCabe for Robbins, Wallace for M.Bermingham, D.Sheedy for Behan, D.Kelly for Morrisey.

Longford E.Daly, P.McGarry, T.Stakem, B.Stakem, C.Egan, T.Roche, D.Corcoran, R.Donnellan, C.Finucane, E.Donnellan, K.Connelly, D.Tanner, K.Murray, J.O'Brien, J.Newman. Subs: M.Doyle for R.Donnellan, M.Farrell for Newman, R.Breslin for Murray, K.Cox for Corcoran.

2014

Longford P.Cullen, C.Egan, B.Stakem, K.Murray, P.Corcoran, C.Flanagan, R.Donnellan, J.Casey, D.Tanner, E.Donnellan, M.Coyle, K.Connelly, J.O'Brien, C.Mullane, J.Newman. Subs: G.Ghee for Newman, C.Kavanagh for Corcoran, T.Stakem for Donnellan.

Fermanagh M.Curry, D.Teague, E.Morrisey, F.Bannon, M.Teague, M.Slevin, J.P.McGarry, R.Bogue, F.McBrien, J.Duffy, B.McGarry, A.Breslin, S.Corrigan, D.McGarry, C.Corrigan. Subs: S.Curran for Bannon, B.Duffy for B.McGarry, M.Beggan for McBrien.

2015

Fermanagh M.Curry, D.Teague, M.Teague, E.Mahon, K.Kehoe, M.Slevin, B.Duffy, J.Duffy, D.Teague, J.P.McGarry, D.McGarry, A.Breslin, S.Corrigan, B.MacLaughlin, C.Corrigan. Subs: F.Barron for Mahon, D.Curran for D.Teague.

Sligo S.Hayes, T.Brennan, M.Davey, R.Redmond, E.McGowan, J.Kenny, A.Morrison, N.Hyland, G.O'Kelly-Lynch, B.McMahon, D.Fahy, K.Redmond, G.Cadden, C.Brennan, G.Waldron. Subs: P.Leonard for Fahy, F.Keown for Redmond, N.Cadden for G.Cadden.

2016

Louth J.Connolly, M.Wallace, B.Minogue, C.Matthews, M.Lyons, R.Maher, A.McCrave, D.O'Hanrahan, S.Callan, G.Smith, N.Stanley, D.Kettle, P.Lynch, L.Dwan, D.Murphy. Subs: N.Cafferkey for Matthews, A.Mackin for Smith, S.Connelly for O'Hanrahan.

Sligo N.McGrath, R.Redmond, J.Kenny, G.Feely, E.Comerford, C.Behan, L.Reidy, R.Cox, K.Raymond, C.Brennan, G.O'Kelly-Lynch, B.O'Loughlin, K.Gilmartin, M.Davey, S.Kenny. Subs: F.Cretaro for K.Gilmartin, M.Gilmartin for Davey, A.Morrison for O'Kelly-Lynch.

2017

Warwickshire M.Cremin, T.Kelly, D.Bruen, M.O'Regan, J.Collins, W.Allen, D.Kennedy, K.Boxwell, P.Uniacke, S.Caulfield, C.Robbins, I.Dwyer, E.McCabe, L.Watson, K.Magee. Subs: C.McBride for Collins, M.McBride for McCabe, S.Hennessy for Magee, J.Meagher for Boxwell, P.Crehan for Dwyer, C.Convery for Uniacke.

Leitrim D.Molloy, K.McGrath, D.Carton, V.McDermott, E.Moreton, C.Byrne, D.McGovern, L.Moreton, J.Glancy, C.O'Donovan, C.Moreton, K.McDermott, P.O'Donnell, C.Cunniffe, Z.Moradi. Subs: M.Quinn for K.McDermott, G.O'Hagan for L.Moreton.

CAPTAINS OF WINNING LORY MEAGHER CUP TEAMS

2009	S.Donnelly (Tyrone)
2010	B.Stakem (Longford)
2011	C.Breathnach (Donegal)
2012	D.Maguire (Tyrone)
2013	C.Maskey (Warwickshire)
2014	M.Coyle (Longford)
2015	J.P.McGarry (Fermanagh)
2016	S.Callan (Louth)
2017	D.Kennedy (Warwickshire)

LORY MEAGHER CUP FINAL REFEREES

2009	T.Carroll (Offaly)
2010	R.Matthews (Antrim)
2011	F.Smith (Meath)
2012	S.Cleere (Kilkenny)
2013	L.McAuley (Antrim)
2014	J.Clarke (Cavan)
2015	C.Cunning (Antrim)
2016	M.Murtagh (Westmeath)
2017	J.Connors (Donegal)

ALL-IRELAND MINOR HURLING FINALS

Year	Winner	Score	Score	Runner-up
1928	Cork	1-8	3-2	Dublin
Replay	Cork	7-6	4-0	Dublin
1929	Waterford	5-0	1-1	Meath
1930	Tipperary	4-1	2-1	Kilkenny
1931	Kilkenny	4-7	2-3	Galway
1932	Tipperary	8-6	5-1	Kilkenny
1933	Tipperary	4-6	2-3	Galway
1934	Tipperary	4-3	3-5	Laois
1935	Kilkenny	4-2	3-3	Tipperary
1936	Kilkenny	2-4	2-3	Cork
1937	Cork	8-5	2-7	Kilkenny
1938	Cork	7-2	5-4	Dublin
1939	Cork	5-2	2-2	Kilkenny
1940	Limerick	6-4	2-4	Antrim
1941	Cork	3-11	1-1	Galway
1942-1944	Suspended			
1945	Dublin	3-14	4-6	Tipperary
1946	Dublin	1-6	0-7	Tipperary
1947	Tipperary	9-5	1-5	Galway
1948	Waterford	3-8	4-2	Kilkenny
1949	Tipperary	6-5	2-4	Kilkenny
1950	Kilkenny	3-4	1-5	Tipperary
1951	Cork	4-5	1-8	Galway
1952	Tipperary	9-9	2-3	Dublin
1953	Tipperary	8-6	3-6	Dublin
1954	Dublin	2-7	2-3	Tipperary
1955	Tipperary	5-15	2-5	Galway
1956	Tipperary	4-16	1-5	Kilkenny
1957	Tipperary	4-7	3-7	Kilkenny
1958	Limerick	5-8	3-10	Galway
1959	Tipperary	2-8	2-7	Kilkenny
1960	Kilkenny	7-12	1-11	Tipperary
1961	Kilkenny	3-13	0-15	Tipperary
1962	Kilkenny	3-6	0-9	Tipperary
1963	Wexford	6-12	5-9	Limerick
1964	Cork	10-7	1-4	Laois
1965	Dublin	4-10	2-7	Limerick
1966	Wexford	6-7	6-7	Cork
Replay	Wexford	4-1	1-8	Cork
1967	Cork	2-15	5-3	Wexford
1968	Wexford	2-13	3-7	Cork
1969	Cork	2-15	3-6	Kilkenny
1970	Cork	5-19	2-9	Galway
1971	Cork	2-11	1-11	Kilkenny
1972	Kilkenny	8-7	3-9	Cork
1973	Kilkenny	4-5	3-7	Galway
1974	Cork	1-10	1-8	Kilkenny
1975	Kilkenny	3-19	1-14	Cork
1976	Tipperary	2-20	1-7	Kilkenny
1977	Kilkenny	4-8	3-11	Cork
Replay	Kilkenny	1-8	0-9	Cork
1978	Cork	1-15	1-8	Kilkenny
1979	Cork	2-11	1-9	Kilkenny
1980	Tipperary	2-15	1-10	Wexford
1981	Kilkenny	1-20	3-9	Galway
1982	Tipperary	2-7	0-4	Galway
1983	Galway	0-10	0-7	Dublin
1984	Limerick	1-14	3-8	Kilkenny
Replay	Limerick	2-5	2-4	Kilkenny
1985	Cork	3-10	0-12	Wexford
1986	Offaly	3-12	3-9	Cork
1987	Offaly	2-8	0-12	Tipperary
1988	Kilkenny	3-13	0-12	Cork
1989	Offaly	2-16	1-12	Clare
1990	Kilkenny	3-14	3-14	Cork
Replay	Kilkenny	3-16	0-11	Cork
1991	Kilkenny	0-15	1-10	Tipperary
1992	Galway	1-13	2-4	Waterford
1993	Kilkenny	1-17	1-12	Galway
1994	Galway	2-10	1-11	Cork
1995	Cork	2-10	1-2	Kilkenny
1996	Tipperary	0-20	3-11	Galway
Replay	Tipperary	2-14	2-12	Galway
1997	Clare	1-11	1-9	Galway
1998	Cork	2-15	1-9	Kilkenny
1999	Galway	0-3	0-10	Tipperary
2000	Galway	2-19	4-10	Cork
2001	Cork	2-10	1-8	Galway
2002	Kilkenny	3-15	1-7	Tipperary
2003	Kilkenny	2-16	2-15	Galway
2004	Galway	3-12	1-18	Kilkenny
Replay	Galway	0-16	1-12	Kilkenny
2005	Galway	3-12	0-17	Limerick
2006	Tipperary	2-18	2-7	Galway
2007	Tipperary	3-14	2-11	Cork
2008	Kilkenny	3-6	0-13	Galway
2009	Galway	2-15	2-11	Kilkenny
2010	Kilkenny	2-10	0-14	Clare
2011	Galway	1-21	1-12	Dublin
2012	Tipperary	2-13	1-16	Dublin

Replay	Tipperary	2-18	1-11	Dublin
2013	Waterford	1-21	0-16	Galway
2014	Kilkenny	2-17	0-19	Limerick
2015	Galway	4-13	1-16	Tipperary
2016	Tipperary	1-21	0-17	Limerick
2017	Galway	2-17	2-15	Cork

ALL-IRELAND MINOR HURLING FINAL TEAMS

1928

Cork   L.Horgan, J.Glavin, F.Cronin, D.Coughlan, C.Sheehan, J.Lee, Der Cogan, C.Murphy, Dan Lynch Denis Lynch, M.Lewis, M.Moloney, M.Finn, G.O'Connor, J.Ryng.
Note: C.Duggan, J.Mannix, J.Healy, J.O'Connor played in drawn game. Dan Lynch, Denis Lynch, J.Ryng and C.Murphy were on for replay.
Dublin   M.Gleeson, J.Lloyd, G.Hughes, M.Kinsella, B.Reynolds, P.Melinn, R.Kavanagh, W.Kells, J.Hannon, M.Collins, G.O'Toole, F.Whelan, P.McHenry, P.Carton, K.O'Toole.
Note: Same team played in drawn game.

1929

Waterford   P.Rellis, F.Pinkert, L.Byrne, D.Wyse, P.Ryan, P.Donnelly (capt.), J.Butler, N.Noonan, J.Dwyer, N.Fardy, P.Sheehan, D.Goode, J.Goode, F.Houlihan, J.Murphy.
Meath   S.Ó Dálaigh, M.Trabbers, S.O'Gibne, P.Ó Lionaird, P.Ó Fearghaill, P.Mac Oireachtaig, P.Donnelláin, P.Pluncéid, T.Cinnéide, S.Moráin, R.Mac Namee, S.Gearóid, G.O'Dare, N.de Bernett, P.Briain.

1930

Tipperary   E.Maher, J.Russell (capt.), Jack Coffey, W.O'Neill, L.Burke, G.Heavey, J.Lanigan, Jimmy Coffey, J.Dunne, J.Semple, E.Wade, P.Ryan, J.Close, T.Harney, J.Quinlan.
Kilkenny   A.Cullen, M.Tyrrell, J.Buggy, W.Burke, T Deneiffe, Milo Kennedy (capt.), W.Ayres, J.Morrissey, J.Shortall, F.Minogue, P.Kelly, M.Byrne, J.Maher, M.Shortall, P.Leahy.

1931

Kilkenny   M.Doyle, D.Hughes, A.Cullen, M.Tyrrell T.Shortall, M.Brennan, J.Murphy, J.Phelan, P.Kelly, J.Shortall (capt.), J.Dwyer, C.Barry, W.Walsh, W.Ayres, P.Shortall.
Galway   P.Comer, M.TuoLy, M.Kelly, M.Loughnane, R.Brogan, M.Donnellan, M.Lane, J.Moore, J.Barrett, J.Killilea, J.J.Darcy, A.Strong, P.J.Walsh, M.Hanniffy (capt.), A.Burke. Sub: J.Kinlen.

1932

Tipperary   T.O'Keeffe, J.Looby, J.O'Dwyer, M.Burke, P.Leahy, C.Downes, J.Cooney, P.Bowe, Ned Barry, P.Purcell, T.Burke, J.Fletcher, D.Gorman (capt.), W.Nolan, J.Maher.
Kilkenny   M.Doyle, W.Wyse, J.McCarthy, J.Dunne, J.Fielding, M.Frisby, R.Teehan, E.Langton, M.Gargan, E.O'Gorman, E.Shortall,D.Roche, M.Foley, P.Larkin, W.Guilfoyle.

1933

Tipperary   J.Moloney, J.Mooney, T.Doyle, Mutt Ryan, M.Condon, M.Everard, P.Duggan,P.Dwyer, Tony Brennan, P.Frazer, M.Burke, J.Farrell, P Callaghan, Tim Maher, Joe Fletcher (capt.)
Galway   J.Keller, M.Loughnane, P.Brogan,F Brogan, T.Molloy, M.Hennessy, T.Coughlan,M.Donnellan, P.J.Walshe, P.Fahy, T B.Murphy, C.Murphy, F.Lahiffe, J.Cox, B.Noone.

1934

Tipperary   C.Maher (capt.), T.Lanigan, J.Noonan, J.Mooney, J.Moloney, Jerry Coffey, Denis Ryan, Tom English, J.Moloney, Tony Brennan, P.Callaghan, Martin Loughnane, M.Mockler, Tom Cawley, P.O'Dwyer.
Laois   J.McCabe, P.O'Connor, W.Brophy, W.O'Neill, A.Bergin, J.Ring, F Moloney, P.Rustchitzko, J.Kelly, T.Carroll, J.Hyland, M.Cahill, W.Delaney, P.Farrell, P.Carroll (capt.). Subs: J.Conroy and F.Matthews.

1935

Kilkenny   Tom Delaney, R.Hinks, P.Grace, (capt.), W.Holohan, P.Boyle, P.Walsh, M.McEvoy, T.Leahy, J.Cahill, E.Tallent, R.Brannigan, J.Langton, J.Mulcahy, T.Prendergast, S.O'Brien. Sub: P.Long.

Tipperary   P Morris, P O'Neill, C.Maher (capt.), T.Walsh, R.Ryan, J.O'Dwyer, T.Leahy, W.Brussels, J.Hennessy, P.Kearns, D.Ryan, M.Loughnane, T.Lanigan, P.Leahy, John Coffey.

1936

Kilkenny   T.Delaney, R.Hinks, P.Kavanagh, E.Fitzpatrick, N.Hyland, J.O'Neill, T.Waldron, R.Brannigan, P.Giles, J.Langton, T.Mahon, E.Tallent (capt.), J.Mulcahy, M.Grace, S.O'Brien.

Cork   M.O'Donovan, M.Healy, R.Murphy, D.Coughlan, M.Goggin, C.Atkinson, P.O'Callaghan, M.Prenderville, P.J.O'Riordan, C.McSweeney, W.Campbell, M.Cahill, R.Dineen, W.Buckley, D.McCarthy.

1937

Cork   D.Coughlan, R.Murphy, R.Dineen, D.O'Sullivan, A.Slattery, J.O'Shea, D.Lynch, J.Burrows, M.Goggin (capt.), M.Warner, D.Hackett, J.P.Creedon, J.O'Mahony, K.McMahon, M.Emphy.

Kilkenny   E.Brett, P.Kavanagh, E.O'Connor, N.Dollard, J.O'Neill, T.Waldron, P.Hennessy, P.Savage, M.Heffernan, P.Burke, J.Dwyer, T.Larkin, T.Murphy, P.Fahy, S.O'Brien.

1938

Cork   P.J.Quinn, J.O'Mahony, A.Lotty, G.Sadlier, C.Ring, P.Hogan, W.Cummins, E.Young, J.Looney, K.O'Keeffe, T.Foley, Luke O'Sullivan, T.Ryan, K.McGrath (capt.), Ted O'Sullivan.

Dublin   C.McCarthy, P Collins, E.Dunphy (capt.), C.Nicholson, M.Hickey, F Flynn, F.Fagan, P.Rafferty, D.Keane, G.Glenn, E.Walsh, M.Keane, R.Molumby, C.Jenkinson, J.Bradley.

1939

Cork   T.McGrath, W.Cummins, D.O'Driscoll, W.Holton P.Hayes, G.Sadlier, S.Murphy, E.Young, T.Crowley, M.Cody, T.Barry (capt.), J.White, P.Keohane, D.Cahalane, K.McGrath. Subs: D.Keating for J.White.

Kilkenny   A.Roberts, E.Quinlan, R.Dowling, P.O'Brien, J.Murphy, K.Grogan, M.Holden, P.O'Neill (capt.), J.Walsh, A.Murray, M.Andrews, K.Ruth, M.Walsh, S.Downey, S.Kelly.

1940

Limerick   P.Healy, K.O'Donoghue, J.Crotty, P.Murphy, M.Culhane, T.Hogan, T.Cregan, M.Fenton, P.McCarthy (Newcastlewest) (capt.), P.McCarthy (Mungret), J.Hayes, W.Deere A.O'Rourke, C.Birrane, J.Blackwell.

Antrim   W.Webb, E.Dick, W.Feeney, M.Flynn, J.Lougheed, F.Fleming, J.Butler, J.Cormican, S.Quinn, W.McGowan, J.Gallagher, T.Lennon, P.Carmichael, J.McCallin, S.Mulholland.

1941

Cork   T.Mulcahy, J.Murphy, J.Looney, D.Lyons, T.Aherne, M.Murphy, C.Flaherty, P.Hill, S.Condon (capt.), D.Twomey, M.Kennefick, P.O'Leary, D.McCarthy, J.Morrison, J.Kelly.

Galway   P.Doyle, P.Murphy, W.Fahy, P.Brady, W.Coen, C.Creane, S.Murphy, R.Beahan, V.Keane, G.McNamee, K.Kennelly, D.Solan, D.Quigley, T.Neary, M.Nestor.

1945

Dublin   J.Copeland, P Whelan, S.McLoughlin, G.Jennings, J.Prendergast, T.McLysaght, B.Clancy, S.McEntaggert, D.Healy (capt.), P.Donnelly, L.Donnelly, N.Maher, F.Tormey, P.McCarthy, P.Lynch. Sub: S.O'Neill tor P McCarthy.

Tipperary   N.Egan, D.Ryan, S.Bannon, T.Tynan, M.Cormack, P Stakelum (capt.), M.Shaughnessy, Jim O'Grady, W.Carroll, J.Harris, M.Maher (Boherlahan), P.Kenny, W.Molloy, J.Byrne, M.Ryan. Subs: W.O'Brien for N.Egan, N.Egan for Jim O'Grady.

1946

Dublin   G.Sutton (capt.), P.Whelan, J.Lavin, S.McLoughlin, J.Butler, N.Fingleton, B.Clancy, J.Guinea, C.McHale, N.Maher, L.Donnelly, J.Finnon, A.Young, C.Kavanagh, W.Fletcher. Sub: S.Molumby for C.McHale.

Tipperary   W.O'Brien, J.Doyle, J.Nolan, H.Sheehy, C.Dalton, J.Ryan, B.McGrath, Jim O'Grady, P.Shanahan, M.Ryan (Éire Óg), M.Shaughnessy, P.Kenny, T.O'Meara, M.Maher, V.Steiglitz. Sub: D.McNulty for C.Dalton.

1947

Tipperary   John O'Gracly, J.Doyle, J.J.McCormack, B.Mockler, C.Keane, J.Ryan, S.Twomey, M.Ryan (Éire Óg), J.Farrell, D.Butler, D. McNulty, P.Kenny (capt.), T.O'Meara, M.Butler, S.McDonnell. Sub: M.Maher (Holycross) for D.McNulty.

Galway   J.Leaper, D.O'Sullivan, P.Daly, S.McGrath, M.McGrath, P.Conroy, M.Power, T.Murphy, J.Salmon, M.Egan, P.Rooney, K.McNamee (capt.), D.Mullaly, S.Marmion, Jimmy Duggan. Sub: S.Ó Coileoin for J.McGrath.

1948

Waterford   S.O'Flynn, M.Morrissey, S.Hayden, M.Hogan, V.Walsh, M.Kelleher, T.Cunningham, J.Conlon, T.Gallagher, W.Conway, M.Flannelly (capt.), M.O'Connor, M.McHugh, P.O'Connor, M.Browne.

Kilkenny   S.Tobin, W.Doyle, K.Crotty, P. Dalton, T.O'Connor, D.Galavan, H.Ryan, M.O'Loughlin, W.Maher, T.Connolly, M.Roche, R.Carroll (capt.), W.Bennett, W.Ronan, R.O'Neill. Sub: W.Hoban for W.Ronan.

1949

Tipperary   John O'Grady (capt.), Jim Moloney, Joe Moloney, S.Browne, D.Maher, J.Finn, S.McGrath, R.Holden, W.Perkins, A.McDonnell, T.Keane, T.Aherne, M.Buckley, M.Ryan (Moyne), G.Doyle. Sub: J.Maher.

Kilkenny   J.Murphy, J.Dobbyn, D.Maher, T.Walton (Capt.), T.O'Connor, M.O'Shaughnessy, J.McGovern, H.Ryan, P.Fitzgerald, T.Dowling, R.O'Neill, T.Prendergast, R.Mahony, P.Horgan, M.Cuggy.

1950

Kilkenny   J.Murphy, J.Doherty, J.Maher, P.Lyng, P.Lennon (capt.), Jim Walsh, J.McGovern, P.Johnston, D.Gorey, M.Gardiner, M.Brophy, T.O'Hanrahan, S.O'Brien, J.Brennan, R.Brennan. Sub: C.Gough for J.Walsh.

Tipperary   G.Butler, P.Mockler, S.Power, M.Hynes, P.Croke, A.Wall, P McGrath, S.Cunningham, G.Doyle (capt.), D.Ryan, D.Nolan, L.McDonnell, W.Moloughney, S.Keaty, D.O'Brien. Subs: W.Quinn, S.Walsh.

1951

Cork   J.Dempsey, J.Coffey, M.Sheehan, P.Dreivers, P.Gaffney, S.O'Regan, F.O'Regan, F.O'Mahony, P.Duggan, P.Crowley, J.O'Donoghue, J.Clifford (capt.), T.Kelly, S.O'Sullivan, E.Goulding. Sub: V.Dorgan for S.O'Regan.

Galway   D.Corrigan, B.Hoare, T.Tarpey, PCallanan, K.Sexton, W.Duffy, J.Larkin, E.Fallon, S.Cullinane, A Hansberry, J.McDonagh, M.Murphy, M.Cullinane, P Finn, S.Trayers. Sub: P.Creaven for S.Cullinane.

1952

Tipperary   E.McLoughney, D.Quinn, E.J.McGrath, E Burke, F.Dyer, W.Hayes, L.Quinn, P.Hennessy, W.Quinn, L.Devaney, A.Wall (capt.), S.McLoughlin, M.Butler, D.Browne, P.Cleary. Sub: S.McGovern for E.Burke.

Dublin   S.O'Neill, S.Hall, B.Campbell, L.Horan, M.Boylan, P.Higgins, S.Doyle, K.McLaughlin, Roger Feeley, O.Haughey, B.Boothman, C.Dolan, M.Doyle, M.O'Connor, V.Bell. Sub: S.Hennessy.

1953

Tipperary   T.McCormack, M.Cleary, T.Kelly, P.Barry, L.Quinn, R.Reidy, S.Kenny, W.Quinn (capt.), M.Kennedy, L.Devaney, J.Murphy, S.McLoughlin, S.Corcoran, M.Stapleton, L.Connolly. Sub: R.Ryan for R.Reidy.

Dublin   M.Meagher, T.Toner, T.O'Neill, S. Murphy, M.Bohan, B.Boothman, S.Darcy, T.Bracken, R.Feely, A.Kavanagh, V.Bell, T.Synott, L.Rowe, E.Clarke, C.Feely. Sub: P.McGuirk for L.Rowe.

1954

Dublin   S.O'Neill, K.Moore, T.O'Neill, M.Bohan, M.Meagher, B.Boothman (capt.), F.Whelan, T.Bracken, P.McGuirk, A.Kavanagh, V.Bell, P.Delaney, P.Hyland, E.Kelly, P.Farnan. Sub: M.Mannion for T.Bracken.

Tipperary   J.Doyle, M.Cleary, D.O'Shea, C.Moloney, R.Ryan, R.Reidy, L.Quinn (capt.), L.Mahony, M.Burns, J.Murphy, T.Gouldsboro, W.O'Donovan, S.Kenny, C.Ahearne, L.Connolly. Subs: K.Dermody for S.Kenny, P.Ryan for Gouldsboro.

1955

Tipperary   S.Ryan, T Gleeson, R.O'Donnell, M.Craddock, D.Ryan, R.Reidy (capt.), S.Warren, C.Foyle, M.Burns, J.Doyle, A.Leahy, M.Gilmartin, W.O'Grady, P.Ryan, P.Dorney. Subs: J.Small for M.Burns, M.O'Gara for J.Small.

Galway   K.Croke, S.Naughton, T.Broderick, S.Keane, P.Davis, A.O'Dwyer, S.Murray, M.Fox, P.J.Lally, N.Murray, T.Ryan, L.Marmion, T.Flanagan, E.Newell, S.Gannon. Sub: N.O'Neill for T Ryan.

1956

Tipperary   A.Tierney, T.Gleeson, M.Dorney, B.Maher, M.Craddock, P.Reynolds, J.Mulooly, S.Warren, S.Mackey, J.Doyle, P.Ryan (capt.), W.O'Grady, T.Flynn, J.Scott, S.Dalton.

Kilkenny   W.Barry, J.Blanchfield, P.Dillon, H.Hickey, J.Cormack, P.Moran, T.Carroll, S.Buckley, T.Brennan, T.Molloy, P.Driscoll, B.Buckley, M.Dunne, S.Leahy, J.Cullinane. Subs: A.Comerford for T.Brennan, R.Dowling for Hickey.

1957

Tipperary
T.Moloney, M.Craddock, M.Lonergan, P.Kearns, M.Stapleton, P.Reynolds, A.Croke, M.Murphy, P Kennedy, S.Ryan, L.Kiely, J.Doyle (capt.), P.Doyle, M.Hogan, P.Butler. Subs: W.Hogan for S.Ryan, P.Woodlock for L.Kiely.

1958 (Kilkenny block at top right)

Kilkenny   W.Barry, P Moran, J.O'Donnell, H.Hickey, L.O'Brien, T.Carroll, N.Hanrahan, L.McCarthy, A.Comerford, P.Maher, R.Walsh(Thomastown) (capt.), E.Keher, T.Bowe, J.Doherty, M.Dunne. Sub: T.O'Connell for A.Comerford.

1958

Limerick   T.Hanley, J.McDonagh, J.Guinane, C.O'Connell, J.J.Bresnihan, J.Leonard, M.Hanrahan, B.Kelleher, P.Hartnett, P.Cobbe (capt.), L.Canty, P.Murphy, E.Carey, J.Hayes, S.Sexton. Sub: D.Dillane for J.J.Bresnihan.

Galway   P.Fahy, D.Robinson, A.McDonnell, S.Francis, S.Corcoran, J.Lyons, P J.Cormican, S.Kelly, C.Stanley, G.Egan, S.Devlin, J.Spillane, P.Jordan, H.Conway, F.Glynn. Sub: G.Loughnane for C.Stanley.

1959

Tipperary   J.O'Donoghue, P.Griffin, G.Kinnane, W.Lonergan, J.Carroll, A.Croke, R.Slevin, T.Ryan (Killenaule), T.Ryan (Toomevara), P.Doyle, W.Carey, M.Duggan, M.Nolan, L.Kiely (capt), J.Ryan. Subs: J.Gleeson for W.Carey, P.Crampton for L.Kiely.

Kilkenny   E.Fitzpatrick, P.Larkin, P.Brett, S.Rafferty, P Grace, A.McGrath, N.Hanrahan, T.Barry, M.Murphy (capt.), J.Ayres, T.Brennan, E.Keher, R.Walsh (Thomastown), J.Nyhan, M.Walsh. Subs: D.Lannon for T.Barry, E.Connolly for P.Larkin.

1960

Kilkenny   P.Dempsey, W.Grace (capt.), P.Brett, N.Rohan, S.O'Brien, A.McGrath, O.Ryan, J.Barry, J.Ayres, R.Walsh (Slieverue), D.Kinsella, P Freaney, P.Ryan, J.Nyhan, T.Murphy.

Tipperary   J.O'Donoghue, J.Kennedy, Christy O'Dwyer, L.Cummins, J.Cummins, Conor Dwyer, W.Greene, P.O'Connell, J.Ryan, W.Nolan, M.Keating, A.McGovern, M.O'Connor, M.Ryan, W.Ryan. Sub: W.Burke for W.Nolan.

1961

Kilkenny   P.Foley, J.McGrath, N.Forrestal, P.Cullen, S.O'Brien, P.Henderson, S.Hanrahan, T.Barry, J.Murphy, T.Walsh, D.Kinsella, P.Freaney, J.Dunphy (capt.), M.Aylward, J.Delaney.

Tipperary   P.O'Sullivan, J.Dillon, L.White, W.Eakins, D.Ryan, N.Lane, P.O'Dwyer, Conor Dwyer, M.Roche, W.Nolan, M.Keating, W.Ryan, N.Hogan (capt.), G.Ryan, T.Brennan.

1962

Kilkenny   N.Skehan, S.Treacy, T.Phelan, J.Walsh, S.Hanrahan, P.Drennan, W.Burke, J.Byrne, S.Muldowney, S.Cooke, T.Walsh, J.Delaney, J.Dunphy (capt.), P.Walsh, M.Aylward. Sub: T.Ryan for P.Walsh.

Tipperary   P Fleming, W.Smith, P.O'Rourke, M.O'Meara, O.Killoran, L.Gaynor, E.Loughnane, P.Delaney, M.O'Brien, W.Nolan, M.Keating (capt.), F.Loughnane, D.Moloney, R.Buckley, T.Brennan. Subs: P.Hayes for D.Moloney, S.Dermody for E.Loughnane, S.Nash for T.Brennan.

1963

Wexford   L.Byrne, J.Hartley, M.Nolan, E.O'Connor, J.Murphy, M.Kinsella, V.Staples, W.Bernie (capt.), C.Rafferty, C.Dowdall, T.Doran, F.Swords, W.Carley, S.Barron, P.Quigley. Sub: B.Gaule for J.Hartley.

Limerick   A.Dunworth, S.O'Brien, J.Egan, S.O'Shaughnessy, P.Heffernan, T.McAuliffe, P.O'Brien, A.Roche, E.Cregan, C.Danagher, B.Savage, M.Graham, S.Geary, G.Cosgrove, B.Cobbe. Subs: E.Grimes for C.Danagher, P.Nash for A.Dunworth, W.O'Gorman for S.O'Shaughnessy.

1964

Cork H.O'Brien, T.Murphy, G.Aherne, P.O'Sullivan, J.O'Callaghan, B.Wylie, W.Murphy, P.O'Riordan, C.Roche, D.Clifford, L.McAuliffe, K.Cummins (capt.), C.McCarthy, A.O'Flynn, M.Kenneally.

Laois E.Bergin, L.Moore, M.McDonnell, F.Byrne, W.Phelan (capt.), L.Purcell, W.Delaney, M.Fennell, P.Dowling, B.Delaney, P.Dillon, P.Payne, D.Conlon, S.Kavanagh, P.Keyes. Subs: S.Sheppard for W.Phelan, P.Kavanagh for P Keyes.

1965

Dublin P.Cunningham, A.Fletcher, L.Deegan, C.Brennan, W.Markey, P.Kennedy, L.Martin (capt.), H.Dalton, F.McDonald, J.Fetherston, E.Davey, T.Grealish, T.McCann, B.Whelan, N.Kinsella. Sub: P.Cassels for C.Brennan, C.Brennan for E.Davey.

Limerick T.Brennan, M.O'Flaherty (capt.), D.Manning, A.Cronin, S.Toomey, E.Boland, J.O'Hehir, P.Doherty, D.Foley, E.Grimes, C.Shanahan, N.Hayes, M.Grace, B.Murnane, S.Burke. Subs: J.Moynihan for N.Hayes, M.Hennessy for B.Murnane.

1966

Wexford H.Butler, J.Quigley, E.Murphy, W.Butler, E.McDonald, E.Buggy, M.Fitzpatrick, D.Howell, T.Kavanagh, T.Furlong, L.Bent, P.Byrne, T.Royce, M.Browne, P.Bernie (capt.). Subs: J.Nangle for M.Fitzpatrick, J.Ryan for P.Byrne.
Note: M.Butler played in drawn game. Tom Kavanagh came on for replay. Subs in drawn game: T.Kavanagh for D.Howell, J.Ryan for T.Royce, T.Royce for M.Butler.

Cork B.Hurley, D.Carroll, P.Geary, N.Norberg, Joe Aherne, J.Horgan, R.Cummins, P.Moylan, W.Walsh, B.Meade, S.Murphy, P.Ring, F.Keane, G.O'Riordan, M.Curley. Subs: L.Comer for G.O'Riordan, C.Kelly for F.Keane.
Note: D.Clifford, L.Comer and C.Kelly played in drawn game. P.Ring, G.O'Riordan and M.Curley were on for replay. Subs in drawn game: F.Hogan for W.Walsh, W.Walsh for F.Hogan.

1967

Cork W.Glavin, M.McCarthy, B.Tobin, M.Bohane, Ted O'Brien, J.Horgan, M.Aherne, P.Moylan (capt.), J.Barrett, S.Murphy, M.Malone, C.Kelly, T.Buckley, B.O'Connor, P.Ring. Subs: M.Ryan for M.Malone, K.Fitzgerald for M.Ryan.

Wexford P.Cox, J.Quigley, J.Royce, E.McDonald, E.Walsh (capt.), L.Byrne, L.Bennett, A.Kavanagh, P.Walsh, James Murphy, M.Butler, P.Byrne, M.Quigley, M.Casey, John Murphy. Sub: D.Lawlor for A.Kavanagh.

1968

Wexford P.Cox, G.O'Connor, J.Russell, P.O'Brien, A.Kerrigan, L.Byrne, L.Bennett, P.Kennedy, T.Byrne (capt.), M.Quigley, P.Walsh, James Murphy, M.Butler, M.Casey, M.Byrne. Subs: L.Kinsella for L.Bennett, T.Walsh for P.Walsh; L.Bennett for M.Byrne.

Cork M.Coleman, J.Horgan, B.Cummins, M.Bohane, B.Coleman, S.Looney, T.O'Shea, K.McSweeney, G.O'Sullivan, M.Ryan, P.Ring, T.Buckley, D.McCarthy (capt.), J.Rothwell, M.Malone. Sub: P.Kavanagh for M.Ryan.

1969

Cork P.Lawton, P.Casey, J.Rothwell, D.O'Sullivan, K.Murray, M.O'Doherty, S.Collins (capt.), N.Crowley, S.O'Farrell, P.Kavanagh, T.Crowley, T.Sheehan, F.Coughlan, G.Hanley, S.O'Leary. Sub: J.Buckley for K.Murray.

Kilkenny A.Condon, P.Boran, P.Butler, T.Teehan, D.McCormack (capt.), G.Burke, G.McCarthy, T.Phelan, T.Waters, P.Bollard, M.O'Shea, M.Buggy, T.Neary, M.Carroll, D.Corcoran. Subs: R.O'Shea for T.Neary, J.O'Brien for D.Corcoran.

1970

Cork D.O'Brien, B.Murphy, L.Kelly, M.Corbett, V.Twomey, M.O'Doherty, J.Buckley, P.Kavanagh (capt.), N.Crowley, G.Hanley, S.O'Farrell, T.Sheehan, D.Relihan, T.Crowley, S.O'Leary.

Galway E.Campbell, S.Cloonan, C.Maher, S.Fahy, I.Clarke, A.Fenton, S.Healy, S.Donoghue, S.Hynes (capt.), M.Donoghue, Joe McDonagh, D.Campbell, P.J.Molloy, C.Fitzgerald, G.Holland. Subs: W.Cummins for I.Clarke, B.Brennan for J.McDonagh, J.Hanniffy for M.Donoghue.

1971

Cork F.O'Sullivan, M.Corbett, L.McNally, D.J.Foley, D.Coakley, J.Buckley, D.O'Keeffe, T.Canavan, D.O'Dwyer, P.Buckley, A.Creagh, V.Twomey (Na Piarsaigh), T.Fogarty, J.Barry Murphy, E.O'Sullivan. Subs: S.Coughlan for J.Barry Murphy; B.Cotter for P.Buckley; S.Ring for D.O'Keeffe.

Kilkenny K.Fennelly, N.Brennan, A.Teehan, S.Brophy, M.Hogan, B.Cody, T.McCormack, T.Barry, J.McCormack, P.Kearney, N.Minogue, E.Holohan, P.Butler (Dunnamaggin), P.Butler (James Stephens), R.Sweeney. Sub: W.Fitzpatrick for R.Sweeney.

1972

Kilkenny K.Fennelly, J.Ryan, J.Burke, P O'Brien, K.Robinson, B.Cody, J.Dowling, G.Woodcock, G.Fennelly, S.O'Brien, M.Tierney, W.Fitzpatrick, P.Butler (James Stephens), M.McCarthy, R.Sweeney. Sub: J.O'Sullivan for S.O'Brien.

Cork F.O'Sullivan, J.Kennefick, L.McNally, J.Barrett, B.Manley, F.Delaney, S.O'Farrell, R.Wilmot, K.Collins, R.Fitzgerald, T.O'Sullivan, B.Óg Murphy, T.Collins, J.Barry Murphy, E.O'Sullivan. Subs: J.Norberg for F.Delaney, B.Gallagher for J.Barrett.

1973

Kilkenny P.Dunphy, R.O'Hara, G.Doheny, K.Robinson (capt.), J.Hennessy, J.Marnell, O.Bergin, G.Devane, B.Waldron, P.Lannon, P.Mulhall, J.Lyng, P.Treacy, S.O'Brien, M.Lyng. Subs: J.Purcell for M.Lyng, M.Lanigan for J.Lyng.

Galway F.Larkin, H.Silke.G.Maher.G.Murphy, J.Dervan (capt.), J.Murphy, G.Lohan, G.Holian, S.Linnane, M.Hanniffy, J.Donoghue, Brian Kelly, F Power, G.Burke, E.Dooley.

1974

Cork J.Cronin, P.Coughlan, W.Geaney (capt.), J.Crowley, C.Brassil, T.Cashman, D.McCurtain, R.O'Mahony, F.Delaney, K.O'Driscoll, D.Ryan, G.McEvoy, T.Murphy, T.Cullinane, D.Buckley. Subs: D.Keane for K.O'Driscoll, D.Murphy for G.McEvoy, Pat Horgan for D.Murphy.

Kilkenny A.Murphy, R.O'Hara, J.Marnell (capt.), G.Stapleton, J.Hennessy, G.Devane, J.Costelloe, B.Waldron, P.Lannon, M.Lyng, J.Walsh, K.Brennan, A.Driscoll, G.Tyrell, B.Fennelly. Subs: M.Kennedy for A.Driscoll, J.Henderson for J.Walsh.

1975

Kilkenny E.Mahon, R.Power, P.Prendergast, J.Henderson, H.Ryan (Capt.), R.O'Hara, G.Stapleton, P.Lannon, J.O'Brien, K.Brennan, J.Wall, K.O'Shea, S.Hennessy, P.Brennan, J.Ryan.

Cork J.Hayes, M.Cronin, F.Walsh, Jerry Murphy, B.Dineen, T.Cashman (capt.), D.McCurtain, D.Herlihy, Pádraig Crowley, Paul Crowley, P.Horgan, J.O'Sullivan, F.Tobin, John Murphy, D.Buckley. Subs: Peter Hogan for D.Herlihy, T Lyons for John Murphy.

1976

Tipperary V.Mullins, P.Loughnane, P.J.Maxwell, A.Slattery, M.Stapleton, G.Stapleton, J.O'Dwyer, J.Hogan (capt.), P.Ryan, E.O'Shea, M.Doyle, T.Grogan, M.Murphy, J.Stone, P.Power. Sub: P.Looby for J.Stone.

Kilkenny E.Mahon (capt.), G.Stapleton, P.Holden, T.Lennon, J.Byrne, P.Prendergast, P.Murphy, S.Hennessy, J.Brennan, L.Fennelly, J.Wall, J.Heffernan, J.Ryan, P.Brennan, J.Waters. Subs: J.Carroll for J.Waters, J.Power for J.Heffernan, E.Deegan for L.Fennelly.

1977
Kilkenny L.Ryan, C.Mackey, M.Meagher, Bill O'Hara, T.Lennon, S.Fennelly (capt.), D.Connolly, G.Ryan, J.Mulcahy, E.Deegan, R.Murphy, E.Crowley, M.Nash, E.Wallace, W.McEvoy. Subs: J.Heffernan for M.Nash, M.Nash For E.Wallace.
Note: J.Heffernan played in drawn game. R.Murphy came on for replay. Sub in drawn game J.Waters for E.Crowley.
Cork J.Hegarty, J.Murphy, S.O'Brien, W.Cashman, S.Hayes (capt.), J.Whooley, A.O'Connell, Tadgh McCarthy, J.Hartnett, R.O'Connor, J.Monaghan, S.O'Gorman, J.Keane, T.Aherne.Sub: D.Murphy for A.O'Connell.
Note: J.Walsh played in clrawn garne. S.O'Mahony was on for replay. Sub in drawn game S.O'Mahony for J.Walsh.

1978
Cork G.Cunningham, W.Cashman, P.Murphy (capt.), J.Hodgins, B.O'Driscoll, J.Murphy, T.McCarthy, D.Walsh, J.Hartnett, L.Lynch, Tom Aherne, G.O'Regan, D.Murphy, S.O'Gorman, S.Cashman.
Kilkenny W.Walton, R.Maloney, W.O'Hara, P.Crowley, L.Hennessy, P.Gannon, M.Cleere, W.Walsh, J.Moriarty, E.Crowley, W.McEvoy, J.Holland, P.Phelan (capt.), M.Heffernan, W.Purcell. Subs: J.J.Long for J.Holland, P.Heffernan for M.Heffernan.

1979
Cork G.Cunningham, W.Cashman, C.O'Connor, J.Hodgins, C.Marshall, K.O'Driscoll, C.Coughlan (capt.), D.Scanlon, D.Walsh, A.O'Sullivan, K.Hennessy, J.Greally, A.Coyne, M O'Sullivan, T.Coakley.Sub: R.Hegarty for J.Greally.
Kilkenny M.Walsh, P.Ryan, E.Aylward, J.Holden, L.Hennessy, P.Heffernan, M.Gaffney, J.Moriarty, J.Mahon W.Purcell, J.O'Dwyer, S.Tyrell (capt.), P Phelan, J.Murphy, T.Moylan. Subs: W.Walton for T.Moylan, M.Walsh (Mooncoin) for M.Gaffney, M.Byrne for J.Murphy.

1980
Tipperary K.Hogan, M.Conway, P Maher, E.Hogan, I.Conroy, J.Maher (capt.), D.Finnerty, J.Hayes, P.Kenny, G.O'Neill, M.McGrath, J.Darcy, A.Browne, W.Peters, N.English. Subs: V.Dooley for M.McGrath, J.Treacy for N.English.
Wexford T.Doyle, W.Keeling, P.Gahan.D.Sheehan, J.Roche (capt.), E.Cleary, J.Grannells, G.Coady, A.Gahan, J.Byrne,J.Codd, T.Morrissey, M.Fitzhenry, J.Barnwell, E.Murphy.

1981
Kilkenny D.Burke, G.O'Neill, E.Kennedy (capt.), E.Wall, D.Hoyne, M.Morrissey, J.O'Hara, P.Ryan, T.Bawle, J McDonald, D.Carroll, R.Heffernan, L.McCarthy, S Delahunty, M.Rafter. Subs: S.Whearty for E.Kennedy, P.Cleere for M.Rafter, J.Donnelly for J.O'Hara.
Galway T.Coen, S.Moylan, P.Finnerty, K.Flannery, J.Grealish, G.Fallon (capt.), T.Helebert, J.Burke, P.Winters, M.McGrath, A.Keady, J.Leahy, P.Burke, E.Ryan, A.Cunningham. Subs: M.Coleman for K.Flannery, S.Brody for J.Burke.

1982
Tipperary J.Leamy, J.Flannery, J.Bergin, Colm Bonnar, B.Everard, D.Kealy, W.Hayes, J.Kennedy (capt.), G.Bradley, N.Sheehy, M.Cunningham, S.Slattery, J.Cormack, L.Stokes M Scully. Subs: M.Corcoran for B.Everard, G.Ryan for L.Stokes, A.Ryan for N.Sheehy.

Galway T.Kenny, S.Murphy, P.Finnerty, P Malone, P.Lynch, T.Helebert, G.McInerney, J.Byrne, M.Kenny, J.Noone, J.Burke, S.Connolly, G.Brehony, T.Moloney, A.Cunningham. Subs: G.Waldron for M.Kenny, D.Murphy for T.Helebert.

1983
Galway J.Commins, M.Killeen, P.Dervan, S.Treacy, P.Brehony, P.Malone, G.Mcinerney, D.Jennings, J.J.Broderick, T.Monaghan, T.Moloney, J.Cooney, S.Keane, A.Cunningham (capt.), P.Higgins. Subs: M.Shiel for J.J.Broderick, G.Elwood for P.Higgins, N.Brody for T.Monaghan.
Dublin T.O'Riordan, N.O'Carroll, E.Clancy, J.P.Byrne, D.Byrne, J.Murphy (capt.), S.Cullen, P.Williams, D.Foley, M.Hayes, R.Collins, P.Confrey, N.Quinn, S.Dalton, B.Gavin. Subs: P.Kearns for D.Foley, A.Spellman for M.Hayes.

1984
Limerick V.Murnane, A.Madden, P.Carey, J.Fitzgerald, G.Hegarty, A.O'Riordan, A.Cunneen, A.Carmody, M.Reale, T.Byrnes, G.Kirby, G.Ryan, J.O'Neill, P.Davern, B.Stapleton. Subs: D.Marren for T.Byrnes, C.Coughlan for J.O'Neill.
Note: D.Flynn played in drawn game. J.Fitzgerald was on for replay. Sub.in drawn game M.O'Brien for J.O'Neill.
Kilkenny A.McCormack, W.Dwyer, B.Bryan, F.Morgan, L.O'Brien, J.Power, D.Mullen, G.Drennan, P.Phelan, P.McEvoy, T.Lennon (capt.), W.Ayres, W.Purcell, M.Frisby, L.Dowling. Subs: L.Egan for G.Drennan, A.Byrne for W.Dwyer, J.Farrell for W.Purcell.
Note: J.Farrell, L.Egan, P.Fennelly and W.Cleere played in drawn game. M.Frisby, W.Purcell, W.Ayres and P.Phelan came on for replay. Subs.in drawn game W.Purcell for W.Cleere, P.Phelan for L.Dowling and W.Ayres for P.Fennelly.

1985
Cork T.Kingston, C.Connery, P.Cahalane, B.Coutts, C.Casey, B.Murphy, K.McGuckian, M.O'Mahony (capt.), L.Kelly, G.O'Riordan, B.Harte, J.Fitzgibbon, G.Manley, M.Foley, M.Mullins.
Wexford P.Nolan, L.O'Gorman, J.Redmond, S.Flood, J.Codd, Ger Cushe, V.Reddy, J.Bolger, J.O'Connor, E.Broders, V.Murphy, P.O'Callaghan, E.Synnott, B.Moran, P.Carton. Subs: S.Wickham for E.Broders, J.Quirke for B.Moran.

1986
Offaly J.Errity, P.Nallen, R.Mannion, D.Sherlock, J.Kilmartin, M.Hogan (Birr) (capt.), B.Kelly, D.Geoghegan, A.Kelly, G.Cahill, D.Regan, R.Byrne, T.Moylan, M.Duignan, D.Pilkington. Sub: B.Dooley for D.Sherlock.
Cork P.Barry, N.Hackett, D.Irwin, K.Keane, R.O'Connor, P.Kenneally, Tony O'Keeffe, J.O'Mahony, J.Corcoran, R.Sheehan, J.Walsh, M.Mullins, B.Cunningham, D.O'Connell, G.Manley. Subs: D.Walsh for G.Manley, P.O'Brien for Tony O'Keeffe.

1987
Offaly John Troy, B.Whelehan, D.Geoghegan, B.Hennessy, Johnny Dooley, J.Errity, A.Cahill, J.Pilkington, T.Dooley, S.Morkam, B.Dooley, K.Egan, T.Moylan (capt.), J.Troy (Kilcormac-Killoughey), D.Pilkington.
Tipperary P.Kearns, L.Sheedy, M.O'Meara (capt.), N.Keane, M.Ryan, Conal Bonnar, B.Corcoran, M.Perdue, J.Quinlan, J.Leahy, S.Bohan, G.Dealey, D.Lyons, Colm Egan, B.Hogan. Subs: S.Quinn for M.Perdue, D.O'Meara for M.Ryan.

1988

Kilkenny J.Conroy, G.Henderson, P.J.O'Connor, D.Roche, P.O'Neill, P.Brophy (capt.), J.Conlon, R.Dooley, D.Bradley, W.O'Keeffe, B.Ryan, P.O'Grady, A.Ronan, C.Carter, D.J.Carey. Subs: P.Treacy for O'Keeffe, J.Buggy for O'Grady.

Cork I.Lynam, T.Twomey, D.Holland, L.Callinan, T.Dineen, D.Quirke, M.Noonan, T.Kelleher, B.Corcoran, T.Hurley, K.Roche, M.Sheehan, P.O'Brien (capt.), B.Cunningham, J.Dillon. Subs: S.Guitheen for Hurley, P.Murray for Dillon.

1989

Offaly John Troy, M.Hogan (Coolderry), F Cullen, H.Rigney, D.Barron, B.Whelahan (capt.), Donal Franks, A.Cahill, R.Dooley, Johnny Dooley, S.Grennan, O.O'Neill, R.McNamara, N.Hand, K.Flynn. Sub: R.Deegan for R.Dooley.

Clare D.Fitzgerald, D.McInerney, P.Lee (capt.), F.Corey, P.Markham, J.O'Gorman, G.Cahill, C.Chaplin, S.Power, P.O'Rourke, G.Moroney, P.Minogue, P.McNamara, C.Clancy, P.Keary. Subs: J.O'Connor for Moroney, K.McNamara for Keary.

1990

Kilkenny A.Behan, M.Holohan, L.Mahony, J.Carroll, D.O'Neill, C.Brennan, P.Larkin, J.McDermott (capt.), P.Long, A.Comerford, J.Shefflin, P.Farrell, P.J.Delaney, S.Ryan, D.Lawlor. Subs: A.Cleere for Long, B.Power for O'Neill.
Note: S.Meally, D.Beirne and A.Cleere played in drawn game. J.Carroll, C.Brennan and P.Long were on for replay. Subs in drawn game B.Power for D.Beirne, C.Brennan for A.Cleere, J.Carroll for S.Meally.

Cork D.O'Mahony, F.Ryan, A.Murphy, A.White, C.Buckley, P.Smith (capt.), B.Sheehan, C.Dillon, R.O'Connell, B.Egan, B.Walsh, L.Meaney, K.Murray, M.Landers, D.Fleming. Subs: B.Corcoran for Buckley, M.Quirke for Ryan, R.Lewis for O'Connell.
Note: B.Corcoran, N.O'Donnell and C.Walsh played in drawn game. A.White, C.Dillon and D.Fleming were on for replay. Subs in drawn game C.Dillon for C.Buckiey, M.Quirke for N.O'Donnell and D.Fleming for C.Walsh.

1991

Kilkenny M.Carey, S.Meally, L.Mahony, B.Power, A.O'Sullivan, E.Dwyer, D.O'Neill (capt.), D.Maher, J.Hickey, S.Dollard, P.J.Delaney, G.Walsh, D.Byrne, M.Owens, R.Shortall. Sub: P.Davis for Walsh.

Tipperary M.Ferncombe, S.O'Donoghue, M.Rabbitte, M.Gleeson, P.Shanahan, B.Gaynor, T.Gleeson, A.Shelly, M.Leonard, T.Dunne, B.O'Meara, A.Hogan (capt.), L.Barrett, T.Fogarty, G.Maguire. Sub: Conor Egan for Barrett.

1992

Galway L.Donoghue, T.Healy, M.Spellman, C.Moore, N.Shaughnessy, C.Donovan (capt.), M.Donoghue, F.Forde, S.Walsh, M.Lynskey, D.Coen, Peter Kelly, S.Corcoran, C.O'Doherty, D.Walsh. Subs: J.Murray for Lynskey, J.Kerins for O'Doherty.

Waterford P.Haran, T.Morrissey, P.O'Donnell (capt.), J.O'Connor, A.Kirwan, G.Harris, T.Feeney, T.Kiely, F.O'Shea, J.P.Fitzpatrick, D.McGrath, J.J.Ronayne, R.Ryan, P.Foley, P.Flynn. Sub: B.McCarthy for Kiely.

1993

Kilkenny O.Blanchfield, T.Hickey, S.Doyle (capt.), J.Ayres, V.O'Brien, B.Lonergan, B.Bolger, K.Grogan, S.Kealy, D.Cleere, L.Smith, E.Mackey, B.Dalton, D.Buggy, O.O'Connor. Sub: J.Young for Kealy.

1994

Galway A.Kerins, G.Kennedy (capt.), P.Huban, O.Canning, M.Healy, F.Gantley, L.Madden, L.Hogan, G.Glynn, K.Broderick, R.Farrell, F.Healy, E.Brady, R.Gantley, D.Fahy. Subs: M.Cullinane for Hogan, B.Carr for Madden, P.Forde for Fahy.

Cork B.Hurley (capt.), P.O'Keeffe, S.Óg Ó hAilpín, P.Walsh, C.Collins, K.Egan, B.McSweeney, A.Cahill, G.Shaw, B.O'Driscoll, J.O'Flynn, A.Walsh, K.Kelleher, D.Ronan, P.Mullaney. Sub: P.O'Connor for A.Walsh.

1995

Cork D.Óg Cusack, A.Kelleher, B.Kidney, P.Walsh, D.Barrett, S.Óg Ó hAilpín, J.O'Dwyer, D.Murphy, A.Walsh, P.Mullaney, T.McCarthy, M.O'Connell, S.O'Farrell, J.Deane, B.O'Keeffe (capt.). Subs: A.Coughlan for P.Mullaney, D.Cott for J.Dwyer.

Kilkenny P.J.Ryan, M.Kavanagh, S.Dowling, A.Hickey, P.Hoyne (capt.), M.Dunphy, D.Carroll, P.J.Coady, R.Mullally, E.Behan, M.Hoyne, G.Kirwan, R.Cahill, T.O'Dowd, S.Millea. Subs: J.Drea for Kirwan, M.Gordan for Behan.

1996

Tipperary F.Horgan, T.Costello, F Heaney, W.Hickey, T.Keane, J.Carroll, J.Teehan, W.Maher (capt.), M.Ryan, D.Browne, D.Fahey, P.Kelly, A.Doyle, E.O'Neill, M.Kennedy. Subs: P.Lonergan for Ryan, P.O'Brien for Kelly, E.Carey for Doyle.
Note: N.Cleere and S.Ryan played in the drawn game. T.Keane and D.Browne were on for replay. Subs in game E.Carey for S.Ryan, T.Keane for N.Cleere, D.Browne for E.Carey.

Galway N.Murray, E.Tannian, M.Healy (capt.), K.Coy, R.Brady, C.O'Reilly, D.Shaughnessy, E.McEntee, C.Coen, R.Cullinane, A.Poinard, D.Loughrey, R.Gantley, E.Cloonan, M.Kerins. Subs: S.McClearn for Coen, E.Donoghue for McEntee.
Note: A.Walsh and P.Kennedy played in the drawn game. R.Gantley and M.Kerins were on for replay. Subs in drawn game M.Kerins for A.Walsh, R.Gantley for P Kennedy and M.Blake for D.Shaughnessy.

1997

Clare G.O'Connell, W.Kennedy, K.Kennedy, D.Duggan, B.McMahon (Newmarketon-Fergus), J.Reddan (capt.), G.Malone, S.Fitzpatrick, G.Considine, P.Moroney, C.Earley, C.Mullen, M.Lennon, D.Madden, B.McMahon (Kilmaley). Subs: Joe O'Meara for Earley, John O'Meara for Lennon.

Galway C.Callanan, E.McDonagh (capt.), D.Cloonan, E.Donoghue, J.Cannon, S.Morgan, A.Walsh, N.Lawlor, J.Hession, D.O'Donoghue, D.Tierney, G.Hurney, O.Deeley, K.Hayes, C.Coen. Subs: E.Hyland for Hession, K.Daniels for Tierney, G.Keary for Hurney.

1998

Cork M.Morrissey, E.O'Sullivan, J.Olden, D.McNamara, B.Murphy, R.Curran, A.Fitzpatrick, A.O'Connor, J.Barrett, J.Egan, G.McCarthy, E.Fitzgerald, C.McCarthy (capt.), B.Lombard, W.Deasy. Subs: N.McCarthy for Deasy, V.Cusack for G.McCarthy, P.Murphy for Fitzgerald.

Kilkenny J.Power, P.Shefflin (capt.), N.Hickey, C.Hickey, C.Herity, J.Morgan, J.Ryall, J.Coogan, K.Moore, K.Power, B.Phelan, D.Walsh, G.Cleere, K.Raher, J.Murray. Subs: E.Walsh for Herity, H.Gannon for Moore.

1999

Galway J.O'Loughlin, B.O'Mahoney, J.Culkin, R.Reilly, F.Moore, C.Dervan, M.J.Quinn, H.Whiriskey, G.Farragher, R.Murray, M.Coughlan, K.Brady, D.Hayes, D.Forde, C.Coen. Subs: B.Gantley for Coen, S.Tierney for Brady.
Tipperary D.Young, C.Everard, P.Curran,D.Maher, C.Ryan, K.Mulryan, L.Kearney, T.King, S.Mason, D.Shelly, Dermot Gleeson, E.Brisbane, J.O'Brien, E.Kelly, K.Cummins. Subs: M.Maher for D.Maher, L.Brett for Cummins, Damien Gleeson for King.

2000

Galway Aidan Diviney, B.O'Mahoney, T.Regan, N.Corcoran, S.Kavanagh, Adrian Diviney, A.Cullinane, G.Farragher, B.Coen, R.Murray, P.Garvey, K.Brady, D.Hayes, T.Kavanagh, D.Greene. Subs: J.Gantley for Brady, F.Moore for Corcoran, J.P.O'Connell for Gantley, K.Brady for Garvey.
Cork Kieran Murphy (Erins' Own), C.Sullivan, J.O'Brien, B.Murphy, J.O'Neill, P.Tierney, G.Calnan, M.O'Connor, B.Carey, G.McLoughlin, C.Brosnan, T.O'Leary, S.Ó hAilpín, E.Collins, Kieran Murphy (Sarsfields). Subs: D.Cashman for McLoughlin, K.Foley for Brosnan, S.O'Sullivan for Carey, R.McCarthy for Calnan.

2001

Cork M.Coleman, J.O'Mahony, C.O'Connor, K.Goggin, M.Prout, J.Gardiner, S.Murphy, K.Hartnett, B.Smiddy, J.O'Connor, Kieran Murphy (Erin's Own), T.O'Leary, F.Murphy, S.Ó hAilpín, Kieran Murphy (Sarsfields). Subs: T.Healy for C.O'Connor, D.O'Riordan for Smiddy.
Galway P.Dullaghan, C.Dervan, T.Óg Regan, C.Finnerty, E.Lynch, S.Kavanagh, J.O'Leary, T.Tierney, G.Farragher, B.Lucas, K.Hayes, A.Cullinane, J.Gantley, J.Maher, K.Burke. Subs: K.Briscoe for O'Leary, A.Smith for Lucas, N.Healy for Hayes.

2002

Kilkenny C.Grant, P.Holden, J.Tennyson, D.Prendergast, K.Nolan, C.Hoyne, P.J.Delaney, M.Rice, S.Maher, R.Power, W.O'Dwyer, S.Coonan, J.Fitzpatrick, E.Reid, A.Healy. Subs: R.Dowling for O'Dwyer, P.Kennedy for Delaney, S.Cadigan for Prendergast.
Tipperary P.McCormack, M.Treacy, D.Bourke, M.Bergin, J.Boland, D.Morrisey, D.Kennedy, W.Cully, C.O'Mahoney, P.Shortt, F.Devanney, W.Ryan, E.Sweeney, T.Scroope, T.Ivors. Subs: D.Sheppard for Sweeney, T.Fitzgerald for Ivors, B.O'Sullivan for Cully, D.Corcoran for Boland, P.Ryan for Morrisey.

2003

Kilkenny C.Grant, J.Dalton, J.Tennyson, S.Cadigan, D.Cody, D.Prendergast, P.O'Donovan, P.Hartley, M.Fennelly, E.McGrath, R.Power, A.Healy, M.Nolan, J.Fitzpatrick, E.Guinan. Subs: A.Murphy for McGrath, R.Wall for Healy, D.McCormack for Hartley.
Galway A.Ryan, T.Linnane, G.Mahon, D.Kennedy, D.Ryan, J.Lee, R.Whyte, C.Burke, D.Kelly, N.Callanan, D.Garvey, N.Coleman, D.Reilly, A.Callanan, N.Healy. Subs: E.Fenton for Burke, K.Hynes for Coleman.

2004

Galway M.Herlihy, P.Loughnane, G.Mahon, C.O'Donovan, M.Ryan, J.Lee, J.Hughes, A.Keary, D.Kennedy, K.Kilkenny, K.Hynes, F.Coone, K.Wade, J.Canning, B.Hanley. Sub: D.White for Ryan. Note: J.Hughes, a sub in the drawn game was retained for the final at the expense of D.White. Other subs used in the drawn game were E.Collins, K.Coen and P.Madden.

1999 (continued) Kilkenny

Kilkenny L.Tierney, J.Maher, K.Joyce, P.Cahill, N.Prendergast, R.Maher, S.Prendergast, P.Hartley, P.Hogan, G.Nolan, M.Nolan, N.Kenny, R.Hogan, E.Guinan, M.Ruth. Sub: E.O'Donoghue for Kenny.
Note: P.Cahill for E.Walsh and M.Ruth for E.O'Donoghue were changes from the drawn final. Ruth and N.Delahunty were subs in the drawn final.

2005

Galway J.Skehill, A.Leech, P.Loughnane, P.Callanan, J.Hughes, C.O'Donovan, K.Kilkenny, A.Keary, K.Coen, S.Glynn, J.Greene, A.Callanan, B.Murphy, C.Kavanagh, J.Canning. Subs: F.Kerrigan for Coen, S.Howley for O'Donovan, T.Flannery for Callanan, J.Gilsen for Murphy, B.Kenny for Leech.
Limerick G.Flynn, S.Brown, L.Hurley, T.Condon, J.Kelly, D.Moloney, G.O'Mahoney, D.Moore, S.Hickey, D.Hanley, J.Ryan, B.O'Sullivan, M.Ryan, E.Ryan, D.O'Sullivan. Subs: G.Allis for D.O'Sullivan, G.Collins for Moore, D.O'Connor for Allis.

2006

Tipperary J.Ryan, M.Cahill, P.Maher, B.Maher, E.Hogan, T.Stapleton, J.O'Keeffe, J.McLoughney, G.Ryan, S.Hennessy, T.McGrath, N.Bergin, P.Bourke, T.Dunne, T.Dalton. Subs: M.Gleeson for Bergin, S.Callinan for Dunne.
Galway J.Skehill, J.Ryan, M.McMahon, A.Moylan, D.Burke, K.Keane, S.Quinn, E.Forde, G.Lally, A.Harte, M.Corcoran, L.Tully, S.Cohen, J.Canning, G.Hennelly. Subs: E.Concannon for Corcoran, K.Killilea for Lally, G.Burke for Harte, N.Lynch for Hennelly.

2007

Tipperary J.Logue, K.O'Gorman, Pádraic Maher, S.O'Brien, J.Barry, J.Coughlin, M.Cahill, B.Maher, N.McGrath, S.Hennessy, C.Lorigan, S.Carey, J.O'Neill, Patrick Maher, M.Heffernan. Subs: P.Murphy for Patrick Maher, J.Gallagher for O'Gorman, D.O'Brien for Lorigan.
Cork D.McCarthy, C.Hurley, A.Kearney, K.Murphy, L.McLoughlin, J.Herlihy, C.O'Donovan, S.Farrell, D.O'Sullivan, P.Gould, M.Bowles, M.O'Mahony, L.O'Farrell, R.White, R.Clifford. Subs: S.McDonnell for Farrell, G.O'Connor for Kearney, D.Stack for Bowles, C.McCarthy for Stack, E.McCarthy for O'Sullivan.

2008

Kilkenny E.Murphy, D.Healy, M.Walsh, A.Cuddihy, M.Moloney, R.Doyle, C.Fogarty, C.Kenny, J.Gannon, J.Brennan, T.Breen, R.Hickey, P.McCarthy, W.Walsh, M.Gaffney. Subs: M.O'Dwyer for Gaffney, D.Purcell for Gannon, C.Maher for Hickey.
Galway F.Flannery, D.Connolly, R.Burke, G.O'Halloran, N.Donoghue, D.Cooney, R.Foy, D.Burke, D.Glennon, N.Quinn, N.Burke, D.Fox, R.Cummins, A.Dolan, B.Burke. Subs: B.Flaherty for Foy, M.Dolphin for Glennon, J.Cannon for Quinn, L.Madden for Fox.

2009

Galway F.Flannery, J.Coen, D.Burke, C.Burke, M.Keating, B.Flaherty, J.Cooney, J.Regan, D.Glennon, D.Fox, N.Burke, J.Grealish, R.Cummins, R.Badger, S.Maloney. Subs: M.Horan for Keating, T.Horan for Badger, N.Keary for Grealish.
Kilkenny J.Power, J.Lyng, D.Kenny, I.Duggan, J.Gannon, R.Doyle, L.Harney, C.Kenny, O.Walsh, G.Brennan, S.Kehoe, C.Buckley, M.Gaffney, W.Walsh, C.Maher. Subs: S.Phelan for Kehoe, G.Aylward for W.Walsh, P.Walsh for Brennan

2010

Kilkenny   D.Walsh, J.Corcoran, W.Phelan, B.Kennedy, P.O'Carroll, L.Harney, D.McGrath, K.Kelly, D.Walsh, J.Power, P.Walsh, C.Buckley, M.Brennan, G.Aylward, T.O'Hanrahan. Subs: P.Buggy for O'Hanrahan, P.Holden for Walsh, R.Reid for Holden.
Clare   R.Taaffe, H.Vaughan, P.Flanagan, S.Morey, E.Boyce, K.Lynch, S.O'Halloran, C.Galvin, T.Kelly, C.Malone, P.Collins, J.Shanahan, D.O'Halloran, N.Arthur, D.Keane. Subs: A.Cunningham for Malone, A.Mulready for Vaughan, D.McInerney for Arthur.

2011

Galway   S.Mannion, C.Diviney, P.Killeen, P.Mannion, A.Tuohy, S.Sweeney, J.Hanbury, P.Brehony, D.Higgins, J.Flynn, J.Glynn, B.Lane, G.O'Donoghue, J.Carr, S.Maloney. Subs: M.Mullins for Hanbury, A.Cullinane for Higgins, D.Dolan for O'Donoghue, P.Flaherty for Carr.
Dublin   C.Ryan, E.Lowdnes, C.O'Callaghan, S.McClelland, C.Crummy, J.Desmond, M.McCaffrey, G.Whelan, C.Cronin, C.McHugh, C.Kilkenny, A.Clabby, C.Costello, E.Ó Conghaile, P.Winters. Subs: D.Gormley for Desmond, D.O'Rorke for McHugh, C.Boland for Winters.

2012

Tipperary   P.Maher, R.Maher, M.Breen, J.Peters, T.Fox, T.Hamill, B.Heffernan, B.Maher, S.Cahill, J.McGrath, D.Fitzell, S.Maher, T.Gallagher, J.Shelly, M.McCarthy. Subs: S.O'Brien for S.Maher, S.Ryan for Cahill, C.Lanigan for Gallagher, J.Loughnane for McCarthy.
(Note: S.O'Brien started the drawn game instead of D.Fitzell. Subs in the drawn game S.Ryan for Shelly, K.Slattery for Gallagher, C.Lanigan for McCarthy)
Dublin   C.Mac Gabhainn, E.Lowndes, C.O'Callaghan, S.Barrett, E.O'Donnell, R.Murphy, S.McClelland, D.Gormley, C.Cronin, C.McHugh, C.Boland, C.Costello, J.Roche, D.O'Rorke, P.Winters. Subs: K.O'Flynn for Murphy, C.Conway for McHugh, S.Treacy for Roche, R.Daly for O'Callaghan.
(Note: C.Conway started the drawn game instead of J.Roche. Sub in the drawn game C.Bennett for Conway)

2013

Waterford   G.Power, W.Hahessy, K.Daly, C.Leamy, M.Harney, A.Gleeson, Shane Bennett, M.O'Brien, T.Devine, Stephen Bennett, D.J.Foran, M.Kearney, A.Farrell, P.Curran, C.Roche. Subs: C.Curran for Foran, C.Gleeson for Farrell, P.O'Connor for C.Roche, S.O'Neill for Hahessy, B.Whelan for Shane Bennett.
Galway   C.Tuohy, M.Ó Conghaile, D.O'Donoghue, M.Conneely, R.Doyle, S.Cooney, E.Burke, S.Linnane, J.Hastings, C.Shaughnessy, D.Dolan, R.O'Meara, A.Morrisey, M.Molloy, C.Whelan. Subs: V.Doyle for R.Doyle, E.Brannigan for Linnane, B.Burke for Whelan, R.Bellew for Hastings, S.Burke for E.Burke.

2014

Kilkenny   D.Brennan, P.Lyng, C.Delaney, C.McGrath, T.Walsh, J.Cleere, D.Joyce, C.Browne, L.Scanlon, S.Morrisey, R.Butler, R.Corcoran, A.Murphy, L.Blanchfield, J.Walsh. Subs: S.Ryan for Butler, E.Kenny for Browne, A.Gaffney for Corcoran.
Limerick   E.McNamara, S.Finn, P.O'Loughlin, L.Lyons, T.Grimes, A.La Touche-Cosgrave, C.Byrnes, R.Hanley, C.Lynch, C.Ryan, B.Nash, R.Lynch, P.Casey, T.Morrisey, S.Flanagan. Subs: C.Fitzgerald for Byrnes, E.Doyle for Fitzgerald, J.Porter for Lyons, B.Murphy for Grimes.

2015

Galway   D.Gilligan, K.O'Connor, J.Fitzpatrick, S.Bannon, C.Mulry, I.O'Brien, A.Greaney, J.Coyne, J.Grealish, B.Concannon, T.Monaghan, F.Burke, C.Fahy, E.Niland, S.Loftus. Subs: L.Forde for Burke, C.Salmon for Fahy, C.McDaid for O'Brien, M.Lynch for Concannon, R.Malone for Greaney.
Tipperary   P.Hayes, E.Heffernan, E.Moloney, J.Quigley, K.Hassett, B.McGrath, D.Peters, S.Quirke, L.McCutcheon, C.Darcy, G.Ryan, A.Tynan, T.Nolan, D.Gleeson, L.Fairbrother. Subs: R.Mulrooney for McCutcheon, J.Skehan for Ryan, M.Connors for Fairbrother, S.Neville for Gleeson.

2016

Tipperary   C.Barrett, K.O'Dwyer, M.Whelan, T.Murphy, C.Flanagan, B.McGrath, J.Cahill, P.Cadell, G.Browne, R.Doody, J.Morris, C.English, C.Darcy, M.Kehoe, L.Fairbrother. Subs: S.Neville for Doody, G.Dunne for Murphy, D.Walsh for Darcy, D.Quirke for Flanagan, C.Stakelum for Browne.
Limerick   M.O'Kelly, B.Nash, C.Nicholas, R.Connolly, J.Adams, C.O'Connor, F.Hourigan, J.Boylan, D.Carroll, M.O'Grady, A.Barrett, B.Ryan, C.Boylan, K.Hayes, C.Magner-Flynn. Subs: P.O'Brien for Magner-Flynn, J.Flynn for Carroll, D.Woulfe for Barrett, M.Bourke for Adams, C.O'Grady for M.O'Grady.

2017

Galway   D.Fahy, C.Killeen, D.Loftus, D Morrissey, R.Glennon, C.Caulfield, M.Gill, M.Colloy, C.Fahy, B.Moran, C.Walsh, M.McManus, S.Bleahene, D.Mannion, J.Canning. Subs: S.Ryan for McManus, S.McArdle for Loftus, M.Kennedy for Moran, E.Fahy for Walsh.
Cork   G.Collins, C.O'Callaghan, S.O'Leary-Hayes, E.Roche, A.Walsh-Barry, J.Keating, G.Millerick, D.Connery, D.Linehan, C.Hanafin, L.O'Shea, B.Roche, E.Sheehan, R.Downey, B.Turnbull. Subs: D.Hannon for Linehan, B.Murphy for Walsh-Barry.

CAPTAINS OF WINNING ALL-IRELAND MINOR HURLING TEAMS

1928	L. Horgan (Cork)
1929	P. Donnelly (Waterford)
1930	J. Russell (Tipperary)
1931	J. Shortall (Kilkenny)
1932	D. O'Gorman (Tipperary)
1933	J. Fletcher (Tipperary)
1934	C. Maher (Tipperary)
1935	P. Grace (Kilkenny)
1936	E. Tallent (Kilkenny)
1937	M. Goggin (Cork)
1938	K. McGrath (Cork)
1939	T. Barry (Cork)
1940	P. McCarthy (Limerick)
1941	S. Condon {Cork)
1942-1944	Suspended
1945	D. Healy (Dublin)
1946	L. Donnelly (Dublin)
1947	P. Kenny (Tipperary)
1948	M. Flannelly (Waterford)
1949	J. O'Grady (Tipperary)
1950	P. Lennon (Kilkenny)
1951	J. Clifford (Cork)
1952	A. Wall (Tipperary)
1953	B. Quinn (Tipperary)
1954	B. Boothman (Dublin)
1955	R. Reidy (Tipperary)
1956	P. Ryan (Tipperary)
1957	J. Doyle (Tipperary)
1958	P. Cobbe (Limerick)
1959	L. Kiely (Tipperary)
1960	W. Grace (Kilkenny)
1961	J. Dunphy (Kilkenny)
1962	J. Dunphy (Kilkenny)
1963	W. Bernie (Wexford)
1964	K. Cummins (Cork)
1965	L. Martin (Dublin)
1966	P. Bernie (Wexford)
1967	P. Moylan (Cork)
1968	T. Byrne (Wexford)
1969	S. Collins (Cork)
1970	P. Kavanagh (Cork)
1971	J. Buckley (Cork)
1972	B. Cody (Kilkenny)
1973	K. Robinson (Kilkenny)
1974	L. Geaney (Cork)
1975	H. Ryan (Kilkenny)
1976	J. Hogan (Tipperary)
1977	S. Fennelly (Kilkenny)
1978	P. Murphy (Cork)
1979	C. Coughlan (Cork)
1980	J. Maher (Tipperary)
1981	E. Kennedy (Kilkenny)
1982	J. Kennedy (Tipperary)
1983	A. Cunningham (Galway)
1984	A. O'Riordan (Limerick)
1985	M. O'Mahony (Cork)
1986	M. Hogan (Offaly)
1987	T Moylan (Offaly)
1988	P. Brophy (Kilkenny)
1989	B. Whelahan (Offaly)
1990	J. McDermott (Kilkenny)
1991	D. O'Neill (Kilkenny)
1992	C. Donovan (Galway)
1993	S. Doyle (Kilkenny)
1994	G. Kennedy (Galway)
1995	B. O'Keeffe (Cork)
1996	W. Maher (Tipperary)
1997	J. Reddan (Clare)
1998	C. McCarthy (Cork)
1999	J. Culkin (Galway)
2000	R. Murray (Galway)
2001	T. O'Leary (Cork)
2002	M. Rice (Kilkenny)
2003	R. Power (Kilkenny)
2004	J. Lee (Galway)
2005	A. Keary (Galway)
2006	J. McLoughney (Tipperary)
2007	B. Maher (Tipperary)
2008	T. Breen (Kilkenny)
2009	R. Cummins (Galway)
2010	C. Buckley (Kilkenny)
2011	S. Maloney (Galway)
2012	B. Maher (Tipperary)
2013	K. Daly (Waterford)
2014	D. Joyce (Kilkenny)
2015	S. Loftus (Galway)
2016	B. McGrath (Tipperary)
2017	D. Morrissey (Galway)

ALL-IRELAND MINOR HURLING FINAL REFEREES

1928	Willie Walsh (Waterford)		1974	Mick Spain (Offaly)
1929	Jim Walsh (Dublin)		1975	Jimmy Rankins (Laois)
1930	Stephen Jordan (Galway)		1976	Paddy Cronin (Cork)
1931	Paddy McNamee (Antrim)		1977	Gerry Kirwan (Offaly)
1932	P. O'Donnell (Waterford)		1978	Jim Joe Landers (Waterford)
1933	Tull Considine (Clare)		1979	Noel O'Donoghue (Dublin)
1934	Sean Robbins (Offaly)		1980	Noel Dalton (Waterford)
1935	Jim O'Regan (Cork)		1981	Michael Kelleher (Kildare)
1936	Ignatius Harney (Galway)		1982	Willie Horgan (Cork)
1937	Dan Ryan (Kerry)		1983	Pascal Long (Kilkenny)
1938	Eugene Kelly (Galway)		1984	Frank Murphy (Cork)
1939	Mick Hennessy (Clare)		1985	Seamus Brennan (Galway)
1940	Dr. Joe Stuart (Dublin)		1986	John Moore (Waterford)
1941	Dr. Joe Stuart (Dublin)		1987	Pascal Long (Kilkenny)
1945	Jim Barry (Cork)		1988	Pat Delaney (Laois)
1946	M. J. Flaherty (Galway)		1989	Willie Horgan (Cork)
1947	John Conroy (Laois)		1990	Willie Barrett (Tipperary)
1948	Gerry Rosengrave (Dublin)		1991	Pat Horan (Offaly)
1949	Gerry Rosengrave (Dublin)		1992	Terence Murray (Limerick)
1950	J. Howard (Dublin)		1993	Seán McMahon (Clare)
1951	M. Feeney (Dublin)		1994	A. Mac Suibhne (Dublin)
1952	John Conroy (Laois)		1995	Pat O'Connor (Limerick)
1953	John Conroy (Laois)		1996	Joe O'Leary (Cork)
1954	Charlie Conway (Cork)		1997	Michael Wadding (Waterford)
1955	M. Leahy (Dublin)		1998	Gerry Devlin (Armagh)
1956	C. McLoughlin (Dublin)		1999	Pat Aherne (Carlow)
1957	C. McLoughlin (Dublin)		2000	Brain Kelly (Westmeath)
1958	G. Rosengrave (Dublin)		2001	T.McIntyre (Antrim)
1959	P. Kelly (Laois)		2002	D.Kirwan (Cork)
1960	Paddy Cronin (Cork)		2003	D.Kirwan (Cork)
1961	Clem Foley (Dublin)		2004	John Sexton (Limerick)
1962	Paddy Cronin (Cork)		Replay	Brian Gavin (Offaly)
1963	Aubrey Higgins (Galway)		2005	Eamonn Morris (Dublin)
1964	Jimmy Duggan (Galway)		2006	D.Connolly (Kilkenny)
1965	Aubrey Higgins (Galway)		2007	James Owens (Wexford)
1966	Tom Foran (Tipperary)		2008	Cathal McAllister (Cork)
Replay	J. Hatton (Wicklow)		2009	James McGrath (Westmeath)
1967	P. Johnson (Kilkenny)		2010	Anthony Stapleton (Laois)
1968	Mick Slattery (Clare)		2011	J.Ryan (Tipperary)
1969	Jimmy Rankins (Laois)		2012	Colm Lyons (Cork)
1970	Clem Foley (Dublin)		Replay	A.Kelly (Galway)
1971	Mick Spain (Offaly)		2013	Cathal McAllister (Cork)
1972	John Moloney (Tipperary)		2014	Fergal Horgan (Tipperary)
1973	Seán O'Connor (Limerick)		2015	P.O'Dwyer (Carlow)
			2016	J.Keenan (Wicklow)
			2017	S.Cleere (Kilkenny)

MUNSTER MINOR HURLING FINALS

1928	Cork	3-4	3-2	Waterford
1929	Waterford	7-5	0-2	Tipperary
1930	Tipperary	4-3	3-0	Cork
1931	Tipperary	6-5	6-3	Waterford
1932	Tipperary	7-8	3-0	Clare
1933	Tipperary	3-1	2-2	Cork
1934	Tipperary	3-6	0-5	Waterford
1935	Tipperary	4-3	2-1	Cork
1936	Cork	6-5	1-4	Tipperary
1937	Cork	8-4	3-2	Limerick
1938	Cork	9-3	0-0	Kerry
1939	Cork	8-3	0-2	Clare
1940	Limerick	8-3	0-4	Clare
1941	Cork	4-6	3-3	Tipperary
1942-1944			No championship	
1945	Tipperary	8-10	0-2	Clare
1946	Tipperary	5-6	4-2	Cork
1947	Tipperary	2-4	1-2	Waterford
1948	Waterford	3-6	0-3	Tipperary
1949	Tipperary	5-6	5-5	Clare
1950	Tipperary	12-3	2-0	Clare
1951	Cork	5-11	1-3	Limerick
1952	Tipperary	10-7	1-2	Clare
1953	Tipperary	3-11	3-3	Limerick
1954	Tipperary	3-5	2-3	Limerick
1955	Tipperary	8-11	2-5	Waterford
1956	Tipperary	10-10	4-4	Waterford
1957	Tipperary	3-8	1-4	Limerick
1958	Limerick	8-9	2-5	Waterford
1959	Tipperary	5-8	1-4	Limerick
1960	Tipperary	6-7	4-3	Galway
1961	Tipperary	7-11	1-6	Cork
1962	Tipperary	4-11	4-1	Cork
1963	Limerick	4-12	5-4	Tipperary
1964	Cork	2-14	2-9	Tipperary
1965	Limerick	5-5	3-9	Tipperary
1966	Cork	6-7	2-8	Galway
1967	Cork	4-10	0-3	Limerick
1968	Cork	7-8	4-2	Waterford
1969	Cork	1-12	2-4	Tipperary
1970	Cork	3-8	4-4	Tipperary
1971	Cork	6-13	3-5	Clare
1972	Cork	4-11	0-3	Limerick
1973	Tipperary	5-12	5-4	Limerick
1974	Cork	3-7	2-10	Tipperary
Replay	Cork	2-11	2-7	Tipperary
1975	Cork	3-16	1-7	Tipperary
1976	Tipperary	5-10	5-6	Limerick
1977	Cork	2-8	2-7	Limerick
1978	Cork	1-14	3-6	Tipperary
1979	Cork	3-17	4-4	Limerick
1980	Tipperary	1-17	1-4	Limerick
1981	Clare	3-13	3-11	Tipperary
1982	Tipperary	1-10	1-7	Limerick
1983	Tipperary	3-15	2-8	Limerick
1984	Limerick	3-6	2-7	Tipperary
1985	Cork	1-13	1-8	Tipperary
1986	Cork	3-10	2-13	Tipperary
Replay	Cork	2-11	1-11	Tipperary
1987	Tipperary	2-1	1-9	Cork
1988	Cork	5-7	1-2	Tipperary
1989	Clare	2-13	2-12	Limerick
1990	Cork	1-9	0-9	Clare
1991	Tipperary	3-13	1-5	Limerick
1992	Waterford	4-7	3-10	Tipperary
Replay	Waterford	2-10	0-14	Tipperary
1993	Tipperary	1-12	1-9	Cork
1994	Cork	2-15	0-9	Waterford
1995	Cork	3-18	0-10	Waterford
1996	Tipperary	2-19	1-11	Waterford
1997	Tipperary	2-13	1-13	Clare
1998	Cork	3-13	0-8	Clare
1999	Tipperary	1-13	2-7	Clare
2000	Cork	2-19	1-10	Limerick
2001	Tipperary	1-13	1-6	Cork
2002	Tipperary	3-7	2-7	Cork
2003	Tipperary	2-12	0-16	Cork
2004	Cork	2-13	3-8	Tipperary
2005	Cork	2-18	1-12	Limerick
2006	Cork	2-20	1-15	Tipperary
2007	Tipperary	0-18	1-11	Cork
2008	Cork	0-19	0-18	Tipperary
2009	Waterford	0-18	1-13	Tipperary
2010	Clare	1-16	1-11	Waterford
2011	Clare	1-20	3-9	Waterford
2012	Tipperary	1-16	1-12	Clare

HURLING

2013	Limerick	2-19	2-19	Waterford
Replay	Limerick	1-20	4-8	Waterford
2014	Limerick	3-14	2-17	Waterford
Replay	Limerick	0-24	0-18	Waterford
2015	Tipperary	0-20	0-17	Limerick
2016	Tipperary	1-24	0-10	Limerick
2017	Cork	4-21	0-16	Clare

LEINSTER MINOR HURLING FINALS

1928	Dublin	6-6	3-2	Offaly
1929	Meath	10-1	6-1	Kilkenny
1930	Kilkenny	6-3	3-5	Laois
1931	Kilkenny	4-9	0-3	Meath
1932	Kilkenny	9-6	6-1	Dublin
1933	Kilkenny	5-8	2-6	Dublin
1934	Laois	8-4	2-0	Dublin
1935	Kilkenny	7-8	1-1	Laois
1936	Kilkenny	3-13	1-1	Dublin
1937	Kilkenny	6-12	2-4	Dublin
1938	Dublin	5-4	1-3	Laois
1939	Kilkenny	3-8	2-2	Dublin
1940	Dublin	10-5	3-3	Laois
	Note: Laois awarded title on objection			
1941	Laois	3-5	2-4	Kilkenny
1942	Kilkenny	3-10	0-4	Dublin
1943-1944	No Championship			
1945	Dublin	5-4	3-1	Kilkenny
1946	Dublin	7-5	0-1	Laois
1947	Dublin	1-5	2-2	Kilkenny
Replay	Dublin	3-2	2-4	Kilkenny
1948	Kilkenny	5-2	3-6	Offaly
1949	Kilkenny	4-6	0-4	Dublin
1950	Kilkenny	4-2	3-2	Offaly
1951	Kilkenny	5-11	2-2	Dublin
1952	Dublin	4-7	4-5	Kilkenny
1953	Dublin	2-6	1-4	Laois
1954	Dublin	4-12	4-7	Kilkenny
1955	Kilkenny	3-10	5-4	Wexford
Replay	Kilkenny	0-11	0-8	Wexford
1956	Kilkenny	4-7	3-7	Wexford
1957	Kilkenny	5-10	4-2	Offaly
1958	Kilkenny	5-11	1-7	Laois
1959	Kilkenny	7-9	3-4	Wexford
1960	Kilkenny	6-14	5-5	Wexford
1961	Kilkenny	4-12	0-7	Dublin
1962	Kilkenny	5-7	5-4	Wexford
1963	Wexford	6-10	6-8	Kilkenny
1964	Laois	4-9	3-8	Kilkenny
1965	Dublin	4-7	1-6	Wexford
1966	Wexford	7-6	1-7	Laois
1967	Wexford	6-7	2-3	Dublin
1968	Wexford	4-11	4-4	Kilkenny
1969	Kilkenny	3-9	2-7	Dublin

1970	Wexford	3-10	1-10	Kilkenny
1971	Kilkenny	7-18	3-5	Wexford
1972	Kilkenny	7-10	0-4	Wexford
1973	Kilkenny	3-10	2-9	Wexford
1974	Kilkenny	8-19	3-5	Dublin
1975	Kilkenny	2-18	3-4	Dublin
1976	Kilkenny	2-14	1-8	Wexford
1977	Kilkenny	5-10	3-6	Wexford
1978	Kilkenny	4-19	2-6	Laois
1979	Kilkenny	5-13	1-9	Antrim
1980	Wexford	1-10	2-6	Dublin
1981	Kilkenny	3-10	3-9	Wexford
1982	Kilkenny	3-16	3-4	Offaly
1983	Dublin	5-14	4-12	Wexford
1984	Kilkenny	2-10	1-11	Wexford
1985	Wexford	0-12	0-8	Kilkenny
1986	Offaly	4-7	1-5	Wexford
1987	Offaly	2-13	0-12	Kilkenny
1988	Kilkenny	2-16	0-6	Offaly
1989	Offaly	0-14	0-14	Kilkenny
Replay	Offaly	4-13	0-13	Kilkenny
1990	Kilkenny	3-15	0-15	Laois
1991	Kilkenny	1-20	0-4	Laois
1992	Kilkenny	1-9	0-11	Wexford
1993	Kilkenny	4-14	0-11	Dublin
1994	Kilkenny	2-13	3-6	Offaly
1995	Kilkenny	4-16	2-6	Offaly
1996	Kilkenny	1-16	1-11	Dublin
1997	Kilkenny	3-16	0-10	Offaly
1998	Kilkenny	1-11	1-11	Wexford
Replay	Kilkenny	2-15	0-6	Wexford
1999	Kilkenny	0-13	0-13	Wexford
Replay	Kilkenny	2-13	1-11	Wexford
2000	Offaly	0-13	0-8	Dublin
2001	Kilkenny	3-16	1-9	Wexford
2002	Kilkenny	2-15	2-8	Wexford
2003	Kilkenny	0-18	0-13	Offaly
2004	Kilkenny	1-15	1-4	Dublin
2005	Dublin	0-17	0-12	Wexford
2006	Kilkenny	4-22	1-5	Carlow
2007	Dublin	2-14	1-10	Kilkenny
2008	Kilkenny	1-19	0-12	Wexford
2009	Kilkenny	1-19	0-11	Wexford
2010	Kilkenny	1-20	0-10	Dublin
2011	Dublin	1-14	1-11	Kilkenny
2012	Dublin	2-15	1-14	Wexford

2013	Kilkenny	1-18	0-8	Laois
2014	Kilkenny	2-19	2-10	Dublin
2015	Kilkenny	1-17	1-15	Dublin
2016	Dublin	2-12	0-12	Wexford
2017	Kilkenny	3-15	1-17	Dublin

ULSTER MINOR HURLING FINALS

Year	Winner			Runner-up
1930	Down	9-7	0-6	Monaghan
1931	Antrim	5-0	3-1	Down
1932	Down	3-5	2-1	Antrim
1933	Antrim	5-4	4-5	Donegal
1934	Down	8-8	0-1	Donegal
1935	Antrim	7-7	3-1	Down
1936	Antrim	6-3	3-0	Down
1937	Antrim	5-7	2-2	Donegal
1938	Antrim w.o.			

Note: Donegal, the other finalists, were disqualified for being late taking the field in the semi-final against Derry.

Year	Winner			Runner-up
1939	Antrim	11-2	0-0	Down
1940	Antrim beat Derry			
1941	Antrim only team to compete			
1942-1944	Abandoned			
1945	Antrim	11-6	1-1	Donegal
1946	Antrim	8-7	0-2	Donegal
1947	Antrim	10-5	0-0	Down
1948	Antrim	15-6	0-0	Donegal
1949	Antrim	13-6	1-1	Donegal
1950	Antrim	4-3	1-3	Armagh
1951	Antrim	12-2	0-1	Down
1952	Antrim	8-8	1-1	Down
1953	Antrim	11-14	1-0	Donegal
1954	Antrim	9-9	1-3	Down
1955	Antrim	5-4	2-2	Armagh
1956	Antrim	7-4	1-3	Down
1957	Down	4-1	3-3	Antrim
1958	Antrim	10-5	0-2	Down
1959	Antrim	12-6	0-2	Donegal
1960	Antrim	16-4	1-0	Donegal
1961	Antrim	11-5	4-4	Donegal
1962	Antrim	12-7	2-3	Donegal
1963	Antrim	6-12	1-1	Donegal
1964	Antrim	11-11	0-0	, Armagh
1965	Antrim	7-3	0-1	Armagh
1966	Antrim	6-6	1-3	Tyrone
1967	Down	5-2	4-2	Tyrone

Note: Special final Down took part in All-Ireland "B" championship in 1967 while Antrim competed in All-Ireland "A" championship.

1968	Antrim only team in "A" championship.			

Note: Down won Special Minor Hurling title and went on to win All-Ireland.

Year	Winner			Runner-up
1969	Antrim	2-11	4-3	Down
1970	Antrim	4-12	0-5	Down
1971	Down	5-11	4-4	Derry

Note: From 1971-83 the Ulster championship was for the weaker counties and winners played in Minor "B"

All-Ireland series. Antrim played in Leinster in 1971 and also 1977-83. They represented Ulster in the All-Ireland "A" championship from 1972-76. After winning the All-Ireland "B" championship in 1978 Down also competed in Leinster from 1979-83.

Year	Winner			Runner-up
1972	Down	4-8	2-4	Armagh
1973	No Competition			
1974	Derry	3-6	2-8	Armagh
1975	Armagh	3-8	3-6	Down
1976	Down	5-12	1-3	Tyrone
1977	No Competition			
1978	Down	4-9	1-11	Derry
1979	Derry	3-8	2-4	Monaghan
1980	Derry	1-5	1-4	Armagh
1981	Derry	3-6	1-4	Armagh
1982	Derry	3-14	2-2	Armagh
1983	Derry	5-10	0-6	Monaghan
1984	Down	3-6	1-11	Antrim
1985	Down	5-4	2-9	Antrim
1986	Antrim	2-9	1-10	Derry
1987	Antrim	5-9	0-6	Down
1988	Antrim	2-10	2-9	Down
1989	Down	2-11	3-8	Antrim
Replay	Down	3-8	2-8	Antrim
1990	Derry	4-11	1-8	Antrim
1991	Derry	3-10	2-11	Antrim
1992	Antrim	0-12	0-7	Down
1993	Antrim	2-13	1-9	Down
1994	Down	3-11	3-10	Antrim
1995	Antrim	2-17	1-4	Derry
1996	Antrim	3-13	2-10	Derry
1997	Antrim	3-14	1-10	Down
1998	Antrim	3-9	0-8	Derry
1999	Antrim	2-13	0-3	Down
2000	Antrim	2-11	1-9	Derry
2001	Derry	0-13	2-5	Antrim
2002	Antrim	1-11	0-4	Derry
2003	Antrim	2-11	2-9	Derry
2004	Antrim	5-15	3-7	Down
2005	Antrim	3-18	2-7	Derry
2006	Antrim	8-18	2-5	Derry
2007	Antrim	2-14	3-8	Down
2008	Antrim	3-18	0-5	Down
2009	Antrim	4-16	0-9	Derry
2010	Antrim	2-19	0-10	Armagh
2011	Antrim	4-17	1-8	Derry
2012	Down	2-13	2-13	Antrim
Replay	Down	0-18	1-12	Antrim
2013	Antrim	2-20	1-12	Down
2014	Antrim	0-17	0-9	Derry
2015	Antrim	2-21	1-9	Derry
2016	Antrim	2-15	0-11	Down
2017	Antrim	3-13	2-8	Derry

CONNACHT MINOR HURLING FINALS

1931	Galway	7-2	1-1	Roscommon
1932	Galway	9-5	0-0	Roscommon
1933	Galway unopposed.			
1934	Galway unopposed.			
1935	Galway	9-4	1-3	Mayo
1936	Galway	7-7	1-1	Roscommon
1937	Galway	4-6	0-2	Roscommon
1938	Galway	7-3	3-0	Roscommon
1939	Galway	5-5	2-2	Roscommon
1940	Galway	7-5	1-2	Roscommon
1941	Galway unopposed.			
1942-1944	No competition.			
1945	Galway unopposed.			
1946	Galway	5-9	0-1	Roscommon
1947	Galway	9-6	1-1	Roscommon
1948	Galway	4-6	5-2	Roscommon
1949	Galway	2-7	3-4	Roscommon
	Galway	6-5	4-4	Roscommon (Replay)
1950	Galway	8-7	2-0	Roscommon
1951	Galway	6-9	2-1	Roscommon
1952	Galway	3-7	2-0	Mayo
1953	Galway	12-10	2-0	Roscommon
1954	Galway	9-9	1-1	Roscommon
1955	Galway	12-11	2-1	Roscommon
1956	Galway	11-20	1-1	Roscommon
1957	Galway w.o. Roscommon scr.			
1958	Galway	12-10	1-1	Roscommon

Note: Galway competed in Munster (1959-1969)

1959	Roscommon 3-8	3-2	Mayo
1960	Roscommon 2-8	2-5	Mayo
1961	No championship		
1962	Roscommon		
1963	Roscommon 1-7	3-0	Mayo
1964	Mayo beat Roscommon		
1965	Leitrim 8-5	0-0	Mayo
1966	Roscommon		
1967	Roscommon beat Leitrim		
	(competed in 'B' minor championship)		
1968	Roscommon		
	(competed in 'B' minor championship)		
1969	Roscommon		
	(competed in 'B' minor championship)		
1970-1988	Galway represented Province in All-Ireland series.		

1989	Galway	2-14	0-6	Roscommon

1990-2017

Galway represented Province in All-Ireland series.

HURLING

U21 HURLING CHAMPIONSHIP FINALS

1964	Tipperary	8-9	3-1	Wexford
1965	Wexford	3-7	1-4	Tipperary
1966	Cork	3-12	5-6	Wexford
Replay	Cork	4-9	4-9	Wexford
Replay	Cork	9-9	5-9	Wexford
1967	Tipperary	1-8	1-7	Dublin
1968	Cork	2-18	3-9	Kilkenny
1969	Cork	5-13	4-7	Wexford
1970	Cork	3-8	2-11	Wexford
Replay	Cork	5-17	0-8	Wexford
1971	Cork	7-8	1-11	Wexford
1972	Galway	2-9	1-10	Dublin
1973	Cork	2-10	4-2	Wexford
1974	Kilkenny	3-8	3-7	Waterford
1975	Kilkenny	5-13	2-19	Cork
1976	Cork	2-17	1-8	Kilkenny
1977	Kilkenny	2-9	1-9	Cork
1978	Galway	3-5	2-8	Tipperary
Replay	Galway	3-15	2-8	Tipperary
1979	Tipperary	2-12	1-9	Galway
1980	Tipperary	2-9	0-14	Kilkenny
1981	Tipperary	2-16	1-10	Kilkenny
1982	Cork	0-12	0-11	Galway
1983	Galway	0-12	1-6	Tipperary
1984	Kilkenny	1-12	0-11	Tipperary
1985	Tipperary	1-10	2-6	Kilkenny
1986	Galway	1-14	2-5	Wexford
1987	Limerick	2-15	3-6	Galway
1988	Cork	4-11	1-5	Kilkenny
1989	Tipperary	4-10	3-11	Offaly
1990	Kilkenny	2-11	1-11	Tipperary
1991	Galway	2-17	1-9	Offaly
1992	Waterford	4-4	0-16	Offaly
Replay	Waterford	0-12	2-3	Offaly
1993	Galway	2-14	3-11	Kilkenny
Replay	Galway	2-9	3-3	Kilkenny
1994	Kilkenny	3-10	0-11	Galway
1995	Tipperary	1-14	1-10	Kilkenny
1996	Galway	1-14	0-7	Wexford
1997	Cork	3-11	0-13	Galway
1998	Cork	2-15	2-10	Galway
1999	Kilkenny	1-13	0-14	Galway
2000	Limerick	1-13	0-13	Galway
2001	Limerick	0-17	2-10	Wexford
2002	Limerick	3-17	0-8	Galway
2003	Kilkenny	2-13	0-12	Galway
2004	Kilkenny	3-21	1-6	Tipperary
2005	Galway	1-15	1-14	Kilkenny
2006	Kilkenny	2-14	2-14	Tipperary
Replay	Kilkenny	1-11	0-11	Tipperary
2007	Galway	5-11	0-12	Dublin
2008	Kilkenny	2-13	0-15	Tipperary
2009	Clare	0-15	0-14	Kilkenny
2010	Tipperary	5-22	0-12	Galway
2011	Galway	3-14	1-10	Dublin
2012	Clare	2-17	2-11	Kilkenny
2013	Clare	2-28	0-12	Antrim
2014	Clare	2-20	3-11	Wexford
2015	Limerick	0-26	1-7	Wexford
2016	Waterford	5-15	0-14	Galway
2017	Limerick	0-17	0-11	Kilkenny

ALL-IRELAND U21 HURLING FINAL TEAMS

1964

Tipperary   P.O'Sullivan, W.Smith, N.O'Gorman, M.O'Meara, O.Killoran, C.Dwyer, L.Gaynor, M.Roche, J.Fogarty, N.Lane, M.Keating, F.Loughnane (capt.), J.Dillon, T.J.Butler, T.Brennan. Sub: P.J.Ryan for M.O'Meara.
Wexford   M.Jacob, J.Dunne, D.Quigley, B.Doyle, V.Staples, Jim Berry (capt.), W.Murphy, M.Byrne, J.Doran, C.Dowdall, C.Jacob, O.Cullen, S.Barron, A.Maher, P.Quigley. Subs: M.Kinsella for J.Dunne, B.Murray for M.Byrne, P.O'Connor for A.Maher.

1965

Wexford   M.Jacob, W.O'Neill (capt.), D.Quigley, A.Somers, V.Staples, M.Kinsella, W.Murphy, E.Ryan, J.Doran, C.Dowdall, P.Quigley, S.Barron, A.Maher, T.Doran, Jack Berry. Sub: C.Jacob.
Tipperary   S.Shinnors, M.Flanagan, J.Costigan, D.Burke, O.Killoran, N.O'Gorman, L.Gaynor, P J.Ryan, J.Quinlan, F.Loughnane, M.Keating, P.Ryan, T.Brennan, T.J.Butler, J.Ryan. Sub: M.O'Meara.

1966

Cork   J.Mitchell, W.Murphy, T.Falvey, P.O'Sullivan, C.Roche, J.Russell, D.Coughlan, J.McCarthy, G.McCarthy (capt.), S.Barry, T.Browne, P.Curley, C.McCarthy, A.O'Flynn, Eddie O'Brien. Subs: A.Maher, B.McKeown.
Note: B.McKeown, K.Farrell, D.Clifford and P.O'Riordan played in first drawn game. T.Falvey, D.Coughlan, G.McCarthy and A.O'Flynn were in for second game. Subs in first game: T.Falvey for B.McKeown, G.McCarthy for J.Russell. Sub in second game: T.Browne for Eddie O'Brien.T .Browne played in third game in place of B.Wylie.
Wexford   H.Butler, W.O'Neill, M.Nolan, A.Somers, W.Bowe, M.Kinsella, V.Staples, M.Jacob, C.Dowdall, S.Barron, P.Quigley, J.Quigley, P.Butler, T.Doran, E.Cousins. Sub: M.Gardiner.
Note: J.Murphy and T.Murphy played in first drawn game. P.O'Brien and B.Ronan were on for second game. Sub in first game: B.Ronan for T.Murphy. Subs in second game: N.Rochford for B.Ronan, B.Ronan for N.Rochford. H.Butler, W.Bowe and P Butler came on for third game in place of P.O'Brien, B.Ronan and M.Gardiner.

1967

Tipperary   H.Condron, S.Ryan, J.Kelly, D.Grady, M.Esmonde, T.O'Connor, S.Hogan, P.J.Ryan (capt.), C.Davitt, P.Lowry, N.O'Dwyer, J.Ryan, J.Walsh, P.O'Connor, J.Flanagan. Subs: M.Nolan, T.Delaney.
Dublin   M.Behan, M.Hannick, P.Martin, C.Brennan, W.Markey, F.Cooney, G.O'Driscoll, H.Dalton, F.McDonnell, E.McGrath, E.Davey, L.Hennebry, T.Grealish, C.Moran, N.Kinsella. Sub: M.Kennedy.

1968

Cork   B.Hurley, W.Murphy, B.Tobin, F.Norberg, N.Dunne, W.Walsh, R.Cummins, D.Clifford, P.Moylan, B.Meade, S.Murphy, P.Hegarty (capt.), H.O'Sullivan, P.Curley, P.Ring. Subs: M.McCarthy, R.Lehane, J.Murphy.
Kilkenny   J.Nolan, L.Byrne, C.O'Brien, M.Leahy, J.O'Shea, N.Morrissey, P.Kealy, F.Cummins, P.Lawlor, W.Harte, F.Farrell, J.Kinsella, P.Dowling, P.Keyes, B.O'Sullivan. Subs: T.Grant, S.Brennan, S.Kearney.

1969

Cork   B.Hurley, M.McCarthy (capt.), B.Tobin, F.Norberg, S.Looney, D.Clifford, Ted O'Brien, S.Murphy, P.Moylan, B.Meade, W.Walsh, N.Dunne, F.Keane, R.Cummins, B.Cummins. Sub: P.McDonnell for S.Looney.
Wexford   P.Cox, E.McDonald, E.Murphy, B.Butler, E.Walsh, J.Russell, L.Bennett, M.Dalton, E.Buggy, T.Royce, M.Quigley, M.Browne, J.Quigley, M.Butler, C.Doran. Subs: T.Byrne for C.Doran, M.Casey.

1970

Cork   M.Coleman, M.McCarthy, P.McDonnell, B.Tobin, S.Murphy, J.Horgan, Ted O'Brien (capt.), S.Looney, P Moylan, C.Kelly, B.Cummins, K.McSweeney, S.O'Leary, J.Barrett, P.Ring.
Note: M.Malone and J.Nodwell played in drawn game. S.O'Leary and C.Kelly were on for replay. Subs in drawn game: S.O'Leary for M.Malone, C.Kelly for J.Nodwell.
Wexford   P.Cox, J.Prendergast, J.Russell, E.McDonald, G.Collins, L.Byrne, L.Bennett (capt.), T.Byrne, C.Doran, B.Murphy M.Quigley, E.Murphy, M.Butler, M.Casey, P.Byrne. Subs: A.Kerrigan for B.Murphy, M.Byrne for P.Byrne, E.Walsh for E.Murphy.
Note: Subs in drawn game: A.Kerrigan for P.Byrne, P.Byrne for B.Murphy. Wexford same team in draw and replay.

1971

Cork   M.Coleman, J.Horgan, P.McDonnell (capt.), B.Murphy, Séamus O'Farrell, M.O'Doherty, B.Coleman, S.Looney, N.Crowley, E.Fitzpatrick, M.Malone, K.McSweeney, B.Cummins, J.Rothwell, S.O'Leary. Subs: P.Casey for S.O'Farrell, D.Collins for E.Fitzpatrick, P.Kavanagh for S.Looney.
Wexford   P.Cox, J.Higgins, G.O'Connor, P.O'Brien, A.Kerrigan, L.Kinsella, L.Bennett, M.Quigley (capt.), A.Dwyer, B.Dunne, T.Byrne, S.Kinsella, P.Flynn, M.Casey, M.Butler. Subs: J.Russell for A.Dwyer, B.Murphy for J.Higgins.

1972

Galway   E.Campbell, L.Glynn, G.Kelly, L.Shields, I.Clarke (capt.), F.Donoghue, A.Brehony, G.Glynn, F.Burke, M.Coen, A.Fenton, M.Donoghue, M.Barrett, T.O'Donoghue, G.Holland. Subs: P.J.Molloy for M.Coen, J.McDonagh for M.Barrett.
Dublin   M.Holden, M.Leonard, N.Quinn, V.Lambe, G.Ryan, J.Brennan, E.Rheinisch, P.J.Holden, M.Greally, P.Lee, V.Holden, J.Kealy (capt.), C.Hennebry, B.Sweeney, J.Whelan. Sub: G.O'Connor for M.Greally, D.O'Donovan for P.Lee.

1973

Cork   F.O'Sullivan, M.Corbett, L.Kelly, B.Murphy, M.O'Doherty (capt.), J.Buckley, D.Burns, T.Crowley, B.Cotter, P.Kavanagh, Seamus O'Farrell, Tony Murphy, D.Relihan, T.Fogarty, S.O'Leary. Subs: T.Sheehan, J.Barry Murphy.
Wexford   J.Nolan, M.Hickey, S.Byrne, M.Dempsey, J.Moloney, E.Breen, R.Lambert, R.Kinsella, P.J.Harris, J.Murphy, A.Dwyer, C.Keogh, N.Walsh, J.Allen, S.Storey. Subs: M.Carty, S.Murphy.

1974

Kilkenny   K.Fennelly, T.McCormack, M.Hogan, J.Dunne, G.Henderson, B.Cody, M.Tierney, J.Dowling, S.Brophy, N.Brennan, G.Woodcock, G.Fennelly (capt.), P.Kearney, A.Teehan, W.Fitzpatrick. Subs: R.Sweeney for A.Teehan, P.Mulcahy for N.Brennan.
Waterford   W.Ryan, F.McCarthy, M.Flynn, K.Ryan, L.O'Brien, J.Galvin, E.Ryan, P.Egan, P.McGrath, B.Mansfield, L.Power, T.Casey, P.O'Keeffe, M.McNamara, P.Moore. Subs: L.Ahearne for P.Moore, E.Kehoe for M.Moore.

1975

Kilkenny K.Fennelly (capt.), J.Marnell, J.Moran, Dick O'Hara, G.Henderson, B.Cody, J.Grace, J.Dowling, G.Fennelly, J.Hennessy, M.Tierney, J.Lyng, Terry Brennan, R.Sweeney, W.Fitzpatrick. Subs: K.Robinson, J.O'Sullivan, G.Woodcock.
Cork F.O'Sullivan, J.Kennefick, D.Hurley, J.O'Herlihy, C.Brassil, K.Murphy, J.Crowley, J.Fenton, F.Delaney, B.Óg Murphy, Seán O'Farrell, Tadhg Murphy, E.O'Sullivan, J.Barry Murphy, Tom Collins. Sub: Tadhg O'Sullivan for T.Collins.

1976

Cork J.Cronin, J.Crowley, W.Geaney, D.McCurtain, J.Fenton, T.Cashman, F.Delaney, S.O'Mahony, C.Brassil, J.Allen, R.McDonnell, P.Horgan, Tadhg Murphy (capt.), K.Murphy, D.Buckley. Sub: W.Reidy.
Kilkenny K.Fennelly, J.Marnell, D.Tyrell, D.O'Hara, H.Ryan, J.Moran, R.Reid, J.Hennessy, K.Robinson, J.Lyng, M.Lyng, K.Brennan, B.Fennelly, G.Tyrell, O.Bergin. Subs: B.Waldron, P.Dunphy, M.Kennedy.

1977

Kilkenny E.Mahon, J.Lennon, J.Henderson, P.Prendergast, J.Hennessy, D.O'Hara, R.Reid, P.Lannon, M.Kennedy, R.Power, M.Lyng (capt.), B.Waldron, B.Fennelly, G.Tyrell, J.Wall. Sub: K.Brennan.
Cork J.Cronin, J.Murphy, J.Crowley, F.Delaney, C.Brassil, T.Cashman, D.McCurtain, D.O'Herlihy, J.O'Brien, P.Horgan, T.Lyons, Paul Crowley, T.Murphy, R.McDonnell, D.Buckley. Subs: D.Keane, G.McEvoy, D.Ryan.

1978

Galway G.Smith, C.Hayes, M.Headd, P.J.Burke, J.Greaney, M.Earls, S.Coen, S.Mahon, M.Kilkenny, G.Kennedy, J.Goode, P.Ryan, B.Forde (capt.), Matty Conneely, J.Ryan.
Note: Subs in drawn game: T.Brehony, J.Coen and S.Forde. G.Linnane played in drawn game. Gerry Kennedy came on for replay.
Tipperary V.Mullins, J.Doyle, J.O'Dwyer, P.Loughnane, M.Stapleton, P.Fitzelle, G.Stapleton, J.Grace, P.Ryan, T.Walsh, M.Doyle, E.O'Shea, T.Ryan, S.Burke, T.Grogan.
Note: Subs: Enda Hogan, K.Fox, A.Slattery, J.Minogue played in drawn game. M.Stapleton was on for replay. Subs in drawn game: K.Fox, M.Murphy, and E.Hogan.

1979

Tipperary V.Mullins, P.Loughnane, J.Ryan, E.Hogan, A.Slattery, J.O'Dwyer, G.Stapleton, G.O'Connor, P.Fox, M.Murphy, E.O'Shea, T.Grogan, B.Mannion, M.Doyle (capt.), P.Looby. Sub: P.Ryan for T.Grogan.
Galway A.Carr, T.Brehony, M.Headd, C.Hayes (capt.), S.Coen M.Earls, E.Reilly, S.Davoren, M.Donoghue, J.Coen, G.Linnane, P.Ryan, S.Dolan, D.Burke, J.Ryan. Subs: G.Dempsey for M.Donoghue, J.Hanlon for G.Linnane, V.Kelly For M.Headd.

1980

Tipperary V.Mullins, M.Ryan, Cormac Bonnar, P.Fox, B.Heffernan, J.O'Dwyer, P.McGrath, M.Kennedy, P.Kennedy (capt.), M.Murphy, B.Ryan, A.Buckley, J.Kennedy, D.O'Connell, P.Power. Sub: A.Kinsella for M.Kennedy.
Kilkenny M.Walsh, M.Morrissey, M.Meagher, W.O'Hara, T.Lennon, W.Doherty, S.Fennelly, E.Wallace, G.Ryan, J Mulcahy, R.Murphy, M.Nash, W.McEvoy, L.Ryan, W.Purcell. Sub: J.Heffernan for R.Murphy.

1981

Tipperary J.Farrell, M.Ryan, P.Brennan, P.Fox, I.Conroy, J.McIntyre, P.McGrath, A.Kinsella, P.Kennedy (capt.), N.English, B.Ryan, M.McGrath, G.O'Neill, D.O'Connell, A.Buckley.
Kilkenny M.Walsh, P.Ryan, E.Aylward, J.Holden, S.Norris, W.O'Hara, M.Cleere, P.Gannon, M.Byrne, W.McEvoy, M.J.Ryan, W.Walton, J.Murphy, J.O'Dwyer, W.Purcell. Subs: S.Tyrrell for J.Holden, E.Crowley for J.Murphy.

1982

Cork G.Cunningham, M.McCarthy (capt.), M.Boylan, J.Hodgins, W.Cashman, K.O'Driscoll, Colm O'Connor, K.Hennessy, D.Curtin, Tony O'Sullivan, Tony Coyne, D.Walsh, E.Brosnan, M.O'Sullivan, Ger Motherway. Subs: P.Deasy for K.O'Driscoll, T.Mulcahy for G.Motherway, Gabriel McCarthy for M.O'Sullivan.
Galway T.Coen, M.Mooney, P.Casserly, D.Burke, P.Healy, T.Nolan, O.Kilkenny, A.Staunton, J.Boland, M.Haverty, P.Piggott, P.Murphy, J.Murphy, M.Grealish, M.McGrath. Subs: N.Morrissey for John Boland, A.Keady for M.Grealish.

1983

Galway T.Coen, B.Dervan, P.Casserly (capt.), M.Donoghue, P.Finnerty, A.Keady, O.Kilkenny, A.Moylan, P.Healy, A.Staunton, M.Coleman, M.Costelloe, G.Burke, J.Murphy, M.McGrath. Subs: E.Ryan for G.Burke, C.Hennebry for M.Costelloe, M.Kenny for C.Hennebry.
Tipperary K.Hogan, Colm Bonnar, P.Maher, E.Hogan, I.Conroy, N.English, D.Finnerty (capt.), J.Hayes, L.Bergin, P.Kenny, C.Donovan, M.McGrath, G.O'Neill, W.Peters, A.Browne. Subs: J.Kennedy for W.Peters, J.Maher for P.Kenny, V.Dooley for J.Hayes.

1984

Kilkenny D.Burke, E.Wall, E.O'Connor, B.Young, D.Hoyne, L.Cleere, L.Walsh, T.Phelan, R.Heffernan, D.Carroll, P.Walsh, J.McDonald, L.McCarthy, R.McCarthy, S.Delahunty (capt.). Subs: P.Ryan for D.Carroll, M.Rafter for D.Carroll.
Tipperary K.Hogan, J.McKenna, Eddie Hogan, Colm Bonnar, R.Stakelum, D.Kealy, J.Leahy, J.Kennedy, J.Hayes, A.Ryan, N.Sheehy, P.Kenny, A.Waters, D.Fogarty, M.Scully. Subs: W.Peters for P.Kenny, M.Cuningham for M.Scully.

1985

Tipperary J.Leamy, N.McDonnell, P.O'Donoghue, Colm Bonnar, M.Corcoran, D.Kealy, P.Delaney, J.Kennedy, A.Ryan, M.Cunningham, J.McGrath, N.Sheehy, J.Cormack, L.Stokes, M.Scully (capt.). Sub: M.Bryan for L.Stokes.
Kilkenny R.Dunne, K.Ryan (capt.), E.O'Connor, P.Healy, T.Lannon, L.Cleere, L.O'Brien, T.Phelan, J.Scott, R.Moran, S.Delahunty, E.Morrissey, M.Dunne, M.Rafter, J.Walsh. Subs: P.Cleere for M.Rafter, T.Bawle for T.Phelan, P.Barron for J.Scott.

1986

Galway J.Commins, P.Dervan, M.Kelly, M.Flaherty, M.Helebert, P.Malone, G.McInerney, T.Monaghan, D.Jennings, M.Connolly, A.Cunningham (capt.), A.Davoren, P.Nolan, Joe Cooney, P.Higgins. Subs: G.Elwood for P.Higgins, S.Keane for T.Monaghan.
Wexford P.Nolan, J.Doyle, M.Foley, P.Bridges, L.O'Gorman, T.Dempsey, K.Murphy, Matt Foley, P.Barden, E.Sinnott, V.Murphy, D.Prendergast, M.Morrissey, P.Carton, R.Murphy. Subs: N.McDonald for M.Foley, J.Murray for D.Prendergast, C.Whelan for L.O'Gorman.

1987
Limerick   V.Murnane, A.Madden, P.Carey, D.Flynn, D.Nash, A.O'Riordan, M.Reale, G.Hegarty, J.O'Neill, G.Kirby, A.Carmody, G.Ryan (capt.), P.Barrett, J.O'Connor, L.O'Connor. Sub: D.Marren for P.Barrett.
Galway   M.Finnerty, B.Cawley, S.Dolphin, B.Cooney, T.Broderick, J.Burke, T.King, D.Cox, G.Coyne, M.Connolly (capt.), K.Coen, H.Davoren, M.Greaney, E.Burke, R.Duane. Subs: E.Lyons for M.Greaney, P.Killilea for T.Broderick, B.Hurney for K.Coen.

1988
Cork   T.Kingston, C.Connery (capt.), D.Irwin, S.O'Leary, C.Casey, P.Kenneally, A.Kealy, P.Delaney, J.Kennedy, A.Ryan, M.Cunningham, J.McGrath, N.Sheehy, J.Cormack, L.Stokes, M.Scully (capt.).Sub M.Bryan for L.Stokes.
Kilkenny   R.Dunne, K.Ryan (Capt.), E.O'Connor, P Healy, T.Lannon, L.Cleere, L.O'Brien, T.Phelan, J.Scott, R.Moran, S.Delahunty, E.Morrissey, M.Dunne, M.Rafter, J.Walsh. Subs:: P.Cleere for M.Rafter, T.Bawle for T.Phelan, P.Barron for J.Scott.

1989
Tipperary   B.Bane, L.Sheedy, M.Ryan, G.Frend, J.Madden, Conal Bonnar, S.Maher, J.Leahy, Declan Ryan (capt.), P.Hogan, C.Stakelum, Dinny Ryan, M.Nolan, D.Quirke, T.Lanigan. Subs: J.Cahill for Maher, D.Lyons for Lanigan, K.Ryan for Cahill.
Offaly   John Troy, B.Whelehan, D.Geoghegan, B.Hennessy, R.Mannion, B.Kelly, G.Cahill, J.Pilkington, A.Cahill, B.Dooley, D.Regan, Johnny Dooley, R.Byrne, D.Pilkington, M.Duignan. Sub: J.Kilmartin for Byrne.

1990
Kilkenny   J.Conroy, J.Holohan, P.O'Neill, D.Carroll, P.Brophy, T.Murphy, J.Conlon, J.Brennan (capt.), B.McGovern, A.Ronan, J.Lawlor, T.Shefflin, D.J.Carey, P.Treacy, C.Carter. Subs: P.O'Grady for Shefflin, J.Walton for McGovern.
Tipperary   B.Bane, L.Fallon, M.Ryan, G.Frend, E.Maher, N.Keane, B.Corcoran, J.Leahy (capt.), Conal Bonnar, C.Egan, L.Sheedy, G.Deely, D.Lyons, P.O'Brien, A.Wall. Subs: M.O'Meara for Egan, K.McCormack for Lyons.

1991
Galway   R.Burke, C.Helebert, B.Feeney (capt.), M.Killilea, G.McGrath, P.Hardiman, N.Power, B.Keogh, N.Larkin, L.Burke, J.Campbell, T.O'Brien, B.Larkin, J.Rabbitte, C.Moran. Subs: P.Egan for Hardiman, M.Curtin for Larkin.
Offaly   Damien Franks, M.Hogan, K.Kinahan, Donal Franks, D.Dooley, H.Rigney, B.Whelehan, J.Pilkington, P.Temple, Johnny Dooley, S.Grennan, A.Cahill, John Troy, J.Brady, E.Mulhare. Subs: O.O'Neill for Cahill, D.Barron for Brady.

1992
Waterford   R.Barry, K.O'Gorman, O.Dunphy, M.O'Sullivan, T.Browne (capt.), P.Fanning, F.Hartley, T.Fives, J.Brenner, A.Fitzgerald, M.Hubbard, Kevin McGrath, N.Dalton, S.Daly, P.Flynn. Sub: P Power for Dalton.
Note: P.Power played in drawn game. P.Flynn was on for replay. Subs: in drawn game: M.Geary for P Power, P.Flynn for M.Geary.
Offaly   Damien Franks, H.Kilmartin, K.Kinahan, Donal Franks, D.Barron, H.Rigney, B.Whelehan (capt.), S.Óg Farrell, M.Hogan, Johnny Dooley, S.Grennan, John Troy, M.Gallagher, N.Hand.O.O'Neill. Sub: A.Cahill for Hogan.
Note: K.Martin played in drawn game. D.Barron was on for replay. Sub in drawn game: B.Gath for M.Hogan.

1993
Galway   M.Darcy.A.Headd, W.Burke, D.Canning, R.Walsh, N.Shaughnessy, M.Donoghue, L.Burke (capt.), Michael Kearns, F.Forde, J.McGrath, A.Kirwan, Peter Kelly, D.Coleman, M.Headd. Subs: C.O'Donovan for Coleman, C.O'Doherty for Kirwan, M.Kilkelly for P.Kelly.
Note: M.Kilkelly played in drawn game.Michael Kearns was on for replay. Subs: in drawn game: C.O'Doherty for N.Shaughnessy, P.Coyne for P.Kelly and N.O'Shaughnessy for P.Kelly.
Kilkenny   J.Dermody, D.Beirne (capt.), M.Holohan, J.Carroll, D.O'Neill, E.Kennedy, P.Larkin, A.Comerford, C.Brennan, P.Farrell, J.McDermott, D.Maher, P.J.Delaney, S.Ryan, D Lawlor. Subs: M.Owens for McDermott, D.Hennessy for Ryan.
Note: J.Shefflin played in drawn game, J.McDermott was on for replay. Subs in drawn game: J.McDermott for J.Shefflin, M.Dowling for D.Maher, M.Owens for S.Ryan.

1994
Kilkenny   M.Carey, S.Meally, E.Drea, B.Power, A.O'Sullivan, E.Dwyer, P.Larkin (capt.), B.McEvoy, D.Maher, S.Dollard, P.Barry, P.J.Delaney, B.Ryan, D.Byrne, R.Shortall. Subs: O.O'Connor for Barry, D.O'Neill for McEvoy.
Galway   L.O'Donoghue, D.Canning, W.Burke, M.Spellman, P.Diviney, N.Shaughnessy, M.Donoghue, C.O'Doherty, C.O'Donovan, F.Forde, J.McGrath, D.Coen, Peter Kelly, O.Fahy, M.Headd. Subs: D.Coleman for Fahy, C.Moore for Headd.

1995
Tipperary   B.Cummins, L.Barron, P.Shelly, P.Shanahan, B.Horgan (capt.), K.Slevin, B.Flannery, A.Butler, Terry Dunne, Thomas Dunne, L.McGrath, E.Enright, K.Tucker, D.O'Connor, D.Bourke. Sub: P.O'Dwyer for Enright.
Kilkenny   M.Carey, B.Lonergan, E.Drea, T.Hickey, V.O'Brien, J.Costelloe, E.Dwyer, D.Maher, P.Barry (capt.), D.Cleere, L.Smith, B.McEvoy, B.Ryan, D.Byrne, D.Buggy. Subs: M.Owens for Buggy, O.O'Connor for Smith.

1996
Galway   E.Cloonan, G.Kennedy, P.Huban (capt.), L.Hodgins, B.Higgins, C.Moore, M.Healy, G.Glynn, O.Fahy, D.Moran, V.Maher, F.Healy, A.Kerins, D.Coen, K.Broderick. Subs: M.Cullinane for Higgins, D.Walsh for F Healy.
Wexford   M.J.Cooper, J.Hegarty, E.Doyle, T.Radford, D.Ruth, J.Purcell, M.O'Leary, R.McCarthy, M.Byrne, J.Lawlor, S.Colfer, E.Cullen, P.Codd, G.Laffan, M.Jordan. Subs: D.Kent for Jordan, D.O'Connor for Laffan, P.J.Carley for Colfer.

1997
Cork   D.Óg Cusack, J.Browne; D.O'Sullivan, W.Sherlock, D.Barrett, D.Murphy (capt.), S.Óg hAilpín, P.Ryan, A.Walsh, B.O'Driscoll, T.McCarthy, M.O'Connell, J.O'Flynn, D.Ronan, J.Deane. Subs: S.O'Farrell for O'Flynn, B.Coleman for McCarthy.
Galway   N.Murray, G.Kennedy, P.Huban, F.Gantley, V.Maher, M.Healy, L.Hodgins, R.Gantley, G.Glynn, F Healy, M.Cullinane, K.Broderick, A.Kerins, E.Cloonan, O.Canning. Subs: D.Shaughnessy for Broderick, B.Higgins for Huban, M.Kerins for O.Canning.

1998
Cork   D.Óg Cusack, M.Prendergast, D.O'Sullivan, W.Sherlock, D.Barrett, D.Murphy (capt.), S.Óg Ó hAilpín, A.Walsh, L.Mannix, N.Ronan, T.McCarthy, M.O'Connell, B.O'Keeffe, S.O'Farrell, J.Deane. Subs: J.Anderson for Mannix, B.O'Connor for O'Farrell.

Galway   T.Grogan, V.Maher, J.Feeney, L.Madden, F.Healy,
M.Healy, G.Lynskey, P.Walsh, A.Kerins, R.Gantley, C.Connaughton,
M.Cullinane, K.Broderick, M.Kerins, E.Cloonan.
Subs: D.Shaughnessy for Connaughton, R.Cullinane for Gantley.

1999
Kilkenny   J.Power, A.Walpole, N.Hickey, M.Kavanagh,
A.Cummins, S.Dowling, R.Mullally, J.O'Neill, J.P.Corcoran,
M.Gordon, J.Coogan, K.Power, A.Geoghegan, H.Shefflin,
E.Brennan. Subs: P.Delaney for A.Geoghegan, J.Barron for
E.Brennan.
Galway   N.Murray, E.McDonagh, D.Cloonan, S.McClearn,
E.Linnane, R.Gantley, D.O'Shaughnessy, E.Tannian, E.Donoghue,
D.Tierney, M.Kerins, D.Loughrey, A.Poniard, E.Cloonan,
D.Donoghue. Subs: S.Lawless for A.Poniard, R.Cullinane for
D.Loughrey, J.Culkin for E.Donoghue.

2000
Limerick   T.Houlihan, D.Reale, E.Mulcahy, P.Reale, P.O'Reilly,
B.Geary, W.Walsh, J.Meskell, S.Lucey, P.O'Grady, S.O'Connor,
D.Stapleton, D.Sheehan, B.Begley, M.Keane. Sub: K.Tobin for
O'Connor.
Galway   K.Callanan, E.McDonagh, D.Cloonan, J.Cannon,
D.Hardiman, C.Dervan, S.Morgan, J.Culkin, S.Donoghue, D.Forde,
E.Hyland, E.Donoghue, D.Joyce, D.Huban, D.Donoghue.
Subs: D.Tierney for Joyce, B.Cunningham for Hyland, M.Greaney
for Huban, G.Keary for E.Donoghue.

2001
Limerick   T.Houlihan, D.Reale, B.Carroll, E.Mulcahy,
M.O'Riordan, B.Geary, M.O'Brien, P.Lawlor, S.Lucey, E.Foley,
K.Tobin, P.Tobin, C.Fitzgerald, N.Moran, M.Keane. Sub
A.O'Shaughnessy for P.Tobin.
Wexford   M.White, N.Maguire, D.O'Connor, R.Kirwan, R.Mallon,
B.McGee, T.Kelly, N.Lambert, D.Stamp, R.Barry, G.Coleman,
R.Jacob, B.Lambert, M.Jacob, D.Lyng. Subs: P.Donoghue for
Kirwan, P.Carley for N.Lambert, N.Lambert for Barry.

2002
Limerick   T.Houlihan, D.Reale, E.Mulcahy, M.Cahill, E.Foley,
P.O'Dwyer, M.O'Brien, P.Lawlor, N.Moran, C.Fitzgerald, J.O'Brien,
K.Tobin, A.O'Shaughnessy, P.Kirby, M.Keane. Subs: P.Tobin for
Fitzgerald, B.Carroll for O'Dwyer, R.Hayes for M.O'Brien.
Galway   A.Diviney, B.O'Mahony, S.Kavanagh, J.Culkin,
F.Moore, C.Dervan, D.Forde, T.Óg Regan, G.Farragher, R.Murray,
M.Coughlan, K.Brady, F.Hayes, A.Cullinane, D.Green.
Subs: J.P.O'Connell for Regan, M.J.Quinn for Coughlan, K.Burke
for Green.

2003
Kilkenny   D.Herity, G.Joyce, C.Hickey, M.Phelan, K.Coogan,
J.Tyrrell, J.J.Delaney, S.Hennessy, T.Walsh, C.Phelan, P.Cleere,
W.O'Dwyer, A.Fogarty, M.Rice, B.Dowling. Subs: S.O'Neill for
Dowling, E.McCormack for Cleere.
Galway   A.Diviney, D.Collins, T.Óg Regan, F.Moore,
S.Kavanagh, E.Lynch, A.Cullinane, K.Brady, B.Mahony, D.Hayes,
T.Tierney, R.Murray, K.Burke, G.Farragher, D.Greene.
Subs: N.Healy for Burke, J.P.O'Connell for Greene, W.Donnellan
for Tierney.

2004
Kilkenny   D.Herity, S.Maher, J.Tennyson, M.Fennelly, T.Walsh,
P.J.Delaney, C.Hoyne, S.Hennessy, P.Cleere, S.O'Neill, W.O'Dwyer,
E.Reid, J.Fitzpatrick, C.Phelan, R.Power. Subs: M.Wright for
Fitzpatrick, B.Dowling for Cleere, E.Larkin for Reid, J.Phelan for
O'Neill, N.Doherty for Delaney.
Tipperary   P.McCormack, A.Morrissey, C.O'Mahony, D.Walton,
E.Hanley, D.Fitzgerald, H.Moloney, J.Caesar, W.Cully, P.Buckley,
S.Sweeney, F.Devanney, E.Sweeney, T.Scroope, M.Farrell.
Subs: W.Ryan for A.Morrisey, D.Sheppard for Buckley, D.Morrissey
for E.Sweeney, T.Fitzgerald for S.Sweeney, P.Shortt for Cully.

2005
Galway   A.Ryan, P.Flynn, A.Gaynor, K.Briscoe, G.Mahon,
B.Cullinane, D.Collins, B.Lucas, A.Garvey, J.Gantley, A.Callanan,
E.Ryan, N.Healy, K.Burke, K.Wade. Subs: F.Coone for Ryan,
C.Dervan for Gantley, D.Kelly for Cullinane.
Kilkenny   D.Fogarty, S.Maher, J.Tennyson, D.Cody, J.Dalton,
P.J.Delaney, C.Hoyne, M.Fennelly, M.Rice, E.Larkin, A.Murphy,
W.O'Dwyer, E.Reid, J.Fitzpatrick, R.Power. Sub: D.McCormack for
Murphy.

2006
Kilkenny   L.Tierney, K.Joyce, J.Tennyson, S.Cummins, P.Hartley,
J.Dalton, D.Fogarty, J.Fitzpatrick, M.Fennelly, T.J.Reid, A.Murphy,
P.Hogan, R.Hogan, R.Power, D.McCormack. Sub: A.Healy for
McCormack.
Tipperary   G.Kennedy, P.Stapleton, A.Byrne, C.O'Brien, D.Young,
J.B.McCarthy, S.Horan, J.Woodlock, S.Lillis, R.O'Dwyer, N.Teehan,
D.Sheppard, R.Ruth, D.O'Hanlon, D.Egan. Subs: P.Austin for
Sheppard, K.Lanigan for Horan, D.Hickey for Teehan, K.Quinlan
for Lillis.
*Note: In the drawn encounter for Kilkenny A.Healy started
for R.Hogan while for Tipperary R.McLoughney started for
D.O'Hanlon. Subs in the drawn match were: Kilkenny R.Hogan
for Healy, M.Nolan for P.Hogan, B.Beckett for Murphy. Tipperary
D.O'Hanlon for McLoughney, D.Hickey for Ruth, K.Quinlan for
McCarthy.*

2007
Galway   J.Skehill, A.Leech, G.Mahon, C.O'Donovan, M.Ryan,
J.Lee, A.Keary, D.Kennedy, K.Kilkenny, S.Glynn, K.Hynes, F.Coone,
C.Cavanagh, J.Canning, K.Wade. Subs: B.Hanley for Glynn,
A.Harte for Kennedy, J.Greene for Coone, N.Kelly for Kavanagh,
P.Loughnane for Leech.
Dublin   P.Curtin, R.Drumgoole, P.O'Callaghan, D.Webster,
K.Dunne, T.Brady, J.Boland, J.McCaffrey, A.McCrabbe, E.Moran,
R.O'Carroll, D.Connolly, P.Carton, D.O'Dwyer, S.Durkin.
Subs: M.McGarry for Webster, I.Fleming for O'Carroll, S.Lehane
for Connolly.

2008
Kilkenny   C.McGrath, P.Murphy, K.Joyce, E.O'Shea, L.Ryan,
P.Hogan, N.Prendergast, J.Dowling, N.Walsh, C.Fennelly, J.Mulhall,
T.J.Reid, M.Ruth, N.Cleere, R.Hogan. Subs: J.J.Farrell for Cleere,
J.Maher for Dowling, M.Bergin for Farrell.
Tipperary   M.Ryan, M.Cahill, P.Maher, K.Maher, K.Lanigan,
T.Stapleton, B.Maher, G.Ryan, S.Hennessy, P.Maher, S.Callanan,
T.McGrath, P.Bourke, M.O'Meara, S.Bourke. Subs: J.O'Keeffe for
Lanigan, D.O'Hanlon for O'Meara, P.Ivors for S.Bourke, J.Ryan for
McGrath.

2009

Clare   D.Tuohy, E.Glynn, C.Dillon, C.O'Doherty, D.O'Donovan, N.O'Connell, J.Gunning, E.Barrett, C.O'Donovan, C.Morey, J.Conlon, S.Collins, C.Tierney, D.Honan, C.Ryan. Subs: C.McGrath for Tierney, P.O'Connor for Morey, E.Hayes for Gunning.

Kilkenny   C.McGrath, P.Murphy, P.Nolan, C.Fogarty, M.Walsh, D.Langton, Lester Ryan, M.Kelly, Liam Ryan, C.Fennelly, M.Bergin, J.Mulhall, R.Hogan, J.J.Farrell, J.Nolan. Sub: N.Cleere for Bergin.

2010

Tipperary   J.Logue, K.O'Gorman, P.Maher, M.Cahill, J.Barry, B.Maher, C.Hough, S.Hennessy, N.McGrath, S.Carey, P.Murphy, P.Maher, M.Heffernan, B.O'Meara, J.O'Dwyer. Subs: C.Coughlan for O'Gorman, J.O'Neill for O'Dwyer, A.Ryan for Murphy, J.Gallagher for McGrath, K.Morris for Heffernan.

Galway   K.Finnegan, D.Connolly, P.Gordan, G.O'Halloran, N.Donoghue, D.Burke, S.Óg Linnane, J.Coen, B.Daly, J.Regan, N.Quinn, E.Forde, R.Cummins, G.Burke, G.Kelly. Subs: J.Cooney for Forde, B.Burke for G.Burke, J.Grealish for Linnane, D.Glennon for Cummins, B.O'Flaherty for Gordan.

2011

Galway   J.Ryan, D.Connolly, N.Donoghue, G.O'Halloran, J.Grealish, P.Gordan, R.Foy, J.Coen, D.Burke, C.Cooney, N.Burke, T.Haran, J.Regan, B.Daly, D.Glennon. Subs: R.Burke for Gordan, B.Burke for Haran, D.Fox for Cooney, N.Quinn for N.Burke, D.Cooney for D.Burke,

Dublin   G.McManus, B.O'Carroll, D.Kelly, J.Doughan, D.Curran, L.Rushe, M.Quilty, C.Gough, D.Suctliffe, K.O'Loughlin, M.Schutte, D.Plunkett, E.Dillon, T.Connolly, N.McMorrow. Subs: F.Clabby for Kelly, S.McGrath for Schutte, R.Mahon for O'Loughlin, B.Quinn for Connolly.

2012

Clare   R.Taaffe, P.Flanagan, D.McInerney, K.Ryan, S.Morey, C.Ryan, P.O'Connor, C.Galvin, S.Golden, A.Cunningham, P.Collins, T.Kelly, C.McInerney, C.McGrath, C.O'Connell. Subs: P.Duggan for Cunningham, N.Arthur for Collins.

Kilkenny   D.Walsh, J.Corcoran, W.Phelan, B.Kennedy, J.Lyng, R.Doyle, L.Harney, G.Brennan, C.Buckley, O.Walsh, J.Power, K.Kelly, W.Walsh, P.Walsh, G.Aylward. Subs: M.Gaffney for O.Walsh, C.Kenny for P.Walsh.

2013

Clare   R.Taaffe, P.Flanagan, D.McInerney, J.Browne, S.Morey, A.O'Neill, S.O'Halloran, C.Galvin, T.Kelly, P.Duggan, P.Collins, C.Malone, C.O'Connell, S.O'Donnell, D.O'Halloran. Subs: J.Colleran for D.McInerney, K.Lynch for Kelly, N.Arthur for Collins, A.Cunningham for O'Donnell, E.Boyce for Galvin.

Antrim   G.Dixon, C.Morgan, M.Donnelly, T.Doyle, T.Ó Ciarain, P.McNaughton, C.McGuinness, J.McGreevy, E.Campbell, S.Dooey, S.McAfee, N.McKenna, D.McKernan, C.McCann, C.Clarke. Subs: D.Kearney for Ó Ciarain, M.Bradley for Donnelly, S.Beatty for Dooey, M.Dudley for McKernan, D.McGuinness for McCann.

2014

Clare   K.Hogan, J.Colleran, J.Browne, S.Morey, G.O'Connell, C.Cleary, J.Shanahan, C.Galvin, E.Enright, B.Duggan, T.Kelly, P.Duggan, S.O'Donnell, A.Cunningham, D.Reidy. Subs: C.O'Connell for G.O'Connell, A.O'Neill for O'Donnell, S.O'Brien for Colleran.

Wexford   O.O'Leary, A.Kenny, L.Ryan, E.Conroy, J.White, S.O'Gorman, J.O'Connor, A.Nolan, C.Devitt, J.Guiney, G.Moore, P.Foley, R.Clarke, C.McDonald, K.Foley. Subs: D.Dunne for O'Connor, J.Cash for White, C.O'Leary for Moore, P.Sutton for Cash.

2015

Limerick   D.McCarthy, S.Finn, R.English, M.Casey, D.Byrnes, B.O'Connell, G.Hegarty, D.O'Donovan, P.Ryan, R.Lynch, C.Lynch, D.Dempsey, C.Ryan, T.Morrisey, B.Nash. Subs: P.Casey for C.Ryan, A.La-Touche Cosgrave for P.Ryan, J.Kelliher for R.Lynch, M.O'Callaghan for Finn, J.Hannon for O'Donovan.

Wexford   O.O'Leary, S.Donohoe, L.Ryan, E.Conroy, J.White, P.Foley, J.O'Connor, C.Devitt, T.French, A.Kenny, K.Foley, J.Cash, C.Dunbar, C.McDonald, P.Sutton. Subs: S.Murphy for French, S.Kenny for Devitt, S.Kelly for K.Foley, J.Firman for Cash.

2016

Waterford   J.Henley, W.Hahessy, C.Gleeson, D.Lyons, M.Harney, A.Gleeson, C.Prunty, M.O'Brien, Shane Bennett, C.Roche, T.Devine, D.J.Foran, M.Kearney, Stephen Bennett, P.Curran. Subs: A.Farrell for Devine, D.Ryan for Lyons, B.O'Keeffe for Harney, B.Whelan for Hahessy, P.Hogan for Shane Bennett.

Galway   C.Tuohy, C.Jennings, D.O'Donoghue, D.Cronin, V.Doyle, S.Cooney, S.Loftus, D.Nevin, D.Dolan, K.McHugo, B.Molloy, S.Linnane, T.Monaghan, C.Whelan, E.Burke. Subs: E.Brannigan for Monaghan, J.Grealish for McHugo, F.Burke for Nevin, C.Burke for Linnane, A.Morrissey for Dolan.

2017

Limerick   E.McNamara, S.Finn, D.Fanning, D.Joy, R.Lynch, K.Hayes, T.Grimes, C.Ryan, R.Hanley, T.Morrissey, B.Nash, C.Lynch, A.Gillane, B.Murphy, P.Casey. Subs: C.Boylan for C.Lynch, A.La-Touche Cosgrave for Morrissey, O.O'Reilly for Murphy, L.Lyons for Nash.

Kilkenny   D.Brennan, M.Cody, C.Delaney, N.McMahon, H.Lawlor, J.Cleere, T.Walsh, B.Ryan, L.Scanlon, L.Blanchfield, S.Morrissey, R.Leahy, S.Walsh, J.Donnelly, J.Walsh. Subs: A.Murphy for Morrissey, P.Lyng for J.Walsh, E.Kenny for S.Walsh, M.Keoghan for Ryan, D.Mullen for Leahy.

CAPTAINS OF WINNING U21 HURLING ALL-IRELAND TEAMS

1964	F. Loughnane (Tipperary)
1965	W. O'Neill (Wexford)
1966	G. McCarthy (Cork)
1967	P J. Ryan (Tipperary)
1968	P. Hegarty (Cork)
1969	M. McCarthy (Cork)
1970	T. O'Brien (Cork)
1971	P. McDonnell (Cork)
1972	I. Clarke (Galway)
1973	M. O'Doherty (Cork)
1974	G. Fennelly (Kilkenny)
1975	K. Fennelly (Kilkenny)
1976	T. Murphy (Cork)
1977	M. Lyng (Kilkenny)
1978	B. Forde (Galway)
1979	M. Doyle (Tipperary)
1980	P. Kennedy (Tipperary)
1981	P. Kennedy (Tipperary)
1982	M. McCarthy (Cork)
1983	P. Casserly (Galway)
1984	S. Delahunty (Kilkenny)
1985	M. Scully (Tipperary)
1986	A. Cunningham (Galway)
1987	G. Ryan (Limerick)
1988	C. Connery (Cork)
1989	D. Ryan (Tipperary)
1990	J. Brennan (Kilkenny)
1991	B. Feeney (Galway)
1992	T. Browne (Waterford)
1993	L. Burke (Galway)
1994	P. Larkin (Kilkenny)
1995	B. Horgan (Tipperary)
1996	P. Huban (Galway)
1997	D. Murphy (Cork)
1998	D. Murphy (Cork)
1999	N. Hickey (Kilkenny)
2000	D. Sheehan (Limerick)
2001	T. Houlihan (Limerick)
2002	P. Lawlor (Limerick)
2003	J. Tyrrell (Kilkenny)
2004	J. Fitzpatrick (Kilkenny)
2005	K. Burke (Galway)
2006	M. Fennelly (Kilkenny)
2007	K. Hynes (Galway)
2008	J. Dowling (Kilkenny)
2009	C. O'Doherty (Clare)
2010	P. Maher (Tipperary)
2011	B. Daly (Galway)
2012	C. McGrath (Clare)
2013	P. Flanagan (Clare)
2014	T. Kelly (Clare)
2015	D. Byrnes (Limerick)
2016	P. Curran (Waterford)
2017	T. Morrissey (Limerick)

U21 HURLING ALL-IRELAND FINAL REFEREES

1964	Aubrey Higgins (Galway)
1965	Jimmy Duggan (Galway)
1966	Donie Nealon (Tipperary)
Replays	G. Fitzgerald (Limerick)
1967	Aubrey Higgins (Galway)
1968	Séamus Power (Waterford)
1969	Paddy Johnson (Kilkenny)
1970	Jim Dunphy (Waterford)
1971	Paddy Buggy (Kilkenny)
1972	Sean O'Grady (Limerick)
1973	John Moloney (Tipperary)
1974	Sean O'Grady (Limerick)
1975	Sean O'Meara (Tipperary)
1976	Gerry Kirwan (Offaly)
1977	Jimmy Rankins (Laois)
1978	Noel O'Donoghue (Dublin)
1979	Noel Dalton (Waterford)
1980	John Denton (Wexford)
1981	Nealie Duggan (Limerick)
1982	Gerry Kirwan (Offaly)
1983	Michael Kelieher (Kildare)
1984	Kevin Walsh (Clare)
1985	John Denton (Wexford)
1986	Gerry Long (Tipperary)
1987	Paschal Long (Kilkenny)
1988	John Moore (Waterford)
1989	Pascal Long (Kilkenny)
1990	Pat Delaney (Laois)
1991	Terence Murray (Limerick)
1992	Willie Barrett (Tipperary)
1993	John McDonnell (Tipperary)
1994	Pat Horan (Offaly)
1995	Terence Murray (Limerick}
1996	Pat O'Connor (Limerick)
1997	Pat Horan (Offaly)
1998	Dickie Murphy (Wexford)
1999	Ger Harrington (Cork)
2000	P.Horan (Offaly)
2001	A.Mac Suibhne (Dublin)
2002	D.Murphy (Wexford)
2003	M.Wadding (Waterford)
2004	B.Kelly (Westmeath)
2005	J.Sexton (Limerick)

2006	M.Haverty (Galway)
Replay	B.Gavin (Offaly)
2007	J.Ryan (Tipperary)
2008	J.Owens (Wexford)
2009	C.McAllister (Cork)
2010	J.McGrath (Westmeath)
2011	T.Carroll (Offaly)
2012	D.Kirwan (Cork)
2013	C.Lyons (Cork)
2014	C.McAllister (Cork)
2015	J.Ryan (Tipperary)
2016	S.Cleere (Kilkenny)
2017	P.O'Dwyer (Carlow)

MUNSTER U21 HURLING FINALS

1964	Tipperary	8-9	3-1	Waterford
1965	Tipperary	4-9	3-3	Galway
1966	Cork	5-12	2-6	Limerick
1967	Tipperary	3-9	3-5	Galway
1968	Cork	4-10	1-13	Tipperary
1969	Cork	3-11	1-5	Tipperary
1970	Cork	3-11	2-7	Tipperary
1971	Cork	5-11	4-9	Tipperary
1972	Tipperary	4-10	3-10	Clare
1973	Cork	4-11	2-7	Limerick
1974	Waterford	2-5	1-3	Clare
1975	Cork	3-12	2-6	Limerick
1976	Cork	2-11	3-6	Clare
1977	Cork	5-9	1-8	Limerick
1978	Tipperary	3-13	4-10	Cork
Replay	Tipperary	3-8	2-9	Cork
1979	Tipperary	1-13	2-7	Cork
1980	Tipperary	4-11	2-9	Cork
1981	Tipperary	1-15	0-10	Cork
1982	Cork	1-14	1-4	Limerick
1983	Tipperary	2-17	3-8	Clare
1984	Tipperary	0-12	1-8	Limenck
1985	Tipperary	1-16	4-5	Clare
1986	Limerick	3-9	3-9	Clare
Replay	Limerick	2-10	0-3	Clare
1987	Limerick	3-14	2-9	Cork
1988	Cork	4-12	1-7	Limerick
1989	Tipperary	5-16	1-6	Limerick
1990	Tipperary	2-21	1-11	Limerick
1991	Cork	0-17	1-7	Limerick
1992	Waterford	0-17	1-12	Clare
1993	Cork	1-18	3-9	Limerick
1994	Waterford	1-12	0-12	Clare
1995	Tipperary	1-17	0-14	Clare
1996	Cork	3-16	2-7	Clare
1997	Cork	1-11	0-13	Tipperary
1998	Cork	3-18	1-10	Tipperary
1999	Tipperary	1-18	1-15	Clare
2000	Limerick	4-18	1-6	Cork
2001	Limerick	3-14	2-16	Tipperary
2002	Limerick	1-20	2-14	Tipperary (aet)
2003	Tipperary	2-14	0-17	Cork (aet)
2004	Tipperary	1-16	1-13	Cork
2005	Cork	4-8	0-13	Tipperary
2006	Tipperary	3-11	0-13	Cork
2007	Cork	1-20	0-10	Waterford
2008	Tipperary	1-16	2-12	Clare
2009	Clare	2-17	2-12	Waterford
2010	Tipperary	1-22	1-17	Clare
2011	Limerick	4-20	1-27	Cork (aet)
2012	Clare	1-16	1-14	Tipperary
2013	Clare	1-17	2-10	Tipperary
2014	Clare	1-28	1-13	Cork
2015	Limerick	0-22	0-19	Clare
2016	Waterford	2-19	0-15	Tipperary
2017	Limerick	0-16	1-11	Cork

LEINSTER U21 HURLING FINALS

1964	Wexford	4-7	2-2	Laois
1965	Wexford	7-9	1-5	Dublin
1966	Wexford	7-10	2-8	Laois
1967	Dublin	2-10	2-9	Offaly
1968	Kilkenny	4-10	5-4	Dublin
1969	Wexford	3-16	4-3	Kilkenny
1970	Wexford	2-15	5-4	Kilkenny
1971	Wexford	2-16	2-9	Kilkenny
1972	Dublin	2-11	0-15	Offaly
1973	Wexford	2-13	2-10	Offaly
1974	Kilkenny	3-8	1-5	Wexford
1975	Kilkenny	3-14	0-8	Wexford
1976	Kilkenny	3-21	0-5	Wexford
1977	Kilkenny	3-11	1-10	Wexford
1978	Offaly	2-14	2-7	Laois
1979	Wexford	0-14	2-8	Kilkenny
Replay	Wexford	1-8	0-10	Kilkenny
1980	Kilkenny	2-14	2-9	Wexford
1981	Kilkenny	6-11	2-10	Wexford
1982	Kilkenny	5-20	2-6	Offaly
1983	Laois	3-13	4-8	Wexford
1984	Kilkenny	0-18	1-10	Wexford
1985	Kilkenny	4-18	1-4	Wexford
1986	Wexford	2-9	2-9	Offaly
Replay	Wexford	1-16	0-10	Offaly
1987	Wexford	4-11	0-5	Offaly
1988	Kilkenny	3-13	2-5	Offaly
1989	Offaly	3-16	3-9	Kilkenny
1990	Kilkenny	2-9	1-10	Laois
1991	Offaly	2-10	0-12	Kilkenny
1992	Offaly	1-15	2-10	Kilkenny
1993	Kilkenny	4-13	2-7	Wexford
1994	Kilkenny	1-14	0-15	Wexford
1995	Kilkenny	2-11	1-12	Wexford
1996	Wexford	1-9	0-12	Offaly
Replay	Wexford	2-16	2-5	Offaly
1997	Wexford	2-13	0-15	Offaly
1998	Kilkenny	2-10	0-12	Dublin
1999	Kilkenny	1-17	1-6	Offaly
2000	Offaly	3-14	2-14	Kilkenny
2001	Wexford	0-10	1-5	Kilkenny
2002	Wexford	1-15	0-15	Dublin (aet)
2003	Kilkenny	0-12	1-4	Dublin
2004	Kilkenny	1-16	2-3	Wexford
2005	Kilkenny	0-17	1-10	Dublin
2006	Kilkenny	2-18	2-10	Dublin
2007	Dublin	2-18	3-9	Offaly
2008	Kilkenny	2-21	2-9	Offaly
2009	Kilkenny	2-20	1-19	Dublin
2010	Dublin	2-15	0-15	Wexford
2011	Dublin	1-18	0-11	Wexford
2012	Kilkenny	4-24	1-13	Laois
2013	Wexford	1-21	0-21	Kilkenny
2014	Wexford	1-20	0-18	Dublin
2015	Wexford	4-17	1-9	Kilkenny
2016	Dublin	2-15	1-10	Offaly
2017	Kilkenny	0-30	1-15	Wexford

ULSTER U21 HURLING FINALS

Year	Winner	Score	Score	Runner-up
1964	Antrim only team entered			
1965	Antrim	5-8	4-7	Down
1966	Antrim	4-5	0-8	Down
1967	Antrim	3-8	2-7	Down
1968	Down	7-6	2-9	Armagh

Note: This was Roinn 'B' final. Antrim represented Province in All-Ireland series.

Year	Winner	Score	Score	Runner-up
1969	Down	5-17	2-11	Antrim
1970	Antrim	6-12	2-10	Down
1971	Down	5-11	2-9	Antrim
1972	Antrim	4-9	1-11	Down
1973	Antrim	1-6	1-6	Down
Replay	Antrim	3-19	3-3	Down
1974	Antrim	3-8	0-3	Down
1975	Down	3-10	1-3	Antrim
1976	Antrim	1-9	0-4	Down
1977	Down	3-7	0-9	Antrim
1978	Antrim	5-18	3-9	Down
1979	Antrim	9-13	2-2	Armagh
1980	Antrim	4-16	0-9	Down
1981	Antrim	2-9	1-5	Down
1982	Antrim	9-14	4-5	Down
1983	Down	2-7	0-7	Antrim
1984	Down	1-14	0-15	Antrim
1985	Down	1-12	1-10	Antrim
1986	Derry	2-9	2-9	Down
Replay	Derry	3-9	1-2	Down
1987	Down	3-12	2-9	Derry
1988	Antrim	6-11	1-4	Down
1989	Antrim	4-18	0-4	Derry
1990	Down	2-9	2-6	Antrim
1991	Antrim	2-19	2-6	Down
1992	Antrim	3-11	3-4	Down
1993	Derry	2-13	1-8	Antrim
1994	Antrim	1-20	1-4	Down
1995	Antrim	2-18	1-7	Derry
1996	Antrim	1-13	1-12	Down
1997	Derry	2-11	0-17	Antrim
Replay	Derry	0-22	1-16	Antrim (aet)
1998	Antrim	3-20	4-8	Down
1999	Antrim	2-14	0-12	Derry
2000	Antrim	2-14	0-3	Derry
2001	Antrim	2-17	1-18	Derry
2002	Antrim	2-13	0-6	Down
2003	Down	3-12	1-12	Derry
2004	Down	5-8	4-7	Derry
2005	No Final			
2006	Antrim	2-15	3-11	Down
2007	Derry	2-16	1-18	Antrim
2008	No Final			
2009	Antrim	1-18	0-9	Derry
2010	Antrim	0-21	0-16	Armagh
2011	Antrim	0-15	2-7	Armagh
2012	Antrim	2-20	1-12	Derry
2013	Antrim	6-22	0-6	Derry
2014	Antrim	7-17	1-5	Down
2015	Antrim	1-19	0-17	Derry
2016	Antrim	0-16	1-9	Derry
2017	Derry	3-17	1-9	Down

ALL-IRELAND JUNIOR HURLING CHAMPIONSHIP FINALS

1912	Cork	3-6	2-1	Westmeath
1913	Tipperary	2-2	0-0	Kilkenny
1914	Clare	6-5	1-1	Laois
1915	Tipperary	1-6	2-2	Offaly
1916	Cork	4-6	3-4	Kilkenny
1917-1922	Suspended			
1923	Offaly	3-4	3-2	Cork
1924	Tipperary	5-5	1-2	Galway
1925	Cork	5-6	1-0	Dublin
1926	Tipperary	6-2	2-3	Galway
1927	Meath	2-3	1-1	Britain
	Home Final: Meath 1-8 3-2 Galway			
	Meath	5-4	3-2	Galway (replay)
1928	Kilkenny	4-6	4-4	Tipperary
1929	Offaly	6-1	2-3	Cork
1930	Tipperary	6-8	3-2	Kilkenny
1931	Waterford	10-7	1-2	Lancashire
	Home Final: Waterford 6-7 0-3 Antrim			
1932	Dublin	8-4	2-0	London
	Home Final: Dublin 6-5 3-3 Galway			
1933	Tipperary	10-1	1-4	London
	Home Final: Tipperary 8-3 1-3 Galway			
1934	Waterford	3-5	3-3	London
	Home Final: Waterford 5-8 1-3 Kildare			
1935	Limerick	4-9	3-3	London
	Home Final: Limerick 2-5 1-2 Galway			
1936	Westmeath 2-5		3-1	Waterford
	Note: Britain did not compete. Instead there was a Junior "International" between Ireland and England.			
1937	Dublin	7-8	3-6	London
	Home Final: Dublin 6-6 3-3 Galway			
1938	London	4-4	4-1	Cork
	Home Final: Cork 6-5 2-4 Antrim			
1939	Galway	2-6	2-2	London
	Home Final: Galway 3-8 3-8 Kilkenny			
	Galway	4-6	4-3	Kilkenny (replay)
1940	Cork	3-3	3-1	Galway
1941	Limerick	8-2	4-1	Galway
1942-1945	Suspended			
1946	Kilkenny	5-4	2-2	London
	Home Final: Kilkenny 4-2 2-3 Galway			
1947	Cork	3-10	2-3	London
	Home Final: Cork 4-10 2-5 Dublin			

1948	Meath	3-5	3-5	London
Replay	Meath	2-7	2-5	London
	Home Final: Meath 5-9 2-1 Limerick			
1949	London	3-7	3-6	Clare
	Home Final: Clare 3-5 3-3 Kilkenny			
1950	Cork	5-5	1-4	London
	Home Final: Cork 3-4 2-5 Dublin			
1951	Kilkenny	3-9	3-5	London
	Home Final: Kilkenny 4-9 4-3 Galway			
1952	Dublin	3-7	2-7	London
	Home Final: Dublin 4-10 2-5 Antrim			
1953	Tipperary	4-10	3-3	Warwickshire
	Home Final: Tipperary 1-7 1-2 Offaly			
1954	Limerick	4-6	2-4	London
	Home Final: Limerick 3-5 1-8 Antrim			
1955	Cork	6-10	0-5	Warwickshire
	Home Final: Cork 3-10 4-5 Galway			
1956	Kilkenny	5-2	2-8	London
	Home Final: Kilkenny 4-8 2-4 Kerry			
1957	Limerick	5-12	2-5	London
	Home Final: Limerick 7-15 5-8 Galway			
1958	Cork	7-10	4-2	Warwickshire
	Home Final: Cork 3-16 2-5 Antrim			
1959	London	5-10	2-10	Antrim
	Home Final: Antrim 3-4 2-3 Cork			
1960	London	2-4	2-4	Carlow
Replay	London	4-8	2-11	Carlow
	Home Final: Carlow 2-15 3-5 Cork			
1961	Kerry	4-14	2-5	London
	Home Final: Kerry 4-9 5-3 Meath			
1962	Kildare	4-7	2-4	London
	Home Final: Kildare 7-15 5-2 Kerry			
1963	London	4-7	3-6	Antrim
	Home Final: Antrim 8-8 6-3 Westmeath			
1964	Down	3-2	1-3	London
	Home Final: Down 9-5 2-7 Kerry			
1965	Roscommon 3-10		2-11	Warwickshire
	Home Final: Roscommon 6-8 1-3 Armagh			
1966	Kildare	4-6	2-9	Warwickshire
	Home Final: Kildare 3-12 2-3 Kerry			
1967	Wicklow	3-15	6-6	London
Replay	Wicklow	3-14	4-7	London
	Home Final: Wicklow 3-7 1-2 Kerry			
1968	Warwickshire 1-14		1-9	Kerry
	Home Final: Kerry 6-9 5-9 Sligo			

1969	Warwickshire 3-6	0-11	Kerry
	Home Final: Kerry 6-11	2-10	Antrim
1970	Meath	1-15	4-6	Hertfordshire
Replay	Meath	3-14	3-7	Hertfordshire
	Home Final: Meath 3-19	1-7	Leitrim
1971	Wicklow	3-9	2-12	Hertfordshire
Replay	Hertfordshire 4-9	3-11	Wicklow
	(Dispute - replay ordered)
Replay	Wicklow	4-6	3-8	Hertfordshire
	Home Final: Wicklow 2-18	1-12	Roscommon
1972	Kerry	5-5	2-9	Warwickshire
	Home Final: Kerry 6-16	3-7	Meath
1973	Warwickshire 6-9	3-8	Louth
	Home Final: Louth 4-11	3-11	Kerry
1974	Roscommon 2-11	2-9	Derry
1975	Derry	5-12	3-5	Louth
1976	Louth	6-8	4-9	Mayo
1977	Louth	1-14	2-4	Fermanagh
1978	Armagh	5-15	2-6	Mayo
1979	Armagh	2-13	2-1	Derry
1980	Mayo	2-13	0-7	Monaghan
1981	Mayo	2-13	1-8	Louth
1982	Derry	0-6	1-10	Monaghan
	Resumed in original format from 1983
1983	Cork	3-14	2-15	Galway
1984	Kilkenny	0-13	2-5	Galway
1985	Wexford	3-9	1-13	Tipperary
1986	Kilkenny	1-17	0-15	Limerick
1987	Cork	3-11	2-13	Wexford
1988	Kilkenny	1-12	0-10	Tipperary
1989	Tipperary	0-12	0-8	Galway
1990	Kilkenny	4-21	2-11	Tipperary
1991	Tipperary	4-17	1-5	London
	Home Final: Tipperary 2-13	0-10	Kilkenny
1992	Wexford	2-7	0-13	Cork
Replay	Wexford	0-13	1-8	Cork
1993	Clare	3-10	0-8	Kilkenny
1994	Cork	2-13	2-11	Kilkenny
1995	Kilkenny	1-20	1-6	Clare
1996	Galway	1-14	2-9	Kilkenny
1997	Monaghan	3-11	0-11	Meath
1998	Meath	1-14	1-9	Monaghan
1999	Meath	2-11	0-9	Tyrone
2000	Armagh	1-11	1-4	Meath
2001	Roscommon 1-18	2-3	Donegal
2002	Antrim	2-7	1-6	Meath
2003	Mayo	1-8	0-9	Donegal
2004	Meath	1-10	1-6	Down

Confined to weaker counties from 1961 to 1973. Stronger counties played in Intermediate Championship. Run in conjunction with Division 3 of National Hurling League 1974-82. Original format restored in 1983. But from 1997 confined to counties graded junior.
Note: There were no Home Finals in 1936, 1940 and 1941.

ALL-IRELAND JUNIOR HURLING CHAMPIONSHIP FINAL TEAMS

1912

Cork C.Hallahan (capt.), J.Long, J.Hallahan, W.Finn, D.Aherne, P.Prior, J.Murphy, W.Lombard, C.Salmon, J.O'Brien, T.O'Riordan, J.Cahill, D.McDonnell, D.Singleton, W.Fitzgerald, P.Vaughan, C.O'Connell.
Westmeath B.Murphy (capt.), J.Buckley, M.Byrne, F.Larkin, J.Blaney, M.Reilly, J.Martin, P.Malynn, H.Hanley, M.Boylan, T.Carty, M.Duffy, F.Nee, M.Kelleghan, H.Grattan, P.Tormey, J.Kearney.

1913

Tipperary Jack Ryan-Lanigan (capt.), Tom Ryan-Lanigan, T.Delaney, J.Hammonds, T.Dwyer, T.Dwan, Pierce Purcell, M.Hammonds, Ned McGrath, P.Leahy, A.O'Donnell, Dick Walsh, J.Power, J.Fitzpatrick, T.Shanahan. Subs: P.Dargan, J.Murphy.
Kilkenny Jim Walton (capt.), T Cummins (goal), J.Holmes, Ned Hally, P.Meighan, P.O'Brien, J.O'Connor, Justin McGrath, NickMullins, T.Murphy, Tom Hanrahan, Larry Dunphy, John Foskin, Matt Corr, Nick Fennelly. Sub: Mick Corr.

1914

Clare D.Minogue (capt.), S.Minogue, D.Flannery, P.Hannon, M.Bolton, T.Daly, J.Quinn, E.Lucid, J.Spellacy, P.Jordan, M.Baker, A.Gleeson, D.Crowe, J.Marrinan, P.Connell.
Laois J.Finlay (capt.), J.Phelan, T.Costigan, J.Phelan, J.Walsh, J.Dunphy, M.Drennan, M.Begadon, M.Carroll, W.Quigley, J.Loughman, J.Dunphy, M.Sheppard, J.Deegan, P.Ryan.

1915

Tipperary T.Dwan (capt.), W.Quinn, M.Leahy, Joe Fitzpatrick, J.Campbell, J.Kennedy, J.Hammonds, W.Dwyer, T.Shanahan, W.Horan, D.Walsh, F.Cronin, M.Leahy, T.Donovan, J.Doore.
Offaly J.Corrigan (capt.), T.O'Donnell, J.Madden, P.Cummins, J.Carroll, F.Reddin, P.Sullivan, M.Cordial, J.O'Meara, H.Corrigan, M.Whelan, M.Kelly, J.Hogan, John Carroll, J.Murphy.

1916

Cork Michael Brophy (capt.), A.Buckley (Cobh), G.Finn, D.Long, C.Neenan, P.Carton, P.Healy, J.O'Driscoll, R.Hunter, D.O'Sullivan, H.Atkins, John Barry-Murphy, Eugene O'Connell, A.Buckley, M.Scannell. Sub: Buckley for J.O'Driscoll.
Kilkenny W.Power, P.Power, J.Sullivan, M.Dermody, E.Donoghue, E.Fennelly, R.Purcell, J.Roberts, J.Walsh, J.Coyne, R.Rockett, T.Mullins, R.Kenneally, J.Hanrahan, J.Whelan.

1923

Offaly M.Cordial, W.Cordial, A.Cordial, J.Halligan (capt.), E.Hayes, P.Lyons, W.Fox, P.Fox, W.Ryan, M.Whelan, N.White, M.Carroll, J.Murphy, J.Horan, J.Carroll. Sub: R.Conway.
Cork R.Canniffe, M.Murphy (capt.), J.Barry, T.Aherne, D.O'Donovan, S.Keane, J.Barry-Murphy, Matt Murphy, M.Ryan, S.Noonan, J.Crotty, F Kelleher, P.McCarthy, D.Barry-Murphy, J.Kenny.

1924

Tipperary P.Purcell (capt.), W.O'Brien, J.O'Loughlin, Stephen Dwan, J.Costelloe, J.Gleeson, T.O'Meara, M.Flanagan, J.Hickey, M.Ryan, T.F.Meagher, P.Kennedy, Martin Kennedy, Rody Nealon, Martin Aherne. Sub: W.O'Meara.

Galway

Galway J.Stanford (capt.), J.Fallon, P.Rooney, P.Kelly, M.Tierney, M.Broderick, J.Morrissey, M.Connaire, J.Cleary, W.Fahy, T.O'Donnell, P.Morgan, M.Houlihan, P.Gilligan, J.Shaughnessy.

1925

Cork M.Kenny (capt.), J.Seymour (goal), E.Lynch, Joe Kearney, Christy Cronin, J.Desmond, J.Barry, D.Barry-Murphy, Dick Geaney, S.Noonon, J.Burke, M.Aherne, J.Hurley, Leo Brady, Jack Egan. Subs: J.Clarke, P.Healy, M.Daly (capt.).
Dublin J.Hyland, W.Higgins, M.Muldoon, P.Cusack, D.McHugh (goal), T.Hennessy, J.Roche, P.McInerney, M.Murphy, E.Dwyer, E.Byrne, M.Treacy, J.Walsh, M.Healy, T.Costigan.

1926

Tipperary T.Butler (goal), J.Moylan, P.Hogan, T.Crowe, P.Harty, J.Hayes, M.Ryan (Newport), M.Ryan (Boherlahan), T.Leahy, T.Treacy (capt.), E.Browne, A.Cleary, E.Walsh, J.O'Gorman, M.F.Cronin.
Galway P.Sheary, M.Cunningham, Conway, T.Fury, Crowe, Griffin, J.Derivan, M.Connaire, J.Deely, T Tierney, T Hackett, M.Nestor, W.Curran, F.Keely, P.Larkin (capt.).

1927

Meath L.Mitchell (capt.), R.Collins, M.Cluskey, T.Irwin, J.Loughran, J.Doherty, E.Giles, M.Madden, W.Smith, T.Browne, S.Finn, C.Doran, T.Loughran, J.Griffin, T.Carrigy.
Note: C.Curley and M.Doherty played in drawn game. J.Loughran and T.Carrigy were on for replay.
Britain J.Ryan (capt.), T.King, J.Butterly, P.Landy, M.Redmond, J.Burke, J.O'Leary, J.Connolly, H.O'Donnell, M.Houlihan, E.Lambert, S.Donoghue, P.Costello, J.Shalloe, G.Moriarty.

1928

Kilkenny M.Bergin, J.Carroll, T.Mullins (capt.), P.Kelly, J.McNamara, T.Grace, P.Butler, T.Cronin, J.Walsh, D.Duggan, M.Brennan, P.Dowling, P.Walsh, P.Dwan, J.Fitzpatrick.
Tipperary A.Foley (capt.), P.O'Keeffe, E.Walsh, P.Guiry, T.Butler, J.Maher, T.Coffey, J.Stapleton, D.Max, R.Dwan, J.Heeney, T.Lowry, W.Matthews, D.Gleeson, Tony McLoughlin.

1929

Offaly M.Corrigan (goal), E.Nolan, J.Kinnarney, W.Guinan, M.Dooley, J.Dooley, T.Dooley, T.Carroll, J.Verney, M.Coughlan, J.Holligan, J.Carroll, P.J.Grogan (capt.), J.King, W.Cordial.
Cork E.O'Connor (capt.), J.Kinsley, D.Cogan, R.Madden, A.Caulfield, S.O'Leary, J.Riordan, P.Dorgan, C.Sheehan, J.Hurley (goal), J.Dermody, J.Callaghan, J.Desmond, J.Quirke M.Walsh.

1930

Tipperary P.Harty (capt.), T.Harty, W.Ryan, T.Connolly, M.McGann, M.Browne, E.Wade, M.Ryan (Clonoulty), J.Dwyer, M.Ryan (Ileigh), D.Looby, P.Furlong, W.Gorman, J.Fletcher, S.Harrington.
Kilkenny Peter O'Reilly, M.Larkin, W.Dalton, Tommy Leahy, M.White, J.Leahy, R.Morrissey, D.Treacy, W.("Lynch") Walsh, J.Malone, Milo Kennedy, W.Meagher, T.Wyse, W.Keane, T.Grace.

1931

Waterford M.Curley (goal), J.O'Donnell, R.Condon (capt.), E.Flynn, G.Kehoe, A.Sandford, W.Sheehan, T.Greaney, P.Hannigan, P.Gough, D.Goode, R.Morrissey, S.Ormond, J.Hunt, N.Condon.
Lancashire T.Collins (goal), M.Campbell, G.Moriarty, J.Connolly, B.Kennelly, M.Redmond, P.Campbell, H.Davis, T.Ward, E.Brennan, T.Hannon, P.Lynch, P.Connolly, S.Donohue, M.Holohan.

1932

Dublin   M.O'Hara (capt.), T.O'Brien, M.Gleeson, J.Kavanagh, B.Reynolds, F.Aherne, C.Sheehan, P.Sexton, W.Flanagan, T.Flanagan, J.Flanagan, J.Moran, T.Dwyer, W.Higgins, D.Sherry.
London   M.Walsh, J.Kearns, M.Cremins (capt.), P Duggan, T.Pyne, W.Scanlon, J.Butterly, P.Nash, M.Collins, J.Ryan, J.Cronin, J.McCarthy, D.O'Brien, J.Holohan, C.O'Neill.

1933

Tipperary   D.Roche, W.Roche, Pat O'Mahony, P.O'Toole, J.Dunne, E.Eade (capt.), P.O'Keeffe, Dave Looby, Dick Hayes, J.Tynan, J.Duggan, D.Gorman, D.Murphy, W.Ryan, D.Gleeson. Subs: M.O'Toole, J.Cooney.
London   J.Desmond, F.Johnson, J.Kinsley, S.Kiely, M.Madden, J.McCarthy, R.Sloan, J.Kearns, P.Duggan, F Trimm, J.Lyons, T.Grant, W.O'Hara, P.Hurney, J.Butterley. Sub: P.Nash for J.McCarthy.

1934

Waterford   M.Curley, W.Hennebry, J.Keane, J.Whelan, J.O'Gorman, M.Ryan, J.Healy, G.Kehoe (capt.), W.Sheehan, B.Doyle, M.Creed, P Sheehan, J.Murphy, J.Walsh, D.Mahony.
London   D.Hoyne, J.Butterly, P Hogan, J.Mahon, G.Pyne, M.Madden, S.Kiely, D.O'Keeffe, H.Burrows, J.Kinsley, M.Cremin, P.McCarthy, E.Foulds, W.Downey, T.Grant.

1935

Limerick   J.McCarthy, J.Curtin, P.O'Carroll, J.Ryan, T.McCarthy, M.Power, M.Cross (capt.), P.McCarthy (Feenagh), J.Sullivan, T.McCarthy, M.Butler, W.Daly, P McSweeney, W.Curtin, Jim O'Sullivan.
London   D.Hoyne, G.Pyne, M.Madden, S.Kiely, J.Hardiman, J.O'Keeffe, W.Galligan, D.O'Keeffe, T.Rainey, T.Grant, A.Noonan, J.Kinsley, E.Foulds, E.Kiely, M.Hynes.

1936

Westmeath   P.Fahy, W.Doyle, J.Mulligan, F.Monaghan, Todd Nugent, F.White (capt.), T.Gavigan, E.Moynihan, P.Lenihan, T.Morgan, M.McCarthy (capt.), S.Skehal, T.McNeice, Tim McGrath, Colm Boland, Sub: Joe Leonard.
Waterford   M.Curley (goal), P.Fanning, D.Hogan, J.O'Gorman, M.Skehan, J.Shortall, J.Plunkett, J.Phelan, P.Greene, J.Murphy, J.Halpin, D.Mahony, P.Gough, M.Hickey, J.Mountain.

1937

Dublin   J.Hennessy, P.Tolan, M.Butler, P.Crowley, P.Horan, D.Hurley, S.Barrett, T.Leahy, R.Ryan, M.Fletcher, P.McCormack, J.Byrne, J.Maher/ P.McMahon (capt.), P.Doody.
London   D.Hoyne, D.Waters, B.Hickey, E.Fox (capt.), J.Hardiman, P.Grant, T.Rainey, P Foley, L.Moran, E.Foulds, M.Doolan, J.Long, P.McDonald, C.Curtin, M.Morris. Sub: P.McCarthy for P.McDonald.

1938

London   E.Shaughnessy, J.Dunne, T.Walker, E.Eade, J.Hickey, E.Foulds, L.Moran, J.Dwyer (capt.), J.Farrell, Mick Regan, J.Hardiman, T Rainey, B.Hickey, N.Noonan, D.Hoyne. Sub: R.Hogan for E.Shaughnessy.
Cork   J.Lynch (capt.), C.Madden, J.Hyde, J.P Creedon, B.Thornhill, Dan Coughlan, D.J.Buckley, R.Dineen, J.Tobin, P.Corbett, D.Cotter, W.Horgan, M.Twomey, T.O'Connell, J.O'Callaghan, Subs: J.O'Mahony for W.Horgan, M.Lucey for J.Tobin.

1939

Galway   T.Nolan, W.Donnellan, J.Fahy, J.Curley, J.Hanney, W.O'Connor, M.Lowry, Joe Costello (capt.), T.Lambert, J.Hanniffy, E.Hogan, T.Cunningham, R.Forae, L.Connaire, M.Mulryan. Subs: P.Fahy for T.Nolan, R.McTigue for M.Mulryan.
London   J.Farrell (goal), J.Heffernan, B.Hickey, P.Walsh, E.O'Brien, K.Odlum, J.Hardiman, W.Galligan, J.Dwyer (capt.), J.Maher, M.Doolan, N.Noonan, J.Dunne, J.Smith, J.Hickey. Subs: P Grant for J.Hardiman, M.Noonan for W.Galligan.

1940

Cork   E.Porter, T.O'Connell, C.Kelly, W.Holton, H.O'Callaghan, G.Sadlier, R.Walsh, P.Aherne, J.Barry–Murphy, E.Riordan, P.J.Riordan, L.Tully, C.Radley, D.Lynch (capt.), P.Corbett.
Galway   A.Reddan, D.Flynn, N.O'Connor, D.Diviney, R.Quinn, T.Fahy, J.Brophy, T.Barry, M.O'Leary, F.Fallon, W.Lambert, P.Thornton, K.Costello, D.Finn, P Robinson. Sub: P.Clarke for W.Lambert.

1941

Limerick   H.Wilson, J.O'Donoghue, S.O'Riordan (capt.), A.O'Donoghue, P Walsh, J.McCarthy, P.McCarthy (Mungret), J.Tobin, T.Toomey, O.O'Brien, T.Murphy, J.Foley, J.Madden, P.McCarthy (Feenagh), K.Foley. Sub: P.Aherne
Galway   S.Duggan, W.O'Connor, P.Ickham, P.Fahy, J.Power, W.Lambert, M.Lowry, J.Brogan, J.Ryan, P.Forde, P.Diviney, C.Corless, B.Mooney, V.McNamee, P.Daly.

1946

Kilkenny   J.Egan, M.Marnell, P.Hayden, P.O'Connor, P.Cahill, P.Prendergast, E.Power, P.Stapleton, P.Dack (capt.), H.Giles, M.Kenny, E.Doyle, P.McEvoy, D.Maher, W.Cahill. Sub: E.Purcell for J.Egan.
London   N.Egan, T.Hayes, M.Regan, S.Murphy, P.O'Brien, M.Ward, S.Fogarty, S.Costelloe, J.Somers, M.Doolan, P.Fouhy, J.Duggan, D.Doyle, W.Guilfoyle, M.Wade (capt.). Sub: J.Dower for M.Wade.

1947

Cork   W.Barry, B.Murphy, W.Holton, D.O'Donovan, D.Lyons, M.Nestor, J.O'Mahony, S.Twomey, J.Thornhill, J.West, M.O'Toole (capt.), W.J.Daly, M.Kearney, T.O'Sullivan, P.Abernethy. Sub: J.O'Grady.
London   E.Maher (goal), T.Hayes, S.Riordan, M.Delaney, M.Ward, M.Regan, S.Fogarty, J.Costelloe, P.Fouhy, N.Egan, J.Donnelly, J.Duggan, D.Doyle, J.Aherne, M.Fletcher. Sub: S.O'Mullane.

1948

Meath   R.Grogan, P.Kane, O.Reilly, N.Collier, S.Kelly, A.Donnelly (capt.), M.Kane, D.Mulligan, P.Donnelly, D.O'Mahony, P.Kelly, A.Foran, L.Wright, M.O'Brien, B.Smyth. Sub: T.Gerrard for L.Wright.
Note: T.Gerrard and J.Loughran played in drawn game. P.Kelly and D.O'Mahony were on for replay. Subs in drawn game: P.Kelly for L.Wright, P.Mitchell for B.Smith.
London   W.Ryan, T.Hayes, G.Aherne, T.Tennyson, W.Miller, E.Wilson, S.Fogarty, J.Costelloe, S.Corcoran, N.Egan, P.Fitzpatrick, J.Duggan, J.Doyle, D.Doyle, M.Fletcher. Sub: R.Ronan for S.Corcoran.
Note: S.Riordan, M.Tuohy, M.Delaney, W.Flanagan, J.Lyons and M.Walsh played in drawn game. T.Hayes, J.Aherne, T.Tennyson, E.Wilson, S.Corcoran and J.Doyle were on for replay.

1949

London W.Ryan, T.Hayes, T.O'Mahony, S.O'Riordan, H.O'Shea, W.Brophy, S.Fogarty (capt.), Sean Costelloe, B.Hoban, P.Fitzpatrick, F.Hogan, J.Duggan, D.Doyle, P.Madden, J.Lawton, Subs: P.Connors for T.O'Shea, J.Lewis for F.Hogan, C.Burke for P.Madden.
Clare M.O'Keeffe, R.McNamara, W.Hogan, T.Casey, Ed.Doyle, P.McNamara, P.Halpin, D.O'Grady, J.Meaney, J.Smith (capt.), P.Greene, P.Leahy, Jas Kenneally, Ed.Hickey, D.Keane. Subs: W.Shanahan for J.Kenneally.

1950

Cork F.Daly, D.Barry, J.Walsh, V.Twomey, P.Walsh, W.O'Neill (capt.), M.Cashman, G.Power, C.O'Neill, D.O'Driscoll, P.Healy, S.Fleming, A.Aherne, M.O'Donoghue, P.O'Riordan.
London W.Ryan, P.McCarthy, T.Mahony, G.O'Brien, Séamus Ó Ceallacháin, W.Brophy (capt.), M.Butler, B.Hoban, S.Costelloe, J.Goggin, C.Burke, J.Duggan, D.Doyle, R.Carew, R.Leahy. Subs: J.Maher for W.Brophy, W.Brophy for J.Maher, J.Maher for G.O'Brien, W.Lewis for R.Leahy, J.Lawton for C.Burke.

1951

Kilkenny R.Rockett, J.Lynch, S.Hokey (capt.), W.Bolger, T.Walsh, P Fitzgerald, J.McGovern, J.Sutton, P.Stapleton, P.Johnson, P.Hennebry, M.Gardiner, T.Ryan, R.Burke, J.Barron.
London E.Moloney, P.McCarthy, A.O'Brien, T.Gleeson, M.Butler, W.Brophy (capt.), P.Connors, S.Costelloe, J.Duggan, J.Goggin, B.Hoban, T.Bergin, C.McDonagh, J.Doyle, J.Lawton Subs: J.Maher for J.Doyle, J.O'Brien for T.Gleeson, S.Costelloe for E.Moloney.

1952

Dublin S.Murphy, J.Duggan, W.Holmes, J.Young, J.Manton, C.Hayes, D.Kelly, L.Skelly (capt.), L.Harding, J.Rodgers, T.Ryan, M.Ryan, W.Fletcher, J.Griffin, S.Daly.
London E.Moloney, M.Fitzpatrick, E.O'Brien, P.Murphy, M.Butler, W.Flanagan, W.Brophy, J.Wade, J.Duggan, D.Bransfield, S.McEntaggart, W.Murphy, E.O'Sullivan, T.Morrissey, T.Murphy, Sub: P.Costelloe for S.McEntaggart.

1953

Tipperary M.Fogarty, T.Kennedy, M.Doheny, S.Kelly, J.Callanan, S.Organ, T.Sweeney, J.Ryan, M.Conway, T.English, M.Kenny (capt.), J.Hannon, T.Foran, E.Hayes, K.McKenna.
Warwickshire M.Leahy, J.Holmes, G.Creighton, P.Walsh, J.Barcoe, P Crowley, T.Ryan, M.Marnell, W.Harkins, S.Collins, D.Fitzgerald, J.Byrne, P.Conway (capt.), W.Hayes, B.Graham. Subs: J.Walsh for W.Harkins, M.O'Mahony for D.Fitzgerald, W.Harkins for P.Walsh, J.McCarthy for J.Byrne.

1954

Limerick P.Cunneen (goal), J.O'Sullivan, Jim Keogh, P.O'Neill, J.Dooley, S.Murphy, Jim Quaid, Jack Quaid, W.Dooley, A.Raleigh, M.Carmody (capt.), V.Cobbe, M.Sheehan, C.Daly, J.Barry.
London E.Moloney, P.Murphy, K.Naughton, M.Butler, M.Lyons, W.Brophy (capt.), M.Fortune, S.Costelloe, Joe Duggan, T.Morrissey, S.O'Sullivan, D.Bransfield, M.Conway, P.Stapleton, S.Marmion. Subs: P.Cleary for M.Fortune, J.Barry for S.Marmion.

1955

Cork L.Ó Tuama, N.Looney, G.Mulcahy, L.Young, S.O'Mahony, C.Moynihan (capt.), P.Dowling, C.Cooney, J.Deasy, J.Browne, M.O'Toole, C.O'Shea, M.Quane, J.Cooney, P.O'Leary.

Warwickshire P.Purcell, P.Foley, P.O'Meara, J.McCarthy, J.Barcoe, T.Ryan, M.Maher, E.Maher, J.Byrne, B.Boothman, J.Jordan, T.Kelly, D.Danagher, J.J.Nevin, B.Graham.

1956

Kilkenny J.Murphy, Tom Walsh, J."Link" Walsh, S.Tyrrell (capt.), Phil Murphy, R.O'Neill, J.Burke, F.McCarthy, D.Gorey, D.Heaslip, Dick Bolger, J.Dunne, M.Fleming, W.Costigan, D.Hogan. Sub: J.Coyne.
London M.Hickey, P Murphy, M.Kersse, M.Kelly, M.Lyons, W.Brophy, P.Ryan, P.Hourigan, J.Ryan, W.Dargan, S.O'Sullivan, E.Murphy, T.Morrissey, M.O'Neill, D.Shanahan (capt.). Subs: M.Fortune for P.Ryan, A.Casey for D.Shanahan.

1957

Limerick G.Casey (goal), T.O Donnell (capt.), P.O'Connor, T.O'Dwyer, D.McCarthy, J.Dooley, J.Nealon, L.Hogan, M.Savage, M.O'Shea, J.Shanahan, M.Sheehan, P.Ryan, J.Enright, J.Barry, Sub.: Dick McGrath.
London G.Sutton, P.Murphy, M.Kersse, M.Shanahan, T.Martin, J.Naughton, L.Friday, W.Dargan, M.O'Connell, E.Murray, W.Brophy, T.Morrissey, M.O'Neill, P.Hourigan, T.Morrissey.

1958

Cork J.Dempsey, S.French, F Maxwell, A.O'Regan, J.Browne, N.Lynam, M.Thompson, C.Cooney, N.Gallagher, W.Galligan, M.O'Brien, S.Kelly, L.McGrath, F.Daly, M.Quane (capt.)
Warwickshire J.Malone, M.Moore, G.Creighton, T.Ryan, M.Maher, M.Cunningham, P.Dalton, D.Curtin, J.Byrne (capt.), P.Thornhill, M.Galvin, B.Finnerty, W.Sheehy, J.J.Nevin, P.O'Connell. Sub: J.Mullins for M.Galvin.

1959

London A.Morrissey, J.Kearns, M.Kersse, P.Murphy, M.Carmody, P.Dwyer, M.Kelly, E.Murray, W.Dargan, S.Sullivan, W.Duffy (capt.), D.Dillon, S.Healy, J.Rabbitte, C.Hickey. Subs: V.O'Halloran for M.Carmody, W.Ryan for S.Healy, J.Hickey for J.Rabbitte, P.Ryan for S.O'Sullivan.
Antrim D.O'Neill, E.Gallagher, G.Walsh, V.Kerr, J.Gibson, S.Wright (capt.), L.McGarry, S.Gallagher, A.Forsythe, P.Mullaney, R.Elliott, O.Campbell, E.McMullan, S.McGuinness, R.McMullan.

1960

London A.Morrisey, J.Kearns, M.Kersse, P.Murphy, F.Spillane, P.Dwyer, A.Moloney, W.Dargan, E.Murray, P.Wilson, W.Duffy, P.Ryan, N.Murphy, J.Hickey, L.Healy. Sub: S.Somers for N.Murphy.
Note: M.O'Connell, J.Fitzgerald and J.Redmond played in drawn game. A.Moloney, P.Ryan and N.Murphy came on for replay. Subs in drawn game W.Ryan for M.O'Connell, Jim Redmond for John Redmond.
Carlow B.Hayden, J.Dermody, P.Somers, W.Walsh, W.Hogan, E.Gladney, T.Nolan, M.O'Brien, M.Morrissey, L.Walsh, W.Walsh (capt.), P.McGovern, J.McCarthy, M.Hogan, E.Long.

1961

Kerry J.O'Donovan, N.Sheehy, N.Quill, T.Kirby, M.Hennessy (capt.), R.McElligott, K.Dermody, S.Lovett, S.Healy, J.Barry, T.Hennessy, P.Sullivan, J.Culloty, W.McCarthy, E.Sullivan.
London W.Barnaville, J.Dermody, J.Twomey, M.O'Dwyer, M.Craddock, P.O'Dwyer, V.O'Halloran, P.Hourigan, T.Delaney, J.Dorgan, J.Tiernan, P.Spillane, W.Barron, S.Somers, C.Hickey, Subs: J.Naughton for J.Dermody, J.Organ for W.Barron, M.O'Connor for P.Hourigan.

1962

Kildare P.Dunny, P.Morris, A.Whelan, P.Sharpe, D.Noonan, T.Connell (capt.), A.Sullivan, P Curley, F.Fogarty, K.O'Malley, M.Wall, J.Barker, M.Leahy, L.Kiely, S.Schwer. Sub: P.Cummins for J.Barker.

London M.Butler, J.Dermody, J.Twomey, M.Butler, M.Craddock, P.Hourigan, L.Murphy, E.Cullen, T.Sheehan, J.Fox, J.Sinnott, T.Delaney, J.J.Dillane, D.Croke, E.Mitchell. Subs: M.O'Connor for L.Murphy, M.Belraine for M.Butler, M.Corcoran for T.Sheehan.

1963

London A.Fayard, T.Connolly, M.Butler, M.O'Brien, M.O'Connor, M.Connolly, V.O'Halloran, T.Sheehan (capt.), M.Murphy, J.J.Browne, E.Murray, J.Barrett, P.Carmody, J.Hickey, J.O'Reilly, Sub: M.Diggins for Carmody.

Antrim J.Kearns, J.Carberry, A.McIntosh, G.Walsh, S.McMullan, D.McNeill, S.Burns, C.Barrett, S.Richmond, C.Brogan, L.McGarry (capt.), P.McShane, B.McGarry, R.Elliott, S.Shannon. Subs: B.Elliott for L.McGarry, J.Hughes For C.Brogan.

1964

Down A.Falloona, Paddy Branniff, H.O'Prey, D.Gilmore, F.Gilmore, H.Dorrian, W.Smith, E.Falloona, Podge Branniff, S.Savage, C.McMullan (capt.), D.Crawford, S.Fitzgerald, H.Sloan, J.McGivern, Subs: G.Gilmore for S.Savage, P.McGratton for Paddy Branniff.

London M.Butler, W.Croke, P.Wiley, T.Morrissey, T.Delaney, C.Hughes, T.Gallagher, D.Henry, L.Murphy, P.O'Donoghue, C.Burke, M.Dunne, T.Barron, J.Dorgan, A.Gordon, Subs: M.Treacy for C.Burke, G.Ryan for A.Gordon.

1965

Roscommon Tony Gavin, T.Moylette, P Lyons, T.Murphy, B.Mitchell, J.Kenny, M.J.Keane, S.Cormican, M.Laffey, G.O'Malley, J.Boland, R.Fallon, M.Hoare (capt.), T.Boyle, J.McDonnell. Sub: M.Glennon for T.Boyle.

Warwickshire J.O'Leary, P.Cullen, M.O'Leary, J.Shine, J.Nolan, J.Burke, T.Ryan, D.Dunne, E.Hanlon, M.Conway, P.Hallinan, W.Hogan, T Buckley, H.Shefflin, M.Murphy.

1966

Kildare J.Curran, C.O'Malley, P.Sharpe, J.Wall, F.Fogarty, P.Dunny (capt.), T.Carew, R.Burke, T.Christian, J.Lalor, D.O'Keeffe, M.Dwane, N.Behan, W.Quinn, M.O'Brien, Sub: L.O'Rourke for J.Lalor.

Warwickshire E.O'Brien, J.Dineen, J.Burke, R.Hayes, T.Ryan, D.Dillane, P.Cullen, E.Hanlon, M.O'Sullivan, R.Dunne, P.Hallinan, W.Hogan, K.Phelan, M.O'Leary, T.Buckley, Subs: P.Gillman for E.O'Brien, J.Byrne for K.Phelan, L.Cullinane for M.O'Leary.

1967

Wicklow J.Torpey, T.Collins, J.Fogarty, Liam Collins, J.Kearns (capt.), T Kelly, Rory O'Shea, S.Doyle, Tony Doyle, P O'Dwyer, L.Jordan, T.Morrissey, M.Jordan, T.Scott, W.Hilliard, Sub: C.Keddy for T.Kelly.
Note: A.Byrne played in drawn game. L.Collins came on for replay. Sub in drawn game C.Keddy for J.Fogarty.

London M.Butler, W.Croke, T.Morrissey, E.Roche, W.Twomey, T.Allen, L.Murphy, M.Dunne, P.O'Neill, N.Peacock, J.Tiernan, J.Barrett, M.Butler, P Spillane, P.Delaney, Sub: T Delaney for L.Murphy.
Note: T.Regan, P.Doherty, J.Holohan, M.Devereaux and K.Dunne

played in drawn game. T.Morrissey, E.Roche, P.Delaney, L.Murphy and M.Butler came on for replay. Subs in drawn game: P.Flynn for P Doherty, L.Murphy for J Holohan.

1968

Warwickshire D.Breen, J.Dineen, J.Quinn, R.Hayes, R.Timmons, D.Dillane, P.Cullen, S.O'Keeffe, C.Danagher, W.Hogan, T.Ryan, M.O'Sullivan, C.Crowe, J.Cronin, D.Dunne. Sub: T.Murphy for J.Cronin.

Kerry J.Breen, Tadgh O'Sullivan, D.Kelleher, W.Kenny, T.Lyons, N.Power, T.Leen, R.O'Sullivan, G.Scollard, Theo O'Sullivan, T Cronin, J O'Sullivan, C.Flaherty, W.McCarthy (capt.), B.Twomey. Sub: M.Griffin for P O'Sullivan.

1969

Warwickshire M.McCarthy, J.O'Brien, P.Grimes, P.Heffernan, M.Hanley, L.Dalton, L.Moore, T.Crowley, L.Moloney, W.Collins, M.Brennan, J.Gilligan, J.McLaughlin, J.Browne (capt.), V.Coffey, Sub: P.Hallinan for J.Gilligan.

Kerry J.Breen, M.J.Quinlan, D.Kelleher, W.Kenny, N.Power, T.Cronin (capt.), P.J.McIntyre, T.B.McCarthy, P Finnegan, P McCarthy, P.Sullivan, J.O'Sullivan, C.Flaherty W.McCarthy, J.Gannon. Subs: B Twomey for C Flaherty T.Fleming for P McCarthy.

1970

Meath P .McGovern T.Troy, T.Reilly, M Doherty, E.Cosgrove, G.Baugh, P.Priest, F.McGann, P.Christie, R.Melia, M.McCabe, S.Carney, F.Gleeson, S.Gohery, N.Costello, Subs: J.Curtis for P.Christie, W.Eiffe for M.Doherty ancd John Doherty.
Note: J.Harty and J Doherty played in drawn game. F Gleeson and S.Gohery were on for replay. Subs in drawn game: F.Gleeson for M.McCabe, S.Goherty for J.Doherty.

Hertsfordshire P Waters, V.Donoghue, N.Kennedy, J.Burke, M.Doherty, T.Cleary, S.McGarry, M.Waters, M.Cuddy (capt.), M.Dollard, J.Cuddy, M.Howley, T.Garret, M.Fennessy, P.Waters, Subs: S.Moriarty for M Howley, S.Burke for M.Dollard, J.Byrne for V.O'Donoghue.
Note: J.Tobin played in drawn game. M.Dollard came in for replay. Subs in drawn game: S Carroll for W.Fennessy; J.Byrne for J.Tobin.

1971

Wicklow J.Byrne, L.O'Loughlin, Tony Reilly, J.O'Shaughnessy, J.Doyle, F.Byrne, M.O'Neill, P.Reilly (capt.), P.Berkerry, P.Sheehan, T.McCarthy, T.Kennedy, G.Delaney, E.Murray, G.Gibbons, Subs: A.Byrne for G.Delaney, D.O'Sullivan for A.Byrne, P O'Connell for G.Gibbons.
Note: P.Doyle and D.O'Sullivan played in first game. G Gibbons and T.Kennedy came on for disputed game and retained their places for third game.

Hertsfordshire P.Waters, M.Doherty, E.Kennedy, Joe Burke, James Burke, T.Cleary, S.McGarry, Peter Waters, M.Fitzgerald, J Cuddy (capt.), E.Walsh, M.Waters, T.Garrett.C.Murphy, J.Carroll. Subs: J.Kennedy for M.Waters, D.Kelly for James Burke, K.Sheridan for J.Cuddy, W.Fennessv for P.Kelly.
Note: K.Sheridan, M.Allen and W.Fennessy played in first game. E.Walsh came on as a sub for K.Sheridan and retained his place for second and third games. C.Murphy for W.Fennessy and M.Fitzgerald for M.Allen came on as subs in second game and retained their places for third game.

1972

Kerry A.Casey, B.Fitzgerald, E.B.Fitzgerald, W.Kenny, E.Canty, T.Cronin, T.Hussey, J.Bunyan, P.Finnegan, C.Nolan, T.Kenny, P.Costello, J.McCarthy, P.Donegan, J.Flanagan (capt.). Sub: M.Fitzgerald for T.Hussey.

Warwickshire D.Breen, J.O'Brien, V.McKenna, T.Conroy, M.Hanley, D.Dillane, J.Scanlon, D.Crowley, L.Moloney, L.Moore, N.McLean, J.Moynihan, C.Danagher, L.Dalton, R.Walsh, Subs: C.Crowe for J.O'Brien, M.Griffin for L.Dalton.

1973

Warwickshire O.Cuddy, V.McKenna, T.Conroy, P.Doherty, L.Dalton, D.Dillane, J.Scanlon, J.Madden, N.McLean (capt.), M.Murphy, L.Moloney, C.Crowe, E.Bergin, J.Ryan, J.Cronin, Subs: T.Crowley for M.Murphy, T.Timmons for J.Scanlan.

Louth P Mulholland, S.Walsh, J.Delaney (capt.), A.Farrelly, D.Callan, L.Toal, J.McGuinness, P.Murphy, M.Rice, P.Rice, T.Rice, S.McEneaney, A.Kinsh, F.Kerrigan, P.Fahy. Subs: T.Lowry for P.Fahy, A.Melia for A.Kinsh.

1974

Roscommon P Dolan, T.Healy, O.Hanley, T.Shaughnessy, C.McConn, S.Farrell, J.Dolan, J.Coyne, F.Mitchell, H.Cox, B.Tansey, D.Cox, B.Mitchell, M.Murphy, R.Fallon (capt.). Sub: J.Kilroy.

Derry A.Crawford, T.McGill, L.Hinphey, Phonsie Boyle, J.O'Kane, S.Stevenson (capt.), A.O'Hara, P.Mellon, P.Stevenson, F.McCluskey, J.McGurk, D.Higgins, C.Ferris, F.Kennedy, B.O'Kane, Sub: C.Hinphey for B.O'Kane, P.Murphy for D.Higgins.

1975

Derry Billy Taylor, T.McGill, L.Hinphey, A.O'Hara, J.O'Kane, S.Stevenson (capt.), P.Stevenson, M.McCloskey, S.Kealy, J.McGurk, P.Mellon, C.Hinphey, F.Kennedy, C.Ferris, L.Moore.

Louth T.Lowry, J.Delaney, A.Byrne, A.Melia, D.O'Gorman, P.Fahy, T.Ryan, M.Rice, L.Geraghty, P.Rice, S.Mulcairns, P.Wright, A.Kerrigan, J.McGuinness, S.McEneaney.

1976

Louth P.Hartnett, J.McGuinness, J.Delaney, S.Walsh, D.Callan, P.Fahy, A.Byrne, L.McKillian, L.Toal, S.McEneaney, T.Rice, P.Murphy, A.Melia, T.Lowry, S.Mulcairns. Subs: M.McGarry for A.Byrne, D.Hegarty for L.McKillian.

Mayo M.Nolan, M.Robinson, M.Keane, E.Freeman, M.Walsh, D.Delaney, M.Molloy, A.Henry, M.Murphy, J.Henry, S.O'Keeffe, V.Henry, M.Connolly, M.Higgins, M.Kenny. Subs: P Clarke for M.Walsh, J.Clarke for D.Delaney.

1977

Louth P.Hartnett, M.Begley, J.Delaney, C.McGinley, D.Callan, P.Fahy, S.Walsh, P.Murphy, A.Kerrigan, T.Ryan, T.Rice, A.Melia, S.Mulcairns, T.Lowry, O.Reilly. Sub: J.McGuinness for C.McGinley.

Fermanagh L.McLoughlin, E.Gallagher, R.Gallagher, O.O'Donnell, T.Rehill, C.Cullen, J.McGoldrick, J.Doran, A.Corrigan, G.Cleary, C.Rehill, B.Corrigan, G.McLoughlin, T.Daly, M.Hughes. Sub: F.Baker for G.McLoughlin.

1978

Armagh P Lavery, S.King, L.McKenna, I.Beattie, G.Devlin, M.Smith, E.Kinsella, C.Casey, B.McNally, J.McCormack, P.Devlin, J.Short, E.Mallon, C.McKeown, J.Corvon.

Mayo M.Nolan, E.Freeman, M.Keane, B.Crowley, M.Robinson, P.Clarke, M.Walsh, M.Murphy, A.Henry, W.Loughnane, J.Henry, V.Henry, J.Hopkins, P.Malone, W.Kelly. Subs: R.Donoghue for J.Hopkins, M.Henry for B.Crowley.

1979

Armagh P.Lavery, S.King (capt.), D.McBride, I.Beattie, G.Devlin, M.Smith, E.Kinsella, C.Casey, B.McNally, J.McCormack, P.Devlin, J.Short, J.Christie, F.Mallon, C.McKeown.

Derry A.Treacy, T.McGill, G.McCullagh, M.McCloskey, J O'Kane, S.Stevenson, P.Murphy, P.Stevenson, J.McCullagh, P.O'Donoghue, E.Hassan, J.McGurk, D.Kealy, C Hinphy, P.Mellon. Sub: P Boyle for G.McCullagh.

1980

Mayo M.Nolan, E.Freernan, M.Keane, M.Walsh, P.Clarke, A.Henry, P.Lynskey, J.Cunnane, V Henry, J.J.Hoban, C.Conlon, C.Murphy, J.Henry, M.Ryan, W.Kelly.

Monaghan L.Freeman, D.Ryan, A.O'Reilly, M.Evans, N.McGuigan, G.Maher, J.Power, W.Connolly, J.Downey, P.Kerr, L.Lenihan, M.O'Dowd (snr.), N.Mullaney; O.Connell, P Bolger.

1981

Mayo D Synnott, M.Walsh, M.Kenny, T.Phillips, P Clarke, A.Henry, P Lynskey, V.Henry, J.Cunnane, C.Conlon, J.Henry, C.Murphy, J.J.Hoban, D.Healy, P Delaney.

Louth P.Hartnett, D.Callan, P.Moran, J.McGuinness, S.Mclnerney, A.Kerrigan, C.McGinley, P Murphy, C.Ross, A.Melia, O.Reilly, T.Murphy, W.Piper, T.Giles, M.McGarry. Subs: S.Mulcairns for P.Hartnett, S.French for W.Piper.

1982

Derry A.Treacy, J.McCullagh, A.O'Hara (capt.), G.McCullagh, C.Kelly, P.Stevenson, D.O'Hara, G.Murphy, B.McGilligan, D.Kealy, S.McCloskey, D.Kealy, P.O'Donoghue, P Murphy, J.A.Mullan. Sub: E.Kealy for S.McCloskey.

Monaghan L.Freeman, D.Ryan, A.O'Reilly, M.Giblin, N.McGuigan, L.Lenihan, B.Lynch, J.Downey, W.Connolly, M.O'Dowd Jnr., P.Egan, P Curran, J.J.Sullivan (capt.), O.Connell, M.O'Dowd Snr. Subs: N.Mullaney for P Curran, P.Hughes for M.O'Dowd Snr., S.O'Gorman for M.Giblin.

1983

Cork J.Cronin, F Walsh, E.Flynn, Dan Relihan, Brendan Coleman, P.Madigan, N.Crowley, W.Walsh, M.Fitzgibbon (capt.), P.O'Connell, D.Walsh, Ned Brosnan, Ray O'Connor, S.O'Gorman, G.Hanley. Subs: A.Jagoe for F.Walsh, M.McDonnell for P.O'Connell.

Galway T.Carr, M.O'Donoghue, P.Finnerty (capt.), T.Riordan, S.Davoren, T.Nolan, T Brehony, N.Uniacke, E.Hanny, J.Murphy, M.Coleman, D.Glennon, J.Kelly, J.Coen, D.Connolly. Subs: E.McLarnan for A.Carr, Mattie Kenny for N.Uniacke, T.Uniacke for J.Kelly.

1984

Kilkenny J.Brennan (capt.) W.O Hara, M.Galway, T.Whelan, P.Power, J Marnell, M.Cleere, D.Hoyne, S.Tyrrell, R.Walsh, P.Walsh, J.McDonald, M.Doyle, J.O'Dwyer, M.Rafter. Subs: John Lawler, J.Kinsella.

Galway M.Gannon, K.Flannery, M.O'Donoghue, S.Treacy, P.Malone, M.Minton, M.Conway, E.Hanny, T.Helebert N.O'Halloran, M.Coleman, R.Haverty, N.Earls.L.Craven, G.Stankard. Subs: T.Moloney, Mattie Kenny, N.Uniacke.

1985

Wexford S.Dunne, J.Prendergast, W.Dunphy, B.Bernie, L.Finn, J.Furlong, J.Weafer, J.Barron, P.Owley, R.Murphy, J.Walsh, M.Murphy, S.Murphy, B.O'Connor, T.Byrne. Subs: P.Barden, P.Bailey, V.Murphy.

Tipperary   P.McLoughney, J.McLoughney, P.Larkin, M.Burke, N.McDonald, J.O'Dwyer, M.Ryan, Colm Bonnar, M.Murphy, J.McGrath, G.O'Brien, D.Darcy, L.Stokes, L.McGrath (capt.), S.Burke, Subs: M.Ryan, D.Aherne

1986

Kilkenny   M.Walsh, J.Lannon, D.Dunne, E.Wall, J.Power, M.Cleere, G.Kenny, M.Morrissey (capt.), K.Hennessy, T.Bawle, T.Lannon, D.Carroll, R.Walsh, L.McCarthy, J.Meaney, Sub: L.Cleere for M.Cleere.

Limerick   J.Cagney, M.Barrett, B.Ryan, M.Keogh, A.Galvin, G.Boyle, J.Burns, P.O'Connor, L.O'Brien, M.O'Brien, T.Burke, M.Ryan, T.Dunne, M.O'Connor (capt.), E.Farrell. Subs: M.J.Coffey for M.Barrett, M.Woulfe for A.Galvin.

1987

Cork   T.Kingston, B.O'Sullivan, P.Redmond, D.Murphy, S.McCarthy, L.Lynch, J.Moynihan, D.Sheehan, M.Fitzpatrick (capt.), T Burke, L.Kelly, T.Barry-Murphy, M.Foley, P Cahill, P.Crowley, Subs: D.McCarthy, D.Relihan, R O'Connor.

Wexford   B.Murphy, J.Weafer, S.Ruth, P.Byrne, L.Finn, A.Fenlon, J.O'Leary, C.Jevans, G.Cody, J.Murphy, J.Byrne, J.Barron (capt.), P.Cleary, S.Murphy, T.Byrne, Sub: J.Higgins.

1988

Kilkenny   D.Burke, J.Marnell, P Holden, J.Lannon, S.Caulfield, P.Dwyer, T.McCluskey, G.Ryan, P.Ryan, T.Bawle, J.Walsh, D.Carroll, M.Rafter, J.O'Dwyer, J.Ronan (capt.). Subs: P Gannon for J.O'Dwyer, D.McCarthy for D.Carroll.

Tipperary   B.Bane, M.Stapleton.M.Bourke (capt.), D.Quinlan, F.McGrath, G.O'Brien, M.Corcoran, M.Kelly, E.Kelly, M.Cunningham, P Delaney, J.Harrington, M.McCormack, J.Sheedy, S.Bourke. Sub: P.Cahill for P.Delaney.

1989

Tipperary   J.Grace, M.Stapleton, Mick Ryan (Ballinahinch), D.Quinlan, G.O'Brien, R.Quirke, L.Sheedy, E.Kelly, K.Laffan (capt.), Dinny Ryan, P.Everard, D.Flannery, M.McCormack, J.Sheedy, S.Nealon. Sub: Colm Egan for S.Nealon.

Galway   R.Burke, P Healy, P.Donoghue, B.Cooney, G.Spellman, S.Treacy, J.Noone (capt.), S.Mahon, P.Killilea, M.Connolly, O.Deely, Mattie Kenny, S.Ruane, T.Grealish, V.Treacy. Subs: P Keane for M.Kenny, D.Flanagan for S.Ruane, E.Keogh for V.Treacy.

1990

Kilkenny   M.Walsh, A.Byrne, P Holden (capt.), L.Simpson, J.Murphy, P.Walsh, J.Mahon, T.Bawle, P.Ryan, M.Dunphy, T.Murphy, C.Carter, M.Rafter, J.Lannon, M.Walsh (Slieverue). Subs: M.Walsh (Mooncoin) for M.Rafter, P Hoban for Lannon.

Tipperary   C.Egan, S.McManus, D.O'Brien, S.Brett, M.Ryan (Fethard), T.Crowe, T.O'Meara, O.Cummins, C.Bryan, L.Stokes, P.O'Brien, E.Maher, J.Harrington, M.Grace, G.Bradley (capt.). Subs: T.Murray for M.Grace, P.Kelly for T.O'Meara, B.Burke for T.Crowe.

1991

Tipperary   J.Leamy, M.Ryan (Fethard), M.Stapleton, D.Quinlan, P.Maguire, G.O'Brien (capt.), S.McManus, O.Cummins, C.Bryan, P.O'Keeffe, L.Sheedy, E.Maher, J.Harrington, E.Kelly, S.Nealon. Sub: M.Ryan (Ballinahinch) for M.Ryan.

London   T.Fahy, G.Maher, L.Weir, P.Maher, A.Fanning, M.Cahill, T.Bergin, G.Ryan, D.O'Hanlon, E.Fanning, J.Scott, P.Lonergan, D.Murphy, M.Rafferty, F.O'Donoghue. Subs: D.Hynes for T.Bergin, J.Hogan for P.Lonergan, F.Dwyer for E.Fanning.

1992

Wexford   M.Quigley, D.Morris, P.McGrath, J.Furlong, P.Nolan, G.Cody (capt.), D.Guiney, P.Owley, R.Guiney, R.O'Callaghan, P.Byrne, R.Quigley, J.Byrne, J.Bolger, S.Conroy. Sub: E.Scallan for R.Quigley.

Note: B.Kavanagh, M.Reck and E.Scallan played in drawn game. P.Owley, R.Guiney and R.Quigiey were on for replay. Subs: in drawn game: P.Walsh for B.Kavanagh, P.J.Kavanagh for E.Scallan

Cork   T.O'Donovan, D.Lucey, D.Holland, D.Motherway, M.Treacy, P.Kenneally, W.Long (capt.), J.O'Mahony, M.Sheehan, A.O'Driscoll, D.O'Leary, M.Mullins, K.Murray, B.Walsh, C.Clancy. Sub: B.Harte for M.Mullins.

Note: B.Sheehan and M.Downing played in drawn game. D.Lucey and M.Mullins were on for replay. Subs in drawn game: M.Mullins for M.Sheehan, B.Harte for M.Downing, P Cahill for J.O'Mahony.

1993

Clare   N.Considine, L.Doyle, F.Corey, B.Lynch, S.Power, T.Kennedy, N.Romer (capt.), D.Considine, C.Chaplin, P.O'Rourke, C.O'Neill, B.Quinn, V.Donnellan, B.McNamara, G.Rogers. Subs: C.Lynch for G.Rogers, J.McKenna for C.Chaplin.

Kilkenny   J.McGarry, J.Holohan, J.Mahon, D.Roche, J.Murphy, D.Shelly, C.Phelan, W.O'Keeffe, Paddy Farrell, T.O'Keeffe, C.Brennan, A.Comerford, C.Carter (capt.), P.Treacy, M.Walsh (Mooncoin). Subs: R.Dooley for J.Murphy, S.Ryan for A.Comerford.

1994

Cork   T.O'Donovan, A.White, J.O'Driscoll, J.Walsh, J.O'Sullivan, J.O'Mahoney, V.Murray (capt.), M.Downing, G.Cummins, M.Sheehan, P.Kenneally, F.McCormack, A.O'Driscoll, K.Morrisson, D.O'Connell. Subs: R.Sheehan for M.Sheehan, B.Sheehan for G.Cummins.

Kilkenny   J.McGarry, J.Holohan, J.Mahon, S.Mealy, J.Murphy, J.Conlon, P.Hennessy, A.Cleere, W.O'Keeffe, Paddy Farrell, B.McGovern, P.Treacy, M.Walsh (Mooncoin), D.Roche (capt.), O.O'Connor. Subs: T.Hickey for J.Holohan, O.Blanchfield for M.Walsh.

1995

Kilkenny   J.McGarry, J.Murphy (capt.), E.Drea, S.Meally, P.Hogan, E.Kennedy, T.Murphy, W.O'Keeffe, A.Cleere, Paddy Farrell, P.Treacy, D.Maher, D.Lawler, S.Ryan, O.O'Connor. Sub: B.McGovern for W.O'Keeffe.

Clare   Leo Doyle, S.Doyle, P.Hayes, S.O'Donnell, L.Hassett, E.Flynn, P.Sheehy, R.O'Halloran (capt.), B.Moloney, D.Forde, D.O'Riordan, F.Flynn, J.McKenna, G.Gleeson, B.Healy. Subs: B.O'Neill, P.McGuane, B.Fitzgerald.

1996

Galway   N.Murphy, K.Rabbitte, W.Burke, J.Feeney, J.Walsh, N.Larkin (capt.), N.Power, B.Carr, L.Hogan, B.Larkin, F.Gantley, F.Healy, A.Kerins, M.Connolly, M.Lynskey. Subs: F.O'Brien for L.Hogan, P.Diviney for J.Walsh, E.Caulfield for F.Gantley.

Kilkenny   J.Dunphy, J.Hickey, M.Holohan, C.Connery, A.Aherne, P.Hoban, M.Fitzgerald, R.Moore, B.Treacy, P.O'Grady, B.Barcoe, B.Phelan, R.Kelly, K.O'Shea (capt.), R.Shortall. Subs: P.Hickey for M.Holohan, M.Moran for B.Treacy, P.Cahill for M.Fitzgerald.

1997

Monaghan O.Connell, D.Connolly, Jim Hayes, T.Gillanders, P.Ward, D.Hanrahan, J.Harding, P.Walsh, B.McShane, R.Healy, C.Connolly (capt.), D.Lennon, M.O'Dowd (jnr.), Joe Hayes, H.Cullen. Subs: P.Cunningham for H.Cullen, D.Reilly for P.Ward, J.O'Rourke for J.Harding.

Meath N.Reilly, A.Heavin, C.Ferguson, D.Maguire, T Shine, C.Connell, P.Tansey, P.Coone, D.Reilly, R.Ferguson, M.Healy, F.Smith, D.Fitzsimons, M.Dineen, E.Dixon. Subs: E.McManus for D.Maguire, V.Maguire for F.Smith.

1998

Meath T.Donoghue, J.Battersby, A.Connell, F.Dunne, E.Dixon, D.Connell (capt.), V.Maguire, F.O'Higgins, J.Burke, P.Coone, M.Healy, F.Smith, N.Reilly, N.McKeague, K.Murray. Subs: A.Snow for F.Smith, O.Gilsenan for F.O'Higgins.

Monaghan O.Connell, N.McGuigan, D.Reilly, C.Curley, P Kelly, D.Connolly, D.Hanrahan, C.Connolly, J.Harding, H.Cullen, P O'Connell, R.Healy, P.Ward, K.Lavelle, P.Cunningham. Subs: M.O'Dowd (jnr.) for J.Harding, C.McEntee for R.Healy, T.Gillanders for P.Cunningham.

1999

Meath D.Bannon, J.Horan, C.Ferguson, J.Curtis, B.Perry, J.Gorry, M.Mullen, D.Reilly, B.Gilsenan, T.McKeown, D.Byrne, S.Myles, M.Smith, P.Kelly, P.J.Walsh. Subs: D.Donnelly for Gilsenan, P.Ferguson for Byrne.

Tyrone M.Ward, S.O'Neill, P.Sweeney, D.Molloy, P.Hughes, E.Hughes, K.Cunningham, N.Hurson, D.McCallion, P.Levery, V.Owens, T.Colton, T.McGowan, E.Devlin, P.Doyle. Subs: P.Hughes for P.Doyle, D.O'Neill for Colton.

2000

Armagh B.McCormack, P.C.Gormley, E.McKee, S.Hughes, M.Fox, N.Traynor, P.Harvey, P.McCormack, M.Lennon, P.McKirk, P.McArdle, G.Enright, M.Grimes, P.McKernan, A.Hatzer. Subs: P.Burke for Grimes, R.Murray for McCann.

Meath R.Flanagan, M.Horan, D.Gaughan, F.Fagan, P.Gannon, B.Ferguson, M.Brennan, V.Maguire, D.McGuinness, F.Smith, M.Hanly, J.O'Connor, D.Smith, A.Doherty, W.Smyth. Subs: J.Flood for O'Connor, N.Watters for Doherty, D.Moran for Flood.

2001

Roscommon D.Casey, M.Keaveney, N.Connolly, M.Flynn, K.Doyle, E.Browne, D.Fallon, T.Lennon, A.Beades, C.Fallon, S.O'Brien, P.Glennon, K.Regan, E.Gormley, B.Mannion. Subs: R.Donohoe for Glennon, F.Carr for Mannion, S.Donohoe for Fallon.

Donegal P.O'Brien, F.Grant, C.Dowds, N.McGavigan, J.M.Wallace, D.McDermott, D.Campbell, A.Wallace, R.McLaughlin, N.Campbell, H.McDermott, M.McCann, S.Murphy, R.Durak, B.Friel. Subs: J.McGrath for Durak, K.McDermott for Friel.

2002

Antrim A.McIlhatton, K.McCann, D.Rooney, J.Friel, C.Turley, P.Nugent, S.McGuiness, S.O'Kane, D.McToal, G.Turley, J.Caulfield, G.McIlhatton, N.McCann, T.Maguire, B.McCann. Subs: S.Burke for McToal, R.Edrahin for Friel, L.Burke for O'Kane.

Meath C.Suher, L.O'Flynn, D.Gaughan, S.Fagan, A.McManus, B.Ferguson, D.Wright, C.Ferguson, M.Geraghty, T.Shine, J.Gorry, J.Mitchell, B.Doherty, E.Duignan, P.Hanley. Subs: C.Doherty for Mitchell, P.Fagan for Duignan, D.Geraghty for B.Doherty, G.Galvin for Gorry.

2003

Mayo M.Walsh, D.Walsh, P.Healy, B.Delaney, D.McDonnell, P.Barrett, G.Whyte, D.McConn, K.Healy, A.Healy, J.Duffy, S.Broderick, O.Shaughnessy, P.Broderick, A.Hession. Subs: C.Ryan for Hession, K.Higgins for Shaughnessy.

Donegal P.McDermott, J.M.Wallace, K.Dowds, M.McGrath, G.Boyle, D.McDermott, A.McDermott, A.Wallace, B.Friel, N.Campbell, E.McDermott, D.Greene, M.McCann, R.McLaughlin, P.O'Brien. Subs: J.Donnelly for Greene, J.O'Brien for E.McDermott.

2004

Meath T.Donoghue, S.Duignan, E.Clancy, B.Flynn, C.Doyle, D.Troy, J.P.Ryan, J.Melia, D.Geraghty, M.Scanlon, P.Donnelly, S.Moran, D.Kirby, P.Tobin, R.Flanagan. Sub: B.Higgins for E.Clancy.

Down G.McMullan, A.McGuinness, B.McAleenan, F.Murray, J.Brown, D.McCuskar, P.McCuskar, J.Murphy, T.Jennings, T.McMahon, K.Courtney, D.McGovern, J.McCuskar, J.McCrickard, A.Brown. Subs: D.Morgan for McGovern, N.Burns for Courtney.

ALL-IRELAND JUNIOR CHAMPIONSHIP
FINAL REFEREES

1912	M. F. Crowe (Dublin)		1965	Jimmy Duggan (Galway)
1913	Fred Cooney (Dublin)		1966	Clem Foley (Dublin)
1914	J. Kirwan (Dublin)		1967	P. Johnson (Kilkenny)
1915	Pat Dunphy (Laois)		1968	Clem Foley (Dublin)
1916	M. F. Crowe (Dublin)		1969	Pat Rankins (Laois)
1923	P. Kenefick (Dublin)		1970	Mick Slattery (Clare)
1924	P. McCullagh (Wexford)		1971	D. Doody (Dublin)
1925	Tim Humphries (Limerick)		1972	P. Byrnes (Gloucestershire)
1926	Tom Hayes (Limerick)		1973	E. Devlin (Tyrone)
1927	S. O'Neill (Dublin)		1974	E. Farrell (Donegal)
1928	Willie Walsh (Waterford)		1975	M. Clarke (Westmeath)
1929	J. J. Callanan (Tipperary)		1976	Gerry Kirwan (Offaly)
1930	Seán Hogan (Waterford)		1977	Clem Foley (Dublin)
1931	Jim Walsh (Dublin)		1978	Noel O'Donoghue (Dublin)
1932	J. Curran (Meath)		1979	Noel O'Donoghue (Dublin)
1933	Tom McGrath (Dublin)		1980	Seamus Brennan (Galway)
1934	S. O'Neill (Dublin)		1981	Clem Foley (Dublin)
1935	Liam Murphy (Dublin)		1982	Clem Foley (Dublin)
1936	T. McGrath (Dublin)		1983	Pat Delaney (Laois)
1937	M. O'Neill (Wexford)		1984	John Moore (Waterford)
1938	J. Ryan (Liverpool)		1985	Jim Joe Landers (Waterford)
1939	E. McMahon (Dublin)		1986	Jim Joe Landers (Waterford)
1940	J. Madigan (Ennis)		1987	Noel O'Donoghue (Dublin)
1941	Mick Hennessy (Clare)		1988	Séamus Brennan (Galway)
1946	Phil Purcell (Tipperary)		1989	Pat Delaney (Laois)
1947	Willie Murphy (Wexford)		1990	M Quinn (Clare)
1948	G. Kelly (Dublin)		1991	Pat Horan (Offaly)
1949	Con Murphy (Galway)		1992	Pat Delaney (Laois)
1950	J. Phelan (Kilkenny)		1993	M. Darcy (Galway)
1951	Hubie Hogan (Tipperary)		1994	Seán O'Meara (Offaly)
1952	J. Keane (Waterford)		1995	John McDonnell (Tipperary)
1953	Jack Mulcahy (Kilkenny)		1996	M. Wadding (Waterford)
1954	M. Leahy (Dublin)		1997	G. Devlin (Armagh)
1955	Moss Pollard (Waterford)		1998	P. Aherne (Carlow)
1956	C. McLoughlin (Dublin)		1999	E. Morris (Dublin)
1957	Mick O'Mahony (Cork)		2000	M.Bodkin (Galway)
1958	F. Sheehan (Wexford)		2001	J. McGrath (Westmeath)
1959	E. Conroy (Laois)		2002	D.O'Donovan (Dublin)
1960	Paddy Cronin (Cork)		2003	J.McGrath (Westmeath)
1961	C. Conway (Cork)		2004	G.Devlin (Armagh)
1962	C. McLoughlin (Dublin)			
1963	Clem Foley (Dublin)			
1964	Clem Foley (Dublin)			

MUNSTER HURLING JUNIOR CHAMPIONSHIP FINALS

1910	Tipperary	5-0	2-0	Clare
	(Unfinished. Refixture ordered.)			
	Tipperary	5-1	1-0	Clare
1911	Tipperary	6-4	2-2	Limerick
1912	Cork	4-5	3-1	Tipperary
1913	Tipperary	3-3	1-6	Cork
1914	Clare	6-2	5-2	Cork
1915	Tipperary	9-1	2-1	Clare
1916	Cork	6-0	4-1	Tipperary
1917-1922	Suspended			
1923	Cork	8-4	5-1	Tipperary
1924	Tipperary	4-3	2-2	Limerick
1925	Cork	6-3	4-2	Clare
1926	Tipperary	3-7	2-3	Cork
1927	Limerick	4-4	2-2	Clare
1928	Tipperary	4-3	0-3	Waterford
1929	Cork	3-3	2-4	Waterford
1930	Tipperary	7-4	1-2	Clare
1931	Waterford	7-3	4-5	Tipperary
1932	Cork	1-4	1-2	Clare
1933	Tipperary	4-2	1-2	Cork
1934	Waterford	7-10	5-2	Cork
1935	Limerick	6-8	2-0	Waterford
1936	Waterford	3-1	1-1	Cork
1937	Cork	5-5	3-1	Limerick
1938	Cork	2-3	1-6	Clare
Replay	Cork	7-5	4-0	Clare
1939	Waterford	4-2	2-4	Limerick
	Limerick awarded title on an objection.			
1940	Cork	5-3	3-3	Tipperary
1941	Limerick	4-8	0-4	Waterford
1942-1945	Suspended			
1946	Limerick	6-6	5-6	Cork
1947	Cork	11-8	1-3	Waterford
1948	Limerick	4-7	4-5	Cork
1949	Clare	3-3	0-6	Cork
1950	Cork	3-7	3-6	Tipperary
1951	Tipperary	4-8	3-2	Limerick
1952	Limerick	6-6	2-6	Cork
1953	Tipperary	4-8	5-5	Cork
Replay	Tipperary	4-7	4-6	Cork
1954	Limerick	5-4	1-7	Tipperary
1956	Kerry	6-7	0-3	Waterford

1957	Limerick	2-10	1-10	Cork
1958	Cork	6-9	3-5	Waterford
1959	Cork	3-9	4-3	Kerry
1960	Cork	4-5	3-4	Kerry
1961-1973	Kerry represented Province in All-Ireland series.			
1974-1982	No team in All-Ireland Junior from Munster.			
1983	Cork	4-19	3-8	Tipperary
1984	Cork	0-14	0-10	Tipperary
1985	Tipperary	3-6	1-10	Limerick
1986	Limerick beat Cork			
1987	Cork	2-16	1-9	Tipperary
1988	Tipperary	5-9	0-15	Cork
1989	Tipperary	2-14	2-8	Clare
1990	Tipperary	0-18	2-6	Cork
1991	Tipperary	4-13	5-10	Cork
Replay	Tipperary	2-20	0-11	Cork
1992	Cork	1-12	1-10	Clare
1993	Clare	2-15	0-10	Waterford
1994	Cork	1-10	1-9	Clare
1995	Clare	4-11	1-9	Waterford
1996	Cork	2-15	2-10	Tipperary
1997-1999	No Munster team in All-Ireland			

HURLING

LEINSTER HURLING JUNIOR CHAMPIONSHIP FINALS

1905	Kildare	3-8	3-5	Westmeath
1906	Kildare	2-6	1-8	Meath
1907	Carlow	2-9	0-9	Meath
1908	Dublin	1-7	1-3	Offaly
	(Unfinished. Dublin awarded title.)			
1909	Kilkenny	4-7	3-3	Dublin
1910	Laois	12-2	2-1	Meath
1911	Kilkenny	5-1	5-1	Dublin
Replay	Kilkenny	3-2	1-3	Dublin
1912	Westmeath	4-3	2-1	Offaly
1913	Kilkenny	7-3	3-3	Wexford
1914	Laois	16-4	0-0	Kildare
1915	Offaly	6-2	3-5	Meath
1916	Kilkenny	12-2	1-1	Westmeath
1917-1921	Suspended			
1922	Offaly	4-3	0-3	Kilkenny
1923	Offaly	4-1	3-2	Laois
1924	Offaly	7-4	5-5	ublin
1925	Dublin	4-4	4-4	Kilkenny
Replay	Dublin	4-4	4-2	Kilkenny
1926	Wexford	4-1	3-1	Laois
1927	Meath	3-4	3-4	Dublin
Replay	Meath	4-6	2-2	Dublin
1928	Kilkenny	3-2	0-2	Laois
1929	Offaly	7-3	1-5	Dublin
1930	Kilkenny	7-3	2-2	Laois
1931	Kilkenny	2-9	1-5	Dublin
	Declared null and void following an objection and counter objection.			
1932	Dublin	6-2	4-5	Kildare
1933	Laois	3-8	4-2	Kilkenny
1934	Kildare	3-7	3-7	Kilkenny
Replay	Kildare	1-8	1-7	Kilkenny
1935	Kilkenny	5-5	1-5	Dublin
1936	Westmeath	4-8	5-2	Laois
1937	Dublin	11-8	5-4	Offaly
1938	Offaly	3-8	1-8	Kilkenny
1939	Kilkenny	6-9	4-3	Dublin
1940	Wexford	4-6	2-7	Dublin
1941	Kilkenny	6-3	2-2	Wexford
1942 -1945	Suspended			
1946	Kilkenny	4-5	1-1	Dublin
1947	Dublin	5-5	1-5	Meath
1948	Meath	2-10	3-5	Kilkenny
1949	Kilkenny	4-3	3-2	Dublin
1950	Dublin	3-7	3-3	Kilkenny
1951	Kilkenny	2-11	2-6	Dublin
1952	Dublin	4-5	2-7	Wicklow
1953	Offaly	3-7	2-2	Kilkenny
1954	Wicklow	4-15	1-3	Westmeath
1955	Dublin	4-12	4-9	Kilkenny
1956	Kilkenny	6-11	1-8	Laois
1957	Wexford	3-11	3-4	Dublin
1958	Kilkenny	2-10	1-5	Meath
1959	Wexford	6-10	0-1	Offaly
1960	Carlow	6-8	3-8	Wexford
1961-1973	Competition confined to weaker counties)			
1961	Meath	1-11	3-3	Wicklow
1962	Kildare	4-10	2-8	Wicklow
1963	Westmeath	4-10	4-7	Wicklow
1964	Wicklow	4-8	2-6	Kildare
1965	Wicklow	3-14	5-8	Kildare
Replay	Wicklow	4-5	2-8	Kildare
1966	Kildare	4-10	4-6	Wicklow
1967	Wicklow	4-13	0-8	Meath
1968	Louth	4-12	5-8	Kildare
1969	Louth	5-8	2-5	Kildare
1970	Meath	6-13	5-9	Wicklow
1971	Wicklow	3-12	0-7	Kildare
1972	Meath	6-9	4-11	Kildare
1973	Louth	8-7	6-5.	Meath
1974-1975	Louth represented Province in All-Ireland series.			
1976-1982	No competition in Leinster.			
1983	Kilkenny	3-13	1-7	Wexford
1984	Kilkenny	2-13	0-7	Wexford
1985	Wexford	4-14	2-6	Dublin
1986	Kilkenny	2-18	0-6	Westmeath
1987	Wexford	6-15	0-9	Dublin
1988	Kilkenny	4-6	3-3	Carlow
1989	Kilkenny	5-12	0-9	Westmeath
1990	Kilkenny	1-9	0-12	Wexford
Replay	Kilkenny	3-10	1-10	Wexford
1991	Kilkenny	3-12	2-6	Wexford
1992	Wexford	2-11	1-12	Laois
1993	Kilkenny	1-15	0-10	Wexford
1994	Kilkenny	2-18	3-8	Wexford
1995	Kilkenny	2-14	4-5	Wexford
1996	Kilkenny	1-13	1-7	Wexford
1997-2002	No Competition			
2003	Meath	0-11	0-9	Longford
2004	Meath	4-14	2-7	Longford

HURLING 'B' CHAMPIONSHIP FINALS

1974	Croke Park, June 23			
	Kildare	*1-26*	*3-13*	*Antrim*
1975	Croke Park, June 15			
	Westmeath 4-16	*3-19*	*London*	
Replay	Croke Park, June 22			
	Westmeath 3-23	*2-7*	*London*	
1976	Croke Park, June 27			
	Kerry	*0-15*	*1-10*	*London*
1977	Croke Park, June 26			
	Laois	*3-21*	*2-9*	*London*
1978	Croke Park, June 25			
	Antrim	*1-16*	*3-7*	*London*
1979	Tullamore, June 17			
	Laois	*2-13*	*3-10*	*London*
Replay	Athy, June 24			
	Laois	*1-20*	*0-17*	*London*
1980	Croke Park, July 6			
	Kildare	*2-20*	*2-14*	*London*
1981	Loughgiel, July 5			
	Antrim	*3-17*	*3-14*	*London*
1982	Ruislip, July 4			
	Antrim	*2-16*	*2-14*	*London*
1983	Tralee, June 26			
	Kerry	*2-8*	*1-7*	*London*
1984	Ruislip, July 8			
	Westmeath 4-10	*1-16*	*London*	
1985	Trim, July 7			
	London	*1-8*	*1-6*	*Meath*
1986	Ruislip, June 29			
	Kerry	*3-10*	*1-9*	*London*
1987	Carlow, July 5			
	London	*0-20*	*1-15*	*Carlow*
1988	Ruislip, July 3			
	London	*2-6*	*1-7*	*Down*
1989	Newbridge, July 2			
	Kildare	*1-13*	*1-12*	*London*
1990	Ruislip, July 8			
	London	*1-15*	*5-2*	*Kildare*
1991	Mullingar, July 7			
	Westmeath 2-12	*2-6*	*London*	
1992	Ruislip, July 12			
	Carlow	*2-15*	*3-10*	*London*
1993	Ruislip, July 11			
	Meath	*2-16*	*1-16*	*London*

1994	Ruislip, July 3			
	Roscommon 1-10	*1-9*	*London*	
1995	Portlaoise, July 2			
	London	*2-7*	*0-8*	*Wicklow*
1996	Croke Park, June 23			
	Derry	*1-14*	*0-10*	*Wicklow*
1997-2001	No competition			
2002	Thurles, July 27			
	Laois	*2-20*	*2-7*	*Wicklow*
2003	Tullamore, July 12			
	Wicklow	*4-16*	*2-13*	*Roscommon*
2004	Croke Park, July 24			
	Kildare	*3-14*	*3-7*	*Mayo*

Note: The All-Ireland "B" winners played in the quarter-final of the Championship proper

ALL-IRELAND INTERMEDIATE HURLING FINALS

1961 17/09/1961, Wexford,
| Wexford | 3-15 | 4-4 | London |
13/08/1961, Kilkenny, Home Final
| Wexford | 5-6 | 5-6 | Tipperary |
20/08/1961, Kilkenny, Home Final, replay
| Wexford | 4-11 | 3-9 | Tipperary |

1962 09/09/1962, Croke Park
| Carlow | 6-15 | 3-3 | London |
26/08/1962, Birr, Home Final
| Carlow | 3-9 | 2-5 | Galway |

1963 08/09/1963, Thurles
| Tipperary | 1-10 | 1-7 | London |
18/08/1963, Waterford, Home Final
| Tipperary | 0-17 | 2-3 | Wexford |

1964 20/09/1964, Enniscorthy
| Wexford | 4-7 | 1-11 | London |
16/08/1964, Waterford, Home Final
| Wexford | 2-8 | 1-5 | Cork |

1965 19/09/1965, Cork
| Cork | 2-20 | 5-5 | London |
15/08/1965, Enniscorthy, Home Final
| Cork | 3-7 | 2-6 | Wexford |

Note: 1966-1973. British winners came in at the semi-final stage.

1966 18/09/1966, Enniscorthy
| Tipperary | 4-11 | 2-12 | Dublin |

1967 17/09/1967, Limerick
| London | 1-9 | 1-5 | Cork |

1968 29/09/1968, Croke Park
| London | 4-15 | 0-3 | Dublin |

1969 12/10/1969, Thurles
| Kildare | 2-8 | 3-4 | Cork |

1970 04/10/1970, Croke Park
| Antrim | 4-18 | 3-6 | Warwickshire |

1971 19/09/1971, Kilkenny
| Tipperary | 3-16 | 3-13 | Wicklow |

1972 17/09/1972, Birr
| Tipperary | 2-13 | 1-9 | Galway |

1973 16/09/1973, Waterford
| Kilkenny | 5-15 | 2-9 | London |

Note: Suspended 1974-1997

1997 11/10/1997, Limerick
| Cork | 2-11 | 1-12 | Galway |

1998 10/10/1998, Thurles
| Limerick | 4-16 | 2-17 | Kilkenny |

1999 25/09/1999, Birr
| Galway | 3-13 | 2-10 | Kilkenny |

2000 23/09/2000, Birr
| Tipperary | 2-17 | 1-10 | Galway |

2001 29/10/2001, Dungarvan
| Cork | 2-17 | 2-8 | Wexford |

2002 21/09/2002, Birr
| Galway | 2-15 | 1-10 | Tipperary |

2003 30/08/2003, Thurles
| Cork | 1-21 | 0-23 | Kilkenny (aet) |

2004 22/08/2004, Thurles
| Cork | 2-11 | 2-11 | Kilkenny |

Replay 04/09/2004, Thurles,
| Cork | 1-16 | 1-10 | Kilkenny |

2005 03/09/2005, Portlaoise
| Wexford | 1-15 | 0-16 | Galway |

2006 26/08/2006, Dungarvan
| Cork | 3-15 | 1-18 | Kilkenny (aet) |

2007 25/08/2007, Kilkenny
| Wexford | 1-11 | 1-9 | Waterford |

2008 30/08/2008, Thurles
| Kilkenny | 1-16 | 0-13 | Limerick |

2009 29/08/2009, Dungarvan
| Cork | 2-23 | 0-16 | Kilkenny |

2010 28/08/2010, Thurles
| Kilkenny | 2-17 | 1-13 | Cork |

2011 27/08/2011, Thurles
| Clare | 2-13 | 1-11 | Kilkenny |

2012 01/09/2012, Thurles
| Tipperary | 3-13 | 1-17 | Kilkenny |

2013 31/08/2013, Kilkenny
| Tipperary | 2-14 | 2-11 | Kilkenny |

2014 09/08/2014, Kilkenny
| Cork | 2-18 | 2-12 | Wexford |

2015 8/8/2015, Limerick
| Galway | 0-23 | 0-14 | Cork |

2016 6/8/2016, Thurles
| Kilkenny | 5-16 | 1-16 | Clare |

2017 23/7/2017, Páirc Uí Chaoimh
| Kilkenny | 2-23 | 2-18 | Cork |

ALL-IRELAND INTERMEDIATE CHAMPIONSHIP FINAL TEAMS

1961

Wexford   J.O'Neill, J.Hyland, W.Ryan, M.Collins, W.Doran, J.Creane, P.Sullivan, L.Byrne (capt.), P.Lynch, J.Walsh, N.Newport, T.Hawkins, L.Creane, J.Coady, S.Whelan. Sub: J.Kehoe for J.Coady.
London   A.Morrissey, P.Murphy, M.Kerrse, A.Moloney, J.Kearns, D.Dillane, M.Cormody, W.Dorgan (capt.), J.Redmond, E.Murray, J.Kiely, P.Egan, L.Healy, W.Duffy, J.Hickey. Subs: P.Ryan for J.Hickey, R.O'Leary for D.Dillane.

1962

Carlow   J.O'Connell, W.Walsh, M.Hogan, A.Fortune, P.McGovern, P.Somers, T.Nolan, M.Morrissey, M.O'Brien, L.Walsh, W.Hogan, P.O'Connell, W.Walsh, E.Gladney, C.Hynes.
London   W.Barnaville, J.Kearns, C.Whelan, B.Neville, P.Dwyer, P Ryan, M.Carmody, J.Daly, R.O'Leary, J.Tiernan, T Cleary, W.Dargan, P.Harney, T.Morrissey, M.Devereaux. Subs M.Collins for P.Dwyer, P.Spillane for W.Dargan, P.Dwyer for M.Collins.

1963

Tipperary   P.O'Sullivan, T.Burke, M.Barry, P.Crampton, W.Boyle, G.Gleeson, P.Dawson, M.Roche, J.Fogarty, M.Kearns, J.Collison, M.Keating, T.Flynn, T.Larkin, J.Lanigan (capt.). Sub: P.J.Grace for T.Flynn.
London   W.Barnaville, J.Kearns, P Dwyer, B.Neville, M.Collins, P.Ryan, M.Carmody, P.Fahy, W.Dargan, J.Tiernan, T.Cleary, M.Devereaux, T.Morrissey, L.Furlong, P.Spillane. Subs: J.Daly for W.Dargan, P.Hourigan for M.Devereaux, M.Craddock for M.Carmody.

1964

Wexford   S.Boggan, N.O'Gorman, E.O'Brien, A.Carty, L.Butler, O.Hearne, J.Murphy, M.Delaney, B.Murray, O.Cullen, S.Whelan, P.Murphy, L.Delaney, L.Kehoe, N.O'Brien. Subs: J.Mannion for P.Murphy, T.Hassey for B.Murray, J.Dunne for J.Mannion.
London   W.Barnaville, J.Kearns, P.Dwyer, B.Neville, M.Collins, P Ryan, M.Carmody, M.Connolly, T.Cleary, E.Murray, T.Connolly, J.J.Browne, J.Barrett, T.Morrissey, L.Furlong. Sub: M.Devereaux for J.J.Browne.

1965

Cork   T.Monaghan, D.Murphy (capt.), John Ryan, M.Garde, J.O'Keeffe, S.Barry-Murphy, F.Sheehan, O.O'Keeffe, J.Hogan, S.Barry, W.Galligan, J.K.Coleman, D.O'Brien, D.O'Keeffe, W.Fitton.
London   W.Barnaville, H.Hickey, B.Neville, M.McGrath, M.Collins, P.Fahy, V.O'Halloran, M.Connolly, W.Dargan, T.Cleary, T.Connolly, M.Devereaux, E.Murray, T.Morrissey, M.Ryan. Subs: J.Curtin for T.Connolly, T.Allen for B.Neville.

1966

Tipperary   S.Shinnors, P.Kennedy, E.Ryan, A.Burke, J.Drohan, N.O'Gorman, P.Dawson, W.O'Grady, J.Fogarty, S.Kenny, M.O'Grady, M.Jones, L.Connolly, S.Noonan, T.Brennan. Subs: D.Dunne for P.Dawson, P.McLoughlin for M.O'Grady.
Dublin   D.Massey, P.Moyles, P Corcoran, B.Dunne, S.Armstrong, T.Burke, S.Moyles, H.Dalton, T.McGrath, N.Kinsella, T.Woods, E.Flynn, T.Cunninghom, B.Sunderland, D.Doody. Sub: W.Markey for S.Armstrong.

1967

London   W.Barnaville, M Hassett, L.Walsh, E.Leary, R.Cashin, M.Connolly, M.Kirwan, P.Fahy, S.Lambe, T.Connolly, T.Cleary, F.Condon, J.Organ, D.O'Keeffe, E.Murray.
Cork   T.Monaghan, D.Murphy, P Dunne, S.Barry, P.Hegarty, J.Hogan, P.O'Sullivon, M.Meaney, J.Keating, T.Ryan, J.K.Coleman, M.Kenneally, D.Coleman, J.O'Connell, D.Doly. Subs: P.Murphy, P.Curley.

1968

London   W.Barnaville, M.Hassett, L.Walsh, C.Wylie, P.Fahy, M.Connolly, R.Cashin, M.Meaney, P.O'Neill, S.Lambe, F.Condon, T.Connolly, M.Loughnane, M.Kirwan, T.Cleary.
Dublin   P Cunningham, W.Devitt, K.Crooks, J.Doody, W.Markey, T.Woods, P.Murphy, T.Flynn, J.Kenny, J.Hackett, C.Ryan, J.Doran, L.Heneberry, W.Lee, D.Doody. Subs: J.Byrne for L.Heneberry, P McCabe for C.Ryan.

1969

Kildare   P.Connolly, S.Malone, C.O'Malley, N.Burke, A.Carew, P.Dunny, M.O'Brien, B.Burke (capt.), J.O'Connell, T.Christian, T.Carew, M.Dwane, N.Behan, M.Mullins, J.Wall. Subs: E.Walsh for T.Carew, P.Connolly for M.Dwane, T.Carew for E.Walsh.
Cork   T.Monaghan, J.Twomey, J.Ryan, J.O'Connell, O.O'Keeffe, J.Hogan, P.McDonnell, Jack Russell, Jim Russell, S.Gillen, M.Malone, F.Kelleher, T.Meaney, D.Daly, D.Coleman. Subs: N.Gallagher For M.Malone, T.O'Mahony for F.Kelleher.

1970

Antrim   J.Coyles, C.Elliott, K.Donnelly, E.Hamill, N.Wheeler, T.Connolly, A.McCamphill, S.Burns (capt.), S.Collins, S.Richmond, E.Donnelly, A.Hamill, B.McGarry, P.McShane, A.McCallin. Subs: A.Connolly for T.Connolly, J.P.McFadden for A.Connolly.
Warwickshire D.Breen, J.O'Brien, P.Grimes, L.Moore, M.Hanley, L.Dalton, T.Ryan, J.Moynihan, D.Dillane, C.Crowe, F.Gantley, W.Hogan, C.Danagher, J.Quinn, V.Coffey. Subs: J.Byrne for J.Quinn, S.O'Keeffe for C.Crowe, P.Shields for V.Coffey.

1971

Tipperary   W.Barnaville, J.Dunlea, P.Kennedy, G.Kehoe, D.Crowe, P.Quinlan, B.Teehan, O.Quinn, J.P.McDonnell, S.Power, J.Noonan, M.Brennan, J.Barry, P.Lowry, E.Butler (capt.).
Wicklow   S.O'Brien, R.O'Shea, W.O'Reilly, J.Kearns, C.Keddy, L.Collins, P.Barry, S.Doyle, S.Brennan, M.O'Brien (capt.), M.Delaney, T.Morrissey, M.Jordan, T.Scott, W.Hilliard. Subs: P.Kennedy for C.Keddy, W.Hilliard for B.Hilliard.

1972

Tipperary   S.Cahalane, J.Costigan, J.Keogh, S.Fitzpatrick, M.Fitzgibbon, N.Seymour, J.Keane, W.Ferncombe, T.Moloney, J.Connors, J.Kennedy, M.Ruth, O.Killeen, J.Seymour, S.Mackey. Subs: J.Darcy for T.Moloney, T.Moloney for W.Ferncombe.
Galway   E.Campbell, P Hobbs, T.Lynch, T.Cloonan, L.Glynn, P.O'Brien, O.Parnell, P.Fahy, P.Ryan, G.Coone, E.Muldoon, M.Barrett, K.Hanniffy, P.Egan, T.O'Hara. Subs: M.Q'Connor for P.O'Brien, K.Lucas for O.Parnell, T.Lane for K.Hanniffy.

1973

Kilkenny   P.Grace (capt.), M.Mason, K.Mahon, M.Hoyne, J.Dunne, T.Murphy, T.Foley, P.Kavanagh, D.Burke, J.Doyle, P.Holden, J.O'Connor, F.Cleere, J.Walsh, S.Muldowney.
London   M.Butler, C.O'Leary, J.Houlihan, M.Ryan, J.Roche, J.Hughes, J.Casey, S.Coughlan, M.Murphy, D.Hallissey, F.Birrane, A.Dwyer, D.McCarthy, P.Fahy, J.McNamara. Subs: C.Danagher for M.Murphy, M.Quinlan for J McNamara, J.Hanley for J.Houlihan.

1997

Cork   D.Óg Cusack, S.Barrett, P.Mulcahy (capt.), J.Walsh, J.O'Sullivan, M.Landers, D.Murphy, G.Cummins, D.Barrett, T.McCarthy, R.Dwane, A.Walsh, D.Maher, S.O'Farrell, J.Smiddy. Subs: P.Cahill for S.Barrett, B.O'Driscoll (Killavullen) for T.McCarthy.
Galway   N.Murphy, P.Diviney, R.Burke, D.Turley, S.Forde, N.Larkin, N.Power (capt.), M.Kenny, L.Hogan, P.Forde, N.Kenny, F.Healy, B.Larkin, M.Connolly (Craughwell), R.Gantley. Subs: K.Rabbitte for P.Diviney, M.Forde for P.Forde, K.Gavin for B.Larkin.

1998

Limerick   P.Horgan, N.Murphy, W.O'Brien, J.Kiely, P.Neenan, G.Galvin, P Cahill, D.Carroll, P.Keyes, D.Murphy, A.Ryan, J.Cormican (capt.), M.O'Brien, O.O'Neill, J.Butler. Sub: M.Quaide for D.Murphy.
Kilkenny   M.Carey, D.Roche, P.Farrell (capt.), J.Walsh, M.Bookle, P.Brophy, S.Moran, D.Maher, J.Bolger, H.Shefflin, A.Cleere, B.Phelan, T.Shefflin, B.Barcoe, R.Shortall. Subs: C.Connery for D.Roche, R.Moore for S.Moran, O.O'Connor for B.Barcoe.

1999

Galway   N.Murphy, P.Diviney, W.Burke, D.Turley, E.Linnane, N.Larkin, N.Power, J.Donnelly, D.O'Brien, G.Glynn, L.Hogan, F.Healy, D.Joyce, M.Connolly, N.Kelly. Subs: D.Donoghue for Kelly, S.Lawless for Donnelly, E.Tannier for O'Brien.
Kilkenny   M.Tyler, S.Kealy, E.Drea, B.Joyce, D.Lyng, M.Bookle, S.Moran, B.O'Keeffe, D.Maher, J.Bolger, J.Carey, P.Farrell, R.Shortall, A.Prendergast, O.O'Connor. Subs: B.Phelan for Bolger, A.Cleere for Corey.

2000

Tipperary   S.Butler, B.Hogan, M.Ryan, M.Gleeson, D.Hackett, C.Bonar, D.Gleeson, S.Maher, J.Teehan, D.O'Connor, C.Morrisey, D.Corcoran, R.Killeen, P.Maguire, D.Browne.
Galway   K.Boyle, R.Brady, E.McEntee, R.Reilly, S.Forde, E.Hyland, S.McClernan, K.Carr, J.Cummins, G.McGlacin, B.Cunningham, S.Tierney, M.Fahy, M.Greaney, M.Headd. Subs: B.Connolly for Fahy, A.Connolly for McClernan, M.Corcoran for Cummins, M.Curtin for Corcoran, M.Lynskey for Curtin.

2001

Cork   B.Rochford, D.Lynch, L.Hayes, B.Lombard, J.Hughes, M.Daly, M.Prendergast, A.O'Connor, R.Dwyer, J.O'Callaghan, T.O'Mahony, S.Hayes, N.Murphy, N.McCarthy, E.Collins. Subs: J.Barrett for Hayes, D.Moher for Murphy.
Wexford   P.Carley, A.Murphy, D.Stafford, T.Walsh, S.Carley, W.Carley, C.Kehoe, J.Simpson, P.Redmond, J.Kenny, M.Murphy, E.Cullen, R.Murphy, M.J.Reck, F.Simpson. Subs: R.Barry for Redmond, J.Maguire for Murphy, M.Jacob for Kenny, B.Redmond for J.Simpson, K.Rooney for Kehoe.

2002

Replay
Galway   N.Murphy, S.McClearn, T.Óg Regan, R.Fahy, E.Tannion, C.Dervan, Adrian Diviney, J.Donnelly, G.Glynn, B.Cunningham, J.Campbell, K.Brady, C.Ryan, J.Conroy, B.Lawless. Subs: Aidan Diviney for Lawless, D.Hayes for Tannion, J.Gantley for Glynn, R.Reilly for Adrian Diviney. (Adrian Diviney, S.Tierney and T.Kavanagh played in the drawn game and were replaced by T.Óg Regan, J.Campbell and C.Ryan for the replay. Subs in the drawn encounter were J.Campbell for Kavanagh, R.Devanney for Aidan Diviney, C.,Ryan for S.Tierney, R.Reilly for McClearn.)
Tipperary   F.Horgan, G.Griffin, M.Peters, B.Gaynor, C.Ryan, C.Morrisey, C.Everard, S.Maher, J.Teehan, B.Hogan, B.Stritch, P.Buckley, G.Maguire, D.Hackett, S.Everard. Subs: T.Connors for Hackett, S.Maher for Teehan, D.Browne for Buckley, P.Morrisey for Hogan. (Subs in the drawn encounter were M.Keeshan for Hackett, T.Connors for S.Everard, K.Hogan for C.Everard, P.Morrisey for Maguire).

2003

Cork   M.Coleman, M.Prout, J.O'Brien, B.Murphy, J.Hughes, B.Lombard, K.Hartnett, A.O'Connor, J.Barrett, J.O'Callaghan, B.Coleman, R.Dwyer, J.Murphy, D.O'Riordan, J.Quinlan. Subs: V.Morrisey for Dwyer, M.Daly for Lombard, V.Hurley for O'Connor, D.Moher for Quinlan, Quinlan for Murphy, Dwyer for Hughes, Lombard for Coleman, Murphy for Quinlan.
Kilkenny   R.O'Neill, P.Costello, S.Lanigan, G.Joyce, E.Mackey, A.Lawlor, J.O'Neill, J.Power, P.Buggy, A.Fogarty, P.Maher, J.Maher, D.Mackey, N.Moloney, P.Sheehan. Subs: D.Lawlor for Buggy, J.P.Corcoran for Sheehan, E.Walsh for P.Maher, N.Doherty for Power.

2004

Cork   A.Nash, J.Crowley, L.Hayes, R.McCarthy, B.Walsh, T.Lorden, D.Fitzgerald, T.Healy, J.Olden, J.Russell, D.Dineen, B.O'Dwyer, S.Hayes, R.Doherty, E.Conway. Subs: J.Masters for Healy, D.McSweeney for Walsh, N.Murphy for Dineen.
Kilkenny   R.O'Neill, J.Tennyson, S.Lanigan, P.Costelloe, S.Kealey, J.Costelloe, J.O'Neill, B.Phelan, C.Herity, D.Mackey, R.Power, J.Power, M.Grace, D.Buggy, E.Walsh. Subs: J.P.Corcoran for Mackey, J.Phelan for B.Phelan.

2005

Wexford   M.White, D.Guiney, B.O'Leary, P.Roche, K.Kavanagh, M.O'Leary, A.Kavanagh, L.Gleeson, C.Kenny, P.Nolan, M.Byrne, S.Doyle, P.Carley, G.Coleman, M.Furlong. Subs: M.Kelly for Coleman, R.Stafford for Gleeson, S.O'Neill for Guiney.
Galway   M.Herlihy, R.Whyte, N.Corcoran, P.Flynn, A.Garvey, E.Tannian, N.Earls, B.Gantley, D.McEvoy, B.Lucas, J.Gantley, E.Ryan, B.Lawless, N.Kenny, K.Burke. Subs: T.Kavanagh for McEvoy, K.Hooban for B.Gantley, J.Fordham for Garvey, R.Reilly for Whyte.

2006

Cork   A.Nash, J.Hughes, W.Twomey, T.Jordan, B.Lombard, D.McSweeney, V.Hurley, M.O'Callaghan, K.Hartnett, R.O'Dwyer, D.Dineen, J.Russell, M.O'Sullivan, R.Doherty, R.Conway. Subs: B.Coleman, S.Hayes, F.O'Leary, M.O'Donovan, B.Dwyer.
Kilkenny   D.Brennan, S.Cummins, G.Joyce, K.Joyce, P.Hartley, D.Carroll, A.McCarthy, P.Hogan, B.Phelan, E.O'Donoghue, A.Murphy, C.O'Loughlin, G.Nolan, M.Murphy, A.Hickey. Subs: E.Walsh, D.Kelly, J.P.Corcoran, D.O'Gorman, R.Hogan.

2007

Wexford   D.Flynn, C.Lawler, B.Kenny, D.Morton, J.O'Connor, B.Malone, L.Prendergast, R.Barry, D.Redmond, J.Roche, J.Breen, P.Doran, N.Kirwan, S.Banville, C.Lyng. Subs: E.Martin for Kirwan, B.O'Connor for Breen, C.O'Connor for Martin, A.Kavanagh for Banville.
Waterford   I.O'Regan, B.Wall, J.O'Leary, T.Molumphy, K.Stafford, S.Kearney, W.Hutchinson, G.Power, E.Bennett, P.Fitzgerald, C.Carey, M.Molumphy, P.Kearney, S.Casey, S.Barron. Subs: D.Power for Bennett, N.Jacob for Carey, J.Hartley for M.Molumphy, B.Foley for Power.

2008

Kilkenny   L.Tierney, M.Phelan, S.Cummins, S.Prendergast, P.Lonergan, P.Hartley, K.Joyce, N.Walsh, D.Fogarty, B.Beckett, C.Phelan, P.Hogan, M.Grace, P.Cleere, Noel Doherty. Subs: Niall Doherty for Walsh, E.Hennebry for Lonergan, J.Nolan for Grace, A.Healy for Noel Doherty, D.Prendergast for Fogarty.

Limerick   B.Hennessy, T.Condon, C.Carey, G.O'Leary, R.O'Neill, M.Keane, S.Walsh, A.Brennan, P.O'Brien, David Moloney, P.O'Reilly, M.McKenna, D.O'Neill, P.McNamara, A.O'Connor. Subs: D.Stapleton for O'Brien, P.Harty for McKenna, P.Browne for David Moloney, N.Maher for D.O'Neill, Damien Moloney for Brennan.

2009

Cork   A.Nash, B.Coleman, D.McSweeney, B.Murphy, J.Carey, R.Cashman, J.Jordan, E.Dillon, L.Desmond, R.Dwyer, Mark O'Sullivan, L.McLoughlin, Maurice O'Sullivan, L.Farrell, S.Moylan. Subs: E.Collins for Maurice O'Sullivan, A.Mannix for Moylan, J.O'Leary for Carey, P.O'Leary for Coleman.

Kilkenny   T.Brophy, K.Mooney, P.Murphy, P.O'Donovan, J.Cottrell, R.Cody, W.Burke, C.Fogarty, N.Kennedy, E.Brennan, J.J.Farrell, B.Lannon, M.Boran, E.Kavanagh, E.Guinan. Subs: J.Cahill for Boran, C.Dunne for Lannon, E.Hickey for Cottrell, N.Cleere for Kavanagh, M.Murphy for Brennan.

2010

Kilkenny   L.Tierney, M.Phelan, P.Murphy, K.Mooney, J.Cotterell, R.Cody, Niall Doherty, P.Hartley, N.Walsh, B.Beckett, R.Dollard, N.Cleere, M.Grace, P.Cleere, A.Healy. Subs: B.Lennon for Cody, Noel Doherty for N.Cleere.

Cork   D.McCarthy, M.Walsh, C.Fogarty, B.Coleman, T.Healy, K.Hartnett, M.Ellis, D.O'Callaghan, B.Fitzgerald, B.Corry, B.Cooper, C.Casey, M.Harrington, E.Conway, M.O'Sullivan. Subs: S.Corr for Fitzgerald, B.Lawton for Conway, J.Halbert for O'Sullivan.

2011

Clare   A.Fahy, M.Earley, P.Kelly, A.Brigdale, K.Moynihan, M.Hayes, J.Fennessy, R.Keane, S.Golden, M.Duggan, T.Carmody, K.Dilleen, J.O'Connor, N.Gilligan, P.Hickey. Subs: D.Keane for Carmody, P.Fitzpatrick for Moynihan, O.O'Rourke for M.Duggan, S.Chaplin for Golden, C.Tierney for Gilligan.

Kilkenny   R.O'Neill, W.Phelan, M.Walsh, S.Phelan, L.Harney, P.J.Rowe, S.Byrne, M.Grace, W.O'Dwyer, P.O'Flynn, S.Kenny, J.J.Farrell, G.Shelly, E.Hickey, A.Stapleton. Subs: G.Aylward for Stapleton, S.Burke for Farrell, O.Walsh for S.Kenny, C.Conway for O'Dwyer, N.Kenny for Hickey.

2012

Tipperary   J.Logue, C.Coughlan, K.O'Gorman, G.Walsh, J.Barry, E.Connolly, R.Sherlock, M.Gleeson, P.White, S.Carey, D.O'Brien, J.Gallagher, K.Morris, M.Heffernan, D.Butler. Subs: R.Ruth for Butler, E.Sweeney for Gallagher, C.Dillon for O'Brien, P.O'Dwyer for White.

Kilkenny   R.O'Neill, M.Phelan, A.Walsh, J.Corcoran, B.Kennedy, B.Beckett, L.Harney, J.Lyng, P.Murphy, N.Walsh, R.Hickey, K.Kelly, R.Walsh, J.J.Farrell, G.Aylward. Subs: P.Hartley for Murphy, N.Malone for R.Walsh, G.Brennan for A.Walsh, C.Kenny for Farrell.

2013

Tipperary   D.Egan, S.O'Brien, M.Butler, T.Treacy, J.O'Keeffe, D.Young, P.Heffernan, B.Fox, W.Ryan, O.Quirke, T.Butler, N.O'Meara, R.Gleeson, D.O'Hanlon, T.Hammersley. Subs: J.McLoughney for Quirke, P.Molloy for O'Hanlon, C.Kenny for M.Butler, P.Shortt for Molloy.

Kilkenny   R.O'Neill, S.Cummins, M.Walsh, S.Prendergast, L.Harney, P.Harltey, M.Moloney, B.Kennedy, D.Langton, B.Beckett, R.Hickey, C.Phelan, J.Brennan, J.Farrell, D.Walton. Subs: J.Lyng for Beckett, P.Holden for Walton, S.Donnelly for Brennan.

2014

Cork   R.Cunningham, J.Callaghan, A.Dennehy, B.O'Sullivan, C.Barry, T.Healy, M.Walsh, N.Kelly, J.Cronin, C.Spillane, P.O'Brien, M.O'Sullivan, C.Casey, D.Drake, A.Spillane. Subs: B.Lawton for Walsh, M.Sugrue for A.Spillane, R.Crowley doe Drake.

Wexford   N.Breen, B.Mulligan, J.Breen, B.Kehoe, P.Naughter, M.Jacob, M.Maloney, B.Jacob, T.O'Dwyer, B.Jordan, J.Berry, P.Murphy, E.Kent, R.Barry, J.Reck. Subs: G.Dolan for Murphy, A.Rochford for Naughter, Dolan for B.Jacob, T.O'Leary for Kent, N.Kirwan for Reck.

2015

Galway   J.Skehill, C.Flynn, D.O'Donoghue, A.Tuohey, P.Flaherty, D.Burke, S.Cooney, K.McHugo, D.Higgins, D.Nevin, T.Haran, E.Burke, B.Molloy, S.Moloney, E.Brannigan. Subs: B.Daly for Brannigan (*blood*), B.Keane for O'Donoghue, J.Kennedy for E.Burke, B.Daly for McHugo, R.O'Meara for Brannigan, K.Lane for Higgins.

Cork   P.Buckley, B.Twomey, E.Finn, G.Murphy, K.Kavanagh, D.O'Donovan, T.Lawrence, K.O'Neill, S.McCarthy, W.Leahy, M.Collins, T.Murphy, N.McNamara, F.O'Leary, D.O'Driscoll. Subs: P.Butler for Finn, M.Brennan for McCarthy, C.O'Brien for G.Murphy, A.Cagney for T.Murphy.

2016

Kilkenny   A.Duggan, E.Cody, T.Aylward, L.Hickey, J.Cleere, C.Delaney, J.Brennan, J.Langton, L.Scanlon, A.Murphy, C.Tobin, R.Leahy, B.Ryan, N.Cleere, J.Walsh. Subs: S.Morrissey for Tobin, J.McGrath for Leahy, S.Donnelly for Murphy.

Clare   D.Vaughan, R.Hayes, E.Quirke, C.Cooney, A.McGuane, S.Taylor, J.McCarthy, D.Conroy, K.Hehir, O.Donnellan, S.McGrath, D.Corry, D.Russell, M.O'Neill, R.Taylor. Subs: D.Walsh for Taylor, E.Enright for Hayes, P.O'Loughlin for Donnellan.

2017

Kilkenny   D.Aylward, N.Doherty, G.Teehan, D.Prendergast, B.Whelan, C.Fleming, J.Cahill, J.P.Treacy, M.Keoghan, P.Holden, D.Brennan, E.Delaney, S.Carey, M.Power, R.Donnelly. Subs: T.Phelan for Fleming, L.Hickey for Carey, J.Power for Delaney, C.Prendiville for Keoghan, D.Walsh for Cahill.

Cork   P.Collins, B.O'Sullivan, S.O'Donovan, S.Hegarty, K.Morrison, D.O'Donovan, K.Kavanagh, D.O'Flynn, M.Collins, D.Casey, N.Kelly, G.O'Neill, S.Hayes, W.Leahy, D.Drake. Subs: T.Lawrence for Morrison, R.O'Shea for Casey, J.Cooper for Flynn, M.Kennefick for Hayes, N.McNamara for O'Neill.

ALL-IRELAND INTERMEDIATE HURLING FINAL REFEREES

1961	Clem Foley (Dublin)
1962	Gerry Fitzgerald (Limerick)
1963	Paddy Johnson (Kilkenny)
1964	Paddy Buggy (Kilkenny)
1965	Gerry Fitzgerald (Limerick)
1966	Paddy Buggy (Kilkenny)
1967	Jimmy Hatton (Wicklow)
1968	John Dowling (Offaly)
1969	Donie Nealon (Tipperary)
1970	Jimmy Hatton (Wicklow)
1971	Noel Dalton (Waterford)
1972	Noel Dalton (Waterford)
1973	Noel Dalton (Waterford)
1997	Seán McMahon (Clare)
1998	Jimmy Cooney (Galway)
1999	Seán McMahon (Clare)
2000	T.McIntyre (Antrim)
2001	M.Bodkin (Galway)
2002	P.Neary (Kilkenny)
2003	T.McIntyre (Antrim)
2004	S.Roche (Tipperary)
2004	P.Ahern (Carlow)
2005	M.Wadding (Waterford)
2006	M.Wadding (Waterford)
2007	E.Morris (Dublin)
2008	J.McGrath (Westmeath)
2009	S.McMahon (Clare)
2010	A.Kelly (Galway)
2011	D.Kirwan (Cork)
2012	J.Owens (Wexford)
2013	T.Carroll (Offaly)
2014	A.Kelly (Galway)
2015	F.Horgan (Tipperary)
2016	P.O'Dwyer (Carlow)
2017	C.Cunning (Antrim)

LEINSTER INTERMEDIATE HURLING FINALS

1961	Wexford	3-11	2-10	Dublin
1962	Carlow	2-11	2-3	Kilkenny
1963	Wexford	3-8	3-6	Kilkenny
1964	Wexford	1-9	2-5	Kilkenny
1965	Wexford	4-16	3-8	Antrim
1966	Dublin	2-9	1-8	Wexford
1967	Kilkenny	6-8	2-8	Kildare
1968	Dublin	2-14	2-12	Carlow
1969	Kildare	3-16	4-6	Wicklow
1970	Dublin	4-9	3-10	Wicklow
1971	Wicklow	1-15	2-9	Dublin
1972	Dublin	3-13	3-4	Wexford
1973	Kilkenny	11-15	1-3	Meath
1997	Kilkenny	5-15	2-11	Carlow
1998	Kilkenny	3-13	0-11	Wexford
1999	Kilkenny	2-15	0-9	Laois
2000	Kilkenny	2-12	1-13	Wexford
2001	Wexford	5-13	1-9	Laois
2002	Wexford	2-16	0-19	Kilkenny
2003	Kilkenny	4-20	1-10	Dublin
2004	Kilkenny	3-17	1-10	Wexford
2005	Wexford	0-14	0-13	Kilkenny
2006	Kilkenny	2-20	0-8	Wexford
2007	Wexford	2-11	1-12	Kilkenny
2008	Kilkenny	4-26	3-15	Dublin (aet)
2009	Kilkenny	0-12	0-11	Wexford
2010	Kilkenny	1-21	0-11	Dublin
2011	Kilkenny	2-19	2-8	Wexford
2012	Kilkenny	3-20	2-14	Wexford
2013	Kilkenny unopposed			
2014	Wexford	2-11	0-14	Kilkenny
2015	Galway	1-20	0-11	Wexford
2016	Kilkenny	3-14	2-14	Wexford
2017	Kilkenny	1-26	1-8	Wexford

MUNSTER INTERMEDIATE HURLING FINALS

1961	Tipperary	3-10	2-12	Cork
1962	Galway	5-4	4-6	Cork
1963	Tipperary	6-10	0-4	Clare
1964	Cork	4-13	1-10	Galway
1965	Cork	1-15	3-2	Waterford
1966	Tipperary	4-2	1-7	Galway
1967	Cork	5-14	2-12	Limerick
1968	Limerick	3-8	1-6	Cork
1969	Cork	4-14	0-6	Galway
1970	Kerry	2-13	2-10	Cork
1971	Tipperary	1-11	2-4	Limerick
1972	Tipperary	4-16	3-12	Kerry
1973	Kerry represented Munster.			
	Note: No competition 1974-1996			
1997	Cork	1-15	1-12	Limerick
1998	Limerick	2-11	0-15	Tipperary
1999	Cork	2-9	1-7	Tipperary
2000	Tipperary	1-19	0-15	Cork
2001	Cork	1-20	1-11	Clare
2002	Tipperary	4-8	2-7	Waterford
2003	Cork	2-12	0-11	Waterford
2004	Cork	0-18	1-9	Tipperary
2005	Cork	2-17	2-11	Tipperary
2006	Cork	2-18	2-13	Tipperary
2007	Waterford	5-11	1-12	Limerick
2008	Limerick	2-16	2-12	Tipperary
2009	Cork	5-24	3-9	Waterford
2010	Cork	0-15	0-13	Waterford
2011	Clare	2-15	2-13	Limerick
2012	Tipperary	1-18	0-17	Clare
2013	Tipperary	0-19	0-18	Cork
2014	Cork	4-15	2-8	Tipperary
2015	Cork	0-20	0-18	Limerick
2016	Clare	1-26	2-18	Limerick (aet)
2017	No Final (Cork nominated)			

CONNACHT INTERMEDIATE HURLING FINALS

1966-1967	Roscommon represented Province			
1968	Roscommon	4-4	3-7	Mayo
	Roscommon	7-11	3-5	Mayo (Replay)
1969	Mayo			

Note: 1970-1972 Galway represented Province. Galway competed in Munster (1961-1969).

1973-1996	No competition			
1997	Galway	7-19	1-7	Roscommon
1998	Galway	2-22	1-11	Roscommon
1999	Galway represented Province in All-Ireland series. Roscommon took part in Open Draw section. They qualified for All-Ireland semi-final in which they lost to Galway.			

ULSTER INTERMEDIATE HURLING FINALS

1966	Antrim 3-11 Down 4-5
1967	Antrim 6-13 Down 2-7
1968	Down 4-5 Antrim 2-9
1969	Antrim 5-6 Down 3-9
1970	Antrim 5-10 Down 3-13
1971	Down 5-8 Antrim 1-12
1972	Down 3-13 Antrim 5-7
	Down 2-9 Antrim 1-10 (Replay)
1973	Antrim 3-11 Down 1-6
1974-1996	No competition
1997	Derry 6-18 Armagh 1-6
1998	Down 3-11 London 2-12
	Note: Antrim competed in Leinster from 1961-'65.
1999	No competition. Down and London took part in Open Draw Section.

NATIONAL HURLING LEAGUE RESULTS

1925/26
Final

Cork	3-7	1-5	Dublin

1926/27
No Competition

1927/28
Tipperary winners on points system: 14 points (from eight games). Draws with Dublin and Laois. Runners-up: *Galway* (with 12 points)

1928/129
Final

Dublin	7-4	5-5	Cork

1929/30
Semi-final

Dublin	8-6	1-0	Clare

Final

Cork	3-5	3-0	Dublin

1930/31
Semi-final

Galway	7-7	3-5	Laois

Final

Galway	4-5	4-4	Tipperary

1931/32
No competition.

1932/33
Final, Kilkenny

Kilkenny	3-8	1-3	Limerick

1933/34
Final, Limerick

Limerick	3-6	3-3	Dublin

1934/35
Limerick: winners on points system: 15 points (from eight games). Runners-up: *Kilkenny* (with 14 points).

1935/36
Limerick: winners on on points system: 15 points (from eight games). Runners-up: *Cork* with 12 points).

1936/137
Limerick: winners on points system: 13 points (from eight games). Runners-up: *Tipperary* with 12 pts.

1937/38
Final

Limerick	5-2	1-1	Tipperary

1938/39
Semi-final
| Waterford | 5-7 | 3-4 | Wexford |
Final
| Dublin | 1-8 | 1-4 | Waterford |

1939/40
Final
| Cork | 8-9 | 6-4 | Tipperary |

1940/41
Final
| Cork | 4-11 | 2-7 | Dublin |

1942-1945
Suspended

1945/46
Semi-final
| Clare | 6-2 | 2-7 | Galway |
Final
| Clare | 1-6 | 1-6 | Dublin |
Replay
| Clare | 2-10 | 2-5 | Dublin |

1946/47
Semi-finals
| Limerick | 5-6 | 4-4 | Laois |
| Kilkenny | 3-12 | 2-6 | Tipperary |
Final
| Limerick | 4-5 | 2-11 | Kilkenny |
Replay
| Limerick | 3-8 | 1-7 | Kilkenny |

1947/48
Final
| Cork | 3-3 | 1-2 | Tipperary |

1948/49
Final
| Tipperary | 3-5 | 3-3 | Cork |

1949/50
Semi-finals
| Tipperary | 9-3 | 0-6 | Meath |
| Kilkenny | 5-6 | 4-6 | Westmeath |
Home Final
| Tipperary | 3-8 | 1-10 | Kilkenny |
Final, New York
| Tipperary | 1-12 | 3-4 | New York |

1950/51
Semi-finals
| Wexford | 6-4 | 2-1 | Meath |
| Galway | 5-14 | 0-4 | Offaly |
Home final
| Galway | 6-7 | 3-4 | Wexford |
Final, New York
| Galway | 2-11 | 2-8 | New York |

1951/52
Home final
| Tipperary | 4-7 | 4-6 | Wexford |
Final, Croke Park
| Tipperary | 6-14 | 2-5 | New York |

1952/53
Final
| Cork | 2-10 | 2-7 | Tipperary |

1953/54
Final
| Tipperary | 3-10 | 1-4 | Kilkenny |

1954/55
Final
| Tipperary | 3-5 | 1-5 | Wexford |

1955/56
Final
| Wexford | 5-9 | 2-14 | Tipperary |

1956/57
Final
| Tipperary | 3-11 | 2-7 | Kilkenny |

1957/58
Final
| Wexford | 5-7 | 4-8 | Limerick |

1958/59
Final
| Tipperary | 0-15 | 0-7 | Waterford |

1959/60
Final
| Tipperary | 2-15 | 3-8 | Cork |

1960/61
Final
| Tipperary | 6-6 | 4-9 | Waterford |

1961/62
Semi-final
| Cork | 6-12 | 1-6 | Dublin |
Final
| Kilkenny | 1-16 | 1-8 | Cork |

1962/63
Semi-finals
| Waterford | 0-9 | 0-7 | Galway |
| Tipperary | 2-12 | 2-9 | Kilkenny |
Home final
| Waterford | 2-15 | 4-7 | Tipperary |
Final, Croke Park
| Waterford | 3-6 | 3-6 | New York |
Replay, Kilkenny
| Waterford | 3-10 | 1-10 | New York |

1963/64
Semi-finals

Tipperary	**3-16**	**2-5**	*Limerick*
Wexford	**2-9**	**2-7**	*Cork*

Home final

Tipperary	**5-12**	**1-4**	*Wexford*

Final, New York

Tipperary	**4-16**	**6-6**	*New York*

1964/65
Semi-finals

Kilkenny	**5-9**	**1-3**	*Wexford*
Tipperary	**2-18**	**1-9**	*Waterford*

Home final

Tipperary	**3-14**	**2-8**	*Kilkenny*

First Leg, New York

Tipperary	**4-10**	**2-11**	*New York*

Second Leg New York

New York	**3-9**	**2-9**	*Tipperary*

Aggregate: Tipperary 6-19, New York 5-20. Tipperary winners by two points on aggregate.

1965/66
Semi-finals

Tipperary	**3-14**	**4-7**	*Clare*
Kilkenny	**4-11**	**1-8**	*Cork*

Home Final

Kilkenny	**0-9**	**0-7**	*Tipperary*

First Leg, Croke Park

Kilkenny	**3-10**	**2-7**	*New York*

Second Leg, Nowlan Park

Kilkenny	**7-5**	**0-8**	*New York*

Aggregate: Kilkenny 10-15, New York 2-15.

1966/67
Semi-finals

Wexford	**6-12**	**1-11**	*Limerick*
Kilkenny	**3-10**	**2-3**	*Clare*

Final

Wexford	**3-10**	**1-9**	*Kilkenny*

1967/68
Semi-finals

Tipperary	**1-15**	**2-7**	*Cork*
Kilkenny	**2-10**	**2-10**	*Clare*
Kilkenny	**3-8**	**3-8**	*Clare* (replay)
Kilkenny	**1-11**	**1-7**	*Clare* (2nd replay)

Home Final

Tipperary	**3-9**	**1-13**	*Kilkenny*

First Leg, New York

New York	**2-14**	**2-13**	*Tipperary*

Second Leg, New York

Tipperary	**4-14**	**2-8**	*New York*

Aggregate: Tipperary 6-27, New York 4-22

1968/69
Semi-finals

Cork	**2-12**	**3-8**	*Tipperary*
Wexford	**2-5**	**1-6**	*Limerick*

Final

Cork	**3-12**	**1-14**	*Wexford*

1969/70
12/04/1969, Semi-final, Thurles

Cork	**2-10**	**2-7**	*Tipperary*

19/04/1969, Semi-final, Thurles

Limerick	**4-15**	**2-8**	*Offaly*

03/05/1969, Home Final, Croke Park

Cork	**2-17**	**0-7**	*Limerick*

Note: League Re-arranged into Two Groups with promotion and relegation)

First Leg, New York

Cork	**4-11**	**4-8**	*New York*

Second Leg, New York

New York	**2-8**	**1-10**	*Cork*

Aggregate: Cork 5-21 (36 points), New York 6-16 (34 points).

1970/71
09/05/1970, Semi-final, Limerick

Tipperary	**2-12**	**2-10**	*Cork*

16/05/1970, Semi-final, Thurles

Limerick	**1-11**	**2-6**	*Clare*

23/05/1970, Final, Cork

Limerick	**3-12**	**3-11**	*Tipperary*

1971/72
16/04/1971, Semi-final, Limerick

Cork	**5-12**	**4-8**	*Tipperary*

23/04/1971, Semi-final, Thurles

Limerick	**3-13**	**2-13**	*Kilkenny*

07/05/1971, Final, Thurles

Cork	**3-14**	**2-14**	*Limerick*

1972/73
15/04/1972, Semi-final, Kilkenny

Limerick	**2-11**	**2-11**	*Tipperary*

22/04/1972, Semi-final, Replay, Birr

Limerick	**5-10**	**3-14**	*Tipperary* (aet)

29/04/1972, Semi-final, Waterford

Wexford	**2-10**	**2-9**	*Kilkenny*

13/05/1973, Final Croke Park

Wexford	**4-13**	**3-7**	*Limerick*

1973/74
21/04/1973, Semi-final, Limerick

Limerick	**1-16**	**3-8**	*Tipperary*

07/04/1973, Semi-final, Croke Park

Cork	**0-18**	**1-11**	*Dublin*

05/05/1974, Final, Limerick

Cork	**6-15**	**1-12**	*Limerick*

1974/75
27/04/1974, Semi-final, Limerick

Tipperary	**1-9**	**0-10**	*Clare*

04/05/1974, Semi-final, Thurles

Galway	**1-9**	**1-6**	*Kilkenny*

25/05/1975, Final, Limerick

Galway	**4-9**	**4-6**	*Tipperary*

1975/76

04/04/1975, Semi-final, Thurles
Cork	*2-11*	*3-8*	*Kilkenny*

25/04/1975, Semi-final, Replay, Thurles
Kilkenny	*2-17*	*3-10*	*Cork*

11/04/1975, Semi-final, Thurles
Wexford	*2-9*	*3-6*	*Clare*

25/04/1975, Semi-final, Replay, Thurles
Clare	*3-24*	*4-16*	*Wexford*

09/05/1975, Final, Thurles
Clare	*2-10*	*0-16*	*Kilkenny*

20/06/1975, Final, Replay Thurles
Kilkenny	*6-14*	*1-14*	*Clare*

1976/77

10/04/1976, Semi-final, Thurles
Clare	*2-15*	*0-7*	*Offaly*

10/04/1976, Semi-final
Kilkenny	*3-12*	*2-9*	*Tipperary*

24/04/1976, Final, Thurles
Clare	*2-8*	*0-9*	*Kilkenny*

1977/78

09/04/1977, Semi-final, Thurles
Clare	*2-16*	*3-6*	*Limerick*

09/04/1977, Semi-final, Carlow
Kilkenny	*3-5*	*2-8*	*Wexford*

16/04/1977, Semi-final, Replay, Carlow
Kilkenny	*5-15*	*5-14*	*Wexford* (aet)

30/04/1977, Final, Thurles
Clare	*3-10*	*1-10*	*Kilkenny*

1978/79

15/04/1978, Semi-final, Thurles
Galway	*1-15*	*4-5*	*Limerick*

16/04/1978, Semi-final, Limerick
Tipperary	*2-13*	*2-12*	*Clare*

06/05/1978, Final, Limerick
Tipperary	*3-15*	*0-8*	*Galway*

1979/80

21/04/1979, Semi-final, Limerick
Cork	*1-12*	*0-12*	*Galway*

21/04/1979, Semi-final
Limerick	*2-13*	*1-11*	*Tipperary*

04/05/1979, Final, Cork
Cork	*2-10*	*2-10*	*Limerick*

18/05/1979, Final, Replay, Cork
Cork	*4-15*	*4-6*	*Limerick*

1980/81

19/04/1980, Semi-final, Kilkenny
Offaly	*2-13*	*4-6*	*Laois*

19/04/1980, Semi-final, Thurles
Cork	*1-19*	*2-10*	*Waterford*

03/05/1980, Final, Thurles
Cork	*3-11*	*2-8*	*Offaly*

1981/82

04/04/1981, Semi-final, Thurles
Wexford	*2-17*	*1-16*	*Cork*

04/04/1981, Semi-final
Kilkenny	*2-14*	*1-17*	*Waterford*

11/04/1981, Semi-final, Replay, Thurles
Kilkenny	*5-14*	*4-6*	*Waterford*

18/04/1981, Final, Croke Park
Kilkenny	*2-14*	*1-11*	*Wexford*

1982/83

03/04/1982, Semi-final, Thurles
Kilkenny	*5-11*	*1-17*	*Laois*

10/04/1982, Semi-final, Thurles
Limerick	*3-10*	*2-6*	*Wexford*

24/04/1982, Final, Thurles
Kilkenny	*2-14*	*2-12*	*Limerick*

1983/84

01/04/1983, Semi-final, Thurles
Limerick	*2-10*	*1-10*	*Tipperary*

01/04/1983, Semi-final
Wexford	*4-9*	*1-14*	*Cork*

08/04/1983, Final, Thurles
Limerick	*3-16*	*1-9*	*Wexford*

1984/85

31/03/1984, Semi-final, Thurles
Limerick	*0-15*	*1-9*	*Offaly*

31/03/1984, Semi-final
Clare	*1-14*	*0-11*	*Galway*

14/04/1984, Final, Thurles
Limerick	*3-12*	*1-7*	*Clare*

1985/86

27/04/1985, Semi-final, Thurles
Kilkenny	*2-15*	*1-8*	*Cork*

27/04/1985, Semi-final
Galway	*1-16*	*3-10*	*Wexford*

04/05/1985, Semi-final, Replay, Thurles
Galway	*3-11*	*2-5*	*Wexford*

11/05/1985, Final, Thurles
Kilkenny	*2-10*	*2-6*	*Galway*

1986/87

19/04/1986, Semi-final, Portlaoise
Galway	*5-16*	*1-12*	*Waterford*

19/04/1986, Semi-final, Cork
Clare	*211*	*1-11*	*Tipperary*

03/05/1986, Final, Thurles
Galway	*3-12*	*3-10*	*Clare*

1987/88

10/04/1988, Semi-Final, Croke Park
Tipperary	*4-19*	*1-8*	*Waterford*

10/04/1988, Semi-Final
Offaly	*2-16*	*3-11*	*Wexford*

24/04/1988, Final, Croke Park
Tipperary	*3-15*	*2-9*	*Offaly*

1988/89

16/04/1989, Semi-final, Croke Park
Tipperary	*0-15*	*1-11*	*Kilkenny*

16/04/1989, Semi-final
Galway	*2-13*	*1-9*	*Dublin*

30/04/1989, Final, Croke Park
Galway	*2-16*	*4-8*	*Tipperary*

1989/90

08/04/1990, Semi-final, Thurles
| Wexford | 2-12 | 2-12 | Cork |

08/04/1990, Semi-final
| Kilkenny | 2-16 | 1-9 | Dublin |

16/04/1990, Semi-final, Replay, Kilkenny
| Wexford | 1-9 | 0-6 | Cork |

22/04/1990, Home Final, Croke Park
| Kilkenny | 3-12 | 1-10 | Wexford |

06/05/1990, Final, Gaelic Park, New York
| Kilkenny | 0-18 | 0-9 | New York |

1990/91

28/04/1991, Semi-final, Croke Park
| Wexford | 2-12 | 2-12 | Kilkenny |

28/04/1991, Semi-final, Limerick
| Offaly | 1-7 | 0-7 | Tipperary |

05/05/1991, Semi-final, Replay, Thurles
| Wexford | 2-14 | 1-12 | Kilkenny |

12/05/1991, Final, Croke Park
| Offaly | 2-6 | 0-10 | Wexford |

1991/92

19/04/1992, Semi-final, Ennis
| Tipperary | 1-15 | 1-8 | Galway |

26/04/1992, Semi-final, Limerick
| Limerick | 2-11 | 1-4 | Cork |

10/05/1992, Final, Limerick
| Limerick | 0-14 | 0-13 | Tipperary |

1992/93

25/04/1993, Semi-final, Thurles
| Cork | 2-11 | 1-13 | Tipperary |

25/04/1993, Semi-final
| Wexford | 3-14 | 1-11 | Limerick |

09/05/1993, Final, Thurles
| Cork | 2-11 | 2-11 | Wexford |

16/05/1993, Final, Replay, Thurles
| Cork | 0-18 | 3-9 | Wexford (aet) |

22/05/1993, Final, 2nd Replay, Thurles
| Cork | 3-11 | 1-12 | Wexford |

1993/94

24/04/1994, Semi-final, Limerick
| Galway | 1-13 | 0-10 | Clare |

30/04/1994, Semi-final, Páirc Uí Chaoimh
| Tipperary | 2-13 | 1-13 | Cork |

108/05/1994, Final, Limerick
| Tipperary | 2-14 | 0-12 | Galway |

1994/95

23/04/1995, Semi-final, Thurles
| Clare | 2-14 | 0-8 | Waterford |

23/04/1995, Semi-final
| Kilkenny | 4-8 | 0-14 | Offaly |

07/05/1995, Final, Thurles
| Kilkenny | 2-12 | 0-9 | Clare |

1995/96

28/04/1996, Semi-final, Kilkenny
| Tipperary | 1-13 | 1-11 | Laois |

28/04/1996, Semi-final, Limerick
| Galway | 2-15 | 1-10 | Wexford |

12/05/1996, Final, Limerick
| Galway | 2-10 | 2-8 | Tipperary |

1997

23/08/1997, Semi-final, Ennis
| Galway | 1-14 | 0-6 | Tipperary |

24/08/1997, Semi-final, Kilkenny
| Limerick | 1-17 | 0-10 | Kilkenny |

05/10/1997, Final, Ennis
| Limerick | 1-12 | 1-9 | Galway |

1998

03/05/1998, Semi-final, Thurles
| Cork | 2-15 | 0-10 | Clare |

03/05/1998, Semi-final, Thurles
| Waterford | 2-17 | 1-11 | Limerick |

17/05/1998, Final, Thurles
| Cork | 2-14 | 0-13 | Waterford |

1999

02/05/1999, Semi-final, Limerick
| Galway | 2-15 | 1-15 | Kilkenny |

02/05/1999, Semi-final, Limerick
| Tipperary | 0-19 | 1-15 | Clare |

16/05/1999, Final, Ennis
| Tipperary | 1-14 | 1-10 | Galway |

2000

30/04/2000, Semi-final, Thurles
| Galway | 2-15 | 1-15 | Waterford |

30/04/2000, Semi-final, Thurles
| Tipperary | 2-18 | 0-17 | Limerick |

14/05/2000, Final, Limerick
| Galway | 2-18 | 2-13 | Tipperary |

2001

28/04/2001, Semi-final, Ennis
| Tipperary | 2-19 | 1-15 | Galway |

29/04/2001, Semi-final, Thurles
| Clare | 2-21 | 3-8 | Kilkenny |

06/05/2001, Final, Limerick
| Tipperary | 1-19 | 0-17 | Clare |

2002

21/04/2002, Semi-final, Páirc Uí Chaoimh
| Cork | 0-21 | 1-10 | Tipperary |

21/04/2002, Semi-final, Limerick
| Kilkenny | 2-14 | 0-15 | Limerick |

05/05/2002, Final, Thurles
| Kilkenny | 2-15 | 2-14 | Cork |

2003

05/05/2003, Final, Croke Park
| Kilkenny | 5-14 | 5-13 | Tipperary |

2004

09/05/2004, Final, Limerick
| Galway | 2-15 | 1-13 | Waterford |

2005

02/05/2005, Final, Thurles
| Kilkenny | 3-20 | 0-15 | Clare |

2006
23/04/2006, Semi-final, Thurles
Limerick   3-23   2-23   Clare (aet)
23/04/2006, Semi-final, Thurles
Kilkenny   3-20   2-11   Tipperary
30/04/2006, Final, Thurles
Kilkenny   3-11   0-14   Limerick

2007
15/04/2007, Semi-final, Thurles
Kilkenny   2-22   2-7   Wexford
15/04/2007, Semi-final, Thurles
Waterford 1-19   1-16   Cork
29/04/2007, Final, Thurles
Waterford 0-20   0-18   Kilkenny

2008
13/04/2008, Semi-final, Nowlan Park
Tipperary   1-15   1-10   Kilkenny
13/04/2008, Semi-final, Gaelic Grounds, Limerick
Galway   2-22   0-24   Cork
20/04/2008, Final, Gaelic Grounds, Limerick
Tipperary   3-18   3-16   Galway

2009
03/05/2009, Final, Thurles
Kilkenny   2-26   4-17   Tipperary (aet)

2010
02/05/2010, Final, Thurles
Galway   2-22   1-17   Cork

2011
01/05/2011, Final, Croke Park
Dublin   0-22   1-7   Kilkenny

2012
22/04/2012, Semi-final, Thurles
Kilkenny   1-20   0-14   Clare
22/04/2012, Semi-final, Thurles
Cork   1-25   2-15   Tipperary
06/05/2012, Final, Thurles
Kilkenny   3-21   0-16   Cork

2013
21/04/2013, Semi-final, Thurles
Tipperary   4-20   0-17   Dublin
21/04/2013, Semi-final, Thurles
Kilkenny   1-24   1-17   Galway
05/05/2013, Final, Kilkenny
Kilkenny   2-17   0-20   Tipperary

2014
20/04/2014, Semi-final, Limerick
Kilkenny   1-16   0-15   Galway
20/04/2014, Semi-final, Limerick
Tipperary   2-24   2-17   Clare
04/05/2014, Final, Thurles
Kilkenny   2-25   1-27   Tipperary (aet)

2015
19/4/2015. Semi-final, Nowlan Park
Cork   1-27   2-23   Dublin
19/4/2015. Semi-final, Nowlan Park
Waterford 1-19   2-15   Tipperary
3/5/2015. Final, Thurles
Waterford 1-24   0-17   Cork

2016
17/4/2016. Semi-final, Thurles
Waterford 3-23   1-18   Limerick
17/4/2016. Semi-final, Thurles
Clare   4-22   2-19   Kilkenny
1/5/2016. Final, Thurles
Clare   0-22   0-22   Waterford (aet)
8/5/2016. Replay, Thurles
Clare   1-23   2-19   Waterford

2017
16/4/2017. Semi-final, Gaelic Grounds
Galway   1-21   1-11   Limerick
16/4/2017. Semi-final, Nowlan Park
Tipperary   5-18   1-19   Wexford
23/4/2017. Final, Gaelic Grounds
Galway   3-21   0-14   Tipperary

HURLING LEAGUE FINAL TEAMS

1925/26
Cork J.Coughlan, Maurice Murphy, S.Óg Murphy (capt.), Mick Murphy, D.Barry Murphy, J.O'Regan, E.O'Connell, J.Hurley, W.Higgins, Matt Murphy, P Aherne, E.Coughlan, D.Aherne, M.Aherne, T.O'Brien.
Dublin E.Tobin (capt.), P.Mcinerney, M.Gill, M.Finn, G.Howard, J.Kirwan, P.Browne, W.Phelan, J.Walsh (Faughs), R.Doherty, T.Barry, J.Bannon, T.Kelly, D.O'Neill, T.Daly.

1926/27
No Competition.

1927/28
Tipperary T.Butler (Sarsfields), S.Moloney, J.Leahy (capt.), M.Ryan, W.Small, J.J.Hayes, P.Purcell, M.Flanagan, T.Treacy, P.Cahill, P.Leahy, P Dwyer, J.J.Callanan, M.Kennedy, M.Cronin.
Note: Played on a league system.The above team played in final game against Laois and clinched the title.

1928/29
Dublin M.Gill (capt.), T.Lawless, T.Burke, G.Howard, M.Power, P.Mcinerney, T.Quinlan, M.Finn, J.Walsh (Faughs), T.Barry, T.O'Meara, C.McMahon, E.Byrne, J.Leeson, S.Tumpane.
Cork M.Casey, M.Madden, W.Donnelly, P.Collins, D.Barry Murphy (capt.), J.O'Regan, T.Barry, J.Hurley, M.O'Connell, E.Coughlan, P.O'Grady, J.Kenneally, P.Aherne, P.Delea, M.Aherne.

1929/30
Cork J.Coughlan, M.Madden, W.Donnelly, J.O'Regan, P.Collins, T.Barry, D.Barry Murphy, E.Coughlan (capt.), J.Hurley, P.Delea, M.O'Connell, S.O'Sullivan, W.Clancy, M.Aherne, W.Stanton. Sub: P O'Grady for M.O'Connell.
Dublin J.O'Dwyer, T.O'Meara, P.McInerney, C.McMahon, E.Campion, T.Teehan, J.Walsh (Faughs), M.Gill (capt.), J.Leeson, T.Quinlan, M.Daniels, S.Hegarty, S.Tumpane, C.Griffin, M.Power. Sub: J.O'Connoll for M.Gill.

1930/31
Galway M.Keating, H.Hodgins, W.Donnelly, M.Broderick, P.Clarke, M.Finn, W.Keane, M.Gill, I.Harney (capt.), R.Donoghue, M.King, M.Cunningham, W.Curran, J.Deely, G.O'Reilly.
Tipperary T.O'Meara, P Byrne, G.Howard, J.Gleeson, T.Treacy, P.Purcell, P.Cahill, J.Donovon, J.O'Loughlin, T.Leahy, T.Harty, W.O'Meara, M.Cronin, M.Kennedy (capt.), M.S.Cronin.

1931/32
No Competition.

1932/33
Kilkenny J.Dermody, P.Larkin, P.O'Reilly, J.Carroll, P.Phelan, P.Byrne, E.Doyle (capt.), E.Byrne, L.Meagher, J.Walsh, Tommy Leahy, Martin Power, J.Fitzpatrick, J.Dunne, Matty Power.
Limerick P.Scanlan, E.Cregan, T.McCarthy, M.Fitzgibbon, D.O'Malley, P.Clohessy, M.Cross, T.Ryan (capt.), M.Quinlivan, J.Mackey, M.Mackey, Martin Ryan, D.Clohessy, C.O'Brien, M.Hough. Subs: P.Joyce for M.Cross, J.J.Moloney for M.Fitzgibbon.

1933/34
Limerick P.Scanlan, E.Cregan, M.Hickey, M.Kennedy (capt.), M.Cross, G.Howard, W.O'Donoghue, T.Ryan, Mick Ryan, J.Mackey, M.Mackey, J.Roche, P.Ryan, C.O'Brien, M.Sexton.
Dublin C.Forde, A.Murphy, J.Bannon, P.Kealy, J.Walsh (Civil Service), D.Canniffe, P.Roche, C.McMahon, E.Wade, S.Hegarty, S.Muldowney, T.Delaney, M.Hough, P Browne, J.O'Connor. Subs: H.Quirke for J.Bannon, T.Quinlan for T.Delaney.

1934/35
Limerick P.Scanlan, E.Cregan, T.McCarthy, M.Kennedy, M.Cross, P.Clohessy, G.Howord, T.Ryan (capt.), Mick Ryan, J.Mackey, M.Mackey, J.Roche, J.O'Connell, P.McMahon, J.Close.
Note: Played on a league system. The above team played in final game against Laois and clinched the title.

1935/36
Limerick T.Shinny, P.Carroll, T.Mccarthy, M.Kennedy, M.Cross, P.Clohessy, G.Howard, T.Ryan (capt.), J.Roche, J.Mackey, M.Mackey, J.Power, D.Clohessy, P McMahon, J.Close.
Note: Played on a league system. The above team played in final game against Dublin and clinched the title.

1936/37
Limerick P.Scanlan, P.Carroll, T.McCarthy, M.Kennedy, M.Cross, P.Clohessy, J.Power, T.Ryan, Mick Ryan, D.Givens, M.Mackey (capt.), J.Roche, D.Clohessy, P.McMahon, J.McCarthy.
Note: Played on a league system. The above team played in final game against Cork and clinched the title.

1937/38
Limerick P.Scanlan, M.Power, T.McCarthy, M.Kennedy, P.Carroll, P.Clohessy, J.Power, T.Ryan, P.Walsh, J.Mackey, M.Mackey (capt.), P.Cregan, D.Givens, J.McCarthy, J.Roche.
Tipperary G.Doyle, D.O'Gorman, G.Cornally, J.Lanigan, Johnny Ryan, J.Maher, T.Kennedy, M.Burke, W.Barry, Jim Coffey, T.Treacy, T.Doyle, W.O'Donnell, D.Murphy, P.Ryan (capt.).

1938/39
Dublin C.Forde, T.Teehan, P.Crowley, C.McMahon, M.Gill (Jnr), J.Gilmartin, J.Byrne, H.Gray, M.Daniels (capt.), P.Flanagan, M.McDonnell, P.Doody, M.Brophy, M.Flynn, W.Loughnane.
Waterford M.Curley, J.Manning, C.Ware, J.Fanning, A.Fleming, J.Keane (capt.), J.Mountain, T.Greaney, C.Moylan, W.Barron, L.Byrne, P.Sheehan, W.Lynch, D.Goode, E.Daly. Sub: J.Butler for P Sheehan.

1939/40
Cork J.Buttimer, W.Murphy, B.Thornhill, A.Lotty, W.Campbell, J.Lynch (capt.), D.J.Buckley, S.Barrett, C.Buckley, C.Ring, J.Quirke, J.Young, R.Ryng, T.O'Sullivan, M.Brennan.
Tipperary W.Ryan, D.O'Gorman, G.Cornally, J.Lanigan, Johnny Ryan, J.Maher (capt.), W.O'Donnell, J.Cooney, D.Mackey, T.Doyle, J.Looby, T Kennedy, P.Maher, T.Treacy, D.Murphy. Sub: P Dwyer for D.Mackey.

1940/41
Cork J.Buttimer, W.Murphy, B.Thornhill, A.Lotty, W.Campbell, J.Quirke, D.J.Buckley, S.Barrett, C.Buckley (capt.), C.Ring, J.Lynch, J.Young, R.Ryng, T.O'Sullivan, M.Brennan.

Dublin C.Forde, C.McMahon, M.Butler, R.O'Brien, M.Prenderville, P.Farrell, J.Byrne, E.Wade (capt.), H.Gray, D.Devitt, C.Downes, P Maher, M.Brophy, P.McSweeney, E.O'Boyle. Sub: G.Glenn for P.Maher.

1942/1945
No Competition.

1945/46
Clare J.Daly, D.McInerney, P.O'Callaghan, T.Byrnes, D.Carroll, D.Solan, B.McMahon, A.Hannon, J.Solan, M.Nugent, R.Frost, M.Daly (capt.), M.O'Halloran, J.Whelan, P.J.Quane. Subs: J.Minogue for M.O'Halloran, P.Lyons for J.Minogue.
Note: G.Frost, P.Byrnes, P.Lyons and A.O'Brien played in drawn game. T.Byrnes, B.McMahon, J.Solan and M.O'Halloran were on for replay.
Dublin M.Banks, Séamus Ó Ceallacháin, E.Dunphy, A.O'Dwyer, G.O'Leary, M.Maher, S.Coughlan, H.Gray, P.O'Brien, E.Wade (capt.), A.Herbert, Seán Óg Ó Ceallacháin, M.McDonnell, E.Daly, J.Prior. Subs: D.Cantwell for M.McDonnell, M.Gill (Jnr) for E.Wade, D.Devitt for M.Maher.
Note: J.O'Neill, P.Flanagan, F.Cummins and D.Cantwell played in drawn game. Séamus Ó Ceallacháin, A.Herbert, M.McDonnell and J.Prior were on for replay. Sub in drawn game: Séamus Ó Ceallacháin for J.O'Neill.

1946/47
Limerick P.Collopy, J.Sadlier, M.Herbert, T.Cregan, S.Herbert, J.Power, T.O'Brien, M.Ryan (Kilteely), P.Fitzgerald (St Patrick's), J.Mulcahy, R.Stokes, M.Dooley, P.Fitzgerald (Askeaton), D.Flanagan, J.Barry. Subs: J.Mackey for M.Dooley, J.O'Donoghue for D.Flanagan.
Note: J.Creamer, T.Murphy, J.Mackey and C.Birrane played in drawn game. M.Ryan, M.Dooley, D.Flanagan and J.Barry were on for replay. Subs in drawn game: C.Crowley for C.Birrane, J.Barry for T.Murphy.
Kilkenny R.Dowling, P.Grace, P.Hayden, M.Marnell, J.Kelly, P.Prendergast, W.Walsh, D.Kennedy (capt.), J.Heffernan, J.Langton, Terry Leahy, L.Reidy, T.Walton, J.Mulcahy, S.Downey. Sub: P.Kenny for P.Prendergast.
Note: Same team played in drawn game. Sub in drawn game: P.O'Brien for D.Kennedy.

1947/48
Cork T.Mulcahy, W.Murphy, C.Murphy, A.Lotty, M.Fouhy, P.O'Donovan, J.Young (capt.), B.Murphy, S.Twomey, M.O'Toole, J.Lynch, W.J.Daly, J.Hartnett, D.Twomey, P.Barry.
Tipperary A.Reddin, Johnny Ryan, W.Wall (capt.), T.Purcell, J.Devitt, P.Furlong, P.Stakelum, Tom Wall, Mick Ryan, R.Stakelum, Jack Ryan, T.Doyle, P.Fahy, P.Kenny, W.Hogan. Sub: John Doyle for Mick Ryan.

1948/49
Tipperary A.Reddin, J.Devitt, A.Brennan, F.Coffey, M.Byrne, P.Furlong, T.Purcell, P.Shanahan, P.Stakelum (capt.), R.Stakelum, W.Carroll, Mick Ryan, Mutt Ryan, S.Maher, Jim Ryan. Sub: Tommy Ryan for Mutt Ryan.
Cork T.Mulcahy, W.Murphy, C.Murphy, J.Young (capt.), M.Fouhy, P.O'Donovan, J.Hartnett, B.Murphy, S.Twomey, C.Ring, J.Lynch, W.J.Daly, M.O'Riordan, G.O'Riordan, D.Twomey. Sub: S.Condon for D.Twomey.

1949/50
Tipperary A.Reddin, M.Byrne, A.Brennan, John Doyle, J.Finn, P.Stakelum, T.Doyle, P.Shanahan, S.Bannon, E.Ryan, Mick Ryan, S.Kenny (capt.), P.Kenny, S.Maher, J.Kennedy.
New York P.Leamy, M.O'Rourke, P.Murphy, J.Looney, T.Flynn, J.Smee (capt.), P.Naughton, P.Grimes, S.Craven, D.Doorley, T.Leahy, B.O'Donoghue, S.Gallagher, J.Kennedy, S.Kelly.

HOME FINAL
Tipperary Same as played in final except Tommy Ryan and Jack Ryan in place of J.Finn and E.Ryan. Sub: J.Finn for P.Stakelum.
Kilkenny R.Dowling, J.Hogan, P.Hayden, M.Marnell, J.Keane (capt.), P.Prendergast, W.Walsh, W.Costigan, S.Downey, J.Heffernan, M.Kenny, L.Reidy, T.Walton, D.Kennedy, P.J.Garvan. Subs: J.Langton for T.Walton, P.Crowley for J.Langton.

1950/51
Galway S.Duggan, C.Corless, F.Flynn, J.Brophy, H.Gordon, Tadgh Kelly, J.Molloy, J.Salmon, T.Moroney, K.McNamee, J.Gallagher, F.Duignan, M.Burke, M.J.Flaherty (capt.), M.Glynn. Sub: John Killeen for F.Duignan.
New York P.Leamy, M.O'Neill, A.Fitzpatrick, P.Murphy, P.Naughton, M.O'Rourke, J.Looney, P.Hoarty, D.Doorley, S.Gallagher, T.Leahy (capt.), M.Loughlin, J.Kennedy, J.Smee, P.Devaney. Subs: S.Craven for M.Loughlin, T.O'Connor for D.Doorley, J.Barrett for S.Craven.

HOME FINAL
Galway Same as played in final. Sub: M.McInerney for M.Glynn.
Wexford A.Foley, W.Rackard, M.Byrne, M.Hanlon, S.Thorpe, R.Rackard, E.Wheeler, M.Codd, J.Morrissey, Podge Kehoe, Paddy Kehoe, T.Russell, D.Aherne, N.Rackard, T.Flood (capt.). Subs: M.Flood for S.Thorpe, P.Shannon for A.Foley, R.Donovan for M.Codd, J.Quinn for T.Russell.

1951/52
Tipperary A.Reddin, Michael Maher, A.Brennan, John Doyle, J.Finn, P.Stakelum (capt.), T.Doyle, P.Shanahan, J.Hough, E.Ryan, Mick Ryan, P.Kenny, Jim Ryan, S.Maher, P.Maher. Sub: R.Mockler for A.Brennan.
New York P.Leamy, M.O'Neill, P.Murphy, J.Looney, P.Moylan, M.O'Rourke, P.Naughton, D.Doorley, A.Galvin, T.Leahy, S.Gallagher (capt.), P.Hoarty, J.Whelan, J.Kennedy, C.O'Leary. Subs: S.Craven for J.Kennedy, A.Fitzpatrick for T.Leahy, T.Leahy for C.O'Leary.

HOME FINAL
Tipperary Same as played in final except S.Bannon and Tim Ryan for J.Finn and P.Kenny.
Wexford A.Foley, S.Thorpe, N.O'Donnell, M.Hanlon, Paddy Kehoe, R.Rackard, W.Rackard, J.Morrissey, E.Wheeler, Podge Kehoe, J.Cummins, M.Flood, D.Aherne, N.Rackard (capt.), T.Flood. Sub: M.Byrne for N.Rackard.

1952/53
Cork D.Creedon, G.O'Riordan, J.Lyons, A.O'Shaughnessy, M.Fouhy, D.O'Leary (capt.), V.Twomey, G.Murphy, J.Twomey, J.Lynam, J.Hartnett, W.J.Daly, C.Ring, L.Dowling, P.Barry. Sub: M.Cashman for D.O'Leary.
Tipperary A.Reddin, M.Byrne, J.Finn, John Doyle, S.Bannon, P.Stakelum, T.Doyle (capt.), P.Shanahan, J.Hough, E.Ryan, A.Wall, Tim Ryan, P.Kenny, P.Maher, Mick Ryan. Subs: Jim Ryan for P.Maher, S.O'Meara for Tim Ryan, Tommy Ryan for Mick Ryan.

1953/54
Tipperary A.Reddin, M.Byrne, J.Finn (capt.), John Doyle, M.Kenny, P.Stakelum, C.Keane, J.Hough, T.English, E.Ryan, Mick Ryan, P.Kenny, M.Seymour, W.Quinn S.Bannon.
Kilkenny M.Rowe, J.Maher, P.Hayden, M.Marnell, P.Buggy, J.Hogan, J.McGovern, J.Sutton, D.Kennedy (capt.), S.Clohosey, P.J.Garvan, M.Kelly, J.Langton, P.Fitzgerald, S.Downey.
Sub: R.Carroll for M.Kelly.

1954/55
Tipperary A.Reddin, M.Byrne, Michael Maher, John Doyle (capt.), C.Keane, J.Finn, J.McGrath, J.Hough, T.English, L.Devaney, P.Stakelum, G.Doyle, S.Bannon, L.Keone, T.Barrett.
Wexford A.Foley, W.Wickham, N.O'Donnell (capt.), M.Hanlon, J.English, J.Morrissey, T.Bolger, E.Wheeler, S.Hearne, Podge Kehoe, T.Dixon, D.Aherne, Paddy Kehoe, T.Ryan, T.Flood.
Subs: M.Codd for E.Wheeler, E.Wheeler for M.Codd.

1955/56
Wexford A.Foley, R.Rackard, N.O'Donnell, M.Hanlon, J.English (capt.), W.Rackard, M.Morrissey, J.Morrissey, S.Hearne, Podge Kehoe, E.Wheeler, T.Flood, T.Ryan, N.Rackard, T.Dixon.
Tipperary A.Reddin, M.Byrne (capt.), Michael Maher, John Doyle, J.Finn, P.Stakelum, A.Wall, J.Hough, S.O'Meara, L.Devaney, L.Skelly, T.English, P.Kenny, W.Quinn, S.Bannon.

1956/57
Tipperary M.Keane, M.Byrne, Michael Maher, John Doyle, J.Finn, P.Stakelum, A.Wall, J.Hough, T.English, Mick Ryan, L.Devaney, Jimmy Doyle, P.Kenny, S.O'Meara, L.Skelly.
Kilkenny O.Walsh, T.Walsh (Dunna- maggin), J.Walsh, J.Maher, P.Buggy, J.Sutton, J.McGovern, W.Walsh, M.Brophy, D.Heaslip, M.Kenny, J.Murphy, R.Rockett, W.Dwyer, S.Clohosey.

1957/58
Wexford P.Nolan, W.Rackard, N.O'Donnell, J.Redmond, J.English, J.Morrissey, M.Morrissey, E.Wheeler, S.Hearne, H.O'Connor (capt.), Podge Kehoe, O.Gough, M.Lyng, T.Flood, M.Codd. Subs: J.O'Brien for H.O'Connor, O.McGrath for M.Lyng.
Limerick G.Casey, D.Kelly (capt.), J.Enright, J.Keogh, T.McGarry, Jim Quaide, S.Quaide, T.Casey, D.Moylan, L.Hogan, N.Stokes, V.Cobbe, J.Shanahan, M.Tynan, L.Moloney. Subs: W.Hogan for M.Tynan, M.Tynan for L.Moloney, L.Moloney for W.Hogan.

1958/59
Tipperary T.Moloney, M.Byrne, Michael Moher, K.Carey, J.Finn, A.Wall (capt.), John Doyle, T.English, D.Nealon, L.Devaney, J.McDonnell, Jimmy Doyle, T.Larkin, Martin Maher, L.Connolly.
Sub: P.Hennessy for T.Larkin.
Waterford E.Power, J.Harney, A.Flynn, J.Barron, M.Óg Morrissey, P.Grimes, Jackie Condon, M.Lacey, S.Power, L.Guinan, T.Cheasty, F.Walsh (capt.), P.Troy, J.Kiely, D.Whelan. Subs: J.Flavin for P.Troy, W.Dunphy for S.Power.

1959/60
Tipperary T.Moloney, M.Byrne, Michael Maher, K.Carey, M.Burns, A.Wall (capt.), John Doyle, T.English, T.Ryan (Killenaule), Jimmy Doyle, L.Devaney, D.Nealon, L.Connolly, W.Moloughney, T.Moloughney. Sub: G.McCarthy for T.Moloughney.
Cork M.Cashman, J.Brohan, D.O'Riordan, S.French, D.Murphy, J.O'Sullivan, M.McCarthy, N.Gallagher, E.Goulding (capt.), P.Harte, T.Kelly, P.Fitzgerald, P.Barry, L.Dowling, C.Ring. Subs: A.Connolly for D.Murphy, M.Horgan for A.Connolly.

1960/61
Tipperary D.O'Brien, M.Hassett (capt.), Michael Maher, K.Carey, M.Burns, A.Wall, John Doyle, T.English, L.Devaney, Jimmy Doyle, D.Nealon, T.Ryan (Killenaule), J.McKenna, W.Moloughney, T.Moloughney. Subs: T.Shanahan for K.Carey, K.Carey for T.Shanahan.
Waterford E.Power, T.Cunningham, A.Flynn, J.Barron, M.Flannelly, M.Óg Morrissey, Joe Condon, S.Power, P.Grimes, M.Murphy, T.Cheasty, F.Walsh, L.Guinan, T.Walsh, D.Whelan. Sub: M.Lacey for D.Whelan.

1961/62
Kilkenny O.Walsh, T.Walsh (Dunnamaggin), J.Walsh, M.Walsh, S.Cleere, A.Hickey (capt.), M.Coogan, A.Comerford, N.Power, E.Keher, R.Carroll, W.Murphy (Carrickshock), D.Heaslip, S.Clohosey, W.Dwyer.
Cork M.Cashman (capt.), J.Brohan, D.Brennan, P.Duggan, J.O'Sullivan, D.Murphy, S.Kennefick, T.Kelly, P.Fitzgerald, P.Harte, D.Sheehan, M.Mortell, L.Dowling, C.Ring, M.Quane. Subs: J.Bennett for M.Mortell, R.Browne for P.Harte.

1962/63
Waterford E.Power, T.Cunningham, A.Flynn, M.Óg Morrissey, L.Guinan, J.Byrne, J.McGrath, Joe Condon, J.Kirwan, J.Meaney (capt.), M.Flannelly, F.Walsh, S.Power, J.Barron, P.Grimes.
Sub: J.Irish for J.McGrath.
Note: J.Irish and C.Ware played in drawn game.J.McGrath and Joe Condon came on for replay. Sub in drawn game: Joe Condon for C.Ware.
New York K.Croke, P.Dowling, C.O'Connell, M.Morrissey, J.Murphy, M.Sweeney, J.O'Donnell, B.Hennessy, J.Keating, S.Ryall, J.Carey (capt.), B.Kelleher, W.Carey, M.Donovan, P.Kirby. Subs: B.McCann for M.Sweeney, J.Naughton for M.Donovan.
Note: D.O'Brien, P.Hennessy and J.Quarry played in drawn game. K.Croke, J.O'Donnell and M.Donovan came on for replay. Subs in drawn game: J.Donoghue for J.Quarry, S.Lakes for J.Murphy, M.Donovan for P Hennessy.

HOME FINAL
Waterford Same as played in final except P.Flynn, M.Dempsey and T.Cheasty for E.Power, J.McGrath and J.Meaney. Subs: J.Meaney for M.Dempsey, E.Power for P.Flynn.
Tipperary R.Mounsey, John Doyle, Michael Maher, K.Carey, M.Burns, A.Wall, M.Murphy, S.English, T.English, Jimmy Doyle, J.McKenna T.Ryan (Killenaule), D.Nealon, L.Devaney, S.McLoughlin (Capt). Sub: T.Moloughney for S.English.

1963/64
Tipperary J.O'Donoghue, John Doyle, Michael Maher, K.Carey, M.Burns, A.Wall, M.Murphy, T.English, M.Roche, Jimmy Doyle, L.Kiely, M.Keating, D.Nealon, T.Ryan (Killenaule), P.Ryan.
New York D.O'Brien, P.Dowling, C.O'Connell, M.Morrissey, J.Murphy, B.Hennessy, P.Hennessy, J.Keating, P.Kelleher, S.Ryall, J.Carney, B.Kelleher, J.Donoghue, J.Carey, P.Kirby.

HOME FINAL
Tipperary Same as played in final except J.McKenna and S.McLoughlin (capt.) for Tom Ryan Killenaule) and M.Keating.
Wexford P.Nolan (capt.), T.Neville, D.Quigley, E.Colfer, P.Wilson, W.Rackard, J.Nolan, J.Kennedy, E.Wheeler, J.O'Brien, R.Shannon, P.Lynch, O.McGrath, Podge Kehoe, J.Foley.

1964/65

Tipperary   J.O'Donoghue, John Doyle, Michael Maher, K.Carey, M.Burns, A.Wall, L.Gaynor, T.English, M.Roche, Jimmy Doyle (capt.), T.Ryan (Toomevara), L.Kiely, D.Nealon, L.Devaney, S.McLoughlin. Sub: P.Doyle for T.English.
Note: M.Keating played in first leg. Tom Ryan (Toomevara) was on for second leg. Sub in first leg: T.Ryan (Toomevara) for M.Keating.
New York   K.Croke, S.Custy, J.Maher, M.Morrissey, P.Hennessy, P.Dowling, J.Murphy, B.Hennessy, P.Donoghue, M.Curtin (capt.), P.Kirby, D.Long, J.Donoghue, J.Naughton, P.Egan. Subs: W.Carey for P.Donoghue, J.Kelly for W.Carey.
Note: M.Butler and P.Kelleher played in first leg.S.Custy and J.Naughton came on for second leg. Subs in first leg B.Kelleher for M.Butler, M.Butler for J.Murphy, B.Aherne for B.Kelleher.

HOME FINAL

Tipperary   Same as played in final except J.McKenna for T.Ryan (Toomevara).
Kilkenny   O.Walsh, P.Henderson, P.Dillon, J.Treacy, P.Drennan, S.Cleere, M.Coogan, P.Moran (capt.), S.Buckley, T.Forristal, P.Carroll, E.Keher, J.Dunphy, J.Lynch, T.Walsh (Thomastown). Subs: J.Teehan for P.Carroll, C.Dunne for T.Walsh.

1965/66

Kilkenny   O.Walsh, T.Carroll, J.Lynch (capt.), J.Treacy, S.Cleere, P.Henderson, M.Coogan, P.Moran, J.Teehan, S.Buckley, J.Bennett, C.Dunne, T.Walsh (Thomastown), P.Dillon, J.Dunphy.
Subs: P.Carroll for J.Dunphy, J.Dunphy for S.Buckley.
Note: P.Carroll played in first leg. P.Dillon was on for second leg.
New York   K.Croke, P.Donoghue, J.Maher, M.Morrissey, P.Hennessy, P.Dowling, J.Murphy, B.Hennessy, B.Aherne, B.Kelleher,J.Donoghue, M.Curtin, D.Long, E.England, S.Forde.
Subs: J.Doherty for M.Curtin, M.Curtin For B.Kelleher, J.Kelly for D.Long.
Note: J.Kelly (Capt) and P.Kelleher played in first leg. E.England and S.Forde were on for second leg. Subs in first leg: A.English for J.Kelly, J.Doherty for P.Hennessy.

HOME FINAL

Kilkenny   Same as played in final except E.Keher and P.Carroll for J.Bennett and C.Dunne.
Tipperary   P.O'Sullivan, John Doyle, K.Carey, J.Gleeson, M.Burns, A.Wall (capt.), L.Gaynor, T.English, M.Roche, Jimmy Doyle, L.Devaney, L.Kiely, D.Nealon, M.Keating, T.Ryan (Toomevara). Subs: J.McKenna For L.Kiely, P. J.Ryan for M.Roche.

1966/67

Wexford   P.Nolan, D.Quigley, M.Collins, E.Colfer, V.Staples, T.Neville, W.Murphy, Joe Murphy, R.Shannon, J.O'Brien, P Lynch, P.Wilson, F.Duff, T.Doran, S.Whelan. Subs: C.Jacob for F.Duff, M.Kinsella for W.Murphy.
Kilkenny   O.Walsh, J.Lynch, P.Dillon, J.Treacy, S.Cleere, P.Henderson, M.Coogan, P.Moran, C.Dunne, T.Walsh (Thomastown), J.Teehan, E.Keher, R.Blanchfield, J.Bennett, Martin Brennan. Sub: F.Cummins for J.Teehan.

1967/68

Tipperary   J.O'Donoghue, J.Costigan, N.O'Gorman, J.Gleeson, M.Burns, M.Roche (capt.), L.Gaynor, J.Flanagan, P.J.Ryan, M.Keating, Jimmy Ryan, Jimmy Doyle, D.Nealon, P.Lowry, S.McLoughlin. Sub: M.Stapleton for N.O'Gorman.
Note: P.Rowland played in first leg. P.Lowry was on for second leg.
New York   K.Croke, P.Donoghue, J.Maher, S.Custy, P.Kirby, P.Dowling, J.Murphy, B.Hennessy, H.McCabe, M.Curtin, M.Mortell, S.Lakes, J.Donoghue, C.O'Connoll, M.Bermingham. Subs: P.Egan for M.Mortell, D.Long for S.Lakes.
Note: P.Egan and B.Kelleher played in first leg. M.Mortell and C.O'Connoll were on for second leg.

HOME FINAL

Tipperary   Same as played in final except L.Devaney for P.Lowry. Sub: J.McKenna for S.McLoughlin.
Kilkenny   O.Walsh, T.Carroll, P.Dillon, J.Treacy, S.Cleere, P.Henderson, M.Coogan, P.Moran, F.Cummins, J.Bennett (capt.), J.Kinsella, C.Dunne, E.Keher, J.Lynch, Martin Brennan. Sub: R.Blanchfield for Martin Brennan.

1968/69

Cork   Paddy Barry, A.Maher, T.O'Donoghue, D.Murphy (capt.), D.Clifford, J.McCarthy, C.Roche, G.McCarthy, R.Touhy, T.Ryan, W.Walsh, P.Hegarty, C.McCarthy, C.Cullinane, E.O'Brien.
Wexford   P.Nolan, T.Neville, J.Furlong, E.Colfer, V.Staples, D.Quigley, W.Murphy, M.Jacob, D.Bernie, J.Quigley, P.Lynch, P.Wilson, T.Doran, S.Whelan, J.Berry.

1969/70

Cork   Paddy Barry, A.Maher, P.McDonnell, J.Horgan, S.Murphy, P.Hegarty, C.Roche, G.McCarthy (Capt), S.Looney, T.Ryan, W.Walsh, D.Clifford, C.McCarthy, R.Cummins, E.O'Brien. Subs: J.O'Sullivan for G.McCarthy, G.McCarthy for J.O'Sullivan.
Note: C.Cullinane played in first leg. D.Clifford came on for second leg.
New York   H.Condron, M.Reynolds, J.Maher, J.O'Neill, P.Donoghue, P.Dowling, P.Dwyer, J.Firth, M.Curtin, T.Corbett, J.Carney, S.Lakes, D.O'Brien, B.Hennessy, P.Kirby.
Subs: J.Foley for P.Kirby, J.Harte for J.Foley, B.Kelleher for J.Carney.
Note: S.Custy played in first leg. M.Reynolds came on for second leg. Subs in first leg: B.Kelleher for J.Carney, J.Harte for P.Dwyer.

HOME FINAL

Cork   Same as played in final except J.O'Sullivan (Capt) and C.Cullinane for S.Murphy and D.Clifford.
Limerick   J.Hogan, J.McDonagh, P.Hartigan, J.O'Brien, Phil Bennis, J.O'Donnell, A.O'Brien, P.J.Keane, B.Hartigan, E.Grimes, R.Bennis, E.Cregan, P.O'Brien, T.Bluett, Peter Bennis. Subs: A.Dunworth for E.Grimes, T.Ryan for P.O'Brien.

1970/71

Limerick   J.Hogan, A.O'Brien (capt.), P.Hartigan, J.O'Brien, C.Campbell, J.O'Donnell, Phil Bennis.S.Foley, M.Graham, R.Bennis, B.Hartigan, E.Grimes, D.Flynn, M.Cregan, E. Cregan. Sub: E.Prenderville for C.Campbell.
Tipperary   P.O'Sullivan, N.Lane, J.Kelly, W.Ryan, J.Fogarty, T.O'Connor, L.Gaynor, M.Roche, M.Jones, F.Loughnane (capt.), J.Flanagan, Jack Ryan, R.Ryan, M.Keating, P.Byrne. Subs: Jimmy Doyle for R.Ryan, J.Gleeson for W.Ryan, M.Nolan for J.Flanagan.

1971/72

Cork Paddy Barry, B.Murphy, P.McDonnell, Paddy Crowley, F Norberg (capt.), S.Looney, C.Roche, J.McCarthy, D.Coughlan, D.Collins, M.Malone, P.Hegarty, C.McCarthy, R.Cummins, S.O'Leary. Subs: S.Murphy for C.Roche.

Limerick J.Hogan (capt.), A.O'Brien, P.Hartigan, J.Allis, Phil Bennis, J.O'Brien, M.Graham, S.Foley, B.Hartigan, F.Nolan, R.Bennis, E.Grimes, D.Flynn, W.Moore, E.Cregan. Subs: C.Campbell for Phil Bennis, S.Burke for E.Cregan.

1972/73

Wexford P.Nolan, J.Prendergast, E.Murphy, J.Quigley (capt.), C.Doran, M.Jacob, W.Murphy, D.Bernie, E.Buggy, C.Keogh, M.Quigley, T.Byrne, H.Gough, T.Doran, J. Berry. Subs: P.Kehoe for J.Prendergast, J.Purcell for H.Gough.

Limerick S.Horgan, P.Hartigan, E.Rea, J.O'Brien, M.Dowling, J.O'Donnell, S.Foley, B.Hartigan, E.Grimes, R.Bennis, E.Cregan, M.Graham, L.O'Donoghue, W.Moore, F.Nolan. Subs: A.Dunworth for M.Graham, Phil Bennis for A.Dunworth, L.Enright for Jim O'Donnell.

1973/74

Cork Paddy Barry, A.Maher, M.O'Doherty, J.Horgan (capt.), Pat Barry, J.Buckley, C.Roche, P.Hegarty, D.Coughlan, T.O'Brien, W.Walsh, G.McCarthy, S.O'Leary, M.Malone, E.O'Donoghue. Sub: C.McCarthy for W.Walsh.

Limerick S.Horgan, P.Herbert, P.Hartigan, J.O'Brien, T.Ryan, E.Cregan, S.Foley, W.Fitzmaurice (capt.), E.Grimes, L.O'Donoghue, R.Bennis, M.Ruth, J.McKenna, E.Rea, F.Nolan. Subs: B.Hartigan for W.Fitzmaurice, M.Dowling for J.McKenna, P.Fitzmaurice for M.Ruth.

1974/75

Galway M.Conneely, N.McInerney, J.Clarke, P Lally, J.McDonagh, S.Silke, I.Clarke, S.Murphy, John Connolly (capt.), G.Coone, F.Burke, P.J.Molloy, M.Barrett, P.J.Qualter, P.Fahy.

Tipperary J.Duggan (capt.), L.King, J.Keogh, J.Bergin, T O'Connor, N.O'Dwyer, J.Dunlea, J.Kehoe, S.Hogan, F.Loughnane, T.Butler, F.Murphy, J.Flanagan, R.Ryan, P.Quinlan.

1975/76

Kilkenny N.Skehan, P.Larkin (capt.), N.Orr, B.Cody, P.Lawlor, P.Henderson, G.Henderson, L.O'Brien, F.Cummins, M.Crotty, M.Ruth, W.Fitzpatrick, Mick Brennan, P.Delaney, E.Keher. Sub: J.Lyng for E.Keher.
Note: T.McCormack and K.Purcell played in drawn game. N.Orr and W.Fitzpatrick were on for replay. Subs in drawn game: W.Fitzpatrick for L.O'Brien, M.Fennelly for K.Purcell, J.Hennessy for T.McCormack.

Clare S.Durack, M.McKeogh, J.Power (capt.), J.McMahon, G.Loughnane, S.Hehir, J.O'Gorman, M.Moroney, S.Stack, J.Callanan, J.McNamara, C.Honan, T.Crowe, N.Casey, E.O'Connor. Sub: C.Woods for S.Hehir.
Note: C.Woods played in drawn game, J.O'Gorman in replay.

1976/77

Clare S.Durack, J.McMahon, J.Power, J.O'Gorman, G.Loughnane, G.Lohan, S.Stack, M.Moroney, C.Honan, J.McNamara (capt.), E.O'Connor, J.Callanan, T.Crowe, N.Casey, P.O'Connor.

Kilkenny N.Skehan, P.Larkin, P.Henderson, D.O'Hara, P.Lawlor, B.Cody, G.Henderson, J.Hennessy, F.Cummins, L.O'Brien, M.Ruth, M.Crotty, Mick Brennan, P Delaney, E.Keher.

1977/78

Clare S.Durack, J.O'Gorman, J.Power, J.McMahon, G.Loughnane, S.Hehir, S.Stack (capt.), M.Moroney, J.Callanan, J.McNamara, N.Casey, C.Honan, P.O'Connor, M.McKeogh, E.O'Connor.

Kilkenny N.Skehan, P.Larkin, D.O'Hara, P.Henderson, J.Hennessy, G.Henderson, R.Reid, L.O'Brien, F.Cummins, Mick Brennan, M.Ruth, K.Brennan, M.Crotty, T.Malone, W.Fitzpatrick.

1978/79

Tipperary P.McLoughney, P.Williams (capt.), J.Keogh, T.O'Connor, K.O'Connor, N O'Dwyer, P.Fitzelle, M.Doyle, G.Stapleton, E.O'Shea, J.Williams, P.Queally, F.Loughnane, J.Kehoe, S.Power.Sub.T.Butler for J.Kehoe.

Galway F.Larkin, N.Mcinerney, J.McDonagh (capt.), I.Clarke, J.Greaney, S.Silke, Jimmy Cooney, John Connolly, S.Mahon, Michael Connolly, Joe Connolly, P.J.Molloy, N.Lane, F Burke, P.Ryan. Subs: M.Earls for S.Silke, F Gantley for M.Connolly.

1979/80

Cork T.Murphy, D.Burns, B.Murphy, J.Crowley, D.Coughlan, T.Cashman, D.McCurtain (capt.), J.Fenton, P.Moylan, T.Crowley, P.Horgan, D.Buckley, S.O'Leary, R.Cummins, E.O'Donoghue.Sub: J.Barry Murphy for D.Buckley.
Note: J.Horgan, J.Barry Murphy and C.McCarthy played in drawn game. P.Moylan, S.O'Leary and J.Fenton were on for replay. Sub in drawn game: S.O'Leary for C.McCarthy.

Limerick T.Quaid, D.Murray, L.Enright, D.Punch, L.O'Donoghue, M.Carroll, S.Foley (capt.), J.Carroll, P.Fitzmaurice, E.Grimes, J.Flanagan, B.Carroll, O.O'Connor, J.McKenna, E.Cregan. Sub: G.Mulcahy for B.Carroll.
Note: G.Mulcahy played in drawn game. S.Foley was on for replay. Sub in drawn game: S.Foley for G.Mulcahy.

1980/81

Cork G.Cunningham, B.Murphy, D.O'Grady (capt.), J.Horgan, D.McCurtain, T.Cashman, N.Kennefick, J.Fenton, P.Moylan, T.Crowley, P.Horgan, Padraig Crowley, S.O'Leary, J.Barry Murphy, E.O'Donohue. Sub: D.Mulcahy for T.Cashman.

Offaly C.King, B.Keeshan, E.Coughlan, P.Fluery, T.Conneely, P.Delaney, G.Coughlan, J.Kelly, L.Currams, M.Corrigan, B.Bermingham, P.Carroll, P.Kirwan, P.Horan (capt.), D.Owens. Sub T.Donoghue for T.Conneely.

1981/82

Kilkenny N.Skehan, J.Henderson, B.Cody (capt.), D.O'Hara, N.Brennan, G.Henderson, P.Prendergast, J.Hennessy, F.Cummins, R.Power, G.Fennelly, K.Brennan, Mick Brennan, L.Fennelly, W.Fitzpatrick. Subs: M.Ruth for R.Power, W.Walton for K.Brennan.

Wexford J.Nolan, B.Murphy, J.Russell, L.Bennett, J.Conran, M.Jacob, C.Doran, P.Courtney, G.O'Connor, J.Fleming, J.Holohan, M.Quigley, S.Kinsella, T.Doran, Johnny Murphy. Sub: E.Walsh for J.Russell.

1982/83

Kilkenny N.Skehan, J.Henderson, D.O'Hara, P.Neary, N.Brennan, G.Henderson, P.Prendergast, F.Cummins, S.Fennelly, R.Power, G.Fennelly, H.Ryan, W.Fitzpatrick, C.Heffernan, L.Fennelly (Capt). Subs: T.McCormack for J.Henderson, P.Lannon for R.Power.

Limerick T.Quaid, P.Fitzmaurice, L.Enright (capt.), P.Herbert, L.O'Donoghue, S.Foley, P.Foley, J.Carroll, D.Fitzgerald, P.Kelly, J.Flanagan, M.J.Coffey, O.O'Connor, J.McKenna, M.Rea. Subs: N.Leonard for P.Fitzmaurice, F.Nolan for S.Foley.

1983/84

Limerick   T.Quaid, P.Fitzmaurice, L.Enright (capt.), P.Herbert, M.Lonergan, M.Carroll, P.Foley, J.Carroll, B.Carroll, L.O'Donoghue, D.Fitzgerald, P.Kelly, O.O'Connor, J.McKenna, M.Rea. Sub: J.Flanagan for O.O'Connor.

Wexford   J.Nolan, E.Cleary, A.Walsh, P.Kenny, J.Conran, G.O'Connor, M.Jacob, P.Courtney, B.Byrne, J.Jordan, James O'Connor, J.McDonald, E.Mythen, M.Quigley, T.Harrington. Subs: J.Walker for E.Mythen, M.O'Connor for J.Conran, Johnny Murphy for B.Byrne.

1984/85

Limerick   T.Quaid, P.Fitzmaurice, L.Enright (capt.), P.Herbert, L.O'Donoghue, M.Carroll, P.Foley, J.Carroll, B.Carroll, P.Kelly, D.Fitzgerald, R.Sampson, O.O'Connor, P.McCarthy, S.Fitzgibbon.

Clare   D.Corry, J.Minogue, S.Hehir, T.Keane, G.Loughnane, M.Meagher, S.Stack, A.Cunningham, D.Coote, C.Lyons, J.Shanahan, J.Callanan, S.Dolan, P.Morey, M.Guilfoyle. Subs: A.Nugent for M.Guilfoyle, P.Lynch for S.Dolan.

1985/86

Kilkenny   K.Fennelly, P.Prendergast, J.Henderson, F.Holohan (capt.), J.Hennessy, G.Henderson, S.Fennelly, G.Fennelly, R.Power, P.Walsh, K.Brennan, J.O'Hara, L.Ryan, L.Fennelly, C.Heffernan. Sub: J.Mulcahy for J.O'Hara.

Galway   P.Murphy, S.Coen, C.Hayes, S.Linnane, O.Kilkenny, P.Piggott, A.Kilkenny, B.Lynskey, S.Mahon, M.Naughton, A. Cunningham, Joe Cooney, B.Forde, N.Lane, P.J.Molloy. Subs: A.Keady for P.Piggott, M.McGrath for B.Forde, M.Connolly (Craughwell) for P.J.Molloy.

1986/87

Galway   P.Murphy, S.Linnane, C.Hayes (capt.), P.Piggott, O.Kilkenny, A.Keady, A.Kilkenny, M.Coleman, S.Mahon, M.McGrath, Joe Cooney, M.Naughton, E.Ryan, B.Lynskey, A.Cunningham. Subs: N.Lane for M.Coleman, M.Coen for S.Mahon.

Clare   E.McMahon, J.Russell, J.Moroney, M.Glynn, G.Loughnane, S.Stack, J.Lee, J.Shanahan, J.Callanan (capt.), G.O'Loughlin, V.O'Loughlin, M.Guilfoyle, C.Lyons, T.Guilfoyle, G.McInerney. Subs: S.Dolan for G.O'Loughlin, A.Cunningham for M.Glynn, V.Donnellan for A.Cunningham.

1987/88

Tipperary   K.Hogan, C.O'Donovan, N.Sheehy, S.Gibson, B.Ryan, J.Kennedy, P.Delaney, J.Hayes, Colm Bonnar, D.Ryan, D.O'Connell, P.O'Neill (capt.), P.Fox, N.English, A.Ryan. Subs: C.Stakelum for D.O'Conneil, J.Leahy for A.Ryan, M.Corcoran for S.Gibson.

Offaly   Jim Troy, J.Miller, A.Fogarty, M.Hanamy, B.Keeshan, M.Coughlan, G.Coughlan, J.Kelly, Joe Dooley, P.O'Connor, D. Fogarty, M.Corrigan, P.Cleary, E.Coughlan, P.Corrigan. Subs: P.J.Martin for M.Coughlan, M.Duignan for P.Corrigan, G.Cahill for P.O'Connor.

1988/89

Galway   J.Commins, S.Linnane, C.Hayes (capt.), O.Kilkenny, P.Finnerty, A.Keady, S.Treacy, M.Coleman, P.Malone, M.McGrath, B.Lynskey, M.Naughton, G.Burke, Joe Cooney, E.Ryan. Subs: N.Lane for B.Lynskey, P.Higgins for P.Finnerty, A.Kilkenny for P.Malone.

Tipperary   K.Hogan, B.Ryan, C.O'Donovan, P.Delaney, R.Stakelum, N.Sheehy, Conal Bonnar, D.Carr, Colm Bonnar, D.Ryan, J.Hayes, J.Leahy, M.Cleary, Cormac Bonnar, P.McGrath (Capt). Subs: J.Cormack for C.O'Donovon, D.O'Connell for J.Hayes.

1989/90

Kilkenny   K.Fennelly (capt.), W.Hennessy, J.Henderson, P.Phelan, J.Power, P.Dwyer, M.Cleere, M.Phelan, L.Ryan, D.J.Carey, R.Power, J.McDonald, E.Morrissey, C.Heffernan, L.Fennelly. Sub: L.McCarthy for L.Fennelly.

New York   J.Duggan, J.Lyons, T.Canty, M.Cosgrove, B.Keeshan, J.Fleming, S.Collison, A.Nugent, S.Donoghue, L.Bergin, I.Conroy, R.Sampson, H.Ryan, W.Lowry, J.McInerney. Sub: M.McCarthy for W.Lowry.

HOME FINAL

Kilkenny   Same as played in final except S.Fennelly (Capt) and W.O'Connor in place of P.Phelan and L.Ryan. Subs: P.Phelan for W.O'Connor, L.Ryan for S.Fennelly.

Wexford   T.Morrissey, N.McDonald, E.Cleary, J.Conran, D.Prendergast, G.O'Connor, L.Dunne, B.Byrne, G.Coady, M.Storey, R.Coleman, James O'Connor, T.Dempsey (capt.), J.Holohan, M.Reck. Subs: M.Fitzhenry for James O'Connor, L.O'Gorman for D.Prendergast.

1990/91

Offaly   Jim Troy, B.Hennessy, S.McGuckian, M.Hanamy, H.Rigney, R.Mannion, B.Whelahan, J.Pilkington, J.Kelly, Johnny Dooley, D.Regan, Joe Dooley, D.Owens (capt.), M.Duignan, M.Corrigan. Subs: B.Dooley for M.Corrigan, B.Kelly for Joe Dooley.

Wexford   T.Morrissey, N.McDonald, G.Cushe, P.Bridges, S.Flood, L.Dunne, L.O'Gorman, B.Byrne, G.O'Connor, M.Storey, E.Synnott, D.Prendergast, T.Dempsey, J.Holohan, S.Wickham. Subs: J.Conran for S.Wickham, D.Guiney for B.Byrne.

1991/92

Limerick   T.Quaid, B.Finn, P.Carey, D.Nash, M.Houlihan, C.Carey, A.Garvey, M.Reale, G.Hegarty, M.Galligan, A.Carmody, G.Kirby, L.Garvey, J.O'Connor, S.Fitzgibbon. Subs: R.Sampson for L.Garvey, P.Davoren for Galligan.

Tipperary   K.Hogan, P.Delaney, N.Sheehy, G.Frend, B.Ryan, C.Bonnar, R.Ryan, D.Carr, E.Ryan, M.Cleary, J.Hayes, C.Stakelum, P.Fox, D.Ryan, N.English. Sub: J.Leahy for Hayes.

1992/93

Cork   G.Cunningham, J.Considine, S.O'Gorman, L.Forde, D.Walsh, J.Cashman, B.Corcoran (capt.), C.Casey, S.McCarthy, T.McCarthy, P.Buckley, T.Mulcahy, G.Manley, P.O'Callaghan, B.Egan. Subs: A.O'Sullivan for J.Cashman, M.Foley for P.O'Callaghan, J.Fitzgibbon for T.Mulcahy.
Note: T.Kingston and K.Hennessy played in first and second games. P.Buckley played in first and third games. P.Hartnett played in first game. G.Cunningham was on for third game. L.Forde and P.O'Callaghan played in second and third games. Subs in second game P.Buckley for P.O'Callaghan, G.Cunningham for T.Kingston, G.Fitzgerald for K.Hennessy.

Wexford   D.Fitzhenry, S.Flood, G.Cushe, N.McDonald, John O'Connor, L.Dunne, T.Dunne, G.O'Connor, T.Dempsey, M.Storey, J.Bolger, L.O'Gorman, E.Scallan, E.Cleary, L.Murphy. Subs: C.McBride for J.Bolger, B.Byrne for E.Cleary.
Note: Wexford played the same team in all three games. Subs in first game: D.Guiney for N.McDonald, B.Byrne for T.Dempsey. Subs in the second game: B.Byrne for J.Bolger, E.Synnott for E.Scallan, C.McBride for E.Synnott, D.Prendergast for L.O'Gorman.

1993/94

Tipperary J.Grace, G.Frend, N.Sheehy, M.Ryan, R.Ryan, M.O'Meara, Conal Bonnar, P.King, J.Hayes, J.Leahy, L.McGrath, A.Ryan, D.Ryan, A.Crosse, M.Cleary. Sub: T.Dunne for A.Ryan.

Galway R.Burke, P.Cooney, S.Treacy, N.Power, P.Kelly, G.McInerney, T.Helebert, M.Coleman, P.Malone, J.Campbell, B.Keogh, J.McGrath, N.Shaughnessy, J.Rabbitte, L.Burke. Subs: M.McGrath for J.McGrath, M.Donoghue for T.Helebert, F Forde for J.Campbell,

1994/95

Kilkenny M.Walsh, E.O'Connor, P.Dwyer, L.Simpson, L.Keoghan, E.Dwyer, W.O'Connor, M.Phelan, W.Hennessy (capt.), A.Ronan, J.Power, P.J.Delaney, E.Morrissey, D.J.Carey, D.Byrne. Subs: C.Brennan for M.Phelan, D.Gaffney for J.Power.

Clare D.Fitzgerald, M.O'Halloran, B.Lohan, F.Lohan, L.Doyle, S.McMahon, A.Daly (capt.), K.Morrissey, S.Sheehy, P.J.O'Connell, C.Clancy, J.O'Connor, J.McInerney, E.Taaffe, G.O'Loughlin. Subs: F.Touhy for C.Clancy, F Hegarty for K.Morrissey, C.Lyons for J.McInerney.

1995/96

Galway M.Darcy, T.Helebert, P.Cooney, G.McInerney, C.O'Donovan, N.Shaughnessy, M.Donoghue, M.Coleman (capt.), B.Keogh, J.Rabbitte, C.Moore, L.Burke, K.Broderick, Joe Cooney, F.Forde. Subs: S.Treacy for P.Cooney, P.Kelly for C.O'Donovon.

Tipperary B.Cummins, G.Frend, P.Shelly, M.Ryan, Conal Bonnar, Colm Bonnar, B.Carroll, C.Gleeson, G.O'Meara, R.Ryan, E.Tucker, J.Leahy, M.Cleary, N.English, L.Cahill. Subs: A.Ryan for E.Tucker, K.Tucker for M.Cleary.

1997

Limerick J.Quaid, S.McDonagh, M.Nash, D.Nash, D.Clarke, T.J.Ryan, J.Foley, C.Carey, S.O'Neill, M.Galligan, M.Foley, B.Foley, J.Moran, O.Moran, G.Kirby (Capt).

Galway P.Costelloe, G.Kennedy, L.Hodgins, V.Maher, B.Keogh, C.Moore, M.Donoghue, L.Burke, N.Shaughnessy, J.Campbell, M.Coleman, J.McGrath, D.Coen, J.Rabbitte, O.Fahy. Subs: A.Kerins for N.Shaughnessy, F.Forde for J.McGrath.

1998

Cork G.Cunningham, F.Ryan, J.Browne, D.O'Sullivan (capt.), M.Landers, B.Corcoron, S.Óg Ó hAilpín, P.Ryan, M.Daly, S.McGrath, F.McCormack, K.Morrison, S.O'Farrell, A.Browne, J.Deane. Sub: B.Egan for M.Daly.

Waterford B.Landers, T.Feeney; S.Cullinane, M.O'Sullivan, S.Frampton (capt.), F.Hartley, B.Greene, A.Browne, P.Queally, D.Shanahan, K.McGrath, D.Bennett, B.O'Sullivan, A.Kirwan, P.Flynn. Sub: M.White for B.O'Sullivan.

1999

Tipperary B.Cummins; D.Fahy, F.Heaney, L.Sheedy; B.Horgan, D.Kennedy, E.Corcoran; E.Enright, D.Carr; T.Dunne (capt.), D.Ryan, B.O'Meara, L.Cahill, P.Shelly, J.Leahy. Subs: Conal Bonner for B.Horgan, C.Gleeson for E.Enright, G.Maguire for P.Shelly.

Galway D.Howe; P.Huban, B.Feeney, L.Hodgins; N.Shaughnessy, F.Flynn, P.Hardiman; T.Kavanagh, L.Burke, A.Kerins, C.Moore (capt.); K.Broderick; O.Fahy, M.Kerins, E.Cloonan. Subs: N.Kenny for T.Kavanagh, F.Healy for C.Moore.

2000

Galway M.Crimmins, L.Hodgins, B.Feeney, V.Maher, F.Gantley, C.Moore, P.Hardiman, A.Kerins, R.Gantley, J.Rabbitte, M.Kerins, D.Tierney, O.Canning, O.Fahy, F.Healy.

Tipperary B.Cummins, L.Sheedy, P.Maher, M.Ryan, P.Ormonde, D.Kennedy, E.Corcoran, J.Carroll, B.O'Meara, M.O'Leary, D.Ryan, T.Dunne, P.O'Brien, P.Shelley, G.Maguire. Subs: D.Fahy for Sheedy, E.O'Neill for Maguire, J.Leahy for O'Meara.

2001

Tipperary B.Cummins, T.Costello, P.Maher, P.Ormonde, J.Leahy, E.Corcoran, M.Ryan, C.Gleeson, T.Dunne, M.O'Leary, E.Enright, L.Cahill, E.Kelly, D.Ryan, L.Corbett. Subs: B.O'Meara for Cahill, E.O'Neill for D.Ryan.

Clare D.Fitzgerald, C.Forde, B.Lohan, F.Lohan, L.Doyle, J.Reddan, G.Quinn, O.Baker, C.Lynch, T.Griffin, J.O'Connor, G.Considine, D.Forde, N.Gilligan, B.Murphy. Subs: A.Markham for Considine, S.McMahon for Doyle, P.J.O'Connell for Griffin.

2002

Kilkenny J.McGarry, M.Kavanagh, N.Hickey, P.Larkin, R.Mullally, P.Barry, J.J.Delaney, D.Lyng, P.Tennyson, J.Hoyne, H.Shefflin, A.Comerford, E.Brennan, M.Comerford, S.Grehan. Subs: K.Power for Grehan, S.Dowling for Tennyson, B.Dowling for Power.

Cork D.Óg Cusack, W.Sherlock, D.O'Sullivan, F.Ryan, D.Barrett, J.Browne, S. Óg Ó hAilpín, A.Cummins, J.Gardiner, J.O'Connor, K.Murphy, N.McCarthy, E.Collins, A.Browne, B.O'Connor. Subs: T.McCarthy for Gardiner, K.Murray for N.McCarthy, P.Ryan for Murphy.

2003

Kilkenny P.J.Ryan, M.Kavanagh, N.Hickey, P.Larkin, R.Mullally, P.Barry, J.J.Delaney, D.Lyng, P.Tennyson, J.Hoyne, H.Shefflin, T.Walsh, D.J.Carey, M.Comerford, E.Brennan. Subs: J.Coogan for Tennyson, A.Cummins for Larkin, C.Carter for Hoyne.

Tipperary B.Cummins, M.Maher, P.Maher, B.Dunne, B.Horgan, D.Kennedy, P.Kelly, T.Dunne, N.Morris, J.Carroll, C.Gleeson, L.Cahill, E.Kelly, G.O'Grady, L.Corbett. Subs: E.Brislane for Morris, J.Devane for P.Maher, E.O'Neill for O'Grady.

2004

Galway L.Donoghue, D.Joyce, D.Cloonan, O.Canning, D.Hardiman, David Hayes, D.Collins, F.Healy, T.Óg Regan, A.Cullinane, D.Forde, A.Kerins, Damien Hayes, E.Cloonan, K.Broderick. Subs: F.Moore for Regan, R.Gantley for Collins, D.Tierney for Cullinane, O.Fahy for Damien Hayes.

Waterford S.Brenner, J.Murray, T.Feeney, E.McGrath, B.Phelan, T.Browne, K.McGrath, M.Walsh, D.Bennett, D.Shanahan, A.Moloney, E.Kelly, S.Prendergast, P.Flynn, J.Mullane. Subs: J.Kennedy for Moloney, P.O'Brien for Kennedy, E.Murphy for Bennett.

2005

Kilkenny J.McGarry, J.Ryall, N.Hickey, J.Tyrrell, R.Mullally, P.Barry, J.J.Delaney, B.Barry, D.Lyng, M.Comerford, E.Larkin, T.Walsh, R.Power, D.J.Carey, H.Shefflin. Subs: E.Brennan for Power, M.Kavanagh for Ryall.

Clare D.Fitzgerald, F.Lohan, B.Lohan, G.O'Grady, A.Markham, S.McMahon, G.Quinn, B.O'Connell, C.Lynch, C.Plunkett, D.McMahon, T.Carmody, T.Griffin, N.Gilligan, A.Quinn. Subs: B.Quinn for F.Lohan, B.Nugent for Plunkett, D.O'Connell for A.Quinn, D.Clancy for B.O'Connell.

2006

Kilkenny   J.McGarry, M.Kavanagh, J.J.Delaney, N.Hickey, J.Tyrrell, J.Tennyson, T.Walsh, D.Lyng, R.Mullally, R.Power, M.Comerford, E.Larkin, J.Fitzpatrick, H.Shefflin, A.Fogarty. Subs: W.O'Dwyer for Power, M.Fennelly for Lyng.

Limerick   B.Murray, D.Reale, T.J.Ryan, M.Foley, O.Moran, B.Geary, D.Moloney, D.Ryan, D.O'Grady, M.O'Brien, S.Lucey, C.Fitzgerald, A.O'Shaughnessy, B.Begley, B.Foley. Subs: N.Moran for O'Brien, S.Hickey for M.Foley, P.O'Grady for D.O'Grady.

2007

Waterford   C.Hennessy, A.Kearney, E.Murphy, D.Prendergast, T.Browne, K.McGrath, J.Murray, M.Walsh, J.Kennedy, D.Shanahan, E.Kelly, S.Molumphy, S.Walsh, S.Prendergast, J.Mullane. Subs: P.Ryan for S.Walsh, E.McGrath for Murray, S.O'Sullivan for Kennedy.

Kilkenny   P.J.Ryan, N.Hickey, B.Hogan, J.J.Delaney, J.Tyrrell, P.J.Delaney, T.Walsh, D.Lyng, W.O'Dwyer, E.Brennan, M.Comerford, R.Power, H.Shefflin, J.Fitzpatrick, A.Fogarty. Subs: E.Larkin for Fitzpatrick, E.McCormack for Fogarty.

2008

Tipperary   B.Cummins, E.Buckley, P.Curran, C.O'Brien, E.Corcoran, C.O'Mahony, S.Maher, B.Dunne, S.McGrath, S.Butler, R.O'Dwyer, J.Woodlock, E.Kelly, L.Corbett, W.Ryan. Subs: S.Callanan for O'Dwyer, J.O'Brien for Dunne, A.Byrne for Corcoran, D.Hickey for Ryan.

Galway   J.Skehill, C.Dervan, T.Óg Regan, F.Moore, S.Kavanagh, J.Lee, A.Cullinane, K.Hynes, R.Murray, G.Farragher, F.Healy, D.Hayes, N.Healy, I.Tannian, J.Canning. Subs: A.Kerins for N.Healy, D.Forde for Farragher, A.Callanan for Murray, K.Wade for Tannian.

2009

Kilkenny   P.J.Ryan, M.Kavanagh, J.J.Delaney, J.Tyrrell, T.Walsh, B.Hogan, J.Ryall, J.Tennyson, M.Rice, R.Hogan, H.Shefflin, E.Larkin, E.Brennan, T.J.Reid, A.Fogarty. Subs: M.Comerford for Hogan, M.Grace for Comerford, J.Fitzpatrick for Shefflin, S.Cummins for Kavanagh.

Tipperary   B.Cummins, P.Stapleton, P.Curran, C.O'Brien, D.Fanning, Pádraic Maher, S.Maher, T.Stapleton, S.McGrath, J.Woodlock, S.Callanan, J.O'Brien, N.McGrath, M.Webster, L.Corbett. Subs: B.Maher for Fanning, H.Maloney for S.Maher, B.Dunne for Maloney, S.Hennessy for Woodlock, D.Fitzgerald for T.Stapleton, Patrick Maher for Webster, E.Buckley for Pádraic Maher.

2010

Galway   C.Callanan, D.Joyce, S.Kavanagh, O.Canning, D.Barry, T.Óg Regan, D.Collins, G.Farragher, D.Burke, A.Harte, C.Donnellan, A.Smith, D.Hayes, J.Canning, I.Tannian. Subs: J.Gantley for Tannian, K.Hynes for Smith, A.Callanan for Burke.

Cork   D.Óg Cusack, S.O'Neill, E.Dillon, B.Murphy, J.Gardiner, R.Curran, S.Óg Ó hAilpin, T.Kenny, L.McLoughlin, M.Cussen, K.Murphy, C.Naughton, B.O'Connor, A.Ó hAilpin, P.Horgan. Subs: J.O'Connor for McLoughlin, M.Walsh for S.Ó hAilpin, P.O'Sullivan for Murphy.

2011

Dublin   G.Maguire, N.Corcoran, T.Brady, P.Kelly, J.McCaffrey, J.Boland, S.Durkin, A.McCrabbe, L.Rushe, C.McCormack, R.O'Dwyer, C.Keaney, D.Plunkett, D.O'Callaghan, P.Ryan. Subs: M.O'Brien for Boland, D.O'Dwyer for Plunkett, D.Treacy for McCrabbe, S.Lambert for Rushe, S.Ryan for O'Callaghan.

Kilkenny   D.Herity, J.Dalton, B.Hogan, N.Hickey, P.Hogan, J.Tyrrell, J.J.Delaney, T.J.Reid, M.Rice, J.Fitzpatrick, M.Ruth, E.Larkin, C.Fennelly, E.Brennan, R.Hogan. Subs: M.Kavanagh for Delaney, J.Mulhall for Fennelly, P.Murphy for Ruth.

2012

Kilkenny   D.Herity, P.Murphy, J.J.Delaney, J.Tyrrell, T.Walsh, B.Hogan, R.Doyle, M.Fennelly, P.Hogan, R.Hogan, T.J.Reid, C.Buckley, C.Fennelly, E.Larkin, M.Ruth. Subs: K.Joyce for Delaney, J.Mulhall for M.Fennelly, M.Bergin for P.Hogan.

Cork   M.Coleman, S.O'Neill, S.McDonnell, B.Murphy, S.Óg Ó hAilpin, E.Cadogan, W.Egan, L.McLoughlin, J.Gardiner, C.Lehane, P.Cronin, N.McCarthy, L.O'Farrell, P.O'Sullivan, P.Horgan. Subs: D.Sweetnam for McLoughlin, C.O'Sullivan for McDonnell, C.Naughton for O'Sullivan, J.Coughlan for McCarthy.

2013

Kilkenny   E.Murphy, P.Murphy, J.J.Delaney, J.Tyrrell, T.Walsh, B.Hogan, K.Joyce, L.Ryan, M.Rice, C.Buckley, M.Fennelly, E.Larkin, C.Fennelly, R.Hogan, A.Fogarty. Sub: M.Ruth for Fogarty.

Tipperary   D.Gleeson, C.O'Brien, P.Curran, M.Cahill, C.O'Mahony, Pádraic Maher, K.Bergin, B.Maher, S.McGrath, S.Callanan, L.Corbett, Patrick Maher, S.Bourke, E.Kelly, N.McGrath. Subs: J.O'Dwyer for Kelly, J.Forde for Callanan, J.O'Brien for S.McGrath, P.Bourke for S.Bourke, J.Woodlock for Patrick Maher.

2014

Kilkenny   E.Murphy, P.Murphy, J.J.Delaney, B.Kennedy, J.Holden, J.Tyrrell, C.Buckley, M.Fennelly, P.Walsh, R.Hogan, C.Fennelly, T.J.Reid, R.Power, M.Kelly, H.Shefflin. Subs: L.Ryan for Holden, W.Walsh for Kelly, E.Larkin for C.Fennelly, C.Fennelly for Shefflin, K.Joyce for Kennedy.

Tipperary   D.Gleeson, C.Barrett, Pádraic Maher, M.Cahill, J.Barry, B.Maher, C.O'Mahony, K.Bergin, J.Woodlock, D.Maher, Patrick Maher, J.O'Dwyer, N.McGrath, S.Callanan, N.O'Meara. Subs: G.Ryan for D.Maher, S.McGrath for Woodlock, S.Bourke for O'Meara, J.O'Brien for Callanan, Callanan for O'Brien, O'Brien for O'Dwyer, O'Dwyer for Bourke.

2015

Waterford   S.O'Keeffe, N.Connors, B.Coughlan, S.Fives, A.Gleeson, T.de Búrca, Philip Mahony, J.Barron, K.Moran, C.Dunford, Pauric Mahony, M.Walsh, J.Dillon, M.Shanahan, S.Bennett. Subs: B.O'Halloran for Dunford, T.Devine for Bennett, S.O'Sullivan for Dillon, M.O'Neill for Gleeson, J.Coughlan for Harnedy.

Cork   A.Nash, S.O'Neill, A.Ryan, S.McDonnell, L.McLoughlin, M.Ellis, C.Murphy, D.Kearney, A.Walsh, B.Cooper, S.Harnedy, R.O'Shea, A.Cadogan, C.Lehane, P.Horgan. Subs: P.O'Sullivan for Cadogan, B.Lawton for Walsh, L.O'Farrell for O'Shea, D.Cahalane for Ryan, G.O'Brien for Barron.

2016

Clare   P.Kelly, O.O'Brien, C.Dillon, P.O'Connor, B.Bugler, C.Cleary, D.Fitzgerald, D.Reidy, C.Galvin, P.Duggan, T.Kelly, A.Cunningham, P.Collins, D.Honan, C.McGrath. Subs: S.O'Donnell for Duggan, C.O'Connell for Honan, C.Ryan for Cunningham, A.Shanahan for Galvin, J.Browne for Cleary, C.Galvin for Collins, S.Morey for Bugler.

Waterford   S.O'Keeffe, S.Fives, B.Coughlan, N.Connors, T.de Búrca, A.Gleeson, Philip Mahony, J.Barron, D.Fives, K.Moran, S.Bennett, M.Walsh, P.Curran, J.Dillon, C.Dunford. Subs: T.Devine for Dunford, M.Shanahan for Dillon, B.O'Halloran for A.Gleeson, C.Gleeson for S.Fives, T.Ryan for Curran, C.Dunford for Bennett, Pauric Mahony for Walsh.

Replay
Clare   P.Kelly, C.Dillon, P.O'Connor, D.Fitzgerald, J.Browne, C.Cleary, B.Bugler, D.Reidy, C Galvin, T.Kelly, C.McGrath, P.Collins, D.Honan, A Cunningham, S.O'Donnell. Subs: C.Ryan for Galvin, C.O'Connell for Collins, A Shanagher for O'Donnell.
Waterford   S.O'Keeffe, B.Coughlan, N.Connors, S.Fives, D.Fives, K.Moran, P.Mahony, T.de Búrca, J.Barron, M.Walsh, A.Gleeson, S.Bennett, J.Dillon, P.Curran, T.Devine. Subs: C.Dunford for Devine, B.O'Halloran for Dillon, M.Shanahan for Bennett, T.Ryan for Walsh.

2017
Galway   C.Callanan, A.Tuohey, Daithí Burke, P.Killeen, P.Mannion, G.McInerney, A.Harte, J.Coen, David Burke, J.Flynn, J.Canning, J.Cooney, C.Whelan, C.Mannion, N.Burke. Subs: J.Glynn for Canning, J.Hanbury for Daithí Burke, C.Donnellan for N.Burke, T.Monaghan for Flynn, S.Loftus for Killeen.
Tipperary   D.Gleeson, C.Barrett, J.Barry, M.Cahill, S.Kennedy, R.Maher, Pádraic Maher, B.Maher, J.Forde, D.McCormack, M.Breen, S.O'Brien, N.McGrath, J.O'Dwyer, J.McGrath. Subs: N.O'Meara for O'Brien, Patrick Maher for O'Dwyer, T.Hamill for Cahill, P.Flynn for Forde, D.Quinn for N.McGrath.

INTERPROVINCIAL HURLING CHAMPIONSHIP 1927-2016

Munster (47)   1928, 1929, 1930, 1931, 1934, 1935, 1937, 1938, 1939, 1940, 1942, 1943, 1944, 1945, 1946, 1948, 1949, 1950, 1951, 1952, 1953, 1955, 1957, 1958, 1959, 1960, 1961, 1963, 1966, 1968, 1969, 1970, 1976, 1978, 1981, 1984, 1985, 1992, 1995, 1996,1997, 2000, 2001, 2005, 2007, 2013, 2016.
Leinster (28)   1927, 1932, 1933, 1936, 1941, 1954, 1956, 1962, 1964, 1965, 1967, 1971, 1972, 1973, 1974, 1975, 1977, 1979, 1988, 1993, 1999, 2002, 2003, 2006, 2008, 2009, 2012, 2014.
Connacht (11)   1947, 1980, 1982, 1983, 1986, 1987, 1989, 1991, 1994, 1998, 2004.

1927
November 21, 1926, Portlaoise.
Leinster	7-6	3-5	Connacht

March 17, 1927, Croke Park
Leinster	1-11	2-6	Munster

1928
February 12, Tuam.
Munster	7-3	2-4	Connacht

March 17, Croke Park.
Munster	2-2	1-2	Leinster

1929
Ulster not competing, Leinster had a bye and Connacht being struck out, Munster got a walk-over.
March 17, Croke Park.
Munster	5-3	3-1	Leinster

1930
March 17, Croke Park.
Munster	4-6	2-7	Leinster

1931
February 8, Birr.
Munster	10-9	1-2	Connacht

March 17, Croke Park.
Munster	1-12	2-6	Leinster

1932
February 28, Birr.
Leinster	6-8	2-4	Connacht

March 17, Croke Park.
Leinster	6-8	4-4	Munster

1933
February 19, Portumna.
Munster	4-5	3-7	Connacht

March 17, Croke Park.
Leinster	4-6	3-6	Munster

1934
February 25, Roscrea.
Leinster	7-6	4-6	Connacht

March 17, Croke Park.
Munster	6-3	3-2	Leinster

1935

February 24, Portumna.
Munster   7-5   4-4   *Connacht*
March 17, Croke Park.
Munster   3-4   3-0   *Leinster*

1936

February 16, Roscrea.
Leinster   2-7   2-4   *Connacht*
March 17, Croke Park.
Leinster   2-8   3-4   *Munster*

1937

February 14, Ennis.
Munster   4-5   3-1   *Connacht*
March 17, Croke Park.
Munster   1-9   3-1   *Leinster*

1938

February 20, Ballinasloe.
Connacht   3-6   3-6   *Leinster*
February 27, Tullamore.
Leinster   4-5   0-3   *Connacht*
March 17, Croke Park.
Munster   6-2   4-3   *Leinster*

1939

February 26, Birr
Munster 8-5   0-2   *Connacht*
March 17, Croke Park
Munster 4-4   1-6   *Leinster*

1940

February 25, Birr.
Leinster   4-5   1-4   *Connacht*
March 17 , Croke Park.
Munster   4-9   5-4   *Leinster*

1941

February 16, Galway.
Munster   7-5   0-6   *Connacht*
March 16, Croke Park.
Leinster   2-5   2-4   *Munster*

1942

February 15, Ballinasloe.
Leinster   7-8   4-7   *Connacht*
March 17, Croke Park.
Munster   4-9   4-5   *Leinster*

1943

February 14, Nenagh.
Munster   3-5   3-2   *Connacht*
March 17, Croke Park.
Munster   4-3   2-4   *Leinster*

1944

February 13, Birr.
Connacht   4-5   1-5   *Leinster*
February 20, Croke Park.
Munster   9-3   3-1   *Ulster*

March 17, Croke Park.
Munster   4-10   4-4   *Connacht*
(Note The year 1944 represented Ulster's first appearance in the competition.)

1945

February 11, Belfast.
Ulster   3-1   2-3   *Leinster*
February 11, Galway.
Munster   2-5   2-5   *Connacht*
March 4 Limerick.
Munster   4-8   3-7   *Connacht*
March 17, Croke Park.
Munster   6-8   2-0   *Ulster*

1946

February 17, Croke Park.
Connacht   4-14   1-7   *Ulster*
February 17, Waterford.
Munster   0-6   1-2   *Leinster*
March 17, Croke Park.
Munster   3-12   4-8   *Connacht*

1947

March 9, Croke Park.
Connacht   2-6   2-5   *Leinster*
March 16, Croke Park.
Munster   9-7   0-0   *Ulster*
April 6, Croke Park.
Connacht   2-5   1-1   *Munster*

1948

February 15, Lurgan.
Leinster   5-5   4-2   *Ulster*
February 15, Ballinasloe.
Munster   6-5   1-4   *Connacht*
March 17, Croke Park.
Munster   3-5   2-5   *Leinster*

1949

February 13, Croke Park.
Munster   2-8   1-8   *Leinster*
February 13, Croke Park.
Connacht   5-7   2-7   *Ulster*
March 17, Croke Park.
Munster   5-3   2-9   *Connacht*

1950

February 12, Croke Park.
Munster   9-4   3-2   *Ulster*
February 12, Ballinasloe.
Leinster   3-10   2-6   *Connacht*
March 17, Croke Park.
Munster   0-9   1-3   *Leinster*

1951

February 18, Croke Park.
Leinster   7-9   0-2   *Ulster*
February 18, Croke Park.
Munster   6-7   2-7   *Connacht*
March 17, Croke Park.
Munster   4-9   3-6   *Leinster*

1952
February 17, Cork.
Munster	**4-8**	**3-5**	*Leinster*

February 17, Corrigan Park
Connacht	**7-6**	**3-0**	*Ulster*

March 17, Croke Park.
Munster	**5-11**	**4-2**	*Connacht*

1953
February 8, Croke Park.
Munster	**8-6**	**1-5**	*Ulster*

February 22, Portlaoise.
Leinster	**7-9**	**4-3**	*Connacht*

March 17, Croke Park.
Munster	**5-7**	**5-5**	*Leinster*

1954
February 21, Croke Park.
Munster	**4-12**	**3-7**	*Connacht*

February 21, Croke Park.
Leinster	**8-7**	**1-1**	*Ulster*

March 17, Croke Park.
Leinster	**0-9**	**0-5**	*Munster*

1955
March 13, Casement Park.
Connacht	**5-10**	*Ulster*	**2-4**

March 17, Croke Park.
Munster	**3-10**	*Leinster*	**2-9**

April 3, Croke Park.
Munster	**6-8**	*Connacht*	**3-4**

1956
February 19, Casement Park.
Munster	**5-13**	**2-6**	*Ulster*

February 26, Ballinsloe.
Leinster	**5-7**	**2-9**	*Connacht*

March 17, Croke Park.
Leinster	**5-11**	**1-7**	*Munster*

1957
February 17, Casement Park.
Leinster	**7-7**	**2-5**	*Ulster*

February 17, Limerick.
Munster	**3-11**	**3-11**	*Connacht*

March 3, Limerick.
Munster	**6-6**	**0-10**	*Connacht*

March 17, Croke Park.
Munster	**5-7**	**2-5**	*Leinster*

1958
February 16, Casement Park.
Leinster	**8-10**	**3-3**	*Ulster*

March 2, Galway.
Munster	**2-15**	**1-8**	*Connacht*

March 17, Croke Park.
Munster	**3-7**	**3-5**	*Leinster*

1959
March 17, Croke Park.
Connacht	**2-14**	**3-7**	*Leinster*

June 7, Croke Park.
Munster	**7-11**	**2-6**	*Connacht*

(Note: Ulster did not compete.)

1960
February 21, Limerick.
Munster	**5-12**	**1-9**	*Connacht*

February 21, Croke Park.
Leinster	**8-6**	**5-3**	*Ulster*

March 17, Croke Park.
Munster	**6-6**	**2-7**	*Leinster*

1961
February 19, Ballinasloe.
Leinster	**5-8**	**3-7**	*Connacht*

February 19, Casement Park.
Munster	**3-13**	**1-2**	*Ulster*

March 17, Croke Park.
Munster	**4-12**	**3-9**	*Leinster*

1962
February 18, Ballinsoloe.
Munster	**6-11**	**1-3**	*Connacht*

February 25, Cavan.
Leinster	**11-4**	**6-3**	*Ulster*

March 17, Croke Park.
Leinster	**1-11**	**1-9**	*Munster*

1963
February 24, Croke Park.
Munster	**9-7**	**3-5**	*Ulster*

February 24, Croke Park.
Leinster	**5-14**	**3-3**	*Connacht*

March 17, Croke Park.
Munster	**5-5**	**5-5**	*Leinster*

April 14, Croke Park, Replay
Munster	**2-8**	**2-7**	*Leinster*

1964
February 16, Limerick.
Munster	**4-9**	**3-5**	*Connacht*

February 16, Croke Park.
Leinster	**8-9**	**1-4**	*Ulster*

March 17, Croke Park.
Leinster	**3-7**	**2-9**	*Munster*

1965
February 28, Casement Park.
Munster	**3-11**	**3-2**	*Ulster*

February 21, Galway.
Leinster	**4-9**	**2-3**	*Connacht*

March 17, Croke Park.
Leinster	**3-11**	**0-9**	*Munster*

1966
February 27, Ballinasloe.
Munster	**6-10**	**3-3**	*Connacht*

March 6, Ballybay.
Leinster	**6-14**	**3-7**	*Ulster*

March 17, Croke Park.
Munster	**3-13**	**3-11**	*Leinster*

1967
February 26, Croke Park.
Leinster	**10-10**	**3-2**	*Connacht*

February 26, Croke Park.
Munster **6-11** 2-6 *Ulster*
March 17, Croke Park.
Leinster **2-14** 3-5 *Munster*

1968

February 25, Thurles.
Munster **3-15** 1-5 *Connacht*
February 25, Navan.
Leinster **5-10** 3-8 *Ulster*
March 17, Croke Park.
Munster **0-14** 0-10 *Leinster*

1969

February 23, Casement Park.
Connacht **3-9** 3-8 *Ulster*
March 2, Ballinasloe.
Connacht **1-11** 2-6 *Leinster*
March 17, Croke Park.
Connacht **2-9** 2-9 *Munster*
April 6, Galway, Replay.
Munster **3-13** 4-4 *Connacht*

1970

February 8, Galway.
Ulster **3-6** 2-6 *Connacht*
February 22, Croke Park.
Munster **6-14** 3-6 *Ulster*
March 17, Croke Park.
Munster **2-15** 0-9 *Leinster*

1971

February 21, Casement Park.
Connacht **4-11** 1-4 *Ulster*
February 28, Athlone.
Leinster **5-13** 4-14 *Connacht*
March 17, Croke Park.
Leinster **2-17** 2-12 *Munster*

1972

January 30, Croke Park.
Combined Universities **0-5** 1-1 *Ulster*
(Note: Abandoned owing to snow.)
February 6, Croke Park.
Combined Universities **0-14** 1-7 *Ulster*
February 20, Croke Park.
Leinster **3-12** 2-13 *Combined Universities*
February 20, Portumna.
Munster **2-10** 2-8 *Connacht*
March 17, Croke Park.
Leinster **3-12** 1-10 *Munster*

1973

January 28, Croke Park.
Combined Universities **6-13** 1-7 *Ulster*
February 18, Croke Park.
Leinster **4-13** 0-9 *Combined Universities*
February 18, Cork.
Munster **3-10** 2-7 *Connacht*
March 17, Croke Park.
Leinster **1-13** 2-8 *Munster*

1974

January 27, Croke Park.
Combined Universities **4-10** 2-7 *Ulster*
February 17, Kilkenny.
Leinster **3-13** 3-6 *Connacht*
February 17, Limerick.
Munster **5-11** 2-7 *Combined Universities*
March 18, Croke Park.
Leinster **2-15** 1-13 *Munster*

1975

February 16, Parnell Park.
Munster **4-16** 2-5 *Ulster*
February 16, Ballinasloe.
Leinster **1-11** 1-7 *Connacht*
March 17, Croke Park.
Leinster **2-9** 1-11 *Munster*

1976

February 15, Croke Park.
Leinster **6-15** 0-12 *Ulster*
February 15, Ballinasloe.
Munster **2-10** 3-6 *Connacht*
March 17, Croke Park.
Munster **4-9** 4-8 *Leinster*

1977

February 13, Enniscorthy.
Leinster 1-12 2-5 *Connacht*
February 13, Croke Park.
Munster 3-17 3-6 *Ulster*
March 17, Croke Park.
Leinster 2-17 1-13 *Munster*

1978

April 16, Páirc Uí Chaoimh.
Munster **0-20** 1-11 *Connacht*
April 23, Corrigan Park.
Leinster **3-17** 1-13 *Ulster*
May 7, Páirc Uí Chaoimh.
Munster **2-13** 1-11 *Leinster*

1979

March 11, Ballinasloe.
Connacht **4-9** 2-7 *Munster*
March 11, Croke Park
Leinster **1-19** 0-11 *Ulster*
April 1, Thurles.
Leinster **1-13** 1-9 *Connacht*

1980

February 17, Ballinsaloe.
Connacht **1-13** 1-10 *Leinster*
February 17, Croke Park.
Munster **4-16** 1-10 *Ulster*
March 17, Croke Park.
Connacht **1-5** 0-7 *Munster*

1981

March 1, Birr.
| *Leinster* | *0-11* | *0-6* | *Connacht* |

March 1, Newbridge.
| *Munster* | *5-13* | *1-8* | *Ulster* |

March 17, Ennis.
| *Munster* | *2-16* | *2-6* | *Leinster* |

1982

February 14, Galway.
| *Connacht* | *1-13* | *2-8* | *Munster* |

February 14, Casement Park.
| *Leinster* | *3-15* | *2-5* | *Ulster* |

March 17, Tullamore.
| *Connacht* | *3-8* | *2-9* | *Leinster* |

1983

February 6, Croke Park.
| *Leinster* | *3-16* | *1-8* | *Ulster* |

February 6, Limerick.
| *Connacht* | *1-9* | *0-9* | *Munster* |

March 17, Cavan.
| *Connacht* | *0-10* | *1-5* | *Leinster* |

1984

March 17, Ballinasloe.
| *Leinster* | *2-10* | *0-5* | *Connacht* |

March 17, Limerick.
| *Munster* | *3-21* | *1-7* | *Ulster* |

March 18, Ennis.
| *Munster* | *1-18* | *2-9* | *Leinster* |

1985

January 27, Birr.
| *Connacht* | *1-12* | *2-6* | *Leinster* |

January 27, Newcastle.
| *Munster* | *3-16* | *2-6* | *Ulster* |

March 18, Thurles.
| *Munster* | *3-6* | *1-11* | *Connacht* |

1986

February 16, Galway.
| *Connacht* | *1-10* | *1-9* | *Leinster* |

February 16, Croke Park.
| *Munster* | *1-19* | *0-11* | *Ulster* |

March 17, Ballinasloe.
| *Connacht* | *3-11* | *0-11* | *Munster* |

1987

October 3, Ennis.
| *Connacht* | *5-13* | *0-15* | *Ulster* |

October 3, Ennis.
| *Leinster* | *1-16* | *1-11* | *Munster* |

October 4, Ennis.
| *Connacht* | *2-14* | *1-14* | *Leinster* |

1988

October 15, Corrigan Park.
| *Connacht* | *4-13* | *2-11* | *Munster* |

October 15, Corrigan Park.
| *Leinster* | *1-13* | *1-8* | *Ulster* |

October 16, Casement Park.
| *Leinster* | *2-14* | *1-12* | *Connacht* |

1989

October 7, Wexford.
| *Munster* | *3-31* | *1-22* | *Ulster* |

October 7, Wexford.
| *Connacht* | *1-19* | *2-15* | *Leinster* |

October 8, Wexford.
| *Connacht* | *4-16* | *3-17* | *Munster* |

1990

No competition.

1991

March 10, Páirc Uí Chaoimh.
| *Munster* | *2-19* | *1-10* | *Leinster* |

March 10, Athenry.
| *Connacht* | *1-11* | *1-6* | *Ulster* |

April 7, Croke Park.
| *Connacht* | *1-13* | *0-12* | *Munster* |

1992

March 14, Kilkenny.
| *Munster* | *1-12* | *0-10* | *Leinster* |

March 14, Kilkenny.
| *Ulster* | *2-6* | *0-7* | *Connacht* |

March 15, Kilkenny.
| *Munster* | *3-12* | *1-8* | *Ulster* |

1993

October 10, Tullamore.
| *Leinster* | *3-13* | *1-9* | *Connacht* |

October 10, Casement Park.
| *Ulster* | *0-21* | *0-18* | *Munster* |

November 7.
| *Leinster* | *1-15* | *2-6* | *Ulster* |

1994

February 6, Kilkenny.
| *Leinster* | *2-17* | *0-8* | *Ulster* |

February 6, Tulla.
| *Connacht* | *1-10* | *0-9* | *Munster* |

February 20, Thurles.
| *Connacht* | *1-11* | *1-10* | *Leinster* |

1995

February 5, Ballinasloe.
| *Ulster* | *2-10* | *0-14* | *Connacht* |

February 5, Limerick.
| *Munster* | *2-25* | *5-12* | *Leinster* |

April 2, Croke Park.
| *Munster* | *0-13* | *1-9* | *Ulster* |

1996

February 25, Ballinasloe.
| *Leinster* | *2-16* | *0-18* | *Connacht* |

February 25, Ennis.
| *Munster* | *5-13* | *0-7* | *Ulster* |

March 18, Ennis.
| *Munster* | *2-20* | *0-10* | *Leinster* |

1997

November 8, Ballinasloe.
| *Leinster* | *2-16* | *1-9* | *Ulster* |

November 8, Ballinasloe.
Munster 1-19 2-15 *Connacht*
November 9, Ballinasloe.
Munster 0-14 0-10 *Leinster*

1998
November 8, Kilkenny.
Leinster 2-15 0-9 *Munster*
November 8, Corrigan Park.
Connacht 3-18 1-12 *Ulster*
November 22, Kilkenny.
Leinster 0-16 2-9 *Connacht*

1999
November 7, Casement Park.
Munster 0-29 3-14 *Ulster*
November 7, Birr.
Connacht 1-14 1-10 *Leinster*
November 25, Thurles.
Connacht 2-13 1-15 *Munster*

2000
November 11, Dicksboro.
Leinster 1-15 1-7 *Ulster*
November 11, Freshford.
Munster 1-19 3-7 *Connacht*
November 12, Nowlan Park.
Munster 3-15 2-15 *Leinster*

2001
November 10, Templemore.
Connacht 4-16 1-9 *Ulster*
November 10, Nenagh.
Munster 2-20 3-12 *Leinster*
November 11, Nenagh.
Munster 1-21 1-15 *Connacht*

2002
November 2, Nowlan Park.
Leinster 3-18 2-13 *Connacht*
November 2, Nowlan Park.
Munster 5-18 0-10 *Ulster*
November 3, Nowlan Park.
Leinster 4-15 3-17 *Munster*

2003
October 18, Limerick.
Connacht 1-20 1-16 *Munster*
October 19, Casement Park.
Leinster 5-16 2-10 *Ulster*
November 8, Rome.
Leinster 4-9 2-12 *Connacht*

2004
October 23, Casement Park.
Connacht 2-24 2-11 *Ulster*
October 24, Croke Park.
Munster 1-21 0-13 *Leinster*
December 5, Salthill.
Connacht 1-15 0-9 *Munster*

2005
October 23 Loughrea.
Leinster 1-25 0-10 *Connacht*
October 23, Casement Park.
Munster 0-25 1-13 *Ulster*
November 6, Boston.
Munster 1-21 2-14 *Leinster*

2006
October 14, Parnell Park.
Leinster 2-19 0-12 *Ulster*
October 15, Ennis.
Connacht 2-17 1-16 *Munster*
October 28, Salthill.
Leinster 1-23 0-17 *Connacht*

2007
October 13, Fermoy.
Munster 1-21 1-13 *Leinster*
October 20, Ballybofey.
Connacht 1-28 4-13 *Ulster*
October 27, Croke Park.
Munster 2-22 2-19 *Connacht*

2008
October 25, Fermoy.
Munster 2-14 1-12 *Ulster*
October 25, Kiltoom.
Leinster 2-11 1-10 *Connacht*
November 1, Portlaoise.
Leinster 1-15 1-12 *Munster*

2009
February 21, Salthill.
Connacht 2-20 2-18 *Munster*
February 21, Casement Park.
Leinster 4-14 0-8 *Ulster*
March 14, Abu Dhabi.
Leinster 3-18 1-17 *Connacht*

2010-2011 No competition

2012
February 19, Nowlan Park.
Leinster 3-14 1-16 *Munster*
February 19, Ballinasloe.
Connacht 3-19 1-15 *Ulster*
March 4, Nowlan Park.
Leinster 2-19 1-15 *Connacht*

2013
February 17, Tullamore.
Connacht 3-13 1-16 *Leinster*
February 17, Armagh.
Munster 3-20 1-14 *Ulster*
March 3, Ennis.
Munster 1-22 0-15 *Connacht*

2014
February 9, Trim.
Leinster 8-18 1-21 *Ulster*
February 9, Ballinasloe.
Connacht 1-18 0-16 *Munster*
March 1, Croke Park.
Leinster 1-23 0-16 *Connacht*

2015
No competition

2016
December 10, Nenagh
Leinster   1-14   1-12   *Connacht*
December 11, Thurles
Munster   3-21   0-15   *Ulster*
December 15, Thurles
Munster   2-20   2-16   *Leinster*

INTERPROVINCIAL HURLING FINAL TEAMS 1927-2016

1927
Leinster   Dr.T.Daly (goal), Ed.Tobin, P.McInerney, G.Howard, M.Gill, D.O'Neill, E.Fahy, Jas.Walsh, M.Power (Dublin), J.Byrne (Laois), W.Dunphy, E.Doyle, L.Meagher, J.Roberts, H.Meagher (Kilkenny).
Munster   Seán Óg Murphy, E.Coughlan, E.O'Connell, M.Murphy, J.Regan, J.Hurley, P.Aherne, M.Aherne (Cork), M.Murphy (goal), J.J.Kinnane, M.Cross, W.Gleeson (Limerick), M.D'Arcy, P.Cahill, M.Kennedy (Tipperary).

1928
Munster   Seán Óg Murphy, E.O'Connell, D.B.Murphy, J.Hurley, E.Coughlan (Cork), T.Shinny (goal), J.J.Kinnane, M.Fitzgibbon, T.Conway (Limerick), P.Cahill, M.Kennedy, J.J.Callanan, P.Purcell, M.Cronin (Tipperary), T.Considine (Clare). Sub.: M.Leahy (Cork).
Leinster   M.Gill, T.Daly (goal), P.McInerney, J.Walsh, E.Tobin, G.Howard, D.O'Neill, M.Power, E.Fahey, T.Barry (Dublin), W.Dunphy, E.Doyle, H.Meagher (Kilkenny), J.Byrne, P.Kelly (Laois).

1929
Munster   Seán Óg Murphy, D.B.Murphy, J.O'Regan, M.O'Connell, E.Coughlan, M.Aherne (Cork), T.Shinny (goal), M.Fitzgibbon, T.Conway, M.Cross (Limerick), J.J.Doyle, T.Considine (Clare), P.Purcell, P.Cahill, M.Kennedy (Tipperary). Sub: C.Keane (Tipperary) for T.Conway.
Leinster   M.Gill, G.Howard, T.Barry, P.McInerney, J.Walsh, M.Power (Dublin), R.Collins (goal) (Meath), J.Byrne, E.Tobin, D.O'Neill, J.Murphy (Laois), P.Byrne, P.Kealy, L.Meagher (Kilkenny), W.Cordial (Offaly).

1930
Munster   D.B.Murphy, J.O'Regan, J.Hurley, M.O'Connell (Cork), T.Shinny (goal), M.Cross, M.Fitzgibbon, T.Conway (Limerick), P.Cahill, P.Purcell, M.Kennedy, T.Treacy (Tipperary), J.J.Doyle, T.Considine (Clare), C.Ware (Waterford).
Leinster   W.Dunphy, P.Phelan (goal), Martin Power, P.Byrne, L.Meagher, P.Walsh (Kilkenny), T.Burke, C.McMahon, E.Byrne, Jim Walsh, M.Gill, M.Power, M.Finn, S.Tumpane (Dublin), E.Giles (Meath). Sub: P.Kelly (Laois).

1931
Munster   T.O'Meara, P.Purcell, P.Cahill, T.Treacy, M.Kennedy (Tipperary), C.Ware (Waterford), J.J.Doyle, T.Considine (Clare), P.Collins, J.Hurley, D.B.Murphy, E Coughlan, P.Aherne (Cork), M.Cross, G.Howard (Limerick).
Leinster   Jas.Walsh, John O'Dwyer (goal), P.McInerney, Chas. McMahon, T.Teehan, M.Gill, S.Tumpane, T.Quinlan, S Hegarty, M.Power (Dublin), P.Byrne, E.Doyle, P.Phelan, J.Roberts, Ecl. Byrne (Kilkenny). Subs: C.Griffin (Dublin) for T.Quinlan, J.O'Meara (Dublin) for T.Teehan.

1932
Leinster   J.Dermody (goal), P.O'Reilly, P.Larkin, P.Phelan, D.Dunne, T.Leahy, M.Power, E.Byrne (Kilkenny), T.Teehan, C.McMahon, J.Walsh, S.Hegarty, D.O'Neill (Dublin), P.Drennan, E.Tobin (Laois). Sub: Jim Grace (Kilkenny) for P.Larkin.
Munster   E.Coughlan, P.Collins, G.Garrett, W.Clancy, D.B.Murphy, M.Aherne (Cork), T.O'Meara (goal), P.Purcell, T.Treacy, P.Cahill, M.Kennedy (Tipperary), J.J.Doyle (Clare), C.Ware, P.Browne (Waterford), M.Cross (Limerick). Sub: P.Clohessy (Limerick) for P.Browne.

1933

Leinster   J.Dermody, P.Larkin, P.O'Reilly, P.Phelan, P.Byrne, E.Doyle, E.Byrne, L.Meagher, J.Walsh, D.Dunne, M.Power (Kilkenny), C.McMahon, E.Wade, J.Walsh, D.O'Neill (Dublin). Subs: Tommy Leahy and Johnny Dunne (Kilkenny) for J.Walsh (Kilkenny) and D.Dunne.

Munster   Tom Daly, J.J.Doyle, J.Houlihan, L.Blake (Clare), G.Garrett, P.Collins, D.B.Murphy, T.McCarthy, W.Clancy (Cork), T.McCarthy, P.Clohessy, Tim Ryan (Limerick), P.Purcell, M.Kennedy (Tipperary), D.Wyse (Waterford). Sub: M.Cross (Limerick) for L.Blake.

1934

Munster   P.Scanlan, E.Cregan, T.McCarthy, M.Cross, P.Clohessy, Tim Ryan, Ml.Mackey (Limerick), G.Garrett, D.B.Murphy, J.Kennealy (Cork), P.Purcell, T.Treacy, M.Kennedy (Tipperary), L.Blake (Clare), D.Wyse (Waterford).

Leinster   C.Forde, C.McMahon, Ed.Wade, S.Hegarty (Dublin), P.Larkin, P.Byrne, P.Phelan, E.Byrne, Tommy Leahy, L.Meagher, Martin Power, J.Walsh, J.Fitzpatrick, J.Dunne, Matty Power (Kilkenny). Sub: J.Cashin (Laois) for P.Larkin.

1935

Munster   T.Ryan, P.Scanlan (goal), T.McCarthy, M.Kennedy, John Mackey, M.Mackey, P.Clohessy (Limerick), C.Ware (Waterford), G.Garrett, J.Barrett, M.Brennan (Cork), L.Blake, M.Hennessy, J.Harrington (Clare), M.Kennedy (Tipperary).

Leinster   C.McMahon, C.Forde (goal), A.Murphy, D.Canniffe, S.Hegarty, E.Wade, J.O'Connell (Dublin), P.Larkin, P.Phelan, Tommy Leahy, E.Byrne, L.Meagher, Matt Power, L.Byrne, J.Dunne (Kilkenny). Subs: T.Treacy (Dublin) for D.Canniffe, J.Walsh (Kilkenny) for S.Hegarty.

1936

Leinster   J.O'Connell (goal), P.Larkin, P.Byrne, P.Blanchfield, Tommy Leahy, Ed.Byrne, P.Phelan, J.Walsh, J.Dunne, M.Power (Kilkenny), T.Teehan, D.Canniffe, C.McMahon, M.Daniels, Ed.Wade (Dublin).

Munster   P.Scanlan (goal), T.McCarthy, M.Kennedy, M.Cross, P.Clohessy, T.Ryan, J.Mackey, M.Mackey, P.McMahon (Limerick), J.Maher, P.Purcell (Tipperary), S.Barrett, M.Brennan (Cork), L.Blake, M.Hennessy (Clare). Subs: J.Cooney (Tipperary) for P.Purcell, J.Quirke (Cork) for P.Clohessy, P.Clohessy for M.Hennessy.

1937

Munster   M.Mackey, P.Scanlan (goal), T.McCarthy, M.Kennedy, P.Clohessy, T.Ryan, J.Mackey, P.McMahon (Limerick), J.Maher, J.Cooney, (Tipperary), J.Keane, C.Moylan (Waterford), J.Quirke, M.Brennan (Cork), L.Blake (Clare).

Leinster   J.O'Connell (goal), P.Larkin, P.Byrne, Tommy Leahy, E.Byrne, P.Phelan, M.White (Kilkenny), T.Teehan, C.McMahon, E.Wade, C.Downes, D.Canniffe (Dublin), A.Bergin, H.Gray, P.Farrell (Laois).

1938

Munster   J.Lanigan, J.Coffey, D.O'Gorman, W.O'Donnell (Tipperary), P.Scanlan (goal), T.McCarthy, P.Clohessy, T.Ryan, M.Mackey, J.Mackey (Limerick), J.Keane, C.Moylan (Waterford), L.Blake (Clare), S.Barrett, J.Quirke (Cork). Sub: J.Lynch (Cork) for L.Blake.

Leinster   P.Larkin, J.O'Connell (goal), W.Burke, P.Blanchfield, Terry Leahy, P.Phelan (Kilkenny), T.Teehan, P.Farrell, C.McMahon, E.Wade, P.MacCormack, M.Daniels (Dublin), J.Brophy (Kilkenny), F.Monaghan (Westmeath), W.Delaney (Laois). Subs: A.Bergin (Laois) for P.Blanchfield, C.Boland (Westmeath) for F.Monaghan.

1939

Munster   M.Curley, J.Keane, C.Moylan, L.Byrne (Waterford), P.Carroll, P.Clohessy, T.Ryan, J.Mackey, M.Mackey (Limerick), S.Barrett, M.Brennan (Cork), D.O'Gorman, E.Wade (Tipperary), T.Loughnane, J.Mullane (Clare).

Leinster   J.O'Connell, P.Larkin, W.Burke, P.Blanchfield, Terry Leahy, P.Phelan, J.Walsh (Kilkenny), M.Gill, P.Farrell, J.Byrne, H.Gray, M.McDonnell, M.Flynn, P.Doody (Dublin), F.White (Westmeath).

1940

Munster   P.Scanlan (goal), P.Clohessy, J.Power, J.Mackey, M.Mackey, P.McMahon (Limerick), W.Murphy, W.Campbell, Seán Barrett, J.Quirke, M.Brennan (Cork), G.Cornally, W.O'Donnell (Tipperary), J.Mullane (Clare), C.Moylan (Waterford). Sub: J.Keane (Waterford) for P.Clohessy.

Leinster   J.O'Connell (goal), P.Grace, W.Burke, P.Blanchfield, R.Hinks, J.Walsh, J.Langton, P.Phelan, J.Kelly, J.Phelan (Kilkenny), A.Bergin, P.Farrell (Laois), M.Gill, H.Gray, M.Brophy (Dublin). Subs: J.Byrne (Dublin) for M.Gill, F.White (Westmeath) for P.Grace, Seán O'Brien (Kilkenny) for A.Bergin.

1941

Leinster   J.O'Connell, P.Grace (Kilkenny), M.Butler (Dublin), P.Blanchfield, R.Hinks (Kilkenny), F.White (Westmeath), P.Phelan (Kilkenny), E.Wade, H.Gray, (Dublin), J.Langton (Kilkenny), P.McSweeney, M.McDonnell (Dublin), J.Mulcahy, S.O'Brien (Kilkenny), Jimmy Phelan (Kilkenny). Sub: J.Kelly (Kilkenny) for M.McDonnell.

Munster   P.Scanlan (Limerick), W.Murphy (Cork), J.Maher (Tipperary), A.Lotty, W.Campbell (Cork), J.Keane (Waterford), P.Cregan, T.Ryan (Limerick), C.Buckley (Cork), J.Power (Limerick), J.Lynch (Cork), R.Stokes (Limerick), J.Mullane (Clare), J.Quirke (Cork), P.Flanagan (Tipperary).

1942

Munster   J.McCarthy (Limerick), D.O'Gorman (Tipperary), B.Thornhill, W.Murphy (Cork), J.Ryan (Tipperary), J.Keane (Waterford), P.Cregan (Limerick), J.Lynch (Cork), C.Moylan (Waterford), W.Barron (Waterford), C.Ring (Cork), R.Stokes (Limerick), J.Quirke (Cork), W.O'Donnell (Tipperary), J.Power (Limerick).

Leinster   D.Conway (Dublin), P.Larkin (Kilkenny), Mick Butler (Dublin), P.Blanchfield (Kilkenny), F.White (Westmeath), W.Burke, P.Phelan, J.Walsh (Kilkenny), H.Gray (Dublin), J.Langton (Kilkenny), M.McDonnell, J.Byrne (Dublin), J.Mulcahy, Jimmy Phelan (Kilkenny), C.Downes (Dublin).

1943

Munster   J.Maher (Tipperary), W.Murphy, B.Thornhill (Cork), P.Cregan (Limerick), A.Fleming, J.Keane (Waterford), J.Young, J.Lynch (Cork), R.Stokes (Limerick), C.Ring (Cork), J.Power (Limerick), T.Doyle (Tipperary), J.Quirke (Cork), W.O'Donnell (Tipperary), M.Mackey (Limerick). Sub: J.Mackey (Limerick) for W.O'Donnell.

Leinster   J.Donegan (Dublin), P.Grace (Kilkenny), M.Butler (Dublin), Joe Bailey (Wexford), F.White (Dublin), W.Burke (Kilkenny), J.Byrne (Dublin), J.Kelly (Kilkenny), D.Dooley (Offaly), M.Ryan (Dublin), N.Rackard (Wexford), J.Farrell (Laois), J.Langton, J.Walsh, Jimmy Phelan (Kilkenny). Sub: Jack Phelan (Kilkenny) for W.Burke, H.Gray (Dublin) for Jack Phelan.

1944
Munster   J.Ware (Waterford), W.Murphy, B.Thornhill (Cork), P.Cregan (Limerick), A.Fleming (Waterford), J.Power (Limerick), C.Cottrell, J.Lynch, S.Condon (Cork), R.Stokes (Limerick), C.Ring, J.Young, J.Quirke (Cork), J.Mackey (Limerick), P.J.Quane (Clare).
Connacht   (All Galway). S.Duggan, P.Forde, M.Forde, P.Brogan, M.Lynch, J.Brophy, D.Flynn, P.Thornton, R.Forde, T.Ryan, M.J.Flaherty, J.Gallagher, M.Nestor, A.Brennan, M.Fennessy. Subs: R.Quinn for P.Brogan, W.Fahy for J.Gallagher.

1945
Munster   J.Ware, A.Fleming (Waterford), W.Murphy (Cork), P.Cregan (Limerick), P.O'Donovan (Cork), J.Power (Limerick), J.Young (Cork), P.McCarthy (Limerick), C.Cottrell (Cork), T.Purcell (Tipperary), C.Ring (Cork), R.Stokes (Limerick), M.Mackey (Limerick), J.Quirke (Cork), P.J.Quane (Clare).
Ulster   M.McKeown, W.Feeney (Antrim), J.Butler, E.O'Toole (Monaghan), P.McKeown (Antrim), B.Denvir (Down), M.Butler (Antrim), O.Keenan (Down), N.Campbell, D.Cormican, K.Armstrong, L.McGrady (Antrim), J.White (Down) C.Mullan, S.Mulholland (Antrim). Subs: T.McAllister (Antrim) for E.O'Toole, J.Butler (Antrim) for J.White.

1946
Munster   J.Maher (Tipperary), W.Murphy (Cork), G.Cornally (Tipperary), A.Fleming (Waterford), J.Devitt (Tipperary), P.Lyons (Clare), M.Hayes (Waterford), R.Stokes, J.Power, S.Herbert (Limerick), C.Ring, J.Young (Cork), P.Fitzgerald (Limerick), A.O'Brien (Clare), T.Doyle (Tipperary).
Connacht   (All Galway). S.Duggan, James Killeen, R.Quinn, D.Flynn, M.J.Flaherty, J.Brophy, W.Faby, John Killeen, P.Gantley, J.Gallagher, P.Jordan, S.Gallagher, M.Doyle, T.Flynn, M.Nestor. Sub: T.Doyle for M.Doyle.

1947
Connacht   (All Galway). S.Duggan, D.Flynn, P.Forde, W.FaLy, M.J.Flaherty, J.Brophy, B.Power, J.Killeen, P.Gantley, J.Gallagher, H.Gordon, P.Jordan, M.Nestor, Tadgh Kelly, S.Gallagher.
Munster   T.Mulcahy, W.Murphy (Cork), J.Keane (Waterford), P.Cregan (Limerick), M.Maher (Tipperary), A.Lotty (Cork), A.Fleming, V.Baston, M.Hayes (Waterford), C.Ring (Cork), J.Power (Limerick), J.Young, M.O'Riordan, G.O Riordan (Cork), T.Doyle (Tipperary). Subs: M.Ryan (Limerick) for M.Hayes and D.Solon (Clare for A.Lotly.

1948
Munster   T.Mulcahy, W.Murphy, C.Murphy (Cork), J.Goode (Waterford), J.Devitt (Tipperary), P.Donovan (Cork), D.Solon (Clare), V.Baston, M.Hayes (Waterford), S.Herbert, J.Power (Limerick), C.Ring (Cork), M.Daly (Clare), E.Daly (Waterford), T.Doyle (Tipperary). Subs: M.Riordan (Cork) for S.Herbert, J.Sadlier (Limerick) for D.Solon.
Leinster   R.Dowling, P.Grace, P.Hayden, M.Marnell, J.Kelly (Kilkenny), P.Brennan (Dublin), J.Mulcahy (Kilkenny), M.Hassett (Dublin), J.Heffernan, J.Langton, Terry Leahy (Kilkenny), A.Herbert (Dublin), N.Rackard (Wexford), J.Prior (Dublin), S.Downey (Kilkenny).

1949
Munster   J.Ware, A.Fleming (Waterford), C.Murphy (Cork), T.Cregan (Limerick), J.Devitt (Tipperary), P.Donovan (Cork), T.Purcell (Tipperary), V.Baston (Waterford), M.Ryan (Limerick), C.Ring (Cork), J.Keane (Waterford), S.Herbert (Limerick), M.Daly (Clare) E.Daly (Waterford), W.O'Carroll (Tipperary). Sub:P.Fitzgerald (Limerick) for W.O'Carroll.
Connacht   S.Duggan, M.Badger, R.Quinn, W.Fahy, M.McInerney, C.Corless, M.J.Flaherty, T.Boyle, J.Killeen, F.Duignan, H.Gordon, T.Moroney, Tadgh Kelly, B.Power, J.Gallagher. Sub: J.Solmon for W.Fahy.
(Note: All Galway with exception of T.Boyle (Roscommon).

1950
Munster   A.Reddan (Tipperary), A.Fleming (Waterford), G.O'Riordan (Cork), J.Sadlier (Limerick), P.Stakelum, (Tipperary), V.Baston (Waterford), M.Fouhy (Cork), S.Bannon, P.Shanahan, J.Kennedy, M.Ryan, S.Kenny (Tipperary), M.Riordan (Cork), W.McAllister (Clare), C.Ring (Cork).
Leinster   T.Fitzpatrick (Laois), S.Cronin (Dublin), P.Hayden, M.Marnell (Kilkenny), J.Kelly (Kilkenny), T.Byrne (Laois), R.Rackard (Wexford), J.Styles (Laois), W.Walsh (Kilkenny), A.Dunne (Laois), A.Herbert (Dublin), J.Langton, S.Downey (Kilkenny), N.Rackard (Wexford), L.Reidy (Kilkenny). Subs: P.Prendergast (Kilkenny) for J.Murray, M.Lyons (Dublin) for N.Rackard.

1951
Munster   A.Reddan (Tipperary), A.Fleming, D.Walsh (Waterford), D.McInerney (Clare), S.Bannon, P.Stakelum (Tipperary), J.Goode (Waterford), M.Fouhy (Cork), S.Kenny (Tipperary), M.Nugent (Clare), M.Ryan (Tipperary), E.Stokes (Limerick), P.Kenny (Tipperary), D.McCarthy (Limerick), C.Ring (Cork). Subs: John Doyle for D.McInerney, P.Shanahan (Tipperary) for S.Kenny, W.J.Daly (Cork) for M.Ryan.
Leinster   R.Dowling (Kilkenny), S.Cronin (Dublin), P.Hayden, M.Marnell (Kilkenny), R.Rackard (Wexford), P.Prendergast, W.Walsh, D.Kennedy (Kilkenny), J.Morrissey, Padge Kehoe (Wexford), J.Prior (Dublin), J.Langton, S.Downey (Kilkenny), N.Rackard, T.Flood (Wexford). Subs.: N.Allen for D.Kennedy, P.Donnelly (Dublin) for W.Walsh, J.Hogan (Kilkenny) for S.Cronin, D.Kennedy for N.Allen.

1952
Munster   A.Reddan (Tipperary), J.Goode, D.Walsh (Waterford), J.Doyle (Tipperary), S.Herbert (Limerick), P.Stakelum (Tipperary), M.Fouhy (Cork), P.Shanahan (Tipperary), J.Kiely (Waterford), M.Nugent (Clare), M.Ryan, S.Bannon, P.Kenny (Tipperary), D.McCarthy (Limerick), C.Ring (Cork).
Connacht   (All Galway). S.Duggan, C.Corless, F.Flynn, J.Brophy, J.Molloy, Tadgh Kelly, H.Gordon, J.Salmon, J.Killeen, F.Duignan, M.Burke, P.Nolan, P.Manton, M.J.Flaherty, J.Gallagher. Subs: T.Moroney for F.Flynn, M.Glynn for F.Dulgnan.

1953
Munster   A.Reddan (Tipperary), J.Goode (Waterford), J.Doyle (Tipperary), A.O'Shaughnessy (Cork), S.Herbert (Limerick), P.Stakelum (Tipperary), D.O'Grady (Clare), G.Murphy (Cork), P.Shanahan (Tipperary), M.Nugent (Clare), W.J.Daly (Cork), S.Bannon, P.Kenny (Tipperary), D.McCarthy (Limerick), C.Ring (Cork). Subs: M.Queally (Waterford) for A.O'Shaughnessy, P.Barry (Cork) for C.Ring.

Leinster K.Matthews (Dublin), J.Hogan, P.Hayden, M.Marnell (Kilkenny), D.Ferguson (Dublin), R.Rackard (Wexford), W.Walsh (Kilkenny), C.Murphy, N.Allen (Dublin), Paddy Kehoe, E.Wheeler (Wexford), T.Maher (Laois), M.Kelly (Kilkenny), N.Rackard, T.Flood (Wexford). Subs: W.Rackard (Wexford) for Tim Maher, Jim Prior (Dublin) for M.Kelly.

1954
Leinster K.Matthews (Dublin), J.Hogan, P.Hayden (Kilkenny), M.Hanlon (Wexford), P.Buggy (Kilkenny), E.Wheeler (Wexford), J.McGovern (Kilkenny), N.Allen (Dublin), J.Sutton (Kilkenny), M.Ryan (Dublin), D.Carroll (Kilkenny), T.Flood (Wexford), J.Langton, P.Fitzgerald, M.Kelly (Kilkenny). Subs: J.Morrissey for M.Ryan, W.Rackard (Wexford) for M.Hanlon.
Munster A.Reddan (Tipperary), G.O'Riordan, J.Lyons (Cork), J.Doyle, J.Finn, P.Stakelum (Tipperary), M.Fouhy (Cork), J.Hough (Tipperary), J.Kiely (Waterford), W.J.Daly (Cork), J.Hartnett (Cork), S.Bannon (Tipperary), J.Smith (Clare), D.McCarthy (Limerick), C.Ring (Cork).

1955
Munster A.Reddan (Tipperary), G.O'Riordan, J.Lyons (Cork), J.Doyle, P.Stakelum (Tipperary), D.O'Grady (Clare), V.Twomey (Cork), J.Smith (Clare), J.Hough (Tipperary), W.J.Daly (Cork), D.Dillon (Clare), J.Hartnett (Cork), S.Power (Waterford), J.Greene (Clare), C.Ring (Cork).
Connacht (All Galway). T.Boland, F.Spillane, B.Power, H.Gordon, M.Murphy, W.Duffy, Tommy Kelly, J.Salmon, J.Duggan, P.Duggan, E.Monahan, M.Cullinane, P.Manton, M.Elwood, J.Fives. Subs: S.Cullinane for Boland, T.Glynn for Murphy.

1956
Leinster A.Foley (Wexford), D.Ferguson (Dublin), N.O'Donnell, R.Rackard, J.English, W.Rackard (Wexford), W.Walsh (Kilkenny), J.Morrissey (Wexford), J.McGrath (Westmeath), S.Clohosey (Kilkenny), E.Wheeler, T.Flood (Wexford), L.Cashin (Dublin), N.Rackard (Wexford), R.Rockett (Kilkenny). Sub: S.Hearne (Wexford) for McGrath.
Munster A.Reddan, M.Byrne (Tipperary), J.Lyons, A.O'Shaughnessy, V.Twomey (Cork), J.Finn, J.Doyle, P.Stakelum (Tipperary), J.O'Connor (Waterford), J.Carney (Clare), D.Kelly (Limerick), J.Smith (Clare), S.Power (Waterford), J.Hartnett, C.Ring (Cork). Sub: T.Casey (Limerick) for O'Shaughnessy.

1957
Munster M.Cashman, J.Brohan, J.Lyons, A.O'Shaughnessy (Cork), M.O'Connor (Waterford), J.Finn (Tipperary), P.Philpott (Cork), M.Ryan (Tipperary), J.O'Connor (Waterford), D.Kelly (Limerick), T.Kelly (Cork), F.Walsh (Waterford), P.Kenny (Tipperary), C.Ring, P.Barry (Cork).
Leinster A.Foley, R.Rackard, N.O'Donnell (Wexford), D.Ferguson (Dublin), J.English, W.Rackard (Wexford), J.McGovern, W.Walsh (Kilkenny), E.Wheeler (Wexford), S.Clohosey, M.Kenny (Kilkenny), T.Flood (Wexford), R.Rockett (Kilkenny), N.Rackard (Wexford), W.Dwyer (Kilkenny). Subs: O.Walsh (Kilkenny) for Foley, L.Cashin (Dublin) for Rockett.

1958
Munster M.Cashman (Cork), J.Finn (Tipperary), J.Lyons (Cork), J.Barron (Waterford), T.McGarry (Limerick), M.Óg Morrissey (Waterford), A.Wall (Tipperary), S.Power, P.Grimes (Waterford), J.Smith (Clare), L.Moloney (Limerick), J.Doyle (Tipperary), P.Barry, C.Ring (Cork), D.Whelan (Waterford). Subs: M.Maher (Tipperary) for Finn, T.Cheasty (Waterford) for Moloney.

Leinster O.Walsh (Kilkenny), N.Drumgoole (Dublin), N.O'Donnell (Wexford), J.Maher (Kilkenny), J.English (Wexford), P.Buggy, J.McGovern, M.Brophy, J.Sutton, D.Heaslip (Kilkenny), E.Wheeler (Wexford), C.O'Brien (Laois), M.Kenny, W.Dwyer, S.Clohosey (Kilkenny). Sub:W.Rackard (Wexford) for Buggy.

1959
Munster M.Cashman, J.Brohan (Cork), M.Maher (Tipperary), J.Barron (Waterford), T.McGarry (Limerick), A.Wall (Tipperary), M.Óg Morrisey (Waterford), T.English (Tipperary), T.Casey (Limerick), D.Nealon (Tipperary), S.Power (Waterford), J.Doyle (Tipperary), J.Smith (Clare), C.Ring (Cork), L.Guinan (Waterford). Sub: T.Kelly (Cork) for Power.
Connacht (All Galway). F.Benson, R.Stanley, P.Burke, S.Cullinane, J.Duggan, J.Fives, M.Sweeney, Tommy Kelly, P.J.Lally, T.Sweeney, P.J.Lawless, S.Gohery, P.Egan, T.Conway, M.Fox. Subs: J.Lyons for Fives, G.Cahill for Kelly.

1960
Munster M.Cashman, J.Brohan (Cork), A.Flynn, J.Barron (Waterford), T.McGarry (Limerick), M.Óg Morrissey (Waterford), John Doyle (Tipperary), S.Power, P.Grimes (Waterford), Jimmy Doyle (Tipperary), T.Cheasty, F.Walsh (Waterford), J.Smith (Clare). C.Ring, P.Barry (Cork). Sub: D.Kelly (Limerick) for McGarry.
Leinster O.Walsh, T.Walsh (Kilkenny), N.O'Donnell (Wexford), P.Croke (Dublin), J.English (Wexford), M.Bohan (Dublin), J.McGovern (Kilkenny), L.Shannon (Dublin), E.Wheeler (Wexford), D.Heaslip, S.Clohosey (Kilkenny), Padge Kehoe (Wexford), C.O'Brien (Laois), W.Dwyer, T.O'Connell (Kilkenny). Subs: J.Byrne (Dublin) for O'Connell, R.Carroll (Kilkenny) for Byrne.

1961
Munster M.Cashman, J.Brohan (Cork), M.Maher (Tipperary), J.Barron (Waterford), T.McGarry (Limerick), A.Wall (Tipperary), M.Morrissey (Waterford), T.English (Tipperary), S.Power (Waterford), Jimmy Doyle (Tipperary), T.Kelly (Cork), F.Walsh (Waterford), J.Smith (Clare), C.Ring (Cork), L.Devaney {Tipperary). Subs: T.Cheasty (Waterford) for Ring, P.Duggan (Cork) for Morrissey.
Leinster O.Walsh, T.Walsh (Kilkenny), N.O'Donnell, T.Neville, J.English, E.Wheeler, J.Nolan (Wexford), D.Foley (Dublin), S.Clohosey (Kilkenny), J.O'Brien, Padge Kehoe (Wexford), E.Keher (Kilkenny), O.McGrath (Wexford), W.Dwyer (Kilkenny), T.Flood (Wexford). Subs: M.Walsh (Kilkenny) for Keher, S.Quaid (Wexford) for Dwyer, O.Fennell (Laois) for Clohosey.

1962
Leinster O.Walsh (Kilkenny), D.Ferguson, N.Drumgoole, L.Foley (Dublin), J.English, W.Rackard (Wexford), O.Fennell (Laois), D.Foley, M.Kennedy, A.Boothman (Dublin), C.O'Brien (Laois), F.Whelan (Dublin), O.McGrath (Wexford), W.Dwyer (Kilkenny), W.Jackson (Dublin). Sub: D.Heaslip (Kilkenny) for Jackson.
Munster M.Cashman, J.Brohan (Cork), M.Maher, K.Carey (Tipperary), J.O'Sullivan (Cork), M.Óg Morrissey (Waterford), M.Burns, T.English, L.Devaney, Jimmy Doyle (Tipperary), T.Kelly (Cork), D.Nealon (Tipperary), J.Smith (Clare), C.Ring (Cork), S.Power (Waterford). Subs: P.J.Keane (Limerick) for Kelly, A.Wall (Tipperary) for English, F.Walsh (Waterford) for Devaney.

1963 REPLAY

Munster   M.Cashman, J.Brohan (Cork), M.Maher, John Doyle (Tipperary), T.McGarry (Limerick), A.Wall (Tipperary) J, J.Byrne (Waterford), P.J.Keane (Lirnerick), J.Condon (Waterford), Jimmy Doyle (Tipperary), T.Cheasty (Waterford), D.Nealon (Tipperary), J.Smith (Clare), C.Ring (Cork), L.Devaney (Tipperary). Subs: F.Walsh (Waterford) for Ring, T.English (Tipperary) for Walsh.
(Note: T.English (Tipperary) played in drawn game. T.Cheasty came on for replay. M.Burns and Tom Ryan (Tipperary) came on as subs in drawn game for T.English and D.Nealon.)

Leinster   O.Walsh (Kilkenny), T.Neville (Wexford), J.Walsh (Kilkenny), L.Foley (Dublin), S.Cleere (Kilkenny), W.Rackard, J.Nolan (Wexford), D.Foley (Dublin), P.Wilson, J.O'Brien (Wexford), C.O'Brien (Laois), F.Whelan (Dublin), W.Hogan (Carlow), E.Wheeler (Wexford), D.Heaslip (Kilkenny). Subs: J.English (Wexford) for Cleere, E.Keher (Kilkenny) for Hogan, O.McGrath (Wexford) for Heaslip.
(Note: E.Keher (Kilkenny) and M.Kennedy (Dublin) played in drawn game. P.Wilson and J.O'Brien came on for replay. Subs in drawn game: O.McGrath (Wexford) for W.Hogan, O.Fennell (Laois) for M.Coogan (Kilkenny), M.Coogan for M.Kennedy.)

1964

Leinster   O.Walsh (Kilkenny), T.Neville, D.Quigley (Wexford), L.Foley (Dublin), S.Cleere (Kilkenny), W.Rackard (Wexford), O.Fennell (Laois), P.Wilson (Wexford), P.Moran (Kilkenny), F.Whelan (Dublin), E.Wheeler (Wexford), E.Keher, T.Walsh (Kilkenny), C.O'Brien (Laois), M.Bermingham (Dublin).
Subs: M.Coogan (Kilkenny) for Fennell, Martin Hogan (Carlow) for Foley, D.Foley (Dublin) for Bermingham.
Munster   J.Hogan (Limerick), John Doyle (Tipperary), A.Flynn (Waterford), D.Murphy (Cork), L.Guinan (Waterford), A.Wall (Tipperary), P.Fitzgerald, J.O'Sullivan (Cork), T.English, Jimmy Doyle (Tipperary), T.Cunningham (Waterford), P.Cronin (Clare), L.Devaney (Tipperary), J.Smith (Clare), P.Grimes (Waterford). Sub: A.O'Brien (Limerick) for Wall.

1965

Leinster   O.Walsh (Kilkenny), T.Neville (Wexford), P.Dillon (Kilkenny), E.Colfer (Wexford), S.Cleere, T.Carroll (Kilkenny), P.Molloy (Offaly), P.Wilson (Wexford), P.Moran (Kilkenny), J.O'Brien (Wexford), D.Foley (Dublin), E.Keher, T.Walsh (Kilkenny), C.O'Brien (Laois), M.Bermingham (Dublin).
Munster   J.O'Donoghue, John Doyle (Tipperary), A.Flynn (Waterford), K.Carey (Tipperary), L.Guinan (Waterford), A.Wall (Tipperary), P.Fitzgerald (Cork), T.English, M.Roche, Jimmy Doyle (Tipperary), P.J.Keane (Limerick), M.Keating (Tipperary), J.Bennett (Cork), L.Devaney, S.McLoughlin (Tipperary). Subs: N.Gallagher (Cork) for English, K.Long (Limerick) for Carey.

1966

Munster   E.Power (Waterford), A.O'Brien (Limerick), A.Flynn (Waterford), D.Murphy, D.O'Riordan (Cork), A.Wall (Tipperary) L.Guinan (Waterford), M.Roche (Tipperary), B.Hartigan (Limerick), L.Danaher (Clare), L.Kiely (Tipperary), F.Walsh (Waterford), D.Nealon, J.McKenna, S.McLoughlin (Tipperary). Subs: P.Fitzgerald (Cork) for O'Riordan, L.Devaney (Tipperary), for Danagher, P.Cronin (Clare) for Nealon.
Leinster   O.Walsh (Kilkenny), T.Neville (Wexford), J.Lynch (Kilkenny), E.Colfer (Wexford), S.Cleere (Kilkenny), D.Quigley, W.Murphy (Wexford), B.Cooney (Dublin), P.Molloy (Offaly), W.Walsh (Carlow), T.Forrestal, E.Keher, T.Walsh, P.Dillon (Kilkenny), J.O'Brien (Wexford). Subs: P.Moran (Kilkenny) for Quigley, J.Foley (Wexford) for Molloy.

1967

Leinster   O.Walsh (Kilkenny), D.Quigley, T.Neville, E.Colfer (Wexford), S.Cleere, P.Henderson, M.Coogan, P.Moran (Kilkenny), H.Dalton (Dublin), E.Keher, J.Teehan, C.Dunne (Kilkenny), P.Molloy (Offaly), J.Bennett, T.Walsh (Kilkenny). Subs: N.Kinsella (Dublin) for Teehan, M.Browne (Wexford) for Dunne.
Munster   P.Barry (Cork), V.Loftus (Clare), A.Flynn (Waterford), D.Murphy (Cork), A.O'Brien, K.Long (Limerick), P.Fitzgerald (Cork), M.Roche (Tipperary), B.Hartigan (Limerick), S.Barry, J.O'Halloran (Cork), P.Cronin (Clare), D.Nealon, J.McKenna (Tipperary), T.Bluett (Limerick).

1968

Munster   M.Foley (Waterford), P.Doolan, T.O'Donoghue (Cork), N.O'Gorman (Tipperary), A.O'Brien (Limerick), J.Cullinane (Clare), L.Gaynor, M.Roche (Tipperary), J.McCarthy (Cork), B.Hartigan (Limerick), L.Guinan (Waterford), E.Cregan (Limerick), S.Barry (Cork), M.Keating, D.Nealon (Tipperary). Subs: C.McCarthy (Cork) for Nealon, P.Cronin (Clare) for Cregan.
Leinster   O.Walsh (Kilkenny), D.Quigley (Wexford), P.Dillon, J.Treacy, S.Cleere, P.Henderson (Kilkenny), W.Murphy (Wexford), P.Moran (Kilkenny), D.Foley (Dublin), E.Keher, C.Dunne (Kilkenny), P.Wilson, J.O'Brien, T.Doran (Wexford), P.Molloy (Offaly). Subs: P.Lynch (Wexford) for Wilson, T.Carroll (Kilkenny) for Murphy.

1969 REPLAY

Munster   J.O'Donoghue (Tipperary), A.O'Brien (Limerick), T.O'Donoghue, D.Murphy (Cork), J.Cullinane (Clare), J.McCarthy (Cork), L.Gaynor, P.J.Ryan (Tipperary), E.Cregan (Limerick), N.Pyne (Clare), N.O'Dwyer, G.McCarthy (Cork), Jimmy Doyle (Tipperary), C.Cullinane (Cork), J.Flanagan (Tipperary).
(Note: J.Kirwan (Waterford) and N.O'Gorman (Tipperary) played in drawn game. N.Pyne (Clare) and C.Cullinane (Cork) came on for replay. C.Cullinane came on a sub in drawn game for E.Cregan.)
Connacht   (All Galway unless stated). A.Gavin, M.Howley, T.Bohan, S.Francis, M.Burke (Sligo), M.McTigue, T.Murphy, J.Connolly, S.Stanley, P.Fahy, B.O'Connor, P.Mitchell, W.Murphy (Sligo), M.O'Connor, D.Coen. Subs: B.Mitchell (Roscommon) for P.Mitchell, C.Muldoon for W.Murphy.
(Note: B.Mitchell (Roscommon) played in drawn game. P.Fahy on for replay.)

1970

Munster   J.O'Donoghue (Tipperary), A.Maher (Cork), M.Considine (Clare), J.O'Brien (Limerick), D.Clifford (Cork), M.Roche, L.Gaynor (Tipperary), G.McCarthy (Cork), B.Hartigan (Limerick), N.O'Dwyer (Tipperary), W.Walsh (Cork), P.Enright (Waterford), Jimmy Doyle (Tipperary), R.Cummins (Cork), M.Keating (Tipperary). Sub: A.O'Brien (Limerick) for Roche.
Leinster   O.Walsh, T.Carroll, P.Dillon (Kilkenny), P.Spellman (Offaly), P.Henderson (Kilkenny), D.Quigley (Wexford), M.Coogan, P.Moran (Kilkenny), D.Haniffy, J.J.Healion (Offaly), P.Wilson (Wexford), E.Keher (Kilkenny), P.Molloy (Offaly), L.Lawlor (Dublin), T.Doran (Wexford). Subs: P.Delaney (Kilkenny) for Healion, F.Cummins (Kilkenny) for Haniffy.

1971

Leinster   P.Nolan, D.Quigley, P.Kavanagh (Wexford), J.Treacy (Kilkenny), M.Browne (Wexford), P.Dunny (Kildare), H.Dalton (Dublin), D.Bernie (Wexford), F.Cummins (Kilkenny), J.Quigley (Wexford), P.Delaney, E.Keher, J.Millea (Kilkenny), T.Doran (Wexford), M.Bermingham (Dublin). Subs: D.Martin (Offaly) for Nolan, P.Henderson (Kilkenny) for Dunny.

Munster P.O'Brien (Clare), A.Maher (Cork), J.Kelly (Tipperary), J.Horgan, C.Roche (Cork), M.Roche, L.Gaynor (Tipperary), B.Hartigan (Limerick), P.J.Ryan, F.Loughnane, N.O'Dwyer (Tipperary), P.Hegarty (Cork), J.Flanagan (Tipperary), R.Cummins (Cork), E.Cregan (Limerick). Subs: G.McCarthy (Cork) for P.J.Ryan; Ryan for Loughnane.

1972

Leinster D.Martin (Offaly), P.Larkin, P.Dillon, J.Treacy (Kilkenny), M.Browne (Wexford), P.Dunny (Kildare), M.Coogan, F.Cummins (Kilkenny), H.Dalton (Dublin), B.Moylan (Offaly), P.Delaney, E.Keher, Mick Brennan (Kilkenny), T.Doran (Wexford), K.Purcell (Kilkenny). Sub: M.Bermingham (Dublin) for Brennan, P.Wilson (Wexford) for Dalton.

Munster P.O'Sullivan, L.King (Tipperary), P.Hartigan, J.O'Brien (Limerick), C.Roche (Cork), J.Kirwan (Waterford), J.O'Gorman (Clare), M.Roche (Tipperary), S.Foley (Limerick), F.Loughnane, N.O'Dwyer (Tipperary), P.Hegarty (Cork), E.Grimes (Limerick), R.Ryan (Tipperary), E.Cregan (Limerick). Subs: J.Flanagan (Tipperary) for Grimes, C.McCarthy (Cork) for Hegarty.

1973

Leinster N.Skehan (Kilkenny), T.O'Connor (Wexford), P.Horan (Offaly), J.Treacy, P.Lawlor, P.Henderson (Kilkenny), M.Mahon (Laois), F.Cummins (Kilkenny), M.Jacob, M.Quigley (Wexford), P.Delaney, K.Purcell (Kilkenny), M.Bermingham (Dublin), T.Doran (Wexford), E.Keher (Kilkenny). Sub: L.O'Brien (Kilkenny) for Cummins, B.Moylan (Offaly) for Bermingham.

Munster S.Durack (Clare), A.Maher (Cork), P.Hartigan (Limerick), J.Gleeson (Tipperary), S.Foley (Limerick), T.O'Connor, L.Gaynor (Tipperary), D.Coughlan (Cork), E.Grimes (Limerick), F.Loughnane, J.Flanagan, N.O'Dwyer (Tipperary), M.Malone, R.Cummins, S.O'Leary (Cork). Subs: J.O'Brien (Limerick) for Grimes, C.McCarthy (Cork) for N.O'Dwyer.

1974

Leinster N.Skehan, P.Larkin (Kilkenny), P.Horan (Offaly), P.Dunny (Kildare), P.Lawlor, P.Henderson (Kilkenny), C.Doran, C.Kehoe (Wexford), F.Cummins (Kilkenny), M.Quigley (Wexford), P.Delaney (Kilkenny), P.Quigley (Dublin), K.Purcell (Kilkenny), T.Doran (Wexford), E.Keher (Kilkenny).

Munster S.Durack (Clare), B.Murphy (Cork), P.Hartigan, J.O'Brien (Limerick), T.O'Connor (Tipperary), E.Cregan (Limerick), C.Roche (Cork), S.Hogan {Tipperary}, S.Foley (Limerick), F.Loughnane (Tipperary), A.Heffernan (Waterford), E.Grimes, L.O'Donoghue, E.Rea, F.Nolan (Limerick). Subs: G.McCarthy (Cork) for Heffernan, M.Hickey {Waterford} for Nolan, P.McGrath (Waterford) for Rea.

1975

Leinster N.Skehan, P.Larkin (Kilkenny), P.Horan (Offaly), P.Dunny (Kildare), P.Lawlor, P.Henderson (Kilkenny), M.Jacob (Wexford), L.O'Brien, F.Cummins (Kilkenny), M.Quigley (Wexford), P.Delaney (Kilkenny), P.Quigley (Dublin), K.Purcell (Kilkenny), T.Doran (Wexford), E.Keher (Kilkenny). Subs: C.Doran (Wexford) for Jacob, J.Quigley (Wexford) for P.Quigley.

Munster S.Durack (Clare), L.King (Tipperary), P.Hartigan (Limerick), S.Hannon (Waterford), G.Loughnane (Clare), E.Cregan (Limerick), P.McGrath (Waterford), G.McCarthy (Cork), S.Hogan, F.Loughnane, N.O'Dwyer, J.Kehoe (Tipperary), E.O'Connor (Clare), W.Walsh (Cork), J.McKenna (Limerick). Sub: J.Barry-Murphy (Cork) for McKenna.

1976

Munster S.Shinnors (Tipperary), P.McDonnell (Cork), P.Hartigan (Limerick), S.Hannon (Waterford), T.O'Connor, N.O'Dwyer (Tipperary), P McGrath (Waterford), G.McCarthy (Cork), J.McKenna (Limerick), F.Loughnane (Tipperary), M.Hickey (Waterford), J.Callinan (Clare), L.O'Donoghue (Limerick), R.Cummins, E.O'Donoghue (Cork). Sub: G.Loughnane (Clare) for O'Connor.

Leinster N.Skehan, P.Larkin (Kilkenny), P.Horan (Offaly), P.Dunny (Kildare), P.Lalor, P.Henderson (Kilkenny), C.Doran, M.Quigley (Wexford), F.Cummins, M.Crotty, M.Ruth (Kilkenny), J.Quigley (Wexford), Mick Brennan (Kilkenny), T.Doran (Wexford), E.Keher (Kilkenny). Subs: B.Cody (Kilkenny) for Dunny. M.Holden (Dublin) for J.Quigley.

1977

Leinster J.Nolan (Wexford), P.Larkin (Kilkenny), W.Murphy (Wexford), P.Henderson, P.Lawlor (Kilkenny), M.Jacob, C.Doran (Wexford), F.Cummins (Kilkenny), N.Buggy (Wexford), L.O'Brien (Kilkenny), M.Quigley (Wexford), M.Ruth, Mick Brennan (Kilkenny), T.Doran (Wexford), E.Keher (Kilkenny).

Munster S.Durack (Clare), N.Cashin (Waterford), P.Hartigan (Limerick), J.Horgan (Cork), G.Loughnane (Clare), N.O'Dwyer (Tipperary), D.Coughlan, G.McCarthy, P.Moylan (Cork), E.O'Connor (Clare), J.Kehoe (Tipperary), J.Callinan (Clare), L.O'Donoghue (Limerick), N.Casey (Clare), P.Moriarty (Kerry). Subs: C.Honan (Clare) for Moriarty, M.Hickey (Waterford) for O'Donoghue.

1978

Munster S.Durack (Clare), N.Cashin (Waterford), M.Doherty, J.Horgan (Cork), G.Loughnane (Clare), P.Hartigan (Limerick), P.McGrath (Waterford), J.Callinan (Clare), T.Cashman (Cork), T.Butler (Tipperary), G.McCarthy (Cork), C.Honan (Clare), C.McCarthy (Cork), J.McKenna (Limerick), N.Casey (Clare).

Leinster N.Skehan, P.Larkin, R.O'Hara (Kilkenny), W.Murphy (Wexford), G.Henderson (Kilkenny), M.Jacob, C.Doran E.Buggy (Wexford), F.Cummins (Kilkenny), M.Walsh (Laois), M.Quigley, M.Butler (Wexford), W.Fitzpatrick (Kilkenny), T.Doran (Wexford), M.Ruth (Kilkenny). Subs: L.O'Brien (Kilkenny) for M.Butler, C.Keogh (Wexford) for M.Ruth.

1979

Leinster N.Skehan.P.Larkin (Kilkenny), W.Murphy, J.Prendergast (Wexford), J.Hennessy (Kilkenny), P.Carton (Dublin), C.Doran (Wexford), G.Henderson (Kilkenny) P.Quirke (Carlow), J.Kelly (Offaly), M.Holden (Dublin), M.Walsh (Laois), W.Fitzpatrick (Kilkenny), T.Doran (Wexford), E.Buggy (Wexford).

Connacht (all Galway, except where stated) F.Larkin, N.McInerney, J.McDonagh, J.Lucas, J.Greaney, C.Hayes, Jimmy Cooney, S.Mahon, John Connolly, N.Lane, Joe Connolly, P.J.Molloy, A.Fenton, F.Gantley, J.Henry (Mayo). Subs: M.Coen for Molloy, F.Burke for Gantley, Molloy for Lucas.

1980

Connacht (all Galway), S.Shinnors, N.McInerney, C.Hayes, Jimmy Cooney, S.Linnane, S.Silke, I.Clarke, S.Mahon John Connolly, M.Kilkenny, Joe Connolly, P.J.Molloy, N.Lane, G.Curtin, F.Gantley.

Munster P.McLoughney (Tipperary), B.Murphy (Cork), J.Keogh, T.O'Connor (Tipperary), D.McCurtain (Cork), M.Carroll (Limerick), G.Loughnane (Clare), T.Cashman (Cork), P.McGrath, M.Walsh (Waterford), J.McKenna (Limerick), J.Callinan (Clare), J.Barry Murphy, R.Cummins (Cork), P.O'Connor (Clare.). Subs: O.O'Connor (Limerick) for Barry Murphy, E.O'Donoghue (Cork) for P.O'Connor, T.Crowley (Cork) for McGrath.

1981

Munster P.McLoughney (Tipperary), G.Loughnane (Clare), B.Murphy (Cork), T.O'Connor (Tipperary), D.McCurtain (Cork), S.Hehir (Clare), L.O'Donoghue (Limerick), J.Fenton, T.Cashman (Cork), J.Callinan (Clare), P.Horgan (Cork), M.Walsh (Waterford), E.O'Donoghue (Cork), J.McKenna, E.Cregan (Limerick). Subs: O.O'Connor (Limerick) for E.O'Donoghue, T.Crowley (Cork) for O'Connor.

Leinster N.Skehan (Kilkenny), C.Doran (Wexford), E.Coughlan, P.Fleury (Offaly), P.Carton (Dublin), P.Delaney (Offaly), C.Jones (Laois), J.Murphy (Wexford), J.Kelly, M.Corrigan (Offaly), P.Quirke (Carlow), P.Carroll (Offaly), Martin Cuddy (Laois), P.Horan (Offaly), M.Walsh (Laois). Sub: J.Hennessy (Kilkenny) for M.Walsh.

1982

Connacht (All Galway except where stated): D.Synnott (Mayo), S.Coen, N.McInerney, J.McDonagh, S.Linnane, S.Silke, I.Clarke, M.Connolly, S.Mahon, J.Henry (Mayo), Joe Connolly, P.Piggott, F.Gantley, B.Lynskey, P.J.Molloy. Subs.Jimmy Cooney for McDonagh, B.Forde for Gantley, N.Lane or Piggott.

Leinster J.Nolan, L.Bennett (Wexford), J.Bohane (Laois) P.Fleury, A.Fogarty, P.Delaney (Offaly), J.Hennessy (Kilkenny), G.O'Connor (Wexford), G.Henderson (Kilkenny), M.Brophy (Laois), B.Bermingham, M.Corrigan, P.Carroll (Offaly), P.J.Cuddy (Laois), W.Fitzpatrick (Kilkenny).

1983

Connacht (all Galway, except where stated). D.Synnott (Mayo), N.McInerney, C.Hayes, S.Coen, S.Linnane, S.Mahon, J.McDonagh, M.Connolly, I.Clarke, A.Staunton, F.Burke, B.Lynskey, B.Forde, N.Lane.P.J.Molloy.

Leinster N.Skehan, J.Henderson (Kilkenny), E.Coughlan (Offaly), L.Bennett (Wexford), A.Fogarty, P.Delaney (Offaly), G.Henderson, G.Fennelly (Kilkenny), J.Kelly, P.Carroll (Offaly), M.Cuddy (Laois), L.Fennelly, W.Fitzpatrick, C.Heffernan (Kilkenny), S.Kinsella (Wexford). Subs: F.Cummins (Kilkenny) for G.Fennelly, J.Conran (Wexford) for Delaney.

1984

Munster G.Cunningham (Cork), S.Hehir (Clare), L.Enright, P.Herbert, L.O'Donoghue (Limerick), S.Stack (Clare) P.Ryan (Waterford), J.Fenton (Cork), J.Carroll (Limerick), N.English (Tipperary), D.Fitzgerald (Limerick), B.Ryan (Tipperary), K.Hennessy (Cork), J.McKenna (Limerick), G.McInerney (Clare). Sub: T.Mulcahy (Cork) for Hennessy.

Leinster N.Skehan, J.Henderson (Kilkenny), E.Coughlan, P.Fleury (Offaly), J.Conran (Wexford), P.Delaney (Laois), A.Fogarty (Offaly), F.Cummins, J.Hennessy (Kilkenny), P.Critchley, M.Cuddy (Laois), G.Fennelly (Kilkenny), P.J.Cuddy (Laois), C.Heffernan, W.Fitzpatrick (Kilkenny). Subs: P.Courtney (Wexford) for Critchley, M.Cosgrove (Westmeath) for Fitzpatrick.

1985

Munster G.Cunningham, (Cork), S.Hehir (Clare), L.Enright, P.Herbert (Limerick), T.Cashman (Cork), S.Stack (Clare), D.MacCurtain (Cork), J.Carroll (Limerick), P.Hartnett (Cork), N.English, D.O'Connell (Tipperary), J.Fenton, T.Mulcahy, K.Hennessy, A.O'Sullivan (Cork). Subs: J.Callinan (Clare) for A.O'Sullivan, S.Power for D.O'Connell, R.Ryan (Tipperary) for N.English.

Connacht (All Galway): P.Murphy, P.Finnerty, C.Hayes, S.Linnane, T.Keady, M.Mooney, Ollie Kilkenny, S.Mahon, T.Kilkenny, M.Haverty, P.Piggott, Joe Cooney, M.McGrath, N.Lane, A.Cunningham. Subs: A.Staunton for A.Kilkenny, B.Forde for M.McGrath.

1986

Connacht (all Galway) P.Murphy, A.Kilkenny, C.Hayes, S.Linnane, P.Finnerty, T.Keady, A.Kilkenny, P.Malone, S.Mahon, M.McGrath, A.Cunningham, Joe Cooney, P.J.Molloy, M.Connolly, N.Lane.

Munster G.Cunningham (Cork), P.Fitzmaurice (Limerick), D.Mulcahy (Cork), T.Keane (Clare), D.Foran (Woterford), J.Carroll (Limerick), B.Ryan (Tipperary), J.Fenton, P.Hartnett (Cork), N.English (Tipperary), K.Hennessy (Cork), C.Lyons (Clare), D.Fitzgerald, P.McCarthy (Limerick), D.O'Connell (Tipperary). Subs: P.Kelly for K.Hennessy, L.O'Donoghue (Limerick) for D.Foran.

1987

Connacht (all Galway) J.Commins, S.Linnane, C.Hayes, O.Kilkenny, P.Malone, P.Piggott, T.Monaghan, S.Mahon, A.Kilkenny, M.Naughton, A.Cunningham, Joe Cooney, M.McGrath, B.Lynskey, E.Ryan. Subs: P.J.Molloy for Naughton: N.Lane for Mahon.

Leinster J.Troy (Offaly), J.Bohane (Laois), P.Prendergast (Kilkenny), J.Henderson (Kilkenny), B.Keeshan (Offaly), G.Henderson (Kilkenny), J.Taylor (Laois), G.Fennelly (Kilkenny), J.Kelly (Offaly) P.Critchley (Laois), B.Byrne (Wexford), L.Ryan (Kilkenny), P.Cleary (Offaly), H.Ryan (Kilkenny), D.Fogarty (Offaly). Subs: R.Power (Kilkenny) for Kelly; T.Dempsey (Wexford) for B.Byrne.

1988

Leinster J.Troy (Offaly), E.Cleary (Wexford), A.Fogarty (Offaly), J.Henderson (Kilkenny), J.O'Connor (Wexford), M.Cleere (Kilkenny), J.Power (Kilkenny), L.Ryan (Kilkenny), S.Dalton (Dublin), V.Teehan (Offaly), B.McMahon (Dublin), M.Corrigan (Offaly), P.J.Cuddy (Laois), C.Heffernan (Kilkenny), D.Kilcoyne (Westmeath).

Connacht (all Galway)—J.Commins, S.Linnane, C.Hayes, M.Helebert, R.Duane, B.Lynskey, T.Monaghan, P.Malone, Joe Cooney, M.Connolly (Craughwell), A.Cunningham, M.Naughton, M.McGrath, E.Dervan, G.Burke, Subs: P.Nolan for Burke.

1989

Connacht (all Galway)—J.Commins, D.Fahy, S.Treacy, S.Dolphin, P.Finnerty, M.Coleman, P.Higgins, J.Hardiman, T.Monaghan, A.Cunningham, J.Cooney, M.Kenny, G.Burke, S.Dolan, E.Ryan. Subs: P.Malone for Hardiman R.Duane for Monaghan.

Munster T.Quaid (Limerick), G.Fitzpatrick (Waterford), C.O'Donovan (Tipperary), J.Heffernan (Tipperary); Conal Bonnar (Tipperary), L.O'Connor (Waterford), B.Finn (Limerick), S.Ahearne (Waterford), A.O'Sullivan (Cork), S.Fitzgibbon (Limerick), G.Kirby (Limerick), M.Cleary (Tipperary), T.Guilfoyle (Clare), Cormac Bonnar (Tipperary), N.English (Tipperary). Subs: C.Stakelum (Tipperary) for O'Sullivan, Colm Bonnar (Tipperary) for Fitzpatrick.

1990

No Competition

1991

Connacht (all Galway)—R.Burke, B.Dervan, P.Finnerty, D.Fahy, A.Keady, M.Coleman, G.Keane, A.Cunningham, P.Malone, M.McGrath, J.Cooney, M.Naughton, G.Burke, B.Lyaskey, J.Rabbitte. Subs: D.Curley for Burke, P.Higgins for Cunningham.

HURLING

Munster G.Cunningham (Cork), D.Byrne (Waterford), P.Carey (Limerick), J.O'Connell (Clare), J.Cashman (Cork), D.Ryan (Tipperary), B.Ryan (Tipperary), M.Houlihan (Limerick) G.Hegarty (Limerick); C.Carey (Limerick), T.Guilfoyle (Clare), J.Leahy (Tipperary), B.O'Sullivan (Waterford), G.Fitzgerald (Cork), M.Cleary (Tipperary). Subs: C.Casey (Cork) for Hegarty, Conal Bonnar (Tipperary) for Cashman, C.Stakelum (Tipperary) for Guilfoyle.

1992
Munster G.Cunningham (Cork), D.Byrne (Waterford), N.Sheehy (Tipperary), P.Delaney (Tipperary), J.O'Connell (Clare), J.Cashman (Cork), D.Walsh (Cork), M.Houlihan (Limerick), D.Carr (Tipperary), M.Cleary (Tipperary), J.Leahy (Tipperary), A.Ryan (Tipperary), B.O'Sullivan (Waterford), G.Kirby (Limerick), C.Carey (Limerick). Subs: C.Walsh (Kerry) for Leahy, B.Ryan (Tipperary) for Delaney, L.Garvey (Limerick) for Cleary.
Ulster P.Gallagher (Antrim), K.Coulter (Down), D.McKinley (Antrim), P.Braniff (Down), M.Mallon (Down), P.Jennings (Antrim), P.McMullan (Down), D.Hughes (Down), C.Mageen (Down), J.Carson (Antrim), A.McCarry (Antnm), S.Downey (Derry), O.McFetridge (Antrim), C.Barr (Antrim), N.Sands (Down). Subs: N.Keith (Down) for Gallagher, M.Baillie (Down) for Carson, G.O'Kane (Antrim) for Coulter, D.McKillop (Antrim) for McCorry.

1993
Leinster J.Troy (Offaly), M.Hanamy (Offaly), C.Duggan (Laois), L.Simpson (Kilkenny), L.Dunne (Wexford), P.O'Neill (Kilkenny), W.O'Connor (Kilkenny), L.O'Gorman (Wexford), M.Phelan (Kilkenny), M.Storey (Wexford), J.Power (Kilkenny), P.Potterton (Meath), E.Morrissey (Kilkenny), D.J.Carey (Kilkenny), A.Ronan (Kilkenny). Sub: T.Dempsey (Wexford) for Storey.
Ulster N.Keith (Down), S.McMullen (Antrim), G.Coulter (Down), P.Branniff (Down), M.Mallon (Down), D.McKinley (Antrim), R.Donnelly (Antrim), P.McKillen (Antrim), C.Mageen (Down), P.O'Prey (Down), Gary O'Kane (Antrim), J.Carson (Antrim), A.Elliott (Antrim), M.Bailie (Down), N.Sands (Down). Sub: S.P.McKillop (Antrim) for Bailie.

1994
Connacht (all Galway)—R.Burke, P.Cooney, S.Treacy, D.Fahy, N.Power, G.McInerney, M.Donoghue, M.Coleman, P.Malone, F.Forde, N.Shaughnessy, B.Keogh, L.Turley, J.Rabbitte, L.Burke. Sub: D.Colemon for Forde.
Leinster J.Troy (Offaly), E.O'Connor (Kilkenny), C.Duggan (Laois), L.Simpson (Kilkenny), L.O'Gorman (Wexford), B.Maher (Laois), L.Keoghan (Kilkenny), T.Dempsey (Wexford), M.Phelan (Kilkenny), M.Storey (Wexford), J.Power (Kilkenny), Johnny Dooley (Offaly), D.J.Carey (Kilkenny), E.Morrissey (Kilkenny), P.Potterton (Meath) Sub: A.Ronan (Kilkenny) for Dooley.

1995
Munster J.Quaid (Limerick), S.McDonagh (Limerick), M.Nash (Limerick), A.Daly (Clare), D.Clarke (Limerick), M.Ryan (Tipperary), D.Nash (Limerick), Colm Bonnar (Tipperary), C.Carey (Limerick), M.Cleary (Tipperary), A.Browne (Waterford), B.Egan (Cork), K.Murray (Cork), G.Kirby (Limerick), D.Quigley (Limerick). Subs: P.Flynn (Waterford) for Browne, J.O'Connor (Clare) for Quigley, J.Brenner (Waterford) for Egan.
Ulster N.Keith (Down), K.Coulter (Down), O.Colgan (Antrim), P.Brannif (Down), M.Mallon (Down), G.Savage (Down), S.P.McKillop (Antrim), P.McKillen (Antrim), C.McCambridge (Antrim), T.McNaughton (Antrim), O.Collins (Derry), D.O'Prey (Down), V.Owens (Tyrone), H.Gilmore (Down), N.Sands (Down). Subs: B.Coulter (Down) for Owens, R.Donnelly (Antrim) for Gilmore.

1996
Munster D.Fitzgerald (Clare), S.McDonagh (Limerick), B.Lohan (Clare), D.Nash (Limerick), A.Browne (Waterford), S.McMahon (Clare), A.Daly (Clare), O.Baker (Clare), C.Carey (Limerick), M.Cleary (Tipperary), D.Ryan (Tipperary), T.Dunne (Tipperary), J.O'Connor (Clare), G.Kirby (Limerick), D.Quigley (Limerick). Subs: L.Doyle (Clare) for McDonagh, B.Corcoran for Dunne, G.Manley (Cork) for Cleary.
Leinster D.Hughes (Offaly), B.Maher (Laois), K.Kinahan (Offaly), M.Hanamy (Offaly), B.Whelahan (Offaly), L.Dunne (Wexford), N.Rigney (Laois), A.Fenlon (Wexford), D.Conroy (Laois), Joe Dooley (Offaly), J.Power (Kilkenny), D.J.Carey (Kilkenny), E.Morrissey (Dublin), J.Troy (Offaly), D.Byrne (Kilkenny). Subs: S.Power (Dublin) for Kinahan, L.Keoghan (Kilkenny) for Conroy, D.Martin (Meath) for Power.

1997
Munster D.Fitzgerald (Clare), S.McDonagh (Limerick), B.Lohan (Clare), M.Ryan (Tipperary), D.Clarke (Limerick), L.Doyle (Clare), A.Browne (Waterford), O.Moran (Limerick), C.Lynch (Clare), T.Dunne (Tipperary), K.McGrath (Waterford), M.Galligan (Limerick), M.Cleary (Tipperary), N.Gilligan (Clare), S.McGrath (Cork). Subs: C.Bonnar (Tipperary) for Moran, D.Forde (Clare) for Cleary.
Leinster R.Cashin (Laois), B.Maher (Laois), S.Power (Dublin), L.Simpson (Kilkenny), N.Rigney (Laois), C.Byrne (Kildare), R.Boland (Dublin), A.Comerford (Kilkenny), O.Dowling (Laois), Johnny Dooley (Offaly), D.Rooney (Laois), C.McCann (Dublin), R.McCarthy (Wexford), C.Brennan (Kilkenny), C.Carter (Kilkenny). Subs: G.Ennis (Dublin) for McCann, C.Cassidy (Offaly) for Byrne, John Troy (Offaly) for Rooney.

1998
Leinster S.Byrne (Offaly), S.Whelahan (Offaly), J.Errity (Offaly), W.O'Connor (Kilkenny), L.Walsh (Dublin), B.Whelahan (Offaly), L.Keoghan (Kilkenny), L.O'Gorman (Wexford), A.Fenlon (Wexford), D.Cuddy (Laois), M.Storey (Wexford), B.McEvoy (Kilkenny), D.J.Carey (Kilkenny), John Troy (Offaly), C.Carter (Kilkenny). Subs: N.Rigney (Laois) for Walsh, N.Moloney (Kilkenny) for O'Gorman.
Connacht (all Galway except where stated)—K.Devine, G.Kennedy, B.Feeney, V.Maher, R.Walsh, N.Shaughnessy, P.Hardiman, T.Kavanagh, M.Cunniffe (Roscommon), J.Rabbitte, C.Moore, N.Kenny, O.Fahy, A.Kelly (Roscommon), K.Broderick. Sub: A.Kerins for Cunniffe.

1999
Connacht (all Galway): M.Crimmins, L.Hodgins, B.Feeney, C.Moore, P.Walsh, N.Larkin, P.Hardiman, R.Gantley, A.Kerins, O.Fahy, J.Rabbitte, O.Canning, E.Cloonan, M.Kerins, K.Broderick.
Munster B.Cummins (Tipperary), F.Ryan (Cork), D.O'Sullivan (Cork), B.Corcoran (Cork), L.Doyle (Clare), O.Moran (Limerick), S.Óg Ó hAilpín (Cork), M.O'Connell (Cork), T.Dunne (Tipperary), A.Markham (Clare), F.McCormack (Cork), K.McGrath (Waterford), L.Cahill (Tipperary), N.Gilligan (Clare), S.McGrath (Cork). Subs: D.Shanahan (Waterford) for T.Dunne, D.Kennedy (Tipperary) for B.Corcoran.

2000
Munster B.Cummins (Tipperary), F.Ryan, D.O'Sullivan (Cork), B.Lohan (Clare), J.Carroll (Tipperary), O.Moran (Limerick), E.Corcoran (Tipperary), P.Queally (Waterford), J.Leahy (Tipperary), A.Markham (Clare), A.Browne (Cork), B.O'Meara (Tipperary), S.McGrath (Cork), P.Flynn (Waterford), J.Deane (Cork). Subs: T.J.Ryan (Limerick) for Markham, D.Barrett (Cork) for Queally, D.Forde (Clare) for Flynn.

Leinster J.McGarry, M.Kavanagh (Kilkenny), K.Kinahan (Offaly), W.O'Connor (Kilkenny), B.Whelahan (Offaly), L.Dunne (Wexford), P.Barry, A.Comerford (Kilkenny), A.Fenlon (Wexford), G.Hanniffy (Offaly), J.Power (Kilkenny), N.Horan (Meath), C.Carter, D.J.Carey, H.Shefflin (Kilkenny). Subs: E.Kennedy (Kilkenny) for Dunne, L.Murphy (Wexford) for Horan, P.Larkin (Kilkenny) for Fenlon.

2001

Munster B.Cummins (Tipperary), T.J.Ryan (Limerick), P.Maher (Tipperary), F.Lohan (Clare), D.Reale, O.Moran (Limerick), P.Kelly (Tipperary), C.Carey (Limerick), P.Queally (Waterford), D.Forde (Clare), K.McGrath (Waterford), S.McGrath (Cork), E.Kelly (Tipperary), A.Browne (Cork), N.Gilligan (Clare). Subs: D.Barrett (Cork) for Queally, Queally for Barrett, B.O'Meara (Tipperary) for S.McGrath, N.Ronan (Cork) for Forde.
Connacht (all Galway) – L.Donoghue, G.Kennedy, M.Healy, C.Moore, P.Walsh, L.Hodgins, D.Hardiman, R.Murray, A.Kerins, N.Hayes, M.Kerins, K.Broderick, D.Coen, O.Fahy, F.Healy. Subs: B.Higgins for Walsh, J.Culkin for Murray, D.Hayes for Healy.

2002

Leinster J.McGarry, M.Kavanagh, N.Hickey (Kilkenny), D.O'Connor (Wexford), R.Mullally, J.J.Delaney (Kilkenny), L.Ryan (Dublin), D.Lyng, A.Comerford, J.Hoyne, H.Shefflin (Kilkenny), C.Keaney (Dublin), J.Coogan, E.Brennan (Kilkenny), B.Murphy (Offaly). Subs: S.Byrne (Offaly) for McGarry, C.Kehoe (Wexford) for O'Connor.
Munster B.Cummins, (Tipperary), B.Greene (Waterford), D.O'Sullivan (Cork), P.Maher (Tipperary), D.Hoey (Clare), E.Corcoran (Tipperary), S.Óg Ó hAilpín (Cork), P.Queally (Waterford), T.Dunne (Tipperary), T.Griffin (Clare), K.McGrath (Waterford), B.O'Connor (Cork), E.McGrath (Waterford), B.Begley (Limerick), J.Deane (Cork). Subs: D.Reale (Limerick) for Greene, A.O'Shaughnessy (Limerick) for Deane, O.Moran (Limerick) for O'Sullivan, E.Kelly (Waterford) for Begley, P.O'Connell (Kerry) for Hoey.

2003

Leinster J.McGarry, M.Kavanagh, N.Hickey (Kilkenny), D.Franks (Offaly), L.Dunne (Wexford), B.Whelahan (Offaly), S.Hiney, C.Keaney (Dublin), D.Lyng, T.Walsh, J.Hoyne (Kilkenny), R.Hanniffy (Offaly), R.Jacob (Wexford), H.Shefflin (Kilkenny), B.Carroll (Offaly). Subs: G.Hanniffy (Offaly) for Jacob, B.Murphy (Offaly) for Carroll, D.O'Connor (Wexford) for Franks, P.Cuddy (Laois) for Whelahan.
Connacht (all Galway) – L.Donoghue, D.Joyce, D.Cloonan, F.Moore, F.Healy, T.Óg Regan, D.Tierney, O.Canning, J.Conroy, A.Kerins, M.Kerins, K.Broderick, D.Forde, E.Cloonan, R.Gantley. Sub: R.Murray for Regan.

2004

Connacht (all Galway) L.Donoghue, D.Joyce, S.Kavanagh, O.Canning, F.Healy, L.Hodgins, F.Moore, D.Collins, D.Tierney, A.Kerins, M.Kerins, K.Broderick, D.Hayes, O.Fahy, D.Donoghue. Subs: T.Óg Regan for Hodgins, G.Farragher for Collins, N.Healy for A.Kerins, K.Higgins for D.Donoghue.
Munster B.Cummins, P.Curran, P.Maher (Tipperary), J.Murray (Waterford), E.Corcoran (Tipperary), R.Curran, J.Gardiner (Cork), T.Browne (Waterford), O.Moran (Limerick), D.Shanahan (Waterford), N.Gilligan (Clare), N.Moran (Limerick), J.Mullane (Waterford), E.Kelly, (Tipperary), J.Deane (Cork). Subs: C.Lynch (Clare) for Browne, K.Murphy (Cork) for Deane, P.O'Brien (Tipperary) for Gilligan.

2005

Munster D.Fitzgerald (Clare), E.Murphy (Waterford), P.Curran (Tipperary), P.Mulcahy (Cork), J.Gardiner (Cork), R.Curran (Cork), D.Fitzgerald (Tipperary), O.Moran (Limerick), P.Kelly (Tipperary), E.Kelly (Waterford), S.Prendergast (Waterford), D.McMahon (Clare), B.O'Connor (Cork), M.Webster (Tipperary), N.Gilligan (Clare). Subs: A.Markham (Clare) for Murphy, D.Óg Cusack (Cork) for Fitzgerald, S.Butler (Tipperary) for Webster, T.Carmody (Clare) for Prendergast.
Leinster J.McGarry (Kilkenny), R.Mullally (Kilkenny), D.Ryan (Wexford), J.Tennyson (Kilkenny), R.Hanniffy (Offaly), D.Ruth (Wexford), J.J.Delaney (Kilkenny), J.Ryall (Kilkenny), B.Barry (Kilkenny), T.Walsh (Kilkenny), R.Power (Kilkenny), J.Young (Laois), E.Brennan (Kilkenny), G.Hanniffy (Offaly), B.Carroll (Offaly). Subs: B.Murphy (Offaly) for Ryall, J.Hoyne (Kilkenny) for Power, M.Comerford (Kilkenny) for Murphy, D.Lyng (Wexford) for Barry, E.Quigley (Wexford) for Carroll.

2006

Leinster B.Mullins (Offaly), R.Mullally (Kilkenny), J.Tennyson (Kilkenny), J.Ryall (Kilkenny), Diarmuid Lyng (Wexford), R.Hanniffy (Offaly), T.Walsh (Kilkenny), Derek Lyng (Kilkenny), G.Hanniffy (Offaly), E.Larkin (Kilkenny), R.Power (Kilkenny), D.Franks (Offaly), E.Brennan (Kilkenny), J.Bergin (Offaly), A.Fogarty (Kilkenny). Subs: M.Jacob (Wexford) for Franks, M.Travers (Wexford) for Mullally, D.McCormack (Westmeath) for Diarmuid Lyng, J.Young (Laois) for Derek Lyng, J.McCormack (Dublin) for Larkin.
Connacht (all Galway) L.Donoghue, D.Joyce, G.Mahon, T.Óg Regan, D.Collins, D.Cloonan, J.Lee, R.Murray, D.Tierney, I.Tannian, M.Kerins, A.Kerins, K.Burke, E.Cloonan, F.Healy. Subs: D.Hayes for Burke, M.J.Quinn for Mahon, N.Healy for A.Kerins, K.Broderick for Murray, G.Farragher for M.Kerins.

2007

Munster B.Murray (Limerick), E.Murphy (Waterford), D.Fanning (Tipperary), G.Quinn (Clare), J.Gardiner (Cork), T.Browne (Waterford), S.Hickey (Limerick), D.O'Grady (Limerick), B.O'Connell (Clare), S.McGrath (Tipperary), O.Moran (Limerick), E.Kelly (Waterford) J.Mullane (Waterford), D.Shanahan (Waterford), L.Corbett (Tipperary). Subs: S.Óg Ó hAilpín (Cork) for O'Connell, N.Gilligan (Clare) for McGrath, G.O'Grady (Tipperary) for Murphy, N.Moran (Limerick) for O.Moran, M.O'Brien (Limerick) for Shanahan.
Connacht (all Galway) J.Skehill, F.Moore, C.Dervan, G.Mahon, D.Collins, J.Lee, A.Keary, F.Healy, R.Murray, A.Kerins, I.Tannian, S.Glynn, D.Hayes, N.Healy, A.Callanan. Subs: D.Joyce for Collins, T.Óg Regan for Mahon, K.Hynes for Glynn, K.Higgins (Mayo) for A.Kerins, G.Kennedy for Moore.

2008

Leinster P.J.Ryan (Kilkenny), J.Dalton (Kilkenny), J.Tyrrell (Kilkenny), D.Franks (Offaly), T.Walsh (Kilkenny), R.Fallon (Dublin), J.O'Connor (Wexford), R.Hanniffy (Offaly), E.Coady (Carlow), M.Rice (Kilkenny), B.Murtagh (Westmeath), E.Larkin (Kilkenny), E.Brennan (Kilkenny), R.Power (Kilkenny), R.Hogan (Kilkenny). Subs: B.Hogan (Kilkenny), A.Fogarty (Kilkenny), D.Horan (Offaly), T.Fitzgerald (Laois).
Munster B.Cummins (Tipperary), C.O'Brien (Tipperary), P.Curran (Tipperary), S.Hickey (Limerick), J.Gardiner (Cork), G.Quinn (Clare), S.Óg Ó hAilpín (Cork), T.Kenny (Cork), B.O'Connell (Clare), P.Kelly (Tipperary), T.Carmody (Clare), B.O'Connor (Cork), A.O'Shaughnessy (Limerick), E.Kelly (Waterford), N.Gilligan (Clare). Subs: D.Óg Cusack (Cork), L.Corbett (Tipperary), D.Fanning (Tipperary), S.Callanan (Tipperary).

2009

Leinster   P.J.Ryan (Kilkenny), D.Franks (Offaly), D.Kenny (Offaly), J.Tyrrell (Kilkenny), T.Walsh (Kilkenny), J.J.Delaney (Kilkenny), M.Jacob (Wexford), R.Hanniffy (Offaly), E.Quigley (Wexford), M.Rice (Kilkenny), H.Shefflin (Kilkenny), D.Lyng (Wexford), D.O'Callaghan (Dublin), J.Bergin (Offaly), E.Brennan (Kilkenny). Subs: A.Fogarty (Kilkenny) for O'Callaghan, S.Hiney (Dublin) for Tyrrell, C.Farrell (Wexford) for Hanniffy, A.McCrabbe (Dublin) for Rice, S.Clynch (Meath) for Lyng.
Connacht   (all Galway unless stated) C.Callanan, M.Ryan, G.McLearn, C.O'Donovan, A.Coen, B.Costello, G.Mahon, A.Cullinane, K.Raymond (Sligo), P.Killilea, M.Kerins, K.Hooban, N.Healy, R.Murray, A.Callanan. Subs: B.Burke for O'Donovan, C.Donnellan for Killilea, F.Healy for Raymond, J.Gantley for Hooban, M.Keaveney (Roscommon) for Mahon.

2012

Leinster   G.Maguire (Dublin), P.Murphy (Kilkenny), K.Rossiter (Wexford), J.Tyrrell (Kilkenny), T.Walsh (Kilkenny), N.Corcoran (Dublin), R.Hanniffy (Offaly), M.Rice (Kilkenny), M.Fennelly (Kilkenny), R.Power (Kilkenny), J.Bergin (Offaly), E.Larkin (Kilkenny), S.Dooley (Offaly), R.O'Dwyer (Dublin), T.J.Reid (Kilkenny). Subs: D.Herity (Kilkenny) for Maguire, B.Murtagh (Westmeath) for O'Dwyer, P.Ryan (Dublin) for Reid, R.Jacob (Wexford) for Dooley, D.Kenny (Offaly) for Corcoran.
Connacht   (all Galway) J.Ryan, P.Shiel, D.Collins, G.O'Halloran, N.Donoghue, F.Moore, J.Cooney, A.Harte, J.Grealish, J.Coen, C.Cooney, I.Tannian, B.Burke, B.Daly, D.Burke. Subs: P.Gordon for Grealish, D.Hayes for Coen, J.Regan for Tannian, D.Glennon for Daly, K.Raymond for Donoghue.

2013

Munster   A.Nash (Cork), S.O'Neill (Cork), T.Condon (Limerick), S.Daniels (Waterford), B.Bugler (Clare), M.Walsh (Waterford), W.McNamara (Limerick), S.O'Sullivan (Waterford), B.Maher (Tipperary), S.Dowling (Limerick), L.Corbett (Tipperary), P.Cronin (Cork), G.Mulcahy (Limerick), P.O'Sullivan (Cork), P.Horgan (Cork). Subs: E.Kelly (Tipperary) for Cronin, T.Kenny (Cork) for O'Sullivan, P.Maher (Tipperary) for Dowling, C.Ryan (Clare) for Corbett, G.O'Mahony (Limerick) for McNamara.
Connacht   (all Galway) C.Callanan, J.Coen, K.Hynes, P.Killeen, B.Flaherty, D.Collins, N.Donoghue, I.Tannian, A.Smith, P.Brehony, N.Burke, C.Donnellan, N.Healy, J.Canning, T.Haran. Subs: D.Glennon for Brehony, J.Glynn for Burke, J.Cooney for Killeen, D.Hayes for Haran, A.Harte for Smith.

2014

Leinster   G.Maguire (Dublin), P.Murphy (Kilkenny), P.Kelly (Dublin), A.Shore (Wexford), T.Walsh (Kilkenny), L.Chin (Wexford), L.Rushe (Dublin), M.Carton (Dublin), R.Hogan (Kilkenny), C.Keaney (Dublin), R.O'Dwyer (Dublin), E.Larkin (Kilkenny), W.Walsh (Kilkenny), D.Currams (Offaly), C.Fennelly (Kilkenny). Subs: M.Hanlon (Wexford) for Shore, T.J.Reid (Kilkenny) for W.Walsh, L.Ryan (Kilkenny) for Carton, J.Guiney (Wexford) for Currams, J.Bergin (Offaly) for Guiney, J.McCaffrey (Dublin) for O'Dwyer.
Connacht   (all Galway) J.Skehill, D.Collins, S.Kavanagh, F.Moore, A.Harte, I.Tannian, D.Burke, D.Burke, P.Brehony, J.Coen, C.Cooney, J.Flynn, R.Commins, N.Healy, C.Mannion. Subs: K.Hynes for Tannian, D.Dolan for Commins, B.Flaherty for Harte, P.Lamders for Flynn, G.McInerney for Coen.

2016

Munster   D.Gleeson (Tipperary), B.Coughlan (Waterford), J.Barry (Tipperary), N.Connors (Waterford), D.Byrnes (Limerick), C.Dillon (Clare), P.Maher (Tipperary), B.Maher (Tipperary), J.Barron (Waterford), D.McCormack (Tipperary), M.Breen (Tipperary), Shane Bennett (Waterford), J.O'Dwyer (Tipperary), S.Callanan (Tipperary), D.Reidy (Clare). Subs: N.McGrath (Tipperary) for Shane Bennett, A.Cadogan (Cork) for B.Maher, B.Nash (Limerick) for McCormack, S.Dowling (Limerick) for O'Dwyer, A.Shanagher (Clare) for Breen, Stephen Bennett (Waterford) for Barron, S.Fives (Waterford) for Coughlan, T.Murnane (Kerry) for Dillon, C.Lynch (Limerick) for Callanan.
Leinster   J.Dempsey (Offaly), M.Whelan (Laois), T.Doyle (Westmeath), L.Ryan (Wexford), P.Walsh (Kilkenny), K.Joyce (Kilkenny), C.Crummey (Dublin), C.Fogarty (Kilkenny), S.Ryan (Offaly), W.Walsh (Kilkenny), L.Chin (Wexford), C.Dwyer (Laois), S.Dooley (Offaly), T.J.Reid (Kilkenny), G.Keegan (Kildare). Subs: M.Kavanagh (Carlow) for Dooley, E.Murphy (Kilkenny) for Keegan, Keegan for S.Ryan.

CAPTAINS OF WINNING INTERPROVINCIAL HURLING TEAMS

1927	Watty Dunphy (Kilkenny)
1928	Seán Óg Murphy (Cork)
1929	Seán Óg Murphy (Cork)
1930	Dinny Barry Murphy (Cork)
1931	Philip Purcell (Tipperary)
1932	Jim Dermody (Kilkenny)
1933	Eddie Doyle (Kilkenny)
1934	Timmy Ryan (Limerick)
1935	Timmy Ryan (Limerick)
1936	Paddy Larkin (Kilkenny)
1937	Mick Mackey (Limerick)
1938	Jim Lanigan (Tipperary)
1939	John Keane (Waterford)
1940	Seán Barret (Cork)
1941	Bobby Hinks (Kilkenny)
1942	Willie O'Donnell (Tipperary)
1943	Jack Lynch (Cork)
1944	Seán Condon (Cork)
1945	Johnny Quirke (Cork)
1946	Ger Cornally (Tipperary)
1947	Seán Duggan (Galway)
1948	Willie Murphy (Cork)
1949	Jim Ware (Waterford)
1950	Pat Stakelum (Tipperary)
1951	Sean Kenny (Tipperary)
1952	Pat Stakelum (Tipperary)
1953	Christy Ring (Cork)
1954	Johnny McGovern (Kilkenny)
1955	Christy Ring (Cork)
1956	Nick O'Donnell (Wexford)
1957	Mick Cashman (Cork)
1958	Phil Grimes (Waterford)
1959	Tony Wall (Tipperary)
1960	Frankie Walsh (Waterford)
1961	Tony Wall (Tipperary)
1962	Noel Dromgoole (Dublin)
1963	Jimmy Doyle (Tipperary)
1964	Seamus Cleere (Kilkenny)
1965	Paddy Moran (Kilkenny)
1966	Jimmy Doyle (Tipperary)
1967	Ollie Walsh (Kilkenny)
1968	Mick Roche (Tipperary)
1969	Len Gaynor (Tipperary)
1970	Gerald McCarthy (Cork)
1971	Tony Doran (Wexford)
1972	Jim Treacy (Kilkenny)
1973	Pat Delaney (Kilkenny)
1974	Pat Henderson (Kilkenny)
1975	Pat Delaney (Kilkenny)
1976	Eamon O'Donoghue (Cork)
1977	Tony Doran (Wexford)
1978	Charlie McCarthy (Cork)
1979	Phil "Fan" Larkin (Kilkenny)
1980	Joe Connolly (Galway)
1981	Joe McKenna (Limerick)
1982	Seán Silke (Galway)
1983	Sylvie Linnane (Galway)
1984	John Fenton (Cork)
1985	Ger Cunningham (Cork)
1986	Noel Lane (Galway)
1987	Conor Hayes (Galway)
1988	Aidan Fogarty (Offaly)
1989	Joe Cooney (Galway)
1990	No competition
1991	Pete Finnerty (Galway)
1992	Declan Carr (Tipperary)
1993	John Power (Kilkenny)
1994	Michael Coleman (Galway)
1995	Gary Kirby (Limerick)
1996	Anthony Daly (Clare)
1997	Brian Lohan (Clare)
1998	Willie O'Connor (Kilkenny)
1999	Brian Feeney (Galway)
2000	Fergal Ryan (Cork)
2001	Brendan Cummins (Tipperary)
2002	Andy Comerford (Kilkenny)
2003	Michael Kavanagh (Kilkenny)
2004	Ollie Fahy (Galway)
2005	John Gardiner (Cork)
2006	Eddie Brennan (Kilkenny)
2007	John Mullane (Waterford)
2008	Tommy Walsh (Kilkenny)
2009	Henry Shefflin (Kilkenny
2010	No competition
2011	No competition
2012	Jackie Tyrrell (Kilkenny)
2013	Brendan Maher (Tipperary)
2014	Conal Keaney (Dublin)
2015	No competition
2016	Brendan Maher (Tipperary)

OIREACHTAS TOURNAMENT

1939 Croke Park, November 5. Final:
Limerick 4-4   2-5   *Kilkenny*

1940 Croke Park, October 27. Final:
Kilkenny 7-11   1-6   *Cork*

1941-1943 Run as football tournament.

1941 Dublin 3-3   2-6   *Kildare*
Newbridge, Replay
Dublin 1-8   1-5   *Kildare*

1942 Dublin 1-6   1-3   *Cavan*

1943 Roscommon 1-6   0-6   *Cavan*

1944 Dublin 6-6   3-6   *Galway*

1945 Croke Park, October 21. Final:
Tipperary 4-6   4-3   *Galway*

1946 Croke Park. Final:
Antrim 2-7   0-10   *Laois*

1947 Croke Park, November 23. Final:
Kilkenny 2-12   2-6   *Galway*

1948 Croke Park, October 17. Final:
Dublin 3-6   2-6   *Waterford*

1949 Croke Park, October 16. Final:
Tipperary 2-8   1-6   *Laois*

1950 Croke Park, October 15. Final:
Galway 2-9   2-6   *Wexford*

1951 Croke Park, October 21. Final:
Wexford 4-7   3-7   *Kilkenny*

1952 Croke Park, October 19. Final:
Galway 3-7   1-10   *Wexford*

1953 Croke Park, October 25. Final:
Wexford 5-11   4-5   *Clare*

1954 Croke Park, October 24. Final:
Clare 2-8   2-8   *Wexford*
Croke Park, November 21. Replay:
Clare 3-6   0-12   *Wexford*

1955 Croke Park, October 23. Final:
Wexford 3-11   3-4   *Kilkenny*

1956 Croke Park, October 21. Final:
Wexford 0-16   1-9   *Kilkenny*

1957 Croke Park, October 20. Final:
Kilkenny 4-10   3-5   *Waterford*

1958 Thurles, October 19: Final:
Galway 5-16   2-4   *Wexford*

1959 Croke Park, October 18. Final:
Kilkenny 6-6   5-8   *Galway*

1960 Croke Park, October 23. Final:
Tipperary 4-11   2-10   *Cork*

1961 Croke Park, October 22. Final:
Tipperary 3-6   2-9   *Wexford*
Croke Park, November 5. Replay:
Tipperary 2-13   3-4   *Wexford*

1962 Croke Park, October 21. Final:
Waterford 4-12   3-9   *Tipperary*

1963 Croke Park, October 20. Final:
Tipperary 4-15   3-12   *Wexford*

1964 Croke Park, October 18. Final:
Tipperary 5-7   4-8   *Kilkenny*

1965 Croke Park, October 18. Final:
Tipperary 2-12   2-7   *Kilkenny*

1966 Croke Park, December 4. Final:
Kilkenny 4-7   1-7   *Wexford*

1967 Croke Park, October 17. Final:
Kilkenny 4-4   1-8   *Clare*

1968 Thurles, October 27. Final:
Tipperary 1-9   1-6   *Cork*

1969 Croke Park, November 2. Final:
Kilkenny 4-14   3-10   *Cork*

1970 Thurles, December 13. Final:
Tipperary 1-12   0-8   *Cork*

1971 Croke Park, October 17. Final:
Limerick 4-12   3-8   *Wexford*

1972 Croke Park, October 15. Final:
Tipperary 2-13   2-13   *Wexford*
Kilkenny, November 26. Replay:
Tipperary 2-13   1-8   *Wexford*

1973 Cork, December 16. Final:
Cork 1-8   1-6   *Kilkenny*

1974 Mardyke,Cork, November 3. Final:
Cork 3-15   1-5   *Waterford*

1975 Croke Park, October 26. Final:
Cork 3-13   2-7   *Wexford*

1976 Croke Park, October 24. Final:
Galway 1-15   2-9   *Cork*

1977 Ballinasloe, March 19, 1978. Final: (no replay)
Galway 2-8   2-8   *Cork*

1978 Wexford, October 22. Final:
Wexford 0-18   1-10   *Galway*

1979 Croke Park, September 23. Final:
Wexford 3-17   5-8   *Offaly*

1980 Birr, October 5. Final:
Wexford 1-19   3-5   *Offaly*

1981 Loughrea, October 18. Final:
Galway 1-15   1-7   *Wexford*

1982 Ennis, November 7. Final:
Clare 3-9   2-9   *Limerick*

1983 Ennis, November 6. Final:
Clare 1-12   1-11   *Kilkenny*

1984 Callan, December 2. Final:
Kilkenny 1-11   1-7   *Cork*

1985 Páirc Uí Chaoimh, November 10. Final:
Cork 2-11   1-10   *Galway*

1986 Athenry, May 31, 1987. Final:
Wexford 3-17   1-22   *Galway (aet)*

1987 No competition

1988 Enniscorthy, April 3. Final:
Galway 4-15   3-11   *Wexford*

1989	Ennis, March 4, 1990. Final:			
	Galway	**1-19**	**0-8**	**Tipperary**
1990	Ennis, November 11. Final:			
	Tipperary	**1-15**	**0-7**	**Galway**
1991	Ballinasloe, November 23. Final:			
	Galway	**2-12**	**3-5**	**Wexford**
1992	Dingle, November 1. Final:			
	Galway	**1-13**	**0-10**	**Waterford**
1993	Athenry, October 25. Final:			
	Galway	**2-19**	**3-9**	**Clare (aet)**
1994	Dungarvan, December 4. Final:			
	Wexford	**2-7**	**1-8**	**Cork**
1995	Wexford, November 25. Final:			
	Offaly	**2-13**	**0-9**	**Wexford**
1996	Ennis, December 1. Final:			
	Clare	**0-11**	**1-4**	**Kilkenny**
1997	Ballinasloe, February 29, 1998. Final:			
	Galway	**0- 14**	**0-8**	**Cork**
1998	Páirc Uí Rinn, Cork, March 14, 1999. Final:			
	Cork	**0-15**	**0-10**	**Galway**
1999	December 3, 2000. Final:			
	Kilkenny	**4-6**	**0-12**	**Galway**

WALSH CUP

Kilkenny (20) — 1955, 1957, 1958, 1959, 1961, 1962, 1963, 1970, 1973, 1974, 1988, 1989, 1992, 2005, 2006, 2007, 2009, 2012, 2014, 2017.

Wexford (15) — 1954, 1956, 1965, 1967, 1968, 1969, 1987, 1995, 1996, 1997, 1998, 1999, 2000, 2001, 2002.

Dublin (7) — 1960, 1964, 1966, 2003, 2011, 2013, 2016

Offaly (5) — 1977, 1981, 1990, 1993, 1994.

Galway (2) — 2010, 2015.

Laois (2) — 1980, 1991.

Westmeath (1) — 1982.

U.C.D. (1) — 2004.

Antrim (1) — 2008.

(Note: No competition 1971,1972, 1975, 1976, 1978, 1979, 1983-1986.)

KEHOE CUP

Meath (8)	1993, 1996, 1997, 2004, 2008, 2011, 2014, 2015.
Westmeath (7)	1978, 1983, 1994, 1995, 2000, 2009, 2010.
Wicklow (6)	1989, 1991, 1998, 2001, 2002, 2003.
Carlow (6)	1986, 1990, 1992, 1999, 2005, 2006.
London (2)	1987, 1988.
Kildare (2)	2013, 2016.
Wexford (1)	1977.
Kilkenny (1)	1980.
Dublin (1)	1981.
Laois (1)	1982.
D.I.T. (1)	2007.
G.M.I.T. (1)	2012.
Maynooth University (1)	2017

(Note: No competition 1979, 1984, 1985.)

THOMOND FEIS

Limerick (14)	1913, 1920, 1922, 1925, 1928, 1932, 1933, 1934, 1935, 1937, 1940, 1944, 1945, 1947.
Tipperary (8)	1915, 1916, 1924, 1927, 1930, 1931, 1949, 1951.
Cork (7)	1914, 1926, 1936, 1941, 1948, 1952, 1954.
Clare (3)	1929, 1946, 1956.

(Note: No competition 1917-1919, 1921, 1923, 1938, 1939, 1942, 1943, 1950-Unfinished. Cork and Tipperary in final. 1953, 1955. Discontinued after 1956.)

CROKE CUP FINALS 1896-1915

1896	Jones's Road, June 27, 1897.			
	Clare	**6-16**	**0-2**	**Wexford**
1897	Thurles, July 9, 1899.			
	Limerick	**3-8**	**1-4**	**Kilkenny**
1898-1901	Cup presented to All-Ireland winners			
1902	Jones's Road, February 19, 1905.			
	Cork	**5-10**	**0-3**	**London**
1903	Dungarvan, May 27, 1906.			
	Cork	**6-9**	**0-5**	**Wexford**

(Note: After the finals of 1896 and 1897 the competition restarted on October 2, 1904. The All Ireland competition had finished on September 11, 1904. It was the 1902 competition with Dungourney having the Cork selection. The following year Blackrock as 1903 champions had the Cork selection.)

1904-1906	None			
1907	Loughrea, October 13, 1907.			
	Galway	**4-5**	**1-8**	**Clare**
1908	Jones's Road, November 22, 1908.			
	Clare	**3-14**	**1-4**	**Galway**
1909	Limerick, October 24.			
	Laois	**3-11**	**3-7**	**Kerry**
1910	Cork, April 23, 1911.			
	Cork	**12-1**	**3-1**	**Galway**
1911	Thurles, April 21, 1912.			
	Tipperary	**6-3**	**4-3**	**Dublin**
1912	Portlaoise, March 30, 1913.			
	Tipperary	**5-3**	**3-2**	**Laois**
1913	Tullamore, May 17, 1914.			
	Cork	**7-8**	**1-1**	**Galway**
1914	Dungarvan, December 18.			
	Cork	**9-1**	**5-1**	**Kilkenny**
1915	Athlone, April 9, 1916.			
	Dublin	**6-5**	**2-0**	**Clare**

(Note: From 1909-1915 the beaten Provincial Finalists played the semi-finals.)

RAILWAY SHIELD FINALS

1905	Limerick, 11 November, 1905.
	Leinster (Kilkenny) 4-10, Connacht (Galway) 4-5
1906	Ennis, 17 February, 1907.
	Munster (Tipperary) 9-14, Connacht (Galway) 1-5
1907	Jones' Road, 29 September, 1907.
	Leinster (Selected) 0-14, Munster (Tipperary) 1-8
1908	St. James Park, Kilkenny. 19 July, 1908.
	Leinster (Kilkenny) 0-14, Munster (Tipperary) 2-5

(Leinster won outright in 1908)

ALL-IRELAND CLUB CHAMPIONSHIPS 1970/71 TO 2016/17

ROLL OF HONOUR - SENIOR HURLING

6   *Ballyhale Shamrocks (Kilkenny)* – 1981, 1984, 1990, 2007, 2010, 2015
4   *Birr (Offaly)* – 1995, 1998, 2002, 2003
    Portumna (Galway) – 2006, 2008, 2009, 2014
3   *Blackrock (Cork)* – 1972, 1974, 1979
    Athenry (Galway) – 1997, 2000, 2001
    James Stephens (Kilkenny) – 1976, 1982, 2005
2   *Glen Rovers (Cork)* – 1973, 1977
    St Finbarr's (Cork) – 1975, 1978
    Sarsfields (Galway) – 1993, 1994
    Loughgiel Shamrocks (Antrim) – 1983, 2012
1   *Roscrea (Tipperary)* – 1971
    Borris-Ileigh (Tipperary) – 1987
    Buffers Alley (Wexford) – 1989
    Castlegar (Galway) – 1980
    Glenmore (Kilkenny) – 1981
    St Martin's (Kilkenny) – 1985
    Kilruane MacDonaghs (Tipperary) – 1986
    Midleton (Cork) – 1988
    Kiltormer (Galway) – 1992
    Sixmilebridge (Clare) – 1996
    St Joseph's Doora-Barefield (Clare) – 1999
    Newtownshandrum (Cork) – 2004
    Clarinbridge (Galway) – 2011
    St Thomas' (Galway) – 2013
    Na Piarsaigh (Limerick) – 2016
    Cuala (Dublin) – 2017

1970/71
PROVINCIAL FINALS
Connacht:
Liam Mellows (Galway) 4-10 Roscommon Gaels 2-5
Ulster:
Loughgiel Shamrocks (Antrim) 6-14 Ballygalget (Down) 2-5
Munster:
Roscrea (Tipperary) 4-11 Clarecastle (Clare) 1-6
Leinster:
St Rynagh's (Offaly) 4-10 Rathnure (Wexford) 2-9
ALL-IRELAND SEMI-FINALS
Roscrea 6-10 Loughgiel Shamrocks 2-8
St Rynagh's WO Liam Mellows Scr
ALL-IRELAND FINAL
Roscrea 4-5 St Rynagh's 2-5

1971/72
PROVINCIAL FINALS
Connacht:
Tommy Larkin's (Galway) 7-14 Four Roads (Roscommon) 0-6
Ulster:
Loughgiel Shamrocks (Antrim) 3-8 Portaferry (Down) 1-12
Munster:
Blackrock (Cork) 4-10 Moyne-Templetuohy (Tipperary) 3-1
Leinster:
Rathnure (Wexford) 2-12 Bennettsbridge (Kilkenny) 1-8
ALL-IRELAND SEMI-FINALS
Rathnure 5-26 Loughgiel Shamrocks 2-4
Blackrock 3-7 Tommy Larkin's 2-8
ALL-IRELAND FINAL
Blackrock 5-13 Rathnure 6-9

1972/73
PROVINCIAL FINALS
Connacht:
Castlegar (Galway) 7-12 Tremane (Roscommon) 2-7
Ulster:
O'Donovan Rossas (Antrim) 2-8 Ballycran (Down) 3-2
Munster:
Glen Rovers (Cork) 2-9 Roscrea (Tipperary) 1-10
Leinster:
St Rynagh's (Offaly) 5-5 Rathnure (Wexford) 2-13
ALL-IRELAND SEMI-FINALS
Glen Rovers 6-9 Castlegar 1-7
St Rynagh's 5-9 O'Donovan Rossas 2-8
ALL-IRELAND FINAL
Glen Rovers 2-18 St Rynagh's 2-8

1973/74
PROVINCIAL FINALS
Connacht:
Castlegar (Galway) 7-8 Tremane (Roscommon) 1-7
Ulster:
St John's (Antrim) wo Dungiven (Derry) scr
Munster:
Blackrock (Cork) 1-13 Newmarket-on-Fergus (Clare) 0-14
Leinster:
Rathnure (Wexford) 1-18 St Rynagh's (Offaly) 2-9
ALL-IRELAND SEMI-FINALS
Blackrock 5-12 St John's 1-5
Rathnure 1-15 Castlegar 1-6
ALL-IRELAND FINAL
Blackrock 2-14 Rathnure 3-11
ALL-IRELAND FINAL REPLAY
Blackrock 3-8 Rathnure 1-9

1974/75
PROVINCIAL FINALS
Connacht:
Ardrahan (Galway) 9-12 Tooreen (Mayo) 1-6
Ulster:
Ballycran (Down) 3-5 Sarsfields (Antrim) 3-2
Munster:
St Finbarr's (Cork) 0-7 Newmarket-on-Fergus (Clare) 0-3
Leinster:
Fenians (Kilkenny) 2-6 St Rynagh's (Offaly) 1-6
ALL-IRELAND SEMI-FINALS
Fenians 2-13 Ardrahan 1-8
St Finbarr's 8-8 Ballycran 3-10
ALL-IRELAND FINAL
St Finbarr's 3-8 Fenians 1-6

1975/76
PROVINCIAL FINALS
Connacht:
Ardrahan (Galway) 2-14 Athleague (Roscommon) 1-4
Ulster:
Ballygalget (Down) 4-6 Ballycastle McOuillans (Antrim) 1-9
Munster:
Blackrock (Cork) 8-12 Mount Sion (Waterford) 3-8
Leinster:
James Stephens (Kilkenny) 1-14 St Rynagh's (Offaly) 2-4
ALL-IRELAND QUARTER-FINAL
Ardrahan 0-7 Brian Boru's (London) 0-5
ALL-IRELAND SEMI-FINALS
Blackrock 2-15 Ardrahan 1-12
James Stephens 4- 15 Ballygalget 1-7
ALL-IRELAND FINAL
James Stephens 2-10 Blackrock 2-4

1976/77
PROVINCIAL FINALS
Connacht:
Tremane (Roscommon) 2-7 Kiltormer (Galway) 1-9
Ulster:
Ballycran (Down) 0-8 O'Donovan Rossa (Antrim) 0-7
Munster:
Glen Rovers (Cork) 2-8 South Liberties (Limerick) 2-4
Leinster:
Camross (Laois) 3-9 James Stephens (Kilkenny) 1-14
ALL-IRELAND QUARTER-FINAL
Glen Rovers 1-13 St Gabriel's (London) 1 -6
ALL-IRELAND SEMI-FINALS
Glen Rovers 7-10 Tremane 0-3
Camross 3-12 Ballycran 0-7
ALL-IRELAND FINAL
Glen Rovers 2-12 Camross 0-8

1977/78
PROVINCIAL FINALS
Connacht:
Four Roads (Roscommon) wo Kiltormer (Galway) scr.
Ulster:
O'Donovan Rossa (Antrim) 1-13 Ballycran (Down) 2-6
Munster:
St Finbarr's (Cork) 3-5 Sixmilebriclge (Clare) 3-5
St Finbarr's 2-8 Sixmilebridge 0-6 (replay)
Leinster:
Rathnure (Wexford) 0-16 Fenians (Kilkenny) 1-10
ALL-IRELAND QUARTER-FINAL
O'Donovan Rossa 2-11 St Gabriel's (London) 1-9
ALL-IRELAND SEMI-FINALS
St Finbarr's 6-12 O'Donovan Rossa 1-16
Rathnure 2-20 Four Roads 2-8
ALL-IRELAND FINAL
St Finbarr's 2-7 Rathnure 0-9

1978/79
PROVINCIAL FINALS
Connacht:
Ardrahan (Galway) 2-9 Tooreen (Mayo) 1-7
Ulster:
Ballycastle McQuillans (Antrim) 2-14 Portaferry (Down) 2-7
Munster:
Blackrock (Cork) 3-8 Newmarket-on- Fergus (Clare) 1-8
Leinster:
Ballyhale Shamrocks (Kilkenny) 1-13 Crumlin (Dublin) 1-6
ALL-IRELAND QUARTER-FINAL
St Gabriel's (London) 2-5 Ardrahan 1-8
St Gabriel's 2-9 Ardrahan 0-10 (replay)
ALL-IRELAND SEMI-FINALS
Ballyhale Shamrocks 4-10 St Gabriel's 1-7
Blackrock 5-12 Ballycastle McQuillan's 2-6
ALL-IRELAND FINAL
Blackrock 5-7 Ballyhale Shamrocks 5-5

1979/80
PROVINCIAL FINALS
Connacht:
Castlegar (Galway) 1-16 Tremane (Roscommon) 1-9
Ulster:
Ballycastle McQuillans (Antrim) 0-11 Ballycran (Down) 0-8
Munster:
Blackrock (Cork) 0-13 Dunhill (Waterford) 1-8

Leinster:
Crumlin (Dublin) 3-5 Camross (Laois) 0-11
ALL-IRELAND QUARTER-FINAL
Blackrock 4-15 Brian Boru's (London) 1-10
ALL-IRELAND SEMI-FINALS
Ballycastle McQuillans 3-9 Crumlin 0-8
Castlegar 2-9 Blackrock 0-9
ALL-IRELAND FINAL
Castlegar 1-11 Ballycastle McQuillans 1-8

1980/81
PROVINCIAL FINALS
Connacht:
Sarsfields (Galway) 4-12 Tremane (Roscommon) 0-5
Ulster:
Ballycastle McQuillans (Antrim) 1-20 Ballycran (Down) 0-13
Munster:
St Finbarr's (Cork) 2-12 Roscrea (Tipperary) 1-14
Leinster:
Ballyhale Shamrocks (Kilkenny) 3-10 Coolderry (Offaly) 1-8
ALL-IRELAND QUARTER-FINAL
Ballycastle McQuillans 1-14 Brian Boru's (London) 2-4
ALL-IRELAND SEMI-FINALS
Ballyhale Shamrocks 2-11 Ballycastle McQuillans 0-12
St Finbarr's 2-11 Sarsfields 1-3
ALL-IRELAND FINAL
Ballyhale Shamrocks 1-15 St Finbarr's 1-11

1981/82
PROVINCIAL FINALS
Connacht:
Gort (Galway) 8-13 Tooreen (Mayo) 0-3
Ulster:
Cushendall (Antrim) 4-17 Portaferry (Down) 0-9
Munster:
Mount Sion (Waterford) 3-9 South Liberties (Limerick) 1-4
Leinster:
James Stephens (Kilkenny) 0-13 Faythe Harriers (Wexford) 1-9
ALL-IRELAND QUARTER-FINAL
Gort 4-12 St Gabriel's (London) 0-9
ALL-IRELAND SEMI-FINALS
James Stephens 1-13 Gort 1-8
Mount Sion 1-14 Cushendall 1-8
ALL-IRELAND FINAL
James Stephens 3-13 Mount Sion 3-8

1982/83
PROVINCIAL FINALS
Connacht:
Kiltormer (Galway) 3-14 Four Roads (Roscommon) 0-6
Ulster:
Loughgiel Shamrocks (Antrim) 1-9 Ballygalget (Down) 0-9
Munster:
Moycarkey-Borris (Tipperary) 1-9 Patrickswell (Limerick) 0-11
Leinster:
St Rynagh's (Offaly) 1-16 Buffers Alley (Wexford) 2-10
ALL-IRELAND QUARTER-FINAL
Moycarkey-Borris 3-5 Brian Boru's (London) 0-5
ALL-IRELAND SEMI-FINALS
St Rynagh's 2-8 Kiltormer 0-8
Loughgiel Shamrocks 2-7 Moycarkey-Borris 1-6
ALL-IRELAND FINAL
Loughgiel Shamrocks 1-8 St Rynagh's 2-5
ALL-IRELAND FINAL REPLAY
Loughgiel Shamrocks 2-12 St Rynagh's 1-12

1983/84
PROVINCIAL FINALS
Connacht:
Gort (Galway) 3-13 Tooreen (Mayo) 1-5
Ulster:
Ballycastle McQuillans (Antrim) 4-12 Ballygalget (Down) 2-3
Munster:
Midleton (Cork) 3-6 Borris-lleigh (Tipperary) 1- 12
Midleton 1-14 Borris-lleigh 1-11 (replay)
Leinster:
Ballyhale Shamrocks (Kilkenny) 3-6 Kinnity (Offaly) 0-9
ALL-IRELAND QUARTER-FINAL
Ballycastle McQuillans 3-7 Desmonds (London) 0-8
ALL-IRELAND SEMI-FINALS
Gort 1-11 Midleton 2-4
Ballyhale Shamrocks 3-14 Ballycastle McQuillans 2-10
ALL-IRELAND FINAL
Ballyhale Shamrocks 1-10 Gort 1-10
ALL-IRELAND FINAL REPLAY
Ballyhale Shamrocks 1-10 Gort 0-7

1984/85
PROVINCIAL FINALS
Connacht:
Castlegar (Galway) 2-14 Tooreen (Mayo) 2-7
Ulster:
Ballycastle McQuillans (Antrim) 1-14 Ballycran (Down) 1-3
Munster:
Sixmilebridge (Clare) 4-10 Patrickswell (Limerick) 2-6
Leinster:
St Martin's (Kilkenny) 2-11 Kinnitty (Offaly) 0-12
ALL-IRELAND QUARTER-FINAL
Castlegar 4-12 St Gabriel's (London) 0-3
ALL-IRELAND SEMI-FINALS
St Martin's 3-15 Ballycastle McQuillans 2-7
Castlegar 3-5 Sixmilebridge 1-5
ALL-IRELAND FINAL
St Martin's 2-9 Castlegar 3-6
ALL-IRELAND FINAL REPLAY
St Martin's 1-13 Castlegar 1-10

1985/86
PROVINCIAL FINALS
Connacht:
Turloughmore (Galway) 1-8 Ballygar (Roscommon) 2-4
Ulster:
Cushendall (Antrim) 0-19 Ballycran (Down) 0-10
Munster:
Kilruane MacDonaghs (Tipperary) 1-8 Blackrock (Cork) 1-8
Kilruane MacDonaghs 0-12 Blackrock 0-6 (replay)
Leinster:
Buffers Alley (Wexford) 3-9 Kinnitty (0ffaly) 0-7
ALL-IRELAND QUARTER-FINAL
Kilruane MacDonaghs 2-9 Desmonds (London) 0-4
ALL-IRELAND SEMI-FINALS
Kilruane MacDonaghs 3-9 Turloughmore 0-9
Buffers Alley 1-10 Cushendall 0-5
ALL-IRELAND FINAL
Kilruane MacDonaghs 1-15 Buffers Alley 2-10

1986/87
PROVINCIAL FINALS
Connacht:
Killimordaly (Galway) 6-16 Tooreen (Mayo) 1-4

Ulster:
Ballycastle McQuillans (Antrim) 1-13 Lavey (Derry) 1-8
Munster:
Borrisoleigh (Tipperary) 1-13 Clarecastle (Clare) 1-9
Leinster:
Rathnure (Wexford) 2-16 Camross (Laois) 3-9
ALL-IRELAND QUARTER-FINAL
Ballycastle McQuillans 4-14 St Gabriel's (London) 1-6
ALL-IRELAND SEMI-FINALS
Rathnure 0-11 Killimordaly 0-9
Borrisoleigh 3-16 Ballycastle McQuillans 3-8
ALL-IRELAND FINAL
Borrisoleigh 2-9 Rathnure 0-9

1987/88
PROVINCIAL FINALS
Connacht:
Athenry (Galway) 4-18 Pádhraic Pearses (Roscommon) 0-7
Ulster:
Cushendall (Antrim) 3-10 Ballycran (Down) 1-6
Munster:
Midleton (Cork) 1-12 Cappawhite (Tipperary) 1-11
Leinster:
Rathnure (Wexford) 3-8 Portlaoise (Laois) 1-13
ALL-IRELAND QUARTER-FINAL
Athenry 2-14 Glen Rovers (Hertfordshire) 0-5
ALL-IRELAND SEMI-FINALS
Athenry 3-12 Rathnure 1-4
Midleton 3-11 Cushendall 2-5
ALL-IRELAND FINAL
Midleton 3-8 Athenry 0-9

1988/89
PROVINCIAL FINALS
Connacht:
Four Roads (Roscommon) 3-5 Abbeyknockmoy (Galway) 1-8
Ulster:
O'Donovan Rossa (Antrim) 0-13 Lavey (Derry) 0-11
Munster:
Patrickswell (Limerick) 3-13 Mount Sion (Waterford) 2-13
Leinster:
Buffers Alley (Wexford) 1-12 Ballyhale Shamrocks (Kilkenny) 1-9
ALL-IRELAND QUARTER-FINAL
Patrickswell 2-15 Desmonds (London) 0-7
ALL-IRELAND SEMI-FINALS
Buffers Alley 2-19 Four Roads 0-9
O'Donovan Rossa 2-9 Patrickswell 2-8
ALL-IRELAND FINAL
Buffers Alley 2-12 O'Donovan Rossa 0- 12

1989/90
PROVINCIAL FINALS
Connacht:
Sarsfields (Galway) 5-14 Tooreen (Mayo) 0-0
Ulster:
Loughgiel Shamrocks (Antrim) 1-14 Portaferry (Down) 2-9
Munster:
Ballybrown (Limerick) 2-12 Sixmilebridge (Clare) 1-8
Leinster:
Ballyhale Shamrocks (Kilkenny) 2-11 Cuala (Dublin) 0-7
ALL-IRELAND QUARTER-FINAL
Loughgiel Shamrocks 3-12 Desmonds (London) 2-10
ALL-IRELAND SEMI-FINALS
Ballyhale Shamrocks 2-8 Sarsfields 0-12
Ballybrown 0-9 Loughgiel Shamrocks 0-8
ALL-IRELAND FINAL
Ballyhale Shamrocks 1-16 Ballybrown 0-16

1990/91
PROVINCIAL FINALS
Connacht:
Kiltormer (Galway) 5-11 Oran (Roscommon) 0-6
Ulster:
Dunloy (Antrim) 0-17 Ballygalget (Down) 2-4
Munster:
Patrickswell (Limerick) 0-8 Éire Óg (Clare) 0-6
Leinster:
Glenmore (Kilkenny) 0-15 Camross (Laois) 1-9
ALL-IRELAND QUARTER-FINAL
St Gabriel's (London) 2-11 Kiltormer 1 -12 (aet)
ALL-IRELAND SEMI-FINALS
Glenmore 1-18 Dunloy 1-10
Patrickswell 8-12 St Gabriel's 3-6
ALL-IRELAND FINAL
Glenmore 1-13 Patrickswell 0-2

1991/92
PROVINCIAL FINALS
Connacht:
Kiltormer (Galway) 2-9 Four Roads (Roscommon) 1-6
Ulster:
Cushendall (Antrim) 1-16 Portaferry (Down) 0-5
Munster:
Cashel King Cormacs (Tipperary) 0-9 Midleton (Cork) 0-6
Leinster:
Birr (Offaly) 2-14 Ballyhale Shamrocks (Kilkenny) 0-3
ALL-IRELAND QUARTER-FINAL
Cashel King Cormacs 0-23 Sean Treacys (London) 0-6
ALL-IRELAND SEMI-FINALS
Birr 2-9 Cushendall 1-6
Kiltormer 1-10 Cashel King Cormacs 2-7
Kiltormer 1-14, Cashel King Cormacs 2-11 (replay) (aet)
Kiltormer 2-8 Cashel King Cormacs 1-8 (2nd replay)
ALL-IRELAND FINAL
Kiltormer 0-15 Birr 1-8

1992/93
PROVINCIAL FINALS
Connacht:
Sarsfields (Galway) 2-15 Oran (Roscommon) 0-7
Ulster:
Cushendall (Antrim) 2-12 Ballygalget (Down) 1-10
Munster:
Kilmallock (Limerick) 3-11 Sixmilebridge (Clare) 2-11
Leinster:
Buffers Alley (Wexford) 2-13 St Rynagh's (Offaly) 0-13
ALL-IRELAND QUARTER-FINAL
Desmonds (London) 2-7 Cushendall 1-8
ALL-IRELAND SEMI-FINALS
Kilmallock 1-16 Desmonds 0-6
Sarafields 4-13 Buffers Alley 1-10
ALL-IRELAND FINAL
Sarsfields 1-17 Kilmallock 2-7

1993/94
PROVINCIAL FINALS
Connacht:
Sarsfields (Galway) 5-15 Four Roads (Roscommon) 0-7
Ulster:
Ballycran (Down) 2-10 Cushendall (Antrim) 0-12
Munster:
Toomevara (Tipperary) 0-15 Sixmilebridge (Clare) 0-7

Leinster:
St Rynagh's (Offaly) 1-14 Dicksboro (Kilkenny) 2-10
ALL-IRELAND QUARTER-FINAL
Sarsfields 2-14 Seán Treacys (London) 0-5
ALL-IRELAND SEMI-FINALS
Toomevara 1-13 Ballycran 1-5
Sarsfields 1-11 St Rynagh's 1-7
ALL-IRELAND FINAL
Sarsfields 1-14 Toomevara 3-6

1994/95
PROVINCIAL FINALS
Connacht:
Athenry (Galway) 3-20 St Dominic's (Roscommon) 2-3
Ulster:
Dunloy (Antrim) 3-9 Lavey (Derry) 1-12
Munster:
Kilmallock (Limerick) 2-11 Toomevara (Tipperary) 1-11
Leinster:
Birr (Offaly) 0-10 Oulart-The Ballagh (Wexford) 1-7
Birr 3-7 Oulart-The Ballagh 2-5 (replay)
ALL-IRELAND QUARTER-FINAL
Kilmallock 1-16 Seán Treacy's (London) 0-10
ALL-IRELAND SEMI-FINALS
Birr 2-8 Kilmallock 0-9
Dunloy 2-10 Athenry 1-11
ALL-IRELAND FINAL
Birr 0-9 Dunloy 0-9
Birr 3-13 Dunloy 2-3 (replay)

1995/96
PROVINCIAL FINALS
Connacht:
Sarsfields (Galway) 2-17 Tooreen (Mayo) 0-5
Ulster:
Dunloy (Antrim) 2- 18 Ballycran (Down) 0-9
Munster:
Sixmilebridge (Clare) 2-18 Eire Óg Nenagh (Tipperary) 1-7
Leinster:
Glenmore (Kilkenny) 2-13 Oulart-The Ballagh (Wexford) 2-10
ALL-IRELAND QUARTER-FINAL
Dunloy 1-16 St Gabriel's (London) 0-9
ALL-IRELAND SEMI-FINALS
Sixmilebridge 5-11 Sarsfields 1-12
Dunloy 2-13 Glenmore 0-7
ALL-IRELAND FINAL
Sixmilebridge 5-10 Dunloy 2-6

1996/97
PROVINCIAL FINALS
Connacht:
Athenry (Galway) 1-15 Four Roads (Roscommon) 1-8
Ulster:
Cushendall (Antrim) 3-9 Portaferry (Down) 2-8
Munster:
Wolfe Tones (Clare) 4-9 Ballygunner (Waterford) 4-8
Leinster:
Camross (Laois) 1-12 O'Tooles (Dublin) 2-5
ALL-IRELAND QUARTER-FINAL
Athenry 3-15 St Gabriel's (London) 1-8
ALL-IRELAND SEMI-FINALS
Wolfe Tones 2-8 Cushendall 1-10
Athenry 4-17 Camross 3-3
ALL-IRELAND FINAL
Athenry 0-14 Wolfe Tones 1-8

1997/98
PROVINCIAL FINALS
Connacht:
Sarsfields (Galway) 5-15 Tooreen (Mayo) 1-5
Ulster:
Dunloy (Antrim) 3-16 Lavey (Derry) 4-10
Munster:
Clarecastle (Clare) 2-11 Patrickswell (Limerick) 0-15
Leinster:
Birr (Offaly) 0-11 Castletown (Laois) 0-5
ALL-IRELAND QUARTER-FINAL
Clarecastle 2-24 St Gabriel's (London) 1-7
ALL-IRELAND SEMI-FINALS
Birr 1-15 Clarecastle 3-9
Birr 0-12 Clarecastle 0-11 (aet)
Sarsfields 3-14 Dunloy 4-11
Sarsfields 1-15 Dunloy 1-11 (replay)
ALL-IRELAND FINAL
Birr 1-13 Sarsfields 0-9

1998/99
PROVINCIAL FINALS
Connacht:
Athenry (Galway) 6-24 Tooreen (Mayo) 0-5
Ulster:
Ballygalget (Down) 1-13 Ballycastle McQuillans (Antrim) 3-7
Ballygalget 1-14 Ballycastle McQuillans 1-12 (replay) (aet)
Munster:
St Joseph's Doora-Barefield (Clare) 0-12 Toomevara (Tipperary) 0-8
Leinster:
Rathnure (Wexford) 1-13 Portlaoise (Laois) 1-6
ALL-IRELAND QUARTER-FINAL
Ballygalget 1-9 Bros Pearse (London) 0-4
ALL-IRELAND SEMI-FINALS
St Joseph's Doora-Barefield 1-13 Athenry 1-12
Rathnure 2-19 Ballygalget 1-8
ALL-IRELAND FINAL
St Joseph's Doora-Barefield 2-14 Rathnure 0-8

1999/00
PROVINCIAL FINALS
Connacht:
Athenry (Galway) 1-13 Tooreen (Mayo) 1-6
Ulster:
Cushendall (Antrim) 1-12 Ballygalget (Down) 1-8
Munster:
St Joseph's Doora-Barefield (Clare) 4-9 Ballygunner (Waterford) 3-8
Leinster:
Birr (Offaly) 1-16 Castletown (Laois) 0-11
ALL-IRELAND QUARTER-FINAL
Athenry 2-20 St Gabriel's (London) 1-9
ALL-IRELAND SEMI-FINALS
Athenry 2-9 Birr 1-10
St Joseph's Doora-Barefield 0-12 Cushendall 0- 12
St Joseph's Doora-Barefield 1-14 Cushendall 1-8 (replay)
ALL-IRELAND FINAL
Athenry 0-16 St Joseph's Doora-Barefield 0-12

2000/01
PROVINCIAL FINALS
Connacht:
Athenry (Galway) 2-16 Four Roads (Roscommon) 1-7
Ulster:
Dunloy (Antrim) 4-14 Slaughtneil (Derry) 0-9

Munster:
Sixmilebridge (Clare) 2-17 Mount Sion (Waterford) 3-8
Leinster:
Graigue-Ballycallan (Kilkenny) 0-14 UCD (Dublin) 1-8
ALL-IRELAND QUARTER-FINAL
Sixmilebridge 2-11 Fr Murphy's (London) 0-6
ALL-IRELAND SEMI-FINALS
Athenry 3-20 Dunloy 1-10
Graigue-Ballycallan 1-16 Sixmilebridge 2-13
Graigue-Ballycallan 1-13 Sixmilebridge 1-12 (replay)
ALL-IRELAND FINAL
Athenry 3-24 Graigue-Ballycallan 2-19 (aet)

2001/02
PROVINCIAL FINALS
Connacht:
Clarinbridge (Galway) 2-18 Four Roads (Roscommon) 1-6
Ulster:
Dunloy (Antrim) 3-11 Lavey (Derry) 1-6
Munster:
Ballygunner (Waterford) 2-14 Blackrock (Cork) 0-12
Leinster:
Birr (Offaly) 0-10 Castletown (Laois) 1-7
Birr 2-10 Castletown 0-5 (replay)
ALL-IRELAND QUARTER-FINAL
Dunloy 6-12 FrMurphy's (London) 1-6
ALL-IRELAND SEMI-FINALS
Clarinbridge 1-15 Ballygunner 2-8
Birr 2-12 Dunloy 1-11
ALL-IRELAND FINAL
Birr 2-10 Clarinbridge 1-5

2002/03
PROVINCIAL FINALS
Connacht:
Athenry (Galway) 1-19 Four Roads (Roscommon) 0-9
Ulster:
Dunloy (Antrim) 0-12 Portaferry (Down) 1-6
Munster:
Mount Sion (Waterford) 0-12 Sixmilebridge (Clare) 0-10
Leinster:
Birr (Offaly) 2-5 Young Irelands (Kilkenny) 1-2
ALL-IRELAND QUARTER-FINAL
Athenry 4-15 Seán Treacy's (London) 0-5
ALL-IRELAND SEMI-FINALS
Dunloy 1-14 Mount Sion 1-13
Birr 0-15 Athenry 0-6
ALL-IRELAND FINAL
Birr 1-19 Dunloy 0-11

2003/04
PROVINCIAL FINALS
Connacht:
Portumna (Galway) 0-17 Athleague (Roscommon) 0-5
Ulster:
Dunloy (Antrim) 3-19 Dungiven (Derry) 0-9
Munster:
Newtownshandrum (Cork) 2-18 Patrickswell (Limerick) 2-9
Leinster:
O'Loughlin Gaels (Kilkenny) 0-15 Birr (Offaly) 0-9
ALL-IRELAND QUARTER-FINAL
Newtownshandrum 1-14 Fr Murphy's (London) 1-5
ALL-IRELAND SEMI-FINALS
Dunloy 2-13 Portumna 2-10

Newtownshandrum 1-16 O'Loughlin Gaels 0-19
Newtownshandrum 0-14 O'Loughlin Gaels 1-8 (replay)
ALL-IRELAND FINAL
Newtownshandrum 0-17 Dunloy 1-6

2004/05
PROVINCIAL FINALS
Connacht:
Athenry (Galway) 2-16 Ballyhaunis (Mayo) 0-7
Ulster:
O'Donovan Rossa (Antrim) 0-16 Ballygalget (Down) 0-14
Munster:
Toomevara (Tipperary) 1-14 Mount Sion (Waterford) 1-13
Leinster:
James Stephens (Kilkenny) 1-13 UCD (Dublin) 1-12
ALL-IRELAND SEMI-FINALS
Athenry 3-12 Toomevara 1-11
James Stephens 0-17 O'Donovan Rossa 1-6
ALL-IRELAND FINAL
James Stephens 0-19 Athenry 0-14

2005/06
PROVINCIAL FINALS
Connacht:
Portumna (Galway) 2-22 Four Roads (Roscommon) 0-6
Ulster: Ballygalget (Down) 1-18 Cushendall (Antrim) 3-8
Munster:
Newtownshandrum (Cork) 0-16 Ballygunner (Waterford) 1-12
Leinster:
James Stephens (Kilkenny) 2-13 UCD (Dublin) 1-12
ALL-IRELAND SEMI-FINALS
Portumna 2-17 James Stephens 0-11
Newtownshandrum 0-14 Ballygalget 1-10
ALL-IRELAND FINAL
Portumna 2-8 Newtownshandrum 1-6

2006/07
PROVINCIAL FINALS
Connacht:
Loughrea (Galway) 2-16 Athleague (Roscommon) 2-3
Ulster:
Cushendall (Antrim) 1-15 Dungiven (Derry) 1-7
Munster:
Toomevara (Tipperary) 2-9 Erin's Own (Cork) 2-8
Leinster:
Ballyhale Shamrocks (Kilkenny) 1-20 Birr (Offaly) 1-8
ALL-IRELAND SEMI-FINALS
Ballyhale Shamrocks 2-20 Toomevara 3-14
Loughrea 1-11 Cushendall 0-9
ALL-IRELAND FINAL
Ballyhale Shamrocks 3-12 Loughrea 2-8

2007/08
PROVINCIAL FINALS
Connacht:
Portumna (Galway) 6-23 James Stephens (Mayo) 0-7
Ulster:
Dunloy (Antrim) 2-14 Dungiven (Derry) 2-8
Munster:
Loughmore/Castleiney (Tipperary) 1-6 Tulla (Clare) 0-7
Leinster:
Birr (Offaly) 1-11 Ballyboden St Enda's (Dublin) 0-13
ALL-IRELAND SEMI-FINALS
Portumna 2-13 Loughmore/Castleiney 2-8
Birr 0-17 Dunloy 0-9
ALL-IRELAND FINAL
Portumna 3-19 Birr 3-9

2008/09
PROVINCIAL FINALS
Connacht:
Portumna (Galway) unopposed
Ulster:
Cushendall (Antrim) 1-14 Ballygalget (Down) 1-13
Munster:
De La Salle (Waterford) 1-9 Adare (Limerick) 0-10
Leinster:
Ballyhale Shamrocks (Kilkenny) 2-13 Birr (Offaly) 1-11
ALL-IRELAND SEMI-FINALS
Portumna 5-11 Ballyhale Shamrocks 1-16
De La Salle 1-21 Cushendall 1-19 (aet)
ALL-IRELAND FINAL
Portumna 2-24 De La Salle 1-8

2009/10
PROVINCIAL FINALS
Connacht:
Portumna (Galway) unopposed
Ulster:
Dunloy (Antrim) 2-16 Ballycran (Down) 2-11
Munster:
Newtownshandrum (Cork) 2-11 Ballygunner (Waterford) 2-9
Leinster:
Ballyhale Shamrocks (Kilkenny) 1-16 Tullamore (Offaly) 1-8
ALL-IRELAND SEMI-FINALS
Ballyhale Shamrocks 0-19 Newtownshandrum 0-17
Portumna 2-18 Dunloy 0-12
ALL-IRELAND FINAL
Ballyhale Shamrocks 1-19 Portumna 0-17

2010/11
PROVINCIAL FINALS
Connacht:
Clarinbridge (Galway) unopposed
Ulster:
Loughgiel Shamrocks (Antrim) 2-24 Keady (Armagh) 0-6
Munster:
De La Salle (Waterford) 0-9 Thurles Sarsfields (Tipperary) 0-8
Leinster:
O'Loughlin Gaels (Kilkenny) 0-14 Oulart-The Ballagh (Wexford) 1-8
ALL-IRELAND SEMI-FINALS
Clarinbridge 3-22 De La Salle 1-27 (aet)
O'Loughlin Gaels 3-10 Loughgiel Shamrocks 0-10
ALL-IRLEAND FINAL
Clarinbridge 2-18 O'Loughlin Gaels 0-12

2011/12
PROVINCIAL FINALS
Connacht:
Gort (Galway) unopposed
Ulster:
Loughgiel Shamrocks (Antrim) 2-18 Ballycran (Down) 0-8
Munster:
Na Piarsaigh (Limerick) 1-11 Crusheen (Clare) 0-14
Na Piarsaigh 1-13 Crusheen 0-9 (replay)
Leinster:
Coolderry (Offaly) 1-15 Oulart-The Ballagh (Wexford) 1-11
ALL-IRELAND SEMI-FINALS
Coolderry 3-16 Gort 0-17
Loughgiel Shamrocks 0-27 Na Piarsaigh 2-13 (aet)
ALL-IRELAND FINAL
Loughgiel Shamrocks 4-13 Coolderry 0-17

2012/13
PROVINCIAL FINALS
Connacht:
St Thomas' (Galway) unopposed
Ulster:
Loughgiel Shamrocks (Antrim) 2-25 Portaferry (Down) 0-12
Munster:
Thurles Sarsfields (Tipperary) 1-21 De La Salle (Waterford) 1-16
Leinster:
Kilcormac/Killoughey (Offaly) 1-12 Oulart-The Ballagh (Wexford) 0-11
ALL-IRELAND SEMI-FINALS
Kilcormac/Killoughey 1-20 Thurles Sarsfields 1-14
St Thomas' 1-25 Loughgiel Shamrocks 3-19 (aet)
St Thomas' 0-15 Loughgiel Shamrocks 0-7 (replay)
ALL-IRELAND FINAL
St Thomas' 1-11 Kilcormac/Killoughey 1-9

2013/14
PROVINCIAL FINALS
Connacht:
Portumna (Galway) unopposed
Ulster:
Loughgiel Shamrocks (Antrim) 3-14 Slaughtneil (Derry) 1-15
Munster:
Na Piarsaigh (Limerick) 4-14 Sixmilebridge (Clare) 0-8
Leinster:
Mount Leinster Rangers (Carlow) 0-11 Oulart-The Ballagh (Wexford) 0-8
ALL-IRELAND SEMI-FINALS
Portumna 1-15 Na Piarsaigh 1-11
Mount Leinster Rangers 0-18 Loughgiel Shamrocks 2-11
ALL-IRELAND FINAL
Portumna 0-19 Mount Leinster Rangers 0-11

2014/15
PROVINCIAL FINALS
Connacht:
Gort (Galway) unopposed
Ulster:
Portaferry (Down) 1-16, Cushendall (Antrim) 0-11
Munster:
Kilmallock (Limerick) 1-32, Cratloe (Clare) 3-18
Leinster:
Ballyhale Shamrocks (Kilkenny) 0-21, Kilcormac/Killoughey (Offaly) 1-14
ALL-IRELAND SEMI-FINALS
Kilmallock 2-19, Portaferry 0-12
Ballyhale Shamrocks 2-17, Gort 1-15
ALL-IRELAND FINAL
Ballyhale Shamrocks 1-18, Kilmallock 1-6

2015/16
PROVINCIAL FINALS
Connacht:
Sarsfields (Galway) unopposed
Ulster:
Cushendall (Antrim) 1-24, Slaughtneil (Derry) 3-17 (aet)
Munster:
Na Piarsaigh (Limerick) 2-18, Ballygunner (Waterford) 2-11
Leinster:
Oulart-The Ballagh (Wexford) 2-13, Cuala (Dublin) 0-13
ALL-IRELAND SEMI-FINALS
Cushendall 3-12, Sarsfields 1-6
Na Piarsaigh 1-22, Oulart-The Ballagh 0-20 (aet)
ALL-IRELAND FINAL
Na Piarsaigh 2-25, Cushendall 2-14

2016/17
PROVINCIAL FINALS
Connacht:
St Thomas' (Galway) unopposed
Ulster:
Slaughtneil (Derry) 2-14, Loughgiel Shamrocks (Antrim) 1-13
Munster:
Ballyea (Clare) 1-21, Glen Rovers (Cork) 2-10
Leinster:
Cuala (Dublin) 3-19, O'Loughlin Gaels (Kilkenny) 1-16
ALL-IRELAND SEMI-FINALS
Ballyea 1-19, St Thomas' 2-14
Cuala 3-21, Slaughtneil 2-11
ALL-IRELAND FINAL
Cuala 2-19, Ballyea 1-10

ALL-IRELAND CLUB HURLING FINAL TEAMS 1971-2017

1971
Roscrea
T.Murphy, M.Hogan, K.Carey, B.Maher, P.Rowland, T.O'Connor, J.Crampton, M.Minogue, D.Moloney (capt.), F.Loughnane, J.Hannon, J.Cunningham, J.Tynan M.Nolan, W.Stapleton.
St.Rynagh's
D.Martin, N.Gallagher, F.Whelehan, A.Horan, P.Moylan, P Horan, S.Moylan, R.Horan, B.Johnson, B.Lyons, P.J.Whelehan, H.Dolan, G.Burke, B.Moylan, P.Mulhare.

1972
Blackrock
B Hurley, P.Casey, P.Geary, J.Horgan (capt), S.Murphy, F.Cummins, F.Norberg, M.Murphy, P.Kavanagh, D.Collins, R.Cummins, P.Moylan, B.Cummins, J.Rothwell, D.Prendergast.
Rathnure
M.Foley, J.Quigley, A.Somers, M.Mooney, J.O'Connor, T.O'Connor, J.Quigley, M.Byrne, J.Mooney, J.Higgins, M.Quigley, J.Murphy, P.Flynn, J.English, D.Quigley. Sub: S.Barron for P Flynn.

1973
Glen Rovers
F.O'Neill, D.O'Riordan, M.O'Doherty, P Barry, J.O'Sullivan, D.Coughlan, M.O'Halloran, J.J.O'Neill P.O'Doherty, P.Harte, R.Crowley, T.Buckley, M.Ryan, T.Collins, J.Young. Sub: M.Corbett for D.O'Riordan.
St Rynagh's
D.Martin, J.Dooley, F.Whelehan, A.Horan, P Moylan, P.Horan, H.Dolan, P.J.Whelehan, B.Johnson, B.Lyons, B.Moylan, J.Horan, R.Horan, P.Mulhare, S.Moylan.

1974
Blackrock
T.Murphy, J.Rothwell, P.Geary, J.Horgan (capt.), F.Cummins, C.O'Brien, F.Norberg, J.Russell, P Moylan, P.Kavanagh, J.O'Halloran, D.Collins, D.Prendergast, R.Cummins, E.O'Donoghue. Subs: S.Kearney for P.Kavanagh, D.Buckley for S.Kearney.
(Note: B.Cummins played in drawn game. C.O'Brien was on for replay.)
Rathnure
M.Foley, P.Quigley, Jim Quigley, M.Mooney, J.O'Connor, T.O'Connor, S.Murphy, M.Quigley, J.Higgins, P Flynn, J.Murphy, M.Byrne, John Quigley, A.Somers, D.Quigley.
(Note: J.Mooney, V.Fenlon played in drawn game. J.Higgins, A.Somers in replay. Subs: J.Higgins for M.Byrne, S.Murphy for J.Mooney in drawn game. Sub: J.Mooney for J.Higgins in replay.)

1975
St Finbarr's J.Power (capt.), A.Maher, S.Canty, C.Barrett, B.O'Brien, D.O'Grady, T.Butler, G.McCarthy, C.Roche, E.Fitzpatrick, J.Barry Murphy, S.Gillen, C.McCarthy, S.Looney, J.O'Shea. Sub: C.Cullinane for S.Long.
The Fenians
P.J.Ryan, S.Delaney, N.Orr, M.Fitzpatrick, G.Murphy, P Henderson, G.Henderson, F.Hawkes, M.Garrett, J.Moriarty, P.Delaney, J.Ryan, W.Fitzpatrick, W.Watson, P Fitzpatrick. Sub: P Murphy for F Hawks.

1976
James Stephens
M.Moore, P.Neary, P.Larkin.N.Morrissey, T.McCormack, B.Cody, J.O'Brien, D.McCormack, M.Taylor, J.Hennessy, L.O'Brien, J.McCormack, M.Crotty, M.Leahy, G.Tyrrell. Sub: M.Neary for J.O'Brien.
Blackrock
T.Murphy, F Norberg, C.O'Brien, D.McCurtain, A.Creagh, J.Horgan, J.Murphy, F.Cummins, J.Rothwell, P.Moylan, D.Collins, P.Kavanagh, E.O'Sullivan, R.Cummins, E.O'Donoghue. Subs: T.Lyons for D.Collins, D.Prendergast for P.Moylan.

1977
Glen Rovers
F.O'Neill (capt.), J.O'Sullivan, M.O'Doherty, T.O'Brien, F.O'Sullivan, D.Clifford, D.Coughlan, R.Crowley, J.J.O'Neill, P Harte, P.Horgan, P O'Doherty, M.Ryan, T.Collins, V.Marshall. Subs: L.McAuliffe, T.O'Neill, F.Cunningham.
Camross
J.Carroll, J.Dooley, T.Cuddy, R.Maloney, J.Doran, J.Fitzpatrick, O.Cuddy, P.Dowling, P.J.Cuddy, Martin Cuddy, G.Cuddy M.Carroll, Michael Cuddy, F.Keenan, S.Cuddy. Subs: Tim Keenan for Michael Cuddy, S.Bergin for P.Dowling, S.Collier for R.Moloney.

1978
St Finbarr's
J.Power, C.Barrett, A.Maher, D.Burns, D.O'Grady, N.Kennefick, G.Murphy, G.McCarthy, J.Cremin, J.Allen, J.Barry Murphy, B.Wiley, E.Fitzpatrick, C.Ryan, C.McCarthy. Sub: B.Meade for G.Murphy.
Rathnure
M.Foley, A.Somers, D.Quigley, T.O'Connor, J.O'Connor, M.Codd, S.Murphy, J.Conran, J.Houlihan, D.O'Connor, M.Quigley, J.Murphy, P.Flynn, J.Quigley, P.Quigley. Sub: L.Byrne for P.Quigley.

1979
Blackrock
T.Murphy, F.Norberg, C.O'Brien, J.Horgan (capt.), D.McCurtain, F.Cummins, A.Creagh, T.Cashman, J.O'Grady, P.Moylan, T.Lyons, D.Collins, E.O'Sullivan, R.Cummins, E.O'Donoghue. Sub: D.Buckley for A.Creagh.
Ballyhale Shamrocks
O.Harrington, D.Shefflin, L.Dalton, R.Reid, W.Phelan, M.Mason, F.Holohan, J.Walsh, S.Fennelly, M.Fennelly, P.Holden, G.Fennelly, L.Fennelly, B.Fennelly, K.Fennelly. Sub: M.Healy for L.Dalton.

1980
Castlegar
T.Grogan, Ted Murphy, Pádraic Connolly, J.Coady, G.Glynn, John Connolly, M.Glynn, T.Murphy, S.Fahy, J.Francis, Joe Connolly, P.O'Connor, Gerry Connolly, Michael Connolly (capt.), L.Mulryan. Sub: P.Burke for P.O'Connor.
Ballycastle
P.Smith, K.Boyle, K.Donnelly (capt.), G.McAuley S.Donnelly, T.Donnelly, D.Donnelly, T.Barton, S.Boyle, B.Donnelly, P.Watson, P.Boyle, P.Dallat, E.Donnelly, O.Laverty.

1981
Ballyhale Shamrocks
K.Fennelly, W.Phelan, L.Dalton, R.Reid (capt.), F.Holohan, M.Mason, D.Connolly, J.Walsh, S.Fennelly, M.Fennelly, P.Holden, G.Fennelly, B.Fennelly, L.Fennelly, M.Kelly. Sub: D.Fennelly for W.Phelan.

St Finbarr's
G.Cunningham, A.Maher, D.O'Grady, J.Blake, D.Burns, B.O'Brien (capt.), N.Kennefick, J.Cremin, J.Meyler, C.Ryan, T.Maher, E.Fitzpatrick, J.Barry Murphy, C.McCarthy, J.Allen. Subs: G.O'Shea for E.Fitzpatrick, F.Scannell for D.Burns, G.Murphy for A.Maher.

1982
James Stephens
M.Moore, P.Neary, B.Cody, P.Larkin, J.Hennessy, M.Hennessy, J.O'Brien (capt.), T.McCormack, D.McCormack, A.Egan, E.Kelly, W.Walton, J.McCormack, M.Crotty, J.J.Cullen. Sub: D.Collins for A.Egan.
Mount Sion
S.Greene, B.Knox, E.Keogh D.Shefflin, P.O'Grady, P.McGrath, P.Ryan, L.Slevin, D.Connolly, A.Cooney, T.Butler, K.Heffernan, M.Geary, P.Kelly, J.Greene. Subs: J.Dalton for K.Heffernan, K.Ryan for P.O'Grady P.O'Grady for M.Geary.

1983
Loughgiel Shamrocks
N.Patterson (capt.), M.Carey, P.J.Mullen, S.Carey, E.Connolly, P.McIlhatton, A.McNaughton, M.O'Connell, G.McKinley, P.Carey (junior), D.McKinley, B.Laverty, P.Carey (senior), A.McCarry, S.McNaughton.
(Note: M.Coyle and B.McCarry played in drawn game. P.Carey (senior) and (junior) subs in drawn match for M.Coyle and B.McCarry, retained for replay.)
St Rynagh's
D.Martin, M.Whelehan, J.Dooley, W.Keane, T.White, A.Fogarty, T Conneely, A.Horan, S.White (capt.), J.Kirwan, P.Horan, D.Devery, J.Horan, F.Kenny, H.Dolan. Subs: G.O'Mahony for A.Horan (draw). J.Cannon for F.Kenny, G.Dolan for J.Kirwan (replay).

1984
Ballyhale Shamrocks
O.Harrington, F.Holohan, L.Dalton, W.Phelan, M.Fennelly, M.Mason, S.Fennelly, J.Walsh, T.Phelan, B.Fennelly, G.Fennelly, M.Kelly, D.Fennelly, K.Fennelly, L.Fennelly. Sub: L.Long for L.Fennelly.
(Note: L.Long, D.Connolly played in drawn game L.Fennelly and T.Phelan were on for replay. Subs in drawn match, T.Phelan for S.Fennelly, R.Keneally for D.Connolly, L.Fennelly for B.Fennelly.)
Gort
J.Commins, S.Linnane, J.Nolan, J.Regan, J.Harte (capt.), P.Piggott, P.Neylon, C.Rock, M.Cahill, P.Hehir, B.Brennan, G.Lally, G.Linnane, K.Fahy, J.Crehan. Subs: M.Murphy for B.Brennan, M.Linnane for M.Murphy, M.Mulcairns for G.Linnane.
(Note: M.Brennan played in draw. J.Regan came on for replay. Subs in drawn game M.Murphy for P.Hehir, M.Mulcairns for B.Brennan.)

1985
St Martin's
B.Shore, J.Kelly, A.Maher, J.J.Dowling, T.Walsh, Jim Moran, M.Maher, P.Lawlor, John Moran, J.Morrissey, J.Brennan (capt.), P.Moran, D.Coonan, T.Moran, R.Moloney. Sub: E.Morrissey for John Moran (draw), and E.Morrissey for P.Lawlor (replay).
Castlegar
T.Grogan, P.Connolly, Ted Murphy, M.Glynn, T.McCormack, S.Murphy, G.Glynn, Tom Murphy, M.Connolly, M.O'Shea, S.Fahy, M.Costelloe, M.Murphy, John Connolly, G.Connolly. Subs: J.Coyne for S.Fahy, Joe Connolly for G.Connolly, J.O'Connor for T.McCormack.
(Note: J.O'Connor and J.Coyne played in drawn game. M.Costelloe for J.Coyne, and M.Glynn for Tom Murphy came on as subs in drawn match and retained their places for replay.)

1986
Kilruane MacDonaghs
A.Sheppard (capt.), J.Cahill, D.O'Meara, S.Gibson, J.Banaghan, J.O'Meara, G.Williams, E.Hogan, D.Cahill, Jerry Williams, Jim Williams, E.O'Shea, Pat Quinlan, P.Williams, Philip Quinlan. Sub: S.Hennessy for E.Hogan.
Buffers Alley
H.Butler, B.Murphy, P.Kenny, C.Doran, J.Donohue, P.Gahan, S.Whelan (capt.), M.Casey, G.Sweeney, T.Dempsey, T.Dwyer, M.Foley, M.Butler, T.Doran, S.O'Leary. Subs: P.Donohue for G.Sweeney, E.Sinnott for M.Foley.

1987
Borris-Ileigh
N.Maher, F.Spillane, T.Stapleton, M.Ryan (capt.), R.Stakelum, G.Stapleton, B.Ryan, T.Ryan, F.Collins, C.Stakelum, N.O'Dwyer, J.McGrath, M.Coen, P.Kenny, A.Ryan. Sub: B.Kenny for T.Ryan.
Rathnure
T.Morrissey, M.Codd, M.Quigley, J.Doyle, D.Sheehan, J.O'Connell (capt.), J.Conran, J.Holohan, L.Ronan, J.Codd, J.Redmond, N.Hearne, P.Codd, J.Murphy, M.Morrissey. Sub: J.Quigley for J.Codd.

1988
Midleton
G.Power, D.Mulcahy, M.Boylan, S.O'Mahony, E.Cleary, S.O'Brien, P.Hartnett, Tadhg McCarthy, M.Crotty, J.Fenton, J.Hartnett, J.Boylan, G.Fitzgerald, C.O'Neill, K.Hennessy. Subs: G.Glavin for M.Crotty, C.O'Neill for J.Boylan, G.Smyth for S.O'Mahony.
Athenry
M.Gannon, D.Monaghan, B.Caulfield, A.Jennings, P Hardiman, M.Cahill, G.Keane, J.Hardiman, P.Healy, G.Dempsey, S.Keane, P.J.Molloy, S.Kearns, P Higgins, D.Higgins. Subs: M.Donoghue for D.Higgins, B.Feeney for S.Keane, J.Rabbitte for G.Dempsey.

1989
Buffers Alley
H.Butler, B.Murphy, P.Kenny (capt.), J.O'Leary, P.Gahan, M.Foley, C.Whelan, E.Sinnott, S.Whelan, T.Dempsey, M.Casey, P.Donoghue, M.Butler, T.Doran, S.O'Laoire.
O'Donovan Rossa
P.Quinn, G.Rogan, D.Murray (capt.), M Barr, A.Murray, M.Reynolds, S.Collins, J.Fagan, J.Close, D.Armstrong, C.Barr, P.Ward, N.Murray, J.Reilly, C.Murphy. Subs: S.Shannon for Ward, P.Rogan for Close, C.Condon for Collins.

1990
Ballyhale Shamrocks
K.Fennelly, M.Fennelly, F.Holohan, W.Phelan, R.Walsh, P.Phelan, S.Fennelly, G.Fennelly, T.Shefflin, T.Phelan, J.Lawlor, D.Fennelly, B.Fennelly, L.Fennelly, B.Mason.
Ballybrown
F O'Reilly, J.Coughlan, J.Kenny, S.Adams, P.O'Connor, J.O'Connor, A.Hall, J.Mann, C.Coughlan, O.O'Connor, P Mulqueen, P.Davoren, C.Keyes, T Kenny, S.Hayes. Subs: E.Cliff for Hayes, G.O'Reilly for Mann.

1991
Glenmore
M.Deady, E.O'Connor E.Aylward, P.J.O'Connor, L.Walsh, W.O'Connor, D.Ennett, R.Heffernan (capt.), D.Heffernan, D.Mullally, M.Phelan, P.Barron, J.Heffernan, C.Heffernan, J.Flynn. Subs: S.Dollard for Ennett, M."Foxy" Phelan for Flynn, M.Aylward for P.J.O'Connor.

Patrickswell
J.Murphy, Philip Foley, Paul Foley, E.Kelleher, David Punch, P.Carey, Pa Foley, S.Carey, A.Carmody, C.Carey, G.Kirby, S.Kirby, N.Carey, S.Foley, L.Enright. Sub: Dom Punch for Kelleher.

1992

Kiltormer
S.McKeigue, B.McManus, C.Hayes, K.Tierney, F.Curley, P.Dervan, G.Kelly, T.Larkin, A.Staunton (capt.), J.Campbell, A.Kilkenny, D.Curley, D.Cox, M.Staunton, S.Kelly. Subs: T.Furey for Dervan, T.Hanrahan for McManus.

Birr
P Kirwan, M.Hogan, D.Geoghegan, B.Hennessy, B.Whelahan (capt.), J.Errity, G.Cahill, J.Pilkington, M.Finnane, D.Regan, P Murphy, D.Pilkington, M.Errity, R.Landy, O.O'Neill. Subs: N.Hogan for M.Errity, J.Carroll for Finnane.

1993

Sarsfields
T.Kenny, Pakie Cooney, B.Cooney, M.Cooney, Padraic Kelly, D.Keane, W.Earls, N.Morrissey, Joe Cooney, M.McGrath, J.McGrath, A.Donohue, Peter Kelly, M.Kenny, Peter Cooney.

Kilmallock
G.Hanly, S.Burchill, J.J.O'Riordan, S.O'Grady, D.Barry, D.Clarke, G.O'Riordan, M.Houlihan, S.Barrett, P.Barrett, M.Nelligan, P.Kelly, P.Tobin, B.Hanley, D.Hanley. Sub: T.Nelligan for M.Nelligan.

1994

Sarsfields
T.Kenny Pakie Cooney, B.Cooney, M.Cooney P.Kelly, D.Keane, W.Earls, N.Morrissey, J.Cooney M.McGrath, J.McGrath, A.Donohue P.Kelly, M.Kenny, Peter Cooney. Sub: J.Keone for Morrissey.

Toomevara
J.Grace P.Meagher, R.Brislane, D.O'Meara G.Frend, M.O'Meara, P.Shanahan T.Delaney, P.King M.Nolan, M.Murphy, L.Flaherty T.Carroll, K.Kennedy, Thomas Dunne. Subs: Terry Dunne for Kennedy L.Nolan for Flaherty.

1995

Birr
R.Shields M.Hogan, J Errity, B.Hennessy B.Whelahan, G.Cahill, N.Hogan J.Pilkington, D.Regan O.O'Neill, C.McGlone, D.Pilkington S.Whelahan, P.Murphy, A.Cahill. Subs: M.Finnane for O'Neill L.Vaughan for C.McGlone R.Landy for M.Hogan.
(Note: Sub in drawn game R.Landy for S.Whelahan.)

Dunloy
S.Elliott B.Óg Cunning, S.McMullan, S.McIlhatton F.McMullan, Gary O'Kane, S.Mullan T.McGrath, C.McGuckian N.Elliott, P.Molloy, J.Elliott E.McKee, Gregory O'Kane, A.Elliott. Sub: J.Cunning for Molloy. (Subs in drawn game: L.Richmond for J.Elliott, S.Boyle for E.McKee, J.Cunning for P.Molloy.)
(Note: Same teams fielded by both clubs in drawn game and replay.)

1996

Sixmilebridge
D.Fitzgerald M.Halloran, K.McInerney M.Toomey, C.Chaplin, J.O'Connell, P.Hayes J.Chaplin, N.Earley David Chaplin, F.Quilligan, M.Conlon: D.McInerney, Danny Chaplin, G.McInerney. Subs: N.Gilligan for Quilligan, N.O'Gorman for Hayes.

Dunloy
S.Elliott N.McCamphill, P.Molloy, S.McIlhatton S.McMullan, Gary O'Kane, S.Mullan F.McMullan, C.McGuckian N.Elliott, T.McGrath, A.Elliott E.McKee, Gregory O'Kane, J.Elliott. Subs: B.Óg Cunning for McCamphill M.Molloy for J.Elliott L.Richmond for S.McMullan.

1997

Athenry
M.Crimmins E.Keogh, G.Keane, J.Feeney B.Higgins, B.Feeney, P.Hardiman P.Healy, B.Keogh, J.Rabbitte, P.Higgins, B.Hanley, A.Poinard, E.Cloonan, C.Moran. Subs: E.Brady for Hanley J.Hardiman for Healy.

Wolfe Tones
D.Garrihy G.McIntyre, B.Lohan, M.Hartigan F.Lohan, S.Power, P.Meaney D.Riordan, Pat O'Rourke, F.Carrig, J.McPhilips, P.Lee Paul O'Rourke, D.Collins, P.Keary. Subs: C.O'Neill for Riordan J.Riordan for Pat O'Rourke.

1998

Birr
B.Mullins S.Whelehan, J.Errity, G.Doorley, Barry Whelahan, Brian Whelahan, N.Claffey J.Pilkington, C.Hanniffy D.Hanniffy, C.McGlone, D.Pilkington G.Cahill, D.Regan, P.Carroll. Subs: O.O'Neill for Carroll L.Power for McGlone.

Sarsfields
T.Kenny, Pádraig Kelly, B.Cooney, G.McGrath M.Stratford, M.Ward, W.Earls N.Morrissey, Joe Cooney, P.Forde, M.McGrath, A.Donohue Peter Kelly, J.McGrath, Peter Cooney. Subs: C.Murray for G.McGrath M.Kenny for Stratford C.Hynes for Morrissey.

1999

St Joseph's Doora-Barefield
C.O'Connor, G.Hoey, D.Cahill, K.Kennedy, D.O'Driscoll, S.McMahon, D.Hoey, O.Baker, J.Considine, J.O'Connor, N.Brodie, L.Hassett, G.Baker, C.O'Neill, A.Whelan. Subs: C.Mullen for G.Baker, F.O'Sullivan for J.Considine.

Rathnure
J.Morrissey, S.Somers, J.Conran, D.Guiney, L.Somers, Joe Mooney, R.Guiney, M.Redmond, M.O'Leary, A.Codd, M.Byrne, P.Codd, M.Morrissey, C.Byrne, B.O'Leary. Subs: N.Higgins for L.Somers, R.Codd for M.Morrissey, J.Holohan for C.Byrne.

2000

Athenry
M.Crimmins, E.Keogh, G.Keane, J.Feeney, B.Higgins, B.Feeney, P.Hardiman, B.Keogh, B.Hanley, J.Rabbitte, P.Higgins, D.Moran, C.Moran, E.Cloonan, D.Donohue. Subs: A.Poniard for C.Moran, P.Healy for Higgins, D.Higgins for Donohue.

St Joseph's Doora-Barefield
C.O'Connor, G.Hoey, D.Cahill, K.Kennedy, D.Hoey, S.McMahon, D.O'Driscoll, O.Baker, J.Considine, J.O'Connor, N.Brodie, L.Hassett, G.Baker, C.O'Neill, A.Whelan. Subs: C.Mullen for Brodie, F.O'Sullivan for Whelan, P.Fahy for O'Neill.

2001

Athenry
M.Crimmins, E.Keogh, G.Keane, J.Feeney, B.Higgins, B.Feeney, P.Hardiman, B.Keogh, B.Hanley, J.Rabbitte, P.Higgins, D.Moran, C.Moran, E.Cloonan, D.Donohue. Subs: D.Burns for C.Moran, S.Donohue for Hanley, D.Cloonan for D.Donohue, D.Donohue for B.Feeney, D.Higgins for P.Higgins.

Graigue-Ballycallan
J.Ronan, J.Butler, P.O'Dwyer, J.Ryall, P.McCluskey, T.Comerford, A.Hoyne, James Young, E.O'Dwyer, D.Byrne, J.Hoyne, M.Hoyne, E.Brennan, T.Dermody, A.Ronan. Subs: D.Hoyne for McCluskey, Joe Young for Dermody, J.Lynch for A.Hoyne.

2002

Birr
B.Mullins, G.Cahill, J.Erritty, J.P.O'Meara, N.Claffey, Brian Whelahan, D.Franks, R.Hanniffy, Barry Whelahan, J.Pilkington, G.Hanniffy, L.Power, S.Browne, S.Whelahan, D.Pilkington. Sub: P.Molloy for Power.

Clarinbridge
L.Donoghue, M.Spellman, A.Quinn, G.Spellman, J.Cannon, M.Donoghue, L.Madden, D.Coen, B.Carr, P.Coen, M.Kerins, A.Kerins, C.Coen, D.Forde, D.Donoghue.

2003

Birr
B.Mullins, G.Cahill, J.Erritty, J.P.O'Meara, N.Claffey, Brian Whelahan, D.Franks, Barry Whelahan, J.Pilkington, R.Hanniffy, G.Hanniffy, L.Power, P.Molloy, S.Whelahan, D.Pilkington. Sub: S.Browne for Power.

Dunloy
G.McGhee, D.McMullan, S.Mullan, F.McMullan, M.Molloy, Gary O'Kane, P.McMullan, C.Cunning, C.McGuckian, L.Richmond, Gregory O'Kane, N.Elliott, P.Richmond, A.Elliott, M.Curry. Sub: E.McKee for Cunning.

2004

Newtownshandrum
P.Morrisey, J.McCarthy, B.Mulcahy, G.O'Mahony, I.Kelleher, P.Mulcahy, P.Noonan, A.T.O'Brien, Jerry O'Connor, D.Mulcahy, B.O'Connor, J.P.King, J.Bowles, D.O'Riordan, M.Farrell. Subs: John O'Connor for Farrell, D.Naughton for King, A.G.O'Brien for O'Mahony.

Dunloy
G.McGhee, S.Mullan, Gary O'Kane, F.McMullan, M.Molloy, M.McClements, D.McMullan, C.Cunning, P.McMullan, P.Richmond, C.McGuckian, L.Richmond, M.Curry, Gregory O'Kane, A.Elliott. Sub: D.Quinn for Curry.

2005

James Stephens
F.Cantwell, D.Cody, M.Phelan, D.Grogan, J.Tyrell, P.Larkin, P.Barry, P.O'Brien, B.McEvoy, J.Murphy, E.Larkin, G.Whelan, E.McCormack, R.Hayes, D.McCormack. Sub: J.Murray for Murphy.

Athenry
M.Crimmins, T.Kelly, P.Hardiman, J.Feeney, B.Higgins, B.Feeney, S.Donohue, L.Howley, B.Hanley, J.Rabbitte, M.J.Quinn, E.Caulfield, D.Moran, E.Cloonan, D.Donohue. Subs: D.Burns for Caulfield, D.Carroll for Hanley, C.O'Donovan for S.Donohue.

2006

Portumna
I.Canning, M.Gill, E.McEntee, O.Canning, G.Heagney, M.Ryan, A.O'Donnell, L.Smith, E.Lynch, D.Canning, K.Hayes, A.Smith, D.Hayes, N.Hayes, J.Canning.

Newtownshandrum
P.Morrisey, M.Farrell, B.Mulcahy, D.Gleeson, A.T.O'Brien, P.Mulcahy, P.Noonan, J.P.King, J.O'Connor, D.Mulcahy, B.O'Connor, J.O'Connor, W.O'Mahony, J.Bowles, C.Naughton.

2007

Ballyhale Shamrocks
J.Connolly, P.Shefflin, E.Walsh, P.Holden, K.Nolan, A.Cummins, B.Aylward, J.Fitzpatrick, M.Fennelly, E.Fitzpatrick, H.Shefflin, T.J.Reid, E.Reid, P.Reid, M.Aylward. Sub: D.Hoyne for E.Fitzpatrick.

Loughrea
N.Murray, T.Regan, D.McLearn, D.Melia, B.Mahony, G.Kennedy, J.Dooley, G.Keary, R.Regan, E.Coen, J.Maher, V.Maher, B.Dooley, J.Loughlin, K.Colleran. Subs: M.Haverty for Loughlin, Loughlin for Dooley, K.Daniels for Coen.

2008

Portumna
I.Canning, M.Gill, E.McEntee, O.Canning, G.Heagney, M.Ryan, P.Smith, L.Smith, E.Lynch, A.Smith, K.Hayes, N.Hayes, D.Hayes, J.Canning, D.Canning. Subs: A.O'Donnell for P.Smith, C.Ryan for D.Canning.

Birr
B.Mullins, J.P.O'Meara, N.Claffey, M.Verney, B.Watkins, P.Cleary, D.Hayden, R.Hanniffy, Barry Whelahan, G.Hanniffy, Brian Whelahan, S.Ryan, P.O'Meara, S.Whelahan, S.Brown. Subs: M.Dwane for Ryan, P.Molloy for P.O'Meara, B.Harding for Hayden.

2009

Portumna
I.Canning, M.Dolphin, E.McEntee, O.Canning, G.Heagney, M.Ryan, A.O'Donnell, E.Lynch, L.Smith, N.Hayes, K.Hayes, A.Smith, D.Hayes, J.Canning, C.Ryan. Subs: D.Canning for C.Ryan, M.Gill for Heagney, P.Smith for L.Smith, P.Treacy for O'Donnell, J.O'Flaherty for McEntee.

De La Salle
S.Brenner, A.Kelly, K.Moran, M.Doherty, D.Russell, I.Flynn, S.Daniels, B.Phelan, C.Watt, P.Nevin, J.Mullane, L.Hayes, D.Twomey, D.McGrath, D.Greene. Subs: B.Farrell for Hayes, T.Kearney for McGrath, J.Quirke for Farrell, A.O'Neill for Watt, D.Dooley for Twomey.

2010

Ballyhale Shamrocks
J.Connolly, A.Cuddihy, A.Cummins, P.Holden, P.Shefflin, E.Walsh, B.Aylward, J.Fitzpatrick, M.Fennelly, C.Fennelly, H.Shefflin, T.J.Reid, E.Reid, P.Reid, D.Hoyne. Subs: J.Holden for M.Fennelly, M.Aylward for P.Reid.

Portumna
I.Canning, A.O'Donnell, E.McEntee, O.Canning, G.Heagney, M.Ryan, P.Smith, L.Smith, E.Lynch, N.Hayes, K.Hayes, A.Smith, D.Hayes, J.Canning, M.Dolphin. Subs: C.Ryan for McEntee, C.Ryan for Hayes.

2011

Clarinbridge
L.Donoghue, C.Forde, B.Burke, P.Callanan, J.Cannon, D.Forde, M.Donoghue, B.Daly, E.Muphry, S.Burke, M.Kerins, S.Forde, E.Forde, A.Kerins, P.Coen. Sub: E.Collins for S.Forde.

O'Loughlin Gaels
S.Murphy, B.Kelly, A.Kearns, E.Kearns, A.O'Brien, B.Hogan, N.Bergin, P.Dowling, M.Nolan, N.McEvoy, M.Bergin, A.Geoghegan, B.Dowling, M.Comerford, D.Loughnane. Subs: S.Cummins for B.Dowling, B.Murphy for Kelly.

2012

Loughgiel Shamrocks
D.D.Quinn, P.Gillan, N.McGarry, R.McCloskey, J.Campbell, M.Scullion, J.Campbell, B.McAuley, M.McFadden, J.Scullion, D.Laverty, E.McCloskey, B.McCarry, L.Watson, S.Casey. Subs: S.Dobbin for McFadden, T.McCloskey for Dobbin, D.McCloskey for Casey.

Coolderry
S.Corcoran, B.Kelly, T.Corcoran, A.Corcoran, K.Brady, J.Brady, B.O'Meara, K.Teehan, D.King, B.Carroll, B.Teehan, C.Parlon, E.Ryan, M.Corcoran, D.Murray. Subs: K.Connolly for T.Corcoran, B.Larkin for Kelly.

2013

St Thomas'
P.Skehill, S.Skehill, Robert Murray, C.Burke, E.Tannion, Darragh Burke, S.Burke, K.Burke, David Burke, S.Cooney, C.Cooney, J.Regan, B.Burke, Richie Murray, A.Kelly. Subs: E.Burke for Kelly, G.Murray for S.Cooney.

Kilcormac/Killoughey
Conor Slevin, J.Grogan, G.Healion, A.McConville, K.Grogan, P.Healion, B.Leonard, D.Kilmartin, K.Leonard, Ciaran Slevin, C.Mahon, P.Geraghty, J.Gorman, T.Fletcher, T.Geraghty. Subs: M.Leonard for Fletcher, C.Guinan for P.Geraghty.

2014

Portumna
J.Keane, C.O'Hare, E.McEntee, G.Heagney, P.Smith, M.Dolphin, E.Lynch, L.Smith, J.Canning, K.Hayes, D.Hayes, O.Canning, R.O'Meara, N.Hayes, A.Smith. Subs: O.Treacy for P.Smith, N.Dolphin for N.Hayes, C.Royston for O'Meara.

Mount Leinster Rangers
F.Foley, M.Doyle, G.Doyle, G.Kelly, Diarmuid Byrne, R.Coady, E.Coady, Derek Byrne, P.Nolan, P.Coady, E.Byrne, D.Phelan, D.Murphy, J.Coady, E.Doyle. Subs: H.P.O'Byrne for J.Coady, J.Murphy for Phelan, W.Hickey for E.Doyle, B.Nolan for Derek Byrne, D.Grennan for Diarmuid Byrne.

2015

Ballyhale Shamrocks
R.Reid, K.Nolan, J.Holden, A.Cuddihy, P.Shefflin, M.Fennelly, A.Cummins, C.Walsh, B.Aylward, J.Fitzpatrick, H.Shefflin, T.J.Reid, P.Reid, C.Fennelly, E.Reid. Subs: M.Aylward for P.Reid, T.Coogan for Nolan, D.Hoyne for Walsh, M.Dermody for P.Shefflin.

Kilmallock
B.Hennessy, L.Hurley, M.O'Loughlin, A.Costello, L.Walsh, Philip O'Loughlin, K.O'Donnell, P.O'Brien, B.O'Sullivan, J.Mulcahy, G.O'Mahony, R.Egan, G.Mulcahy, K.Kenneally, E.Ryan. Subs: Paddy O'Loughlin for Kenneally, R.Hanley for Egan, C.Barry for O'Sullivan, A.O'Shaughnessy for E.Ryan.

2016

Na Piarsaigh
P.Kennedy, M.Casey, K.Breen, K.Kennedy, M.Foley, R.Lynch, C.King, A.Dempsey, W.O'Donoghue, S.Dowling, K.Breen, A.Breen, K.Downes, D.Dempsey, P.Casey. Subs: K.Ryan for D.Breen, P.Gleeson for O'Donoghue.

Cushendall
E.Gillan, R.McCambridge, M.Burke, A.Graffin, D.Kearney, E.Campbell, S.Delargy, S.McNaughton, A.Delargy, C.Carson, N.McManus, S.McAfee, P.McGill, D.McNaughton, C.McNaughton. Subs: C.Boylan for McManus, P.Burke for S.Delargy, K.McKeegan for D.McNaughton, A.McNaughton, for C.McNaughton, E.McKillop for Graffin, E.Laverty for McGill.

2017

Cuala
S.Brennan, P.Schutte, Cian O'Callaghan, S.Timlin, O.Gough, S.Moran, J.Malone, J.Sheanon, D.O'Connell, D.Treacy, C.Cronin, S.Treacy, C.Waldron, Con O'Callaghan, M.Schutte. Subs: C.Sheanon for Waldron, R.Tierney for Timlin, N.Kenny for Cronin.

Ballyea
K.Sheehan, B.Carrig, J.Browne, J.Neylon, P.Flanagan, G.O'Connell, J.Murphy, T.Kelly, S.Lineen, N.Deasy, P.Connolly, C.Doohan, P.Lillis, G.Brennan, D.Burke. Subs: M.O'Leary for Connolly, D.Egan for Burke, B.Murphy for Neylon, M.Coughlan for Lineen.

CAPTAINS OF WINNING ALL-IRELAND CLUB HURLING TEAMS

1971	D . Moloney (Roscrea)
1972	J. Horgan (Blackrock)
1973	D. Coughlan (Glen Rovers)
1974	J. Horgan (Blockrock)
1975	J. Power (St. Finbarr's)
1976	P. Larkin (James Stephens)
1977	M. Doherty (Glen Rovers)
1978	D. Burns (St. Finbarr's)
1979	J. Horgan (Blackrock)
1980	M. Connolly (Castlegar)
1981	R. Reid (Ballyhale Shamrocks)
1982	J. O'Brien (James Stephens)
1983	N. Patterson (Loughgiel Shamrocks)
1984	K. Fennelly (Ballyhale Shamrocks)
1985	J. Brennan (St. Martin's)
1986	T. Sheppard (Kiluane McDonagh's)
1987	M. Ryan (Borris-Ileigh)
1988	G. Power (Midleton)
1989	P. Kenny (Buffer's Alley)
1990	W. Phelan (Ballyhale Shamrocks)
1991	R . Heffernan (Glenmore)
1992	A. Staunton (Kiltormer)
1993	P. Cooney (Sarsfields)
1994	P. Cooney (Sarsfields)
1995	J. Pilkington (Birr)
1996	G. McInerney (Sixmilebridge)
1997	B. Feeney (Athenry)
1998	J. Errity (Birr)
1999	L. Hassett (St. Joseph's Doora-Barefield)
2000	J.Rabbitte (Athenry)
2001	J.Rabbitte (Athenry)
2002	S.Whelahan (Birr)
2003	G.Hanniffy (Birr)
2004	J.McCarthy (Newtownshandrum)
2005	P.Barry (James Stephens)
2006	E.McEntee (Portumna)
2007	T.Coogan (Ballyhale Shamrocks)
2008	O.Canning (Portumna)
2009	O.Canning (Portumna)
2010	E. Walsh (Ballyhale Shamrocks)
2011	P.Callanan (Clarinbridge)
2012	J.Campbell (Loighgiel Shamrocks)
2013	R.Murray (St Thomas')
2014	O.Canning (Portumna)
2015	T.J.Reid (Ballyhale Shamrocks)
2016	C.King (Na Piarsaigh)
2017	O.Gough (Cuala)

CLUB HURLING FINAL REFEREES

1971	Frank Murphy (Cork)
1972	Noel Dalton (Waterford)
1973	Sean O'Grady (Limerick)
1974	Paddy Johnson (Kilkenny)
1975	Mick Spain (Offaly)
1976	Jimmy Rankins (Laois)
1977	John Moloney (Tipperary)
1978	Noel O'Donoghue (Dublin)
1979	Seamus Brennan (Galway)
1980	Nealie Duggan (Limerick)
1981	Noel O'Donoghue (Dublin)
1982	George Ryan (Tipperary)
1983	N. O'Donoghue/J. Rankins
1984	George Ryan (Tipperary)
1985	George Ryan (Tipperary)
1986	Terence Murray (Limerick)
1987	Gerry Kirwan (Offaly)
1988	Gerry Kirwan (Offaly)
1989	Willie Horgan (Cork)
1990	Willie Horgan (Cork)
1991	Willie Barrett (Tipperary)
1992	Dickie Murphy (Wexford)
1993	Pat Horan (Offaly)
1994	Pat Horan (Offaly)
1995	Pat O'Connor (Limerick)
1996	Dickie Murphy (Wexford)
1997	Dickie Murphy (Wexford)
1998	Willie Barrett (Wexford)
1999	Pat O'Connor (Limerick)
2000	M Wadding (Waterford)
2001	J McDonnell (Tipperary)
2002	G Harrington (Cork)
2003	S McMahon (Clare)
2004	B Kelly (Westmeath)
2005	S Roche (Tipperary)
2006	B.Gavin (Offaly)
2007	D.Kirwan (Cork)
2008	J.Sexton (Cork)
2009	J.McGrath (Westmeath)
2010	C.McAllister (Cork)
2011	J.Ryan (Tipperary)
2012	A.Kelly (Galway)
2013	J.Sexton (Cork)
2014	B.Kelly (Westmeath)
2015	J.Owens (Wexford)
2016	D.Kirwan (Cork)
2017	F.Horgan (Tipperary)

ALL-STAR HURLING TEAMS

1971
D.Martin (Offaly), A.Maher (Cork), P.Hartigan (Limerick), J.Treacy (Kilkenny), T.O'Connor (Tipperary), M.Roche (Tipperary), M.Coogan (Kilkenny), F.Cummins (Kilkenny), John Connolly (Galway), F.Loughnane (Tipperary), M.Keating (Tipperary), E.Keher (Kilkenny), M.Bermingham (Dublin), R.Cummins (Cork), E.Cregan (Limerick).

1972
N.Skehan (Kilkenny), A.Maher (Cork), P.Hartigan (Limerick), J.Treacy (Kilkenny), P.Lawlor (Kilkenny), M.Jacob (Wexford), C.Roche (Cork), F.Cummins (Kilkenny), D.Coughlan (Cork), F.Loughnane (Tipperary), P.Delaney (Kilkenny), E.Keher (Kilkenny), C.McCarthy (Cork), R.Cummins (Cork), E.Cregan (Limerick).

1973
N.Skehan (Kilkenny), P.Larkin (Kilkenny), P.Hartigan (Limerick), J.O'Brien (Limerick), C.Doran (Wexford), P.Henderson (Kilkenny), S.Foley (Limerick), R.Bennis (Limerick), L.O'Brien (Kilkenny), F.Loughnane (Tipperary), P.Delaney (Kilkenny), E.Grimes (Limerick), M.Quigley (Wexford), K.Purcell (Kilkenny), E.Keher (Kilkenny).

1974
N.Skehan (Kilkenny), P.Larkin (Kilkenny), P.Hartigan (Limerick), J.Horgan (Cork), G.Loughnane (Clare), P.Henderson (Kilkenny), C.Roche (Cork), L.O'Brien, (Kilkenny), J.Galvin (Waterford), J.McKenna (Limerick), M.Quigley (Wexford), M.Crotty (Kilkenny), J.Quigley (Wexford), K.Purcell (Kilkenny), E.Keher (Kilkenny).

1975
N.Skehan (Kilkenny), N.McInerney (Galway), P.Hartigan (Limerick), B.Cody (Kilkenny), T.O'Connor (Tipperary), S.Silke (Galway), I.Clarke (Galway), L.O'Brien (Kilkenny), G.McCarthy (Cork), M.Quigley (Wexford), J.McKenna (Limerick), E.Grimes (Limerick), M.Brennan (Kilkenny), K.Purcell (Kilkenny), E.Keher (Kilkenny).

1976
N.Skehan (Kilkenny), P.Larkin (Kilkenny), W.Murphy (Wexford), J.McMahon (Clare), J.McDonagh (Galway), M.Jacob (Wexford), D.Coughlan (Cork), F.Burke (Galway), P.Moylan (Cork), M.Malone (Cork), M.Quigley (Wexford), J.Barry Murphy (Cork), M.Brennan (Kilkenny), T.Doran (Wexford), S.O'Leary (Cork).

1977
S.Durack (Clare), J.McMahon (CLare), M.O'Doherty (Cork), J.Horgan (Cork), G.Loughnane (Clare), M.Jacob (Wexford), D.Coughlan (Cork), T.Cashman (Cork), M.Moroney (Clare), C.Keogh (Wexford), J.Barry Murphy (Cork), P.J.Molloy (Galway), C.McCarthy (Cork), R.Cummins (Cork), S.O'Leary (Cork).

1978
S.Durack (Clare), P.Larkin (Kilkenny), M.O'Doherty (Cork), J.Horgan (Cork), J.Hennessy (Kilkenny), G.Henderson (Kilkenny), D.Coughlan (Cork), T.Cashman (Cork), I.Clarke (Galway), J.Barry Murphy (Cork), N.Casey (Clare), C.Honan (Clare), C.McCarthy (Cork), J.McKenna (Limerick), T.Butler (Tipperary).

1979
P.McLoughney (Tipperary), B.Murphy (Cork), M.O'Doherty (Cork), T.O'Connor (Tipperary), D.McCurtain (Cork), G.Henderson (Kilkenny), I.Clarke (Galway), John Connolly (Galway), J.Hennessy (Kilkenny), J.Callinan (Clare), F.Burke (Galway), L.O'Brien (Kilkenny), M.Brennan (Kilkenny), J.McKenna (Limerick), E.Buggy (Wexford).

1980
P.McLoughney (Tipperary), N.McInerney (Galway), L.Enright (Limerick), Jimmy Cooney (Galway), D.McCurtain (Cork), S.Silke (Galway), I.Clarke (Galway), J.Kelly (Offaly), M.Walsh (Waterford), Joe Connolly (Galway), P.Horgan (Cork), P Carroll (Offaly), B.Forde (Galway), J.McKenna (Limerick), E.Cregan (Limerick).

1981
S.Durack (Clare), B.Murphy (Cork), L.Enright (Limerick), Jimmy Cooney (Galway), L.O'Donoghue (Limerick), S.Stack (Clare), G.Coughlan (Offaly), S.Mahon (Galway), L Currams (Offaly), J.Callinan (Clare), G.O'Connor (Wexford) M Corrigan (Offaly), P.Carroll (Offaly), J.McKenna (Limerick), J Flaherty (Offaly).

1982
N.Skehan (Kilkenny), J.Galvin (Waterford), B.Cody (Kilkenny), P.Fleury (Offaly), A.Fogarty (Offaly), G.Henderson (Kilkenny), P.Prendergast (Kilkenny), T.Crowley (Cork), F.Cummins (Kilkenny), A.O'Sullivan (Cork), P.Horgan (Cork), R.Power (Kilkenny), W.Fitzpatrick (Kilkenny), C.Heffernan (Kilkenny), J Greene (Waterford).

1983
N.Skehan (Kilkenny), J.Henderson (Kilkenny), L.Enright (Limerick), D.O'Hara (Kilkenny), J.Hennessy (Kilkenny), G.Henderson (Kilkenny), T.Cashman (Cork), F.Cummins (Kilkenny), J.Fenton (Cork), N.English (Tipperary), G.Fennelly (Kilkenny), N.Lane (Galway), W.Fitzpatrick (Kilkenny), J.Barry Murphy (Cork), L.Fennelly (Kilkenny).

1984
G.Cunningham (Cork), P.Fitzmaurice (Limerick), E.Coughlan (Offaly), P.Fleury (Offaly), J.Hennessy (Kilkenny), J.Crowley (Cork), D.MacCurtain (Cork), J.Fenton (Cork), J.Kelly (Offaly), N.English (Tipperary), K.Brennan (Kilkenny), P.Kelly (Limerick), T.Mulcahy (Cork), N.Lane (Galway), S.O'Leary (Cork).

1985
G.Cunningham (Cork), S.Coen (Galway), E.Coughlan (Offaly), S.Linnane (Galway), P.Finnerty (Galway), P.Delaney (Offaly), G.Coughlan (Offaly), P.Critchley (Laois), J Fenton (Cork), N.English (Tipperary), B.Lynskey (Galway), Joe Cooney (Galway), P.Cleary (Offaly), P.Horan (Offaly), L.Fennelly (Kilkenny).

1986
G.Cunningham {Cork), D.Mulcahy (Cork), C.Hayes (Galway), S.Linnane (Galway), P Finnerty (Galway), A.Keady (Galway), B.Ryan (Tipperary), R.Power (Kilkenny), J.Fenton (Cork), A.O'Sullivan (Cork), T.Mulcahy (Cork), Joe Cooney (Galway), D.Kilcoyne (Westmeath), J.Barry Murphy (Cork), K.Hennessy (Cork).

1987

K.Hogan (Tipperary), J.Hennessy (Kilkenny), C.Hayes (Galway), O.Kilkenny
(Galway), P.Finnerty (Galway), G.Henderson (Kilkenny), J.Conran (Wexford), S.Mohan (Galway), J.Fenton (Cork), M.McGrath (Galway), Joe Cooney (Galway), A.Ryan (Tipperary), P.Fox (Tipperary), N.English (Tipperary), L.Fennelly (Kilkenny).

1988

J.Commins (Galway), S.Linnane (Galway), C.Hayes (Galway), M.Hanamy (Offaly), P.Finnerty (Galway), A.Keady (Galway), B.Ryan (Tipperary), Colm Bonnar (Tipperary), G.O'Connor (Wexford), D.Ryan (Tipperary), C.Barr (Antrim), M.Naughton (Galway), M.McGrath (Galway), N.English (Tipperary), A.O'Sullivan (Cork).

1989

J.Commins (Galway), A.Fogarty (Offaly), E.Cleary (Wexford), D.Donnelly (Antrim), Conal Bonnar (Tipperary), B.Ryan (Tipperary), S.Treacy (Galway), M.Coleman (Galway), D.Carr (Tipperary), E.Ryan (Galway), Joe Cooney (Galway), O.McFetridge (Antrim), P Fox (Tipperary), Cormac Bonnar (Tipperary), N.English (Tipperary).

1990

G.Cunningham (Cork), J.Considine (Cork), N.Sheehy (Tipperary), S.O'Gorman (Cork), P.Finnerty (Galway), J.Cashman (Cork), L.Dunne (Wexford), M.Coleman (Galway), J.Pilkington (Offaly), M.Cleary (Tipperary), Joe Cooney (Galway), A.O'Sullivan (Cork), E.Morrissey (Kilkenny), B.McMahon (Dublin), J.Fitzgibbon (Cork).

1991

M.Walsh (Kilkenny), P.Delaney (Tipperary), N.Sheehy (Tipperary), S.Treacy (Galway), Conal Bonnar (Tipperary), J.Cashman (Cork), C.Casey (Cork), T.McNaughten (Antrim), J.Leahy (Tipperary), M.Cleary (Tipperary), G.Kirby (Limerick), D.J.Carey (Kilkenny), P.Fox (Tipperary), Cormac Bonnar (Tipperary), J.Fitzgibbon (Cork).

1992

T.Quaid (Limerick), B.Corcoran (Cork), P.Dwyer (Kilkenny), L.Simpson (Kilkenny), B.Whelehan (Offaly), C.Carey (Limerick), W.O'Connor (Kilkenny), M.Phelan (Kilkenny), S.McCarthy (Cork), G.McGrattan (Down), J.Power (Kilkenny), A.O'Sullivan (Cork), M.Cleary (Tipperary), L.Fennelly (Kilkenny), D.J.Carey (Kilkenny).

1993

M.Walsh (Kilkenny), E.O'Connor (Kilkenny), S.O'Gorman (Cork), L.Simpson (Kilkenny), L.Dunne (Wexford), P.O'Neill (Kilkenny), P.Kelly (Galway), P.Malone (Galway), P.McKillen (Antrim), M.Storey (Wexford), J.Power (Kilkenny), D.J.Carey (Kilkenny), M.Cleary (Tipperary), J.Rabbitte (Galway), B.Egan (Cork).

1994

Joe Quaid (Limerick), A.Daly (Clare), K.Kinahan (Offaly), M.Hanamy (Offaly), D.Clarke (Limerick), H.Rigney (Offaly), K.Martin (Offaly), C.Carey (Limerick), M.Houlihan (Limerick), Johnny Dooley (Offaly), G.Kirby (Limerick), J.Leahy (Tipperary), B.Dooley (Offaly), D.J.Carey (Kilkenny), D.Quigley (Limerick).

1995

D.Fitzgerald (Clare), K.Kinahan (Offaly), B.Lohan (Clare), L.Doyle (Clare), B.Whelehan (Offaly), S.McMahon (Clare), Anthony Daly (Clare), O.Baker (Clare), M.Coleman (Galway), Johnny Dooley (Offaly), G.Kirby (Limerick), J.O'Connor (Clare), B.Dooley (Offaly), D.J.Carey (Kilkenny), G.O'Loughlin (Clare).

1996

Joe Quaid (Limerick), T.Helebert (Galway), B.Lohan (Clare), L.O'Gorman (Wexford), L.Dunne (Wexford), C.Carey (Limerick), M.Foley (Limerick), A.Fenlon (Wexford), M.Houlihan (Limerick), R.McCarthy (Wexford), M.Storey (Wexford), L.Murphy (Wexford), L.Cahill (Tipperary), G.Kirby Limerick), T.Dempsey (Wexford).

1997

D.Fitzhenry (Wexford), P Shelly (Tipperary), B.Lohan (Clare), W.O'Connor (Kilkenny), L.Doyle (Clare), S.McMahon (Clare), L.Keoghan (Kilkenny), C.Lynch (Clare), T.Dunne (Tipperary), J.O'Connor (Clare), D.Ryan (Tipperary), J.Leahy (Tipperary), K.Broderick (Galway), G.O'Loughlin (Clare), D.J.Carey (Kilkenny).

1998

S.Byrne (Offaly), W.O'Connor (Kilkenny), K.Kinahan (Offaly), M.Hanamy (Offaly), A.Daly (Clare), S.McMahon (Clare), K.Martin (Offaly), Tony Browne (Waterford), O.Baker (Clare), M.Duignan (Offaly), M.Storey (Wexford), J.O'Connor (Clare), Joe Dooley (Offaly), B.Whelahan (Offaly), C.Carter (Kilkenny).

1999

Donal Óg Cusack (Cork), Fergal Ryan (Cork), Diarmuid O'Sullivan (Cork), Frank Lohan (Clare), Brian Whelahan (Offaly), Brian Corcoran (Cork), Peter Barry (Kilkenny), Andy Comerford (Kilkenny), Tommy Dunne (Tipperary), DJ Carey (Kilkenny), John Troy (Offaly), Brian McEvoy (Kilkenny), Sean McGrath (Cork), Joe Deane (Cork), Niall Gilligan (Clare).

2000

Brendan Cummins (Tipperary), Noel Hickey (Kilkenny), Diarmuid O'Sullivan (Cork), Willie O'Connor (Kilkenny), John Carroll (Tipperary), Eamonn Kennedy (Tipperary), Peter Barry (Kilkenny), Johnny Dooley (Offaly), Andy Comerford (Kilkenny), Denis Byrne (Kilkenny), Joe Rabbitte (Galway), Henry Shefflin (Kilkenny), Charlie Carter (Kilkenny), DJ Carey (Kilkenny), Joe Deane (Cork).

2001

Brendan Cummins (Tipperary), Darragh Ryan (Wexford), Philip Maher (Tipperary), Ollie Canning (Galway), Eamonn Corcoran (Tipperary), Liam Hodgins (Galway), Mark Foley (Limerick), Thomas Dunne (Tipperary), Eddie Enright (Tipperary), Mark O'Leary (Tipperary), James O'Connor (Clare), Kevin Broderick (Galway), Charlie Carter (Kilkenny), Eugene Cloonan (Galway), Eoin Kelly (Tipperary).

2002

David Fitzgerald (Clare), Michael Kavanagh (Kilkenny), Brian Lohan (Clare), Philip Larkin (Kilkenny), Fergal Healy (Waterford), Peter Barry (Kilkenny), Paul Kelly (Tipperary), Colin Lynch (Clare), Derek Lyng (Kilkenny), Eoin Kelly (Waterford), Henry Shefflin (Kilkenny), Ken McGrath (Waterford), Eoin Kelly (Tipperary), Martin Comerford (Kilkenny), DJ Carey (Kilkenny).

2003

Brendan Cummins (Tipperary), Michael Kavanagh (Kilkenny), Noel Hickey (Kilkenny), Ollie Canning (Galway), Seán Óg Ó hAilpín (Cork), Ronan Curran (Cork), JJ Delaney (Kilkenny), Derek Lyng (Kilkenny), Tommy Walsh (Kilkenny), John Mullane (Waterford), Henry Shefflin (Kilkenny), Eddie Brennan (Kilkenny), Setanta Ó hAilpín (Cork), Martin Comerford (Kilkenny), Joe Deane (Cork).

2004

Damien Fitzhenry (Wexford), Wayne Sherlock (Cork), Diarmuid O'Sullivan (Cork), Tommy Walsh (Kilkenny), JJ Delaney (Kilkenny), Ronan Curran (Cork), Seán Óg Ó hAilpín (Cork), Ken McGrath (Waterford), Jerry O'Connor (Cork), Dan Shanahan (Waterford), Niall McCarthy (Cork), Henry Shefflin (Kilkenny), Eoin Kelly (Tipperary), Brian Corcoran (Cork), Paul Flynn (Waterford).

2005

Davy Fitzgerald (Clare), Pat Mulcahy (Cork), Diarmuid O'Sullivan (Cork), Ollie Canning (Galway), Derek Hardiman (Galway), John Gardiner (Cork), Sean Óg Ó hAilpín (Cork), Jerry O'Connor (Cork), Paul Kelly (Tipperary), Ben O'Connor (Cork), Henry Shefflin (Kilkenny), Tommy Walsh (Kilkenny), Ger Farragher (Galway), Eoin Kelly (Tipperary), Damien Hayes (Galway).

2006

Donal Óg Cusack (Cork), Eoin Murphy (Waterford), JJ Delaney (Kilkenny), Brian Murphy (Cork), Tony Browne (Waterford), Ronan Curran (Cork), Tommy Walsh (Kilkenny), Jerry O'Connor (Cork), James Fitzpatrick (Kilkenny), Dan Shanahan (Waterford), Henry Shefflin (Kilkenny), Eddie Brennan (Kilkenny), Eoin Kelly (Tipperary), Martin Comerford (Kilkenny), Tony Griffin (Clare).

2007

Brian Murray (Limerick), Michael Kavanagh (Kilkenny), Declan Fanning (Tipperary), Jackie Tyrrell (Kilkenny), Tommy Walsh (Kilkenny), Ken McGrath (Waterford), Tony Browne (Waterford), Michael Walsh (Waterford), James Fitzpatrick (Kilkenny), Dan Shanahan (Waterford), Ollie Moran (Limerick), Stephen Molumphy (Waterford), Andrew O'Shaughnessy (Limerick), Henry Shefflin (Kilkenny), Eddie Brennan (Kilkenny).

2008

Brendan Cummins (Tipperary), Michael Kavanagh (Kilkenny), Noel Hickey (Kilkenny), Jackie Tyrrell (Kilkenny), Tommy Walsh (Kilkenny), Conor O'Mahony (Tipperary), JJ Delaney (Kilkenny), James Fitzpatrick (Kilkenny), Shane McGrath (Tipperary), Ben O'Connor (Cork), Henry Shefflin (Kilkenny), Eoin Larkin (Kilkenny), Eddie Brennan (Kilkenny), Eoin Kelly (Waterford), Joe Canning (Galway).

2009

P J Ryan (Kilkenny), Ollie Canning (Galway), Padraig Maher (Tipperary), Jackie Tyrrell (Kilkenny), Tommy Walsh (Kilkenny), Michael Walsh (Waterford), Conor O'Mahony (Tipperary), Michael Rice (Kilkenny), Alan McCrabbe (Dublin), Lar Corbett (Tipperary), Henry Shefflin (Kilkenny), Eoin Larkin (Kilkenny), Noel McGrath (Tipperary), Joe Canning (Galway), John Mullane (Waterford).

2010

Brendan Cummins (Tipperary), Noel Connors (Waterford), Paul Curran (Tipperary), Jackie Tyrrell (Kilkenny), Tommy Walsh (Kilkenny), Michael Walsh (Kilkenny), JJ Delaney (Kilkenny), Brendan Maher (Tipperary), Michael Fennelly (Kilkenny), Damien Hayes (Galway), Noel McGrath (Tipperary), Lar Corbett (Tipperary), John Mullane (Waterford), Richie Power (Kilkenny), Eoin Kelly (Tipperary).

2011

Gary Maguire (Dublin), Paul Murphy (Kilkenny), Paul Curran (Tipperary), Michael Cahill (Tipperary), Tommy Walsh (Kilkenny), Brian Hogan (Kilkenny), Pádraic Maher (Tipperary), Liam Rushe (Dublin), Michael Fennelly (Kilkenny), Michael Rice (Kilkenny), Richie Power (Kilkenny), Henry Shefflin (Kilkenny), John Mullane (Waterford), Lar Corbett (Tipperary), Richie Hogan (Kilkenny).

2012

Anthony Nash (Cork), Paul Murphy (Kilkenny), JJ Delaney (Kilkenny), Fergal Moore (Galway), Brendan Bugler (Clare), Brian Hogan (Kilkenny), David Collins (Galway), Iarla Tannian (Galway), Kevin Moran (Waterford), T.J.Reid (Kilkenny), Henry Shefflin (Kilkenny), Damien Hayes (Galway), John Mullane (Waterford), Joe Canning (Galway), David Burke (Galway).

2013

Anthony Nash (Cork), Richie McCarthy (Limerick), Peter Kelly (Dublin), David McInerney (Clare), Brendan Bugler (Clare), Liam Rushe (Dublin), Patrick Donnellan (Clare), Colm Galvin (Clare), Conor Ryan (Clare), Seamus Harnedy (Cork), Tony Kelly (Clare), Danny Sutcliffe (Dublin), Pádraic Collins (Clare), Patrick Horgan (Cork), Conor McGrath (Clare).

2014

Darren Gleeson (Tipperary), Paul Murphy (Kilkenny), JJ Delaney (Kilkenny), Seamus Hickey (Limerick), Brendan Maher (Tipperary), Pádraic Maher (Tipperary), Cillian Buckley (Kilkenny), Richie Hogan (Kilkenny), Shane McGrath (Tipperary), John O'Dwyer (Tipperary), Patrick Maher (Tipperary), T.H.Reid (Kilkenny), Colin Fennelly (Kilkenny), Séamus Callanan (Tipperary), Shane Dowling (Limerick).

2015

Colm Callanan (Galway), Paul Murphy (Kilkenny), Joey Holden (Kilkenny), Noel Connors (Waterford), Daithí Burke (Galway), Tadhg de Búrca (Waterford), Cillian Buckley (Kilkenny), Michael Fennelly (Kilkenny), David Burke (Galway), Cathal Mannion (Galway), Richie Hogan (Kilkenny), T.J.Reid (Kilkenny), Ger Aylward (Kilkenny), Séamus Callanan (Tipperary), Maurice Shanahan (Waterford).

2016

Eoin Murphy (Kilkenny), Cathal Barrett (Tipperary), James Barry (Tipperary), Daithí Burke (Galway), Pádraig Walsh (Kilkenny), Ronan Maher (Tipperary), Pádraic Maher (Tipperary), Jamie Barron (Waterford), David Burke (Galway), Walter Walsh (Kilkenny), Austin Gleeson (Waterford), Patrick Maher (Tipperary), Richie Hogan (Kilkenny), Séamus Callanan (Tipperary), John McGrath (Tipperary).

2017

Stephen O'Keeffe (Waterford), Pádraic Mannion (Galway), Daithí Burke (Galway), Noel Connors (Waterford), Pádraic Maher (Tipperary), Gearóid McInerney (Galway), Mark Coleman (Cork), Jamie Barron (Waterford), David Burke (Galway), Kevin Moran (Waterford), Joe Canning (Galway), Michael Walsh (Waterford), Conor Whelan (Galway), Conor Cooney (Galway), Patrick Horgan (Cork).

LEADING AWARD WINNERS

Henry Shefflin (Kilkenny) 11
2000, 2002, 2003, 2004, 2005, 2006, 2007, 2008, 2009, 2011, 2012.
D. J. Carey (Kilkenny) 9
1991, 1992, 1993, 1994, 1995, 1997, 1999, 2000, 2002.
Tommy Walsh (Kilkenny) 9
2003, 2004, 2005, 2006, 2007, 2008, 2009, 2010, 2011.
Noel Skehan (Kilkenny) 7
1972, 1973, 1974, 1975, 1976, 1982, 1983.
J.J.Delaney (Kilkenny) 7
2003, 2004, 2006, 2008, 2010, 2012, 2014.
Joe McKenna (Limerick) 6
1974, 1975, 1978, 1979, 1980, 1981
Nicholas English (Tipperary) 6
1983, 1984, 1985, 1987, 1988, 1989.

ALL-TIME HURLING ALL-STAR AWARD WINNERS

1980	Mick Mackey (Limerick)
1981	Jack Lynch (Cork)
1982	Garrett Howard (Limerick)
1983	Fowler McInerney (Clare)
1984	Jim Langton (Kilkenny)
1985	Eudie Coughlan (Cork)
1986	Tommy Doyle (Tipperary)
1987	Christy Moylan (Waterford)
1988	Paddy "Fox" Collins (Cork)
1989	M. J. "Inky" Flaherty (Galway)
1990	John Joe Doyle (Clare)
1991	Jackie Power (Limerick)
1992	Bobby and Billy Rackard (Wexford)
1993	Pat Stakelum (Tipperary)
1994	Martin White (Kilkenny)

Discontinued

HURLER OF THE YEAR AWARD

The following are the Hurling stars who have been awarded
Texaco Trophies by the Sports Editors since the inauguration of
the award in 1958 by the sponsors Texaco. Also listed are the
Hall of Fame winners in hurling since the introduction of this
category in 1960.

1958	Tony Wall Tipperary.
1959	Christy Ring (Cork).
1960	Nick O'Donnell (Wexford).
1961	Liam Devaney (Tipperary).
1962	Donie Nealon (Tipperary).
1963	Seamus Cleere (Kilkenny).
1964	John Doyle (Tipperary).
1965	Jimmy Doyle (Tipperary).
1966	Justin McCarthy (Cork).
1967	Ollie Walsh (Kilkenny).
1968	Dan Qulgley (Wexford).
1969	Ted Carroll (Kilkenny).
1970	Pat McDonnell (Cork).
1971	Michael Keating (Tipperary).
1972	Eddie Keher (Kilkenny).
1973	Eamonn Grimes (Limerick).
1974	Pat Henderson (Kilkenny).
1975	Liam O'Brien (Kilkenny).
1976	Tony Doran (Wexford).
1977	Denis Coughlan (Cork).
1978	John Horgan (Cork).
1979	Ger Henderson (Kilkenny).
1980	John Connolly (Galway).
1981	Pat Delaney (Offaly).
1982	Noel Skehan (Kilkenny).
1983	Frank Cummins (Kilkenny).
1984	John Fenton (Cork).
1985	Eugene Coughlan (Offaly).
1986	Ger Cunningham (Cork).
1987	Joe Cooney (Galway).
1988	Tony Keady (Galway).
1989	Nicholas English (Tipperary).
1990	Tony O'Sullivan (Cork).
1991	Pat Fox (Tipperary).
1992	Brian Corcoran (Cork).
1993	D.J.Carey (Kilkenny).
1994	Brian Whelehan (Offaly).
1995	Seán McMahon (Clare).
1996	Larry O'Gorman (Wexford).
1997	Jamesie O'Connor (Clare).
1998	Brian Whelehan (Offaly).
1999	Brian Corcoran (Cork).
2000	D.J.Carey (Kilkenny).
2001	Thomas Dunne (Tipperary).
2002	Henry Shefflin (Kilkenny).
2003	J.J.Delaney (Kilkenny).
2004	Seán Óg Ó hAilpín (Cork).
2005	Jerry O'Connor (Cork).
2006	Henry Shefflin (Kilkenny).
2007	Dan Shanahan (Waterford).
2008	Eoin Larkin (Kilkenny).
2009	Tommy Walsh (Kilkenny).
2010	Lar Corbett (Tipperary).
2011	Michael Fennelly (Kilkenny).
2012	Henry Shefflin (Kilkenny).
2013	Tony Kelly (Clare).
2014	Richie Hogan (Kilkenny)
2015	T.J.Reid (Kilkenny)
2016	Austin Gleeson (Waterford)
2017	Joe Canning (Galway)

HALL OF FAME

1961 Mick Mackey, Limerick.
1971 Christy Ring, Cork.
1992 John Doyle, Tipperary.
2001 Willie Rackard, Wexford.

THOSE HONOURED BETWEEN 1963 AND 1967

Before the All-Star Awards were officially formalised in 1971 and took on a new importance, the now-defunct Gaelic Weekly sponsored the selection of All-Star teams from 1963 to 1967 (inclusive) in both hurling and football. Here are the hurling teams:

1963
O.Walsh (Kilkenny), T.Neville (Wexford), A.Flynn (Waterford), John Doyle (Tipperary), S.Cleere (Kilkenny), Billy Rackarcl (Wexford), L.Guinan (Waterford), T.English (Tipperary), D.Foley (Dublin), Jimmy Doyle (Tipperary), M.Flannelly (Waterford), E.Keher (Kilkenny), L.Devaney (Tipperary), J.Smith (Clare), P.Grimes (Waterford).

1964
O.Walsh (Kilkenny), John Doyle (Tipperary), P.Dillon (Kilkenny), T.Neville (Wexford), S.Cleere (Kilkenny), Tony Wall (Tipperary), P.Henderson (Kilkenny), M.Roche (Tipperary), P.Moran (Kilkenny), Jimmy Doyle (Tipperary), M.Keating (Tipperary), E.Keher (Kilkenny), T.Walsh (Kilkenny), J.McKenna (Tipperary), D.Nealon (Tipperary).

1965
J.O'Donoghue (Tipperary), T.Neville (Wexford), A.Flynn (Waterford), K.Carey (Tipperary), D.O'Riordan (Cork), Tony Wall (Tipperary), J.Duggan (Galway), P.Wilson (Wexford), M.Roche (Tipperary), Jimmy Doyle (Tipperary), P.Carroll (Kilkenny), P.Cronin (Clare), D.Nealon (Tipperary), John McKenna (Tipperary), S.McLoughlin (Tipperary).

1966
P.Barry (Cork), P.Henderson (Kilkenny), A.Flynn (Waterford), D.Murphy (Cork), S.Cleere (Kilkenny), K.Long (Limerick), M.Coogan (Kilkenny), B.Hartigan (Limerick), T.English (Tipperary), S.Barry (Cork), E.Keher (Kilkenny), P.Cronin (Clare), P.Molloy (Offaly), John McKenna (Tipperary), M.Fox (Galway).

1967
O.Walsh (Kilkenny), P.Henderson (Kilkenny), P.Dillon (Kilkenny), J.Treacy (Kilkenny), S.Cleere (Kilkenny), J.Cullinan (Clare), L.Gaynor (Tipperary), M.Roche (Tipperary), P.Moran (Kilkenny), E.Keher (Kilkenny), T.Walsh (Kilkenny), P.Cronin (Clare), D.Nealon (Tipperary), Tony Doran (Wexford), M.Keating (Tipperary).

1968-1970 No All-Star Teams

ATTENDANCE FIGURES

ALL-IRELAND FINALS

1931	Cork v Kilkenny	26,460
Replay	Cork v Kilkenny	33,124
Replay	Cork v Kilkenny	31,935
1932	Kilkenny v Clare	34,372
1933	Kilkenny v Limerick	45,176
1934	Limerick v Dublin	34,867
Replay	Limerick v Dublin	30,250
1935	Kilkenny v Limerick	46,591
1936	Limerick v Kilkenny	51,235
1937	Tipperary v Kilkenny	43,638
1938	Dublin v Waterford	37,129
1939	Kilkenny v Cork	39,302
1940	Limerick v Kilkenny	39,260
1941	Cork (nominated) v Dublin	26,150
1942	Cork v Dublin	27,313
1943	Cork v Antrim	48,843
1944	Cork v Dublin	26,896
1945	Tipperary v Kilkenny	69,459
1946	Cork v Kilkenny	64,415
1947	Kilkenny v Cork	61,510
1948	N.A.	
1949	Tipperary v Laois	67,168
1950	Tipperary v Kilkenny	67,629
1951	Tipperary v Wexford	68,515
1952	Cork v Dublin	64,332
1953	Cork v Galway	71,195
1954	Cork v Wexford	84,856
1955	Wexford v Galway	77,854
1956	Wexford v Cork	83,096
1957	Kilkenny v Waterford	70,594
1958	Tipperary v Galway	47,276
1959	Waterford v Kilkenny	73,707
Replay	Waterford v Kilkenny	77,285
1960	Wexford v Tipperary	77,154
1961	Tipperary v Dublin	67,866
1962	Tipperary v Wexford	75,039
1963	Kilkenny v Waterford	73,123
1964	Tipperary v Kilkenny	71,282
1965	Tipperary v Wexford	67,498
1966	Cork v Kilkenny	68,249
1967	Kilkenny v Tipperary	64,241
1968	Wexford v Tipperary	63,461

1969	Kilkenny v Cork	66,844
1970	Corkv v Wexford	65,062
1971	Tipperary v Kilkenny	61,393
1972	Kilkenny v Cork	66,135
1973	Limerick v Kilkenny	58,009
1974	Kilkenny v Limerick	62,071
1975	Kilkenny v Galway	63,711
1976	Corkv v Wexford	62,071
1977	Cork v Wexford	63,168
1978	Cork v Kilkenny	64,155
1979	Kilkenny v Galway	63,711
1980	Galwayv v Limerick	64,384
1981	Offaly v Galway	71,384
1982	Kilkenny v Cork	59,550
1983	Kilkenny v Cork	58,381
1984	Cork v Offaly	58,814
1985	Offaly v Galway	61,814
1986	Cork v Galway	43,451
1987	Galway v Kilkenny	59,550
1988	Galway v Tipperary	63,545
1989	Tipperary v Antrim	65,496
1990	Cork v Galway	63,954
1991	Tipperary v Kilkenny	64,500
1992	Kilkenny v Cork	64,354
1993	Kilkenny v Galway	63,460
1994	Offaly v Limerick	56,458
1995	Clare v Offaly	65,092
1996	Wexford v Limerick	65,849
1997	Clare v Tipperary	65,575
1998	Offaly v Kilkenny	65,491
1999	Cork v Kilkenny	62,989
2000	Kilkenny v Offaly	61,493
2001	Tipperary v Galway	68,512
2002	Kilkenny v Clare	76,254
2003	Kilkenny v Cork	79,383
2004	Cork v Kilkenny	78,212
2005	Cork v Galway	81,136
2006	Kilkenny v Cork	82,275
2007	Kilkenny v Limerick	82,127
2008	Kilkenny v Waterford	82,186
2009	Kilkenny v Tipperary	82,104
2010	Tipperary v Kilkenny	81,765
2011	Kilkenny v Tipperary	81,214
2012	Kilkenny v Galway	81,932
Replay	Kilkenny v Galway	82,274
2013	Clare v Cork	81,651

Replay	Clare v Cork	82,276
2014	Kilkenny v Tipperary	82,179
Replay	Kilkenny v Tipperary	81,753
2015	Kilkenny v Galway	82,300
2016	Tipperary v Kilkenny	82,106
2017	Galway v Waterford	82,300

LEINSTER FINAL ATTENDANCES

1950	Kilkenny v Wexford	36,494
1951	Wexford v Laois	29,692
1952	Dublin v Wexford	30,500
1953	Kilkenny v Wexford	37,533
1954	Wexford v Dublin	28,592
1955	Wexford v Kilkenny	37,079
Replay	Wexford v Kilkenny	41,226
1956	Wexford v Kilkenny	52,077
1957	Kilkenny v Wexford	52,272
1958	Kilkenny v Wexford	41,729
1959	Kilkenny v Dublin	31,312
1960	Wexford v Kilkenny	42,332
1961	Dublin v Wexford	27,446
1962	Wexford v Kilkenny	45,303
1963	Kilkenny v Dublin	33,438
1964	Kilkenny v Dublin	30,103
1965	Wexford v Kilkenny	28,000
1966	Kilkenny v Wexford	35,000
1967	Kilkenny v Wexford	25,242
1968	Wexford v Kilkenny	25,000
1969	Kilkenny v Offaly	24,800
1970	Wexford v Kilkenny	19,306
1971	Kilkenny v Wexford	19,344
1972	Kilkenny v Wexford	22,745
Replay	Kilkenny v Wexford	18,611
1973	Kilkenny v Wexford	24,000
1974	Kilkenny v Wexford	20,742
1975	Kilkenny v Wexford	26,228
1976	Wexford v Kilkenny	23,500
1977	Wexford v Kilkenny	30,614
1978	Kilkenny v Wexford	27,371
1979	Kilkenny v Wexford	24,991
1980	Offaly v Kilkenny	9,613
1981	Offaly v Wexford	29,053
1982	Kilkenny v Offaly	32,093
1983	Kilkenny v Offaly	35,707
1984	Offaly v Wexford	30,016
1985	Offaly v Laois	32,123
1986	Kilkenny v Offaly	28,635
1987	Kilkenny v Offaly	29,133
1988	Offaly v Wexford	28,234
1989	Offaly v Kilkenny	24,519
1990	Offaly v Dublin	20,383
1991	Kilkenny v Dublin	41,215

1992	Kilkenny v Wexford	41,097
1993	Kilkenny v Wexford	37,715
Replay	Kilkenny v Wexford	41,833
1994	Offaly v Wexford	32,141
1995	Offaly v Kilkenny	31,950
1996	Wexford v Offaly	34,365
1997	Wexford v Kilkenny	55,492
1998	Kilkenny v Offaly	32,490
1999	Kilkenny v Offaly	38,310
2000	Kilkenny v Offaly	32,802
2001	Kilkenny v Wexford	41,146
2002	Kilkenny v Wexford	37,567
2003	Kilkenny v Wexford	50,000
2004	Wexford v Offaly	46,820
2005	Kilkenny v Wexford	35,010
2006	Kilkenny v Wexford	44,081
2007	Kilkenny v Wexford	34,872
2008	Kilkenny v Wexford	18,855
2009	Kilkenny v Dublin	29,427
2010	Kilkenny v Galway	31,376
2011	Kilkenny v Dublin	33,814
2012	Galway v Kilkenny	22,171
2013	Dublin v Galway	36,657
2014	Kilkenny v Dublin	32,567
2015	Kilkenny v Galway	31,954
2016	Kilkenny v Galway	29,377
2017	Galway v Wexford	60,032

HURLING

MUNSTER FINAL ATTENDANCES

Year	Match	Attendance
1950	Tipperary v Cork	38,733
1951	Tipperary v Cork	42,337
1952	Cork v Tipperary	42,326
1953	Corkv v Tipperary	46,265
1954	Cork v Tipperary	50,071
1955	Limerick v Clare	23,125
1956	Cork v Limerick	47,017
1957	Waterford v Cork	40,368
1958	Tipperary v Waterford	41,384
1959	Waterford v Cork	55,174
1960	Tipperary v Cork	49,670
1961	Tipperary v Cork	61,175
1962	Tipperary v Waterford	31,000
1963	Waterford v Tipperary	36,000
1964	Tipperary v Cork	44,245
1965	Tipperary v Cork	40,687
1966	Cork v Waterford	31,352
1967	Tipperary v Clare	34,940
1968	Tipperary v Cork	43,238
1969	Cork v Tipperary	43,569
1970	Cork v Tipperary	33,900
1971	Tipperary v Limerick	31,118
1972	Cork v Clare	25,048
1973	Limerick v Tipperary	41,723
1974	Limerick v Clare	36,446
1975	Cork v Limerick	46,851
1976	Cork v Limerick	46,800
1977	Cork v Clare	44,586
1978	Cork v Clare	54,981
1979	Cork v Limerick	47,849
1980	Limerick v Cork	43,090
1981	Limerick v Clare	40,205
1982	Cork v Waterford	38,558
1983	Cork v Waterford	20,816
1984	Cork v Tipperary	50,093
1985	Cork v Tipperary	49,691
1986	Cork v Clare	39,975
1987	Tipperary v Cork	56,005
Replay	Tipperary v Cork	45,000
1988	Tipperary v Cork	50,000
1989	Tipperary v Waterford	30,241
1990	Cork v Tipperary	45,000
1991	Tipperary v Cork	47,500
Replay	Tipperary v Cork	55,600
1992	Cork v Limerick	48,036
1993	Tipperary v Clare	41,557
1994	Limerick v Clare	43,638
1995	Clare v Limerick	46,361
1996	Limerick v Tipperary	43,525
Replay	Limerick v Tipperary	40,000
1997	Clare v Tipperary	43,560
1998	Clare v Waterford	51,417
Replay	Clare v Waterford	51,731
1999	Cork v Clare	54,000
2000	Cork v Tipperary	54,586
2001	Tipperary v Limerick	43,500
2002	Waterford v Tipperary	40,276
2003	Cork v Waterford	52,833
2004	Waterford v Cork	53,000
2005	Cork v Tipperary	43,500
2006	Cork v Tipperary	53,286
2007	Waterford v Limerick	48,371
2008	Tipperary v Clare	48,076
2009	Tipperary v Waterford	40,330
2010	Waterford v Cork	35,962
Replay	Waterford v Cork	22,763
2011	Tipperary v Waterford	36,654
2012	Tipperary v Waterford	26,438
2013	Limerick v Cork	42,730
2014	Cork v Limerick	36,075
2015	Tipperary v Waterford	43,084
2016	Tipperary v Waterford	26,508
2017	Cork v Clare	45,558

FOOTBALL

ROLL OF HONOUR

SENIOR

Kerry *(37)* 1903, 1904, 1909, 1913, 1914, 1924, 1926, 1929, 1930, 1931, 1932, 1937, 1939, 1940, 1941, 1946, 1953, 1955, 1959, 1962, 1969, 1970, 1975, 1978, 1979, 1980, 1981, 1984, 1985, 1986, 1997, 2000, 2004, 2006, 2007, 2009, 2014.

Dublin *(27)* 1891, 1892, 1894, 1897, 1898, 1899, 1901, 1902, 1906, 1907, 1908, 1921, 1922, 1923, 1942, 1958, 1963, 1974, 1976, 1977, 1983, 1995, 2011, 2013, 2015, 2016, 2017.

Galway *(9)* 1925, 1934, 1938, 1956, 1964, 1965, 1966, 1998, 2001.

Meath *(7)* 1949, 1954, 1967, 1987, 1988, 1996, 1999.

Cork *(7)* 1890, 1911, 1945, 1973, 1989, 1990, 2010.

Wexford *(5)* 1893, 1915, 1916, 1917, 1918.

Cavan *(5)* 1933, 1935, 1947, 1948, 1952.

Down *(5)* 1960, 1961, 1968, 1991, 1994.

Tipperary *(4)* 1889, 1895, 1900, 1920.

Kildare *(4)* 1905, 1919, 1927, 1928.

Louth *(3)* 1910, 1912, 1957.

Mayo *(3)* 1936, 1950, 1951.

Offaly *(3)* 1971, 1972, 1982.

Tyrone *(3)* 2003, 2005, 2008.

Limerick *(2)* 1887, 1896.

Roscommon *(2)* 1943, 1944.

Donegal *(2)* 1992, 2012.

Derry *(1)* 1993.

Armagh *(1)* 2002.
(Note: No Championship in 1888, U.S. Invasion)

MINOR

Kerry *(15)* 1931, 1932, 1933, 1946, 1950, 1962, 1963, 1975, 1980, 1988, 1994, 2014, 2015, 2016, 2017.

Dublin *(11)* 1930, 1945, 1954, 1955, 1956, 1958, 1959, 1979, 1982, 1984, 2012.

Cork *(10)* 1961, 1967, 1968, 1969, 1972, 1974, 1981, 1991, 1993, 2000.

Tyrone *(8)* 1947, 1948, 1973, 1998, 2001, 2004, 2008, 2010.

Mayo *(7)* 1935, 1953, 1966, 1971, 1978, 1985, 2013.

Galway *(6)* 1952, 1960, 1970, 1976, 1986, 2007.

Derry *(4)* 1965, 1983, 1989, 2002.

Down *(4)* 1977, 1987, 1999, 2005.

Roscommon *(4)* 1939, 1941, 1951, 2006.

Meath *(3)* 1957, 1990, 1992.

Laois *(3)* 1996, 1997, 2003.

Cavan *(2)* 1937, 1938.

Louth *(2)* 1936, 1940.

Armagh *(2)* 1949, 2009.

Tipperary *(2)* 1934, 2011

Clare *(1)* 1929.

Offaly *(1)* 1964.

Westmeath *(1)* 1995.
(Note: Suspended 1942-1944 inclusive).

U21

Cork *(11)* 1970, 1971, 1980, 1981, 1984, 1985, 1986, 1989, 1994, 2007, 2009.

Kerry *(10)* 1964, 1973, 1975, 1976, 1977, 1990, 1995, 1996, 1998, 2008.

Galway *(5)* 1972, 2002, 2005, 2011, 2013.

Tyrone *(5)* 1991, 1992, 2000, 2001, 2015.

Mayo *(5)* 1967, 1974, 1983, 2006, 2016.

Dublin *(5)* 2003, 2010, 2012, 2014, 2017.

Roscommon *(2)* 1966, 1978.

Donegal *(2)* 1982, 1987.

Derry *(2)* 1968, 1997.

Kildare *(1)* 1965.

Antrim *(1)* 1969.

Down *(1)* 1979.

Offaly *(1)* 1988.

Meath *(1)* 1993.

Westmeath *(1)* 1999.

Armagh *(1)* 2004.

JUNIOR

Kerry *(18)* 1913, 1915, 1924, 1928, 1930, 1941, 1949, 1954, 1963, 1967, 1983, 1991, 1994, 2006, 2012, 2015, 2016, 2017.

Cork *(17)* 1951, 1953, 1955, 1964, 1972, 1984, 1987, 1989, 1990, 1993, 1996, 2001, 2005, 2007, 2009, 2011, 2013.

London *(6)* 1938, 1966, 1969, 1970, 1971, 1986.

Dublin *(6)* 1914, 1916, 1939, 1948, 1960, 2008.

Mayo *(5)* 1933, 1950, 1957, 1995, 1997.

Meath *(5)* 1947, 1952, 1962, 1988, 2003.

Louth *(4)* 1925, 1932, 1934, 1961.

Galway *(4)* 1931, 1958, 1965, 1985.

Tipperary *(3)* 1912, 1923, 1998.

Roscommon *(2)* 1940, 2000.

Wicklow *(2)* 1936, 2002.

Waterford *(2)* 1999, 2004.

Sligo *(2)* 1935, 2010.

Cavan *(2)* 1927, 2014.

Armagh *(1)* 1926.

Westmeath *(1)* 1929.

Longford *(1)* 1937.

Down *(1)* 1946.

Monaghan *(1)* 1956.

Fermanagh *(1)* 1959.

Tyrone *(1)* 1968.

Laois *(1)* 1973.

Wexford *(1)* 1992.

(Note: Junior Football suspended in 1917-1922 and 1974-1982 inclusive).

SENIOR "B" FOOTBALL

Leitrim *(1)* 1990.
Clare *(1)* 1991.
Wicklow *(1)* 1992.
Laois *(1)* 1993.
Carlow *(1)* 1994.
Tipperary *(1)* 1995.
Fermanagh *(1)* 1996.
Louth *(1)* 1997.
Monaghan *(1)* 1998.

ALL-IRELAND SENIOR FOOTBALL CHAMPIONSHIP RESULTS

(Note: Teams 21-a-side. A goal outweighted any number of points)

1887

Open draw. Counties represented by county champions.
Inchicore, August 28.
Louth (Dundalk Young Irelands) 0-7 Wexford (Castlebridge) 0-4
Limerick Junction, October 22.
Tipperary (Templemore) 0-3 Limerick (Commercials) 0-3
Tipperary Town, March 11 1888, Replay
Limerick (Commercials) 1-9 Tipperary (Templemore) 0-4
Clonskeagh, April 29 1888. Final:
Limerick (Commercials) 1-4 Louth (Dundalk Young Irelands) 0-3

1888

Championship unfinished owing to U.S.A. invasion by GAA athletes.

1889

No semi-finals.
Inchicore, October 20. Final:
Tipperary (Bohercrowe) 3-6 Laois (Maryborough) 0-0

1890

Clonturk Park, November 16.
Cork (Midleton) 1-15 Armagh (Harps) 0-0
Wexford (Blues & Whites) W.O. from Galway (Cahirlistrane)
Clonturk Park, June 26 1892. Final:
Cork (Midleton) 2-4 Wexford (Blues & Whites) 0-1

1891

No Connacht representatives.
Clonturk Park, February 28 1892.
Dublin (Young Irelands) 3-7 Cavan (Slashers) 0-3
Clonturk Park February 281892. Final:
Dublin (Young Irelands) 2-1 Cork (Clondrohid) 1-9

(Note: Teams reduced to 17-a-side. A goal made equal to 5 Points from 1892)

1892

At the Annual Congress county champions were granted permission to select players from other clubs within the county. No Ulster representatives.
Clonturk Park, March 19 1893.
Dublin 1-9 Roscommon 1-1
Clonturk Park March 26 1893. Final:
Dublin (Young Irelands) 1-4 Kerry (Laune Rangers) 0-3

(Note: With no representation from Ulster and Connacht there were no semi-finals from 1893 to 1899)

1893

Phoenix Park, June 24 1894. Final:
Wexford (Young Irelands) 1-1 Cork (Dromtariffe) 0-1
(Note: Game unfinished. Wexford declared champions).

1894

Clonturk Park, March 24 1895. Final:
Dublin (Young Irelands) 0-6 Cork (Nils) 1-1
Thurles, April 21 1895. Replay:
Dublin 0-5 Cork 1-2
(Note: Unfinished. Dublin awarded title.
The final was replayed at Thurles on 21 May 1895. Cork were leading 1-2 to 0-5 when a dispute arose and Dublin walked off before the finish. When Cork refused to play a third time the title was awarded to Dublin.)

1895

Jones's Road, March 15 1896. Final:
Tipperary (Arravale Rovers) 0-4 Meath (Pierce O'Mahony's) 0-3

(Note: Goal made equal to 3 Points from 1896 and the parallelogram introduced.)

1896

Jones's Road February 6 1898. Final:
Limerick (Commercials) 1-5 Dublin (Young Irelands) 0-7

1897

Jones's Road, February 5 1899. Final:
Dublin (Kickhams) 2-6 Cork (Dunmanway) 0-2

1898

Tipperary Town, April 8 1900. Final:
Dublin (Geraldines) 2-8 Waterford (Erin's Hope) 0-4

1899

Jones's Road, February 10 1901. Final:
Dublin (Geraldines) 1-10 Cork (Nils) 0-6

1900

Galway W.O. from Antrim
Carrick-on-Suir, June 30 1902.
Kilkenny 1-6 Tipperary 0-7
(Note: An objection by Tipperary resulted in the Central Council ordering a replay. Kilkenny refused to replay the game which was awarded to Tipperary.)
Terenure, September 21 1902. Home Final:
Tipperary 2-17 Galway (Krugers Tuam) 0-1
Jones's Road, October 26 1902. Final:
Tipperary (Clonmel Shamrocks) 3-7 London (Hibernians) 0-2

1901

Jones's Road, April 12 1903.
Dublin 1-12 Antrim 0-3
Limerick, May 17 1903.
Cork 4-16 Mayo 0-1
Tipperary, July 5 1903. Home Final:
Dublin 1-2 (Isles of the Sea) Cork (Nils) 0-4
Jones's Road, August 2 1903. Final:
Dublin 0-14 London (Hibernians) 0-2

1902

Athenry, April 24 1904.
Tipperary 2-5 Galway 0-4
Drogheda, June 11 1904
Dublin 4-16 Armagh 1-6

Kilkenny, July 24 1904. Home Final:
Dublin 0-6   **Tipperary 0-5**
Cork, September 11 1904. Final:
Dublin (Bray Emmets) 2-8   **London (Hibernians) 0-4**

1903
Limerick, May 7 1905.
Kerry 2-7   **Mayo 0-4**
Jones's Road, June 18 1905.
Kildare 0-8   **Cavan 0-0**
Tipperary July 23 1905. Home Final:
Kerry 1-4   **Kildare (Clane) 1-3**
(Disputed)
Cork, August 27 1905. Replay:
Kerry 0-7   **Kildare 1-4**
Cork, October 13 1905. 2nd Replay:
Kerry 0-8   **Kildare 0-2**
Jones's Road, November 121905. Final:
Kerry (Tralee Mitchels) 0-11   **London (Hibernians) 0-3**

1904
Jones's Road, May 6 1906.
Kerry 4-10   **Cavan 0-1**
Athlone, May 13 1906.
Dublin 0-8   **Mayo 1-4**
Cork, July 1 1906. Final:
Kerry (Tralee Mitchels) 0-5   **Dublin (Kickhams) 0-2**

1905
Jones's Road, August 5 1906.
Dublin 1-9   **London 1-4**
Limerick, September 2 1906.
Kerry 2-10 Roscommon 1-3
Jones's Road September 30.
Kildare 4-15   **Cavan 1-6**
(Note: Kildare qualified for All-Ireland final by beating Dublin and Louth (final) in Leinster championship.)
Thurles June 16 1907. Final:
Kildare 1-7   **Kerry 0-5**

1906
Belfast, May 19 1907.
Kildare 2-10   **Monaghan 1-3**
Wexford, August 4 1907.
Dublin 2-7   **London 0-3**
Limerick, September 8 1907.
Cork 0-10   **Mayo 0-6**
(Note: Dublin qualified for All-Ireland final by beating Kildare in Leinster final).
Athy, October 20 1907. Final:
Dublin (Kickhams) 0-5 Cork (Fermoy) 0-4

1907
Jones's Road, March 15 1908.
Dublin 1- 5   **Monaghan 0-2**
Limerick, May 10 1908.
Cork 2-10   **Mayo 0-2**
Cork, June 7 1908.
Cork 1-14   **London 1-5**
Tipperary, July 5 1908. Final:
Dublin (Kickhams) 0-6 Cork (Lees) 0-2

1908
Jones's Road, February 21 1909.
Dublin 1-8   **Antrim 0-2**
Limerick, February 14 1909.
Kerry 2-4   **Mayo 0-1**
Thurles, May 9 1909. Home Final:
Dublin 0-10   **Kerry (Mitchels) 0-3**
Jones's Road, August 1 1909. Final:
Dublin (Geraldines) 1-10   **London (Hibernians) 0-4**

1909
Ennis, November 21 1909.
Kerry 2-12   **Mayo 0-6**
Belfast, October 10 1909.
Louth 2-13   **Antrim 0-15**
Jones's Road, December 5. Final:
Kerry (Tralee Mitchels) 1-9   **Louth (Tredaghs) 0-6**

1910
Tuam, August 21 1910.
Kerry 1-7   **Mayo 0-4**
Dundalk, September 11 1910.
Louth 3-4   **London 2-2**
Jones's Road, October 2 1910.
Dublin 3-5   **Antrim 0-2**
(Note: Louth qualified for the final by beating Dublin in the Leinster championship). Final fixed for Jones's Road. Louth (Tredaghs) W.O. from Kerry (Tralee Mitchels) who refused to travel.)

1911
Jones's Road, December 10.
Antrim 3-1   **Kilkenny 1-1**
Portlaoise, December 3.
Cork 3-4   **Galway 0-2**
Jones's Road, January 14 1912. Final:
Cork (Lees) 6-6   **Antrim (Shauns) 1-2**

1912
Jones's Road, August 25 1912.
Antrim 3-5   **Kerry 0-2**
Jones's Road, September 29 1912.
Dublin 2-4   **Roscommon 1-1**
(Note: Louth qualified by beating Dublin in the Leinster championship).
Jones's Road, November 3. Final:
Louth (Tredaghs) 1-7 Antrim (Mitchels) 1-2
(Note: Teams reduced to 15-a-side from 1913.)

1913
London, August 4 1913.
Louth 3-6   **London 1-2**
(Note: Wexford qualified by beating Louth in the Leinster final).
Jones's Road, October 5 1913.
Wexford 4-4   **Antrim 0-1**
Portlaoise, November 9 1913.
Kerry 1-8   **Galway 0-1**
Croke Park, December 14 1913. Final:
Kerry (Killarney) 2-2   **Wexford (Rapparees) 0-3**

1914
Portlaoise, September 6 1914.
Kerry 2-4   Roscommon 0-1
Croke Park, September 13 1914.
Wexford 2-6   Monaghan 0-1
Croke Park, November 1 1914. Final:
Kerry 1-3   Wexford 2-0
Croke Park, November 29 1914. Replay:
Kerry (Killarney) 2-3   Wexford (Blues & Whites) 0-6

1915
Portlaoise, September 19 1915.
Kerry 2-3   Roscommon 1-1
Croke Park, October 17 1915.
Wexford 3-7   Cavan 2-2
Croke Park, November 7 1915. Final:
Wexford (Blues & Whites) 2-4   Kerry (Selection) 2-1

1916
Carrickmacross, October 22 1916.
Wexford 0-9   Monaghan 1-1
Athlone, October 22 1916.
Mayo 1-2   Cork 0-2
(Objection replay ordered.)
Croke Park, November 19 1916.
Mayo 1-2   Cork 1-1
Croke Park, December 17 1916. Final:
Wexford (Blues & Whites) 3-4   Mayo (Stephenites Ballina) 1-2

1917
Athlone, November 18 1917.
Clare 2-1   Galway 0-4
Wexford, November 18 1917.
Wexford 6-6   Monaghan 1-3
Croke Park, December 9 1917. Final:
Wexford (Blues & Whites) 0-9   Clare (Selection) 0-5

1918
Croke Park, January 12 1919.
Tipperary 2-2   Mayo 1-4
Belturbet, October 20 1918.
Louth 2-4   Cavan 0-4
(Note: Wexford qualified for final by beating Louth in Leinster final.)
Croke Park, February 16 1919. Final:
Wexford (Blues & Whites) 0-5 Tipperary (Fethard) 0-4

1919
Croke Park, August 24 1919.
Galway 2-6   Kerry 3-3
Croke Park, September 14 1919. Replay:
Galway 4-2   Kerry 2-2
Navan, September 14 1919.
Kildare 3-2   Cavan 1-3
Croke Park, September 28 1919. Final:
Kildare (Caragh) 2-5   Galway (Selection) 0-1

1920
Navan, September 26 1920.
Dublin 3-6   Cavan 1-3
Croke Park, May 7 1922.
Tipperary 1-5   Mayo 1-0
Croke Park, June 11 1992. Final:
Tipperary 1-6   Dublin (O'Toole's) 1-2

1921
Dundalk, June 18 1922.
Dublin 2-8   Monaghan 2-2
Mayo W.O. from Tipperary
Croke Park, June 17 1923. Final:
Dublin (St Mary's) 1-9 Mayo (Stephenites Ballina) 0-2

1922
Dundalk, July 15 1923.
Dublin 2-5   Monaghan 0-0
Croke Park, September 9 1923.
Sligo 1-8   Tipperary 0-7
(Note: Galway qualified by beating Sligo in replay of Connacht final.)
Croke Park, October 7 1923. Final:
Dublin (O'Toole's) 0-6 Galway (Ballinasloe) 0-4

1923
Croke Park, April 27 1924. Semi-Final:
Kerry   1-3   1-2   Cavan
Croke Park, May 18 1924n Semi-Final:
Dublin   1-6   1-2   Mayo
Croke Park, September 28. 1924 Final:
Dublin   1-5   1-3   Kerry

1924
Croke Park, December 7. Semi-final.
Kerry   1-4   0-1   Mayo
Croke Park, January 18 1925. Semi-final:
Dublin   0-6   1-1   Cavan
Croke Park, April 26 1925. Final:
Kerry   0-4   0-3   Dublin

1925
Galway declared champions.

Games in lieu of Championship:
Croke Park, December 6 1925.
Galway   3-4   1-1   Wexford
Croke Park, January 10 1926.
Galway   3-2   1-2   Cavan
(Kerry, Munster Champions refused to compete.)
The results of the Championship semi-finals were:
Tralee, August 23.
Kerry   1-7   2-3   Cavan
Croke Park, August 30.
Mayo   2-4   1-4   Wexford

1926
Croke Park, August 8. Semi-final:
Kerry   1-6   0-1   Cavan
Croke Park, August 22. Semi-final:
Kildare   2-5   0-2   Galway
Croke Park, September 5. Final:
Kerry   1-3   0-6   Kildare
Croke Park, October 17. Replay:
Kerry   1-4   0-4   Kildare

1927
Tuam, August 28. Semi-final:
Kerry   0-4   0-2   Leitrim
Drogheda, August 28. Semi-final:
Kildare   1-7   0-2   Monaghan
Croke Park, September 25. Final:
Kildare   0-5   0-3   Kerry

1928
Cavan, August 26. Semi-final:
| *Cavan* | **2-5** | **0-4** | *Sligo* |

Cork, September 2. Semi-final:
| *Kildare* | **3-7** | **0-2** | *Cork* |

Croke, Park September 30. Final:
| *Kildare* | **2-6** | **2-5** | *Cavan* |

1929
Roscommon, August 18. Semi-final:
| *Kerry* | **3-8** | **1-1** | *Mayo* |

Croke Park, August 25. Semi-final:
| *Kildare* | **0-9** | **0-1** | *Monaghan* |

Croke Park, September 22. Final:
| *Kerry* | **1-8** | **1-5** | *Kildare* |

1930
Croke Park, August 24. Semi-final:
| *Monaghan* | **1-6** | **1-4** | *Kildare* |

Roscommon, August 24. Semi-final:
| *Kerry* | **1-9** | **0-4** | *Mayo* |

Croke Park, September 28. Final:
| *Kerry* | **3-11** | **0-2** | *Monaghan* |

1931
Tuam, August 30. Semi-final:
| *Kerry* | **1-6** | **1-4** | *Mayo* |

Cavan, August 30. Semi-final:
| *Kildare* | **0-10** | **1-5** | *Cavan* |

Croke Park, September 27. Final:
| *Kerry* | **1-11** | **0-8** | *Kildare* |

1932
Croke Park August 21. Semi-final:
| *Mayo* | **2-4** | **0-8** | *Cavan* |

Croke Park August 21. Semi-final:
| *Kerry* | **1-3** | **1-1** | *Dublin* |

Croke Park September 25. Final:
| *Kerry* | **2-7** | **2-4** | *Mayo* |

1933
Mullingar, August 20. Semi-final:
| *Galway* | **0-8** | **1-4** | *Dublin* |

Cavan, August 27. Semi-final:
| *Cavan* | **1-5** | **0-5** | *Kerry* |

Croke Park, September 24. Final:
| *Cavan* | **2-5** | **1-4** | *Galway* |

1934
Tuam, August 12. Semi-final:
| *Galway* | **1-8** | **0-8** | *Cavan* |

Tralee, September 9. Semi-final:
| *Dublin* | **3-8** | **0-6** | *Kerry* |

Croke Park, September 23. Final:
| *Galway* | **3-5** | **1-9** | *Dublin* |

1935
Croke Park, August 18. Semi-final:
| *Cavan* | **1-7** | **0-8** | *Tipperary* |

Croke Park, August 25. Semi-final:
| *Kildare* | **2-6** | **0-7** | *Mayo* |

Croke Park, September 22. Final:
| *Cavan* | **3-6** | **2-5** | *Kildare* |

1936
Roscommon, August 9. Semi-final:
| *Mayo* | **1-5** | **0-6** | *Kerry* |

Croke Park, August 23. Semi-final:
| *Laois* | **2-6** | **1-5** | *Cavan* |

Croke Park, September 27. Final:
| *Mayo* | **4-11** | **0-5** | *Laois* |

1937
Cork, August 15. Semi-final:
| *Kerry* | **2-3** | **1-6** | *Laois* |

Mullingar, August 22. Semi-final:
| *Cavan* | **2-5** | **1-7** | *Mayo* |

Waterford, August 29. Replay:
| *Kerry* | **2-2** | **1-4** | *Laois* |

Croke Park, September 26. Final:
| *Kerry* | **2-5** | **1-8** | *Cavan* |

Croke Park, October 17. Replay:
| *Kerry* | **4-4** | **1-7** | *Cavan* |

1938
Mullingar, August 14. Semi-final:
| *Galway* | **2-10** | **2-3** | *Monaghan* |

Croke Park, August 21. Semi-final:
| *Kerry* | **2-6** | **2-4** | *Laois* |

Croke Park, September 25. Final:
| *Galway* | **3-3** | **2-6** | *Kerry* |

Croke Park, October 23. Replay:
| *Galway* | **2-4** | **0-7** | *Kerry* |

1939
Croke Park, August 13. Semi-final:
| *Kerry* | **0-4** | **0-4** | *Mayo* |

Croke Park, August 20. Semi-final:
| *Meath* | **1-9** | **1-1** | *Cavan* |

Croke Park, September 10. Replay:
| *Kerry* | **3-8** | **1-4** | *Mayo* |

Croke Park, September 24. Final:
| *Kerry* | **2-5** | **2-3** | *Meath* |

1940
Croke Park, August 18. Semi-final:
| *Galway* | **3-8** | **2-5** | *Meath* |

Croke Park, August 18. Semi-final:
| *Kerry* | **3-4** | **0-8** | *Cavan* |

Croke Park, September 22. Final:
| *Kerry* | **0-7** | **1-3** | *Galway* |

1941
Croke Park, August 10. Semi-final:
| *Kerry* | **0-4** | **0-4** | *Dublin* |

Tralee, August 17. Replay:
| *Kerry* | **2-9** | **0-3** | *Dublin* |

Croke Park, August 17. Semi-final:
| *Galway* | **1- 12** | **1-4** | *Cavan* |

Croke Park, September 7. Final:
| *Kerry* | **1-8** | **0-7** | *Galway* |

1942
Croke Park, August 2. Semi-final:
Dublin   1-6   1-3   *Cavan*
Croke Park, August 9. Semi-final:
Galway   1-3   0-3   *Kerry*
Croke Park, September 20. Final:
Dublin   1-10   1-8   *Galway*

1943
Croke Park, August 8. Semi-final:
Roscommon   3-10   3-6   *Louth*
Croke Park, August 15. Semi-final:
Cavan   1-8   1-7   *Cork*
Croke Park, September 26. Final:
Roscommon   1-6   1-6   *Cavan*
Croke Park, October 10. Replay:
Roscommon   2-7   2-2   *Cavan*

1944
Croke Park, August 20. Semi-final:
Roscommon   5-8   1-3   *Cavan*
Croke Park, August 27. Semi-final:
Kerry   3-3   0-10   *Carlow*
Croke Park, September 24. Final:
Roscommon   1-9   2-4   *Kerry*

1945
Croke Park, August 12. Semi-final:
Cork   2-12   2-8   *Galway*
Croke Park, August 19. Semi-final:
Cavan   1-4   0-5   *Wexford*
Croke Park, September 23. Final:
Cork   2-5   0-7   *Cavan*

1946
Croke Park, August 18. Semi-final:
Kerry   2-7   0-10   *Antrim*
Croke Park, August 25. Semi-final:
Roscommon   3-5   2-6   *Laois*
Croke Park, October 6. Final:
Kerry   2-4   1-7   *Roscommon*
Croke Park, October 27. Replay:
Kerry   2-8   0-10   *Roscommon*

1947
Croke Park, August 3. Semi-final:
Cavan   2-4   0-0   *Roscommon*
Croke Park, August 10. Semi-final:
Kerry   1-11   0-5   *Meath*
Polo Grounds, New York, September 14. Final:
Cavan   2-11   2-7   *Kerry*

1948
Croke Park, August 22. Semi-final:
Cavan   1-14   4-2   *Louth*
Croke Park, August 29. Semi-final:
Mayo   0-13   0-3   *Kerry*
Croke Park, September 26. Final:
Cavan   4-5   4-4   *Mayo*

1949
Croke Park, August 14. Semi-final:
Meath   3-10   1-10   *Mayo*
Croke Park, August 21. Semi-final:
Cavan   1-9   2-3   *Cork*
Croke Park, September 25. Final:
Meath   1-10   1-6   *Cavan*

1950
Croke Park, August 13. Semi-final:
Mayo   3-9   0-6   *Armagh*
Croke Park, August 20. Semi-final:
Louth   1-7   0-8   *Kerry*
Croke Park, September 24. Final:
Mayo   2-5   1-6   *Louth*

1951
Croke Park, August 12. Semi-final:
Kerry   1-5   1-5   *Mayo*
Croke Park, August 19. Semi-final:
Meath   2-6   1-7   *Antrim*
Croke Park, September 9. Replay:
Mayo   2-4   1-5   *Kerry*
Croke Park, September 23. Final:
Mayo   2-8   0-9   *Meath*

1952
Croke Park, August 3. Semi-final:
Meath   1-6   0-7   *Roscommon*
Croke Park, August 17. Semi-final:
Cavan   0-10   2-3   *Cork*
Croke Park, September 28. Final:
Cavan   2-4   1-7   *Meath*
Croke Park, October 12. Replay:
Cavan   0-9   0-5   *Meath*

1953
Croke Park, August 9. Semi-final:
Armagh   0-8   0-7   *Roscommon*
Croke Park, August 23. Semi-final:
Kerry   3-6   0-10   *Louth*
Croke Park, September 27. Final:
Kerry   0-13   1-6   *Armagh*

1954
Croke Park, August 1. Semi-final:
Meath   1-5   0-7   *Cavan*
Croke Park, August 15. Semi-final:
Kerry   2-6   1-6   *Galway*
Croke Park, September 26. Final:
Meath   1-13   1-7   *Kerry*

1955
Croke Park, August 14. Semi-final:
Kerry   2-10   1-13   *Cavan*
Croke Park, August 21. Semi-final:
Dublin   0-7   1-4   *Mayo*
Croke Park, September 11. Replay:
Kerry   4-7   0-5   *Cavan*
Croke Park, September 11. Replay:
Dublin   1-8   1-7   *Mayo*
Croke Park, September 25. Final:
Kerry   0-12   1-6   *Dublin*

1956
Croke Park, August 5. Semi-final:
Cork 0-9 0-5 *Kildare*
Croke Park, August 12. Semi-final:
Galway 0-8 0-6 *Tyrone*
Croke Park, October 7: Final:
Galway 2-13 3-7 *Cork*

1957
Croke Park, August 11. Semi-final:
Cork 2-4 0-9 *Galway*
Croke Park, August 18. Semi-final:
Louth 0-13 0-7 *Tyrone*
Croke Park, September 22. Final:
Louth 1-9 1-7 *Cork*

1958
Croke Park, August 17. Semi-final:
Dublin 2-7 1-9 *Galway*
Croke Park, August 24. Semi-final:
Derry 2-6 2-5 *Kerry*
Croke Park, September 28. Final:
Dublin 2-12 1-9 *Derry*

1959
Croke Park, August 16. Semi-final:
Kerry 1-10 2-5 *Dublin*
Croke Park, August 23. Semi-final:
Galway 1-11 1-4 *Down*
Croke Park, September 27. Final:
Kerry 3-7 1-4 *Galway*

1960
Croke Park, August 7. Semi-final:
Kerry 1-8 0-8 *Galway*
Croke Park, August 21. Semi-final:
Down 1-10 2-7 *Offaly*
Croke Park, September 11. Replay:
Down 1-7 1-5 *Offaly*
Croke Park, September 25. Final:
Down 2-10 0-8 *Kerry*

1961
Croke Park, August 6. Semi-final:
Down 1-12 0-9 *Kerry*
Croke Park, August 20. Semi-final:
Offaly 3-6 0-6 *Roscommon*
Croke Park, September 24. Final:
Down 3-6 2-8 *Offaly*

1962
Croke Park, August 5. Semi-final:
Kerry 2-12 0-10 *Dublin*
Croke Park, August 19. Semi-final:
Roscommon 1-8 1-6 *Cavan*
Croke Park, September 23. Final:
Kerry 1-12 1-6 *Roscommon*

1963
Croke Park, August 4. Semi-final:
Galway 1-7 0-8 *Kerry*

Croke Park, August 18. Semi-final:
Dublin 2-11 0-7 *Down*
Croke Park, September 22. Final:
Dublin 1-9 0-10 *Galway*

1964
Croke Park, August 9. Semi-final:
Galway 1-8 0-9 *Meath*
Croke Park, August 23. Semi-final:
Kerry 2-12 0-6 *Cavan*
Croke Park, September 27. Final:
Galway 0-15 0-10 *Kerry*

1965
Croke Park, August 8. Semi-final:
Kerry 4-8 2-6 *Dublin*
Croke Park, August 22. Semi-final:
Galway 0-10 0-7 *Down*
Croke Park, September 26. Final:
Galway 0-12 0-9 *Kerry*

1966
Croke Park, August 7. Semi-final:
Galway 1-11 1-9 *Cork*
Croke Park, August 21. Semi-final:
Meath 2-16 1-9 *Down*
Croke Park, September 25. Final:
Galway 1-10 0-7 *Meath*

1967
Croke Park, August 6. Semi-final:
Cork 2-7 0-12 *Cavan*
Croke Park, August 20. Semi-final:
Meath 3-14 1-14 *Mayo*
Croke Park, September 24. Final:
Meath 1-9 0-9 *Cork*

1968
Croke Park, August 4. Semi-final:
Kerry 2-13 2-11 *Longford*
Croke Park, August 18. Semi-final:
Down 2-10 2-8 *Galway*
Croke Park, September 22. Final:
Down 2-12 1-13 *Kerry*

1969
Croke Park, August 10. Semi-final:
Kerry 0-14 1-10 *Mayo*
Croke Park, August 24. Semi-final:
Cavan 1-9 0-12 *Offaly*
Croke Park, September 14. Replay:
Offaly 3-8 1-10 *Cavan*
Croke Park, September 28. Final:
Kerry 0-10 0-7 *Offaly*

(Note: First 80-minute Final was introduced in 1970)

1970
Croke Park, August 9. Semi-final:
| Meath | 0-15 | 0-11 | Galway |

Croke Park, August 23. Semi-final:
| Kerry | 0-23 | 0-10 | Derry |

Croke Park, September 27. Final:
| Kerry | 2-19 | 0-18 | Meath |

1971
Croke Park, August 8. Semi-final:
| Galway | 3-11 | 2-7 | Down |

Croke Park, August 22. Semi-final:
| Offaly | 1-16 | 1-11 | Cork |

Croke Park, September 26. Final:
| Offaly | 1-14 | 2-8 | Galway |

1972
Croke Park, August 13. Semi-final:
| Kerry | 1-22 | 1-12 | Roscommon |

Croke Park, August 20. Semi-final:
| Offaly | 1-17 | 2-10 | Donegal |

Croke Park, September 24. Final:
| Offaly | 1-13 | 1-13 | Kerry |

Croke Park, October 15. Replay:
| Offaly | 1-19 | 0-13 | Kerry |

1973
Croke Park, August 12. Semi-final:
| Galway | 0-16 | 2-8 | Offaly |

Croke Park, August 19. Semi-final:
| Cork | 5-10 | 2-4 | Tyrone |

Croke Park, September 23. Final:
| Cork | 3-17 | 2-13 | Galway |

1974
Croke Park, August 11. Semi-final:
| Dublin | 2-11 | 1-8 | Cork |

Croke Park, August 18. Semi-final:
| Galway | 3-13 | 1-14 | Donegal |

Croke Park, September 22. Final:
| Dublin | 0-14 | 1-6 | Galway |

(Note: The 70-minute Final was introduced in 1975)

1975
Croke Park, August 10. Semi-final:
| Kerry | 3-13 | 0-5 | Sligo |

Croke Park, August 24. Semi-final:
| Dublin | 3-13 | 3-8 | Derry |

Croke Park, September 28. Final:
| Kerry | 2-12 | 0-11 | Dublin |

1976
Croke Park, August 8. Semi-final:
| Kerry | 5-14 | 1-10 | Derry |

Croke Park, August 29. Semi-final:
| Dublin | 1-8 | 0-8 | Galway |

Croke Park, September 26. Final:
| Dublin | 3-8 | 0-10 | Kerry |

1977
Croke Park, August 14. Semi-final:
| Armagh | 3-9 | 2-12 | Roscommon |

Croke Park, August 21. Semi-final:
| Dublin | 3-12 | 1-13 | Kerry |

Croke Park, August 28. Replay:
| Armagh | 0-15 | 0-14 | Roscommon |

Croke Park, September 25. Final:
| Dublin | 5-12 | 3-6 | Armagh |

1978
Croke Park, August 13. Semi-final:
| Kerry | 3-11 | 0-8 | Roscommon |

Croke Park, August 20. Semi-final:
| Dublin | 1-16 | 0-8 | Down |

Croke Park, September 24. Final:
| Kerry | 5-11 | 0-9 | Dublin |

1979
Croke Park, August 12. Semi-final:
| Kerry | 5-14 | 0-7 | Monaghan |

Croke Park, August 19. Semi-final:
| Dublin | 0-14 | 1-10 | Roscommon |

Croke Park, September 16. Final:
| Kerry | 3-13 | 1-8 | Dublin |

1980
Croke Park, August 10. Semi-final:
| Roscommon 2-20 | 3-11 | Armagh |

Croke Park, August 24. Semi-final:
| Kerry | 4-15 | 4-10 | Offaly |

Croke Park, September 21. Final:
| Kerry | 1-9 | 1-6 | Roscommon |

1981
Croke Park, August 9. Semi-final:
| Kerry | 2-19 | 1-6 | Mayo |

Croke Park, August 23. Semi-final:
| Offaly | 0-12 | 0-6 | Down |

Croke Park, September 20. Final:
| Kerry | 1-12 | 0-8 | Offaly |

1982
Croke Park, August 15. Semi-final:
| Kerry | 3-15 | 1-11 | Armagh |

Croke Park, August 22. Semi-final:
| Offaly | 1-12 | 1-11 | Galway |

Croke Park, September 19. Final:
| Offaly | 1-15 | 0-17 | Kerry |

1983
Croke Park, August 14. Semi-final:
| Galway | 1-12 | 1-11 | Donegal |

Croke Park, August 21. Semi-final:
| Dublin | 2-11 | 2-11 | Cork |

Páirc Uí Chaoimh, August 28. Replay:
| Dublin | 4-15 | 2-10 | Cork |

Croke Park, September 18. Final:
| Dublin | 1-10 | 1-8 | Galway |

1984
Croke Park, August 12. Semi-final:
| Kerry | 2-17 | 0-11 | Galway |
Croke Park, August 19 Semi-final:
| Dublin | 2-11 | 0-8 | Tyrone |
Croke Park, September 23. Final:
| Kerry | 0-14 | 1-6 | Dublin |

1985
Croke Park, August 11. Semi-final:
| Kerry | 1-12 | 2-9 | Monaghan |
Croke Park, August 18. Semi-final:
| Dublin | 1-13 | 1-13 | Mayo |
Croke Park, August 25. Replay:
| Kerry | 2-9 | 0-10 | Monaghan |
Croke Park, September 8. Replay:
| Dublin | 2-12 | 1-7 | Mayo |
Croke Park, September 22. Final:
| Kerry | 2-12 | 2-8 | Dublin |

1986
Croke Park, August 17. Semi-final:
| Tyrone | 1-12 | 1-9 | Galway |
Croke Park, August 24. Semi-final:
| Kerry | 2-13 | 0-12 | Meath |
Croke Park , September 21. Final:
| Kerry | 2-15 | 1-10 | Tyrone |

1987
Croke Park, August 16. Semi-final:
| Cork | 1-11 | 1-11 | Galway |
Croke Park, August 23. Semi-final:
| Meath | 0-15 | 0-8 | Derry |
Croke Park, August 30. Replay:
| Cork | 0-18 | 1-4 | Galway |
Croke Park, September 20. Final:
| Meath | 1-14 | 0-11 | Cork |

1988
Croke Park, August 14. Semi-final:
| Cork | 1-14 | 0-6 | Monaghan |
Croke Park, August 21. Semi-final:
| Meath | 0-16 | 2-5 | Mayo |
Croke Park, September 18. Final:
| Meath | 0-12 | 1-9 | Cork |
Croke Park, October 9. Replay:
| Meath | 0-13 | 0-12 | Cork |

1989
Croke Park, August 13. Semi-final:
| Mayo | 0-12 | 1-6 | Tyrone |
Croke Park, August 20. Semi-final:
| Cork | 2-10 | 1-9 | Dublin |
Croke Park, September 17. Final:
| Cork | 0-17 | 1-11 | Mayo |

1990
Croke Park, August 12. Semi-final:
| Cork | 0-17 | 0-10 | Roscommon |
Croke Park, August 19. Semi-final:
| Meath | 3-9 | 1-7 | Donegal |
Croke Park, September 16. Final:
| Cork | 0-11 | 0-9 | Meath |

1991
Croke Park, August 11. Semi-final:
| Down | 2-9 | 0-8 | Kerry |
Croke Park, August 18. Semi-final:
| Meath | 0-15 | 1-11 | Roscommon |
Croke Park, September 15. Final:
| Down | 1-16 | 1-14 | Meath |

1992
Croke Park, August 16. Semi-final:
| Donegal | 0-13 | 0-9 | Mayo |
Croke Park, August 23. Semi-final:
| Dublin | 3-14 | 2-12 | Clare |
Croke Park, September 20. Final:
| Donegal | 0-18 | 0-14 | Dublin |

1993
Croke Park, August 15. Semi-final:
| Cork | 5-15 | 0-10 | Mayo |
Croke Park, August 22. Semi-final:
| Derry | 0-15 | 0-14 | Dublin |
Croke Park, September 19. Final:
| Derry | 1-14 | 2-8 | Cork |

1994
Croke Park, August 14. Semi-final:
| Down | 1-13 | 0-11 | Cork |
Croke Park, August 21. Semi-final:
| Dublin | 3-15 | 1-9 | Leitrim |
Croke Park, September 18. Final:
| Down | 1-12 | 0-13 | Dublin |

1995
Croke Park, August 13. Semi-final:
| Tyrone | 1-13 | 0-13 | Galway |
Croke Park, August 20. Semi-final:
| Dublin | 1-12 | 0-12 | Cork |
Croke Park, September 17. Final:
| Dublin | 1-10 | 0-12 | Tyrone |

1996
Croke Park, August 11. Semi-final:
| Mayo | 2-13 | 1-10 | Kerry |
Croke Park, August 18. Semi-final:
| Meath | 2-15 | 0-12 | Tyrone |
Croke Park, September 15. Final:
| Meath | 0-12 | 1-9 | Mayo |
Croke Park, September 29. Replay:
| Meath | 2-9 | 1-11 | Mayo |

1997
Croke Park, August 24. Semi-final:
| Kerry | 1-17 | 1-10 | Cavan |
Croke Park, August 31. Semi-final:
| Mayo | 0-13 | 0-7 | Offaly |
Croke Park, September 28. Final:
| Kerry | 0-13 | 1-7 | Mayo |

1998
Croke Park, August 23. Semi-final:
| Galway | 0-16 | 1-8 | Derry |

Croke Park, August 30. Semi-final:
| Kildare | 0-13 | 1-9 | Kerry |

Croke Park, September 27. Final:
| Galway | 1-14 | 1-10 | Kildare |

1999
Croke Park, August 22. Semi-final:
| Cork | 2-12 | 0-12 | Mayo |

Croke Park, August 29. Semi-final:
| Meath | 0-15 | 2-5 | Armagh |

Croke Park, September 26. Final:
| Meath | 1-11 | 1-8 | Cork |

2000
Croke Park, August 20. Semi-final:
| Kerry | 2-11 | 2-11 | Armagh |

Croke Park, August 27. Semi-final:
| Galway | 0-15 | 2-6 | Kildare |

Croke Park, September 2. Replay:
| Kerry | 2-15 | 1-15 | Armagh (aet) |

Croke Park, September 24. Final:
| Kerry | 0-14 | 0-14 | Galway |

Croke Park, October 7. Replay:
| Kerry | 0-17 | 1-10 | Galway |

2001
Thurles, August 4. Quarter-final:
| Kerry | 1-14 | 2-11 | Dublin |

Castlebar, August 4. Quarter-final:
| Galway | 0-14 | 1-5 | Roscommon |

Croke Park, August 5. Quarter-final:
| Meath | 2-12 | 3-9 | Westmeath |

Clones, August 5. Quarter-final:
| Derry | 1-9 | 0-7 | Tyrone |

Thurles, August 11. Replay:
| Kerry | 2-12 | 1-12 | Dublin |

Croke Park, August 11. Replay:
| Meath | 2-10 | 0-11 | Westmeath |

Croke Park, August 26. Semi-final:
| Galway | 1-14 | 1-11 | Derry |

Croke Park, September 2. Semi-final:
| Meath | 2-14 | 0-5 | Kerry |

Croke Park, September 23. Final:
| Galway | 0-17 | 0-8 | Meath |

2002
Croke Park, August 4. Quarter-final:
| Kerry | 2-17 | 1-12 | Galway |

Croke Park, August 4. Quarter-final:
| Armagh | 2-9 | 0-15 | Sligo |

Croke Park, August 5. Quarter-final:
| Cork | 0-16 | 1-10 | Mayo |

Croke Park, August 5. Quarter-final:
| Dublin | 2-8 | 0-14 | Donegal |

Croke Park, August 17. Replay:
| Dublin | 1-14 | 0-7 | Donegal |

Navan, August 18. Replay:
| Armagh | 1-16 | 0-17 | Sligo |

Croke Park, August 25. Semi-final:
| Kerry | 3-19 | 2-7 | Cork |

Croke Park, September 1. Semi-final:
| Armagh | 1-14 | 1-13 | Dublin |

Croke Park, September 22. Final:
| Armagh | 1-12 | 0-14 | Kerry |

2003
Croke Park, August 3. Quarter-final:
| Armagh | 0-15 | 0-13 | Laois |

Croke Park, August 3. Quarter-final:
| Tyrone | 1-21 | 0-5 | Fermanagh |

Croke Park, August 4. Quarter-final:
| Kerry | 1-21 | 3-10 | Roscommon |

Croke Park, August 4. Quarter-final:
| Donegal | 0-14 | 1-11 | Galway |

Castlebar, August 10. Replay:
| Donegal | 0-14 | 0-11 | Galway |

Croke Park, August 24. Semi-final:
| Tyrone | 0-13 | 0-6 | Kerry |

Croke Park, August 31. Semi-final:
| Armagh | 2-10 | 1-9 | Donegal |

Croke Park, September 28. Final:
| Tyrone | 0-12 | 0-9 | Armagh |

2004
Croke Park, August 7. Quarter-final:
| Fermanagh | 0-12 | 0-11 | Armagh |

Croke Park, August 7. Quarter-final:
| Mayo | 0-16 | 1-9 | Tyrone |

Croke Park, August 14. Quarter-final:
| Derry | 2-9 | 0-13 | Westmeath |

Croke Park, August 14. Quarter-final:
| Kerry | 1-15 | 1-8 | Dublin |

Croke Park, August 22. Semi-final:
| Mayo | 0-9 | 0-9 | Fermanagh |

Croke Park, August 28. Replay:
| Mayo | 0-13 | 1-8 | Fermanagh |

Croke Park, August 29. Semi-final:
| Kerry | 1-17 | 1-11 | Derry |

Croke Park, September 26. Final:
| Kerry | 1-20 | 2-9 | Mayo |

2005
Croke Park, August 7. Quarter-final:
| Cork | 2-14 | 2-11 | Galway |

Croke Park, August 7. Quarter-final:
| Kerry | 2-15 | 0-18 | Mayo |

Croke Park, August 13. Quarter-final:
| Tyrone | 1-14 | 1-14 | Dublin |

Croke Park, August 20. Quarter-final:
| Armagh | 2-17 | 1-11 | Laois |

Croke Park, August 27. Replay:
| Tyrone | 2-18 | 1-14 | Dublin |

Croke Park, August 28. Semi-final:
| Kerry | 1-19 | 0-9 | Cork |

Croke Park, September 4. Semi-final:
| Tyrone | 1-13 | 1-12 | Armagh |

Croke Park, September 25. Final:
| Tyrone | 1-16 | 2-10 | Kerry |

2006
Croke Park, August 5. Quarter-final:
| Kerry | 3-15 | 1-13 | Armagh |

Croke Park, August 5. Quarter-final:
| Cork | 1-11 | 1-10 | Donegal |

Croke Park, August 12. Quarter-final:
| Dublin | 1-12 | 0-5 | Westmeath |

Croke Park, August 13. Quarter-final:
| Mayo | 0-15 | 0-15 | Laois |

Croke Park, August 20. Replay:
| Mayo | 0-14 | 0-11 | Laois |

Croke Park, August 20. Semi-final:
| Kerry | 0-16 | 0-10 | Cork |

Croke Park, August 27. Semi-final:
Mayo   1-16   2-12   *Dublin*
Croke Park, September 17. Final:
Kerry   4-15   3-5   *Mayo*

2007

Croke Park, August 4. Quarter-final:
Cork   1-11   0-8   *Sligo*
Croke Park, August 4. Quarter-final:
Meath   1-13   2-8   *Tyrone*
Croke Park, August 11. Quarter-final:
Dublin   0-18   0-15   *Derry*
Croke Park, August 12. Quarter-final:
Kerry   1-12   1-11   *Monaghan*
Croke Park, August 19. Semi-final:
Cork   1-16   0-9   *Meath*
Croke Park, August 26. Semi-final:
Kerry   1-15   0-16   *Dublin*
Croke Park, September 16. Final:
Kerry   3-13   1-9   *Cork*

2008

Croke Park, August 9. Quarter-final:
Wexford   1-14   0-12   *Armagh*
Croke Park, August 9. Quarter-final:
Kerry   1-21   1-16   *Galway*
Croke Park, August 10. Quarter-final:
Cork   2-11   1-11   *Kildare*
Croke Park, August 16. Quarter-final:
Tyrone   3-14   1-8   *Dublin*
Croke Park, August 24. Semi-final:
Kerry   1-13   3-7   *Cork*
Croke Park, August 31. Replay:
Kerry   3-14   2-13   *Cork*
Croke Park, August 31. Semi-final:
Tyrone   0-23   1-14   *Wexford*
Croke Park, September 21. Final:
Tyrone   1-15   0-14   *Kerry*

2009

Croke Park, August 2. Quarter-final:
Tyrone   0-16   1-11   *Kildare*
Croke Park, August 2. Quarter-final:
Cork   1-27   2-10   *Donegal*
Croke Park, August 3. Quarter-final:
Kerry   1-24   1-7   *Dublin*
Croke Park, August 9. Quarter-final:
Meath   2-15   1-15   *Mayo*
Croke Park, August 23. Semi-final:
Cork   1-13   0-11   *Tyrone*
Croke Park, August 30. Semi-final:
Kerry   2-8   1-7   *Meath*
Croke Park, September 20. Final:
Kerry   0-16   1-9   *Cork*

2010

Croke Park, July 31. Quarter-final:
Down   1-16   1-10   *Kerry*
Croke Park, July 31. Quarter-final:
Dublin   1-15   0-13   *Tyrone*
Croke Park, August 1. Quarter-final:
Cork   1-16   0-10   *Roscommon*
Croke Park, August 1. Quarter-final:
Kildare   2-17   1-12   *Meath*
Croke Park, August 22. Semi-final:
Cork   1-15   1-14   *Dublin*
Croke Park, August 29. Semi-final:
Down   1-16   1-14   *Kildare*
Croke Park, September 19. Final:
Cork   0-16   0-15   *Down*

2011

Croke Park, July 30. Quarter-final:
Donegal   1-12   0-14   *Kildare*
Croke Park, July 31. Quarter-final:
Kerry   1-20   0-10   *Limerick*
Croke Park, July 31. Quarter-final:
Mayo   1-13   2-6   *Cork*
Croke Park, August 7. Quarter-final:
Dublin   0-22   0-15   *Tyrone*
Croke Park, August 21. Semi-final:
Kerry   1-20   1-11   *Mayo*
Croke Park, August 28. Semi-final:
Dublin   0-8   0-6   *Donegal*
Croke Park, September 18. Final:
Dublin   1-12   1-11   *Kerry*

2012

Croke Park, August 4. Quarter-final:
Mayo   3-18   2-9   *Down*
Croke Park, August 4. Quarter-final:
Dublin   1-12   0-12   *Laois*
Croke Park, August 5. Quarter-final:
Cork   2-19   0-12   *Kildare*
Croke Park, August 5. Quarter-final:
Donegal   1-12   1-10   *Kerry*
Croke Park, August 26. Semi-final:
Donegal   0-16   1-11   *Cork*
Croke Park, September 2. Semi-final:
Mayo   0-19   0-16   *Dublin*
Croke Park, September 23 Final:
Donegal   2-11   0-13   *Mayo*

2013

Croke Park, August 3. Quarter-final:
Tyrone   0-14   0-12   *Monaghan*
Croke Park, August 3. Quarter-final:
Dublin   1-16   0-14   *Cork*
Croke Park, August 4. Quarter-final:
Kerry   0-15   0-9   *Cavan*
Croke Park, August 4. Quarter-final:
Mayo   4-17   1-10   *Donegal*
Croke Park, August 25. Semi-final:
Mayo   1-16   0-13   *Tyrone*
Croke Park, September 1. Semi-final:
Dublin   3-18   3-11   *Kerry*
Croke Park, September 22. Final:
Dublin   2-12   1-14   *Mayo*

2014

Croke Park, August 3. Quarter-final:
Kerry   1-20   2-10   *Galway*
Croke Park, August 3. Quarter-final:
Mayo   1-19   2-15   *Cork*
Croke Park, August 9. Quarter-final:
Donegal   1-12   1-11   *Armagh*
Croke Park, August 9. Quarter-final:
Dublin   2-22   0-11   *Monaghan*
Croke Park, August 24. Semi-final:
Kerry   1-16   1-16   *Mayo*
Limerick August 30. Replay:
Kerry   3-16   3-13   *Mayo (aet)*
Croke Park, August 31. Semi-final:
Donegal   3-14   0-17   *Dublin*
Croke Park, September 21. Final:
Kerry   2-9   0-12   *Donegal*

FOOTBALL

2015

Croke Park, August 2. Quarter-final:
| *Kerry* | **7-16** | **0-10** | *Kildare* |

Croke Park, August 2. Quarter-final:
| *Dublin* | **2-23** | **2-15** | *Fermanagh* |

Croke Park, August 8. Quarter-final:
| *Tyrone* | **0-18** | **0-14** | *Monaghan* |

Croke Park, August 8. Quarter-final:
| *Mayo* | **2-13** | **0-11** | *Donegal* |

Croke Park, August 23. Semi-final:
| *Kerry* | **0-18** | **1-11** | *Tyrone* |

Croke Park, August 30. Semi-final:
| *Dublin* | **2-12** | **1-15** | *Mayo* |

Croke Park, September 5. Replay:
| *Dublin* | **3-15** | **1-14** | *Mayo* |

Croke Park, September 20. Final:
| *Dublin* | **0-12** | **0-9** | *Kerry* |

2016

Croke Park, July 31. Quarter-final:
| *Kerry* | **2-16** | **0-11** | *Clare* |

Croke Park, July 31. Quarter-final:
| *Tipperary* | **3-13** | **1-10** | *Galway* |

Croke Park, August 6. Quarter-final:
| *Mayo* | **0-13** | **0-12** | *Tyrone* |

Croke Park, August 6. Quarter-final:
| *Dublin* | **1-15** | **1-10** | *Donegal* |

Croke Park, August 21. Semi-final:
| *Mayo* | **2-13** | **0-14** | *Tipperary* |

Croke Park, August 28. Semi-final:
| *Dublin* | **0-22** | **2-14** | *Kerry* |

Croke Park, September 18. Final:
| *Dublin* | **2-9** | **0-15** | *Mayo* |

Croke Park, October 1. Replay:
| *Dublin* | **1-15** | **1-14** | *Mayo* |

2017

Croke Park, July 30. Quarter-final:
| *Kerry* | **1-18** | **0-13** | *Galway* |

Croke Park, July 30. Quarter-final:
| *Mayo* | **1-12** | **2-9** | *Roscommon* |

Croke Park, August 5. Quarter-final:
| *Tyrone* | **3-17** | **0-8** | *Armagh* |

Croke Park, August 5. Quarter-final:
| *Dublin* | **1-19** | **0-12** | *Monaghan* |

Croke Park, August 7. Replay:
| *Mayo* | **4-19** | **0-9** | *Roscommon* |

Croke Park, August 20. Semi-final:
| *Mayo* | **2-14** | **2-14** | *Kerry* |

Croke Park, August 26. Replay:
| *Mayo* | **2-16** | **0-17** | *Kerry* |

Croke Park, August 27. Semi-final:
| *Dublin* | **2-17** | **0-11** | *Tyrone* |

Croke Park, September 17. Final:
| *Dublin* | **1-17** | **1-16** | *Mayo* |

ALL-IRELAND FINAL FOOTBALL TEAMS

(Author's note. Despite checking with a number of sources allowance must still be made for possible errors in early teams as records are not reliable from these times. It must be noted too that teams were not given in line-out order until the 1930s.)

1887

Limerick   Denis Corbett (capt.), P.Reeves, J.Mulqueen, M.Slattery, T.McNamara, T.Fitzgibbon, P.Kelly, P.J.Corbett, T.Kennedy, E.Nicholas, J.Hyland, M.O'Brien, E.Casey, R Normoyle, T.Keeting, W.J.Spain, J.R.Kennedy, W.Gunning, P.Keating, W.Cleery, R.Breen.

Louth   M.J.Carroll (capt.), E.Goodman, J.Dowdall, N.Fagan, R.Clarke, T.McGrane, T.O'Connor, P.McGuinness, J.McGuire, A.O'Hagan, T.Campbell, R.Morgan, P.Jackson, J.Keating, T.Murphy, E.Murphy, W.Wheetley, P.McGuinn, E.Fealy, T.O'Rourke, T.Lowry.

1888

No final played owing to visit of hurlers and athletes to the USA, known as "The American Invasion".

1889

Tipperary   Gil Kavanagh (capt.), J.Cranley, P.Glasheen, T.Dwyer, P.Finn, W.O'Shea, P.Buckley, D.Whelan, J.Daly, J.Ronan, P.Hall, J.Carey, M.Wade, B.O'Brien, L.Fox, W.Ryan, Joe Ryan, Jack Ryan, Wm.Ryan, P.Ryan, J.Keating.

Laois   J.Delaney (capt.), J.Whelan, J.Fleming, J.Walsh, J.Murphy, N.Maher, P.Brady, D.Drennan, T.McDonnell, M.Culleton, J.Troy, D.Teehan, J.Conroy, J.Dunne, J.Teehan, J.O'Connor, Tom Cushion, Tim Cushion, P.Cushion, D.Cushion, M.Cushion.

1890

Cork   Jim Power (capt.), J.Downey, P.Moore, J.Leahy, R.Kelleher, M.Coleman, T.Lucey, Jack Fitzgerald, Jim Fitzgerald, M.Riordan, T.Downey, R.Power, J.D.O'Brien, M.Hennessy, M.Egan, J.Aherne, M.Murphy, M.Buckley, W.Buckley, W.Hennessy, P.O'Sullivan.

Wexford   P.Keating (capt.), J.McGrath, J.French, J.Meyler, D.Phillips, T.Gaffney, P.Byrne, T.Byrne, A.Furlong, T.Hayes, J.Kenny, M.Clancy, M.Murphy, J.Monaghan, M.O'Neill, J.Keegan, J.Doyle, P.Curran, J.O'Connor, J.Hayes, N.Meyler.

1891

Dublin   John Kennedy (capt.), G.Charlemont (goal), G.Roche, J.Scully, T.Lyons, J.Roche, J.Silke, P.Heslin, J.Mahony, A.O'Hagan, P.O'Hagan, Dick Curtis, S.Hughes, S.Flood, T.Murphy, J.Geraghty, T.Halpin, M.Cooney, P.Kelly, R.Flood, M.Condon.

Cork   Con O'Leary (capt.), Denis O'Leary, J.O'Leary, Dan O'Leary, D.J.Kelleher, J.Kelleher, Con Kelleher, Jer Kelleher, C.Duggan, J.Duggan, A.Desmond, P.Desmond T.O'Riordan, M.O'Riordan, M.Quill, J.O'Sullivan, J.Murphy, D.O'Sullivan, T.O'Shea, J.Ahern, M.Kelleher.

1892

Dublin   John Kennedy (capt.), G.Roche, G.Charlemont, J.Roche, J.Geraghty, R.Flood, S.Flood, S.Hughes, F.O'Malley, T.Doran, L.Kelly, P.Kelly, P.Heslin, M.Byrne, J.Silke, T.("Darby") Errity, R.Curtis.

Kerry   J.P.O'Sullivan (capt.), J.J.O'Sullivan, J.Curran, T Curran, J.Murphy, P.Sugrue, F.Doherty, D.P.Murphy, M.O'Brien, W.O'Sullivan, M.Flynn, W.Fleming, M.Hayes, J.O'Reilly, P.O'Regan, D.Clifford, P.Teahan.

1893

Wexford   Thomas Hayes (capt.), James Maloney Redmond, T.("Hoey") Redmond, P.Curran, M.Curran, J.McGinn, J.Doyle, N.Leahy, J.Bolger, J.O'Neill, W.O'Leary, A.Furlong, T.O'Connor, J.O'Connor, P.O'Connor, F.Boggan, J.Phelan.
Cork   Jack ("Fox") O'Keeffe (capt.), D.O'Hanlon, T.Burton, T.Forrest, D.Doherty T.Irwin, J.O'Leary, J.Mulcahy, M.Buckley, M.O'Keeffe, T.Healy, J.Vaughan, J.Riordan, J.Coughlan, J.O'Sullivan, E.Mulcahy, W.Riordan.

1894

Dublin   John Kennedy (capt.), G.Charlemont, Dick Curtis, G.Roche, P.Heslin, T.Lyons, J.Geraghty, L.Kelly, P.Kelly, T.Hughes, T.O'Mahony, M.Condon, M.Byrne, T.("Darby") Errity, P.O'Toole, J.Kirwan, F.O'Malley.
Cork   J.O'Leary (capt.), J.Mulcahy, P.J.Walsh, D.Kelleher, T.Houlihan, D.McSweeney, M.Coleman, M.McCarthy, W.Riordan, D.Coughlan, F.Joyce, W.Burgess, P.Coughlan, D.O'Connell, M.Downey, T.Irwin, J.Riordan.

1895

Tipperary   Paddy Finn (capt.), Willie Ryan, R.Quane, J.Riordan, M.Finn, P.Glasheen, M.("Terry") McInerney, J.Carew, M.Conroy, J.Carey, D.Butler, W.P.Ryan, J.Heffernan, P.Daly, J.O'Brien, B.Finn, P.Dwyer.
Meath   M.Murray (capt.), H.Pendleton, P.Clarke, J.Hegarty, J.Russell, J.W.Toombe, J.A.Shaw, M.McCabe, P.Fox, J.Elliott, M.Rogers, C.Curtis, J.Sharkey, P.Daly, J.Quinn, V.McDermott, J.Fitzpatrick.

1896

Limerick   Con Fitzgerald (capt.), D.Birrane, W.Guiry, J.O'Riordan, L.Roche, J.O'Riordan, L.Sheehan, P.Roche, A.Quillinan, J.Buttimer, T.Campion, J.Dalton, B.Murphy, W.McNamara, J.Murphy, J.Nash, M.Ryan.Sub: J.Griffin.
Dublin   George Roche (capt.), J.Kirwan, L.Kelly, W.Conlon, J.Teeling, T.Hession, J.Gannon, Dick Curtis, S.Mooney, R.Graham, P.O'Toole, J.Brady, T.Doran, T.("Darby") Errity, P.Heslin, M.Byrne, J.Ledwidge.

1897

Dublin   P.J.Walsh (capt.), W.Guiry, R.Scanlon, L.Kelly, W.Callaghan, E.Downey, Dick Curtis, D.O'Donnell, M.Chambers, V.Kelly, C.Cannon, P.O'Donoghue, R.O'Brien, P.Redmond, J.Matthews, W.Flynn, J.O'Brien.
Cork   D.O'Donovan (capt.), F.J.Crowley, J.Fuller, J.O'Kelly-Lynch, D.Crowley, T.Lordan, P.Lordan, T.Coughlan, C.Coughlan, D.Bernard, F.Searles, T.Twohill, T.Crowley, T.Mullane, D.Coughlan, J.Murphy, J.Aherne.

1898

Dublin   Matt Rea (capt.), J.J.Keane, T.H.Redmond, W.Sherry, J.Heslin, D.O'Callaghan, P.Levey, C.Sargent, P.Redmond, P.McCann, T.Norton, T.("Darby") Errity, P.Fitzsimmons, P.Smith, J.Ryan, J.Ledwidge.
Waterford   M Cullinan, J.Nagle, W.Meade, P.Sullivan, J.Nestor J.C.Heelan, P.Kirwan, J.Hogan, J.F.Flynn, J.Power, T.Power, J.Kennedy, R.Rockett, D.F.Flynn, S.Curran, M.Dunworth, G.Cummin. Sub W.O'Brien for T.Power.

1899

Dublin   Matt Rea (capt.), J.Lane, P.McCann, D.Smith, W.Sherry, T.("Darby") Errity, G.Brady, John Ryan, J.Norton, J.J.Keane, J.Farrelly, P.Leary, P.Fitzsimons, D.O'Callaghan, J.Heslin, J.Ledwidge, T.H.Redmond.
Cork   R.Coughlan (capt.), W.Mackessy, S.Murphy, J.Clifford, D.Coughlan, W.O'Neill, J.Long, J.Cronin, M.Howard, Tom Irwin, M.Aherne, M.Sullivan, J.Collins, C.Walsh, J.Murphy, J.Kelleher, M.Barrett.

1900

Tipperary   J.Tobin (capt.), P.Moloney, W.McReil, J.Dwan, D.Myers, M.Walsh, J.O'Brien, R.Quane, R.Hourigan, P.Wall, W.O'Toole, D.Harney, J.O'Shea, J.Cooney, D.Smyth, P.Cox, J.Hayes.
London   M.J.Hayes, S.Maguire, J.Maguire, J.Hooper, D.Donovan, M.Reidy, T.Corcoran, J.Gaffney, T.J.Quilter, J.Crowley, P.J.Crotty, F.Collins, M.J.O'Grady, T.Lyons, D.Cronin, J.Hayes, T.Brown.

'Home' Final:

Tipperary   J.Tobin (capt.), P.Moloney, J.Long, R.Hourigan, M.Kiely, D.Smith, P.Cox, J.Hayes, P.Sweeny, M.Alyward, J.Dwan, D.Myers, M.Walsh, J.O'Brien, R.Quane, L.Tobin, P.Moroney.
Galway   J.Hosty, W.Kennedy, S.Bourke, T.Hannon, F.Walsh (capt.), M.Farrell, J.Kilkenny, T.Handlebury, M.Connor, J.O'Brien, C.Whyte, D.Hession, S.Barry, M.(Tom) Connolly, J.Ridge, J.O'Brien, M.Muldowney.

1901

Dublin   J.Darcy (capt.), J.McCullagh, J.Fahy, D.Holland, T.Doyle, J.O'Brien, B.Connor, P.Daly, M.Madigan, L.Kelly, J.Grace, P.Redmond, M.O'Brien P.McCann, J.Whelan, T.Lawless, V.Harris.
London   S.Maguire (capt.), J.Maguire, D.Donovan, J.Hooper, M.J.Hayes, J.O'Driscoll, W.Morrissey, T.Corcoran, J.O'Dwyer, J.Griffin, M.Roddy, J.Scanlon, J.Fitzgerald, T.Twomey, M.J.O'Grady, D.Cronin, J.Shouldice.

'Home' Final:

Dublin   J.Darcy (capt.), M.McCullagh, D.Brady, P.McCann, J.Fahy, J.O'Brien, M.Madigan, J.Grace, T.Doyle, J.Whelan, T.Lawless, M.O'Brien, L.Kelly, V.Harris, P.McCann, P.Redmond, P.Daly.
Cork   J.Murphy (capt.), Gus Groegor, T.Hartigan, S.Murphy, J.McCarthy, J.Long, C.Walsh, J.Morrissey, W.Mackessy, C.McCarthy, J.McCarthy, W.O'Neill, P.Spillane, P.Daly, M.O'Connor, J.Desmond, T.Mahony.

1902

Dublin   J.Dempsey (capt.), S.Mulvey, D.Brady, W.Casey, W.Sherry, A.Wall, J.Brennan, P.Weymess, P.D.Breen, J.McCann, T.Errity, J.Fahy, J.Grace, J.Keane, P.Brady, E.Brady, P.Daly.
London   J.Maguire, M.Hayes, D.Donovan, J.O'Driscoll, J.Fitzpatrick, P.Sheehan, J.Heffernan, J.Heffernan, M.Roddy, J.Shouldice, C.Shine, J.Kavanagh, J.Dwyer, J.Griffin, D.O'Leary, J.O'Grady, J.Fitzgerald.

'Home' Final:

Dublin   J.Dempsey, S.Mulvey, D.Brady, M.Casey, W.Sherry, J.McCann, T.Errity, J.Keane, J.Grace, C.Brady, P.Daly, J.Brennan, P.Weymess, P.Archdeacon, P.D.Breen, - Dunne.
Tipperary   R.Quane (capt.), W.P.Ryan, R.Butler, D.Quane, J.Noonan, J.Wyse, J.Butler, J.Bohan, J.Ryan, D.Smith, D.Myers, W.Barrett, P.Moloney, E.Kelly, P.Wall, J.O'Shea, J.Hayes.

1903

Kerry T.O'Gorman (capt.), J.O'Gorman, D.Curran, Mce. McCarthy, J.Buckley, C.Healy, A.Stack, R.Fitzgerald, P.Dillon, W.Lynch, D.McCarthy, J.Myers, D.Kissane, F.O'Sullivan, R.Kirwan, D.Breen, J.T.Fitzgerald.

London S.Maguire (capt.), D.Donovan, J.O'Driscoll, A.Leary, T.Doody, T.Quilter, J.Griffin, J.Shouldice, M.J.Collins, J.Heffernan, J.Walsh, J.P.McKeever, C.Shine, J.Dwyer, T.O'Neill, M.Sheehan, J.Scanlan.

'Home' Final:

Kerry (Third match) Same as above, except that E.O'Neill played instead of F.O'Sullivan. C.Duggan played instead of F.O'Sullivan in first two games.

Kildare Jos.Rafferty (capt.), W.Merriman, L.Cribben, W.Losty, J.Wright, J.Dunne, W.Bracken, J.Murray, M.Murray, M.Kennedy, J.Scott, M.Donnelly, F."Joyce" Conlon, J.Gorman, M.Fitzgerald, J.Fitzgerald, E.Kennedy.

1904

Kerry A.Stack (capt.), M.McCarthy, J.T.Fitzgerald, J.O'Gorman, T.O'Gorman, C.Healy, P.J.Cahill, J.Buckley, D.Curran, J.O'Sullivan, P.Dillon, J.Myers, D.McCarthy, R.Fitzgerald, W.Lynch, F.O'Sullivan, D.Breen.

Dublin J.Lynch (capt.), P.McCann, M.Kelly, P.Daly, J.Brennan, J.Dempsey, D.Brady, J.Grace, M.Keane, P.O'Callaghan, T.Murphy, M.Barry, J.Chadwick, L.Sheehan, T.Walsh, P.Casey, J.Fahy.

1905

Kildare J.Murray (capt.), M.Murray, J.Fikgerald, M.Kennedy, J.Rafferty, J.Gorman, T.Keogh, F."Joyce" Conlon, J.Scott, W.Merriman, L.Cribben, W.Bracken, W.Losty, J.Connolly, E.Kennedy, T.Kelly, M.Fitzgerald.

Kerry M.McCarthy (capt.), P.J.Cahill, J.T.Fitzgerald, T.O'Gorman, J.O'Gorman, J.O'Sullivan, C.Healy, T.Costello, D.Curran, R.Fitzgerald, P.Dillon, J.Myers, C.Murphy, J.Spillane, R.Kirwan, D.Breen, J.Wrenn.

1906

Dublin J.Grace (capt.), D.Brady, J.Dempsey, D.Kelleher, J.Brennan, M.Kelly, M.Keane, M.Curry, M.Barry, P.O'Callaghan, P.Casey, H.Hilliard, M.Madigan, T.Quane, T.Walsh, P.Grace, L.Sheehan.

Cork M.O'Connor (capt.), P.Daly, P.Lenihan, C.Paye, J.Kent, R.O'Sullivan, W.Mackessy, M.Mehigan, M.Twomey, T.Breen, T.O'Donoghue, J.McCarthy, J.Morrissey, C.McCarthy, J.Murphy, F.Searles, R.Flavin.

1907

Dublin D.Kelleher, D.Brady, J.Brennan, J.Grace (capt.), J.Lynch, H.Hilliard, T.Quane, J.Dempsey, P.Casey, M.Curry, M.Barry, M.Madigan, P.O'Callaghan, T.Walsh, M.Kelly, D.Kavanagh, P.Grace.

Cork W.Mackessy (capt.), J.McCarthy, J.Morrissey, M.Mehigan, P.O'Neill, J.Ryan, T.Breen, J.Beckett, J.Shorten, C.O'Shea, J.Driscoll, J.Lehane, J.Kelleher, J.Kent, R.O'Sullivan, Jerh. Murphy, R.Flavin.

1908

Dublin D.Kelleher (capt.), J.Grace, H.Hilliard, T.Walsh, J.Lynch, D.Cavanagh, J.S.Brennan, T.Healy, F.Cooney, J.Brennan, P.Daly, T.McAuley, P.Whelan, P.Fallon, M.Collins, M.Power, J.Shouldice.

London E.O'Sullivan (capt.), J.Kerin, D.Daly, J.B.Kavanagh, D.P.Cremin, M.Hickey, W.O'Brien, S.Black, T.Ambrose, C.Shine, J.Griffin, J.Walsh, J.Maguire, E.O'Leary, P.M.Attridge, C.Tobin, M.O'Donoghue.

'Home' Final:

Dublin Same as final.

Kerry J.T.Fitzgerald (capt.), P.Dillon, R.Fitzgerald, J.Sullivan, J.O'Riordan, J.Lawlor, M.Mahony, P.Mullane, B.O'Connor, C.Murphy, F.Cronin, E.Spillane, J.McCarthy, C.Healy, T.Costello, D.Breen, J.Casey. Sub: J.Condon for J.O'Riordan.

1909

Kerry T.Costello (capt.), M.McCarthy, C.Healy, T.Rice, J.O'Sullivan, D.Breen, M.J.Quinlan, R.Fitzgerald, C.Murphy, E.Spillane, J.Skinner, P.Mullane, J.Kennelly, B.O'Connor, J.McCarthy, F.J.Cronin, P.Dillon.

Louth J.Carvin (capt.), W.Byrne, Joe Quinn, C.Clarke, Joe Donnelly, Jim Clarke, E.Burke, Joe Mulligan, J.Brennan, J.Hanlon, Joe Matthews, O.Markey, J.Bannon, L.McCormack, J.Hand, J.Donegan, T.Morgan.

1910

No final: Louth awarded walk-over from Kerry. (The following is the Louth team that beat Dublin in the Leinster final and would no doubt have contested the All-Ireland final if it had gone ahead: M.Byrne, J.Mulligan, J.Donnelly, J.Brennan, O.Markey, T.Matthews, L.McCormack, J.Bannon, M.Hand, P.O'Reilly, J.McDonnell, J.Clarke, J.Quinn, E.Burke, J.Smith, J.Carvin, T.Morgan)

1911

Cork M.Mehigan (capt.), M.O'Shea, E.Barrett, J.A.Beckett, J.O'Driscoll, J.Donovan, W.Mackessy, M.Cotter, T.Murphy, J.Lehane, W.Lehane, J.Lynch, C.Kelleher, J.Young, P.Connell, C.Paye, J.O'Neill. Subs: P.McSweeney for J.O'Neill, T.Breen for C.Paye.

Antrim H.Sheehan (capt.), H.Kane, J.Murphy, P.Barnes, J.Mulvihill, P.Moylan, P.L.Kelly, J.M.Darby, C.McCurry, J.Fegan, J.Mullen, E.Gorman, J.Healy, J.Coburn, W.Manning, P.Meany, W.Williams.

1912

Louth J.Smith (capt.), M.Byrne, J.Clarke, J.Quinn, J.Fitzsimmons, J.Mulligan, E.Burke, L.McCormack, J.Reilly, J.Bannon, D.Warren, J.Johnstone, O.Markey, T.Matthews, J.Campbell, J.Brennan, S.Fitzsimons.

Antrim J.Coburn (capt.), J.Monaghan, P.Moylan, T.Meany, H.Sheehan, P.L.Kelly, W.Manning, J.Murphy, M.Goggan, L.Waters, J.Mulvihill, E.Ward, J.Mullen, J.Gorman, P.Barnes, M.Maguire, J.Gallagher.

1913

Kerry R.Fitzgerald (capt.), J.Skinner, D.Doyle, C.Murphy, P.Healy, J.O'Mahony, C.Clifford, T.Rice, J.J.Rice, M.McCarthy, T.Costelloe, J.Lawlor, D.Mullins, P.O'Shea, P.Kennelly.

Wexford T.Doyle (capt.), T.Mernagh, A.Doyle, J.Cullen (goal), E.Black, T.Murphy, J.Doyle, J.Kennedy, P.Mackey, G.Kennedy, J.Mullally, R.Reynolds, F.Furlong, J.Byrne, J.Rossiter.

1914 REPLAY

Kerry R.Fitzgerald (capt.), M.McCarthy, D.Doyle, J.Skinner, J.Mahony, C.Murphy, P.Healy, C.Clifford, P.Breen, T.Rice, J.J.Rice, J.Lawlor, D.Mullins (goal), T.Costelloe, P.O'Shea. (Note: H.Murphy and W.Keating played in drawn game. M.McCarthy and J.J.Rice came in for replay.)

Wexford Seán Kennedy (capt.), T.McGrath (goal), T.Murphy, P.Mackey, J.Byrne, P.D.Breen, T.Doyle, T.Mernagh, P.Murphy, J.Doyle, J.Mullally, R.Reynolds, A.Doyle, G.Kennedy, J.Rossitor.

1915
Wexford Seán Kennedy (capt.), Gus Kennedy, P.Mackey, T.Murphy, F.Furlong, J.Wall, Fr.E.Wheeler, T.Mernagh, T.Doyle, E.Black, A.Doyle, James Byrne, M.Howlett, R.Reynolds, T.McGrath (goal).
Kerry R.Fitzgerald (capt.), M.McCarthy, J.Lawlor, T.Costelloe, T.Rice, H.Murphy, P.Healy, C.Clifford, Con Murphy, P.O'Shea, M.Donovan, J.Rice, D.Doyle, M.Carroll, D.Mullins (goal).

1916
Wexford Seán Kennedy (capt.), T.McGrath (goal), P.Mackey, Fr.E.Wheeler, Jas.Byrne, T.Murphy, T.Mernagh, M.Howlett, F.Furlong, Tom Doyle, J.Crowley, R.Reynolds, J.Wall, A.Doyle, Gus Kennedy.
Mayo P.Loftus, T.Gibson, J.Waldron, J.E.McEllin, G.Delaney, P.Robinson, J.Lydon, H.Hession, D.F.Courell, M.Murray, T.Boshell, P.Kelly, J.Reilly, A.Lyons, P.Smith.

1917
Wexford Seán Kennedy (capt.), G.Kennedy, P.Mackey, A.Doyle, T.Mernagh, T.McGrath (goal), T.Murphy, W.Hodgins, J.Quinn, J.Byrne, J.Crowley, F.Furlong, M.Howlett, T.Doyle, R.Reynolds.
Clare M.Conole, P.Hennessy, J.Foran, E.McNamara, P.O'Brien, M.McMahon, J.Fitzgerald, M.McNamara, J.Marrinan, P.O'Donoghue, J.Spellissy, E.Carroll, M.Malone, E.Roche, T.Considine.

1918
Wexford T.McGrath (goal), N.Stuart, P.Mackey, J.Byrne (capt.), T.Murphy, T.Doyle, M.Howlett, W.Hodgins, J.Doran, J.Crowley, R.Reynolds, T.Pierse, A.Doyle, G.Kennedy, J.Redmond.
Tipperary A.Carroll, J.McNamara, E.O'Shea, J.Shelly, W.Ryan, E.Egan, T.Powell, J.Quinlan, J.Ryan, W.Grant, J.Skinner, R.Heffernan, G.McCarthy, J.O'Shea.

1919
Kildare L.Stanley (capt.), L.Cribben, J.Conlon, J.Moran, T.Goulding, M.Buckley, J.O'Connor, P Doyle, M.Sammon, G.Magan, J.Stanley, C.Flynn, B.McGlade, James O'Connor, F."Joyce" Conlon.
Galway T.Egan (capt.), D.Egan, J.Egan, Peter Higgins, M."Knacker" Walsh, P.Roche, J.Hanniffy, G.Jennings, L.Rahery, M.Flannelly, H.Burke, G.Feeney, M.Walsh, T.McDonnell, M.Cawley.

1920
Tipperary A.Carroll (goal), J.McNamara, Edwd.O'Shea, R.Lanigan, Bill Ryan, J.Shelly (capt.), W.Grant, W.Barrett, M.Tobin, J.Ryan, J.Doran, G.McCarthy, V.Vaughan, M.Arrigan, T.Powell.
Dublin J.McDonnell (goal), W.Robbins, Joe Joyce, P.Carey, Joe Synott, Joe Norris, John Reilly, J.Murphy, W.Donovan, J.Carey, P.McDonnell, Ger Doyle, John Synnod, F.Burke, S.Synott.

1921
Dublin E.Carroll (capt.), John Reilly, Joe Norris, P.Carey, John Synnott, P.Kirwan, W.Donovan, P.Fallon (goal), John Murphy, Thomas Pierse, F.Burke, C.McDonald, A.Belmain, J.O'Grady, W.Fitzsimons.
Mayo B.Durkin (capt.), J.White, Geo.Delaney, M.Barrett, W.Boshell, P.McLean, J.Lavin, P.Robinson, F.Doherty, J.E.McEllin, P.O'Beirne, M.McNicholas, K.Dillon (goal), J.Forde, P.Colleran. Sub: P.Moran for B.Durkin.

1922
Dublin P.Carey (capt.), J.McDonnell (goal), P.McDonnell, W.Robbins, A.Gibbons, Joe Synnott, John Synnott, Joe Norris, John Reilly, W.Rooney, C.McDonald, Wm.Donovan, P.Kirwan, F Burke, Tom Pierse.
Galway M.Walsh (capt.), W.Flanagan (goal), D.Egan, J.Egan, T.Molloy, T.Hession, J.Hanniffy, L.McGrath, J.Kirwan, P.Roche, G.Jennings, P.Jennings, Wm.Walsh, M.Donnellan, P.Kilroy.

1923
Dublin John Reilly, P.McDonnell (capt.), John Murphy, Joseph Norris, Joe Synott, Patk.Carey, P.Kirwan, J.Stynes, Frank Burke, John McDonnell (goal), John Synnott, M.Shanahan, J.Sherlock, P.O'Beirne, L.Stanley.
Kerry J.Sheehy (goal), J.Barrett, P.Sullivan, E.Moriarty, P.Russell, T.Kelleher, J.Moriarty (capt.), C.Brosnan, P.McKenna, John Ryan, John J.Sheehy, D.Donoghue, John Baily, Jas.Baily, W.Landers.

1924
Kerry J.Moriarty, John Sheehy (goal), Phil Sullivan (capt.), Joe Barrett, John Murphy, Paul Russell, Jack Walsh, Con Brosnan, R.Stack, John Ryan, John J.Sheehy, R.Prenderville, John Baily, Jas. Baily, W.Landers.
Dublin P.McDonnell (capt.), J.McDonnell (goal), P.Carey, W.O'Reilly, Joe Synott, Joe Norris, John Reilly, Peter Synnott, M.O'Brien, P.O'Beirne, John Murphy, M.Shanahan, F.Burke, G.Madigan, P.J.Kirwan.

1925
Galway declared champions
(Note: No football final played. Kerry and Cavan were declared illegal. Mayo, nominated by Connacht Council, beat Wexford, and then lost the Connacht final to Galway, who were declared champions.)
The Galway team which beat Mayo was: M.Walsh (capt.), T.Molloy, J.Egan, D.Egan, H.Burke, F.Benson, W.Smyth, T Leech, M.Bannerton, Leonard McGrath, P.Roche, G.Jennings, P.Ganley, Lar McGrath, M.Donnellan.

1926
Kerry John J.Sheehy (capt.), John Riordan (goal), P.Clifford, Joe Barrett, Jack Walsh, Paul Russell, J.Moriarty, John Slattery, Con Brosnan, Robt.Stack, John Ryan, D.O'Connell, Tom Mahony, Jas. Baily, Wm.Gorman.
Kildare Jos.Loughlin (capt.), Jas.Cummins (goal), Ml.Buckley, Matt.Goff, B.Graham, F.Malone, Jack Higgins, John Hayes, P.Martin, Gus Fitzpatrick, L.Stanley, Paul Doyle, Wm.Gannon, T.Donoghue, Joe Curtis.
(Note: The Kerry and Kildare players given are those who did duty in the replay. D.O'Connell, J.Slattery and P.Clifford replaced J.Murphy, Joe O'Sullivan and Phil O'Sullivan on the Kerry side, while T.Donoghue and Gus Fitzpatrick replaced A.O'Neill and G.Higgins on the Kildare side.
J.Slattery and P.Clifford came on as subs in drawn game.)

1927

Kildare   M.Buckley (capt.), M.Walsh (goal), Gus Fitzpatrick, F.Malone, J.Higgins, J.Hayes, J.Loughlin, W.Gannon, J.Curtis, P.Martin, P.Doyle, W.Mangan, P.Loughlin, T.Keogh, M.Goff. Sub: P.Ryan.
Kerry   J.J.Sheehy (capt.), J.O'Riordan (goal), D.O'Connor, J.Barrett, J.Walsh, D.O'Connell, P.O'Sullivan, J.Slattery, C.Brosnan, R.Stack, J.Ryan, E.Fitzgeraid, T.Mahony, Jas.Baily, J.J.Landers.

1928

Kildare   W.("Squires") Gannon (capt.), M.Walshe, M.Buckley, M.Goff, Gus Fitzpatrick, F.Malone, J.Higgins, J.Hayes, Joe Loughlin, P.Martin, P.Loughlin, P.Doyle, W.Mangan, J.Curtis, T.Keogh.
Cavan   J.Smith (capt.), J.Morgan, T.Campbell, H.Clegg, J.J.Clarke, H.Mulvany, P.Lynch, H.O'Reilly, P.Devlin, Jas.Murphy, A.Conlon, J.Farrell, W.Young, W.A.Higgins, G.Malcolmson. Sub: T.Crowe.

1929

Kerry   J.Riordan (goal), D.O'Connor, Joe Barrett (capt.), Jack Walsh, Paul Russell, Joe O'Sullivan, T.O'Donnell, Con Brosnan, R.Stack, J.Ryan, M.Doyle, J.J.Landers, E.Sweeney, Jas.Baily, J.J.Sheehy.
Kildare   J.Higgins (capt.), J.O'Reilly (goal), J.Hayes, M.Goff, Gus Fitzpatrick, M.Fenerall, F.Malone, P.Loughlin, Joe Loughlin, P.Martin, Wm.Hynam, Paul Doyle, T.Wheeler, P.Pringle, W.Gannon.

1930

Kerry   J.J.Sheehy (capt.), J.Riordan (goal), D.O'Connor, J.Barrett, Jack Walsh, P.Russell, J.O'Sullivan, T.O'Donnell, C.Brosnan, R.Stack, J.Ryan, M.Doyle, E.Fitzgerald, E.Sweeney, J.J.Landers.
Monaghan   P.Kilroy (capt.), T.Bradley (goal), T.Shevlin, J.Farrell, P.Duffy, P.Heeran, J.Duffy, P.Lambe, W.Mason, M.McAleer, C.Fisher, J.O'Carroll, P.McConnon, J.Sexton, H.Brannigan. Sub: P.J.Duffy.

1931

Kerry   Con Brosnan (capt.), D.O'Keeffe (goa), D.O'Connor, J.Barrett, Jack Walsh, P.Russell, J.O'Sullivan, T.Landers, R.Stack, J.J.Landers, M.Doyle, E.Fitzgerald, J.Ryan, P.Whitty, M.Regan.
Kildare   M.Walsh (capt.) (goal), J.Meany, M.Goff, F.Malone, P.Miles, J.Higgins, W.Hynam, P.Watters, P.Loughlin, J.Maguire, P.Martin, P.Byrne, H.Burke, D.Burke, P.Doyle.

1932

Kerry   D.O'Keeffe, D.O'Connor, Joe Barrett (capt), Jack Walsh, P.Russell, Joe O'Sullivan, P.Whitty, R.Stack, J.Walsh, C.Geaney, M.Doyle, T.Landers, J.Ryan, C.Brosnan, J.J.Landers. Sub: W.Landers for C.Geaney.
Mayo   T.Burke, J.Gannon, P.Quinn, P.Kelly, T.Tunney, S.O'Malley, G.Ormsby, M.Mulderrig, M.Ormsby, P.Munnelly, T.Hanley, P.Flannelly, G.Courell, P.Moclair, J.Forde.

1933

Cavan   J.Smith (capt.), W.Young (goal), M.Denneny, P.Phair, T.O'Reilly, P.Lynch, H.O'Reilly, W.Connolly, T.Coyle, L.Blessing, P.Devlin, D.Morgan, J.Smallhorn, V.McGovern, M.J.Magee. Subs: T.Crowe, P.W.Connolly, T.O'Reilly (Mullahoran).
Galway   M.Donnellan (capt.), F.Fox, B.Nestor, M.Brennan (goal), H.Carey, M.Connaire, J.Dunne, J.Kelleher, M.Kelly, T.McCarthy, F.Burke, M.Higgins, D.O'Sullivan, T.Hughes, D.Mitchell.

1934

Galway   M.Higgins (capt.), M.Brennan (goal), P.J.McDonnell, M.Ferriter, H.Carey, D.O'Sullivan, T.Hughes, T.McCarthy, F.Fox, J.Dunne, M.Connaire, R.Griffin, M.Kelly, D.Mitchell, B.Nestor.
Dublin   J.McDonnell (goal), G.Comerford, M.O'Brien, D.Brennan, M.Casey, F.Cavanagh, P.Cavanagh, P.Hickey, W.Dowling, R.Beggs, M.Wellington, G.Fitzgerald, M.Kelly, M.Keating (capt.), E.McCann.

1935

Cavan   W.Young, W.Connolly, J.Smith, M.Denney, T.Dolan, T.O'Reilly (Mullahoran), P.Phair, H.O'Reilly (capt.), T.O'Reilly, D.Morgan, P.Devlin, J.Smallhorn, P.Boylan, L.Blessing, M.J.Magee.
Kildare   J.Maguire (goal), W.Mangan, M.Goff, J.Byrne, P.Watters, J.Higgins, F.Dowling, P.Mathews, C.Higgins, T.Mulhall, P.Byrne, P.Martin, J.Dowling, M.Geraghty, T.Keogh. Sub: J.Dalton for C.Higgins.

1936

Mayo   T.Burke (goal), J.McGowan, P.Quinn, "Purty" Kelly, T.Regan, S.O'Malley (capt.), G.Ormsby, P.Flannelly, H.Kenny, J.Carney, P.Laffey, T.Grier, J.Munnelly, P.Moclair, P.Munnelly.
Laois   J.McDonnell (capt.), T.Delaney (goal), T.Delaney, J.Brennan, T.O'Brien, P.Swayne, D.Walsh, C.Delaney, W.Delaney, D.Douglas, J.Delaney, M.Delaney, T.Keogh, J.Keating, J.O'Reilly. Sub: J.Moran for D.Walsh.

1937 REPLAY

Kerry   D.O'Keeffe (goal), W.Kinnerk, J.Keohane, W.Myers, T.O'Donnell, W.Dillon, T.Healy, J.Walsh, S.Brosnan, J.Flavin, C.O'Sullivan, T.Landers, J.J.Landers, M.Doyle (capt.), T.O'Leary. Sub: T.O'Connor for T.O'Donnell.
Gearóid Fitzgerald and Paddy Kennedy played in drawn game. J.Flavin and T.O'Leary came in for replay. Sub: S.McCarthy.
Cavan   W.Young (goal), E.Finnegan, J.Smith, M.Denneny, D.Kerrigan, T.O'Reilly (capt.), J.J.O'Reilly, V.White, P.Smith, D.Morgan, P.Deviin, J.Smallhorn, P.Boylan, L.Blessing, M.Magee. Subs: T.O'Reilly (Mullahorn), J.White, W.Carroll, J.Mitchell. W.Carroll and J.White played in drawn game. D.Kerrigan and J.Smallhorn were on for replay.

1938 REPLAY

Galway   J.McGauran (goal), M.Raftery, M.Connaire, D.O'Sullivan, F.Cunniffe, R.Beggs, C.Connolly, J.Burke, J.Dunne (capt.), J.Flavin, M.Higgins, R.Griffin, E.Mulholland, M.Kelly, B.Nestor. Subs: M.Ryder for E.Mulholland, P.McDonagh for J.Burke.
Kerry   W.Kinnerk (capt.), D.O'Keeffe, P.B.Brosnan, W.Myers, W.Dillon, M.Casey, T.O'Connor, J.Walsh, S.Brosnan, P.Kennedy, A.McAuliffe, C.O'Sullivan, M.Regan, M.Doyle, T.O'Leary. Sub: J.J.Landers for J.Walsh.
J.J.Landers and Joe Keohane played in drawn game. P.B.Brosnan and M.Regan came on for replay.

1939

Kerry   D.O'Keeffe, W.Myers, J.Keohane, T.Healy, W.Dillon, W.Casey, E.Walsh, P.Kennedy, J.O'Gorman, M.Kelly, T.O'Connor (capt.), J.Walsh, C.O'Sullivan, D.Spring, T.Landers.
Meath   H.McEnroe, P.Beggan, T.McGuinness, P.Donnelly, T.Meade, C.O'Reilly, J.Kearney, M.O'Toole, J.Loughran, M.Gilsenan (capt.), A.Donnelly, J.Clarke, W.Brien, J.Cummins, K.Devin. Subs: H.Lynch for W.Brien, M.Clinton for M.O'Toole.

1940

Kerry   D.O'Keeffe, W.Myers, J.Keohane, T.Healy, W.Dillon, W.Casey, E.Walsh, S.Brosnan, J.Walsh, J.O'Gorman, T.O'Connor, P.Kennedy, M.Kelly, D.Spring (capt.), C.O'Sullivan. Sub: P.B.Brosnan.
Galway   J.McGauran, M.Raftery, M.Connaire, D.O'Sullivan, F.Cunniffe, R.Beggs, C.Connolly, J.Dunne (capt.), J.Duggan, J.Flavin, J.Burke, J.Canavan, M.Higgins, E.Mulholland, B.Nestor.

1941

Kerry   D.O'Keeffe, W.Myers, Joe Keohane, T.Healy, W.Dillon (capt.), W.Casey, E.Walsh, S.Brosnan, P.Kennedy, J.Walsh, T.O'Connor, P.B.Brosnan, J.O'Gorman, M.Kelly, C.O'Sullivan. Subs: T.Landers for W.Myers, M.Lyne for J.Walsh.
Galway   J.McGauran, M.Raftery, P.McDonagh, D.O'Sullivan (capt.), F.Cunniffe, R.Beggs, J.Duggan, C.Connolly, D.Kavanagh, J.Hanniffy, J.Dunne, J.Canavan, E.Mulholland, P.McDonagh, J.Burke. Sub: P.Thornton for J.Canavan.

1942

Dublin   C.Kelly, R.Beggs, P.Kennedy, C.Crone, P.Henry, P.O'Reilly, B.Quinn, M.Falvey, Joe Fitzgerald (capt.), J.Joy, P.Bermingham, Gerry Fitzgerald, M.Fletcher, P.O'Connor, T.Banks.
Galway   J.McGauran, F.Cunniffe, M.Connaire, P.McDonagh, J.Duggan, J.Casey, Tom O'Sullivan, D.Kavanagh, C.Connolly (capt.), J.Clifford, M.Fallon, J.Canavan, J.Flavin, P.Thornton, Seán Thornton. Subs: E.Mulholland for Clifford; Seán Walsh for J.Flavin).

1943 REPLAY

Roscommon F.Glynn, L.Cummins, J.P.O'Callaghan, W.Jackson, B.Lynch, W.Carlos, O.Hoare, E.Boland, L.Gilmartin, P.Murray, J.Murray (capt.), D.Keenan, D.McDermott, J.McQuillan, F.Kinlough. W.Heavey, who played in the drawn game, was replaced by O.Hoare for replay.
Cavan   J.D.Benson, E.Finnegan, B.Cully, P.P.Galligan, G.Smith, T.O'Reilly (capt.), J.J.O'Reilly, S.Deignan, T.P.O'Reilly, D.Morgan, P.Smith, M Higgins, P.Boylan, Joe Stafford, H.Rogers. Sub: J.Keegan for H.Rogers.
J.Maguire, who played in drawn was replaced by H.Rogers for replay.

1944

Roscommon O.Hoare, W.Jackson, J.P.O'Callaghan, J.Casserly, B.Lynch, W.Carlos, P.Murray, E.Boland, L.Gilmartin, F.Kinlough, J.Murray (capt.), D.Keenan, H.Gibbons, J.McQuillan, J.J.Nerney. Sub: D.McDermott for J.J.Nerney.
Kerry   D.O'Keeffe, T.Healy, J.Keohane, T.Brosnan, W.Dillon, M.McCarthy, E.Walsh, P.Kennedy, S.Brosnan, J.Clifford, J.Lyne, P.B.Brosnan (capt.), D.Lyne, M.Kelly, E.Dunne. Subs: D.Kavanagh for P.Kennedy; J.Walsh for P.B.Brosnan.
Referee P.Mythen (Wexford).

1945

Cork   M.O'Driscoll, D.Magnier, P.A.Murphy, C.Crone, P.Cronin, T.Crowley (capt.), D.O'Connor, F.O'Donovan, E.Young, E.Casey, H.O'Neill, M.Tubridy, J.Lynch, J.Cronin, D.Beckett. Sub: J.Ahern for E.Casey.
Cavan   B.Kelly, T.O'Reilly (capt.), B.Cully, P.P.Galligan, J.Wilson, J.J.O'Reilly, P.Smith, A.Tighe, S.Deignan, A.Commiskey, J.Boylan, T.P.O'Reilly, J.Stafford, P.Donohue, P.J.Duke.

1946 REPLAY

Kerry   D.O'Keeffe, D.Lyne, J.Keohane, P.B.Brosnan, J.Lyne, W.Casey, E.Walsh, Teddy O'Connor, P.Kennedy (capt.), J.Falvey, Tom O'Connor, B.Grvey, F.O'Keeffe, P.Burke, D.Kavanagh.
Gus Cremins (capt.) and Willie O'Donnell played in drawn game. F.O'Keeffe and J.Falvey came on for replay. Gus Cremin replaced J.Falvey as sub during replay.
Subs in drawn game: E.Dowling for P.Kennedy, B.Kelleher for J.Lyne.
Roscommon G.Dolan, W.Jackson, J.Casserly, O.Hoare, B.Lynch, W.Carlos, T.Collins, P.Murray, E.Boland, F.Kinlough, J.Murray (capt.), D.Keenan, J.McQuillan, J.J.Fallon, J.J.Nerney. Sub: D.McDermott for B.Lynch.
Vincent Beirne came on as a sub in drawn game for J.Murray.

1947

Cavan   V.Gannon, W.Doonan, B.O'Reilly, P.Smith, J.Wilson, J.J.O'Reilly (capt.), S.Deignan, P.J.Duke, P.Brady, A.Tighe, M.Higgins, C.McDyer, J.Stafford, P.Donohoe, T.P.O'Reilly.
Kerry   D.O'Keeffe, D.Lyne (capt.), J.Keohane, P.Brosnan, J.Lyne, W.Casey, E.Walsh, E.Dowling, E.O'Connor, E.O'Sullivan, D.Kavanagh, B.Garvey, F.O'Keeffe, T.O'Connor, P.Kennedy. Subs: W.O'Donnell for E.Dowling; M.Finucane for E.Walsh; T.Brosnan for W.O'Donnell; G.Teehan for P.Kennedy.

1948

Cavan   J.D.Benson, W.Doonan, B.O'Reilly, P.Smith, P.J.Duke, J.J.Reilly (capt.), S.Deignan, P.Brady, V.Sherlock, A.Tighe, M.Higgins, J.J.Cassidy, J.Stafford, P.Donohoe, E.Carolan. Sub: O.R.McGovern for J.J.O'Reilly.
Mayo   T.Byrne, P.Quinn, P.Prendergast, S.Flanagan J.Forde (capt.), P.McAndrew, Jn.Gilvarry, E.Mongey, P.Carney, W.Kenny, T.Langan, Joe Gilvarry, T.Acton, P.Solon, S.Mulderrig.

1949

Meath   K.Smith, M.O'Brien, P.O'Brien, K.McConnell, S.Heery, P.Dixon, C.Hand, P.Connell, J.Kearney, F.Byrne, B.Smyth (capt.), M.McDonnell, P.Meegan, W.Halpenny, P.McDermott. Sub: P.Carolan for F.Byrne.
Cavan   J.Morris, J.McCabe, P.Smith, O.R.McGovern, P.J.Duke, J.J.O'Reilly (capt.), S.Deignan, P.Brady, V.Sherlock, A.Tighe, M.Higgins, J.J.Cassidy, J.Stafford, P.Donohoe, E.Carolan.

1950

Mayo   W.Durkin, J.Forde, P.Prendergast, S.Flanagan (capt.), P.Quinn, H.Dixon, J.McAndrew, P.Carney, E.Mongey, M.Flanagan, W.Kenny, J.Gilvarry, M.Mulderrig, T.Langan, P.Solon. Subs: S.Wynne for W.Durkin; M.Caulfield for W.Kenny; S.Mulderrig for M.Caulfield.
Louth   S.Thornton, M.Byrne, T.Conlon (capt.), J.Tuft, S.Boyle, P.Markey, P.McArdle, J.Regan, F.Reid, J.McDonnell, N.Roe, S.White, R.Lynch, H.Reynolds, M.Reynolds. Subs: R.Mooney for N.Roe; M.McDonnell for P.McArdle.

1951

Mayo   S.Wynne, J.Forde, P.Prendergast, S.Flanagan (capt.), J.Staunton, H.Dixon, P.Quinn, E.Mongey, J.McAndrew, P.Irwin, P.Carney, S.Mulderrig, M.Flanogan, T.Langan, J.Gilvarry. Sub: L.Hastings for H.Dixon.
Meath   K.Smyth, M.O'Brien, P.O'Brien, K.McConnell, S.Heery (capt.), C.Kelly, C.Hand, D.Taaffe, P.Connell, F.Byrne M.McDonnell, P.Meegan, B.Smyth, J.Reilly, P.McDermott. Subs: P.Dixon for C.Hand; C.Hand for S.Heery.

1952 REPLAY

Cavan S.Morris, J.McCabe, P.Brady, D.Maguire, P.Carolan, L.Maguire, B.O'Reilly, V.Sherlock, T.Hardy, S.Hetherton, M.Higgins (capt.), E.Carolan, J.J.Cassidy, A.Tighe, J.Cusack.
P.Fitzsimons played in drawn game. J.Cusack came on for replay. P.Fitzsimmons was introduced as sub for J.J.Cassidy in replay.
Meath K.Smyth, M.O'Brien, P.O'Brien, K.McConnell, T.O'Brien, C.Kelly, C.Hand, B.Maguire, D.Taaffe, D.Brennan, B.Smith, P.Meegan (capt.), M.McDonnell, J.Reilly, P.McDermott.
P.McGearty and P.Connell played in drawn game. T.O'Brien and D.Brennan came on for replay.

1953

Kerry J.Foley, J.Murphy (capt.), E.Roche, D.Murphy, C.Kennelly, J.Cronin, J.M.Palmer, Seán Murphy, D.Hanifin, J.Brosnan, J.J.Sheehan, T.Lyne, T.Ashe, S.Kelly, J.Lyne. Sub: G.O'Sullivan for Hannifin.
Armagh E.McMahon, E Morgan, J.Bratten, J.McKnight, F.Kernan, P.O'Neill, S.Quinn (capt.), M.O'Hanlon, M.McEvoy, J.Cunningham, B.Seeley, W.McCorry, P.Campbell, A.O'Hagan, G.O'Neill. Subs: G.Wilson for McMahon; G.Murphy for Wilson; J.O'Hare for Quinn.

1954

Meath P.McGearty, M.O'Brien, P.O'Brien, K.McConnell, K.Lenehan, J.Reilly, E.Durnin, P.Connell, T.O'Brien, M.Grace, B.Smyth, M.McDonnell, P.Meegan, T.Moriarty, P.McDermott. (capt.).
Kerry G.O'Mahony, J.M.Palmer, E.Roche, D.Murphy, Seán Murphy, J.Cronin, C.Kennelly, John Dowling (capt.), T.Moriarty, R.Buckley, J.J.Sheehan, P.Sheehy, J.Brosnan, S.Kelly, T.Lyne.

1955

Kerry G.O'Mahony, J.O'Shea, E.Roche, J.M.Palmer, Seán Murphy, J.Cronin, T.Moriarty, J.Dowling (capt.), D.O'Shea, P.Sheehy, T.Costelloe, T.Lyne, J.Culloty, M.Murphy, J.Brosnan. Sub: J.J.Sheehan for Moriarty.
Dublin P.O'Flaherty, D.Mahony (capt.), J.Lavin, M.Moylan, Maurice Whelan, J.Crowley, N.Maher, J.McGuinness, C.O'Leary, D.Ferguson, O.Freaney, J.Boyle, P.Haughey, K.Heffernan, C.Freaney. Subs: T.Jennings for McGuinness; W.Monks for Jennings.

1956

Galway J.Mangan (capt.), J.Keeley, G.Daly, T.Dillon, J.Kissane, J.Mahon, M.Greally, F.Evers, Matly McDonagh, J.Coyle, S.Purcell, W.O'Neill, J.Young, F.Stockwell, G.Kirwan. Sub: A.Swords for Young.
Cork P.Tyres, P.Driscoll, D.O'Sullivan (capt.), D.Murray, P.Harrington, D.Bernard, M.Gould, S.Moore, E.Ryan, D.Kelleher, C.Duggan, P.Murphy, T.Furlong, N.Fitzgerald, J.Creedon. Sub: E.Goulding for Murphy.

1957

Louth S.Flood, O.Reilly, T.Conlon, J.Meehan, P.Coleman, P.Smith, S.White, K.Beahan, D.O'Neill, S.O'Donnell, D.O'Brien (capt.), F.Lynch, S.Cunningham, J.McDonnell, J.Roe.
Cork L.Power, M.Gould, D.Bernard, D.Murray, P.Harrington, P.O'Driscoll, J.J.Henchion, E.Ryan, S.Moore, J.O'Sullivan, N.Fitzgerald, T.Furlong, E.Goulding, C.Duggan (capt.), D.Kelleher. Sub: F.McAuliffe for J.O'Sullivan.

1958

Dublin P.O'Flaherty, L.Foley, M.Wilson, Joe Timmons, C.O'Leary, J.Crowley, J.Boyle, John Timmons, S.Murray, P.Haughey, O.Freaney, D.Ferguson, P.Farnan, J.Joyce, K.Heffernan (capt.). Subs: Maurice Whelan for Murray; P.Downey for John Timmons.
Derry P.Gormley, P.McLarnon, H.F.McGribben, T.Doherty, P.Breen, C.Mulholland, P.Smith, J.McKeever (capt.), P.Stuart, S.O'Connell, B.Murray, D.McKeever, B.Mullan, O.Gribben, C.Higgins. Subs: R.Gribben for Higgins; L.O'Neill for Mullan; C.O'Neill for Breen.

1959

Kerry J.Culloty, J.O'Shea, N.Sheehy, T.Lyons, Seán Murphy, K.Coffey, M.O'Dwyer, M.O'Connell (capt.), Seamus Murphy, D.McAuliffe, T.Long, P.Sheehy, D.Geaney, John Dowling, T.Lyne. Subs: Jack Dowling for Lyons; Moss O'Connell for Mick O'Connell; G.McMahon for Geaney.
Galway J.Farrell, J.Kissane, S.Meade, M.Greally, M.Garrett, J.Mahon, S.Colleran, F.Evers, Matty McDonagh, J.Young, S.Purcell (capt), Ml.McDonagh, M.Laide, F.Stockwell, J.Nallen. Subs: J.Keeley for Nallen, P.Dunne for Greally.

1960

Down E.McKay, G.Lavery, L.Murphy, P.Rice, K.Mussen (capt.), D.McCartan, K.O'Neill, J.Lennon, J.Carey, S.O'Neill, J.McCartan, P.Doherty, A.Hadden, P.O'Hagan, B.Morgan. Sub: K.Denvir for Lennon.
Kerry J.Culloty, J.O'Shea, N.Sheehy, T.Lyons, Seán Murphy, K.Coffey, M.O'Dwyer, M.O'Connell, J.D.O'Connor, Seamus Murphy, T.Long, P.Sheehy (capt.), G.McMahon, John Dowling, T.Lyne. Subs: Jack Dowling for John Dowling; J.Brosnan for McMahon; D.McAuliffe for Lyne.

1961

Down E.McKay, G.Lavery, L.Murphy, P.Rice, P.O'Hagan, D.McCartan, J.Smith, J.Carey, J.Lennon, S.O'Neill, J.McCartan, P.Doherty (capt.), A.Hadden, P.J.McIlroy, B.Morgan. Subs: K.O'Neill for P.Rice; Denvir for G.Lavery.
Offaly W.Nolan (capt.), P.McCormack, G.Hughes, J.Egan, P.O'Reilly, M.Brady, C.Wrenn, S.Brereton, S.Ryan, T.Cullen, P.Daly, T.Greene, M.Casey, D.O'Hanlon, H.Donnelly. Subs: F.Weir for M.Casey, S.Foran for S.Ryan, F.Higgins for P.O'Reilly.

1962

Kerry J.Culloty, Seamus Murphy, N.Sheehy, T.Lyons, S.Óg Sheehy (capt.), N.Lucey, M.O'Dwyer, M.O'Connell, J.Lucy, D.McAuliffe, T.O'Sullivan, J.O'Riordan, G.McMahon, T.Long, P.Sheehy. Subs: J.J.Barrett for T.Lyons, K.Coffey for D.McAuliffe.
Roscommon A.Brady, J.J.Breslin, J.Lynch, J.O.Moran, R.Creaven, G.O'Malley (capt.), G.Reilly, B.Kyne, J.Kelly, G.Geraghty, E.Curley, A.Whyte, Don Feely, C.Mahon, Des Feely. Subs: T.Turley for G.Reilly, A.Kenny for T.Turley.

1963

Dublin P.Flynn, L.Hickey, L.Foley, W.Casey, D.McKane, P.Holden, M.Kissane, D.Foley (capt.), John Timmons, B.McDonald, Mickie Whelan, G.Davey, S.Behan, D.Ferguson, N.Fox. Sub: P.Downey for P.Holden.
Galway M.Moore, E.Colleran, N.Tierney, S.Meade, J.B.McDermott, J.Donnellan, M.Newell, M.Garrett (capt.), M.Reynolds, C.Dunne, Matly McDonagh, P.Donnellan, J.Keenan, S.Cleary, S.Leydon. Sub: B.Geraghty for S.Cleary.

1964

Galway   J.Geraghty, E.Colleran, N.Tierney, J.B.McDermott, J.Donnellan (capt.), S.Meade, M.Newell, M.Garrett, M.Reynolds, C.Dunne, M.McDonagh, S.Leydon, C.Tyrrell, S.Cleary, J.Keenan.
Kerry   J.Culloty, M.Morris, N.Sheehy (capt.), P.Donoghue, Denis O'Sullivan, Seamus Murphy, J.D.O'Connor, M.Fleming, Donie O'Sullivan, P.Griffin, M.O'Dwyer, M.O'Connell, F.O'Leary, T.Long, J.J.Barrett. Subs: J.McCarthy for J.D.O'Connor, B.O'Callaghan for F.O'Leary, K.Coffey for J.McCarthy.

1965

Galway   J.Geraghty, E.Colleran (capt.), N.Tierney, J.B.McDermott, J.Donnellan, S.Meade, M.Newell, P.Donnellan, M.Garrett, C.Dunne, Matty McDonagh, S.Leydon, C.Tyrrell, S.Cleary, J.Keenan. Sub: M.Reynolds.
Kerry   J.Culloty, Donie O'Sullivan, N.Sheehy, M.Morris, Seamus Murphy, P.O'Donoghue, J.D.O'Connor (capt.), Denis O'Sullivan, M.O'Connell, V.Lucey, P.Griffin, D.O'Shea, B.O'Callaghan, M.O'Dwyer, J.J.Barrett. Subs: D.Geaney for V.Lucey, J.O'Shea for J.J.Barrett.

1966

Galway   J.Geraghty, E.Colleran (capt.), N.Tierney, J.B.McDermott, C.McDonagh, S.Meade, M.Newell, J.Duggan, P.Donnellan, C.Dunne, Matty McDonagh, S.Leydon, L.Sammon, S.Cleary, J.Keenan. Sub: J.Donnellan for S.Meade.
Meath   S.McCormack, D.Donnelly, J.Quinn, P.Darby, P.Collier, B.Cunningham, P.Reynolds, P.Moore, T.Brown, A.Brennan, M.O'Sullivan, D.Carty (capt.), G.Quinn, N.Curran, O.Shanley. Subs: M.White for D.Donnelly, J.Fagan for D.Carty, M.Quinn for J.Fagan.

1967

Meath   S.McCormack, M.White, J.Quinn, P.Darby (capt.), P.Collier, B.Cunningham, P.Reynolds, P.Moore, T.Kearns, A.Brennan, M.Kerrigan, M.Mellett, P.Mulvaney, N.Curran, O.Shanley.
Cork   W.Morgan, B.Murphy, J.Lucey, J.O'Mahony, F.Cogan, D.Coughlan, K.Dillon, M.Burke, M.O'Loughlin, E.Philpott, E.McCarthy, B.O'Neill, E.Ryan, C.O'Sullivan, F.Hayes. Subs: J.Carroll for M.Burke, J.Downing for E.McCarthy, J.J.Murphy for J.Downing.

1968

Down   D.Kelly, B.Sloan, D.McCartan, T.O'Hare, R.McConville, W.Doyle, J.Lennon (capt.), J.Milligan, C.McAlarney, M.Cole, P.Doherty, J.Murphy, P.Rooney, S.O'Neill, J.Purdy. Subs: L.Powell for J.Lennon, G.Glynn for L.Powell.
Kerry   J.Culloty, Seamus Murphy, P.O'Donoghue, S.Burrows, Denis O'Sullivan, M.Morris, Donie O'Sullivan, M.O'Connell, M.Fleming, B.Lynch, P.Griffin (capt.), E.O'Donoghue, T.Prendergast, D.J.Crowley, M.O'Dwyer. Subs: P.Moynihan for T.Prendergast, S.Fitzgerald for S.Burrows.

1969

Kerry   J.Culloty (capt.), Seamus Murphy, P.O'Donoghue, S.Fitzgerald, T.Prendergast, M.Morris, M.O'Shea, M.O'Connell, D.J.Crowley, B.Lynch, P.Griffin, E.O'Donoghue, M.Gleeson, L.Higgins, M.O'Dwyer.
Offaly   M.Furlong, P.McCormack, G.Hughes, J.Egan (capt.), E.Mulligan, N.Clavin, M.Ryan, L.Coughlan, W.Bryan, P.Keenan, A.Hickey, A.McTague, S.Kilroy, S.Evans, J.Cooney. Subs: F.Costelloe for A.Hickey, K.Kilmurray for P.Keenan, P.Monaghan for S.Kilroy.

1970

Kerry   J.Culloty, Seamus Murphy, P.O'Donoghue, Donie O'Sullivan (capt.), T.Prendergast, J.O'Keeffe, M.O'Shea, M.O'Connell, D.J.Crowley, B.Lynch, P.Griffin, E.O'Donoghue, M.Gleeson, L.Higgins, M.O'Dwyer. Sub: S.Fitzgerald for Donie O'Sullivan.
Meath   S.McCormack, M.White, J.Quinn (capt.), B.Cunningham, O.Shanley, T.Kearns, P.Reynolds, V.Foley, V.Lynch, A.Brennan, M.Kerrigan, M.Mellett, K.Rennicks, J.Murphy, M.Fay. Subs: P.Moore for M.Mellette, W.Bligh for T.Kearns.

1971

Offaly   M.Furlong, M.Ryan, P.McCormack, M.O'Rourke, E.Mulligan, N.Clavin, M.Heavey, W.Bryan (capt.), K.Claffey, J.Cooney, K.Kilmurray, A.McTague, J.Gunning, S.Evans, Murt Connor. Subs: J.Smith for N.Clavin; P.Fenning for J.Gunning.
Galway   P.J.Smyth, B.Colleran, J.Cosgrove, N.Colleran, L.O'Neill, T.J.Gilmore, C.McDonagh, L.Sammon (capt.), W.Joyce, P.Burke, J.Duggan, M.Rooney, E.Farrell, F.Canavan.S.Leydon. Subs: T.Divilly for M.Rooney; M.Feerick for P.Burke.

1972 REPLAY

Offaly   M.Furlong, M.Ryan, P.McCormack, L.Coughlan, E.Mulligan, S.Lowry, M.Heavey, W.Bryan, S.Evans, J.Cooney, K.Kilmurray, A.McTague (capt.), S.Darby, J.Smith, P.Fenning. Subs: Murt Connor for J.Cooney; N.Clavin for E.Mulligan; M.Wright for L.Coughlan.
Murt Connor played in drawn game. Seamus Darby came on for replay. Jody Gunning came on as a sub in drawn game for E.Mulligan.
Kerry   E.Fitzgerald, Donie O'Suillvan, P.O'Donoghue, S.Fitzgerald, T.Prendergast (capt.), M.O'Shea, P.Lynch, M.O'Connell, J.O'Keeffe, B.Lynch, D.Kavanagh, E.O'Donoghue, M.Gleeson, L.Higgins, M.O'Dwyer. Subs: Derry Crowley for S.Fitzgerald; P.Griffin for M.Gleeson; J.Walsh for B.Lynch. Kerry fielded same team in both games. Derry Crowley and Pat Griffin came on as subs in drawn game for S.Fitzgerald and L.Higgins.

1973

Cork   W.Morgan (capt.), F.Cogan, H.Kelleher, B.Murphy (Nemo Rangers), K.J.O'Sullivan, J.Coleman, C.Hartnett, D.Long, D.Coughlan, E.Kirby, D.Barron, D.McCarthy, J.Barry Murphy, R.Cummins, J.Barrett. Subs: S.Coughlan for J.Coleman; D.Hunt for McCarthy; M.Scannell for D.Kelleher.
Galway   G.Mitchell, J.Waldron, J.Cosgrove, B.Colleran, L.O'Neill, T.J.Gilmore, J.Hughes, W.Joyce, J.Duggan, M.Burke, L.Sammon (capt.), M.Rooney, J.Coughlan, T.Naughton, M.Hughes. Subs: F.Canavan for J.Coughlan; C.McDonagh for M.Burke.

1974

Dublin   P.Cullen, G.O'Driscoll, S.Doherty (capt.), R.Kelleher, P.Reilly, A.Larkin, G.Wilson, S.Rooney, B.Mullins, B.Doyle, A.Hanahoe, D.Hickey, J.McCarthy, J.Keaveney, A.O'Toole.
Galway   G.Mitchell (capt.), J.Waldron, J.Cosgrove, B.Colleran, L.O'Neill, T.J.Gilmore, J.Hughes, W.Joyce, M.Rooney, T.Naughton, J.Duggan, P.Sands, C.McDonagh, L.Sammon, J.Tobin. Sub: J.Burke for C.McDonagh.

1975

Kerry P.O'Mahony, G.O'Keeffe, J.O'Keeffe, J.Deenihan, P.Ó Sé, T.Kennelly, G.Power, P.Lynch, P.McCarthy, B.Lynch, D.''Ogie'' Moran, M.O'Sullivan (capt.), J.Egan, M.Sheehy, P.Spillane. Sub: G.O'Driscoll for M.O'Sullivan.

Dublin P.Cullen, G.O'Driscoll, S.Doherty (capt.), R.Kelleher, P.Reilly, A.Larkin, G.Wilson, B.Mullins, B.Brogan, A.O'Toole, A.Hanahoe, D.Hickey, J.McCarthy, J.Keaveney, P.Gogarty. Subs: B.Doyle for B.Brogan; P.O'Neill for J.McCarthy; B.Pocock for P.Reilly.

1976

Dublin P.Cullen, G.O'Driscoll, S.Doherty, R.Kelleher, T.Drumm, K.Moran, P.O'Neill, B.Mullins, B.Brogan, A.O'Toole, A.Hanahoe (capt.), D.Hickey, B.Doyle, J.Keaveney, J.McCarthy. Subs: F.Ryder for A.Hanahoe; P.Gogarty for B.Doyle.

Kerry P.O'Mahony, G.O'Keeffe, J.O'Keeffe (capt.), J.Deenihan, P.Ó Sé, T.Kennelly, G.Power, P.Lynch, P.McCarthy, D.''Ogie'' Moran, M.Sheehy, M.O'Sullivan, B.Lynch, J.Egan, P.Spillane. Subs: C.Nelligan for P.O'Mahony; S.Walsh for P.McCarthy; G.O'Driscoll for M.O'Sullivan.

1977

Dublin P.Cullen, G.O'Driscoll, S.Doherty, R.Kelleher, T.Drumm, K.Moran, P.O'Neill, B.Mullins, B.Brogan, A.O'Toole, A.Hanahoe (capt.), D.Hickey, B.Doyle, J.Keaveney, J.McCarthy. Subs: P.Reilly for P.O'Neill; A.Larkin for B.Brogan; J.Brogan for R.Kelleher.

Armagh B.McAlinden, D.Stevenson, T.McCreesh, J.McKerr, K.Rafferty, P.Moriarty, J.Donnelly, J.Kernan, C.McKinistry, L.Kearns, J.Smyth, N.Marley, S.Devlin, P.Trainor, P.Loughran. Subs: J.Loughran for J.Donnelly; S.Daly for N.Marley; F.Toman for J.McKerr.

1978

Kerry C.Nelligan, J.Deenihan, J.O'Keeffe, M.Spillane, P.Ó Sé, T.Kennelly, P.Lynch, J.O'Shea, S.Walsh, G.Power, D.''Ogie'' Moran (capt.), P.Spillane, M.Sheehy, E.Liston, J.Egan. Sub: P.O'Mahony for J.Deenihan.

Dublin P.Cullen, G.O'Driscoll, S.Doherty, R.Kelleher, T.Drumm, K.Moran, P.O'Neill, B.Mullins, B.Brogan, A.O'Toole, A.Hanahoe (capt.), D.Hickey, B.Doyle, J.Keaveney, J.McCarthy.

1979

Kerry C.Nelligan, J.Deenihan, J.O'Keeffe, M.Spillane, P.Ó Sé, T.Kennelly (capt.), P.Lynch, J.O'Shea, S.Walsh, T.Doyle, D.''Ogie'' Moran, P.Spillane, M.Sheehy, E.Liston, J.Egan. Subs: V.O'Connor for J.O'Keeffe.

Dublin P.Cullen, M.Kennedy, M.Holden, D.Foran, T.Drumm, F.Ryder, P.O'Neill, B.Mullins, B.Brogan, A.O'Toole, A.Hanahoe (capt.), D.Hickey, M.Hickey, B.Doyle, J.McCarthy. Subs: J.Ronayne for M.Hickey; G.O'Driscoll for McCarthy; B.Pocock for A.O'Toole.

1980

Kerry C.Nelligan, J.Deenihan, J.O'Keeffe, P.Lynch, P.Ó Sé, T.Kennelly, G.O'Keeffe, J.O'Shea, S.Walsh, G.Power (capt.), D.''Ogie'' Moran, P.Spillane.M.Sheehy, T.Doyle, J.Egan. Sub: G.O'Driscoll for G.Power.

Roscommon G.Sheerin, H.Keegan, P.Lindsay, G.Connellan, G.Fitzmaurice, T.Donlon.D.Murray (capt.), D.Earley, S.Hayden, J.O'Connor, J.O'Gara, A.Dooley, M.Finneran, A.McManus, E.McManus. Subs: M.Dolphin for A.Dooley, M.McDermott for S.Hayden.

1981

Kerry C.Nelligan, J.Deenihan (capt.).J.O'Keeffe.P.Lynch, P.Ó Sé, T.Kennelly, M.Spillane, S.Walsh, J.O'Shea, G.Power, D.''Ogie'' Moran, T.Doyle, M.Sheehy, E.Liston, J.Egan. Subs: P.Spillane for J.Egan, G.O'Keeffe for M.Spillane.

Offaly M.Furlong, M.Fitzgerald, L.Connor, C.Conroy, P.Fitzgerald, R.Connor (capt.), L.Currams, T.Connor, P.Dunne, V.Henry, G.Carroll, A.O'Halloran, Matt Connor, S.Lowry, B.Lowry. Subs: J.Mooney for T.Connor, J.Moran for V.Henry.

1982

Offaly M.Furlong, M.Lowry, L.Connor, M.Fitzgerald, P.Fitzgerald, S.Lowry, L.Currams, T.Connor, P.Dunne, J.Guinan, R.Connor (capt.), G.Carroll, J.Mooney, Matt Connor, B.Lowry. Subs: Stephen Darby for M.Lowry; Seamus Darby for J.Guinan.

Kerry C.Nelligan, G.O'Keeffe, J.O'Keeffe, P.Lynch, P.Ó Sé, T.Kennelly, T.Doyle, J.O'Shea, S.Walsh, G.Power, T.Spillane, D.''Ogie'' Moran, M.Sheehy, E.Liston, J.Egan (capt.). Sub: P.Spillane for D.Moran.

1983

Dublin J.O'Leary, M.Holden, G.Hargan, R.Hazley, P.Canavan, T.Drumm (capt.), P.J.Buckley, J.Ronayne, B.Mullins, B.Rock, T.Conroy, C.Duff, J.Caffrey, A.O'Toole, J.McNally. Subs: J.Kearns for T.Conroy; K.Maher for J.Caffrey.

Galway P.Coyne, J.Hughes, S.Kinneavy, M.Coleman, P.O'Neill, P.Lee, S.McHugh (capt.), B.Talty, R.Lee, B.Brennan, V.Daly, B.O'Donnell, T.Tierney, G.McManus, S.Joyce. Subs: M.Brennan for B.Talty; W.Joyce for P.Lee; J.Tobin for J.Hughes.

1984

Kerry C.Nelligan, P.Ó Sé, S.Walsh, M.Spillane, T.Doyle, T.Spillane, G.Lynch, J.O'Shea, A.O'Donovan (capt.), J.Kennedy, D.''Ogie'' Moran, P.Spillane, G.Power, E.Liston, J.Egan. Sub: T.O'Dowd for J.Egan.

Dublin J.O'Leary, M.Holden, G.Hargan, M.Kennedy, P.Canavan, T.Drumm (capt.), P.J.Buckley, J.Ronayne, B.Mullins, B.Rock, T.Conroy, K.Duff, J.Kearns, A.O'Toole J.McNally. Subs: M.O'Callaghan for J.McNally; C.Sutton for J.Ronayne.

Referee P.Collins (Westmeath).

1985

Kerry C.Nelligan, P.Ó Sé (capt.), S.Walsh, M.Spillane, T.Doyle, T.Spillane, G.Lynch, J.O'Shea, A.O'Donovan, T.O'Dowd, D.''Ogie'' Moran, P Spillane, M.Sheehy, E.Liston, G.Power. Sub: J.Kennedy for G.Power.

Dublin J.O'Leary, M.Kennedy, G.Hargan, R.Hazley, P.Canavan, N.McCaffrey, D.Synnott, J.Roynane, B.Mullins (capt.), B.Rock, T.Conroy, C.Redmond, J.Kearns, J.McNally, K.Duff. Subs: T.Carr for Redmond; P.J.Buckley for B.Mullins.

1986

Kerry C.Nelligan, P.Ó Sé, S.Walsh, M.Spillane, T.Doyle (capt.), T.Spillane, G.Lynch, J.O'Shea, A.O'Donovan, W.Maher, D.''Ogie'' Moran, P.Spillane, M.Sheehy, E.Liston, G.Power. Sub: T.O'Dowd for A.O'Donovan.

Tyrone A.Skelton, J.Mallon, C.McGarvey, J.Lynch, K.McCabe, N.McGinn, P.Ball, P.Donaghy, H.McClure, M.McClure, E.McKenna (capt.), S.McNally, M.Mallon, D.O'Hagan, P.Quinn. Subs: S.Conway for J.Lynch; S.Rice for E.McKenna; A.O'Hagan for M.Mallon.

1987
Meath   M.McQuillan, R.O'Malley, M.Lyons (capt.),
T.Ferguson, K.Foley, L.Harnan, M.O'Connell, L.Hayes, G.McEntee,
D.Beggy, J.Cassells, P.J.Gillic, C.O'Rourke, B.Stafford, B.Flynn.
Subs: C Coyle for J.Cassells; P.Lyons for M.O'Connell.
Cork   J.Kerins, A.Davis, C.Corrigan, D.Walsh, A.Nation,
C.Counihan (capt.), N.Cahalane, S.Fahy, T.McCarthy, J.O'Driscoll,
L.Tompkins, J.Kerrigan, C.O'Neill, C.Ryan, J.Cleary. Subs: J.Evans
for C.Corrigan; T.Leahy for S.Fahy; P.Hayes for C.Ryan.

1988 REPLAY
Meath   M.McQuillan, R.O'Malley, M.Lyons, T.Ferguson,
C.Coyle, L.Harnan, M.O'Connell, L.Hayes, G.McEntee, D.Beggy,
J.Cassells (capt.), P.J.Gillic, C.O'Rourke, B.Stafford, B.Flynn. Sub:
M.McCabe for Gillic.
Páraic Lyons, Kevin Foley and Mattie McCabe played in drawn
game when Colm Coyle (for M.McCabe), Terry Ferguson (for
K.Foley) and Joe Cassells (for B.Flynn) came on as subs and were
on the team for the replay. Mick Lyons was captain in the drawn
game.
Cork   J.Kerins, N.Cahalane, C.Corrigan, S.O'Brien, A.Davis,
C.Counihan, A.Nation (capt.), S.Fahy, T.McCarthy P.McGrath,
L.Tompkins, B.Coffey, D.Allen.D.Barry, M McCarthy. Subs: C
O'Neill for McCarthy; J.O'Driscoll for McGrath.
Note: Stephen O'Brien, who came on as a sub for Denis Walsh in
the first half of the drawn game retained his place for the replay.

1989
Cork   J.Kerins, N.Cahalane, S.O'Brien, J.Kerrigan, M.Slocum,
C.Counihan, A.Davis, T.McCarthy, S.Fahy, D.Barry, L.Tompkins,
B.Coffey, P.McGrath, D.Allen (capt.), J.Cleary. Subs: J.O'Driscoll for
Coffey; M.McCarthy for S.Fahy; Danny Culloty for J.Cleary.
Mayo   G.Irwin, J.Browne (capt.).P.Forde, D.Flanagan,
M.Collins, T.J.Kilgallon, J.Finn, S.Maher, L.McHale, G.Maher,
W.J.Padden, N.Durkin, M.Fitzmaurice, J.Burke, K.McStay. Subs:
A.Finnerty for J.Burke; R.Dempsey for S.Maher; B.Kilkelly for
G.Maher.

1990
Cork   J.Kerins, A.Nation, S.O'Brien, N.Cahalane, M.Slocum,
C.Counihan, B.Coffey, S.Fahy, D.Culloty, D.Barry, L.Tompkins
(capt.), T.McCarthy, P.McGrath, C.O'Neill, M.McCarthy. Subs:
J.O'Driscoll for M.McCarthy; P.Hayes for D.Barry; J.Cleary for
P.McGrath.
Meath   D.Smyth, R.O'Malley, M.Lyons, T.Ferguson, B.Reilly,
K.Foley, M.O'Connell, L.Hayes, G.McEntee, D.Beggy, P.J.Gillic,
C.Brady, C.O'Rourke (capt.), B.Stafford, B.Flynn. Subs: C.Coyle for
C.Brady; J.Cassells for G.McEntee; T.Dowd for D.Beggy

1991
Down   N.Collins, B.McKernan, C.Deegan, P.Higgins,
P.O'Rourke (capt.), J.Kelly, D.J.Kane, B.Breen, E.Burns, R.Carr,
G.Blaney, G.Mason, M.Linden, P.Withnell, J.McCartan. Subs:
L.Austin for B.Breen, A.Rodgers for P.Withnell.
Meath   M.McQuillan, B.Reilly, M.Lyons, T.Ferguson, K.Foley,
L.Harnan, M.O'Connell, L.Hayes (capt.), G.McEntee, D.Beggy,
T.Dowd, C.Coyle, P.J.Gillic, B.Stafford, B.Flynn. Subs: C.O'Rourke
for C.Coyle; A.Browne for M.Lyons; M.McCabe for P.J.Gillic.

1992
Donegal   G.Walsh, B.McGowan, M.Gallagher, N.Hegarty,
D.Reid, M.Gavigan, J.J.Doherty, A.Molloy (capt.), B.Murray,
J.McHugh, M.McHugh, J.McMullan, D.Bonner, T.Boyle, M.Boyle.
Sub: B.Cunningham for B.Murray.

Dublin   J.O'Leary, M.Deegan, G.Hargan, T.Carr (capt.),
P.Curran, K.Barr, E.Heery, P.Clarke, D.Foran, C.Redmond, J.Sheedy,
N.Guiden, D.Farrell, V.Murphy, M.Galvin. Sub: P.Bealan for
D.Foran.

1993
Derry   D.McCusker, K.McKeever, A.Scullion, F.McCusker,
J.McGurk, H.Downey (capt.), G.Coleman, A.Tohill, B.McGilligan,
D.Heaney, D.Barton, D.Cassidy, J.Brolly, S.Downey, E.Gormley.
Subs: D.McNicholl for D.Cassidy; E.Burns for S.Downey.
Cork   J.Kerins, N.Cahalane, M.O'Connor, B.Corcoran,
C.O'Sullivan, S.O'Brien, A.Davis, S.Fahy, T.McCarthy, D.Davis,
J.Kavanagh, B.Coffey, C.Corkery, J.O'Driscoll, M.McCarthy
(capt.), Subs: D.Culloty for T.McCarthy; J.Cleary for M.McCarthy;
C.Counihan for C.Corkery.

1994
Down   N.Collins, M.Magill, B.Burns, P.Higgins, E.Burns,
B.Breen, D.J.Kane (capt.), G.McCartan, C.Deegan, R.Carr,
G.Blaney, J.McCortan, M.Linden, A.Farrell, G.Mason. Sub:
G.Colgan for C.Deegan.
Dublin   J.O'Leary (capt.), P.Moran, D.Deasy, P.Curran,
P.Clarke, K.Barr, M.Deegan, B.Stynes, P.Gilroy, J.Sheedy, V.Murphy,
N.Guiden, D.Farrell, M.Galvin, C.Redmond. Subs: P.Bealin for
P.Gilroy, S.Cahill for M.Galvin, J.Barr for N.Guiden.

1995
Dublin   J.O'Leary (capt.), P.Moran, C.Walsh, K.Galvin,
P.Curran, K.Barr, M.Deegan, P.Bealin, B.Stynes, J.Gavin, D.Farrell,
P.Clarke, M.Galvin, J.Sherlock, C.Redmond. Subs: P.Gilroy for
K.Galvin, R.Boyle for M.Galvin, V.Murphy for D.Farrell.
Tyrone   F.McConnell, P.Devlin, C.Lawn, F.Devlin, R.McGarrity,
S.McCallan, S.McLoughlin, F.Logan, J.Gormley, C.Corr (capt),
Pascal Canavan, C.Loughran, C.McBride, Peter Canavan, S.Lawn.
Subs: M.McGlennon for C.Loughran, B.Gormley for S.Lawn,
P.Donnolly for S.McCallan.

1996 REPLAY
Meath   C.Martin, M.O'Reilly, D.Fay, M.O'Connell, C.Coyle,
E.McManus, P.Reynolds, J.McGuinness, J.McDermott, T.Giles,
T.Dowd (capt.), G.Geraghty, C.Brady, B.Reilly, B.Callaghan. Subs:
J.Devine for B.Callaghan, O.Murphy for M.O'Reilly.
Evan Kelly played in drawn game. C.Brady came on for
replay. Subs in drawn game C.Brady for E.Kelly, J.Devine for
J.McGuinness, D.Curtis for P.Reynolds.
Mayo   J.Madden, D.Flanagan, K.Cahill, K.Mortimer,
P.Holmes, J.Nallen, N.Connelly (capt.), L.McHale, D.Brady,
M.Sheridan, C.McManamon, J.Horan, R.Dempsey, J.Casey,
A.Finnerty. Subs: P.J.Loftus for R.Dempsey, P.Fallon for
D.Flanagan, T.Reilly for A.Finnerty.
D.Nestor played in drawn game. A.Finnerty came on for replay.
Subs in drawn game P.J.Loftus for D.Nestor, A.Finnerty for J.Casey,
K.O'Neill for J.Horan.

1997
Kerry   D.O'Keeffe, K.Burns, B.O'Shea, S.Stack, S.Moynihan,
L.O'Flaherty, E.Breen, Darragh Ó Sé, W.Kirby, P.Laide, L.Hassett
(capt.), D.O'Dwyer, B.O'Shea, D.Ó Cinnéide, M.Fitzgerald. Subs:
J.Crowley for B.O'Shea, D.Daly for W.Kirby, M.F.Russell for D.Ó
Cinnéide.
Mayo   P.Burke, P.Holmes, K.Mortimer, D.Flanagan,
F.Costelloe, J.Nallen, N.Connelly (capt.), P.Fallon, D.Heaney,
M.Sheridan, C.McManamon, J.Casey, K.McDonald, L.McHale,
D.Nestor. Subs: J.Horan for D.Flanagan, D.Byrne for M.Sheridan,
P.J.Loftus for D.Nestor.

1998

Galway M.McNamara, T.Meehan, G.Fahy, T.Mannion, R.Silke (capt.), J.Divilly, S.Óg de Paor, K.Walsh, S.Ó Domhnaill, M.Donnellan, S.Walsh, J.Fallon, S.Walsh, D.Savage, P.Joyce, N.Finnegan. Sub: P.Clancy for S.Walsh.

Kildare C.Byrne, B.Lacey, J.Finn, K.Doyle, S.Dowling, G.Ryan (capt.), A.Rainbow, N.Buckley, W.McCreery, E.McCormack, D.Kerrigan, D.Earley, M.Lynch, K.O'Dwyer, P.Gravin. Subs: P.Brennon for P.Gravin, B.Murphy for M.Lynch.

1999

Meath C.O'Sullivan, M.O'Reilly, D.Fay, C.Murphy, P.Reynolds, E.McManus, H.Traynor, N.Crawford, J.McDermott, N.Nestor, T.Giles, D.Curtis, E.Kelly, G.Geraghty (capt.), O.Murphy. Subs: R.Kealy for N.Nestor, B.Callaghan for H.Traynor, T.Dowd for E.Kelly.

Cork K.O'Dwyer, R.McCarthy, S.Óg Ó hAilpín, A.Lynch, C.O'Sullivan, O.Sexton, M.Cronin, N.Murphy, M.O'Sullivan, M.Cronin, J.Kavanagh, P.O'Mahony, P.Clifford (capt.), D.Davis, M.O'Sullivan. Subs: F.Murray for M.O'Sullivan, F.Collins for M.Cronin and M.Donovan for P.O'Mahony.

2000 REPLAY

Kerry D.O'Keeffe, M.Hassett, S.Moynihan, M.McCarthy, T.Ó Sé, E.Fitzmaurice, T.O'Sullivan, D.Ó Sé, D.Daly, A.MacGearailt, L.Hassett, N.Kennelly, M.F.Russell, D.Ó Cinnéide, J.Crowley, Subs: M.Fitzgerald for Kennelly, T.Griffin for O'Sullivan.
Kerry started with the same 15 as in the drawn encounter. Subs used in the drawn final were M.Fitzgerald for Crowley, D.Dwyer for Kennelly.

Galway M.McNamara, T.Meehan, G.Fahy, R.Fahy, D.Meehan, J.Divilly, S.Óg dePaor, K.Walsh, S.Ó Domhnaill, P.Clancy, M.Donnellan, T.Joyce, D.Savage, P.Joyce, N.Finnegan. Subs: J.Bergin for K.Walsh, K.Walsh for Ó Domhnaill, J.Donnellan for T.Joyce, S.Walsh for Clancy.
R.Silke and J.Bergin started the drawn final but not the replay. Subs used in the drawn final were – K.Walsh for Bergin, R.Fahy for Silke, J.Donnellan for T.Joyce.

2001

Galway A.Keane, K.Fitzgerald, G.Fahy, R.Fahy, D.Meehan, T.Mannion, S.Óg dePaor, K.Walsh, M.Donnellan, J.Bergin, P.Clancy, J.Fallon, P.Joyce, D.Savage, T.Joyce. Subs: A.Kerins for Bergin, K.Comer for dePaor.

Meath C.Sullivan, M.O'Reilly, D.Fay, C.Murphy, D.Curtis, M.Nestor, H.Traynor, N.Crawford, J.McDermott, E.Kelly, T.Giles, R.Kealy, O.Murphy, G.Geraghty, R.Magee. Subs: P.Reynolds for Murphy, J.Cullinane for Kealy, N.Kelly for Murphy, A.Kenny for Magee.

2002

Armagh B.Tierney, E.McNulty, J.McNulty, F.Bellew, A.O'Rourke, K.McGeeney, A.McCann, J.Toal, P.McGrane, P.McKeever, J.McEntee, O.McConville, S.McDonnell, R.Clarke, D.Marsden. Subs: B.O'Hagan for J.McEntee, T.McEntee for McKeever.

Kerry D.O'Keeffe, M.Ó Sé, S.Moynihan, M.McCarthy, T.Ó Sé, E.Fitzmaurice, J.Sheehan, D.Ó Sé, D.Daly, S.O'Sullivan, E.Brosnan, L.Hassett, M.F.Russell, D.Ó Cinnéide, C.Cooper. Subs: A.MacGearailt for O'Sullivan, T.O'Sullivan for M.Ó Sé, J.Crowley for Hassett, B.O'Shea for Daly.

2003

Tyrone J.Devine, C.Gourley, C.McAnallen, R.McMenamin, C.Gormley, G.Devlin, P.Jordan, K.Hughes, S.Cavanagh, B.Dooher, B.McGuigan, G.Cavlan, E.McGinley, P.Canavan, O.Mulligan. Subs: S.O'Neill for McGuigan, McGuigan for Canavan, C.Holmes for Gourley, Canavan for Cavlan, C.Lawn for Gormley.

Armagh P.Hearty, F.Bellew, E.McNulty, A.Mallon, A.O'Rourke, K.McGeeney, A.McCann, P.Loughran, P.McGrane, R.Clarke, J.McEntee, O.McConville, S.McDonnell, D.Marsden, T.McEntee. Subs: P.McKeever for Marsden, K.Hughes for Mallon, Marsden for Clarke, B.O'Hagan for J.McEntee.

2004

Kerry D.Murphy, A.O'Mahony, M.McCarthy, T.O'Sullivan, M.Ó Sé, E.Fitzmaurice, T.Ó Sé, W.Kirby, E.Brosnan, L.Hassett, D.O'Sullivan, P.Galvin, C.Cooper, D.Ó Cinnéide, J.Crowley. Subs: S.Moynihan for Hassett, M.F.Russell for Crowley, R.O'Connor for Ó Cinnéide, P.Kelly for Galvin, B.Guiney for T.Ó Sé.

Mayo P.Burke, D.Geraghty, D.Heaney, G.Ruane, P.Gardiner, J.Nallen, P.Kelly, M.McGarrity, F.Kelly, T.Mortimer, C.McDonald, B.Maloney, C.Mortimer, J.Gill, A.Dillon. Subs: D.Brady for F.Kelly, C.Moran for Geraghty, M.Conroy for Gill, A.Moran for C.Mortimer, P.Navin for Heaney.

2005

Tyrone P.McConnell, R.McMenamin, J.McMahon, M.McGee, D.Harte, C.Gormley, P.Jordan, E.McGinley, S.Cavanagh, B.Dooher, B.McGuigan, R.Mellon, P.Canavan, S.O'Neill, O.Mulligan. Subs: C.Homles for Canavan, C.Lawn for McMahon, Canavan for McGinley.

Kerry D.Murphy, M.McCarthy, A.O'Mahony, T.O'Sullivan, T.Ó Sé, S.Moynihan, D.Ó Sé, W.Kirby, L.Hassett, E.Brosnan, P.Galvin, C.Cooper, Declan O'Sullivan, D.Ó Cinnéide. Subs: M.F.Russell for Hassett, Darran O'Sullivan for Ó Cinnéide, E.Fitzmaurice for Moynihan, B.Sheehan for Galvin.

2006

Kerry D.Murphy, M.McCarthy, T.O'Sullivan, A.O'Mahony, S.Moynihan, M.Ó Sé, T.Ó Sé, D.O'Se, T.Griffin, S.O'Sullivan, Declan O'Sullivan, P.Galvin, C.Cooper, K.Donaghy, M.F.Russell. Subs: E.Brosnan for T.O'Se, Darran O'Sullivan for S.O'Sullivan, B.Sheehan for Russell, E.Fitzmaurice for Griffin, B.Guiney for O'Mahony.

Mayo D.Clarke, D.Geraghty, D.Heaney, K.Higgins, A.Higgins, J.Nallen, P.Gardiner, R.McGarrity, P.Harte, B.J.Padden, G.Brady, A.Dillon, K.O'Neill, C.Mortimer, C.McDonald. Subs: D.Brady for Nallen, T.Mortimer for Dillon, B.Moran for O'Neill, A.Kilcoyne for Padden, A.Moran for Gardiner.

2007

Kerry D.Murphy, M.Ó Sé, T.O'Sullivan, P.Reidy, A.O'Mahony, T.Ó Sé, K.Young, D.Ó Sé, S.Scanlon, P.Galvin, Declan O'Sullivan, E.Brosnan, C.Cooper, K.Donaghy, B.Sheehan. Subs: S.O'Sullivan for Galvin, Darran O'Sullivan for Brosnan, T.Griffin for Young, M.F.Russell for Sheehan, M.Lyons for Reidy.

Cork A.Quirke, M.Shields, G.Canty, K.O'Connor, N.O'Leary, G.Spillane, J.Miskella, D.Kavanagh, N.Murphy, C.McCarthy, P.O'Neill, K.McMahon, J.Masters, M.Cussen, D.O'Connor. Subs: D.Goulding for Masters, A.Lynch for Miskella, F.Gould for McMahon, K.O'Sullivan for McCarthy.

2008

Tyrone P.McConnell, Joseph McMahon, Justin McMahon, C.Gormley, D.Harte, P.Jordan, R.McMenamin, C.Holmes, E.McGinley, B.Dooher, M.Penrose, R.Mellon, T.McGuigan, S.Cavanagh, C.McCullagh. Subs: S.O'Neill for McCullagh, K.Hughes for Holmes, B.McGuigan for Penrose, O.Mulligan for Mellon, C.Cavanagh for T.McGuigan.

Kerry D.Murphy, M.Ó Sé, T.O'Sullivan, P.Reidy, T.Ó Sé, A.O'Mahony, K.Young, D.Ó Sé, S.Scanlon, B.Sheehan, Declan O'Sullivan, E.Brosnan, C.Cooper, K.Donaghy, T.Walsh. Subs: Darran O'Sullivan for Brosnan, T.Griffin for Scanlon, P.Galvin for Walsh, D.Moran for Sheehan.

2009
Kerry D.Murphy, M.Ó Sé, T.Griffin, T.O'Sullivan, T.Ó Sé, M.McCarthy, K.Young, D.Ó Sé, S.Scanlon, Darran O'Sullivan, T.Kennelly, P.Galvin, C.Cooper, Declan O'Sullivan, T.Walsh. Subs: D.Walsh for Kennelly, M.Quirke for D.Ó Sé, K.Donaghy for Darran O'Sullivan, D.Moran for T.Walsh, A.O'Mahony for Young.
Cork A.Quirke, K.O'Connor, M.Shields, A.Lynch, N.O'Leary, G.Canty, J.Miskella, A.O'Connor, N.Murphy, P.Kelly, P.O'Neill, P.Kerrigan, D.Goulding, C.O'Neill, D.O'Connor. Subs: E.Cadogan for K.O'Connor, F.Goold for Kerrigan, D.Kavanagh for Lynch, J.Masters for Goulding, M.Cussen for A.O'Connor.

2010
Cork A.Quirke, E.Cadogan, M.Shields, R.Carey, N.O'Leary, G.Canty, P.Kissane, A.O'Connor, A.Walsh, C.Sheehan, P.O'Neill, P.Kelly, D.Goulding, D.O'Connor, P.Kerrigan. Subs: N.Murphy for A.O'Connor, G.Canty for Kissane, C.O'Neill for P.O'Neill, D.Kavanagh for O'Leary, J.Hayes for Kerrigan.
Down B.McVeigh, D.McCartan, D.Gordon, D.Rafferty, D.Rooney, K.McKernan, C.Garvey, K.King, P.Fitzpatrick, D.Hughes, M.Poland, B.Coulter, P.McComiskey, J.Clarke, M.Clarke. Subs: C.Maginn for J.Clarke, R.Murtagh for McComiskey, B.McArdle for Rafferty, C.Laverty for Poland.

2011
Dublin S.Cluxton, C.O'Sullivan, R.O'Carroll, M.Fitzsimons, J.McCarthy, G.Brennan, K.Nolan, D.Bastick, M.D.Macauley, P.Flynn, B.Cahill, B.Cullen, A.Brogan, D.Connolly, B.Brogan. Subs: P.McMahon for McCarthy, K.McManamon for Flynn, E.O'Gara for Cahill, E.Fennell for Bastick.
Kerry B.Kealy, M.Ó Sé, T.o'Sullivan, K.Young, T.Ó Sé, E.Brosnan, A.O'Mahony, A.Maher, B.Sheehan, D.Walsh, Darran O'Sullivan, K.Donaghy, C.Cooper, Declan O'Sullivan, K.O'Leary. Subs: P.Galvin for O'Leary, B.J.Keane for Walsh, D.Bohan for Brosnan.

2012
Donegal P.Durcan, P.McGrath, N.McGee, F.McGlynn, E.McGee, K.Lacey, A.Thompson, N.Gallagher, R.Kavanagh, R.Bradley, L.McLoone, M.McHugh, P.McBrearty, M.Murphy, C.McFadden. Subs: D.Walsh for Bradley, M.McElhinney for McBrearty, C.Toye for McLoone.
Mayo D.Clarke, K.Keane, G.Cafferkey, K.Higgins, L.Keegan, D.Vaughan, C.Boyle, B.Moran, A.O'Shea, K.McLoughlin, J.Doherty, A.Dillon, E.Varley, C.O'Connor, M.Conroy. Subs: A.Freeman for Doherty, J.Gibbons for Conroy, R.Feeney for Varley, S.O'Shea for Moran.

2013
Dublin S.Cluxton, P.McMahon, R.O'Carroll, J.Cooper, J.McCarthy, G.Brennan, J.McCaffrey, M.D.Macauley, C.O'Sullivan, P.Flynn, C.Kilkenny, D.Connolly, P.Mannion, P.Andrews, B.Brogan. Subs: E.O'Gara for Mannion, D.Daly for McCaffrey, D.Rock for Kilkenny, K.McManamon for Andrews, D.Bastick for Cooper.
Mayo R.Hennelly, T.Cunniffe, G.Cafferkey, C.Barrett, L.Keegan, D.Vaughan, C.Boyle, A.O'Shea, S.O'Shea, K.McLoughlin, K.Higgins, A.Dillon, C.O"Connor, A.Freeman, A.Moran. Subs: M.Conroy for Freeman, E.Varley for Dillon, B.Moran for S.O'Shea, J.Doherty for Moran.

2014
Kerry B.Kelly, M.Ó Sé, A.O'Mahony, F.Fitzgerald, P.Murphy, P.Crowley, K.Young, A.Maher, D.Moran, S.O'Brien, J.Buckley, D.Walsh, P.Geaney, K.Donaghy, J.O'Donoghue. Subs: M.Geaney for O'Brien, B.J.Keane for P.Geaney, S.Enright for Fitzgerald, D.O'Sllivan for Walsh, B.Sheehan for Moran, K.O'Leary for Donaghy.

Donegal P.Durcan, E.McGee, N.McGee, P.McGrath, A.Thompson, K.Lacey, F.McGlynn, N.Gallagher, O.Mac Niallais, R.Kavanagh, L.McLoone, R.McHugh, D.O'Connor, M.Murphy, C.McFadden. Subs: C.Toye for O'Connor, P.McBrearty for McHugh, M.McElhinney for Mac Niallais, D.Walsh for McLoone, D.Molloy for Kavanagh.

2015
Dublin S.Cluxton, P. McMahon, R.O'Carroll, J.Cooper, J.McCarthy, C.O'Sullivan, J.McCaffrey, B.Fenton, D.Bastick, P.Flynn, D.Connolly, C.Kilkenny, P.Andrews, D.Rock, B.Brogan. Subs: K.McManamon for Rock, M.D.Macauley for Bastick, M.Fitzsimons for Cooper, J.Small for McCaffrey, D.Daly for O'Sullivan, A.Brogan for Fenton.
Kerry B.Kealy, F.Fitzgerald, A.O'Mahony, S.Enright, J.Lyne, P.Crowley, K.Young, A.Maher, D.Moran, S.O'Brien, J.Buckley, D.Walsh, C.Cooper, P.Geaney, J.O'Donoghue. Subs: D.O'Sullivan for O'Brien, B.Sheehan for Buckley, K.Donaghy for Geaney, P.Galvin for Moran, P.Murphy for O'Mahony, B.J.Keane for O'Donoghue.

2016
Dublin S.Cluxton, P.McMahon, J.Cooper, D.Byrne, J.McCarthy, C.O'Sullivan, J.Small, B.Fenton, M.D.Macauley, P.Flynn, K.McManamon, C.Kilkenny, D.Rock, D.Connolly, B.Brogan. Subs: P.Andrews for McCarthy, P.Mannion for McManamon, M.Fitzsimons for Macauley, E.O'Gara for Brogan, D.Daly for Byrne, D.Bastick for Flynn.
Mayo D.Clarke, B.Harrison, D.Vaughan, K.Higgins, L.Keegan, C.Boyle, P.Durcan, S.O'Shea, T.Parsons, K.McLoughlin, A.O'Shea, D.O'Connor, J.Doherty, A.Moran, C.O'Connor. Subs: A.Dillon for S.O'Shea, C.Barrett for Boyle, B.Moran for Dillon, S.Coen for D.O'Connor, E.Regan for A.Moran, C.Loftus for Regan.

REPLAY
Dublin S.Cluxton, M.Fitzsimons, P.McMahon, J.Cooper, J.McCarthy, C.O'Sullivan, J.Small, B.Fenton, P.Flynn, C.Kilkenny, K.McManamon, D.Connolly, P.Mannion, D.Rock, P.Andrews. Subs: D.Byrne for Cooper, B.Brogan for Andrews, M.D.Macauley for Mannion, C.Costello for McManamon, E.Lowndes for Small, D.Daly for O'Sullivan.
Mayo R.Hennelly, P.Durcan, K.Higgins, B.Harrison, L.Keegan, C.Boyle, D.Vaughan, S.O'Shea, T.Parsons, D.O'Connor, K.McLoughlin, J.Doherty, A.Moran, A.O'Shea, C.O'Connor. Subs: S.Coen for Keegan, B.Moran for Parsons, C.O'Shea for Vaughan, D.Clarke for Hennelly, B.Moran for A.Moran, A.Dillon for Doherty, C.Barrett for Boyle.

2017
Dublin S.Cluxton, M.Fitzsimons, P.McMahon, J.Cooper, J.Small, C.O'Sullivan, J.McCaffrey, B.Fenton, J.McCarthy, D.Rock, C.O'Callaghan, C.Kilkenny, P.Mannion, E.O'Gara, P.Andrews. Subs: P.Flynn for McCaffrey, D.Connolly for Andrews, K.McManamon for O'Gara, B.Brogan for Flynn, N.Scully for O'Callaghan, C.Costello for Mannion.
Mayo D.Clarke, C.Barrett, B.Harrison, P.Durcan, L.Keegan, C.Boyle, K.Higgins, S.O'Shea, T.Parsons, K.McLoughlin, A.O'Shea, D.Vaughan, J.Doherty, C.O'Connor, A.Moran. Subs: D.O'Connor for S.O'Shea, S.Coen for Durcan, C.Loftus for Moran, D.Drake for Doherty, D.Kirby for McLoughlin, G.Cafferkey for Higgins.

CAPTAINS OF WINNING ALL-IRELAND SENIOR FOOTBALL TEAMS

1887	D.Corbett (Limerick)
1888	No Final.
1889	G.Kavanagh (Tipperary)
1890	J.Power (Cork)
1891	J.Kennedy (Dublin)
1892	J.Kennedy (Dublin)
1893	T.Hayes (Wexford)
1894	J.Kennedy (Dublin)
1895	P.Finn (Tipperary)
1896	C.Fitzgerald (Limerick)
1897	P.J.Walsh (Dublin)
1898	M.Rea (Dublin)
1899	M.Rea (Dublin)
1900	J.Tobin (Tipperary)
1901	J.Darcy (Dublin)
1902	J.Dempsey (Dublin)
1903	T.O'Connor (Kerry)
1904	A.Stack (Kerry)
1905	J.Murray (Kildare)
1906	J.Grace (Dublin)
1907	J.Grace (Dublin)
1908	D.Kelleher (Dublin)
1909	T.Costello (Kerry)
1910	No Final. Louth awarded walk-over from Kerry.
1911	M.Mehigan (Cork)
1912	J.Smith (Louth)
1913	R.Fitzgerald (Kerry)
1914	R.Fitzgerald (Kerry)
1915	S.Kennedy (Wexford)
1916	S.Kennedy (Wexford)
1917	S.Kennedy (Wexford)
1918	J.Byrne (Wexford)
1919	L.Stanley (Kildare)
1920	J.Shelly (Tipperary)
1921	E.Carroll (Dublin)
1922	P.Carey (Dublin)
1923	P.McDonnell (Dublin)
1924	P.Sullivan (Kerry)
1925	No Final
1926	J.J.Sheehy (Kerry)
1927	M.Buckley (Kildare)
1928	W."Squires" Gannon (Kildare)
1929	J.Barrett (Kerry)
1930	J.J.Sheehy (Kerry)
1931	C.Brosnan (Kerry)
1932	J.Barrett (Kerry)
1933	J.Smith (Cavan)
1934	M.Higgins (Galway)
1935	H.O'Reilly (Cavan)
1936	S.O'Malley (Mayo)
1937	M.Doyle (Kerry)
1938	J.Dunne (Galway)
1939	T.O'Connor (Kerry)
1940	D.Spring (Kerry)
1941	W.Dillon (Kerry)
1942	J.Fitzgerald (Dublin)
1943	J.Murray (Roscommon)
1944	J.Murray (Roscommon)
1945	T.Crowley (Cork)
1946	P.Kennedy (Kerry)
1947	J.J.O'Reilly (Cavan)
1948	J.J.O'Reilly (Cavan)
1949	B.Smyth (Meath)
1950	S.Flanagan (Mayo)
1951	S.Flanagan (Mayo)
1952	M.Higgins (Cavan)
1953	J.Murphy (Kerry)
1954	P.McDermott (Meath)
1955	J.Dowling (Kerry)
1956	J.Mangan (Galway)
1957	D.O'Brien (Louth)
1958	K.Heffernan (Dublin)
1959	M.O'Connell (Kerry)
1960	K.Mussen (Down)
1961	P.Doherty (Down)
1962	S.Óg Sheehy (Kerry)
1963	D.Foley (Dublin)
1964	J.Donnellan (Galway)
1965	E.Colleran (Galway)
1966	E.Colleran (Galway)
1967	P.Darby (Meath)
1968	J.Lennon (Down)
1969	J.Culloty (Kerry)
1970	D.O'Sullivan (Kerry)
1971	W.Bryan (Offaly)
1972	A.McTague (Offaly)
1973	W.Morgan (Cork)
1974	S.Doherty (Dublin)
1975	M.O'Sullivan (Kerry)

1976	T.Hanahoe (Dublin)
1977	T.Hanahoe (Dublin)
1978	D."Ogie" Moran (Kerry)
1979	T.Kennelly (Kerry)
1980	G.Power (Kerry)
1981	J.Deenihan (Kerry)
1982	R.Connor (Offaly)
1983	T.Drumm (Dublin)
1984	A.O'Donovan (Kerry)
1985	P.Ó Sé (Kerry)
1986	T.Doyle (Kerry)
1987	M.Lyons (Meath)
1988	J.Cassells (Meath)
1989	D.Allen (Cork)
1990	L.Tompkins (Cork)
1991	P.O'Rourke (Down)
1992	A.Molloy (Donegal)
1993	H.Downey (Derry)
1994	D.J.Kane (Down)
1995	J.O'Leary (Dublin)
1996	T.Dowd (Meath)
1997	L.Hassett (Kerry)
1998	R.Silke (Galway)
1999	G.Geraghty (Meath)
2000	S.Moynihan (Kerry)
2001	G.Fahy (Galway)
2002	K.McGeeney (Armagh)
2003	P.Canavan (Tyrone)
2004	D.Ó Cinnéide (Kerry)
2005	B.Dooher (Tyrone)
2006	Declan O'Sullivan (Kerry)
2007	P.Galvin (Kerry)
2008	B.Dooher (Tyrone)
2009	Darran O'Sullivan (Kerry)
2010	G.Canty (Cork)
2011	B.Cullen (Dublin)
2012	M.Murphy (Donegal)
2013	S.Cluxton (Dublin)
2014	F.Fitzgerald (Kerry)
2015	S.Cluxton (Dublin)
2016	S.Cluxton (Dublin)
2017	S.Cluxton (Dublin)

SENIOR FOOTBALL FINAL REFEREES

1887	J.Cullinane (Tipperary)
1888	No Final
1889	F.T.O'Driscoll (Cork)
1890	J.J.Kenny (Dublin)
1891	F.J.Whelan (Laois)
1892	D.Fraher (Waterford)
1893	T.Gilligan (Dublin)
1894	R.T.Blake (Meath)
1895	J.J.Kenny (Dublin)
1896	T.Dooley (Cork)
1897	D.S.Lyons (Limerick)
1898	J.McCarthy (Kilkenny)
1899	L.Stanley (Laois)
1900	T.H.Redmond (Dublin)
1901	J.McCarthy (Kilkenny)
1902	T.F.O'Sullivan (Kerry)
1903	J.McCarthy (Kilkenny)
1904	J.Fitzgerald (Cork)
1905	M.F.Crowe (Limerick)
1906	J.Fitzgerald (Kildare)
1907	J.Fitzgerald (Kildare)
1908	M.Conroy (Dublin)
1909	M.F.Crowe (Limerick)
1910	No Final
1911	M.O'Brennan (Roscommon)
1912	T.Irwin (Cork)
1913	M.F.Crowe (Limerick)
1914	H.Boland (Dublin) Draw and replay
1915	P.Dunphy (Laois)
1916	P.Dunphy (Laois)
1917	P.Dunphy (Laois)
1918	P.Dunphy (Laois)
1919	P.Dunphy (Laois)
1920	W.Walsh (Waterford)
1921	W.Walsh (Waterford)
1922	P.Dunphy (Laois)
1923	J.Byrne (Wexford)
1924	T.Shevlin (Roscommon)
1925	No Final
1926	T.Shevlin (Roscommon) Draw and replay
1927	T.Shevlin (Roscommon)
1928	T.Burke (Louth)
1929	P.O'Farrell (Roscommon)
1930	J.Byrne (Wexford)

FOOTBALL

1931	T.Keating (Tipperary)
1932	M.O'Neill (Wexford)
1933	M.O'Neill (Wexford)
1934	J.McCarthy (Kerry)
1935	S.Jordan (Galway)
1936	J.McCarthy (Kerry)
1937	M.Hennessy (Clare) Draw and replay
1938	T.Culhane (Limerick)
Replay	P.Waters (Kildare)
1939	J.Flaherty (Offaly)
1940	S.Burke (Kildare)
1941	P.McKenna (Limerick)
1942	S.Kennedy (Donegal)
1943	P.McKenna (Limerick)
Replay	P.Mythen (Wexford)
1944	P.Mythen (Wexford)
1945	J.Dunne (Galway)
1946	W.Delaney (Laois)
Replay	P.Mythen (Wexford)
1947	M.O'Neill (Wexford)
1948	J.Flaherty (Offaly)
1949	D.Ryan (Kerry)
1950	S.Deignan (Cavan)
1951	W.Delaney (Laois)
1952	S.Hayes (Tipperary) Draw and replay
1953	P.McDermott (Meath)
1954	S.Deignan (Cavan)
1955	W.Goodison (Wexford)
1956	P.McDermott (Meath)
1957	P.Geraghty (Galway)
1958	S.Deignan (Cavan)
1959	J.Dowling (Offaly)
1960	J.Dowling (Offaly)
1961	L.Maguire (Cavan)
1962	E.Moules (Wicklow)
1963	E.Moules (Wicklow)
1964	J.Hatton (Wicklow)
1965	M.Loftus (Mayo)
1966	J.Hatton (Wicklow)
1967	J.Moloney (Tipperary)
1968	M.Loftus (Mayo)
1969	J.Moloney (Tipperary)
1970	P.Kelly (Dublin)
1971	P.Kelly (Dublin)
1972	P.Devlin (Tyrone)
Replay	F.Tierney (Cavan)
1973	J.Moloney (Tipperary)
1974	P.Devlin (Tyrone)
1975	J.Moloney (Tipperary)
1976	P.Collins (Westmeath)
1977	J.Moloney (Tipperary)
1978	S.Aldridge (Kildare)
1979	H.Duggan (Armagh)
1980	S.Murray (Monaghan)
1981	P.Collins (Westmeath)
1982	P.J.McGrath (Mayo)
1983	J.Gough (Antrim)
1984	P.Collins (Westmeath)
1985	P.Kavanagh (Meath)
1986	J.Dennigan (Cork)
1987	P.Lane (Limerick)
1988	T.Sugrue (Kerry) Draw and replay
1989	P.Collins (Westmeath)
1990	P .Russell (Tipperary)
1991	S.Prior (Leitrim)
1992	T.Sugrue (Kerry)
1993	T.Howard (Kildare)
1994	T.Sugrue (Kerry)
1995	P .Russell (Tipperary)
1996	P.McEneaney (Monaghan) Draw and replay
1997	B.White (Wexford)
1998	J.Bannon (Longford)
1999	M.Curley (Galway)
2000	P.McEneaney (Monaghan)
Replay	B.White (Wexford)
2001	M.Collins (Cork)
2002	J.Bannon (Longford)
2003	B.White (Wexford)
2004	P.McEneaney (Monaghan)
2005	M.Monahan (Kildare)
2006	B.Crowe (Cavan)
2007	D.Coldrick (Meath)
2008	M.Deegan (Laois)
2009	M.Duffy (Sligo)
2010	D.Coldrick (Meath)
2011	J.McQuillan (Cavan)
2012	M.Deegan (Laois)
2013	J.McQuillan (Cavan)
2014	E.Kinsella (Laois)
2015	D.Coldrick (Meath)
2016	C.Lane (Cork)
Replay	M.Deegan (Laois)
2017	J.McQuillan (Cavan)

MUNSTER SENIOR FOOTBALL FINALS

1888	Tipperary w.o. Limerick (scratched)			
1889	Tipperary	1-2	0-3	Cork
1890	Cork	1-4	0-1	Kerry (refixture)
	Cork	0-1	0-0	Kerry
	(abandoned after 57 minutes when football burst)			
1891	Cork	3-2	1-1	Waterford
1892	Kerry	0-12	0-0	Waterford
1893	Cork w.o. Kerry scr.			
1894	Cork	0-6	0-2	Tipperary
	(objection)			
	Cork	2-4	0-1	Tipperary
	(refixture)			
1895	Tipperary	0-5	0-2	Limerick
1896	Limerick	0-4	0-1	Waterford
	(Unfinished. Title awarded to Limerick)			
1897	Cork	0-5	0-3	Limerick
1898	Waterford	1-11	1-3	Cork
1899	Tipperary	2-1	0-1	Cork
	(first game abandoned at half-time, no ball available)			
	Cork	1-2	0-1	Tipperary
	(refixture abandoned half time, dispute over score)			
	Cork	3-11	0-1	Tipperary
	(third match)			
1900	Tipperary	1-13	1-4	Kerry
1901	Cork	1-9	1-6	Limerick
1902	Tipperary	1-4	1-4	Kerry
Replay	Tipperary	1-6	1-5	Kerry
1903	Kerry	1-7	0-3	Cork
1904	Kerry	0-3	0-3	Waterford
Replay	Kerry	2-3	0-2	Waterford
1905	Kerry	2-10	1-6	Limerick
1906	Cork	1-10	0-3	Kerry
1907	Cork	1-7	0-1	Tipperary
1908	Kerry	0-7	0-2	Waterford
1909	Cork	2-8	1-7	Kerry
	(objection)			
	Kerry	1-5	0-6	Cork
1910	Kerry	0-4	0-2	Cork
1911	Cork	2-5	0-1	Waterford
1912	Kerry	0-3	0-1	Clare
1913	Kerry	1-6	0-1	Cork
1914	Kerry	0-5	0-1	Cork
1915	Kerry	4-3	0-1	Clare
1916	Cork	2-2	1-4	Clare
1917	Clare	5-4	0-1	Cork
1918	Tipperary	1-1	0-1	Kerry
1919	Kerry	6-11	2-0	Clare
1920	Tipperary	2-2	0-2	Kerry

1921	No Championship. Tipperary nominated to represent Munster but gave a walk-over to Mayo in All-Ireland semi-final.)			
1922	Tipperary	1-7	0-1	Limerick
1923	Kerry	0-5	0-3	Tipperary
1924	Kerry	5-8	2-2	Clare
1925	Kerry	5-5	0-0	Clare
1926	Kerry	0-11	1-4	Tipperary
1927	Kerry	4-4	1-3	Clare
1928	Cork	4-3	0-4	Tipperary
1929	Kerry	1-14	1-2	Clare
1930	Kerry	3-4	1-2	Tipperary
1931	Kerry	5-8	0-2	Tipperary
1932	Kerry	3-10	1-4	Tipperary
1933	Kerry	2-8	1-4	Tipperary
1934	Kerry	1-14	1-2	Limerick
1935	Tipperary	2-8	1-2	Cork
1936	Kerry	1-11	2-2	Clare
1937	Kerry	4-9	1-1	Clare
1938	Kerry	4-14	0-6	Cork
1939	Kerry	2-11	0-4	Tipperary
1940	Kerry	1-10	0-6	Waterford
1941	Kerry	2-9	0-6	Clare
1942	Kerry	3-7	0-8	Cork
1943	Cork	1-7	1-4	Tipperary
1944	Kerry	1-6	0-5	Tipperary
1945	Cork	1-11	1-6	Kerry
1946	Kerry	2-15	2-1	Waterford
1947	Kerry	3-8	2-6	Cork
1948	Kerry	2-9	2-6	Cork
1949	Cork	3-6	0-7	Clare
1950	Kerry	2-5	1-5	Cork
1951	Kerry	1-6	0-4	Cork
1952	Cork	0-11	0-2	Kerry
1953	Kerry	2-7	2-3	Cork
1954	Kerry	4-9	2-3	Cork
1955	Kerry	0-14	2-6	Cork
1956	Cork	0-8	2-2	Kerry
Replay	Cork	1-8	1-7	Kerry
1957	Cork	0-16	1-2	Waterford
1958	Kerry	2-7	0-3	Cork
1959	Kerry	2-15	2-8	Cork
1960	Kerry	3-15	0-8	Waterford
1961	Kerry	0-10	1-7	Cork
Replay	Kerry	2-13	1-4	Cork
1962	Kerry	4-8	0-4	Cork

1963	Kerry	1-18	3-7	Cork
1964	Kerry	2-11	1-8	Cork
1965	Kerry	2-16	2-7	Limerick
1966	Cork	2-7	1-7	Kerry
1967	Cork	0-8	0-7	Kerry
1968	Kerry	1-21	3-8	Cork
1969	Kerry	0-16	1-4	Cork
1970	Kerry	2-22	2-9	Cork
1971	Cork	0-25	0-14	Kerry
1972	Kerry	2-21	2-15	Cork
1973	Cork	5-12	1-15	Kerry
1974	Cork	1-11	0-7	Kerry
1975	Kerry	1-14	0-7	Cork
1976	Kerry	0-10	0-10	Cork
Replay	Kerry	3-20	2-19	Cork (aet)
1977	Kerry	3-15	0-9	Cork
1978	Kerry	3-14	3-7	Cork
1979	Kerry	2-14	2-4	Cork
1980	Kerry	3-13	0-12	Cork
1981	Kerry	1-11	0-3	Cork
1982	Kerry	0-9	0-9	Cork
Replay	Kerry	2-18	0-12	Cork
1983	Cork	3-10	3-9	Kerry
1984	Kerry	3-14	2-10	Cork
1985	Kerry	2-11	0-11	Cork
1986	Kerry	0-12	0-8	Cork
1987	Cork	1-10	2-7	Kerry
Replay	Cork	0-13	1-5	Kerry
1988	Cork	1-14	0-16	Kerry
1989	Cork	1-12	1-9	Kerry
1990	Cork	2-23	1-11	Kerry
1991	Kerry	0-23	3-12	Limerick
1992	Clare	2-10	0-12	Kerry
1993	Cork	1-16	1-8	Tipperary
1994	Cork	2-19	3-9	Tipperary
1995	Cork	0-15	1-9	Kerry
1996	Kerry	0-14	0-11	Cork
1997	Kerry	1-13	0-11	Clare
1998	Kerry	0-17	1-10	Tipperary
1999	Cork	2-10	2-4	Kerry
2000	Kerry	3-15	0-8	Clare
2001	Kerry	0-19	1-13	Cork
2002	Cork	2-11	1-14	Tipperary
Replay	Cork	1-23	0-7	Tipperary
2003	Kerry	1-11	0-9	Limerick
2004	Kerry	1-10	1-10	Limerick

Replay	Kerry	3-10	2-9	Limerick
2005	Kerry	0-10	0-10	Cork
Replay	Kerry	1-11	0-11	Cork
2006	Cork	1-12	0-9	Kerry
2007	Kerry	1-15	1-13	Cork
2008	Cork	1-16	1-11	Kerry
2009	Cork	2-6	0-11	Limerick
2010	Kerry	1-17	1-14	Limerick
2011	Kerry	1-15	1-12	Cork
2012	Cork	3-16	0-13	Clare
2013	Kerry	1-16	0-17	Cork
2014	Kerry	0-24	0-12	Cork
2015	Kerry	2-15	3-12	Cork
Replay	Kerry	1-11	1-6	Cork
2016	Kerry	3-17	2-10	Tipperary
2017	Kerry	1-23	0-15	Cork

LEINSTER SENIOR FOOTBALL FINALS

1887	No Final open draw			
1888	Kilkenny	1-4	0-2	Wexford
1889	Laois	0-3	0-2	Louth
1890	Wexford	1-3	1-2	Dublin
1891	Dublin w.o. Kildare scr.			
1892	Dublin w.o. Louth scr.			
1893	Kilkenny	0-5	0-1	Wexford
	(unfinished – Wexford awarded title)			
1894	Dublin	0-4	0-4	Meath
Replay	Dublin	0-2	0-2	Meath
Replay	Dublin	1-8	1-2	Meath
1895	Meath	0-6	0-2	Dublin
1896	Dublin	2-4	1-5	Meath
1897	Dublin	1-9	0-3	Wicklow
1898	Dublin	2-6	0-0	Wexford
1899	Dublin	1-7	0-3	Wexford
1900	Kilkenny	0-12	0-0	Louth
1901	Dublin	1-9	0-1	Wexford
1902	Dublin	2-4	0-2	Wexford
	(unfinished replay ordered)			
Replay	Dublin	1-5	0-5	Wexford
1903	Kildare	1-2	0-5	Kilkenny
Replay	Kildare	1-6	1-5	Kilkenny
	(point disputed, replay ordered)			
	Kildare	0-9	0-1	Kilkenny
1904	Dublin	0-5	0-1	Kilkenny
1905	Kildare	0-12	1-7	Louth
1906	Dublin	1-9	0-8	Kildare
1907	Dublin	1-11	0-4	Offaly
1908	Dublin	1-7	0-3	Kildare
1909	Louth	2-9	0-4	Kilkenny
1910	Louth	0-3	0-0	Dublin
1911	Kilkenny	2-4	1-1	Meath
1912	Louth	1-2	1-1	Dublin
1913	Wexford	2-3	2-2	Louth
1914	Wexford	3-6	0-1	Louth
1915	Wexford	2-2	2-2	Dublin
Replay	Wexford	3-5	1-3	Dublin
1916	Wexford	1-7	1-0	Kildare
1917	Wexford	1-3	1-1	Dublin
1918	Wexford	2-5	1-4	Louth
1919	Kildare	1-3	1-2	Dublin
1920	Dublin	1-3	0-3	Kildare
1921	Dublin	0-6	1-3	Kildare
Replay	Dublin	3-3	1-2	Kildare

1922	Dublin	1-7	0-2	Kilkenny
1923	Dublin	3-5	0-0	Meath
1924	Dublin	1-4	1-4	Wexford
Replay	Dublin	3-5	2-3	Wexford
1925	Wexford	2-7	0-3	Kildare
1926	Kildare	2-8	1-5	Wexford
1927	Kildare	0-5	0-3	Dublin
1928	Kildare	0-10	1-6	Dublin
1929	Kildare	2-3	0-6	Laois
1930	Kildare	0-6	1-3	Meath
Replay	Kildare	2-6	1-2	Meath
1931	Kildare	2-9	1-6	Westmeath
1932	Dublin	0-8	1-5	Wexford
Replay	Dublin	4-6	1-5	Wexford
1933	Dublin	0-9	1-4	Wexford
1934	Dublin	1-2	0-5	Louth
Replay	Dublin	3-2	2-5	Louth
Replay	Dublin	2-9	1-10	Louth
1935	Kildare	0-8	0-6	Louth
1936	Laois	3-3	0-8	Kildare
1937	Laois	0-12	0-4	Louth
1938	Laois	2-8	1-3	Kildare
1939	Meath	2-7	2-3	Wexford
1940	Meath	2-7	1-7	Laois
1941	Dublin	4-6	1-4	Carlow
1942	Dublin	0-8	0-6	Carlow
1943	Louth	3-16	2-4	Laois
1944	Carlow	2-6	1-6	Dublin
1945	Wexford	1-9	1-4	Offaly
1946	Laois	0-11	1-6	Kildare
1947	Meath	3-7	1-7	Laois
1948	Louth	2-10	2-5	Wexford
1949	Meath	4-5	0-6	Westmeath
1950	Louth	1-3	1-3	Meath
Replay	Louth	3-5	0-13	Meath
1951	Meath	4-9	0-3	Laois
1952	Meath	1-6	0-8	Louth
1953	Louth	1-7	0-7	Wexford
1954	Meath	4-7	2-10	Offaly
1955	Dublin	5-12	0-7	Meath
1956	Kildare	2-11	1-8	Wexford
1957	Louth	2-9	1-7	Dublin
1958	Dublin	1-11	1-6	Louth
1959	Dublin	1-18	2-8	Laois
1960	Offaly	0-10	1-6	Louth
1961	Offaly	1-13	1-8	Dublin

FOOTBALL

1962	Dublin	2-8	1-7	Offaly
1963	Dublin	2-11	2-9	Laois
1964	Meath	2-12	1-7	Dublin
1965	Dublin	3-6	0-9	Longford
1966	Meath	1-9	1-8	Kildare
1967	Meath	0-8	0-6	Offaly
1968	Longford	3-9	1-4	Laois
1969	Offaly	3-7	1-8	Kildare
1970	Meath	2-22	5-12	Offaly
1971	Offaly	2-14	0-6	Kildare
1972	Offaly	1-18	2-8	Kildare
1973	Offaly	3-21	2-12	Meath
1974	Dublin	1-14	1-9	Meath
1975	Dublin	3-13	0-8	Kildare
1976	Dublin	2-8	1-9	Meath
1977	Dublin	1-9	0-8	Meath
1978	Dublin	1-17	1-6	Kildare
1979	Dublin	1-8	0-9	Offaly
1980	Offaly	1-10	1-8	Dublin
1981	Offaly	1-18	3-9	Laois
1982	Offaly	1-16	1-7	Dublin
1983	Dublin	2-13	1-11	Offaly
1984	Dublin	2-10	1-9	Meath
1985	Dublin	0-10	0-4	Laois
1986	Meath	0-9	0-7	Dublin
1987	Meath	1-13	0-12	Dublin
1988	Meath	2-5	0-9	Dublin
1989	Dublin	2-12	1-10	Meath
1990	Meath	1-14	0-14	Dublin
1991	Meath	1-11	0-8	Laois
1992	Dublin	1-13	0-10	Kildare
1993	Dublin	0-11	0-7	Kildare
1994	Dublin	1-9	1-8	Meath
1995	Dublin	1-18	1-8	Meath
1996	Meath	0-10	0-8	Dublin
1997	Offoly	3-17	1-15	Meath
1998	Kildare	1-12	0-10	Meath
1999	Meath	1-14	0-12	Dublin
2000	Kildare	0-14	0-14	Dublin
Replay	Kildare	2-11	0-12	Dublin
2001	Meath	2-11	0-14	Dublin
2002	Dublin	2-13	2-11	Kildare
2003	Laois	2-13	1-13	Kildare
2004	Westmeath	0-13	0-13	Laois
Replay	Westmeath	0-12	0-10	Laois
2005	Dublin	0-14	0-13	Laois

2006	Dublin	1-15	0-9	Offaly
2007	Dublin	3-14	1-14	Laois
2008	Dublin	3-23	0-9	Wexford
2009	Dublin	2-15	0-18	Kildare
2010	Meath	1-12	1-10	Louth
2011	Dublin	2-12	1-12	Wexford
2012	Dublin	2-13	1-13	Meath
2013	Dublin	2-15	0-14	Meath
2014	Dublin	3-20	1-10	Meath
2015	Dublin	2-13	0-6	Westmeath
2016	Dublin	2-19	0-10	Westmeath
2017	Dublin	2-23	1-17	Kildare

CONNACHT SENIOR FOOTBALL FINALS

| 1892 | Roscommon represented Province in All-Ireland series. | | | |

1888-1891 and 1893-1899:
No Connacht representatives in All-Ireland series.

1900	Galway unopposed			
1901	Mayo	2-4	0-3	Galway
1902	Mayo	2-2	0-6	Galway
1903	Roscommon	1-1	0-3	Mayo
1904	Mayo	3-6	0-1	Roscommon
1905	Roscommon	0-7	0-5	Mayo
1906	Mayo	2-13	0-5	Roscommon
1907	Mayo	3-9	0-1	Galway
1908	Mayo	1-4	0-3	Galway
1909	Mayo	1-4	0-5	Galway
1910	Galway	1-3	1-2	Roscommon
1911	Galway nominated			
1912	Roscommon	0-2	0-0	Galway
1913	Galway	1-2	0-3	Mayo
1914	Roscommon	1-2	0-1	Leitrim
1915	Mayo	3-1	1-3	Roscommon
1916	Mayo	1-5	0-3	Roscommon
1917	Galway	1-4	1-1	Mayo
1918	Mayo	0-4	0-1	Galway
1919	Galway	1-6	0-5	Roscommon
1920	Mayo	2-3	1-4	Sligo
1921	Mayo	1-4	0-1	Roscommon
1922	Sligo	3-2	1-7	Galway
	(objection replay ordered)			
	Galway	2-4	2-2	Sligo (replay)
1923	Mayo	0-3	0-2	Galway
1924	Mayo	0-1	0-1	Galway
Replay	Mayo	2-6	0-5	Galway
1925	Galway	1-5	1-3	Mayo
1926	Galway	3-2	1-2	Mayo
1927	Leitrim	2-4	0-3	Galway
1928	Sligo	1-4	0-6	Mayo
1929	Mayo	1-6	0-4	Galway
1930	Mayo	1-7	1-2	Sligo
1931	Mayo	2-10	3-2	Roscommon
1932	Mayo	2-6	0-7	Sligo
1933	Galway	1-7	1-5	Mayo
1934	Galway	2-4	0-5	Mayo
1935	Mayo	0-12	0-5	Galway
1936	Mayo	2-4	1-7	Galway
Replay	Mayo	2-7	1-4	Galway
1937	Mayo	3-5	0-8	Galway

1938	Galway	0-8	0-5	Mayo
1939	Awarded to Mayo			
	(Mayo 2-6 Galway 0-3. Match unfinished.)			
1940	Galway	1-7	0-5	Mayo
1941	Galway	0-8	1-4	Roscommon
1942	Galway	2-6	3-2	Roscommon
1943	Roscommon	2-6	0-8	Galway
1944	Roscommon	2-11	1-6	Mayo
1945	Galway	2-6	1-7	Mayo
1946	Roscommon	1-4	0-6	Mayo
	(objection and counter-objection, replay ordered)			
Replay	Roscommon	1-9	1-2	Mayo
1947	Roscommon	2-12	1-8	Sligo
1948	Mayo	2-4	1-7	Galway
Replay	Mayo	2-10	2-7	Galway (aet)
1949	Mayo	4-6	0-3	Leitrim
1950	Mayo	1-7	0-4	Roscommon
1951	Mayo	4-13	2-3	Galway
1952	Roscommon	3-5	0-6	Mayo
1953	Roscommon	1-6	0-6	Mayo
1954	Galway	2-10	3-4	Sligo
1955	Mayo	3-11	1-3	Roscommon
1956	Galway	3-12	1-5	Sligo
1957	Galway	4-8	0-4	Leitrim
1958	Galway	2-10	1-11	Leitrim
1959	Galway	5-8	0-12	Leitrim
1960	Galway	2-5	0-5	Leitrim
1961	Roscommon	1-11	2-7	Galway
1962	Roscommon	3-7	2-9	Galway
1963	Galway	4-11	1-6	Leitrim
1964	Galway	2-12	1-5	Mayo
1965	Galway	1-12	2-6	Sligo
1966	Galway	0-12	1-8	Mayo
1967	Mayo	4-15	0-7	Leitrim
1968	Galway	2-10	2-9	Mayo
1969	Mayo	0-11	1-8	Galway
Replay	Mayo	1-11	1-8	Galway
1970	Galway	2-15	1-8	Roscommon
1971	Galway	2-15	2-15	Sligo
Replay	Galway	1-17	3-10	Sligo
1972	Roscommon	5-8	3-10	Mayo
1973	Galway	1-17	2-12	Mayo
1974	Galway	2-14	0-8	Roscommon
1975	Sligo	2-10	1-13	Mayo
Replay	Sligo	2-10	0-15	Mayo
1976	Galway	1-8	1-8	Roscommon

Replay	Galway	1-14	0-9	Roscommon
1977	Roscommon	1-12	2-8	Galway
1978	Roscommon	2-7	0-9	Galway
1979	Roscommon	3-15	2-10	Mayo
1980	Roscommon	3-13	0-8	Mayo
1981	Mayo	0-12	0-4	Sligo
1982	Galway	3-17	0-10	Mayo
1983	Galway	1-13	1-10	Mayo
1984	Galway	2-13	2-9	Mayo
1985	Mayo	2-11	0-8	Roscommon
1986	Galway	1-8	1-5	Roscommon
1987	Galway	0-8	0-7	Mayo
1988	Mayo	1-12	0-8	Roscommon
1989	Mayo	0-12	1-9	Roscommon
Replay	Mayo	3-14	2-13	Roscommon (aet)
1990	Roscommon	0-16	1-11	Galway
1991	Roscommon	0-14	0-14	Mayo
Replay	Roscommon	0-13	1-9	Mayo
1992	Mayo	1-14	0-10	Roscommon
1993	Mayo	1-5	0-7	Roscommon
1994	Leitrim	0-12	2-4	Mayo
1995	Galway	0-17	1-7	Mayo
1996	Mayo	3-9	1-11	Galway
1997	Mayo	0-11	1-7	Sligo
1998	Galway	0-11	0-11	Roscommon
Replay	Galway	1-17	0-17	Roscommon (aet)
1999	Mayo	1-14	1-10	Galway
2000	Galway	1-13	0-8	Leitrim
2001	Roscommon	2-10	1-12	Mayo
2002	Galway	1-11	0-11	Sligo
2003	Galway	1-14	0-13	Mayo
2004	Mayo	2-13	0-9	Roscommon
2005	Galway	0-10	0-8	Mayo
2006	Mayo	0-12	1-8	Galway
2007	Sligo	1-10	0-12	Galway
2008	Galway	2-12	1-14	Mayo
2009	Mayo	2-12	1-14	Galway
2010	Roscommon	0-14	0-13	Sligo
2011	Mayo	0-13	0-11	Roscommon
2012	Mayo	0-12	0-10	Sligo
2013	Mayo	5-11	0-10	London
2014	Mayo	3-14	0-16	Galway
2015	Mayo	6-25	2-11	Sligo
2016	Galway	0-13	1-10	Roscommon
Replay	Galway	3-16	0-14	Roscommon
2017	Roscommon	2-15	0-12	Galway

ULSTER SENIOR FOOTBALL FINALS

1887	No Ulster championship			
1888	Monaghan	0-2	0-2	Cavan
Replay	Monaghan	0-3	0-1	Cavan
1889	No Ulster championship			
1890	Armagh	2-8	1-2	Tyrone
1891	Cavan	1-11	0-0	Armagh
	(Note: First game unfinished disputed goal).			
1892-1900	No Ulster championship			
	Cavan played in Leinster in 1895.			
1900	Antrim were to have represented Ulster but gave walk-over to Galway.			
1901	Antrim	3-5	2-5	Armagh
1902	Armagh	2-2	1-4	Antrim
1903	Cavan	0-5	0-5	Armagh
Replay	Cavan	0-5	0-5	Armagh
Replay	Cavan	0-8	0-4	Armagh
1904	Cavan	0-7	0-4	Monaghan
1905	Cavan	0-7	0-3	Monaghan
1906	Monaghan	2-10	1-2	Antrim
1907	No Final result in records			
1908	Antrim	1-8	0-4	Cavan
1909	Antrim	1-9	0-5	Cavan
1910	Antrim	3-4	0-1	Cavan
1911	Antrim	2-8	0-4	Cavan
1912	Antrim	2-2	0-1	Armagh
1913	Antrim	2-1	1-2	Monaghan
1914	Monaghan	2-4	0-2	Fermanagh
1915	Cavan	3-2	2-5	Monaghan
Replay	Cavan	0-4	0-3	Monaghan
1916	Monaghan	2-3	0-2	Antrim
1917	Monaghan	4-2	0-4	Armagh
1918	Cavan	3-2	0-0	Antrim
1919	Cavan	5-6	0-2	Antrim
1920	Cavan	4-6	1-4	Armagh
1921	Monaghan	2-2	0-1	Derry
1922	Cavan	2-3	2-3	Monaghan
Replay	Cavan	3-4	3-3	Monaghan
1923	Cavan	5-10	1-1	Monaghan
1924	Cavan	1-3	0-6	Monaghan
Replay	Cavan	2-3	1-3	Monaghan
1925	Cavan	2-3	3-0	Antrim
Replay	Cavan	3-6	0-1	Antrim
1926	Cavan	5-3	0-6	Antrim
1927	Monaghan	3-5	2-5	Armagh
1928	Cavan	2-6	1-4	Armagh
1929	Monaghan	1-4	1-4	Cavan
Replay	Monaghan	1-10	0-7	Cavan

Year	Winner	Score	Score	Loser
1930	Monaghan	4-3	1-5	Cavan
1931	Cavan	0-8	2-1	Armagh
1932	Cavan	2-4	0-2	Armagh
1933	Cavan	6-13	1-2	Tyrone
1934	Cavan	3-8	0-2	Armagh
1935	Cavan	2-6	2-1	Fermanagh
1936	Cavan	1-7	0-7	Monaghan
1937	Cavan	0-13	0-3	Armagh
1938	Monaghan	2-5	2-2	Armagh
1939	Cavan	2-3	1-3	Armagh
	(first game unfinished. Replay ordered)			
Replay	Cavan	2-3	1-4	Armagh
1940	Cavan	4-10	1-5	Down
1941	Cavan	3-9	0-5	Tyrone
1942	Cavan	5-11	1-3	Down
1943	Cavan	2-3	0-5	Monaghan
1944	Cavan	1-9	1-6	Monaghan
1945	Cavan	4-10	1-4	Fermanagh
1946	Antrim	2-8	1-7	Cavan
1947	Cavan	3-4	1-6	Antrim
1948	Cavan	2-12	2-4	Antrim
1949	Cavan	1-7	1-6	Armagh
1950	Armagh	1-11	1-7	Cavan
1951	Antrim	1-7	2-3	Cavan
1952	Cavan	1-8	0-8	Monaghan
1953	Armagh	1-6	0-5	Cavan
1954	Cavan	2-10	2-5	Armagh
1955	Cavan	0-11	0-8	Derry
1956	Tyrone	3-5	0-4	Cavan
1957	Tyrone	1-9	0-10	Derry
1958	Derry	1-11	2-4	Down
1959	Down	2-16	0-7	Cavan
1960	Down	3-7	1-8	Cavan
1961	Down	2-10	1-10	Armagh
1962	Cavan	3-6	0-5	Down
1963	Down	2-11	1-4	Donegal
1964	Cavan	2-10	1-10	Down
1965	Down	3-5	1-8	Cavan
1966	Down	1-7	0-8	Donegal
1967	Cavan	2-12	0-8	Down
1968	Down	0-16	1-8	Cavan
1969	Cavan	2-13	2-6	Down
1970	Derry	2-13	1-12	Antrim
1971	Down	4-15	4-11	Derry
1972	Donegal	2-13	1-11	Tyrone
1973	Tyrone	3-13	1-11	Down
1974	Donegal	1-14	2-11	Down
Replay	Donegal	3-9	1-12	Down
1975	Derry	1-16	2-6	Down
1976	Derry	1-8	1-8	Cavan
Replay	Derry	0-22	1-16	Cavan (aet)
1977	Armagh	3-10	1-5	Derry
1978	Down	2-19	2-12	Cavan
1979	Monaghan	1-15	0-11	Donegal
1980	Armagh	4-10	4-7	Tyrone
1981	Down	3-12	1-10	Armagh
1982	Armagh	0-10	1-4	Fermanagh
1983	Donegal	1-14	1-11	Cavan
1984	Tyrone	0-15	1-7	Armagh
1985	Monaghan	2-9	0-8	Derry
1986	Tyrone	1-11	0-10	Down
1987	Derry	0-11	0-9	Armagh
1988	Monaghan	1-10	0-11	Tyrone
1989	Tyrone	0-11	0-11	Donegal
Replay	Tyrone	2-13	0-7	Donegal
1990	Donegal	0-15	0-14	Armagh
1991	Down	1-15	0-10	Donegal
1992	Donegal	0-14	1-9	Derry
1993	Derry	0-8	0-6	Donegal
1994	Down	1-17	1-11	Tyrone
1995	Tyrone	2-13	0-10	Cavan
1996	Tyrone	1-9	0-9	Down
1997	Cavan	1-14	0-16	Derry
1998	Derry	1-7	0-8	Donegal
1999	Armagh	3-12	0-10	Down
2000	Armagh	1-12	1-11	Derry
2001	Tyrone	1-13	1-11	Cavan
2002	Armagh	1-14	1-10	Donegal
2003	Tyrone	1-17	4-8	Down
Replay	Tyrone	0-23	1-5	Down
2004	Armagh	3-15	0-11	Donegal
2005	Armagh	2-8	0-14	Tyrone
Replay	Armagh	0-13	0-11	Tyrone
2006	Armagh	1-9	0-9	Donegal
2007	Tyrone	1-15	1-13	Monaghan
2008	Armagh	2-8	1-11	Fermanagh
Replay	Armagh	1-11	0-8	Fermanagh
2009	Tyrone	1-18	0-15	Antrim
2010	Tyrone	1-14	0-7	Monaghan
2011	Donegal	1-11	0-8	Derry
2012	Donegal	2-18	0-13	Down
2013	Monaghan	0-13	0-7	Donegal
2014	Donegal	0-15	1-9	Monaghan
2015	Monaghan	0-11	0-10	Donegal
2016	Tyrone	0-13	0-11	Donegal
2017	Tyrone	2-17	0-15	Down

FOOTBALL

ALL-IRELAND MINOR FOOTBALL FINALS

1929	Clare	5-3	3-5	Longford
1930	Dublin	1-3	0-5	Mayo
1931	Kerry	3-4	0-4	Louth
1932	Kerry	3-8	1-3	Laois
1933	Kerry	4-1	0-9	Mayo
1934	Tipperary awarded title.			
	(Note: Dublin and Tyrone the semi-finalists			
	were disqualified.)			
1935	Mayo	1-6	1-1	Tipperary
1936	Louth	5-1	1-8	Kerry
1937	Cavan	1-11	1-5	Wexford
1938	Cavan	3-3	0-8	Kerry
1939	Roscommon	1-9	1-7	Monaghan
1940	Louth	5-5	2-7	Mayo
1941	Roscommon	3-6	0-7	Louth
1942-1944	No competition			
1945	Dublin	4-7	0-4	Leitrim
1946	Kerry	3-7	2-3	Dublin
1947	Tyrone	4-4	4-3	Mayo
1948	Tyrone	0-11	1-5	Dublin
1949	Armagh	1-7	1-5	Kerry
1950	Kerry	3-6	1-4	Wexford
1951	Roscommon	2-7	1-5	Armagh
1952	Galway	2-9	1-6	Cavan
1953	Mayo	2-11	1-6	Clare
1954	Dublin	3-3	1-8	Kerry
1955	Dublin	5-4	2-7	Tipperary
1956	Dublin	5-14	2-2	Leitrim
1957	Meath	3-9	0-4	Armagh
1958	Dublin	2-10	0-8	Mayo
1959	Dublin	0-11	1-4	Cavan
1960	Galway	4-9	1-5	Cork
1961	Cork	3-7	0-5	Mayo
1962	Kerry	6-5	0-7	Mayo
1963	Kerry	1-10	0-2	Westmeath
1964	Offaly	0-15	1-11	Cork
1965	Derry	2-8	2-4	Kerry
1966	Mayo	1-12	1-8	Down
1967	Cork	5-14	2-3	Laois
1968	Cork	3-5	1-10	Sligo
1969	Cork	2-7	0-11	Derry
1970	Galway	1-8	2-5	Kerry
Replay	Galway	1-11	1-10	Kerry
1971	Mayo	2-15	2-7	Cork
1972	Cork	3-11	2-11	Tyrone
1973	Tyrone	2-11	1-6	Kildare
1974	Cork	1-10	1-6	Mayo
1975	Kerry	1-10	0-4	Tyrone
1976	Galway	1-10	0-6	Cork
1977	Down	2-6	0-4	Meath
1978	Mayo	4-9	3-8	Dublin
1979	Dublin	0-10	1-6	Kerry
1980	Kerry	3-12	0-11	Derry
1981	Cork	4-9	2-7	Derry
1982	Dublin	1-11	1-5	Kerry
1983	Derry	0-8	1-3	Cork
1984	Dublin	1-9	0-4	Tipperary
1985	Mayo	3-3	0-9	Cork
1986	Galway	3-8	2-7	Cork
1987	Down	1-12	1-5	Cork
1988	Kerry	2-5	0-5	Dublin
1989	Derry	3-9	1-6	Offaly
1990	Meath	2-11	2-9	Kerry
1991	Cork	1-9	1-7	Mayo
1992	Meath	2-5	0-10	Armagh
1993	Cork	2-7	0-9	Meath
1994	Kerry	0-16	1-7	Galway
1995	Westmeath	1-10	0-11	Derry
1996	Laois	2-11	1-11	Kerry
1997	Laois	3-11	1-14	Tyrone
1998	Tyrone	2-11	0-11	Laois
1999	Down	1-14	0-14	Mayo
2000	Cork	2-12	0-13	Mayo
2001	Tyrone	0-15	1-12	Dublin
Replay	Tyrone	2-11	0-6	Dublin
2002	Derry	1-12	0-8	Meath
2003	Laois	1-11	1-11	Dublin
Replay	Laois	2-10	1-9	Dublin
2004	Tyrone	0-12	0-10	Kerry
2005	Down	1-15	0-8	Mayo
2006	Roscommon	0-15	0-15	Kerry
Replay	Roscommon	1-10	0-9	Kerry
2007	Galway	1-10	1-9	Derry
2008	Tyrone	0-14	0-14	Mayo
Replay	Tyrone	1-20	1-15	Mayo (aet)
2009	Armagh	0-10	0-7	Mayo
2010	Tyrone	1-13	1-12	Cork
2011	Tipperary	3-9	1-14	Dublin
2012	Dublin	0-14	1-5	Meath
2013	Mayo	2-13	1-13	Tyrone
2014	Kerry	0-17	1-10	Donegal
2015	Kerry	4-14	0-6	Tipperary
2016	Kerry	3-7	0-9	Galway
2017	Kerry	6-17	1-8	Derry

ALL-IRELAND MINOR FOOTBALL FINAL TEAMS

1929
Clare T.Crowe, J.O'Leary, G.Comerford, E.Kelly, J.McMahon, D.Twomey, J.Keane, L.Conlon, J.Morgan, J.Kilmartin, J.Lucey, P.Keane, P.Lucey, P.Stack, J.Brown.
Longford B.Phipps, A.Vaughan, J.Mulvey, J.Lyons, J.Quinn, J.Sheridan, P.Keenan, P.Farrell, J.Barden, W.Clarke, T.McHale, P.McLoughlin, M.Barden, W.Farrell, J.Smith.

1930
Dublin B.Synott, G.McLoughlin, T.Sharkey, K.Barry, S.O'Toole, T.Markham, T.Lawless, J.Scott, P.Diffney, W.Fallon, W.Bastow, B.Murphy, M.Grimes, J.Pearse, P.Castian, F.Williams, J.Brady, P.Crummey.
(Note: Only Dublin panel of 18 listed in media but not the final 15.)
Mayo John O'Gara, C.Gannon, C.Ward, G.Ormsby, C.McHale, John Acton, J.O'Donoghue, M.Flannery, C.O'Boyle, Jas.McGowan, T.Burke, W.Dever, P.McGoff, B.Scanlon, Martin O'Connor.

1931
Kerry B.Reidy, F.O'Neill, P.Walsh, E.Mahony, D.J.McCarthy, J.O'Keeffe, T.O'Sullivan, J.O'Gorman, P.McMahon, T.Murphy, P.O'Sullivan, M.Buckley, T.Chute, C.O'Sullivan, B.Healy.
Louth P.McDonnell, J.Tiernan, J.Hearty, J.Beirne, L.Dyas, G.Marley, J.Kelly, J.Caffrey, K.McArdle, P.Collier, Fearon, A.Dempsey, G.Watters, J.Harlin, A.Bradley.

1932
Kerry B.Reidy, F.O'Neill, E.Healy, J.P.Doyle, P.McMahon, P.Ronan, S.McCarthy, J.O'Sullivan, T.Weir, P.McMahon (Listowel), T.Wrenn, P.Ferriter, M.Brosnan, T.Leary, C.O'Sullivan. Sub: P.Lawlor.
Laois E.Roche, J.Hinchion, M.Hyland, W.Troy, J.Nolan, M.Fanning, S.Shortt, S.Harkins, M.McGough, W.Delaney, J.J.Delaney, J.J.Reilly, S.Meehan, M.Cahill, T.Kehoe.

1933
Kerry B.Reidy, M.O'Gorman, M.McCarthy, L.Crowley, S.Sullivan, W.Myers, T.O'Leary, W.Dillon, S.Brosnan, E.Buckley, B.Cronin, D.Griffin, W.Fitzgibbon, P.Kennedy, J.Counihan.
Mayo W.McHale, Joe Murphy, J.O'Neill, J.O'Donoghue, B.Duggan, J.Munnelly, J.Wright, P.Murphy, W.Mongey, M.Gallagher, J.Bracken, R.Winters, J.J.Kilroy, T Hoban, M.Griffin.

1934
Tipperary A.Greensmith, J.O'Connor, W.Power, M.Byrne, H.O'Donnell, J.Hickey, M.Lawlor, H.McGrath, T.Kenny, C.Dillon, M.Gavin, J.Maher, M.Power, P.Blanchfield, B.Kissane.
(Note: No final. Dublin/Tyrone disqualified for illegalities. Tipperary beat Mayo 4-9 to 2-5 in semi-final. Tipperary declared champions)

1935
Mayo T.Hannon, P.J.Irwin, D.Egan, M.J.Kearney, D.McNamara, W.Durkin, P.O'Malley, P.J.Judge, J.Galvin, J.McLoughlin, P.J.Roche, M.O'Malley, P.McNicholls, J.Keane, P.Quinn.

Tipperary M.Gavin, E.O'Meara, W.Treacy, H.Greensmith, E.Smith, P.Quinn, M.Flynn, W.McCarthy, P.Dillon, J.Hickey, P.Rafferty, T.Kenny, W.Hennessy, W.O'Donoghue, W.Power.

1936
Louth F.Rock, A.Lynn, P.Tuite, B.O'Dowda, L.Byrne, M.Cunningham, L.McEntee, L.Waller, J.O'Reilly, G.Hall, E.McGrath, D.Brady, K.O'Dowda, J.Cunningham, M.McArdle.
Kerry G.Teahan, P.Dowling, P.Kennedy, T.Healy, J.Keohane, S.O'Sullivan, T.Lyne, T.O'Connor, D.J.Healy, T.O'Sullivan, P.Breen, P.Sexton, B.Scannell, T.Brosnan, W.Casey.

1937
Cavan J.J.Brady, M.Argue, B.Cully, T.Cully, P.Clarke, M.O'Reilly, T.P.O'Reilly, P.O'Reilly, D.Brady, P.Conaty, H.Bouchier, P.McDonnell, J.McCormack, M.Farrell, P.Fay.
Wexford M.Kehoe, J.Dwyer, M.Butler, H.Kenny, D.Hall, T.Hurley, J.Morris, J.Murphy, P.Foley, P.Dunbar, T.Redmond, W.Howlin, J.Williams, S.Roice, S.Thorpe.

1938
Cavan J.D.Benson, W.Doonan, B.Cully, P.P.Galligan, M.Reilly, P.Coyle, S.Deignan, J.Maguire, J.McCormack, K.O'Reilly, P.Conaty, M.Fitzsimons, F.Coyle, J.Johnson, P.Doyle.
Kerry P.O'Brien, P.Burke, E.Dunne, T.Long, P.O'Donnell, M.Farrell, D.Kavanagh, T.O'Connor, T.Flavin, D.Rice, M.O'Shea, J.Bailey, T.Lyne, P.Fitzgerald, M.Kennedy.

1939
Roscommon S.Naughton, L.Cummins, W.Carlos, D.Boyd, T.Cox, L.Gilmartin, A.Murray, T.Lynch (Oran), S.Lavin, C.O'Beirne, J.Tiernan, J.McDermott, J.Bambrick, G.Kilduff, H.Winston. Sub: W.Penny for H.Winston.
Monaghan P.Farrell, D.Hughes, Phil Donoghue, D.Marron, J.McGeogh, O.King, V.Flanagan, P.Ruttledge, D.Rice, F.McCormack, J.McGeogh, P.McCarney, J.Woods, P.McKenna, J.McHugh.

1940
Louth C.Brown, B.Breen, B.Burke, M.Flanagan, B.Fretwell, E.Reay, O.Mohan, L.Murphy, P.J.Kelly, A.Cahill, S.McGivern, P.Corr, P.McCourt, J.Kiernan, G.Brennan.
Mayo A.Breslin, M.Galvin, C.Long, J.McLaughlin, T.Acton, F.Mongey, S.Durkin, M.Langan, J.Forkin, J.Ralph, J.J.McGowan, A.McNally, J.Jennings, T.Byrne, D.Loughrey. Sub: P.Browne.

1941
Roscommon G.Dolan, T.F.Bannon, T.J.Lynch (Boyle), L.Kelly, P.Donnelly, B.Lynch, P.Hoare, W.Carlos, E.Curran, B.O'Gara, P.Duignan, B.O'Rourke, C.Murray, G.Kilduff, P.Hannelly.
Louth J.Allen, J.P.Grist, J.Mulligan, W.Pigott, J.Larkin, M.O'Grady, J.Clarke, B.O'Dowda, P.McCourt, P.Corr, J.MacArtain, A.Cahill, E.Boyle, M.Hardy, J.O'Reilly. Sub: P.Kelly.

1945
Dublin C.Feeney, D.O'Mahony, J.Sharry, G.Jennings, N.Maher, D.Healy, T.Nolan, S.McEntaggert, S.Guinea, L.Donnelly, O.Freaney, J.Nugent, J.Copeland, P.McCarthy, C.Dignam.
Leitrim P.Heeran, T.P.Reynolds, J.Bohan, M.Dolan, J.Brennan, S.Mulvey, T.Cryan, J.Heslin, R.O'Beirne, P.Dolan, M.Fallon, B.McTiernan, M.J.McKeon, K.Herity, C.Cassidy. Sub: F.Canning.

1946

Kerry   J.Ryan, S.McCarthy, B.O'Sullivan, D.Murphy, S.O'Sullivan, D.Sheehan, J.Fenton, T.Moriarty, T.Ashe, M.Lynch, D.O'Regan, P.O'Sullivan, J.O'Brien, J.Madden, P.Godley.
Dublin   C.Feeney, D.Mahony, P.Lawlor, P.Cloonan, J.Butler, J.Lavin, B.Clancy, N.Fingleton, N.Maher, L.Donnelly, O.Freaney, D.Stanley, K.Heffernan, A.Clohessy, C.Mehigan. Subs: P.Bates for P.Cloonan, T.Mulligan for Mahony.

1947

Tyrone   M.Bradley, L.Campbell, R.McNulty, V.Cullen, M.Vaughan, E.Devlin, M.Cushenan, S.McGrath, J.Poyntz, H.Hartop, M.Dargan, J.McConnell, D.McCafferty, T.Sullivan, P Donnelly.
Mayo   A.O'Toole, M.Kinnane, P.Flanagan, M.Jordan, A.McMorris, P.Doherty, N.Keane, N.McDonnell, T.Walsh, M.Loughnane, P.Carroll, C.McHale, L.Flynn, P.Solan, M.O'Connell.

1948

Tyrone   J.McGahern, D.Donnelly, Mal Connolly, E.Knox, Louis Campbell, E.Devlin, P.O'Hanlon, S.McGrath, H.Hartop, J.O'Reilly, M.Dargan, B.Eastwood, Leo Devlin, J.J.O'Hagan, J.Twomey. Sub: S.Donnelly.
Dublin   P.King, P.Connolly, K.Lougheed, G.Brogan, W.Fleming, S.Page, P.McGahan, T.Jennings, C.Freaney, B.Conboy, D.Ferguson, J.Kelly, P.Ryan, D.Carney, B.Redmond. Sub: J.Guidon.

1949

Armagh   L.McCorry, E.McCann, J.Bratton, J.McKnight, F.Kernan, B.O'Neill, T.McConville, E.Mee, S.Collins, T.Connolly, S.Blaney, J.Cunningham, S.Smith, P.J.McKeever B.McGrane. Sub: M.McKnight for S.Collins.
Kerry   J.Foley, J.O'Shea, P.Colgan, M.Galway, M.Kerins, J.Moriarty, P.Costello, S.Murphy, D.Falvey, P.Coleman, P.O'Donnell, P.Sheehy, B.Galvin, C.Kennelly, R.Miller.

1950

Kerry   D.O'Neill, M.Galway, M.Brosnan, J.Collins, T.Murphy, P.O'Donnell, J.Kerins, S.Murphy, P.Sheehy, R.Millar, C.Kennelly, C.O'Riordan, B.Galvin, T.Lawlor, P.Fitzgerald.
Wexford   T.O'Sullivan, M.O'Donoghue, R.McCabe, M.Hyde, M.Culliton, A.Doyle, J.Synott, P.O'Kennedy, B.McGuinness, W.Bennett, L.Larkin, P.Sheehan, J.O'Sullivan, P.Jordan, J.Doran.

1951

Roscommon   P Muldoon, O.Murray, J.Lynch, E.O'Connor, B.Molloy, T.Finnegan, G.Healy, H.Connolly, J.Rafferty, J.O'Brien, J.Campbell, E.Duignan, L.Duffy, M.Shivnan, H.Penny. Sub: M.Kelly for E.Duignan.
Armagh   G.Murphy, G.Donnelly, B.Seeley, P.Moore, D.Skelton, E.Quinn, M.Grimley, B.O'Neill, S.McCresh, A.Dilllon, S.Hanratty, S.Crossey, P.Kierans, P.McArdle, D.McCorry. Sub. S.McMahon for A.Dillon.

1952

Galway   M.Ryan, B.Naughton, S.Kyne, S.Hoban, M.Lohan, E.Dunleavy, M.Hawkshaw, M.Kelly, B.Mahon, T.Brosnan, S.Mitchell, L.Manning, B.Waldron, G.Kirwan, M.Geraghty.
Cavan   S.Frawley, P.O'Hare, S.Farrelly, P.A.Farrell, D.Kelly, B.Brady, S.Keoghan, T.Maguire, G.Keyes, S.Farrelly, G.Smythe, V.Blythe, G.Fitzpatrick, M.McKenna, S.McDonnell.

1953

Mayo   S.Stewart, P.Gavin, S.Veldon, F.Fahy, W Joyce, J.Jennings, B.Keane, D.Keane, M.Stewart, E.Neilan, T.Treacy, V.Blyth, V.Kilcullen, C.McDonnell, E.Walsh. Sub: M.Tuohy for J.Jennings.
Clare   M.Garry, J.Carmody, T.Griffin, D.Fitzgerald, J.Power, T.Mangan, S.Barrett, P.O'Dea, M.Greene, P.Griffin, F.Cassidy, J.Drury, T.Flynn, C.Comer, M.McGrath. Sub: P.Daly for M.Greene.

1954

Dublin   R.Brady, M.Bohan, B.O'Boyle, D.Sweeney, T.Bracken, N.Boylan, M.Cronin, B.McLaughlin, P.Heron, V.Bell, P.Farnan, A.Kavanagh, G.O'Reilly, P.Feeney, D.Waters. Subs: E.Gilbert for P.Farnan, V.Lyons G.O'Reilly.
Kerry   M.Cournane, T.Barrett, J.Dowling, L.Cloghlan, B.Kennelly, P.Shea, F.O'Leary, T.Long, J.Foley, T.O'Dowd J.Cullotty, F.Lynch, T.Garvey, B.Sheehy, G.White. Sub: T.Foley for G.White.

1955

Dublin   S.Denigan, V.Murphy, D.Sweeney, D.Hearns, R.Doherty, S.Graham, C.Jones, P.Heron, L.Foley, E.Burgess, S.Linehan, C.McSweeney, J.Joyce, G.Wolfe, C.Leaney. Sub: L.Boyle for G.Wolfe.
Tipperary   S.Ryan, G.King, S.Condon, P.Burke, S.Connolly, T.Walsh, D.Stapleton, P.Tobin, L.Boland, A.Danagher, E.Casey, M.Moroney, M.Ryan, S.Ferris, S.Brennan. Sub: P.Nolan for S.Ryan.

1956

Dublin   D.Creed, A.Talbot, P.Lacey, D.Hearns, R.Doherty, D.Cashel, V.Kavanagh, L.Foley, S.Lenihan, J.Brogan, D.Foley, N.Fox, R.McCrea, G.Wolfe, C.Leaney. Sub: P.Dennis for G.Wolfe.
Leitrim   L.Feehily, S.Bredin, T.Fallon, P.McGloin, W.McWeeney, P.McGowan, S.Fallon, P.Heslin, J.Murray, L.Foran, J.O'Donnell, P.Dolan, P.McIntyre, F.Canning, P.Conboy. Sub: J.Clyne for S.Fallon.

1957

Meath   P.J.O'Reilly, T.Gibney, J.Kelleher, B.Cunningham, J.Fagan, T.Fitzsimons, M.Clerkin, J.Halpin, S.Clinch, P.Hanley, J.Grey, B.Cahill, T.Monaghan, M.Greville, L.Drumm.
Armagh   J.Finnegan, S.McConville, A.Bennett, B.Connolly, F.Toal, B.Donaghy, A.Casey, O.Agnew, R.Dowds, S.Mallon, S.Murphy, H.Loughran, B.McGeary, K.Halpenny, S.Toner. Subs: N.Greene for O.Agnew, C.McNiece for F.Toal.

1958

Dublin   K.Donnelly, N.Joyce, P.Holden, D.Mulligan, D.Jones, A.Whelan, M.Kissane, D.Foley, A.O'Reilly, P.Taylor, N.Fox, B.McDonald, J.Sweeney, J.Gilroy, B.Beggs. Sub: S.Behan for P.Taylor.
Mayo   K.Doherty, M.O'Boyle, M.Sweeney, M.Tighe, J.Rowe, L.Doherty, C.Maguire, T.Rochford, J.Rowe, J.Corcoran, T.Gibbons, J.Cosgrove, M.Lyons, J.Langan, P.Sheridan. Subs: A.O'Connell for M.Lyons, P.Griffin for J.Cosgrove.

1959

Dublin   P.Talbot, E.Grainger, A.Doran, F.McCourt, M.Campion, M.Kissane, F.Byrne, S.Behan, J.Levins, P.Delaney, B.McDonald, J.Dowling, J.McKettrick, G.McCabe, S.Coen. Subs: B.Cooney for T.McKettrick, P.Taylor for S.Behan.
Cavan   S.Boyle, F.Cafferty, F.McKiernan, F.O'Reilly, P.Flood, T.Morris, F.Kennedy, B.Morris, D.McCluskey, B.Sherlock, D.Brady, K.Blessing, L.McCluskey, K.McCormack, P.Murray. Subs: T.McKiernan for D.McCluskey, G.O'Reilly for L.McCluskey, L.McCluskey for G.O'Reilly.

1960

Galway M.King, G.Lohan, N.Tierney, L.O'Brien, E.Colleran, A.Ryan, J.Smith, H.Anderson, S.Cleary, C.Tyrrell, G.Prendergast, S.Leydon, J.Gavin, E.Slattery, A.Donnelly.

Cork T.Hegarty, J.Burke, J.McGrath, V.Cronin, P.Pyne, E.O'Connor, G.Harrington, M.O'Brien, P.Curley, J.Travers, B.Coughlan, B.Larkin, T.Burke, D.Moynihan, L.O'Hanrahan. Subs: D.Buckley for P.Pyne, D.Nangle for J.McGrath.

1961

Cork R.Cawley, D.Nangle, J.McGrath, V.Cronin, G.Harrington, B.Larkin, J.O'Donoghue, F.Cogan, E.Coughlan, F.Hayes, D.Barrett, D.Philpott, T.Burke, M.Archer, T.Monaghan.

Mayo H.O'Brien, C.Hanley, B.Reape, S.Murphy, E.Carroll, G.Nicholson, V.Nally, J.Langan, J.Madden, D.McSweeney, M.Connaughton, P.J.McLoughlin, J.Nealon, E.Maguire, J.Warde. Subs: D.Carroll for G.Nicholson, M.O'Malley for D.McSweeney.

1962

Kerry S.Fitzgerald, D.Lovett, C.O'Connor, S.Burrowes, T.Fitzgerald, P.O'Donoghue, A.Burrowes, D.O'Sullivan, T.Doyle, S.O'Mahony, A.Barrett, D.O'Shea, S.Flavin, R.O'Donnell, T.Mulvihill. Subs: S.Corridon for T.Doyle, T.Kenneally for T.Mulvihill.

Mayo L.McEllin, A.Brett, J.Early, D.O'Leary, N.Golden, M.Brennan, E.Carroll, M.Connaughton, M.O'Malley, F.McDonald, P.Costello, C.Dolan, N.Maguire, D.McSweeney, J.J.Cribben. Sub: T.Staunton for L.McEllin.

1963

Kerry S.Fitzgerald, A.Behan, J.McCarthy, S.Burrowes, T.O'Shea, B.Burrowes, C.O'Riordan, D.O'Sullivan, G.Curran, T.O'Hanlon, A.Spring, J.Saunders, T.Kelleher, H.McKinney, C.Donnelly. Subs: M.O'Sullivan, S.O'Shea.

Westmeath K.Higgins, B.Glynn, P.Malone, T.King, J.Murray, P.Bradley, R.Cornally, G.Frawley, R.Niland, P.Buckley, F.Connaughton, C.Kelly, J.V.Costello, K.Coffey, M.Fagan. Subs: T.Reeves, D.Hamm.

1964

Offaly M.Furlong, S.Coughlan, J.Smith, M.Ryan, E.Mulligan, S.Grogan, L.Duffy, O.Kilmurray, F.Greene, W.Bryan, A.McTague, J.Gunning, E.Kennedy, D.Mcintyre, M.Byrne. Sub: M.O'Rourke for W.Bryan.

Cork T.Murphy, R.Kelly, J.Cawley, P.Lyne, B.O'Brien, N O'Donovan, Colman McCarthy, J.Cogan, J.Downing, E.Philpott, T.F.Hayes, C.Roche, B.O'Leary, L.McAuliffe, Charlie McCarthy. Sub: D.Bermingham for Charlie McCarthy.

1965

Derry E.McCaul, A.Burke, T.Quinn, M.Kelly, C.Mullen, M.McAfee, A.McGuckian, T.Diamond, S.Lagan, B.Mullen, M.Niblock, E.Coleman, S.Kearney, S.McCluskey, P.Friel.

Kerry B.Lynch, J.O'Sullivan, J.Coughlan, T.Crean, P.O'Donovan, M.Aherne, P.Scanlon, P.O'Connell, F.Moroney, R.Geaney, D.Moriarty, B.McCarthy, K.Griffin, G.O'Donnell, T.Kelleher. Sub: S.O'Connor for T.Crean.

1966

Mayo E.Rooney, S.Hughes, T.Snee, B.Meenehan, G.Nevin, T.Cafferkey, B.McHale, S.O'Dowd, A.Joyce, J.Timoney, T.Fitzgerald, D.Griffith, P.Glavey, J.Smyth, A.Kelly. Sub: S.Kilbride for P.Glavey.

1967

Cork M.Cotter, S.Looney, Ted Murphy, J.Fahy, Der Cogan, S.Murphy, K.Kehilly, Donal Aherne, D.Long, Jerry Horgan, D.Hunt, J.Barrett, D.Morley, N.Kirby, Ted O'Brien. Sub: David Aherne for S.Looney.

Laois A.Burke, M.Murphy, P.Fingleton, J.Mangan, J.Kavanagh, W.Monaghan, C.Murphy, S.Fleming, I.Houlihan, S.Furey, R.Millar, S.Allen, E.Condron, J.Lawlor, T.Keane. Sub: C.McEvoy for C.Murphy.

1968

Cork D.O'Mahony, Jerry Coleman, F.Cronin, S.Looney, D.Cogan, R.O'Sullivan, C.Hartnett, Donal Aherne, Barry Murphy, Tony Murphy, John Coleman, H.O'Sullivan, F.Twomey, M.O'Doherty, B.Cummins. Sub: D.McCarthy for H.O'Sullivan.

Sligo P.McLoughlin, R.Lipsett, J.Brennan, N.Kellegher, J.Kilgallon, J.Gilmartin, K.Conway, G.Hegarty, A.Richardson, D.Kerins, R.Henry, H.Quinn, R.Sherlock, R.Boland, P.Kearins. Sub. J.Kilgallon for R.Sherlock.

1969

Cork B.O'Brien, P.Barry, G.B.O'Sullivan, D.Moloney, Brian Murphy, M.O'Doherty, C.Hartnett, E.Hallinan, J.Coleman, D.Curran, E.Fitzparick, H.O'Sullivan, J.Courtney, D.Barron, P.Lonergan.

Derry K.McGahon, P.Burke, L.Murphy, P.McGuckian, B.Kearney, M.Moran, R.Hasson, E.Laverty, H.McGoldrick, S.Mullan, B.Ward, T.McWilliams, M.O'Neill, S.McGeehan, G.O'Neill. Subs: M.Bradley for T.McWilliams, S.Coyle for E.Lavery.

1970

Galway J.Higgins, S.Cloonan, A.Marren, J.Kemple, P.J.Burke, M.Geraghty, J.Corcoran, T.O'Connor, P.Silke, I.Barrett, M.Rooney, J.Lardner, M.Burke, S.Meehan, J.Tobin. Sub: M.Walsh who played in drawn game for S.Meehon. S.Meehan came on as sub in drawn game for M.Walsh.

Kerry P.O'Mahony, B.O'Shea, S.Clifford, J.Deenihan, D.Healy, M.O'Sullivan, G.O'Keeffe, P.Lynch, J.Long, C.O'Connell, J.Egan, G.Power, P.B.Brosnan, S.Fitzgerald, A.Moore. Subs: M.O'Connor for D.Healy, R.Casey for G.O'Keeffe.T.McEllistrim and A.Moore came on as subs in drawn game. S.Fitzgerald and A.Moore were on for replay. J.Murphy and G.Dillon played in drawn game.

1971

Mayo M.Griffin, J.O'Mahony, S.Reilly, A.Durkan, G.Feeney, C.Moynihan, J.Culkin, J.Quinn, R.McNicholas, M.Gannon, J.P.Kean, M.Higgins, G.Farragher, F.Harty, M.Maloney. Sub: M.Fahy for J.Quinn.

Cork G.Stanton, K.Collins, J.O'Shea, K.Murphy, M.Corbett, C.Kelleher, R.Wilmot, J.Lynch, S.Fitzgerald, D.Crowley, S.Coughlan, S.Murphy, D.Philpott, J.Barry Murphy, A.Fahy. Subs: V.Twomey for S.Fitzgerald, D.O'Sullivan for R.Wilmot, G.Aherne for S.Murphy.

1966

1972
Cork   T.O'Sullivan, D.Keohane, Conor Barrett, T.Creedon, S.O'Farrell, S.O'Sullivan, R.Wilmot, K.Murphy, K.Collins, L.Gould, D.O'Hare, G.Aherne, Liam Good, J.Barry Murphy, S.O'Shea. Sub: B.Óg Murphy for S.O'Shea.
Tyrone   P.Kerlin, G.Goodwin, H.Mooney, D.Daly, P.O'Neill, C.McAleer, J.Doherty, F.McGuigan, D.McKenna, M.Quinn, J.Hughes, B.O'Neill, T.Campbell, M.Harte, P.Quinn. Subs: D.Kennedy for T.Campbell, M.Coyle for P.Quinn.

1973
Tyrone   B.Campbell, G.Goodwin, M.Lennon, H.Mooney S.Gormley, C.McAleer, J.O'Doherty, P.Kerlin, D.McKenna S.O'Kane, E.McKenna, J.Cunningham, M.Quinn, B.O'Neill, K.Currie. Sub: S.Coyne for K.Currie.
Kildare   A.Dunne, J.Clancy, J.Grehan, S.Ryan, J.Jacob, P.Archibald, T.Browne, N.Fennelly, P.Winders, P.Mulhearn, J.Geoghegan, J.Delaney, E.Delahunt, N.Fahy, B.Whelan. Subs: P.Lyons, J.Dooley.

1974
Cork   F.Delaney, W.Lynch, J.Slattery, E.Desmond, B.Twomey, J.Crowley, T.Cashman, D.Good, R.Kenny, Declan Murphy, Diarmuid McCarthy, Don McCarthy, G.O'Sullivan, M.O'Regan, T.Murphy. Subs: M.Carey for J.Crowley, D.McCurtain for Don McCarthy, W.O'Driscoll for R.Kenny.
Mayo   J.Cuddy, S.Sweeney, D.Conway, J.Gallagher, E.Brett, V.Ryan, J.Brennan, P.Mohan, W.Nally, K.Geraghty, M.Burke, S.Moran, G.Hennigan, J.Burke, M.Mannion. Subs: J.Nally for S.Sweeney, G.Reilly for G.Hennigan, M.McCormack for M.Mannion.

1975
Kerry   C.Nelligan, V.O'Connor, M.O'Sullivan, M.Colgan, J.J.O'Connor, M.Spillane, G.Casey, S.Walsh, N.O'Donovan, F.Scannell, J.Mulvihill, R.Bunyan, C.O'Connor, J.O'Shea, P.Sheehan.
Tyrone   A.Skelton, B.Campbell, K.McGarvey P.McCallan, P.J.Trainor, K.McCabe, J.J.Campbell, T.O'Rourke, G.McCallan, P.Teague, M.McCoy, P.Donnelly, D O'Hagan, M.McAnneny, S.Daly. Subs: S.Donnelly for T.O'Rourke, E.McCann for S.Daly.

1976
Galway   P.Coyne, M.Coleman, O.Burke, C.Ó Fatharta, J.Kelly, R.Bermingham, G.Forde, G.Burke, L.Higgins, B.Brennan, S.Ruane, P.Conroy, K.O'Sullivan, G.McManus, F.Rooney. Sub: K.Donnellan for B.Brennan.
Cork   S.Martin, T.Healy, J.Murphy, M.Moloney, D.Buckley, J.Cremin, J.Nolan, P.McCarthy, B.McSweeney, T.Dalton, M.Mullins, P.Smith, K.O'Leary, G.Mulcahy, J.O'Sullivan Subs: M.Shinnick for K.O'Leary, J.Wilmot for T.Dalton.

1977
Down   P.Donnan, S.McNulty, A.McAulfield, Seán Brunker, P.O'Rourke, M.Sands, B.McGovern, John McCartan, P.Kennedy, E.Toner, A.Rogers, M.McCann, T.Bradley, B.Loughran, J.Digney Subs: E.McGivern for T.Bradley, F.Rooney for B.McGovern.
Meath   M.McQuillan, L.Harnan, B.Cullen, C.O'Reilly, G.Gough, C.Brazil, M.Sheilds, A.Tormey, J.Butler, G.Cooney, N.O'Sullivan, P.Finnerty, J.McCluskey, F.O'Sullivan, B.Reddy. Sub: J.Tallon.

1978
Mayo   S.Warde, M.Maloney, G.Golden, M.Walsh, N.Heffernan, A.Garvey, E.Melvin, M.Joyce, T.J.Kilgallon, S.Clarke, J.Maughan, A.McNicholas, K.O'Malley, J.Lyons, E.Griffin. Subs: L.Lyons for S.Clarke, T.Byrne for J.Lyons, C.Gilmartin for M.Maloney.
Dublin   P.O'Toole, F.Walsh, P.Canavan, C.Finnegan, K.Byrne, S.Fleming, T.Mannion, J.Kelly, A.White, C.Duff, M.Loftus, C.Griffin, N.Gaffney, B.Rock, K.Barry. Sub: D.Deasy for J.Kelly.

1979
Dublin   J.O'Leary, J.Grace, V.Conroy, S.Wade, C.Eustace, C.Finnegan, Derek Murphy, B.Kavanagh, P.Boylan, B.Jordan, M.Loftus, C.Duff, Dermot Murphy, B.Rock, K.Barry. Subs: T.Kelly for J.Grace, P.McCabe Derek Murphy.
Kerry   N.Cronin, S.Keane, B.Lavin, C.Bambury, D.Keane, P.Sheehan, A.Shannon, A.O'Donovan, T.Dee, J.Chute, L.Kearns, D.Kennelly, W.O'Connor, T.Spillane, G.O'Donnell.

1980
Kerry   R.O'Brien, D.Keane, M.Crowley, M.Counihan, J.O'Sullivan, T.Sheehy, J.T.O'Sullivan, P.O'Donoghue, A.O'Donovan, T.Dee, J.Shannon, L.Kearns, T.Parker, W.Maher, M.McAuliffe. Sub: T.Spillane for L.Kearns.
Derry   J.Mackle, B.McNabb, M.O'Brien, M.Tully, M.Convery, O.McKee, D.McCluskey, D.Barton, D.O'Kane, L.McElhinny, B.McErlean, J.McErlean, P.McKiernan, T.McGuckian, R.McCusker. Subs: M.Bradley for M.O'Brien, D.McNicholl for T.McGuckian.

1981
Cork   M.Maguire, D.O'Brien, J.Murphy, N.Cahalane, C.Hannon, V.Hedderman, A.Davis, A.Leahy, T.Mannix, Tony O'Sullivan, E.O'Mahony, P.Fitzgerald, P.Healy, C.O'Neill, J.Cleary. Sub: T.Cole for T.Mannix.
Derry   L.Peoples, B.McNabb, K.Rafferty, E.Reilly, C.Kelly, B.McPeake, M.Tully, L.McElhinny, M.Bradley, Eunan Rafferty, D.O'Kane, T.McGuckian, Dermot McNicholl, J.McErlean, J.A.Mullen. Subs: J.McGrath for B.McNabb, P.McCormack for M.Bradley.

1982
Dublin   J.McNally, C.Sage, F.McGrath, L.O'Rourke, E.Heary, T.Delaney, M.Deegan, D.Sheehan, B.Cooke, M.Coffey, M.Egan, S.O'Brien, P.O'Carroll, T.McCormack, B.Redmond. Sub: T.Murphy for T.McCormack.
Kerry   D.O'Neill, D.Cremin, J.Keane, J.O'Connell, J.Moriarty, J.O'Donnell, J.Rice, T.Brosnan, S.Wight, D.O'Donoghue, M.Keating, P.Galvin, B.Keane, E.Fitzgerald, M.McAuliffe. Subs: P.J.O'Leary for P.Galvin, T.O'Connor for J.Keane, E.Marey for J.O'Connell.

1983
Derry   D.Kelly, P.O'Donnell, P.Bradley, J.McGurk, R.Conway, B.Kealy, N.Mullon, P.Young, C.Barton, C.McNicholl, D.McNicholl, E.McElhinny, E.Lynch, D.Cassidy, Tony McKiernan.
Cork   R.Duffy, M.Maguire, T.Minihane, K.Scanlon, M.Slocum, B.Searles, J.Moynihan, B.Coffey, B.Stack, M.McCarthy, Teddy McCarthy, D.Kennedy, J.Cashman, M.Kelleher; P.Harrington. Subs: I.Breen for J.Cashman, E.Kenneally for D.Kennedy, T.Power for P.Harrington.

1984

Dublin   M.Broderick, G.Walsh, J.Barry, Ciarán Walsh, A.Martin, J.Power, B.McKeon, J.Stynes, P.Clarke, D.de Lappe, A.McClean, J.Fahy, N.Clancy, M.Crowley, C.Crowley. Subs: P.Daly for C.Walsh, D.Whelan for A.McClean.

Tipperary   G.Enright, D.Walsh, R.Quirke, D.Williams, J.Owens, F.Howlin, M.Holland, B.Burke, G.Ryan, M.Goonan, J.O'Meara, K.Farrelly, T.Sheehan, A.Crosse, S.Brett. Subs.: D.Pyke for K.Farrelly, J.Hackett for S.Brett.

1985

Mayo   J.Cummins, K.Beirne, E.Gilvarry, M.Coyle, D.Burke, D.Fitzgerald, J.French, M.Fitzmaurice, G.Maher, Tony Munnelly, P.Walsh, T.O'Grady, P.Kerrane, M.J.Mullen, J.Gallagher. Sub: M.MullagLy for Tony Munnelly.

Cork   J.O'Mahony, M.Murphy, D.Duggan, J.Allen, N.Creedon, B.Murphy, T.Griffin, K.Kiely, J.O'Driscoll, B.Harte, D.O'Connell, G.O'Regan, P Cahill, P.Collins, R.Sheehan. Sub: K.Nagle for R.Sheehan.

1986

Galway   A.Brennan, B.Silke, F.McWalter, G.Farrell, P.Fallon, A.Mulholland, M.Tarpey, J.Joyce, K.Walsh, T.Kilcommins, F.O'Neill, M.McDonagh, T.Mannion, P.Maher, T.Finnerty. Subs: B.Walsh for B.Silke, N.Costelloe for T.Kilcommins, J.Mitchell for M.McDonagh.

Cork   P.Hayes S.O'Brien M.O'Connor S.O'Rourke, N.Murphy, M.Crowley, D.Burke, F.Corrigan, G.Lally, P.Davis, M.Mullins, P.Coleman, N.Twomey, D.Larkin, I.Aherne. Subs: M.Farr for S.O'Rourke, R.Sheehan for G.Lally.

1987

Down   D.Hawkins, N.Caulfield, L.Duggan, M.McGivern, M.Quinn, C.Deegan, C.Mason, B.McCartan, P.Hannaway, C.Murray, R.Haughean, G.Breen, R.Fitzpatrick, T.Fagan, J.McCartan.

Cork   J.J.Sweeney, D.O'Callaghan, B.Cooney, M.Lyons, S.Coughlan, S.O'Brien, D.Burke, L.Honohan, S.Dineen, G.McPolin, M.Burke, D.Davis, J.J.Barrett, D.O'Sullivan, N.Twomey. Subs: F.Fitzgerald for G.McPolin, J.Corcoran for L.Honohan, S.Calnan for D.O'Sullivan.

1988

Kerry   P.O'Leary, P.Lenihan, N.Savage, J.B.O'Brien, L.Flaherty, V.Knightly, S.Walsh, E.Stack.F.Ashe, P.Laide, D.Cahill, S.O'Sullivan, C.Geaney, D.Farrell, B.O'Sullivan. Sub: F.Doherty for D.Farrell.

Dublin   D.O'Farrell, P.McManus, J.Jordan, C.Kavanagh, T.O'Boyle, B.Murray, G.O'Regan, D.Quinlivan, P.Cassells, D.Howard, B.Stynes, T.Keogh, D.Farrell, S.Moylan, B.Barnes. Subs: S.Cahill for Cassells, T.Gavigan for O'Boyle.

1989

Derry   M.O'Connor, J.Martin, P.McAllister, G.Simpson, B.McGonigle, G.Coleman, R.Skelly, J.Mulholland, A.Tohill, R.McEldowney, J.Lynn, E.Burns, E.O'Kane, D.Heaney, D.Boteson. Subs: K.Diamond for Martin, R.Murphy for Lynn, J.O'Connor for E.O'Kane.

Offaly   D.Scully, K.Flynn, C.Maher, P.Dunne, B.Daly, F.Cullen, P.Moran, S.Grennan, B.O'Brien, A.Hogan, N.Hand, D.McKeon, W.Reynolds, S.Kellaghan, C.McTeague. Subs: F.Kinnally for Daly, J.Hiney for Reynolds, P.Carroll for Dunne.

1990

Meath   C.Martin, V.Ryan, E.McManus, N.Collier, R.McGrath, G.Geraghty, T.Hanley, J.Hendrick, J.McCarthy, T.Byrne, D.Martin, B.Kealy, H.Carolan, T.O'Connor, C.Sheridan. Sub: C.Macken for Ryan.

Kerry   D.O'Keeffe, F.Stack, J.Cronin, J.O'Driscoll, O.Joy, S.Moynihan, B.O'Shea, C.Kennedy, S.O'Driscoll, J.Bowler W.O'Donnell, K.O'Shea, C.O'Grady, J.Wieboltt, G.Farrell. Sub: S.Curtin for S.O'Driscoll.

1991

Cork   K.O'Dwyer, D.O'Callaghan, B.Corcoran, B.Murphy G.McCullagh, T.Lynch, A.McCarthy, F.Collins, P.Hegarty, S.Barrett, M.O'Sullivan, P.O'Mahony, K.Harrington, J.Kavanagh, P.O'Rourke. Subs: F.O'Mahony for O'Rourke, D.O'Neill for Barrett.

Mayo   B.Heffernan, T.Burke, J.McSharry, K.Mortimer, P.Cunney, D.Leyden, F.Costello, M.Smith, P.McNamara, T.J.McHugh, K.O'Neill, R.Golding, D.Burke, T.Walkin, D.McDonagh. Subs: S.Brady for McDonagh, C.Deacy for McHugh.

1992

Meath   B.Murphy, K.Cantwell, J.Brady, J.Smith, P.Shankey, J.Tighe, B.Sheridan, D.Hunt, N.Dunne, K.Harten, C.Hall, G.Bell, P.Duff, P.O'Sullivan, T.Giles. Subs: P.Nestor for Duff, M.Farrelly for Harten.

Armagh   D.Whitmarsh, E.Fearon, E.Martin, E.Bratten, C.Wilson, M.Hanratty, K.O'Hagan, B.O'Hagan, P.McGrane, B.Hughes, D.Marsden, P.McNulty, D.Toner, D.Mackin, N.McGleenan. Subs: J.Rafferty for McGleenan, A.McCann for Fearon, K.Mallie for Bratten.

1993

Cork   D.McAuley; T.O'Mahony, K.O'Connell, J.Kingston; A.O'Shea, E.Sexton, S.Prendeville, J.O'Connell, D.Dempsey; M.Cronin, A.O'Regan, J.Buckley; S.Collins, P.O'Flynn, B.Cuthbert. Sub: J.McCarthy for Dempsey.

Meath   N.Craven, N.Kearney, C.Woods, H.Traynor; P.Reynolds, D.Fay, B.Sheridan; T.Giles, A.Finnegan; N.Farrelly, J.Lacy, N.Walsh; O.Murphy, B.Callaghan, P.Nestor. Subs: P.Duff for Nestor, N.Regan for Walsh, J.Farrelly for Finnegan.

1994

Kerry   B.Murphy, K.O'Driscoll, B.O'Shea, S.O'Mahony, T.Fleming, T.McCarthy, F.O'Connor, D.Dwyer, G.O'Keeffe, J.Ferriter (capt.), L.Brosnan, G.Lynch, J.O'Shea, P.Sullivan, G.Murphy. Sub: M.Russell for G.Murphy.

Galway   L.Kelly, R.Fahy, K.Keane, T.Meehan, J.Divilly, D.Meehan, J.Lardner, A.Donnellan (capt.), M.Higgins, P.Clancy, M.Donnellan, P.Joyce, D.Savage, J.Concannon, D.Reilly. Subs: M.Waldron for J.Lardner, T.Reilly for D.Savage.

1995

Westmeath   A.Lennon, D.Phelan, K.Hickey, F.Murray, M.Murtagh, K.McKinley, S.Deering, D.Gavin (capt.), J.Casey, J.Deehan, T.Cleary, T.Stuart-Trainor, D.Martin, C.Keane, J.Glennon. Sub: C.Lyons for D.Martin.

Derry   D.Hopkins, J.Heaney, M.Kelly, E.McGilloway, P.McFlynn, C.McNally, P.Diamond, J.McBride (capt.), G.Doyle, G.Coleman, E.Muldoon, A.McGuckin, G.Cushnehan, J.Cassidy, G.Cassidy. Subs: D.McGrillis for G.Coleman, P.Wilson for G.Doyle, E.Farren for G.Cushnahan.

1996

Laois R.Darby, P.Langton, M.Buggy, D.O'Hara, N.Collins, D.Conroy, C.Parkinson, M.Delaney (capt.), N.Garvin, O.Delaney, C.Conway, S.Kelly, B.McDonald, D.Doogue, K.Fitzpatrick.
Kerry K.O'Keeffe, K.Leen, M.McCarthy, O.O'Connell, P.McCarthy, T.Ó Sé, P.Murphy, J.Lynch (capt.), J.Sugrue, N.Kenneally, B.O'Connor, L.Murphy, M.Cahill, G.Clifford, J.Twiss. Subs: A.Mac Gearailt for J.Lynch, M.Beckett for J.Sugrue, R.Lynch for M.Cahill.

1997

Laois M.Leigh, P.McDonald, E.Bland, T.Mulligan, D.Mullins, J.Higgins, J.P.Kehoe, B.Fitzpatrick, D.Rooney, M.Lambe, S.Kelly, T.Kelly, K.Kelly (capt.), B.McDonald, M.Hovendon.
Tyrone G.Maguire, K.O'Brien, G.Gourley, B.Donnelly, A.Ball, D.McCrossan (capt.), G.Hetherington, C.McAnallen, K.Hughes, J.Campbell, B.McGuigan, C.Martin, M.Harte, R.Thornton, S.O'Neill. Subs: B.O'Neill for C.Martink, C.McGinley for G.Hetherington.

1998

Tyrone P.McConnell; G.Devlin, M.McGee, F.Loughran; C.Meenagh, D.O'Hanlon, P.O'Neill; C.McAnallen, K.Hughes; G.Wylie, M.Hughes, S.O'Neill; A.Lynch, E.McGinley, E.Mulligan. Subs: B.McGuigan for M.Hughes, R.O'Neill for K.Hughes.
Laois J.Graham; R.Jones, B.Gaynor, C.Clear; A.Fennelly, P.Leonard, B.McCormack; B.Fitzpatrick, J.Behan; M.Dunne, B.McDonald, K.Kelly, J.M.McDonald, P.Clancy, M.Clancy. Subs: B.O'Connell for M.Clancy, J.Moran for J.M.McDonald, D.Walsh for M.Dunne.

1999

Down J.Sloan, J.Clarke, B.Grant, M.Doran, B.Kearney, L.Doyle, C.Murtagh, L.Sloan, B.Coulter, D.McGrady, M.Walsh, R.Murtagh, P.J.McAlinden, J.Fegan, R.Sexton.
Mayo J.O'Hara, M.J.Meenaghan, P.Kelly, J.Brogan, R.Keane, P.Coady, C.Moran, J.Gill, G.Duffy, R.Moran, B.J.Padden, B.Loftus, G.Dillon, A.Dillon, E.Gallagher. Subs: D.Costelloe for E.Gallagher, J.Moran for B.Loftus.

2000

Cork Kevin Murphy, N.O'Donovan, P.Deane, E.Bourke, N.O'Leary, D.O'Hare, P.McCarthy, G.McLoughlin, Kieran Murphy, M.O'Connor, C.Murphy, J.Collins, J.Masters, K.McMahon, C.Brosnan. Subs: D.Barron for O'Connor, D.Burns for McLoughlin.
Mayo D.Clarke, R.Keane, R.Walshe, D.Geraghty, D.Costello, E.Devenney, C.Moran, E.Barrett, A.Burke, P.Prenty, C.Mortimer, D.Flynn, P.Carey, A.Dillon, T.Geraghty. Subs: S.Drake for Devenney, J.Morrin for T.Geraghty.

2001

Tyrone J.Devine, R.O'Neill, D.Carlin, N.McStravog, J.McMahon, K.McCrory, P.Quinn, P.Donnelly, S.Cavanagh, C.Donnelly, B.Mulligan, T.McGuigan, L.Meenan, M.Penrose, G.Toner. Sub: N.Gormley for Meenan.
(Note: Tyrone started with the same 15 as in the drawn final Subs used in the drawn final were – A.Donaghy for Mulligan, P.Rafferty for Toner.)
Dublin P.Copeland, D.McCann, M.Fitzpatrick, D.Galvin, P.Griffin, B.Cullen, B.Lyons, P.Brennan, D.O'Mahony, N.McAuliffe, G.Cullen, G.Brennan, D.O'Callaghan, D.Farrell, J.Noonan. Subs: M.Whelan for G.Brennan, N.Clarke for Galvin, M.Taylor for P.Brennan.
(Note: G.Dent and M.Taylor started the drawn final but not the replay. Subs used in the drawn final were – M.Whelan for P.Brennan, C.Corrigan for Taylor, D.McCann for Dent.)

2002

Derry E.McNicholl, M.McGoldrick, G.O'Kane, J.Keenan, C.McCallon, M.Lynch, P.O'Hea, P.Bradley, R.Convery, B.McGoldrick, C.O'Kane, C.Moran, J.Bateson, P.Young, C.Mullan.
Meath M.Brennan, B.O'Reilly, T.O'Connor, D.O'Halloran, S.Stephens, C.King, E.Dunne, J.Melia, F.Murphy, D.Murtagh, P.Murray, G.McCullagh, B.Regan, J.Sheridan, B.Farrell. Subs: R.Brennan for O'Halloran, M.Whearty for Regan, T.Farrelly for Murray, A.Reynolds for McCullagh, A.Johnson for Dunne.

2003

Laois C.Gorman, C.Healy, C.Ryan, R.Stapleton, P.O'Leary, C.Begley, N.Donagher, B.Quigley, C.Rogers, D.Bergin, Colm Kelly (Stradbally), P.McNulty, M.Tierney, D.Brennan, Colm Kelly (St. Joseph's). Subs: I.Fleming for C.Kelly (Stradbally), D.Murphy for Tierney.
(Note: Laois used the same starting 15 in the drawn final. Subs in the drawn final were – B.Fitzgerald for C.Kelly (Stradbally), D.Murphy for McNulty)
Dublin K.Walsh, A.Downes, K.Cleere, W.Lowry, C.Murtagh, G.Brennan, I.Ward, B.Phelan, J.Coughlan, M.Vaughan, F.Fitzgerald, G.O'Meara, J.O'Hara, K.Leahy, B.Kennedy. Subs: J.Brogan for O'Hara, D.Walsh for Downes, M.Hallows for Murtagh, W.Moore for Fitzgerald.
(Note: D.Reilly, F.Fitzgerald and A.Relihan started in the drawn final, but not in the replay. Subs in the drawn final were – F.Fitzgerald for Brennan, J.O'Brien for Kennedy, C.Moore for O'Hara)

2004

Tyrone J.Curran, N.McGinn, P.Marlow, D.Burke, J.Gilmore, N.Kerr, M.Murray, R.Mulgrew, S.O'Hagan, C.O'Neill, M.Cunningham, R.McRory, G.Devlin, C.Cavanagh, A.Cassidy. Subs: P.J.Quinn for Murray, C.McCarron for Cavanagh, J.Kelly for O'Neill, S.O'Neill for Burke, S.Donaghy for O'Hagan.
Kerry B.Kealy, P.Reidy, L.Quinn, K.Young, D.Doyle, C.Kelliher, D.O'Connor, B.Moran, A.Kennelly, D.O'Sullivan, S.Murphy, M.O'Donoghue, M.Evans, R.Keating, P.O'Connor. Subs: P.Curran for Keating, E.Mangan for O'Donoghue, D.Culloty for Kelliher, B.Looney for Murphy.

2005

Down M.McAllister, G.Magee, C.Garvey, H.Magee, G.McCartan, E.McConville, K.Duffin, J.Colgan, P.Fitzpatrick, D.Lavery, M.Clarke, S.Grant, C.Brannigan, R.Kelly, P.McCumiskey. Subs: R.Kerr for Grant, C.Murney for Duffin, C.Clerkin for Lavery, K.McKernan for Fitzpatrick, G.Joyce for McAllister.
Mayo S.Nallen, J.Burke, G.Cafferkey, P.Healy, C.Barrett, T.Cuniffe, D.Hughes, P.Collins, D.O'Connor, P.Hanley, A.Campbell, D.Kilcullen, R.O'Boyle, P.O'Connor, M.Sweeney. Subs: S.O'Shea for Burke, G.O'Boyle for P.O'Connor, K.Barnicle for Nallen, J.Noone for O'Boyle, S.Kelly for Kilcullen.

2006

Roscommon M.Miley, P.Domican, P.Gleeson, S.Ormsby, N.Carty, D.Flynn, C.Garvey, D.Keenan, D.Shine, F.Cregg, D.O'Hara, C.Devaney, P.Garvey, J.McKeague, K.Waldron. Subs: C.McHugh for McKeague, A.O'Hara for P.Garvey. Subs: N.Carty for McLoughlin, K.Waldron for Higgins, A.O'Hara for P.Garvey, C.Smith for McKeague.

Kerry T.Mac an tSaoir, B.Russell, M.Maloney, D.Ó Sé, S.Enright, A.Greadey, B.Costello, T.Walsh, D.Moran, P.Curtin, G.O'Driscoll, J.Buckley, G.Sayers, P.Curran, E.Kennedy. Subs: D.O'Shea for Buckley, S.Browne for Costello, J.Doolan for Curtin. Subs: P.Curtin for Ó Sé, S.Brown for Russell, J.Doolan for Sayers, W.Devane for Buckley.
(Note: In the drawn encounter for Roscommon M.McLoughlin and K.Higgins started for N.Carty and K.Waldron while for Kerry D.O'Shea started for J.Buckley.)

2007
Galway O.Higgins, E.Glynn, C.Forde, K.Kelly, C.Doherty, D.O'Reilly, T.Fahy, P.Conroy, A.Griffin, J.J.Greaney, M.Martyn, J.O'Brien, J.Ryan, T.Walsh, D.Reddington. Subs: J.Burke for Ryan, O.O'Brien for Greaney.
Derry A.Warnock, M.McKinney, C.McWilliams, D.Bell, N.Forrester, J.F.Bradley, B.Henry, C.McKaigue, C.O'Boyle, J.Kielt, S.Cleary, D.Mullan, A.Heron, G.McGeehan, L.Moore. Subs: D.Heavron for Forrester, C.McFeely for Cleary, L.Kennedy for Heron.

2008
Tyrone T.Harney, S.McRory, G.Teague, F.McQuaid, R.McNabb, P.Harte, R.Tierney, N.McKenna, R.Keenan, C.Gervin, D.McNulty, M.Donnelly, K.Coney, P.McNiece, C.O'Neill. Subs: K.Mossey for McRory, S.Warnock for McNulty, B.McGarvey for Tierney.
Mayo R.Hennelly, D.Dolan, K.Keane, J.Broderick, S.McHale, E.Reilly, S.Nally, J.Cafferty, G.McDonagh, C.Freeman, A.O'Shea, R.Geraghty, K.Charlton, A.Walsh, A.Corduff. Subs: D.O'Hara for Charlton, D.Gavin for Geraghty, J.Carney for McHale.
(Note: In the drawn encounter for Tyrone R.Pickering and M.Rogers started for R.Tierney and R.Keenan. Mayo started with the same 15. Subs in the drawn match were; Tyrone: R.Tierney for McRory, S.Warnock for Rogers, B.McGarvey for McNabb. Mayo: D.Galvin for Charlton, D.O'Hara for Geraghty.)

2009
Armagh S.O'Reilly, K.Downey, R.Finnegan, D.McKenna, K.Nugent, N.Rowland, J.Morgan, P.Carragher, A.Murnin, R.Grugan, J.Donnelly, C.King, R.Tasker, E.McVerry, G.McPartland. Subs: C.McCafferty for Finnegan, T.McAlinden for McVerry.
Mayo M.Schlingermann, D.Gavin, K.Rogers, M.Walsh, C.Charlton, S.McDermott, C.Crowe, D.Kirby, A.Walsh, D.Coen, A.Farrell, F.Durkan, B.Ruttledge, A.Corduff, C.O'Connor. Subs: J.Carney for Farrell, J.McDonnell for Coen.

2010
Tyrone C.Spiers, S.McGarrity, C.Clarke, H.P.McGeary, N.Sludden, M.Donaghy, E.Deeney, H.Óg Conlon, C.Grugan, R.Donnelly, T.Canavan, R.Devlin, S.Tierney, J.McCullagh, R.O'Neill. Subs: P.McNulty for Donaghy, L.Girvan for Devlin, D.Donnelly for Tierney.
Cork D.Hanrahan, J.Wall, T.Clancy, A.Cronin, K.Fulignati, M.O'Shea, C.O'Sullivan, J.Burns, D.Cahalane, K.Hallisey, T.Hegarty, J.O'Rourke, D.McEoin, M.Sugure, B.Hurley. Subs: D.Fitzgerald for Hegarty, L.Connolly for Sugure, D.O'Donovan, for Filignati, S.O'Mahony for O'Sullivan, K.Sheehan for O'Rourke.

2011
Tipperary E.Comerford, N.O'Sullivan, J.Meagher, C.O'Sullivan, C.O'Riordan, D.Fitzelle, S.Kennedy, S.O'Brien, I.Fahey, G.Henry, J.McGrath, B.Maher, L.McGrath, M.Quinlivan, T.J.Ryan. Subs: P.Quirke for J.McGrath, C.Kennedy for Ryan, A.McGuire for O'Riordan, J.Lonergan for Henry, J.Martin for Maher.
Dublin R.O'Hanlon, G.Hannigan, R.McDaid, R.Real, E.Lowndes, J.Small, J.McCaffrey, P.O'Higgins, E.Ó Conghaile, C.Costello, C.Kilkenny, G.Ivory, S.Fulham, P.Mannion, C.Meaney. Subs: D.Campbell for Meaney, D.Byrne for Hannigan, N.Scully for Fulham.

2012
Dublin L.Molloy, E.Mullan, D.Byrne, R.McGowan, E.Lowndes, C.Mullally, M.McDonncha, S.Cunningham, S.Carthy, G.Burke, C.McHugh, N.Walsh, R.Gaughan, C.Costello, N.Scully. Subs: D.Gormley for Burke, D.Campbell for Walsh, M.Deegan for Scully.
Meath R.Burlingham, R.Ó Coileann, B.Power, S.Gallagher, D.Smyth, P.Harnan, S.Lavin, S.McEntee, A.Flanagan, C.O'Sullivan, J.Daly, J.McEntee, B.Dardis, F.Ward, S.Coogan. Subs: P.Kennelly for Dardis, H.Rooney for Coogan, C.Carlton for Smyth, C.O'Griofa for Ward, C.O'Brien for Daly.

2013
Mayo M.Mulligan, E.Doran, S.Cunniffe, D.Kenny, M.Hall, S.Coen, S.Conlon, V.Roughneen, D.O'Connor, C.Loftus, M.Plunkett, P.Prendergast, D.Doherty, L.Irwin, T.Conroy. Subs: C.Byrne for Doherty, H.Cafferty for Plunkett.
Tyrone S.Fox, C.Byrne, R.Quinn, C.McCann, S.Hamill, C.Morris, P.McGirr, R.Nugent, F.Burns, D.Mulgrew, C.McKenna, R.McGlone, L.Brennan, D.Gallagher, S.McGrath. Subs: C.McShane for McGlone, P.Donnelly for McGrath, M.Lynn for McGirr, C.O'Donnell for Gallagher.

2014
Kerry S.Ryan, D.O'Donoghue, B.Ó Beaglaoich, T.O'Sullivan, B.Sugrue, A.Barry, C.Coffey, B.O'Sullivan, M.O'Connor, M.Burns, B.Rayel, M.Flaherty, K.Spillane, L.Kearney, T.Ó Sé. Subs: L.Carey for Coffey, J.Kiely for Kearney, R.Wahrton for Sugrue, S.O'Sullivan for Ó Sé, I.Parker for Rayel.
Donegal D.Rodgers, D.Monagle, C.Gillespie, C.Kelly, S.McMenamin, T.McCleneghan, C.Mulligan, E.Gallagher, M.McGonagle, S.McBrearty, L.Connor, M.Carroll, J.Brennan, J.Campbell, E.O'Donnell. Subs: N.Harley for Kelly, G.McBride for O'Donnell, C.Bonner for Gallagher, C.Diver for Harley.

2015
Kerry B.Courtney, D.Brosnan, J.Foley, T.O'Sullivan, J.Moran, A.Barry, G.White, M.O'Connor, J.M.Foley, B.Ó Seanachain, S.O'Shea, B.Barrett, N.Foley, B.Sweeney, C.Geaney. Subs: S.O'Sullivan for Barrett, J.Duggan for J.Foley, M.Breen for J.M.Foley, D.O'Brien for T.O'Sullivan, D.Ó Sé for Brosnan, G.O'Sullivam for Morgan.
Tipperary C.Manton, T.Fitzgerald, J.Sheehan, T.Lowry, D.Owens, L.Fahy, E.Moloney, J.Kennedy, T.Nolan, A.Buckley, A.Tynan, C.English, S.Quirke, B.McGrath, B.Martin. Subs: J.Bergin for English, R.Peters for Buckley, M.Irwin for Fitzgerald, M.Kehoe for McGrath, G.Whelan for Moloney, C.Cashman for Martin.

2016

Kerry B.Courtney, D.Naughten, N.Collins, G.O'Sullivan, M.Potts, D.O'Brien, M.Foley, M.Breen, M.Ryan, D.O'Connor, S.O'Shea, D.Moynihan, B.Friel, D.Clifford, D.Shaw. Subs: C.Linnane for Friel, C.Teahan for Collins, B.Sweeney for Shaw, K.Dwyer for Foley, S.Okunbor for O'Connor.

Galway C.Haslam, L.Boyle, S.Mulkerrin, E.McFadden, A.Quirke, E.McDonagh, F.Garvey, C.Darcy, J.Maher, F.Ó Laoi, E.Murphy, R.Forde, R.Finnerty, S.Raftery, D.Connelly. Subs: B.Goldrick for E.Murphy, R.Murphy for Raftery, R.Cunningham for Finnerty, E.Deely for Garvey.

2017

Kerry D.Uosis, C.O'Donoghue, M.Potts, S.O'Leary, C.Gammell, P.Warren, N.Donohue, B.Mahony, D.O'Connor, A.Donoghue, B.Friel, F.Clifford, J.Griffin, D.Clifford, Donal O'Sullivan. Subs: E.Horan for Griffin, Donnchadh O'Sullivan for Donal O'Sullivan, C.O'Reilly for F.Clifford, M.O'Leary for Gammell, R.O'Neill for Donohue, M.Slattery for Donoghue.

Derry O.Hartin, O.McGill, C.McCluskey, S.McKeever, C.McShane, S.McErlain, P.McGrogan, O.McWilliams, D.Rafferty, R.Mullan, M.Bradley, P.Quigg, M.McGrogan, L.McWilliams, B.McCarron. Subs: C.Brown for Rafferty, C.Quinn for McCarron, D.Cassidy for McCluskey, O.Quinn for McShane, T.McHugh for Mullan, P.Devlin for McGrogan.

CAPTAINS OF WINNING ALL-IRELAND MINOR FOOTBALL TEAMS

1929	G.Comerford (Clare)
1930	B.Synott (Dublin)
1931	J.O'Gorman (Kerry)
1932	C.O'Sullivan (Kerry)
1933	T.O'Leary (Kerry)
1934	A.Greensmith (Tipperary)
1935	W.Durkin (Mayo)
1936	L.McEntee (Louth)
1937	J.J.McCormack (Cavan)
1938	P.Conaty (Cavan)
1939	L.Gilmartin (Roscommon)
1940	B.Burke (Louth)
1941	W.Carlos {Roscommon)
1942-1944	Suspended
1945	S.McEntaggart (Dublin)
1946	T.Moriarty (Kerry)
1947	E.Devlin (Tyrone)
1948	E.Devlin (Tyrone)
1949	S.Blaney (Armagh)
1950	M.Brosnan (Kerry)
1951	B.Molloy (Roscommon)
1952	B.Mahon (Galway)
1953	E.Walsh (Mayo)
1955	P.Heron (Dublin)
1956	L.Foley (Dublin)
1957	B.Cahill (Meath)
1958	D.Foley (Dublin)
1959	M.Kissane (Dublin)
1960	S.Cleary (Galway)
1961	E.Coughlan (Cork)
1962	S.O'Mahony (Kerry)
1963	T.O'Hanlon (Kerry)
1964	S.Grogan (Offaly)
1965	T.Diamond (Derry)
1966	S.O'Dowd (Mayo)
1967	D.Aherne (Cork)
1968	D.Aherne (Cork)
1969	E.Fitzpatrick (Cork)
1970	J.Corcoran (Galway)
1971	J.P.Kean (Mayo)
1972	G.Aherne (Cork)
1973	D.McKenna (Tyrone)
1974	E.Desmond (Cork)

1975	R.Bunyan (Kerry)
1976	G.Burke (Galway)
1977	J.McCartan (Down)
1978	A.Garvey (Mayo)
1979	M.Loftus (Dublin)
1980	T.Dee (Kerry)
1981	V.Hedderman (Cork)
1982	L.O'Rourke (Dublin)
1983	D.McNicholl (Derry)
1984	P.Clarke (Dublin)
1985	M.Fitzmaurice (Mayo)
1986	J.Joyce (Galway)
1987	M.Quinn (Down)
1988	D.Cahill (Kerry)
1989	G.Coleman (Derry)
1990	E.McManus (Meath)
1991	A.McCarthy (Cork)
1992	P.O'Sullivan (Meath)
1993	B.Cuthbert (Cork
1994	J.Ferriter (Kerry)
1995	D.Gavin (Westmeath)
1996	M.Delaney (Laois)
1997	K.Kelly (Laois)
1998	C.McAnallen {Tyrone)
1999	L.Doyle (Down)
2000	J.Masters (Cork)
2001	P.Donnelly (Tyrone)
2002	G.O'Kane (Derry)
2003	C.Rogers (Laois)
2004	M.Cunningham (Tyrone)
2005	J.Colgan (Down)
2006	D.Flynn (Roscommon)
2007	P.Conroy (Galway)
2008	R.Pickering (Tyrone)
2009	D.McKenna (Armagh)
2010	S.McGarrity (Tyrone)
2011	L.McGrath (Tipperary)
2012	D.Byrne (Dublin)
2013	S.Coen (Mayo)
2014	L.Kearney (Kerry)
2015	M.O'Connor (Kerry)
2016	S.O'Shea (Kerry)
2017	D.Clifford (Kerry)

ALL-IRELAND MINOR FOOTBALL FINAL REFEREES

1929	Seán Robbins (Offaly)
1930	Jack McCarthy (Kerry)
1931	Patsy Fearon (Armagh)
1932	Seán Robbins (Offaly)
1933	John Doyle (Dublin)
1934	No final – Tipperary awarded title.
1935	P. J. Masterson (Cavan)
1936	Tom Shevlin (Roscommon)
1937	Stephen Synott (Dublin)
1938	P. Ratty (Meath)
1939	P. Ratty (Meath)
1940	P. J. Masterson (Cavan)
1941	Seán Kennedy (Dublinl
1945	P. J. Masterson {Cavan)
1946	Brendan Nestor (Galway)
1947	J. Dowling (Kildare)
1948	John Dunne (Galway)
1949	Gerald Courell (Mayo)
1950	J. Shanely (Leitrim)
1951	Peter McDermott (Meath)
1952	Seán Óg Ó Ceallacháin (Dublin)
1953	D. King (Down)
1954	Bill Jackson (Roscommon)
1955	Patsy Geraghty (Galway)
1956	Gus Cremins (Kerry)
1957	C. Costello (Galway)
1958	P. Silke (Galway)
1959	P. Geraghty (Galway)
1960	M. McArdle (Louth)
1961	Brian Smith (Meath)
1962	Jimmy Hatton (Wicklow)
1963	Jackie Martin (Tyrone)
1964	Mick Loftus (Mayo)
1965	Jimmy Hatton (Wicklow)
1966	Eamon Moules (Wicklow)
1967	Patsy Devlin (Tyrone)
1968	Liam Maguire (Monaghan)
1969	Brendan Louth (Dublin)
1970	P. Greene (Antrim)
1971	Fintan Tierney (Cavan)
1972	M. Hynes (Roscommon)
1973	P. O'Gorman (Sligo)
1974	Paddy Collins (Westmeath)

1975	P. J. McGrath (Mayo)
1976	Martin Meally (Kilkenny)
1977	Tommy Moran (Leitrim)
1978	Jimmy Dennigan (Cork)
1979	P. J. McGrath (Mayo)
1980	Seamus Murray (Monaghan)
1981	Tony Jordan (Dublin)
1982	J. Keaney (Tyrone)
1983	P. Kavanagh (Meath)
1984	J. Mullaney (Roscommon)
1985	Gerry McGlory (Antrim)
1986	Carthage Buckley (Offaly)
1987	Seamus Prior (Leitrim)
1988	Michael Greenan (Cavan)
1989	Paddy Russell (Tipperary)
1990	Damien Campbell (Fermanagh)
1991	Tommy McDermott (Cavan)
1992	Seamus Prior (Leitrim)
1993	Michael Cranny (Down)
1994	Pat Casserly (Westmeath)
1995	Michael Curley (Galway)
1996	Brian White (Wexford)
1997	John Bannon (Longford)
1998	Michael Curley (Galway)
1999	Seamus McCormack (Meath)
2000	M.Monaghan (Kildare)
2001	M.Daly (Mayo)
Replay	D.Joyce (Galway)
2002	M.Ryan (Limerick)
2003	J.Geany (Cork)
Replay	M.Hughes (Tyrone)
2004	T.Quigley (Wexford)
2005	M.Deegan (Laois)
2006	S.Doyle (Wexford)
Replay	P.Hughes (Armagh)
2007	D.Fahy (Longford).
2008	R.Hickey (Clare)
Replay	C.Reilly (Meath)
2009	E.Kinsella (Laois)
2010	M.Duffy (Sligo)
2011	P.Hughes (Armagh)
2012	B.Cassidy (Derry)
2013	C.Lane (Cork)
2014	F.Kelly (Longford)
2015	D.Gough (Meath)
2016	C.Branagan (Down)
2017	A.Nolan (Wicklow)

MUNSTER MINOR FOOTBALL FINALS

1929	Clare	1-6	0-4	Waterford
1930	Clare	2-3	1-3	Tipperary
1931	Kerry	3-6	0-7	Tipperary
1932	Kerry	4-5	2-5	Cork
1933	Kerry	2-9	3-4	Cork
1934	Tipperary	3-10	0-5	Waterford
1935	Tipperary	3-5	0-4	Cork
1936	Kerry	1-5	1-2	Tipperary
1937	Kerry	3-8	1-2	Clare
1938	Kerry	8-9	1-2	Cork
1939	Cork	3-3	3-2	Kerry
1940	Kerry	1-3	1-2	Clare
1941	Kerry	7-5	2-1	Waterford
1942-1944	Championship suspended			
1945	Kerry	2-4	2-3	Cork
1946	Kerry	4-7	0-2	Tipperary
1947	Kerry	0-7	1-3	Cork
1948	Kerry	3-4	1-5	Cork
1949	Kerry	0-7	0-5	Cork
1950	Kerry	4-10	1-5	Limerick
1951	Kerry	0-7	1-3	Cork
1952	Cork	3-9	1-1	Clare
1953	Clare	0-7	0-2	Cork
1954	Kerry	4-10	1-3	Cork
1955	Tipperary	0-9	1-6	Kerry
Replay	Tipperary	0-9	1-5	Kerry
1956	Limerick	1-7	1-5	Kerry
1957	Kerry	1-5	0-5	Cork
1958	Kerry	3-11	0-4	Waterford
1959	Cork	2-7	0-7	Kerry
1960	Cork	3-8	0-7	Kerry
1961	Cork	2-12	0-2	Clare
1962	Kerry	2-9	0-9	Cork
1963	Kerry	0-8	0-8	Cork
Replay	Kerry	0-11	0-4	Cork
1964	Cork	4-11	0-5	Clare
1965	Kerry	3-11	1-5	Cork
1966	Cork	5-12	1-7	Kerry
1967	Cork	2-8	0-3	Kerry
1968	Cork	2-13	0-2	Kerry
1969	Cork	3-11	0-12	Kerry
1970	Kerry	4-9	1-11	Cork
1971	Cork	2-13	1-2	Kerry
1972	Cork	2-14	1-14	Kerry
1973	Cork	1-13	3-5	Kerry
1974	Cork	0-13	1-6	Kerry
1975	Kerry	3-7	1-11	Cork
1976	Cork	0-10	1-5	Kerry

1977	Cork	1-7	1-3	Kerry
1978	Kerry	1-4	0-6	Cork
1979	Kerry	3-6	2-9	Cork
Replay	Kerry	1-11	1-5	Cork
1980	Kerry	1-12	1-10	Cork
1981	Cork	0-9	1-5	Kerry
1982	Kerry	1-11	0-5	Cork
1983	Cork	1-11	1-5	Tipperary
1984	Tipperary	2-3	0-8	Kerry
1985	Cork	1-8	0-4	Kerry
1986	Cork	2-12	0-4	Kerry
1987	Cork	0-8	0-8	Kerry
Replay	Cork	0-12	1-8	Kerry
1988	Kerry	1-8	0-10	Cork
1989	Kerry	2-10	2-9	Cork
1990	Kerry	1-10	0-3	Cork
1991	Cork	0-10	0-8	Kerry
1992	Cork	0-11	2-5	Kerry
Replay	Cork	3-6	2-7	Kerry
1993	Cork	2-15	2-7	Tipperary
1994	Kerry	2-11	3-5	Clare
1995	Tipperary	2-6	0-10	Cork
1996	Kerry	3-9	2-6	Cork
1997	Kerry	4-12	1-7	Limerick
1998	Kerry	2-11	0-8	Limerick
1999	Cork	2-16	1-9	Kerry
2000	Cork	1-13	0-14	Kerry
2001	Kerry	0-15	0-12	Cork
2002	Kerry	3-16	2-6	Tipperary
2003	Kerry	1-14	0-10	Cork
2004	Kerry	0-9	0-9	Cork
Replay	Kerry	0-13	1-7	Cork
2005	Cork	3-8	1-11	Kerry
2006	Kerry	1-13	0-8	Tipperary
2007	Cork	1-16	2-8	Kerry
2008	Kerry	1-9	1-9	Tipperary
Replay	Kerry	2-12	0-8	Tipperary
2009	Kerry	0-12	0-6	Tipperary
2010	Cork	1-8	1-7	Kerry
2011	Tipperary	3-11	1-9	Cork
2012	Tipperary	2-14	1-14	Kerry
2013	Kerry	0-15	0-10	Tipperary
2014	Kerry	2-17	2-13	Cork
2015	Kerry	2-14	1-11	Tipperary
2016	Kerry	3-14	3-8	Cork
2017	Kerry	2-21	0-3	Clare

LEINSTER MINOR FOOTBALL FINALS

1929	Longford	3-4	1-4	Dublin
1930	Dublin	1-6	0-4	Longford
1931	Louth	1-5	0-3	Wexford
1932	Laois	3-2	1-7	Louth
1933	Dublin	3-7	0-6	Laois
1934	Dublin	0-5	0-2	Kildare
1935	Louth	1-7	1-6	Dublin
1936	Louth	3-6	2-1	Wexford
1937	Wexford	2-7	2-5	Louth
1938	Longford	3-6	2-8	Louth
1939	Westmeath	1-2	0-2	Louth
1940	Louth	3-5	1-6	Kildare
1941	Louth	4-4	1-6	Wexford
1942	Louth	5-10	0-6	Kildare
1943-1944	Championship suspended			
1945	Dublin	3-5	1-0	Wexford
1946	Dublin	4-6	0-3	Meath
1947	Offaly	1-7	1-7	Dublin
Replay	Offaly	1-7	1-5	Dublin
1948	Dublin	2-5	1-6	Offaly
1949	Dublin	3-10	1-5	Kildare
1950	Wexford	3-6	2-8	Dublin
1951	Louth	3-9	2-5	Westmeath
1952	Westmeath	3-14	3-3	Wicklow
1953	Louth	1-6	0-6	Kildare
1954	Dublin	2-7	0-11	Meath
1955	Dublin	2-11	1-4	Meath
1956	Dublin	1-10	1-9	Meath
1957	Meath	0-8	0-5	Offaly
1958	Dublin	2-10	1-6	Louth
1959	Dublin	3-13	1-7	Offaly
1960	Offaly	1-12	1-5	Louth
1961	Dublin	2-8	1-8	Offaly
1962	Offaly	2-8	1-4	Dublin
1963	Westmeath	2-14	3-7	Dublin
1964	Offaly	1-7	1-6	Laois
1965	Offaly	2-11	1-5	Kildare
1966	Laois	1-10	0-7	Offaly
1967	Laois	1-8	2-4	Dublin
1968	Dublin	1-11	0-8	Laois
1969	Wexford	0-11	0-7	Dublin
1970	Dublin	2-8	0-13	Meath
1971	Dublin	2-7	0-4	Louth
1972	Meath	3-8	1-10	Dublin
1973	Kildare	4-11	0-10	Laois
1974	Wicklow	5-6	1-9	Longford
1975	Kildare	2-9	3-5	Meath
1976	Dublin	2-8	0-13	Offaly

FOOTBALL

1977	Meath	1-7	0-9	Dublin
1978	Dublin	3-12	0-11	Wexford
1979	Dublin	2-13	0-8	Meath
1980	Meath	1-12	1-9	Kildare
1981	Dublin	1-8	0-9	Meath
1982	Dublin	0-10	0-4	Westmeath
1983	Kildare	1-11	1-6	Meath
1984	Dublin	0-12	1-6	Westmeath
1985	Meath	0-11	1-4	Offaly
1986	Dublin	2-16	0-6	Meath
1987	Kildare	0-13	2-5	Dublin
1988	Dublin	4-6	0-8	Meath
1989	Offaly	2-11	0-7	Kildare
1990	Meath	1-19	1-6	Kildare
1991	Kildare	2-8	0-12	Dublin
1992	Meath	1-8	1-5	Westmeath
1993	Meath	1-16	3-3	Wicklow
1994	Dublin	2-12	2-6	Wexford
1995	Westmeath	0-12	1-9	Laois
Replay	Westmeath	3-12	2-15	Laois (aet)
Replay	Westmeath	1-10	0-9	Laois
1996	Laois	0-15	2-9	Dublin
Replay	Laois	2-18	1-8	Dublin
1997	Laois	2-11	0-10	Wicklow
1998	Laois	2-9	0-12	Dublin
1999	Dublin	1-13	2-10	Wexford
Replay	Dublin	2-13	1-12	Wexford
2000	Westmeath	2-9	1-10	Dublin
2001	Dublin	1-17	0-6	Offaly
2002	Longford	3-8	3-5	Meath
2003	Dublin	1-11	1-9	Laois
2004	Laois	0-10	0-6	Kildare
2005	Laois	1-12	1-7	Offaly
2006	Meath	1-16	2-5	Offaly
2007	Laois	3-8	1-12	Carlow
2008	Meath	1-14	2-10	Offaly
2009	Dublin	1-10	1-10	Kildare
Replay	Dublin	1-15	1-10	Kildare (aet)
2010	Longford	0-14	0-8	Offaly
2011	Dublin	2-18	1-11	Meath
2012	Dublin	3-17	1-11	Meath
2013	Kildare	2-15	2-7	Westmeath
2014	Dublin	3-16	1-12	Kildare
2015	Kildare	2-15	1-9	Longford
2016	Kildare	1-18	0-10	Laois
2017	Dublin	2-19	0-12	Louth

CONNACHT MINOR FOOTBALL FINALS

1930	Mayo	3-4	1-1	Sligo
1931	Mayo	2-7	0-3	Sligo
1932	Galway	2-5	2-3	Mayo
1933	Mayo	5-7	0-6	Roscommon
1934	Mayo	2-13	0-5	Galway
1935	Mayo	2-2	1-4	Sligo
1936	Mayo	4-9	1-8	Sligo
1937	Galway	2-8	1-3	Mayo
1938	Galway	6-5	1-6	Leitrim
1939	Roscommon	1-10	1-3	Mayo
1940	Mayo	8-5	1-6	Leitrim
1941	Roscommon	2-6	0-6	Galway
1942-1944	Championship suspended			
1945	Leitrim	1-5	2-2	Sligo
Replay	Leitrim	2-6	1-5	Sligo
1946	Mayo	4-9	1-5	Galway
1947	Mayo	3-6	2-5	Sligo
1948	Galway	3-6	1-3	Sligo
1949	Roscommon	2-4	1-7	Sligo
Replay	Roscommon	3-10	2-7	Sligo
	(Sligo awarded title on objection)			
1950	Mayo	3-7	1-4	Roscommon
1951	Galway	1-8	2-4	Roscommon
	(Roscommon awarded title on objection)			
1952	Galway	4-11	0-3	Sligo
1953	Mayo	1-9	1-3	Roscommon
1954	Mayo	9-16	0-4	Sligo
1955	Mayo	2-5	1-5	Galway
1956	Leitrim	2-7	1-6	Roscommon
1957	Mayo	4-4	2-5	Leitrim
1958	Mayo	1-8	1-4	Roscommon
1959	Galway	3-9	1-8	Mayo
1960	Galway	4-11	0-3	Roscommon
1961	Mayo	5-8	0-5	Sligo
1962	Mayo	7-8	0-10	Galway
1963	Mayo	3-5	1-5	Roscommon
1964	Mayo	2-7	1-3	Galway
1965	Roscommon	2-10	1-10	Mayo
1966	Mayo	1-9	0-7	Roscommon
1967	Roscommon	2-5	1-5	Mayo
1968	Sligo	1-8	0-7	Galway
1969	Galway	3-3	0-8	Mayo
1970	Galway	2-11	1-6	Mayo
1971	Mayo	2-12	1-8	Roscommon
1972	Galway	4-11	1-11	Roscommon
1973	Mayo	3-7	0-3	Galway
1974	Mayo	4-12	2-3	Roscommon
1975	Roscommon	1-15	0-5	Galway

1976	Galway	6-16	3-3	Sligo
1977	Mayo	2-20	0-7	Leitrim
1978	Mayo	2-6	0-4	Galway
1979	Mayo	5-11	3-7	Galway
1980	Mayo	3-8	2-9	Roscommon
1981	Roscommon	2-8	3-4	Mayo
1982	Galway	1-7	0-7	Leitrim
1983	Galway	2-10	2-5	Roscommon
1984	Roscommon	1-11	2-8	Mayo
Replay	Roscommon	3-9	2-8	Mayo
1985	Mayo	0-6	1-1	Galway
1986	Galway	1-9	2-1	Mayo
1987	Galway	2-8	2-4	Mayo
1988	Galway	2-9	3-4	Mayo
1989	Galway	2-8	0-13	Roscommon

(Provincial Council decides to replay due to disputed penalty goal).

Replay	Roscommon	2-11	0-15	Galway (aet)
1990	Galway	1-18	2-3	Roscommon
1991	Mayo	4-9	0-6	Leitrim
1992	Roscommon	0-10	0-9	Mayo
1993	Galway	0-11	1-8	Mayo
Replay	Galway	3-8	1-10	Mayo
1994	Galway	2-11	0-9	Mayo
1995	Galway	2-14	2-11	Mayo
1996	Mayo	0-10	0-10	Sligo
Replay	Mayo	2-3	0-8	Sligo
1997	Mayo	0-13	0-9	Roscommon
1998	Leitrim	0-8	0-7	Sligo
1999	Mayo	3-3	1-6	Galway
2000	Mayo	1-12	1-8	Roscommon
2001	Mayo	0-15	0-11	Galway
2002	Galway	1-12	0-6	Leitrim
2003	Galway	1-9	0-9	Mayo
2004	Galway	3-10	2-10	Roscommon
2005	Galway	0-10	0-9	Mayo
2006	Roscommon	0-12	0-9	Mayo
2007	Galway	2-7	0-9	Roscommon
2008	Mayo	0-10	0-7	Roscommon
2009	Mayo	1-5	0-8	Roscommon
Replay	Mayo	1-8	0-5	Roscommon
2010	Mayo	3-9	1-10	Galway
2011	Roscommon	1-9	0-6	Galway
2012	Roscommon	0-10	0-8	Mayo
2013	Mayo	3-7	1-10	Roscommon
2014	Mayo	2-16	0-14	Roscommon
2015	Galway	0-7	1-4	Sligo
Replay	Galway	4-12	1-8	Sligo
2016	Galway	1-9	0-6	Mayo
2017	Galway	3-11	0-10	Sligo

ULSTER MINOR FOOTBALL FINALS

1930	Armagh	3-4	0-10	Monaghan
1931	Tyrone	0-7	0-4	Armagh
1932	Antrim	2-7	1-2	Tyrone
1933	Antrim	2-7	1-1	Armagh
1934	Tyrone	1-4	1-3	Down
1935	Tyrone	2-2	2-1	Donegal

Objection and counter-objection.
Competition declared null and void.

1936	Antrim	2-7	2-4	Tyrone
1937	Cavan	1-10	0-3	Armagh
1938	Cavan	2-7	2-4	Antrim
1939	Monaghan	0-5	0-5	Cavan
Replay	Monaghan	1-8	1-7	Cavan
1940	Monaghan	0-8	0-4	Antrim
1941	Antrim	2-5	1-7	Cavan
1942-1944		Championship suspended		
1945	Monaghan	1-7	0-7	Down
1946	Tyrone	1-4	0-5	Monaghan
1947	Tyrone	3-6	2-8	Armagh
1948	Tyrone	5-7	2-3	Monaghan
1949	Armagh	4-6	1-4	Donegal
1950	Antrim	1-8	1-8	Armagh
Replay	Antrim	1-9	1-1	Armagh
1951	Armagh	3-1	1-4	Cavan
1952	Cavan	1-5	1-3	Down
1953	Armagh	2-15	3-2	Tyrone
1954	Armagh	2-8	0-9	Down
1955	Antrim	4-3	2-6	Cavan
1956	Donegal	2-5	0-6	Armagh
1957	Armagh	3-6	0-10	Donegal
1958	Down	3-9	3-1	Cavan
1959	Cavan	2-11	2-7	Antrim
1960	Down	2-7	1-4	Monaghan
1961	Armagh	3-8	1-4	Monaghan
1962	Down	2-5	0-8	Armagh
1963	Down	4-6	2-11	Donegal
1964	Antrim	2-10	0-6	Cavan
1965	Derry	3-11	2-4	Cavan
1966	Down	1-12	1-9	Derry
1967	Tyrone	0-16	2-5	Fermanagh
1968	Armagh	4-8	1-7	Derry
1969	Derry	1-9	0-5	Tyrone
1970	Derry	1-14	0-11	Fermanagh
1971	Tyrone	0-19	0-7	Fermanagh
1972	Tyrone	3-6	1-6	Cavan
1973	Tyrone	1-13	0-9	Down
1974	Cavan	3-9	1-4	Derry

1975	Tyrone	0-10	0-7	Cavan
1976	Tyrone	5-7	1-9	Cavan
1977	Down	0-8	1-5	Armagh
Replay	Down	0-11	1-6	Armagh
1978	Tyrone	3-11	2-9	Monaghan
1979	Down	1-7	0-6	Tyrone
1980	Derry	3-14	1-2	Armagh
1981	Derry	0-11	1-2	Armagh
1982	Antrim	2-10	3-5	Down
1983	Derry	3-9	0-4	Monaghan
1984	Derry	1-4	0-3	Armagh
1985	Donegal	2-11	1-3	Cavan
1986	Down	1-12	0-10	Derry
1987	Down	1-7	0-4	Armagh
1988	Tyrone	2-7	0-3	Cavan
1989	Derry	2-15	2-3	Armagh
1990	Derry	2-10	2-8	Down
1991	Donegal	1-10	1-9	Tyrone
1992	Armagh	0-13	0-9	Donegal
1993	Tyrone	1-9	1-5	Derry
1994	Armagh	3-13	1-7	Down
1995	Derry	2-12	1-7	Down
1996	Donegal	0-9	0-9	Derry
Replay	Donegal	0-9	1-5	Derry
1997	Tyrone	3-13	2-10	Antrim
1998	Tyrone	4-9	2-2	Antrim
1999	Down	0-10	0-10	Donegal
Replay	Down	2-7	0-9	Donegal
2000	Derry	2-11	1-11	Tyrone
2001	Tyrone	2-13	0-13	Monaghan
2002	Derry	0-12	0-11	Tyrone
2003	Tyrone	3-9	0-9	Fermanagh
2004	Tyrone	0-11	0-11	Down
Replay	Tyrone	0-15	0-8	Down
2005	Armagh	0-11	0-10	Down
2006	Donegal	2-12	1-5	Antrim
2007	Tyrone	0-10	1-6	Derry
2008	Tyrone	0-13	0-10	Monaghan
2009	Armagh	1-8	1-5	Down
2010	Tyrone	1-14	0-5	Armagh
2011	Cavan	0-12	1-6	Armagh
2012	Tyrone	0-14	1-8	Monaghan
2013	Monaghan	4-10	2-14	Tyrone
2014	Donegal	2-12	0-10	Armagh
2015	Derry	1-11	0-11	Cavan
2016	Donegal	2-10	1-11	Derry
2017	Derry	1-22	2-12	Cavan

ALL-IRELAND U21 FOOTBALL FINALS

1964	Kerry	1-10	1-3	Laois
1965	Kildare	2-11	1-7	Cork
1966	Roscommon	2-10	1-12	Kildare
1967	Mayo	2-10	2-10	Kerry
Replay	Mayo	4-9	1-7	Kerry
1968	Derry	3-9	1-9	Offaly
1969	Antrim	1-8	0-10	Roscommon
1970	Cork	2-11	0-9	Fermanagh
1971	Cork	3-10	0-3	Fermanagh
1972	Galway	2-6	0-7	Kerry
1973	Kerry	2-13	0-13	Mayo
1974	Mayo	0-9	0-9	Antrim
Replay	Mayo	2-10	2-8	Antrim
1975	Kerry	1-15	0-10	Dublin
1976	Kerry	0-14	1-3	Kildare
1977	Kerry	1-11	1-5	Down
1978	Roscommon	1-9	1-8	Kerry
1979	Down	1-9	0-7	Cork
1980	Cork	2-8	1-5	Dublin
1981	Cork	0-14	2-8	Galway
Replay	Cork	2-9	1-6	Galway
1982	Donegal	0-8	0-5	Roscommon
1983	Mayo	2-5	1-8	Derry
Replay	Mayo	1-8	1-5	Derry
1984	Cork	0-9	0-6	Mayo
1985	Cork	0-14	1-8	Derry
1986	Cork	3-16	0-12	Offaly
1987	Donegal	1-7	0-10	Kerry
Replay	Donegal	1-12	2-4	Kerry
1988	Offaly	0-11	0-9	Cavan
1989	Cork	2-8	1-10	Galway
1990	Kerry	5-12	2-11	Tyrone
1991	Tyrone	4-16	1-5	Kerry
1992	Tyrone	1-10	1-7	Galway
1993	Meath	1-8	0-10	Kerry
1994	Cork	1-12	1-5	Mayo
1995	Kerry	2-12	3-9	Mayo
Replay	Kerry	3-10	1-12	Mayo
1996	Kerry	1-17	2-10	Cavan
1997	Derry	1-12	0-5	Meath
1998	Kerry	2-8	0-11	Laois
1999	Westmeath	0-12	0-9	Kerry
2000	Tyrone	3-12	0-13	Limerick
2001	Tyrone	0-13	0-10	Mayo

2002	Galway	0-15	0-7	Dublin
2003	Dublin	0-12	0-7	Tyrone
2004	Armagh	2-8	1-9	Mayo
2005	Galway	6-5	4-6	Down
2006	Mayo	1-13	1-11	Cork
2007	Cork	2-10	0-15	Laois
2008	Kerry	2-12	0-11	Kildare
2009	Cork	1-13	2-9	Down
2010	Dublin	1-10	1-8	Donegal
2011	Galway	2-16	1-9	Cavan
2012	Dublin	2-12	0-11	Roscommon
2013	Galway	1-14	1-11	Cork
2014	Dublin	1-21	3-6	Roscommon
2015	Tyrone	1-11	0-13	Tipperary
2016	Mayo	5-7	1-14	Cork
2017	Dublin	2-13	2-7	Galway

ALL-IRELAND U21 FOOTBALL FINAL TEAMS

1964
Kerry   S.Fitzgerald, M.Morris, P.O'Donoghue, D.Lovett, S.McCarthy, V.Lucey, Donie O'Sullivan, Denis O'Sullivan, P.Griffin, H.McKinney, A.Barrett, D.O'Shea, D.O'Donnell (capt.), J.J.Barrett, S.Burrowes. Subs: P.Cahill for M.Morris, T.Fitzgerald for P.Griffin.
Laois   T.Miller, E.Fennelly, A.Maher, J.Conway, G.Lawlor, J.Leonard, S.Harkins, G.Brennan, E.Mulhall, J.Fennell, M.Fennell, D.Brennan, C.O'Connor, P.Delaney, B.Delaney. Subs: R.Miller for C.O'Connor, J.Heenan for E.Mulhall, E.Mulhall for J.Heenan.

1965
Kildare   O.Crinnigan, D.Wynne, S.Cash, J.McTeague, S.Reilly, P.Nally, J.Millar, J.Donnelly, P.Mangan, T.Carew, P.Dunny (capt.), K.Kelly, T.Walsh, P.Newins, N.Behan. Subs: T.Keogh for M.Behan, P.Harman for P.Nally.
Cork   W.Morgan, D.Kehilly, J.Lucey, J.Crowley, D.Dineen, F.Cogan, J.Dunlea, D.Couglan, J.Dowling, E.Philpott, M.O'Loughlin, J.Cogan, Batt O'Keeffe, B.O'Neill, Brendan O'Keeffe. Sub: C.Roche for D.Coughlan.

1966
Roscommon   P.Reynolds, P.Clarke, P.Nicholson, C.Shine (capt.), G.Mannion, P.Moclair, T.Heneghan, M.J.Keane, J.O'Connor, J.Finnegan, D.Earley, J.Cox, M.Cummins, J.Keane, J.Kelly. Sub: M.O'Gara for M.Cummins.
Kildare   O.Crinnigan, D.Wynne, S.Cash, J.McTeague, J.O'Reilly, P.Nally, T.Keogh, P.Mangan, L.Casey, T.Carew, P.Dunny, T.Walsh, K.Kelly, M.Mullins, N.Behan. Sub: M.Mannion for L.Casey.

1967
Mayo   E.Rooney, J.Earley, C.Loftus, N.McDonald, J.Ryan, T.Cafferkey, M.Flatley, W.Loftus (capt.), T.Keane, S.O'Dowd, J.Gibbons, W.McGee, T.Fitzgerald, D.Griffith, J.Smith. Sub: J.Clark for N.McDonald.
(Note: M.Nally played in drawn game.)
Kerry   J.O'Brien, P.Sweeney, G.McCarthy, C.O'Sullivan, D.Crowley, S.Burrowes, T.O'Callaghan, P.O'Connell, M.Aherne, B.McCarthy, P.Finnegan, P.O'Connor, E.O'Donoghue, W.Kennedy, B.Lynch. Subs: P.Joy for P.O'Connor, V.McDyer for B.McCarthy.

1968
Derry   J.Somers, M.Trolan, T.Quinn, M.P.Kelly, T.Diamond (capt.), M.McAfee, G.O'Loughlin, T.McGuinness, S.Lagan, E.Coleman, M.Niblock, J.J.Kearney, A.McGuickan, S.McCloskey, K.Teague. Subs: A.McGurk for G.O'Loughlin, C.O'Donnell for J.J.Kearney.
Offaly   N.Kinnarney, L.Pender, J.Smith, P.Byrne, E.Mulligan, N.Clavin, P.Monaghan, W.Bryan, S.Evans, C.Daly, L.Flynn, G.Grehan, M.Feehan, S.Kilroy, P.Keegan. Subs: J.Dunne for L.Pender, P.Fenning for C.Daly.

1969
Antrim   R.McIlroy, D.Burns, S.Killough, M.McGranaghan, J.Mullan, L.Millar, M.Colbert, L.Boyle (capt.), T.Dunlop, A.Hamill, G.McCann, G.Mellis, A.McCallin, G.Dillon, D.McGrogan. Sub: G.Pollock for M.Colbert.
Roscommon W.Gallagher, T.Mahon, E.Beades, W.Feeley, P.Tiernan, A.O'Sullivan, J.Kerrane, D.Earley (capt.), M.Cox, T.Hunt, J.Kelly, M.Freyne, M.O'Hara, J.Cox, M.O'Gara.

1970

Cork   D.O'Mahony, M.O'Doherty, M.Scannell, S.Looney, S.Murphy, K.Kehilly, C.Hartnett, D.Hunt (capt.), D.Long, Tony Murphy, E.Kirby, John Coleman, J.Barrett, D.Barron, T.O'Brien. Subs: F.Twomey for S.Murphy, Donal Aherne for D.Hunt.

Fermanagh P.Sheridan, P.Reilly, C.Campbell, J.Courtney, M.McGarrity, S.Sheridan, S.Flanagan, D.Campbell, D.McKenna, T.McGrath, A.Campbell, E.McPartland (capt.), E.Treacy, G.Gallagher, P.McGinnitty. Sub: T.Boyle for E.McPartland, E.McPartland for T.Boyle, T.Boyle for D.McKenna.

1971

Cork   D.O'Mahony, P.Barry, M.O'Doherty, S.Looney (capt.), D.Cogan, B.Murphy, C.Hartnett, J.Coleman, D.Aherne, T.Murphy, B.Daly, F.Twomey, B.Cogan, D.Barron, D.Curran. Sub: J.Lynch for B.Daly.

Fermanagh P.Sheridan, P.O'Reilly, C.Campbell, P.Burns, B.McGovern, S.Flanagan, G.Lynch, D.McKenna, C.Gallagher, P.McGinnitly, A.Campbell, M.Cassidy, E.Treacy, T.McGrath, B.O'Reilly. Subs: H.Kelly for A.Campbell, M.McGarritly for G.Lynch.

1972

Galway   M.Noonan, J.Waldron (capt.), J.Dillon, B.Costelloe, P.J.Burke, M.Geraghty, S.Stephens, M.Walsh, M.Rooney, P.Burke, T.Naughton, M.Burke, J.Lardner, F.Rushe, J.Tobin. Sub: E.Monaghan for J.Lardner.

Kerry   J.Crean, S.O'Donovan, J.Deenihan, D.O'Keeffe, M.Murphy, P.Lynch, G.O'Keeffe, N.O'Sullivan, J.O'Keeffe, M.McEllistrim, M.O'Sullivan, J.Walsh (capt.), P.Horan, M.Ferris, G.Power. Subs: J.Egan for M.Ferris, M.O'Connor for P.Horan.

1973

Kerry   P.O'Mahony, B.Harman, J.Deenihan, B.O'Shea, G.O'Keeffe, G.Power, K.O'Donoghue, J.Long, P.Lynch, J.Coffey (capt.), M.O'Sullivan, P.O'Shea, M.O'Shea, J.Egan, M.Sheehy. Subs: M.Ferris for M.O'Shea, N.Brosnan for P.Lynch.

Mayo   S.Langan, P.Cunningham, S.Reilly, J.O'Mahony, G.Feeney (capt.), C.Moynihan, J.Culkin, R.McNicholas, G.Farragher, M.Gannon, T.Webb, R.Bell, E.Ralph, S.McGrath, M.Flannery. Subs: S.Barrett for M.Flannery, S.Weir for E.Ralph.

1974

Mayo   I.Heffernan, A.Durkin, S.Reilly, J.O'Mahony, G.Feeney, C.Moynihan, J.Culkin (capt.), R.Bell, G.Farragher, M.Flannery, J.P.Kean, T.Webb, M.Moloney, D.McGrath, M.Higgins. Subs: D.McGrath for M.Flannery in draw game; J.Burke for M.Moloney, M.O'Malley for A.Durcan in replay; J.Burke played in drawn game. D.McGrath came in for replay.

Antrim   C.Moore, N.Madden, P.McKiernan, J.McAllister, G.McHugh, J.P.O'Kane, C.Smith, L.Jennings, J.McKiernan, K.Gough, P.Armstrong, B.Growcott, H.McRory, J.O'Hare, D.Cormican. Subs: J.McAllister, K.Young draw; K.Young replay; R.Carlin played in drawn game.

1975

Kerry   C.Nelligan, K.O'Donoghue (capt.), P.Ó Sé, G.Leahy, M.Spillane, T.Kennelly, D.(Ogie) Moran, G.O'Driscoll, S.Walsh, B.Walsh, M.Sheehy, D.Murphy, T.Doyle, J.O'Shea, P.Spillane.

Dublin   A.Fayne, B.Fitzpatrick, L.Egan, G.McCaul, K.Bruton J.Thompson, M.Holden, F.Ryder, J.Corcoran, P.Connellan, B.Mullins, P.J.Buckley, P.Reaney, C.Fitzpatrick, S.McCarthy. Subs: D.O'Reilly for J.Corcoran, A.Cunningham for K.Bruton, P.Rooney for P.Connellan.

1976

Kerry   C.Nelligan, M.Colgan, P.Ó Sé, G.Leahy, M.Spillane, D."Ogie" Moran, V.O'Connor, S.Walsh, J.O'Shea, N.O'Donovan, P.Spillane, G.Murphy (capt.), B.Walsh, G.O'Sullivan, P.Foley.

Kildare   A.Dunne, C.Farrell, P.O'Donoghue, F.Mulligan, D.O'Reilly, J.Crofton, P.Kenny, J.Geoghegan, M.Fennelly, T.Shaw, M.Condon, P.Mulhern, N.Fahy, M.O'Gorman, B.Whelan. Subs: S.Ryan for C.Farrell, P.Lyons for N.Fahy, P.Carr for P.Mulhern.

1977

Kerry   C.Nelligan, M.Keane, V.O'Connor, M.Spillane, D.(Ogie) Moran (capt.), J.Mulvihill, G.Casey, J.O'Shea, E.Liston, T.Doyle, S.Walsh, P.Foley, D.Moran, T.Bridgman, D.Coffey. Sub: G.O'Sullivan for D.Moran.

Down   J.Carr, M.Sands, D.Carey, H.Trainor, J.McCartan, T.McGovern, P.O'Rourke, J.Wright, L.Austin, D.Watson, R.Mathews, V.McGovern, B.Loughran, J.McCartan, M.McCann. Subs: E.McGivern for P.O'Rourke, A.McAulfield for B.Loughran.

1978

Roscommon B.Kenny, D.Newton, P.Dolan, S.Tighe, G.Connellan, R.O'Beirne, E.Egan, S.Hayden (capt.), G.Fitzmaurice, M.Finneran, G.Emmett, C.Reynolds, A.McHugh, H.Crowley, T.McManus. Sub: A.Dooley for A.McHugh.

Kerry   C.Nelligan, M.Keane, V.O'Connor, M.Spillane, G.Lynch, J.Mulvihill, G.Casey, J.O'Shea, S.Walsh, T.Bridgman, D.Higgins, J.L.McElligot, P.Foley, E.Liston, P.Sheehan. Sub: D.Coffey for P.Sheehan.

1979

Down   Pat Donnan, E.King, A.McAulfield, M.Sands, G.Murdock, P.O'Rourke, B.McGovern, P.Kennedy, L.Austin, J.McCartan (capt.), M.Burns, G.Blaney, Peter Donnan, G.O'Hare, J.Digney. Sub: M.McCann for G.O'Hare.

Cork   B.O'Driscoll, T.Healy, M.Healy, J.Murphy, L.Forde, M.Moloney, J.Kerrigan, R.Lotty, D.O'Mahony, T.Dalton, M.Mullins, B.McSweeney, S.Hayes, G.Mulcahy, F.O'Mahony. Subs: D.Kelleher for D.O'Mahoney, D.Philpott for R.Lotty, J.Nolan for T.Healy.

1980

Cork   M.Creedon, J.Fouhy, M.Healy, C.Counihan, B.McSweeney, T.Hennebry, J.Kerrigan, D.Philpott, Brian Lotty, D.Barry, S.Hayes, T.Dalton (capt.), E.Fitzgerald, N.O'Connor, F.O'Mahony. Sub: M.Burns for B.McSweeney.

Dublin   J.O'Leary, F.Walsh, V.Conroy, D.Foran, P.Canavan, S.Wade, C.Eustace, J.Ronayne, P.Boylan, D.O'Brien, M.Loftus, C.Duff, W.Hughes, B.Rock, A.McCaul. Subs: S.Fleming for C.Eustace, V.Kearney for W.Hughes, G.O'Neill for A.McCaul.

1981

Cork   M.Creedon, J.Fouhy, M.Healy, P.Buckley, M.Hannon, M.Burns, C.Corrigan, Brian Lotty, D.Murphy, D.Barry, S.Hayes (capt.), M.Connolly, A.O'Sullivan, N.O'Connor, E.Fitzgerald. (Note: C.Hartnett and D.Kelleher played in drawn game. P.Buckley and A.O'Sullivan came on for replay.) Subs: P.Buckley for C.Hartnett, T.Ross for D.Murphy in drawn game; T.Ross for D.Murphy, D.Kelleher for M.Connolly in replay.

Galway   P.Coyne, S.Cronin, P.Connolly, S.Rhattigan, H.Heskin, T.Tierney, M.Gleeson, A.Murphy, P.Kelly, V.Daly, M.McDonagh, M Brennan, P.O'Dea, C.O'Dea, C.Gibbons. (Note: S.Kelly, P.Clancy, H.Blehein, B.O'Donnell played in drawn game. S.Rhattigan, G.Gibbons, P.Kelly and H.Heskin came on for replay.) Subs: H.Heskin for M.Gleeson, P.Kelly for C.McDonagh in drawn game; M.Sweeney for M.McDonagh, M.McDonagh for C.O'Dea in replay.

1982

Donegal   M.Kelly, M.McBrearty, S.Bonnar, M.Gallagher, E.McIntyre, T.McDermott, B.Tuohy, A.Molloy, D.Reid, M.McHugh, C.Mulgrew, J.McMullen, S.Meehan, P.Carr, P.McGroarty. Subs: P.Gallagher for Bonnar, S.Maguire for McGroarty.
Roscommon G.Cunniffe, G.Wynne, G.Collins, M.Shanahan, P.McNeill, M.Tiernan, P.Rogers, E.Glancy, T.Corcoran, E.McManus, P.Hickey, J.Connellan, P.Earley, R.McPhillips, P.Doorey (capt.). Subs: J.Kelly for R.McPhillips, S.Killoran for E.Glancy.

1983

Mayo   G.Irwin, P.Forde, J.Maughan, E.Gibbons (capt.), J.McNabb, M.Feeney, J.Finn, G.Geraghty, S.Maher, P.Brogan, J.Lindsay, N.Durkin, B.Kilkelly, T.Grogan, P.Duffy.
(Note: M.Kerins played in draw and came on as a sub in replay for T.Grogan. Kevin McStay replaced P.Duffy in draw and J.Lindsay in replay. P.Brogan was on for replay.)
Derry   J.Mackle, K.Rafferty, F.Burke, T.Scullion, J.McErlean, B.McPeake, C.Keenan, C.Quinn, D.Barton, L.McIlhenny, D.McNicholl, P.McCann, T.McGuinness, R.McCusker, T.McGuckian.
(Note: E.Cassidy, B.McErlean played in drawn game. Subs: R.McCusker for E.Cassidy, P.McCann for J.McErlean in drawn game (they retained their places for the replay).D.O'Kane for T.McGuiness, M.Tully B.McPeake, E.Cassidy for C.Quinn subs in replay.)

1984

Cork   M.Maguire, John Murphy (Passage), N.Cahalane (capt.), A.Davis, D.Cleary, M.Slocum, T.Nation, D.Cullotty, T.Leahy, B.Coffey, T.Mannix, M.McCarthy, K.McCarthy, C.O'Neill, A.O'Sullivan. Subs: T.McCarthy for A.O'Sullivan, J.Cleary for K.McCarthy, B.Stack for D.Cullotty.
Mayo   G.Irwin, C.Dever, J.Gilmore, E.Gibbons, A.McGarry, J.McNabb, J.Finn, P.Brogan, S.Maher, J.Dooley, P.Duffy, N.Durkin, B.Kilkelly, L.McHale, P.O'Reilly. Sub: T.Morgan for P.O'Reilly.

1985

Cork   J.O'Mahony, K.Scanlon, A.Davis (capt.), D.Walsh, D.Cleary, B.Stack, M.Slocum, D.Cullotty, P.Hayes, M.McCarthy, T.McCarthy, B.Coffey, S.O'Donovan, C.O'Neill, P.McGrath. Sub: B.Lane for D.Cullotty.
Derry   D.McCusker, B.Young, F.Bourke, P.McCann, J.McGurk, B.McPeake, N.Mullen, D.O'Kane, D.Healy, Declan McNicholl, D.Cassidy, M.McGurk, Dermot McNicholl, Cathal McNicholl, T.McKiernan. Subs: P.Bradley for F.Bourke, C.Barton for M.McGurk, J.Mulholland for N.Mullen.

1986

Cork   J.O'Mahony, K.Scanlon, J.Murphy (Glanmire), D.Walsh, M.Slocum (capt.), M.Maguire, A.Griffin, P.Hayes, T.McCarthy, C.O'Connell, M.McCarthy, B.Coffey, P.Harrington, J.O'Driscoll, P.McGrath. Subs: J.O'Brien for J.O'Mahony, A.McCarthy for M.Maguire, B.Stack for A.Griffin.
Offaly   A.Daly, J.Owens, C.Higgins, K.Corcoran, A.Stewart, K.Rigney, B.Scully, G.O'Brien, P.Brady, V.Claffey, D.Claffey, C.Ryan, R.Scully, M.Casey, V.Brady. Subs: G.Blong for J.Owens, K.Brasil for K.Rigney, G.Galvin for G.O'Brien.

1987

Donegal   D.Gallagher, J.J.Doherty, J.Connors, T.Maguire, P.Carr, J.Cunningham (capt.), D.Keon, B.Cunningham, J.Gallagher, P.Hegarty, T.Ryan, B.McGowan, D.Ward, M.Boyle, L.Gavigan. Sub: S.Ward for J.Gallagher in replay.
(Note: Donegal played same team in drawn game. Subs in drawn game: C.White for P.Hegarty, J.McDermott for D.Ward.)
Kerry   C.Moran, K.Savage, M.Brosnan, M.Nix, S.Stack, N.O'Leary, P.Coughlan, M.Galway, J.Brosnan, P.J.Gaine, G.Looney, D.McEvoy, G.Murphy, P.Hoare, M.Dennehy.
(Note: M.Downey played in draw. Subs: G.Murphy for M.Dennehy in drawn game (he retained his place for replay); D.Moynihan for G.Looney, T.Walsh for P.Coughlan, M.Downey for M.Dennehy in replay.)

1988

Offaly   D.O'Neill, P.Moran, G.O'Brien (capt.), T.Coffey, J.Stewart, A.Bracken, P.O'Reilly, M.Plunkett, K.Kelleghan, G.Daly, V.Claffey, N.O'Shea, M.Casey, J.Mullan, B.Flynn. Subs: B.Scully for G.Daly, V.Daly for V.Claffey.
Cavan   J.Reilly, G.Smith, D.O'Reilly, B.Sweeney, J.Donnellan, J.Brady, P.Sharkey, L.Brady, M.Fegan, F.Cahill, S.Donoghue, D.Brady, V.Kelly, V.Dowd, F.Mooney. Sub: C.Murtagh for L.Brady.

1989

Cork   A.Cawley, M.Lyons, M.O'Connor, D.Burke, S.Coughlan, S.O'Brien (capt.), N.Murphy, D.Fitzgerald, L.Honohan, I.Ahearne, M.Mullins, D.Davis, J.Barrett, D.O'Sullivan, N.Twomey. Subs: S.Calnan for Ahearne, C.Corkerry for Barrett.
Galway   A.Brennan, J.Kilraine, F.McWalter, B.Walsh, P.Fallon, A.Mulholland, N.O Neachtain, B.Moylan, A.O'Connor, S.De Paor, T.Mannion, F.O'Neill, T.Kilcommins, K.Walsh, T.Finnerty. Subs: B.Silke for Kilraine, J.Joyce for de Paor, E.Geraghty for Mannion.

1990

Kerry   P.O'Leary, J.B.O'Brien, S.Burke, L.Flaherty, P.Slattery, V.Knightley (capt.), E.Breen, M.Fitzgerald, N.O'Mahony, P.Laide, P.McKenna, G.O'Driscoll, P.Dennehy, D.Farrell, W.O'Sullivan. Sub: P.Griffin for Dennehy.
Tyrone   C.Blee, F.Devlin, A.McGinn, P.Devlin, P.Donnelly, B.McGinn, A.Morris, A.Kilpatrick, D.Barr, A.Cush, M.Cummings, P.Canavan, L.Strain, C.McElduff, C.Loughran. Sub: E.McCaffrey for Cummings.

1991

Tyrone   C.Blee, D.Hagan, C.Lawn, F.Devlin, P.Donnelly, B.McGinn, T.O'Neill, A.Kilpatrick, D.Barr, A.Cush, E.McCaffrey, P.Canavan (capt.), C.Loughran, C.McBride, B.Gormley. Subs: S.Lawn for Donnelly, J.Cassidy for Blee.
Kerry   P.O'Leary, J.O'Brien, N.Savage, J.Cronin, L.Flaherty, V.Knightley, S.Walsh, F.Ashe, C.Kearney, P.Laide, G.O'Driscoll, S.O'Sullivan, G.Farrell, D.Farrell, W.O'Sullivan. Subs: E.Stack for Kearney, D.Cahill for Walsh, T.Byrnes for Laide.

1992

Tyrone   B.McConnell, E.Martin, C.Lawn, F.Devlin, S.Lawn, J.Gormley, C.Hughes, A.Kilpatrick, S.McCallan, E.McCaffrey, C.Donnelly, P.Canavan (capt.), K.Loughran, C.McBride, B.Gormley. Sub: M.Slevin for C.Lawn.
Galway   D.O Flaharta, K.Fallon, G.Fahy, E.Godwin, I.O'Donoghue, P.Crowley, D.Cronin, F.Gavin, P.Boyce, J.Wilson, C.McGauran, T.Wilson, B.Forde, J.Fallon, N.Finnegan. Subs: F.Keenan for Crowley, A.Feerick for Forde.

1993

Meath C.Martin, V.Ryan, E.McManus, R.McGrath, J.McCarthy, G.Geraghty, T.Hanley (capt.), J.Hendrick, J.McGuinness, T.Shine, H.Carolan, T.Byrne, P.O'Sullivan, T.O'Connor, C.Sheridan. Subs: B.Kealy for Hendrick, T.Giles for O'Connor, N.Collier for McCarthy.

Kerry D.O'Keeffe, M.Hassett, G.McGrath, N.Mangan, S.Curtin, F.Stack, J.O'Connell, S.Moynihan, J.Quirke, C.O'Grady, B.O'Shea, P.O'Driscoll, E.Hennessy, J.O'Shea, S.Culloty. Subs: D.O'Shea for Quirke, K.Scanlon For McGrath, S.O'Driscoll for J.O'Shea.

1994

Cork K.O'Dwyer, D.O'Callaghan, B.Corcoran, T.Óg Lynch M.O'Donovan, B.Murphy, P.O'Regan, F.Collins, D.O'Neill, J.Buckley, J.Kavanagh, P.O'Mahony, J.Clifford, P.Hegarty, P.O'Rourke. Subs: M.O'Sullivan for Buckley, M.Moran for O'Rourke.

Mayo B.Heffernan, F.Costello, K.Morley, J.Nallen, P.Cunney, K.Mortimer, J.Casey, P.McNamara, D.O'Loughlin, R.Ruane, D.Jennings, R.Golding, K.O'Neill, K.McDonald, M.Sheridan. Subs: D.Byrne for O'Loughlin, M.Smith for Jennings, J.McHugh for P.McNamara.

1995

Kerry D.Murphy (capt.), N.Mangan, B.McCarthy, B.O'Shea, K.Burns, M.Hassett, C.McCarthy, D.Ó Sé, D.Daly, D.Dwyer, J.Crowley, M.Moynihan, J.Ferriter, L.Hassett, D.Ó Cinnéide. Subs: K.O'Driscoll for O'Shea, C.Drummond for Mangan, D.Dennehy for Dwyer. W.Kirby went in as a sub in the drawn game for D.Ó Sé. *(Note: Kerry played same team in both games.)*

Mayo J.Madden, F.Costello, L.Moffat, R.Connelly, T.Corcoran, K.Mortimer (capt.), S.Moffat, D.Brady, J.Casey, D.O'Loughlin, J.Mitchell, E.McDonagh, M.Horan, D.Byrne, D.Nestor. Subs: D.Tierney for McDonagh, D.Sweeney for Mitchell, B.Forde for O'Loughlin.
(R.Connelly, E.McDonagh and M.Horan replaced D.Mulligan, P.Whitaker and K.McDonald who played in draw. M.Higgins, D.Sweeney and C.Deacy went on as subs in drawn game for P.Whitaker, J.Mitchell and D.Mulligan.)

1996

Kerry D.Murphy, K.O'Driscoll, B.McCarthy, M.O'Shea, K.Burns, C.Drummond, E.Fitzmaurice, D.Ó Sé, W.Kirby, D.Dwyer, L.Hassett (capt.), D.Ó Cinnéide, J.O'Shea, B.Clarke, M.F.Russell. Subs: J.Brennan for Clarke, R.O'Rahilly for Brennan, J.Ferriter for J.O'Shea.

Cavan A.Donohoe, P.Murphy, M.Reilly, C.McCarey, P.Brady, P.Reilly, M.McGauran, D.McCabe, T.Farrelly, D.Fagan, R.Brennan, A.Forde, J.Reilly, L.Reilly, M.Graham. Sub: B.Mulvaney for Fagan.

1997

Derry S.O'Kane, S.Donnelly, D.O'Neill, M.Kelly, P.McFlynn, S.M.Lockhart, E.McGillowey, E.Muldoon, G.Doyle, B.Murray, J.McBride, S.McGuckin, J.Cassidy, A.McGuckin, M.Gribbin.

Meath C.O'Sullivan, S.Carolan, D.Fay, A.Meade, N.Kearney, M.Reilly, P.Reynolds, S.O'Rourke, J.Cullinane, B.Smyth, S.Dillon, K.Dowd, R.McGee, B.Callaghan, R.Farrelly. Subs: C.McGrath for Carolan, E.Grogan for Dowd, F.Owens for O'Rourke.

1998

Kerry D.Moloney, M.McCarthy, T.O'Sullivan, K.Leen, J.Sheehan, T.Ó Sé, M.Beckett, T.Griffin, E.Fitzmaurice, A.Mac Gearailt, P.O'Sullivan, L.Brosnan, M.F.Russell, N.Kennelly, B.Scanlon. Subs: I.Twiss for Scanlon, M.Burke for Beckett.

Laois D.O'Mahony, J.P.Kehoe, M.Buggy, J.Higgins, N.Collins, D.Conroy, C.Parkinson, M.Delaney, N.Garvan, G.Ramsbottom, I.Fitzgerald, C.Conway, B.McDonald, D.Doogue, K.Fitzpatrick. Subs: S.Kelly for Delaney, T.Kelly for Doogue.

1999

Westmeath C.Mullin, P.Mullen, J.Galvin, F.Murray, B.Lambden, A.Canning (capt.), M.Burke, K.Burke, D.O'Shaughnessy, S.Deering, F.Wilson, R.Browne, J.Fallon, M.Ennis, D.Dolan. Sub: D.Heavin for J.Galvin.

Kerry K.Cremin, S.O'Sullivan, T.O'Sullivan, M.McCarthy, S.Hegarty, T.Ó Sé, E.Galvin, T.Griffin, J.Sugrue, N.Kennelly (capt.), A.Mac Gearailt, T.Kennelly, P.Galvin, L.Murphy, I.Twiss. Subs: S.O'Sullivan for P.Galvin, M.D.Cahill for Twiss.

2000

Tyrone P.McConnell, G.Devlin, D.O'Hanlon, M.McGee, C.McGinley, C.Gourley, D.McCrossan, C.McAnallen, K.Hughes, J.Campbell, B.McGuigan, S.O'Neill, M.Harte, R.Thornton, O.Mulligan. Subs: E.McGinley for McAnallen, A.Ball for McCrossan.

Limerick M.Keogh, M.O'Riordan, P.Fitzgerald, B.Geary, C.Mullane, S.Lucey, T.Stack, J.Stokes, J.Galvin, P.Ahern, M.Culhane, T.Carroll, C.Fitzgerald, B.Begley, C.Hickey. Sub: S.Byrne for Culhane.

2001

Tyrone P.McConnell, C.Gormley, D.O'Hanlon, M.McGee, C.Meenagh, G.Devlin, P.Jordan, P.Donnelly, C.McAnallen, R.Mellon, B.McGuigan, S.O'Neill, E.McGinley, K.Hughes, O.Mulligan. Sub: G.Wylie for Donnelly.

Mayo D.Clarke, M.J.Meenaghan, P.Kelly, K.Deignan, E.Casey, B.Prendergast, G.Brady, J.Gill, S.Grimes, C.Lyons, A.Dillon, T.Mortimer, M.Keane, B.Maloney, C.Mortimer. Subs: M.McNicholas for Lyons, B.Padden for Dillon, R.Loftus for Grimes, R.Walsh for Meenagh.

2002

Galway D.Morris, C.Monaghan, K.Fitzgerald, M.Comer, R.Murray, D.Blake, K.Brady, J.Bergin, K.Comer, M.Clancy, J.Devane, D.Burke, M.Meehan, D.O'Brien, N.Joyce. Sub: D.Hanley for Burke.

Dublin S.Cluxton, N.Kane, D.Corcoran, P.Griffin, P.Casey, B.Cullen, N.O'Driscoll, D.Magee, C.Murphy, L.Óg Ó hEineacháin, C.Keaney, D.Lally, A.Brogan, G.Cullen, T.Quinn. Subs: D.O'Callaghan for Keaney, D.O'Mahony for G.Cullen, S.Walsh for Corcoran, M.Lyons for Lally, G.Smith for Murphy.

2003

Dublin P.Copeland, N.Kane, M.Fitzpatrick, P.Griffin, N.Cooper, B.Cullen, C.Prenderville, D.O'Mahony, P.Brennan, C.Keaney, L.Óg Ó hEineacháin, D.Lally, A.Brogan, G.Cullen, J.Noonan. Subs: D.Murray for Cooper, M.Lyons for Ó hEineacháin, S.Walsh for G.Cullen.

Tyrone J.Devine, S.Sweeney, K.McCrory, D.Carlin, O.Devine, M.Garry, P.O'Farrell, P.Donnelly, S.Cavanagh, K.Hughes, L.Meenan, J.McMahon, M.Penrose, A.McCarron, R.McCann. Subs: T.McGuigan for McCann, P.Armour for O'Farrell, D.McDermott for Penrose.

2004

Armagh   P.Wilson, G.Smyth, F.Moriarty, A.Mallon, A.Kernan, C.McKeever, B.McDonald, M.Mackin, G.Swift, G.Loughran, S.Kernan, P.Toal, M.McNamee, R.Austin, B.Mallon. Subs: P.Duffy for McDonald, B.Toner for Loughran, J.Murtagh for Austin, M.Moore for A.Kernan, S.O'Neill for Mackin.

Mayo   F.Ruddy, D.Geraghty, P.Navin, T.Howley, M.Carey, L.O'Malley, S.Drake, B.Moran, C.Barrett, A.Kilcoyne, R.McNamara, A.Moran, A.Costello, D.Munnelly, M.Conroy. Subs: P.Casey for Kilcoyne, P.Lydon for Drake, P.Doherty for Carey, J.Prenty for Munnelly, N.Lydon for Conroy.

2005

Galway   M.Killilea, A.Burke, F.Hanley, M.Flannery, D.Mullahy, N.Coyne, G.Sice, N.Coleman, B.Cullinane, B.Faherty, D.Dunleavy, F.Breathnach, M.Meehan, C.Blake, S.Armstrong. Subs: J.Murphy for Mullahy, A.Glynn for Coyne.

Down   D.Alder, N.McEvoy, M.Rooney, E.Henry, D.Neeson, J.Colgan, D.Cunningham, A.Rogers, M.McClean, C.Laverty, A.Carr, N.McArdle, M.Poland, J.McGovern, J.Brown. Subs: J.Ireland for Henry, M.Clarke for McGovern, J.Patterson for McArdle, N.Miskelly for Brown, G.Dobbin for Rooney.

2006

Mayo   K.O'Malley, T.Howley, G.Cafferkey, K.Higgins, C.Barrett, T.Cunniffe, C.Boyle, S.O'Shea, B.Moran, A.Campbell, J.Dillon, A.Kilcoyne, M.Ronaldson, M.Hannick, M.Conroy. Subs: S.Ryder for Boyle, K.Costello for Dillon, E.Varley for Hannick.

Cork   K.O'Halloran, R.Carey, C.Murphy, S.O'Donoghue, D.Limerick, M.Shields, E.Cadogan, A.O'Connor, F.Gould, P.Kelly, C.Keane, P.Kerrigan, D.Goulding, P.O'Flynn, J.Hayes. Subs: G.O'Shea for Hayes, F.Lynch for Kelly.

2007

Cork   K.O'Halloran, R.Carey, M.Shields, K.Harrington, S.O'Donoghue, D.Limerick, E.Cadogan, F.Gould, A.O'Sullivan, F.Lynch, C.Keane, P.Kerrigan, C.O'Neill, D.Goulding, S.Cahalane. Subs: R.Leahy for Cahalane, G.O'Shea for Keane, S.McCarthy for Lynch.

Laois   C.Munnelly, C.Healy, M.Timmons, B.Meredith, S.Lalor, J.O'Loughlin, N.Donoher, B.Quigley, C.Og Greene, D.Brennan, C.Rogers, S.O'Leary, M.Tierney, S.O'Neill, D.Conway. Subs: D.Kingston for O'Neill, I.Fleming for O'Leary.

2008

Kerry   T.Mac an tSaoir, C.O'Mahony, M.Maloney, S.Enright, Aidan O'Sullivan, K.Young, G.Duffy, D.Moran, Alan O'Sullivan, K.O'Leary, J.Buckley, M.O'Donoghue, P.Curran, T.Walsh, P.O'Connor. Subs: K.Brennan for Duffy, E.Hickson for Aidan O'Sullivan, B.Looney for Buckley, J.Doolan for Walsh, E.O'Neill for O'Donoghue.

Kildare   N.McConnell, C.Brophy, D.Brennan, S.Murphy, J.Browne, G.White, T.Byrne, M.Waters, N.Higgins, D.Whyte, E.O'Flaitheartaigh, K.Kelly, S.Fahy, A.Smith, G.Smullen. Subs: N.Clynch for Brophy, J.Fogarty for Kelly, J.Cocoman for Whyte, M.O'Sullivan for Fahy.

2009

Cork   A.Seymour, S.McLoughlin, L.Jennings, N.Galvin, Conor O'Driscoll, A.Walsh, B.Daly, C.O'Donovan, K.O'Driscoll, C.Sheehan, M.Collins, Colm O'Driscoll, C.O'Neill, D.Goold, P.Honohan. Subs: J.Fitzpatrick for Sheehan, B.Lombard for Jennings, B.O'Driscoll for Honohan, L.McLoughlin for K.O'Driscoll.

Down   G.Joyce, M.Digney, C.Murney, D.Turley, T.Hanna, J.Fitzpatrick, J.Murphy, M.Magee, O.Fitzpatrick, E.Toner, C.Maginn, J.O'Reilly, P.Devlin, P.McComiskey, C.Poland. Sub: N.Higgins for Digney.

2010

Dublin   V.Whelan, E.Culligan, R.O'Carroll, D.Nelson, JCooper, J.McCarthy, N.Devereux, S.Murray, C.Mullins, M.Coughlan, T.Furman, G.Sweeney, R.McCarthy, D.Rock, C.Dorney. Subs: D.Quinn for R.McCarthy, C.Reddin for J.McCarthy, B.O'Rourke for Furman, S.McGuinness for Nelson, N.Brogan for Dorney.

Donegal   P.Boyle, D.Walsh, P.McGrath, C.Boyle, K.Mulhern, D.Curran, E.Doherty, C.Classon, M.Murphy, A.McFadden, D.Molloy, T.McKinley, L.McLoone, J.Carroll, M.McHugh. Subs: C.Morrison for McFadden, D.Murphy for McKinley, C.McGinley for Carroll, S.O'Kennedy for Curran.

2011

Galway   M.Breathnach, G.Sweeney, C.Forde, A.Tierney, J.Moore, J.Duane, T.Fahy, F.Ó Curraoin, T.Flynn, M.Boyle, M.Hehir, C.Doherty, D.Cummins, P.Sweeney, E.Monaghan. Subs: A.Murphy for P.Sweeney, M.Farragher for Monaghan, B.Flaherty for Boyle, C.Halloran for Fahy, C.Silke for Tierney.

Cavan   A.O'Mara, M.Leddy, O.Minagh, D.Tighe, K.Meehan, D.Barkey, M.Brady, G.McKiernan, F.Flanagan, N.Smith, N.Murray, B.Reilly, J.Brady, N.McDermott, P.Leddy. Subs: P.King for M.Leddy, T.Mooney for Tighe, K.Tierney for Reilly, N.McKiernan for King, C.McCleary for Meehan.

2012

Dublin   J.Carthy, M.Concarr, K.O'Brien, S.George, L.Fletcher, J.Kelly, J.McCaffrey, E.Ó Conghaile, C.Reddin, D.Byrne, G.Sweeney, M.Schutte, C.Kilkenny, P.Ryan, P.Hudson. Subs: P.Maguire for Schutte, G.Seaver for Byrne, H.Dawson for Ryan, P.O'Higgins for Reddin, P.Mannion for Hudson.

Roscommon   T.Lowe, C.Cafferkey, C.Duignan, D.Murray, C.Daly, P.Brogan, R.Stack, C.Shine, N.Daly, S.Oates, N.Kilroy, D.Keane, C.Connolly, C.Compton, D.Smith. Subs: J.McManus for Keane, F.Cregg for Stack, C.Murtagh for Connolly, F.Kelly for Kilroy.

2013

Galway   T.Healy, D.Cunnane, J.Shaughnessy, M.Loughnane, P.Varley, D.Burke, E.Walsh, F.Ó Curraoin, T.Flynn, C.Mulryan, S.Moran, D.Comer, S.Walsh, A.Varley, I.Burke. Subs: C.Rabbitte for Moran, J.Healy for T.Healy, P.Ezergailis for Cunnane, G.Kelly for Burke, S.Maughan for A.Varley.

Cork   D.Hanrahan, C.Dorman, D.Cahalane, A.Cronin, B.O'Driscoll, T.Clancy, J.Wall, S.Kiely, I.Maguire, A.Cadogan, J.O'Rourke, M.Sugure, D.MacEoin, B.Hurley, L.Connolly. Subs: J.Burns for Kiely, C.Vaughan for Sugrue, T.J.Brosnan for Wall, K.Hallisey for Cadogan.

2014

Dublin   L.Molloy, R.McGowan, D.Byrne, R.McDaid, C.Mullally, J.Small, J.McCaffrey, P.O'Higgins, B.Fenton, S.Boland, E.Lowndes, N.Scully, P.Mannion, C.Costello, C.McHugh. Subs: E.Ó Conghaile for Byrne, G.Hannigan for Boland, G.Ivory for O'Higgins, S.Cunningham for Costello, N.Walsh for Mannion.

Roscommon   C.Lavin, S.Mullooly, C.Kenny, D.Murray, C.Daly, J.McManus, R.Daly, U.Harney, T.Corcoran, C.Kilcline, M.Healy, E.Smith, M.Nally, D.Murtagh, D.Smith. Subs: M.Gunning for Nally, T.Featherston for Kenny, N.McInerney for C.Daly, A.Gleeson for Gunning, S.Flynn for R.Daly, S.Killoran for Healy.

2015

Tyrone   S.Fox, R.Mullan, P.Hampsey, C.McLaughlin, M.Cassidy, R.Brennan, K.McGeary, C.McShane, D.McNulty, M.Kavanagh, C.Meyler, M.Walsh, L.Brennan, F.Burns, M.Bradley. Subs: R.McGlone for Walsh, R.Kelly for McShane, P.McKenna for L.Brennan.

Tipperary   E.Comerford, K.Fahey, J.Feehan, C.O'Shaughnessy, R.Mulcahy, L.Boland, B.Maher, S.O'Brien, C.O'Riordan, J.Lonergan, I.Fahey, L.Casey, K.O'Halloran, J.Keane, P.Maher. Sub: J.McGrath for P.Maher.

2016

Mayo   M.Flanagan, E.O'Donoghue, S.Cunniffe, D.Kenny, S.Akram, M.Hall, J.Kelly, M.Ruane, S.Coen, F.Boland, C.Loftus, D.O'Connor, L.Irwin, F.Duffy, M.Plunkett. Subs: J.Carr for F.Duffy, B.Duffy for Kelly, M.Lyons for Plunkett.

Cork   A.Casey, M.McSweeney, J.Mullins, E.Lavers, K.Flahive, S.Cronin, K.Histon, S.White, R.O'Toole, S.O'Donoghue, S.Powter, R.Harkin, B.Coakley, P.Kelleher, M.Hurley. Subs: S.O'Leary for O'Toole, D.Ó Duinnin for White, C.Kiely for Harkin, S.Sherlock for Hurley, D.Quinn for McSweeney.

2017

Dublin   E.Comerford, D.Byrne, S.McMahon, D.Monaghan, C.O'Shea, E.Murchan, C.Murphy, A.Foley, B.Howard, D.O'Brien, G.O'Reilly, A.Byrne, T.Fox, C.Basquel, C.O'Callaghan. Subs: D.Gavin for Foley, D.Spillane for Fox, C.Sallier for O'Reilly, A.McGowan for McMahon, P.Small for Basquel, S.Smith for A.Byrne.

Galway   R Ó Beoláin, L Kelly, S.A.Ó Ceallaigh, R.Greene, C.McDaid, D.McHugh, K.Molloy, P.Cooke, C.D'Arcy, P.Mannion, M.Daly, S.Kelly, R.Finnerty, E Finnerty, D.Conneely. Subs: C.Brady for R.Finnerty, C.Brennan for D'Arcy, M.Boyle for Conneely, E.Lee for Kelly, A.Ó Laoi for Mannion, P.Ó Curraoin for Molloy.

CAPTAINS OF WINNING ALL-IRELAND U21 FOOTBALL TEAMS

1964	D. O'Donnell (Kerry)
1965	P. Dunny (Kildare)
1966	C. Shine (Roscommon)
1967	W. Loftus (Mayo)
1968	T. Diamond (Derry)
1969	L. Boyle (Antrim)
1970	D. Hunt (Cork)
1971	S . Looney (Cork)
1972	J. Waldron (Galway)
1973	J. Coffey (Kerry)
1974	J. Culkin (Mayo)
1975	K. O'Donoghue (Kerry)
1976	G. Murphy (Kerry)
1977	D. "Ogie" Moran (Kerry)
1978	S. Hayden (Roscommon)
1979	Ned King (Down)
1980	T. Dalton (Cork)
1981	S. Hayes (Cork)
1982	B. Tuohy (Donegal)
1983	E. Gibbons (Mayo)
1984	N. Cahalane (Cork)
1985	A. Davis (Cork)
1986	M. Slocum (Cork)
1987	J. Cunningham (Donegal)
1988	G. O'Brien (Offaly)
1989	S. O'Brien (Cork)
1990	V. Knightley (Kerry)
1991	Peter Canavan (Tyrone)
1992	Peter Canavan (Tyrone)
1993	Thomas Hanley (Meath)
1994	Damien O'Neill (Cork)
1995	Diarmuid Murphy (Kerry)
1996	Liam Hassett (Kerry)
1997	John McBride (Derry)
1998	Brian Scanlon (Kerry)
1999	Aiden Canning (Westmeath)
2000	C.McAnallen (Tyrone)
2001	C.McAnallen (Tyrone)
2002	J.Bergin (Galway)
2003	A.Brogan (Dublin)
2004	C.McKeever (Armagh)
2005	A.Burke (Galway)
2006	K.Higgins (Mayo)

2007	A.O'Sullivan (Cork)
2008	K.Young (Kerry)
2009	C.O'Neill (Cork)
2010	J.Cooper (Dublin)
2011	C.Forde (Galway)
2012	K.O'Brien (Dublin)
2013	F.Ó Curraoin (Galway)
2014	J.McCaffrey (Dublin)
2015	K.McGeary (Tyrone)
2016	S.Coen (Mayo)
2017	C.O'Shea/C.O'Callaghan (Dublin)

U21 FOOTBALL FINAL REFEREES

1964	J.Martin (Roscommon)
1965	J.Martin (Tyrone)
1966	J.Martin (Tyrone)
1967	J.Moloney (Tipperary)
1968	J.Hatton (Wicklow)
1969	B.Lowth (Dublin)
1970	P.Kelly (Dublin)
1971	S.Campbell (Kildare)
1972	D.Barry (Meath)
1973	M.Spain (Offaly)
1974	G.Hoey (Louth)
1975	B.Hayden (Carlow)
1976	G.Fagan (Armagh)
1977	M.Meally (Kilkenny)
1978	S.Murray (Monaghan)
1979	G.McCabe (Tyrone)
1980	W.Fogarty (Kerry)
1981	K.Campbell (Fermanagh)
1982	T.Moran (Leitrim)
1983	P.O'Gorman (Sligo)
1984	P.Kavanagh (Meath)
1985	C.Buckley (Offaly)
1986	J.Gough (Antrim)
1987	M.Kearns (Sligo)
1988	T.Sugrue (Kerry)
1989	P.Moran (Laois)
1990	P.Collins (Westmeath)
1991	C.Conlon (Westmeath)
1992	T.Howard (Kildare)
1993	D.Campbell (Fermanagh)
1994	P.McEnaney (Monaghan)
1995	P.McEnaney (Monaghan)
1996	P.Casserley (Westmeath)
1997	M.Curley (Galway)
1998	P.McEnaney (Monaghan)
1999	B.Gorman (Armagh)
2000	S.McCormack (Meath)
2001	A.Mangan (Kerry)
2002	M.McGrath (Donegal)
2003	G.Kinneavy (Roscommon)
2004	A.Mangan (Kerry)
2005	M.Deegan (Laois)
2006	J.McQuillan (Cavan)
2007	V.Neary (Mayo)

FOOTBALL

2008	M.Duffy (Sligo)
2009	C.Reilly (Meath)
2010	M.Duffy (Sligo)
2011	E.Kinsella (Laois)
2012	P.O'Sullivan (Kerry)
2013	D.Gough (Meath)
2014	B.Cassidy (Derry)
2015	F.Kelly (Longford)
2016	P.Hughes (Armagh)
2017	C.Branagan (Down)

MUNSTER U21 FOOTBALL FINALS

1962	Kerry	2-7	1-4	Cork
1963	Cork	2-3	1-4	Kerry
1964	Kerry	0-15	1-2	Tipperary
1965	Cork	2-14	1-6	Tipperary
1966	Kerry	3-8	0-14	Cork
1967	Kerry	2-12	1-7	Clare
1968	Kerry	5-7	2-9	Clare
1969	Cork	1-14	1-11	Kerry
1970	Cork	5-12	1-7	Clare
1971	Cork	1-10	2-5	Waterford
1972	Kerry	1-11	2-7	Cork
1973	Kerry	2-12	1-12	Cork
1974	Cork	3-5	1-10	Kerry
1975	Kerry	0-17	1-5	Waterford
1976	Kerry	2-16	1-6	Cork
1977	Kerry	2-8	0-8	Cork
1978	Kerry	0-14	0-9	Cork
1979	Cork	1-11	1-9	Clare
1980	Cork	3-15	0-4	Clare
1981	Cork	0-11	0-6	Kerry
1982	Cork	2-12	0-4	Kerry
1983	Kerry	1-10	0-12	Cork
1984	Cork	1-18	0-4	Limerick
1985	Cork	1-18	1-7	Clare
1986	Cork	0-8	0-7	Tipperary
1987	Kerry	0-7	0-7	Tipperary
Replay	Kerry	0-15	1-11	Tipperary (aet)
1988	Kerry	0-14	2-6	Clare
1989	Cork	3-15	1-7	Clare
1990	Kerry	2-9	0-9	Cork
1991	Kerry	1-8	0-10	Cork
1992	Kerry	3-12	1-8	Cork
1993	Kerry	1-21	3-5	Waterford
1994	Cork	2-11	0-4	Waterford
1995	Kerry	1-21	2-5	Waterford
1996	Kerry	3-14	0-6	Clare
1997	Kerry	2-11	3-8	Cork
Replay	Kerry	0-12	1-7	Cork
1998	Kerry	3-10	1-11	Tipperary
1999	Kerry	1-10	0-7	Cork
2000	Limerick	0-7	0-4	Waterford
2001	Cork	1-12	0-8	Limerick
2002	Kerry	3-15	2-11	Clare
2003	Waterford	2-8	1-9	Kerry

2004	Cork	0-13	0-12	Kerry
2005	Cork	1-14	1-11	Limerick
2006	Cork	4-14	1-6	Waterford
2007	Cork	3-19	3-12	Tipperary
2008	Kerry	0-15	2-7	Tipperary
2009	Cork	1-9	2-5	Tipperary
2010	Tipperary	1-7	1-6	Kerry
2011	Cork	2-24	0-8	Kerry
2012	Cork	2-12	1-14	Kerry
2013	Cork	1-17	0-9	Tipperary
2014	Cork	1-18	3-8	Tipperary
2015	Tipperary	1-15	3-8	Cork
2016	Cork	3-9	1-14	Kerry
2017	Kerry	2-16	0-6	Cork

LEINSTER U21 FOOTBALL FINALS

1964	Laois	1-8	0-8	Offaly
1965	Kildare	1-11	0-10	Offaly
1966	Kildare	4-14	2-5	Longford
1967	Kildare	3-11	0-4	Wicklow
1968	Offaly	2-13	0-7	Wexford
1969	Laois	2-7	2-6	Wicklow
1970	Louth	2-13	3-9	Offaly
1971	Offaly	1-9	0-11	Meath
1972	Kildare	0-14	2-8	Offaly
Replay	Kildare	2-9	0-6	Offaly
1973	Offaly	3-8	3-6	Kildare
1974	Dublin	1-10	0-8	Wexford
1975	Dublin	0-12	1-6	Laois
1976	Kildare	1-12	0-9	Dublin
1977	Offaly	0-12	0-4	Kildare
1978	Louth	2-8	2-7	Offaly
1979	Offaly	4-14	5-4	Louth
1980	Dublin	2-7	1-10	Kildare
Replay	Dublin	0-10	0-8	Kildare
1981	Louth	2-8	0-6	Longford
1982	Laois	2-11	0-3	Longford
1983	Kildare	1-13	1-8	Louth
1984	Dublin	0-9	1-5	Carlow
1985	Meath	2-7	0-12	Kildare
1986	Offaly	1-11	2-8	Laois
Replay	Offaly	1-10	0-9	Laois
1987	Laois	1-12	1-8	Meath
1988	Offaly	0-8	1-5	Wexford
Replay	Offaly	0-12	2-6	Wexford (aet)
Replay	Offaly	1-12	1-12	Wexford (aet)
Replay	Offaly	2-7	2-5	Wexford
1989	Meath	2-5	0-9	Kildare
1990	Meath	1-14	0-6	Wicklow
1991	Meath	0-9	1-5	Wicklow
1992	Kildare	2-12	0-9	Dublin
1993	Meath	2-11	2-9	Dublin
1994	Laois	2-4	1-7	Meath
Replay	Laois	1-17	1-13	Meath (aet)
1995	Offaly	0-14	0-8	Westmeath
1996	Meath	1-8	0-8	Louth
1997	Meath	1-11	0-7	Westmeath
1998	Laois	1-13	1-7	Dublin
1999	Westmeath	1-12	2-9	Laois
Replay	Westmeath	1-9	0-10	Laois

2000	Westmeath	0-7	0-6	Meath
2001	Meath	0-10	0-5	Dublin
2002	Dublin	1-17	2-4	Wicklow
2003	Dublin	3-13	1-6	Longford
2004	Kildare	0-7	1-4	Dublin
Replay	Kildare	1-10	0-12	Dublin
2005	Dublin	1-10	1-10	Kildare
Replay	Dublin	0-13	0-11	Kildare
2006	Laois	0-9	0-7	Longford
2007	Laois	0-13	1-7	Offaly
2008	Kildare	0-10	0-6	Wexford
2009	Dublin	0-12	0-9	Laois
2010	Dublin	1-12	0-9	Westmeath
2011	Wexford	1-9	0-11	Longford
2012	Dublin	1-16	0-8	Louth
2013	Kildare	1-12	0-12	Longford
2014	Dublin	0-15	0-10	Meath
2015	Dublin	3-10	1-12	Kildare
2016	Dublin	2-14	0-17	Kildare
2017	Dublin	2-14	0-8	Offaly

CONNACHT U21 FOOTBALL FINALS

1964	Galway	3-6	3-5	Mayo
1965	Galway	3-9	1-13	Mayo
1966	Roscommon	1-15	0-9	Mayo
1967	Mayo	3-11	2-8	Roscommon
1968	Mayo	1-13	2-3	Roscommon
1969	Roscommon	1-9	0-12	Galway
Replay	Roscommon	1-10	2-3	Galway (aet)
1970	Mayo	0-14	1-10	Roscommon
1971	Mayo	5-10	0-8	Roscommon
1972	Galway	0-16	0-5	Roscommon
1973	Mayo	1-7	0-5	Galway
1974	Mayo	1-12	0-9	Roscommon
1975	Mayo	2-10	0-9	Galway
1976	Mayo	1-8	0-2	Galway
1977	Leitrim	1-3	0-5	Roscommon
1978	Roscommon	3-9	2-11	Galway
1979	Galway	0-12	0-9	Sligo
1980	Mayo	4-11	1-5	Galway
1981	Galway	0-9	0-8	Mayo
1982	Roscommon	1-10	0-5	Galway
1983	Mayo	1-19	1-6	Roscommon
1984	Mayo	2-7	2-4	Galway
1985	Mayo	2-6	0-7	Galway
1986	Mayo	0-12	0-5	Leitrim
1987	Galway	1-10	0-10	Roscommon
1988	Galway	0-10	0-6	Roscommon
1989	Galway	1-13	0-3	Roscommon
1990	Galway	0-9	0-5	Leitrim
1991	Leitrim	1-7	0-9	Galway
1992	Galway	1-10	0-12	Mayo
1993	Galway	0-14	0-9	Roscommon
1994	Mayo	0-12	0-6	Sligo
1995	Mayo	1-10	1-10	Sligo
Replay	Mayo	1-16	3-4	Sligo
1996	Galway	0-12	0-5	Mayo
1997	Mayo	0-7	0-6	Galway
1998	Galway	0-13	1-7	Leitrim
1999	Roscommon	1-12	0-9	Sligo
2000	Galway	1-12	0-12	Mayo
2001	Mayo	0-15	0-7	Sligo
2002	Galway	1-9	1-8	Mayo
2003	Mayo	1-9	0-11	Galway
2004	Mayo	0-16	0-13	Roscommon
2005	Galway	1-13	0-4	Mayo

2006	Mayo	0-15	1-5	Galway
2007	Mayo	1-22	1-8	Roscommon
2008	Mayo	1-14	0-14	Roscommon
2009	Mayo	3-14	1-8	Sligo
2010	Roscommon	1-6	0-4	Sligo
2011	Galway	1-10	0-4	Roscommon
2012	Roscommon	1-13	0-8	Sligo
2013	Galway	1-17	2-11	Roscommon
2014	Roscommon	0-19	1-3	Leitrim
2015	Roscommon	3-14	3-11	Galway
2016	Mayo	1-11	1-10	Roscommon
2017	Galway	3-20	2-14	Sligo

ULSTER U21 FOOTBALL FINALS

1963	Donegal	3-6	1-3	Cavan
1964	Donegal	2-14	0-4	Monaghan
1965	Down	0-9	1-2	Cavan
1966	Donegal	2-12	1-6	Down
1967	Derry	1-11	1-4	Monaghan
1968	Derry	4-9	2-4	Monaghan
1969	Antrim	2-8	1-9	Down
1970	Fermanagh	0-13	0-8	Cavan
1971	Fermanagh	2-12	1-8	Tyrone
1972	Derry	1-7	1-7	Tyrone
Replay	Tyrone	3-13	1-6	Derry
1973	Tyrone	2-14	2-5	Monaghan
1974	Antrim	2-6	1-8	Tyrone
1975	Antrim	2-7	0-7	Tyrone
1976	Derry	1-6	1-4	Down
1977	Down	3-5	0-10	Cavan
1978	Down	0-11	1-6	Cavan
1979	Down	1-9	0-5	Tyrone
1980	Tyrone	4-4	2-5	Down
1981	Monaghan	0-8	0-6	Donegal
1982	Donegal	0-10	1-5	Derry
1983	Derry	3-13	1-3	Donegal
1984	Down	1-10	1-8	Antrim
1985	Derry	3-7	0-7	Tyrone
1986	Derry	4-7	0-6	Donegal
1987	Donegal	0-7	1-4	Monaghan
Replay	Donegal	1-11	0-8	Monaghan
1988	Cavan	3-10	0-6	Antrim
1989	Antrim	1-6	1-5	Down
1990	Tyrone	2-8	0-11	Down
1991	Tyrone	3-10	0-8	Down
1992	Tyrone	0-14	2-6	Monaghan
1993	Derry	1-9	1-8	Down
1994	Fermanagh	2-8	0-8	Derry
1995	Donegal	1-9	1-9	Cavan
Replay	Donegal	3-11	1-11	Cavan
1996	Cavan	1-11	1-5	Derry
1997	Derry	1-12	1-6	Fermanagh
1998	Armagh	1-8	0-10	Derry
1999	Monaghan	0-12	1-8	Donegal
2000	Tyrone	1-18	1-4	Donegal
2001	Tyrone	1-19	0-10	Fermanagh
2002	Tyrone	0-13	1-7	Cavan
2003	Tyrone	2-8	0-11	Monaghan

Year	Winner			Runner-up
2004	Armagh	2-12	0-4	Derry
2005	Down	2-14	2-12	Cavan (aet)
2006	Tyrone	0-12	1-7	Derry
2007	Armagh	1-16	1-9	Monaghan
2008	Down	3-11	1-14	Derry
2009	Down	1-14	2-10	Armagh
2010	Donegal	2-8	0-7	Cavan
2011	Cavan	1-10	0-10	Tyrone
2012	Cavan	1-10	0-10	Tyrone
2013	Cavan	0-13	1-6	Donegal
2014	Cavan	2-6	0-8	Donegal
2015	Tyrone	1-11	0-13	Donegal
2016	Monaghan	0-13	0-11	Tyrone
2017	Donegal	3-17	0-13	Derry

ALL-IRELAND JUNIOR FOOTBALL FINALS

1912	Tipperary	1-4	1-3	Louth
1913	Kerry	0-7	1-2	Carlow
1914	Dublin	5-4	1-6	Mayo
1915	Kerry	0-6	1-2	Westmeath
1916	Dublin	1-2	1-2	Limerick
Replay	Dublin	6-4	0-3	Limerick
1917-1922	Suspended			
1923	Tipperary	2-6	1-1	Carlow
1924	Kerry	1-6	0-4	Longford
1925	Louth	2-6	2-5	Mayo
1926	Armagh	4-11	0-4	Dublin
1927	Cavan	4-1	1-1	Britain
	'Home' Final:			
	Cavan	0-7	1-3	Kildare
1928	Kerry	2-8	2-3	Louth
1929	Westmeath	0-9	1-2	London
	'Home' Final:			
	Westmeath	3-3	0-3	Limerick
1930	Kerry	2-2	1-4	Dublin
	No 'Home' Final.			
	London competed at quarter-final stage.			
1931	Galway	3-3	1-5	London
	'Home' Final:			
	Galway	1-8	1-7	Kildare
1932	Louth	0-6	0-4	London
	'Home' Final:			
	Louth	1-12	0-4	Roscommon
1933	Mayo	3-7	2-4	London
	'Home' Final			
	Mayo	2-15	2-2	Donegal
1934	Louth	1-3	0-3	London
	'Home' Final:			
	Louth	0-9	1-4	Kerry
1935	Sligo	5-8	0-3	London
	'Home' Final:			
	Sligo	4-2	2-5	Tipperary
1936	Wicklow	3-3	2-5	Mayo
1937	Longford	0-9	0-7	London
	'Home' Final:			
	Longford	1-7	1-6	Mayo
1938	London	5-7	2-9	Leitrim
	'Home' Final:			
	Leitrim	1-8	0-5	Kildare
1939	Dublin	2-14	0-4	London
	'Home' Final:			
	Dublin	2-9	1-9	Roscommon
1940	Roscommon	2-9	0-5	Westmeath
1941	Kerry	0-9	0-4	Cavan
1942-1945	Suspended			
1946	Down	2-10	1-9	Warwickshire

	'Home' Final:			
	Down	2-7	2-3	Leitrim
1947	Meath	2-11	2-6	London
	'Home' Final:			
	Meath	1-12	3-3	Kerry
1948	Dublin	2-11	1-5	London
	'Home' Final:			
	Dublin	2-6	2-3	Armagh
	(unfinished). Replay ordered.			
	Dublin	3-8	2-6	Armagh
1949	Kerry	2-14	0-6	Lancashire
	'Home' Final:			
	Kerry	3-11	3-5	Down
1950	Mayo	2-4	0-3	London
	'Home' Final:			
	Mayo	4-3	2-7	Derry
1951	Cork	5-11	1-3	Warwickshire
	'Home' Final:			
	Cork	1-5	1-2	Mayo
1952	Meath	3-9	0-4	London
	'Home' Final:			
	Meath	0-11	0-2	Leitrim
1953	Cork	1-11	1-4	Lancashire
	'Home' Final:			
	Cork	2-9	0-4	Longford
1954	Kerry	1-7	1-5	London
	'Home' Final:			
	Kerry	3-6	1-6	Donegal
1955	Cork	3-9	1-5	Warwickshire
	'Home' Final:			
	Cork	3-10	1-7	Derry
1956	Monaghan	3-7	2-6	London
	'Home' Final:			
	Monaghan	1-8	0-5	Kildare
1957	Mayo	2-7	2-5	Warwickshire
	'Home' Final:			
	Mayo	1-11	1-3	Cork
1958	Galway	4-5	3-1	Lancashire
	'Home' Final:			
	Galway	1-10	0-7	Meath
1959	Fermanagh	1-11	2-4	London
	'Home' Final:			
	Fermanagh	1-13	2-3	Kerry
1960	Dublin	2-5	0-5	London
	'Home' Final:			
	Dublin	1-12	0-9	Galway
1961	Louth	1-13	1-10	Yorkshire
	'Home' Final:			
	Louth	0-11	1-7	Galway
1962	Meath	1-13	3-5	London
	'Home' Final:			
	Meath	1-11	3-4	Cavan
1963	Kerry	3-5	2-5	Lancashire
	'Home' Final:			
	Kerry	1-12	2-7	Wexford
1964	Cork	1-8	2-4	London
	'Home' Final:			
	Cork	2-5	1-8	Meath
	Cork	2-9	0-10	Meath (replay)
1965	Galway	1-8	0-4	Hertfordshire
	'Home' Final:			
	Galway	1-15	2-4	Kildare
1966	London	1-6	0-8	Cork
	'Home' Final:			
	Cork	2-12	0-9	Down
1967	Kerry	0-9	0-4	London
	'Home' Final:			
	Kerry	1-10	1-3	Mayo
1968	Tyrone	3-8	0-7	London
	'Home' Final:			
	Tyrone	3-9	2-11	Mayo
1969	London	3-9	1-12	Wicklow
	'Home' Final:			
	Wicklow	0-12	1-8	Kerry
1970	London	1-12	0-11	Kildare
	'Home' Final:			
	Kildare	1-12	1-10	Cork
1971	London	1-9	0-9	Dublin
	'Home' Final:			
	Dublin	1-14	2-5	Cork
1972	Cork	5-16	0-3	Hertfordshire
	'Home' Final:			
	Cork	1-10	0-8	Galway
1973	Laois	0-12	1-8	London
	'Home' Final:			
	Laois	2-13	1-5	Sligo
1974-1982	Suspended			
1983	Kerry	0-15	0-2	Yorkshire
	'Home' Final:			
	Kerry	1-9	0-5	Dublin
1984	Cork	3-20	0-7	Warwickshire
	'Home' Final:			
	Cork	1-10	0-9	Wexford
1985	Galway	4-17	0-4	Warwickshire
	'Home' Final:			
	Galway	0-9	0-9	Kerry
	Galway	0-11	0-7	Kerry (replay)
1986	London	1-9	0-7	Cork
	'Home' Final:			
	Cork	0-9	1-6	Meath
	Cork	0-11	1-4	Meath (replay)
1987	Cork	0-14	0-3	Warwickshire
	'Home' Final:			
	Cork	2-7	0-8	Dublin
1988	Meath	1-10	0-3	London
	'Home' Final:			
	Meath	1-9	1-5	Cork
1989	Cork	0-18	0-3	Warwickshire
	'Home' Final:			
	Cork	1-11	0-3	Kildare
1990	Cork	3-16	0-8	Warwickshire
	'Home' Final:			
	Cork	1-12	1-10	Meath
1991	Kerry	2-14	0-5	London
	'Home' Final:			
	Kerry	1-15	0-12	Meath
1992	Wexford	1-9	0-11	Cork
1993	Cork	0-11	2-3	Laois

1994	Kerry	0-15	0-4	Galway
1995	Mayo	3-9	0-10	London
1996	Cork	4-11	0-10	Meath
1997	Mayo	2-8	1-10	Kerry
1998	Tipperary	2-9	0-6	Offaly
1999	Waterford	2-12	2-11	Meath
2000	Roscommon	0-14	0-11	Kerry
2001	Cork	1-15	3-7	Mayo
2002	Wicklow	4-9	2-12	Kerry
2003	Meath	0-16	1-7	Galway
2004	Waterford	1-10	1-10	Leitrim
Replay	Waterford	2-12	2-9	Leitrim
2005	Cork	0-10	1-4	Meath
2006	Kerry	1-9	0-10	Roscommon
2007	Cork	1-14	3-2	Wexford
2008	Dublin	0-13	0-7	Roscommon
2009	Cork	0-15	0-12	Roscommon
2010	Sligo	2-10	1-7	Kerry
2011	Cork	1-12	0-13	Kildare
2012	Kerry	0-19	1-7	Mayo
2013	Cork	0-13	1-7	Kildare
2014	Cavan	2-14	0-14	Kerry
2015	Kerry	2-18	0-10	Mayo
2016	Kerry	2-18	2-11	Mayo
2017	Kerry	2-19	1-14	Meath

JUNIOR FOOTBALL FINALISTS

1912

Tipperary Ned O'Shea, John O'Shea, L.Gorman, Ned Delahunty, F.O'Brien, Ned Egan, N.Vaughan, T.Connors, M.Devitt, H.Kennedy, J.Quinn, D.Stapleton, Dick Heffernan, P.Dwyer, J.Shelly, Bill Scully, P.Egan.

Louth M.Carolan, M.Tinnelly, J.McGann, S.Reilly, J.Burke, P.Kirk, J.Naughton, E.McCormack, P.McLoughlin, T.Burke, J.Matthews, P.O'Hanlon, P.Mulholland, P.McGeogh, W.Wiley, M.Heeney, B.Lennon.

1913

Kerry A.Callaghan (goal), P.Foley, J.Keating, J.McGaley, J.Kennedy, P.O'Donnell, J.Courtney, H.Murphy, E.Murphy, T.King, E.Hogan, M.Daly, J.Connell, J.Collins, J.McCarthy.

Carlow W.Mulhall (capt.), M.Lawlor, D.Fitzpatrick, Millett, W.Cooney, F.Shaw, J.Murphy, A.Murphy, P.Haughney, P.Hogan, Hennessy, M.Haughney, M.Hogan, Tobin, W.Murphy.

1914

Dublin P.Carey, S.Synott, T.Corr, M.Nolan, P.Smith, D.Kiely, D.Kelly, P.Kearns, F.Burke, F.McGann, J.Cromien, P.McDonnell, J.Coogan, J.McAdams, P.Whelan.

Mayo J.O'Reilly, J.Gavin, J.Jordan, J.Robinson, Jas.Robinson, P.Cowley, T.Ruane, M.Murray, T.Gibson, J.Brennan, J.McNally, E.McEllin, J.Reilly, P.Galvin, J.McNulty.

1915

Kerry R.Power, W.Sheehan, J.Cronin, M.Carroll, P.Sullivan, J.Dunne, T.Doherty, M.Moriarty, J.Connor, T King (capt.), P.Slattery, M.Daly, J.Walsh, B.Hickey, J.McGaley.

Westmeath L.Leech, P Whelehan, J.McKeogh, M.McKeon, J.Cooney, R.O'Reilly, P.Arthur, J.Moran, Rochford, J.Reilly, Bob Reilly, J.McGuinness, Early, P.Ledwith, Mallory.

1916

Dublin J.Maguire (capt.), F.McGann, H.O'Neill, N.Sheridan, J.O'Reilly, P.McDonnell, J.Molloy, P White, J.O'Donovan, P.McCarville, F.Burke, B.Joyce, J.Hayden, J.Treacy, J.Byrne.

Limerick C.Kiely (capt.), P.O'Donnell, M.Walsh, M.Osborne (goal), M.Davoren, D.O'Grady, J.J.O'Keeffe, T.Butler, J.Lyons, M.McGrath, D.Breen, A.Dalton, J.O'Donovan, D.Casey, J.Crowley.

1923

Tipperary Ned Cummins (capt.), T Hogan, P.Walsh, H.Dillon, Gus Dwyer, M.Barry, M.Nolan, D.Mullins, T Tubridy, G.McCarthy, J.Delaney, T.Dunne, J.Davy, T.Armitage, P.Dwan.

Carlow B.Hennessy, M.Murray, B.Nolan, W.Cooney, W.Doyle, W.Hogan, W.Qulgley, M.Hogan, J.Moore, P.Haughney T.Nolan, E.Wall, M.Hanley, R.McDonnell, T.Dillon.

1924

Kerry J.Riordan (goal), J.McCarthy (capt.), D.O'Connell, W.Riordan, J.Slattery, P.Clifford, T.Graham, M.Graham, T.Mahony, Paud Sullivan, T.O'Donnell, S.Kerins, E.Fitzgerald, D.O'Connor, T.O'Connor.

Longford F.Gaffney (capt.), J.Brennan, P.Bates, F.Canning, P.McWade, C.Heuston, J.McWade, M.Deane, E.Gaffney, M.Grehan, P Reilly, M.Burke, M.Cawley, M.O'Toole, H.Greene. Subs: F.Beirne, J.Gavigan.

FOOTBALL

1925
Louth   S.Hughes, M.Tuite, J.Traynor, J.Lynch (capt.), M.Lynch, J.McMahon, W.Doyle, T.Rath, M.McKeown, J.Heaney, J.Halligan, E.Kane, J.Murray, F.Penthony, P Butterley.
Mayo   P.Hoban, J.Courell, R.Coleman, M.J.Moran, J.McGahern, J.Gallagher (capt.), M.Barrett, J.Carr, J.Burke, T.Carty, M.Chambers, J.Biggins, E.Hogan, C.Armstrong, M.J.Horan.

1926
Armagh   C.Morgan, H.Cumiskey, Gene Hanratty (capt.), J.Vallely, Joe Harney, J.Maguire, Owen Connolly, J.Corrigan, F.McAvinchey, F.Toner, P.Fearon, J.Kernan, H.Arthurs, J.Donaghy, J.McCusker. Sub: J.McEntee for F.McAvinchey.
Dublin   H.Kelly (goal), T.Kavanagh (capt.), E.Rice, D.Nolan, J.Rodgers, M.Langton, J.Corcoran, W.Finlay, S.Banim, A.Doyle, D.Murphy, Joe Sherlock, S.Nolan, J.Doran, M.Gill.

1927
Cavan   P.Lynch, J.Morgan, J.P.Dolan, T.Crowe, G.Malcolson, P.Leddy, F.Gilsenan, L.Mallon, P.Fox, H.O'Reilly, F.Fitzpatrick J.Young, P.Devlin, A.Conlon, P.J.O'Reilly.
Britain   P.J.Kane, P.Darby, E.O'Hourigan, M.Fitzgerald, P.O'Malley, M.Kelly, L.Hartnett, R.Mackey, J.Burns, G.Keevans, J.Farrell, J.Cox, P.Gallagher, L.Duffy, S.Marshall.

1928
Kerry   Billy McSweeney, R.O'Donoghue (capt) T.Barrett, M.Healy, J.Price, M.Doyle, J.Quill, J.Murphy, T.Landers, R.Savage, T.Curran, J.Horan, T.O'Donnell, R.Clifford, J.Sullivan.
Louth   Callaghan, Roche, Downey, Corroway, Cluskey, Bishop, Canavan, MaHhews, Connor, Byrne, Byrne, Hearty, Gunning, Mullan, Bailey.

1929
Westmeath F.McGuinness (capt.), S.Bracken (goal), M.McCarthy, A.Mullen, T.Finneran, J.Dunican, A.Dunne, J.Austin, D.Breen, J.Byrne, P.Bracken, J.Guilfoyle, J.Smyth, J.Coughlan, T.Seery.
London   J.Farrell (capt.), C.Finnegan (goal), D.Fitzpatrick, R.Smith, J.Shalloe, J.Dillon, R.Tuite, L.Hartnett, G.Murphy, H.Murphy, P.Mulpeter, T.Morgan, L.Cunningham, J.Reilly, C.Traynor.

1930
Kerry   D.O'Keeffe, P.Murphy, D.O'Donoghue, J.O'Connor, S.Moynihan, J.O'Connor (Cahirciveen), L.Powell, C.Geaney, D.Spring, J.Flavin, J.Price, W.Quill, M.O'Regan, M.Healy, T.Landers.
Dublin   J.Begley, Hugh Kelly, P.Rogers, F.Kavanagh, P.Byrne, P.Hickey, J.O'Rourke, P.Kavanagh, C.Duffy, E.Lee, A.Dixon, G.O'Reilly.E.Hunston, Dr.S.Lavan, M.Brennan.

1931
Galway   J.O'Rourke, M.Connaire, W.Mannion, P.Morris, J.Mitchell, M.Mannion, P.Daly, F.Fox, J.Dunne, M.Stewart, J.Kelleher (capt.), W.Birrell, F.Morris, Martin Donnellan, B.Nestor.
London   C.Finnegan, D.Fitzpatrick, R.Smith, J.Murphy, J.Dillon, P.O'Malley (capt.), C.Murray, J.Fitzpatrick, G.Murphy, J.O'Brien, M.Lennon, P.Mulpeter, J.Power, M.Reilly, C.Traynor.

1932
Louth   P.Byrne (capt.), M.Leech, P.Dunne, W.Crilly, T.McArdle, V.Kerr, P.Cluskey, P.Martin, P.Devlin, J.Culligan, P.Moore, J.Mullan, T.Tiernan, P.Downey, J.Moonen. Sub: J.Byrne for P.Devlin.
London   D.Fitzpatrick (capt.), M.Murphy, M.Fitzpatrick, M.Lennon, C.Corpenter, C.Finnegan, J.Dillon, J.Fitzpatrick, J.Murphy, P.Mulpeter, G.Murphy, H.Murphy, D.Loughlin, J.J.Power, J.McGrath. Sub: Joe Murphy for C.Murray.

1933
Mayo   T.Grier (capt.), J.O'Gara, P.O'Loughtin, P.J.Coffey, B.Frazer, P.J.Walsh, M.Raftery, P.Collins, T.Regan, J.Carney, P.Conboy, P.Laffey, H.O'Brien, T.Kelly, T.Culkin.
London   C.Finnegan, L.Murphy, M.Murphy, G.Murphy, J.Roche, J.J.Keogh, P.Mulpeter, W.Kelly, T.Keyes, J.Dillon, J.Fitzpatrick (capt.), H.Murphy, J.O'Brien, C.Carpenter, J.Murphy. Sub: R.Smith for J.Fitzpatrick.

1934
Louth   H.Callan (goal), J.Doyle (capt.), P.Tuite, T.Tiernan, J.Collins, J.McKevitt, P.Cluskey, M.Callaghan, J.Beirne, P.Byrne, J.Clarke, P.Mullen, P.Moore, V.Kerr, P.McKevitt.
London   J.Smith, R.Kelly, H.Murphy, T.Behan, T.Shields, P.Mulpeter, G.Murphy, J.Roche, J.Fitzpatrick, Walsh, C.Carpenter, P.Buckley, P.Devlin, J.Murphy, P.Carroll.

1935
Sligo   J.Scanlon (capt.), S.Scanlon, P.McGovern, J.Carty, M.Kennedy, O.Harte, P.Tiernan, F.Henry, M.Waters, C.Curran, P.Brennan, M.Stenson, J.O'Donnell, S.Tansey, J.Quinn.
(Note: The Sligo team listed is the one that is on all the papers. However according to the photograph three of those listed, M.Kennedy, P.Brennan and J.Quinn were not on.The three players in the photograph were F.Cavanagh, M.Snee and M.O'Dowd.
London   D.Buckley (capt.), J.Smith, W.Higgins, P.Grant, K.Hughes, P.Hartley, T.Shiels, P.Carroll, G.Murphy, P.Mulpeter, L.Murphy, R.Murphy, J.O'Loughlin, J.Murtagh, J.Reilly.

1936
Wicklow   J.Kelly, T.Sullivan, P.Nolan, M.O'Brien, Bob Elliot, J.Dalton, J.Deering, M.Byrne, D.Kerrigan, M.Keating, P.Sullivan, T.Tyrell, M.O'Neill (capt.), Ned Byrne, G.Kealy.M.Frawley for M.Byrne, R.Walsh.
Mayo   J.Acton, A.Golden, W.Frazer, W.Durkin, J.Robinson, M.Collins, W.Mongey, P.Bennett, J.McLoughlin, T.Grier, D.Sullivan, M.O'Malley, P.O'Malley, P.Judge, M.Heaney.

1937
Longford   G.Marsden, J.Lyons, J.McDermott, J.Murphy, E.Reilly, J.Regan, B.Sheridan, J.McCarthy, J.Keenan, W.Keenan, H.Rogers, J.Rogers, F.Marsden, B.Reilly, J.Murphy.
London   J.Smith, C.Feeney, D.Larkin, T.Shields, J.Sweeney, D.Fitzmaurice, C.Murphy, P.McEnroe, J.O'Sullivan, H.Murphy, M.O'Sullivan, P.Conboy, P.Mulpeter, M.Moore, R.Baker, E.Stenson. Sub: J.Sweeney.

1938
London   J.Smith, C.Murphy, T.Shields, J.Sweeney, D.Fitzmaurice, J.Sullivan (capt.), J.Byrne, P.Conboy, H.Murphy, E.Stenson, W.Kelly, P.Rosney, O.McKeown, R.Baker, P.Mulpeter. Subs: J.Grennan, P.Burke, D.Larkin.

Leitrim   F.McGoldrick, P.Reynolds, E.O'Reilly, M.Kilkenny (capt.), F.Carter, J.F.McGuinness, P.Rogan, G.Shanley, M.Moran, J.Shanley, E.Dolan, J.Keegan, J.Molohan, J.Turbitt, J.Mitchell. Sub: H.Turbitt.

1939

Dublin   P.Dowling, B.Murphy, C.Donnellan, W.Rayburn, F.Harford, H.Donnelly, D.Smyth, R.Smyth, J.Farrell, T.Dowling, M.Richardson, M.Meehan, T. Markey, J.Sweeney, M.O'Reilly. Sub: P.Kennedy For J.Sweeney.
London   J.Smith, C.Murphy, T.Shiels, F.Feeney, E.Stenson, J.O'Sullivan, J.Kennedy, H.Murphy, J.Byrne, P.Burke, E.Monaghan, W.Williams, O.McKeown, R.Baker, P.Mulpeter.

1940

Roscommon   F.Glynn, J.F.Comer, J.P.O'Callaghan, O.Hoare, H.Connor, P.Kelly, W.Heavey, J.Murray, E.Boland, P.Kenny, K.Winston, D.Keenan, G.Beirne, H.Gibbons (capt.), P.McManus. Sub: P.Murray, K.Heavey.
Westmeath   S.Bracken, E.Martin, C.Fagan, A.Carr, P.J.O'Neill, J.Carbury (capt.), M.Dunne, J.Lawlor, J.Leech, V.Gillick, P.McCormack, M.Devaney, E.McCormack, P.Mullen, G.Wallace. Subs: M.Daly for J.Leech, A.Mullen for V.Gillick, M.Keogh.

1941

Kerry   J.Sheehy, T.Brosnan (capt.), T.O'Sullivan, T.Long, T.Barrett, D.Lyne, T.Lyne, J.Sexton, J.Murphy, M.McCarthy, D.J.Healy, J.Kennington, W.O'Donnell, P.Donoghue, P.McCarthy.
Cavan   J.D.Benson, T.Cahill, J.F.McGahern, M.Argue, J.O'Reilly, P.Coyle, J.Greenan, J.Maguire, W.Doonan, T.Hennessy, B.Hunt, J.Devlin, P.Coyle, J.Coyle, P.J.Clarke. Sub: J.J.Cassidy.

1946

Down   E.McGivern, P.O'Hagan, A.Murnin, H.Downey, G.Browne, E.Grant, Noel McCarthy, G.Carr (capt.), J.Haughian, G.Doherty, T.Brown, D.Downey, D.Kennedy, H.Brown, J.Heaney. Subs: K.O'Hare, M.Short.
Warwickshire   R.Tumulty, R.Green, P.J.Foran, J.Lonergan, T.Geraghty, W.Halton, M.Hartney, P.Hartnett, A.Green, P.Mooney, P.Judge, J.McDermott, J.Casey, M.O'Dowd, J.O'Neill.

1947

Meath   T.Tuite, E.McCabe, W.Rispin, J.Donegan, P.Connell, M.O'Brien, G.McArdle, D.Taaffe, E.Daly, W.Snow, J.Johnson, J.Sampson, J.Carolan, L.McGuinness (capt.), J.Hand. Subs: J.Casserley for J.Sampson, A.O'Reilly for T.Tuite, M.McCaffrey for W.Rispin.
London   F.Finnesson, J.Poppenwell, S.Melotte, S.Mulderrig, P.Casey, E.McQuillan, P.Dolan, M.Wrenn, F.Moore, R.Allen, D.Mulvihill, M.Kilcullen, F.Cummins, J.Farrelly, P.Traynor. Sub: D.O'Shea for J.Farrelly.

1948

Dublin   V.Russell, L.Ledwidge, G.Donoghue, N.Fingleton, M.Richardson, E.Lyons, M.Scanlon, S.Farrell, J.Tunney, P.Walsh (capt.), J.O'Toole, J.McDonnell, J.Copeland, E.Kenneally, K.Heffernan.
London   F.Fennison, F.Cummins, E.McQuillan, T.Crean, P.Casey, J.Owens, D.Mulvihill, F.P.Forkin, C.Carroll, T.Dunne, P.Dolan, F.Bambrick, J.Murray, D.Curran, J.Moriarty.

1949

Kerry   L.Fitzgerald, J.O'Connor, T.Flynn, D.Dowling, M.Lynch, P.Shanahan, M.McElligott, Seán Murphy, J.Dowling, P.Murphy, P.McCarthy, T.Long (capt.), J.C.Cooper, M.J.Palmer, J.Kennedy.
Lancashire   J.Duffy, T.Heffernan, P.McDermott, J.Brett, J.Regan, Jas.Duffy, M.Kilkenny (capt.), J.Fitzgerald, R.Harrison, J.Keane, P.J.Wright, F.Flynn, J.Tiernan, P.Carroll, M.Mullally. Sub: R.O'Rafferty for J.Fitzgerald.

1950

Mayo   T.Byrne, P.Gilvarry, P.Doherty, T.Quinn, J.Staunton, J.O'Sullivan, C.Hegarty, S.Hennigan, P.Jordan, T.Canavan, S.Mellotte (capt.), M.Loftus, F.McGovern, M.McDonnell, J.J.McGowan. Sub: A.O'Toole for T.Canavan.
London   M.Minchin, J.Owens, T.Crean, J.Butler, F.Canavan, M.Lynch, P.Brennan, J.Leahy, P.McConnan, S.Shields, R.Murphy, M.Barry, F.Stockwell, P.Quinn, J.Barton. Sub: J.Griffin for F Canavan

1951

Cork   C.Kearney, W.Barry, Noel Fitzgerald, P.J.Kelly, S.O'Connell, D.Bernard, J.Downing, T.Moriarty, J.J.Henchion (capt.), Ted Kelleher, M.Galvin, G.Hurley, E.Prendergast, S.Condon, P.O'Regan. Subs: M.O'Shea for J.Downing, F.Scanlan for T.Moriarty.
Warwickshire   F.Conroy, F.Daly, P.O'Reilly, P.Kinsella, A.O'Neill, J.Turner, T.O'Brien, H.Burke, D.Regan (capt.), P.Reynolds, W.Holton, P.Clarke, J.Johnson, P.O'Sullivan, P.Clarke. Subs: T.Skahill for F.Daly, M.Walsh for P.Clarke.

1952

Meath   P.Watters, P.McKeever, J.Donegan, E.Mee, F.Clare, K.Lenehan, B.Conlon, T.O'Brien, S.Duff, L.O'Brien, D.Brennan, S.O'Brien, P.Whelan (capt.), T.Moriarly, P.Ratty. Subs: J.Smith for B.Conlon, J.McHugh for J.Smith.
London   P.Fall, H.O'Donnell, J.O'Sullivan, T.Crean, P.Brennan, J.Butler, T.O'Connell, J.Walsh, J.Leahy, S.Boyle, J.Barton, S.Shiels, J.Moriarty, P.Fitzgerald, M.Lowrey. Sub: S.Henry for J.Butler.

1953

Cork   J.Lyons (capt.), J.Finnegan, G.Linehan, E.Downey, D.O'Herlihy, D.Murray, J.Lowney, J.Collins, D.Madden, T.Furlong, G.Brennan, J.O'Donovon, E.Goulding, J.Creedon, J.Barry. Sub: J.O'Keeffe for D.Madden.
Lancashire   E.McDermott, J.McCabe, P.McDermott, J.Cahill, J.Harrison, E.Bartley, S.Keane, J.Quirke, P.J.Wright, M.McDermott, J.Corr, J.Burns, T.Shiel, C.Johnson, V.Wymes. Sub: J.Flynn.

1954

Kerry   N.Hussey, T.Spillane, J.O'Connor, T.Healy, T.Costello, J.Spillone, D.Falvey, E.Fitzgerald, D.Dillon, J.Cullotly, T.Collins, S.Lovett, P.P.Fitzgerald, E.Dowling, B.Galvin.
London   P.Casey, J.McHugh, T.Crehan, P.Hinson, J.Glennon, E.Moran, C.Carroll, K.Mulderrig, J.Walsh, M.Lowry, P.McGlennon, M.O'Malley, J.Sugrue, J.Murrihy, S.Shields. Sub: J.McGurk for J.Murrihy.

1955

Cork   L.Power, T.Moynihan, Dermot O'Sullivan, T.O'Callaghan, T.Connolly, B.O'Sullivan, Paddy Murphy, J.Collins, T.Furlong, D.Murphy, Dermot O'Donovan, Bob Troy, D.J.O'Sullivan, R.Nutly, O.McAuliffe (capt.). Subs: P.J.Kelly for P.Murphy, P.Murphy for T.Moynihan.

Warwickshire   D.McMahon, J.Gately, J.Turner, T.Quinn,
A.O'Neill, P.Duggan, P.Holton, W.Wynne, J.Wynne, P.O'Flynn,
P.Murphy, P.Burke, J.Johnson, R.Malone, C.Deeney.

1956
Monaghan T.McArdle, G.McArdle, O.O'Rourke, B.Hamill,
D.McGuigan, D.Ward, P.McGuigan, J.Byrne, S.McElroy, S.Mulligan,
T.Duffy, P.Murphy, P.Clarke (capt.), N.Ward, E.McCooey. Sub:
E.Murphy for S.M.McElroy.
London J.J.Minihan, J.McHugh, P.Dooley, J.Clarke, D.McCarthy,
J.Spillane, A.Cunningham, J.Lynn (capt.), C.Greene, M.Lowry,
P.McGlennon, M.Vesey, J.Lyons, S.Mulderrig, E.Nealon. Subs:
W.Cantillon for D.McCarthy, A.McWade for J.M McHugh.

1957
Mayo   E.Waters, I.McCaffrey, C.O'Toole, J.Healy, T.Lyons,
J.McAndrew, P.Gannon, T.Quigley, P.Maye, D.McManus,
P.McManamon, J.Biesty, J.Munnelly, M.Lokus (capt.) J McGrath.
Sub: P.Fallon for P.Maye.
Warwickshire   M.Flaherty, R.Burke, J.Wynne, J.Gately,
T.O'Donoghue, E.Conway, B.Kennecly, A.O'Neill, P.McMurrough,
J.O'Malley, M.Wynne, M.West, C.McGuigan, L.Brogan, P.Burke.
Sub: T.Quinn for B.Kennedy.

1958
Galway   K.Cummins, B.Naughton, P.Davin, S.Meade,
J.Donnellan, F.Cloonan, P.Dunne, J.Mannion, J.Glavey,
M."Hauleen" McDonagh, P.Coyle, E.Sharkey, M.Walsh, L.Mannion
(capt.), M.Costello.
Lancashire P.McCabe, J.Harrison, E.Smith, S.Houricane,
P.Fox, C.Smith, S.Harte, J.Gargan, M.Reynolds, P.O'Brien,
S.Goff, P.Farrelly 1capt.), J.St.John, M.O'Connor, S.Keane. Sub:
C.McLoughlin.

1959
Fermanagh J.O'Neill, O.O'Callaghan, I.McQuillan (capt.),
J.Collins, J.J.Treacy, J.Cassidy, L.McMahon, J.Maguire, M.Brewster,
D.O'Rourke, P.T.Treacy, K.Sreenan, F.McGurn, O.Clerkin,
D.Devanney. Sub: H.Murphy for H.McGurn.
London   M.Nolan, J.Jennings, S.Mulderrig, P.McDonnell,
R.Doherty, M.Freyne, S.Murphy, S.O'Sullivan, A.Cunningham,
L.McLoughlin, P.Whelan, S.Harrison, S.McCormack, T.O'Connell,
D.Waters. Subs: J.Garvey for S.O'Sullivan, E.Barrett for
P.McDonnell, S.Moran for M.Freyne, T.O'Sullivan for J.Garvey.

1960
Dublin   F.McPhillips, C.Kane, J.Farrell, F.McHugh, C.Carroll,
D.Mulligan, O.Callaghan, S.Murray, P.Hallinan, P.Delaney,
V.Murphy, S.Coen, B.McDonald, J.Kirwan, F.McCourt.
London   C.Galligan, F.Tiernan, S.Hendry, F.Hurley, T.Crohon,
J.Jennings, S.Murphy, T.Egan, J.Moffatt, M.Vesey, P.Wilson, P.Kane,
J.Myles, T.Connell, S.Harrison. Subs: S.Mulderrig for M.Vesey,
M.Burke for J.Myles.

1961
Louth   J.Clifford, O.Coombes, J.Butterly, A.Kirwan, A.Sheelan
(capt.), M.Kelly, P.Dixon, F.Fegan, P.Jordan, J.Sheelan, M.McKeown,
J.Judge, S.Goodman, H.Donnelly, F.Kirk. Subs: J.Mallon for
O.Coombes, L.Toal for P.Jordan.
Yorkshire   M.Courtney, D.Grennan, L.Daly, T.Fox, P.Donlon,
P.Beirne, P.O'Hara, M.Jordan, J.Kelly, H.Marron, M.Keegan (capt.),
M.Kelly, P.Burke, M.Neary, J.Shields.

1962
Meath   M.Clarke, S.McCormack, J.Ryan, J.Quinn, W.Eiffe,
T.Gibney, P.Price, T.Muldoon, T.Monaghan, P.McCormack,
P.Hanley, J.Walsh (capt.), P.Christie, O.Kealy, T.Mongey.
Subs: G.Quinn for P.Hanly, J.Kane for T.Muldoon, P.Black for
T.Monaghan.
London   J.Kelly, P.McLarnon, S.Hendry, S.Mulderrig, P.Russell,
J.Jennings, W.Flaherty, S.McCowell, N.O'Reilly, R.Doherty,
P.Long, D.Sheehan, D.Mullins, J.Ashe, F.Smith. Subs: J.Hughes for
P.McLarnon, J.Sharkey for W.Flaherty, P.Burke for N.O'Reilly.

1963
Kerry   A.Guerin, P.Kerins, J.Dowling, P.Sayers, T.Sheehan,
M.Morris, J.Driscoll, J.D.O'Connor, D.O'Sullivan, T.Burke, B.Sheehy,
D.O'Shea, T.O'Dowd, J.Burke, D.O'Donnell.
Lancashire M.O'Donoghue, R.Henderson, E.Smith, P.Osborne,
B.Harrington, C.Smith, M.O'Connell, O.Agnew, S.Corridan,
M.McGeaney, P.J.Gilmartin, E.Fullan, T.Brennan, S.Goff, E.Hogan.
Subs: R.Reidy for P.J.Gilmartin, P.Farrelly for E.Fullan.

1964
Cork   B.Murphy, D.Kehilly, J.McGrath, D.Coughlan,
J.Dunlea, F.Kehilly, J.Crowley, D.McCarthy, M.O'Loughlin, T.Burke,
C.Kelliher (capt.), M.Coughlan, H.Casey, S.McCarthy, Dermot
O'Donovan. Sub: R Honohan.
London   J.Kelly, T.Fox, S.Hendry, C.O'Connor, E.O'Connor,
E.O'Driscoll, J.Madden, T.Dowling, S.McCowell, J.Devine,
P.Fitzmaurice, R.Doherty, D.Mullins, D.O'Connor, M.Doran. Sub:
F.Gaughan for D.Mullins, A.Heaphy for C.O'Connor, H.Sheehan
for R.Doherty.

1965
Galway   Greg Higgins, K.O'Connor, M.Kane, M.Tarpey, Coleen
McDonagh, T.Brennan, T.Kelly, F.Canavan, J.Glynn, T.Sands,
F.Heaney, T.Keenan, B.Geraghty, E.Geraghty, P.Crisham.
Hertsfordshire L.O'Leary, P.Forde, P.Davin, M.McNicholas,
J.Fitzpatrick, J.Lonergan, H.Hegarty, J.Connors, N.Ging,
A.Rothwell, M.Connors, M.Smith, M.Trainor, E.McCruaden,
T.O'Rourke. Subs: M.Lonergan for P.Forde, S.Daly for J.Lonergan,
M.Donoghue for E.McCrudden.

1966
London   M.Nally, N.Lucey, S.O'Sullivan, P.Flynn, J.Kilcommins,
J.Harrison, J.Madden, N.O'Reilly, J.Langan, P.McKenna,
T.O'Sullivan, E.Glennon, P.Grainger, R.Dowd, T.Roche. Sub:
M.Moffatt for J.Langan.
Cork   G.McCarthy, J.O'Flynn, T.Bermingham, A.Burke,
M.Healy, J.O'Halloran, J.O'Leary, P.J.O'Sullivan, R.Evans, T.Burke,
D.Sheehan, R.Honohan, C.Kelleher, Denis McCarthy (Kilmurray),
B.O'Keeffe. Sub: J.Downing, J.Allen.

1967
Kerry   A.Fogarty, D.Lovett, D.O'Sullivan, G.McCarthy,
D.Crowley, M.Gleeson, P.Aherne, M.O'Shea, M.Aherne,
P.O'Connor, P.O'Connell, W.Doran, P.Finnegan, B.Kennedy,
P.J.McIntyre. Sub: B.McCarthy for P.O'Connor.
London   P.Patton, M.Moffatt, S.Hendry, E.O'Connor,
A.McDonagh, S.Keane, M.O'Meara, B.Morris, J.Kelly, L.Octagen,
C.O'Malley, N.Peacock, H.Sheehan, M.Cahill, M.Doran. Subs:
J.Allen for H.Sheehan, P.Russell for J.Kelly.

1968

Tyrone A.Gallagher, D.O'Neill, S.Graham, P.Coyle, M.Jordan, A.McRory, F.McCartan, P.O'Neill (capt.), C.O'Hagan, P.McGonagle, S.Donaghy, K.Teague, F.Donnelly, B.Dolan, J.Early.
London M.Nally, E.O'Connor, J.McDonagh, M.Moffatt, A.McDonagh, J.Madden, T.McGovern, P.McKenna, J.Gallagher, C.O'Meara, G.Driscoll, E.Glennon, P.J.Fitzpatrick, E.Slattery, F.Doherty. Subs: K.Kelly, M.Doran, R.O'Hare.

1969

London M.Nally, J.Madden, F.Tiernan, M.Doran, J.Fenton, J.Harrison, M.Newell, P.McKenna, T.Dowling, P.J.Fitzpatrick, J.Meeney, H.Sheehan, G.Driscoll, M.Cahill, T.Greene. Subs: J.Toner for Harrison, M.Cooney for Fenton.
Wicklow P.Cronin, W.Whelan, C.Keogh, P.Hedderman, M.Behan, G.Moran, J.Cullen, T.Foley, M.Coffey, T.Humphries, M.O'Toole, J.McDonald, L.Keogh, N.Carthy (capt.), W.Wall. Subs: S.Doyle for J.Cullen, P.Carty for G.Moran.

1970

London M.Nally, J.Madden, J.McDonagh, J.Fenton, A.McDonagh, J.Harrison, M.Doran, P.McKenna, W.McAuliffe, B.Haipin, G.Mahony, E.Glennon, G.Driscoll, M.Cahill, T.Dowds. Subs: J.Toner, M.Fennell for M.Cahill.
Kildare J.Leahy, D.Dalton, M.Cullen, T.Foley, T.Brereton, S.Dowling, K.O'Brien, J.O'Connell, H.Hyland, M.Mannion, P.Kinihan, J.J.Walsh, J.O'Reilly, T.Christian, D.Flanagan. Sub: J.Goulding for J.J.Walsh.

1971

London M.Nally, C.Kelly, J.McDonagh, J.Behan, M.McMenamin, J.Harrison, M.Doran (capt.), P.McKenna, G.O'Mahony, J.Fennell, I.Donnelly, John O'Mahony, T.Meany, M.Fennell, T.Dowd. Sub: J.Thompson for J.Behan.
Dublin A.Milner, L.Hickey, J.O'Neill, S.O'Hare, D.O'Donovan, F.Kavanagh, P.Farran, P.Wilson, F.Farren, C.Hanley, A.O'Toole, W.McCabe, F.Hutchinson, B.Keenan, J.Clarke. Subs: M.McMenamon for J.O'Neill, J.Kelly for J.Clarke.

1972

Cork N.Murphy, Ted Murphy, J.Fahy, M.O'Doherty, Der Cogan, D.Kehilly, N.Crowley, M.Mehigan, S.Daly, Tony Murphy, S.O'Connor, D.Curran, Colmon Twomey, M.Sloane, T.Monaghan.
Hertsfordshire M.English, P.Murphy (capt.), B.Cahill, F.O'Connor, M.Lawlor, S.Daly, J.Sherry, J.Mulvaney, J.Kellett, J.McGinley, F.Tynan, R.Sherlock, M.J.O'Sullivan, B.Flynn, E.McNelis. Subs: T.Clifford for B.Cahill, P.J.Galligan for P.Murphy, N.Deane for M.J.O'Sullivan.

1973

Laois S.Whelan, P.Lalor, E.Harte, D.Lutterel, T.Clancy, J.Miller, P.Dunne, E.Whelan (capt.), B.Nerney, N.Flynn, S.Fleming, M.Dooley, D.Doogue, A.Fennell, D.Booth. Sub: T Dowling for D.Doogue.
London M.Nally, J.Freyne, J.Hickey, M.Whelan, C.Kelly, F.Dolan, A.Flavin, M.Carolan, P.McKenna, M.McManamon, J.O'Mahony, N.McCarthy, T.Meany, B.Devlin, B.O'Connell. Subs: S.Corridan for M.Carolan, R.Munnelly for P.McKenna, J.Donnelly for S.Corridan.

1983

Kerry J.Kennelly, M.Colgan, B.O'Sullivan, P.Brosnan, P.Sheehan, D.Hartnett, J.Stack, Ger O'Driscoll, T.O'Connell, J.Walsh, R.O'Donoghue, P.O'Mahony, J.Doyle, J.O'Sullivan, P.Sheehan. Subs: G.Casey for J.O'Sullivan, D.Higgins for P.Sheehan.
Yorkshire B.Grogan, A.Beggs, D.McGuigan, S.Kennedy, B.O'Carroll, B.Coleman, P.Kissane, P.J.O'Reilly, H.Ruane, T.Cormelly, D.Murphy, G.Mills, P.J.Cullen, M.O'Connor, G.Molloy.

1984

Cork W.McCarthy, D.O'Sullivan, J.Murphy, C.Counihan, B.Stack, D.Mulcahy, A.Davis, C.Collins, D Culloty, T.Cole, C.O'Reilly (capt.), M.McCarthy, N.O'Connor, P.Barrett, G.O'Rourke. Subs: P.O'Connor for N.O'Connor, J.O'Sullivan for D.Culloty, B.Daly for A.Davis.
Warwickshire F.Quinn, K.McEvoy, M.Cunningham, A.Cairns, B.Higgins, P.Moran (capt.), E.Dowd, T.Tolan, B.McDonnell, S.Dunne, N.McLean, D.Brennan, A.Smith, B.Nannery, A.Tolan. Subs: J.McDonagh for M.Cunningham, J.McKinney for B.Higgins, M.Cunningham for A.Smith.

1985

Galway P.Coyne, T.Heavey, G.Dolan, C.Faherty, G.Daly, M.Melia, S.Glynn, P.Greaney, H.Bleahen, P.O'Dea, G.Burke, T.McHugh, S.Burke, C.O'Dea (capt.), F.Stockwell. Subs:P.Hynes for S.Burke, G.Kinneavy for P.Coyne, J.Morley for G.Dolan.
Warwickshire F.Quinn, G.Dowd, J.McDonagh, C.Conway, P.Moran, T.Hourihane, P.Power, T.Tolan, G.Byrne, D.Brennan, S.Dunne, D.Cooke, E.Tolan, N.McLeane, A.Connellan. Subs: M.Cunningham for T.Hourihane, J.King for G.Byrne, E.Sheridan for A.Connellan.

1986

London G.Doyle, F.Glynn, T.Finnerty, R.Harran, S.Hussey, A.Wolfe, A.Hanley, M.Duggan, T.Walsh, J.O'Sullivan, B.O'Herlihy, J.Sheridan, M.Gallagher, L.Hughes, T.Parker.
Cork J.O'Brien, D.O'Sullivan, S.Bowes, D.O'Connor, G.O'Connell, Gene O'Driscoll, T.O'Callaghan, D.Creedon, M.Spillane, M.Hannon, L.O'Callaghan, C.O'Connell, W.O'Riordan, T.Murphy, D.J.O'Shea. Sub: B.O'Herlihy.

1987

Cork N.Gallagher, M.Walsh, S.Bowes, D.O'Connor, K.Creed, G.O'Driscoll, T.O'Callaghan, M.Spillane, G.Lally, W.O'Riordan, M.Kelleher (capt.), C.O'Connell, P.Harrington, T.Murphy, J.Dennehy. Sub: B.Lotty.
Warwickshire F.Quinn, K.Kerr, P.Walsh, B.Carolan, K.Brennan, T.Tolan, P.Cooke, P.McLoughlin, E.Sheridan, E.Tolan, P.Higgins, D.Cooke, J.Butler, J.O'Donoghue, R.Doherty. Subs: N.McLean, J.O'Hanlon, M.Corcoran.

1988

Meath R.O'Connell, P.Mcintyre, P.Fay, D.Mullen, D.Lynch, J.McEnroe (capt.), L.McEnroe, T.Kane, J.Cunningham, P.Henry, P.Curran, J.Devine, M.Kirk, T.Mullen, N.Rennick. Sub: H.Gilsennan for T.Mullen.
London P.J.Burke, M.Grant, D.Carville, R.Heraty, J.Breen, M.Somers, A.Hanley, P.Pidgeon, P.Dreelan, R.Haran, C.White, S.Cassidy, B.Murphy, J.Linden, M.Hession. Subs: P.Reynolds for B.Murphy, D.Duggan for J.Linden.

1989

Cork M.Creedon, P.Kenneally G.O'Connell, D.O'Connor, K.Creed, P.Buckley, B.Herlihy, M.Murphy, M.O'Connor, J.Casey, T.Buckley, D.McCarthy (capt.), O.Riordan, N.O'Connor, N.Twomey. Subs: C.O'Connell for M.Murphy, G.Ring for N.O'Connor, O.O'Sullivan for K.Creed.

Warwickshire F.Quinn, S.Quigley, G.Dowd, P.McLaughlin, B.Carolan, J.King, T.Rafferty, E.Sheridan, D.Sheridan, D.Cooke, E.O'Loughlin, C.Folan, T.Tolan, G.Butler, A.Connellan. Subs: E.Tolan, L.Dundass, P.McLoughlin.

1990

Cork J.Collins (capt.), M.Lyons, M.Farr, A.Devoy, S.Coughlan, P.Coleman, D.Burke, D.Fitzgerald, C.O'Sullivan, G.McPolin, A.Barry, G.Manley, M.Lewis, T.O'Reilly, J.Caulfield. Subs: D.Lynch, Martin Kelleher.

Warwickshire F.Quinn, S.Daly, D.Sheridan, P.Kinnally, P.O'Connor, A.Connellan, D.Cooke, N.McMenamin, M.Laverty, C.Folan, J.Mooney, E.Tolan, S.Crowe, J.O'Donoghue, T.Tolan. Sub: M.Corcoran.

1991

Kerry K.Moran, T.Hanafin, L.Burns, T.Dennehy, R.O'Dwyer, V.Knightly, P.Dillane, F.Ashe, T.Harrington (capt.), D.Moynihan, G.O'Driscoll, J.Kennedy, M.McAuliffe, T.Brosnan, S.O'Sullivan. Subs: T.Evans, S.Tuohy, J.Murphy.

London M.Kelly, P.Murray, G.McDaid, T.Rooney, J.Flaherty, M.Somers, G.McColgan, S.McLoughlin, S.O'Brien, P.Goggins, P.Dreelan, D.Murray, P.Coleman, S.McDonald, R.Haran. Subs: M.Lavery, V.O'Neill, P.Doyle.

1992

Wexford J.Cooper, S.O'Neill, T.Gorman, M.Caulfield, J.Casey, J.Dunne, P.Courtney, P.Walsh, B.Kavanagh, J.Byrne, N.Guinan, N.Darcy, S.Dunne, M.Furlong, G.Byrne. Subs: M.Darcy for S.Dunne, M.Mahon for M.Darcy.

Cork J.O'Brien, A.Devoy, P.Coleman, M.Farr, S.Coughlan, Niall Murphy, Mark O'Connor, C.O'Sullivan, D.Devoy, R.Sheehan, G.Manley, D.Lynch, N.O'Connor, E.O'Mahony, M.Lewis. Subs: A.Berry for R.Sheehan, G.Cooney for D.Lynch.

1993

Cork J.O'Brien, D.Walsh, P.Hanley, D.Burke, O.O'Sullivan, B.Murphy, D.McIlhenny, F.Collins, G.Ring, D.Fitzgerald, G.McPolin, P.Buckley, M.Harrington, K.Harrington, R.Sheehan (capt.).

Laois E.Burke, B.Kerwin, D.Cryan, K.Dennis, B.Keville, J.O'Reilly, J.Buggy, A.Phelan, P.J.Dempsey, T.Bowe, L.Ramsbottom, T.Gorman, P.Coffey, M.Behan, M.O'Brien. Subs: D.Sweeney, D.Delaney.

1994

Kerry D.O'Keeffe, P.Lenihan, L.Burns, J.B.O'Brien, J.Stack, K.Scanlon, S.Stack, D.Daly, D.Ó Cinnéide, J.Crowley, M.Keating (capt.), D.Moynihon, S.Murphy, S.Fitzgerald, P.O'Donoghue. Subs: J.Daly for D.Daly, C.O'Donnell for Keating, J.Walsh for K.Scanlon.

Galway C.McGinley, T.Ryder, P.Crowley, D.Geraghty, R.Doyle, D.Carr, F.Keenan, D.Cronin, D.Gilmartin, P.Duffy, K.Collins, L.Colleran, L.Ó Flatharta, T.Morgan, J.Dooley. Subs: N.Ó Neachtáin for K.Collins, T.Screen for F.Keenan, J.Donnellan for P.Duffy.

1995

Mayo N.O'Brien, S.Grealish, K.Byrne, B.Henihan, P.Touhy, G.McNicholas, D.O'Loughlin, P.McNamara, J.Heshin, G.Butler, M.Butler, O.Walsh, W.Fitzpatrick, V.Keane, D.Nestor. Subs: N.Loftus, N.Jennings, J.Commins.

London M.O'Connor, C.Byrne, M.Moclair, P.Sheehy, C.Murphy, J.Sharvin, G.Barrett, S.McLoughlin, P.Coleman, O.Joy, P.McNamee, M.Byrne, T.Coakley, P.Coggins, J.Coffey. Sub: G.O'Shea.

1996

Cork K.Farr, K.Creed (capt.), R.Walsh, P.Murray, J.O'Leary, Donal Óg Liatháin, M.O'Donovan, P.Murphy, O.O'Sullivan, J.Clifford, J.McCarthy, M.Harrington, J.Whooley, P.Hayes, N.Twomey. Subs: E.Barrett for P.Murphy, J.Dennehy for N.Twomey.

Meath J.O'Sullivan, A.Coffey, D.Lane, A.Kealy, N.Collier, N.Kearney, S.Murphy, N.Nestor, J.Henry, R.Keely, S.Duff, K.Barry, P.O'Sullivan, T.O'Connor, B.Healy. Subs: M.Kirk for K.Barry, L.Rennicks for N.Collier.

1997

Mayo J.Dunne, D.Costello, J.McCallion, J.Fallon, F.Touhy, V.Keane, G.Ruane, J.Hession, K.Comer, D.O'Loughlin, J.Commins, O.Walsh, W.Fitzpatrick, M.Smith, A.Morley. Subs: S.Grealish, D.Jennings.

Kerry D.Murphy, A.Morris, M.O'Donoghue, D.Moynihan, K.Scanlon, M.O'Connor, S.O'Mahony, J.Daly, G.O'Connor, L.Brosnan, E.Fitzpatrick, J.J.Corduff, S.McElligott, J.Quirke, P.O'Donoghue. Subs: O.Doherty for Morris, D.Dennehy for Corduff.

1998

Tipperary S.Delahunty, D.Byrne, F.Clifford, M.O'Mahony, P.J.Lanigan, D.Peters, W.Morrissey, P.Ormond, M.Leonard, P.Cahill, M.O'Shea, B.Maguire, K.Coonan, A.Crosse, T.Sheehan. Subs: D.O'Brien for B.Maguire, J.McAuliffe for M.Leonard.

Offaly K.Furlong, J.Hurst, A.Murphy, B.Wynne, M.Kennedy, P.Mulvihill, D.Quinn, D.Kelly, P.Connolly, G.Comerford, N.Bryant, C.Brazil, J.Kennedy, M.Keenaghan, D.Connolly. Subs: S.Manley for G.Comerford, K.Slattery for C.Brazil.

1999

Waterford A.Kirwan (capt.), D.Ryan, R.Power, M.Byrne, N.Guiry, P.Walsh, A.Reynolds, S.Bergin, P.Queally, C.Power, K.Walsh, D.Wyse, P.Ferncombe, J.Kiely, D.Whelan. Subs: C.O'Keeffe for K.Walsh, G.Walsh for P.Ferncombe.

Meath J.Curry, M.Briody, A.Coffey, N.Collier, P.Curran, N.Horan, D.Davis, J.Cullinane, E.Grogan, P.Nestor, J.Carey, M.Crampton, N.Walsh, S.Duff, F.McMahon. Subs: S.Murphy for M.Briody, J.Mitchell for N.Walsh, B.Shaw for P.Nestor.

2000

Roscommon S.Curran, I.Daly, G.Mockler, N.Galvin, B.Mannion, P.Noone, A.McPadden, K.Keane, D.Gillooly, G.Cox, B.O'Brien, C.Lynch, J.Neary, K.Mannion, R.O'Donoghue. Sub: J.Heneghan for Lynch.

Kerry D.Murphy, D.McNamara, M.O'Donoghue, L.Harty, N.Sheedy, K.Scanlon, S.O'Mahony, P.Somers, J.Daly, J.Shanahan, D.Moynihan, L.Murphy, J.Dennehy, J.Quirke, B.Scanlon. Subs: E.Hennessy for Murphy, L.Brosnan for J.Quirke, M.Quirke for Daly.

2001
Cork   P.Mackey, D.Duggan, M.Daly, J.Honohan, N.O'Leary, G.Spillane, T.Kenny, M.Kelleher, M.Monaghan, P.Connolly, B.Coleman, A.O'Driscoll, B.O'Sullivan, G.Kelleher, P.Dunlea. Subs: J.Buckley for Connolly, S.Levis for Daly.
Mayo   N.O'Brien, A.Costello, B.Heneghan, B.Burke, S.Grimes, J.Fallon, J.Rafter, D.O'Loughlin, P.Kelly, J.Mitchell, A.O'Malley, K.Malone, D.Quinn, B.Maloney, M.Horan. Subs: N.Dunne for Horan, D.McDonagh for Malone.

2002
Wicklow   K.Quirke, A.Byrne, H.Kenny, R.Doyle, C.Foley, A.Jameson, C.Davis, D.Doran, B.O'Keeffe, J.Doyle, D.McGillycuddy, J.P.Davis, W.O'Gorman, S.Byrne, K.O'Brien. Subs: S.Corrigan for Doran, J.Murphy for J.Doyle, S.Miley for J.P.Davis.
Kerry   K.Cremin, D.McNamara, S.O'Sullivan, Don Murphy, B.Fitzgerald, C.Scanlon, S.Flynn, P.Somers, E.O'Donoghue, A.Constable, J.Ferriter, M.Cooper, B.Scanlon, P.Kennedy, C.Foley. Subs: R.Donovan for Somers, N.Sheehy for McNamara, Damien Murphy for Don Murphy.

2003
Meath   J.Curry, C.McLoughlin, T.Bannon, P.Nugent, N.Horan, F.McMahon, B.Kieran, I.McManus, J.Gallagher, C.Sheridan, P.Duff, S.Bray, B.Farrell, B.Lynch, R.Russell. Subs: W.Byrne for Russell, S.Smith for Gallagher.
Galway   D.O'Dowd, C.Monaghan, R.Gibbons, P.Fahy, M.Conroy, J.Flaherty, D.O'Brien, P.Gilmore, B.Cullinane, S.Mannion, B.Moran, D.Ward, B.Colleran, M.Costello, C.Bane. Subs: C.McHugh for Ward, S.Cloherty for Gilmore, S.Kenny for Conroy.

2004
Waterford   A.Kirwan, D.Ryan, R.Power, M.Boyne, N.Barrie, L.Hurney, J.Phelan, D.Kirwan, M.O'Brien, K.Wheelan, M.Kiely, R.Hennessy, E.Doherty, P.Foley, J.Kiely. Subs: A.Power for A.Kirwan, T.Kirwan for Phelan, S.Dempsey for O'Brien, J.Power for J.Kiely, S.McGrath for J.Power.
(S.Dempsey started the drawn final. Subs in the drawn final were A.Ahern for Dempsey, J.Power for Hennessy)
Leitrim   K.Ludlow, K.Kennedy, O.McBride, B.Butler, F.Holohan, D.McHugh, D.Duignan, K.Scollan, J.Kilbane, J.Cullen, D.O'Donnell, B.McWeeney, S.Maguire, O.Maguire, J.Holohan. Subs: P.McGarry for McHugh, S.Foley for Scollan, G.McWeeney for O'Donnell, S.Doorigan for J.Cullen.(S.Maguire started the drawn final. Subs in the drawn final were B.McWeeney for Kennedy, S.Foley for Munnelly, P.McGarry for Scollan, G.McWeeney for S.Maguire)

2005
Cork   A.Quirke, C.Murphy, D.Wiseman, M.Prout, K.Kehilly, G.Spillane, E.Wiseman, A.O'Connor, S.O'Sullivan, J.Buckley, S.Hayes, J.Russell, D.Goulding, V.Hurley, P.Dunlea. Subs: D.O'Connor for Hurley, N.O'Riordan for Hayes.
Meath   J.Curry, T.Bannon, C.McLoughlin, P.Nugent, B.Kiernan, J.Donoghue, G.Hynes, B.Lynch, S.Dillon, P.Curran, I.McManus, G.McCullagh, J.McGee, J.Gallagher, R.Maguire. Subs: C.Brennan for McManus, W.Reilly for Curran.

2006
Kerry   S.Óg Ciardabháin, S.Hegarty, J.Costello, D.Doyle, D.O'Sullivan, B.Hickey, J.King, J.P.Brosnan, A.Garnett, N.Fleming, M.Murphy, C.Daly, R.McAuliffe, S.Wallace, J.Buckley. Subs: K.Foley for Fleming, F.O'Sullivan for Brosnan, F.Griffin for King.
Roscommon David Moran, T.Bannon, D.Donnellan, A.Murtagh, B.Goode, N.Moran, G.Mockler, D.McNulty, R.O'Connor, R.Cox, P.Moran, S.Purcell, Derek Moran, M.Connolly, S.Heneghan. Subs: M.O'Keeffe for Bannon, S.Sharkey for Mockler, J.Callery for Heneghan, M.Killilea for O'Connor.

2007
Cork   K.Murphy, D.Wiseman, E.Wiseman, D.O'Riordan, P.Kissane, B.Cogan, M.Feehily, A.O'Sullivan, A.O'Connor, F.Lynch, V.Hurley, S.O'Sullivan, C.Brosnan, N.O'Sullivan, P.Dunlea. Subs: J.Russell for N.O'Sullivan, P.Cahill for Brosnan.
Wexford   A.Masterson, D.Walsh, M.Gahan, C.Molloy, T.Wall, J.Waters, S.Cousins, P.Murphy, B.Doyle, M.Flynn- O'Connor, D.Farrell, W.Hudson, J.O'Shaughnessy, D.Foran, P.Sinnott. Subs: P.Atkinson for Flynn-O'Connor, G.Jacob for O'Shaughnessy, K.Kennedy for Waters, P.Hughes for Hudson.

2008
Dublin   C.Clarke, D.Daly, M.Fitzsimons, C.Prenderville, M.White, A.Dennis, N.Brogan, D.Bastick, C.Daly, R.Joyce, K.Connolly, J.Cooper, W.Finnegan, E.O'Gara, A.Darcy. Subs: D.Homan for Joyce, C.Norton for Finnegan, N.Tormey for Connolly.
Roscommon M.Miley, N.Carty, R.Cox, J.Whyte, E.Towey, J.Harte, C.Garvey, B.Higgins, M.Reynolds, D.Moran, J.McKeague, K.Higgins, F.Dolan, F.Cregg, P.Garvey. Subs: R.Brady for Whyte, M.O'Donoghue for P.Garvey, D.Ward for Towey, C.McHugh for K.Higgins, M.Killilea for McKeague.

2009
Cork   P.O'Shea, P.Gayer, E.Wiseman, J.McLoughlin, R.O'Sullivan, G.Healy, M.Fehilly, A.O'Sullivan, C.O'Donovan, D.O'Donovan, S.O'Sullivan, C.O'Driscoll, V.Hurley, R.O'Mahony, J.P.Murphy. Subs: M.Prout for Fehilly, P.O'Cahill for Hurley, N.O'Riordan for A.O'Sullivan.
Roscommon M.Miley, K.Kilcline, M.McLoughlin, E.Towey, N.Carthy, D.McGarry, C.Dineen, P.Freeman, M.Reynolds, C.McCormack, D.Keenehan, R.Cox, P.Garvey, R.Kelly, D.McDermott. Subs: S.Ormsby, T.Mahon for McCormack, B.Mullen for Kelly.

2010
Sligo   J.Farrell, O.McLynn, D.Rooney, L.Bree, E.McHugh, A.McIntyre, K.Gallagher, J.Murphy, P.McTiernan, K.Finan, P.McGoldrick, B.Egan, C.McNamara, S.Stenson, D.Maye. Subs: B.McDonagh for McTiernan, N.Walsh for Stenson, J.Quinn for McGoldrick.
Kerry   S.Óg Ó Ciardubhain, G.O'Connor, F.Griffin, A.Cahill, E.Hickson, A.Greaney, B.Guiney, M.Coakley, D.Murphy, M.Murphy, M.O'Donoghue, A.O'Sullivan, G.Sayers, A.Mac Gearailt, J.Buckley. Subs: B.Poff for Mac Gearailt, C.O'Mahony for O'Connor, A.Fitzgerald for Coakley, T.McGoldrick for Cahill, J.McGoldrick for Buckley.

2011

Cork   T.O'Connor, E.Wiseman, O.O'Mahony, K.Harrington, S.Kiely, R.O'Sullivan, A.J.O'Connor, A.O'Sullivan, D.O'Donovan, T.Clancy, C.Keane, B.Coughlan, K.Hallisey, A.O'Brien, L.Shorten. Subs: B.Daly for O'Mahony, M.Dilworth for Keane, P.Gayer for O'Connor, Keane for Dilworth, P.Daley for Clancy, O'Connor for O'Sullivan.

Kildare   R.Eyres, D.McEvoy, K.Fitzpatrick, R.Walsh, M.Kelly, J.Doyle, T.Archibald, P.Dunne, E.Carew, C.Murphy, T.Moolick, C.Kelly, D.Mulhall, P.Meagher, J.Gately. Subs: D.Campbell for Gately, J.Comerford for Kelly, J.Lambe for Meagher, E.Hyland for Mulhall, M.Fitzharris for Crew, C.Bolton for Lambe, Meagher for Archibald, Carew for Murphy, Mulhall for Campbell, D.Barker for Doyle.

2012

Kerry   S.Óg Ó Ciardubhain, K.Quirke, B.O'Mahony, K.O'Dwyer, M.Mangan, J.Sherwood, J.Walsh, A.Garnett, A.O'Sullivan, N.O'Mahony, N.Ó Sé, P.O'Donoghue, D.O'Callaghan, M.O'Donoghue, C.Cox. Subs: E.Hickson for Quirke, M.Brennan for Garnett, C.Kerins for O'Callaghan, B.Poff for P.O'Donoghue, P.Carridan for Mangan.

Mayo   P.Mannion, M.Walsh, L.O'Malley, B.Leonard, M.Forde, O.Feeney, O.Quinn, R.McNamara, P.Collins, P.McManamon, E.McManamon, S.Cloherty, A.McTigue, C.Dempsey, A.Egan. Subs: M.Moran for McNamara, K.Gibbons for McTigue, C.Horan for P.McManamon, G.McDonagh for Cloherty.

2013

Cork   D.Hanrahan, A.J.O'Connor, E.O'Mahony, K.Harrington, Richard O'Sullivan, Rory O'Sullivan, S.Kiely, R.Deane, M.Ó Laoire, C.Vaughan, A.O'Brien, C.O'Driscoll, K.O'Driscoll, F.Lynch, D.Harrington. Subs: P.Daly for O'Mahony, Daly for Rory O'Sullivan, M.Vaughan for Harrington, E.Buckley for O'Brien.

Kildare   C.Heneghan, J.O'Connor, W.Burke, P.Warren, D.Barker, C.Fitzpatrick, C.O'Shea, K.Cribbin, S.Darcy, C.Fagan, S.Hanafin, H.Mahon, P.Mahon, C.Bolton, M.McNally. Subs: G.Waters for Warren, G.Farrell for Darcy, D.Grehan for P.Mahon, D.Duke for H.Mahon.

2014

Cavan   J.Farrelly, D.Barkey, J.Morris, F.Reilly, C.Brady, B.Sankey, P.Smith, L.Buchanan, P.Leddy, C.P.Moynagh, C.Conroy, E.Reilly, T.Hayes, E.Hessin, P.O'Connor. Subs: N.Smith for O'Connor, D.Hyland for Conroy, B.Doyle for Leddy, N.Clerkin for Reilly, C.Caffrey for Hessin, T.Moore for Moynagh.

Kerry   S.Murphy, M.Brennan, K.O'Dwyer, D.Wren, G.Gibson, D.Daly, G.Crowley, A.Garnett, B.O'Sullivan, P.O'Connor, C.Keating, B.Crowley, G.O'Grady, P.Kennelly, T.Hickey. Subs: S.Moloney for Wren, A.O'Donoghue for Daly, E.Walsh for G.Crowley, P.Óg Ó Sé for O'Connor, D.Roche for Garnett.

2015

Kerry   S.Murphy, D.O'Donoghue, J.McGuire, D.Culhane, T.Morley, J.Walsh, G.Crowley, B.O'Sullivan, L.Kearney, P.O'Connor, B.Crowley, K.Spillane, A.O'Donoghue, C.Cox, T.Hickey. Subs: E.Sugrue for McGuire, J.O'Donoghue for Cox, G.O'Sullivan for Spillane, M.Brennan for O'Sullivan, E.Kiely for Kearney, D.Griffin for B.Crowley.

Mayo   B.Forkan, P.Barrett, B.Moran, B.Leonard, E.Collins, D.McHugh, E.O'Donoghue, P.Collins, P.Feerick, G.Conway, C.Freeman, D.Durcan, D.McGing, J.Hutton, R.Malee. Subs: A.Farrell for Malee, S.Gaughan for Leonard, M.Barrett for Gaughan, M.Forde for Durcan, D.Healy for Moran, M.Togher for Collins.

2016

Kerry   Darragh O'Shea, F.Clifford, J.Foley, C.Ó Luing, P.Clifford, A.Barry, R.Wharton, A.Spillane, J.O'Connor, B.Ó Seanacháin, P.O'Donoghue, D.Foran, N.O'Shea, K.Hurley, S.M.Ó Conchúir. Subs: K.O'Sullivan for Clifford, D.Roche for Hurley, L.Bastible for Foley, Dara O'Shea for Ó Seanacháin, M.O'Donnell for Spillane, A.Barry for Foran.

Mayo   M.Flanagan, J.Forkan, N.Freeman, E.O'Donoghue, B.Duffy, J.Kelly, P.Feerick, M.Togher, P.Collins, B.Reape, M.Forde, K.Gibbons, D.Coen, A.Farrell, C.Keane. Subs: S.Gaughan for Collins, R.Malee for Farrell, R.Holian for Reape, S.Akram for O'Donoghue, R.Doherty for Feerick.

2017

Kerry   T.Mac an tSaoir, E.Kiely, J.McGuire, B.Sugrue, J.Walsh, P.Kilkenny, D.O'Brien, R.Ó Sé, B.O'Sullivan, P.O'Connor, J.O'Donoghue, E.Ó Conchuir, K.Spillane, C.Cox, T.Ó Sé. Subs: L.Carey for O'Donoghue, M.Foley for Kilkenny, S.O'Sullivan for Cox, I.Parker for O'Sullivan, P.J.Mac Laimh for Walsh, D.Murphy for Kiely.

Meath   J.Lynch, L.Moran, M.Flood, A.Lynch, D.Toner, W.Carry, D.Healy, A.Flanagan, C.Farrell, N.Shorthall, K.Ross, C.McConnell, J.Scully, D.Rowe, B.Brennan. Subs: J.Conlon for Scully, S.Coogan for Ross, S.Reilly for Farrell, C.O'Rourke for Carry, C.Moriarty for Shorthall, S.Coogan for Rowe.

ALL-IRELAND JUNIOR FOOTBALL FINAL REFEREES

1912	Tom Irwin (Cork)
1913	M. F. Crowe (Dublin)
1914	E. Tarrant (Laois)
1915	P. Dunphy (Laois)
1916	P. D. Breen (Wexford) (draw)/A. Rogers (Louth) (replay)
1923	Mick Sammon (Dublin)
1924	P. Kilduff (Kildare)
1925	M. Shanahan (Dublin)
1926	Tom Burke (Louth)
1927	Tom Burke (Louth)
1928	Tom Shevlin (Roscommon)
1929	Seán O'Connor (Dublin)
1930	W. P. Aherne (Cork)
1931	Seán O'Connor (Dublin)
1932	J. Giles (Meath)
1933	S. O'Neill (Dublin)
1934	P. Waters (Kildare)
1935	P. Waters (Kildare)
1936	D. Ryan (Kerry)
1937	John Ryan (Liverpool)
1938	D. Hamilton (Dublin)
1939	P. J. Masterson (Cavan)
1940	P. McKenna (Limerick)
1941	Jimmy Flaherty (Offaly)
1946	F. Brophy (Dublin)
1947	Paddy Mythen (Wexford)
1948	Paul Russell (Kerry)
1949	Simon Deignan (Cavan)
1950	J. Moran (Tuam)
1951	Moss Colbert (Limerick)
1952	P. McGooey (Monaghan)
1953	Capt. J. O'Boyle (Donegal)
1954	Seán Hayes (Tipperary)
1955	Simon Deignan (Cavan)
1956	Michael McArdle (Louth)
1957	Peter McDermott (Meath)
1958	Mick Higgins (Cavan)
1959	John Dowling (Offaly)
1960	Jimmy Martin (Roscommon)
1961	Brian Smith (Meath)
1962	Michael McArdle (Louth)
1963	Jimmy Martin (Roscommon)
1964	A. Coleman (Laois)
1965	Eamon Moules (Wicklow)
1966	Tom Cunningham (Galway)
1967	Tom Cunningham (Galway)
1968	Paul Kelly (Dublin)
1969	Fintan Tierney (Cavan)
1970	Mick Spain (Offaly)
1971	Jimmy Martin (Roscommon)
1972	Martin Meally (Kilkenny)
1973	Hugh McPoland (Antrim)
1974-1982	Suspended
1983	Ray Moloney (Limerick)
1984	Tommy Moran (Leitrim)
1985	Paddy Lane (Limerick)
1986	Tommy Moran (Leitrim)
1987	Tommy Sugrue (Kerry)
1988	Pat Egan (Leitrim)
1989	Michael Cranny (Down)
1990	Tommy Howard (Kildare)
1991	Joe Kearney (Roscommon)
1992	Seán McHale (Mayo)
1993	Joe Kearney (Roscommon)
1994	Tommy McDermott (Cavan)
1995	Muiris O'Sullivan (Kerry)
1996	Michael McGrath (Donegal)
1997	Martin McBrien (Tyrone)
1998	Des Joyce (Galway)
1999	Haulie Beirne (Roscommon)
2000	E.Murtagh (Longford)
2001	E.Whelan (Laois)
2002	M.Hughes (Tyrone)
2003	S.McGonigle (Donegal)
2004	E.Whelan (Laois) (draw)/P.Fox (Westmeath) (replay)
2005	P.Carney (Roscommon)
2006	F.Barrett (Kildare)
2007	B.Tyrell (Tipperary)
2008	M.Sludden (Tyrone)
2009	T.Quigley (Dublin)
2010	D.Brazil (Offaly)
2011	D.O'Mahoney (Tipperary)
2012	M.Condon (Waterford)
2013	G.McCormack (Dublin)
2014	J.Henry (Mayo)
2015	N.Mooney (Cavan)
2016	S.McLaughlin (Donegal)
2017	J.Hickey (Carlow)

MUNSTER JUNIOR FOOTBALL FINALS

1910	Tipperary	1-1	0-0	Limerick
1911	Cork	3-1	3-0	Waterford
1912	Tipperary	0-5	0-2	Cork
1913	Kerry	1-3	1-2	Limerick
	(Note: Replay ordered following an objection)			
Replay	Kerry	1-4	0-0	Limerick
1914	Kerry	0-7	0-0	Waterford
1915	Kerry	2-3	1-5	Waterford
1916	Limerick awarded title on an objection after Cork had won final 1-0 to 0-2.			
1917-1922	Suspended			
1923	Tipperary	2-5	1-3	Cork
1924	Kerry	2-2	1-1	Clare
1925	Clare	0-6	0-5	Cork
1926	Kerry	1-5	2-1	Tipperary
1927	Kerry	1-10	3-2	Clare
1928	Kerry	3-2	0-4	Waterford
1929	Limerick	2-6	0-3	Clare
1930	Kerry	2-2	1-1	Clare
1931	Kerry	2-5	2-3	Cork
1932	Cork	1-5	1-3	Kerry
1933	Cork	2-2	1-3	Kerry
1934	Kerry	2-12	0-1	Waterford
1935	Tipperary	4-10	0-3	Cork
1936	Kerry	4-14	3-1	Waterford
1937	Tipperary	3-6	0-6	Limerick
1938	Kerry	2-4	1-0	Limerick
1939	Limerick	1-7	1-2	Kerry
1940	Cork	1-6	0-3	Tipperary
1941	Kerry	1-10	0-3	Tipperary
1942-1945	Suspended			
1946	Kerry	3-3	1-7	Cork
1947	Kerry	3-7	3-5	Limerick
1948	Waterford	2-8	1-7	Limerick
1949	Kerry	2-5	0-6	Waterford
1950	Limerick	3-6	1-6	Cork
1951	Cork	3-6	1-4	Kerry
1952	Tipperary	0-15	2-9	Kerry
Replay	Tipperary	0-8	0-6	Kerry
1953	Cork	1-10	0-10	Tipperary
1954	Kerry	1-9	2-2	Cork
1955	Cork	3-7	0-5	Limerick
1956	Kerry	4-10	1-4	Waterford
1957	Cork	1-7	0-7	Limerick
1958	Kerry	3-11	2-4	Waterford
1959	Kerry	3-8	0-6	Cork

1960	Kerry	2-6	1-8	Cork
1961	Kerry	2-4	0-6	Cork
1962	Cork	3-6	0-8	Limerick
1963	Kerry	2-4	0-6	Limerick
1964	Cork	2-5	1-4	Clare
1965	Kerry	3-13	0-6	Clare
1966	Cork	1-7	0-7	Clare
1967	Kerry	2-7	0-9	Cork
1968	Kerry	3-11	2-6	Clare
1969	Kerry	1-11	1-5	Tipperary
1970	Cork	2-10	2-9	Kerry
1971	Cork	2-7	1-5	Clare
1972	Cork	2-13	0-9	Kerry
1973-1982	Suspended			
1983	Kerry	2-10	0-9	Cork
1984	Cork	1-12	0-9	Kerry
1985	Kerry	0-7	0-7	Tipperary
Replay	Kerry	1-5	1-4	Tipperary
1986	Cork	1-12	1-6	Tipperary
1987	Cork	1-12	1-5	Tipperary
1988	Cork beat Tipperary			
1989	Cork	0-10	0-9	Kerry
1990	Cork	1-9	1-6	Kerry
1991	Kerry	1-12	3-4	Waterford
1992	Cork	0-13	1-9	Clare
1993	Cork	1-10	0-9	Tipperary
1994	Kerry	1-6	0-8	Clare
1995	Kerry	1-21	0-19	Cork (aet)
1996	Cork	1-10	1-8	Kerry
1997	Kerry	1-15	0-9	Clare
1998	Tipperary	0-6	0-5	Cork
1999	Waterford	0-9	0-7	Clare
2000	Kerry	1-15	1-6	Clare
2001	Cork	0-17	0-11	Tipperary
2002	Kerry	2-14	0-15	Tipperary
2003	Kerry	2-9	0-14	Cork
2004	Waterford	1-7	0-9	Cork
2005	Cork	2-13	0-8	Kerry
2006	Kerry	0-12	1-8	Cork
2007	Cork	0-12	0-11	Clare
2008	Kerry	1-11	1-9	Cork
2009	Cork	1-21	0-13	Clare
2010	Kerry	3-12	1-6	Limerick
2011	Cork	0-10	1-6	Kerry
2012	Kerry	3-17	3-7	Clare
2013	Cork	1-18	0-9	Waterford
2014	Kerry	3-14	0-13	Cork
2015	Kerry	1-20	0-11	Cork
2016	Kerry	0-14	0-13	Cork
2017	Kerry	4-24	3-20	Cork

FOOTBALL

LEINSTER JUNIOR FOOTBALL FINALS

1905	Westmeath	1-4	1-3	Carlow
1906	Wicklow	1-11	0-0	Westmeath
1907	Laois	2-11	0-5	Westmeath
1908	Dublin	1-8	0-3	Meath
1909	Wicklow	1-10	0-3	Westmeath
1910	Louth	1-5	1-1	Laois
1911	Wexford	3-1	0-2	Dublin
1912	Louth	3-1	2-2	Carlow
1913	Carlow	3-4	0-0	Meath
1914	Dublin	2-2	0-3	Kilkenny
1915	Westmeath	3-0	2-1	Wexford
1916	Dublin	2-7	0-2	Wexford
1917-1921	Suspended			
1922	Dublin	0-3	0-3	Wicklow
Replay	Dublin	2-2	0-3	Wicklow)
1923	Carlow	2-5	1-1	Dublin
1924	Meath	1-3	0-2	Longford

Longford awarded the title on an objection.

1925	Louth	1-3	0-4	Dublin
1926	Dublin	0-4	0-3	Kildare
1927	Kildare	3-3	2-3	Offaly
1928	Louth	1-5	1-4	Dublin
1929	Westmeath	1-2	0-2	Laois
1930	Dublin	3-3	0-2	Carlow
1931	Kildare	1-6	1-4	Dublin
1932	Louth	2-7	1-5	Carlow
1933	Carlow	5-3	4-5	Wicklow
1934	Louth	2-4	1-7	Kildare
Replay	Louth	1-7	0-5	Kildare
1935	Offaly	1-6	1-6	Dublin
Replay	Offaly	2-3	0-2	Dublin
1936	Wicklow	5-5	0-3	Kildare
1937	Longford	3-7	4-1	Offaly
1938	Kildare	1-3	0-5	Westmeath
1939	Dublin	2-4	1-7	Meath
Replay	Dublin	2-12	0-7	Meath
1940	Westmeath	5-7	0-5	Kildare
1941	Laois	2-7	2-5	Louth
1942-1945	Suspended			
1946	Louth	3-5	0-1	Wexford
1947	Meath	2-3	1-4	Dublin
1948	Dublin	3-6	4-3	Wexford
Replay	Dublin	6-3	2-4	Wexford
1949	Wicklow	5-2	2-10	Meath
1950	Dublin	1-15	2-8	Wexford
1951	Dublin	5-7	0-7	Carlow
1952	Meath	2-6	0-1	Wicklow
1953	Longford	3-5	1-5	Kilkenny
1954	Dublin	0-10	0-10	Louth
Replay	Dublin	2-11	2-4	Louth
1955	Dublin	1-12	4-3	Meath
Replay	Dublin	1-8	0-5	Meath
1956	Kildare	2-8	2-3	Wexford
1957	Louth	2-6	1-5	Kilkenny
1958	Meath	1-5	1-3	Dublin
1959	Dublin	2-16	0-5	Longford
1960	Dublin	2-9	0-5	Meath
1961	Louth	2-4	0-8	Dublin
1962	Meath	2-11	1-4	Wexford
1963	Wexford	0-14	1-6	Westmeath
1964	Meath	3-10	1-13	Kildare
1965	Kildare	2-7	0-7	Laois
1966	Louth	3-14	3-12	Kildare (aet)
1967	Kildare	0-11	1-7	Offaly
1968	Laois	2-7	3-4	Westmeath
Replay	Laois	0-9	0-4	Westmeath
1969	Wicklow	2-5	0-5	Meath
1970	Kildare	3-13	1-11	Dublin
1971	Dublin	2-9	0-5	Kilkenny
1972	Offaly	3-8	1-3	Wexford
1973	Laois	1-9	0-9	Meath
1974-1982	Suspended			
1983	Dublin	2-8	0-5	Meath
1984	Wexford	0-8	0-6	Louth
1985	Dublin	3-16	2-4	Louth
1986	Meath	1-10	1-5	Kildare
1987	Dublin	1-8	0-4	Meath
1988	Meath	0-10	1-4	Dublin
1989	Kildare	1-7	1-6	Louth
1990	Meath	0-15	0-11	Dublin
1991	Meath	1-10	1-10	Dublin
Replay	Meath	1-14	2-2	Dublin
1992	Wexford	1-16	2-10	Meath
1993	Laois	2-8	0-11	Carlow
1994	Dublin	0-9	0-5	Louth
1995	Meath	2-11	1-5	Offaly
1996	Meath	1-13	2-7	Laois
1997	Meath	0-16	1-8	Louth
1998	Offaly	1-18	0-8	Kildare

1999	Meath	1-9	1-6	Dublin
2000	Wexford	1-9	1-5	Dublin
2001	Offaly	2-9	1-11	Meath
2002	Wicklow	3-6	0-9	Kildare
2003	Meath	1-15	0-7	Wexford
2004	Kildare	0-9	0-8	Dublin
2005	Meath	1-9	0-5	Louth
2006	Meath	1-12	0-11	Louth
2007	Wexford	1-10	1-8	Dublin
2008	Dublin	1-13	1-9	Meath
2009	Louth	1-8	0-11	Longford
Replay	Louth	1-12	0-10	Longford
2010	Louth	0-13	2-6	Cavan
2011	Kildare	5-8	1-9	Cavan
2012	Cavan	1-13	0-9	Kildare
2013	Kildare	2-15	3-8	Longford
2014	Cavan	1-11	1-7	Longford
2015	Wexford	1-10	0-12	Meath
2016	Wexford	2-12	0-9	Louth
2017	Meath	0-19	0-10	Louth

CONNACHT JUNIOR FOOTBALL FINALS

1907	Mayo	2-9	0-4	Galway
1908-1912	Suspended			
1913	Mayo	2-6	0-0	Galway
1914	Mayo	1-3	1-2	Galway
1915	Galway	2-5	1-4	Mayo
1916-1918	Suspended			
1919	Galway	5-0	1-2	Leitrim
1920-1923	Suspended			
1924	Mayo	1-4	0-1	Galway
1925	Mayo	3-5	1-0	Leitrim
1926	Sligo	1-3	0-1	Roscommon
1927	Mayo	3-12	0-4	Leitrim
1928	Sligo	1-3	0-1	Mayo
1929	Galway	1-7	0-6	Roscommon

Refixture following an objection. Roscommon w.o. Galway scr.

1930	Mayo	2-9	3-2	Roscommon
1931	Galway	3-8	0-3	Leitrim
1932	Roscommon	4-6	0-5	Sligo
1933	Mayo	3-0	1-5	Galway
1934	Mayo	2-5	1-6	Roscommon
1935	Sligo	2-2	1-4	Mayo
1936	Mayo	3-7	2-3	Sligo
1937	Mayo	3-10	3-7	Galway
1938	Leitrim	0-9	1-5	Galway
1939	Roscommon	2-6	1-4	Mayo
1940	Roscommon	1-7	2-1	Mayo
1941	Leitrim	3-9	1-7	Galway
1942-1945	Suspended			
1946	Leitrim	2-9	0-4	Galway
1947	Galway	4-10	2-6	Roscommon
1948	Galway	4-11	1-4	Sligo
1949	Galway	3-9	1-9	Mayo
1950	Mayo	4-7	1-5	Roscommon
1951	Mayo	3-4	2-4	Leitrim
1952	Leitrim	2-7	1-3	Mayo
1953	Mayo	6-7	1-1	Galway
1954	Galway	2-6	1-8	Roscommon
1955	Mayo	3-6	0-2	Galway
1956	Sligo	3-2	2-3	Mayo
1957	Mayo	2-8	2-6	Galway
1958	Galway	3-11	0-2	Sligo
1959	Roscommon	2-5	1-6	Galway

FOOTBALL

1960	Galway	3-5	0-10	Leitrim
1961	Galway	2-12	0-9	Mayo
1962	Leitrim	2-11	2-7	Mayo
1963	Mayo	3-4	1-5	Galway
1964	Roscommon	2-6	2-6	Galway
Replay	Roscommon	0-8	0-7	Galway
1965	Galway	6-17	0-1	Leitrim
1966	Galway	2-5	0-7	Roscommon
1967	Mayo	1-11	2-5	Galway
1968	Mayo	3-10	1-10	Roscommon
1969	Galway	2-8	0-4	Sligo
1970	Mayo	1-11	1-10	Roscommon
1971	Mayo	0-6	0-4	Leitrim
1972	Galway	1-9	1-4	Mayo
1973	Sligo	4-8	1-4	Leitrim
1974-1982	Suspended			
1983	Galway	2-13	3-9	Leitrim
1984	Galway	2-7	0-7	Mayo
1985	Galway	1-9	0-6	Leitrim
1986-1991	Suspended			
1992	Mayo represented province in All-Ireland series			
1993	Mayo	1-9	0-11	Leitrim
1994	Galway	0-12	1-9	Mayo
Replay	Galway	0-11	0-8	Mayo
1995	Mayo	1-15	1-9	Galway
1996	Galway	1-10	2-5	Mayo
1997	Mayo	1-15	0-8	Roscommon
1998	Sligo	3-13	3-5	Roscommon
1999	Roscommon	2-7	0-10	Galway
2000	Roscommon	2-8	0-8	Leitrim
2001	Mayo	1-16	0-9	Leitrim
2002	Mayo	2-14	1-4	Leitrim
2003	Galway	1-7	0-4	Roscommon
2004	Leitrim	0-12	1-8	Roscommon
2005	Sligo	0-12	0-11	Mayo
2006	Roscommon	1-10	0-11	Mayo
2007	Mayo	3-10	2-7	Sligo
2008	Roscommon	2-10	0-13	Leitrim (aet)
2009	Roscommon	2-9	0-10	Mayo
2010	Sligo	0-9	0-8	Galway
2011	Sligo	1-10	1-9	Mayo
2012	Mayo	2-12	0-10	Galway
2013	Sligo	0-15	1-11	Mayo
2014	Sligo	0-9	0-6	Leitrim
2015	Mayo	1-12	0-13	Galway
2016	Mayo	1-11	0-12	Galway
2017	Leitrim	1-16	0-16	Mayo

ULSTER JUNIOR FOOTBALL FINALS

1914	Cavan beat Antrim			
1915	Cavan	2-3	1-3	Antrim
1916	Cavan	0-7	0-0	Monaghan
1917-1922	Suspended			
1923	Antrim	1-3	1-2	Cavan
1924	Cavan	3-7	2-0	Antrim
1925	Armagh	2-3	2-1	Cavan
1926	Armagh	0-3	0-2	Tyrone
1927	Cavan	4-8	1-2	Armagh
1928	No competition			
1929	Armagh	3-14	1-2	Derry
1930	Donegal w.o. Cavan scr.			
1931	Down	1-3	0-5	Cavan
1932	Cavan	2-5	1-1	Down
1933	Donegal	3-7	1-3	Derry
1934	Donegal	0-9	1-4	Down
	Replay ordered following an objection.			
Replay	Down	4-6	3-5	Donegal
1935	Armagh	3-6	3-2	Derry
1936	Cavan	4-7	4-2	Down
1937	Antrim	2-6	1-6	Tyrone
1938	Cavan	2-3	2-1	Armagh
1939	Donegal	2-8	3-4	Cavan
1940	Cavan	3-5	1-8	Antrim
1941	Cavan	2-7	1-8	Armagh
1942	Antrim	3-10	1-6	Fermanagh
1943	Fermanagh	3-8	2-6	Antrim
1944	Cavan	0-10	0-5	Donegal
1945	Derry	4-2	0-6	Armagh
1946	Down	2-5	0-7	Donegal
1947	Down	5-4	0-7	Derry
1948	Armagh	1-12	3-2	Antrim
1949	Down	2-4	1-3	Fermanagh
1950	Derry	2-7	1-4	Antrim
1951	Armagh	3-6	0-6	Down
1952	Donegal	4-5	1-8	Tyrone
1953	Derry	3-6	1-5	Cavan
1954	Donegal	1-7	0-8	Tyrone
1955	Derry	0-13	0-6	Down
1956	Monaghan	0-10	0-2	Cavan
1957	Cavan	3-6	2-2	Donegal
1958	Down	0-10	1-5	Antrim
1959	Fermanagh	2-13	1-4	Antrim

1960	Antrim	1-7	1-6	Derry
1961	Monaghan	2-8	1-6	Antrim
1962	Cavan	0-8	0-7	Down
1963	Antrim	5-8	1-3	Donegal
1964	Derry	2-13	0-8	Antrim
1965	Down	3-8	2-8	Derry
1966	Down	2-6	0-8	Monaghan
1967	Derry	2-8	0-4	Cavan
1968	Tyrone	2-6	0-3	Armagh
1969	Derry	3-9	2-5	Down
1970	Antrim	3-8	3-5	Donegal
1971	Down	3-10	1-1	Fermanagh
1972	Antrim	3-8	1-6	Monaghan
1973–1982	Suspended			
1983	Tyrone	5-7	1-8	Monaghan
1984	Cavan	2-7	0-10	Monaghan
1985	Armagh	2-9	0-12	Donegal
1986	Tyrone	1-7	0-4	Monaghan
1987–2017	No competition			

TOMMY MURPHY CUP FINALS

2004	Croke Park August 22:			
	Clare	*1-11*	*0-11*	*Sligo*
2005	Croke Park September 4:			
	Tipperary	*3-10*	*0-15*	*Wexford*
2006	Croke Park August 27:			
	Louth	*3-14*	*1-11*	*Leitrim*
2007	Croke Park August 4:			
	Wicklow	*3-13*	*1-17*	*Antrim (aet)*
2008	Croke Park August 2:			
	Antrim	*3-12*	*1-15*	*Wicklow*

FOOTBALL

NATIONAL FOOTBALL LEAGUE RESULTS

1925/26
Laois beat Sligo (replay 4-6 to 1-4) and Kerry (1-6 to 1-5) and Dublin (2-1 to 1-0) in Final

1926/27
No League

1927/28
Deciders: Kildare (0-8 to 0-5) and Kerry (0-6 to 0-4) beat Mayo and Kerry beat Kildare (2-4 to 1-6) in Final

1928/29
Deciders: Kildare (4-5) beat Monaghan (0-5); Sligo (1 -5) beat Westmeath (0-4); Kerry (1-5) beat Sligo (1-2) and in Final Kildare (1-7 to 2-3)

1929/30
Final:

Kerry	**1-3**	**1-2**	**Cavan**

Division II Northern-Donegal Midland A-Kilkenny Midland B-Westmeath

1930/31
Semi-finals:

Kerry	**2-5**	**1-6**	**Mayo**
Cork	**wo**	**scr**	**Meath**

Final:

Kerry	**5-2**	**3-3**	**Cork**

1931/32
No competition

1932/33
Final at Croke Park:

Meath	**0-10**	**1-6**	**Cavan**

Special Division Final:

Wexford	**3- 5**	**1-8**	**Cork**

1933/34
Division 1, Inter-Group Test, May 13 1934 at Castlebar:

Mayo	**2-3**	**1-6**	**Dublin**

Replay, October 15 Croke Park:

Mayo	**2-4**	**1-5**	**Dublin**

Division ll Inter-Group Test, October 14 1934 at Tuam:

Offaly	**3-6**	**1-6**	**Sligo**

1934/35
Division 1, Inter-Group Tests, June 9 1935, Clonmel:

Mayo	**6-8**	**2-5**	**Tipperary**

August 4 1935 Castlebar:

Mayo	**5-8**	**0-2**	**Fermanagh**

Tipperary were winners of McGrath Cup in Munster and Fermanagh in Ulster tournaments.
Division II, Final at Armagh October 27 1935:

Armagh	**3-1**	**0-9**	**Westmeath**

1935/36
Division 1:
Winners: **Mayo** (12 points from eight games)
Runners-up: **Dublin and Cavan** (with 10 points)

Division 2, Final at Mullingar, March 29 1936:

Offaly	**3-3**	**1-6**	**Longford**

1936/37
Division 1, Decider, April 11 1937, Croke Park:

Mayo	**5-4**	**1-8**	**Meath**

Division 2, Decider, March 7 1937, Ardara:

Longford	**1-7**	**1-3**	**Donegal**

1937/38
Division 1, Decider, Castlebar, July 3 1938:

Mayo	**3-9**	**1-3**	**Wexford**

Division 2: **Tipperary**
Connacht League: **Sligo**

1938/39
Final at Ballina:

Mayo	**5-9**	**0- 6**	**Meath**

(Twenty-seven counties took part in this season's League)

1939/40
Final at Croke Park:

Galway	**2-5**	**1-5**	**Meath**

(Mayo (holders) did not compete Twenty-three counties participated)

1940/41
Group Winners:
Final at Croke Park:

Mayo	**3-7**	**0-7**	**Dublin**

1941/42
National Leagues suspended
Substitute Competitions:
South Leinster: **Laois**
Connacht: **Roscommon**
Ulster: **Antrim**
North Leinster: **Dublin**

1943/44
Leinster League:
Meath

1944/45
Leinster League:
Meath

1944
Ulster Minor League: **Armagh**
Connacht League: **Galway**

1945
Connacht League: **Sligo**

1945/46
Final:

Meath	**2-2**	**0-6**	**Wexford**

1946/47
Final:

Derry	2-9	2-5	Clare

1947/48
Final:

Cavan	2-11	3-8	Cork

Replay:

Cavan	5-9	2-8	Cork

1948/49
Final:

Mayo	1-8	1-6	Louth

1949/50
'Home' Final:

Cavan	2-8	1-6	Meath

Final, Croke Park:

New York	2-8	0-12	Cavan

1950/51
'Home' Final:

Meath	0-6	0-3	Mayo

Final, New York:

Meath	1-10	0-10	New York

1951/52
'Home' Final:

Cork	2-3	1-5	Dublin

Final, Croke Park:

Cork	1-12	0-3	New York

1952/53
Final:

Dublin	4-6	0-9	Cavan

1953/54
Final:

Mayo	2-10	0-3	Carlow

1954/55
Final:

Dublin	2-12	1-3	Meath

1955/56
Final:

Cork	0-8	0-7	Meath

1956/57
Final:

Galway	1-8	0-6	Kerry

1957/58
Final:

Dublin	3-13	3-8	Kildare

1958/59
Final:

Kerry	2-8	1-8	Derry

1959/60
Final:

Down	0-12	0-9	Cavan

1960/61
Final:

Kerry	4-16	1-5	Derry

1961/62
Final:

Down	2-5	1-7	Dublin

1962/63
'Home' Final:

Kerry	0-9	1-5	Down

Final, Croke Park:

Kerry	1-18	0-10	New York

1963/64
'Home' Final:

Dublin	2-9	0-7	Down

Final, New York:

New York	2-12	1-13	Dublin

1964/65
'Home' Final:

Galway	1-7	0-8	Kerry

New York, 27/6/65:

Galway	1-4	0-8	New York

New York, 4/7/65:

Galway	3-8	0-9	New York

Aggregate:

Galway	4-12	0-17	New York

1965/66
'Home' Final:

Longford	0-9	0-8	Galway

Longford, 2/10/66:

Longford	1-9	0-7	New York

Croke Park, 9/10/66:

Longford	0-9	0-10	New York

Aggregate:

Longford	1-18	0-17	New York

1966/67
'Home' Final:

Galway	0-12	1-7	Dublin

New York, 14/5/67:

New York	3-5	1-6	Galway

New York, 21/5/67:

New York	4-3	0-10	Galway

Aggregate:

New York	7-8	1-16	Galway

1967/68
Croke Park, 26/5/68:

Down	2-14	2-11	Kildare

1968/69

'Home' Final, 18/5/69:

Kerry	3-11	0-8	Offaly

New York, 22/6/69:

Kerry	0-12	0-12	New York

29/6/69:

Kerry	2-21	2-12	New York (aet)

Aggregate:

Kerry	2-33	2-24	New York

1969/70

Croke Park, April 5, Semi-final:

Mayo	0-10	1-5	Kerry

Croke Park, April 12, Semi-final:

Down	1-11	2-3	Kildare

Croke Park, April 19, Final:

Mayo	4-7	0-10	Down

1970/71

Croke Park, May 16, Semi-final:

Kerry	1-11	1-10	Derry

Croke Park, May 23, Semi-final:

Mayo	1-9	0-8	Dublin

Croke Park, June 20, Final:

Kerry	0-11	0-8	Mayo

1971/72

Croke Park, April 9, Semi-final:

Kerry	0-17	0-13	Derry

Croke Park, April 16, Semi-final:

Mayo	2-10	0-16	Offaly

Croke Park, April 30, Replay:

Mayo	1-9	0-6	Offaly

Croke Park, May 14, Final:

Kerry	2-11	1-9	Mayo

1972/73

Croke Park, April 8, Semi-final:

Kerry	0-11	2-5	Derry

No replay, Derry conceded walkover

Croke Park, April 15, Semi-final:

Offaly	0-11	0-6	Sligo

Croke Park, May 6, Final:

Kerry	2-12	0-14	Offaly

1973/74

Croke Park, April 7, Semi-final:

Kerry	2-14	0-12	Tyrone

Croke Park, April 28, Semi-final:

Roscommon	0-12	0-12	Sligo

Castlebar, May 5, Replay:

Roscommon	0-16	0-10	Sligo

Croke Park, May 19, Final:

Kerry	1-6	0-9	Roscommon

Croke Park, May 26, Replay:

Kerry	0-14	0-8	Roscommon

1974/75

Croke Park, April 27, Semi-final:

Meath	4-6	0-8	Mayo

Croke Park, May 4, Semi-final:

Dublin	3-12	1-7	Tyrone

Croke Park, May 18, Final:

Meath	0-16	1-9	Dublin

1975/76

Croke Park, April 4, Semi-final:

Dublin	1-11	0-12	Galway

Croke Park, April 11, Semi-final:

Derry	0-17	1-6	Cork

Croke Park, May 2, Final:

Dublin	2-10	0-15	Derry

1976/77

Croke Park, March 27, Semi-final:

Dublin	2-12	0-5	Mayo

Croke Park, April 3, Semi-final:

Kerry	2-13	0-8	Roscommon

Croke Park, April 17, Final:

Kerry	1-8	1-6	Dublin

1977/78

Croke Park, April 2, Semi-final:

Dublin	0-12	0-7	Laois

Croke Park, April 9, Semi-final:

Mayo	0-10	0-6	Down

Croke Park, April 23, Final:

Dublin	2-18	2-13	Mayo

1978/79

Croke Park, April 15, Semi-final:

Roscommon	1-14	0-12	Offaly

Croke Park, April 22, Semi-final:

Cork	2-9	0-4	Kildare

Croke Park, May 13, Final:

Roscommon	0-15	1-3	Cork

1979/80

Croke Park, April 6, Semi-final:

Kerry	1-11	1-6	Armagh

Croke Park, April 13, Semi-final:

Cork	1-16	1-6	Galway

Páirc Uí Chaoimh, April 27, Final:

Cork	0-11	0-10	Kerry

1980/81

Ennis, April 26, Semi-final:

Galway	0-10	0-8	Kerry

Roscommon, April 26, Semi-final:

Roscommon	1-11	1-6	Mayo

Croke Park, May 10, Final:

Galway	1-11	1-3	Roscommon

1981/82

Croke Park, April 11, Semi-final:

Cork	1-15	1-10	Offaly

Croke Park, April 11, Semi-final:

Kerry	3-4	1-5	Armagh

Killarney, April 25, Final:

Kerry	0-11	0-11	Cork

Páirc Uí Chaoimh, May 9, Replay:

Kerry	1-9	0-5	Cork

1982/83
Croke Park, April 10, Semi-final:
| **Down** | 1-9 | 0-4 | *Kildare* |
Croke Park April 10, Semi-final:
| **Armagh** | 2-8 | 1-7 | *Meath* |
Croke Park, April 24, Final:
| **Down** | 1-8 | 0-8 | *Armagh* |

1983/84
Croke Park, April 1, Semi-final:
| **Kerry** | 0-12 | 1-6 | *Down* |
Croke Park, April 1, Semi-final:
| **Galway** | 1-10 | 0-13 | *Meath* |
Croke Park April 15, Replay:
| **Galway** | 0-10 | 0-9 | *Meath* |
Limerick, April 29, Final:
| **Kerry** | 1-11 | 0-11 | *Galway* |

1984/85
Croke Park, March 24, Semi-final:
| **Armagh** | 1-9 | 0-6 | *Down* |
Croke Park, March 24, Semi-final:
| **Monaghan** | 1-6 | 0-9 | *Tyrone* |
Armagh, March 31, Replay:
| **Monaghan** | 1-8 | 0-8 | *Tyrone (aet)* |
Croke Park, April 7, Final:
| **Monaghan** | 1-11 | 0-9 | *Armagh* |

1985/86
Croke Park, April 20, Semi-final:
| **Laois** | 0-12 | 1-7 | *Dublin* |
Croke Park, April 20, Semi-final:
| **Monaghan** | 0-10 | 1-6 | *Mayo* |
Croke Park, May 4, Final:
| **Laois** | 2-6 | 2-5 | *Monaghan* |

1986/87
Croke Park, April 12, Semi-final:
| **Kerry** | 2-11 | 2-9 | *Monaghan* |
Croke Park, April 19, Semi-final:
| **Dublin** | 1-8 | 0-8 | *Galway* |
Croke Park, April 26, Final:
| **Dublin** | 1-11 | 0-11 | *Kerry* |

1987/88
Croke Park, April 3, Semi-final:
| **Dublin** | 4-12 | 1-8 | *Monaghan* |
Croke Park, April 3, Semi-final:
| **Meath** | 0-13 | 1-9 | *Down* |
Croke Park, April 17, Final:
| **Meath** | 0-11 | 1-8 | *Dublin* |
Croke Park, May 22, Replay:
| **Meath** | 2-13 | 0-11 | *Dublin* |

1988/89
Croke Park, April 9, Semi-final:
| **Dublin** | 1-10 | 1-9 | *Cavan* |
Páirc Uí Chaoimh, April 9, Semi-final:
| **Cork** | 0-10 | 0-4 | *Kerry* |
Croke Park, April 23, 'Home' Final:
| **Cork** | 0-15 | 0-12 | *Dublin* |
Gaelic Park, New York, May 7, Final 1st leg:
| **Cork** | 1-12 | 1-5 | *New York* |

Gaelic Park, New York, May 14, Final 2nd leg:
| **Cork** | 2-9 | 1-9 | *New York* |
Aggregate:
| **Cork** | 3-21 | 2-14 | *New York* |

1989/90
Croke Park, April 15, Semi-final:
| **Meath** | 0-14 | 0-10 | *Cork* |
Croke Park, April 15, Semi-final:
| **Down** | 4-8 | 0-11 | *Roscommon* |
Croke Park, April 29, Final:
| **Meath** | 2-7 | 0-11 | *Down* |

1990/91
Croke Park, April 21, Semi-final:
| **Kildare** | 0-14 | 0-10 | *Donegal* |
Croke Park, April 21, Semi-final:
| **Dublin** | 1-18 | 0-11 | *Roscommon* |
Croke Park, May 5, Final:
| **Dublin** | 1-9 | 0-10 | *Kildare* |

1991/92
Croke Park, April 19, Semi-final:
| **Derry** | 0-12 | 1-8 | *Meath* |
Croke Park, April 19, Semi-final:
| **Tyrone** | 0-13 | 1-9 | *Dublin* |
Croke Park, May 3, Final:
| **Derry** | 1-10 | 1-8 | *Tyrone* |

1992/93
Croke Park, April 18, Semi-final:
| **Donegal** | 1-12 | 1-7 | *Clare* |
Croke Park, April 18, Semi-final:
| **Dublin** | 1-10 | 0-11 | *Kerry* |
Croke Park, May 2, Final:
| **Dublin** | 0-9 | 0-9 | *Donegal* |
Croke Park, May 9, Replay:
| **Dublin** | 0-10 | 0-6 | *Donegal* |

1993/94
Croke Park, April 17, Semi-final:
| **Armagh** | 3-11 | 1-9 | *Laois* |
Croke Park, April 17, Semi-final:
| **Meath** | 0-15 | 0-11 | *Westmeath* |
Croke Park, May 1, Final:
| **Meath** | 2-11 | 0-8 | *Armagh* |

1994/95
Croke Park, April 30, Semi-final:
| **Derry** | 1-8 | 2-3 | *Tyrone* |
Croke Park, April 30, Semi-final:
| **Donegal** | 1-14 | 2-8 | *Laois* |
Croke Park, May 14, Final:
| **Derry** | 0-12 | 0-8 | *Donegal* |

FOOTBALL

1995/96
Croke Park, April 21, Semi-final:
Derry	*1-12*	*0-7*	*Mayo*

Croke Park, April 21, Semi-final:
Donegal	*0-10*	*0-9*	*Cork*

Croke Park, May 5, Final:
Derry	*1-16*	*1-9*	*Donegal*

1996/97
Croke Park, April 20, Semi-final:
Kerry	*2-13*	*1-10*	*Laois*

Croke Park, April 20, Semi-final:
Cork	*2-10*	*1-9*	*Kildare*

Páirc Uí Chaoimh, May 4, Final:
Kerry	*3-7*	*1-8*	*Cork*

1997/98
Croke Park, April 12, Semi-final:
Derry	*1-12*	*0-8*	*Monaghan*

Croke Park, April 12, Semi-final:
Offaly	*3-10*	*1-14*	*Donegal*

Croke Park, April 26, Final:
Offaly	*0-9*	*0-7*	*Derry*

1998/99
Croke Park, April 2, Semi-final:
Cork	*0-6*	*0-3*	*Meath*

Croke Park, April 25, Semi-final:
Dublin	*0-11*	*0-11*	*Armagh*

Croke Park, May 2, Replay:
Dublin	*1-14*	*0-12*	*Armagh*

Páirc Uí Chaoimh, May 9, Final:
Cork	*0-12*	*1-7*	*Dublin*

1999/00
Clones, April 23, Semi-final:
Derry	*0-15*	*0-8*	*Roscommon*

Thurles, April 23, Semi-final:
Meath	*4-11*	*1-18*	*Kerry*

Croke Park, May 7, Final:
Derry	*1-12*	*1-12*	*Meath*

Clones, May 20, Replay:
Derry	*1-8*	*0-9*	*Meath*

2000/01
Roscommon, April 21, Semi-final:
Galway	*2-12*	*0-11*	*Sligo*

Sligo, April 22, Semi-final:
Mayo	*0-16*	*1-10*	*Roscommon*

Croke Park, April, 29, Final:
Mayo	*0-13*	*0-12*	*Galway*

2002
Enniskillen, April 14, Semi-final:
Tyrone	*3-12*	*0-11*	*Mayo*

Mullingar, April 14, Semi-final:
Cavan	*5-13*	*3-12*	*Roscommon*

Clones, April 28, Final:
Tyrone	*0-16*	*0-7*	*Cavan*

2003
Croke Park, April 20, Semi-final:
Laois	*1-14*	*1-11*	*Armagh*

Croke Park, April 20, Semi-final:
Tyrone	*4-11*	*1-11*	*Fermanagh*

Croke Park, May 4, Final:
Tyrone	*0-21*	*1-8*	*Laois*

2004
Limerick, April 18, Semi-final:
Kerry	*0-12*	*0-10*	*Limerick*

Omagh, April 18, Semi-final:
Galway	*1-16*	*1-16*	*Tyrone (aet)*

Galway, April 25, Replay:
Galway	*2-18*	*1-19*	*Tyrone (aet)*

Croke Park, May 2, Final:
Kerry	*3-11*	*1-16*	*Galway*

2005
Portlaoise, April 17, Semi-final:
Wexford	*1-8*	*1-7*	*Tyrone*

Croke Park, April 24, Semi-final:
Armagh	*0-19*	*0-14*	*Mayo*

Croke Park, May 1, Final:
Armagh	*1-21*	*1-14*	*Wexford*

2006
Killarney, April 16, Semi-final:
Kerry	*1-15*	*0-10*	*Laois*

Castlebar, April 16, Semi-final:
Galway	*1-11*	*1-6*	*Mayo*

Gaelic Grounds, April, 23 Final:
Kerry	*2-12*	*0-10*	*Galway*

2007
Croke Park, April 15, Semi-final:
Donegal	*1-13*	*1-11*	*Kildare*

Croke Park, April 15, Semi-final:
Mayo	*2-10*	*1-12*	*Galway*

Croke Park, April 22, Final:
Donegal	*0-13*	*0-10*	*Mayo*

2008
Parnell Park, April 27, Final:
Derry	*2-13*	*2-9*	*Kerry*

2009
Croke Park, April 26, Final:
Kerry	*1-15*	*0-15*	*Derry*

2010
Croke Park, April 25, Final:
Cork	*1-17*	*0-12*	*Mayo*

2011
Croke Park, April 24, Final:
Cork	*0-21*	*2-14*	*Dublin*

2012

Croke Park, April 15, Semi-final:
| Mayo | 2-15 | 1-17 | Kerry (aet) |

Croke Park, April 15, Semi-final:
| Cork | 2-17 | 1-12 | Down |

Croke Park, April 29, Final:
| Cork | 2-10 | 0-11 | Mayo |

2013

Croke Park, April 14, Semi-final:
| Dublin | 2-16 | 0-16 | Mayo |

Croke Park, April 14, Semi-final:
| Tyrone | 2-15 | 2-11 | Kildare |

Croke Park, April 28, Final:
| Dublin | 0-18 | 0-17 | Tyrone |

2014

Croke Park, April 13, Semi-final:
| Derry | 2-15 | 1-16 | Mayo |

Croke Park, April 13, Semi-final:
| Dublin | 2-20 | 2-13 | Cork |

Croke Park, April 27, Final:
| Dublin | 3-19 | 1-10 | Derry |

2015

Croke Park, April 12. Semi-final:
| Cork | 4-11 | 0-19 | Donegal |

Croke Park, April 12. Semi-final:
| Dublin | 0-17 | 0-16 | Monaghan |

Croke Park, April 26. Final:
| Dublin | 1-21 | 2-7 | Cork |

2016

Croke Park, April 10. Semi-final:
| Kerry | 3-15 | 0-14 | Roscommon |

Croke Park, April 10. Semi-final:
| Dublin | 1-20 | 0-13 | Donegal |

Croke Park, April 24. Final:
| Dublin | 2-18 | 0-13 | Kerry |

2017

Croke Park, April 9. Final:
| Kerry | 0-20 | 1-16 | Dublin |

NATIONAL FOOTBALL LEAGUE FINALISTS

1925/26

Laois   R.Miller (capt.), W.Irwin, P.Bates, J.Browne, Matt Delaney, T.Cribben, J.Ward, C.Miller, W.Whelan, Jim Miller, P.Whelan, J.O'Shea, J.Delaney, John Miller, T.Costelloe.
Dublin   P.McDonnell, J.McDonnell, Joe Synnott, John Synnott, J.Reilly, J.Kirwan, M.Durnin, P.Molloy, Jim Norris, P.Carey, M.Lennon, P.Mohan, Joe Norris, C.McDonald, P.Stynes.

1926/27   NO COMPETITON

1927/28

Kerry   J.Riordan, D.O'Connor, J.Barrett Jack Walsh, P.Russell, Joe O'Sullivan, James O'Sullivan, C.Brosnan, R.Stack, J.Ryan, J.J.Sheehy (capt.), E.Fitzgerald, E.Sweeney, James Baily, J.J.Landers.
Kildare   M.Walsh, M.Buckley, M.Goff, A.Fitzpatrick, F.Malone, J.Higgins, J.Hayes, J.Loughlin, W.Gannon, J.Curtis, P.Martin, P.Doyle, W.Mangan, P.Loughlin, T.Keogh. Subs: A.O'Neill for J.Curtis.

1928/29

Kerry   J.Riordan, D.O'Connor, J.Barrett (capt.), Jack Walsh, P.Russell, Joe O'Sullivan, T.O'Donnell, C.Brosnan, R.Stack, J.Ryan, J.J.Sheehy, M.Doyle, E.Sweeney, James Baily, J.J.Landers.
Kildare   J.O'Reilly, M.Buckley, M.Goff, C.Graham, W.Hynan, J.Higgins (capt.), J.Hayes, P.Loughlin, F.Malone, P.Martin, P.Plant, P.Doyle, P.Byrne, P.Pringle, A.O'Neill.

1929/30

Kerry   J.Riordan (capt.), T.O'Donnell, P.Whitty, Jack Walsh, P.Russell, Joe O'Sullivan, E.Fitzgerald, C.Brosnan, R.Stack, C.Geaney, M.Doyle, J.Flavin, E.Sweeney, J.J.Landers, T.Landers. Sub: E.Barrett for R.Stack.
Cavan   W.Young, T.Campbell, T.Crowe, M.Dinneny, J.Molloy, P.Lynch, F.Fitzpatrick, J.Smith (capt.), H.O'Reilly, P.McNamee, O.Fay, J.Smallhorne, L.Blessing, T.J.Weymns, T.Coyle. Subs: T.O'Reilly (Cornafean) for W.Young, W.Young for T.Coyle.

1930/31

Kerry   D.O'Keeffe, D.O'Connor, P.Whitty, Jack Walsh, T.O'Donnell, W.Kinnerk, M.Healy, R.Stack, J.J.Landers, T.Landers, M.Doyle (capt.), J.Ryan, J.Quill, W.Landers, C.Brosnan.
Cork   P.J.Downing, C.Cronin, M.O'Flynn, D.Kiely, J.Lynch, J.Dunlea, T.Kiely, D.Burke, Tim Cotter, M.O'Connor, W.Lynch, L.Flanagan, G.Harrington, J.McKenna, J.O'Regan (capt.).

1931/32   NO COMPETITION

1932/33

Meath   P.Browne, R.Cassidy, W.Dillon, W.Clynch, P.Geraghty, T.Meade, T.Smith, J.Loughran, R.Durnin, A.Donnelly, W.Shaw (capt.), M.Rogers, M.Brennan, P.McEnroe, P.Mooney.
Cavan   W.Young, W.Connolly, P.Lynch, M.Dinneny, T.Coyle, J.Smith (capt.), P.Phair, H.O'Reilly, T.O'Reilly (Cornafean), D.Morgan, P.Devlin, J Smallhorne, V.McGovern, L.Blessing, M.J.Magee. Sub: T.O'Reilly (Mullahoran) for M.J.Magee.

1933/34

Mayo   T.Burke, J.Gannon, P.Quinn, P.Kelly, T.Regan, H.Kenny, P.Brett, P.Flannelly, G.Ormsby, J.Carney, P.O'Malley, P.Laffey, G.Courell (capt.), P.Moclair, P.Munnelly.
(Note: P.O'Loughlin, M.Raftery and P.Collins played in drawn game. J.Gannon, P.O'Malley and P.Brett came on for replay.)
Dublin   J.McDonnell, D.Brennan, S.Lambe, F.Cavanagh, P.Hickey, E.McCann, P.Cavanagh, R.Beggs, M.Kelly, W.Dowling, G.Fitzgerald, M.O'Brien, M.Wellington, M.Keating (capt.), H.Farnan.
(Note: J.O'Shea, C.McMahon and P.Perry played in drawn game. S.Lambe, M.Kelly and H.Farnan came on for replay.)

1934/35

Mayo   T.Burke, T.McNicholas, P.Quinn, P.Kelly, T.Regan, H.Kenny, P.Brett, P.Flannelly, G.Ormsby, J.Carney, J.Munnelly, P.Laffey, G.Courell (capt.), P.Moclair, P.Munnelly. Sub: J.Gannon for T.McNicholas.
Fermanagh   P.Donaghy, E.Lennon, W.Carty, P.Burns, H.Darcy, E.McDonnell, H.McPike, J.McCullagh, T.McDonnell, G.Magee, P.McGrane, J.Monaghan, C.McDonnell, W.Maguire, F.Johnston.

1935/36

Mayo   D.Acton, J.McGowan, P.Quinn, P.Kelly, T.Regan, G.Ormsby, P.Collins, P.Flannelly, H.Kenny, J.Carney, J.Munnelly, P Laffey, G.Courell (capt.), P.Moclair, P.Munnelly.
(Note: Played on a league system. The above is the team, which beat Cavan and clinchecl the title.)

1936/37

Mayo   T.Burke, J.McGowan, P.Quinn, P.Kelly, T.Regan, G.Ormsby, P.Robinson, P.Flannelly, H.Kenny, J.Carney, T.Grier, P.Laffey, J.Munnelly, P Moclair (capt.), P.Munnelly.
Meath   P.Browne, R.Cassidy, P.Beggan, H.McEnroe, P.Geraghty (capt.), K.Murray, P.Duffy, M.Casey, J.Cummins, T.Burns, A.Donnelly, M.Gilsenan, T.Coogan, T.McGuinness, M.Rogers.

1937/38

Mayo   T.Burke, J.McGowan, P.Quinn, P.Kelly, T.Regan, G.Ormsby, T.McNicholas, Patsy Flannelly, H.Kenny, J.Laffey, P.J.Judge, P.Laffey, J.Munnelly, P.Moclair (capt.), M.Hannon. Subs: M.O'Malley for T.McNicholas, S.Melody for T.Regan.
Wexford   P.Lynch, J.Furlong, P Hayes (capt.), F.Clancy, P.Boggan, D.Morris, P.Mythen, J.Donoghue, P.Quinn, J.Moriarty, J.Nolan, M.Roche, F.Walsh, T.Roche, W.Howlin.

1938/39

Mayo   T.Burke, J.McGowan, P.Quinn, J.Sammon, T.Regan, G.Ormsby, T.Robinson, C.O'Toole, H.Kenny, J.Carney, P.J.Judge, P.Laffey, J.Munnelly, P.Moclair (capt.), T.Hoban.
Meath   H.McEnroe, C.Coleman, M.O'Toole, M.Clinton, K.Johnston, C.O'Reilly, P Donnelly, J.Loughran, J.Kearney, J.Clarke, A Donnelly, M.Gilsenan (capt.), W.Brien, J.Cummins, H.Lynch.

1939/40

Galway   J.McGauran, M.Raftery, C.Connolly, P McDonagh, F.Cunniffe, R.Beggs, J.Casey, P.Mitchell, J.Dunne (capt.), J.Flavin, E.Mulholland, J.Burke, M.Higgins, C.McGovern, B.Nestor.
Meath   H.McEnroe, P.Beggan, M.O'Toole, P.Donnelly, K.Johnston, C.O'Reilly, J.Kearney, J.Loughran, P.Ward, P.McDermott, A.Donnelly, M.Gilsenan (capt.), W.Brien, T.McGuinness, K.Devin. Sub: J.Cummins for K.Devin.

1940/41

Mayo   D.Acton, J.McGowan, R.Winters, J.Laffey, T.Regan, G.Ormsby, T.Robinson, H.Kenny (capt.), J.Munnelly (Ballycastle), J.Carney, P.J.Judge, P.Laffey, M.O'Malley, J.Munnelly, T.Hoban.
Dublin   C.Kelly, T.Moore, G.McLoughlin, B.Murphy, P.O'Reilly, M.Falvey, B.Quinn, P.Holly (capt.), S.O Dubhda, J.Joy, G.Fitzgerald, T.Banks, M.Fletcher, P.Bermingham, J.Buckley.

1942/1945   NO COMPETITION

1945/46

Meath   K.Smith, J.Kearney, M.O'Toole (capt.), J.Byrne, P.Gogan, A.Donnelly, C.Hand, M.O'Brien, P.O'Brien, F.Byrne, P.McDermott, V.Sherlock, P.Meegan, W.Halpenny, J.Clarke.
Wexford   M.Kehoe, T.Doyle, G.Kavanagh, J.Coady, J.Culleton, W.Goodison, J.Morris, D.Clancy, P.Kehoe, D.O'Neill, N.Rackard, T.Somers, S.Thorpe, T.O'Leary, J.O'Connor. Subs: M.Hanlon for G.Kavanagh, G.Kavanagh for M.Hanlon.

1946/47

Derry   C.Moran, S.Keenan, J.Convery, J.Hurley, J.Murphy, S.McCann, T.E.McCloskey, M.McNaught, R.Gribben, P.Keenan (capt.), F.Niblock, L.Higgins, P.McErlean, J.E.Mullan, J.Cassidy.
Clare   P.Gallagher, D.Hogan, F.Keane, M.Collins, D.Fitzgerald, J.Murrihy, R.Bradley, E.J.Carroll, P.Power, P.Daly, S.Guinnane, P.J.Griffin, J.Hill, R.Fitzpatrick, N.Crowley.

1947/48

Cavan   S.Morris, W.Doonan, B.O'Reilly, P.Smith, O.R.McGovern, J.J.O'Reilly (capt.), S.Deignan, P.J.Duke, P.Brady, A.Tighe, M.Higgins, J.J.Cassidy, J.Stafford, P.Donohoe, E.Carolan. Sub: T.P.O'Reilly for E.Carolan.
(Note: J.D.Benson, B.Cully and T.P.O'Reilly played in drawn game. S.Morris, B.O'Reilly and E.Carolan came on for replay.)
Cork   M.O'Driscoll, D.O'Connor, P.A.Murphy, C.Crone, J.Hartnett, T.Crowley, T.O'Driscoll, C.McGrath, B.Murphy, D.O'Donovan, C.Duggan, T.Daly, J.Lynam, Jim Cronin, E.Young. Subs: F.O'Donovan for B.Murphy, H.O'Neill for C.Crone.
(Note: J.Murphy, C.Power, F.O'Donovan, N.Ryan and J.Aherne played in drawn game. J.Hartnett, T.O'Driscoll, B.Murphy, T.Daly and E.Young came on for replay. Subs in drawn game: J.Hartnett for N.Ryan, C.O'Connor for C.Power.)

1948/49

Mayo   T.Byrne (capt.), P.Gilvarry, P.Prendergast, J.Forde, W.Kenny, E.Mongey, S.Mulderrig, P.Carney, H.Dixon, L.Hastings, T.Langan, Joe Gilvarry, T.Acton, P.Solan, M.Flanagan.
Louth   S.Thornton, J.Bell, J.Malone, T.Mulligan, S.Boyle, P.Markey, P.McArdle, J.Regan, H.Reynolds, F.Fegan, J.Quigley, S.White, H.O'Rourke, T.Walsh, M.Reynolds.

1949/50

New York   P.O'Reilly, J.Quinn, T.Gallagher, D.O'Connor, J.Redican, W.Carlos, E.Kenny, P.McAndrew, P.Ryan, M.O'Sullivan (capt.), J.Hughes, F.Quinn, P.Holly, S.Keane, J.Corcoran.
Cavan   S.Morris, S.Deignan, J.McCabe, P.Smith, P.Carolan, J.J.O'Reilly (capt.), J.J.Cassidy, P.Brady, V.Sherlock, A.Tighe, M.Higgins, T.Hardy, E.Carolan, P.Donohoe, J.Cusack.

'HOME' FINAL
Cavan   Same as played in final except L.Maguire in place of J.McCabe. Sub: J.Stafford for S.Morris.

Meath   K.Smith, M.O'Brien, P.O'Brien, K.McConnell, S.Heery, P.Dixon, C.Hand, D.Taaffe, P.Connell, F.Byrne, B.Smith (capt.), P.Meegan, P.Carolan, J.Meehan, M.McDonnell.

1950/51

Meath   K.Smith, M.O'Brien, P.O'Brien, K.McConnell, C.Kelly, P.Dixon, C.Hand, D.Taaffe, P.Connell, F.Byrne, M.McDonnell, P.Meegan (capt.), B.Smith, J.Reilly, P.McDermott. Subs: L.McGuinness for B.Smith, B.Smith for P.Connell.
New York   T.Sheehan, D.O'Connor, T.Gallagher, J.Foley, J.Redican, W.Carlos, E.Kenny, P.McAndrew, E.Austin, M.O'Sullivan, T.O'Connor (capt.), J.Hughes, F.Quinn, M.Culhane, J.Corcoran. Subs: F.Driscoll for E.Austin, D.Danagher for J.Corcoran.

'HOME' FINAL
Meath   Same as played in final except S.Heery in place of K.McConnell. Sub: K.McConnell for C.Hand.
Mayo   S.Wynne, J.Forde, P.Prendergast, S.Flanagan (capt.), J.Staunton, H.Dixon, J.McAndrew, E.Mongey, P.Irwin, M.Flanagan, S.Mulderrig, Joe Gilvarry, M.Mulderrig, T.Langan, P.Solan.

1951/52

Cork   D.O'Keeffe, C.Dineen, P.A.Murphy, J.O'Brien, D.O'Donovan, D.Bernard, M.Gould, D.Kelleher, C.Duggan, T.Moriarty, C.McGrath, E.Young (capt.), M.Cahill, J.J.Henchion, Jim Cronin.
New York   T.Sheehan, D.O'Connor, T.Gallagher, J.Foley, J.Redican, W.Carlos, E.Kenny, P.McAndrew, F.Driscoll, M.O'Sullivan, J.Hughes, P.Ryan, F.Quinn, J.McElligott, T.O'Connor (capt.). Subs: J.Looney for J.Redican, E.Driscoll for W.Carlos, T.Conway for D.O'Connor, E.Lyons for J.Looney, W.Carlos for J.McElligoff

'HOME' FINAL
Cork   Same as played in final except P.O'Driscoll and John Cronin in place of D.Kelleher and Jim Cronin. Sub: D.Kelleher for M.Gould.
Dublin   G.O'Toole, M.Moylan, J.Lavin, N.Allen, S.Scally, D.Sullivan, F.McCready, J.Crowley, Mossy Whelan, C.O'Leary, O.Freaney, M.Murphy, D.Ferguson, A.Young, K.Heffernan. Subs: D.Mahony for F.McCready.

1952/53

Dublin   A.O'Grady, D.Mahony, M.Moylan, M.Wilson, J.Lavin, N.Allen, N.Maher, J.Crowley, Mossy Whelan (capt.), D.Ferguson, O.Freaney, C.Freaney, B.Atkins, A.Young, K.Heffernan.
Cavan   S.Morris, J.McCabe, P.Brady, V.Clarke, T.Hardy, L.Maguire, S.Keogan, P.Carolan, P.Fitzsimons, B.Gallagher, M.Higgins (capt.), E.Carolan, S.Deignan, A.Tighe, J.Cusack. Subs: G.Keyes for P.Carolan, D.Smith for V.Clarke, P.Carolan for S.Keogan, D.McCaffrey for J.McCabe.

1953/54

Mayo   S.Wynne, J.Forde, P.Prendergast, S.Flanagan, F.Fleming, J.McAndrew, E.Moriarty, J.Nallen, P.Irwin, S.O'Donnell, P.Carney (capt.), E.Mongey, M.Flanagan, T.Langan, D.O'Neill.
Carlow   A.Magee, L.Murphy, W.Canavan, P.Connolly, M.Molloy, A.Murphy, P.Delaney, J.Fogarty, E.Kehoe, W.Magill (capt.), E.Doogue, W.Whelan, W.Walsh, J.Hayes, L.Quigley. Sub: P.Metcalf for P.Delaney.

1954/55
Dublin   P.O'Flaherty, D.Mahony (capt.), J.Lavin, M.Moylan, W.Monks, N.Allen, N.Maher, J.Crowley, S.McGuinness, D.Ferguson, O.Freaney, C.O'Leary, P.Haughey, K.Heffernan, S.O'Boyle. Sub: M.Whelan for McGuinness.
Meath   P.McGearty, M.O'Brien, P.O'Brien, K.McConnell, K.Lenehan, J.Reilly, E.Durnin, T.O'Brien, P.Connell, M.Grace, B.Smith, W.Rattigan, M.McDonnell, T.Moriarty, P.Ratty (capt.). Subs: L.O'Brien for Smith, J.Ryan for P.O'Brien.

1955/56
Cork   P.Tyers, P.O'Driscoll, D.O'Sullivan (capt.), D.Murray, P.Harrington, D.Bernard, M.Gould, E.Ryan, S.Moore, D.Kelleher, C.Duggan, P.Murphy, T.Furlong, N.Fitzgerald, J.Creedon.
Meath   P.McGearty, K.Lenihan, J.Ryan, W.McGurk, T.O'Brien (capt.), P.McKeever, E.Durnin, M.Dunican, T.Duff, L.O'Brien, M.McDonnell, W.Rattigan, B.Smith, S.Duff, P.Ratty. Subs: M.Grace for L.O'Brien, T.Smith for W.Rattigan.

1956/57
Galway   J.O'Neill, S.Keeley, G.Daly, T.Dillon, J.Kissane, J.Mahon (capt.), M.Greally, F.Evers, M.McDonagh, J.Coyle, S.Purcell, W.O'Neill, J.Young, F.Stockwell G.Kirwan.
Kerry   D.O'Neill, J.O'Shea (capt.), E.Roche, T.Lyons, Seán Murphy, John Dowling, C.Kennelly, D.O'Shea, T.Long, P.Sheehy, T.Moriarty, T.Lyne, T.Collins, M.Murphy, D.McAuliffe. Sub: P.Fitzgerald for T.Collins.

1957/58
Dublin   P.O'Flaherty, M.Wilson, Joe Timmons, J.Brennan, C.O'Leary, J.Crowley, S.O'Boyle, S.Murray, P.Downey, P.Haughey, O.Freaney, D.Ferguson, P.Farnan, J.Joyce, K.Heffernan (capt.). Subs: L.Foley for P.Downey, C.Leaney for D.Ferguson.
Kildare   M.Nolan, S.McCormack, D.Flood, P.Connolly, P.Gibbons, M.Carolan, P.Maguire, P.Moore, T.Connolly, C.Kelly, L.McCormack (capt.), K.O'Malley, E.Treacy, J.Dowling, E.Hogan. Subs: P.Timmons for P.Maguire, M.Doyle for P.Connolly.

1958/59
Kerry   J.Culloty, J.O'Shea, Jack Dowling, T.Lyons, Seán Murphy, K.Coffey, M.O'Dwyer, M.O'Connell, Seamus Murphy, D.McAuliffe, T.Long, P.Sheehy, D.Geaney, John Dowling, J.Brosnan.
Derry   P.Gormley, P.McLarnon, H.F.Gribben, T.Doherty, P.Breen, C.Mulholland, P.Smith, J.McKeever, L.O'Neill, S.O'Connell, B.Murray, D.McKeever, B.Mullan, O.Gribben, P.Stuart.

1959/60
Down   E.McKay, G.Lavery, L.Murphy, P.Rice, K.Mussen (capt.), D.McCartan, K.O'Neill, P.J.McElroy, P.O'Hagan, S.O'Neill, J.Carey, P.Doherty, A.Hadden, J.McCartan, B.Morgan. Subs: K.Denvir for J.Carey, E.Lundy for L.Murphy, L.Murphy for E.Lundy, E.Lundy for A.Hadden
Cavan   B.O'Reilly, N.O'Reilly, G.Kelly, M.Brady, H.Gaffney, T.Maguire (capt.), J.Meehan, J.McDonnell, H.B.O'Donoghue, C.Smith, T.Galligan, C.Gallagher, M.Shiels, J.Brady, J.Sheridan. Subs: S.Conaty for T.Galligan, T.Galligan for J.McDonnell.

1960/61
Kerry   J.Culloty, Jack Dowling, N.Sheehy (capt.), T.Lyons, K.Coffey, T.Long, M.O'Dwyer, M.O'Connell, Seamus Murphy, D.McAuliffe, B.Sheehy, J.Sheehy, T.O'Dowd, John Dowling, D.Geaney

Derry   P.Gormley, P.McLarnon, B.Devlin, H.F.Gribben, C.Mulholland, T.Scullion, P.Smith, P.Stuart, B.Murray, J.McKeever (capt.), S.O'Connell, L.O'Neill, D.McKeever, W.O'Kane, C.O'Connor. Subs: G.Magee for C.O'Connor, G.O'Neill for P.Stuart, C.O'Connor for P.Gormley.

1961/62
Down   E.McKay, G.Lavery, L.Murphy, P.Rice, K.Mussen, P.O'Hagan, K.O'Neill, J.Carey, J.Lennon, S.O'Neill, J.McCartan, P.Doherty (capt.), A.Hadden, D.McCartan, B.Morgan. Sub: P.Hamill for K.O'Neill.
Dublin   P.Flynn, L.Hickey, L.Foley, W.Casey, C.O'Leary, P.Holden, C.Kane, John Timmons, D.McKane, Micky Whelan, P.Farnan, A.Donnelly, E.Burgess, J.Joyce, K.Heffernan (capt.). Subs: N.Fox for Timmons, Timmons for P.Farnan.

1962/63
Kerry   S.Fitzgerald, K.Coffey, N.Sheehy (capt.), Donie O'Sullivan, J.J.Barrett, S.Murphy, J.D.O'Connor, J.O'Riordan, M.Fleming, B.O'Callaghan, M.O'Dwyer, D. O'Shea, P.Aherne, T.Burke, Denis O'Sullivan.
New York   J.Duffy, J.Lowrey, D.Bernard, S.McElligott, P.Lynch, J.Foley, M.Foley, J.Halpin, T.Feighery, S.Kenna, G.McCarthy, M.Moynihan, P.Boyle, B.O'Donnell, P.Carey. Sub: P.Flood for P.Lynch.

'HOME' FINAL
Kerry   Same as played in final except J.Culloty, T.Lyons, M.O'Connell, J.Lucey, S.Óg Sheehy, W.Doran and T.Long for S.Fitzgerald, J.J.Barrett, M.Fleming, D.O'Shea, P.Aherne, T.Burke and Denis O'Sullivan. Subs: D.Geaney for J.O'Riordan, P.Aherne for S.Óg Sheehy, J.J.Barrett for T.Lyons.
Down   P.McAlinden, G.Lavery, L.Murphy, P.Rice, P.O'Hagan, D.McCartan, K.O'Neill, J.Lennon, A.Hadden, B.Morgan, B.Johnston, S.O'Neill, K.Mussen, P.J.McElroy, P.Doherty. Subs: P.Hamill for P.J.McElroy, T.O'Hare for K.Mussen.

1963/64
New York   J.Duffy, H.Coyle, P.Nolan, S.McElligott, B.Hennessy, E.McCarthy, P.Barden, M.Moynihan, D.Finn, P.Cummins, P.Casey, J.Foley, T.Hennessy (capt.), B.O'Donnell, P.Casey.
Dublin   P.Flynn, L.Hickey, L.Foley, C.Kane, D.McKane, P.Holden, M.Kissane, D.Foley, John Timmons, B.McDonald, Micky Whelan (capt.), N.Fox, G.Davey, W.Casey, D.Ferguson. Sub: M.Keane for L.Hickey.

'HOME' FINAL
Dublin   Same as played in final except E.Breslin and J.Gilroy for D.McKane and N.Fox.
Down   P.McAlinden, G.Lavery (capt.), L.Murphy, T.O'Hare, P.O'Hagan, D.McCartan, K.O'Neill, B.Johnston, L.Powell, S.O'Neill, J.McCartan, P.Doherty, J.Lennon, P.Rice, V.Kane. Subs: B.Morgan for J.Rice, P.Hamill for P.O'Hagan, J.Smith for L.Murphy.

1964/65
Galway   J, Geraghty, J.B.McDermott, N.Tierney, S.Meade, J.Donnellan (capt.), E.Colleran, M.Newell, M.Reynolds, P.Donnellan, C.Dunne, M.McDonagh, S.Leydon, C.Tyrrell, S.Cleary, J.Keenan. Subs: T.Sands for S.Meade, B.Geraghty for J.Keenan. (Note: M.Garrett played in first leg. P.Donnellan was on for second leg. Subs in first leg: P.Donnellan for M.Garrett, M.Tarpey for S.Meade.)

New York   J.Duffy, M.Foley, P.Nolan, K.Finn, D.Finn, G.McCarthy, P.Barden, T.Feighery, J.Halpin, P.Cummins, J.Foley, T.Foley, S.Nugent, B.O'Donnell, P.Casey. Subs: B.Tumulty for, D.Ryan, S.Kenna.
(Note: H.Coyle and M.Moynihan played in first leg. M.Foley and T.Furlong were on for second leg. Sub in first leg: T.Furlong.)

'HOME' FINAL
Galway   Same as played in final except M.Garrett for P.Donnellan. Sub: P.Donnellan for M.Reynolds.
Kerry   J.Culloty, Donie O'Sullivan, P.O'Donoghue, M.Morris (capt.), Denis O'Sullivan, J.D.O'Connor, Seamus Murphy, J.Lucey, M.Fleming, B.O'Callaghan, M.O'Connell, P.Griffin, J.J.Barrett, V.Lucey, M.O'Dwyer.

1965/66

Longford   J.Heneghan, Seamus Flynn, L.Gillen, B.Gilmore, B.Barden (capt.), J.Donlon, P.Barden, Jimmy Flynn, T.Mulvihill, J.Devine, M.Hopkins, J.Hanniffy, S.Murray, R.Burns, S.Donnelly. Subs: T.McGovern for L.Gillen, L.Gillen for T.McGovern.
(Note: M.Burns played in first leg. T.Mulvihill was on for second leg. Sub in first leg T.Mulvihill for M.Burns.)
New York   W.Nolan, P.Maguire, P.Nolan, K.Finn, D.Finn, S.Nugent, G.Driscoll, J.Foley, B.Tumulty, D.Byrne, M.Moynihan, K.McNamee, P.Cummins (capt.), S.Brogan, J.Halpin.
(Note: S.Kenna, B.O'Donnell and J.O'Brien played in first leg. D.Byrne, M.Moynihan and S.Brogan were on for second leg. Subs in first leg: G.McCarthy for B.O'Donnell, D.Ryan for J.O'Brien, T.Frawley for S.Kenna.)

'HOME' FINAL
Longford   Same as played in final except T.McGovern and M.Burns for P.Barden and T.Mulvihill.
Galway   J.Geraghty, S.Meade, N.Tierney, J.B.McDermott, E.Colleran (capt.), J.Donnellan, M.Newell, T.Sands, M.Reynolds, C.Dunne, F.Canavan, S.Leydon, C.Tyrrell, M.McDonagh, J.Keenan.

1966/67

New York   W.Nolan, K.Finn (capt.), P.Nolan, P.Maguire, D.Finn, S.Nugent, S.Kenna, B.Tumulty, J.Foley, P.Cummins, M.Moynihan, P.Caulfield, T.Furlong, B.O'Donnell, J.Halpin. Subs: T.Feighery for P.Caulfield, A.Brady for J.Halpin.
(Note: T.Feighery and D.Ryan played in first leg. P.Cummins and P.Caulfield came on for second leg. Sub in first leg: P.Cummins for D.Ryan.)
Galway   J.Geraghty, E.Colleran (capt.), S.Meade, J.B.McDermott, J.Donnellan, N.Tierney, C.McDonagh, J.Duggan, J.Glynn, C.Dunne, M.McDonagh, S.Leydon, L.Sammon, F.Canavan, P.Donnellan. Subs: J.Keenan for L.Sammon, M.Reynolds for J.Duggan.
(Note: J.Keenan played in first leg. M.McDonagh was on for second leg. Subs in first leg: M.McDonagh for F.Canavan, F.Canavan for L.Sammon.)

'HOME' FINAL
Galway   Same as played in final except M.Newell, S.Cleary and J Keenan for S.Meade, M.McDonagh and F.Canavan. Subs: S.Meade for N.Tierney, M.McDonagh for S.Cleary.
Dublin   P.Cullen, W.Casey, L.Hickey, C.Kane, M.Kissane, M.Kelleher, G.Davey, S.O'Connor, A.Donnelly, Micky Whelan, J.Keaveney (capt.), M.Cranny, B.Dowling, J.Eivers, L.Deegan. Subs: S.Lee for M.Cranny, D.Foley for M.Kissane.

1967/68

Down   D.Kelly, B.Sloan, D.McCartan, T.O'Hare, R.McConville, L.Powell, J.Lennon (capt.), J.Milligan, C.McAlarney, M.Cole, P.Doherty, J.Murphy, P.Rooney, S.O'Neill, J.Purdy. Subs: R.Murphy for L.Powell.
Kildare   O.Crinnigan, J.McTeague, N.Ryan, J.Cummins, T.Keogh, P.Mangan, J.Doyle, K.Maguire, L.Casey, J.Donnelly, P.Dunny, T.Carew, K.Kelly, P.Connolly (capt.), M.Mullins. Subs: M.Carolan for K.Maguire, L.Gleeson for L.Casey.

1968/69

Kerry   J.Culloty (capt.), Seamus Murphy, P.O'Donoghue, S.Fitzgerald, Donie O'Sullivan, M.Morris, M.O'Shea, M.Fleming, D.J.Crowley, B.Lynch, C.O'Sullivan, E.O'Donoghue, T.Prendergast, L.Higgins, M.O'Dwyer. Subs: M.O'Connell for C.O'Sullivan, Derry Crowley for L.Higgins.
(Note: M.O'Connell and D.O'Donnell played in first leg. C.O'Sullivan and T.Prendergast were on for second leg. Subs in first leg: P.Moynihan for M.O'Connell, T.Prendergast for D.O'Donnell, C.O'Sullivan for P.Moynihan.)
New York   W.Nolan, D.Finn, P.Nolan, P.Maguire, M.Moore, K.Finn, S.Nugent, T.Feighery, D.Duff, M.Gannon, J.Foley, M.Moynihan (capt.), D.Ryan, T.Furlong, J.Halpin. Subs: M.Fitzgerald for P.Nolan, B.O'Donnell for T.Furlong, P.Cummins for M.Gannon.
(Note: M.Fitzgerald played in first leg. J.Halpin was on for second leg. Subs in first leg: P.Cummins for M.Fitzgerald, J.Halpin for D.Duffy.)

'HOME' FINAL
Kerry   Same as played in final except Denis O'Sullivan, M.O'Connell, P.Griffin (capt.) and D.O'Donnell for Seamus Murphy, Donie O'Sullivan, C.O'Sullivan and T.Prendergast.
Offaly   M.Furlong, M.Ryan, G.Hughes, P.McCormack, E.Mulligan, J.Smith, N.Clavin, L.Coughlan, A.Hickey, P.Monaghan (capt.), W.Bryan, A.McTague, M.O'Rourke, J.Cooney, S.Kilroy. Subs: J.Egan for N.Clavin, B.Guinan for W.Bryan, W.Bryan for A.Hickey.

1969/70

Mayo   E.Rooney, S.Hughes, R.Prendergast, R.Niland, J.Corey (capt.), J.Morley, J.Earley, P.J.Loftus, J.Langan, T.Fitzgerald, J.Gibbons, J.Corcoran, D.Griffith, W.McGee, J.J.Cribben. Sub: S.O'Grady for P.J.Loftus.
Down   D.Kelly, B.Sloan, D.McCartan, T.O'Hare (capt.), R.McConville, J.Fitzsimons, H.McGrath, J.Milligan, J.Lennon, J.Murphy, J.Morgan, M.Cole, P.Rooney, S.O'Neill, J.Purdy. Subs: C.McAlarney for J.Fitzsimons, N.Millar for H.McGrath.

1970/71

Kerry   J.Culloty, Donie O'Sullivan (capt.), P.O'Donoghue, S.Fitzgerald, T.Prendergast, J.O'Keeffe, M.O'Shea, P.Lynch, D.J.Crowley, B.Lynch, P.Griffin, E.O'Donoghue, M.Gleeson, L.Higgins, M.O'Dwyer. Sub: Derry Crowley for S.Fitzgerald.
Mayo   E.Rooney, S.Hughes, R.Prendergast, J.Earley, J.Carey, J.Morley, B.O'Reilly, S.Kilbride, P.J.Loftus, T.Fitzgerald, J.Gibbons, J.Corcoran, W.McGee, J.J.Cribben, D.Griffith. Subs: S.O'Grady for S.Kilbride, R.Niland for B.O'Reilly.

1971/72

Kerry E.Fitzgerald, Donie O'Sullivan, P.O'Donoghue, S.Fitzgerald, T.Prendergast, Derry Crowley, M.O'Shea, M.O'Connell, J.O'Keeffe, P.Lynch, D.Kavanagh, E.O'Donoghue, M.Gleeson (capt.), L.Higgins, M.O'Dwyer. Subs: B.Lynch for E.O'Donoghue, J.Walsh for Derry Crowley, M.O'Sullivan for S.Fitzgerald.

Mayo J.J.Costelloe, M.Begley, R.Prendergast (capt.), T.Keane, M.Higgins, J.Morley, B.O'Reilly, S.O'Grady, S.Kilbride, T.Fitzgerald, J.Gibbons, J.Corcoran, T.O'Malley, W.McGee, J.J.Cribben. Subs: F.Burns for B.O'Reilly, D.Griffith for J.J.Cribben.

1972/73

Kerry E.Fitzgerald, Donie O'Sullivan, P.O'Donoghue, J.Deenihan, G.O'Keeffe, Derry Crowley, M.O'Shea, D.Kavanagh, J.O'Keeffe, B.Lynch (capt.), L.Higgins, E.O'Donoghue, J.Egan, M.O'Dwyer, J.Walsh. Subs: M.O'Sullivan for L.Higgins, G.Power for M.O'Shea.

Offaly M.Furlong, S.Lowry, M.Ryan, M.O'Rourke, E.Mulligan, L.Coughlan, M.Wright, W.Bryan, S.Evans, P.Fenning, K.Kilmurray, A.McTague, Murt Connor, J.Smith, J.Cooney. Subs: N.Kelly for E.Mulligan, K.Claffey for Murt Connor.

1973/74

Kerry P.O'Mahony, Donie O'Sullivan, P.O'Donoghue, Derry Crowley, P.Ó Sé, P.Lynch, G.O'Keeffe, J.O'Keeffe, J.Long, E.O'Donoghue, M.O'Sullivan, G.Power, J.Egan, S.Fitzgerald, M.Sheehy.
(Note: P.Spillane and J.Walsh played in drawn game. P.Ó Sé and E.O'Donoghue were on for replay. Subs in drawn game: E.O'Donoghue for P.Spillane, P.Ó Sé for S.Fitzgerald.)

Roscommon J.McDermott, H.Keegan, P.Linsday, G.Mannion, A.Regan, D.Watson, J.Kerrane, M.Freyne, J.O'Gara, J.Kelly, D.Earley, J.Mannion, J.Finnegan, T.Heneghan, T.Donlon. Subs: G.Beirne for D.Watson, H.Griffin for J.Mannion.
(Note: P P.White and M.McNamara played in drawn game. J.McDermott and J.Mannion were on for replay. Subs in drawn game: M.Griffin for J.Kelly, P.O'Callaghan for M.McNamara.)

1974/75

Meath R.Giles (capt.), M.Collins, J.Quinn, B.Murray, P.Smith, P.Reynolds, P.J.O'Halloran, J.Cassells, M.Ryan, E.O'Brien, K.Rennicks, P.Traynor, M.Kerrigan, C.Rowe, O.O'Brien.

Dublin P.Cullen, G.O'Driscoll, S.Doherty, R.Kelleher, P.O'Reilly, A.Larkin, G.Wilson, B.Mullins, S.Rooney, R.Doyle, A.Hanahoe, D.Hickey, J.McCarthy, J.Keaveney, A.O'Toole. Sub P.Gogarty for D.Hickey.

1975/76

Dublin P.Cullen, G.O'Driscoll, S.Doherty, R.Kelleher, B.Pocock, P.O'Neill, K.Synnott, B.Mullins, K.Moran, A.O'Toole, A.Hanahoe, D.Hickey, R.Doyle, J.Keaveney, P.Gogarty. Sub: B.Brogan for P.O'Neill.

Derry M.McFeely, L.Murphy, T.Quinn, P.Stevenson, G.O'Loughlin, A.McGurk, M.Moran, T.McGuinness, S.Lagan, G.McElhinney, M.Lynch, G.Bradley, B.Kelly, S.O'Connell, J.O'Leary. Subs: F.McCloskey for S.Lagan, A.McGuckian for G.Bradley.

1976/77

Kerry C.Nelligan, J.Deenihan, P.Lynch, G.O'Keeffe, P.Ó Sé, T.Kennelly, G.Power, J.O'Keeffe, J.O'Shea, S.Walsh, D.Moran, M.Sheehy, B.Walsh, P.Spillane, J.Egan.

Dublin P.Cullen, G.O'Driscoll, S.Doherty, R.Kelleher, T.Drumm, K.Moran, P.O'Neill, B.Brogan, A.Larkin, A.O'Toole, A.Hanahoe, D.Hickey, R.Doyle, J.Keaveney, J.McCarthy. Subs: M.Hickey for B.Brogan, F.Ryder for A.Larkin.

1977/78

Dublin P.Cullen, G.O'Driscoll, S.Doherty, R.Kelleher, F.Ryder, J.Brogan, P.O'Neill, B.Mullins, B.Brogan, A.O'Toole, A.Hanahoe, D.Hickey, R.Doyle, J.Keaveney, J.McCarthy.

Mayo E.Lavin, S.Minogue, G.King, P.Burke, G.Feeney, S.Sweeney, H.Gavin, A.Egan, D.Dolan, J.P.Kean, W.Nally, L.Donoghue, T.O'Malley, W.J.Padden, W.Fitzpatrick. Subs: R.Bell for J.P.Kean, M.Gavin for P.Burke.

1978/79

Roscommon J.McDermott, S.Tighe, P.Lindsay, T.Heneghan, G.Fitzmaurice, T.Donlon, D.Murray, D.Earley, S.Hayden, A.McManus, J.O'Gara, S.Kilbride, M.Finneran, M.Freyne, E.McManus. Sub: R.Beirne for T.Heneghan.

Cork W.Morgan, S.O'Sullivan, K.Kehily, B.Murphy, J.Crowley, C.Ryan, J.Kerrigan, J.Courtney, V.Coakley, D.McCarthy, J.Barry Murphy, D.Allen, P.Kavanagh, D.Barron, C.Kearney. Subs: T.O'Reilly for V.Coakley, M.Mullins for D.McCarthy, J.Coleman for J.Crowley.

1979/80

Cork W.Morgan, S.O'Sullivan, K.Kehily, J.Evans, J.O'Sullivan, C.Ryan, J.Kerrigan, T.Creedon, V.Coakley, S.Murphy, D.Allen, T.Dalton, J.Barry Murphy, J.Allen, D.Barron. Subs: A.Creagh for V.Coakley, C.Kearney for A.Creagh, J.Lynch for S.Murphy.

Kerry P.O'Mahony, J.Deenihan, J.O'Keeffe, M.Spillane, P.Ó Sé, T.Kennelly, P.Lynch, J.Ó Sé, S.Walsh, D.Moran, T.Doyle, P.Spillane, G.Power, E.Liston, J.Egan. Sub: V.O'Connor for P.Spillane.

1980/81

Galway P.Coyne, J.Hughes, S.Kinneavy, P.Moran, P.O'Neill, P.Lee, S.McHugh, B.Talty, W.Joyce, B.Brennan (capt.), D.Smith, S.Joyce, T.Naughton, T.J.Gilmore, G.McManus. Subs: G.Burke for T.J.Gilmore, P.Conroy for D.Smith,

Roscommon G.Sheerin, H.Keegan, P.Lindsay, J.McManus, G.Connellan, T.Donlon, D.Murray, S.Hayden, J.O'Gara, E.McManus, A.McManus, D.Earley, J.O'Connor, M.Finneran, G.Emmett. Subs: M.McDermott for J.O'Gara, M.Dolphin for J.O'Connor.

1981/82

Kerry C.Nelligan, J.Deenihan, J.O'Keeffe, G.O'Keeffe, P.Ó Sé, T.Kennelly.G.Lynch, J.O'Shea, S.Walsh, J.L McElligott, D.Moran, T.Doyle, G.Power, E.Liston, J.Egan.
(Note: P V.O'Connor and M.Spillane played in drawn game. P.Ó Sé and T.Doyle were on for replay. Subs in drawn game: P.Ó Sé for V.O'Connor, P.Spillane for M.Spillane.)

Cork M.Creedon, M.Healy, K.Kehily, J.Evans, M.Moloney, T.Creedon, J.Kerrigan, M.Burns, D.Creedon, D.Barry, D.Allen, T.O'Reilly, D.McCarthy, C.Ryan, E.Fitzgerald. Sub: T.Murphy for E.Fitzgerald.
(Note: P M.Connolly played in drawn game. T.O'Reilly was on for replay. Subs in drawn game: T.Murphy for M.Connolly, S.Hayes for E.Fitzgerald.)

1982/83

Down   J.McAleavy, E.King, T.McGovern, M.Turley (capt.), P.Kennedy, P.O'Rourke, B.McGovern, L.Austin, B.Toner, John McCartan, D.Bell, G.Blaney, M.Linden, A.Rogers, B.Mason.
Armagh   B.McAlinden, D.Stevenson, J.McKerr (capt.), K.McNally, B.Canavan, P.Moriarty, J.Donnelly, N.Marley, F.McMahon, J.Murphy, J.Kernan, S.Devlin, J.Corvan, B.McGeown, M.McDonald. Subs: D.McCoy for J.Kernan, K.McGurk for D.Stevenson, C.Harney for B.McGeown.

1983/84

Kerry   C.Nelligan, P.Ó Sé, V.O'Connor, M.Spillane, T.Doyle, J.Higgins, G.Power, J.O'Shea, S.Walsh, T.O'Dowd, D.Moran, P.Spillane, D.O'Donoghue, T.Spillane, M.Sheehy. Subs: E.Liston for T.O'Dowd, W.Maher for D.O'Donoghue.
Galway   P.Coyne, S.McHugh, S.Kinneavy, P.Lee, P.O'Neill, T.Tierney, M.Coleman, B.Talty, R.Lee, B.O'Donnell, G.McManus, S.Joyce, V.Daly, M.Brennan, K.Clancy. Subs: H.Bleahen for R.Lee, P.O'Dea for K.Clancy, L.Higgins for G.McManus.

1984/85

Monaghan   P.Linden, E.Sherry, G.McCarville, F.Caulfield, G.Hoey, C.Murray, Brendan Murray, H.Clerkin, D.Byrne, D.Flanagan, E.McEneaney, Bernie Murray, R.McCarron, E.Murphy, E.Hughes.
Armagh   B.McAlinden, D.Stevenson, T.Cassidy, J.Murphy, B.Canavan, K.McNally, J.Donnelly, J.McCorry, F.McMahon, A.Short, C.Harney, K.McGurk, J.Corvan, D.Seely, J.Cunningham. Subs: J.Kernan for J.Cunningham, P.Rafferty for K.McGurk, J.McKerr for B.Canavan.

1985/86

Laois   M.Conroy, P.Dunne, Martin Dempsey, E.Kelly, M.Aherne, P.Brophy, C.Browne (capt.), J.Costelloe, L.Irwin, G.Browne, W.Brennan, T.Prendergast, Michael Dempsey, E.Whelan, C.Maguire. Subs: N.Prendergast for C.Maguire, G.Lalor for W.Brennan, B.Nerney for N.Prendergast.
Monaghan   P.Linden, E.Sherry, G.McCarville, F.Caulfield, Brendan Murray, C.Murray, D.Loughman, H.Clerkin, K.Carragher, R.McCarron, M.O'Dowd, E.Hughes, M.Caulfield, E.Murphy, G.Hoey. Subs: E.McEneaney for M.O'Dowd, D.Byrne for D.Loughman.

1986/87

Dublin   J.O'Leary, D.Carroll, G.Hargan, M.Kennedy, D.Synnott, G.O'Neill, N.McCaffrey, J.Roynane, D.Bolger, B.Rock, J.McNally, K.Duff, D.De Lappe, M.Galvin, A.McCaul. Sub: D.Sheehan for D.De Lappe.
Kerry   C.Nelligan, P.Ó Sé, T.Spillane, M.Spillane, S.Stack, T.Doyle, G.Lynch, J.O'Shea, T.O'Dowd, J.Kennedy, D.Moran, P.Spillane, W.Maher, M.Sheehy, G.Power. Subs: J.Higgins for S.Stack, E.Liston for W.Maher.

1987/88

Meath   M.McQuillan, R.O'Malley, M.Lyons (capt.), P.Lyons, K.Foley, L.Harnan, M.O'Connell, L.Hayes, G.McEntee, B.Reilly, P.J.Gillic, M.McCabe, C.O'Rourke, B.Stafford, B.Flynn.
(Note: P T.Ferguson, D.Beggy and J.Cassells played in drawn game. P.Lyons, B.Reilly and M.McCabe were on for replay. Subs in drawn game: M.McCabe for J.Cassells, P.Lyons for T.Ferguson.)
Dublin   J.O'Leary, D.Carroll, G.Hargan, M.Kennedy, D.Synnott, N.McCaffrey, P.Clarke, J.Bissett, D.Bolger, V.Murphy, C.Redmond, K.Duff, D.De Lappe, J.McNally, B.Rock. Subs: T.O'Driscoll for D.Synnott, B.O'Hagan for D.Carroll, J.Prendergast for T.O'Driscoll.

(Note: P E.Heery, T.Conroy and M.Galvin played in drawn game. P.Clarke, C.Redmond and B.Rock were on for replay. Sub in drawn game: P.Clarke for D.Bolger.)

1988/89

Cork   J.Kerins, N.Cahalane, C.Corrigan, J.Kerrigan, M.Slocum, C.Counihan, A.Davis, L.Tompkins, B.Coffey, S.O'Brien, D.Barry, A.Nation (capt.), P.McGrath, D.Allen, J.Cleary. Subs: E.O'Mahony for C.Corrigan, D.Culloty for E.O'Mahony, M.Maguire for J.Kerins.
(Note: P T.McCarthy and J.O'Driscoll played in first leg. C.Corrigan and D.Barry were on for second leg. Subs in first leg: C.Corrigan for J.O'Driscoll, C.O'Neill for P.McGrath.)
New York   K.Nolan, A.Wiseman, V.Hatton, J.Donoghue, J.Owens, E.McNulty, E.McIntyre, P.Dunne (capt.), D.McSweeney, T.Connaughton, J.P.O'Kane, M.McEntee, M.Connolly, W.Doyle, W.Lowry. Subs: K.O'Reilly for W.Doyle, J.Cassidy for D.McSweeney, D.O'Connell for A.Wiseman.
(Note: P J.Lyons and K.O'Reilly played in first leg. E.McNulty and W.Doyle were on for second leg. Subs in first leg: W.Doyle for K.O'Reilly, L.Molloy for T.Connaughton, P.O'Toole for D McSweeney.)

'HOME' FINAL

Cork   Same as played in final except T.McCarthy for A.Nation.
Dublin   J.O'Leary, E.Heery, G.Hargan, M.Kennedy, N.McCaffrey, T.Carr, M.Deegan, J.Roynane, P.Bealin, V.Murphy, C.Redmond, K.Duff, B.Rock, M.Galvin, A.McNally. Sub: D.Carroll for P.Bealin.

1989/90

Meath   D.Smith, K.Foley, M.Lyons, T.Ferguson, B.Reilly, L.Harnan, M.O'Connell, L.Hayes, C.Brady, D.Beggy, C.Coyle, P.J.Gillic, C.O'Rourke (capt.), B.Stafford, B.Flynn. Subs: J.Cassells for C.Coyle, S.Kelly for L.Harnan.
Down   N.Collins, P.Higgins, C.Deegan, B.Breen, J.Kelly, P.O'Rourke (capt.), D.J.Kane, R.Carr, E.Burns, A.Rogers, G.Blaney, C.Burns, C.Murray, M.Linden, James McCartan. Subs: B.Mason for A.Rogers.M.McCartan for C.Burns.

1990/91

Dublin   J.O'Leary, M.Deegan, C.Walsh, M.Kennedy, T.Carr (capt.), K.Barr, E.Heery, D.Foran, P.Clarke, C.Redmond, P.Curran, N.Guiden, J.Sheehy, V.Murphy, D.McCarthy. Subs: M.Galvin for D.McCarthy, K.Duff for N.Guiden.
Kildare   N.Connolly, D.Dalton, J.Crofton, S.Dowling, G.Ryan, P.O'Donoghue, W.Sex, M.Lynch, S.McGovern, D.Kerrigan, T.Harris, J.McDonald, P.McLoughlin, D.McKevitt, J.Gilroy. Subs: S.Ryan for W.Sex, N.Donlon for J.McDonald.

1991/92

Derry   D.McCusker, K.McKeever, D.Quinn, A.Scullion, H.Downey, C.Rafferty, G.Coleman, B.McGilligan, D.Heaney, A.Tohill, D.McNicholl, G.McGill, J.Brolly, F.McCusker, E.Gormley. Subs: S.Downey for D.McNicholl, J.McGurk for C.Rafferty, D.Bateson for G.McGill.
Tyrone   F.McConnell, S.Meyler, C.Lawn, P.Donnelly, F.Devlin, E.Kilpatrick, N.Donnelly, C.Corr, P.Donaghy, A.Cush, E.McCaffrey, B.Gormley, M.McGleenan, D.O'Hagan, Peter Canavan. Sub: P.Devlin for S.Meyler.

1992/93

Dublin J.O'Leary (capt.), C.Walsh, D.Deasy, P.Moran, E.Heery, P.Curran, M.Deegan, J.Sheedy, P.Bealin, J.Gavin, T.Carr, N.Guiden, P.Clarke, V.Murphy, M.Doran.
(Note: P J.Calvert and C.Redmond played in drawn game. J.Gavin and P.Clarke were on for replay. Subs in drawn game: K.Barr for J.Calvert, M.Galvin for M.Doran.)
Donegal G.Walsh, J.J.Doherty, M.Gallagher, B.McGowan, D.Reid, N.Hegarty, M.Shovlin, A.Molloy, B.Murray, J.McHugh, B.Cunningham, J.McMullan, D.Bonner, A.Boyle, M.Boyle. Subs: S.Maguire for J.McMullan, M.Gavigan for M.Shovlin, M.McHugh for B.Cunningham.
(Note: P M.Gavigan and M.McHugh played in drawn game. N.Hegarty and J.McMullan were on for replay. Sub in drawn game: N.Hegarty for M.Gavigan.)

1993/94

Meath D.Smith, R.O'Malley (capt.), M.O'Connell, T.Hanley, G.Geraghty, C.Murphy, B.Reilly, J.McGuinness, P.J.Gillic, N.Dunne, C.O'Rourke, T.Giles, B.Flynn, T.Dowd, J.Devine. Sub: B.Stafford for N.Dunne.
Armagh B.Tierney, D.Clarke, G.Hoey, J.Rafferty, D.Horish, K.McGeeney, M.McQuillan, N.Smith, J.Burns, C.O'Rourke, K.McGurk, D.Marsden, B.O'Hagan, G.Houlahan (capt.), J.McConville. Subs: J.Grimley for B.O'Hagan, D.Macken for D.Marsden, J.Toner for C.O'Rourke.

1994/95

Derry D.McCusker, K.McKeever, A.Scullion, G.Coleman, J.McGurk, H.Downey, F.McCusker, A.Tohill, B.McGilligan, D.Heaney, D.Barton, E.Burns, J.Brolly, S.Downey, E.Gormley. Sub: D.Bateson for J.Brolly.
Donegal G.Walsh, J.J.Doherty, M.Gallagher, B.McGowan, M.Crossan, M.Gavigan, M.Shovlin, M.McShane, B.Murray, P.Hegarty, N.Hegarty, J.McHugh, J.Duffy, A.Boyle, M.Boyle. Sub: D.Bonner for A.Boyle.

1995/96

Derry J.Kelly, K.McKeever, G.Coleman, A.Scullion, K.Diamond, H.Downey, F.McCusker, A.Tohill, B.McGilligan, E.Burns, D.Barton, S.M.Lockhart, J.Brolly, S.Downey, E.Gormley. Subs: D.Dougan for E.Burns, G.McGill for S.Downey.
Donegal G.Walsh, M.Gallagher, J.J.Doherty, M.Crossan, B.McGowan, J.Cunningham, M.Shovlin, J.Ruane, B.Murray, P.Hegarty, N.Hegarty, J.B.Gallagher, B.Roper, A.Boyle, M.Boyle. Subs: J.McHugh for J.B.Gallagher, D.McNamara for B.Roper.

1996/97

Kerry D.O'Keeffe, K.Burns, B.O'Shea, M.Hassett (capt.), S.Moynihan, L.Flaherty, E.Breen, D.Ó Sé, W.Kirby, P.Laide, L.Hassett, D.O'Dwyer, D.Ó Cinnéide, B.Clarke, M.Fitzgerald. Subs: M.F.Russell for D.Ó Cinneide.
Cork K.O'Dwyer, M.O'Connor, R.McCarthy, E.Sexton, S.Óg Ó hAilpín, N.Cahalane, M.O'Donovan, C.O'Sullivan, D.O'Neill, M.Cronin, B.Corcoran, O.O'Sullivan, C.Corkery, S.O'Brien, A.Dorgan. Subs: J.Kavanagh for C.Corkery, P.Griffin for B.Corcoran, B.Murphy for M.Cronin.

1997/98

Offaly P.Kelly, C.Daly, J.Ryan, D.Foley, J.Kenny, F.Cullen (capt.), J.Brady, R.Mooney, James Grennan, C.Quinn, J.Stewart, C.McManus, V.Claffey, R.Malone, P.O'Reilly. Subs: S.Grennan for R.Malone, B.Mooney for P.O'Reilly.

Derry E.McCloskey, P.Diamond, S.M.Lockart, K.McKeever, P.McFlynn, H.Downey, J.McBride, A.Tohill, F.McCusker, G.McGill, G.Coleman, D.Dougan, J.Brolly, B.Murray, J.Cassidy. Sub: S.McLarnon for J.Cassidy.

1998/99

Cork K.O'Dwyer; M.O'Donovan, S.Óg Ó hAilpín, A.Lynch; C.O'Sullivan, E.Sexton, M.Cronin; Michael O'Sullivan, N.Murphy; A.Dorgan, J.Kavanagh, P.O'Mahony; P.Clifford (capt.), Mark O'Sullivan, A.O'Regan. Subs: D.Davis for O'Regan, R.McCarthy for Murphy.
Dublin D.Byrne; P.Moran, P.Christie, S.Ryan; T.Lynch, P.Curran, K.Galvin; C.Whelan, E.Sheehy; J.Gavin, D.Darcy, B.Stynes; B.O'Brien, D.Farrell (capt.), N.O'Donoghue. Subs: D.Homan for O'Donoghue, J.Sherlock for O'Brien.

1999/00

Derry M.Conlon, G.Coleman, S.M.Lockhart, D.O'Neill, H.Downey, P.McFlynn, A.Tohill, D.Heaney, N.McOscar, D.Dougan, R.Rocks, P.Bradley, E.Muldoon, J.McBride. Subs: C.Gilligan for Rocks, G.McGonigle for Gilligan, S.McLarnon for Bradley.
(Note: P E.McCloskey, K.McKeever, B.Murray and E.Burns played in the drawn final, but didn't line out in the replay. Subs in the drawn encounter were G.McGonigle for McBride, R.Dougan for Coleman, S.Downey for Burns, F.McCusker for Murray.)
Meath C.Sullivan, M.O'Reilly, D.Fay, C.Murphy, N.Nestor, A.Moyles, R.Kealy, N.Crawford, J.McDermott, E.Kelly, T.Giles, D.Curtis, O.Murphy, R.Fitzsimons, J.Devine. Subs: B.Callaghan for Devine, T.Dowd for Curtis, S.Dillon for Kelly.
(Note: P H.Traynor, P.Reynolds and G.Geraghty played in the drawn final, but didn't line out in the replay. Subs in the drawn encounter were N.Nestor for Kealy, J.Devine for Fitzsimons.)

2000/01

Mayo P.Burke, R.Connelly, T.Nallen, K.Cahill, F.Costello, A.Roche, N.Connelly, C.McManamon, D.Brady, J.Gill, D.McDonagh, S.Carolan, M.McNicholas, R.Loftus, T.Mortimer. Subs: M.Moyles for Mortimer, J.Nallen for Roche, M.Sheridan for Loftus, D.Nestor for Moyles.
Galway P.Lally, M.Comer, K.Fitzgerald, M.Colleran, D.Meehan, J.Divilly, S. Óg de Paor, M.Donnellan, J.Bergin, M.Clancy, K.Comer, L.Colleran, D.Savage, P.Joyce, J.Donnellan. Subs: S.Walsh for Clancy, R.Fahy for M.Comer, T.Mannion for Colleran, J.Fallon for K.Comer, S.Ó Domhnaill for Bergin.

2002

Tyrone P.Ward, C.Gormley, C.Lawn, B.Robinson, R.McMenamin, C.Gourley, P.Jordan, C.McAnallen, C.Holmes, B.Dooher, S.O'Neill, G.Cavlan, B.McGuigan, K.Hughes, Peter Canavan. Subs: S.Cavanagh for Hughes, Pascal Canavan for McGuigan, D.McCrossan for Jordan.
Cavan A.Donohue, E.Reilly, T.Prior, C.Hannon, M.Brides, A.Forde, J.Doonan, P.McKenna, C.Collins, P.Galligan, P.Reilly, F.O'Reilly, L.Reilly, J.Reilly, M.Graham. Subs: E.Reilly for Graham, E.Jackson for Doonan, R.Rogers for L.Reilly.

2003

Tyrone J.Devine, R.McMenamin, C.Holmes, M.McGee, C.Gormley, G.Devlin, P.Jordan, C.McAnallen, S.Cavanagh, B.Dooher, B.McGuigan, S.O'Neill, E.McGinley, P.Canavan, O.Mulligan. Subs: G.Cavlan for McGinley, R.Mellon for McGuigan, C.Lawn for McMenamin, D.McCrossan for Gormley.

Laois   F.Byron, T.Kelly, C.Byrne, J.Higgins, D.Rooney, K.Fitzpatrick, D.Conroy, P.Clancy, N.Garvan, C.Parkinson, I.Fitzgerald, M.Lawlor, B.McDonald, D.Delaney, S.Kelly. Subs: R.Munnelly for Lawlor, C.Conway for Delaney, D.Miller for Garvan, D.Sweeney for S.Kelly, A.Fennelly for Fitzgerald.

2004
Kerry   D.Murphy, T.O'Sullivan, M.McCarthy, A.O'Mahony, T.Ó Sé, E.Fitzmaurice, S.Moynihan, E.Brosnan, W.Kirby, P.Galvin, D.O'Sullivan, L.Hassett, C.Cooper, J.Crowley, M.F.Russell. Subs: D.O'Cinneide for Crowley, M.Ó Sé for Galvin.
Galway   A.Keane, K.Fitzgerald, G.Fahy, M.Comer, D.Meehan, P.Clancy, S.Óg de Paor, J.Bergin, S.Ó Domhnaill, M.Clancy, M.Donnellan, J.Devane, M.Meehan, P.Joyce, T.Joyce. Subs: N.Joyce for Devane, C.Monaghan for Comer, D.Savage for M.Clancy.

2005
Armagh   P.Hearty, A.Mallon, F.Bellew, P.McCormack, A.Kernan, K.McGeeney, C.McKeever, J.Toal, P.McGrane, M.O'Rourke, J.McEntee, O.McConville, S.McDonnell, R.Clarke, B.Mallon. Subs: P.McKeever for O'Rourke, A.McCann for Kernan, J.McNulty for Bellew, P.Loughran for McGrane, A.O'Rourke for McKeever.
Wexford   J.Cooper, C.Morris, P.Wallace, N.Murphy, D.Breen, D.Murphy, S.Cullen, D.Fogarty, N.Lambert, D.Kinsella, P.Colfer, J.Hegarty, R.Barry, J.Hudson, M.Forde. Subs: P.Forde for Hegarty, J.Darcy for Colfer, D.Foran for Darcy, P.Curtis for N.Murphy.

2006
Kerry   D.Murphy, A.O'Mahony, M.Ó Sé, T.O'Sullivan, S.Moynihan, T.Ó Sé, M.Lyons, D.Ó Sé, K.Donaghy, P.Galvin, E.Fitzmaurice, B.Sheehan, C.Cooper, Declan O'Sullivan, R.O'Connor. Subs: Darran O'Sullivan for O'Connor, E.Brosnan for Fitzmaurice, T.Griffin for O'Mahony, M.F.Russell for Cooper.
Galway   A.Keane, D.Meehan, K.Fitzgerald, D.Burke, A.Burke, D.Blake, M.Comer, P.Clancy, N.Coleman, M.Clancy, D.Savage, M.Donnellan, M.Meehan, P.Joyce, S.Armstrong. Subs: P.Geraghty for Armstrong, B.Cullinane for Savage, F.Hanley for D.Burke.

2007
Donegal   P.Durcan, N.McGee, K.Lacey, P.Campbell, B.Dunnion, B.Monaghan, P.McConagley, N.Gallagher, K.Cassidy, B.Roper, C.Bonner, C.Toye, C.McFadden, B.Devenney, M.Hegarty. Subs: K.McMenamin for Devenney, E.McGee for McGee, T.Donoghue for McConagley, R.Kavanagh for Gallagher, A.Sweeney for Bonner.
Mayo   D.Clarke, K.Higgins, J.Kilcullen, L.O'Malley, E.Devenney, B.J.Padden, P.Gardiner, D.Heaney, J.Nallen, P.Harte, G.Brady, A.Dillon, A.Moran, C.Mortimer, M.Conroy. Subs: A.Higgins for Kilcullen, K.O'Neill for Conroy, T.Howley for A.Higgins, A.Kilcoyne for Dillon, A.Campbell for Nallen.

2008
Derry   B.Gillis, K.McGuckin, N.McCusker, F.McEldowney, L.Hinphey, G.O'Kane, M.McIvor, F.Doherty, J.Diver, M.Lynch, B.McGoldrick, E.Muldoon, C.Gilligan, P.Bradley, E.Bradley. Subs: S.M.Lockhart for McEldowney, P.Murphy for E.Bradley, K.McCloy for Hinphey, J.Keenan for McIvor, C.Mullan for Gilligan.
Kerry   D.Murphy, P.Reidy, M.Ó Sé, T.O'Sullivan, T.Ó Sé, A.O'Mahony, R.Flaharta, D.Ó Sé, S.Scanlon, Declan O'Sullivan, D.Walsh, E.Brosnan, Darran O'Sullivan, K.Donaghy, M.F.Russell. Subs: C.Cooper for Declan O'Sullivan, M.Quirke for Scanlon, D.Bohane for O'Flaharta, A.Maher for Russell.

2009
Kerry   D.Murphy, P.Reidy, T.O'Sullivan, K.Young, T.Ó Sé, A.O'Mahony, T.Griffin, A.Maher, M.Quirke, Darren O'Sullivan, Declan O'Sullivan, D.Walsh, C.Cooper, K.Donaghy, T.Walsh. Subs: D.Ó Sé for Quirke, T.Kennelly for D.Walsh, D.Moran for Maher, B.Sheehan for Donaghy, D.Bohan for Griffin, S.O'Sullivan for Darran O'Sullivan.
Derry   B.Gillis, K.McGuckin, K.McCloy, G.O'Kane, C.McKaigue, B.McGuigan, S.L.McGoldrick, F.Doherty, J.Diver, E.Lynn, P.Murphy, B.Mullan, E.Bradley, P.Bradley, M.Lynch. Subs: J.Kielt for P.Bradley, P.Bradley for Mullan, D.McBride for O'Kane, S.Bradley for Murphy, R.Dillon for McKaigue.

2010
Cork   P.O'Shea, R.Carey, M.Shields, E.Cotter, N.O'Leary, P.Kissane, J.O'Sullivan, A.O'Connor, A.Walsh, F.Goold, D.O'Connor, P.Kelly, D.Goulding, C.Sheehan, P.Kerrigan. Subs: N.Murphy for Goold, D.Kavanagh for Walsh, C.O'Neill for D.O'Connor, J.Hayes for Goulding, G.Spillane for Shields.
Mayo   D.Clarke, C.Barrett, G.Cafferkey, L.O'Malley, D.Vaughan, T.Howley, K.McLoughlin, T.Parsons, S.O'Shea, A.Moran, A.Dillon, T.Mortimer, A.O'Shea, M.Ronaldson. Subs: R.McGarrity for Ronaldson, A.Kilcoyne for T.Mortimer, A.Freeman for Parsons, B.Moran for C.Mortimer, P.Harte for A.O'Shea.

2011
Cork   K.O'Halloran, J.O'Sullivan, R.Carey, M.Shields, N.O'Leary, J.Miskella, P.Kissane, A.O'Connor, P.O'Neill, C.Sheehan, P.Kelly, F.Goold, D.Goulding, D.O'Connor, P.Kerrigan. Subs: F.Lynch for F.Goold, D.O'Sullivan for Miskella, D.Goold for Kerrigan, N.Murphy for A.O'Connor.
Dublin   S.Cluxton, M.Fitzsimons, P.Brogan, P.McMahon, B.Cahill, G.Brennan, K.Nolan, D.Bastick, M.D.Macauley, B.Cullen, K.McManamon, P.Flynn, B.Brogan, D.Connolly, T.Quinn. Subs: D.Daly for Cullen, P.Burke for B.Brogan, D.Kelly for Connolly, P.Andrews for Daly, D.Lally for Cahill.

2012
Cork   A.Quirke, R.Carey, M.Shields, E.Cadogan, N.O'Leary, G.Canty, P.Kissane, P.O'Neill, A.O'Connor, F.Goold, P.Kelly, P.Kerrigan, C.O'Neill, A.Walsh, D.O'Connor. Subs: B.O'Driscoll for Walsh, D.Goulding for C.O'Neill, N.Murphy for A.O'Connor, B.O'Driscoll for P.O'Neill.
Mayo   D.Clarke, K.Keane, G.Cafferkey, K.Higgins, L.Keegan, D.Vaughan, C.Boyle, B.Moran, J.Gibbons, K.McLoughlin, A.Moran, A.Dillon, C.Mortimer, C.O'Connor, M.Conroy. Subs: P.Harte for Gibbons, E.Varley for Conroy, D.Geraghty for Harte, Geraghty for B.Moran, J.Doherty for O'Connor, R.Feeney for Dillon.

2013
Dublin   S.Cluxton, K.O'Brien, J.Cooper, D.Daly, J.McCarthy, G.Brennan, J.McCaffrey, M.D.Macauley, C.O'Sullivan, J.Whelan, D.Connolly, B.Cullen, P.Mannion, P.Andrews, B.Brogan. Subs: S.Carthy for Whelan, K.McMenamon for Cullen, D.Bastick for O'Sullivan, P.McMahon for Macauley, D.Rock for Brogan.
Tyrone   N.Morgan, P.J.Quinn, C.Clarke, C.mcCarron, C.Gormley, D.Carlin, Justin McMahon, C.Cavanagh, S.Cavanagh, Matthew Donnelly, Mark Donnelly, Joe McMahon, M.Penrose, C.McAliskey, P.McNiece. Subs: A.Cassidy for Carlin, P.Kane for Justin McMahon, K.Coney for McNiece, R.McKenna for Gormley, A.McCrory for Cassidy.

2014
Dublin   S.Cluxton, P.McMahon, R.O'Carroll, J.Cooper,
J.McCarthy, N.Devereux, K.Nolan, M.D.Macauley, C.O'Sullivan,
P.Flynn, P.Andrews, D.Connolly, A.Brogan, E.O'Gara, B.Brogan.
Subs: K.McManamon for Andrews, D.Byrne for Nolan,
M.Fitzsimons for O'Carroll, C.Reddin for O'Gara, D.Nelson for
O'Sullivan, T.Brady for A.Brogan.
Derry   T.Mallon, O.Duffy, C.McKaigue, D.McBride,
K.Johnson, G.O'Kane, A.McAlynn, F.Doherty, P.Bradley, E.Lynn,
M.Lynch, C.McFaul, B.Herron, E,McGuckin, C.O'Boyle. Subs:
E.Bradley for Heron, D.Mullen for P.Bradley, D.Brown for Duffy,
M.Craig for Johnson, N.Holly for Lynn.

2015
Dublin   S.Cluxton, P.McMahon, R.O'Carroll, J.Cooper,
J.McCarthy, C.O'Sullivan, J.McCaffrey, D.Bastick, B.Fenton,
T.Brady, C.Kilkenny, D.Connolly, D.Rock, K.McManamon,
B.Brogan. Subs: M.Fitzsimons for O'Carroll, P.Andrews for Brady,
E.Ó Conghaile for Bastick, C.Costello for Connolly, J.Small for
McMahon, D.Daly for Fenton.
Cork   K.O'Halloran, N.Galvin, M.Shields, J.Loughrey,
J.O'Sullivan, C.Dorman, T.Clancy, E.Cadogan, F.Goold,
K.O'Driscoll, J.O'Rourke, C.O'Driscoll, C.O'Neill, M.Collins,
B.Hurley. Subs: P.Kerrigan for Dorman, D.Goulding for O'Rourke,
B.O'Driscoll for C.O'Driscoll, D.Óg Hodnett for O'Sullivan, J.Hayes
for Collins, S.Cronin for Galvin.

2016
Dublin   S.Cluxton, P.McMahon, J.Cooper, D.Byrne,
J.McCarthy, C.O'Sullivan, J.Small, B.Fenton, D.Bastick, P Flynn,
D.Rock, C.Kilkenny, P.Mannion, D.Connolly, B.Brogan. Subs:
M.D.Macauley for Bastick, K.McManamon for Connolly,
C.Costello for Rock, M.Fitzsimons for McMahon, E.Lowndes for
Mannion, D.Daly for Small.
Kerry   B.Kealy, M.Ó Sé, M.Griffin, S.Enright, P.Crowley,
A.O'Mahony, F.Fitzgerald, K.Donaghy, D.Moran, B.Sheehan,
P.Murphy, D.Walsh, D.O'Sullivan, C.Cooper, S.O'Brien. Subs:
K.Young for Fitzgerald, B.O'Sullivan for Walsh, J.Lyne for Griffin,
B.J.Keane for O'Brien, P.O'Connor for Crowley, M.Geaney for
Murphy.

2017
Kerry   B.Kealy, F.Fitzgerald, M.Griffin, R.Shanahan,
P.Crowley, T.Morley, P.Murphy, D.Moran, J.Barry, J.Lyne, M.Geaney,
D.Walsh, K.McCarthy, P.Geaney, J.Savage. Subs: G.Crowley for
Lyne, D.O'Sullivan for Savage, B.J.Keane for McCarthy, B.Sheehan
for Walsh, A.Maher for Barry, A.Spillane for Geaney.
Dublin   S.Cluxton, P.McMahon, M.Fitzsimons, D.Daly,
J.McCarthy, C.O'Sullivan, E.Lowndes, B.Fenton, C.Reddin, P.Flynn,
C.Kilkenny, D.Connolly, D.Rock, P.Andrews, B.Brogan. Subs:
N.Scully for Connolly, P.Mannion for Andrews, M.D.Macauley
for Reddin, K.McManamon for O'Sullivan, D.Byrne for Lowndes,
E.O'Gara for Flynn.

INTERPROVINCIAL FOOTBALL CHAMPIONSHIP

Ulster (31) – 1942, 1943, 1947, 1950, 1956, 1960, 1963, 1964,
1965, 1966, 1968, 1970, 1971, 1979, 1980, 1983, 1984, 1989,
1991, 1992, 1993, 1994, 1995, 1998, 2000, 2003, 2004, 2007,
2012, 2013, 2016.
Leinster (28) – 1928, 1929, 1930, 1932, 1933, 1935, 1939,
1940, 1944, 1945, 1952, 1953, 1954, 1955, 1959, 1961, 1962,
1974, 1985, 1986, 1987, 1988, 1996, 1997, 2001, 2002, 2005,
2006.
Munster (15) – 1927, 1931, 1941, 1946, 1948, 1949, 1972,
1975, 1976, 1977, 1978, 1981, 1982, 1999, 2008.
Connacht (10) – 1934, 1936, 1937, 1938, 1951, 1957, 1958,
1967, 1969, 2014.
Combined Universities (1) – 1973.

Note: No competition in 1990, 2010, 2011 and 2015.

1927
November 14 1926, Cavan:

Munster	1-8	3-1	Ulster

November 14 1926, Ballinasloe:

Connacht	1-4	1-3	Leinster

March 17 1927, Croke Park:

Munster	2-3	0-5	Connacht

1928
February 19 Portlaoise:

Leinster	1-9	1-5	Connacht

February 26 Croke Park:

Ulster	2-8	2-6	Munster (unfinished)

March 17 Croke Park:

Leinster	1-8	2-4	Ulster

1929
February 10 Cavan:

Leinster	2-8	1-2	Ulster

(Connacht were struck out and Munster got a bye)
March 17 Croke Park:

Leinster	1-7	1-3	Munster

1930
February 23 Croke Park:

Leinster	0-8	0-3	Connacht

February 23 Croke Park:

Munster	2-13	1-3	Ulster

March 17 Croke Park:

Leinster	2-3	0-6	Munster

1931
February 1 Athlone:

Munster	4-5	1-7	Connacht

February 8 Navan:

Leinster	1-8	1-2	Ulster

March 17 Croke Park:

Munster	2-2	0-6	Leinster

1932
February 14 Mardyke, Cork:

Munster 1-9		0-5	Connacht

February 14 Drogheda:
Leinster *4-11* *1-3* *Ulster*
March 17 Croke Park:
Leinster *2-10* *3-5* *Munster*

1933
February 12 Mardyke, Cork:
Leinster *2-4* *1-2* *Munster*
February 12 Monaghan:
Connacht *1-5* *0-5* *Ulster*
March 17 Croke Park:
Leinster *0-12* *2-5* *Connacht*

1934
February 11 Mardyke, Cork:
Leinster *2-6* *1-5* *Munster*
February 18 Castlebar:
Connacht *0-8* *0-6* *Ulster*
March 17 Croke Park:
Connacht *2-9* *2-8* *Leinster*

1935
February 17 Mullingar:
Leinster *1-6* *1-3* *Connacht*
February 24 Croke Park:
Munster *0-10* *1-5* *Ulster*
March 17 Croke Park:
Leinster *2-9* *0-7* *Munster*

1936
February 9 Castlebar:
Connacht *1-7* *2-2* *Munster*
February 9 Dundalk:
Leinster *0-2* *0-2* *Ulster*
March 1 Cavan, Replay:
Ulster *1-7* *1-5* *Leinster*
March 17 Croke Park:
Connacht *3-11* *2-3* *Ulster*

1937
February 7 Carrick-on-Shannon:
Connacht *4-6* *1-4* *Ulster*
February 21 Portlaoise:
Munster *5-6* *1-1* *Leinster*
March 17 Croke Park:
Connacht *2-4* *0-5* *Munster*

1938
February 13 Croke Park:
Munster *0-8* *1-4* *Leinster*
February 13 Cavan:
Connacht *2-8* *0-3* *Ulster*
March 17 Croke Park:
Connacht *2-6* *1-5* *Munster*

1939
February 19 Croke Park:
Ulster *2-8* *1-6* *Munster*
February 19 Ballinasloe:
Leinster *3-4* *2-5* *Connacht*
March 17 Croke Park:
Leinster *3-8* *3-3* *Ulster*

1940
February 11 Ballinasloe:
Munster *3-4* *2-5* *Connacht*
February 11 Dundalk:
Leinster *2-4* *0-6* *Ulster*
March 1 7 Croke Park:
Leinster *3-7* *0-2* *Munster*

1941
February 9 Killarney:
Munster *1-9* *0-6* *Connacht*
February 9 Cavan:
Ulster *1-9* *2-5* *Leinster*
March 16 Croke Park:
Munster *1-8* *1-8* *Ulster*
April 14 Croke Park:
Munster *2-6* *1-6* *Ulster*

1942
February 22 Wexford:
Munster *2-7* *0-6* *Leinster*
February 22 Longford:
Ulster *3-7* *2-6* *Connacht*
March 17 Croke Park:
Ulster *1-10* *1-5* *Munster*

1943
February 21 Croke Park:
Ulster *3-8* *0-8* *Connacht*
February 28 Tralee:
Leinster *1-3* *0-4* *Munster*
March 17 Croke Park:
Ulster *3-7* *2-9* *Leinster*

1944
February 20 Croke Park:
Ulster *2-10* *1-7* *Munster*
February 27 Croke Park:
Leinster *2-11* *1-8* *Connacht*
March 17 Croke Park:
Leinster *1-10* *1-3* *Ulster*

1945
February 18 Ballinasloe:
Connacht *2-8* *1-6* *Munster*
February 25 Croke Park:
Leinster *4-3* *2-9* *Ulster*
March 4 Croke Park:
Leinster *4-9* *3-6* *Ulster*
March 17 Croke Park:
Leinster *2-5* *0-6* *Connacht*

1946
February 24 Cork:
Munster *1-6* *0-5* *Connacht*
February 24 Cavan:
Leinster *2-5* *1-5* *Ulster*
March 17 Croke Park:
Munster *3-5* *1-9* *Leinster*

1947

February 16 Croke Park:
Ulster   0-11   1-3   *Munster*
March 9 Croke Park:
Leinster   3-7   1-7   *Connacht*
March 17 Croke Park:
Ulster   1-6   0-3   *Leinster*

1948

February 22 Tralee:
Munster   3-5   2-6   *Connacht*
February 29 Croke Park:
Ulster   2-10   1-12   *Leinster*
March 17 Croke Park:
Munster   4-5   2-6   *Ulster*

1949

February 20 Ballinasloe:
Munster   4-7   1-11   *Connacht*
February 20 Clones:
Leinster   3-5   2-2   *Ulster*
March 17 Croke Park:
Munster   2-7   2-7   *Leinster*
March 20 Croke Park:
Munster   4-9   1-4   *Leinster*

1950

February 12 Croke Park:
Ulster   2-9   2-6   *Connacht*
February 19 Navan:
Leinster   2-6   1-5   *Munster*
March 17 Croke Park:
Ulster   4-11   1-7   *Leinster*

1951

February 25 Tralee:
Munster   2-8   1-9   *Leinster*
February 25 Croke Park:
Connacht   3-6   2-8   *Ulster*
March 17 Croke Park:
Connacht   1-9   1-8   *Munster*

1952

February 24 Croke Park:
Munster   1-7   0-3   *Ulster*
February 24 Ballinasloe:
Leinster   1-8   1-7   *Connacht*
March 17 Croke Park:
Leinster   0-5   0-3   *Munster*

1953

February 8 Croke Park:
Leinster   2-11   2-7   *Connacht*
February 15 Croke Park:
Munster   2-5   2-5   *Ulster*
February 22 Croke Park:
Munster   1-12   2-7   *Ulster*
March 17 Croke Park:
Leinster   2-9   0-6   *Munster*

1954

February 14 Croke Park:
Leinster   3-14   3-6   *Ulster*
February 14 Tralee:
Connacht   2-9   2-8   *Munster*
March 1 7 Croke Park:
Leinster   1-7   1-5   *Connacht*

1955

February 13 Cavan:
Leinster   2-9   2-4   *Ulster*
February 13 Castlebar:
Connacht   1-6   1-5   *Munster*
March 17 Croke Park:
Leinster   1-14   1-10   *Connacht*

1956

February 19 Casement Park:
Ulster   3-8   1-4   *Connacht*
March 4 Croke Park:
Munster   3-4   0-9   *Leinster*
March 17 Croke Park:
Ulster   0-12   0-4   *Munster*

1957

February 10 Cork:
Munster   2-5   0-9   *Leinster*
February 10 Markievicz Park:
Connacht   2-8   0-8   *Ulster*
March 17 Croke Park:
Connacht   2-9   1-6   *Munster*

1958

February 16 Ballinasloe:
Connacht   1-11   0-7   *Leinster*
February 23 Cavan:
Munster   1-6   0-8   *Ulster*
March 17 Croke Park:
Connacht   2-7   0-8   *Munster*

1959

February 15 Tullamore:
Leinster   0-10   0-8   *Connacht*
March 8 Tralee:
Munster   2-12   0-7   *Ulster*
March 17 Croke Park:
Leinster   2-7   0-7   *Munster*

1960

February 21 Croke Park:
Ulster   2-9   1-5   *Leinster*
February 28 Tralee:
Munster   4-9   2-3   *Connacht*
March 17 Croke Park:
Ulster   2-12   3-8   *Munster*

1961

February 19 Casement Park:
Leinster   2-5   1-7   *Ulster*
February 26 Tuam:
Munster   0-6   1-3   *Connacht*

March 12 Croke Park:
Munster   *4-7*   *1-6*   **Connacht**
March 17 Croke Park:
Leinster *4-5*   *0-4*   **Munster**

1962
February 18 Tullamore:
Leinster *2-17*   *0-6*   **Munster**
February 25 Cavan:
Ulster   *5-6*   *1-7*   **Connacht**
March 17 Croke Park:
Leinster *1-11*   *0-11*   **Ulster**

1963
February 17 Tralee:
Leinster *2-6*   *1-8*   **Munster**
February 17 Sligo:
Ulster   *2-8*   *1-5*   **Connacht**
March 17 Croke Park:
Ulster   *2-8*   *1-9*   **Leinster**

1964
February 16 Croke Park:
Ulster   *3-6*   *0-11*   **Munster**
February 23 Ballinasloe:
Leinster *3-7*   *0-9*   **Connacht**
March 17 Croke Park:
Ulster   *0-12*   *1-6*   **Leinster**

1965
Febuary 21 Croke Park:
Ulster   *0-14*   *0-9*   **Munster**
February 28 Navan:
Connacht *1-7*   *0-8*   **Leinster**
March 17 Croke Park:
Ulster   *0-19*   *0-15*   **Connacht**

1966
February 27 Tralee:
Munster   *0-11*   *0-11*   **Connacht**
March 13 Nenagh:
Munster   *2-8*   *2-6*   **Connacht**
February 27 Croke Park:
Ulster   *1-8*   *1-4*   **Leinster**
March 17 Croke Park:
Ulster   *2-5*   *1-5*   **Munster**

1967
February 26 Galway:
Connacht *0-11*   *0-6*   **Munster**
February 26 Casement Park:
Ulster   *0-9*   *0-8*   **Leinster**
March 17 Croke Park:
Connacht *1-9*   *0-11*   **Ulster**

1968
February 25 Navan:
Leinster *0-11*   *0-6*   **Munster**
March 3 Cavan:
Ulster   *4-8*   *1-10*   **Connacht**
March 17 Croke Park:
Ulster   *1-10*   *0-8*   **Leinster**

1969
February 16 Tuam:
Connacht *1-11*   *2-4*   **Ulster**
February 23 Killarney:
Munster   *2-11*   *1-9*   **Leinster**
March 17 Croke Park:
Connacht *1-12*   *0-6*   **Munster**

1970
February 22 Croke Park:
Ulster   *2-12*   *0-6*   **Munster**
Februray 22 Crossmolina:
Connacht *1-11*   *1-4*   **Leinster**
March 17 Croke Park:
Ulster   *2-11*   *0-10*   **Connacht**

1971
February 21 Navan:
Connacht *1-9*   *0-9*   **Leinster**
February 28 Croke Park:
Ulster   *2-7*   *1-7*   **Munster**
March 17 Croke Park:
Ulster   *3-11*   *2-11*   **Connacht**

1972
Roscommon February 13:
Connacht *1-15*   *1-9*   **Combined Universities**
February 20 Croke Park:
Munster   *1-9*   *0-9*   **Connacht**
February 20 Croke Park:
Leinster *0-13*   *1-9*   **Ulster**
March 17 Croke Park:
Munster   *1-15*   *1-15*   **Leinster**
April 23 Cork:
Munster   *2-14*   *0-10*   **Leinster**

1973
Cavan January 28:
Combined Universities *2-7* *0-12* **Ulster**
February 18 Roscommon:
Connacht *3-10*   *2-10*   **Munster**
February 18 Croke Park:
Combined Universities *0-11* *0-8* **Leinster**
March 17 Croke Park:
Combined Universities *2-12* *0-18* **Connacht**
April 23 Athlone, Replay:
Combined Universities *4-9* *1-11* **Connacht**

1974
Mardyke January 26:
Combined Univerities *1-7* *1-4* **Munster**
February 10 Tullamore:
Leinster *0-12*   *0-9*   **Combined Universities**
February 10 Ballybay:
Connacht *2-11*   *4-4*   **Ulster**
March 17 Croke Park:
Leinster *2-10*   *1-7*   **Connacht**

1975
February 16 Cork (Mardyke):
Munster *1-9* *0-8* *Leinster*
February 16 Carrick-on-Shannon:
Ulster *5-13* *1-12* *Connacht*
March 17 Croke Park:
Munster *6-7* *0-15* *Ulster*

1976
February 15 Ballina:
Leinster *2-9* *1-10* *Connacht*
February 15 Croke Park:
Munster *3-7* *0-9* *Ulster*
March 17 Croke Park:
Munster *2-15* *2-8* *Leinster*

1977
February 13 Croke Park:
Munster *0-14* *0-8* *Ulster*
February 13 Navan:
Connacht *2-13* *1-8* *Leinster*
March 17 Croke Park:
Munster *1-14* *1-9* *Connacht*

1978
March 19 Sligo:
Munster *2-6* *0-7* *Connacht*
March 19 Cavan:
Ulster *1-7* *0-7* *Leinster*
March 27 Croke Park:
Munster *2-7* *2-7* *Ulster*
April 16 Croke Park:
Munster *4-12* *0-19* *Ulster (aet)*

1979
March 11 Croke Park:
Ulster *5-8* *1-13* *Leinster*
March 11 Tralee:
Munster *4-7* *1-6* *Connacht*
March 18 Croke Park:
Ulster *1-7* *0-6* *Munster*

1980
March 2 Newbridge:
Munster *2-10* *1-11* *Leinster*
March 2 Cavan:
Ulster *0-17* *1-3* *Connacht*
March 17 Croke Park:
Ulster *2-10* *1-9* *Munster*

1981
March 8 Roscommon:
Connacht *2-19* *2-14* *Ulster (aet)*
March 8 Killarney:
Munster *2-12* *0-10* *Leinster*
March 17 Ennis:
Munster *3-10* *1-9* *Connacht*

1982
February 14 Croke Park:
Munster *4-5* *0-10* *Ulster*

February 14 Galway:
Connacht *0-8* *0-2* *Leinster*
March 17 Tullamore:
Munster *1-8* *0-10* *Connacht*

1983
February 6 Tullamore:
Leinster *1-9* *0-7* *Connacht*
February 6 Croke Park:
Ulster *2-10* *2-4* *Munster*
March 17 Cavan:
Ulster *0-24* *2-10* *Leinster (aet)*

1984
March 17 Ballinasloe:
Connacht *0-15* *1-9* *Leinster*
March 17 Limerick:
Ulster *0-12* *0-7* *Munster*
March 18 Ennis:
Ulster *1-12* *1-7* *Connacht*

1985
January 27 Croke Park:
Leinster *2-8* *2-7* *Ulster*
January 27 Roscommon:
Munster *3-7* *0-12* *Connacht*
March 17 Croke Park:
Leinster *0-9* *0-5* *Munster*

1986
February 16 Tralee:
Connacht *2-6* *0-7* *Munster*
February 16 Cavan:
Leinster *3-7* *1-9* *Ulster*
March 17 Ballinasloe:
Leinster *2-8* *2-5* *Connacht*

1987
October 3 Newbridge:
Munster *3-12* *1-9* *Ulster*
October 3 Newbridge:
Leinster *2-10* *1-9* *Connacht*
October 4 Newbridge:
Leinster *1-13* *0-9* *Munster*

1988
October 15 Ballina:
Leinster *2-11* *0-8* *Munster*
Octiber 15 Ballina:
Ulster *3-12* *1-10* *Connacht*
October 16 Ballina:
Leinster *2-9* *0-12* *Ulster*

1989
October 7 Macroom:
Munster *0-8* *0-7* *Leinster*
October 7 Mitchelstown:
Ulster *4-8* *0-7* *Connacht*
October 8 Páirc Uí Chaoimh:
Ulster *1-11* *1-8* *Munster*

1990
No competition

1991
March 24 Ballybofey:

Ulster	1-15	1-13	Connacht (aet)

March 24 Navan:

Munster	1-10	0-11	Leinster

April 7 Croke Park:

Ulster	1-11	1-8	Munster

1992
March 1 Tralee:

Munster	2-7	1-9	Leinster

March 1 Carrick-on-Shannon:

Ulster	0-11	0-7	Connacht

March 15 Newry:

Ulster	2-7	0-8	Munster

1993
October 17 Newry:

Ulster	3-17	0-8	Munster

October 17 Roscommon:

Leinster	3-11	2-8	Connacht

October 31 Longford:

Ulster	1-12	0-12	Leinster

1994
February 13 Ballinasloe:

Munster	1-15	0-10	Connacht

February 13 Armagh:

Ulster	0-9	1-5	Leinster

March 6 Ennis:

Ulster	1-6	1-4	Munster

1995
February 5 Newbridge:

Leinster	3-14	1-9	Munster

February 5 Clones:

Ulster	0-16	0-8	Connacht

February 26 Clones:

Ulster	1-9	0-8	Leinster

1996
February 18 Navan:

Leinster	1-8	1-6	Connacht

March 10 Clones:

Munster	2-17	1-20	Ulster (aet)

March 18 Ennis:

Munster	0-13	0-12	Ulster

April 14 Newbridge:

Leinster	1-13	0-9	Munster

1997
January 26 Navan:

Leinster	3-14	1-10	Ulster

January 26 Ennis:

Connacht	2-15	1-17	Munster (aet)

Final February 9 Castlebar:

Leinster	2-14	0-12	Connacht

1998
January 25 Roscommon:

Ulster	0-15	0-15	Connacht (aet)

February 1 Clones, Replay:

Ulster	0-20	1-14	Connacht (aet)

January 25 Killarney:

Leinster	2-8	0-12	Munster

February 8 Clones:

Ulster	0-20	0-17	Leinster (aet)

1999
April 4 Tuam:

Connacht	4-7	1-8	Leinster

April 4 Killarney:

Munster	1-20	3-14	Ulster (aet)

April 18 Omagh:

Munster	2-19	3-13	Ulster (aet)

May 2 Tuam:

Munster	0-10	0-6	Connacht

2000
January 30 Castlebar:

Connacht	2-10	1-3	Munster

January 30 Casement Park:

Ulster	1-14	0-10	Leinster

February 6 Sligo:

Ulster	1-9	0-3	Connacht

2001
November 10 Tralee:

Leinster	2-11	0-16	Munster (aet)

November 10 Killarney:

Connacht	0-15	1-10	Ulster

November 11 Killarney:

Leinster	1-10	0-10	Connacht

2002
November 2 Ballindereen:

Ulster	0-17	0-15	Munster

November 2 Ballindereen:

Leinster	1-15	2-9	Connacht

November 3 Galway:

Leinster	1-14	2-9	Ulster

2003
November 15 Enniskillen:

Ulster	2-13	0-16	Leinster (aet)

November 15 Enniskillen:

Connacht	1-13	1-9	Munster

November 16 Enniskillen:

Ulster	0-14	0-9	Connacht

2004
October 31 Portlaoise:

Leinster	1-10	1-9	Munster

October 31 Castlebar:

Ulster	0-15	1-6	Connacht

November 13 Paris:

Ulster	1-13	1-8	Leinster

2005

October 29 Parnell Park:
Leinster **1-14** **3-7** *Connacht*
October 30 Crossmaglen:
Ulster **2-13** **0-9** *Munster*
November 12 Parnell Park:
Leinster **0-20** **0-18** *Ulster (aet)*

2006

October 6 Ballyforan:
Connacht **1-15** **2-10** *Munster (aet)*
October 7 Breffni Park:
Leinster **2-13** **2-10** *Ulster*
October 22 Boston:
Leinster **2-14** **2-11** *Connacht*

2007

October 13 Fermoy:
Munster **2-11** **0-12** *Leinster*
October 20 Ballybofey:
Ulster **1-15** **2-9** *Connacht*
October 27 Croke Park:
Ulster **1-12** **1-8** *Munster*

2008

October 25 Fermoy:
Munster **1-5** **0-5** *Ulster*
October 25 Kiltoom:
Connacht **2-15** **0-11** *Leinster*
November 1 Portlaoise:
Munster **1-9** **0-7** *Connacht*

2009

October 24 Crossmaglen:
Ulster **1-14** **1-10** *Leinster*
October 24 Gaelic Grounds:
Munster **1-13** **1-10** *Connacht*
November 8 Ruislip:
Ulster **0-15** **1-8** *Munster*

2010–2011

No Competition

2012

February 19 Sligo:
Ulster **3-16** **0-13** *Connacht*
February 19 Parnell Park:
Munster **1-16** **1-13** *Leinster*
February 26 Armagh:
Ulster **3-11** **1-15** *Munster*

2013

February 17 Longford:
Ulster **1-14** **1-13** *Munster*
February 17 Armagh:
Leinster **1-21** **1-20** *Connacht*
February 24 Croke Park:
Ulster **3-12** **0-17** *Leinster*

2014

February 16 Tuam:
Connacht **3-19** **2-16** *Munster*
February 16 Navan:
Ulster **2-26** **3-21** *Leinster (aet)*
February 23 Tuam:
Connacht **2-19** **1-7** *Ulster*

2015

No Competition

2016

December 10, Parnell Park:
Connacht **2-17** **1-18** *Leinster*
December 11, Parnell Park:
Ulster **3-17** **1-15** *Munster*
December 17, Carrick-on-Shannon:
Ulster **2-16** **3-10** *Connacht*

INTERPROVINCIAL FOOTBALL FINAL TEAMS

1927

Munster J.Riordan (goal), John J.Sheehy, Joe Barrett, J.Walsh, Paul Russell, E.Fitzgerald, J.Slattery, C.Brosnan, R.Stack, J.Ryan, Joe Sullivan, T.Mahony, James Baily, Frank Sheehy, P.Clifford (all Kerry).
Connacht T.Molloy, M.Walsh, M.Bonnerton, T.Leech, T.Hegarty, Mick Donnellan (Galway), R.Creagh, John Forde, M.Mulderrig (Mayo), G.Higgins (goal), Thos.Shevlin, M.Murphy (Roscommon), P.Colleran (Sligo), W.Martin, M.Dolan (Leitrim).

1928

Leinster M.Walsh (goal), M.Goff, J.Higgins, F.Malone, P.Martin, P.Doyle (Kildare), P.Russell, P.McDonnell (Dublin), M.O'Neill, N.Walsh (Wexford), M.McKeown, W.Lawless (Louth), P.Bates, W.Whelan (Laois), M.Keoghan (Meath). Sub: J.Delaney (Laois).
(Paul Russell selected for both Munster and Leinster, Central Council ruled that he play for Leinster).
Ulster P.Kilroy, T.Bradley (goal), F.Farrell, J.Brannigan, J.Duffy, J.Treanor (Monaghan), G.Hanratty, J.Maguire, P.Fearon, J.McCusker (Armagh), J.P.Murphy, J.Smith (Cavan), P.Cunning, J.C.McDonnell (Antrim), C.Fisher (Monaghan).

1929

Leinster W.Gannon, M.Goff, A.Fitzpatrick, J.Higgins, P.Doyle, P.Martin (Kildare), J.McDonnell (goal), J.Norris, M.O'Brien, P.McDonnell (Dublin), P.Bates, J.Delaney (Laois), M.McKeown (Louth), N.Walsh, M.O'Neill (Wexford).
Munster Dr.J.Kearney, M.Murphy, M.Donegan (Cork), J.Riordan (goal), J.Barrett, J.Walsh, P.Russell, J.O'Sullivan, C.Brosnan, E.Fitzgerald, J.J.Sheehy, J.Landers (Kerry), M.Keating (Limerick), T.Lee, C.Keane (Tipperary).

1930

Leinster John Higgins, M.Goff, W.Hynan, F.Malone, P.Loughlin, P.Doyle, P.Martin (Kildare), John McDonnell (goal), P.McDonnell, M.O'Brien (Dublin), D.Walsh, D.Douglas, J.Delaney (Laois), P.Byrne (Wexford), M.Rogers (Meath). Sub: M.O'Neill (Wexford).
Munster J.Barrett, J.Riordan (goal), J.Walsh, J.O'Sullivan, P.Russell, T.O'Donnell, C.Brosnan, R.Stack, J.Ryan, M.Doyle, E.Sweeney, J.J.Sheehy, M.O'Rourke, T.Barrett (Kerry), M.Donegan (Cork).

1931

Munster J.O'Riordan, D.O'Connor, J.Barrett, J.Walsh, P.Russell, J.O'Sullivan, T.O'Donnell, C.Brosnan, R.Stack, E.Fitzgerald, M.Doyle, J.J.Landers, E.Sweeney, T.Landers, J.J.Sheehy (all Kerry).

FOOTBALL

Leinster   M.Goff, J.Hayes, F.Malone, J.Higgins, W.Hynan, P.Loughlin, P.Martin (Kildare), John McDonnell M.O'Brien, T.O'Dowd (Dublin), T.Nulty, M.Rogers (Meath), D.Walsh, D.Douglas, J.Delaney (Laois).

1932

Leinster   J.Higgins, M.Goff, P.Martin, P.Byrne, D.Burke (Kildare), J.McDonnell (goal), P.Hickey, T.O'Dowd (Dublin), M.Nulty, T.Meade, M.Rogers, T.McGuinness (Meath), D.Walsh, J.Delaney, D.Douglas (Laois).
Munster   D.O'Keeffe (goal), D.O'Connor, P.Whitty, John Walsh, P.Russell, T.Landers, C.Brosnan, R.Stack, M.Doyle J.Landers, J.Ryan, C.Geaney (Kerry), G.Comerford (Clare), J.Duggan (Limerick), P.Arrigan (Tipperary).

1933

Leinster   J.McDonnell, P.Hickey, C.McLoughlin, D.Brennan, E.McCann, T.O'Dowd (Dublin), T.Meade, W.Shaw (Meath), J.Higgins, P.Martin, P.Byrne (Kildare), N.Walsh, P.Spillane (Wexford), D.Douglas, J.Delaney (Laois).
Connacht   T.Burke, P.Kelly, P.Quinn, S.O'Malley, G.Courell, P.Moclair, J.Forde, M.Mulderrig (Mayo), H.Carey, Ml.Donnellan, Ml.Higgins, L.Colleran, M.Kilcoyne, M.Noone (Sligo), J.Creighton (Roscommon).

1934

Connacht   T.Burke (goal), P.Quinn, P.Kelly, P.Flannelly, G.Ormsby, J.Carney, G.Courell, P.Moclair (Mayo), H.Carey, M.Connaire, F.Fox, J.Dunne, M.Donnellan, M.Higgins, B.Nestor (Galway).
Leinster   J.McDonnell (goal), D.Brennan, P.Synnott, M.Kelly (Dublin), T.Meade, J.Loughran (Meath), M.McKeown (Louth), P.Fane, P.Mythen, N.Walsh (Wexford), J.Higgins, P.Martin, P.Byrne (Kildare), D.Douglas, J.Delaney (Laois).

1935

Leinster   J.McDonnell (goal), R.Beggs, P.Cavanagh, G.Comerford (Dublin), E.Boyle, J.Coyle (Louth), T.McGuinness, W.Shaw, A.Donnelly (Meath), J.Byrne, P.Watters, P.Byrne (Kildare), W.Delaney, John Delaney, D.Douglas (Laois).
Munster   P.Russell, T.O'Donnell, P.Whitty, P.O'Connor (Kerry), M.O'Sullivan (goal), J.Lonergan, T.O'Keeffe, R.Power, R.Allen B.McGann (Tipperary), M.Studdert (Clare), T.Greany, P.O'Donnell (Waterford), T.Culhane (Limerick), T.Cotter (Cork).

1936

Connacht   T.Burke (goal), P.Kelly, T.Regan, G.Ormsby, H.Kenny, P.Flannelly, J.Carney, P.Moclair (Mayo), M.Connaire, F.Fox, R.Beggs, M.Higgins, R.Griffin, B.Nestor (Galway), F.Cavanagh (Sligo). Sub: F.Cunniffe (Golway) for F.Cavanagh.
Ulster   W.Young (goal), T.Dolan, M.Denneny, T.O'Reilly, P.Phair, H.O'Reilly, T.O'Reilly, D.Morgan, P.Devlin, J.Smallhorn, P.Boylan, L.Blessing, M.J.Magee (Cavan), J.Vallely, J.McCullagh (Armagh).

1937

Connacht   T.Burke (goal), T.Regan, P.Quinn, P.Kelly, P.Flannelly, H.Kenny, J.Carney, P.Laffey, J.Munnelly, P.Moclair (Mayo), M.Connaire, J.Dunne, D.O'Sullivan, B.Nestor, R.Beggs (Galway). Sub: J.McGowan (Mayo) for P.Quinn.
Munster   D.O'Keeffe (goal), J.O'Gorman, J.Walsh, P.Kennedy, M.Doyle, G.Fitzgerald, T.Landers, M.Kelly (Kerry), W.McMahon, M.Casey, G.Comerford, J.Burke (Clare), W.Scott, R.Power (Tipperary), T.Culhane (Limerick). Sub: A.Slattery (Clare) for R.Power.

1938

Connacht   P.Moclair, T.Burke (goal), J.McGowan, T.Regan, H.Kenny, J.Carney, P.Laffey, J.Munnelly, P.Kelly (Mayo), M.Connaire, C.Connolly, D.O'Sullivan, J.Dunne, M.Higgins, B.Nestor (Galway). Sub: P.Flannelly (Mayo) for J.Carney.
Munster   J.Keohane, D.O'Keeffe (goal), W.Myers, W.Kinnerk, W.Dillon, T.Healy, J.Walsh, P.Kennedy, J.J.Landers, C.O'Sullivan (Kerry), T.Culhane (Limerick), G.Comerford, J.Burke, M.Casey (Clare), T.Cotter (Cork). Sub: A.Slattery (Clare) for M.Casey.

1939

Leinster   M.Farrell, D.Walsh, M.Delaney, J.Slator, W.Delaney, C.Delaney (Laois), E.Boyle, E.Callan, J.Coyle (Louth), T.McEvoy (Offaly), J.Loughran, A.Donneliy (Meath), P.Bermingham (Dublin), P.O'Sullivan (Wicklow), T.Mulhall (Kildare). Sub: J.Delaney (Laois).
Ulster   A.Lynn, R.Keelaghan, J.Crawley, V.Duffy (Monaghan), E.McMahon, E.McLoughlin, J.McCullagh, A.Murray, J.Fitzpatrick (Armagh), P.Smith, T.O'Reilly, J.J.O'Reilly, V.White (Cavan), J.Doherty (Donegal), E.Thornbury (Antrim).

1940

Leinster   P.Dowling (goal), P.Bermingham (Dublin), E.Boyle (Louth), T.McEvoy, W.Mulhall (Offaly), D.Walsh, M.Delaney, W.Delaney, T.Murphy, C.Delaney (Laois) J.Kearney, M.Gilsenan, A.Donnelly (Meath), P.O'Sullivan (Wicklow), T.Mulhall (Kildare).
Munster   D.O'Keeffe (goal), W.Myers, J.Keohane, T.Healy, W.Dillon, W.Casey, E.Walsh, P.Kennedy, T.O'Connor, M.Kelly, Sean Brosnan, J.Walsh, J.Gorman, D.Spring, T.Landers. Subs: P.B.Brosnan for W.Casey, C.O'Sullivan for E.Walsh (all Kerry).

1941 REPLAY

Munster   D.O'Keeffe, W.Myers, Joe Keohane, T.Healy (Kerry), R.Harnedy (Cork), W.Casey, E.Walsh, S.Brosnan, P.Kennedy, J.Walsh, T.O'Connor (Kerry), E.Young (Cork), M.Kelly, P.Brosnan, J.O'Gorman (Kerry).
Ulster   B.Kelly (Cavan), E.McLoughlin, E.McMahon (Armagh), J.McGlory (Down), G.Smith (Cavan), J.McCullagh (Armagh), T.O'Reilly, J.J.O'Reilly, P.Smith, D.Morgan (Cavan), A.Murray (Armagh), T.P.O'Reilly (Cavan), J.Carr, M.Lynch (Down), V.Duffy (Monaghan). Sub: B.Cully (Cavan) for E.McMahon.
(P.B.Brosnan (Kerry) replaced C.O'Sullivan (Kerry) on the Munster team, while T.P.O'Reilly (Cavan) and M.Lynch (Down) replaced P.Conaty (Cavan) and J.Gallagher (Donegal) on the Ulster team, which played in the drawn game.)

1942

Ulster   B.Kelly (Cavan), E.McLoughlin (Armagh), B.Cully, T.O'Reilly, G.Smith (Cavan), J.McCullagh (Armagh), V.Duffy (Monaghan), C.McDyer (Donegal), J.J.O'Reilly (Cavan), K.Armstrong (Antrim), A.Murray (Armagh), T.P.O'Reilly (Cavan), B.Cullen (Tyrone), S.Deignan (Cavan), H.Gallagher (Donegal).
Munster   D.O'Keeffe, W.Myers, J.Keohane, T.Healy, W.Dillon, W.Casey, E.Walsh, S.Brosnan, P.Kenneoy, John Walsh, T.O'Connor (Kerry), E.Young (Cork), J.O'Gorman, M.Kelly, P.B.Brosnan (Kerry). Sub: R.Harnedy (Cork) for E.Walsh.

1943

Ulster   J.D.Benson (Cavan), E.McLoughlin (Armagh), B.Cully, T.O'Reilly, G.Smith (Cavan), J.McCullagh (Armagh), V.Duffy (Monaghan), J.J.O'Reilly (Cavan), C.McDyer (Donegal), K.Armstrong (Antrim).A.Murray (Armagh), P.Maguire (Derry), P.McCarney (Monaghan), S.Deignan (Cavan), H.Gallagher (Donegal). Sub: T.McCann (Down).

Leinster   P.Lynch (Wexford), J.Murphy, P.Kennedy, C.Crone, P.Henry, P.O'Reilly (Dublin), J.Clarke (Meath), J.Fitzgerald (Dublin), T.Murphy (Loois), J.Joy (Dublin), W.Delaney (Laois), P.Berminghom (Dublin), M.Gilsenan (Meath), P.O'Connor, T.Banks (Dublin).

1944

Leinster   P.Larkin (Louth), J.Archbold (Carlow), E.Boyle (Louth), C.Crone, P.O'Reilly (Dublin), J.Quigley (Louth), M.Geraghty (Kildare), W.Delaney (Laois), J.Thornton (Louth), D.O'Neill (Wicklow), O.Halpin (Louth), P.McDermott (Meath), P.Bermingham (Dublin), C.Delaney (Laois), J.Rea (Carlow).

Ulster   H.Vernon (Antrim), E.McLoughlin, J.McCullagh (Armagh), E.Finnegan, G.Smith (Cavan), E.McDonald (Monaghan), J.J.O'Reilly, L.McAlinden (Armagh), S.Deignan (Cavan), K.Armstrong (Antrim), A.Murray (Armagh), P.Maguire (Derry), P.McCarney (Monaghan), B.McAteer (Antrim), H.Gallagher (Donegal). Sub: F.Hamill (Antrim) for E.Finnegan.

1945

Leinster   P.Larkin, S.Boyle, E.Boyle (Louth), P.McIntyre (Dublin), P.Whelan (Carlow), P.O'Reilly (Dublin), M.Geraghty (Kildare), J.Morris (Carlow), J.Hanniffy (Longford), F.Byrne (Meath), W.Delaney (Laois), D.O'Neill (Wicklow), P.Meegan (Meath), C.Delaney (Laois), J.Rea (Carlow). Sub: T Murphy (Laois) for J.Hanniffy.

Connacht   T.Byrne (Mayo), W.Jackson (Roscommon), T.Dunleavy (Sligo), C.Connolly (Galway), B.Lynch, W.Carlos (Roscommon), T.O'Sullivan (Galway), E.Boland (Roscommon), C.McDyer (Sligo), M.Fallon (Galway), J.Murray, D.Keenan, P.Murray, J.McQuillan Roscommon), T.Hoban (Mayo). Subs: L.McAlinden (Leitrim) for C.McDyer, J.Munnelly (Mayo) for E.Boland.

1946

Munster   J.Williams (Tipperary), D.Magnier, P.Murphy, C.Crone, P.Cronin, T.Crowley (Cork), E.Walsh, P.Kennedy (Kerry), M.Cahill (Tipperary), M.Tubridy (Cork), W.O'Donnell (Kerry), E.Young (Cork), D.Kavanagh (Kerry), J.Cronin (Cork), J.Lyne (Kerry).

Leinster   P.Larkin, S.Boyle, E.Boyle (Louth), J.Cody, J.Culleton, W.Goodison (Wexford), M.Geraghty (Kildare), M.O'Brien (Wicklow), J.Morris (Carlow), F.Byrne (Meath), W.Delaney (Laois), D.O'Neill (Wexford), P.Meegan (Meath), N.Rackard (Wexford), J.Rea (Carlow).

1947

Ulster   J.O'Hare (Down), W.Feeney, G.Watterson (Antrim), J.McCullagh (Armagh), E.McDonnell (Monaghan), J.J.O'Reilly, S.Deignan (Cavan), H.O'Neill, S.Gallagher, K.Armstrong (Antrim), M.Higgins (Cavan), F.Niblock (Derry), S.Gibson, B.McAteer, S.McCallin (Antrim). Sub: H.Brown (Down).

Leinster   K.Smyth (Meath), M.O'Brien (Kildare), E.Boyle (Louth), J.Cody (Wexford), P.O'Reilly (Dublin), W.Goodison (Wexford), M.Geraghty (Kildare), M.Haughney, D.Connolly (Laois), F.Byrne, P.McDermott (Meath), D.O'Neill (Wexford), P.Meegan (Meath), P.Lennon, R.Byrne (Wicklow).

1948

Munster   D.O'Keeffe (Kerry), P.A.Murphy (Cork), J.Keohane, P.B.Brosnan, J.Lyne (Kerry), T.Crowley (Cork), E.O'Connor, T.Spillane (Kerry), M.Cahill (Tipperary), C.McGrath (Cork), W.O'Donnell, B.Garvey (Kerry), N.Crowley (Clare), J.Cronin, J.Aherne (Cork). Subs: T.O'Sullivan (Kerry) for T.Crowley and F.O'Keeffe (Kerry) for W.O 'Donnell.

Ulster   J.O'Hare (Down), W.Doonan (Cavan), G.Watterson (Antrim), P.Smith, P.J.Duke, J.J.O'Reilly, S.Deignan (Cavan), E.McDonald (Monaghan), S.Gallagher, K.Armstrong (Antrim), M.Higgins (Cavan), S.Gallagher (Donegal), S.Gibson (Antrim), P.Donohoe, A.Tighe (Cavan). Subs: H.O'Neill (Antrim) for M.Higgins and M.Higgins later for W.Doonan .

1949 REPLAY

Munster   M.O'Driscoll (Cork), E.O'Connor (Kerry), P.A.Murphy (Cork), P.B.Brosnan, M.Finucane, J.Lyne (Kerry), M.Cahill (Tipperary), C.McGrath (Cork), E.Dowling (Kerry), D.O'Donovan, C.Duggan (Cork), B.Garvey (Kerry), N.Crowley (Clare), J.Cronin (Cork), P.Brennan (Tipperary). Sub: T.Spillane (Kerry) for E.O'Connor.

(Tom O'Connor (Kerry) played in drawn game. Packie Brennan (Tipperary) came on for replay.)

Leinster   K.Smith (Meath), J.Bell (Louth), A.Murphy (Carlow), J.Coady (Wexford), S.Boyle, P.Markey (Louth), S.Brennan (Kildare), J.Donegan (Offaly), P.O'Brien (Meath), F.Fegan (Louth), P.White (Kildare), D.Connolly (Laois), W.Halpenny (Meath), W.Kelly (Wexford), P.McDermott (Meath). Subs: A.Burke (Kildare), S.White (Louth) and J.Quigley (Louth) for A.Murphy, J.Donegan and W.Halpenny.

(Des Connolly (Laois) who came on as sub in first game for Kevin Heffernan (Dublin) retained his place for the replay.)

1950

Ulster   J.O'Hare (Down), J.J.O'Reilly (Cavan), M.Moyna (Monaghan), P.Smith, P.J.Duke (Cavan), P.O'Neill, S.Quinn (Armagh), P.Brady (Cavan), W.McCorry (Armagh), A.Tighe, M.Higgins, V.Sherlock (Cavan), K.Armstrong (Antrim), P.Donohue (Cavan), H.McKearney (Monaghan). Sub: S.Gallagher (Antrim) for V.Sherlock.

Leinster   K, Smith (Meath), J.Bell (Louth), N.Redmond (Wexford), K.McConnell (Meath), W.Geraghty (Kildare), W.Goodison (Wexford), C.Hand, P.Connell (Meath), J.McDonnell (Louth), F.Byrne, B.Smyth (Meath), S.White (Louth), W.Kelly, N.Rackard (Wexford), P.McDermott (Meath). Sub: S.Brennan (Kildare) for W.Geraghty.

1951

Connacht   J.Mangan (Galway), W.McQuillan (Roscommon), P.Prendergast, S.Flanagan (Mayo), E.Boland (Roscommon), H.Dixon, E.Mongey (Mayo), S.Purcell (Galway), G.O'Malley (Roscommon), E.Keogh (Galway), P.Carney, J.Gilvarry, M.Mulderrig, T.Langan, P.Solon (Mayo). Subs: M.Flanagan (Mayo) for P.Carney, F.White (Sligo) for M.Flanagan.

Munster   L.Fitzgerald, J.Murphy (Kerry), P.A.Murphy (Cork), P.B.Brosnan (Kerry), P.Driscoll (Cork), J.Lyne (Kerry), S.Cronin (Cork), S.Connolly (Clare), C.Duggan (Cork), T.McGrath (Waterford), C.McGrath (Cork), P.J.O'Dea (Clare), P.Brennan (Tipperary), J.M.Palmer (Kerry), D.O'Donovan (Cork). Sub: D.Murphy (Kerry) for S.Connolly.

1952

Leinster   T.Malone (Kildare), M.O'Brien (Meath), T.Conlon, J.Tuft (Louth), G.O'Reilly (Wicklow), P.Dunne (Laois), S.Brennan (Kildare), D.Taaffe (Meath), J.Rogers (Wicklow), P.Meegan (Meath), O.Freaney (Dublin), S.White (Louth), M.McDonnell (Meath), H.Reynolds (Louth), K.Heffernan (Dublin). Subs: K.McConnell (Meath) for Tuft, J.Crowley (Dublin) for Taaffe and C.O'Leary (Dublin) for McDonnell.
Munster   D.O'Keeffe (Cork), J.Murphy (Kerry), P.A.Murphy (Cork), P.B.Brosnan, S.Murphy (Kerry), J.Cronin (Cork), J.M.Palmer (Kerry), C.McGrath, C.Duggan (Cork), J.Brosnan (Kerry), E.Young (Cork), J.J.Sheehan (Kerry), T.Ashe (Kerry), M.Cahill (Cork), P.J.O'Dea (Clare). Sub: P.Sheehy (Kerry) for M.Cahill.

1953

Leinster   T.Malone (Kildare), M.O'Brien, P.O'Brien, K.McConnell (Meath), G.O'Reilly (Wicklow), P.Dunne (Laois), A.Murphy (Carlow), S.Brennan (Kildare), J.Rogers (Wicklow), P.Meegan (Meath), V.Tierney (Longford), S.White (Louth), O.Freaney (Dublin), J.McDonnell (Louth), K.Heffernan (Dublin).
Munster   D.Roche (Cork), J.Murphy, E.Roche, J.O'Shea (Kerry), P.O'Driscoll (Cork), J.Cronin, C.Kennelly, B.O'Shea (Kerry), D.Kelleher, D.O'Donovan (Cork), T.Lyne (Kerry), W.Kirwan (Waterford), M.Cahill (Cork), S.Kelly (Kerry), P.Brennan (Tipperary). Sub: F.Meany (Clare) for B.O'Shea.

1954

Leinster   J.O'Neill (Wexford), M.O'Brien, P.O'Brien, K.McConnell (Meath), G.O'Reilly (Wicklow), P.Dunne (Laois), A.Murphy (Carlow), J.Rogers (Wicklow), S.White (Louth), J.Reilly (Meath), O.Freaney, C.O'Leary (Dublin), P.Meegan (Meath), J.McDonnell (Louth), K.Heffernan (Dublin).
Connacht   A.Brady, P.English (Roscommon), P.Prendergast, S.Flanagan (Mayo), B.Lynch (Roscommon), T.Dillon (Galway), F.Kelly, G.O'Malley (Roscommon), J.Nallen (Mayo), I.O'Dowd (Sligo), S.Purcell (Galway), E.O'Donohue (Roscommon), T.Hayden (Leitrim), T.Langan (Mayo), P.McGarty (Leitrim).

1955

Leinster   P.McGearty, M.O'Brien, P.O'Brien, K.McConnell (Meath), A.Murphy (Carlow), J.Fitzparick (Wicklow), S.White (Louth), J.Rogers (Wicklow), P.Casey (Offaly), J.McDonnell (Louth), O.Freaney, C.O'Leary (Dublin), M.McDonnell, T.Moriarty (Meath), K.Heffernan (Dublin).
Connacht   A.Brady (Roscommon), F.White (Sligo), P.Prendergast, S.Flanagan (Mayo), J.Mahon, T.Dillon (Galway), F.Kelly, G.O'Malley (Roscommon), I.O'Dowd (Sligo), P.Irwin (Mayo), S.Purcell, W.O'Neill (Galway), E.O'Donohue (Roscommon), M.Gaffney (Sligo), P.McGarty (Leitrim). Sub: T.Langan (Mayo) for O'Donohue.

1956

Ulster   S.Morris, N.O'Reilly (Cavan), J.Bratten, J.McKnight (Armagh), K.Mussen (Down), J.Rice (Monaghan), J.McDonnell (Cavan), J.McKeever (Derry), T.Maguire (Cavan), K.Denvir (Down), J.Taggart (Tyrone), J.Cunningham, P.Campbell (Armagh), V.Sherlock (Cavan), Rody Gribben (Derry).
Munster   P.Tyers (Cork), J.O'Shea (Kerry), D.O'Sullivan, P.Driscoll (Cork), T.Moriarty (Kerry), D.Bernard, D.Murray (Cork), J.Dowling (Kerry), E.Ryan (Cork), P.Sheehy (Kerry), C.Duggan (Cork), T.Lyne, J.Culloty, M.Murphy (Kerry), T.Cunningham (Waterford). Sub: Seán Murphy (Kerry) for Culloty.

1957

Connacht   J.Mangan (Galway), W.Casey (Mayo), I.O'Dowd (Sligo), T.Dillon (Galway), G.O'Malley (Roscommon), J.Mahon (Galway), E.Moriarty (Mayo), N.Blessing (Leitrim), J.Nallen (Mayo), F.Evers, S.Purcell (Galway), P.McGarty (Leitrim), J.Young, F.Stockwell (Galway), M.Christie (Sligo).
Munster   D.O'Neill (Kerry), P.O'Driscoll (Cork), E.Roche, J.O'Shea, S.Murphy (Kerry), D.Bernard, D.Murray, S.Moore (Cork), T.Long (Kerry), E.Ryan, C.Duggan (Cork), T.Lyne, J.Brosnan, M.Murphy (Kerry), D.Kelleher (Cork). Subs: N.Fitzgerald (Cork) for Brosnan, T.Moriarty (Kerry) for Long.

1958

Connacht   A.Brady (Roscommon), W.Casey (Mayo), I.O'Dowd (Sligo), T.Dillon, J.Mahon (Galway), G.O'Malley (Roscommon), M.Greally (Galway), J.Nallen (Mayo), F.Evers, M.McDonagh, S.Purcell (Galway), P.McGarty (Leitrim), G.Kirwan, F.Stockwell (Galway), C.Flynn (Leitrim).
Munster   L.Power (Cork), J.O'Shea, T.Lyons (Kerry), P.Driscoll, P.Harrington (Cork), T.Cunningham (Waterford), D.Murray (Cork), M.O'Connell (Kerry), S.Moore, N.Fitzgerald (Cork), J.Dowling (Kerry), E.Ryan (Cork), P.Sheehy, M.Murphy (Kerry), D.Kelleher (Cork).

1959

Leinster   S.Flood (Louth), G.Hughes (Offaly), A.Doyle (Wexford), J.Timmons, J.Boyle (Dublin), P.Nolan (Offaly), M.Grace (Meath), F.Walsh (Laois), C.O'Leary (Dublin), S.Brereton (Offaly), O.Freaney (Dublin), J.Kenna (Laois), P.Farnan, J.Joyce, K.Keffernan (Dublin).
Munster   L.Power (Cork), Jack Dowling, T.Lyons (Kerry), D.Murray (Cork), Sean Murphy, J.O'Shea, M.O'Dwyer (Kerry), P.Harrington (Cork), Seamus Murphy (Kerry), T.Mangan (Clare), N.Fitzgerald (Cork), P.Sheehy (Kerry), T.Furlong (Cork), John Dowling, T.Long (Kerry). Sub: E.Ryan (Cork) for Seamus Murphy.

1960

Ulster   T.Turbett (Tyrone), G.Kelly (Cavan), H.F.Gribben (Derry), P.Rice (Down), P.Breen (Derry), T.Maguire (Cavan) J.McDonnell (Cavan), J.Lennon (Down), J.O'Neill (Tyrone), S.O'Neill (Down), J.McKeever (Derry), P.Doherty (Down), J.Whan (Armagh), J.Brady (Cavan), A.Hadden (Down). Sub: K.Mussen (Down) for Breen.
Munster   L.Power (Cork), J.O'Shea (Kerry), C.O'Sullivan (Cork), N.Sheehy (Kerry), P.Harrington (Cork), K.Coffey, M.O'Dwyer, M.O'Connell, Seamus Murphy, D.McAuliffe (Kerry), E.Ryan (Cork), T.Long (Kerry), J.O'Sullivan (Cork), J.Dowling (Kerry), E.McCarthy (Cork).

1961

Leinster   W.Nolan, P.McCormack, G.Hughes, J.Egan, M.Brady (Offaly), P.Holden (Dublin), C.Wrenn (Offaly), M.Carley (Westmeath), S.Foran (Offaly), K.Beahan, F.Lynch (Louth), J.Kenna (Laois), S.Brereton (Offaly), J.Joyce, K.Heffernan (Dublin).
Munster   J.Culloty (Kerry), P.Harrington (Cork), T.Lyons, N.Sheehy, K.Coffey, T.Long, M.O'Dwyer, Seamus Murphy (Kerry), C.O'Sullivan, E.McCarthy (Cork), J.Keating (Tipperary), P.Sheehy (Kerry), T.Power (Waterford), J.Dowling, G.McMahon (Kerry). Subs: D.McAuliffe (Kerry) for Power, J.O'Sullivan (Cork) for Keating.

1962

Leinster   A.Phillips (Wicklow), P.McCormack, G.Hughes (Offaly), M.Carolan (Kildare), B.Barden (Longford), P.Holden (Dublin), C.Wrenn (Offaly), D.Foley (Dublin), M.Carley (Westmeath), S.Brereton (Offaly), M.Whelan (Dublin), T.Greene (Offaly), P.Gearty (Longford), J.Timmons, K.Heffernan (Dublin). Sub: F.Lynch (Louth) for T.Greene.

Ulster   T.McArdle (Monaghan), G.Kelly (Cavan), L.Murphy, P.Rice (Down), B.Mone (Monaghan), D.McCartan (Down), J.McDonnell (Cavan), J.Carey (Down), E.Larkin (Armagh), S.O'Neill, J.McCartan, P.Doherty (Down), S.O'Connell (Derry), J.Whan (Armagh), B.Morgan (Down). Subs: T.Hadden (Down) for J.Carey, M.Donaghy (Tyrone) for S.O'Connell.

1963

Ulster   T.Turbett (Tyrone), G.Kelly (Cavan), L.Murphy, P.Rice (Down), P.J.Flood (Donegal), T.Maguire, J.McDonnell (Cavan), S.Ferriter (Donegal), R.Carolan (Cavan), S.O'Neill (Down), F.McFeeley (Donegal), P.Doherty (Down), J.Whan (Armagh), P.T.Treacy (Fermanagh), B.Morgan (Down). Subs: J.O'Neill (Tyrone) for S.Ferriter, J.McCartan (Down) for R.Carolan.

Leinster   A.Phillips (Wicklow), P.McCormack, G.Hughes (Offaly), P.Connolly (Offaly), W.Casey, P.Holden (Dublin), C.Wrenn (Offaly), M.Carley (Westmeath), M.Carolan (Kildare), F.Walsh (Laois), D.Foley, M.Whelan (Dublin), P.Cummins (Kildare), N.Delaney (Laois), S.Brereton (Offaly). Subs: L.Foley (Dublin) for M.Carley, F.Lynch (Louth) for D.Foley, T.Browne (Laois) for S.Brereton.

1964

Ulster   S.Hoare (Donegal), G.Kelly (Cavan), L.Murphy (Down), B.Brady (Donegal), D.McCartan (Down), T.Maguire J.McDonnell (Cavan), J.Lennon (Down), S.Ferriter (Donegal), S.O'Neill, J.McCartan, P.Doherty (Down), J.Whan (Armagh), P.Treacy (Fermanagh), F.Donnelly (Tyrone). Subs: C.Gallagher (Cavan) for F.Donnelly, J.O'Neill (Tyrone) for Joe Lennon.

Leinster   A.Phillips (Wicklow), P.McCormack, G.Hughes (Offaly), W.Casey, M.Kissane, P.Holden (Dublin), F.Lynch (Louth), D.Foley (Dublin), T.Browne (Laois), J.Mulroy (Louth), J.Timmons, M.Whelan (Dublin), S.Murray, B.Burns (Longford), G.Kane (Westmeath). Subs: L.Foley (Dublin) for G.Kane, M.Carley (Westmeath) for T.Browne, B.McDonald (Dublin) for J.Mulroy.

1965

Ulster   S.Hoare (Donegal), G.Kelly (Cavan), B.Brady (Donegal), A.Morris (Cavan), D.McCartan (Down), T.Maguire (Cavan), P.Kelly, S.Ferriter (Donegal), R.Carolan (Cavan), S.O'Connell (Derry), J.O'Neill (Tyrone), P.Doherty (Down), C.Gallagher (Cavan), S.O'Neill (Down), P.T.Treacy (Fermanagh). Sub: J.Carroll (Monaghan) for S.Ferriter.

Connacht   J.Geraghty, E.Colleran, S.Meade (Galway), J Murray (Leitrim), J.Donnellan (Galway), C.Cawley (Sligo), M Newell (Galway), J.Langan (Mayo), M.Reynolds, C.Dunne (Galway), P.McGarty (Leitrim), M.Kearins (Sligo), M.McDonagh, S.Cleary, S.Leydon (Galway).

1966

Ulster   S.Hoare, P.Kelly (Donegal), T.McCreesh (Armagh), T.O'Hare, P.O'Hagan, D.McCartan (Down), P.J.Flood (Donegal), R.Carolan (Cavan), J.O'Neill (Tyrone), J.Lennon J.McCartan, P.Doherty (Down), C.Gallagher (Cavan), S.O'Neill (Down), P.T.Treacy (Fermanagh). Subs: A.Morris (Cavan), S.O'Connell (Derry).

Munster   J.Culloty, Donie O'Sullivan (Kerry), S.Downes (Clare), M.Morris, Denis O'Sullivan (Kerry), A.Fitzgerald (Limerick), J.D.O'Connor, M.Fleming (Kerry), M.Burke (Cork), P.McMahon (Clare), P.Moynihan, D.Geaney, B.O'Callaghan (Kerry), C.O'Sullivan (Cork), M.Keating (Tipperary). Subs: M.Tynan (Limerick), J.Lucey (Cork).

1967

Connacht   J.Geraghty, E.Colleran, N.Tierney, J.B.McDermott, J.Donnellan (Galway), J.Morley (Mayo), R.Craven (Roscommon), P.Donnellan (Galway), J.Langan (Mayo), C.Dunne, J.Duggan (Galway), M.Kearins (Sligo), J.Keenan (Galway), J.Corcoran (Mayo), S.Leydon (Roscommon) for J.Langan.

Ulster   S.Hoare (Donegal), G.Kelly (Cavan), B.Brady (Donegal), T.O'Hare, D.McCartan (Down), P.J.Flood (Donegal), J.Lennon (Down), R.Carolan (Cavan), A.McAtamney (Antrim), M.Brewster (Fermanagh) J.McCartan (Down), S.O'Connell (Derry), M.McLoone (Donegal), S.O'Neill (Down), M.Griffin (Donegal). Subs: J.O'Neill (Tyrone) for A.McAtamney, S.Ferriter (Donegal) for M.Brewster.

1968

Ulster   S.Hoare (Donegal), G.Kelly (Cavan), B.Brady (Donegal), T.O'Hare, J.Lennon, D.McCartan (Down), P.Pritchard, R.Carolan (Cavan), C.McAlarney (Down), M.Niblock (Derry), J.J.O'Reilly (Cavan), N.Gallagher (Donegal), S.O'Connell (Derry), S.O'Neill (Down), C.Gallagher (Cavan). Sub: D.O'Carroll (Donegal).

Leinster   M.Furlong (Offaly), P.Cole (Westmeath), L.Gillen (Longford), J.Smith (Offaly), J.Donlon (Longford), L.Toal (louth), G.Davey (Dublin), J.Donnelly (Kildare), L.Coughlan (Offaly), B.Gaughran (Louth), J.Hannify (Longford), A.McTague (Offaly), D.Dolan (Westmeath), M.Whelan (Dublin), S.Donnelly (Longford). Subs: J.Conway (Laois), W.Bryan (Offaly).

1969

Connacht   P.Brennan (Sligo), N.Colleran, N.Tierney (Galway), R.Craven (Roscommon), J.Morley, J.Carey (Mayo), L.Caffrey (Sligo), J.Duggan (Galway), D.Earley (Roscommon), H.O'Carroll (Leitrim), J.Colleary, M.Kearins (Sligo), J.Corcoran, W.McGee (Mayo), J.Keenan (Galway). Sub: S.Leydon (Galway) for M.Kearins.

Munster   W.Morgan, B.Murphy (Cork), S.Downes (Clare), Donie O'Sullivan (Kerry), F.Cogan (Cork), M.Morris (Kerry), B.Hartigan (Limerick), M.Fleming (Kerry), B.O'Neill (Cork) B.Lynch, P.Griffin (Kerry), M.Haugh (Clare), M.O'Connell (Kerry), R.Cummins (Cork), E.O'Donoghue (Kerry). Sub: P.McMahon (Clare) for M.Fleming.

1970

Ulster   A.Gallagher (Tyrone), A.McCabe (Cavan), T.McCreesh (Armagh), T.O'Hare (Down), B.McEniff (Donegal), M.McAfee (Derry), E.McGowan, R.Carolan (Cavan), A.McAtamney (Antrim), J.Murphy (Down), M.Niblock (Derry), S.Duggan, G.Cusack (Cavan), S.O'Neill (Down), S.O'Connell (Derry).

Connacht   E.Rooney, J.Carey, R.Prendergast (Mayo), N.Colleran (Galway), G.Mannion (Roscommon), J.Morley (Mayo), L.Caffrey (Sligo), D.Earley (Roscommon), J.Duggan (Galway), H.O'Carroll (Leitrim), J.Colleary, M.Kearins (Sligo), J.Kelly (Roscommon), W.McGee (Mayo), J.Keenan (Galway).

1971

Ulster   P.McCarthy (Monaghan), J.Burns (Antrim), H.Diamond (Derry), A.McCabe (Cavan), B.McEniff (Donegal), M McAfee (Derry), E.McGowan, R.Carolan (Cavan), F.Fitzsimmons (Antrim), S.O'Connell (Derry), C.McAlarney (Down), M.Niblock

(Derry), G.Cusack (Cavan), S.O'Neill (Down), A.McCallin (Antrim). Subs: E.Coleman (Derry) for F.Fitzsimons, J.Murphy (Down) for G.Cusack.
Connacht E.Rooney, J.Carey (Mayo), N.Colleran (Galway), T.Colleary (Sligo), G.Mannion (Roscommon), J.Morley (Mayo), L.O'Neill, J.Duggan (Galway), D.Earley (Roscommon), B.Wynne (Leitrim), J.Colleary, M.Kearins (Sligo), L.Sammon (Galway), W.McGee (Mayo), J.Corcoran (Mayo).

1972 REPLAY

Munster B.Morgan (Cork), D.O'Sullivan (Kerry), J.Wall (Waterford), S.Fitzgerald, T.Prendergast, J.O'Keeffe (Kerry), K.J.O'Sullivan (Cork), M.O'Connell (Kerry), F.Cogan, D.Hunt, D.Coughlan (Cork), E.O'Donoghue (Kerry), M.Keating (Tipperary), R.Cummins (Cork), M.O'Dwyer (Kerry). Sub: J Barrett (Cork) for O'Donoghue.
Leinster M.Furlong, M.Ryan, P.McCormack (Offaly), J.Conway (Laois), E.Mulligan, N.Clavin (Offaly), P.Mangan (Kildare), W.Bryan (Offaly), B.Millar (Laois), K.Rennicks (Meath), K.Kilmurray, A.McTague, J.Cooney (Offaly), T.Carew (Kildare), M.Fay (Meath). Subs: Murt Connor (Offaly) for Fay.P.Reynolds (Meath) for Millar.
(Mick Scannell (Cork) came on as a sub in drawn game. Murt Connor (Offaly) played in drawn game. Mick Fay was selected for replay.Jim Mulroy (Louth) and John Smith (Offaly) came on as subs in drawn game.)

1973 REPLAY

Combined Universities N.Murphy (U.C.C.& Cork), J.Waldron (U.C.D.& Galway), S.Killough (Queens & Antrim), J.Stafford (U.C.D.& Cavan), G.McHugh (Queens & Antrim), P.O'Neill (U.C.D.& Dublin), T.Regan (U.C.G.& Roscommon), J.O'Keeffe (U.C.D.& Kerry), K.Kilmurray (U.C.D.& Offaly), B.Lynch (U.C.C.& Kerry), D.McCarthy (U.C.D.& Cork), M.Carney (U.C.G.& Donegal), P.Moriarty (Queens & Armagh), D.Kavanagh (U.C.C.& Kerry), A.McGuirk (Queens & Derry).
(Note: P.Lynch (U.C.C.& Kerry), J.Rainey (Queens and Antrim) and C.Hughes (Maynooth and Carlow) played in drawn game. J.Stafford, P.O'Neill and M.Carney came on for replay. Sub (drawn game) J.P.Kane (U.C.D.and Mayo).
Connacht J.Neill, T.Heneghan (Roscommon), J.Brennan (Sligo), J.Morley (Mayo), B.Murphy (Sligo), T.J.Gilmore, L.O'Neill (Galway), D.Earley (Roscommon), S.Kilbride (Mayo), B.Wynne (Leitrim), L.Sammon (Galway), M.Kearins (Sligo), M.Burke (Galway), M.Freyne (Roscommon), J.Duggan (Galway). Subs: J.Kelly (Roscommon) for Burke; J.Gibbons (Mayo) for Wynne.
(Matty Brennan (Sligo) and John Kelly (Roscommon) played in drawn game. T.J.Gilmore and Jimmy Duggan came on for replay. Sub (drawn game) Jimmy Duggan)

1974

Leinster M.Furlong (Offaly), D.Dalton (Kildare), M.Ryan, M.O'Rourke, E.Mulligan, S.Lowry (Offaly), G.Wilson (Dublin), P.Mangan (Kildare), R.Millar (Laois), P.Fenning (Offaly), S.Allen (Laois), K.Rennicks (Meath), J.Cooney, W.Bryan (Offaly), B.Gaughran (Louth). Subs: D.Nugent (Louth) for Wilson, P.Dunny (Kildare) for Gaughran.
Connacht N.Crossan (Leitrim), J.Waldron (Galway), J.Brennan (Sligo), H.Keegan, J.Kerrane (Roscommon), T.J.Gilmore (Galway), P.Henry (Sligo), D.Earley (Roscommon), S.Kilbride (Mayo), L.Sammon, J.Duggan (Galway), M.Kearins (Sligo), T.O'Malley (Mayo), M.Freyne (Roscommon), J.Tobin (Galway). Subs: M.Brennan (Sligo) for Henry, J.Morley (Mayo) For Kilbride, M.Burke (Galway) for Tobin.

1975

Munster W.Morgan (Cork), E.Webster (Tipperary), H.Kelleher (Cork), J.Deenihan (Kerry), K.J.O'Sullivan (Cork), J.O'Keeffe, G.Power (Kerry), D.Long, D.McCarthy (Cork), B.Lynch (Kerry), J.Barrett (Cork), M.O'Sullivan (Kerry), J.Barry-Murphy (Cork), S.Kearney (Tipperary), J.Egan (Kerry). Sub: D.Hunt (Cork) for Long.
Ulster L.Turbett (Tyrone), D.Monaghan, P.McShea (Donegal), P.Mulgrew (Tyrone), P.Kerr (Monaghan), J.P.O'Kane (Antrim), E.Tavey (Monaghan), T.McGuinness (Derry), P.McGinnity (Fermanagh), F.McGuigan (Tyrone), C.McAlarney (Down), M.Carney (Donegal), P.Rooney (Down), S.Bonner (Donegal), S.O'Neill (Down). Subs: A.Curran (Donegal) for Mulgrew, M.Slevin (Down) for Kerr, B.Donnelly (Tyrone) for Rooney.

1976

Munster P.O'Mahoney (Kerry), E.Webster (Tipperary), B.Murphy (Cork), J.Deenihan, P.Ó Sé (Kerry), K.Kehily (Cork), G.Power(Kerry), D.Long (Cork), D.Moran (Kerry), D.Allen (Cork), M.Sheehy, M.O'Sullivan, J.Egan (Kerry), J.Barry-Murphy (Cork), P.Spillane (Kerry). Sub: G.O'Keeffe (Kerry) for Webster.
Leinster P.Cullen, G.O'Driscoll (Dublin), J.Conway (Laois), R.Kelleher (Dublin), J.Balfe (Kildare), S.Lowry (Offaly), K.Brennan (Laois), B.Mullins (Dublin), K.Rennicks (Meath), R.Doyle, A.Hanahoe, D.Hickey (Dublin) P.Fenning (Offaly), J.Keaveney, A.O'Toole (Dublin). Subs: M.O'Rourke (Offaly) for Balfe. S.Doherty (Dublin) for O'Rourke.

1977

Munster W.Morgan, K.Kehily (Cork), J.O'Keeffe (Kerry), B.Murphy (Cork), D.Moran, T.Kennelly, G.Power (Kerry), D.Long, D.McCarthy, S.O'Shea (Cork), M.Sheehy, P.Spillane (Kerry), J.Barry-Murphy (Cork), S.Walsh, J.Egan (Kerry). Subs: J.O'Shea (Kerry) for D.McCarthy (Cork), D.Allen (Cork) for S.O'Shea.
Connacht G.Mitchell (Galway), G.Kirrane (Mayo), M.J.Judge, S.McHugh (Galway), G.Feeney (Mayo), J.Hughes (Galway), P.Henry (Sligo), T.J.Gilmore, W.Joyce (Galway), R.Bell, J.P.Kean (Mayo), M.Martin (Leitrim), T.O'Malley (Mayo), J.Duggan, L.Sammon (Galway). Subs: T.Naughton (Galway) for Gilmore, H.Keegan (Roscommon) for McHugh.

1978

Munster B.Morgan, B.Murphy (Cork), J.O'Keeffe, J.Deenihan, P.Ó Sé, T.Kennelly (Kerry), M.Murphy (Clare), G.McGrath (Tipperary), M.Quish (Limerick), P.Spillane, M.Sheehy, G.Power (Kerry), J.Barry-Murphy (Cork), S.Walsh (Kerry), J.Hennessy (Waterford). Subs: J.O'Shea (Kerry) for Quish.G.O'Driscoll (Kerry) for Spillane.D.Moran (Kerry) for Hennessy
(K.Kehilly, D.Allen, D.McCarthy (all Cork) and Ger O'Driscoll (Kerry) played in drawn game. B.Murphy, M.Quish, J.B.Murphy and M.Sheehy came on for replay.)
Ulster J.Somers (Derry), D.Stevenson (Armagh), P.Mulgrew (Tyrone), E.McGowan (Cavan), P.Moriarty (Armagh), A.McGurk, M.Moran (Derry), C.McAlarney (Down), P.McGinnity (Fermanagh), L.Austin (Down), E.McKenna (Tyrone), J.Kernan (Armagh), J.Byrne (Down), P.Rooney (Down), P.Traynor (Armagh). Subs: K.McCabe (Tyrone) for Moriarty.N.Marley (Armagh) for Traynor.B.Kelly (Derry) for Byrne, J.Smith (Armagh) for Austin. The game went to extra time.
(Kevin McCabe (Tyrone) and J.Smith (Armagh) played in drawn game. P.Moriarty and Joe Kernan came on for replay. Subs (drawn game) N.Marley (Armagh) for L.Austin, D.Watson (Down) for K.McCabe, J.Kernan (Armagh) for P.Traynor.)

FOOTBALL

1979

Ulster B.McAlinden, D.Stevenson (Armagh), T.McGovern (Down), F.Ward (Donegal), K.McCabe (Tyrone), P.Moriarty (Armagh), M.Moran (Derry), P.McGinnity (Fermanagh), L.Austin, C.McAlarney (Down), J.Kernan (Armagh), B.Donnelly (Tyrone) P.Loughran (Armagh), P.Rooney (Down), S.Devlin (Armagh). Subs: C.Digney (Down) for Moran, P.McNamee (Cavan) for Loughran. J.Smyth (Armagh) for Donnelly.

Munster C.Nelligan (Kerry), K.Kehily (Cork), J.O'Keeffe (Kerry), T.Creedon (Cork), P.Ó Sé, T.Kennelly, P.Lynch, J.O'Shea, S.Walsh (Kerry), P.Leahy (Limerick), M.Sheehy, G.Power (Kerry), J.Barry-Murphy (Cork), E.Liston, J.Egan (Kerry). Subs: P.Spillane (Kerry) for Leahy, D.Moran (Kerry) for Egan.

1980

Ulster B.McAlinden (Armagh), E.Hughes (Monaghan), T.McGovern (Down), F.Ward (Donegal), K.McCabe (Tyrone), P.Moriarty (Armagh), S.McCarville (Monaghan), P.McGinnitty (Fermanagh), L.Austin, C.McAlarney (Down), J.Kernan (Armagh), E.Young (Derry), P.McNamee (Cavan), P.Rooney (Down), P.Loughran (Armagh). Sub: M.Moran (Derry) for Loughran.

Munster C.Nelligan, J.Deenihan, J.O'Keeffe (Kerry), K.Kehily (Cork), P.Ó Sé, T.Kennelly (Kerry), T.Creedon (Cork), S.Walsh (Kerry), C.Ryan (Cork), G.Power, M.Sheehy, P.Spillane (Kerry), D.Allen (Cork), E.Liston, J.Egan (Kerry). Sub: J.Barry-Murphy (Cork) for Power.

1981

Munster C.Nelligan, J.Deenihan, J.O'Keeffe (Kerry), K Kehily (Cork), P.Ó Sé, T.Kennelly, D.Moran, S.Walsh, J O'Shea, G.Power (Kerry), D.Allen (Cork), P.Spillane, M Sheehy, E.Liston, J.Egan (Kerry).

Connacht M.Webb (Mayo), J.Hughes (Galway), P.Lindsay, J.McManus (Roscommon), S.McHugh (Galway), T.Donnellan, D.Murray, S.Hayden (Roscommon), M.McCorrick (Sligo), B.Brennan (Galway), J.Kent (Sligo), D.Earley, M.Finneran, A.McManus (Roscommon), M.Carney (Mayo). Subs: H.Gavin (Mayo) for Hughes, G.McManus (Galway) for Finneran.

1982

Munster C.Nelligan (Kerry), J.Evans (Cork), J.O'Keeffe (Kerry), K.Kehily (Cork), P.O'Shea, T.Kennelly (Kerry), M.Moloney (Cork), J.O'Shea, S.Walsh, G.Power (Kerry), C.Ryan (Cork), D.Moran (Kerry), S.Moloney (Clare), E.Liston (Kerry), D.Allen (Cork). Subs: J.Kerrigan (Cork) for M.Moloney, N.Normoyle (Clare) for Power.

Connacht M.Webb (Mayo), M.Gavin (Mayo), P.Lindsay (Roscommon), M.O'Toole (Mayo), P.O'Neill, M.Coleman, S.McHugh, B.Talty (Galway), J.Lyons (Mayo), D.Earley, A.McManus (Roscommon), J.Kent (Sligo), B.Brennan (Galway), J.Burke (Mayo), G.McManus (Galway). Subs: S.Hayden (Roscommon) for Lyons, M.Carney (Mayo) for Brennan.

1983

Ulster B.McAlinden (Armagh), P.Kennedy (Down), G.McCarville (Monaghan), J.Irwin (Derry), E.Hughes (Monaghan), P.Moriarty (Armagh), J.Reilly (Cavan), L.Austin (Down), F.McMahon (Armagh), P.McGinnitty (Fermanagh), G.Blaney, M.McCartan (Down), J.Corvan (Armagh), E.McKenna (Tyrone), M.McHugh (Donegal). Subs: P.O'Rourke (Down) for McCarville, P.McNamee (Cavan) for McCartan, D.Stevenson (Armagh) for Hughes, G.McCarville for McHugh.

Leinster M.Furlong (Offaly), T.Foley (Wexford), L.O'Connor, M.Fitzgerald, P.Fitzgerald (Offaly), P.O'Donoghue (Kildare), M.Casey (Longford), T.Connor (Offaly), T.O'Dwyer (Carlow), P.Dunne, R.Connor, G.Carroll (Offaly), C.O'Rourke (Meath), M.Connor (Offaly), S.Fahy (Kildare). Subs: L.Tompkins (Kildare) for O'Dwyer, G.McEntee (Meath) for T.Connor, B.Rock (Dublin) for O'Rourke, A.Wiseman (Louth) for O'Donoghue, T.Connor for McEntee, J.Crofton (Kildare) for P.Fitzgerald. This final went to extra time.

1984

Ulster B.McAlinden (Armagh), P.Kennedy (Down), G.McCarville (Monaghan), J.Irwin (Derry), M.Carr, M.Lafferty (Donegal), J.Reilly (Cavan), L.Austin (Down), E.McKenna (Tyrone), P.McGinnity (Fermanagh), J.Kernan (Armagh), G.Blaney (Down), M.McHugh (Donegal), F McGuigan (Tyrone), E.Hughes (Monaghan). Subs: T.McDermott (Donegal) for Irwin, F.McMahon (Armagh) for Austin, P.O'Rourke (Down) for Carr.

Connacht P.Coyne (Galway), H.Keegan (Roscommon), S.Kinneavy, S.McHugh, P.O'Neill, T.Tierney (Galway), D.Flanagan (Mayo), M.Quinn (Leitrim), M.McCarrick (Sligo), B.Talty (Galway), D.Earley (Roscommon), M.Martin (Leitrim), J.Kent (Sligo), S.Mulhern (Leitrim), S.Joyce (Galway). Subs: T.J.Kilgallon (Mayo) for Quinn, B.O'Donnell (Galway) for McCarrick

1985

Leinster J.O'L.eary, M.Holden (Dublin), M.Lyons (Meath), M.Drennan (Laois), P.Canavan (Dublin), J.Cassells (Meath), C.Browne (Laois), B.Mullins (Dublin), P.Dunne (Offaly), L.Tompkins (Kildare), T.Conroy, C.Duff, B.Rock (Dublin), C.O'Rourke (Meath), J.Mooney (Offaly). Sub.S.Fitzhenry (Wexford) for B.Rock.

Munster C.Nelligan, P.Ó Sé, T.Spillane, M.Spillane (Kerry), N.Roche (Clare), J.Kerrigan (Cork), G.Lynch, J.O'Shea, A.O'Donovan, J.Kennedy, G.Power (Kerry), C.O'Neill, E.O'Mahony (Cork), E.Liston (Kerry), F.Kelly (Tipperary). Subs: G.McGrath (Tipperary) for C.O'Neill, E.O'Brien (Waterford) for F.Kelly.

1986

Leinster J.O'Leary (Dublin), P.Dunne (Laois), G.Hargan (Dublin), P.Lyons (Meath), C.Browne (Laois), N.McCaffrey, D.Synnott (Dublin), L.Hayes, J.Cassells (Meath), B.Rock (Dublin), K.O'Brien (Wicklow), G.Browne (Laois), J.Mooney (Offaly), T.Conroy, C.Duff (Dublin).

Connacht G.Sheerin (Roscommon), M.Carney (Mayo), H.Keegan (Roscommon), S.McHugh (Galway), F.Noone (Mayo), V.Daly (Galway), D.Flanagan (Mayo), T.Tierney (Galway), T.J.Kilgallon (Mayo), P.Kelly (Galway), J.Kent (Sligo), N.Durkin, J.Burke (Mayo), P.Earley (Roscommon), M.Martin (Leitrim). Subs: K.McStay (Mayo) for J.Kent, P.Brogan (Mayo) for T.J.Kilgallon, M.McCarrick (Sligo) for P.Earley.

1987

Leinster J.O'Leary (Dublin), R.O'Malley (Meath), G.Hargan (Dublin), S.Dowling (Kildare), C.Browne (Laois), L.Harnan (Meath), N.McCaffrey (Dublin), G.McEntee (Meath), L.Hayes (Meath), P.J.Gillic (Meath), J.McNally (Dublin), K.Duff (Dublin), B.Lowry (Offaly), B.Stafford (Meath), B.Flynn (Meath). Subs: G.Browne (Laois) for McNally; Mick Lyons (Meath) for G.Browne.

Munster J.Kearns (Cork), A.Davis (Cork), A.Moloney (Clare), N.Roche (Clare), N.Cahalane (Cork), C.Counihan (Cork), G.Lynch (Kerry), A.Leahy (Cork), L.O'Connor (Waterford), T.Brown (Limerick), D.Fitzgibbon (Limerick), F.Griffin (Clare), J.Cleary (Cork), F.Ryan (Limerick), J.McGrath (Waterford). Subs: M.McAuliffe (Kerry for McGrath, D.Culloty (Cork) for Brown, P.Ivers (Limerick) for Cahalane.

1988

Leinster   M.McQuillan (Meath), D.Synnott (Dublin), J.O'Gorman (Wexford), M.Kennedy (Dublin), D.Kelly (Offaly), L.Harnan (Meath), K.Foley (Meath), D.Kavanagh (Offaly), D.Bolger (Dublin), C.Coyle (Meath), V.Murphy (Dublin), C.Duff (Dublin), P.Brady (Offaly), B.Stafford (Meath), D.Barry (Longford). Subs: E.Heery (Dublin) for Synnott and M.McCabe (Meath) for Murphy.
Ulster   P.Linden (Monaghan), J.Lynch (Tyrone), E.Sherry (Monaghan), A.Scullion (Derry), C.Murray (Monaghan), D.Loughman (Monaghan), J.Reilly (Cavan), B.McGilligan (Derry), P.Donaghy (Tyrone), K.McCabe (Tyrone), G.Blaney (Down), D.McNicholl (Derry), N.Hughes (Monaghan), E.Murphy (Monaghan), M.McHugh (Donegal). Subs: F.Cahill (Cavan) for McNicholl.

1989

Ulster   P.Linden (Monaghan), C.Hamill (Antrim), E.Sherry (Monaghan), A.Scullion (Derry), M.McQuillan (Armagh), D.Loughman (Monaghan), J.Reilly (Cavan), M.Grimley (Armagh), P.Donaghy (Tyrone), J.McMullan (Donegal), D.O'Hagan (Tyrone), G.Blaney (Down), M.McHugh (Donegal), E.McKenna (Tyrone), J.McConville (Armagh). Subs: P McErlean (Antrim) for McMullan, A.Molloy (Donegal) for Donaghy.
Munster   C.Nelligan (Kerry), C.Murphy (Kerry), M.O'Connor (Cork), N.Roche (Clare), J.Costello (Tipperary), S.Counihan (Cork), A Davis (Cork), T.McCarthy (Cork), A.O'Donovan (Kerry), P.McGrath (Cork), M.McCarthy (Cork), B.Coffey (Cork), C.O'Neill (Cork), J.O'Driscoll (Cork), M.McAuliffe (Kerry). Subs: M.Fitzgerald (Kerry) for McAuliffe, D.Culloty (Cork) for McCarthy, D.Fitzgibbon (Limerick) for McGrath.

1990

No Competition.

1991

Ulster   G.Walsh (Donegal), J.J.Doherty (Donegal), C.Deegan (Down), A.Scullion (Derry), M.McQuillan (Armagh), D.Loughman (Monaghan), M.Shovlin (Donegal), B.McGilligan (Derry), P.Donaghy (Tyrone), A.Cush (Tyrone), N.Smith (Armagh), D Bonner (Donegal), P.Canavan (Tyrone), G.Blaney (Down), J.McCartan (Down). Subs: D.McNicholl (Derry) for Cush, E.Kilpatrick (Tyrone) for Deegan, K.McGurk (Armagh) for Bonner.
Munster   J.Kerins (Cork), N.Roche (Clare), N.Cahalane (Cork), C.Murphy (Kerry), M.Slocum (Cork), C.Counihan (Cork), A.Davis (Cork), D.Culloty (Cork), N.O'Mahony (Kerry), D.Barry (Cork), J.Costello (Tipperary), S.O'Brien (Cork), C.O'Neill (Cork), F.McInerney (Clare), E.O'Brien (Waterford). Subs: D.Fitzgibbon (Limerick) for Costello, P.Vaughan (Clare) for O'Mahony.

1992

Ulster   N.Collins (Down), M.Gallagher (Donegal), C.Deegan (Down), T.Scullion (Derry), M.McQuillan (Armagh), E.Kilpatrick (Tyrone), B.Breen (Down), S.King (Cavan), P.Brogan (Donegal), R.Carr (Down), N.Smith (Armagh), A.Cush (Tyrone), M.Linden (Down), T.Boyle (Donegal), R.Carolan (Cavan). Subs: B.McGilligan (Derry) for Brogan, M.McHugh (Donegal) for Cush.
Munster   P.O'Leary (Kerry), N.Roche (Clare), P.Coleman (Cork), A.Davis (Cork), E.Breen (Kerry), C.Counihan (Cork), L.Flaherty (Kerry), D.Culloty (Cork), A.O'Donovan (Kerry), J.O'Driscoll (Cork), T.Fleming (Kerry), G.Killeen (Clare), J.Cronin (Kerry), D.Fitzgerald (Limerick), F.Kelly (Tipperary). Subs: D.Fitzgibbon (Limerick) for Killeen, A.Moloney (Clare) for Counihan, M.McCarthy (Cork) for Fitzgerald.

1993

Ulster   D.McCusker (Derry), K.McKeever (Derry), M.Gallagher (Donegal), A.Scullion (Derry), M.McQuillan (Armagh), N.Hegarty (Donegal), D.J.Kane (Down), A.Tohill (Derry), B.McGilligan (Derry), D.Heaney (Derry), M.McHugh (Donegal), N.Smyth (Armagh), J.McCartan (Down), G.Houlihan (Armagh), E.Gormley (Derry). Subs: F.Cahill (Cavan) for McHugh, F.Devlin (Tyrone) for McQuillan.
Leinster   J.O'Leary (Dublin), R.O'Malley (Meath), D.Deasy (Dublin), H.Kenny (Wicklow), G.Geraghty (Meath), G.Ryan (Kildare), S.Melia (Louth), F.Daly (Wicklow), P.Bealin (Dublin), M.Lynch (Kildare), R.Danne (Wicklow), V.Murphy (Dublin), S.White (Louth), K.O'Brien (Wicklow), C.Redmond (Dublin). Subs: P.O'Byrne (Wicklow) for Murphy, C.Hayden (Carlow) for White.

1994

Ulster   D.McCusker (Derry), J.J.Doherty (Donegal), M.Gallagher (Donegal), A.Scullion (Derry), M.McQuillan (Armagh), D.Loughman (Monaghan), D.J.Kane (Down), B.McGilligan (Derry), A.Tohill (Derry), J.McHugh (Donegal), N.Smyth (Armagh), R.Carr (Down), G.Houlihan (Armagh), D.Heaney (Derry), J.McCartan (Down). Subs: H.Downey (Derry) for Loughman, P.Canavan (Tyrone) for McHugh, B.Murray (Donegal) for Heaney.
Munster   P.O'Leary (Kerry), P.Coleman (Cork), M.O'Connor (Cork), A.Gleeson (Kerry), C.O'Sullivan (Cork), A.Moloney (Clare), J.Owens (Tipperary), J.Quane (Limerick), D.Culloty (Cork), J.Costello (Tipperary), W.O'Shea (Kerry), F.McInerney (Clare), M.Fitzgerald (Kerry), D.Fitzgibbon Limerick, J.O'Driscoll (Cork). Sub: T.Morrissey (Clare) for Culloty.

1995

Ulster   F.McConnell (Tyrone), K.McKeever (Derry), A.Scullion (Derry), M.Gallagher (Donegal), M.McQuillan (Armagh), D.J.Kane (Down), F.Devlin (Tyrone), P.Brewster (Fermanagh), B.Murray (Donegal), R.Carolan (Cavan), G.Blaney (Down), J.McCartan (Down), M.Linden (Down), A.Boyle (Donegal), P.Canavan (Tyrone). Subs: H.Downey (Derry) for McQuillan, A.Tohill (Derry) for Brewster, R.Carr (Down) for Boyle.
Leinster   J.O'Leary (Dublin), D.Dalton (Kildare), H.Kenny (Wicklow), P.Moran (Dublin), D.Lalor (Laois), G.Ryan (Kildare), P.Curran (Dublin), P.Bealin (Dublin), A.Maher (Laois), H.Emerson (Laois), J.Sheedy (Dublin), N.Buckley (Kildare), D.Farrell (Dublin), T.Dowd (Meath), C.Kelly (Louth). Subs: S.Doran (Wexford) for Farrell, K.O'Brien (Wicklow) for Kelly.

1996

Leinster   C.Byrne (Kildare), G.O'Neill (Louth), H.Kenny (Wicklow), E.Heery (Dublin), P.Curran (Dublin), G.Ryan (Kildare), D.Lalor (Laois), P.Bealin (Dublin), J.McDermott (Meath), S.O'Hanlon (Louth), A.Maher (Laois), G.Geraghty (Meath), K.O'Brien (Wicklow), B.Stynes (Dublin), C.Kelly (Louth). Sub: N.Buckley (Kildare) for O'Hanlon.
Munster   K.O'Dwyer (Cork), B.Corcoran (Cork), M.O'Connor (Cork), B.Rouine (Clare), C.O'Sullivan (Cork), S.Burke (Kerry), S.Stack (Kerry), D.Foley (Tipperary), D.Ó Sé (Kerry), W.O'Shea (Kerry), J.Kavanagh (Cork), B.Burke (Tipperary), M.Daly (Clare), C.Corkery (Cork), D.Ó Cinnéide (Kerry). Subs: M.O'Sullivan (Cork) for Burke, D.Culloty (Cork) for Ó Sé.

1997

Leinster   C.Byrne (Kildare), D.Brady (Westmeath), H.Kenny (Wicklow), D.Lalor (Laois), P.Curran (Dublin), G.Ryan (Kildare), J.Donaldson (Louth), J.McDermott (Meath), A.Maher (Laois), S.O'Hanlon (Louth), B.Stynes (Dublin), J.McDonald (Kildare), G.Geraghty (Meath), T.Dowd (Meath), C.Kelly (Louth). Subs: C.Whelan (Dublin) for McDonald, G.O'Neill (Louth) for Brady, S.Doran (Wexford) for Geraghty.
Connacht   P.Comer (Galway), K.Mortimer (Mayo), G.Fahy (Galway), E.Gavin (Roscommon), N.Connelly (Mayo), D.Mitchell (Galway), S.de Paor (Galway), J.Nallen (Mayo), L.McHale (Mayo), E.O'Hara (Sligo), D.Darcy (Leitrim), T.Ryan (Roscommon), C.McManamon (Mayo), N.Dineen (Roscommon), N.Finnegan (Galway). Subs: J.Casey (Mayo) for Mitchell, J.Horan (Mayo) for McHale, P.Kenny (Leitrim) for Dineen.

1998

Ulster   F.McConnell (Tyrone), J.J.Doherty (Donegal), C.Lawn (Tyrone), P.Devlin (Tyrone), K.McGeeney (Armagh), H.Downey (Derry), N.Hegarty (Donegal), J.Burns (Armagh), A.Tohill (Derry), J.McGuinness (Donegal), G.Cavlan (Tyrone), P.McGrane (Armagh), D.McCabe (Cavan), A.Boyle (Donegal), P.Canavan (Tyrone). Subs: G.Coleman (Derry) for Lawn, P.Brewster (Fermanagh) for Burns, M.Linden (Down) for McGuinness. In extra time McGuinness for McGrane, D.Marsden (Armagh) for Boyle.
Leinster   C.Byrne (Kildare), C.Daly (Offaly), D.Fay (Meath), M.O'Reilly (Meath), D.Lalor (Laois), G.O'Neill (Louth), F.Cullen (Offaly), J.McDermott (Meath), N.Buckley (Kildare), C.Whelan (Dublin), B.Stynes (Dublin), T.Giles (Dublin), T.Dowd (Meath), D.Darcy (Dublin), K.O'Brien (Wicklow). Subs: Seán Grennan (Offaly) for Stynes, G.Geraghty (Meath) for Whelan, P.Brady for Darcy. In extra time K.Reilly (Louth) for Buckley, V.Claffey (Offaly) for Grennan, J.Kenny (Offaly) for M.O'Reilly.

1999

Munster   D.O'Keeffe (Kerry); M.O'Donovan, S.Óg Ó hAilpín (Cork), A.Malone (Clare); C.O'Sullivan (Cork), S.Moynihan, E.Breen; D.Ó Sé (Kerry), J.Quane (Limerick); P.O'Mahoney, J.Kavanagh (Cork), D.Ó Cinnéide (Kerry); P.Lambert (Tipperary), M.O'Sullivan, A.Dorgan (Cork). Subs: L.Hassett (Kerry) for D.Ó Cinnéide, A.Lynch (Cork) for M.O'Donovan.
Connacht   P.Burke (Mayo); R.Silke (Galway), D.Donlan (Roscommon), K.Mortimer (Mayo), M.Ryan (Roscommon), J.Nallen (Mayo), S.Óg de Paor (capt.); S.Ó Domhnaill (Galway), P.Fallon (Mayo); M.Donnellan (Galway), E.O'Hara (Sligo), P.Joyce (Galway); L.Dowd (Roscommon), P.Taylor (Sligo), N.Finnegan (Galway). Subs: J.Fallon (Galway) for P.Joyce, F.Costelloe (Mayo) for M.Ryan, D.Sloyan (Sligo) for P.Fallon.

2000

Ulster   F.McConnell (Tyrone), M.Crossan (Donegal), S.M.Lockhart, G.Coleman, P.McFlynn, H.Downey (Derry), M.Magill (Down), P.Brewster (Fermanagh), G.McCartan (Down), J.McGuinness (Donegal), S.Mulholland (Down), O.McConville (Armagh), B.Devenney (Donegal), E.Gormley, Peter Canavan (Tyrone). Subs: D.Heaney (Derry) for McGuinness, T.Blake (Donegal) for McConnell, Pascal Canavan (Tyrone) for McConville, B.Dooher (Donegal) for Gormley, R.Gallagher (Fermanagh) for Mullholland.
Connacht   P.Burke, K.Mortimer (Mayo), G.Fahy (Galway), D.Gavin (Roscommon), D.Heaney (Mayo), J.Divilly (Galway), M.Ryan (Roscommon), S.Ó Domhnaill (Galway), P.Fallon (Mayo), J.Fallon (Galway), D.Duggan (Roscommon), E.O'Hara, D.Sloyane (Sligo), P.Joyce, N.Finnegan (Galway). Subs: K.O'Neill (Mayo) for Finnegan, A.Higgins (Mayo) for Mortimer, S.Davey (Sligo) for P.Fallon.

2001

Leinster   C.O'Sullivan, M.O'Reilly (Meath), D.Mitchell (Westmeath), C.Daly (Offaly), D.Healy (Westmeath), N.Nestor, (Meath), K.Doyle (Kildare), R.O'Connell (Westmeath), N.Garvan (Laois), C.McManus (Offaly), P.Barden (Longford), E.Kelly (Meath), C.Quinn (Offaly), G.Geraghty (Meath), G.Heavin (Westmeath). Subs: J.Higgins (Laois) for Doyle, J.Hegarty (Wexford) for Quinn, M.Stanfield (Louth) for Garvan, P.Conway (Laois) for Barden.
Connacht   A.Keane (Galway), D.Galvin (Roscommon), K.Fitzgerald, R.Fahy, T.Joyce (Galway), F.Grehan (Roscommon), M.Colleran, K.Walsh, J.Bergin (Galway), C.Connelly (Roscommon), E.O'Hara (Sligo), P.Clancy, D.Savage, P.Joyce (Galway), F.Dolan (Roscommon). Subs: S.O'Neill (Roscommon) for O'Hara, J.Dunning (Roscommon) for Dolan, T.Mortimer (Mayo) for Connelly.

2002

Leinster   E.Murphy, B.Lacey (Kildare), P.Christie (Dublin), A.Hoey (Louth), K.Slattery (Offaly), P.Andrews (Dublin), A.Rainbow (Kildare), C.McManus (Offaly), C.Whelan (Dublin), M.Farrelly (Louth), P.Barden (Longford), E.Kelly (Meath), J.P.Rooney (Louth), R.Cosgrove (Dublin), D.Dolan (Westmeath). Subs: T.Gill (Wicklow) for Rooney, M.Stanfield (Louth) for Farrelly, R.O'Connell (Westmeath) for Barden, T.Kelly (Laois) for Lacey.
Ulster   S.McGreevy (Antrim), E.McNulty (Armagh), C.Lawn, C.Gormley, R.McMenamin (Tyrone), C.McGeeney, A.McCann, P.McGrane (Armagh), J.McGuinness (Donegal), K.Hughes (Tyrone), R.Gallagher (Fermanagh), M.Hegarty, A.Sweeney (Donegal), R.Clarke, D.Marsden (Armagh). Subs: L.Doyle (Down) for McMenamin, T.Freeman (Monaghan) for Sweeney, M.Walsh (Down) for Hegarty, P.Reilly (Cavan) for Gallagher.

2003

Ulster   M.McVeigh (Down), E.McNulty (Armagh), N.McCusker (Derry), N.McCready (Donegal), A.Forde (Cavan), B.Monaghan (Donegal), R.McMenamin (Tyrone), G.McCartan (Down), P.McGrane (Armagh), T.Brewster (Fermanagh), S.Cavanagh (Tyrone), L.Doyle (Down), S.McDonnell (Armagh),
Connacht   S.Curran (Roscommon), K.Fitzgerald, G.Fahy (Galway), M.McGuinness (Leitrim), S.Og dePaor (Galway), F.Grehan (Roscommon), J.Nallen (Mayo), K.Walsh, J.Bergin (Galway), G.Cox (Roscommon), P.Joyce, D.Savage, M.Clancy (Galway), C.Mortimer (Mayo), F.Dolan (Roscommon). Subs: J.Gill (Mayo) for Cox, T.Mortimer (Mayo) for C.Mortimer, S.O'Neill (Roscommon) for Walsh, D.Casey (Roscommon) for Fitzgerald, G.McGowan (Sligo) for Gill.

2004

Ulster   M.McVeigh (Down), N.McCready, R.Sweeney (Donegal), E.McNulty (Armagh), P.McFlynn (Derry), B.Monaghan (Donegal), R.McMenamin (Tyrone), D.Gordon (Down), M.McGrath (Fermanagh), B.Dooher, B.McGuigan, S.Cavanagh, S.O'Neill (Tyrone), P.Bradley, E.Muldoon (Derry). Subs: P.Loughran (Armagh) for McGrath, R.Johnston (Fermanagh) for McFlynn, K.Madden (Antrim) for Bradley.
Leinster   G.Connaughton, D.O'Donoghue (Westmeath), T.Kelly (Laois), N.McKeigue (Meath), K.Fitzpatrick (Laois), B.Cullen (Dublin), K.Slattery (Offaly), N.Garvan (Laois), N.Crawford, E.Kelly (Meath), P.Barden (Longford), J.Doyle (Kildare), A.Brogan (Dublin), P.Kellaghan (Offaly), M.Forde (Wexford). Subs: P.Davis (Longford) for Forde, T.Walsh (Carlow) for Fitzpatrick, P.Keenan (Louth) for Kellaghan, T.Smullen (Longford) for Slattery.

2005

Leinster F.Byron (Laois), M.Ennis (Westmeath), T.Kelly (Laois), D.Healy (Westmeath), B.Cahill (Dublin), C.Moran (Dublin), P.Andrews (Dublin), T.Walsh (Carlow), N.Garvan (Laois), A.Mangan (Westmeath), R.Munnelly (Laois), P.Clancy (Laois), D.Dolan (Westmeath), G.Geraghty (Meath), J.Sherlock (Dublin). Subs: M.Forde (Wexford) for Walsh, J.Doyle (Kildare) for Munnelly, B.Sheehan (Laois) for Mangan, S.Ryan (Dublin) for Garvan, Garvan for Sherlock, D.Regan (Meath) for Forde.

Ulster J.Reilly (Cavan), K.McGuckin (Derry), K.McCloy (Derry), E.McNulty (Armagh), A.Kernan (Armagh), C.Gormley (Tyrone), A.Mallon (Armagh), D.Gordon (Down), S.Cavanagh (Tyrone), B.Dooher (Tyrone), C.Toye (Donegal), D.Clerkin (Monaghan), T.Freeman (Monaghan), P.Bradley (Derry), S.McDonnell (Armagh). Subs: A.O'Rourke (Armagh) for McCloy, D.Diver (Donegal) for Gormley, R.Mellon (Tyrone) for Bradley, P.Hearty (Armagh) for Reilly, R.Clarke (Armagh) for Mellon.

2006

Leinster G.Connaughton (Westmeath), A.Fennelly (Laois), B.Cahill (Dublin), M.Ennis (Westmeath), C.King (Meath), C.Moran (Dublin), K.Slattery (Offaly), B.Quigley (Laois), P.Clancy (Laois), D.Lally (Dublin), J.Doyle (Kildare), M.Carpenter (Carlow), C.Keaney (Dublin), J.Sheridan (Meath), B.Kavanagh (Longford). Subs: A.Mangan (Westmeath) for Kavanagh, T.Walsh (Carlow) for Clancy, D.Clarke (Louth) for Lally.

Connacht D.Clarke (Mayo), D.Burke (Galway), F.Hanley (Galway), S.McDermott (Roscommon), S.Daly (Roscommon), D.Blake (Galway), D.Heaney (Mayo), P.Harte (Mayo), D.Brady (Mayo), A.Kerins (Galway), G.Brady (Mayo), A.Dillon (Mayo), C.Mortimer (Mayo), M.Meehan (Galway), D.Savage (Galway). Subs: K.Mannion (Roscommon) for G.Brady, S.Davey (Sligo) for Harte, K.O'Neill (Mayo) for Kerins.

2007

Ulster J.Reilly (Cavan), B.Owens (Fermanagh), K.McCloy (Derry), K.Lacey (Donegal), C.McKeever (Armagh), C.Gormley (Tyrone), K.Cassidy (Donegal), E.Lennon (Monaghan), D.Gordon (Down), D.Clerkin (Monaghan), S.Cavanagh (Tyrone), P.Finlay (Monaghan), T.Freeman (Monaghan), P.Bradley (Derry), E.Muldoon (Derry). Subs: B.Monaghan (Donegal) for McCloy, S.McDonnell (Armagh) for Bradley, J.Crozier (Antrim) for Lacey, B.Coulter (Down) for Gordon, S.Goan (Fermanagh) for McKeever.

Munster A.Quirke (Cork), T.O'Gorman (Waterford), T.O'Sullivan (Kerry), K.O'Connor (Cork), T.O'Se (Kerry), M.Shields (Cork), G.Spillane (Cork), D.O'Se (Cork), S.Scanlon (Kerry), E.Brosnan (Kerry), P.O'Neill (Cork), J.Miskella (Cork), M.F.Russell (Kerry), K.Donaghy (Kerry), D.O'Connor (Cork). Subs: G.Canty (Cork) for O'Gorman, F.Gould (Cork) for D.O'Se, M.D.O'Sullivan (Kerry) for Miskella, G.Hurney (Waterford) for Brosnan.

2008

Munster P.Fitzgerald (Tipperary), D.Duggan (Cork), J.McCarthy (Limerick), P.Reidy (Kerry), T.Ó Sé (Kerry), S.Lavin (Limerick), T.O'Gorman (Waterford), J.Galvin (Limerick), N.Murphy (Cork), P.Kelly (Cork), D.O'Connor (Cork), M.O'Gorman (Waterford), D.Goulding (Cork), A.O'Connor (Cork), I.Ryan (Limerick). Subs: R.Costigan (Cork), J.Hayes (Cork), S.O'Donoghue (Cork), E.Rockett (Waterford).

Connacht D.Clarke (Mayo), G.Bradshaw (Galway), T.Cunniffe (Mayo), C.Harrison (Sligo), P.Gardiner (Mayo), D.Blake (Galway), J.Nallen (Mayo), R.McGarrity (Roscommon), M.Finneran (Roscommon), A.Moran (Mayo), P.Harte (Mayo), A.Dillon (Mayo), C.Mortimer (Mayo), D.Maxwell (Leitrim), E.Mulligan (Leitrim). Subs: J.Bergin (Galway), G.Heneghan (Roscommon), D.Kelly (Sligo).

2009

Ulster J.Devine (Tyrone), K.Lacey (Donegal), Justin McMahon (Tyrone), G.O'Kane (Derry), A.Kernan (Armagh), C.McKeever (Armagh), R.Flanagan (Cavan), K.Hughes (Tyrone), E.McGinley (Tyrone), P.Finlay (Monaghan), B.Coulter (Down), Joe McMahon (Tyrone), P.Bradley (Derry), S.O'Neill (Tyrone), M.Murphy (Donegal). Subs: C.Gormley (Tyrone) for McKeever, R.McCloskey (Fermanagh) for Lacey, D.Hughes (Down) for Joe McMahon, D.Gordon (Down) for Murphy, T.Freeman (Monaghan) for Hughes.

Munster P.Fitzgerald (Tipperary), T.O'Gorman (Waterford), J.McCarthy (Limerick), P.Reidy (Kerry), M.O'Gorman (Waterford), M.Shields (Cork), P.Ranahan (Limerick), N.Murphy (Cork), P.O'Neill (Cork), P.Kelly (Cork), D.O'Connor (Cork), P.Kerrigan (Cork), G.Hurney (Waterford), D.Goulding (Cork), L.Ó Lionnáin (Waterford). Subs: R.Costigan (Tipperary) for M.O'Gorman, J.Ryan (Limerick) for Kerrigan, S.Scanlon (Kerry) for O'Neill, A.Walsh (Cork) for Ó Lionnáin.

2010

No Competition.

2011

No Competition.

2012

Ulster B.McVeigh (Down), B.Donaghy (Armagh), N.McGee (Donegal), K.Lacey (Donegal), J.Loughrey (Antrim), D.Hughes (Monaghan), C.McKeever (Armagh), D.Gordon (Down), R.Kavanagh (Donegal), P.Harte (Tyrone), M.Poland (Down), M.Penrose (Tyrone), C.Gilligan (Derry), B.Coulter (Down), O.Mulligan (Tyrone). Subs: J.McMahon (Tyrone) for Gilligan, O.Lennon (Monaghan) for Kavanagh, V.Corey (Monaghan) for Loughrey.

Munster A.Quirke (Cork), A.O'Mahony (Kerry), J.McCarthy (Limerick), S.Lavin (Limerick), T.Ó Sé (Kerry), G.Canty (Cork), P.Kissane (Cork), G.Brennan (Clare), S.Scanlon (Kerry), P.Kelly (Cork), P.Kerrigan (Cork), J.Cooke (Limerick), D.Tubridy (Claere), G.Hurney (Waterford), I.Ryan (Limerick). Subs: P.O'Neill (Cork) for Cooke, R.Donnelly (Clare) for Kelly, M.Collins (Cork) for Ryan.

2013

Ulster P.McConnell (Tyrone), C.McKaigue (Derry), E.McGee (Donegal), C.McKeever (Armagh), A.Kernan (Armagh), D.Hughes (Monaghan), P.Harte (Tyrone), S.Cavanagh (Tyrone), D.Givney (Cavan), M.McHugh (Donegal), M.Penrose (Tyrone), Joe McMahon (Tyrone), J.Clarke (Armagh), K.Niblock (Antrim), C.McManus (Monaghan). Subs: M.Murphy (Donegal) for Niblock, G.McKiernan (Cavan) for Givney, Justin McMahon (Tyrone) for McKeever, M.Poland (Down) for Penrose, K.Hughes (Monaghan) for McHugh.

Leinster S.Cluxton (Dublin), K Lillis (Laois), G.Molloy (Wexford), B.Malone (Wexford), M.Quinn (Longford), G.Brennan (Dublin), A.Flynn (Wexford), M.D.Macauley (Dublin), J.Heslin (Westmeath), B.Connor (Offaly), R.Barry (Wexford), C.O'Sullivan (Dublin), B.Brogan (Dublin), J.Sheridan (Meath), B.Murphy (Carlow). Subs: P.Keenan (Louth) for O'Connor, R.O'Carroll (Dublin) for Lillis, K.McMenamon (Dublin) for Barry, S.McCormack (Longford) for Sheridan, J.Stafford (Meath) for Murphy.

2014

Connacht R.Hennelly (Mayo), S.McDermott (Roscommon), J.Moore (Galway), K.Higgins (Mayo), G.Bradshaw (Galway), N.Daly (Roscommon), K.McLoughlin (Mayo), A.O'Shea (Mayo), J.Gibbons (Mayo), S.Armstrong (Galway), E.Mulligan (Leitrim), C.Cregg (Roscommon), M.Conroy (Mayo), P.Conroy (Galway), D.Kelly (Sligo). Subs: T.Flynn (Galway) for O'Shea, O'Shea for Flynn, D.Cummins (Galway) for Kelly, Kelly for Cummins, M.Brehony (Sligo) for Kelly, E.Concannon (Galway) for M.Conroy, G.Reynolds (Leitrim) for Bradshaw, N.Ewing (Sligo) for McDermott.

Ulster N.Morgan (Tyrone), E.Mcgee (Donegal), N.McGee (Donegal), C.Clarke (Tyrone), S.L.McGoldrick (Derry), R.McCluskey (Fermanagh), P.Harte (Tyrone), S.Cavanagh (Tyrone), E.Donnelly (Fermanagh), C.Mackey (Cavan), M.Poland (Down), C.Cavanagh (Tyrone), E.Keating (Cavan), M.Murphy (Donegal), C.McManus (Monaghan). Subs: K.Hughes (Monaghan) for Keating, M.McHugh (Donegal) for Mackey, C.McKaigue (Derry) for McCluskey, D.Givney (Cavan) for Donnelly, K.McKernan (Down) for Cavanagh.

2015

No Competition.

2016

Ulster N.Morgan (Tyrone), M.Jones (Fermanagh), K.Clarke (Cavan), D.O'Hagan (Down), T.McCann (Tyrone), C.Moynagh (Cavan), A.Breen (Fermanagh), E.Donnelly (Fermanagh), C.Vernon (Armagh), K.Niblock (Antrim), P.Harte (Tyrone), E.Lynn (Derry), N.Sludden (Tyrone), S.Campbell (Armagh), T.Corrigan (Fermanagh). Subs: R.Johnston (Down) for Niblock, C.McKaigue (Derry) for Moynagh, B.Rogers (Derry) for McKaigue, D.McCusker (Fermanagh) for Clarke, M.Donnelly (Tyrone) for Campbell, T.Kernan (Armagh) for Vernon.

Connacht D.Clarke (Mayo), K.McDonnell (Sligo), J.Duane (Galway), D.Wynne (Galway), N.Daly (Roscommon), G.O'Donnell (Galway), J.Heaney (Galway), E.Smith (Roscommon), K.Higgins (Roscommon), F.Cregg (Roscommon), D.Cummins (Galway), C.Murtagh (Roscommon), N.Murphy (Sligo), D.Comer (Galway), J.Doherty (Mayo). Subs: P.Conroy (Galway) for Cummins, D.Wrynn (Leitrim) for Higgins, G.Bradshaw (Galway) for Doherty, E.Mulligan (Leitrim) for Conroy, J.McManus (Roscommon) for McDonnell, D.Murtagh (Roscommon) for Murphy, C.O'Shea (Mayo) for Smith.

CAPTAINS OF WINNING INTERPROVINCIAL FOOTBALL TEAMS

1927	John Joe Sheehy (Kerry)
1928	Matt Goff (Kildare)
1929	Bill Gannon (Kildare)
1930	John Higgins (Kildare)
1931	Joe Barrett (Kerry)
1932	John Higgins (Kildare)
1933	John McDonnell (Dublin)
1934	Mick Donnellan (Galway)
1935	John McDonnell (Dublin)
1936	Paddy Moclair (Mayo)
1937	Purty Kelly (Mayo)
1938	Paddy Moclair (Mayo)
1939	Bill Delaney (Laois)
1940	Matty Gilsenan (Meath)
1941	Danno Keeffe (Kerry)
1942	John J. O'Reilly (Cavan)
1943	John J. O'Reilly (Cavan)
1944	Jim Thornton (Louth)
1945	Peeny Whelan (Carlow)
1946	Tadgh Crowley (Cork)
1947	Kevin Armstrong (Antrim)
1948	Jackie Lyne (Kerry)
1949	Batt Garvey (Kerry)
1950	John J. O'Reilly (Cavan)
1951	Seán Flanagan (Mayo)
1952	Paddy Meegan (Meath)
1953	Paddy Meegan (Meath)
1954	Stephen White (Louth)
1955	Paddy O'Brien (Meath}
1956	Seamus Morris (Cavan)
1957	Jack Mangan (Galway)
1958	Seán Purcell (Galway)
1959	Kevin Heffernan (Dublin)
1960	Seán O'Neill (Down)
1961	Willie Nolan (Offaly)
1962	Greg Hughes (Offaly)
1963	Jim McDonnell (Cavan)
1964	Paddy Doherty (Down)
1965	Tom Maguire (Cavan)
1966	Jim McCartan (Down}
1967	Enda Colleran (Galway)
1968	Joe Lennon (Down)
1969	Noel Tierney (Galway)

1970	Ray Carolan (Cavan
1971	Mal McAfee (Derry)
1972	Donal Hunt (Cork)
1973	Brendan Lynch (U.C.C. and Kerry)
1974	Martin Furlong (Offaly)
1975	Billy Morgan (Cork)
1976	Michael O'Sullivan (Kerry)
1977	John O'Keeffe (Kerry)
1978	John O'Keeffe (Kerry)
1979	Colm McAlarney (Down)
1980	Peter McGinnitty (Fermanagh)
1981	Ger Power (Kerry)
1982	Tim Kennelly (Kerry)
1983	Peter McGinnitty (Fermanagh)
1984	Eugene McKenna (Tyrone)
1985	Brian Mullins (Dublin)
1986	John O'Leary (Dublin)
1987	Ger McEntee (Meath)
1988	Michael McQuillan (Meath)
1989	Jim Reilly (Cavan)
1990	No competition
1991	Tony Scullion (Derry)
1992	Greg Blaney (Down)
1993	Martin McHugh (Donegal)
1994	Brian McGilligan (Derry)
1995	Mickey Linden (Down)
1996	Paul Curran (Dublin)
1997	Tommy Dowd (Meath)
1998	Peter Canavan (Tyrone)
1999	Seamus Moynihan (Kerry)
2000	Henry Downey (Derry)
2001	Mark O'Reilly (Meath)
2002	N.A.
2003	Paul McGrane (Armagh)
2004	Michael McVeigh (Down)
2005	Ciarán Whelan (Dublin)
2006	Colin Moran (Dublin)
2007	Conor Gormley (Tyrone)
2008	Nicholas Murphy (Cork)
2009	Stephen O'Neill (Tyrone)
2010	No Competition
2011	No Competition
2012	Darren Hughes (Monaghan)
2013	Darren Hughes (Monaghan)
2014	Aidan O'Shea (Mayo)
2015	No Competition
2016	Eoin Donnelly (Fermanagh)

ALL-IRELAND CLUB SENIOR CHAMPIONSHIPS

7 *Nemo Rangers (Cork)* – 1973, 1979, 1982, 1984, 1989, 1994, 2003.
6 *Crossmaglen Rangers (Armagh)* – 1997, 1999, 2000, 2007, 2011, 2012.
3 *St Finbarr's (Cork)* – 1980, 1981, 1987.
 St Vincent's (Dublin) – 1976 2008, 2014.
2 *UCD (Dublin)* – 1974, 1975.
 Burren (Down) – 1986, 1988.
 Kilmacud Crokes (Dublin) – 1995, 2009.
 Corofin (Galway) – 1998, 2015.
 Dr. Crokes (Kerry) – 1992, 2017.
1 *East Kerry* – 1971.
 Bellaghy (Derry) – 1972.
 Austin Stacks (Kerry) – 1977.
 Thomond College (Limerick) – 1978.
 Portlaoise (Laois) – 1983.
 Castleisland Desmonds (Kerry) – 1985.
 Baltinglass (Wicklow) – 1990.
 Lavey (Derry) – 1991.
 O'Donovan Rossa (Cork) – 1993.
 Laune Rangers (Kerry) – 1996.
 Crossmolina (Mayo) – 2001.
 Ballinderry (Derry) – 2002.
 Caltra (Galway) – 2004.
 Ballina Stephenites (Mayo) – 2005.
 Salthill-Knocknacarra (Galway) – 2006.
 St Gall's (Antrim) – 2010.
 St Brigid's (Roscommon) – 2013.
 Ballyboden St. Enda's (Dublin) – 2016.

1970/71
PROVINCIAL FINALS
Connacht:
Fr Griffin's (Galway) 2-9 Castlebar (Mayo) 1-10
Ulster:
Bryansford (Down) 0-6 Newbridge (Derry) 0-3
Munster:
East Kerry (Kerry) 0-7 Muskerry (Cork) 0-6
Leinster:
Gracefield (Offaly) 0-12 Newtown Blues (Louth) 0-9
ALL-IRELAND SEMI-FINALS
East Kerry 0-12 Gracefield 0-7
Bryansford wo FrGriffin's scr
(Fr Griffin's did not play because Liam Sammon was unavailable owing to San Francisco exhibition v Kerry)
ALL-IRELAND FINAL
East Kerry 5-9 Bryansford 2-7

1971/72
PROVINCIAL FINALS
Connacht:
Claremorris (Mayo) 0-10 Milltown (Galway) 1-5
Ulster:
Bellaghy (Derry) 1-11 Clan na Gael (Armagh) 0-5
Munster:
UCC 2-9 Clonmel Commercials (Tipperary) 1-8
Leinster:
Portlaoise (Laois) 2-11 Athlone (Westmeath) 2-9
ALL-IRELAND SEMI-FINALS
UCC 3-12 Claremorris 1-7
Bellaghy 1-11 Portlaoise 1-10
ALL-IRELAND FINAL
Bellaghy 0-15 UCC 1-11

FOOTBALL

1972/73
PROVINCIAL FINALS
Connacht:
Fr Griffin's (Galway) 1-8 Ballaghaderreen (Mayo) 0-6
Ulster:
Clan na Gael (Armagh) 0-8 Ardboe (Tyrone) 1-3
Munster:
Nemo Rangers (Cork) 3-9 Doonbeg (Clare) 0-5
Leinster:
St Vincent's (Dublin) 6-10 The Downs (Westmeath) 2-5
ALL-IRELAND SEMI-FINALS
Nemo Rangers 0-17 Fr Griffin's 0-9
StVincent's 2-8 Clan na Gael 0-7
ALL-IRELAND FINAL
Nemo Rangers 2-11 St Vincent's 2-11
Nemo Rangers 4-6 St Vincent's 0-10 (replay)

1973/74
PROVINCIAL FINALS
Connacht:
Knockmore (Mayo) 4-10 Seán O'Heslin's (Leitrim) 0-8
Ulster:
Clan na Gael (Armagh) 1-10 St Joseph's (Donegal) 0-3
Munster:
UCC 2-8 Loughmore-Castleiney (Tipperary) 1-5
Leinster:
UCD 1-6 Cooley Kickham's (Louth) 0-7
ALL-IRELAND SEMI-FINALS
Clan na Gael 3-7 UCC1-10
UCD 4-13 Knockmore 0-4
ALL-IRELAND FINAL
UCD 1-6 Clan na Gael 1-6
UCD 0-14 Clan na Gael 1-4 (replay)

1974/75
PROVINCIAL FINALS
Connacht:
Roscommon Gaels (Roscommon) 0-11 Garrymore (Mayo) 0-11
Roscommon Gaels 1-12 Garrymore 0-7 (replay)
Ulster:
Clan na Gael (Armagh) 1-7 Trillick (Tyrone) 1-4
Munster:
Nemo Rangers (Cork) 2-6 Austin Stacks (Kerry) 1-7
Leinster:
UCD 2-7 Ferbane (Offaly) 1-9
ALL-IRELAND SEMI-FINALS
UCD 0-12 Roscommon Gaels 1-2
Nemo Rangers 1-3 Clan na Gael 1-3
Nemo Rangers 2-5 Clan na Gael 0-6 (replay)
ALL-IRELAND FINAL
UCD 1-11 Nemo Rangers 0-12

1975/76
PROVINCIAL FINALS
Connacht:
Roscommon Gaels (Roscommon) 0-6 Fr Griffin's (Galway) 0-5
Ulster:
St Joseph's (Donegal) 3-6 Castleblaney Faughs (Monaghan) 1-8
Munster:
Nemo Rangers (Cork) 2-7 Austin Stacks (Kerry) 2-7
Nemo Rangers 1-9 Austin Stacks 2-6 (replay)
Nemo Rangers 1-9 Austin Stacks 0-10 (2nd replay)

Leinster:
St Vincent's (Dublin) 3-9 St Joseph's (Laois) 1-8
ALL-IRELAND QUARTER FINAL
Roscommon Gaels 1-7 Seán McDermott's (London) 0-8
ALL-IRELAND SEMI-FINALS
Roscommon Gaels 1-7 St Joseph's 0-3
St Vincent's 0-10 Nemo Rangers 0-3
ALL-IRELAND FINAL
St Vincent's 4-10 Roscommon Gaels 0-5

1976/77
PROVINCIAL FINALS
Connacht:
Killererin (Galway) 3-8 Garrymore (Mayo) 0-5
Ulster:
Ballerin (Derry) 2-8 Clan na Gael (Armagh) 2-3
Munster:
Austin Stack's (Kerry) 1-7 St Finbarr's (Cork) 0-8
Leinster:
Portlaoise 1-12 Cooley Kickham's (Louth) 0-8
ALL-IRELAND QUARTER FINAL
Austin Stack's 2-16 Kingdom (London) 0-7
ALL-IRELAND SEMI-FINALS
Austin Stack's 1-14 Portlaoise 2-6
Ballerin 5-9 Killererin 1-4
ALL-IRELAND FINAL
Austin Stack's 1-13 Ballerin 2-7

1977/78
PROVINCIAL FINALS
Connacht:
St Mary's (Sligo) 4-6 Corofin (Galway) 1-9
Ulster:
St John's (Antrim) 2-10 Cavan Gaels 2-2
Munster:
Thomond College (Limerick) 0-12 Nemo Rangers (Cork) 1-3
Leinster:
Summerhill (Meath) 5-4 St Vincent's (Dublin) 0-6
ALL-IRELAND QUARTER FINAL
St John's 4-9 Kingdom (London) 1-8
ALL-IRELAND SEMI-FINALS
Thomond College 1-12 St Mary's 1-8
St John's 4-12 Summerhill 1-8
ALL-IRELAND FINAL
Thomond College 2-14 St John's 1-3

1978/79
PROVINCIAL FINALS
Connacht:
Killererin (Galway) 1-11 Castlebar Mitchels (Mayo) 1-4
Ulster:
Scotstown (Monaghan) 1-8 StJohn's (Antrim) 1-4
Munster:
Nemo Rangers (Cork) 0-8 Kilrush Shamrocks (Clare) 0-5
Leinster:
Walsh Island (Offaly) 2-9 St Joseph's (Laois) 3-5
ALL-IRELAND QUARTER FINAL
Killererin wo Kingdom (London) scr
Note: Kingdom withdrew because of a spate of injuries
ALL-IRELAND SEMI-FINALS
Nemo Rangers 3-6 Killererin 1-6
Scotstown 3-4 Walsh Island 0-8
ALL-IRELAND FINAL
Nemo Rangers 2-9 Scotstown 1-3

1979/80
PROVINCIAL FINALS
Connacht:
St Grellan's (Galway) 0-4 St Mary's (Sligo) 0- 4
St Grellan's 0-9 St Mary's 0-8 (replay)
Ulster:
Scotstown (Monaghan) 0-9 Carrickcruppin (Armagh) 0-8
Munster:
St Finbarr's (Cork) 0-10 Kilrush Shamrocks (Clare) 0-4
Leinster:
Walsh Island (Offaly) 3-2 Portlaoise (Laois) 1-6
ALL-IRELAND QUARTER FINAL
St Finbarr's 3-17 Kingdom (London) 1-3
ALL-IRELAND SEMI-FINALS
St Grellan's Ballinasloe 1-11 Walsh Island 1-8
St Finbarr's 0-7 Scotstown 0-4
ALL-IRELAND FINAL
St Finbarr's 3-9 St Grellan's Ballinasloe 0-8

1980/81
PROVINCIAL FINALS
Connacht:
St Mary's (Sligo) 3-6 St Grellan's Ballinasloe (Galway) 3-3
Ulster:
Scotstown (Monaghan) 1-4 St John's (Antrim) 1-3
Munster:
St Finbarr's (Cork) 3-12 Stradbally (Waterford) 1-8
Leinster:
Walterstown (Meath) 2-9 Éire Óg (Carlow) 2-8
ALL-IRELAND QUARTER FINAL
Scotstown 1-8 Tara (London) 0-5
ALL-IRELAND SEMI-FINALS
Walterstown 2-12 St Mary's 1-5
St Finbarr's 0-8 Scotstown 0-4
ALL-IRELAND FINAL
St Finbarr's 1-8 Walterstown 0-6

1981/82
PROVINCIAL FINALS
Connacht:
Garrymore (Mayo) 0-9 St Mary's (Sligo) 1-5
Ulster:
Ballinderry (Derry) 2-3 Burren (Down) 0-5
Munster:
Nemo Rangers (Cork) 3-9 Kilrush Shamrocks (Clare) 1-6
Leinster:
Raheens (Kildare) 1-7 Portlaoise (Laois) 0-6
ALL-IRELAND QUARTER FINAL
Garrymore 0-9 Parnell's (London) 0-8
ALL-IRELAND SEMI-FINALS
Nemo Rangers 1-10 Raheens 0-7
Garrymore 0-8 Ballinderry 1-4
ALL-IRELAND FINAL
Nemo Rangers 6-11 Garrymore 1-8

1982/83
PROVINCIAL FINALS
Connacht:
Clann na nGael (Roscommon) 2-6 Tourlestrane (Sligo) 1-3
Ulster:
St Gall's (Antrim) 0-15 Roslea (Fermanagh) 2-5
Munster:
St Finbarr's (Cork) 0-11 Castleisland Desmonds (Kerry) 1-8
St Finbarr's 2-6 Castleisland Desmonds 0-6 (replay)

Leinster:
Portlaoise (Laois) 1-8 Ballymun Kickham's (Dublin) 0-7
ALL-IRELAND QUARTER FINAL
St Finbarr's 5-21 Hugh O'Neill's (Yorkshire) 1-6
ALL-IRELAND SEMI-FINALS
Portlaoise 0-7 St Finbarr's 0-6
Clann na nGael 3-6 St Gall's 2-8
ALL-IRELAND FINAL
Portlaoise 0-12 Clann na nGael 2-0

1983/84
PROVINCIAL FINALS
Connacht:
St Mary's (Sligo) 1-7 Knockmore (Mayo) 0-5
Ulster:
Burren (Down) 0-7 St Gall's (Antrim) 0-7
Burren 1-4 St Gall's 0-5 (replay)
Munster:
Nemo Rangers (Cork) 2-10 Doonbeg (Clare) 0-3
Leinster:
Walterstown (Meath) 3-9 Walsh Island (Offaly) 2-11
ALL-IRELAND QUARTER FINAL
Burren 3-12 Tír Conaill Gaels (London) 0-2
ALL-IRELAND SEMI-FINALS
Walterstown 3-6 Burren 0-8
Nemo Rangers 2-10 St Mary's 1-7
ALL-IRELAND FINAL
Nemo Rangers 2-10 Walterstown 0-5

1984/85
PROVINCIAL FINALS
Connacht:
Clann na nGael (Roscommon) 1-6 St Mary's (Sligo) 0-9
Clann na nGael 1-7 St Mary's 0-9 (replay)
Ulster:
Burren (Down) 0-10 St John's (Antrim) 2-2
Munster:
Castleisland Desmonds (Kerry) 2-6 St Finbarr's (Cork) 0-9
Leinster:
St Vincent's (Dublin) 1-13 Tinahely (Wicklow) 1-3
ALL-IRELAND QUARTER FINAL
Clann na nGael 0-11 Parnell's (London) 0-5
ALL-IRELAND SEMI-FINALS
St Vincent's 2-5 Burren 0-8
Castleisland Desmonds 1-4 Clann na nGael 0-7
Castleisland Desmonds 2-6 Clann na Gael 0-8 (replay)
ALL-IRELAND FINAL
Castleisland Desmonds 2-2 St Vincent's 0-7

1985/86
PROVINCIAL FINALS
Connacht:
Clann na Gael (Roscommon) 0-10 Ballina Stephenites (Mayo) 1-5
Ulster:
Burren (Down) 0-6 Scotstown (Monaghan) 1-2
Munster:
Castleisland Desmonds (Kerry) 1-11 St Finbarr's (Cork) 0-5
Leinster:
Portlaoise (Laois) 1-8 Baltingloss (Wicklow) 1-8
Portlaoise (Laois) 2-8 Baltinglass (Wicklow) 1-9 (replay)
ALL-IRELAND QUARTER FINAL
Castleisland Desmonds 5-12 Kingdom (London) 2-4
ALL-IRELAND SEMI-FINALS
Burren 2-13 Portlaoise 0-6
Castleisland Desmonds 0-11 Clann na nGael 1-8
Castleisland Desmonds 2-9 Clann na Gael 1-6 (replay)
ALL-IRELAND FINAL
Burren 1-10 Castleisland Desmonds 1-6

1986/87
PROVINCIAL FINALS
Connacht:
Clann na nGael (Roscommon) 2-9 Seán O'Heslin's (Leitrim) 2-4
Ulster:
Castleblaney Faughs (Monaghan) 0-4 Burren (Down) 0-3
Munster:
St Finbarr's (Cork) 2-15 Kilrossanty (Waterford) 1-5
Leinster:
Ferbane (Offaly) 3-5 Portlaoise (Laois) 1-10
ALL-IRELAND QUARTER FINAL
Castleblaney Faughs 2-10 Kingdom (London) 0-7
ALL-IRELAND SEMI-FINALS
Clann na nGael 0-13 Ferbane 1-5
St Finbarr's 2-9 Castleblaney Faughs 1-12
St Finbarr's 3-5 Castleblaney Faughs 2-7 (replay)
ALL-IRELAND FINAL
St Finbarr's 0-10 Clann na nGael 0-7

1987/88
PROVINCIAL FINALS
Connacht:
Clann na nGael (Roscommon) 0-9 Ballina Stephenites (Mayo) 0-8
Ulster:
Burren (Down) 0-8 Kingscourt (Cavan) 0-6
Munster:
Nemo Rangers (Cork) 5-15 Newcastlewest (Limerick) 2-3
Leinster:
Portlaoise (Laois) 1-8 Parnell's (Dublin) 1-8
Portlaoise 1-7 Parnell's 1-5 (replay)
ALL-IRELAND QUARTER FINAL
Clann na nGael 0-16 Kingdom (London) 0-7
ALL-IRELAND SEMI-FINALS
Burren 1-5 Nemo Rangers 0-6
Clann na nGael 1-9 Portlaoise 0-9
ALL-IRELAND FINAL
Burren 1-9 Clann na nGael 0-8

1988/89
PROVINCIAL FINALS
Connacht:
Clann na nGael (Roscommon) 1-8 Castlebar Mitchels (Mayo) 0-9
Ulster:
Burren (Down) 0-8 Pearse Óg (Armagh) 0-3
Munster:
Nemo Rangers (Cork) 1-6 Kilrossanty (Waterford) 1-2
Leinster:
Parnell's (Dublin) 2-5 Ferbane (Offaly) 1-8
Parnell's 1-4 Ferbane 0-6 (replay)
ALL-IRELAND QUARTER FINAL
Nemo Rangers 3-15 John Mitchel's (Birmingham) 0-2
ALL-IRELAND SEMI-FINALS
Clann na nGael 1-6 Burren 1-5
Nemo Rangers 1-4 Parnell's 0-5
ALL-IRELAND FINAL
Nemo Rangers 1-13 Clann na nGael 1-3

1989/90
PROVINCIAL FINALS
Connacht:
Clann na nGael (Roscommon) 3-10 Knockmore (Mayo) 0-7
Ulster:
Scotstown (Monaghan) 2-9 Coalisland (Tyrone) 0-5

Munster:
Castlehaven (Cork) 0-13 St Senan's Kilkee (Clare) 1-8
Leinster:
Baltinglass (Wicklow) 1-6 Thomas Davis (Dublin) 1-6
Baltinglass 1-9 Thomas Davis 0-11 (replay)
ALL-IRELAND QUARTER FINAL
Clann na nGael 2-9 Kingdom (London) 1-4
ALL-IRELAND SEMI-FINALS
Clann na Gael 1-8 Scotstown 0-6
Baltinglass 1-5 Castlehaven 0-6
ALL-IRELAND FINAL
Baltinglass 2-7 Clann na nGael 0-7

1990/91
PROVINCIAL FLNALS
Connacht:
Salthill (Galway) 0-11 Seán O'Heslin's (Leitrim) 0-5
Ulster:
Lavey (Derry) 2-10 Kingscourt (Cavan) 0-4
Munster:
Dr Crokes (Kerry) 0-8 Clonmel Commercials (Tipperary) 0-8
Dr Crokes 0-15 Clonmel Commercials 0-10 (replay) (aet)
Leinster:
Thomas Davis (Dublin) 0-8 Baltinglass (Wicklow) 1-5
Thomas Davis 1-8 Baltinglass 0-8 (replay)
ALL-IRELAND QUARTER FINAL
Lavey 2-11 Tir Conaill Gaels (London) 1-12 (aet)
ALL-IRELAND SEMI-FINALS
Salthill 3-9 Dr Crokes 2-6
Lavey 2-6 Thomas Davis 0-10
ALL-IRELAND FINAL
Lavey 2-9 Salthill 0-10

1991/92
PROVINCIAL FINALS
Connacht:
Corofin (Galway) 2-5 Clann na nGael (Roscommon) 0-9
Ulster:
Castleblaney Faughs (Monaghan) 0-8 Killybegs (Donegal) 0-6
Munster:
Dr Crokes (Kerry) 2-10 Doonbeg (Clare) 0-8
Leinster:
Thomas Davis (Dublin) 1-7 Clara (Offaly) 1-5
ALL-IRELAND QUARTER FINAL
Dr Crokes (Killarney) 3-9 Parnell's (London) 1-7
ALL-IRELAND SEMI-FINALS
Thomas Davis 2-9 Castleblaney Faughs 1-7
Dr Crokes 3-4 Corofin 1-5
ALL-IRELAND FINAL
Dr Crokes 1-11 Thomas Davis 0-13

1992/93
PROVINCIAL FINALS
Connacht:
Knockmore (Mayo) 4-4 Aughawillan (Leitrim) 0-7
Ulster:
Lavey (Derry) 0-10 Burrren (Down) 0-10
Lavey 0-11 Burren 1-5 (replay)
Munster:
O'Donovan Rossa (Cork) 2-13 St Senan's (Clare) 0-12
Leinster:
Éire Óg (Carlow) 2-5 Ballyroan (Laois) 1-7
ALL-IRELAND QUARTER FINAL
Lavey 0-12 Tír Conaill Gaels 1-7

ALL-IRELAND SEMI-FINALS
Éire Óg 2-5 Knockmore 0-9
O'Donovan Rossa 2-10 Lavey 0-4
ALL-IRELAND FINAL
O'Donovan Rossa 1-12 Éire Óg 3-6
O'Donovan Rossa 1-7 Eire Óg 0-8 (replay)

1993/94
PROVINCIAL FINALS
Connacht:
Castlebar Mitchels (Mayo) 1-9 Clann na Gael (Roscommon) 0-12
Castlebar Mitchels 1-7 Clann na nGael 0-9 (replay)
Ulster:
Errigal Chiarán (Tyrone) 3-7 Downpatrick (Down) 1-8
Munster:
Nemo Rangers (Cork) 1-17 Kilmurray-Ibrickane (Clare) 0-4
Leinster:
Éire Óg (Carlow) 3-7 Erin's Isle (Dublin) 0-11
ALL-IRELAND QUARTER FINAL
Castlebar Mitchels 0-11 Tír Conaill Gaels (London) 0-8
ALL-IRELAND SEMI-FINALS
Castlebar Mitchels 1-9 Éire Óg 1-9
Castlebar Mitchels 0-8 Éire Óg 0-7 (replay)
Nemo Rangers 1-13 Errigal Chiarán 0-11 (aet)
ALL-IRELAND FINAL
Nemo Rangers 3-11 Castlebar Mitchels 0-8

1994/95
PROVINCIAL FINALS
Connacht:
Tuam Stars (Galway) 2-9 Aughawillan (Leitrim) 1-8
Ulster:
Bellaghy (Derry) 0-11 Clontibret O'Neill's (Monaghan) 0-10
Munster:
Castlehaven (Cork) 2-14 CLonmel Commercials (Tipperary) 1-4
Leinster:
Kilmacud Crokes (Dublin) 0-12 Seneschalstown (Meath) 1-8
ALL-IRELAND QUARTER FINAL
Castlehaven 3-18 Oisín (Manchester) 0-3
ALL-IRELAND SEMI-FINALS
Kilmacud Crokes 1-11 Castlehaven 1-7
Bellaghy 0-13 Tuam Stars 1-6
ALL-IRELAND FINAL
Kilmacud Crokes 0-8 Bellaghy 0-5

1995/96
PROVINCIAL FINALS
Connacht:
Corofin (Galway) 2-11 St Mary's (Leitrim) 0-10
Ulster:
Mullaghbawn (Armagh) 1-11 Bailieboro (Cavan) 2-5
Munster:
Laune Rangers (Kerry) 3-19 Moyle Rovers (Tipperary) 2-4
Leinster:
Éire Óg (Carlow) 2-9 An Tochar (Wicklow) 0- 15
Éire Óg 0-15 An Tóchar 1-6 (replay)
ALL-IRELAND QUARTER FINAL
Mullaghbawn 0-11 Tara (London) 0-5
ALL-IRELAND SEMI-FINALS
Éire Óg 0-12 Mullaghbawn 0-6
Laune Rangers 0-8 Corofin 0-6
ALL-IRELAND FINAL
Laune Rangers 4-5 Éire Óg 0-11

1996/97
PROVINCIAL FINALS
Connacht:
Knockmore (Mayo) 1-5 Clann na nGael (Roscommon) 0-6
Ulster:
Crossmaglen Rangers (Armagh) 1-7 Bellaghy (Derry) 1-7
Crossmaglen Rangers 2-5 Bellaghy 0-8 (replay)
Munster:
Laune Rangers (Kerry) 0-13 Clonakilty (Cork) 0-10
Leinster:
Éire Óg (Carlow) 1-10 St Sylvester's (Dublin) 0-8
ALL-IRELAND QUARTER FINAL
Knockmore (Mayo) 1-11 Tír Conaill Gaels (London) 2-6
ALL-IRELAND SEMI-FINALS
Knockmore 3-14 Éire Óg 0-5
Crossmaglen Rangers 1-8 Laune Rangers 1-7
ALL-IRELAND FINAL
Crossmaglen Rangers 2-13 Knockmore 0-11

1997/98
PROVINCIAL FINALS
Connacht:
Corofin (Galway) 2-10 Allen Gaels (Leitrim) 0-11
Ulster:
Dungiven (Derry) 0-14 Errigal Chiarán (Tyrone) 1-8
Munster:
Castlehaven (Cork) 1-14 Fethard (Tipperary) 1-8
Leinster:
Erin's Isle (Dublin) 2-11 Clane (Kildare) 1-11
ALL-IRELAND QUARTER FINAL
Castlehaven 0-15 Tír Conaill Gaels (London) 0-8
ALL-IRELAND SEMI-FINALS
Corofin 0-11 Dungiven 0-9
Erin's Isle 2-12 Castlehaven 0-17
ALL-IRELAND FINAL
Corofin 0-15 Erin's Isle 0-10

1998/99
PROVINCIAL FINALS
Connacht:
Ballina Stephenites (Mayo) 1-10: Roscommon Gaels (Roscommon) 0-6
Ulster:
Crossmaglen Rangers (Armagh) 1-11 Bellaghy (Derry) 1-10
Munster:
Doonbeg (Clare) 1-8 Moyle Rovers (Tipperary) 2-5
Doonbeg 0-7 Moyle Rovers 0-4 (replay)
Leinster:
Éire Óg (Carlow) 1-6 Kilmacud Crokes (Dublin) 0-9
Éire Óg 0-7 Kilmacud Crokes 0-7 (replay)
Éire Óg 1-11 Kilmacud Crokes 0-11 (2nd replay)
ALL-IRELAND QUARTER FINAL
Crossmaglen Rangers 1-18 Tír Conaill Gaels (London) 0-8
ALL-IRELAND SEMI-FINALS
Crossmaglen Rangers 1-10 Éire Óg 1-5
Ballina Stephenites 0-8 Doonbeg 0-4
ALL-IRELAND FINAL
Crossmaglen Rangers 0-9 Ballina Stephenites 0-8

FOOTBALL

1999/00

PROVINCIAL FINALS
Connacht:
Crossmolina (Mayo) 0-9 Roscommon Gaels (Roscommon) 0-9
Crossmolina 1-7 Roscommon Gaels 0-5 (replay)
Ulster:
Crossmaglen Rangers (Armagh) 0-10 Enniskillen Gaels (Fermanagh) 0-9
Munster:
UCC 1-17 Doonbeg (Clare) 0-7
Leinster:
Na Fianna (Dublin) 1-11 Sarsfields (Kildare) 0-8
ALL-IRELAND QUARTER-FINAL
Crossmolina 8-15 Hugh O'Neill's (Yorkshire) 0-4
ALL-IRELAND SEMI-FINALS
Na Fianna 1-10 Crossmolina 2-3
Crossmaglen Rangers 2-16 UCC 3-6
ALL-IRELAND FINAL
Crossmaglen Rangers 1-14 Na Fianna 0-12

2000/01

PROVINCIAL FINALS
Connacht:
Crossmolina (Mayo) 1-10 Corofin (Galway) 0-5
Ulster:
Bellaghy (Derry) 1-10 Errigal Chiarán (Tyrone) 1-4
Munster:
Nemo Rangers (Cork) 0-11 Glenflesk (Kerry) 0-7
Leinster:
O'Hanrahan's (Carlow) 1-7 Na Fianna (Dublin) 1-5
ALL-IRELAND QUARTER-FINAL
Nemo Rangers 2-8 Tír Chonaill Gaels (London) 0-6
ALL-IRELAND SEMI-FINALS
Nemo Rangers 0-12 O'Hanrahan's 1-7
Crossmolina 1-8 Bellaghy 0-7
ALL-IRELAND FINAL
Crossmolina 0-16 Nemo Rangers 1-12

2001/02

PROVINCIAL FINALS
Connacht:
Charlestown (Mayo) 2-9 Annaghdown (Galway) 2-7
Ulster:
Ballinderry (Derry) 1-10 Mayobridge (Down) 1-7
Munster:
Nemo Rangers (Cork) 1-11 Fethard (Tipperary) 0-10
Leinster:
Rathnew (Wicklow) 0-9 Na Fianna (Dublin) 1-6
Rathnew 2-16 Na Fianna 1-10 (replay)
ALL-IRELAND QUARTER-FINAL
Ballinderry 2-14 Tír Chonaill Gaels (London) 0-6
ALL-IRELAND SEMI-FINALS
Ballinderry 1-9 Rathnew 0-7
Nemo Rangers 0-9 Charlestown 0-7
ALL-IRELAND FINAL
Ballinderry 2-10 Nemo Rangers 0-9

2002/03

PROVINCIAL FINALS
Connacht:
Crossmolina (Mayo) 1-11 Strokestown (Roscommon) 0-10
Ulster:
Errigal Chiarán (Tyrone) 0-8 Enniskillen Gaels (Fermanagh) 1-3
Munster:
Nemo Rangers (Cork) 4-15 Monaleen (Limerick) 0-6

Leinster:
Dunshaughlin (Meath) 0-13 Mattock Rangers (Louth) 0-7
ALL-IRELAND SEMI-FINALS
Crossmolina 3-10 Dunshaughlin 1-12
Nemo Rangers 1-12 Errigal Chiarán 0-11
ALL-IRELAND FINAL
Nemo Rangers 0-14 Crossmolina 1-9

2003/04

PROVINCIAL FINALS
Connacht:
Caltra (Galway) 1-6 Curry (Sligo) 0-6
Ulster:
Loup (Derry) 0-11 St Gall's (Antrim) 1-5
Munster:
An Ghaeltacht (Kerry) 1-8 St Senan's (Clare) 1-6
Leinster:
St Brigid's (Dublin) 3-11 Round Towers (Kildare) 1-10
ALL-IRELAND QUARTER-FINAL
An Ghaeltacht 3-12 Tara (London) 1-8
ALL-IRELAND SEMI-FINALS
An Ghaeltacht 1-9 St Brigid's 2-3
Caltra 2-9 Loup 0-9
ALL-IRELAND FINAL
Caltra 0-13 An Ghaeltacht 0-12

2004/05

PROVINCIAL FINALS
Connacht:
Ballina Stephenties (Mayo) 1-13 Killererin (Galway) 2-6
Ulster:
Crossmaglen Rangers (Armagh) 0-14 Mayobridge (Down) 0-9
Munster:
Kilmurry-Ibrickane (Clare) 0-9 Stradbally (Waterford) 0-9
Kilmurry-Ibrickane 0-9 Stradbally 0-8 (replay)
Leinster:
Portlaoise (Laois) 1-11 Skryne (Meath) 2-4
ALL-IRELAND QUARTER-FINAL
Crossmaglen Rangers 2-10 Kingdom Kerry Gaels (London) 1-9
ALL-IRELAND SEMI-FINALS
Ballina Stephenites 0-10 Kilmurry-Ibrickane 0-8
Portlaoise 0-8 Crossmaglen Rangers 0-7
ALL-IRELAND FINAL
Ballina Stephenites 1-12 Portlaoise 2-8

2005/06

PROVINCIAL FINALS
Connacht:
Salthill-Knocknacarra (Galway) 1-10 St Brigid's (Roscommon) 0-5
Ulster:
St Gall's (Antrim) 1-8 Bellaghy (Derry) 0-8
Munster:
Nemo Rangers (Cork) 2-12 St Senan's (Clare) 1-6
Leinster:
Kilmacud Crokes (Dublin) 0-10 Sarsfields (Kildare) 0-9
ALL-IRELAND QUARTER-FINAL
Salthill-Knocknacarra 0-9 Tír Chonaill Gaels (London) 0-5
ALL-IRELAND SEMI-FINALS
Salthill-Knocknacarra 1-9 Kilmacud Crokes 1-7
St Gall's 0-10 Nemo Rangers 1-6
ALL-IRELAND FINAL
Salthill-Knocknacarra 0-7 St Gall's 0-6

2006/07
PROVINCIAL FINALS
Connacht:
St Brigid's (Roscommon) 1-10 Corofin (Galway) 3-3
Ulster:
Crossmaglen Rangers (Armagh) 0-5 Ballinderry (Derry) 0-3
Munster:
Dr Crokes (Kerry) 2-5 The Nire (Waterford) 0-8
Leinster:
Moorefield (Kildare) 3-6 Rhode (Offaly) 0-8
ALL-IRELAND QUARTER-FINAL
Dr Crokes 2-12 St Brendan's (London) 0-5
ALL-IRELAND SEMI-FINALS
Crossmaglen Rangers 1-11 St Brigid's 0-11
Dr Crokes 1-9 Moorefield 0-12
Dr Crokes 2-9 Moorefield 0-8 (replay)
ALL-IRELAND FINAL
Crossmaglen Rangers 1-9 Dr Crokes 1-9
Crossmaglen Rangers 0-13 Dr Crokes 1-5 (replay)

2007/08
PROVINCIAL FINALS
Connacht:
Ballina Stephenites (Mayo) 2-8 St Brigid's (Roscommon) 0-12
Ulster:
Crossmaglen Rangers (Armagh) 1-9 St Gall's (Antrim) 1-6
Munster:
Nemo Rangers (Cork) 1-10 Ballinacourty (Waterford) 1-7
Leinster:
St Vincent's (Dublin) 2-8 Tyrrellspass (Westmeath) 0-7
ALL-IRELAND QUARTER-FINAL
Crossmaglen Rangers 0-10 Tír Chonaill Gaels (London) 0-6
ALL-IRELAND SEMI-FINALS
St Vincent's 2-9 Crossmaglen Rangers 0-11
Nemo Rangers 0-14 Ballina Stephenites 1-4
ALL-IRELAND FINAL
St Vincent's 1-11 Nemo Rangers 0-13

2008/09
PROVINCIAL FINALS
Connacht:
Corofin (Galway) 0-11 Eastern Harps (Sligo) 0- 6
Ulster:
Crossmaglen Rangers (Armagh) 1-10 Ballinderry (Derry) 1-10
Crossmaglen Rangers 0-12 Ballinderry 1-4 (replay)
Munster:
Dromcollogher-Broadford (Limerick) 0-6 Kilmurry-Ibrickane (Clare) 0-5
Leinster:
Kilmacud Crokes (Dublin) 2-7 Rhode (Offaly) 1-7
ALL-IRELAND QUARTER-FINAL
Corofin 2-7 Tír Chonaill Gaels (London) 0-6
ALL-IRELAND SEMI-FINALS
Kilmacud Crokes 2-11 Corofin 0-11
Crossmaglen Rangers 4-11 Dromcollogher-Broadford 0-6
ALL-IRELAND FINAL
Kilmacud Crokes 1-9 Crossmaglen Rangers 0-7

2009/10
PROVINCIAL FINALS
Connacht:
Corofin (Galway) 2-14 Charlestown (Mayo) 0-7
Ulster:
St Gall's (Antrim) 0-16 Loup (Derry) 0-5

Munster:
Kilmurry-Ibrickane (Clare) 0-7 Kerins O'Rahillys (Kerry) 0-6
Leinster:
Portlaoise (Laois) 1-9 Garrycastle (Westmeath) 1-5
ALL-IRELAND QUARTER-FINAL
Kilmurry-Ibrickane 1-4 Tír Chonaill Gaels (London) 0-3
ALL-IRELAND SEMI-FINALS
Kilmurry-Ibrickae 1-14 Portlaoise 0-8
St Gall's 1-15 Corofin 1-11
ALL-IRELAND FINAL
St Gall's 0-13 Kilmurry-Ibrickane 1-5

2010/11
PROVINCIAL FINALS
Connacht:
St Brigid's (Roscommon) 2-14 Killererin (Galway) 1-10
Ulster:
Crossmaglen Rangers (Armagh) 2-9 Naomh Conaill (Donegal) 0-10
Munster:
Nemo Rangers (Cork) 1-15 Dr Crokes (Kerry) 1-13
Leinster:
Kilmacud Crokes (Dublin) 0-15 Rhode (Offaly) 1-7
ALL-IRELAND QUARTER-FINAL
Crossmaglen Rangers 1-8 Neasden Gaels (London) 0-5
ALL-IRELAND SEMI-FINALS
St Brigid's 0-13 Nemo Rangers 1-8
Crossmaglen Rangers 2-11 Kilmacud Crokes 1-12
ALL-IRELAND FINAL
Crossmaglen Rangers 2-11 St Brigid's 1-11

2011/12
PROVINCIAL FINALS
Connacht:
St Brigid's (Roscommon) 0-11 Corofin (Galway) 0-10
Ulster:
Crossmaglen Rangers (Armagh) 2-11 Burren (Down) 0-10
Munster:
Dr Crokes (Kerry) 3-14 UCC (Cork) 2-10
Leinster:
Garrycastle (Westmeath) 1-8 St Brigid's (Dublin) 0-10
ALL-IRELAND QUARTER-FINAL
St Brigid's 1-12 Fulham Irish (London) 0-7
ALL-IRELAND SEMI-FINALS
Crossmaglen Rangers 3-8 Dr Crokes 2-8
Garrycastle 1-11 St Brigid's 1-9
ALL-IRELAND FINAL
Crossmaglen Rangers 0-15 Garrycastle 1-12
Crossmaglen Rangers 2-19 Garrycastle 1-7 (replay)

2012/13
PROVINCIAL FINALS
Connacht:
St Brigid's (Roscommon) 1-12 Ballaghaderreen (Mayo) 0-6
Ulster:
Crossmaglen Rangers (Armagh) 3-9 Kilcoo (Down) 1-9
Munster:
Dr Crokes (Kerry) 0-19 Castlehaven (Cork) 0-12
Leinster:
Ballymun Kickhams (Dublin) 0-11 Portlaoise (Laois) 0-8
ALL-IRELAND QUARTER-FINAL
Dr Crokes 3-12 Tír Chonaill Gaels (London) 0-6
ALL-IRELAND SEMI-FINALS
Ballymun Kickhams 1-10 Dr Crokes 0-9
St Brigid's 2-7 Crossmaglen Rangers 1-9
ALL-IRELAND FINAL
St Brigid's 2-11 Ballymun Kickhams 2-10

2013/14
PROVINCIAL FINALS
Connacht:
Castlebar Mitchels (Mayo) 3-13 St Brigid's (Roscommon) 2-12
Ulster:
Ballinderry (Derry) 1-13 Glenswilly (Donegal) 2-6
Munster:
Dr Crokes (Kerry) 0-13 Cratloe (Clare) 0-12
Leinster:
St Vincent's (Dublin) 3-12 Portlaoise (Laois) 3-9
ALL-IRELAND QUARTER-FINAL
Ballinderry 3-9 Kingdom Kerry Gaels (London) 2-7
ALL-IRELAND SEMI-FINALS
St Vincent's 2-14 Ballinderry 1-13
Castlebar Mitchels 3-13 Dr Crokes 1-11
ALL-IRELAND FINAL
St Vincent's 4-12 Castlebar Mitchels 2-11

2014/15
PROVINCIAL FINALS
Connacht:
Corofin (Galway) 2-13 Ballintubber (Mayo) 1-7
Ulster:
Slaughtneil (Derry) 1-10 Omagh (Tyrone) 1-9
Munster:
Austin Stacks (Kerry) 3-5 The Nire (Waterford) 2-4
Leinster:
St Vincent's (Dublin) 1-13 Rhode (Offaly) 0-6
ALL-IRELAND QUARTER-FINAL
Corofin 0-9 Tír Chonaill Gaels (London) 0-2
ALL-IRELAND SEMI-FINALS
Corofin 1-13 St Vincent's 1-9
Slaughtneil 1-14 Austin Stacks 2-10
ALL-IRELAND FINAL
Corofin 1-14 Slaughtneil 0-7

2015/16
PROVINCIAL FINALS
Connacht:
Castlebar Mitchels (Mayo) 2-10 Corofin (Galway) 0-11
Ulster:
Crossmaglen Rangers (Armagh) 2-17 Scotstown (Monaghan) 2-12
Munster:
Clonmel Commercials (Tipperary) 1-7 Nemo Rangers (Cork) 0-9
Leinster:
Ballyboden St Enda's (Dublin) 2-9 Portlaoise (Laois) 1-11
ALL-IRELAND QUARTER-FINAL
Clonmel Commercials 2-12 Tír Chonaill Gaels (London) 0-9
ALL-IRELAND SEMI-FINALS
Ballyboden St Enda's 0-15 Clonmel Commercials 0-10
Castlebar Mitchels 0-13 Crossmaglen Rangers 0-12
ALL-IRELAND FINAL
Ballyboden St Enda's 2-14 Castlebar Mitchels 0-7

2016/17
PROVINCIAL FINALS
Connacht:
Corofin (Galway) 2-13 St Brigid's (Roscommon) 0-5
Ulster:
Slaughtneil (Derry) 0-12 Kilcoo (Down) 0-9
Munster:
Dr. Crokes (Kerry) 3-15 The Nire (Waterford) 0-6
Leinster:
St Vincent's (Dublin) 1-16 Rhode (Offaly) 0-12

ALL-IRELAND QUARTER-FINAL
Slaughtneil 2-11 St Kiernan's (London) 0-5
ALL-IRELAND SEMI-FINALS
Dr. Crokes 2-11 Corofin 0-8
Slaughtneil 0-12 St Vincent's 0-10
ALL-IRELAND FINAL
Dr. Crokes 1-9 Slaughtneil 1-7

ALL-IRELAND CLUB FOOTBALL
FINAL TEAMS

1971

East Kerry
E.Fitzgerald, D.O'Sullivan, D.Crowley, J.Gleeson, G.Cullinane,
N.Power, J.O'Donoghue, P.Moynihan, P.Casey, P.O'Donoghue,
D.O'Keeffe, D.Healy, D.Coffey, M.Gleeson, D.Kavanagh. Sub:
T.Looney for P.Casey.

Bryansford
J.Boden, B.Cunningham, O.Burns, J.Neeson, D.McNamara,
P.Cunningham, S.Cunningham, B.Ward, P.Neeson, W.Kane,
M.Cunningham, K.Bailie, S.O'Hare, B.Neeson, E.Grant. Subs:
F.McGinn for D.McNamara, J.McGinn for K.Bailie.

1972

Bellaghy
P.McTaggart, T.Scullion, A.Mulholland, F.Cassidy, T.Diamond,
H.McGoldrick, C.Browne, L.Diamond, P.Doherty, F.Downey,
B.Cassidy, F.O'Loane, H Donnelly, T.Quinn, K.Cassidy.

U.C.C.
N.Murphy, J.Gleeson, M.Keane, J.Coughlan, J.O'Grady,
S.Looney, T.Looney, N.O'Sullivan, P.Lynch, B.Lynch, R.Bambury,
D.Murray, D.Coffey, D.Kavanagh, N.Brosnan. Sub: S.Murphy for
N.Brosnan.

1973

Nemo Rangers
B.Morgan, J.Corcoran, E.Brophy, B.Murphy, R.Twomey, F.Cogan,
D.O'Driscoll, D.Barrett, M.O'Donoghue, K.Collins, S.Coughlan,
B.Cogan, L.Good, J.Barrett, C.Murphy.(Note: D.Cogan played in
drawn game.)

St Vincent's
T.O'Byrne, L.Ferguson, G.O'Driscoll, M.Hannick, M.Behan,
D.Billings, E.Brady, P.Hallinan, P.J.Reid, B.Doyle, T.Hanahoe,
B.Mullins, C.Keaney, D.Foley, J.Keaveney.(Note: G.Keavey,
S.Mullins played in drawn game.) Subs: L.Foley, D.Redmond
drawn game.L.Foley, D.Redmond, S.Mullins replay.

1974

U.C.D.
I.Heffernan, M.Judge, G.O'Reilly, P.Gilroy, F.O'Donoghue,
E.O'Donoghue, P.Kerr, K.Kilmurray, B.Gaughran, E.Condron,
O.Leddy, J.Walsh, J.P.Keane, D.O'Connor, P.Duggan.
(Note: J.Waldron, P.J.O'Halloran, J.O'Keeffe played in drawn game.
Sub: D.O'Connor in drawn match.)

Clann na Gael
P.Scullion, K.France, J.O'Hagan, T.Moore, O.Crewe, J.Greene,
S.Lavelle, S.O'Hagan, C.McKinstry, M.O'Neill, J.Smyth,
T.McCaughey, G.Hamill, N.O.Hagan, P.McGuinness. Subs:
J.McKenna and J.Moore in replay.(Note: J.McKenna and J.Byrne
played in drawn game.)

1975

U.C.D.
I.Heffernan, M.Judge, G.O'Reilly, C.Moynihan, P.J.O'Halloran,
E.O'Donoghue, F.O'Donoghue, M.Carty, P.O'Neill, B.Dunleavy,
J.P.Keane, J.Walsh, B.Walsh, P.Duggan, B.Heneghan. Sub:
E.Condron.

Nemo Rangers
W.Morgan, J.Corcoran, E.Brophy, D.O'Sullivan, D.Cogan,
B.Murphy, D.O'Driscoll, K.Collins, K.Murphy, L.Goode, S.Coughlan,
S.Leydon, N.Morgan, J.Barrett, C.Murphy. Subs: Declan Murphy,
M.O'Donoghue.

1976

St Vincent's
N.Bernard, D.Billings, G.O'Driscoll, M.Hennrick, M.Behan,
V.Lambe, B.Pocock, B.Mullins, F.Ryder, B.Reddy, T.Hanahoe,
M.Whelan, L.Deegan, J.Keaveney, B.Doyle. Sub: P.Reid for
M.Hennrick.

Roscommon Gaels
T.O'Connor, P.Kelly, P.Dolan, S.Hunt, M.Menton, M.McNeela, A.de
Paoli, J.O'Gara, J.Donlon, J.Martin, M.McNamara, H.Griffin, F.Daly,
L.O'Gara, P.Shaughnessy. Sub: M.Moloney for F.Daly.

1977

Austin Stacks
T.Brick, G.Scollard, N.Power, P.Lucey, F.Lawlor, A.O'Keeffe,
G.Power, G.O'Keeffe, J.O'Keeffe, F.Ryan, D.Long, T.Sheehan,
J.Power, P.McCarthy, M.Sheehy. Sub: C.Mangan.

Ballerin
S.Deighan, E.Moloney, S.McGahan, G.Forrest, V.Moloney,
P.Stevenson, B.O'Kane, M.McAfee, J.Scullion, G.O'Connell,
G.Keane, J.McAfee, C.Faulkner, S.O'Connell, P.M.Deighan.

1978

Thomond College
L.Murphy, M.Heuston, S.O'Shea, E.Mahon, M.Spillane,
B.McSweeney, M.Connolly, T.Harkin, B.Talty, J.Dunne, R.Bell,
D.Smyth, M.Kilcoyne, P.Spillane, J.O'Connell. Sub: D.O'Boyle for
M.Connolly.

St John's
P.McCann, D.McNeill, K.McFerran, G.McCann, J.Rainey,
J.McGuinness, J.Donnelly, L.Jennings, P.McGinnitty, K.Gough,
H.McRory, A.McCallin, M.Darragh, S.McFerran, P.McFaul. Subs:
J.McGranaghan, J.Cunningham.

1979

Nemo Rangers
W.Morgan, F.Cogan, F.Stone, K.Murphy, J.Kerrigan, B.Murphy,
D.O'Driscoll, K.Brady, D.Linehan, J.Barrett, D.Allen, T.Dalton,
N.Morgan, K.Collins, C.Murphy. Sub: D.Murphy for C.Murphy.

Scottstown
E.Keenan, M.McCarville, G.McCarville, F.Caulfield, D.Stirratt,
S.McCarville, J.Treanor, B.Lillis, S.McCrudden, B.Morgan,
Seamus McCarville, C.Morgan, J.McCabe, J.Moyna, B.Rice. Sub:
R.McDermott for B.Rice.

1980

St.Finbarr's
B.O'Brien, D.O'Grady, E.Desmond, N.Aherne, D.Brosnan, M.Lynch,
M.Carey, C.Ryan, D.Philpott, F.Twomey, R.Kenny, F.O'Mahony,
J.Barry Murphy, J.Allen, J.O'Callaghan. Sub: D.Barry for D.Philpott.

St Grellan's
W.Devlin, N.Jennings, J.Kelly, J.Boswell, P.Cunningham,
E.Flanagan, K.Mitchell, B.Brennan, P.McGettigan, M.Cunningham,
J.Manton, G.Gibbons, J.Whelan, C.Loftus, S.Riddell. Subs: P.Ryan,
L.White.

1981

St.Finbarr's
B.O'Brien, J.Cremin, M.Healy,
E.Desmond, M.Carey, C.Ryan, D.O'Grady, T.Holland, M.Lynch,
D.Barry, R.Kenny, F.O'Mahony, J.Barry Murphy, J.Allen,
J.O'Callaghan. Sub: J.Barry for T.Holland.

Walterstown
S.Reilly, P.Smith, W.Clarke, M.Sheils, E.Ward, C.Bowens, G.Reynolds, C Reynolds, N.O'Sullivan, E.O'Brien, E.Barry, G.McLaughlin, G.Cooney, O.O'Brien, F.O'Sullivan. Subs: M.Barry for P.Smith, T.Clarke for G.McLaughlin.

1982
Nemo Rangers
D.Bevan, F.Cogan, B.Murphy, A.Keane, D.O'Driscoll, T.Hennebry, J.Kerrigan, M.Niblock, T.Dalton, S.Coughlan, D.Allen, S.Hayes, C.Murphy, E.Fitzgerald, M.Dorgan. Subs: Charlie Murphy for D.Allen, K.Murphy for D.O'Driscoll, D.Linehan for S.Hayes.
Garrymore
M.J.Connolly, P.Nally, D.Conway, J.Nally, P.Flannery, D.Mellett, G.Farragher, J.Monaghan, P.Mohan, T.Walsh, P.Dixon, D.Dolan, T.Connolly, L.Dolan, B.Fitzpatrick. Subs: P.Monaghan for D.Conway, M.Walsh for P.Nally.

1983
Portlaoise
M.Mulhall, J.Bohane, J.Bergin, M.Kavanagh, C.Browne, M.Lillis, B.Conroy, E.Whelan, M.Dooley, N.Prendergast, L.Scully, P.Critchley, T.Prendergast, J.Keenan, G.Browne. Subs: W.Bohane for J.Keenan, J.Keenan for W.Bohane.
Clan na nGael
J.O'Neill, W.Harney, L.O'Neill, C.Deignan, G.Petitt, M.Keegan, J.McManus, E.McManus, F.Nicholson, E.McManus (Jnr), M.McManus, O.McManus, P.J.Glynn, T.McManus, D.Shine. Subs: L.Dunne for G.Petitt, V.Harney for P.J.Glynn.

1984
Nemo Rangers
D.Bevan, A.Keane, B.Murphy, K.Murphy, J.Kerrigan, M.Lynch, T.Nation, M.Niblock, T.Dalton, S.Coughlan, S.Hayes, C.Murphy, E.Fitzgerald, D.Allen, M.Dorgan. Sub: Charlie Murphy for S.Hayes.
Walterstown
C.Bowen, G.McLaughlin, W.Clarke, P.Smith, P.Carr, E.O'Brien, G.Reynolds, C.Reynolds, N.O'Sullivan, J.Barry, E.Barry, M.Barry, F.O'Sullivan, O.O'Brien, G.Cooney. Subs: O.Clynch for M.Barry, K.McLoughlin for O.Clynch.

1985
Castleisland Desmonds
C.Nelligan, D.Ciarubhain, B.Lyons, W.King, D.Lyons, M.J Kearney, P.Callaghan, M.O'Connor, D.Hannafin, W.O'Connor, C.Kearney, D.Lyne, J O'Connor, D.Buckley, P.Horan. Subs: M.Downey for J.O'Connor, J.Lyons for D.Lyne.
St.Vincent's
N.Bernard, T.Diamond, V.Conroy, S.Wade, R.Hazley, S.Fleming, A.Devlin, P.Canavan, B.Mullins, T.Conroy, B.Jordan, S.McDermott, C.Buffini, M.Loftus, P.McLoughlin. Sub: E.Heery for C.Buffini.

1986
Burren
D.Murdock, B.McKernan, A.Murdock, M.Murdock, K, McConville, W.McMahon, B.McGovern, T.McGovern, P.O'Rourke, L.Fitzpatrick, J.Treanor, P.McKay, J.McGreevy, V.McGovern, T.McArdle. Sub: C.Doyle for J.McGreevy.
Castleisland Desmonds
C.Nelligan, D.Ó Ciarubhain, B.Lyons, W.King, J.O'Connor, M.J.Kearney, P.O'Callaghan, M.O'Connor, D.Hannafin, W.O'Connor, C.Kearney, D.Lyne, P.Horan, D.Buckley, J.Lordan. Sub: M.Downey for P.Horan.

1987
St Finbarr's
J.Kerins, J.Cremin, J.Meyler, E.Desmond, M.Carey, K.Scanlon, B.O'Connell, P.Hayes, T.Leahy, K McCarthy, C.Ryan, M.Slocum, T.Power, D.O'Mahony, J Allen. Sub: M.Barry for T.Power.
Clan na nGael
T.Seery, J.Dowling, M.Keegan, J McManus, O.McManus, F.Nicholson, A.McManus, P McManus, E.McManus (Snr), K.Pettit, P.Naughton, E McManus (Jnr), T.Lennon, T.McManus, E.Durney. Subs: H.Moody for P.Naughton, J.Connaughton for M.Petitt.

1988
Burren
D.Murdock, B.McKernan, A.Murdock, M.Murdock, K.McConville, L.Fitzpatrick, B.McGovern, B.Laverty, T.McGovern, T.McArdle, J.Traenor, P.McKay, R.Fitzpatrick, V.McGovern, T.Fegan. Sub: P.Fegan for B.Laverty.
Clan na nGael
T.Seery, J.Dowling, M.Keegan, V.Harney, O.McManus, F.Nicholson, A.McManus, P.McManus, J McManus, J.Connaughton, G.Lennon, E.McManus (Jnr), P.Naughton, T.Lennon, J.McManus. Subs: E.McManus (Snr) for G.Lennon, E.Durney for P.Naughton.

1989
Nemo Rangers
J.O'Mahoney, A.Keane, N.Creedon, M.Lynch, J.Kerrigan, T.Griffin, D.Creedon, D.O'Sullivan, T.Dalton, S.O'Brien, E.O'Mahoney, T.Nation, S.Calnan, D.Allen, M.Dargan. Subs: P.O'Donovan for Dalton, S.Hayes for Calnan.
Clan na nGael
P.Naughton, J.Dowling, J.McManus, D.Rock.O.McManus, J.Lennon, A.McManus, P.McManus, G.Lennon, J.Connaughton, E.McManus (Snr), E.McManus (Jnr), P.Naughton, T.McManus, E.Durney. Subs: L.Dunne for E.Durney, M.Keegan for J.Lennon.

1990
Baltinglass
D.Leigh, S.O'Brien, H.Kenny, T.Donohue, H.Fitzpatrick, P.Murphy, B.Kilcoyne, R.Danne, B.Kenny, P.Kenny, R.McHugh, L.Horgan, C.Murphy, K.O'Brien, T.Murphy. Sub: B.Timmons for P.Kenny.
Clan na nGael
Paul Naughton, D.Rock, M.Keegan, F.Nicholson, J.Connaughton, J.McManus, A.McManus, P.McManus, Eamonn McManus, Eoin McManus, Eamonn McManus (Jnr), E.Durney, Pauric Naughton, T.Lennon, T.McManus. Subs: D.Kenny for Pauric Naughton, D.Nolan for Durney.

1991
Lavey
B.Regan, D.Doherty, A.Scullion, B.Scullion, J.McGurk, H.Downey, Ciaran McGurk, D.O'Boyle, J.Chivers, F.Rafferty, B.McCormack, H.M.McGurk, D.Mulholland, S.Downey, Colm McGurk. Sub: A.McGurk for Colm McGurk.
Salthill
C.McGinley, J.Kilraine, E.O'Donnellan, G.O'Farrell, F.Mitchell, E.O'Donoghue, M.Tarpey, A.Mulholland, M.Gibbs, P.J.Kelly, M.Butler, J.McDonagh, N.Costelloe, P.Comer, N.Finnegan, Subs: C.McGauran for Kelly, M.Ruane for McDonagh.

1992

Dr.Croke's
P.O'Brien, D.Keogh, L.Hartnett, S.Clarke, J.Clifford, J.Galvin,
C.O'Shea, C.Murphy, N.O'Leary, C.Doherty, D.Cooper, S.O'Shea,
P.O'Shea, V.Casey, G.O'Shea.

Thomas Davis
F.Troy, D.Nugent, J.J.Martin, E.O'Toole; J.Fadian, P.Curran,
G.Kilmartin, D.Foran, P.Godson, P.Waldron, P.Nugent, S.Grealis,
P.Joyce, L.Adamson, V.Corney. Subs: K.O'Donovon for O'Toole,
P.Dwane for Joyce.

1993

O'Donovan Rossa
K.O'Dwyer, J.Evans, J.O'Donovan, F.McCarthy, G.O'Driscoll,
A.Davis, I.Breen, D.O'Driscoll, B.O'Donovan, B.Carmody,
J.O'Driscoll, D.Davis, N.Murphy, M.McCarthy, P.Davis. Sub:
M.McCarthy for G.O'Driscoll.*(In drawn game, sub.: D.Whooley for
Murphy).*

Éire Óg
J.Kearns, J.Wynne, R.Moore, J.Dooley, B.Hayden, A.Callinan,
N.Fallon, G.Ware, H.Brennan, J.Hayden, J.Morrissey, T.Nolan,
J.Murphy, C.Hayden, A.Keating. Sub: D.Moore for Nolan.*(In drawn
game, D.Wynne at full-back, D.Walker centre half-back.)*

1994

Nemo Rangers
D.Bevan; J.Kerrigan, N.Creedon, P.Dorgan; K.Cowhie, T.Griffin,
T.Nation; S.Fahy, S.O'Brien; J.Kavanagh, T.Dalton, S.Calnan;
P.Lambert, C.Corkery, E.Fitzgerald. Subs: L.Kavanagh for Dorgan,
A.Quinlivan for Nation, N.Corkery for Fitzgerald.

Castlebar Mitchels
J.Cuddy; W.Flynn, J.McCabe, A.Waldron; D.Shaw, J.Maughan,
D.Noone; R.Ruane, P.Holmes; S.Murphy, T.Reilly, P.Jordan;
B.Kilkelly, D.Byrne, K.Lydon. Subs: F.Joyce for Jordan, M.Feeney for
Ruane, H.Gavin for Kilkelly.

1995

Kilmacud Crokes
M.Pender; R.Ward, C.Cleary, R.Leahy; J.O'Callaghan, J.Sweeney,
P.Burke; M.Dillon, Mick Leahy; P.Dalton, S.Morris, P.Ward;
N.Clancy, Maurice Leahy, P.O'Donoghue. Sub: T.Gunning for
Maurice Leahy.

Bellaghy
M.Kearns; S.Birt, P.Downey, P.Diamond; D.Brown, K.Diamond,
G.McPeake; D.Quinn, J.Mulholland; L.McPeake, B.Lee, G.Doherty;
J.Donnelly, D.Cassidy, E.Cassidy. Subs: C.Scullion for Donnelly,
M.Diamond for E.Cassidy.

1996

Laune Rangers
P.Lyons; A.Hassett, P.Sheahan, M.O'Connor; M.Hassett, T.Byrne,
S.O'Sullivan; T.Fleming, P.Prendiville; G.Murphy, C.Kearney,
J.Shannon; P.Griffin, L.Hassett, B.O'Shea. Subs: B.O'Sullivan for
Griffin, J.O'Shea for Prendiville.

Éire Óg
J.Kearns; J.Wynne, D.Wynne, J.Murphy; B.Hayden, D.Moore,
A.Callinan; J.Morrissey, H.Brennan; J.Hayden, G.Ware, W.Quinlan;
P.McCarthy, C.Hayden, A.Keating. Subs: J.Owens for Morrissey,
K.Haughney for McCarthy.

1997

Crossmaglen Rangers
Jarlath McConville; M.Califf, D.Murtagh, P.McKeown; J.Fitzpatrick,
F.Bellew, G.McShane; J.McEntee, A.Cunningham; C.Short,
A.McEntee, O.McConville; Jim McConville, G.Cumiskey, C.O'Neill.
Sub: M.Moley for J.McEntee.

Knockmore
P.Reape; F.Sweeney, C.Naughton, T.Bourke; G.O'Hora, P.Butler,
J.Davis; K.Staunton, D.Dempsey; P.Cawley, D.Sweeney, S.Sweeney;
K.O'Neill, R.Dempsey, P.Brogan. Subs: T.Holmes for Dempsey,
H.Langan for O'Hora.

1998

Corofin
M.McNamara; O.Burke, J.Killeen, J.Lardner; A.Fahy, R.Silke,
T.Greaney; G.Burke, A.Donnellan; S.Conlisk, M.Donnellan,
T.Burke; M.Kenny, E.Steede, D.Reilly. Subs: K.Newell for Killeen,
K.Comer for Kenny, K.Treacy for Steede.

Erin's Isle
T.Quinn; K.Murray, K.Spratt, M.Naughton; D.Collins, M.Deegan,
G.O'Connell; K.Barr, J.Barr; E.Barr, P.Cunningham, T.Gorman;
C.O'Hare, R.Boyle, N.Crossan. Subs: S.McCormack for Gorman,
F.Brown for O'Connell.

1999

Crossmaglen Rangers
P.Hearty, M.Califf, D.Murtagh, C.Dooley, F.Shields, F.Bellew,
J.Fitzpatrick, J.McEntee, A.Cunningham, C.Short, T.McEntee,
O.McConville, J.McConville, G.Cummiskey, C.O'Neill. Subs:
G.McShea for M.Califf, M.Moley for C.O'Neill.

Ballina Stephenites
J.Healy, K.Golden, J.Devenney, D.Leydon, B.Ruane, B.Heffernan,
S.Sweeney, L.McHale, D.Brady, B.McStay, D.Coen, M.McGrath,
G.Brady, P.McGarry, K.Lynn. Subs: L.Brady for D.Coen, C.Deacy for
M.McGrath, P.McStay for B.McStay.

2000

Crossmaglen Rangers
P.Hearty, M.Califf, D.Murtagh, G.McShane, J.Fitzpatrick, F.Bellew,
J.Donaldson, J.McEntee, A.Cunningham, C.Shortt, T.McEntee,
O.McConville, J.McConville, G.Cumiskey, C.O'Neill. Sub – M.Moley
for J.McConville.

Na Fianna
S.Gray, S.McGlinchey, B.Quinn, M.Foley, S.Connell, T.Lynch,
P.McCarthy, S.Forde, K.McGeeney, M.Galvin, D.Farrell, K.Donnelly,
D.Mackin, J.Sherlock, A.Shearer. Subs – D.Keegan for Forde,
I.Foley for Shearer, N.O'Murchu for Foley.

2001

Crossmolina
B.Heffernan, S.Rochford, T.Nallen, C.Reilly, P.Gardiner,
D.Mulligan, P.McAndrew, J.Nallen, M.Moyles, J.Keane,
K.McDonald, E.Lavelle, P.McGuinness, L.Moffatt, J.Leonard. Subs
– G.O'Malley for Leonard, T.Loftus for Keane.

Nemo Rangers
D.Heaphy, L.Kavanagh, N.Geary, I.Gibbons, K.Connolly, S.O'Brien,
M.Cronin, D.Kavanagh, K.Cahill, S.O'Brien, L.O'Sullivan,
D.Niblock, J.Kavanagh, C.Corkery, A.Cronin. Subs – J.P.O'Neill for
Niblock, M.McCarthy for Cahill, A.Morgan for O'Sullivan.

2002

Ballinderry
M.Conlan, K.McGuckin, N.McCusker, J.Bell, P.Wilson, R.McGuckin, D.Crozier, S.Donnelly, B.McCusker, A.McGuckin, C.Gilligan, D.Conway, D.Bateson, E.Muldoon, G.Cassidy. Sub – M.Harney for B.McCusker.

Nemo Rangers
D.Heaphy, L.Kavanagh, Steven O'Brien, Sean O'Brien, G.Murphy, N.Geary, M.Cronin, K.Cahill, D.Kavanagh, D.Meighan, J.P.O'Neill, M.McCarthy, J.Kavanagh, C.Corkery, A.Cronin. Subs – S.Calnan for Meighan, L.O'Sullivan for O'Neill.

2003

Nemo Rangers
D.Heaphy, L.Kavanagh, N.Geary, Sean O'Brien, G.Murphy, M.Cronin, M.Daly, K.Cahill, D.Kavanagh, A.Cronin, Steven O'Brien, M.McCarthy, J.Kavanagh, C.Corkery, W.Morgan. Subs – P.Brophy for Geary, B.O'Regan for Cronin, D.Mehigan for D.Kavanagh, J.P.O'Neill for Steven O'Brien.

Crossmolina
B.Heffernan, S.Rochford, T.Nallen, C.Reilly, P.Gardiner, D.Mulligan, G.O'Malley, G.Walsh, J.Nallen, M.Moyles, C.McDonald, E.Lavelle, L.Moffatt, J.Keane, P.McGuinness. Subs – J.Leonard for Lavelle, P.McAndrew for O'Malley.

2004

Caltra
K.Kilroy, J.Murray, E.Meehan, B.Kilroy, D.Meehan, K.Gavin, O.Kelly, T.Meehan, D.Cunniffe, J.Galvin, B.Laffey, M.Killilea, M.Meehan, N.Meehan, S.Hogan. Subs – C.Kilroy for Laffey, O.Hennelly for Hogan.

An Ghaeltacht
P.Ó hEalaithe, D.MacGearailt, S.MacSithigh, M.Ó Sé, R.Ó Flatharta, T.Ó Sé, B.Breathnach, D.Ó Sé, P.Ó Cuinn, C.Ó Dubhda, R. MacGearailt, T.Conchúir, C.Ó Cruadhlaoich, D.Ó Cinnéide, A.MacGearailt. Subs – M.MacGearailt for Ó Cruadhlaoich, F.Ó Sé for MacSithigh.

2005

Ballina
J.Healy, J.Devenney, M.Wynne, C.Leonard, B.Ruane, S.Sweeney, S.Melia, R.McGarrity, D.Brady, P.Harte, G.Brady, E.Casey, P.McGarry, L.Brady, S.Hughes. Subs – P.McHale for Melia, E.Devenney for McGarry, A.Tighe for Leonard.

Portlaoise
M.Nolan, T.Fitzgerald, C.Byrne, E.Bland, B.Mulligan, C.Healy, A.Fennelly, M.Delaney, K.Fitzpatrick, B.McCormack, I.Fitzgerald, C.Rogers, P.McNulty, C.Parkinson, B.Fitzgerald. Sub – M.Fennelly for Delaney.

2006

Salthill-Knocknacarra
C.McGinley, R.McTiernan, F.Hanley, C.Begley, M.O'Connell, G.Morley, B.Geraghty, M.Sheridan, B.Dooney, A.Kerins, M.Donnellan, S.Rabbitte, S.Crowe, J.Boylan, S.Armstrong. Subs – A.Callanan for Boylan, D.Burke for Kerins, P.J.Kelly for Callanan, F.McCann for Crowe, A.McDermott for Geraghty.

St.Gall's
R.Gallagher, S.Kennedy, Kieran McGourty, C.Brady, A.Healey, G.McGirr, S.Kelly, M.McCrory, C.McCrossan, P.Gribbin, S.Burns, A.Gallagher, K.Stewart, Kevin McGourty, K.Niblock. Subs – A.McLean for McCrossan, T.O'Neill for Stewart, C.McGourty for Kieran McGourty.

2007

Crossmaglen Rangers
P.Hearty, S.McNamee, F.Bellew, P.Kernan, A.Kernan, J.Donaldson, B.McKeown, D.McKenna, T.McEntee, M.Ahern, J.McEntee, J.Murtagh, M.McNamee, J.Hanratty, O.McConville. Subs – S.Kernan for M.McNamee, S.Clarke for J.McEntee, C.Short for Ahern, A.Finnegan for S.McNamee.

Dr. Crokes
K.Cremin, K.McMahon, L.Quinn, M.Moloney, B.Moriarty, B.McMahon, E.Cavanagh, A.O'Donovan, E.Brosnan, B.Looney, S.Doolan, J.Fleming, C.Cooper, D.Moloney, K.O'Leary. Subs – J.Cahillane for B.McMahon, B.McMahon for Doolan, K.Brosnan for Looney. *In the drawn encounter for Crossmaglen S.Clarke started for P.Kernan. Dr.Crokes started with the same fifteen. *Subs in the drawn game were – Crossmaglen; S.Kernan for Aherne, P.Kernan for Clarke, C.Short for Hanratty, T.Kernan for McNamee. Dr.Crokes; J.Cahillane for McMahon, K.Brosnan for E.Brosnan V.Cooper for Doolan.*

2008

St Vincent's
M.Savage, P.Conlon, E.Brady, H.Gill, T.Doyle, G.Brennan, P.Kelly, H.Coughlan, M.O'Shea, K.Golden, T.Diamond, D.Connolly, B.Maloney, P.Gilroy, T.Quinn. Subs – R.Traynor for Gilroy, C.Brady for Coughlan, R.Fallon for Gill, W.Lowry for O'Shea.

Nemo Rangers
B.Morgan, N.Geary, D.Kavanagh, D.Breen, G.O'Shea, M.Cronin, B.O'Regan, P.Morgan, M.McCarthy, R.Kenny, D.Meighan, A.Cronin, D.Kearney, J.Masters, P.Kerrigan. Subs – S.O'Brien for Kenny, C.O'Brien for O'Shea, D.Niblock for P.Morgan, B.O'Driscoll for A.Cronin.

2009

Kilmacud Crokes
D.Nestor, Ross O'Carroll, Rory O'Carroll, K.Nolan, B.McGrath, P.Griffin, C.O'Sullivan, D.Magee, N.Corkery, L.Og O'hEineachainn, B.Kavanagh, A.Morrisey, M.Vaughan, M.Davoren, P.Burke. Subs – J.Magee for O'hEineachainn, R.Cosgrove for Kavanagh.

Crossmaglen Rangers
P.Hearty, B.McKeown, P.Kernan, P.McKeown, A.Kernan, F.Bellew, J.Donaldson, T.McEntee, D.McKenna, M.McEntee, J.McEntee, T.Kernan, J.Clarke, J.Murtagh, O.McConville. Subs – S.Kernan for M.McEntee, K.Carragher for Murtagh, S.Finnegan for B.McKeown, R.O'Kelly for Donaldson, C.Short for J.McEntee.

2010

St Gall's
Ronan Gallagher, P.Veronica, A.McClean, C.Brady, S.Kelly, A.Healy, M.Kelly, S.Burke, A.Gallagher, T.O'Neill, Kieran McGourty, Kevin McGourty, C.McGourty, K.Niblock, Rory Gallagher. Subs – K.Stewart for O'Neill, S.Burns for Burke, S.Kennedy for Veronica.

Kilmurry-Ibrickane
D.O'Brien, D.Hickey, M.Killeen, M.McMahon, S.Hickey, E.Coughlan, D.Callinan, P.O'Connor, P.O'Dwyer, I.McInerney, M.Hogan, S.Moloney, M.O'Dwyer, J.Daly, N.Downes. Subs – E.Talty for Hogan, O.O'Dwyer for Talty, M.McCarthy for O'Connor, B.Moloney for Killeen, P.O'Dwyer for Downes.

2011

Crossmaglen Rangers
P.Hearty, P.McKeown, P.Kernan, J.Morgan, A.Kernan, D.O'Callaghan, S.Finnegan, J.Hanratty, D.McKenna, T.Kernan, A.Cunningham, F.Hanratty, J.Clarke, S.Kernan, O.McConville. Subs – J.McEntee for F.Hanratty, M.McNamee for Cunningham, M.Aherne for T.Kernan, K.Carragher for Finnegan, F.Bellew for S.Kernan.

St Brigid's
P.Martin, R.Kelly, D.Donnelly, D.Sheedy, I.Kilbride, P.Domican, G.Cunniffe, G.Dolan, K.Mannion, E.Sheedy, D.Dolan, Cathal McHugh, Conor McHugh, S.Kilbride, F.Dolan. Subs – J.Tiernan for Cathal McHugh, D.Kelleher for Conor McHugh, D.O'Connor for Tiernan.

2012

Crossmaglen Rangers
P.Hearty, J.Morgan, P.Kernan, P.McKeown, A.Kernan, D.O'Callaghan, S.Finnegan, J.Hanratty, D.McKenna, T.Kernan, S.Kernan, A.Cunningham, J.Clarke, F.Hanratty, O.McConville. Subs – M.McNamee for F.Hanratty, M.Aherne for T.Kernan, K.Carragher for Cunningham, G.Carragher for P.Kernan, K.Brennan for McConville.

Garrycastle
C.Mullin, M.McCallon, J.Gaffey, T.McHugh, K.Henson, D.Harte, E.Mulvihill, S.O'Donoghue, D.O'Shaughnessy, P.Dillon, D.Dolan, J.Dolan, G.Dolan, P.Mulvihill, J.Duignan. Subs – A.Fox for McHugh, A.Browne for Duignan, C.Cosgrove for Henson, J.O'Shaughnessy for E.Mulvihill.

(Note: In the drawn encounter Crossmaglen started B.McKeown, M.McNamee, K.Brennan instead of S.Finnegan, T.Kernan and F.Hanratty. Garrycastle started with the same 15. Subs in the drawn game were: Crossmaglen – S.Finnegan for B.McKeown, K.Carragher for Brennan, M.Ahern for McNamee. Garrycastle – R.McGowan for Duignan, A.Browne for G.Dolan, A.Fox for Henson, A.Daly for Dillon)

2013

St Brigid's
S.Curran, J.Murray, D.Donnelly, G.Cunniffe, N.Grehan, P.Domican, R.Stack, K.Mannion, I.Kilbride, D.Kelleher, F.Dolan, D.Dolan, Cathal McHugh, S.Kilbride, R.Blaine. Subs – G.Dolan for Kelleher, E.Sheehy for McHugh, Conor McHugh for Blaine, Kelleher for D.Dolan.

Ballymun Kickhams
S.Currie, E.Daly, S.George, E.Dolan, A.Hubbard, K.Connolly, J.Burke, J.McCarthy, Davy Byrne, E.Reilly, K.Leahy, J.Whelan, T.Furman, P.McMahon, D.Rock. Subs – Derek Byrne for Leahy, C.Weir for George, J.Small for Reilly.

2014

St Vincent's
M.Savage, K.Bonnie, J.Curley, H.Gill, B.Egan, G.Brennan, M.Concarr, D.Murphy, E.Fennell, G.Burke, D.Connolly, S.Carthy, R.Trainor, C.Dorney, T.Quinn. Subs – T.Diamond for Burke, C.Diamond for Fennell, K.Golden for Trainor, A.Baxter for Dorney, N.Mullins for Carthy.

Castlebar Mitchels
C.Naughton, T.Cunniffe, A.Feeney, R.O'Malley, P.Durcan, E.O'Reilly, D.Newcombe, D.Kirby, A.Walsh, N.Douglas, R.Feeney, G.McDonagh, N.Lydon, B.Moran, T.King. Subs – F.Durcan for R.Feeney, J.Durcan, for Douglas, D.Joyce for O'Malley, S.Hopkins for McDonagh, K.Filan for F.Durcan.

2015

Corofin
T.Healy, C.McGrath, K.Fitzgerald, C.Silke, G.Higgins, L.Silke, A.Burke, D.Burke, R.Steede, G.Sice, Michael Farragher, G.Delaney, I.Burke, M.Lundy, Martin Farragher. Subs: D.Wall for Martin Farragher, J.Burke for Steede, M.Comer for C.Silke, C.Cunningham for Higgins, K.Murphy for Delaney, J.Canney for I.Burke.

Slaughtneil
A.McMullan, K.McKaigue, B.Rodgers, Francis McEldowney, C.McKaigue, B.McGuigan, C.Cassidy, Patsy Bradley, P.McGuigan, P.Kelly, C.Bradley, R.Bradley, G.Bradley, Paul Bradley, C.O'Doherty. Subs: P.McNeill for C.Cassidy, S.McGuigan for R.Bradley, P.Cassidy for P.Kelly, S.Kelly for P.McGuigan, Fergal McEldowney for C.Bradley, P.Kearney for B.McGuigan.

2016

Ballyboden St. Enda's
P.Durcan, S.Clayton, S.Hiney, B.Dwan, S.O'Connor, D.Nelson, S.Durkin, A.Waters, M.D.Macauley, D.O'Reilly, C.Basquel, R.McDaid, R.Basquel, C.Keaney, A.Kerin. Subs: C.Flaherty for Nelson, S.Lambert for Macauley, S.Molony for R.Basquel, D.Davey for O'Reilly, D.McCabe for Waters, S.Gibbons for McDaid.

Castlebar Mitchels
R.Byrne, T.Cunniffe, A.Feeney, D.Newcombe, P.Durkan, E.O'Reilly, R.O'Malley, G.McDonagh, E.Moran, S.Hopkins, N.Lydon, N.Douglas, S.Keane, D.Kirby, R.Feeney. Subs: F.Durkan for Hopkins, J.Durkan for R.Feeney, C.Costello for Keane, A.Walsh for Douglas, S.Conlon for O'Malley, R.Burke for Newcombe.

2017

Dr. Crokes
S.Murphy, J.Payne, M.Moloney, L.Quinn, D.O'Leary, G.White, F.Fitzgerald, A.O'Donovan, A.O'Sullivan, J.Buckley, G.O'Shea, B.Looney, C.Cooper, D.Casey, K.O'Leary. Subs: J.Kiely for O'Sullivan, M.Burns for O'Shea, S.Doolan for D.O'Leary, T.Brosnan for Looney, E.Brosnan for Casey, C.Brady for K.O'Leary.

Slaughtneil
A.McMullan, F.McEldowney, B.Rodgers, K.McKaigue, P.O'Neill, D.McKaigue, K.Feeney, Patsy Bradley, P.Cassidy, Shane McGuigan, Paul Bradley, M.McGrath, C.Bradley, Sé McGuigan, C.O'Doherty. Subs: B.Cassidy for O'Doherty, R.Bradley for McGrath, B.McGuigan for Feeney, G.Bradley for Sé McGuigan, S.Cassidy for Patsy Bradley.

CAPTAINS OF WINNING ALL-IRELAND CLUB FOOTBALL TEAMS

1971   M. Gleeson (East Kerry)
1972   T. Scullion (Ballaghy)
1973   W. Morgan (Nemo Rangers)
1974   P. Kerr (U.C.D.)
1975   M. Carty (U.C.D.)
1976   T. Hanahoe (St. Vincent's)
1977   J. O'Keeffe (Austin Stacks)
1978   R. Bell (Thomond College)
1979   B. Murphy (Nemo Rangers)
1980   N. Aherne (St. Finbarr's)
1981   B. O'Brien (St. Finbarr's)
1982   C. Murphy (Nemo Rangers)
1983   L. Scully (Portlaoise)
1984   J. Kerrigan (Nemo Rangers)
1985   B. Lyons (Castleisland Desmonds)
1986   T. McGovern (Burren)
1987   J. Meyler (St. Finbarr's)
1988   V. McGovern (Burren)
1989   Tony Nation (Nemo Rangers)
1990   Brian Fitzpatrick (Baltinglass)
1991   John McGurk (Lavey)
1992   Seán O'Shea (Dr. Croke's)
1993   Mick McCarthy (O'Donovan Rossa)
1994   Steven O'Brien (Nemo Rangers)
1995   Mick Dillon (Kilmacud Crokes)
1996   Gerard Murphy (Laune Rangers)
1997   Jim McConville (Crossmaglen Rangers)
1998   Ray Silke (Corofin)
1999   John McEntee (Crossmaglen Rangers)
2000   A.Cunningham (Crossmaglen Rangers)
2001   T.Nallen (Crossmolina)
2002   A.McGuckin (Ballinderry)
2003   C.Corkery (Nemo Rangers)
2004   N.Meehan (Caltra)
2005   B.Ruane (Ballina)
2006   M.Sheridan (Salthill-Knocknacarra)
2007   O.McConville (Crossmaglen Rangers)
2008   T.Quinn (St.Vincent's)
2009   J.Magee (Kilmacud Crokes)
2010   C.Brady (St. Gall's)
2011   P.McKeown (Crossmaglen Rangers)
2012   S.Kernan (Crossmaglen Rangers)
2013   G.Cunniffe/D.Donnelly (St. Brigid's)
2014   G.Brennan (St. Vincent's)
2015   Martin Farragher (Corofin)
2016   D.Nelson (Ballyboden St. Enda's)
2017   J.Buckley (Dr. Crokes)

ALL-IRELAND CLUB FOOTBALL FINAL REFEREES

1971   Jimmy Hatton (Wicklow)
1972   D. Guerin (Dublin)
1973   Mick Spain (Offaly)
1974   Mick Spain (Offaly)
1975   P. J. McGrath (Mayo)
1976   Paddy Collins (Westmeath)
1977   Seamus Aldridge (Kildare)
1978   Seamus Aldridge (Kildare)
1979   Tommy Moran (Leitrim)
1980   Weeshy Fogarty (Kerry)
1981   Seamus Aldridge (Kildare)
1982   Tony Jordan (Dublin)
1983   John Moloney (Tipperary)
1984   Seamus Aldridge (Kildare)
1985   Pat Kavanagh (Meath)
1986   Mickey Kearns (Sligo)
1987   Michael Greenan (Cavan)
1988   D. Guerin (Dublin)
1989   Gerry McGlory (Antrim)
1990   Tommy Sugrue (Kerry)
1991   Tommy Howard (Kildare)
1992   T. McDermott (Cavan)
1993   Jimmy Curran (Tyrone)
1994   Pat Casserly (Westmeath)
1995   Paddy Russell (Tipperary)
1996   Pat McEneaney (Monaghan)
1997   Brian White (Wexford)
1998   Pat Casserly (Westmeath)
1999   John Bannon (Longford)
2000   M.Curley (Galway)
2001   J.Bannon (Longford)
2002   S.McCormack (Meath)
2003   B.Crowe (Cavan)
2004   M.Monahan (Kildare)
2005   B.Crowe (Cavan)
2006   D.Coldrick (Meath)
2007   S.Doyle (Wexford)
Replay   S.Doyle (Wexford)
2008   J.McQuillan (Cavan)
2009   G.Ó Conamha (Galway)
2010   D.Fahy (Longford)
2011   C.Reilly (Meath)
2012   R.Hickey (Clare)
Replay   M.Duffy (Sligo)
2013   P.Hughes (Armagh)
2014   E.Kinsella (Laois)
2015   D.Coldrick (Meath)
2016   C.Lane (Cork)
2017   M.Deegan (Laois)

REPRESENTATIVE GAMES

1950
February 26 Croke Park.
Ireland   1-12 2-3 *Combined Universities*

1951
March 4 Croke Park.
Ireland beat Combined Universities

1952
March 2 Croke Park.
Ireland   2-4 1-5 *Combined Universities*

1953
March 1 Croke Park.
Ireland beat Combined Universities

1954
March 7 Croke Park.
Combined Universities 2-8 1-8 Ireland

1955
March 6 Croke Park.
Ireland   1-10 2-5 *Combined Universities*

1956
March 18 Croke Park.
Ireland   2-14 3-10 *Combined Universities*

1957
March 18 Croke Park.
Ireland   3-10 3-6 *Combined Universities*

1958
May 4 Croke Park.
Combined Universities 0-12 0-10 Ireland

1959
Not played because of re-construction work at Croke Park.

1960
March 20 Croke Park.
Ireland   4-5 3-2 *Combined Universities*

1961
March 12 Croke Park.
Combined Universities 2-10 1-7 The Army

1962
March 18 Croke Park.
Combined Universities 1-8 1-6 Ireland

1963
March 24 Croke Park.
Kerry   4-7 1-7 *Combined Universities*

1950
Ireland
K.Smyth (Meath), J.Bell (Louth), P.O'Brien (Meath), S.Flanagan (Mayo), J.Lyne (Kerry), W.Goodison (Wexford), S.Quinn (Armagh), C.McGrath (Cork), W.McCorry (Armagh), A.Tighe (Cavan), B.Smyth (Meath), V.Sherlock (Cavan), N.Crowley (Clare), P.O'Donohoe (Cavan), B.Garvey (Kerry)
Combined Universities
M.O'Malley (UCG), N.Redmond (UCD), W.McQuillan (UCG), J.O'Brien (UCD), PJ Duke (UCD), P.O'Neill (QUB), C.Garvey (UCG), P.Carney (UCD), W.Kenny (UCG), P.O'Regan (UCC), H.McKearney (UCD), J.Brosnan (UCC), T.L'Estrange (QUB), P.Solan (UCG), E.Carolan (UCD)

1951
Ireland
S.Thornton (Louth), J.Murphy (Kerry), P.O'Brien (Meath), S.Flanagan (Mayo), J.Lyne (Kerry), H.Dixon (Mayo), S.Quinn (Armagh), C.McGrath (Cork), E.Mongey (Mayo), A.Tighe (Cavan), M.Higgins (Cavan), J.McDonnell (Louth), B.Smyth (Meath), T.Langan (Mayo), E.Carolan (Cavan)
Combined Universities
M.O'Malley (UCG), P.Bernard (UCC), N.Redmond (UCD), D.Murphy (UCD), P.Markey (UCD), P.O'Neill (QUB), M.Gould (UCD), S.Purcell (UCG), J.Brosnan (UCC), N.Redmond (UCD), D.Murphy (UCD), P.Markey (UCD), P.O'Neill (QUB), M.Gould (UCD), S.Purcell (UCG), J.Brosnan (UCC), E.Devlin (UCD), H.McKearney (UCD), M.Brosnan (UCC), P.O'Regan (UCC), T.L'Estrange (QUB), P.Solan (UCG)

1952
Ireland
S.Wynne (Mayo), M.O'Brien (Meath), P.Prendergast (Mayo), S.Flanagan (Mayo), L.Lyne (Kerry), R.Beirne (Antrim); C.Hand (Meath), C.Duggan (Cork), E.Mongey (Mayo), S.Purcell (Galway), P.Carney (Mayo), P.Meegan (Meath), M.Flanagan (Mayo), T.Langan (Mayo), M.Higgins (Cavan)
Combined Universities
G.Stack (UCG), J.O'Brien (UCC), M.Costello (UCG), D.Bernard (UCC), M.Gould (UCD), P.O'Neill (QUB), C.Garvey (UCG), E.Devlin (UCD), J.Galvin (UCC), J.Brosnan (UCC), H.McKearney (UCD), P.Sheehy (UCC), E.Carolan (UCD), T.L'Estrange (QUB), P.Solan (UCG)

1953
Ireland
S.Morris (Cavan), M.O'Brien (Meath), P.O'Brien (Meath), S.Flanagan (Mayo), P.Driscoll (Cork), G.O'Malley (Roscommon), J.Cronin (Kerry), P.Carney (Mayo), V.Sherlock (Cavan), S.Purcell (Galway), M.Higgins (Cavan), P.Meegan (Meath), O.Freaney (Dublin), T.Langan (Mayo), J.McDonnell (Louth)
Combined Universities
P.McGearty (UCD), I.Hanniffy (UCG), J.McArdle (UCD), C.Garvey (UCG), T.Hardy (UCD), S.Gallagher (QUB), K.Mussen (QUB), E.O'Donoghue (UCG), E.Devlin (UCD), J.Cunningham (QUB), R.Buckley (UCC), P.Sheehy (UCC), M.Walsh (QUB), P.Kearns (UCG), P.Brennan (DU)

1954
Combined Universities
A.Brady (UCD), M.Gould (UCD), D.Bernard (UCC), J.McKnight (UCD), T.Hardy (UCD), G.O'Malley (UCG), S.Murphy (UCD), E.Devlin (UCD), PJ McElroy (UCD), J.Brosnan (UCC), P.Carolan (UCD), E.Donoghue (UCG), O.Freaney (UCD), P.Fenelon (UCD), K.Heffernan (DU)

Ireland
P.McGearty (Meath), E.Morgan (Armagh), T.Conlon (Louth),
K.McConnell (Meath), P.Driscoll (Cork), M.O'Hanlon (Armagh),
B.Lynch (Roscommon), I.O'Dowd (Sligo), D.Kelleher (Cork), T.Lyne
(Kerry), JJ Sheehan (Kerry), S.White (Louth), T.Langan (Mayo),
A.O'Hagan (Armagh), I.Jones (Tyrone)

1955
Ireland
J.Mangan (Galway), W.Casey (Mayo), P.O'Brien (Meath),
D.Murphy (Kerry), P.Casey (Offaly), T.Dillon (Galway), N.Maher
Dublin), M.McEvoy (Armagh), I.O'Dowd (Sligo), T.Lyne (Kerry),
M.McDonnell (Meath), S.White (Louth), M.Grace (Meath),
A.O'Hagan (Armagh), P.Sheehy (Kerry). Subs: J.Teggart (Tyrone)
for Lyne, J.Mahon (Galway) for O'Brien
Combined Universities
O.R.O'Neill (UCG), J.McCabe (UCC), S.Purcell (UCG), J.McKnight
(UCD), S.Murphy (UCD), D.Bernard (UCC), K.Swords (UCG),
G.O'Malley (UCG), J.Nangle (UCC), J.Cunningham (QUB), K.Denvir
(UCD), O.Freaney (UCD), J.O'Donovan (UCC), P.Carolan (UCD),
K.Heffernan (DU). Subs: J.McArdle (UCD) For McCabe, P.Kearns
(UCG) for Nangle

1956
Ireland
A.Brady (Roscommon), W.Casey (Mayo), P.Prendergast (Mayo),
J.M Palmer (Kerry), P.Casey (Offaly), J.Crowley (Dublin), E.Moriarty
(Mayo), J.Dowling (Kerry), J.Nallen (Mayo), J.McKeever (Derry),
M.McDonnell (Meath), T.Lyne (Kerry), D.Ferguson (Dublin),
M.Murphy (Kerry), J.Boyle (Dublin). Subs: E.Ryan for Dowling,
J.O'Shea for W Casey
Combined Universities
O.R.O'Neill (UCG), D.Murray (UCC), T.Lyons (UCD), J.McKnight
(UCD), S.Murphy (UCD), J.Mahon (UCG), D.Bernard (UCC),
G.O'Malley (UCG), J.McDonnell (UCD), P.Sheehy (UCC), S.Purcell
(UCG), J.Cunningham (QUB), S.O'Donnell (UCC), O.Freaney (UCD),
K.Heffernan (DU)

1957
Ireland
J.Mangan (Galway), P.Driscoll (Cork), J.Devlin (Tyrone), T.Dillon
(Galway), P.Harrington (Cork), J.Rice (Monaghan), G.O'Reilly
(Wicklow), S.Moore (Cork), F.Evers (Galway), J.McKeever (Derry),
L.McCormack (Kildare), P.McGarty (Leitrim), D.Ferguson (Dublin),
F.Stockwell (Galway), D.Kelleher (Cork) Sub: N.Fitzgerald (Cork)
for McCormack
Combined Universities
J.O'Neill (QUB), C.Mallon (QUB), T.Lyons (UCD), C.O'Toole (UCG),
S.Murphy (UCD), J.Ryan (UCD), D.Murray (UCG), G.O'Malley (UCG),
J.McDonnell (UCD), E.Devlin (UCD), S.Purcell (UCG), M.Stewart
(UCG), M.Moroney (UCC), F.Higgins (QUB), K.Keffernan (DU)

1958
Combined Universities
J.O'Neill (QUB), D.Murray (UCC), J.Ryan (UCD), T.Lyons (UCD),
S.Murphy (UCD, capt), J.Mahon (UCG), J.McDonnell (UCD),
G.O'Malley (UCG), S.Moore (UCC), H.O'Kane (QUB), S.Purcell
(UCG), M.O'Connell (UCC), J.Brady (UCD), K.Heffernan (DU),
P.Sheehy (UCC)
Ireland
T.Turbett (Tyrone), P.Driscoll (Cork), T.Conlon (Louth), T.Dillon
(Galway), M.Greally (Galway), P.Nolan (Offaly), S.White (Louth),
J.McKeever (Derry), E.Ryan (Cork), K.Beahan (Louth), J.Nallen
(Mayo), P.McGarty (Leitrim), D.O'Brien (Louth, capt), F.Stockwell
(Galway), F.Donnelly (Tyrone). Sub: J Boyle (Dublin) for Stockwell

1960
Ireland
A.Brady (Roscommon), W.Casey (Mayo), G.Hughes (Offaly), P.Rice
(Down), K.Mussen (Down), C.O'Leary (Dublin), M.O'Dwyer (Kerry),
F.Evers (Galway), D.Foley (Dublin), J.McKeever (Derry), T.Long
(Kerry), J.Kenna (Laois), D.McAuliffe (Kerry), J.Joyce (Dublin),
C.Flynn (Leitrim)
Combined Universities
J.O'Neill (QUB), F.McKnight (UCD), N.Sheehy (UCC), M.Brewster
(QUB), L.O'Neill (QUB), J.Mahon (UCG), E.Curley (UCG),
M.O'Connell (UCC), J.McDonnell (UCD), S.O'Neill (QUB),
G.O'Malley (UCG), P.Sheehy (UCC), C.Gallagher (UCD), J.Brady
(UCD), K.Heffernan (DU) Sub: J.Healy (UCC) for Mahon

1961
Combined Universities
J.Boyle (QUB), B.O'Callaghan (UCC), F.McKnight (UCD), S.Murray
(UCD), M.Laide (UCG), B.Donaghy (QUB), M.Newell (UCG), G.Glynn
(UCG), F.O'Leary (UCD), P.Donnellan (UCG), P.Kelly (UCD), D.Feely
(UCG), D.Geaney (UCG), S.Donnelly (UCG), A.Kenny (UCG) Sub:
J.Healy (UCD) for O'Leary
The Army
R.Bennett (CTC), P.McCaffrey (Air Corps), D.Flood (Western),
B.Kavanagh (CTC), B.Bardon (AC), J.Harold (Eastern), C.Wrenn
(AC), C.O'Leary (Eastern), M.Coughlan (AC), S.Kilgannon
(Western), P.Daly (CTC), T.Gunn (Western), N.Fitzgerald
(Southern), S.O'Keeffe (AC), H.Donnelly (AC) Sub: C.Leaney (CTC)
for Kilgannon

1962
Combined Universities
J.Finn (UCD), B.O'Callaghan (UCC), F.McKnight (UCD), S.Murray
(UCD), K.O'Neill (UCD), G.O'Malley (UCG), M.Newell (UCG),
J.McDonnell (UCD), G.B.McDermott (UCG), S.O'Neill (QUB),
B.Geraghty (UCG), P.Kelly (UCD), G.Kane (UCD), S.Donnelly (USG),
D.Geaney (UCC)
Ireland
J.Culloty (Kerry), J.Lynch (Roscommon), L.Murphy (Down),
P.McCormack (Offaly), M.O'Dwyer (Kerry), D.McCartan (Down),
P.Doherty (Down), S.Brereton (Offaly), J.Timmons (Dublin),
B.Morgan (Down) Subs: J.Whan (Armagh), E.McCarthy (Cork)

1963
Kerry
J.Culloty, P.O'Donoghue, N.Sheehy, T.Lyons, JJ Barrett,
D.O'Sullivan, J.O'Driscoll, S.Murphy, J.O'Riordan, B.O'Callaghan,
S.Roche, W.Doran, T.Long, P.Ahearn
Combined Universities
S.Gannon (UCG), B.O'Callaghan (UCC), H.McGonigle (UCG),
H.Toner (QUB), E.Colleran (UCG), K.Coffey (DU), M.Fleming (UCC),
M.O'Shea (UCG), F.McFeeley (UCD), D.Philpott (UCC), E.McGuire
(UCC), P.Donnellan (UCG), P.Harte (QUB), B.Brady (UCD),
S.Donnelly (UCG)

O'BYRNE CUP (LEINSTER FOOTBALL)

Kildare (11)	1962, 1968, 1970, 1973, 1976, 1982, 1989, 2003., 2011, 2013, 2014.
Meath (9)	1967, 1974, 1977, 1983, 1992, 2001, 2004, 2006, 2016.
Dublin (9)	1956, 1958, 1960, 1966, 1999, 2007, 2008, 2015, 2017.
Offaly (6)	1954, 1961, 1981, 1993, 1997, 1998.
Laois (5)	1978, 1987, 1991, 1994, 2005.
Wicklow (4)	1955, 1957, 1986, 1996.
Louth (4)	1963, 1980, 1990, 2009.
Westmeath (3)	1959, 1964, 1988.
Longford (2)	1965, 2000.
DCU (2)	2010, 2012.
Wexford (1)	1995.
Carlow (1)	2002.

No competition: 1969, 1971, 1972, 1975, 1979, 1984, 1985.

DR. McKENNA CUP (ULSTER FOOTBALL)

Tyrone (15)	1957, 1973, 1978, 1982, 1984, 2004, 2005, 2006, 2007, 2012, 2013, 2014, 2015, 2016, 2017.
Monaghan (14)	1927, 1928, 1932, 1935, 1936, 1937, 1948, 1952, 1976, 1979, 1980, 1983, 1995, 2003.
Cavan (11)	1936, 1940, 1943, 1951, 1953, 1955, 1956, 1962, 1968, 1988, 2000.
Down (11)	1944, 1959, 1961, 1964, 1972, 1987, 1989, 1993, 1996, 1998, 2008.
Derry (11)	1947, 1954, 1958, 1960, 1969, 1970, 1971, 1974, 1993, 1999, 2011.
Armagh (9)	1929, 1931, 1938, 1939, 1949, 1950, 1986, 1990, 1994.
Donegal (8)	1963, 1965, 1967, 1975, 1985, 1991, 2009, 2010.
Antrim (7)	1926, 1941, 1942, 1945, 1946, 1966, 1981.
Fermanagh (4)	1930, 1934, 1977, 1997.

DR. LAGAN CUP (ULSTER FOOTBALL)

Derry (6)	1945, 1947, 1950, 1953, 1959, 1961.
Down (5)	1949, 1960, 1962, 1963, 1964.
Donegal (4)	1952, 1965, 1966, 1967.
Antrim (3)	1944, 1946, 1948.
Tyrone (3)	1943, 1957, 1958.
Armagh (3)	1954, 1955, 1956.
Monaghan (1)	1951.
(Discontinued)	

RAILWAY SHIELD FINALS

1905
Limerick 11 November.
Leinster: (Kildare) 1-8 Connacht (Mayo) 0-5

1906
Ennis 17 February 1907.
Munster (Kerry) 2-10 Connacht (Roscommon) 2-2

1907
Tipperary 22 September.
Munster: (Kerry) 1-7 Leinster (Selected) 1-6.

GROUNDS TOURNAMENT (1961-1973)

1961
Tullamore October 3.
Offaly	2-12	1-7	**Kerry**

Belfast October 3.
Down	0-11	0-7	**Roscommon**

Croke Park October 29. Final:
Offaly	0-11	0-8	**Down**

1962
Croke Park October 7.
Dublin	0-8	0-7	**Roscommon**

Croke Park October 7.
Kerry	2-7	1-10	**Cavan**

October 21.
Kerry	5-4	1-10	**Cavan (replay)**

Croke Park November 4. Final:
Kerry	0-14	0-7	**Dublin**

1963
Croke Park October 13.
Dublin	1-12	2-7	**Kerry**

Croke Park October 13.
Galway	0-10	0-8	**Down**

Croke Park November 3. Final:
Dublin	2-10	0-8	**Galway**

1964
Croke Park October 11.
Galway	3-10	0-9	**Cavan**

Croke Park October 11.
Meath	2-7	0-7	**Cork**

(Meath withdrew and were replaced by Dublin in final)
Croke Park November 8. Final:
Galway	0-13	0-10	**Dublin**

1965
Croke Park October 24.
Down	0-11	1-7	**Kerry**

Croke Park October 24.
Galway	2-11	1-6	**Dublin**

Croke Park November 7. Final:
Down	3-10	0-7	**Galway**

1966
Croke Park October 24.
Cork	1-14	1-11	**Meath**

Croke Park October 24.
Galway	2-15	0-10	**Down**

Croke Park November 7. Final:
Galway	0-15	1-6	**Cork**

1967
Croke Park October 22.
Mayo	2-9	1-8	**Cork**

Croke Park October 22.
Cavan	2-8	1-11	**Meath**

November 5.
Cavan	1-8	2-4	**Meath (replay)**

Croke Park May 19 1968. Final:
Mayo	1-10	1-7	**Cavan**

1968
Croke Park October 6.
Galway   *2-12*   *1-14*   *Kerry*
Croke Park October 6.
Longford   *3-9*   *1-12*   *Down*
Croke Park November 18. Final:
Galway   *2-8*   *0-7*   *Longford*

1969
Croke Park October 12.
Kerry   *3-15*   *0-8*   *Cavan*
Croke Park October 12.
Offaly   *2-7*   *0-13*   *Mayo*
Croke Park October 26.
Offaly   *3-9*   *2-7*   *Mayo (replay)*
Croke Park November 30. Final:
Kerry   *2-17*   *1-9*   *Offaly*

1970
Croke Park October 11.
Derry   *2-13*   *1-7*   *Meath*
Croke Park October 25.
Kerry   *3-9*   *0-11*   *Galway*
Croke Park November 8. Final:
Kerry   *2-6*   *1-8*   *Derry*

1971
Croke Park October 24.
Offaly   *1-12*   *0-8*   *Down*
Croke Park October 24.
Galway   *2-15*   *1-6*   *Cork*
Croke Park November 7. Final:
Offaly   *5-7*   *1-7*   *Galway*

1972
Croke Park October 22.
Donegal   *1-12*   *1-11*   *Roscommon*
(Offaly qualified by their All-Ireland win over Kerry)
Croke Park November 5. Final:
Offaly   *4-11*   *0-7*   *Donegal*

1973
Croke Park November 3.
Offaly   *1-8*   *0-8*   *Cork*
Croke Park November 4.
Tyrone   *0-12*   *1-6*   *Galway*
Croke Park November 18. Final:
Offaly   *3-9*   *2-6*   *Tyrone*
(Suspended)

CROKE CUP FINALS (1896-1915)

1896
Jones's Road June 1 1897.
Dublin   *0-4*   *0-3*   *Tipperary*

1897
Jones's Road May 28 1899.
Wexford   *1-11*   *0-2*   *Cork*

1898-1901 Cup presented to All-Ireland winners

1902
Jones's Road February 19 1905.
Tipperary   *0-5*   *0-2*   *London*

1903
Jones's Road April 1906.
Kildare   *1-9*   *0-0*   *Mayo*

1904-1905 None

1906
Ennis November 17 1907.
Kerry   *2-6*   *2-3*   *Mayo*

1907
Jones's Road November 22 1908.
Mayo   *1-8*   *0-5*   *Kerry*

1908
Athlone August 29 1909.
Kildare   *0-7*   *0-4*   *Mayo*

1909
Limerick November 14.
Mayo   *1-8*   *0-5*   *Waterford*

1910
Cork April 23 1911.
Cork   *3-3*   *0-1*   *Galway*

1911
Jones's Road May 26 1912.
Meath   *1-4*   *0-3*   *Waterford*

1912
Jones's Road February 12 1913.
Dublin   *3-4*   *0-1*   *Clare*

1913
Croke Park June 28 1914.
Louth   *2-2*   *1-1*   *Cork*

1914
Croke Park February 28 1915.
Cork   *2-1*   *0-3*   *Louth*

1915
Athlone April 9 1916.
Dublin   *1-8*   *2-1*   *Roscommon*

ALL-STAR FOOTBALL TEAMS

1971

P. J. Smyth (Galway); Johnny Carey (Mayo), Jack Cosgrove (Galway), Donie O'Sullivan (Kerry); Eugene Mulligan (Offaly), Nicholas Clavin (Offaly), Pat Reynolds (Meath); Liam Sammon (Galway), Willie Bryan (Offaly), Tony McTague (Offaly), Ray Cummins (Cork), Mickey Kearns (Sligo); Andy McCallin (Antrim), Seán O'Neill (Down), Seamus Leydon (Galway).

1972

Martin Furlong (Offaly); Mick Ryan (Offaly), Paddy McCormack (Offaly), Donie O'Sullivan (Kerry); Brian McEniff (Donegal), Tommy Joe Gilmore (Galway), Kevin Jer O'Sullivan (Cork); Willie Bryan (Offaly), Mick O'Connell (Kerry); Johnny Cooney (Offaly), Kevin Kilmurray (Offaly), Tony McTague (Offaly); Mickey Freyne (Roscommon), Seán O'Neill (Down), Paddy Moriarty (Armagh).

1973

Billy Morgan (Cork); Frank Cogan (Cork), Mick Ryan (Offaly), Brian Murphy (Cork); Liam O'Neill (Galway), Tommy Joe Gilmore (Galway), Kevin Jer O'Sullivan (Cork); John O'Keeffe (Kerry), Denis Long (Cork); Johnny Cooney (Offaly), Kevin Kilmurray (Offaly), Liam Sammon (Galway); Jimmy Barry Murphy (Cork), Ray Cummins (Cork), Anthony McGurk (Derry).

1974

Paddy Cullen (Dublin); Donal Monaghan (Donegal), Seán Doherty (Dublin), Robbie Kelleher (Dublin); Paddy Reilly (Dublin), Barnes Murphy (Sligo), Johnny Hughes (Galway); Dermot Earley (Roscommon), Paud Lynch (Kerry); Tom Naughton (Galway), Declan Barron (Cork), David Hickey (Dublin); Jimmy Barry Murphy (Cork), Jimmy Keaveney (Dublin), Johnny Tobin (Galway).

1975

Paud O'Mahony (Kerry); Gay O'Driscoll (Dublin), John O'Keeffe (Kerry), Robbie Kelleher (Dublin); Peter Stevenson (Derry), Anthony McGurk (Derry), Ger Power (Kerry); Denis Long (Cork), Colm McAlarney (Down); Gerry McElhinney (Derry), Ken Rennicks (Meath), Mickey O'Sullivan (Kerry); John Egan (Kerry), Matt Kerrigan (Meath), Anton O'Toole (Dublin).

1976

Paddy Cullen (Dublin); Ger O'Keeffe (Kerry), John O'Keeffe (Kerry), Brian Murphy (Cork); Johnny Hughes (Galway), Kevin Moran (Dublin), Ger Power (Kerry); Brian Mullins (Dublin), Dave McCarthy (Cork); Anton O'Toole (Dublin), Tony Hanahoe (Dublin), David Hickey (Dublin); Bobby Doyle (Dublin), Mike Sheehy (Kerry), Pat Spillane (Kerry).

1977

Paddy Cullen (Dublin); Gay O'Driscoll (Dublin), Pat Lindsay (Roscommon), Robbie Kelleher (Dublin); Tommy Drumm (Dublin), Paddy Moriarty (Armagh), Pat O'Neill (Dublin); Brian Mullins (Dublin), Joe Kernan (Armagh); Anton O'Toole (Dublin), Jimmy Smyth (Armagh), Pat Spillane (Kerry); Bobby Doyle (Dublin), Jimmy Keaveney (Dublin), John Egan (Kerry).

1978

Ollie Crinnigan (Kildare); Harry Keegan (Roscommon), John O'Keeffe (Kerry), Robbie Kelleher (Dublin); Tommy Drumm (Dublin), Ollie Brady (Cavan), Paud Lynch (Kerry); Colm McAlarney (Down), Tomás Connor (Offaly); Ger Power (Kerry), Declan Barron (Cork), Pat Spillane (Kerry); Mike Sheehy (Kerry), Jimmy Keaveney (Dublin), John Egan (Kerry).

1979

Paddy Cullen (Dublin); Eugene Hughes (Monaghan), John O'Keeffe (Kerry), Tom Heneghan (Roscommon); Tommy Drumm (Dublin), Tim Kennelly (Kerry), Danny Murray (Roscommon); Dermot Earley (Roscommon), Bernard Brogan (Dublin); Ger Power (Kerry), Seán Walsh (Kerry), Pat Spillane (Kerry); Mike Sheehy (Kerry), Seán Lowry (Offaly), Joe McGrath (Mayo).

1980

Charlie Nelligan (Kerry); Harry Keegan (Roscommon), Kevin Kehily (Cork), Gerry Connellan (Roscommon); Kevin McCabe (Tyrone), Tim Kennelly (Kerry), Danny Murray (Roscommon); Jack O'Shea (Kerry), Colm McKinstry (Armagh); Ger Power (Kerry), Denis Allen (Cork), Pat Spillane (Kerry); Matt Connor (Offaly), Eoin Liston (Kerry), John Egan (Kerry).

1981

Martin Furlong (Offaly); Jimmy Deenihan (Kerry), Paddy Kennedy (Down), Paud Lynch (Kerry); Páidí Ó Sé (Kerry), Richie Connor (Offaly), Seamus McHugh (Galway); Jack O'Shea (Kerry), Seán Walsh (Kerry); Barry Brennan (Galway), Denis "Ogie" Moran (Kerry), Pat Spillane (Kerry); Mike Sheehy (Kerry), Eoin Liston (Kerry), Brendan Lowry (Offaly).

1982

Martin Furlong (Offaly); Mick Fitzgerald (Offaly), Liam Connor (Offaly), Kevin Kehily (Cork); Páidí Ó Sé (Kerry), Seán Lowry (Offaly), Liam Currams (Offaly); Jack O'Shea (Kerry), Padraig Dunne (Offaly); Peter McGinnity (Fermanagh), Joe Kernan (Armagh), Matt Connor (Offaly); Mike Sheehy (Kerry), Eoin Liston (Kerry), John Egan (Kerry).

1983

Martin Furlong (Offaly); Páidí Ó Sé (Kerry), Stephen Kinneavy (Galway), John Evans (Cork); Pat Canavan (Dublin), Tommy Drumm (Dublin), Jimmy Kerrigan (Cork); Jack O'Shea (Kerry), Liam Austin (Down); Barney Rock (Dublin), Matt Connor (Offaly), Greg Blaney (Down); Martin McHugh (Donegal), Colm O'Rourke (Meath), Joe McNally (Dublin).

1984

John O'Leary (Dublin); Páidí Ó Sé (Kerry), Mick Lyons (Meath), Seamus McHugh (Galway); Tommy Doyle (Kerry), Tom Spillane (Kerry), P. J. Buckley (Dublin); Jack O'Shea (Kerry), Eugene McKenna (Tyrone); Barney Rock (Dublin), Eoin Liston (Kerry), Pat Spillane (Kerry); Mike Sheehy (Kerry), Frank McGuigan (Tyrone), Dermot McNicholl (Derry).

1985

John O'Leary (Dublin); Páidí Ó Sé (Kerry), Gerry Hargan (Dublin), Mick Spillane (Kerry); Tommy Doyle (Kerry), Ciarán Murray (Monaghan), Dermot Flanagan (Mayo); Jack O'Shea (Kerry), Willie Joe Padden (Mayo); Barney Rock (Dublin), Tommy Conroy (Dublin), Pat Spillane (Kerry); Kevin McStay (Mayo), Paul Earley (Roscommon), Eugene Hughes (Monaghan).

FOOTBALL

1986

Charlie Nelligan (Kerry); Harry Keegan (Roscommon), Mick Lyons (Meath), John Lynch (Tyrone); Tommy Doyle (Kerry), Tom Spillane (Kerry), Colm Browne (Laois); Plunkett Donaghy (Tyrone), Liam Irwin (Laois); Ray McCarron (Monaghan), Eugene McKenna (Tyrone), Pat Spillane (Kerry); Mike Sheehy (Kerry), Damian O'Hagan (Tyrone), Ger Power (Kerry).

1987

John Kearns (Cork); Robbie O'Malley (Meath), Colman Corrigan (Cork), Tony Scullion (Derry); Niall Cahalane (Cork), Tom Spillane (Kerry), Ger Lynch (Kerry); Gerry McEntee (Meath), Brian McGilligan (Derry); David Beggy (Meath), Larry Tompkins (Cork), Kieran Duff (Dublin); Val Daly (Galway), Brian Stafford (Meath), Bernard Flynn (Meath).

1988

Paddy Linden (Monaghan); Bobby O'Malley (Meath), Colman Corrigan (Cork), Mick Kennedy (Dublin); Niall Cahalane (Cork), Noel McCaffrey (Dublin), Martin O'Connell (Meath); Shea Fahy (Cork), Liam Hayes (Meath); Maurice Fitzgerald (Kerry), Larry Tompkins (Cork), Kieran Duff (Dublin); Colm O'Rourke (Meath), Brian Stafford (Meath), Eugene Hughes (Monaghan).

1989

Gabriel Irwin (Mayo), Jimmy Browne (Mayo), Gerry Hargan (Dublin), Dermot Flanagan (Mayo); Connie Murphy (Kerry), Conor Counihan (Cork), Anthony Davis (Cork); Teddy McCarthy (Cork), Willie Joe Padden (Mayo); Dave Barry (Cork) Larry Tompkins (Cork), Noel Durkin (Mayo); Paul McGrath (Cork), Eugene McKenna (Tyrone), Tony McManus (Roscommon).

1990

John Kerins (Cork); Bobby O'Malley (Meath), Stephen O'Brien (Cork), Terry Ferguson (Meath); Michael Slocum (Cork), Conor Counihan (Cork), Martin O'Connell (Meath); Shea Fahy (Cork), Mickey Quinn (Leitrim); David Beggy (Meath), Val Daly (Galway), Joyce McMullan (Donegal); Paul McGrath (Cork), Kevin O'Brien (Wicklow), James McCartan (Down).

1991

Michael McQuillan (Meath); Mick Deegan (Dublin), Conor Deegan (Down), Enon Gavin (Roscommon); Tommy Carr (Dublin), Keith Barr (Dublin), Martin O'Connell (Meath); Barry Breen (Down), Martin Lynch (Kildare); Ross Carr (Down), Greg Blaney (Down), Tommy Dowd (Meath); Colm O'Rourke (Meath), Brian Stafford (Meath), Bernard Flynn (Meath).

1992

Gary Walsh (Donegal); Seamus Clancy (Clare), Matt Gallagher (Donegal), Tony Scullion (Derry); Paul Curran (Dublin), Martin Gavigan (Donegal), Eamonn Heery (Dublin); Anthony Molloy (Donegal), T. J. Kilgallon (Mayo); Anthony Tohill (Derry), Martin McHugh (Donegal), James McHugh (Donegal); Tony Boyle (Donegal), Vinny Murphy (Dublin), Enda Gormley (Derry).

1993

J. O'Leary (Dublin); J. J. Doherty (Donegal), D. Deasy (Dublin), T. Scullion (Derry); McGuirk (Derry), H. Downey (Derry), G. Coleman (Derry); A. Tohill (Derry), B. McGilligan (Derry); Kevin O'Neill (Mayo), Joe Kavanagh (Cork), C. Redmond (Dublin); C. Corkery (Cork), G. Houlihan (Armagh), E. Gormley (Derry).

1994

J. O'Leary (Dublin); M. Magill (Down), S. Quinn (Leitrim), P. Higgins (Down); G. Geraghty (Meath), S. O'Brien (Cork), D. J. Kane (Down); J. Sheedy (Dublin), G. McCartan (Down); Peter Canavan (Tyrone), G. Blayney (Down), J. McCartan (Down); M. Linden (Down), T. Dowd (Meath), C. Redmond (Dublin).

1995

J. O'Leary (Dublin); T. Scullion (Derry), M. O'Connor (Cork), F. Devlin (Tyrone); P. Curran (Dublin), K. Barr (Dublin), S. O'Brien (Cork); B. Stynes (Dublin), A. Tohill (Derry); J. Fallon (Galway), D. Farrell (Dublin), P. Clarke (Dublin); T. Dowd (Meath), Peter Canavan (Tyrone), C. Redmond (Dublin).

1996

F. McConnell (Tyrone); K. Mortimer (Mayo), D. Fay (Meath), M. O'Connell (Meath); P. Holmes (Mayo), J. Nallen (Mayo), P. Curran (Dublin); L. McHale (Mayo), J. McDermott (Meath); T. Giles (Meath), T. Dowd (Meath), J. Horan (Mayo); J. Brolly (Derry), Peter Canavan (Tyrone), M. Fitzgerald (Kerry).

1997

D. O'Keeffe (Kerry); K. Mortimer (Mayo), D. Dalton (Kildare), C. Daly (Offaly); S. Moynihan (Kerry), G. Ryan (Kildare), E. Breen (Kerry); P. Fallon (Mayo), N. Buckley (Kildare); P. Laide (Kerry), T. Giles (Meath), D. McCabe (Cavan); J. Brolly (Derry), B. Reilly (Meath), M. Fitzgerald (Kerry).

1998

M. McNamara (Galway), B. Lacey (Kildare), S. M. Lockhart (Derry), T. Mannion (Galway); J. Finn (Kildare), G. Ryan (Kildare), S. Óg de Paor (Galway); K. Walsh (Galway), J. McDermott (Meath), M. Donnellan (Galway), J. Fallon (Galway), D. Earley (Kildare); K. O'Dwyer (Kildare), P. Joyce (Galway), D. Browne (Tipperary).

1999

Kevin O'Dwyer (Cork), Mark O'Reilly (Meath), Darren Fay (Meath), Anthony Lynch (Cork), Ciaran O'Sullivan (Cork), Kieran McGeeney (Armagh), Paddy Reynolds (Meath), John McDermott (Meath), Ciaran Whelan (Dublin), Diarmuid Marsden (Armagh), Trevor Giles (Meath), James Horan (Mayo), Philip Clifford (Cork), Graham Geraghty (Meath), Ollie Murphy (Meath).

2000

Declan O'Keeffe (Kerry), Kieran McKeever (Derry), Seamus Moynihan (Kerry), Michael McCarthy (Kerry), Declan Meehan (Galway), Kieran McGeeney (Armagh), Anthony Rainbow (Kildare), Anthony Tohill (Derry), Darragh Ó Sé (Kerry), Michael Donnellan (Galway), Liam Hassett (Kerry), Oisín McConville (Armagh), Mike Frank Russell (Kerry), Padraig Joyce (Galway), Derek Savage (Galway).

2001

Cormac Sullivan (Meath), Kieran Fitzgerald (Galway), Darren Fay (Meath), Coman Goggins (Dublin), Declan Meehan (Galway), Francie Grehan (Roscommon), Seán Óg de Paor (Galway), Kevin Walsh (Galway), Rory O'Connell (Westmeath), Evan Kelly (Meath), Stephen O'Neill (Tyrone), Michael Donnellan (Galway), Ollie Murphy (Meath), Padraig Joyce (Galway), John Crowley (Kerry).

2002

Stephen Cluxton (Dublin), Enda McNulty (Armagh), Paddy Christie (Dublin), Anthony Lynch (Cork), Aidan O'Rourke (Armagh), Kieran McGeeney (Armagh), Kevin Cassidy (Donegal), Darragh Ó Sé (Kerry), Paul McGrane (Armagh), Steven McDonnell (Armagh), Eamonn O'Hara (Sligo), Oisín McConville (Armagh), Peter Canavan (Tyrone), Ray Cosgrove (Dublin), Colm Cooper (Kerry).

2003

Fergal Byron (Laois), Francie Bellew (Armagh), Cormac McAnallen (Tyrone), Joe Higgins (Laois), Conor Gormley (Tyrone), Tom Kelly (Laois), Philip Jordan (Tyrone), Kevin Walsh (Galway), Seán Cavanagh (Tyrone), Brian Dooher (Tyrone), Brian McGuigan (Tyrone), Declan Browne (Tipperary), Steven McDonnell (Armagh), Peter Canavan (Tyrone), Adrian Sweeney (Donegal).

2004

Diarmuid Murphy (Kerry), Tom O'Sullivan (Kerry), Barry Owens (Fermanagh), Michael McCarthy (Kerry), Tomas Ó Sé (Kerry), James Nallen (Mayo), John Keane (Westmeath), Martin McGrath (Fermanagh), Seán Cavanagh (Tyrone), Paul Galvin (Kerry), Ciaran McDonald (Mayo), Dessie Dolan (Westmeath), Colm Cooper (Kerry), Enda Muldoon (Derry), Matty Forde (Wexford).

2005

Diarmuid Murphy (Kerry), Ryan McMenamin (Tyrone), Mike McCarthy (Kerry), Andy Mallon (Armagh), Tomás Ó Sé (Kerry), Conor Gormley (Tyrone), Philip Jordan (Tyrone), Seán Cavanagh (Tyrone), Paul McGrane (Armagh), Brian Dooher (Tyrone), Peter Canavan (Tyrone), Eoin Mulligan (Tyrone), Colm Cooper (Kerry), Stephen O'Neill (Tyrone), Steven McDonnell (Armagh).

2006

Stephen Cluxton (Dublin), Marc Ó Sé (Kerry), Barry Owens (Fermanagh), Karl Lacey (Donegal), Seamus Moynihan (Kerry), Ger Spillane (Cork), Aidan O'Mahony (Kerry), Darragh Ó Sé (Kerry), Nicholas Murphy (Cork), Paul Galvin (Kerry), Alan Brogan (Dublin), Alan Dillon (Mayo), Conor Mortimer (Mayo), Kieran Donaghy (Kerry), Ronan Clarke (Armagh).

2007

Stephen Cluxton (Dublin), Marc Ó Sé (Kerry), Kevin McCloy (Derry), Graham Canty (Cork), Tomás Ó Sé (Kerry), Aidan O'Mahony (Kerry), Barry Cahill (Dublin), Ciarán Whelan (Dublin), Darragh Ó Sé (Kerry), Stephen Bray (Meath), Declan O'Sullivan (Kerry), Alan Brogan (Dublin), Colm Cooper (Kerry), Paddy Bradley (Derry), Thomas Freeman (Monaghan).

2008

Gary Connaughton (Westmeath), Conor Gormley (Tyrone), Justin McMahon (Tyrone), John Keane (Westmeath), Davy Harte (Tyrone), Tomás Ó Sé (Kerry), Philip Jordan (Tyrone), Enda McGinley (Tyrone), Shane Ryan (Dublin), Brian Dooher (Tyrone), Declan O'Sullivan (Kerry), Seán Cavanagh (Tyrone), Colm Cooper (Kerry), Kieran Donaghy (Kerry), Ronan Clarke (Armagh).

2009

Diarmuid Murphy (Kerry), Karl Lacey (Donegal), Michael Shields (Cork), Tom O'Sullivan (Kerry), Tomás Ó Sé (Kerry), Graham Canty (Cork), John Miskella (Cork), Dermot Earley (Kildare), Seamus Scanlon (Kerry), Paul Galvin (Kerry), Pearse O'Neill (Cork), Tadhg Kennelly (Kerry), Daniel Goulding (Cork), Declan O'Sullivan (Kerry), Stephen O'Neill (Tyrone).

2010

Brendan McVeigh (Down), Peter Kelly (Kildare), Michael Shields (Cork), Charlie Harrison (Sligo), Paudie Kissane (Cork), Graham Canty (Cork), Philip Jordan (Tyrone), Paddy Keenan (Louth), Aidan Walsh (Cork), Daniel Hughes (Down), Martin Clarke (Down), Johnny Doyle (Kildare), Colm Cooper (Kerry), Bernard Brogan (Dublin), Benny Coulter (Down).

2011

Stephen Cluxton (Dublin), Marc Ó Sé (Kerry), Neil McGee (Donegal), Michael Foley (Kildare), Kevin Cassidy (Donegal), Karl Lacey (Donegal), Kevin Nolan (Dublin), Bryan Sheehan (Kerry), Michael Darragh Macauley (Dublin), Darran O'Sullivan (Kerry), Alan Brogan (Dublin), Paul Flynn (Dublin), Colm Cooper (Kerry), Andy Moran (Mayo), Bernard Brogan (Dublin)

2012

Paul Durcan (Donegal), Neil McGee (Donegal), Ger Cafferkey (Mayo), Keith Higgins (Mayo), Lee Keegan (Mayo), Karl Lacey (Donegal), Frank McGlynn (Donegal), Neil Gallagher (Donegal), Aidan Walsh (Cork), Paul Flynn (Dublin), Alan Dillon (Mayo), Mark McHugh (Donegal), Colm O'Neill (Cork), Michael Murphy (Donegal), Colm McFadden (Donegal).

2013

Stephen Cluxton (Dublin), Colin Walshe (Monaghan), Rory O'Carroll (Dublin), Keith Higgins (Mayo), Lee Keegan (Mayo), Cian O'Sullivan (Dublin), Colm Boyle (Mayo), Michael Darragh Macauley (Dublin), Aidan O'Shea (Mayo), Paul Flynn (Dublin), Colm Cooper (Kerry), Seán Cavanagh (Tyrone), James O'Donoghue (Kerry), Bernard Brogan (Dublin), Conor McManus (Monaghan).

2014

Paul Durcan (Donegal), Paul Murphy (Kerry), Neil McGee (Donegal), Keith Higgins (Mayo), James McCarthy (Dublin), Peter Crowley (Kerry), Colm Boyle (Mayo), Neil Gallagher (Donegal), David Moran (Kerry), Paul Flynn (Dublin), Michael Murphy (Donegal), Diarmuid Connolly (Dublin), Cillian O'Connor (Mayo), Kieran Donaghy (Kerry), James O'Donoghue (Kerry)

2015

Brendan Kealy (Kerry), Shane Enright (Kerry), Rory O'Carroll (Dublin), Philly McMahon (Dublin), Lee Keegan (Mayo), Cian O'Sullivan (Dublin), Jack McCaffrey (Dublin), Brian Fenton (Dublin), Anthony Maher (Kerry), Mattie Donnelly (Tyrone), Ciaran Kilkenny (Dublin), Donnchadh Walsh (Kerry), Conor McManus (Monaghan), Aidan O'Shea (Mayo), Bernard Brogan (Dublin).

2016

David Clarke (Mayo), Brendan Harrison (Mayo), Jonny Cooper (Dublin), Philly McMahon (Dublin), Lee Keegan (Mayo), Colm Boyle (Mayo), Ryan McHugh (Donegal), Brian Fenton (Dublin), Mattie Donnelly (Tyrone), Peter Harte (Tyrone), Diarmuid Connolly (Dublin), Ciarán Kilkenny (Dublin), Dean Rock (Dublin), Michael Quinlivan (Tipperary), Paul Geaney (Kerry).

2017

David Clarke (Mayo), Chris Barrett (Mayo), Michael Fitzsimons (Dublin), Keith Higgins (Mayo), Colm Boyle (Mayo), Cian O'Sullivan (Dublin), Jack McCaffrey (Dublin), Colm Cavanagh (Tyrone), James McCarthy (Dublin), Dean Rock (Dublin), Aidan O'Shea (Mayo), Con O'Callaghan (Dublin), Paul Mannion (Dublin), Paul Geaney (Kerry), Andy Moran (Mayo).

LEADING AWARD WINNERS

Pat Spillane (Kerry) 9   1976, 1977, 1978, 1979, 1980, 1981, 1984, 1985, 1986.
Mike Sheehy (Kerry) 7   1976, 1978, 1979, 1981, 1982, 1984, 1986.
Jack O'Shea (Kerry) 6   1980, 1981, 1982, 1983, 1984, 1985.
Ger Power (Kerry) 6   1975, 1976, 1978, 1979, 1980, 1986.

ALL-TIME ALL-STAR AWARD WINNERS FOOTBALL

1980	Larry Stanley (Kildare).
1981	Tommy Murphy (Laois).
1982	Paddy Moclair (Mayo).
1983	Jim McCullogh (Armagh).
1984	John Dunne (Galway).
1985	J. J. (Purty) Landers and Tim (Roundy) Landers (Kerry).
1986	Alf Murray (Armagh).
1987	Mick Higgins (Cavan).
1988	Kevin Armstrong (Antrim).
1989	Peter McDermott (Meath).
1990	Eddie Boyle (Louth).
1991	Seán Purcell (Galway).
1992	Seán Flanagan (Mayo).
1993	Jimmy Murray (Roscommon).
1994	Bill Delaney (Laois). Discontinued.

FOOTBALLER OF THE YEAR AWARD

The following are the football stars who have been awarded Texaco Trophies by the Sports Editors since the inauguration of the award in 1958. Also listed are the Hall of Fame winners in football since the introduction of this category in 1960.

1958	Jim McKeever, Derry.
1959	Seán Murphy, Kerry.
1960	Jim McCartan, Down.
1961	Jim McCartan, Down.
1962	Mick O'Connell, Kerry.
1963	Lar Foley, Dublin.
1964	Noel Tierney, Galway.
1965	Martin Newell, Galway.
1966	Mattie McDonagh, Galway.
1967	Bertie Cunningham, Meath.
1968	Seán O'Neill, Down.
1969	Mick O'Dwyer, Kerry.
1970	Tom Prendergast, Kerry.
1971	Eugene Mulligan, Offaly.
1972	Willie Bryan, Offaly.

1973	Billy Morgan, Cork.
1974	Kevin Heffernan, Dublin (coach/manager).
1975	John O'Keeffe, Kerry.
1976	Jimmy Keaveney, Dublin.
1977	Jimmy Keaveney, Dublin.
1978	Pat Spillane, Kerry.
1979	Mike Sheehy, Kerry.
1980	Jack O'Shea, Kerry.
1981	Jack O'Shea, Kerry.
1982	Martin Furlong, Offaly.
1983	Tommy Drumm, Dublin.
1984	Jack O'Shea, Kerry.
1985	Jack O'Shea, Kerry.
1986	Pat Spillane, Kerry.
1987	Brian Stafford, Meath.
1988	Bobby O'Malley, Meath.
1989	Teddy McCarthy, Cork.
1990	Shay Fahy, Cork.
1991	Colm O'Rourke, Meath.
1992	Martin McHugh, Donegal.
1993	Henry Downey, Derry.
1994	Mickey Linden, Down.
1995	Paul Curran, Dublin.
1996	Martin O'Connell, Meath.
1997	Maurice Fitzgerald, Kerry.
1998	Michael Donnellan, Galway.
1999	Trevor Giles, Meath.
2000	Seamus Moynihan, Kerry.
2001	Pádraic Joyce, Galway.
2002	Kieran McGeeney, Armagh.
2003	Peter Canavan, Tyrone.
2004	Colm Cooper, Kerry.
2005	Stephen O'Neill, Tyrone.
2006	Kieran Donaghy, Kerry.
2007	Marc Ó Sé, Kerry.
2008	Seán Cavanagh, Tyrone.
2009	Paul Galvin, Kerry.
2010	Bernard Brogan, Dublin.
2011	Alan Brogan, Dublin.
2012	Karl Lacey, Donegal.
2013	Michael Darragh Macauley, Dublin.
2014	James O'Donoghue, Kerry.
2015	Jack McCaffrey, Dublin.
2016	Lee Keegan, Mayo.
2017	Andy Moran, Mayo.

HALL OF FAME

1963	John Joe Sheehy (Kerry)
1970	Larry Stanley (Kildare)
1989	Mick Higgins (Cavan)
1992	John Doyle (Tipperary)
1998	Kevin Heffernan (Dublin)

In 1993 Jack Lynch (Cork) was given the Hall of Fame award under the heading Gaelic Sport as he had won five All-Ireland senior hurling medals with Cork (1941-'44 and '46) and one senior football medal in 1945.

ATTENDANCE FIGURES
ALL-IRELAND FINALS

1933	Cavan v Galway	45,188
1934	Galway v Dublin	36,143
1935	Cavan v Kildare	50,380
1936	Mayo v Laois	50,168
1937	Kerry v Cavan	52,325
Replay	Kerry v Cavan	51,234
1938	Galway v Kerry	68,950
Replay	Galway v Kerry	47,581
1939	Kerry v Meath	46,828
1940	Kerry v Galway	60,824
1941	Kerry v Galway	45,512
1942	Dublin v Galway	37,105
1943	Roscommon v Cavan	68,023
Replay	Roscommon v Cavan	47,193
1944	Roscommon v Kerry	79,245
1945	Cork v Cavan	67,329
1946	Kerry v Roscommon	75,771
1947	Cavan v Kerry	34,941
1948	Cavan v Mayo	74,645
1949	Meath v Cavan	79,460
1950	Mayo v Louth	76,174
1951	Mayo v Meath	78,201
1952	Cavan v Meath	60,020
Replay	Cavan v Meath	62,515
1953	Kerry v Armagh	86,155
1954	Meath v Kerry	72,276
1955	Kerry v Dublin	87,102
1956	Galway v Cork	70,772
1957	Louth v Cork	72,732
1958	Dublin v Derry	73,371
1959	Kerry v Galway	85,897
1960	Down v Kerry	87,768
1961	Down v Offaly	90,556
1962	Kerry v Roscommon	75,771
1963	Dublin v Galway	87,106
1964	Galway v Kerry	76,498
1965	Galway v Kerry	77,735
1966	Galway v Meath	71,569
1967	Meath v Cork	70,343
1968	Down v Kerry	71,294
1969	Kerry v Offaly	67,828
1970	Kerry v Meath	71,775
1971	Offaly v Galway	70,798

FOOTBALL

1972	Offaly v Kerry	72,032
Replay	Offaly v Kerry	66,136
1973	Cork v Galway	73,309
1974	Dublin v Galway	71,898
1975	Kerry v Dublin	66,346
1976	Dublin v Kerry	73,588
1977	Dublin v Armagh	66,542
1978	Kerry v Dublin	71,503
1979	Kerry v Dublin	72,185
1980	Kerry v Roscommon	63,854
1981	Kerry v Offaly	61,489
1982	Offaly v Kerry	62,309
1983	Dublin v Galway	71,988
1984	Kerry v Dublin	68,365
1985	Kerry v Dublin	69,389
1986	Kerry v Tyrone	68,628
1987	Meath v Cork	68,431
1988	Meath v Cork	65,000
Replay	Meath v Cork	64,067
1989	Cork v Mayo	65,519
1990	Cork v Meath	65,723
1991	Down v Meath	64,500
1992	Donegal v Dublin	64,547
1993	Derry v Cork	64,500
1994	Down v Dublin	58,684
1995	Dublin v Tyrone	65,983
1996	Meath v Mayo	65,898
Replay	Meath v Mayo	65,802
1997	Kerry v Mayo	65,601
1998	Galway v Kildare	65,886
1999	Meath v Cork	62,989
2000	Kerry v Galway	63,349
Replay	Kerry v Galway	64,094
2001	Galway v Meath	70,482
2002	Armagh v Kerry	79,500
2003	Tyrone v Armagh	79,391
2004	Kerry v Mayo	79,749
2005	Tyrone v Kerry	82,112
2006	Kerry v Mayo	82,289
2007	Kerry v Cork	82,126
2008	Tyrone v Kerry	82,204
2009	Kerry v Cork	82,286
2010	Cork v Down	81,604
2011	Dublin v Kerry	82,300
2012	Donegal v Mayo	82,269
2013	Dublin v Mayo	82,274
2014	Kerry v Donegal	82,184

2015	Dublin v Kerry	82,300
2016	Dublin v Mayo	82,257
Replay	Dublin v Mayo	82,249
2017	Dublin v Mayo	82,300

The 1933 figures set up a new record the previous highest being an attendance of 43,839 at the 1929 final in which Kerry defeated Kildare. The 1947 football final between Cavan and Kerry was played in the Polo Grounds New York.

The attendance of 73,588 at the Dublin-Kerry game in 1976 was the highest at a final since the capacity of Croke Park was reduced with the installation of the seats under the old Cusack Stand in 1966 (the previous best for the altered Croke Park was set in 1973 when 73,308 saw the Cork-Galway final).

Note: The first Cusack Stand was officially opened on August 21 1938 with 5,000 upperdeck seats. In 1996 seating for 9,000 was installed on the terraces underneath to form the lower deck. This reduced the capacity of Croke Park to 75,000. The first Hogan Stand (capacity 900) was opened in 1924 and replaced with the new structure which was officially opened on June 7 1959 with accommodation for 16,000. The first phase of the modernisation of the stadium began in October 1993 with the demolition of the Cusack Stand. It was replaced with a 26,000 seater structure the first in Irish sport to offer corporate boxes and premier seating; it was first in use on July 31 1994 for the Leinster football final and was offically opened on June 5 1996. Phase 2 of the re-development – a new stand at the Canal end of the ground – commenced in October 1998. This and the new Hogan Stand were officially opened in March 2003 and the redevelopment was completed in 2005 with the opening of the new Hill 16. This brings the capacity to 83,000.

DUAL ALL-IRELAND SENIOR MEDALISTS

W. J. Spain (Tipperary): Hurling 1889. Football (Limerick) 1887.
Bill Mackessey (Cork): Hurling 1903. Football 1911.
Pierce Grace (Kilkenny): Hurling 1911, 1912, 1913. Football (Dublin) 1908.
Seán O'Kennedy (Wexford): Hurling 1910. Football 1915-'17.
Paddy Mackey (Wexford): Hurling 1910. Football 1915-'18.
Frank Burke (Kildare): Hurling (Dublin) 1917, 1920. Football (Dublin) 1921 -'23.
Leonard McGrath (Galway): Hurling 1923. Football 1925.
Jack Lynch (Cork): Hurling 1941, 1942, 1943, 1944, 1946. Football 1945.
Derry Beckett (Cork): Hurling 1942. Football 1945.
Ray Cummins (Cork): Hurling 1970, 1976, 1977, 1978. Football 1973.
Denis Coughlan (Cork): Hurling 1970 (sub), 1976, 1977, 1978. Football 1973.
Brian Murphy (Cork): Hurling 1976, 1977, 1978. Football 1973.
Jimmy Barry-Murphy (Cork): Hurling 1976, 1977, 1978, 1984, 1986. Football 1973.
Liam Currams (Offaly): Hurling 1981. Football 1982.
Teddy McCarthy (Cork): Hurling 1986, 1990. Football 1989, 1990.
Denis Walsh (Cork): Hurling 1986. Football 1989 (sub).
Paddy Healy (Cork): Hurling 1944, 1946. Football 1945 (sub).
Teddy O'Brien (Cork): Football 1973 (sub). Hurling 1976 (sub).

Teddy McCarthy is the only player to win two senior All-Ireland medals in the same year. That record was achieved in 1990 when he was on the victorious Cork hurling and football teams.

COLLEGES

COLLEGES

ALL-IRELAND CHAMPIONSHIPS
HURLING FINALS

1944	St Flannan's Ennis 5-5, St Kieran's Kilkenny 3-3
1945	St Flannan's Ennis 7-10, St Joseph's Marino 2-3
1946	St Flannan's Ennis 5-7, O'Connell Schools Dublin 5-2
1947	St Flannan's Ennis 6-8, St Joseph's Roscrea 3-1
1948	St Kieran's Kilkenny 2-12, St Colman's Fermoy 2-2
1949-1956	Suspended
1957	St Kieran's Kilkenny 4- 2, St Flannan's Ennis 2-7
1958	St Flannan's Ennis 3-10, St Kieran's Kilkenny 0-2
1959	St Kieran's Kilkenny 2- 13, Tipperary CBS 4-2
1960	North Mon Cork 1-9, St Peter's Wexford 1-4
1961	St Kieran's Kilkenny 8- 8, North Mon Cork 1-4
1962	St Peter's Wexford 0-10, Ennis CBS 2-4
Replay	St Peter's Wexford 4-11, Ennis CBS 2-4
1963	St Finbarr's Cork 4-8, Ballyfin Laois 3-4
1964	Limerick CBS 6-7, St Peter's, Wexford 4-5
1965	St Kieran's Kilkenny 6- 9, Limerick CBS 6-1
1966	Limerick CBS 8-9, St Mary's Galway 2-2
1967	St Peter's Wexford 5-13, Limerick CBS 5-13
Replay	St Peter's Wexford 5-11, Limerick CBS 3-6
1968	St Peter's Wexford 4-3, Col Chríost Rí Cork 3-6
Replay	St Peter's Wexford 5-10, Col Chríost Rí Cork 4-5
1969	St Finbarr's Cork 5-15, St Kieran's Kilkenny 2-1
1970	North Mon Cork 2- 13, Kilkenny CBS 2-8
1971	St Kieran's Kilkenny 8-6, St Finbarr's Cork 5-8
1972	St Finbarr's Cork 3-7, St Kieran's Kilkenny 2-5
1973	St Peter's Wexford 2-6, Our Lady's Gort 2-6
Replay	St Peter's Wexford 4-15, Our Lady's Gort 1-5
1974	St Finbarr's Cork 2- 11, St Kieran's Kilkenny 1-12
1975	St Kieran's Kilkenny 6- 9, Col Iognáid Rís 2-3
1976	St Flannan's, Ennis 3-7, Presentation Athenry 4-4
Replay	St Flannan's, Ennis 3-9, Presentation Athenry 1-7
1977	St Colman's Fermoy 2-13, St Kieran's Kilkenny 1-9
1978	Templemore CBS 2-11, St Peter's Wexford 1-4
1979	St Flannan's, Ennis 3-15, Presentation (Birr) 2-3
1980	North Mon Cork 5-11, Birr Community 3-7
1981	Kilkenny CBS 3-5, North Mon Cork 1-8
1982	St Flannan's, Ennis 1-4, St Peter's Wexford 1-4
Replay	St Flannan's, Ennis 2-9, St Peter's Wexford 0-10
1983	St Flannan's, Ennis 0-16, Kilkenny CBS 2-4
1984	St Finbarr's Farrenferris 1-15, St Kieran's 0-8
1985	North Mon Cork 2-7, Birr Community School 3-4
Replay	North Mon Cork 4-11, Birr Community School 1-5
1986	Birr CS 5-8, North Mon Cork 1-8
1987	St Flannan's, Ennis 4-11, St Kieran's Kilkenny 1-7
1988	St Kieran's Kilkenny 3- 10, Midleton CBS 2-7
1989	St Kieran's Kilkenny 3-5, St Flannan's, Ennis 1-9
1990	St Kieran's Kilkenny 2-10, St Flannan's, Ennis 0-7
1991	St Flannan's, Ennis 1-15, St Kieran's Kilkenny 1-9
1992	St Kieran's Kilkenny 1- 7, St Colman's Fermoy 0-8
1993	St Kieran's Kilkenny 3- 15, Our Lady's Gort 1-10
1994	North Mon 1-10, St Mary's, Galway 1-6
1995	St Raphael's Loughrea 3-10, Midleton CBS 3-5
1996	St Kieran's Kilkenny 1-14, St Colman's, Fermoy 2-6
1997	St Colman's Fermoy 4-20, Good Counsel, New Ross 0-9
1998	St Flannan's, Ennis 2- 16, St Raphael's, Loughrea 1-11
1999	St Flannan's, Ennis 2- 15, St Kieran's Kilkenny 2-10
2000	St Kieran's Kilkenny 1- 10, St Flannan's Ennis 0-9
2001	St Colman's Fermoy 2- 10, Gort CS 2-7
2002	St Colman's Fermoy 0- 11, St Kieran's Kilkenny 2-4
2003	St Kieran's Kilkenny 1-15, St Colman's Fermoy 1-4
2004	St Kieran's Kilkenny 3-20, St Raphael's Loughrea 1-6
2005	St Flannan's Ennis 2-15, St Kieran's Kilkenny 2-12
2006	Dublin Colleges 1-11, St Flannan's Ennis 0-1
2007	De La Salle Waterford 0-13, Kilkenny CBS 1-9
2008	De La Salle Waterford 2-12, Thurles CBS 1-15
Replay	De La Salle Waterford 2- 9, Thurles CBS 2-8
2009	Thurles CBS 1-17, Good Counsel, New Ross 1-15
2010	St Kieran's Kilkenny 2-11, Ardscoil Rís Limerick 2-8
2011	St Kieran's Kilkenny 2-10, Ardscoil Rís Limerick 1-11
2012	Nenagh CBS 3-10, Kilkenny CBS 2-11
2013	Dungarvan Colleges 1-12, Kilkenny CBS 1-7
2014	St Kieran's Kilkenny 2-16, Kilkenny CBS 0-13
2015	St Kieran's Kilkenny 1-15, Thurles CBS 1-12
2016	St Kieran's Kilkenny 1-15 Ardscoil Rís Limerick 1-13
2017	Our Lady's Templemore 3-13, St Kieran's Kilkenny 3-11

MUNSTER SENIOR HURLING
CHAMPIONS (DR. HARTY CUP)

1918	Rockwell College
1919	North Monastery, Cork
1920	Limerick CBS
1921	None
1922	St. Munchin's, Limerick
1923	Rockwell College
1924	Rockwell College
1925	Limerick CBS
1926	Limerick CBS
1927	Limerick CBS
1928	No Competition
1929	North Monastery, Cork
1930	Rockwell College
1931	Rockwell College
1932	Limerick CBS
1933	Thurles CBS
1934	North Monastery, Cork
1935	North Monastery, Cork
1936	North Monastery, Cork
1937	North Monastery, Cork
1938	Thurles CBS
1939	Thurles CBS
1940	North Monastery, Cork
1941	North Monastery, Cork
1942	North Monastery, Cork
1943	North Monastery, Cork
1944	St. Flannan's, Ennis
1945	St. Flannan's, Ennis
1946	St. Flannan's, Ennis
1947	St. Flannan's, Ennis
1948	St. Colman's, Fermoy
1949	St. Colman's, Fermoy
1950	Thurles CBS
1951	Thurles CBS
1952	St. Flannan's, Ennis
1953	Mount Sion, Waterford
1954	St. Flannan's, Ennis
1955	North Monastery, Cork
1956	Thurles CBS
1957	St. Flannan's, Ennis
1958	St. Flannan's, Ennis
1959	Tipperary CBS
1960	North Monastery, Cork
1961	North Monastery, Cork
1962	Ennis CBS
1963	St. Finbarr's, Farranferris
1964	Limerick CBS
1965	Limerick CBS
1966	Limerick CBS
1967	Limerick CBS
1968	Col. Chríost Rí, Cork
1969	St. Finbarr's, Farranferris
1970	North Monastery, Cork
1971	St. Finbarr's, Farranferris
1972	St. Finbarr's, Farranferris
1973	St. Finbarr's, Farranferris
1974	St. Finbarr's, Farranferris
1975	Col. Iognaid Rís, Cork
1976	St. Flannan's, Ennis
1977	St. Coleman's, Fermoy
1978	Templemore CBS
1979	St. Flannan's, Ennis
1980	North Monastery, Cork
1981	North Monastery, Cork
1982	St. Flannan's, Ennis
1983	St. Flannan's, Ennis
1984	St. Finbarr's, Farranferris
1985	North Monastery, Cork
1986	North Monastery, Cork
1987	St. Flannan's, Ennis
1988	Midleton CBS
1989	St. Flannan's, Ennis
1990	St. Flannan's, Ennis
1991	St. Flannan's, Ennis
1992	St. Colman's, Fermoy
1993	St. Michael's CBS, Limerick
1994	North Monastery, Cork
1995	Midleton CBS, Cork
1996	St. Colman's, Fermoy
1997	St. Colman's, Fermoy
1998	St. Flannan's, Ennis
1999	St. Flannan's, Ennis
2000	St. Flannan's, Ennis
2001	St. Colman's, Fermoy
2002	St. Colman's, Fermoy
2003	St. Colman's, Fermoy
2004	St. Flannan's, Ennis
2005	St. Flannan's, Ennis
2006	Midleton CBS, Cork
2007	De La Salle, Waterford
2008	De La Salle, Waterford
2009	Thurles CBS
2010	Ardscoil Rís, Limerick
2011	St. Colman's, Fermoy
2012	Dungarvan Colleges
2013	Ardscoil Rís, Limerick
2014	Ardscoil Rís, Limerick
2015	Thurles CBS
2016	Ardscoil Rís, Limerick
2017	Our Lady's, Templemore

COLLEGES

LEINSTER SENIOR HURLING CHAMPIONS

1918	Castleknock College, Dublin		1967	St. Peter's, Wexford
1919	No Competition		1968	St. Peter's, Wexford
1920	Mount St. Joseph's, Roscrea		1969	St. Kieran's, Kilkenny
1921	Mount St. Joseph's, Roscrea		1970	Kilkenny CBS
1922	St. Kieran, Kilkenny		1971	St. Kieran's, Kilkenny
1923	Mount St. Joseph's, Roscrea		1972	St. Kieran's, Kilkenny
1924	Mount St. Joseph's, Roscrea		1973	St. Peter's, Wexford
1925	St. Kieran's, Kilkenny		1974	St. Kieran's, Kilkenny
1926	St. Kieran's, Kilkenny		1975	St. Kieran's, Kilkenny
1927	St. Kieran's, Kilkenny		1976	Kilkenny CBS
1928	St. Kieran's, Kilkenny		1977	St. Kieran's, Kilkenny
1929	St. Kieran's, Kilkenny		1978	St. Peter's, Wexford
1930	Col. Caoimhghin, Dublin		1979	Presentation, Birr
1931	St. Kieran's, Kilkenny		1980	Birr Community School
1932	St. Kieran's, Kilkenny		1981	Kilkenny CBS
1933	St. Kieran's, Kilkenny		1982	St. Peter's, Wexford
1934	Col. Caoimhghin, Dublin		1983	Kilkenny CBS
1935	Blackrock College, Dublin		1984	St. Kieran's, Kilkenny
1936	Kilkenny CBS		1985	Birr Community School
1937	St. Kieran's, Kilkenny		1986	Birr Community School
1938	St. Kieran's, Kilkenny		1987	St. Kieran's, Kilkenny
1939	St. Kieran's, Kilkenny		1988	St. Kieran's, Kilkenny
1940	St. Kieran's, Kilkenny		1989	St. Kieran's, Kilkenny
1941	St. Kieran's, Kilkenny		1990	St. Kieran's, Kilkenny
1942	Patrician College, Ballyfin		1991	St. Kieran's, Kilkenny
1943	St. Kieran's, Kilkenny		1992	St. Kieran's, Kilkenny
1944	St. Kieran's, Kilkenny		1993	St. Kieran's, Kilkenny
1945	St. Joseph's, Marino, Dublin		1994	St. Kieran's, Kilkenny
1946	O'Connell's School, Dublin		1995	Good Counsel, New Ross
1947	Mount St. Joseph's, Roscrea		1996	St. Kieran's, Kilkenny
1948	St. Kieran's, Kilkenny		1997	Good Counsel, New Ross
1949	St. Kieran's, Kilkenny		1998	Coláiste Eamon Rís, Callan
1950	St. Kieran's, Kilkenny		1999	St. Kieran's, Kilkenny
1951	St. Kieran's, Kilkenny		2000	St. Kieran's, Kilkenny
1952	Patrician College, Ballyfin		2001	Dublin Colleges
1953	St. Kieran's, Kilkenny		2002	St. Kieran's, Kilkenny
1954	O'Connell Schools, Dublin		2003	St. Kieran's, Kilkenny
1955	Knockbeg College, Carlow		2004	St. Kieran's, Kilkenny
1956	Patrician College, Ballyfin		2005	St. Kieran's, Kilkenny
1957	St. Kieran's, Kilkenny		2006	Kilkenny CBS
1958	St. Kieran's, Kilkenny		2007	Castlecomer CS
1959	St. Kieran's, Kilkenny		2008	Dublin Colleges
1960	St. Kieran's, Kilkenny		2009	Good Counsel, New Ross
1961	St. Kieran's, Kilkenny		2010	St. Kieran's, Kilkenny
1962	St. Peter's, Wexford		2011	St. Kieran's, Kilkenny
1963	Patrician College, Ballyfin		2012	St. Kieran's, Kilkenny
1964	St. Peter's, Wexford		2013	Kilkenny CBS
1965	St. Kieran's, Kilkenny		2014	Kilkenny CBS
1966	St. Kieran's, Kilkenny		2015	St Kieran's, Kilkenny
			2016	St Kieran's, Kilkenny
			2017	St Kieran's, Kilkenny

CONNACHT SENIOR HURLING CHAMPIONS

1938	Roscommon CBS
1939	Roscommon CBS
1940	St. Mary's, Galway
1941	St. Mary's, Galway
1942	St. Mary's, Galway
1943-1945	None
1946	St. Mary's, Galway
1947	St. Mary's, Galway
1948	De La Salle, Loughrea
1949	St. Mary's, Galway
1950	St. Mary's, Galway
1951	St. Mary's, Galway
1952	St. Mary's, Galway
1953	St. Mary's, Galway
1954	St. Mary's, Galway
1955	St. Mary's, Galway
1956	St. Mary's, Galway
1957	St. Mary's, Galway
1958	St. Joseph's, Galway
1959	St. Joseph's, Gorbally
1960	St. Marys, Galway
1961	St. Molaises', Portumna
1962	St. Molaises', Portumna
1963	St. Mary's, Galway
1964	St. Mary's, Galway
1965	St. Mary's, Galway
1966	St. Mary's, Galway
1967	St. Mary's, Galway
1968	St. Joseph's, Garbally
1969	Our Ladys, Gort
1970	Presentation, Athenry
1971	Presentation, Athenry
1972	Our Lady's, Gort
1973	Our Lady's, Gort
1974	Our Lady's, Gort
1975	Our Lady's, Gort
1976	Presentation, Athenry
1977	Presentation, Athenry
1978	Our Lady's, Gort
1979	St. Mary's, Galway
1980	St. Joseph's, Garbally
1981	Our Ladys, Gort
1982	Our Ladys, Gort
1983	St. Joseph's, Garbally
1984	Our Ladys, Gort
1985	St. Joseph's, Garbally
1986	St. Joseph's, Garbally
1987	St. Joseph's, Garbally
1988	St. Mary's, Galway
1989	St. Mary's, Galway
1990	St. Mary's, Galway
1991	St. Raphael's, Loughrea
1992	St. Raphael's, Loughrea
1993	Our Lady's, Gort
1994	St. Mary's, Galway
1995	St. Raphael's, Loughrea
1996	St. Raphael's, Loughrea
1997	Presentation, Athenry
1998	St. Raphael's, Loughrea
1999	Gort C.S.
2000	Gort C.C.
2001	Gort C.S.
2002	Mercy College, Woodford
2003	Gort C.S.
2004	St. Raphael's, Loughrea
2005	Gort C.C.
2006	Gort C.C.
2007	Gort C.C.
2008	Gort C.C.
2009	Gort C.C.
2010	Gort C.C.
2011	Presentation, Athenry
2012	Portumna
2013	Mercy College (Woodford and St Raphael's)
2014	Presentation, Athenry
2015	Presentation, Athenry
2016	Presentation, Athenry
2017	St Brigid's, Loughrea

COLLEGES

ALL-IRELAND CHAMPIONSHIPS
FOOTBALL FINALS

1946	St Patrick's, Armagh 3- 11; St Jarlath's, Tuam 4-7
1947	St Jarlath's, Tuam 4- 10; St Patrick's, Armagh 3-8
1948	St Mel's, Longford 4-7; St Patrick's, Cavan 3-3
1949-1956	Suspended
1957	St Nathy's, Ballaghadereen 1-7; St Colman's, Newry 0-4
1958	St Jarlath's, Tuam 1-7; Franciscan College, Gormanston 2-3
1959	St Joseph's, Fairview 3-9; St Nathy's, Ballaghaderreen 2-8
1960	St Jarlath's, Tuam 3-10; St Finian's, Mullingar 3-7
1961	St Jarlath's, Tuam 2-8; St Mel's, Longford 1-8
1962	St Mel's, Longford 3- 11; St Jarlath's, Tuam 2-12
1963	St Mel's, Longford 1- 6; St Brendan's, Killarney 2-2
1964	St Jarlath's, Tuam 0-11; St Mel's, Longford 1-8
Replay	St Jarlath's, Tuam 1-10; St Mel's, Longford 0-4
1965	St Columb's, Derry 0-9; Belcamp OMI Dublin 0-9
Replay	St Columb's, Derry 0-11; Belcamp OMI Dublin 1-7
1966	St Jarlath's, Tuam 1-10; St Finian's, Mullingar 1-9
1967	St Colman's, Newry 1- 8; St Jarlath's, Tuam 1-7
1968	Col Críost Rí, Cork 3- 11; Belcamp OMI Dublin 1-10
1969	St Brendan's, Killarney 1- 13; St Mary's, Galway 3-3
1970	Col Críost Rí, Cork 4-5; St Malachy's, Belfast 1-13
1971	St Mary's CBS, Belfast 1-13; Col Iosagáin Ballyvourney 1-7
1972	St Patrick's, Cavan 2- 11; St Brendan's, Killarney 1-5
1973	Franciscan College Gormanston 1-7; St Jarlath's, Tuam 0-8
1974	St Jarlath's, Tuam 4-11; Franciscan Col. Gormanston 2-11
1975	St Colman's, Newry 1- 7; Carmelite College Moate 2-3
1976	Carmelite College Moate 1-10; St Jarlath's, Tuam 0-11
1977	St Colman's, Claremorris 1-11; Carmelite Col. Moate 1-10
1978	St Jarlath's, Tuam 2- 11; St Colman's, Newry 2-4
1979	Ard Scoil Rís Dublin 0-10; St Jarlath's, Tuam 0-10
Replay	Ard Scoil Rís Dublin 2-9; St Jarlath's, Tuam 1-10
1980	Carmelite College Moate 0-12; St Patrick's, Maghera 1-8
1981	Carmelite Coll. Moate 2-2; St Colman's, Claremorris 1-4
1982	St Jarlath's, Tuam 1-7; St Fachtna's, Skibbereen 1-7
Replay	St Jarlath's, Tuam 1-8; St Fachtna's, Skibbereen 0-7
1983	Col Críost Rí, Cork 3- 6; St Jarlath's, Tuam 2-5
1984	St Jarlath's, Tuam 0-10; St Patrick's, Maghera 2-3
1985	Col Críost Rí, Cork 1-9; Summerhill 0-9
1986	St Colman's, Newry 3-10; St David's, Artane 0-7
1987	St Mel's, Longford 0- 8; St Mary's, Galway 1-4
1988	St Colman's, Newry 1-11; St Mel's, Longford 1-7
1989	St Patrick's, Maghera 1-5; Col Críost Rí, Cork 0-8
Replay	St Patrick's, Maghera 2-15; Col Críost Rí, Cork 1-6
1990	St Patrick's, Maghera 1-4; St Jarlath's, Tuam 0-7
Replay	St Patrick's, Maghera 1-11; St Jarlath's, Tuam 0- 13
1991	St Fachtna's, Skibereen 2-9; St Patrick's, Dungannon 0-7
1992	St Brendan's, Killarney 0-9, St Jarlath's, Tuam 0-5
1993	St Colman's, Newry 2-10, St Jarlath's, Tuam 1-9
1994	St Jarlath's, Tuam 3- 11, St Patrick's, Maghera 0-9
1995	St Patrick's, Maghera 2- 11, Good Counsel, New Ross 1-6
1996	Intermediate School Killorglin 4-8, St Patrick's 1-14
1997	St Patrick's, Dungannon 1-10, St Gerard's, Castlebar 0-3
1998	St Colman's, Newry 2- 14, Coláiste Eoin, Stillorgan 1-7
1999	Good Counsel New Ross 1-11, St Jarlath's, Tuam 1-7
2000	St Patrick's, Navan 0-11, St Patrick's, Armagh 1-6
2001	St Patrick's, Navan 2- 10, St Jarlath's, Tuam 2-8
2002	St Jarlath's, Tuam 3-13, St Michael's, Enniskillen 0-6
2003	St Patrick's, Maghera 1-9, St Jarlath's, Tuam 2-4
2004	St Patrick's, Navan 1-11, St Patrick's, Dungannon 1-10
2005	Knockbeg College Carlow 2-8, St Mary's, Galway 0-11
2006	Abbey CBS, Newry 2-15; St Patrick's Navan 2-13
2007	Omagh CBS 0-16; Tralee CBS 0-7
2008	St Patrick's Dungannon 1-9; St Brendan's Killarney 1-7
2009	Coláiste na Scéilge 1-9; St Mary's SS Edenderry 0-10
2010	StColman's, Newry 1-18, St Brendan's, Killarney 3-5
2011	St Colman's, Newry 2-10, St Jarlath's, Tuam 0-15
2012	St Mary's, Edenderry 1-16, St Michael's Coll., Enniskillen 0-6
2013	St Patrick's, Maghera 1-20, St Patrick's, Navan 1-10
2014	Pobalscoil Chorca Dhuibhne 1-8, St Patrick's Maghera 1-6
2015	Pobalscoil Chorca Dhuibhne 1-12, Roscommon CBS 2-5
2016	St Brendan's Killarney 2-13, St Patrick's Maghera 2-6
2017	St Brendan's Killarney 0-18, St Peter's Wexford 0-10

MUNSTER SENIOR FOOTBALL CHAMPIONS

1928	High School, Clonmel
1929	St. Brendan's, Killarney
1930	St. Brendan's, Killarney
1931	Tralee CBS
1932	Tralee CBS
1933	Tralee CBS
1934	Tralee CBS
1935	North Monastery, Cork
1936	North Monastery, Cork
1937	St. Brendan's, Killarney
1938	St. Brendan's, Killarney
1939	Col. na Mumban, Mallow
1940	Tralee CBS
1941	Tralee CBS
1942	Tralee CBS
1943	St. Brendan's, Killarney
1944	Tralee CBS
1945	Tralee CBS
1946	St. Brendan's, Killarney
1947	St. Brendan's, Killarney
1948	Tralee CBS
1949	Col. Iosagáin, Ballyvourney
1950	Rochestown College, Cork
1951	Col. Iosagáin, Ballyvourney
1952	Col. Iosagáin, Ballyvourney
1953	Tralee CBS
1954	Col. Iosagáin, Ballyvourney
1955	Tralee CBS
1956	Limerick CBS
1957	Col. Iosagáin, Ballyvourney
1958	De La Salle, Waterford
1959	St. Flannan's, Ennis
1960	Limerick CBS
1961	De La Salle, Waterford
1962	De La Salle, Waterford
1963	De La Salle, Waterford
1964	De La Salle, Waterford
1965	De La Salle, Waterford
1966	St. Brendan's, Killarney
1967	Col. Chríost Rí, Cork
1968	Col. Chríost Rí, Cork
1969	St. Brendan's, Killarney
1970	Col. Chríost Rí, Cork
1971	Col. Iosagáin, Ballyvourney
1972	St. Brendan's, Killarney
1973	St. Brendan's, Killarney
1974	St. Brendan's, Killarney
1975	Col. Iognáid Rís, Cork
1976	Tralee CBS
1977	St. Brendan's, Killarney
1978	Col. Chríost Rí, Cork
1979	Col. Chríost Rí, Cork
1980	Col. Chríost Rí, Cork
1981	Col. Iosagáin, Ballyvourney
1982	St. Fachtna's, Skibbereen
1983	Col. Chríost Rí, Cork
1984	Col. Chríost Rí, Cork
1985	Col. Chríost Rí, Cork
1986	St. Brendan's, Killarney
1987	Col. Chríost Rí, Cork
1988	North Monastery, Cork
1989	Col. Chríost Rí, Cork
1990	St. Fachtna's, Skibbereen
1991	St. Fachtna's, Skibbereen
1992	St. Brendan's, Killarney
1993	St. Flannan's, Ennis
1994	St. Brendan's, Killarney
1995	St. Flannan's, Ennis
1996	Intermediate School, Killorglin
1997	Col. Chríost Rí, Cork
1998	Col. Chríost Rí, Cork
1999	Tralee CBS
2000	Tralee CBS
2001	Coláiste na Sceilige
2002	Coláiste na Sceilige
2003	Coláiste na Sceilige
2004	Col. Chroist Rí, Cork
2005	Spioraid Naomh
2006	De La Salle, Macroom
2007	Tralee CBS
2008	St Brendan's, Killarney
2009	Coláiste na Sceilige
2010	St. Brendan's, Killarney
2011	Col. Chríost Rí, Cork
2012	Pobalscoil Chorca Dhuibhne
2013	Pobalscoil Chorca Dhuibhne
2014	Pobalscoil Chorca Dhuibhne
2015	Pobalscoil Chorca Dhuibhne
2016	St Brendan's, Killarney
2017	St Brendan's, Killarney

LEINSTER SENIOR FOOTBALL CHAMPIONS

1920	Knockbeg College, Carlow
1921	Belcamp College, Dublin
1922	St. Kieran's, Kilkenny
1923	St. Thomas' College, Newbridge
1924	St. Joseph's, Roscrea
1925	St. Finian's, Mullingar
1926	St. Finian's, Mullingar
1927	St. Finian's, Mullingar
1928	St. Mel's, Longford
1929	Col. Caoimhghin, Dublin
1930	Col. Caoimhghin, Dublin
1931	Col. Caoimhghin, Dublin
1932	Knockbeg College
1933	St. Mel's, Longford
1934	St. Mel's, Longford
1935	St. Mel's, Longford
1936	St. Mel's, Longford
1937	St. Mel's, Longford
1938	St. Mel's, Longford
1939	St Finian's. Mullingar
1940	St. Mel's, Longford
1941	St. Mel's, Longford
1942	St. Mel's, Longford
1943	St. Mel's, Longford
1944	St. Finian's, Mullingar
1945	St. Mel's, Longford
1946	St. Mel's, Longford
1947	St. Mel's, Longford
1948	St. Mel's, Longford
1949	St. Finian's, Mullingar
1950	St. Finian's, Mullingar
1951	St. Mel's, Longford
1952	Franciscan College, Multyfarnham
1953	St. Finian's, Mullingar
1954	Knockbeg College, Carlow
1955	Knockbeg College, Carlow
1956	St. Joseph's, Fairview
1957	Patrician College, Ballyfin
1958	Franciscan College, Gormanston
1959	St. Joseph's, Fairview
1960	St. Finian's, Mullingar
1961	St. Mel's, Longford
1962	St. Mel's, Longford
1963	St. Mel's, Longford
1964	St. Mel's, Longford
1965	Belcamp O.M.I., Dublin
1966	St Finian's, Mullingar
1967	Belcamp O.M.I., Dublin
1968	Belcamp O.M.I., Dublin
1969	St. Mel's, Longford
1970	Franciscan College, Gormanston
1971	St. Mel's, Longford
1972	Franciscan College, Gormanston
1973	Franciscan College, Gormanston
1974	Franciscan College, Gormanston
1975	Carmelite College, Moate
1976	Carmelite College, Moate
1977	Carmelite College, Moate
1978	Carmelite College, Moate
1979	Ard Scoil Rís, Dublin
1980	Carmelite College, Moate
1981	Carmelite College, Moate
1982	St. Mel's, Longford
1983	St. Mary's, Mullingar
1984	Portarlington CBS
1985	Dundalk CBS
1986	St. David's, Artaine
1987	St. Mel's, Longford
1988	St. Mel's, Longford
1989	St. Mel's, Longford
1990	St. Mel's, Longford
1991	St. Patrick's, Navan
1992	St. Peter's, Wexford
1993	St. Patrick's, Navan
1994	St. Mel's, Longford
1995	Good Counsel, New Ross
1996	Good Counsel, New Ross
1997	St. Patrick's, Navan
1998	Coláiste Eoin, Stillorgan, Dublin
1999	Good Counsel, New Ross
2000	St. Patrick's, Navan
2001	St. Patrick's, Navan
2002	Dundalk Schools
2003	St. Mel's, Longford
2004	St. Patrick's, Navan
2005	Knockbeg College (Carlow)
2006	St. Patrick's, Navan
2007	St. Patrick's, Navan
2008	Athlone CC
2009	St. Mary's SS, Edenderry
2010	St. Patrick's, Navan
2011	Dundalk Colleges
2012	St Mary's, Edenderry
2013	St. Patrick's, Navan
2014	Coláiste Eoin, Dublin
2015	Good Counsel, New Ross
2016	St Benidus, Dublin
2017	St Peter's, Wexford

CONNACHT SENIOR FOOTBALL CHAMPIONS

1929	St. Gerard's, Castlebar
1930	Summerhill, Sligo
1931	Summerhill, Sligo
1932	St. Jarlath's, Tuam
1933	St. Jarlath's, Tuam
1934	St. Jarlath's, Tuam
1935	St. Jarlath's, Tuam
1936	St. Jarlath's, Tuam
1937	St. Jarlath's, Tuam
1938	St. Jarlath's, Tuam
1939	St. Jarlath's, Tuam
1940	Roscommon CBS
1941	Roscommon C.B.S
1942	Roscommon CBS
1943	St. Jarlath's, Tuam
1944	St. Jarlath's, Tuam
1945	St. Jarlath's, Tuam
1946	St. Jarlath's, Tuam
1947	St. Jarlath's, Tuam
1948	Roscommon CBS
1949	St. Nathy's, Ballaghaderreen
1950	St. Jarlath's Tuam
1951	St. Jarlath's, Tuam
1952	St. Mary's, Galway
1953	St. Jarlath's, Tuam
1954	Summerhill, Sligo
1955	Summerhill, Sligo
1956	St. Jarlath's, Tuam
1957	St. Nathy's, Ballaghaderreen
1958	St. Jarlath's, Tuam
1959	St. Nathy's, Ballaghaderreen
1960	St. Jarlath's, Tuam
1961	St. Jarlath's, Tuam
1962	St. Jarlath's, Tuam
1963	St. Jarlath's, Tuam
1964	St. Jarlath's, Tuam
1965	St. Jarlath's, Tuam
1966	St. Jarlath's, Tuam
1967	St. Jarlath's, Tuam
1968	St. Nathy's, Ballaghaderreen
1969	St. Mary's, Galway
1970	St. Colman's, Claremorris
1971	Summerhill, Sligo
1972	St. Jarlath's, Tuam
1973	St. Jarlath's, Tuam
1974	St. Jarlath's, Tuam
1975	Summerhill, Sligo
1976	St. Jarlath's, Tuam
1977	St. Colman's, Claremorris
1978	St. Jarlath's, Tuam
1979	St. Jarlath's, Tuam
1980	Tuam CBS
1981	St. Colman's, Claremorris
1982	St. Jarlath's, Tuam
1983	St. Jarlath's, Tuam
1984	St. Jarlath's, Tuam
1985	Summerhill, Sligo
1986	St. Mary's, Galway
1987	St. Mary's, Galway
1988	St. Mary's, Galway
1989	Tuam CBS
1990	St. Jarlath's, Tuam
1991	St Mary's, Galway
1992	St. Jarlath's, Tuam
1993	St. Jarlath's, Tuam
1994	St. Jarlath's, Tuam
1995	St. Patrick's, Tuam
1996	St. Gerard's, Castlebar
1997	St. Gerard's, Castlebar
1998	Roscommon CBS
1999	St. Jarlath's, Tuam
2000	St. Jarlath's, Tuam
2001	St. Jarlath's, Tuam
2002	St. Jarlath's, Tuam
2003	St. Jarlath's, Tuam
2004	St. Mary's, Galway
2005	St. Mary's, Galway
2006	St. Mary's, Galway
2007	St. Jarlath's, Tuam
2008	St. Jarlath's, Tuam
2009	St. Colman's, Claremorris
2010	St. Gerard's, Castlebar
2011	St. Jarlath's, Tuam
2012	St. Jarlath's, Tuam
2013	St. Gerard's, Castlebar
2014	St. Gerard's, Castlebar
2015	Roscommon CBS
2016	Summerhill, Sligo
2017	St Colman's, Claremorris

COLLEGES

ULSTER SENIOR FOOTBALL CHAMPIONS

1919	St. Patrick's, Armagh
1920-1923	Suspended
1924	St. Patrick's, Armagh
1925	Unfinished
1926	St. Patrick's, Armagh
1927	St. Patrick's, Armagh
1928	St. Patrick's, Armagh
1929	St. Malachy's, Belfast
1930	St. McCartan's, Monaghan
1931	St. Patrick's, Armagh
1932	St. McCartan's, Monaghan
1933	St. McCartan's, Monaghan
1934	St. McCartan's, Monaghan, St. Patrick's, Armagh (joint holders)
1935	St. Patrick's, Cavan
1936	St. Patrick's, Cavan
1937	St. Patrick's, Cavan
1938	St. Mary's, Dundalk
1939	St. Patrick's, Covan
1940	St. McCartan's, Monaghan
1941	St. Mary's, Dundalk
1942	St. McCartan's, Monaghan
1943	St. Patrick's, Cavan
1944	St. Patrick's, Armagh
1945	St. Patrick's, Armagh
1946	St. Patrick's, Armagh
1947	St. Patrick's, Armagh
1948	St. Patrick's, Cavan
1949	St. Colman's, Newry
1950	St. Colman's, Newry
1951	St. Patrick's, Cavan
1952	St. McCartan's, Monaghan
1953	St. Patrick's, Armagh
1954	Newry CBS
1955	St. Patrick's, Cavan
1956	St. McCartan's, Monaghan
1957	St. Colman's, Newry
1958	St. Colman's, Newry
1959	Newry CBS
1960	St. Colman's' Newry
1961	St. Patrick's, Cavan
1962	St. Colman's, Newry
1963	St. Colman's, Newry
1964	Newry CBS
1965	St. Columb's, Derry
1966	St. Columb's, Derry
1967	St. Colman's, Newry
1968	St. Colman's, Newry
1969	St. Colman's, Newry
1970	St. Malachy's, Belfast
1971	St. Mary's CBS, Belfast
1972	St. Patrick's, Cavan
1973	St. Michael's, Enniskillen
1974	Omagh CBS
1975	St. Colman's, Newry
1976	St. Colman's, Newry
1977	St. Patrick's, Maghera
1978	St. Colman's, Newry
1979	St. Colman's, Newry
1980	St. Patrick's, Maghera
1981	St. Colman's, Newry
1982	St. Patrick's, Maghera
1983	St. Patrick's, Maghera
1984	St. Patrick's, Maghera
1985	St. Patrick's, Maghera
1986	St. Colman's, Newry
1987	Abbey CBS, Newry
1988	St. Colman's, Newry
1989	St. Patrick's, Maghera
1990	St. Patrick's, Maghera
1991	St. Patrick's, Dungannon
1992	St. Michael's, Enniskillen
1993	St. Colman's, Newry
1994	St. Patrick's, Maghera
1995	St. Patrick's, Maghera
1996	St. Patrick's, Maghera
1997	St. Patrick's, Dungannon
1998	St. Colman's, Newry
1999	St. Michael's, Enniskillen
2000	St. Patrick's, Armagh
2001	St. Michael's, Enniskillen
2002	St. Michael's, Enniskillen
2003	St. Patrick's, Maghera
2004	St. Patrick's, Dungannon
2005	Omagh CBS
2006	Abbey CBS, Newry
2007	Omagh CBS
2008	St. Patrick's, Dungannon
2009	St. Patrick's, Dungannon
2010	St. Colman's, Newry
2011	St. Colman's, Newry
2012	St. Michael's, Enniskillen
2013	St. Patrick's, Maghera
2014	St. Patrick's, Maghera
2015	St Patrick's, Cavan
2016	St Patrick's, Maghera
2017	St Mary's, Magherafelt

HIGHER EDUCATION

HIGHER EDUCATION

UCD	University College Dublin.
UCC	University College Cork.
UCG	University College Galway.
QUB	Queen's University Belfast.
TCD	Trinity College Dublin.
NUU	New University of Ulster (Coleraine), which changed to UUC (University of Ulster, Coleraine) in 1985.
UUJ	University of Ulster, Jordanstown
NIHEL /UL	National Institute of Higher Education, Limerick, which became UL (University of Limerick) in 1990.
TRTC / ITT	Tralee Regional Technical College, which became Institute of Technology, Tralee in 1997.
ARTC/AIT	Athlone Regional Technical College, which became Institute of Technology in 1997.
ITS	Institute of Technology, Sligo.
WRTC / WIT	Waterford Institute of Technology.
GMIT	Galway-Mayo Institute of Technology.
DCU	Dublin City University.
DIT	Dublin Institute of Technology.

FITZGIBBON CUP FINALS/RESULTS

Note: From the start and in most years up to 1948/49 the competition was played on a league basis over one weekend and the college that collected the most league points won the championship.

1911/12
UCD champions with four league points.

1912/13
UCC champions with four league points.

1913/14
UCC champions with four league points.

Note: In the years 1914/15 to 1917/18 UCG did not take part.

1914/15
Terenure, 2 March. Final:

UCD	6-0	3-0	**UCC**

1915/16
Cork Athletic Grounds, 27 February. Final:

UCD	7-2	1-2	**UCC**

1916/17
Terenure, 18 February. Final:

UCD	3-2	2-1	**UCC**

1917/18
Date unknown. Final:
UCC beat UCD.

1918/19
UCG champions by conceding fewest scores.

Note: In the years 1919/20 to 1921/22 UCG did not take part.

1919/20
Terenure, 12 May. Final:

UCC	3-4	3-3	**UCD**

1920/21
Not played.

1921/22
Mardyke, 3 May. Final:

UCC	6-1	3-2	**UCD**

1922/23
UCD champions with four league points.

1923/24
UCD champions with four league points.

1924/25
UCC champions with four league points.

1925/26
UCG champions with highest aggregate score.

Note: In the years 1926/27 and 1927/28 UCG did not take part.

1926/27
Terenure, 8 May. Final:

| **UCD** | **5-4** | **1-3** | **UCC** |

1927/28
Mardyke, 26 February. Final:

| **UCC** | **10-5** | **2-0** | **UCD** |

1928/29
UCC champions with four league points.

1929/30
UCC champions with four league points.

1930/31
UCC champions with four league points.

1931/32
UCD champions with four league points.

1932/33
UCC awarded title on objection, after **UCD** topped league with four points.

1933/34
Limerick, 25 March, Final Play-off:

| **UCD** | **6-1** | **2-2** | **UCC** |

1934/35
UCD champions with four league points.

1935/36
UCD champions with four league points.

1936/37
UCC champions with four league points.

1937/38
UCD champions with four league points.

1938/39
UCC champions with four league points.

1939/40
UCC champions with four league points.

1940/41
UCD champions with four league points.

1941/42
UCG champions with four league points.

1942/43
Not played.

1943/44
UCD champions with four league points.

1944/45
UCG champions with highest aggregate score.

1945/46
UCG champions with six league points.

1946/47
UCC champions with six league points.

1947/48
UCD champions with six league points.

Note: From 1948/49 onwards the competition adopted a straight knock-out format.

1948/49
Corrigan Park, 30 January:

| **UCG** | **4-8** | **3-1** | **UCD** |

1949/50
Galway, 5 February:

| **UCD** | **4-6** | **2-3** | **UCG** |

1950/51
Mardyke, 28 January:

| **UCD** | **2-6** | **1-3** | **UCC** |

1951/52
Croke Park, 27 January:

| **UCD** | **2-12** | **2-2** | **UCC** |

1952/53
Corrigan Park, 26 April:

| **QUB** | **1-3** | **0-5** | **UCD** |

1953/54
Fahy's Field, 14 February:

| **UCG** | **5-3** | **0-3** | **UCD** |

Competition declared null and void

1954/55
Mardyke, 13 February:

| **UCC** | **7-3** | **1-1** | **UCG** |

1955/56
Nenagh, 26 February:

| **UCC** | **4- 6** | **3-5** | **UCD** |

Note: From 1956/57 to 1965/66 (except for 1963/64) the Fitzgibbon Cup competition was played during the first term of the academic year (Michaelmas), chiefly in November and December.

1956/57
Fahy's Field, 18 November:

| **UCC** | **3-8** | **2-6** | **UCG** |

1957/58
1 December:

| **UCD** | **7-9** | **2-1** | **UCG** |

1958/59
Casement Park, 16 November.
UCC 4-8 3-2 **UCD**

1959/60
Croke Park, 29 November.
UCD 4-10 4-3 **UCC**

1960/61
Pearse Stadium, 4 December.
UCD 3-6 3-4 **UCG**

1961/62
Mardyke, 19 November.
UCC 5-9 1-6 **UCG**

1962/63
Casement Park, 18 November.
UCC 3-5 2-2 **UCD**

1963/64
Croke Park, 8 March:
UCD 4-7 4-3 **UCC**

1964/65
Pearse Stadium, 22 November.
UCD 4-8 4-2 **UCG**

1965/66
Mardyke, 21 November:
UCC 5-5 3-3 **UCD**

Note: From 1966/67 to the present day the Fitzgibbon Cup was
played in the second term (Hilary), chiefly in February and March.

1966/67
Croke Park, 5 March:
UCC 3-17 2-5 **UCG**

1967/68
Casement Park, 3 March:
UCD 1-15 2-1 **UCC**

1968/69
Croke Park, 23 February:
UCD 1-12 1-10 **UCC**

1969/70
Pearse Stadium, 8 March:
UCG 4-8 2-12 **UCD (aet)**

1970/71
Mardyke, 28 February:
UCC 2-16 2-6 **UCG**

1971/72
Croke Park, 12 March:
UCC 3-11 0-6 **UCG**

1972/73
Pearse Stadium, 11 March:
Maynooth 2-12 4-4 **UCG**

1973/74
Ballycastle, 3 March:
Maynooth 2-10 1-7 **UCD**

1974/75
O'Toole Park, 2 March:
UCD 4-8 2-7 **Maynooth**

1975/76
Mardyke, 22 February:
UCC 3-5 0-10 **Maynooth**

1976/77
Maynooth College, 6 March:
UCG 1-14 1-12 **Maynooth**

1977/78
Corrigan Park, 5 March:
UCD 3-15 2-7 **UCC**

1978/79
Croke Park, 25 March:
UCD 4-21 1-8 **Maynooth**

1979/80
Galway, 2 March:
UCG 0-10 1-5 **UCC**

1980/81
Croke Park, 1 March:
UCC 2-9 0-8 **UCD**

1981/82
Páirc Uí Chaoimh, 21 February:
UCC 0-14 3-3 **UCG**

1982/83
Bellaghy, 27 February:
UCC 3-12 1-3 **UCG**

1983/84
Highfield, 19 February:
UCC 0-7 0-5 **UCD**

1984/85
Malone, 3 March:
UCC 1-15 1-7 **UCG**

1985/86
Croke Park, 2 March:
UCC 3-10 0-12 **QUB**

1986/87
Castlegar, 22 February:
UCC 1-11 0-11 **UCD**

1987/88
Corrigan Park, 28 February:
UCC 1-14 1-3 **UCG**

1988/89
Belfield, 26 February:
NIHEL 2-9 1-9 **UCD**

1989/90
Páirc Uí Chaoimh, 18 March:
| UCC | 3-10 | 0-12 | WRTC |

1990/91
Corrigan Park, 10 March:
| UCC | 1-14 | 1-6 | UCD |

1991/92
Limerick Gaelic Grounds, 8 March:
| WRTC | 1-19 | UL | 1-8 |

1992/93
Walsh Park, 14 March:
| UCD | 2-21 | 4-14 | UCC (aet) |

1993/94
Clarinbridge, 13 March:
| UL | 2- 12 | 1-11 | WRTC (aet) |

1994/95
Clane, 5 March:
| WRTC | 3- 15 | 1-4 | UCD |

1995/96
Belfield, 10 March:
| UCC | 3- 16 | 0-16 | UL |

1996/97
Páirc Uí Rinn, 2 March:
| UCC | 0-14 | 1-8 | Garda |

1997/98
Limerick Gaelic Grounds, 1 March:
| UCC | 2-17 | 0-13 | WIT |

1998/99
Templemore, 28 February:
| WIT | 4-15 | 3-12 | UCC |

1999/00
Walsh Park, 5 March:
| WIT | 2-10 | 1-6 | UCD |

2000/01
Parnell Park, 11 April:
| UCD | 0- 15 | 0-15 | UCC (aet) |

Nenagh, 18 April:
| UCD | 2-10 | 1-9 | UCC (replay) |

2001/02
Castlegar, 3 March:
| UL | 2-14 | 2-11 | WIT |

2002/03
Ragg, 1 March:
| WIT | 0-13 | 0-7 | CIT |

2003/04
Athlone, 6 March:
| WIT | 0-11 | 0-9 | Cork IT |

2004/05
Limerick Gaelic Grounds, 5 March:
| LIT | 2-13 | 3-6 | UL |

2005/06
Páirc Uí Rinn, 4 March:
| WIT | 4-13 | 0-8 | UCD |

2006/07
Dr Cullen Park, 10 March:
| LIT | 2-15 | 0-13 | NUIG |

2007/08
Cork IT, 1 March:
| WIT | 1-29 | 1-24 | LIT (aet – 2 periods) |

2008/09
Parnell Park, 7 March:
| UCC | 2-17 | 0-14 | UL |

2009/10
Pearse Stadium, 6 March:
| NUIG | 1-17 | 1-16 | WIT (aet) |

2010/11
WIT Sports Complex, 28 February:
| UL | 1-17 | 2-11 | LIT |

2011/12
Mardyke, 3 March:
| UCC | 2-15 | 2-14 | CIT (aet) |

2012/13
Pearse Stadium, 2 March:
| UCC | 2-17 | 2-12 | Mary Immaculate College |

2013/14
The Dub, 1 March:
| WIT | 0-17 | 0-12 | CIT |

2014/15
Gaelic Grounds, 28 February
| UL | 0-21 | 3-12 | WIT (aet) |

Páirc Uí Rinn, 1 March
| UL | 2-18 | 1-14 | WIT |

2015/16
Cork IT Grounds Bishopstown, 27 February
Mary Immaculate College 1-30 3-22 UL (aet)

2016/17
Pearse Stadium, February 25
Mary Immaculate College 3-24 1-19 Carlow IT

FITZGIBBON CUP FINAL TEAMS

Note: Although in most years up to 1948/49 there was no Fitzgibbon Cup final per se, the following list includes the runner-up college team where available.

1911/12
U.C.D. B.Hynes, P.Salmon, John Ryan (Limerick & Dublin), J. O'Keeffe, M.O'Hanlon, M.Heenan, J.Pollard, P.D. Murphy, Patrick Stokes (Tipperary), D.Kennedy, P.Fitzpatrick, D.Chadwick, J.Dwan (capt.), R.Hennessy, T.F.Connolly, C.Ryan, Éamon Bulfin (Offaly).
U.C.C. Peter M.Murphy (Cork) (capt.), T.Lynch, Jim Reidy (Limerick), Dan Boohan (Limerick), John Hickey (Tipperary), Bill Fitzgerald (Cork), T.Kelleher, E.Hartnett, D.O'Keeffe, T.O'Keeffe, William Lehane (Cork), Patrick Joseph Burke (Tipperary), J.O'Mullane, Denny Pa Lucey, Jack O'Sullivan, Hugh Whelan, Davy Ring (Cork).

1912/13
U.C.C. (16 players listed) – T O'Keeffe, Jim Reidy (Limerick), T Lynch, Peter M Murphy (Cork) (capt.), Patrick Joseph Burke (Tipperary), J Nunan, Bill Fitzgerald (Cork), Davy Ring (Cork), J Connolly, Tommy Richardson (Cork), J O'Brien, Denny Pa Lucey, Hugh Whelan, D O'Keeffe, P Hayes, George O'Mahoney.
U.C.D. (15 players listed) – John Ryan (Limerick & Dublin) (capt.), Éamon Bulfin (Offaly), P.D. Murphy, Solomon Lawlor (Kerry & Dublin), J.Dwan, M.Heenan, R.Hennessy, W.Chadwick, P.Fitzgerald, B.Hynes, Pierce Walton (Kilkenny), Frank Burke (Kildare & Dublin), J.O'Keeffe, D.Fury, J.Duffy.

1913/14
U.C.C. A.McGuinness (Cork) (goal), Jim Reidy (Limerick), John Hickey (Tipperary), Charlie O'Riordan (Cork), T.Flynn, George Mahony, Dan Boohan (Limerick), Peter M Murphy (Cork), David Coleman, Hugh Whelan, M.'Hawk' O'Brien (Tipperary), Denny Pa Lucey, Cornie O'Neill, T.Dwane (Tipperary), Dan Joe Murphy. J.Nunan also played over weekend.
U.C.D. B.Hayes, Pierce Walton (Kilkenny), John Ryan (Dublin), M.Heenan, P.O'Brien, P.Fitzpatrick, Eimar O'Duffy (Dublin), N.Maher, L.Flynn, D.Murphy, E.Finn, Éamon Bulfin (Offaly), Thomas O'Hickey, Solomon Lawlor (Kerry & Dublin), Frank Burke (Kildare & Dublin).

1914/15
U.C.D. Éamon Bulfin (Offaly) (capt.), John Ryan (Dublin), E.Coogan, Charlie Stuart (Clare), Eimar O'Duffy (Dublin), Pierce Walton (Kilkenny), D.Kennedy, Tommy Daly (Clare & Dublin) (goal), Solomon Lawlor (Kerry & Dublin), Brian Joyce (Galway), Thomas O'Hickey, D.Sullivan, N.Maher, Frank Burke (Kildare & Dublin), T.Cummins.
U.C.C. John Hickey (Tipperary), Dan Boohan (Limerick), Peter M Murphy (Cork), T.Dwane (Tipperary), J.McCarthy, J Maher, E.Dwyer, Harry St. John Atkins (Cork), Davy Ring (Cork), D.J.O'Sullivan, Dick F O'Brien, M.Hurley, George O'Mahoney, Dan O'Driscoll, R.B.O'Brien, Jack Saunders, J.Looney.

1915/16
U.C.D. John Ryan (Dublin) (capt.), Tommy Daly (Clare & Dublin), Solomon Lawlor (Kerry & Dublin), P.Harte, P.Cummins, Charlie Stuart (Clare), P.O'Brien, Thomas O'Hickey, J.P.Nolan, Frank Burke (Dublin), E.Coogan, W.Murphy, N.Cooney, D.Sullivan.
U.C.C. team-list not available.

1916/17
U.C.D. John Ryan (Dublin) (capt.), Tommy Daly (Clare & Dublin) (goal), Solomon Lawlor (Kerry & Dublin), P.Harte, Pierce Walton (Kilkenny), E.Coogan, P.Cummins, D.Sullivan, Brian Joyce (Galway & Dublin), Joe Phelan (Kilkenny & Dublin), Frank Burke (Dublin), P.J.O'Brien, Charlie Stuart (Clare), N.Cooney, D.Downey.
U.C.C. Con Lucey (Cork) (capt.), Tim Sheehan (goal), Willie Moore (Kilkenny), T.Dwane (Tipperary), R.Lahiffe, Donovan, O'Brien, J.McCarthy, John Breen, Harry St. John Atkins (Cork), Eugene 'Nudge' Callanan (Tipperary), Jack Falvey (Cork), Christopher T.O'Neill, Curran, Murphy.

1917/18
U.C.C. (as listed in a non-Fitzgibbon Cup game) – James G Lahiff, P.O'Keeffe, Willie Moore (Kilkenny & Cork), P.F.Fitzpatrick, J.McCarthy, J.Meagher, Jack Falvey (Cork), E.Lahiff, T.Blake, J.J.Lucy, T.O'Driscoll, M.C.O'Mahony, S.Kelleher, C.Moloney, William S Nunan. Subs.: C.Bastible.
U.C.D. team-list not available.

1918/19
U.C.G. Martin Fahy (capt.), J.Darcy, M.O'Keeffe, M.O'Farrell, M.Kyne, Leonard? McGrath, Tom Fahy (Galway), Andrew Sexton, Edward Brennan, Arthur de B Joyce, Joseph Sexton, D.Clune, G.H.Joyce, J.Jordan, P.Fahy (Galway).
U.C.D. team-list not available.

1919/20
U.C.C. team-list not available.
U.C.D. team-list not unavailable.

1920/21
No Competition

1921/22
U.C.C. J.O'Donnell, Maurice O'Brien, William Fortune (Cork), M.C.O'Mahony, Bernie Flynn (Cork), Harry St. John Atkins (Cork), Wille Cotter (Cork), Eugene 'Nudge' Callanan (Tipperary), R.Lahiffe, M.Cotter, R.Kelly, Con Lucey (Cork), Finian O'Shea (Cork), Pat Nyhan (Cork), Joe Kearney (Cork).
U.C.D. M.O'Brien (goal), J.Hogan, J.Godfrey, Tommy Daly (Clare & Dublin) (capt.), G.Conway, M.McManus, Mick D'Arcy (Tipperary & Dublin), J.O'Neill, F.O'Dea, Tom Pierse (Wexford), J.Pierce, Timothy J Kirby, John Kennedy, T.Fanning, John Joe Callanan (Tipperary & Dublin).

1922/23
U.C.D. Tommy Daly (Clare & Dublin) (capt.), Mick D'Arcy (Tipperary), Tom Pierse (Wexford), S.Conway, J.Pierce, E.MacMahon, Joe Phelan (Kilkenny & Dublin), Paul Power (Tipperary), Michael Waldron, Paddy McDonald (Cavan), J O'Neill, T.Fanning, John Kennedy, Timothy J Kirby, J.Hogan.
U.C.C. Finian O'Shea (Cork) (capt.), Tom Lee (Tipperary), M.O'Sullivan, J.O'Sullivan, J.Breen, Dan Walsh (Cork), Dinny Barry-Murphy (Cork), M.C.O'Mahony, J.O'Mahony, Michael O'Toole, R.Hazel, Seán Forde, B.Kelly, M.O'Donnell, Pat Nyhan (Cork).

1923/24
U.C.D. Tommy Daly (Clare & Dublin) (goal) (capt.), William Small (Tipperary & Dublin), Conway, Paddy McDonald (Cavan), Conway, Mick D'Arcy (Tipperary), Flanagan, Paul Power (Tipperary), Myles J Shelly, Joe Phelan (Kilkenny & Dublin), Frank Burke (Dublin), Tom Pierse (Wexford), D.Smith, Donovan, D.Kennedy.
U.C.C. Pat Nyhan (Cork) (goal), William Fortune (Cork) (capt.), Maurice O'Brien (Cork), M O'Donnell, John Barry-Murphy (Cork), Dinny Barry-Murphy (Cork), Matt Murphy (Cork), Frank Creedon (Cork), Bernie Flynn (Cork), Donovan, Joe Kearney (Cork), Callaghan, Finian O'Shea (Cork), Dan Walsh (Cork), O'Mahony.

1924/25
U.C.C. Pat Nyhan (Cork) (goal), Maurice O'Brien (Cork), J.Barry (Cork), M O'Donnell, Seán Forde, Dinny Barry-Murphy (Cork), John Barry-Murphy (Cork), Tom Lee (Tipperary) (capt.), Jim Hurley (Cork), M.Ryan (Cork), Bernie Flynn (Cork), Dan Walsh (Cork), William Fortune (Cork), J.O'Shea, Joe Kearney (Cork).
U.C.D. Tommy Daly (Clare & Dublin) (goal) (capt.), Mick D'Arcy (Tipperary), J.Lowery, Phil Sullivan (Kerry), T.Maguire, T.Lyng, Michael Waldron (Dublin), Paddy McDonald (Cavan), Denis Finn (Tipperary), Jim Smith (Cavan), Andrew Cooney (Tipperary), Paul Power (Tipperary), J.O'Neill, W.Ryan.

1925/26
U.C.G. T.O'Grady (capt.), Nicholas J Bodkin, M.O'Toole, P.J.Hanley, P.Lenihan, P.Kelly, B.Roland, P.Barry, Andy Kelly (Galway), P.Finn, M.King (Galway), Peadar Ó Maille, Bernard F.S.McKiernan, W.Keane, D.Kelleher, T.Cunningham.
U.C.D. team-list not available.

1926/27
U.C.D. O.O'Neill (capt.), Tommy Daly (Clare & Dublin), William Small (Tipperary & Dublin), Joe Stuart (Clare), Myles J.Shelly, Mick D'Arcy (Tipperary & Dublin), Michael Waldron (Dublin), Patrick G.Collier, Denis Finn (Tipperary), Andrew Cooney (Tipperary), P.O'Meara, Frank Sheehy (Kerry), D.Smith, J.Gleeson, P.Muldowney.
U.C.C. Donal McCarthy (capt.), Paddy O'Donovan (Cork), Tom Lee (Tipperary), John Barry-Murphy (Cork), B.Farrell, William Finlay (Tipperary), Dinny Barry-Murphy (Cork), Bernie Flynn (Cork), Pat Nyhan (Cork), J.Dargan, Eugene 'Nudge' Callanan (Cork), T.O'Brien, Dan Walsh (Cork), Mossie Donegan (Cork), J.Barry (Cork).

1927/28
U.C.C. Richard Molloy (Cork) (capt.), Donal McCarthy (Cork), Batt Daly, Patrick O'Donnell, R.Coughlan, Dinny Barry-Murphy (Cork), John J.Dorgan, Mossie Donegan (Cork), Jack Russell (Cork), J Benson, Bernie Flynn (Cork), William Finlay (Tipperary), C.Creegan, Paddy O'Donovan (Cork), Tony Hennerty (Cork).
U.C.D. Denis Finn (Tipperary) (capt.), William Small (Tipperary & Dublin), Joe Stuart (Clare), P.Teehan, Frank Sheehy (Kerry), Andrew Cooney (Tipperary), F.Fanning, Andrew Quinn (Tipperary), M.Quirke, Joseph Canning (Cork), V.Corcoran, T.Mitchell, T.McConnell, Michael Waldron (Dublin), Patrick G.Collier.

1928/29
U.C.C. Paddy O'Donovan (Cork) (capt.), Richard Molloy (Cork), Donal McCarthy (Cork), Batt Daly, Denis W.Harvey, William Finlay (Tipperary), Mossie Donegan (Cork), B.Farrell, M.Queally, J.Barry (Cork), Jim O'Regan (Cork), Tony Hennerty (Cork), T.Hegarty, Patrick O'Donnell, R.Coughlan.
U.C.D. team-list not available.

1929/30
U.C.C. Daniel O'Connell Keating (Cork), Patrick O'Donnell (capt.), Richard Molloy (Cork), Batt Daly, William Finlay (Tipperary), Tony Hennerty (Cork), Paddy O'Donovan (Cork), Gus Kelleher (Cork), J.A.Costelloe, P.Condon, D.Murphy, C.Sheehan, T.McCarthy, J.Murphy, Jim Hurley (Cork).
U.C.D. James Flanagan (Tipperary), Frank Sheehy (Kerry) (capt.), P.McDonnell, Andrew Quinn (Tipperary), Mick D'Arcy (Tipperary), Joe Stuart (Clare), J.Walsh, Michael Falvey (Clare), John Bourke, Thomas Costelloe (Clare), T.Mitchell, V.Ryan, P.Barron, P.O'Connor, Kevin McNeill (Dublin).

1930/31
U.C.C. Richard Molloy (Cork), P.Condon, D.Murphy, J.Murphy, J.Casey, Gus Kelleher (Cork), Patrick O'Donnell, Jim Hurley (Cork), William Finlay (Tipperary), Ted Vaughan (Cork), Paddy O'Donovan (Cork), M.Teehan, Luke Tully (Cork), T.Calthorpe, T.O'Neill. Sub.: J.A.Costelloe.
U.C.D. James Flanagan (Tipperary), Terry McCarthy (Cork), Michael Falvey (Clare), Mick D'Arcy (Tipperary), Paddy Bresnihan (Limerick), P.O'Neill, Martin Waldron, M.Walsh, Andrew Quinn (Tipperary), E.T.Lundren, Jack Walsh, Thomas Costelloe (Clare), Tom Loughnane (Clare), Joseph Canning (Cork), L.Cooney. John Durkin (Mayo), McMahon & Kenny also played over the weekend.

1931/32
U.C.D. Jack Walsh (capt.), James Flanagan (Tipperary) (goal), Paddy Bresnihan (Limerick), Tom Loughnane (Clare), Patrick Devaney (Clare), Kevin McNeill (Dublin), T.Hogan, W.Walsh, Michael Falvey (Clare), Terry McCarthy (Cork), Thomas Costelloe (Clare), J.O'Dea, Joseph Canning (Cork), Dennis Madigan (Limerick), W.F.Dwyer.
U.C.G. John Langan (capt.), Michael Lee (Galway), H.Casey, Christopher McKeown, Joseph Madden, J.Harrington (Clare), Michael Kennedy (Tipperary), William Kennedy, Tom Gill, John O'Leary (Clare), Pádraic Fahy, John Bourke, J.Sweeney, Seán O'Donovan, Maurice Moynihan. Sub.: J.Leydon.

1932/33
U.C.C. (18-man squad) Richard Cronin (Cork) (capt.), Richard Molloy (Cork), Donal McCarthy (Cork), William Finlay (Tipperary), G.Gleeson, Tony Hennerty (Cork), Paddy O'Donovan (Cork), Tom Murphy (Cork), Martin Cronin (Cork), M.Franklin, C.Ronan, Con McGrath (Cork), Gus Kelleher (Cork), P.Nunan, John McCarthy (Cork), Tom O'Reilly (Cork), T.O'Neill, P.O'Keeffe.
U.C.D. James Flanagan (Tipperary) (capt.), Tom Loughnane (Clare), Séamus Hogan (Clare), Terry McCarthy (Cork), Michael Falvey (Clare), Colm Boland (Westmeath & Dublin), Dennis Madigan (Limerick), Paddy Bresnihan (Limerick), Kevin McNeill (Dublin), Thomas Costelloe (Clare), Joseph Canning (Cork), Patrick Devaney (Tipperary), J.Lynch (Cork), Andrew Quinn (Tipperary), John Durkin (Mayo). T.Lee also played over the weekend.

1933/34
U.C.D. (as in first final) James O'Flanagan (Tipperary), Paddy C Bresnihan (Limerick), Tom Loughnane (Clare), Matt Hawe (Cork), Larry M.Hayes (Kilkenny), Séamus Hogan (Clare), Jer Lynch (Cork), Terry McCarthy (Cork), Jimmy Cooney (Tipperary), Tony MacSullivan (Limerick), John T.Ryan (Kilkenny), Joseph Canning (Cork & Dublin), Colm Boland (Westmeath & Dublin), Thomas J.Butler (Kilkenny), Bill Loughnane (Clare).
U.C.C. (as in first final) Tom O'Reilly (Cork), P.O'Keeffe, Con McGrath (Cork), Martin Cronin (Cork), Tom Murphy (Cork), Donal McCarthy (Cork), John McCarthy (Cork), Paddy O'Donovan (Cork), C.Ronan, Joe Roche (Cork), Luke Tully (Cork), D.Conroy, Derry Beckett (Cork), Ted Vaughan (Cork), J.Sullivan.

1934/35
U.C.D. Toddy Walsh (Kerry), Mickey Griffin (Clare), Tom Loughnane (Clare), Patrick Devaney (Tipperary), Larry M.Hayes (Kilkenny), Paddy C Bresnihan (Limerick), Tony MacSullivan (Limerick), Jimmy Cooney (Tipperary), Seán Feeney (Waterford & Dublin), Dick Foley, Colm Boland (Westmeath & Dublin), Peter Flanagan (Clare), Thomas J Butler (Kilkenny), Bill Loughnane (Clare), John T.Ryan (Kilkenny).
U.C.G. team-list not available.

1935/36

U.C.D. Toddy Walsh (Kerry), Mickey Griffin (Clare), Tom Loughnane (Clare), Tony MacSullivan (Limerick), Larry M.Hayes (Kilkenny), Paddy Bresnihan (Limerick), PÓ.Flaithinn, Jimmy Cooney (Tipperary), Seán Feeney (Waterford & Dublin), Dick Foley, Colm Boland (Westmeath & Dublin), Peter Flanagan (Clare), Michael Falvey (Clare), Bill Loughnane (Clare & Dublin), Jim McCarthy (Dublin). M.Franklin also played over the weekend.

1936/37

U.C.C. Tom O'Reilly (Cork), Eddie O'Donovan (Cork), Mícheál Cranitch (Cork), D.Gavin (Cork), Tommy Magner (Cork), Tom Murphy (Cork), Jackie Spencer (Cork), Mossie Roche (Limerick), Gus Kelleher (Cork), P.J.McCarthy, John McCarthy (Cork), Joe Roche (Cork), M.Moriarty, Gerry Madden (Limerick), Paddy Reid (Cork). Theo Lynch (Cork) & T.O'Sullivan (Cork) also played.

U.C.D. Toddy Walsh (Kerry), Dave Hurley (Limerick), Frank Lahiffe (Galway), Tony MacSullivan (Limerick), Larry M Hayes (Kilkenny), Seán Feeney (Waterford & Dublin), Mickey Griffin (Clare), T.Healy, Jimmy Cooney (Tipperary), Roger Hayes (Limerick), Colm Boland (Westmeath & Dublin), Peter Flanagan (Clare), M.Sheehy, Jim McCarthy (Dublin), W.Herlihy. Sub.: D Fitzgerald for Boland.

1937/38

U.C.D. Toddy Walsh (Kerry), W.Herlihy, M.Sheehy, Frank Lahiffe (Galway), Larry M Hayes (Kilkenny), Dave Hurley (Limerick), Tony MacSullivan (Limerick), Jimmy Cooney (Tipperary), Roger Hayes (Limerick), T.Healy (Cork), Bill Loughnane (Clare), Liam White (Kilkenny), T.Fitzgerald, Toddy Walsh (Kerry), Jim McCarthy (Dublin).

U.C.C. Tom O'Reilly (Cork), Mícheál Cranitch (Cork), Seán Houlihan (Laois), Eddie O'Donovan (Cork), Tommy Magner (Cork), Tom Murphy (Cork), Jackie Spencer (Cork), Mossie Roche (Limerick), P.J.McCarthy (Cork), John McCarthy (Cork), M.McGrath. (Only 11 players listed in reports.)

1938/39

U.C.C. Tom O'Reilly (Cork), James O'Neill (Cork), Seán Houlihan (Laois), Mícheál Cranitch (Cork), Dan Coughlan (Cork), Tom Murphy (Cork), Kevin Flynn (Clare), Jim Young (Cork), McCarthy, Prendergast, Jackie Spencer (Cork), Roche, Peadar Garvan (Cork), Gerry Madden (Limerick), Derry Beckett (Cork).

U.C.D. team-list not available.

1939/40

U.C.C. Paddy Moynihan (Cork), James O'Neill (Cork), Mícheál Cranitch (Cork), Jim Duggan (Cork), Tommy Magner (Cork), Tom Murphy (Cork), Dan Coughlan (Cork), Jim Young (Cork), Jackie Spencer (Cork), P.J.McCarthy (Cork), Paddy Reid (Cork), Joe Roche (Cork), Peadar Garvan (Cork), Gerry Madden (Limerick), Derry Beckett (Cork). Sub.: D.O'Mahony.

U.C.D. T.Hennessy, Dave Hurley (Limerick), Jim McCarthy (Limerick), Johnny Wall (Limerick), J./ Billy O'Neill (Kilkenny), Kevin Flynn (Clare), Liam White (Kilkenny), Dick Stokes (Limerick), Roger Hayes (Limerick), M.Healy (Cork), Bill Loughnane (Clare & Dublin), Fintan Flynn (Clare), Éamonn O'Boyle (Offaly), T Walsh, M Walsh.

1940/41

U.C.D. Gerry Fitzgerald (Clare), Billy O'Connell (Limerick), Jim McCarthy (Limerick), Johnny Wall (Limerick), Billy O'Neill (Kilkenny), Kevin Jones (Clare), Jimmy Hurley (Tipperary), Luke O'Sullivan (Cork), Dick Stokes (Limerick), J.Phelan, Éamonn O'Boyle (Offaly), Fintan Flynn (Clare), Roger Hayes (Limerick), "Jumbo" Maher (Tipperary), Bill Loughnane (Clare & Dublin).

U.C.C. Paddy Moynihan (Cork), Peadar Garvan (Cork), C.Healy, Jim Duggan (Cork), Tom Murphy (Cork), James O'Neill (Cork), Tom Fleming, Jim Young (Cork), Arthur Beckett (Cork), J.McCarthy, Derry Beckett (Cork), J.Healy (Cork), T.Riordan, J.O'Mahony, Luke Tully (Cork).

1941/42

U.C.G. Tom Nolan (Galway), M.Walsh, Donal Flynn (Cork & Galway), Pat Hehir (Galway), Stephen Fahy (Galway), Jimmy Brophy (Kilkenny & Galway), Michael McDermott (Galway), Paddy Donnellan (Galway), Pierce Thornton (Galway), Tommy Doyle (Galway), Bob Forde (Galway), Bill Trayers (Galway), J.Lynch, Seán Thornton (Galway), T.Donohue. Sub.: Martin Kelly.

U.C.D. Gerry Fitzgerald (Clare), Seán Doohan (Offaly), Johnny Wall (Limerick), Kevin Jones (Clare), G.Fitzgerald (Limerick), Billy O'Neill (Kilkenny), Jimmy Hurley (Tipperary), Dick Stokes (Limerick), Roger Hayes (Limerick), L.Keating (Kilkenny), Ned Daly (Waterford), Mickey Feeney (Waterford), Brendan White (Tipperary), Éamonn O'Boyle (Offaly & Dublin), Luke O'Sullivan (Cork).

1942/43

NO COMPETITION

1943/44

U.C.D. Peter O'Keeffe (Laois), Seán Doohan (Offaly), Davy Walsh (Kilkenny), Kieran Maloney (Clare), George Frost (Clare), Bob Frost (Clare), Mick Maher (Tipperary), Dick Stokes (Limerick), Mick Hassett (Dublin), ?????, Ned Daly (Waterford), Mickey Feeney (Waterford), Brendan White (Tipperary), Éamonn O'Boyle (Offaly), Frank Commons (Tipperary), D.McInerney. Luke O'Sullivan also played.

U.C.C. Paddy Moynihan (Cork), C.Healy, J.Duggan, Bernie Murphy, Con Murphy, Tom Fleming, J.O'Mahony, S.J.Keane, D.Keating, T.Joyce, J.Healy, Derry Beckett, A.Power, Jim Young (Cork), Liam Moriarty, T.Aherne, J.McNamara, B.Murphy, R.Brennan, J.Daly. (20- man squad.)

1944/45

U.C.G. Seánie Duggan (Galway), Seán Thornton (Galway), Pat Hehir (Galway), Tom Hanley (Limerick), Joe Glynn (Galway), Vincent Baston (Waterford & Galway), Paul Murphy (Galway), Pierce Thornton (Galway), Michael "Hockey" Nestor (Galway), Bob Forde (Galway), Tony Dervan (Galway), Michael "Miko" Doyle (Galway), Johnny Scanlon (Galway), Eugene Lee (Clare), Dinny McMahon (Clare). Tim Regan (Galway), Cathal O'Connor (Galway) & Tommy Doyle (Galway) also played over the weekend.

U.C.C. team-list not available.

1945/46

U.C.G. Seánie Duggan (Galway), Tom Hanley (Limerick), Donal Flynn (Cork), Pat Hehir (Galway), Joe Glynn (Galway), Jimmy Brophy (Kilkenny & Galway), Paddy Donnellan (Galway), Bob Forde (Galway), Tony Dervan (Galway), Johnny Scanlon (Galway), Josie Gallagher (Galway), Michael "Miko" Doyle (Galway), Vincent Doyle (Galway), Gerry Fahy (Galway), Dinny McMahon (Clare). Sub.: Finian Fahy (Galway).

U.C.D. Peter O'Keeffe (Laois), Harry Boland (Dublin), Davy Walsh (Kilkenny), Mick Maher (Tipperary), George Frost (Clare), Bob Frost (Clare), Brian McMahon (Clare), Mick Hassett (Dublin), Des Dillon (Clare), Jimmy Kennedy (Tipperary & Dublin), Ned Daly (Waterford), Mickey Feeney (Waterford), Brendan White (Offaly), Dan McInerney (Clare), Frank Commons (Tipperary). Sub.: Kieran Maloney (Clare).

1946/47

U.C.C. Dinny Houlihan (Kilkenny), Tony Daly (Cork), Ted O'Driscoll (Cork), Frank Coughlan (Cork), Paddy Tyers (Waterford), Bernie Murphy (Cork), Jackie Houlihan (Limerick), Bill Carroll (Tipperary), Paddy Gallagher (Clare), (i.e. Fr. Paddy Gantley (Galway)) Jackie Harris (Tipperary), Michael O'Shaughnessy (Tipperary), Mick Herlihy (Cork), Bill Cahill (Kilkenny), Arthur Beckett (Cork), Derry Beckett (Cork) Nicky Purcell (Kilkenny) and Mick Phelan (Waterford) also played over the weekend.

U.C.D. Peter O'Keeffe (Laois), Seán Doohan (Tipperary), Davy Walsh (Kilkenny & Dublin), Kieran Maloney (Clare), Mick Maher (Tipperary), Pierce Thornton (Galway), Brian McMahon (Clare), Des Dillon (Clare), Phil Bartley (Limerick), Jimmy Kennedy (Tipperary & Dublin), Ned Daly (Waterford), Willie Harty (Tipperary), Joby Maher (Tipperary), Ned Ryan (Limerick), Frank Commons (Tipperary).

1947/48

U.C.D. Tadhg Hurley (Kerry), Seán Doohan (Offaly), Davy Walsh (Kilkenny & Dublin), Mick Maher (Boharlahan), Paddy Enright (Clare), Pierce Thornton (Galway & Dublin), Joby Maher (Tipperary), Mick Hassett (Dublin), Phil Bartley (Limerick), Jimmy Kennedy (Tipperary), Ned Daly (Waterford), Mickey Feeney (Waterford), Willie Harty (Tipperary), Ned Ryan (Limerick), Frank Commons (Tipperary & Dublin). Des Dillon (Clare) also played in the tournament.

U.C.C. Gary Fleming (Cork), Tony Daly (Cork), Ted O'Driscoll (Cork), Frank Coughlan (Cork), Paddy Tyers (Waterford), Bernie Murphy (Cork), Jimmy O'Reilly (Cork), Brendan Hanniffy (Galway), Bill Carroll (Tipperary), Dave O'Connor (Cork), Humphrey O'Neill (Cork), Seán McCarthy (Cork), Mick Fennelly (Kilkenny), Tony Brennan (Kilkenny), B.Herlihy (Cork).

1948/49

U.C.G. Bernie Egan (Galway), Joe Glynn (Galway), Pat Hehir (Galway), Billy Glynn (Galway), Harry Crowley (Galway), Mick Costello (Galway), Paul Murphy (Galway), Joe Salmon (Galway), Michael McInerney (Galway), Frank Duignan (Galway), Dick Leonard (Limerick), Jack O'Brien (Clare), Johnny Scanlon (Galway), John Joe Coyne (Galway), Donal Donovan (Galway). Sub.: Paddy Greally (Galway) for McInerney.

U.C.D. Tadhg Hurley (Kerry), Seán Doohan (Offaly), Frank Flynn (Galway), Mick Maher (Boharlahan), Finian Fahy (Galway), Dick Stokes (Limerick), Joby Maher (Tipperary), Peter Fitzgerald (Tipperary), Maurice Queally (Waterford), Jimmy Kennedy (Tipperary), Frank Commons (Tipperary & Dublin), Ned Ryan (Limerick), Willie Harty (Tipperary), Harry Murphy (Kilkenny), Gerry Fahy (Galway).

1949/50

U.C.D. Ray Brennan (Wexford), A.McCarthy, Frank Flynn (Galway), Mick Maher (Boharlahan), Finian Fahy (Galway), Maurice Queally (Waterford), Mick O'Shaughnessy (Cork), Des Dillon (Clare & Dublin), Martin Fitzgerald (Tipperary & Dublin), Gerry Kelly (Tipperary & Dublin), M.O'Connell, Johnny Ryan (Tipperary), Tim O'Sullivan (Kerry), Harry Murphy (Kilkenny), Danny Mehigan (Cork).

U.C.G. Bernie Egan (Galway), Joe Glynn (Galway), Ned Quinn (Galway), Billy Glynn (Galway), Paul Murphy (Galway), Mick Costello (Galway), Paddy Daly (Galway), Dick Leonard (Limerick), Joe Salmon (Galway), Kevin Maher (Tipperary), Michael McInerney (Galway), S.Murphy, John Joe Coyne (Galway), Donie Murphy (Kerry), Fergie McDonagh (Westmeath). Sub.: Jack O'Brien (Clare) for Daly.

1950/51

U.C.D. Ray Brennan (Wexford), Martin McDonnell (Wexford), Mick Maher (Holycross), Mick Maher (Boharlahan), Pat Tynan (Kilkenny), Mick O'Shaughnessy (Cork), Maurice Queally

(Waterford), Des Dillon (Clare & Dublin), Martin Fitzgerald (Tipperary & Dublin), Danny Mehigan (Cork), Gerry Kelly (Tipperary & Dublin), Joe Conlon (Waterford), Dick O'Neill (Kilkenny), Harry Murphy (Kilkenny), Johnny Ryan (Tipperary).

U.C.C. John O'Grady (Tipperary), Jimmy Leahy (Tipperary), J.J.O'Brien (Cork), Paddy Hayes (Cork), Tom Barry (Waterford), Denis McCarthy (Cork), Paddy O'Regan (Cork), Mickey 'Jinx' Ryan (Tipperary), Tom Crotty (Cork), Seán Boyle (Tipperary), Bill Lineen (Waterford), Willie Walsh (Cork), S.McSweeney (Cork), Pat O'Grady (Clare), Paddy Horgan (Cork). Subs.: Vilem Steiglitz (Tipperary) for Boyle, Tom Cavanagh (Cork) for O'Regan.

1951/52

U.C.D. Ray Brennan (Wexford), Pat Tynan (Kilkenny), Mick Maher (Holycross), Ted Hurley (Cork), Éamonn 'Ned' Hallahan (Waterford), Jim White (Clare), Maurice Queally (Waterford), Martin Fitzgerald (Tipperary & Dublin), Des Dillon (Clare & Dublin), Gerry Kelly (Tipperary & Dublin), Seán Kennedy (Tipperary), Mick Gardiner (Cork), Johnny Ryan (Tipperary), Dick O'Neill (Kilkenny), Donal Mehigan (Cork).

U.C.C. John O'Grady (Tipperary), Tom O'Connor (Kilkenny), Ted O'Driscoll (Cork), J.J.O'Brien (Cork), Paddy Hayes (Cork), Denis McCarthy (Cork), John Joe O'Sullivan (Cork), Gerry Murphy (Cork), Willie O'Driscoll (Cork), Mickey 'Jinx' Ryan (Tipperary), Tom Barry (Waterford), Vincent Walsh (Waterford), Paddy Horgan (Cork), P.Walsh (Waterford), Tom Crotty (Cork).

1952/53

Q.U.B. Brendan Trainor (Antrim), Vincent Kelly (Antrim), John Butler (Antrim), John Flanagan (Antrim), Danny Gilmartin (Antrim), Des Cormican (Antrim), Paddy Duggan (Antrim), Séamus "Stout" McDonald (Antrim), Jack Savage (Antrim), Ted McConnell (Antrim), Bobby McMullen (Antrim), Brendan McAleenan (Down), Paul Crilly (Antrim), Donal Anglin (Antrim), Gerry Treacy (Antrim).

U.C.D. Todd Comerford (Kilkenny), Bill English (Tipperary), Éamonn McGrath (Tipperary), Ted Hurley (Cork), Éamonn 'Ned' Hallahan (Waterford), Jim White (Clare), Michael Doyle (Kilkenny), Pat Tynan (Kilkenny), Jim O'Keeffe, Des Dillon (Clare & Dublin), Gerry Kelly (Tipperary & Dublin), Danny Mehigan (Cork), J.Buckley, John Daly (Cork), Larry Power (Tipperary). Sub.: P.Ryan for O'Keeffe.

1953/54

U.C.G. Phil Waldron (Clare), Gerry Meehan (Galway), Frank Daly (Cork), John Naughton (Laois), Eddie Kelly (Limerick), Séamus Cullinane (Galway), Tom O'Toole (Galway), Eddie Fallon (Galway), Pádraic Keane (Galway), Eddie Abberton (Galway), Michael McInerney (Galway), Paddy O'Donoghue (Waterford), Séamus Trayers (Galway), Jimmy Haverty (Galway), Noel McMahon (Offaly). Sub.: Máirtín Fallon (Galway) for Cullinane.

U.C.D. Todd Comerford (Kilkenny), Bill English (Tipperary), Éamonn McGrath (Tipperary), John O'Mahony (Tipperary), Éamonn 'Ned' Hallahan (Waterford), Jim White (Clare), Michael Doyle (Kilkenny), Nicky Stokes (Limerick), Declan O'Sullivan (Westmeath), Ted Hurley (Cork), Des Dillon (Dublin), Bill Hartley (Wexford), Jimmy Barrett (Kilkenny), Bernard Hoey (Clare), Danny Mehigan (Cork). Sub.: Martin Gibbons (Kilkenny) for Mehigan.

1954/55

U.C.C. Tony Murphy (Cork), Leo Young (Cork), Paddy Maloney (Tipperary), Jim Forrestal (Kilkenny), Tommy Ryan (Tipperary), Liam Shalloe (Waterford), Pat Teehan (Waterford), Donal 'Duck' Whelan (Waterford), Dick Troy (Cork), Mick Hanley (Clare), Cathal Hurley (Cork), Dan Kennefick (Cork), Tom Crotty (Cork), Billy McCarthy (Kerry), Johnny Dwane (Cork).

U.C.G. Des Nolan (Galway), Tony O'Gorman (Galway), Frank Daly (Cork), Tom Brennan (Waterford), Tom O'Toole (Galway), Séamus Cullinane (Cork), John Hassett (Clare), Mickey Cullinane (Galway), F Fahy (Galway), Séamus Trayers (Galway), Eddie Fallon (Galway), Paddy O'Donoghue (Waterford), Pádraic Cummins (Galway), Niall McInerney (Galway), Noel McMahon (Offaly).

1955/56
U.C.C. Tony Murphy (Cork), Leo Young (Cork), George O'Sullivan (Cork), Dan Kelleher (Cork), Tom Gallagher (Waterford), Johnny Vaughan (Cork), Seán Browne (Cork), Dick Troy (Cork), Bernie Cotter (Cork), Gerry McCarthy (Cork), Steve Long (Limerick), Seán Moore (Cork), Paddy Horgan (Cork), Kevin Twomey (Cork), Johnny Dwane (Cork). Subs.: Cathal O'Keeffe for Long, Long for O'Keeffe.
U.C.D. Phil Waldron (Clare), Bill English (Tipperary), Bernard Hoey (Clare), Ted Hurley (Cork), Seán Dunne (Kilkenny), Éamonn McGrath (Tipperary), Jim McDonnell (Tipperary), Gerry Murphy (Cork), Declan O'Sullivan (Westmeath), Nicky Stokes (Limerick), Billy O'Donovan (Tipperary), Dan Delaney (Tipperary), Jimmy Barrett (Tipperary), Mick Cowhig (Cork), Billy McCarthy (Kerry). Sub.: Maurice Begley (Limerick) for Delaney.

1956/57
U.C.C. Tony Murphy (Cork), Leo Young (Cork), George O'Sullivan (Cork), Dan Kelleher (Cork), Tom Gallagher (Waterford), Seán O'Riordan (Cork), Gerry O'Meara (Tipperary), Dick Troy (Cork), Liam Shalloe (Waterford), Gerry McCarthy (Cork), Jim McGrath (Limerick), Joe Phelan (Limerick), Bernie Cotter (Cork), Joe Rabbitte (Galway), Seán Moore (Cork).
U.C.G. Alphonsus Tully (Roscommon), Máirtín Nestor (Galway), Tony O'Gorman (Galway), Pádraic Keane (Galway), Owen Lynch (Cork), Tom Brennan (Waterford), John Dunne (Galway), Bobby Curran (Waterford), Jim Hassett (Clare), Dennis McSweeney (Galway), Mickey Cullinane (Galway), Michael Greene (Clare), Pádraic Cummins (Galway), Eddie Fallon (Galway), John White (Cork). Sub.: Paschal Finn (Galway) for Nestor.

1957/58
U.C.D. Dan Delaney (Tipperary), Roger O'Donnell (Tipperary), Bernard Hoey (Clare), Dan Kelleher (Cork), Billy O'Donovan (Tipperary), Dennis Kelleher (Cork), Mick Cowhig (Cork), Jim McDonnell (Tipperary), Johnny O'Connor (Waterford), Seán Dunne (Kilkenny), Mickey Cullinane (Galway), Donie Nealon (Tipperary), Tommy Ryan (Tipperary), Nicky Stokes (Limerick), Ted Hurley (Cork). Sub.: Ted Carroll (Kilkenny) for Denis Kelleher.
U.C.G. Enda O'Flaherty (Galway), Máirtín Nestor (Galway), Tony O'Gorman (Galway), Pádraic Keane (Galway), Owen Lynch (Cork), Tom Brennan (Waterford), John Dunne (Galway), Bobby Curran (Waterford), Jim Hassett (Clare), Dennis McSweeney (Galway), Liam Gilmartin (Offaly), John White (Cork), Richie Queally (Waterford), Jack Daly (Clare), Pádraig Cummins (Galway). Sub.: Donal Murphy (Limerick) for Cummins.

1958/59
U.C.C. Billy Moroney (Tipperary), Donie Murphy (Cork), Des Kiely (Tipperary), Seán O'Riordan (Cork), Tom Gallagher (Waterford), Liam Shalloe (Waterford), Mickey Horgan (Cork), Noel Gallagher (Cork), Pat O'Shea (Tipperary), Ollie Harrington (Kilkenny), Jim McGrath (Limerick), Pat Henchy (Clare), John Joe Browne (Cork), Tom Riordan (Cork), Steve Long (Limerick).
U.C.D. Dan Delaney (Tipperary), Harry Hickey (Kilkenny), Billy O'Donovan (Tipperary), Dan Kelleher (Cork), Seán Moore (Cork), Dennis Kelleher (Cork), Ted Carroll (Kilkenny), Jim McDonnell (Tipperary), Seán Dunne (Kilkenny), Donie Nealon (Tipperary), Mick Leahy (Cork), John Joe O'Keeffe (Limerick), Patsy Nealon (Tipperary), Nicky Stokes (Limerick), Billy McCarthy (Kerry).

1959/60
U.C.D. Dan Delaney (Tipperary), Tom Nolan (Carlow), Dick O'Donnell (Tipperary), Louis Foyle (Tipperary), Brian McDonnell (Tipperary), Ted Carroll (Kilkenny), Seán Kinsella (Wexford), Seán Quinlivan (Clare), Gus Danaher (Tipperary), Pat Henchy (Clare), Jim Kissane (Wexford), Donie Nealon (Tipperary), Mick Leahy (Cork), Owen O'Neill (Limerick), Patsy Nealon (Tipperary). Sub.: R Reynolds for Danaher.
U.C.C. Ollie Harrington (Kilkenny), Cormac Flynn (Limerick), Des Kiely (Tipperary), Robert Galvin (Cork), Mickey Horgan (Cork), George Walsh (Cork), Jimmy Byrne (Waterford), Pat O'Shea (Tipperary), Noel Phelan (Limerick), Mick Mortell (Cork), John Joe Browne (Cork), Joe Flynn (Cork), Danny McDonnell (Cork), Tom Riordan (Cork), Steve Long (Limerick). Subs.: Donie Cregan (Limerick) for McDonnell, Ciaran Kelly (Cork) for Walsh.

1960/61
U.C.D. Owen Hurley (Cork), Seán Kinsella (Wexford), Tom Melody (Clare), Louis Foyle (Tipperary), John Joe O'Keeffe (Limerick), Ted Carroll (Kilkenny), Richard Walsh (Kilkenny), Brian McDonnell (Tipperary), Seán Quinlivan (Limerick), Pat Henchy (Clare), Mick Carroll (Kilkenny), Donie Nealon (Tipperary), Patsy Nealon (Tipperary), Owen O'Neill (Limerick), Murt Duggan (Tipperary). Sub.: Dick Dowling (Kilkenny) for Duggan.
U.C.G. John O'Mahony (Galway), Séamus Hayes (Waterford), Pat Hassett (Clare), Pádraic Keane (Galway), Joe Lyons (Galway), Tony O'Gorman (Galway), Kevin Smyth (Clare), Paddy Fahy (Galway), John Whiriskey (Galway), Séamus Gohery (Galway), Leo Gardiner (Galway), Seán Devlin (Galway), Gerry Gardiner (Galway), Mick Shaughnessy (Galway), E.Burke (Galway). Sub.: Séamus Fallon (Galway) for Burke.

1961/62
U.C.C. John O'Donoghue (Tipperary), Tom Conway (Limerick), Des Kiely (Tipperary), Noel Phelan (Limerick), Jimmy Byrne (Waterford), Dan Kelleher (Cork), John Alley (Laois), Ollie Harrington (Kilkenny), Mick Waters (Cork), John O'Halloran (Cork), Jimmy Blake (Limerick), Mick Mortell (Cork), George Allen (Cork), Donie Flynn (Limerick), Gerry Gleeson (Limerick). Sub.: Mícheál Óg Murphy (Cork) for Mortell.
U.C.G. John O'Mahony (Galway), Séamus Hayes (Waterford), Paddy Hassett (Clare), Bernie Diviney (Galway), Joe Lyons (Galway), Mick Shaughnessy (Galway), Kevin Smyth (Galway), John Whiriskey (Galway), Tom Gilmore (Galway), P.J.Qualter (Galway), Leo Gardiner (Galway), Seán Devlin (Galway), M Niland, Tom Brennan (Waterford), Gerry Gardiner (Galway). Subs.: Séamus Fallon (Galway) for Diviney, J.Greally for G.Gardiner, Diviney for Hayes.

1962/63
U.C.C. John O'Donoghue (Tipperary), Tom Conway (Limerick), Des Kiely (Tipperary), Mick McCormack (Tipperary), Ollie Harrington (Kilkenny), Jimmy Byrne (Waterford), John Alley (Laois), Mícheál Óg Murphy (Cork), Donie Flynn (Limerick), John O'Halloran (Cork), Jimmy Blake (Limerick), Mick Mortell (Cork), George Allen (Cork), Maurice Fahy (Cork), Donal Murphy (Cork).
U.C.D. Murt Duggan (Tipperary), Noel Rohan (Kilkenny), Pat Hassett (Clare), Dick Dowling (Kilkenny), Nicky Hanrahan (Kilkenny), Phil Murray (Tipperary), Richard Walsh (Kilkenny), Brian McDonnell (Tipperary), Seán Quinlivan (Clare), Tom Forrestal (Kilkenny), Hugh McDonnell (Tipperary), Donie Nealon (Tipperary), Patsy Nealon (Tipperary), Owen O'Neill (Limerick), Pat Carroll (Kilkenny).

1963/64

U.C.D. Murt Duggan (Tipperary), Willie Smith (Tipperary), Dick Dowling (Kilkenny), John Dowling (Kilkenny), Michael Browne (Wexford), Phil Murray (Tipperary), Nicky Hanrahan (Kilkenny), Seán Quinlivan (Clare), Tom Barry (Kilkenny), Pat Henchy (Clare), Donal Walsh (Wexford), Pat Murphy (Limerick), Tony Loughnane (Clare), Tom Forrestal (Kilkenny), Pat Kennedy (Tipperary). Subs.: Pat Hassett (Clare) for Murphy, Eddie Walsh (Wexford) for Browne.
U.C.C. Jerry O'Callaghan (Cork), Tom Kavanagh (Wexford), Eamonn "Ned" Rea (Limerick), Mick McCormack (Tipperary), Jimmy Byrne (Waterford), Tony O'Brien (Limerick), John Alley (Laois), Mícheál Óg Murphy (Cork), Dermot Mulcahy (Limerick), Donie Flynn (Limerick), John O'Halloran (Cork), Dan Harnedy (Cork), Noel Phelan (Limerick), Jimmy Blake (Limerick), Ollie Harrington (Kilkenny). Subs.: Michael Fahy (Cork) for Phelan, Phelan for Fahy, Jerry Gleeson (Limerick) for Mulcahy.

1964/65

U.C.D. Murt Duggan (Tipperary), Willie Smith (Tipperary), Eddie Walsh (Wexford), Dick Dowling (Kilkenny), Brian McDonnell (Tipperary), Phil Murray (Tipperary), John Murphy (Wexford), Tom Barry (Kilkenny), Phil Ryan (Tipperary), Peadar Murphy (Wexford), Kevin Long (Limerick), Pat Murphy (Limerick), Tony Loughnane (Clare), Tom Forrestal (Kilkenny), Paudie Kennedy (Tipperary). Subs.: Jimmy Cummins (Tipperary) for Peadar Murphy, Caimin Jones (Clare) for Cummins.
U.C.G. Pat O'Neill (Galway), Oliver Dolly (Galway), John Egan (Limerick), Michael Walsh (Galway), Coilín McDonagh (Galway), Tom Canavan (Galway), Séamus Fallon (Galway), Frank Coffey (Galway), Ray Gilmore (Galway), Ray Niland (Westmeath & Galway), Richard Pyne (Clare), Jimmy Rabbitte (Galway), Seán Murphy (Galway), Austin Costelloe (Galway), Frank Hassett (Clare). Subs.: Bernie Diviney (Galway) for Walsh, P.J.Qualter (Galway) for McDonagh, Tom Holton (Galway) for Fallon.

1965/66

U.C.C. T O'Shea (Kilkenny), Tom Field (Cork), Mick McCormack (Tipperary), Éamonn 'Ned' Rea (Limerick), Ger O'Herlihy (Cork), John O'Keeffe (Cork), Tom Walsh (Waterford), Willie Cronin (Cork), Pat O'Connell (Tipperary), Donal Clifford (Cork), John O'Halloran (Cork), Seánie Barry (Cork), Richard Lehane (Cork), Jimmy Blake (Limerick), Brendan Kenneally (Cork). Sub.: Pierce Dooley (Laois) for Lehane.
U.C.D. Murt Duggan (Tipperary), Willie Smith (Tipperary), Willie Hoyne (Kilkenny), Jim Furlong (Wexford), Pat Drennan (Kilkenny), Kevin Long (Limerick), John Murphy (Wexford), Pat Kavanagh (Kilkenny), Phil Dillon (Laois), Frank Smith (Tipperary), Jim O'Neill (Wexford), Derry O'Connor (Tipperary), Tony Loughnane (Dublin), Dermot Kavanagh (Kilkenny), Joe Carroll (Limerick). Sub.: Caimin Jones (Clare) for O'Connor.

1966/67

U.C.C. John Mitchell (Cork), Tom Field (Cork), Mick McCormack (Tipperary), Éamonn 'Ned' Rea (Limerick), Ger O'Herlihy Cork), John O'Keeffe (Cork), Noel Dunne (Cork), Pat O'Connell (Tipperary), Pierce Dooley (Laois), Seánie Barry (Cork), John O'Halloran (Cork), Donal Clifford (Cork), Richard Lehane (Cork), Denis Philpott (Cork), Noel Morgan (Cork). Subs.: Ray Cummins (Cork) for Morgan, Jimmy McCarthy (Cork) for O'Connell.
U.C.G. Peter Cosgrave (Galway), Tom McGarry (Tipperary), John Egan (Limerick), Bernie Diviney (Galway), Tom Canavan (Galway), Sam Stanley (Galway), John Kenny (Galway), Frank Coffey (Galway), Séamus Hogan (Tipperary), Ray Niland (Galway), Brendan Shaughnessy (Galway), Pádraig Fahy (Galway), Michael Keane (Galway), Gus Costello (Galway), Brendan Barry (Offaly). Subs.: Niall O'Halloran (Galway) for Kenny, Kenny for O'Halloran, O'Halloran for Shaughnessy, Pat Tobin (Tipperary) for McGarry.

1967/68

U.C.D. Éamonn Kennedy (Tipperary), Willie Smyth (Tipperary), Jim Furlong (Wexford), Jim O'Neill (Wexford), Donal Kavanagh (Kilkenny), Pat Drennan (Kilkenny), Jimmy Rabbitte (Galway), Phil Dillon (Laois), Willie Cronin (Cork), Pat Kavanagh (Kilkenny), Gerry Quinlan (Tipperary), Frank Smyth (Tipperary), Jack Ryan (Tipperary), Nicky Walsh (Wexford), Colm Muldoon (Galway). Subs.: Tony Loughnane (Dublin) for Muldoon, Mattie Ryan (Limerick) for D.Kavanagh, Tony Henry (Mayo) for Cronin.
U.C.C. John Mitchell (Cork), Tom Field (Cork), John Kelly (Tipperary), Simon O'Leary (Cork), Ger O'Herlihy (Cork), Seán O'Keeffe (Cork), Noel Dunne (Cork), Mick Watters (Cork), Pierce Dooley (Laois), Kevin Cummins (Cork), Ray Cummins (Cork), Donal Motherway (Cork), S Meade (Cork), Henry O'Sullivan (Cork), Noel Rochford (Wexford). Subs.: Michael Bond (Galway) for Rochford, Richard Lehane (Cork) for Meade, Mick Murphy (Cork) for Motherway.

1968/69

U.C.D. Éamonn Kennedy (Tipperary), Jim O'Neill (Wexford), Mattie Ryan (Limerick), Kevin Kehilly (Cork), Donal Kavanagh (Kilkenny), Conor O'Brien (Kilkenny), Tony Henry (Mayo), Phil Dillon (Laois), Tim Delaney (Tipperary), Pat Kavanagh (Kilkenny), Tom Crowe (Clare), Donal Carroll (Limerick), Pat O'Connor (Tipperary), Tony Loughnane (Dublin), Jack Ryan (Tipperary). Sub.: Denis Burke (Tipperary) for Crowe.
U.C.C. John Mitchell (Cork), Mick McCarthy (Cork), Pat McDonnell (Cork), Paddy Crowley (Cork), Gabriel Daly (Waterford), Donal Clifford (Cork), Séamus Looney (Cork), Michael Murphy (Cork), Seán Walsh (Kilkenny), Noel Dunne (Cork), Jimmy Barrett (Cork), John O'Halloran (Cork), Noel Morgan (Cork), Henry O'Sullivan (Cork), Tom Buckley (Cork). Subs.: Pat Doherty (Limerick) for Barrett, Mick Dowling (Limerick) for Murphy, Murphy for Walsh.

1969/70

U.C.G. Peter Cosgrave (Galway), Niall McInerney (Clare), Richard Walsh (Wexford), Terry Crowe (Clare), Tom Cloonan (Galway), Éamonn Corcoran (Galway), Jim Goulding (Waterford), Séamus Hogan (Tipperary), Colm O'Flaherty (Galway), Seán Ó Broudar (Limerick), Austin Costello (Galway), Paul McNamee (Galway), Tim Burns (Galway), Michael Keane (Galway), Seán Burke (Limerick). Subs.: Des O'Halloran (Galway) for Burns, Pat Sheedy (Tipperary) for McNamee, John O'Donoghue (Clare) for Crowe.
U.C.D. Éamonn Kennedy (Tipperary), Kevin O'Connell (Cork), Enda Murphy (Wexford), Willie Dwyer (Tipperary), Donal Kavanagh (Kilkenny), Conor O'Brien (Kilkenny), Willie Murphy (Kilkenny), Jack Russell (Wexford), Eugene Moore (Laois), Gerry McCarthy (Kilkenny), Aidan Spooner (Tipperary), Tony Henry (Mayo), Jack Ryan (Tipperary), Phil Ryan (Tipperary), Pat O'Connor (Tipperary). Sub.: Dermot Kavanagh (Kilkenny) for Murphy.

1970/71

U.C.C. Jer Cremin (Cork), Mick McCarthy (Cork), Pat McDonnell (Cork), Willie Moore (Limerick), Simon Murphy (Cork), John O'Grady (Kerry), Jim Darcy (Tipperary), Mick Dowling (Limerick), Donie Walsh (Kilkenny), Mick Crotty (Kilkenny), Séamus Looney (Cork), Seán Twomey (Cork), Pat Lucey (Cork), Henry O'Sullivan (Cork), Éamonn Fitzpatrick (Cork). Subs.: Jim Geoghegan (Waterford) for O'Sullivan, O'Sullivan for Geoghegan, Pat McCarthy for Lucey.
U.C.G. Frank Fahy (Galway), Niall McInerney (Clare), Richard Walsh (Wexford), Éamonn Corcoran (Galway), Michael Bond (Galway), Donal Ahern (Cork), Jim Goulding (Waterford), Mick O'Shea (Kilkenny), Frank Burke (Galway), Seán Ó Broudar (Limerick), Michael Hanniffy (Galway), Paul McNamee (Galway), Pat Sheedy (Galway), Michael Keane (Galway), Seán Burke (Limerick).

1971/72

U.C.C. Tony Smith (Cork), Mick McCarthy (Cork), Pat McDonnell (Cork), Paddy Geary (Cork), Paddy Crowley (Cork), John Buckley (Cork), Liam Kearney (Cork), Michael Murphy (Cork), John O'Grady (Kerry), Seán Twomey (Cork), Séamus Looney (Cork), Mick Crotty (Kilkenny), Henry O'Sullivan (Cork), Willie Moore (Limerick), Seán Burke (Limerick). Sub.: Éamonn Fitzpatrick (Cork) for O'Sullivan.

U.C.G. Michael Kennedy (Galway), Luke Glynn (Galway), Tom Cloonan (Galway), John O'Donoghue (Clare), Paul McNamee (Galway), Niall McInerney (Clare), Jim Goulding (Waterford), Séamus Hogan (Tipperary), Joe McDonagh (Galway), Mick O'Shea (Kilkenny), Jody Spooner (Tipperary), Martin Barrett (Galway), Pat Sheedy (Tipperary), John Cremin (Kilkenny), Seán Ó Broadar (Limerick). Subs.: Brendan Forde (Galway) for Cremin, Frank Burke (Galway) for Barrett, Michael Hanniffy (Galway) for Sheedy.

1972/73

Maynooth Dick Browne (Tipperary), Paddy Barry (Cork), Oliver Perkins (Tipperary), Michael Ryan (Tipperary), Mick Brennan (Galway), Seán Silke (Galway), Seán Stack (Clare), Iggy Clarke (Galway), Andy Fenton (Galway), Willie Fitzmaurice (Limerick), Paudie Fitmaurice (Limerick), Joe Condon (Limerick), Gus O'Driscoll (Cork), Larry Byrne (Wexford), Henry Goff (Wexford). Sub.: Aidan Kerrigan (Wexford) for Stack.

U.C.G. Frank Fahy (Galway), Luke Glynn (Galway), John O'Donoghue (Clare), Nicky O'Connor (Clare), Mick O'Shea (Kilkenny), Niall McInerney (Clare), Joe McDonagh (Galway), Séamus Hogan (Tipperary), Joe Larkin (Galway), Mattie Murphy (Galway), Jody Spooner (Tipperary), Seán Ó Broadar (Limerick), Pat Sheedy (Tipperary), Frank Burke (Galway), Pat Moroney (Clare). Sub.: John Cremin (Kilkenny) for Larkin.

1973/74

Maynooth Dick Browne (Tipperary), Paddy Barry (Cork), Oliver Perkins (Tipperary), Joe Clarke (Galway), Seán Stack (Clare), Seán Silke (Galway), Mick Brennan (Galway), Iggy Clarke (Galway), Paddy Ballard (Kilkenny), Henry Goff (Wexford), Paudie Fitzmaurice (Limerick), Fachtna O'Driscoll (Cork), Gus O'Driscoll (Cork), Andy Fenton (Galway), Liam Everard (Tipperary). Sub.: Séamus Fitzgerald (Tipperary) for F.O'Driscoll.

U.C.D. Dave Behan (Waterford), Timmy Cleary (Tipperary), Matt Ryan (Limerick & Laois), Pat Flynn (Clare), Martin Bohan (Tipperary), Dennis Burns (Cork), Eugene Ryan (Tipperary), Tom Barry (Kilkenny), Séamus Ryan (Tipperary), Martin Troy (Tipperary), John O'Leary (Kildare), John Callinan (Clare), Jimmy Duggan (Tipperary), Dick O'Shea (Kilkenny), Seán Liddy (Clare). Sub.: Mick Hennessy (Tipperary) for Duggan.

1974/75

U.C.D. Jimmy Duggan (Tipperary), Martin Quirke (Tipperary), Matt Ryan (Tipperary), Timmy Cleary (Tipperary), John Killeen (Laois), Tom Walsh (Wexford), Eugene Ryan (Tipperary), Mick Brophy (Tipperary), Séamus Ryan (Tipperary), Matt Ruth (Kilkenny), Mick Reidy (Dublin), Pat White (Kildare), Martin Barrett (Galway), Hugh Dolan (Offaly), Martin Troy (Tipperary). Subs.: Jack Ryan (Tipperary) for Troy.

Maynooth Fachtna O'Driscoll (Cork), Paddy Barry (Cork), Martin Downey (Laois), Joe Clarke (Galway), Tony Kelly (Galway), Seán Silke (Galway), Seán Stack (Clare), Iggy Clarke (Galway), Christy Kennedy (Offaly), Tony Brennan (Cork), Paudie Fitzmaurice (Limerick), Liam Everard (Tipperary), Gus O'Driscoll (Cork), Henry Goff (Wexford), Tommy Ryan (Tipperary). Sub.: Mick O'Mahoney (Cork) for T.Ryan.

1975/76

U.C.C. Gerry Cronin (Cork), Billy Reidy (Cork), Pat Quigley (Wexford), John Roche (Cork), Andrew O'Regan (Cork), Donal McGovern (Cork), Gerard McEvoy (Cork), Sylvester O'Mahony

(Cork), Dave Keane (Cork), John Higgins (Cork), Martin McDonnell (Cork), Brian Waldron (Kilkenny), Tadhg O'Sullivan (Cork), Oliver Cussen (Cork), Patsy O'Keeffe (Waterford). Subs.: Eamonn Coakley (Cork) for McEvoy, Willie Vereker (Kilkenny) for Waldron.

Maynooth Frank O'Neill (Cork), Anthony Kelly (Galway), Joe Clarke (Galway), Seán Clarke (Offaly), Pat Greene (Tipperary), Seán Silke (Galway), Austin McNamara (Limerick), Seán Stack (Clare), Iggy Clarke (Galway), Liam Everard (Tipperary), Paddy Barry (Cork), Liam Lynch (Monaghan), Tommy Ryan (Tipperary), Gus O'Driscoll (Cork), Fachtna O'Driscoll (Cork).

1976/77

U.C.G. Brendan Kenny (Clare), Hugh O'Donovan (Cork), Tom Cloonan (Galway), Conor Hayes (Galway), Niall McInerney (Galway), Pat Fleury (Offaly), Pat Leahy (Galway), Joe McDonagh (Galway), Frank Holohan (Kilkenny), Pat Costello (Galway), Martin Quilty (Limerick), Gerry P.Fahy (Galway), Jody Spooner (Galway), Joe Connolly (Galway), Cyril Farrell (Galway). Subs.: Seán Flaherty (Galway) for Quigley, Alfie Barrett (Galway) for Costello.

Maynooth Finbarr Crowley (Cork), Tony Kelly (Galway), Joe Clarke (Galway), Austin McNamara (Limerick), Seán Clarke (Offaly), Iggy Clarke (Galway), Con Woods (Clare), Anthony Brennan (Galway), Seán Stack (Clare), Noel Foynes (Laois), Fachtna O'Driscoll (Cork), Dick Marnell (Kilkenny), Tommy Ryan (Tipperary), Gus O'Driscoll (Cork), Liam Everard (Tipperary). Subs.: Willie Allen (Dublin) for Foynes, Henry Goff (Wexford) for Allen.

1977/78

U.C.D. Jack Ryan (Tipperary), Tom Breen (Wexford), Michael Meagher (Kilkenny), Andy Doyle (Wexford), John Killeen (Laois), John Martin (Kilkenny), Mick Maher (Tipperary), Mick Brophy (Tipperary), Gerry Lohan (Galway), Matt Ruth (Kilkenny), Sylvie Lester (Kilkenny), Pat White (Kildare), Tom Browne (Down), Tom Crowe (Clare), Séamus Burke (Tipperary).

U.C.C. Matt Shortt (Tipperary), Seán Feehan (Waterford), Martin O'Doherty (Cork), John Roche (Cork), Brian Dineen (Cork), Martin McDonnell (Cork), Timmy O'Callaghan (Cork), Dave Keane (Cork), John Minogue (Clare), Patsy Corbett (Cork), John Higgins (Cork), Brian Waldron (Kilkenny), Terry Brennan (Kilkenny), Theo Cullinane (Cork), Gerard McEvoy (Cork).

1978/79

U.C.D. Jack Ryan (Tipperary), John Martin (Kilkenny), Michael Meagher (Kilkenny), Andy Doyle (Wexford), Paul Redmond (Cork), Tom Breen (Wexford), Mick Maher (Tipperary), Gerry Lohan (Galway), John Kennedy (Cork), Pat Quigley (Tipperary), Peadar Queally (Tipperary), Pat White (Kildare), Tom Browne (Down), Jim McCarthy (Kilkenny), Séamus Burke (Tipperary).

Maynooth Jim Doyle (Wexford), Frank O'Neill (Cork), Michael Kennedy (Offaly), Denis Forde (Cork), Pat Greene (Tipperary), Seán Clarke (Offaly), Austin McNamara (Limerick), John Curtis (Wexford), Bill Doherty (Kilkenny), Henry Goff (Wexford), Finbar Crowley (Cork), John Kennedy (Tipperary), Jack Caesar (Tipperary), Fachtna O'Driscoll (Cork), Noel Foynes (Laois). Sub.: Phil Stack for O'Driscoll.

1979/80

U.C.G. Billy Reilly (Galway), Mick McGuane (Galway), Conor Hayes (Galway), Willie Burke (Limerick), John Costello (Kilkenny), Seánie McMahon (Clare), Pat Ryan (Clare), John Boland (Galway), Ian Barrett (Galway), Leo Quinlan (Clare), Vincent Daly (Clare), Noel Colleran (Galway), Gerry Dempsey (Galway), Seán Forde (Galway), Mick Clohessy (Clare). Subs.: Kevin Menton (Galway) for Clohessy, Billy Loughnane (Clare) for Daly, Éamonn Burke (Galway) for Menton.

U.C.C. Tom Abernethy (Cork), John Minogue (Clare), John Murphy (Cork), Seán Feehan (Waterford), Noel Wall (Tipperary), Billy Farrell (Cork), Frank Houlihan (Limerick), Kieran White (Cork), Noel Leonard (Limerick), David Boylan (Cork), Jimmy

Greally (Cork), Danny Buckley (Cork), Michael Kelleher (Cork), Pat O'Leary (Cork), Michael Walsh (Waterford). Subs.: Eddie Murphy (Cork) for Walsh, Pat Curran (Waterford) for White.

1980/81

U.C.C. John Farrell (Tipperary), John Minogue (Clare), Michael Boylan (Cork), Billy Farrell (Cork), Pat O'Leary (Cork), Noel Leonard (Limerick), Brian Dineen (Cork), Mick Lyons (Cork), Maurice O'Donoghue (Kerry), Danny Buckley (Cork), Michael Kilcoyne (Westmeath), Nicholas English (Tipperary), Michael Kelleher (Cork), Ger Motherway (Cork), Tadhg Coakley (Cork).

U.C.D. Denis Corry (Clare), Tom Hogan (Kilkenny), Michael Meagher (Kilkenny), P.J.Burke (Galway), Willie Burke (Limerick), Cormac Bonner (Tipperary), Liam Grogan (Offaly), John Kennedy (Cork), Dennis O'Driscoll (Cork), Éamonn O'Shea (Tipperary), Peadar Queally (Tipperary), Pat Quigley (Tipperary), Pat Power (Tipperary), Andy Doyle (Wexford), Mick Kelly (Kilkenny).

1981/82

U.C.C. John Farrell (Tipperary), John Minogue (Clare), Mick Boylan (Cork), Jim Murray (Cork), Michael Allen (Cork), Noel Leonard (Limerick), Brian Dineen (Cork), Mick Lyons (Cork), Paul O'Connor (Cork), Danny Buckley (Cork), Dennis O'Driscoll (Cork), Nicholas English (Tipperary), Michael Kelleher (Cork), Ger Motherway (Cork), Tim Finn (Cork). Sub.: Tadhg Coakley (Cork) for Finn.

U.C.G. Billy Reilly (Galway), Michael Morrissey (Galway), Peter Casserley (Galway), Ger Costello (Galway), Dermot Monaghan (Galway), Noel Colleran (Clare), Tom Nolan (Galway), Michael Molyneaux (Limerick), Brian Ryan (Limerick), Leo Quinlan (Clare), Martin Raftery (Galway), Derek Fahy (Galway), Gerry Dempsey (Galway), John Boland (Galway), Brendan Kenny (Clare). Sub.: Albert Moylan (Galway) for Raftery.

1982/83

U.C.C. John Farrell (Tipperary), Michael Allen (Cork), Mick Boylan (Cork), Jim Murray (Cork), John Grainger (Cork), John O'Connor (Wexford), Kieran White (Cork), Maurice O'Donoghue (Kerry), Mick Lyons (Cork), Paul O'Connor (Cork), Nicholas English (Tipperary), Tadhg Coakley (Cork), Michael Walsh (Waterford), Mick Quaide (Limerick), Tim Finn (Cork).

U.C.G. Billy Reilly (Galway), Damien Kennedy (Galway), Peter Casserley (Galway), Tom Phillips (Mayo), John Barry (Tipperary), Tom Nolan (Galway), Aidan Bellew (Galway), Alan Cunningham (Clare), John Joe Flaherty (Galway), John Leahy (Galway), Peter Leydon (Clare), Michael Coleman (Galway), Joe Byrne (Galway), Michael Keane (Galway), Anthony Cunningham (Galway).

1983/84

U.C.C. Ger Cotter (Cork), Mick Boylan (Cork), Richard Browne (Cork), John Grainger (Cork), Oliver Kearney (Cork), Seán O'Gorman (Cork), Tadhg Coakley (Cork), Paul O'Connor (Cork), Ian Conroy (Tipperary), Jerry Sheehan (Limerick), Colm O'Neill (Cork), Nicholas English (Tipperary), Christy Ring (Cork), Mick Quaide (Limerick), John O'Connor (Wexford). Sub.: Rory Dwan (Tipperary).

U.C.D. Denis Corry (Clare), Austin Finn (Wexford), Richie Healy (Cork), Gerry Morrissey (Kilkenny), Frank O'Donoghue (Galway), Mick Glynn (Clare), Willie Burke (Limerick), Richie Walsh (Waterford), Mick Ronayne (Cork), Brian Slattery (Waterford), Jim Kinsella (Kilkenny), Ed Prendergast (Kilkenny), Danny O'Donoghue (Kerry), Aidan Stafford (Wexford), Gerry Drennan (Kilkenny).

1984/85

U.C.C. Michael Hartnett (Cork), Mick Quaide (Limerick), Richard Browne (Cork), Rory Dwan (Tipperary), John O'Connor (Wexford), John Grainger (Cork), Pat Hartnett (Cork), Paul O'Connor (Cork), Ian Conroy (Tipperary), Kevin Coakley (Cork), Colm O'Neill (Cork), Nicholas English (Tipperary), Mark Foley

(Cork), Mick Crowe (Limerick), Niall Sheehan (Limerick). Sub.: John O'Leary (Cork) for John O'Connor.

U.C.G. Richard Woulfe (Limerick), Seán Williams (Tipperary), Tony Henderson (Kilkenny), Jim Ryan (Limerick), Michael Nash (Limerick), Michael Coleman (Galway), Joe Byrne (Galway), Alan Cunningham (Clare), Gerry Brennan (Kilkenny), Séamie Kearns (Galway), Paddy Maher (Laois), Dave Cowhig (Kilkenny), Pat Ryan (Limerick), Brian Ryan (Limerick), Anthony Cunningham (Galway). Subs.: Joe O'Rourke (Galway) for Brennan, Damien Kennedy (Galway) for Cowhig, Bobby Power (Clare) for C.Ryan.

1985/86

U.C.C. Ger Cotter (Cork), Andy O'Callaghan (Cork), Shane O'Connell (Cork), John Grainger (Cork), Mick Coakley (Cork), John O'Connor (Cork), Denis O'Mahony (Cork), Paul O'Connor (Cork), Kieran Looney (Cork), Mick Crowe (Limerick), Michael Walsh (Kilkenny), Bill O'Connell (Cork), Martin Everard (Cork), Mark Foley (Cork), Tomás Fitzgibbon (Cork). Sub.: Rory McInerney (Limerick) for O'Connell.

Q.U.B. Conor McGurk (Derry), Peter Flynn (Antrim), Ciarán Cooper (Antrim), Bernard McKay (Antrim), Colm McGurk (Derry), Pádraig Devlin (Tyrone), Joe McClintock (Derry), Ciarán Barr (Antrim), Liam Coulter (Down), Joe Cunningham (Meath), David Ross (Down), Henry Downey (Derry), David Maguire (Antrim), Declan McLoughlin (Antrim), John McGurk (Derry).

1986/87

U.C.C. Ger Cotter (Cork), Andy O'Callaghan (Cork), Shane O'Connell (Cork), John Grainger (Cork), Trevor Cooney (Cork), John O'Connor (Cork), John Considine (Cork), Mick Coakley (Cork), Cathal Casey (Cork), Kieran Looney (Cork), Michael Walsh (Kilkenny), Tomás Fitzgibbon (Cork), Mark Foley (Cork), Mick Crowe (Limerick), Barry Harte (Cork).

U.C.D. Philly Ryan (Tipperary), Mick Brady (Cork), Liam Kinsella (Kilkenny), John Herbert (Limerick), Séamie O'Shea (Tipperary), Andy Dunne (Laois), Austin Finn (Wexford), Conor Stakelum (Tipperary), Jim Bolger (Wexford), Gerry Drennan (Kilkenny), Joe Walsh (Kilkenny), Tom Callan (Kilkenny), Charlie Purcell (Kilkenny), Éamon Kehir (Kilkenny), Vincent Teehan (Offaly).

1987/88

U.C.C. Ger Cotter (Cork), Andy O'Callaghan (Cork), Shane O'Connell (Cork), David Quinlan (Tipperary), Trevor Cooney (Cork), John Considine (Cork), Damien Keane (Cork), Cathal Casey (Cork), Anthony O'Sullivan (Cork), Pat Heffernan (Limerick), John O'Connor (Cork), Colm Egan (Tipperary), Mark Foley (Cork), Mick Crowe (Limerick), Tomás Fitzgibbon (Cork). Sub.: Tim Cummins (Cork) for J.O'Connor.

U.C.G. Billy Curley (Waterford), Ken Corless (Galway), Martin Dowd (Galway), John O'Dwyer (Tipperary), Andrew Hanley (Clare), John Lee (Clare), Seánie McCarthy (Clare), Séamus Grealish (Galway), Rory O'Connor (Cork), John Bates (Laois), Fergus Fleming (Kilkenny), Dave Cowhig (Kilkenny), Frank Keane (Cork), Séamie Kearns (Galway), Michael O'Doherty (Galway).

1988/89

N.I.H.E.L. Paul Brennan (Kilkenny), Shane McManus (Tipperary), Paddy Carter (Limerick), Vincent Morrissey (Waterford), Pádraic Hogan (Tipperary), Eoin O'Shaughnessy (Galway), Daragh O'Neill (Limerick), Dan Tracey (Clare), Dave Quinlan (Tipperary), Brendan Corcoran (Tipperary), Michael Hogan (Clare), Eoin Cleary (Clare), Brian Stapleton (Tipperary), Vincent Reddy (Wexford), Brendan Ryan (Tipperary). Sub.: T.J.O'Dwyer (Tipperary) for M.Hogan.

U.C.D. Philly Ryan (Tipperary), Fergal Finn (Wexford), John Herbert (Limerick), Shane McGuckian (Offaly), Paddy O'Brien (Limerick), Séamie O'Shea (Tipperary), Nicky Farrell (Limerick), Jim Bolger (Wexford), Conal Bonnar (Tipperary), Joe Walsh (Kilkenny), Derek Gaffney (Kilkenny), Conor Stakelum (Tipperary), Gerry Drennan (Kilkenny), Vincent Teehan (Offaly), Charlie Purcell (Kilkenny).

1989/90

U.C.C. Ger Cotter (Cork), Eddie Burke (Waterford), Brian Murphy (Cork), David Quinlan (Tipperary), Pat Kenneally (Cork), Noel O'Leary (Cork), John Considine (Cork), Cathal Casey (Cork), Derry Murphy (Cork), Brian Cunningham (Cork), Adrian Kelly (Roscommon), Mick Crowe (Limerick), Anthony O'Sullivan (Cork), Niall Aherne (Cork), Kevin Roche (Cork). Sub.: Johnny Ryan (Cork) for Kelly.

W.R.T.C. Liam Slevin (Kilkenny), Donncha O'Donnell (Cork), Paudie Coffey (Waterford), John Houlihan (Kilkenny), Denis Mullally (Kilkenny), Damien Hernon (Dublin), Ger Crosse (Tipperary), Owen Cummins (Tipperary), Phil O'Callaghan (Wexford), Noel Dalton (Waterford), Kevin Byrne (Wexford), Billy O'Sullivan (Waterford), Ger Scully (Cork), Michael O'Mahony (Waterford), Damien Curley (Galway). Subs.: Anthony Qualter (Waterford) for Byrne, Tony O'Meara (Tipperary) for Dalton, James Aherne (Cork) for Scully.

1990/91

U.C.C. Pat Looney (Cork), Eddie Burke (Waterford), Garret Kavanagh (Wexford), Noel O'Leary (Cork), John Considine (Cork), Brian Murphy (Cork), Pat Hartnett (Cork), Cathal Casey (Cork), Derry Murphy (Cork), Brian Cunningham (Cork), Adrian Kelly (Roscommon), Brian Kehoe (Wexford), Johnny Ryan (Cork), Pat Heffernan (Limerick), John Magner (Cork). Sub.: Kevin Roche (Cork) for Kehoe.

U.C.D. Pádraig Delaney (Dublin), Mick Cullen (Wexford), Shane McGuckian (Offaly), Ray Cullinane (Wexford), Dave O'Mahony (Wexford), Pat O'Callaghan (Cork), Nicky O'Farrell (Limerick), John Pilkington (Offaly), Conal Bonnar (Tipperary), Danny Curran (Wicklow), Tom Ryan (Tipperary), Barry O'Brien (Tipperary), Pat Leahy (Tipperary), Ciarán Carroll (Tipperary), Jim Byrne (Wexford). Subs.: Mick Quigley (Tipperary) for Cullen, Brendan Carroll (Tipperary) for Byrne, Niall Murphy (Dublin) for Carroll.

1991/92

W.R.T.C. Alan Hickey (Cork), John Houlihan (Kilkenny), Paul Lee (Clare), Denis Mullally (Kilkenny), David Beirne (Kilkenny), Ger Crosse (Tipperary), Donncha O'Donnell (Cork), Owen Cummins (Tipperary), Paudie O'Keeffe (Tipperary), Michael Hubbard (Waterford), Pádraic Fanning (Waterford), PJ Delaney (Kilkenny), Noel Dalton (Waterford), Seán Ryan (Kilkenny), James Aherne (Cork).

U.L. Alan Quirke (Tipperary), Alby Quinlan (Tipperary), Willie Burke (Galway), Mark Kenny (Offaly), Paul Hardiman (Galway), Daragh O'Neill (Limerick), Ger Moroney (Clare), Damien Considine (Clare), Jack Griffin (Tipperary), Ray Dooley (Offaly), John Fitzgerald (Limerick), Pat Maguire (Tipperary), Ger Rodgers (Clare), David O'Driscoll (Limerick), T.J.O'Dwyer (Tipperary). Subs.: Andrew Ryan (Limerick) for Griffin, Mark Scanlon (Clare) for Fitzgerald.

1992/93

U.C.D. Jim Conroy (Kilkenny), Pádraig Dolan (Galway), Mick Cullen (Wexford), Paul Finnegan (Galway), Andy Dunne (Laois), Tim Cronin (Cork), Dan O'Neill (Kilkenny), John Pilkington (Offaly), Brendan Carroll (Tipperary), Paul Maher (Tipperary), Joe Walsh (Kilkenny), Colmáin Ó Drisceoill (Dublin), Éamonn Scallan (Wexford), Séamus Hughes (Wexford), Jim Byrne (Wexford). Sub.: Dave O'Mahony (Wexford) for Cronin.

U.C.C. Pat Looney (Cork), Diarmaid McInerney (Wexford), Andrew Murphy (Cork), Frank Lohan (Clare), Kieran Murphy (Cork), Pat Kenneally (Cork), Colman Dillon (Cork), Johnny Brenner (Waterford), Damien Quigley (Limerick), Declan O'Sullivan (Cork), Alan Browne (Cork), Vincent O'Neill (Cork), Donal O'Mahony (Cork), Tony Doolan (Cork), Gerry Maguire (Tipperary). Subs.: Pat Hartnett (Cork) for O'Sullivan, Tom O'Connell (Kerry) for Dillon, Dillon for O'Connell, O'Sullivan for Murphy, Murphy for Quigley.

1993/94

U.L. Damien Garrihy (Clare), Brian Lohan (Clare), Willie Burke (Galway), Conor Galvin (Clare), Shane Doyle (Kilkenny), Daragh O'Neill (Limerick), Seán McMahon (Clare), Fergal Hartley (Waterford), Pat Maguire (Tipperary), Colm O'Doherty (Galway), John O'Halloran (Limerick), Pat Divinney (Galway), Darren O'Donoghue (Cork), Alan Quirke (Tipperary), Fionán O'Sullivan (Laois). Subs.: Con Murphy (Clare) for Hartley, Barry White (Cork) for Quirke, Quirke for White, Kevin McCarthy (Cork) for Quirke.

W.R.T.C. Brendan Cummins (Tipperary), Tomás Keane (Tipperary), Paul Lee (Clare), Brian Flannery (Tipperary), Ollie Moran (Limerick), Fergal McCormack (Cork), Tom Feeney (Waterford), Pádraic Fanning (Waterford), Peter Barry (Kilkenny), Tommy Dunne (Tipperary), Brian O'Meara (Tipperary), Ollie O'Connor (Kilkenny), James Moran (Limerick), Anthony Qualter (Waterford), P.J.Delaney (Kilkenny). Subs.: Paudie O'Keeffe (Tipperary) for O'Connor, Tom Kavanagh (Galway) for Fanning, O'Connor for Kavanagh.

1994/95

W.R.T.C. Patrick Harnan (Waterford), Brian Kelly (Kilkenny), Paul Lee (Clare), Tom Feeney (Waterford), Colm O'Flaherty (Tipperary), Fergal McCormack (Cork), Patrick Mullally (Kilkenny), Colm Bonnar (Tipperary), Peter Barry (Kilkenny), Tommy Dunne (Tipperary), P.J.Delaney (Kilkenny), James Moran (Limerick), Barry Walsh (Waterford), Michael Hubbard (Waterford), Ollie O'Connor (Kilkenny). Subs.: Aidan Flanagan (Tipperary) for Mullally, Martin Morrissey (Wexford) for O'Connor, Richie Murphy (Wexford) for Hubbard.

U.C.D. Myles Byrne (Meath), Dave Larkin (Dublin), John Dowling (Kilkenny), Kevin Harrington (Dublin), Hugh Sisk (Kildare), Barry O'Connell (Limerick), Brendan Bolger (Kilkenny), Dan O'Neill (Kilkenny), Seán Kealy (Kilkenny), Jarlath Bolger (Kilkenny), John Ryan (Tipperary), Noel Carr (Tipperary), Máirtín Óg Corrigan (Cork), Adrian Donoghue (Dublin), John Morris (Dublin). Subs.: Pat O'Keeffe (Cork) for O'Connell, Ciaran Collins (Cork) for Kerrigan.

1995/96

U.C.C. John O'Brien (Limerick), Denis Twomey (Cork), Frank Lohan (Clare), Niall Murphy (Limerick), Dan Murphy (Cork), Johnny Collins (Cork), Tim Cronin (Cork), Alan Cummins (Cork), Tim Coffey (Cork), Donal O'Mahony (Cork), Eddie Enright (Tipperary), John Enright (Tipperary), Eoin O'Neill (Limerick), Kieran Morrison (Cork), Joe Deane (Cork). Sub.: Richard Woods (Cork) for Cronin.

U.L. Damien Garrihy (Clare), Michael Healy (Galway), Shane Doyle (Kilkenny), Tom Hickey (Kilkenny), Noel Finnerty (Galway), Seán McMahon (Clare), Conor Hanniffy (Offaly), Pat Divinney (Galway), Rory McCarthy (Wexford), David Forde (Clare), Darren O'Connor (Tipperary), Colm O'Doherty (Galway), Darren O'Donoghue (Cork), Gerry Maguire (Tipperary), Brian O'Driscoll (Cork). Subs.: John Kiely (Limerick) for McCarthy, Niall Hayes (Galway) for Diviney.

1996/97

U.C.C. Brendan Kelly (Cork), Denis Twomey (Cork), Tom Bambury (Cork), Niall Murphy (Limerick), Dan Murphy (Cork), Richard Woods (Cork), John Browne (Cork), Martin Hayes (Cork), Colm O'Brien (Limerick), Derek McGrath (Waterford), Eddie Enright (Tipperary), Seánie McGrath (Cork), John Enright (Tipperary), Kieran Morrison (Cork), Joe Deane (Cork).

Garda Cathal Jordan (Galway), Niall O'Donnell (Cork), Séamus McIntyre (Kerry), John Finnegan (Dublin), Kevin Long (Cork), Conor Gleeson (Tipperary), Stephen Hogan (Tipperary), Ollie Baker (Clare), Tommy Kennedy (Tipperary), Damien Cleere (Kilkenny), Brian O'Dwyer (Tipperary), Tom Kavanagh (Galway), Niall Maloney (Kilkenny), Denis Byrne (Kilkenny), Aidan Flanagan (Tipperary). Subs.: Jimmy Smiddy (Cork) for Flanagan, Séamus Maher (Tipperary) for O'Dwyer, Nigel Carey (Limerick) for Kennedy.

1997/98

U.C.C. Brendan Kelly (Cork), Pat Mahon (Laois), Tom Bambury (Cork), Luke Mannix (Cork), Mark O'Sullivan (Waterford), Dan Murphy (Cork), Liam Harte (Cork), James Murray (Waterford), Eddie Enright (Tipperary), John Enright (Tipperary), John O'Brien (Limerick), Seánie McGrath (Cork), Dave Bennett (Waterford), Kieran Morrison (Cork), Joe Deane (Cork). Subs.: Seán Ryan (Tipperary) for O'Brien, Colm O'Brien (Limerick) for McGrath, Niall Murphy (Limerick) for E.Enright.

W.I.T. Anthony McCormack (Kilkenny), Cathal Murray (Galway), Michael Kavanagh (Kilkenny), Alan Kelleher (Cork), Brian Forde (Clare), Éamonn Corcoran (Tipperary), Declan Ruth (Wexford), Fergus Flynn (Clare), Colm Cassidy (Offaly), Liam Walsh (Kilkenny), William Maher (Tipperary), Andy Moloney (Tipperary), Chris McGrath (Wexford), Henry Shefflin (Kilkenny), Mark O'Leary (Tipperary). Subs.: Michael O'Dowd (Tipperary) for Ruth, Pádraig Delaney (Kilkenny) for Cassidy, Dara O'Sullivan (Waterford) for McGrath.

1998/99

W.I.T. Kevin O'Brien (Tipperary), Michael Kavanagh (Kilkenny), Eric Flynn (Clare), Alan Kelleher (Cork), Brian Forde (Clare), Éamonn Corcoran (Tipperary), Colm Cassidy (Offaly), Shane McClaren (Galway), Alan Geoghegan (Kilkenny), Michael Bevans (Tipperary), Andy Moloney (Tipperary), Dave Bennett (Waterford), Neil Ronan (Cork), Henry Shefflin (Kilkenny), Declan Browne (Waterford). Subs.: Derek Lyng (Kilkenny) for Flynn, Alan Ahearne (Kilkenny) for Geoghegan, Pádraig Delaney (Kilkenny) for Forde.

U.C.C. Jim McDonald (Tipperary), Pat Mahon (Laois), Tom Bambury (Cork), Niall Murphy (Limerick), James Murray (Waterford), John Browne (Cork), Liam Harte (Cork), Stefan Fitzpatrick (Clare), Luke Mannix (Cork), John Enright (Tipperary), Richie Flannery (Tipperary), Eoin Bennett (Waterford), Donagh Sheehan (Limerick), John Kingston (Cork), John Murphy (Cork). Subs.: Shane Killeen (Cork) for Sheehan, Michael Hartigan (Clare) for Mahon.

1999/00

W.I.T. Damien Young (Tipperary), Cathal Murray (Galway), Paul Curran (Tipperary), Alan Kelleher (Cork), Brian Forde (Clare), Éamonn Corcoran (Tipperary), Michael Kavanagh (Kilkenny), John O'Neill (Kilkenny), Andy Moloney (Tipperary), Alan Geoghegan (Kilkenny), William Maher (Tipperary), Damien Joyce (Galway), Michael Bevans (Tipperary), Henry Shefflin (Kilkenny), Declan Browne (Tipperary). Sub: Leigh O'Brien (Wexford) for Maher.

U.C.D. Michael Lyons (Offaly), Brian Walton (Tipperary), Stephen Lucey (Limerick), Cathal Murphy (Offaly), Conor O'Donovan (Galway), David Hegarty (Clare), Hugh Flannery (Tipperary), Seán O'Neill (Limerick), Paul Ormonde (Tipperary), Paddy O'Brien (Tipperary), Noel Murphy (Offaly), Pat Fitzgerald (Waterford), Michael Gordon (Kilkenny), Jim Byrne (Wexford), Brendan Murphy (Offaly). Subs.: Alan Barry (Kilkenny) for O'Donovan, John Berkery (Wicklow) for Byrne.

2000/01

U.C.D. Mattie White (Wexford), Brian Walton (Tipperary), David O'Connor (Wexford), Robbie Kirwan (Wexford), Hugh Flannery (Tipperary), David Hegarty (Clare), Colm Everard (Tipperary), Gary Mernagh (Tipperary), Stephen Lucey (Limerick), Pat Fitzgerald (Waterford), Seán O'Neill (Limerick), Redmond Barry (Wexford), John Culkin (Galway), Alan Barry (Kilkenny), Brendan Murphy (Offaly). Subs.: Tim Murphy (Kilkenny) for Lucey, Pat Tennyson (Kilkenny) for Culkin, Paddy O'Brien (Tipperary) for Mernagh. Tim Murphy, Martin Bergin (Kilkenny) and Tennyson all started the first match, and were replaced by Mernagh, O'Neill and Alan Barry respectively. Hugh Gannon (Kilkenny) and Aidan Power (Dublin) also appeared as substitutes in the drawn game.

U.C.C. Richie O'Neill (Kilkenny), John Browne (Cork), John Crowley (Cork), Alan Kirwan (Waterford), Rory O'Doherty (Cork), Richie Flannery (Tipperary), Jonathan Olden (Cork), Eoin Murphy (Waterford), Eoin Morrissey (Tipperary), Brian Phelan (Kilkenny), Stiofán Fitzpatrick (Clare), Noel Brodie (Clare), Donncha Sheehan (Limerick), John Kingston (Cork), John Murphy (Cork). Subs: Éamonn Collins (Cork) for Kingston, Victor Cusack (Cork) for Sheehan. Tom Kenny (Cork) and Mark O'Connor (Cork) started the first game, and were replaced by Olden and Brodie respectively. David Niblock (Cork), Jim McDonnell (Tipperary), Niall Murphy (Limerick) also appeared as substitutes in the drawn match.

2001/02

U.L. Timmy Houlihan (Limerick), Brian O'Mahony (Galway), John Devane (Tipperary), Dermot Gleeson (Tipperary), Colm Forde (Clare), Brian Geary (Limerick), Conor Earley (Clare), Richie Murray (Galway), John Barron (Kilkenny), Conor Fitzgerald (Cork), Niall Moran (Limerick), Eoin Fitzgerald (Cork), David Donohoe (Galway), David Forde (Galway), Donncha Sheehan (Limerick). Sub.: Paul O'Reilly (Limerick) for Gleeson, Mick O'Hara (Offaly) for Donohoe.

W.I.T. Damien Young (Tipperary), Damien Joyce (Galway), Paul Curran (Tipperary), J.J.Delaney (Kilkenny), Mick Fitzgerald (Cork), Joe Brady (Offaly), John O'Neill (Kilkenny), Alan Geoghegan (Kilkenny), Ger Coleman (Wexford), Mick Jacob (Wexford), Fergus Flynn (Clare), Setanta Ó hAilpín (Cork), Brian Dowling (Kilkenny), Henry Shefflin (Kilkenny), Damien Murray (Offaly). Subs.: Stephen Brown (Offaly) for Dowling, Niall Murphy (Cork) for Flynn.

2002/03

W.I.T. Damien Young (Tipperary), Brian Lynch (Clare), Paul Curran (Tipperary), J.J.Delaney (Kilkenny), Mick Fitzgerald (Cork), Joe Brady (Offaly), Ken Coogan (Kilkenny), Ollie Moran (Limerick), Fergus Flynn (Clare), Brian Dowling (Kilkenny), Mick Jacob (Wexford), M.J. Furlong (Wexford), Setanta Ó hAilpín (Cork), Conor Phelan (Kilkenny), Damien Murray (Offaly). Subs.: Shane Hennessy (Kilkenny) for Phelan, Rory Jacob (Wexford) for Murray, C. Phelan for Ó hAilpín.

C.I.T. Martin Coleman (Cork), Brian Murphy (Cork), Jackie Tyrrell (Kilkenny), Michael Prout (Cork), Vincent Hurley (Cork), Ronan Curran (Cork), Pat Sloane (Cork), Stephen O'Sullivan (Cork), John Gardiner (Cork), Garvan McCarthy (Cork), Colin O'Leary (Cork), John O'Connor (Cork), Aidan Fogarty (Kilkenny), Diarmuid O'Riordan (Cork), Kieran Murphy (Cork). Subs.: Paul Tierney (Cork) for O'Leary, Gary McLoughlin (Cork) for O'Riordan, Garvan McCarthy (Cork) for O'Connor.

2003/04

W.I.T. Philip Brennan (Clare), Chris O'Neill (Kilkenny), Ken Coogan (Kilkenny), J.J.Delaney (Kilkenny), Tommy Holland (Clare), Keith Rossiter (Wexford), Hugh Maloney (Tipperary), David Hayes (Galway), Michael Walsh (Waterford), Conor Phelan (Kilkenny), Peter Garvey (Galway), John Phelan (Kilkenny), Rory Jacob (Wexford), Anthony Owens (Kilkenny), Brian Dowling (Kilkenny). Subs.: P.J..Delaney (Kilkenny) for Rossiter, Conor Burns (Cork) for Owens, Adrian Cullinane (Galway).

U.C.C. Richie O'Neill (Kilkenny), John Tennyson (Kilkenny), Canice Hickey (Kilkenny), Michael Phelan (Kilkenny), Tom Kenny (Cork), Kevin Hartnett (Cork), Evan Hanley (Tipperary), Tommy Walsh (Kilkenny), Mark O'Connor (Cork), Mark O'Leary (Tipperary), Eoin Conway (Cork), Shane O'Sullivan (Waterford), James 'Cha' Fitzpatrick (Kilkenny), Éamonn Collins (Cork), Noel Moloney (Tipperary). Subs.: Paul O'Brien (Waterford) for Moloney, Donagh O'Sullivan (Limerick) for Conway.

2004/05

L.I.T. Aidan Ryan (Galway), Enda Collins (Clare), John Coen (Clare), Conor O'Mahony (Tipperary), Shane McGrath (Tipperary), Fergus Flynn (Clare), David Morrissey (Tipperary), Jackie Tyrrell (Kilkenny), John Reddan (Clare), Aengus Callanan (Galway), Barry Nugent (Clare), Iarla Tannian (Galway), Niall Healy (Galway), Eoin Kelly (Tipperary), Kieran Murphy (Cork). Subs.: Donal O'Reilly (Galway) for Murphy.

U.L. Tadhg Flynn (Kerry), Brendan Bugler (Clare), John Devane (Tipperary), Aidan Murphy (Wexford), Robert Conlon (Clare), Raymond Hayes (Limerick), Ger Flood (Wexford), Niall Moran (Limerick), Barry Coleman (Cork), Paul O'Flynn (Kilkenny), Joe Gantley (Galway), David McCormack (Kilkenny), Brian Carroll (Limerick), David Greene (Galway), Nicky Kenny (Kilkenny). Subs.: Tadhg Healy (Cork) for Coleman, Peter Dowling (Kilkenny) for Gantley, John Heneghan (Waterford) for McCormack.

2005/06

W.I.T. Philip Brennan (Clare), Keith Rossiter (Wexford), Kevin Moran (Waterford), Alan Kirwan (Waterford), Daniel Hoctor (Offaly), Kevin Brady (Offaly), Hugh Maloney (Tipperary), Ger Mahon (Galway), Michael Walsh (Waterford), Conor Phelan (Kilkenny), Adrian Cullinane (Galway), Eoin Reid (Kilkenny), Brian Dowling (Kilkenny), Willie Ryan (Tipperary), Rory Jacob (Wexford). Subs.: Liam Lawlor (Waterford) for Hayes, Cathal Parlon (Offaly) for Cullinane, Conor O'Brien (Tipperary) for Hoctor, Pat Hartley (Kilkenny) for Walsh, Mark Heffernan (Kilkenny) for Kirwan.

U.C.D. Mattie White (Wexford), Diarmaid Fitzgerald (Tipperary), Michael Fitzgerald (Cork), Eddie Campion (Kilkenny), David Prendergast (Kilkenny), Éamon Ryan (Tipperary), Seán Cummins (Kilkenny), Bryan Barry (Kilkenny), David Hayes (Galway), Éamon O'Gorman (Kilkenny), John McCarthy (Limerick), Brendan Murphy (Offaly), Andy Smith (Galway), Tommy Fitzgerald (Tipperary), John O'Connor (Wexford). Subs.: Paul Ormond (Tipperary) for Hayes, Stephen Nolan (Wexford) for Fitzgerald, P.J.Nolan (Wexford) for O'Connor, Kieran Breen (Limerick) for Nolan.

2006/07

L.I.T. James Skehill (Galway), Michael Walsh (Cork), Jackie Tyrrell (Kilkenny), Alan Byrne (Tipperary), Shane McGrath (Tipperary), Conor O'Mahony (Tipperary), Maurice O'Brien (Limerick), Jonathan Clancy (Clare), Kieran Murphy (Cork), Eoin Cadogan (Cork), Austin Murphy (Kilkenny), Iarla Tannian (Galway), Aonghus Callanan (Galway), Joe Canning (Galway), James McInerney (Clare). Subs.: Bernard Gaffney (Clare) for Cadogan.

N.U.I.G. David Woods (Clare), Roderick Whyte (Galway), Martin Ryan (Galway), Liam Geraghty (Galway), James Dunphy (Kilkenny), John Lee (Galway), Enda Barrett (Clare), Colin Ryan (Clare), Stephen Molumphy (Waterford), Peter O'Brien (Cork), David Barrett (Clare), Finian Coone (Galway), David Kenny (Offaly), Darragh Egan (Tipperary), Seán Glynn (Galway). Subs.: Vinny Faherty (Galway) for O'Brien, Pádraic Kennedy (Limerick) for Ryan.

2007/08

W.I.T. Adrian Power (Waterford), Kevin Lanigan (Tipperary), John Dalton (Kilkenny), Conor Cooney (Clare), Shane Fives (Waterford), Pat Hartley (Kilkenny), Kevin Moran (Waterford), Stephen Lillis (Tipperary), Pat Kelly (Clare), Fintan O'Leary (Cork), T.J.Reid (Kilkenny), Ronan Good (Cork), Ray McLoughney (Tipperary), Eoin Reid (Kilkenny), Shane O'Sullivan (Waterford). Subs.: Mark Gorman (Waterford) for Good, Shane Kelly (Cork) for Fives, Gavin Nolan (Kilkenny) for S.Kelly, Kieran Grehan (Kilkenny) for Gorman.

L.I.T. Matthew Ryan (Tipperary), Michael Walsh (Cork), Alan Byrne (Tipperary), Enda Collins (Clare), Gary O'Connell (Clare), Shane Maher (Tipperary), Maurice O'Brien (Limerick), Jonathan Clancy (Clare), Wayne McNamara (Limerick), Willie Hyland (Laois), Cyril Donnellan (Galway), James McInerney (Clare), Paudie O'Brien (Limerick), Joe Canning (Galway), Niall Healy (Galway). Subs.: Blaine Earley (Clare) for P O'Brien, Austin Murphy (Kilkenny) for Clancy, Clancy for Healy, Healy for McInerney.

2008/09

U.C.C. Anthony Nash (Cork), Shane O'Neill (Cork), Darragh McSweeney (Cork), Conor O'Sullivan (Cork), Richie Foley (Waterford), Joe Jordan (Cork), Kevin Hartnett (Cork), Bryan O'Sullivan (Limerick), Michael Cahill (Tipperary), Don Hanley (Limerick), Bill Beckett (Kilkenny), John Mulhall (Kilkenny), Stephen Moylan (Cork), Shane Burke (Tipperary), Tadhg Óg Murphy (Cork). Subs: Éanna Martin (Wexford) for Hanley, Damien Browne (Clare) for Cahill, William Kearney for C.O'Sullivan, Michael Grace (Kilkenny) for O'Neill, Conor O'Driscoll for Burke.

U.L. Patrick McCormack (Tipperary), Brian Fox (Tipperary), Kieran Joyce (Kilkenny), Michael Verney (Offaly), Jim Bob McCarthy (Tipperary), Tom Stapleton (Tipperary), Martin Walsh (Kilkenny), Séamus Hickey (Limerick), Michael Gleeson (Tipperary), Seán Ryan (Offaly), Ryan O'Dwyer (Tipperary), John Greene (Galway), Brian Carroll (Offaly), Matt Ruth (Kilkenny), Alan Egan (Offaly). Subs used: Noel Ó Murchú (Waterford) for Greene, Shane O'Brien (Clare) for Fox, Dylan Hayden (Offaly) for Stapleton, David Burke (Galway) for O'Dwyer, Kevin Lanigan (Tipperary) for Egan.

2009/10

N.U.I.G. D.Tuohy, D.Nash, J.Lee, D.Connolly, P.Gordon, S.Hennessy, P.Kelly, B.Daly, D.O'Donovan, J.Conlon, K.Keehan, C.O'Donovan, G.Kelly, C.Morey, F.Coone. Subs: J.P.O'Connell for C.O'Donovan, S.Quinlan for Keehan, J.O'Gorman for Conlon, Conlon for G.Kelly.

W.I.T. A.Power, B.Kenny, R.McCarthy, N.Connors, W.Hutchinson, S.Fives, P.J.Rowe, E.Barrett, M.Molloy, F.O'Leary, R.McLoughney, R.Good, T.Hammersley, B.O'Meara, K.Grehan. Subs: K.Reade for Good, S.Power for Grehan, W.O'Dwyer for Molloy, H.Vaughan for Power.

2010/11

U.L. T.Lowry, P.Stapleton, M.Walsh, S.Hickey, P.J.Delaney, B.Bugler, K.Joyce, P.Cronin, D.Burke, B.Carroll, B.Beckett, P.Murphy, K.Morris, P.Kelly, A.Quinn. Subs: M.Boran for Murphy, T.Connors for Boran, T.O'Brien for Beckett.

L.I.T. M.Ryan, E.Glynn, C.Cowan, C.Cooney, J.Hayes, J.McInerney, J.O'Keeffe, S.Collins, P.Browne, S.Lambert, W.Hyland, P.O'Brien, B.Gaffney, S.Tobin, D.Reale. Sub: C.Madden for Gaffney.

2011/12

U.C.C. D.McCarthy, S.Maher, J.O'Callaghan, K.Murphy, J.Barry, D.Fives, W.Egan, Philip Mahony, B.Murray, Pauric Mahony, D.McCormack, S.Harnedy, S.Bourke, S.Moylan, B.O'Sullivan. Subs: S.Corry for Murray, R.White for Harnedy, B.Hartnett for O'Sullivan, D.Brosnan for McCormack, M.Grace for Maher, Murray for Brosnan.

C.I.T. K.Roche, B.Weathers, S.McDonnell, E.Keane, S.White, L.McLoughlin, P.O'Connor, J.Coughlan, M.O'Sullivan, J.Cronin, D.Drake, P.Gould, C.Fennelly, P.O'Sullivan, T.Quaid. Subs: A.Walsh for Quaid, C.Casey for Gould, N.Kelly for M.O'Sullivan, S.Daniels for Keane, P.Gould for Drake, O'Sullivan for Cronin.

2012/13

U.C.C. D.McCarthy, S.Maher, D.Glynn, K.Murphy, J.Barry, D.Fives, W.Egan, P.Haughney, B.Murray, S.Harnedy, D.McCormack, Brian Lawton, B.O'Sullivan, C.Lehane, B.Hartnett. Subs: Barry Lawton for Murray, A.Breen for McCormack, D.Kearns for O'Halloran.

Mary Immaculate College S.Nolan, C.Fennessy, R.O'Donnell, A.Ryan, J.Wall, D.Hannon, Eanna Hogan, C.Galvin, N.O'Meara, B.O'Halloran, W.Hickey, C.Cooney, S.Curran, J.Conlon, L.O'Farrell. Subs: Eoin Hogan for Hickey, L.Considine for Eanna Hogan.

2013/14

W.I.T. S.O'Keeffe, G.Teehan, P.Gahan, J.Maher, T.Hamill, J.O'Dwyer, J.Langton, S.Roche, C.Kenny, H.Kehoe, P.Mahony, E.Murphy, L.McGrath, J.Dillon, G.O'Brien. Subs: J.Hayes for McGrath, A.Kenny for O'Dwyer, M.Power for Kenny.
C.I.T.S. Nylan, S.Murphy, A.Dennehy, T.Lawrence, E.Keane, M.Ellis, P.Butler, W.Murphy, J.Coughlan, J.O'Dwyer, J.Cronin, C.Hammersley, B.Cooper, D.Dooley, D.Drake. Subs: K.O'Connor for Coughlan, K.Hallissey for Drake, D.Corbett for Murphy, D.Brosnan for Corbett, S.Murray for Cooper.

2014/15 REPLAY

UL P.Maher, J.Browne, G.Ryan, B.Troy, D.Quinn, D.McInerney, B.Stapleton, T.Kelly, D.Morrissey, K.O'Brien, C.Martin, T.Heffernan, C.McInerney, J.McGrath, J.Forde. Subs: S.Bennett for C.McInerney, P.J.Scully for O'Brien, S.O'Gorman for Morrissey, K.Walsh for Heffernan, E.Moriarty for Forde.
WIT D.Stapleton, O.McGrath, G.Teehan, J.Maher, T.Hamill, M.O'Neill, T.Fox, J.Langton, S.Roche, P.Mahony, L.McGrath, H.Kehoe, A.Gleeson, J.Dillon, G.O'Brien. Subs: J.Hayes for Gleeson, G.Malone for L.McGrath, C.O'Brien for Roche, J.O'Dwyer for Hamill.

2015/16

Mary Immaculate College M.Ó Conghaile, E.Quirke, R.English, A.Ryan, R.Maher, T.Stapleton, J.Meagher, C.Galvin, D.O'Donovan, S.Linnane, C.Lynch, D.Reidy, D.Hannon, N.O'Meara, D.Corry. Subs: M.O'Neill for Galvin, T.Gallagher for Corry, S.Cahill for O'Donovan, S.Kennedy for Linnane, Corry for Quirke, O'Donovan for O'Meara, Linnane for Gallagher, Gallagher for Hannon.
UL P.Maher, G.Ryan, J.Browne, S.Roche, B.Heffernan, J.Forde, B.Stapleton, A.McGuane, K.Hehir, D.Fitzgerald, J.McGrath, C.Martin, K.O'Brien, T.Morrissey, C.McInerney. Subs: T.Heffernan for Fitzgerald, G.Hegarty for Stapleton, A.Murphy for O'Brien, M.Casey for Hehir, P.Ryan for Forde, B.Maher for McGuane.

2016/17

Mary Immaculate College C.Barrett, D.Sweeney, R.English, E.Quirke, C.Twomey, R.Maher, A.Flynn, C.Galvin, S.Cahill, D.O'Donovan, M.O'Neill, A.Gillane, T.Gallagher, C.Lynch, L.Meade. Subs: T.Monaghan for Gallagher, P.Ryan for O'Neill, S.Burke for Gillane.
Carlow IT E.Rowland, D.Palmer, K.Hannafin, R.Browne, R.Moran, D.Healy, D.O'Hanlon, J.Doyle, C.Dunford, M.Kavanagh, C.Dwyer, S.Maher, C.Bolger, M.Russell, J.Fagan. Sub: T.Nolan for Russell.

FITZGIBBON CUP WINNING CAPTAINS

1911/12	J Dwan (UCD)
1912/13	Peter M Murphy (UCC & Cork)
1913/14	Jim Reidy (UCC & Limerick)
1914/15	Éamon Bulfin (UCD & Offaly)
1915/16	John Ryan (UCD, Limerick & Dublin)
1916/17	John Ryan (UCD, Limerick & Dublin)
1917/18	(UCC captain's name not available)
1918/19	Martin Fahy (UCG)
1919/20	R Lahiffe (UCC)
1920/21	Not played
1921/22	(UCC captain's name not available)
1922/23	Tommy Daly (UCD & Clare & Dublin)
1923/24	Tommy Daly (UCD & Clare & Dublin)
1924/25	Tom Lee (UCC & Tipperary)
1925/26	T O'Grady (UCG)
1926/27	O O'Neill (UCD)
1927/28	Richard Molloy (UCC & Cork)
1928/29	Paddy O'Donovan (UCC & Cork)
1929/30	Patrick O'Donnell (UCC)
1930/31	William Finlay (UCC & Tipperary)
1931/32	Jack Walsh (UCD)
1932/33	Richard Cronin (UCC & Cork)
1933/34	Séamus Hogan (UCD & Clare)
1934/35	Tom Loughnane (UCD & Clare)
1935/36	Tony MacSullivan (UCD & Limerick)
1936/37	Mossie Roche (UCD & Limerick)
1937/38	Jimmy Cooney (UCD & Tipperary)
1938/39	Jackie Spencer (UCC & Cork)
1939/40	Jim Young (UCC & Cork)
1940/41	Billy O'Neill (UCC & Kilkenny)
1941/42	Pat Hehir (UCG & Galway)
1942/43	Not played
1943/44	Dick Stokes (UCD & Limerick)
1944/45	Michael "Miko" Doyle (UCG & Galway)
1945/46	Michael "Miko" Doyle (UCG & Galway)
1946/47	Mick Herlihy (UCC & Cork)
1947/48	Frank Commons (UCD & Tipperary & Dublin)
1948/49	Johnny Scanlon (UCG & Galway)
1949/50	Mick Maher (UCD & Boharlahan, Tipperary)
1950/51	Martin Fitzgerald (UCD & Tipperary & Dublin)
1951/52	Des Dillon (UCD & Clare & Dublin)
1952/53	Ted McConnell (QUB & Antrim)
1953/54	Declared null & void
1954/55	Pat Teehan (UCD & Waterford)

1955/56	Johnny Dwane (UCC & Cork)	2001/02	Eoin Fitzgerald (UL & Cork)
1956/57	Tony Murphy (UCC & Cork)	2002/03	Paul Curran (WIT & Tipperary)
1957/58	Bernard Hoey (UCD & Clare)	2003/04	J.J.Delaney (WIT & Kilkenny)
1958/59	Steve Long (UCC & Limerick)	2004/05	Eoin Kelly (LIT & Tipperary)
1959/60	Donie Nealon (UCD & Tipperary)	2005/06	Brian Dowling (WIT & Kilkenny), Hugh Maloney (WIT & Tipperary)
1960/61	Owen O'Neill (UCD & Limerick)	2006/07	Kieran Murphy (LIT & Cork)
1961/62	Jimmy Byrne (UCC & Waterford)	2007/08	Kevin Moran (WIT & Waterford)
1962/63	Des Kiely (UCC & Tipperary)	2008/09	Kevin Hartnett (UCC & Cork)
1963/64	Seán Quinlivan (UCD & Clare)	2009/10	Finian Coone (NUI & Galway)
1964/65	Murt Duggan (UCD & Tipperary)	2010/11	Kieran Joyce (UL & Kilkenny)
1965/66	Willie Cronin (UCC & Cork)	2011/12	Shane Bourke (UCC & Tipperary)
1966/67	Seánie Barry (UCC & Cork)	2012/13	Darren McCarthy (UCC & Cork)
1967/68	Jim Furlong (UCD & Wexford)	2013/14	Eoin Murphy (WIT & Kilkenny)
1968/69	Pat Kavanagh (UCD & Kilkenny)	2014/15	David McInerney (UL & Clare)
1969/70	Séamus Hogan (UCG & Tipperary)	2015/16	Richard English (Mary Immaculate & Limerick)
1970/71	Pat McDonnell (UCC & Cork)	2016/17	Eoin Quirke (Mary Immaculate & Clare)
1971/72	Mick McCarthy (UCC & Cork)		
1972/73	Paudie Fitzmaurice (Maynooth & Limerick)		
1973/74	Paddy Barry (Maynooth & Cork)		
1974/75	Séamus Ryan (UCD & Tipperary)		
1975/76	Donal McGovern (UCC & Cork)		
1976/77	Pat Fleury (UCG & Offaly)		
1977/78	John Martin (UCD & Kilkenny)		
1978/79	Tom Breen (UCD & Wexford)		
1979/80	Vincent Daly (UCG & Clare)		
1980/81	John Minogue (UCC & Clare)		
1981/82	John Farrell (UCC & Tipperary)		
1982/83	Tadhg Coakley (UCC & Cork)		
1983/84	Mick Boylan (UCC & Cork)		
1984/85	Nicholas English (UCC & Tipperary)		
1985/86	Paul O'Connor (UCC & Cork)		
1986/87	John Grainger (UCC & Cork)		
1987/88	Andy O'Callaghan (UCC & Cork)		
1988/89	Dan Treacy (NIHEL & Clare)		
1989/90	Mick Crowe (UCC & Limerick)		
1990/91	Pat Heffernan (UCC & Limerick)		
1991/92	Pádraic Fanning (WRTC & Tipperary)		
1992/93	Jim Byrne (UCD & Wexford)		
1993/94	Daragh O'Neill (UL & Limerick)		
1994/95	Colm Bonnar (WRTC & Tipperary)		
1995/96	Frank Lohan (UCC & Clare)		
1996/97	Kieran Morrison (UCC & Cork)		
1997/98	Eddie Enright (UCC & Tipperary)		
1998/99	Andy Moloney (WIT & Tipperary)		
1999/00	Andy Moloney (WIT & Tipperary)		
2000/01	David Hegarty (UCD & Clare)		

FITZGIBBON CUP FINAL TOP SCORERS 1949-2017

Note: The competition was played on a league basis up until 1947/48 inclusive.

1948/49	John L Coyne (UCG & Galway) 2-0
1949/50	S Murphy (UCG) 2-1
1950/51	Johnny Ryan (UCD & Tipperary) 1-1
1951/52	Johnny Ryan (UCD & Tipperary) 1-2
1952/53	Séamus "Stout" McDonald (QUB & Antrim) 1-1
1953/54	Paddy O'Donoghue (UCG & Waterford) 2-0;
	Noel McMahon (UCG & Offaly) 2-0;
	*result declared void
1954/55	Mick Hanley (UCC & Clare) 3-1
1955/56	Dick Troy (UCC & Cork) 1-5
1956/57	Dick Troy (UCC & Cork) 1-6
1957/58	Nicky Stokes (UCD & Limerick) 2-4
1958/59	Tom Riordan (UCC & Cork) 2-0;
	John Joe Browne (UCC & Cork) 2-0;
	Donie Nealon (UCD & Tipperary) 2-0
1959/60	Donie Nealon (UCD & Tipperary) 2-3
1960/61	Pat Henchy (UCD & Clare) 2-0
1961/62	Ollie Harrington (UCC & Kilkenny) 1-4
1962/63	Donie Nealon (UCD & Tipperary) 2-1
1963/64	Pat Henchy (UCD & Clare) 4-3
1964/65	Tom Forrestal (UCD & Kilkenny) 3-2
1965/66	Brendan Kenneally (UCC & Cork) 2-1
1966/67	Séamus Hogan (UCG & Tipperary) 2-2;
	Dennis Philpott (UCC & Cork) 2-2
1967/68	Pat Kavanagh (UCD & Kilkenny) 1-7
1968/69	Pat Kavanagh (UCD & Kilkenny) 0-7
1969/70	Gerry McCarthy (UCD & Kilkenny) 1-8
1970/71	Seán Twomey (UCC & Cork) 1-10
1971/72	Seán Twomey (UCC & Cork) 1-6
1972/73	Henry Goff (Maynooth & Wexford) 2-0
1973/74	Paudie Fitzmaurice (Maynooth & Limerick) 0-7
1974/75	Matt Ruth (UCD & Kilkenny) 2-2
1975/76	Gus O'Driscoll (Maynooth & Cork) 0-7
1976/77	Fachtna O'Driscoll (Maynooth & Cork) 0-9
1977/78	Dave Keane (UCC & Cork) 2-3
1978/79	Peadar Queally (UCD & Tipperary) 3-2
1979/80	Seán Forde (UCG & Galway) 0-4;
	Gerry Dempsey (UCG & Galway) 0-4
1980/81	Michael Kelleher (UCC & Cork) 1-2
1981/82	Nicholas English (UCC & Tipperary) 0-10
1982/83	Mick Quaide (UCC & Limerick) 3-2
1983/84	Colm O'Neill (UCC & Cork) 0-4;
	Jim Kinsella (UCD & Kilkenny) 0-4
1984/85	Colm O'Neill (UCC & Cork) 0-5
1985/86	Mick Walsh (UCC & Kilkenny) 2-1

1986/87	Mark Foley (UCC & Cork) 0-5;
	Vincent Teehan (UCD & Offaly) 0-5;
	Jim Bolger (UCD & Wexford) 0-5
1987/88	Tony O'Sullivan (UCC & Cork) 0-5
1988/89	Derek Gaffney (UCD & Kilkenny) 1-4
1989/90	Damien Curley (WRTC & Galway) 0-10
1990/91	Brian Cunningham (UCC & Cork) 0-5;
	Johnny Ryan (UCC & Cork) 1-2
1991/92	Noel Dalton (WRTC & Waterford) 0-9
1992/93	Jim Byrne (UCD & Wexford) 2-7
1993/94	Colm O'Doherty (UL & Galway) 1-5
1994/95	Barry Walsh (WRTC & Waterford) 2-1
1995/96	John Enright (UCC & Tipperary) 0-7
1996/97	John Enright (UCC & Tipperary) 0-9
1997/98	Seánie McGrath (UCC & Cork) 1-4;
	Henry Shefflin (WIT & Kilkenny) 0-7
1998/99	John Enright (UCC & Tipperary) 1-7
1999/00	Henry Shefflin (WIT & Kilkenny) 1-5
2000/01	Pat Fitzgerald (UCD & Waterford) 0-9
Replay	John Murphy (UCC & Cork) 0-6;
	Alan Barry (UCD & Kilkenny) 2-0;
	Pat Fitzgerald (UCD & Waterford) 0-6
2001/02	Conor Fitzgerald (UL & Cork) 0-7
2002/03	Aidan Fogarty (Cork IT & Kilkenny) 0-4
2003/04	James Fitzpatrick (UCC & Kilkenny) 0-5
2004/05	Eoin Kelly (LIT & Tipperary) 1-9
2005/06	Willie Ryan (WIT & Tipperary 3-0
2006/07	Joe Canning (LIT & Galway) 1-8
2007/08	Joe Canning (LIT & Galway) 1-16
2008/09	John Mulhall (UCC & Kilkenny) 1-3
2009/10	Timmy Hammersley (WIT & Tipperary) 1-11
2010/11	David Burke (UL & Galway) 0-4;
	Pa Cronin (UL & Cork) 0-4,
	Andrew Quinn (UL & Clare) 0-4
2011/12	Jamie Coughlan (CIT & Cork) 1-4
2012/13	Conor Lehane (UCC & Cork) 1-9
2013/14	John O'Dwyer (CIT & Tipperary) 0-5
2014/15	Pauric Mahony (WIT & Waterford) 0-8
Replay	Tony Kelly (UL & Clare) 0-6
	John McGrath (UL & Tipperary) 0-6
2015/16	Declan Hannon (Mary Immaculate & Limerick) 1-12
2016/17	Stephen Maher (CIT & Laois) 1-13

HIGHER EDUCATION

SIGERSON CUP FINALS/RESULTS

1910/11
UCC champions with four league points.

1911/12
UCG champions with three league points.

1912/13
UCD champions with highest aggregate score.

1913/14
UCC champions with four league points.

1914/15
UCD champions by conceding fewest scores.

1915/16
UCC champions with four league points.

1916/17
UCD champions with four league points.

1917/18
UCD beat UCG; **UCC** beat UCD; **UCD** beat UCG.

1918/19
UCC champions with four league points.

Note: from 1919/20 to 1925/26 the competition was played as a straight knock-out.

1919/20
Terenure, 22 February:

UCD	1-7	1-4	UCC

1920/21
No competition.

Note: from 1921/22 to 1966/67 the Sigerson Cup competition was held in the first academic term of the year (Michaelmas), chiefly in November and December.

1921/22
19 December, South Park:

UCG	0-1	0-0	UCC

1922/23

UCC	3-1	0-8	UCD

1923/24
Terenure, 16 December:

UCD	2-4	0-2	UCC

1924/25
Galway, 21 December:

UCC	1-2	0-2	UCG

1925/26
Mardyke, 13 December:

UCC	4-3	0-2	UCD

Note: From 1926/27 to 1932/33 the competition reverted to a league format.

1926/27
UCD champions with four league points.

1927/28
UCC champions with four league points.

1928/29

UCD	5-6	0-0	UCC

1929/30
UCD champions with highest scoring aggregate.

1930/31
UCD champions with four league points.

1931/32
UCD champions with three league points.

1932/33
UCD champions with four league points.

Note: From 1933/34 onwards the competition was played as a straight knock-out.

1933/34
Galway Sports Ground, 10 December:

UCG	5-6	2-3	UCD

1934/35
Mardyke, 9 December:

UCG	1-6	0-2	UCC

1935/36
Corrigan Park, 8 December:

UCD	2-3	0-1	QUB

1936/37
Croke Park, 6 December:

UCG	4-6	1-3	UCD

1937/38
Galway Sports Ground, 5 December:

UCG	0-7	1-2	UCD

1938/39
Mardyke, 4 December:

UCG	2-3	0-0	UCC

1939/40
Galway:

UCG	2-6	1-3	UCD

1940/41
Belfield, 15 December:
| UCG | 3-5 | 1-2 | UCD |

1941/42
Galway Sports Ground, 14 December:
| UCG | 0-8 | 2-1 | UCD |

1942/43
Not played.

1943/44
Mardyke, 28 November:
| UCC | 2-5 | 3-1 | UCD |

1944/45
Belfield, 10 December:
| UCD | 3-8 | 0-2 | UCC |

1945/46
Corrigan Park, 9 December:
| UCD | 4-5 | 2-6 | QUB |

1946/47
Galway Sports Ground, 10 December:
| UCC | 2-3 | 0-4 | UCD |

1947/48
Mardyke, 23 November:
| UCD | 0-3 | 0-2 | UCC |

1948/49
Corrigan Park, 14 November:
| UCG | 2-5 | 2-4 | UCD |

1949/50
Croke Park, 6 November:
| UCD | 1-8 | 1-7 | UCG |

1950/51
Galway Sports Ground, 26 November:
| UCG | 1-12 | UCC | 1-2 |

1951/52
Mardyke, 11 November:
| UCC | 0-5 | 0-3 | UCG |

1952/53
Corrigan Park, 9 November:
| UCC | 3-4 | 0-3 | UCD |

1953/54
Croke Park, 29 November:
| UCD | 2-7 | 0-4 | UCG |

1954/55
Galway Sports Ground, 14 November:
| UCG | 2-6 | 1-9 | UCD |

Fahy's Field, 30 January 1955:
| UCG | 1-10 | 2-6 | UCD (replay) (aet) |

1955/56
Mardyke, 20 November:
| UCD | 3-5 | 2-4 | UCC |

1956/57
Casement Park, 2 December:
| UCD | 1-8 | 1-4 | UCC |

1957/58
Croke Park, 24 November:
| UCD | 0-9 | 2-2 | UCC |

1958/59
Fahy's Field, 23 November:
| QUB | 2-7 | 2-7 | UCD |

Ballybay, 15 February 1959:
| QUB | 0-10 | 0-9 | UCD (replay) |

1959/60
Mardyke, 7 December:
| UCD | 3-8 | 1-4 | UCC |

1960/61
Casement Park, 20 November:
| UCG | 1-9 | 2-3 | UCD |

1961/62
Croke Park, 26 November:
| UCD | 3-7 | 2-7 | UCG |

1962/63
Pearse Stadium, 25 November:
| UCG | 1-9 | 1-3 | UCC |

1963/64
Mardyke, 1 December:
| UCG | 2-10 | 0-5 | UCC |

1964/65
Casement Park, 29 November:
| QUB | 3-5 | 0-8 | UCD |

1965/66
Croke Park, 5 December:
| UCC | 3-9 | 0-2 | UCG |

1966/67
Pearse Stadium, 27 November:
| UCC | 0-9 | 1-5 | UCG |

Note: From 1967/68 onwards the Sigerson Cup competition was held during the second term (Hilary), chiefly in February and March.

1967/68
Croke Park, 28 January:
| UCD | 1-10 | 0-4 | UCG |

1968/69
Mardyke, 2 March:
| UCC | 5-12 | 0-3 | UCG |

1969/70
Newry, 16 March:
UCC 1-10 1- 5 **QUB**

1970/71
Pearse Stadium, 7 March:
QUB 0-7 0-6 **UCC**

1971/72
O'Toole Park, 5 March:
UCC 5-7 3-8 **UCG**

1972/73
Cork Athletic Grounds, 4 March:
UCD 1-9 1-5 **Maynooth**

1973/74
Newbridge, 24 February:
UCD 0-14 1-5 **UCG**

1974/75
Corrigan Park, 9 March:
UCD 0-18 0-10 **QUB**

1975/76
Croke Park, 29 February:
Maynooth 2-5 0-9 **UCD**

1976/77
Pearse Stadium, 27 February:
UCD 1-8 1-8 **UCG**
Final replay at Pearse Stadium, 10 April:
UCD 1-11 0-6 **UCG**

1977/78
Croke Park, 26 February:
UCD 1-13 0-7 **UCG**

1978/79
Páirc Uí Chaoimh, 25 February:
UCD 2-15 0-2 **UCG**

1979/80
Bellaghy, 9 March:
UCG 1-8 0-7 **UCD**

1980/81
Maynooth College, 22 February:
UCG 1-12 0-6 **TCD**

1981/82
Malone, 28 February:
QUB 0- 12 1-7 **UCG (aet)**

1982/83
Santry, 20 February:
UCG 2-8 2-5 **QUB**

1983/84
Pearse Stadium, 4 March:
UCG 1-11 0-6 **UCC**

1984/85
Croke Park, 24 February:
UCD 0- 10 0-5 **QUB**

1985/86
Mardyke, 9 March:
UUJ 1-8 1-5 **UCC**

1986/87
Bellaghy, 1 March:
UUJ 0-6 **UCC** 0-4

1987/88
Summerhill, 6 March:
UCC 0-8 0-5 **UCG**

1988/89
Malone, 5 March:
St. Mary's 3-13 1-5 **UCC**

1989/90
Santry, 24 February:
QUB 3-8 1-9 **St. Mary's**

1990/91
Enniskillen, 24 March:
UUJ 0-7 0-6 **UCG**

1991/92
Pearse Stadium, 15 March:
UCG 2-8 0-11 **QUB**

1992/93
Casement Park, 21 March:
QUB 1-12 0-4 **St. Mary's**

1993/94
Belfield, 27 February:
UCC 1-9 2-5 **QUB**

1994/95
Páirc Uí Rinn, 12 March:
UCC 0-12 1-7 **UCG**

1995/96
UL Grounds, 3 March:
UCD 2-11 3-5 **Garda**

1996/97
UUC, 9 March:
TRTC 1-13 1-6 **UL**

1997/98
Austin Stack Park, 8 March:
ITT 0-10 0-8 **UUJ**

1998/99
Malone, 7 March:
ITT 1-8 0- 7 **Garda**

1999/00
Maigh Cuilinn, 27 February:
QUB 1-8 0-8 **UCD (aet)**

2000/01
Scotstown, 11 April:

| **UUJ** | **1-14** | **1-9** | UCD |

2001/02
Markiewicz Park, 23 February:

| **ITS** | **0-6** | **0-5** | UCC |

2002/03
Páirc Uí Rinn, 9 March:

| **NUIG** | **1-8** | **0-8** | UCD |

2003/04
Corrigan Park, 28 February:

| **ITS** | **1-10** | **1-7** | QUB |

2004/05
Dundalk IT, 26 February:

| **ITS** | **0-10** | **0-7** | QUB (aet) |

2005/06
Parnell Park, 25 February:

| **DCU** | **0-11** | **1-4** | QUB |

2006/07
Malone, 3 March:

| **QUB** | **0- 15** | **0-14** | UUJ (aet) |

2007/08
ITC, 22 April:

| **UUJ** | **1-16** | **1-14** | Garda (aet) |

2008/09
Cork IT Grounds, Bishopstown, 28 February:

| **Cork** | **1- 15** | **1-10** | DIT |

2009/10
Maynooth, 27 February:

| **DCU** | **1-11** | **0-10** | UCC |

2010/11
Belfield, 5 March:

| **UCC** | **0-10** | **0-7** | UUJ |

2011/12
Dangan, 25 February:

| **DCU** | **2-17** | **0-7** | NUIM |

2012/13
Athlone, 23 February:

| **DIT** | **3-8** | **0-7** | UCC |

2013/14
The Dub, Belfast: 22 February:

| **UCC** | **0-10** | **0-9** | UUJ |

2014/15
Mardyke, 21 February

| **DCU** | **1-14** | **2-10** | UCC (aet) |

2015/16
Jordanstown, 20 February

| **UCD** | **0-10** | **2-2** | DCU |

2016/17
Connacht GAA Centre Bekan, 18 February

| **St Mary's** | **0-13** | **2-6** | UCD |

SIGERSON CUP FINAL TEAMS

Note: Although in most years up to 1933/34 there was no Sigerson Cup final per se, the following list includes the runner-up college team where available.

1910/11
U.C.C.   W.John Riordan (Cork) (capt.), T.Nunan, Charlie Delea, Bill Fitzgerald (Cork), William Lehane (Cork), W.O'Brien, J.J.O'Keeffe, D.J.Burke, E.Hartnett, W.Walsh, Tommy Richardson (Cork), D.Saunders, Eddie Cotter (Cork), C.Collins, T.Buckley, D.O'Keeffe, J.Barry.

U.C.G. (as listed for a non-Sigerson Cup game)   D.Morrin (capt.), J.F.McDermott, Mick Martin (Galway), T.McGowan, J.Collins, Toss Heneghan, J.Eaton, T.Doyle, Brian Cusack, J.Devine, F.Ronayne, T.Curtin, J.Doyle, D.Flannery, C.Farrell, J.Sheills, Conor O'Malley (Galway).

1911/12
U.C.G.   Joseph F Donegan (Sligo) (capt.), Mick Martin (Galway), Jack Sheehy, Tom Flannery, Hubert O'Connor, T.Goff, Conor O'Malley (Galway), B.Barrett, Geoff Collins, J.Marron, Michael Keane (Galway), J.F.McDermott, T.McGowan, Tommy Quinn (Galway), Toss Heneghan, P.Dempsey, J.Doherty.

U.C.D.   team-list not available.

1912/13
U.C.D.   L.Murray, J.Murray, Solomon Lawlor (Kerry & Dublin), J.F.Kearney (Kerry), Redihan, Finnegan, Fitzmaurice, Joseph McGrath, Ward, P.Fitzpatrick, Kelly, J.Marron, Heavey, Éamon Bulfin (Offaly), Finnegan.

U.C.G.   O.Leonard (goal), Peter O'Farrell (Roscommon), Joseph F Donegan (Sligo) (capt.), Toss Heneghan, Casey, Michael Keane (Galway), Mick Martin (Galway), Doherty, Conor O'Malley (Galway), Thompson, T.Goff, Tom Flannery, J.F.McDermott, J.Marron, Jack Sheehy.

1913/14
U.C.C.   Tom Nunan (Cork) (capt.), Patrick O'Donnell, W.John Riordan (Cork), Michael 'Charlie' Troy (Kerry), Tommy Richardson (Cork), William Lehane (Cork), Dick F.O'Brien (Cork), James J.Mulvihill (Kerry), Jack Lynch (Cork), Jeremiah J.Creed (Cork), C.Collins, E.Hartnett, Denny Pa Lucy, T.Brien, M.Kelly, T.McCarthy, C.Delea.

U.C.D.   Éamon Bulfin (Offaly), P.Fitzpatrick (capt.), J.Ward, Heneghan, Pierce Walton (Kilkenny), J.F.Kearney (Kerry), Sheehan, Joseph McGrath, Stokes, Ward, James McPhillips, Thomas O'Hickey, J.Marron, Solomon Lawlor (Kerry & Dublin), Frank Burke (Kildare & Dublin).

1914/15
U.C.D.   Solomon Lawlor (Kerry & Dublin), Éamon Bulfin (Offaly) (goal), John Ryan (Limerick & Dublin), P.Fitzpatrick, Pierce Walton (Kilkenny), T.Hassett, P.Purcell, Thomas Joyce, Thomas Hickey, M.McGuinness, Frank Burke (Kildare & Dublin), James McPhillips, J.Marron, J.F.Kearney (Kerry), P.Conway.

U.C.G. (14 players listed)   T.Goff, Fred O'Doherty, Peter O'Farrell (Roscommon), O.Leonard, Burke, B.Barrett, T.P.Flanagan, Jimmy Collins (capt.), J.Drury, D.Rowland, Tom Flannery, M.Whelan, J.McEvoy, O'Sullivan.

1915/16

U.C.C. E.Michael 'Charlie' Troy (goal), P.J.Moloney, Jack Lynch (Cork), L.O'Connor, James Mulvihill (Kerry), R.Evans, Willie Moore (Kilkenny), Patrick O'Donnell, Willie Murphy (Cork), William Richardson (Cork), D.J.O'Sullivan, Jeremiah J.Creed (Cork), Con Lucey (Cork), D.Mulcahy, Larry O'Brien (Cork), James Murphy-O'Connor (Cork). C.Collins also played.

U.C.D. Solomon Lawlor (Kerry & Dublin) (capt.), Deignan, Young, P.McGuinness, Brian Joyce (Galway & Dublin), P.Fitzpatrick, Harte, Pierce Walton (Kilkenny), Pat O'Shea, Joe Phelan (Kilkenny & Dublin, P.J.O'Brien, Fanning, Thomas O'Hickey, John Ryan (Dublin), P.Purcell.

1916/17

U.C.D. Solomon Lawlor (Kerry & Dublin) (capt.), Éamon Bulfin (Offaly) (goal), James P McNulty, Michael 'Charlie' Troy, P.Purcell, J.Keating, P.McGuinness, Brian Joyce (Galway & Dublin), Pierce Walton (Kilkenny), Patrick Concannon, Maurice Collins, Patrick McCarvill (Monaghan), P.J.O'Brien, Joe Phelan (Kilkenny & Dublin), Frank Burke (Dublin).

U.C.C. James J.Mulvihill (Kerry & Cork) (capt.), Jack Lynch (Cork) (goal), Roger O'Connor (Cork), James Lynch (Cork), Willie Moore (Kilkenny), R.Evans, James Carver, D.J.O'Sullivan, Willie Murphy (Cork), William Richardson (Cork), Andrew McCarthy, Dick F.O'Brien (Cork), James Murphy-O'Connor (Cork), Con Lucey (Cork), P.O'Sullivan.

1917/18

U.C.D. (16 players listed) Solomon Lawlor (Dublin) (capt.), Brian Joyce (Galway & Dublin), Frank Burke (Dublin), P.Purcell, P.McGuinness, Patrick McCarvill (Monaghan), P.Fitzpatrick, T.Long, P.Collins, J.Keating, Johnny Keohane, J.Cullen, F.McGinley, Joe Phelan (Kilkenny & Dublin), J.O'Connor, D.Healy.

U.C.C. team-list not available.

1918/19

U.C.C. (16 players listed) Con Lucey (Cork), Roger O'Connor (Cork), Willie Moore (Kilkenny & Cork), Willie Murphy (Cork), James Murphy-O'Connor (Cork), J.Fenton, William S Nunan, Joe Kearney (Cork), Richard O'Brien (Cork), John Kiely (Waterford), Eugene 'Nudge' Callanan (Tipperary), Michael Breen, T.O'Sullivan, Jack Murphy (Kerry), Jack Falvey (Cork), F.Fitzpatrick.

U.C.D. team-list not available.

1919/20

U.C.D. T.Long (goal), Tom Pierse (Wexford) (capt.), John A.Henry (Mayo), P.Lenihan, Joe Phelan (Kilkenny & Dublin), Frank Burke (Dublin), Garrett Scanlan, Patrick Moran (Roscommon), Patrick Caffrey (Dublin), John A.Cusack, Mick J.Mullen (Mayo), D.Purcell, W.Doyle, Éamonn N.M.O'Sullivan (Kerry), T.O'Sullivan.

U.C.C. J.Fenton (capt.), C.Balty (goal), Roger O'Connor, H.Johnson, Jack Murphy (Kerry), William S.Nunan, Eugene 'Nudge' Callanan (Tipperary), Willie Murphy (Cork), J.Kennedy, T.Fitzpatrick, P.O'Sullivan, M.Bastible (Cork), John Kiely (Waterford), Finian O'Shea (Cork).

1920/21

NO COMPETITION.

1921/22

U.C.G. W.McDonald (capt.), Michael Greene (goal), Fred O 'Doherty, M.J.Ring, J Scott, J.F.Glavey, C.O'Connor, T.Jordan, M.Dalton, Arthur de B.Joyce, T.McDonagh/ld, T.Linehan, Michael Dolan, E.Moran, C.E.Flynn.

U.C.C. Joe Kearney (Cork) (capt.), Willie Moore (Kilkenny & Cork), Willie Cotter (Cork), Frank Creedon (Cork), Tom Nunan (Cork), Michael Breen (goal), Eugene 'Nudge' Callanan (Tipperary), Finian O'Shea (Cork), Donal O'Donoghue (Kerry), John Kiely (Waterford), William Fortune (Cork), R.Bastible, J.Fenton, Con Lucey (Cork), Harry St. John Atkins (Cork).

1922/23

U.C.C. Tom Nunan (Cork) (capt.), Michael Breen, Tom Lee (Tipperary), R.Mulcahy, Jack Murphy (Kerry), Harry St. John Atkins (Cork), Murphy, Finian O'Shea (Cork), M.C.O'Mahony, J.O'Connor, William Fleming (Cork), T.Fitzgerald, E.Scanlan, J.Kirwan, T.Quinlan. Subs.: T.Fitzgerald, T.O'Toole.

U.C.D. Éamonn N.M.O'Sullivan (Kerry) (capt.), Garrett Scanlan, Séamus Gardiner (Tipperary & Dublin), P.Groarke, Thomas Gardiner (Clare), T.O'Sullivan, James D.Grant, Éamonn O'Doherty (Clare), Gerard A.Conway, B.McGowan, Seán Lavan (Mayo), Tom Pierse (Wexford), John A.Henry (Mayo), George Madigan, Éamonn Mongey (Mayo). Subs.: B.McDonnell, John Kennedy, Mick D'Arcy (Tipperary).

1923/24

U.C.D. Séamus Gardiner (Tipperary & Dublin) (captain), Thomas Gardiner (Clare) (goal), Éamonn O'Doherty (Clare), John A.Henry (Mayo), James D.Grant, Mick Kilcoyne (Sligo), P.Mannix, M.McQuaide, George Madigan, G.Hurlay, Éamonn O'Sullivan (Kerry), Tom Pierse (Wexford), B.McGowan, Jim Smith (Cavan), Frank Burke (Dublin).

U.C.C. Michael Breen (goal), Finian O'Shea (Cork) (capt.), Tom Nunan (Cork), Jack Murphy (Kerry), R.Mulcahy, Donal O'Donoghue (Kerry), Tom Lee (Tipperary), Frank Creedon (Cork), Joe Kearney (Cork), William Fleming (Cork), M.Murphy, Éamonn Fitzgerald (Kerry), J.O'Connor, Harry St. John Atkins (Cork), J.Powell.

1924/25

U.C.C. Michael Murphy (Kerry) (capt.), Jack Murphy (Kerry), J.O'Sullivan, Tom Nunan (Cork), Frank Hurley, Donal O'Donoghue (Kerry), Matt Murphy (Cork), Harry St. John Atkins (Cork), Tom Lee (Tipperary), Patrick O'Sullivan, David Barry, Pat Nyhan (Cork), Joe Kearney (Cork), Frank Creedon (Cork), Peter Coughlan (Kerry & Cork). Subs.: Patrick O'Donoghue (Kerry), W.McLaughlin, D.O'Keeffe.

U.C.G. J.M.Treacy, J.H.Higgins, C.E.Flynn, W.T.Hession (Galway), M.Moloney, M.Mannion (Galway), R.Donnellan, E.Donnelly, T.Jordan, J.Walsh (Galway), T.Collian, W.Croyne, P.Molloy, C.Macken, D.Walshe. Sub.: J.P.Caffrey.

1925/26

U.C.C. Seán O'Sullivan (goal), Tom Nunan (Cork), Eugene 'Nudge' Callanan (Tipperary & Cork), Dan Lynch (Cork), William Fleming (Cork), Frank Creedon (Cork), Tom Lee (Tipperary), Donal O'Donoghue (Kerry), M.Murphy, David Barry, Patrick O'Sullivan, Peter Coughlan (Kerry & Cork), Michael Powell (Kerry), Joe Kearney (Cork), J.O'Connor.

U.C.D. Drury (goal), Éamonn O'Doherty (Clare), R.Mulcahy, Paddy McDonald (Cavan), Brown, Francis Friel, Éamonn Fitzgerald (Kerry), Mick J Mullen (Mayo), Seán Lavan (Mayo), M.McQuaid, Balfe, George Madigan, John A.Henry (Mayo), T.Mullen. Sub.: Daly for Devine.

1926/27

U.C.D. Paddy McDonald (Cavan) (goal), R.Mulcahy, Éamonn O'Doherty (Clare), J.Stack, J.Duffy, Éamonn Fitzgerald (Kerry), Bernard F.Leavy, Joe O'Sullivan (Kerry), Mick J.Mullen (Mayo), Seán Lavan (Mayo), Patrick Casey, J.T.O'Connell, T.Mullen, Frank Sheehy (Kerry), John A.Henry (Mayo).
U.C.G. team-list not available.

1927/28

U.C.C. Michael Lane, Tom Nunan (Cork), Seán Russell, Richard Molloy (Cork), Donal McCarthy (Cork), N.Matthew, Matt Murphy (Cork), Dennis O'Keeffe, Michael Murphy (Kerry), Mossie Donegan (Cork), Peter Coughlan (Kerry & Cork), Eugene 'Nudge' Callanan (Cork), David Barry, Patrick O'Sullivan, Patrick Moynihan (Kerry). Donal O'Donoghue (Kerry) & Michael Powell (Kerry) also played over weekend.
U.C.D. team-list not available.

1928/29

U.C.D. K.Mallin, Éamonn O'Doherty (Clare), James J.O'Shea, J.Duffy, Mick O'Gorman (Monaghan), Joe O'Sullivan (Kerry), Michael 'Al' Moroney (Clare), Mick J.Mullen (Mayo), B.Quigley, Laurence Marron (Monaghan), Éamonn Fitzgerald (Kerry), Seán Lavan (Mayo), Michael Falvey (Clare), Frank Sheehy (Kerry), T.P.O'Callaghan.
U.C.C. Denis W Harvey, Tom Nunan (Cork), Richard Molloy (Cork), Jim O'Regan (Cork), J.Murphy, Dennis O'Keeffe, Mossie Donegan (Cork), H.O'Leary (Cork), Seán Vaughan (Cork), D.Coughlan, Michael Murphy (Kerry & Cork), Donal McCarthy (Cork), Eugene 'Nudge' Callanan (Cork), Donal O'Donoghue (Kerry), Anthony O'Callaghan.

1929/30

U.C.D. Con O'Leary (goal), Joe O'Sullivan (Kerry), N.Devine, Mick J.Mullen (Mayo), Jack Walsh (Kerry), Mick O'Gorman (Monaghan), Séamus Duffy, J.Quigley, Éamonn Fitzgerald (Kerry), P.Jordan, Bernard Higgins, Seán Lavan (Mayo), Patrick Flynn, Michael Falvey (Clare), Peter J.Duffy (Monaghan).
U.C.C. team-list not available.

1930/31

U.C.D. B.Winston (goal), Mick O'Gorman (Monaghan), James J.O'Shea, Jack Walsh (Kerry), Joe O'Sullivan (Kerry), John Kennedy, George Powell (Kerry), Éamonn Fitzgerald (Kerry), B.Quigley, Bernard Higgins, Patrick Flynn, Johnny O'Donnell (Donegal), B.Sullivan, Colm Connolly (Galway), Thomas Walsh.
U.C.G. Jack Langan (Mayo) (goal), Séamus O'Malley (Mayo), Kelly (Mayo), J.Egan, P.J.Dempsey, John O'Leary (Clare), Paddy Stephens (Galway), Dermot Mitchell (Galway) (capt.), Paddy Quinn (Mayo), Mick Higgins (Galway), Frank Burke (Galway), Michael Naughton (Mayo), Tom Gill (Mayo), John Donnellan (Galway), James P.("Tot") McGowan (Mayo). Sub.: Éamonn "Ned" Murphy (Mayo). B.Mannion, T.McCarthy & Glynn also played over the weekend.

1931/32

U.C.D. J.Doyle, Mick O'Gorman (Monaghan), Jack Walsh (Kerry), John Kennedy, George Powell (Kerry), J.Colleran, Colm Connolly (Galway), Byrne, P.Fitzgibbon, J.Lynch, Seán Flood (Meath), MacNamara, McGillicuddy, Johnny O'Donnell (Donegal), Mick Casey (Clare).

U.C.G. Jack Langan (Mayo), Patrick Colleran (Sligo), Tom Gill (Mayo), Séamus O'Malley (Mayo), Paddy Quinn (Mayo), Dermot Mitchell (Galway), Mick Ferriter (Galway), James Patrick ("Tot") McGowan (Mayo), Brian Scanlon (Mayo), Éamonn "Ned" Murphy (Mayo), John O'Leary (Clare), Mick Higgins (Galway), John Egan (Mayo), Michael Naughton (Mayo), Mulvihill.

1932/33

U.C.D. J.Doyle, Mick Casey (Clare), Mick O'Gorman (Monaghan), Jack Walsh (Kerry), James J.O'Shea, Stephen Barrett, Toddy Walsh (Kerry), Seán Flood (Meath), Johnny Walsh (Kerry), James J.Dore, Maurice McKenna (Kerry), Colm Boland (Westmeath & Dublin), Colm Connolly (Galway), Dermot Bourke (Kildare), George Powell (Kerry & Dublin).
U.C.C. Daniel Buckley, E.O'Mahony (Kerry & Cork), M.Lillis (Cork), J.T Connolly (Cork), Luke Flanagan (Cork), Richard Molloy (Cork), M.Finnucane (Kerry), Martin Cronin (Cork), Thomas O'Reilly (Cork), B.Herlihy, Donal McCarthy (Cork), Gus Kelleher (Cork), Michael Murphy (Cork), J.Flanagan, William Finlay (Tipperary).

1933/34

U.C.G. Mícheál Conneely (Galway), Mick Raftery (Mayo), Paddy Quinn (Mayo), Vinny Kelly (Mayo), Tony Regan (Galway), Séamus O'Malley (Mayo), John O'Leary (Clare), Dinny O'Sullivan (Galway), Mick Higgins (Galway), Mick Ferriter (Kerry), Brendan Nestor (Galway), J.Cummins (Mayo), Vincent McDarby (Galway), Brian Scanlon (Mayo), James Patrick ('Tot') McGowan (Mayo). Sub.: James Laffey (Mayo) for Cummins.
U.C.D. J.Doyle, Paddy McMahon (Kerry), James J.O'Shea, A.Moran, Colm Boland (Dublin), Mick Casey (Clare), George Powell (Kerry & Dublin), Seán Flood (Meath), Patrick M Farrell (Longford), Vincent McGovern (Cavan), Maurice McKenna (Kerry), J.Lynham (Dublin), Colm Connolly (Galway), Dermot Bourke (Kildare), T.O'Gorman.

1934/35

U.C.G. Mícheál Conneely (Galway), Mick Raftery (Mayo), Paddy Quinn (Mayo), Ned Murphy (Mayo), Tony Regan (Galway), Dinny O'Sullivan (Galway), John O'Leary (Clare), Donal McCarthy (Kerry), Diarmaid O'Connell (Cork), James Laffey (Mayo), Hugh Gibbons (Roscommon), Mick Higgins (Galway), Brian Scanlon (Mayo), Vincent McDarby (Galway), Mick Ferriter (Kerry & Galway). Sub: Andy Laffey (Mayo) for McCarthy.
U.C.C. Denis W.Harvey, Gus Kelleher (Cork), C.Ryan (Kerry), H.O'Leary (Cork), D.Crowley, Thomas O'Reilly (Cork), F.O'Donovan (Cork), Michael Geaney, J.Sullivan, M.Collins, Donal McCarthy (Cork), Joe Roche (Cork), Brendan Flahive, Liam Tierney (Cork), C.Greaney.

1935/36

U.C.D. John "Roger" Horan (Kerry), Gerry O'Leary (Cork), Paddy McMahon (Kerry), Rex Keelaghan (Monaghan), Jack O'Connor (Kerry), Joe Hughes (Galway), Paddy O'Loughlin (Mayo), Patrick Henry (Offaly), George Powell (Kerry & Dublin), J.Lynham (Dublin), Kevin Maher (Carlow), Toddy Walsh (Kerry), Éamonn Gavin (Westmeath), Vincent McGovern (Cavan), Peter Carney (Westmeath).
Q.U.B. Joe McNamee (Antrim), Frank Murray (Antrim), Hugh Albert McCaffrey (Tyrone), Seán Arthurs (Armagh), Felix O'Kane (Antrim), Terence McLornan (Antrim), John A.Macaulay (Antrim), Brendan Murray (Armagh), Jimmy Burns (Down), Tom Fee (Fermanagh), Kevin Flynn (Armagh), Larry Higgins (Derry), Phil Bradley (Antrim), Frank Martin (Antrim), Jerry Hicks (Armagh). Sub.: William Steele (Antrim) for Higgins.

1936/37

U.C.G. Jimmy McGauran (Roscommon), John O'Leary (Clare), Mick Raftery (Mayo), Joe Salmon (Mayo), Tony Regan (Galway), Henry Kenny (Mayo), Charlie O'Sullivan (Galway), Eugene O'Sullivan (Kerry), Donal McCarthy (Kerry), Joe Fitzgerald (Galway), Hugh Gibbons (Roscommon), Dick Winters (Mayo), Dennis Egan (Mayo), Brian Scanlon (Mayo), Gerry O'Beirne (Roscommon).

U.C.D. John "Roger" Horan (Kerry), V.Moran (Mayo), Gerry O'Leary (Cork), Robert O'Connor (Roscommon), Jack O'Connor (Kerry), Rex Keelaghan (Monaghan), Paddy O'Loughlin (Mayo), Thomas Canning (Cavan), J.Lynham (Dublin), M.McGahey (Monaghan), Toddy Walsh (Kerry), Paddy McEllin (Mayo), Patrick O'Riordan (Carlow), Vincent McGovern (Cavan), W.O'Brien (Kerry).

1937/38

U.C.G. Jimmy McGauran (Roscommon), John O'Leary (Clare), Mick Raftery (Mayo & Galway), Joe Salmon (Mayo & Galway), Tony Regan (Galway), Henry Kenny (Mayo), Charlie O'Sullivan (Galway), James Laffey (Mayo),
Eugene O'Sullivan (Kerry), Con McGovern (Longford & Galway), Hugh Gibbons (Roscommon), Brendan Houlihan (Kerry), Dennis Egan (Mayo), Joe Joe Carney (Mayo), Gerry O'Beirne (Roscommon).

U.C.D. John "Roger" Horan (Kerry), Dinny Cullinan (Limerick), Gerry O'Leary (Cork), Rex Keelaghan (Monaghan), Jack O'Connor (Kerry), Paddy Lynch (Clare), Robert O'Connor (Roscommon), Paddy Smith (Cavan), Thomas Canning (Cavan), Jim Clarke (Meath), Vincent McGovern (Cavan), Paddy McEllin (Mayo), Patrick O'Riordan (Carlow), Lar McEntee (Meath), Dick Winters (Mayo).

1938/39

U.C.G. Jimmy McGauran (Roscommon & Galway), Jim Bohan (Leitrim), Mick Raftery (Galway), Joe Salmon (Galway), Charlie O'Sullivan (Galway), John O'Leary (Clare), Hugh Gibbons (Roscommon), Con McGovern (Longford & Galway), Pat Mitchell (Galway), James Laffey (Mayo), Jack Bracken (Mayo), P.J.Carroll (Mayo), Dennis Egan (Mayo), Joe Joe Carney (Mayo), Gerry O'Beirne (Roscommon).

U.C.C. Steve O'Donoghue (Kerry), Tim Foley (Kerry), M.Murphy (Kerry), D.McCarthy (Cork), Jackie Spencer (Cork), T.Mangan, Arthur Beckett (Cork), Dick Walsh (Kerry), Jim Young (Cork), P.O'Sullivan (Kerry), Johnny Daly (Kerry), Joe Roche (Cork), P.Dowling (Kerry), D.Cotter (Limerick), Derry Beckett (Cork).

1939/40

N.B. - U.C.G. & U.C.D. listed as in "replay" final, Q.U.B. as in Belfast "final".

U.C.G. Jimmy McGauran (Roscommon), Jim Bohan (Leitrim), Mick Raftery (Mayo & Galway), Joe Salmon (Mayo & Galway), Hugh Gibbons (Roscommon), Henry Kenny (Mayo), Paddy Dixon (Mayo), Pat Mitchell (Galway), Con McGovern (Galway), James Laffey (Mayo), Seán Mitchell (Leitrim), Dermot McDermott (Roscommon), Joe Joe Carney (Mayo), Jack Bracken (Mayo), Gerry O'Beirne (Roscommon). In the Belfast final, Dan Kavanagh (Kerry) was centre-forward, and Eugene Heavey (Roscommon) no.13.

Q.U.B. Johnny Tohill (Antrim), John A Macaulay (Antrim), Eddie McLaughlin (Armagh), Paddy O'Neill (Antrim), George Watterson (Antrim), Danny MacRandal (Antrim), T.Byrne (Antrim), Gene Thornbury (Antrim), Peter Lenfesty (Antrim), Brian O'Kane (Antrim), Alf Murray (Armagh), Austin Colohan (Armagh), Gerard Quigley (Derry), Hugh Glancy (Armagh), Jarlath Gibbons (Down).

U.C.D. Aloysius 'Wishie' Lynn (Monaghan), Billy Durkan (Mayo), Gerry O'Leary (Cork), Rex Keelaghan (Monaghan), Cornelius Murphy (Limerick), Paddy Lynch (Clare & Dublin), Joe O'Leary (Cork), Jim Clarke (Meath), Dinny Cullinan (Limerick), Tom P.O'Reilly (Cavan), Vincent White (Cavan), Vincent Duffy (Monaghan), Eugene 'Silky' Smith (Dublin), Robert O'Connor (Roscommon), Seán Mullarkey (Sligo). N.B. - John 'Roger' Horan, U.C.D. goalkeeper in their drawn match against U.C.G. in 1939, died between then and the "replay".

1940/41

U.C.G. Jimmy McGauran (Roscommon), Jim Bohan (Leitrim), Mick Raftery (Galway), Joe Salmon (Galway), Pat McDonagh (Galway), Henry Kenny (Mayo), Pat Mitchell (Galway), Joe Duggan (Galway), Dan Kavanagh (Kerry), Dermot McDermott (Roscommon), Oliver Clarke (Mayo), Pierce Thornton (Galway), Bernie Egan (Mayo), Tom Walsh (Kerry), Seán Thornton (Galway). Sub.: Evan Kennedy (Galway) for Walsh.

U.C.D. Aloysius 'Wishie' Lynn (Monaghan), J.O'Kane (Clare), Gerry O'Leary (Cork), Rex Keelaghan (Monaghan), Cyril Hayes (Clare), Barney Cully (Cavan), Jim Clarke (Meath), Vincent Duffy (Monaghan), Joe O'Leary (Cork), Eugene 'Silky' Smith (Dublin), Tom P O'Reilly (Cavan), Donal Keenan (Roscommon), Brendan Devlin (Tyrone), Seán Mullarkey (Sligo), Vincent White (Cavan). Sub.: Bernard Burbage (Longford) for Cully.

1941/42

U.C.G. Jack Morahan (Mayo), Pat McDonagh (Galway), Mick Raftery (Galway), Joe Salmon (Galway), Oliver Clarke (Mayo), Kevin Forde (Roscommon), Paddy Fitzgerald (Galway), Dan Kavanagh (Kerry & Galway), Henry Kenny (Mayo), Vincent Keane (Kerry), Dermot McDermott (Roscommon), Evan Kennedy (Galway), Bernie Egan (Mayo), Pierce Thornton (Galway), Seán Thornton (Galway). Sub: Séamus Sweeney (Mayo) for Keane.

U.C.D. John Desmond Benson (Cavan), Jim Bohan (Leitrim), Jack Culleton (Wexford), Dennis O'Driscoll (Cork), Jim Clarke (Meath), Barney Cully (Cavan), Vincent Duffy (Monaghan & Dublin), Seán Brosnan (Kerry), Tom P.O'Reilly (Cavan), Eugene 'Silky' Smith (Dublin), Donal Keenan (Roscommon), Murt Kelly (Kerry), Brendan Devlin (Tyrone), Walsh, Bernard Burbage (Longford).

1942/43

NO COMPETITION.

1943/44

U.C.C. Dessie Lucey (Kerry), Tom McElligott (Kerry), William Gavin (Tipperary), Jim Carr (Limerick), Paddy Fitzgerald (Limerick), Martin McCarthy (Kerry), Jack Lyne (Kerry), Frank McGovern (Leitrim), Donagh Keating (Cork), Mick Casey (Tipperary), Hugh McNeill, Jim Young (Cork), Paddy O'Keeffe (Cork), George Cashell (Cork), Derry Beckett (Cork). Sub.: Anthony Power (Waterford) for O'Keeffe.

U.C.D. John Desmond Benson (Cavan), Niall Kennedy (Offaly), Dennis O'Driscoll (Cork), Jack Culleton (Wexford), Tom Staunton (Mayo), Vincent Duffy (Monaghan), Jim Clarke (Meath), Phelim Murray (Roscommon), Tom P.O'Reilly (Cavan), Des O'Neill (Wicklow), Tadhg Brennan (Kildare), Donal Keenan (Roscommon), Charlie Brennan (Monaghan), Pearse O'Connor (Tyrone), Dick Stokes (Limerick).

1944/45

U.C.D. J.Greenan, Seán Flanagan (Mayo), Jack Culleton (Wexford), Tom Deignan (Longford), Jim Clarke (Meath), Seán Mitchell (Leitrim), Vincent Duffy (Monaghan), Phelim Murray (Roscommon), Tom Lawlor (Roscommon), Des O'Neill (Wicklow), Frank Kinlough (Roscommon), Donal Keenan (Roscommon), Brendan Devlin (Tyrone), Dick Stokes (Limerick), Charlie Brennan (Monaghan). Subs.: Colm Kelleher (Leitrim), Pierce Thornton (Galway).

U.C.C. Dessie Lucey (Kerry), J.Glynn, Tom McElligott (Kerry), Donagh Keating (Cork), Jack Lyne (Kerry), Martin McCarthy (Kerry), Paddy Fitzgerald (Limerick), Frank McGovern (Leitrim & Cork), Arthur Beckett (Cork), Martin Murtagh (Leitrim), Mick Casey (Tipperary), Jim Young (Cork), Anthony Power (Waterford), Denny Burke (Kerry), Derry Beckett (Cork).

1945/46

U.C.D. John Shorten (Cork), Seán Flanagan (Mayo), Barney Cully (Cavan), Jim Clarke (Meath), Pádraic Carney (Mayo), Jack Culleton (Wexford), Charlie Coughlan (Kerry), Brendan Lunney (Fermanagh), P.J.Duke (Cavan), Joe Gilvarry (Mayo), Frank Kinlough (Roscommon), Donal Keenan (Roscommon), Charlie Brennan (Monaghan), Seán Mitchell (Leitrim), Paddy Kelly (Westmeath).

Q.U.B. Mannix McAllister (Antrim), Colm Murphy (Antrim), Harry McPartland (Armagh), John Joe McKenna (Tyrone), Seán Carey (Down), Brian Gallagher (Fermanagh), Donal Kelly (Antrim), Danny MacRandal (Antrim), John Gallagher (Antrim), Seán Gibson (Antrim), Kevin Armstrong (Antrim), Joe McCallin (Antrim), Harry Greenwood (Antrim), Peter Lenfesty (Antrim), Brendan Mullan (Tyrone).

1946/47

U.C.C. Tony Daly (Cork), Paddy Fitzgerald (Limerick), Tom McElligott (Kerry), Frank O'Brien (Waterford), Paddy Tyers (Waterford), James 'Mixie' Palmer (Kerry), Humphrey O'Neill (Cork), Bernie Murphy (Cork), Frank McGovern (Leitrim & Cork), Paddy O'Regan (Cork), Derry Burke (Kerry), Nioclás Mac Craith (Waterford), Jim Young (Cork), Paddy Burke (Kerry), Derry Beckett (Cork).

U.C.D. Peter Conlon (Roscommon), Pat Walsh (Carlow), Seán Flanagan (Mayo), Christy Garvey (Roscommon), P.J.Duke (Cavan), Jack Lyne (Kerry), Pádraic Carney (Mayo), Liam Hastings (Mayo), Brendan Lunney (Fermanagh), Paddy Kelly (Westmeath), Pierce Thornton (Galway), Donal Keenan (Roscommon), Frank Kinlough (Roscommon), Seán Mitchell (Leitrim), Augustine Waldron (Mayo). Sub.: Éamonn Quinn (Leitrim) for Kinlough.

1947/48

U.C.D. Peter Conlon (Roscommon), Jim Fox (Leitrim), John O'Brien (Meath), Éamonn Quinn (Leitrim), Mick Costello (Galway), Paddy Henry (Sligo), John Lynch (Cork), Pádraic Carney (Mayo), P.J.Duke (Cavan), Mick Flanagan (Mayo), Des McEvoy (Galway & Dublin), Mick McCormack (Monaghan), Edwin Carolan (Cavan), Jimmy Adams (Offaly), Dick Corcoran (Dublin).

U.C.C. Tony Daly (Cork), Gerry Murray (Cork), Bernie Murphy (Cork), Con Power (Cork), Paddy Tyers (Waterford), James 'Mixie' Palmer (Kerry), Humphrey O'Neill (Cork), Gerald O'Sullivan (Kerry), Steve Gavin (Offaly), P Marron (Cork), Paddy O'Regan (Cork), Brendan Hanniffy (Galway), Gerry Byrne (Kerry), Derry Burke (Kerry), Donal Murphy (Tipperary).

1948/49

U.C.G. Mick O'Malley (Mayo), Willie McQuillan (Roscommon), Mick Costello (Galway), Donie Murphy (Kerry), Christy Garvey (Roscommon), Pat McAndrew (Mayo), Iggy Hanniffy (Galway), Con McGrath (Cork), Billy Kenny (Mayo), Peadar "Pat" McGowan (Mayo), Brian O'Rourke (Roscommon), Mick Loftus (Mayo), Pat Fenelon (Offaly), Peter Solan (Mayo), John Joe McGowan (Mayo).

U.C.D. Gerry Gearty (Longford), B.Carroll (Monaghan), Nicky Redmond (Wexford), John O'Brien (Meath), Seán F.Heslin (Leitrim), P.J.Duke (Cavan), John Lynch (Cork), Pádraic Carney (Mayo), Des McEvoy (Galway & Dublin), Pat Harrington (Dublin), Eddie Devlin (Tyrone), Mick Flanagan (Mayo), Frank Deady (Kilkenny), Brian Sharkey (Monaghan), Brendan Duffy (Monaghan).

1949/50

U.C.D. Gerry Gearty (Longford), Jim McDonnell (Louth), Nicky Redmond (Wexford), John O'Brien (Meath), Séamus O'Connor (Monaghan), P J Duke (Cavan), John Lynch (Cork), Pádraic Carney (Mayo), Frank Deady (Kilkenny), Mick Flanagan (Mayo), Hugh McKearney (Monaghan), Tom Hardy (Cavan), Brendan Duffy (Monaghan), Edwin Carolan (Cavan), Anton Rodgers (Donegal).

U.C.G. Mick O'Malley (Mayo), Willie McQuillan (Roscommon), Mick Costello (Galway), John Trant (Kerry), John Fitzpatrick (Westmeath), Christy Garvey (Roscommon), Iggy Hanniffy (Galway), Billy Kenny (Mayo), Donie Murphy (Kerry), Peadar "Pat" McGowan (Mayo), John Joe McGowan (Mayo), Mick Loftus (Mayo), Mick Greaney (Galway), Peter Solan (Mayo), Tony O'Toole (Mayo).

1950/51

U.C.G. Mick O'Malley (Mayo), Willie McQuillan (Roscommon), Gerry Stack (Kerry), John Trant (Kerry), Kevin Weir (Westmeath), Christy Garvey (Roscommon), Pat O'Malley (Galway), Seán Purcell (Galway), Mick Loftus (Mayo), Peadar "Pat" McGowan (Mayo), John Joe McGowan (Mayo), Peadar Kearns (Roscommon), Gussie O'Malley (Mayo), Tom O'Toole (Galway), Peter Solan (Mayo).

U.C.C. Tony Daly (Cork), Tom Cavanagh (Cork), Jim O'Brien (Cork) (i.e. Fr. Jim White), Kevin O'Sullivan (Cork), Mick Brosnan (Kerry), Denis Bernard (Cork), Con Murray (Cork), Jim Galvin (Cork), Jim Brosnan (Kerry), Paddy O'Regan (Cork), Tom Barry (Waterford), Paudie Sheehy (Kerry), Ted Downey (Cork), Mick Galvin (Cork), Tom Lawlor (Kerry). Sub.: Joe Kelly (Cork) for O'Sulivan.

1951/52

U.C.C. Ted Downey (Cork), Paddy Tyers (Waterford), Jim O'Brien (i.e. Fr. Jim White) (Cork), Kevin O'Sullivan (Cork), Tom Cavanagh (Cork), Denis Bernard (Cork), Jim Brosnan (Kerry), Jim Galvin (Cork), Tom Barry (Waterford), Tom Lawlor (Kerry), Paddy O'Regan (Cork), Paudie Sheehy (Kerry), Mick Galvin (Cork), Dick Murphy (Cork), John Sugrue (Kerry). Subs.: Tomás Murphy (Kerry) for Lawlor, Justin Graham (Westmeath) for Cavanagh.

U.C.G. Gerry Stack (Kerry), Pat O'Malley (Galway), Mick Costello (Galway), Seán Downes (Mayo), Joe O'Donoghue (Mayo), Christy Garvey (Roscommon), Brian Mahon (Galway), Mick Galvin (Mayo), Iggy Hanniffy (Galway), Peadar McGowan (Mayo), Peadar Kearns (Roscommon), Liam Hanniffy (Galway), Mick Mellotte (Mayo), Seán Collearry (Mayo), Peter Solan (Mayo). Sub.: T.Griffin (Westmeath) for Mellotte.

1952/53

U.C.C. Pat Dineen (Cork), Jim Bennett (Cork), Denis Bernard (Cork), Paddy Gallagher (Clare) (i.e. Fr. Paddy Gantley (Galway)) Tom Cavanagh (Cork), John Holland (Mayo), Walter Cleary (Tipperary), Tom Barry (Waterford), Bobby Buckley (Kerry), Jim Brosnan (Kerry), Mick Brosnan (Kerry), Paudie Sheehy (Kerry), Tom Lawlor (Kerry), Tom Connolly (Tipperary), Tomás Murphy (Kerry).

U.C.D. Gerry Stack (Kerry), Paddy O'Donnell (Donegal), John O'Brien (Meath), Seán Collins (Kerry), Leo Heslin (Leitrim), Mick Gould (Cork), Kieran Mulderrig (Mayo), Jim McArdle (Louth), P.J.McElroy (Down), Kieran Denvir (Down), Eddie Devlin (Tyrone), Pádraig Gearty (Longford), John McKnight (Armagh), Pat Fenelon (Offaly), Tom Crotty (Cavan).

1953/54

U.C.D. Pádraig Gearty (Longford), Jim McArdle (Louth), Tim Lyons (Kerry), John McKnight (Armagh), Seán Collins (Kerry), Mick Gould (Cork), Tom Hardy (Cavan), P.J.McElroy (Down), Eddie Devlin (Tyrone), Tom McEvoy (Monaghan), Paddy Carolan (Cavan), Kieran Denvir (Down), David Sheeran (Longford), Pat Fenelon (Offaly), Mick Murphy (Cork).

U.C.G. Eoghan Roe O'Neill (Mayo), Iggy Hanniffy (Galway), Colm O'Toole (Mayo), Maurice Hegarty (Galway), Paddy Dockery (Sligo), Christy Garvey (Roscommon), Brian Mahon (Galway), Seán Purcell (Galway), Art Thornberry (Westmeath), Kevin Swords (Mayo), Éamonn O'Donoghue (Roscommon), Con McAuley (Donegal), Peadar Kearns (Roscommon), Séamus "Sam" Breslin (Donegal), Séamus Mannion (Galway).

1954/55 REPLAY

U.C.G. Eoghan Roe O'Neill (Mayo), Maurice Hegarty (Galway), Colm O'Toole (Mayo), Colm Toland (Donegal), Kevin Swords (Mayo), Christy Garvey (Roscommon), Paddy Hoare (Galway), Mick Hanley (Sligo), Mick Loftus (Mayo), Francis McGovern (Sligo), Peadar Kearns (Roscommon), Peadar "Pat" McGowan (Mayo), Éamonn McTigue (Mayo), Frank Daly (Cork), Aidan Swords (Galway). Sub.: Séamus "Sam" Breslin (Donegal) for Hegarty.

U.C.D. Pádraig Gearty (Longford), Dan O'Donovan (Limerick), Jim McArdle (Louth), John McKnight (Armagh), Seán Murphy (Kerry), Tom Hardy (Cavan), Paddy Dockery (Sligo), Eddie Duffy (Leitrim), Art Thornberry (Westmeath), Jim McDonnell (Cavan), J.Lovett (Kerry), Kieran Denvir (Down), Johnny Maguire (Fermanagh), Paddy Carolan (Cavan), Paul McMurrough (Monaghan). Subs.: Tom Crotty (Cavan) for McMurrough.

1954/55 DRAW

U.C.G. Eoghan Roe O'Neill (Mayo), Maurice Hegarty (Galway), Colm O'Toole (Mayo), Colm Toland (Donegal), Kevin Swords (Mayo), Christy Garvey (Roscommon), Brian Mahon (Galway), Francis McGovern (Sligo), Paddy Hoare (Galway), Peadar 'Pat' McGowan (Mayo), Mick Loftus (Mayo), Éamonn McTigue (Mayo), Peadar Kearns (Roscommon), Tom O'Toole (Galway), Liam Hanniffy (Galway).

U.C.D. Pádraig Gearty (Longford), Colm O'Shea (Kerry), John McKnight (Armagh), Paddy Dockery (Sligo), Tom Hardy (Cavan), Leo Heslin (Leitrim), Seán Murphy (Kerry), Eddie Duffy (Leitrim), Jim McDonnell (Cavan), Art Thornberry (Westmeath), Kieran Denvir (Down), Johnny Maguire (Fermanagh), Paddy Carolan (Cavan), Paul McMurrough (Monaghan), Jim McArdle (Louth).

1955/56

U.C.D. Pádraig Gearty (Longford), Felix McKnight (Armagh), Tim Lyons (Kerry), Jim Ryan (Meath), Seán Murphy (Kerry), John McKnight (Armagh), Paddy Dockery (Sligo), Art Thornberry (Westmeath), Jim McDonnell (Cavan), James Brady (Cavan), Kieran Denvir (Down), Séamus Murphy (Kerry), Johnny Maguire (Fermanagh), Colm Swords (Mayo), Tom Crotty (Cavan). Sub.: Mick Murphy (Cork) for Maguire.

U.C.C. Ted Murphy (Kerry), Dermot O'Sullivan (Cork), Donal O'Sullivan (Cork), Dan Murray (Cork), Séamus O'Donoghue (Kerry), Jack Dowling (Kerry), Liam Coughlan (Kerry), Mick O'Connell (Kerry), Paddy Murphy (Cork), Mick Moroney (Tipperary), Mick Brosnan (Kerry), Tom Costelloe (Kerry), Seán O'Donnell (Mayo), Dave O'Donovan (Cork), Jim O'Donovan (Cork).

1956/57

U.C.D. Brian O'Reilly (Cavan), Felix McKnight (Armagh), Tim Lyons (Kerry), Dermot O'Sullivan (Cork), Seán Murphy (Kerry), Jim Ryan (Meath), Eddie Duffy (Leitrim), Frank O'Leary (Westmeath), Jim McDonnell (Cavan), Des Keane (Mayo), Kieran Denvir (Down), Paddy Murphy (Cork), Jim Brosnan (Kerry), Colm Swords (Mayo), James Brady (Cavan). Sub.: Séamus Conaty (Cavan) for O'Leary.

U.C.C. Gerry O'Sullivan (Cork), Tony O'Sullivan (Kerry), Jack Dowling (Kerry), Liam Coughlan (Cork), Liam Shalloe (Waterford), Séamus O'Donoghue (Kerry), Dan Murray (Cork), Tom Stapleton (Limerick), Dick Troy (Cork), Mick Moroney (Tipperary), Pat O'Shea (Kerry), Dennis Corrigan (Cork), Seán O'Donnell (Mayo), John Burke (Kerry), Dan Kennefick (Cork).

1957/58

U.C.D. Brian O'Reilly (Cavan), Felix McKnight (Armagh), Dermot O'Sullivan (Cork), Joe Fingleton (Laois), Seán Murphy (Kerry), Eddie Duffy (Leitrim), Jim McDonnell (Cavan), Paddy Murphy (Cork), James Brady (Cavan), Don Feeley (Roscommon), Kieran Denvir (Down), Séamus Murphy (Kerry), Ted Duffy (Monaghan), Colm Swords (Mayo), Cathal Young (Cavan). Sub.: Dennis Brosnan (Kerry) for Young.

U.C.C. Tom Fitzgerald (Kerry), Noel Mullins (Cork), Tony O'Sullivan (Kerry), Mick Garvey (Limerick), Éamonn Horan (Kerry), Liam Shalloe (Waterford), Éamonn O'Connor (Limerick), Barry Studdart (Cork), Mick Lovett (Kerry), Mick Moroney (Tipperary), Seán Murphy (Cork), Dick Troy (Cork), Pat Whelan (Galway), John Joe Sheehan (Kerry), Dan Corrigan (Cork). Sub.: Frankie Sawyers (Kerry) for Corrigan.

1958/59

Q.U.B. John O'Neill (Fermanagh), Charles Murphy (Antrim), Mick Brewster (Fermanagh), Christy Mallon (Tyrone), Leo O'Neill (Derry), Brendan Donaghy (Armagh), Peter Smith (Derry), Hugh O'Kane (Antrim), Phil Stuart (Derry), Tom Scullion (Derry), Frank Higgins (Tyrone), Seán O'Neill (Down), Barney McNally (Antrim), Séamus Mallon (Armagh), Kevin Halpenny (Armagh).

U.C.D. (1st game) Anthony Leavey (Westmeath), Joe Fingleton (Laois), Felix McKnight (Armagh), Seán Murray (Longford), Seán Murphy (Kerry), Jim McDonnell (Cavan), John L'Estrange (Westmeath), Tom Stapleton (Limerick), Frank O'Leary (Westmeath & Mayo), Harry McGann (Longford), Don Feeley (Roscommon), Séamus Murphy (Kerry), Willie McCarthy (Kerry), James Brady (Cavan), Charlie Gallagher (Cavan). Subs.: Plunkett Devlin (Tyrone) for O'Leary, O'Leary for Stapleton.

U.C.D. (replay) Anthony Leavey, Jim Flynn (Longford), Felix McKnight, John Vesey (Mayo), Seán Murphy, Joe Fingleton, John L'Estrange, Jim McDonnell, Frank O'Leary, Don Feeley, Ted Duffy, Séamus Murphy, Colm Stanley (Dublin), Willie McCarthy, Charlie Gallagher. Sub.: James Brady for O'Leary.

1959/60

U.C.D. Noel Sammon (Mayo), Felix McKnight (Armagh), Peadar Kealey (Derry), Seán Murray (Longford), Paddy McMenamin (Mayo), Joe Fingleton (Laois), John Vesey (Mayo), Tom Stapleton (Limerick), Frank O'Leary (Mayo), Aidan Swords (Mayo), Charlie Gallagher (Cavan), Kieran O'Malley (Kildare), George Keane (Westmeath), James Brady (Cavan), Paul Kelly (Donegal).

U.C.C. Tony Guerin (Kerry), Brian O'Callaghan (Tipperary), Mick Brosnan (Kerry), Éamonn O'Connor (Limerick), Mick Crowley (Cork), Liam Shalloe (Waterford), Éamonn Horan (Kerry), Séan Sheehy (Kerry), John Healy (Kerry), Mick O'Sullivan (Cork), Seán Murphy (Cork), Paudie Sheehy (Kerry), Liam Scully (Kerry), John Joe Sheehan (Kerry), Dave Geaney (Kerry). Subs.: 'Jasper' McAuliffe (Kerry) for Shalloe, Bob Honohan (Cork) for Geaney.

1960/61

U.C.G. Aidan Kilbane (Mayo), Willie Loftus (Mayo), Hubert McGonigle (Sligo), Alan Delaney (Roscommon), Tony Ryan (Galway), Mick Laide (Kerry & Galway), Martin Newell (Galway), George Glynn (Galway), John Kelly (Limerick), Pat Donnellan (Galway), Brian Geraghty (Galway), Des Feeley (Roscommon), Joe Langan (Mayo), Seán Donnelly (Longford), Tony Kenny (Roscommon).

U.C.D. Anthony Leavey (Westmeath), Paddy McMenamin (Mayo), Felix McKnight (Armagh), Seán Murray (Longford), Éamonn Curley (Roscommon), Johnny Healy (Kerry), Seán Woods (Louth), Frank O'Leary (Mayo), Dave McCarthy (Kerry), Paul Kelly (Donegal), Brendan McFeeley (Donegal), George Keane (Westmeath), Bobby Burns (Longford), Aidan Swords (Mayo).

1961/62

U.C.D. Jimmy Finn (Tipperary), Connor Maguire (Cavan), Kevin O'Neill (Down), Seán Murray (Longford), Paddy McMenamin (Mayo), Bernard Brady (Donegal), Brian McMahon (Kerry), Frank O'Leary (Mayo), Seán O'Loughlin (Kildare), Paul Kelly (Donegal), Eddie Melvin (Mayo), Mick O'Brien (Cork), George Kane (Westmeath), Seán Cleary (Galway), Leo McEldowney (Derry).

U.C.G. Aidan Kilbane (Mayo), Willie Loftus (Mayo), Hubert McGonigle (Sligo), Enda Colleran (Galway), Kevin Moyles (Mayo), Bosco McDermott (Galway), Martin Newell (Galway), George Glynn (Galway), John Stafford Kelly (Roscommon), Joe Langan (Mayo), Brian Geraghty (Galway), Pat Donnellan (Galway), Des Feeley (Roscommon), Seán Donnelly (Longford), Tony Kenny (Roscommon). Subs.: Mick O'Shea (Kerry) for Colleran, Pat McGee for Moyles.

1962/63

U.C.G. Seán Gannon (Galway), Mick Moylett (Mayo), Hubert McGonigle (Sligo), Enda Colleran (Galway), Kevin Moyles (Mayo), Kieran O'Connor (Galway), Martin Newell (Galway), Mick O'Shea (Kerry), Tom Gilmore (Galway), Jimmy Jordan (Louth), Éamonn Slattery (Galway), Pat Donnellan (Galway), Christy Tyrrell (Galway), Seán Donnelly (Longford), Séamus Kilraine (Roscommon).

U.C.C. John O'Donoghue (Tipperary), Brian O'Callaghan (Tipperary), Jim Harmon (Kerry), Derry Spillane (Kerry), Séanie Condon (Kerry), Jim Blake (Tipperary), Liam Scully (Kerry), Mick Fleming (Kerry), Fergus O'Rourke (Leitrim), Dave Geaney (Kerry), Eddie Maguire (Mayo), Denis Philpott (Cork), Dan Harnedy (Cork), Frank Heslin (Leitrim), Olly Whitson (Kerry). Subs.: Cillian O'Neill (Clare) for Philpott, Dan Mangan (Kerry) for O'Rourke.

1963/64

U.C.C. Johnny Geraghty (Galway), John Bonner (Donegal), Kieran O'Connor (Galway), Mick O'Malley (Mayo), Kevin Moyles (Mayo), Enda Colleran (Galway), Ray Niland (Westmeath), Pat Donnellan (Galway), Joe Langan (Mayo), Jimmy Jordan (Louth), Éamonn Slattery (Galway), Pat Sheridan (Mayo), Christy Tyrrell (Galway), Seán Donnelly (Longford), Tony McDevitt (Donegal).

U.C.C. Gabriel Lohan (Galway), Brian O'Callaghan (Tipperary), Mick McCormack (Tipperary), Derry Spillane (Kerry), Finbarr O'Reilly (Cavan), Jim Blake (Limerick), Seán McCarthy (Kerry), Mick Fleming (Kerry), Frank Cogan (Cork), Dave Geaney (Kerry), John O'Sullivan (Cork), Dan Harnedy (Cork), Éamonn Ryan (Cork), Fergus O'Rourke (Leitrim), Olly Whitson (Kerry). Sub.: Denis Philpott (Cork) for Ryan.

1964/65

Q.U.B. Des Sharkey (Antrim), Pat Loughran (Armagh), Leonard McEvoy (Armagh), Niall McEnhill (Tyrone), Paddy Diamond (Derry), James McKenny (Down), Phil McCotter (Derry), Terry Gilmore (Antrim), Jimmy Hughes (Tyrone), Oliver McDonald (Armagh), Gerry McCrory (Antrim), Jackie Fitzsimmons (Down), Jimmy Beggs (Tyrone), Seán O'Neill (Down), Éamonn Flanagan (Fermanagh). Subs.: Stephen Fitzpatrick (Antrim) for Loughran.

U.C.D. Matt McHugh (Cavan), Paddy O'Hanlon (Armagh), Paud O'Donoghue (Kerry), Paul Kelly (Donegal), Peadar McGee (Mayo), Bernard Brady (Donegal), Frank Kennedy (Cavan), Mick O'Shea (Kerry), Mick O'Brien (Cork), Benny Gaughran (Louth), Davy Doris (Mayo), George Kane (Westmeath), Brian Kennedy (Cavan), Jim Hennigan (Mayo), Brendan O'Rourke (Kerry).

1965/66

U.C.C. Billy Morgan (Cork), Christy O'Sullivan (Kerry), Jerry Lucey (Cork), John McCarthy (Kerry), John O'Halloran (Cork), Mick Morris (Kerry), Frank Cogan (Cork), Mick Fleming (Kerry), Pat Moynihan (Kerry), Pat O'Connell (Tipperary), Éamonn Ryan (Cork), Denis Philpott (Cork), Dan Harnedy (Cork), Dave Geaney (Kerry), Brendan O'Keeffe (Cork).

U.C.G. Seán Gannon (Galway), Mick O'Sullivan (Galway), Kieran O'Connor (Galway), Mick O'Malley (Mayo), Kevin Moyles (Mayo), Enda Colleran (Galway), Cóilín McDonagh (Galway), Ray Gilmore (Galway), Pat Donnellan (Galway), Christy Tyrrell (Galway), Liam Sammon (Galway), Ray Niland (Westmeath & Galway), Billy Doran (Kerry), Éamonn Maguire (Mayo), Frank Canny (Galway). Sub.: Pat Sheridan (Mayo) for Sammon.

1966/67

U.C.C. Billy Morgan (Cork), Ger O'Herlihy (Cork), Mick McCormack (Tipperary), Christy O'Sullivan (Kerry), John O'Halloran (Cork), Mick Morris (Kerry), John McGrath (Fermanagh), Mick Fleming (Kerry), Pat Moynihan (Kerry), Éamonn Ryan (Cork), Pat O'Connell (Tipperary), Denis Philpott (Cork), Eric Philpott (Cork), Brian Hurley (Cork), Dick Geaney (Kerry). Subs.: P.J.Gormley (Tyrone) for Moynihan, Brendan O'Keeffe (Cork) for Geaney.

U.C.G. Michael Moore (Galway), Martin Flatley (Mayo), Mick Moylett (Mayo), Ray Niland (Galway), Joe Earley (Mayo), Ray Gilmore (Galway), Cóilín McDonagh (Galway), Adrian O'Sullivan (Roscommon), Jimmy Hanniffy (Longford), Christy Tyrrell (Galway), Seán McGhee (Donegal), Pat Sheridan (Mayo), Joe McLoughlin (Galway), Éamonn Maguire (Mayo), Noel McCormack (Galway). Subs.: Jimmy Langan (Mayo) for Magee, Liam Sammon (Galway) for Maguire.

1967/68

U.C.D. Willie Howlett (Wexford), Jim McElwee (Donegal), Garret O'Reilly (Cavan), Denis Burke (Tipperary), Tom O'Callaghan (Kerry), Gerry Mannion (Roscommon), Anton Carroll (Donegal), Donie O'Sullivan (Kerry), Tom Mulvihill (Longford), Benny Gaughran (Louth), Frank Canavan (Galway), John Purdy (Down), Tony Barrett (Kerry), Mick Gleeson (Kerry), John Kelly (Roscommon).

U.C.G. Michael Moore (Galway), Seán McGhee (Donegal), Mick Moylett (Mayo), Ray Niland (Galway), Joe Earley (Mayo), Ray Gilmore (Galway), Cóilín McDonagh (Galway), Martin Flatley (Mayo), Adrian O'Sullivan (Roscommon), Kevin Lavelle (Mayo), Joe McLoughlin (Galway), Jimmy Hanniffy (Longford), Alo Conneely (Galway), Liam Sammon (Galway), Lorcan Geoghegan (Galway). Subs.: Jimmy Langan (Mayo) for O'Sullivan, Jerry Conway (Sligo) for Geoghegan.

1968/69

U.C.C. Jim Carroll (Dublin), Jim Gleeson (Kerry), Moss Keane (Kerry), Jim Coughlan (Kerry), Séamus Looney (Cork), Mick Morris (Kerry), Ted Murphy (Cork), Paddy Doherty (Limerick), Mick Power (Waterford), Brendan Lynch (Kerry), Christy O'Sullivan (Kerry), Richie Bambury (Kerry), Eric Philpott (Cork), Ray Cummins (Cork), Dick Geaney (Kerry).

U.C.G. Mick Deegan (Galway), Jimmy Langan (Mayo), Mick Moylett (Mayo), Ray Niland (Galway), Tony Geraghty (Galway), Adrian O'Sullivan (Roscommon), Seán McGhee (Donegal), Christy Scanlan (Galway), Johnny Coughlan (Mayo), Aidan Kelly (Mayo), Joe McLoughlin (Galway), Anthony Canny (Galway), Enda Bonner (Donegal), Johnny Kilbane (Mayo), Colm O'Flaherty (Tipperary). Sub.: Rory Kilfeather (Donegal) for O'Sullivan.

1969/70

U.C.C. Jim Carroll (Dublin), Jim Gleeson (Kerry), Jim Coughlan (Kerry), Tony Mahon (Roscommon), John O'Grady (Kerry), Moss Keane (Kerry), John O'Halloran (Cork), Paddy Doherty (Cork), Séamus Looney (Cork), Dan Kavanagh (Kerry), Jimmy Barrett (Cork), Richie Bambury (Kerry), Denis Coffey (Kerry), Ray Cummins (Cork), Barry Hanley (Cork). Sub.: Noel Sullivan (Kerry) for Bambury.

Q.U.B. Ciaran Lewis (Armagh), Liam Murphy (Derry), Séamus Killough (Antrim), Michael P Kelly (Derry), Barney McKibbon (Down), Noel Moore (Armagh), Seán McMullan (Down), Anthony McGurk (Derry), Pat Turley (Down), Fionn Sherry (Fermanagh), Brendan Neeson (Down), Kevin Teague (Tyrone), Paddy Park (Tyrone), Séamus Woods (Tyrone), Aidan Hamill (Antrim). Sub.: Martin McAleese (Antrim) for Neeson.

1970/71

Q.U.B. Ciarán Lewis (Armagh), Liam Murphy (Derry), Seamus Killough (Antrim), Malachy McDonald (Antrim), Malachy Duffin (Antrim), Maurice Denvir (Down), Kevin Stevenson (Armagh), J.J.O'Reilly (Fermanagh), Pat Turley (Down), Paddy Park (Tyrone), Kevin Teague (Tyrone), Fionn Sherry (Fermanagh), Martin McAleese (Antrim), Anthony McGurk (Derry), John Rainey (Antrim). Sub.: Séamus Mullan (Derry) for O'Reilly.

U.C.C. Noel Murphy (Cork), Jim Gleeson (Kerry), Moss Keane (Kerry), Jim Coughlan (Kerry), John O'Grady (Kerry), Séamus Looney (Cork), Tony Mahon (Roscommon), Paudie Lynch (Kerry), Dan Kavanagh (Kerry), Brendan Lynch (Kerry), Richie Bambury (Kerry), Donie Murray (Cork), Billy Field (Cork), Denis Coffey (Kerry), Brendan O'Keeffe (Kerry). Subs.: Tom Looney (Kerry) for O'Keeffe, Seán Kavanagh (Kerry) for Mahon.

1971/72

U.C.C. Noel Murphy (Cork), Jim Gleeson (Kerry), Moss Keane (Kerry), Mick Scannell (Cork), John O'Grady (Kerry), Séamus Looney (Cork), Tom Looney (Kerry), Flan Groarke (Kerry), Paudie Lynch (Kerry), Brendan Lynch (Kerry), Richie Bambury (Kerry), Donie Murray (Cork), Denis Coffey (Kerry), Dan Kavanagh (Kerry), Billy Field (Cork). Subs.: Pat O'Connell (Tipperary), Mick Fleming (Kerry).

U.C.G. Paudie O'Mahony (Kerry), Colm O'Flaherty (Tipperary), Bernie Jennings (Mayo), Tony Dolan (Leitrim), Martin Carney (Donegal), Ger O'Keeffe (Kerry), Tony Regan (Roscommon), Jimmy Mannion (Roscommon), Martin Flatley (Mayo), Tommy O'Malley (Roscommon), Dan Ahern (Cork), Aidan Kelly (Mayo), Mark O'Gara (Roscommon), Mick Sweeney (Mayo), John Tobin (Galway). Subs.: Eddie O'Sullivan (Galway) for O'Flaherty, Jimmy Langan (Mayo) for Dolan.

1972/73

U.C.D. Tom Hunt (Waterford), Joe Waldron (Galway), Alfie Marron (Galway), Jimmy Stafford (Cavan), Frank Donoghue (Galway), Éamonn O'Donoghue (Kildare), Pat O'Neill (Dublin), John O'Keeffe (Kerry), Dave McCarthy (Cork), Paddy Kerr (Monaghan), Kevin Kilmurray (Offaly), Jackie Walsh (Kerry), Enda Condron (Laois), Pat Duggan (Dublin), John P Kean (Mayo). Sub.: Bernie Geraghty (Kildare) for Marron.

Maynooth Kieran McGovern (Leitrim), Bob Casey (Kerry), John O'Mahony (Mayo), Dan O'Mahony (Mayo), Pat Henry (Sligo), Tony O'Keeffe (Kerry), Louis Walsh (Donegal), Cyril Hughes (Carlow), Seán McCarthy (Cork), Frank Murray (Longford), Peter Burke (Longford), Jimmy Kennelly (Cork), Seán McKeown (Kildare), Mel Flanagan (Roscommon), Frank McCann (Meath). Sub.: Terry McElvanney (Monaghan) for Henry.

1973/74

U.C.D. Ivan Heffernan (Mayo), Mick Judge (Sligo), Bernie Jennings (Mayo), Gerry McCaul (Dublin), P J O'Halloran (Meath), Éamonn O'Donoghue (Kildare), Paddy Kerr (Monaghan), John O'Keeffe (Kerry), Mick Carty (Wexford), Enda Condron (Laois), Kevin Kilmurray (Offaly), Jackie Walsh (Kerry), John P Kean (Mayo), Oliver Leddy (Cavan), Pat Duggan (Dublin). Sub: Barry Walsh (Kerry) for Duggan.

U.C.G. Paudie O'Mahony (Kerry), Joe McDonagh (Galway), Jim Miller (Laois), Christy McCann (Mayo), Jimmy O'Dowd (Roscommon), Martin Carney (Donegal), Tony Regan (Roscommon), Jimmy Mannion (Roscommon), Benny Wilkinson (Sligo), Morgan Hughes (Galway), Michael McNamara (Roscommon), Hugh Griffin (Roscommon), Ger Aherne (Cork), Mick Sweeney (Mayo), Mickey Fox (Westmeath). Sub: Kevin Clancy (Galway) for Wilkinson.

1974/75

U.C.D. Ivan Heffernan (Mayo), Con Moynihan (Mayo), Éamonn O'Donoghue (Kildare), Gerry McCaul (Dublin), P J O'Halloran (Meath), Mick Carty (Wexford), Frank Donoghue (Galway), Denis "Ogie" Moran (Kerry), John O'Keeffe (Kerry), Benny Wilkinson (Sligo), John P Kean (Mayo), Jackie Walsh (Kerry), Barry Walsh (Kerry), Pat Duggan (Dublin), Paddy Gray (Meath). Sub.: Finian Mac an Bhaird (Donegal) for McCaul, Brendan Dunleavy (Donegal) for Wilkinson.

Q.U.B. Gerry Moore (Antrim), Kevin McFerran (Antrim), Canice Woods (Tyrone), John Killen (Down), Seán Sands (Down), Gerry McHugh (Antrim), Joe McGrade (Tyrone), Pat Armstrong (Antrim), Peter McGinnity (Fermanagh), Brendan Kelly (Derry), Paddy Moriarty (Armagh), Con McAllister (Antrim), Kieran O'Toole (Down), Brendan Donnelly (Tyrone), Denis Stevenson (Armagh).

1975/76

Maynooth Jack Fitzgerald (Cork), Tony O'Keeffe (Kerry), Dan O'Mahony (Mayo), Tom Barden (Longford), Larry Kelly (Kerry), Mick McElvanney (Longford), Francie Henry (Mayo), Éamonn Whelan (Laois), Paddy Henry (Sligo), Donal Brennan (Sligo), Martin Nugent (Offaly), Paddy McGovern (Cavan), Pat Donellan (Galway), John McPartland (Down), Peter Burke (Longford). Sub: Seán McKeown (Kildare) for McGovern.

U.C.D. Ivan Heffernan (Mayo), Finian Ward (Donegal), Bernie Jennings (Mayo), Gerry McCaul (Dublin), P J O'Halloran (Meath), Mick Carty (Wexford), Denis 'Ogie' Moran (Kerry), Éamonn O'Donoghue (Kildare), Gerry McEntee (Meath), Colm O'Rourke (Meath), John P Kean (Mayo), Jackie Walsh (Kerry), Barry Walsh (Kerry), Pat Duggan (Dublin), Paddy Gray (Meath). Subs.: Oliver Leddy (Cavan) for O'Rourke, Tony McManus (Roscommon) for Gray.

1976/77 REPLAY

U.C.D. Ivan Heffernan (Mayo), Dave Billings (Dublin), Bernie Jennings (Mayo), Séamus Hunt (Roscommon), P.J.O'Halloran (Meath), Mick Carty (Wexford), Pat O'Neill (Dublin), Gerry McEntee (Meath), Denis 'Ogie' Moran (Kerry), Adge King (Cavan), John P Kean (Mayo), Tony McManus (Roscommon), Barry Walsh (Kerry), Tommy Murphy (Wicklow), Pat Duggan (Dublin). Sub.: P.J.Finlay (Monaghan) for Billings.

N.B. - In the drawn game, Ger Griffin (Kerry) started as No.15, and was substituted by Oliver Leddy (Cavan), and Kean came on as a sub for King. McManus lined out the first day as No.11, Murphy as No.12, and Duggan as No.14.

U.C.G. Gay Mitchell (Galway), Paddy Tunney (Donegal), Joe McDonagh (Galway), Breandán Ó Callaráin (Galway), John Costello (Kilkenny), M.J.Reddington (Galway), Tony Regan (Roscommon), Martin McCarrick (Sligo), Martin Carney (Donegal), Paul McGettigan (Donegal), Kevin Clancy (Galway), Tony O'Connor (Mayo), Brendan Dooley (Wicklow), Gay McManus (Galway), John Tobin (Galway). Sub: Paul Griffin (Kerry) for O'Connor, O'Connor for Griffin.

N.B. - In the drawn match, Frank Morris (Galway) began at full-back, but McDonagh was brought on as a sub in his place. Carney lined out at No.12 that day, while McGettigan was at midfield and O'Connor at No.12. Morgan Hughes (Galway) and Colm Loftus (Sligo) were also used as replacements in the drawn game.

1977/78

U.C.D. Johnny Murphy (Sligo), Séamus Hunt (Roscommon), Brendan Dunleavy (Donegal), Gerry McCaul (Dublin), Declan Carey (Down), Mick Carty (Wexford), Pat O'Neill (Dublin), Paddy O'Donoghue (Kildare), Vincent O'Connor (Kerry), Tony McManus (Roscommon), Mick Hickey (Dublin), Jackie Walsh (Kerry), Mick Fennelly (Kildare), Tommy Murphy (Wicklow), Mícheál Flannery (Mayo). Sub.: Mickey O'Sullivan (Kerry) for Fennelly.

U.C.G. Gay Mitchell (Galway), Bernard O'Sullivan (Kerry), Gerry King (Mayo), Breandán Ó Callaráin (Galway), John Costello (Kilkenny), Richie Lee (Galway), Brendan Walsh (Galway), Martin Dolphin (Roscommon), Colm Brogan (Galway), Paul McGettigan (Donegal), Pádraig Mitchell (Galway), Kevin Clancy (Galway), Micksey Clarke (Westmeath), Gay McManus (Galway), Conor Richardson (Dublin).

1978/79

U.C.D. Johnny Murphy (Sligo), Joe Joe O'Connor (Kerry), Paddy O'Donoghue (Kildare), Séan O'Doherty (Tyrone), Declan Carey (Down), P J Finlay (Monaghan), Barry O'Donoghue (Kildare), Colm O'Rourke (Meath), John Caffrey (Dublin), Andy Roche (Dublin), Tony McManus (Roscommon), Morgan Hughes (Galway), Jimmy Lyons (Mayo), Tommy Murphy (Wicklow), Frank O'Sullivan (Meath). Sub.: Finn McDonagh (Cavan) for Lyons.

U.C.G. Joe Cuddy (Mayo), Bernard O'Sullivan (Kerry), Gerry King (Mayo), Brendan Colleran (Galway), Seán Luskin (Mayo), Joe Kelly (Galway), John Costello (Kilkenny), Richie Lee (Galway), Seán Forde (Galway), Conor Richardson (Dublin), Pádraig Mitchell (Galway), Martin Joyce (Mayo), Paudie O'Riordan (Laois), Gay McManus (Galway), Mícheál Flannery (Mayo). Subs.: Des Bergin (Kildare) for Forde, Kieran O'Malley (Mayo) for O'Riordan, John Hayes (Galway) for King.

1979/80

U.C.G. Gay Mitchell (Galway), Joe Kelly (Galway), Christy McCutcheon (Cavan), Seán Luskin (Mayo), John Costello (Kilkenny), Pádraig Monaghan (Mayo), Séamus McHugh (Galway), Richie Lee (Galway), T.J.Kilgallon (Mayo), Jimmy Ward (Leitrim), Gay McManus (Galway), Pádraig Mitchell (Galway), Micksey Clarke (Westmeath), Seán Forde (Galway), Paudie O'Riordan (Laois). Subs.: Colm Brogan (Galway) for Forde, Kieran O'Malley (Mayo) for Ward, Breandán Ó Callaráin (Galway) for Costello.

U.C.D. Johnny Murphy (Sligo), Séamus Hunt (Roscommon), Cormac Bonner (Tipperary), Joe Joe O'Connor (Kerry), Declan Carey (Down), Austin Finnegan (Galway), Barry O'Donoghue (Kildare), Gerry McEntee (Meath), Colm O'Rourke (Meath), Jimmy Lyons (Mayo), Tony McManus (Roscommon), Morgan Hughes (Galway), Tony O'Connor (Mayo), Tommy Murphy (Wicklow), Finn McDonagh (Cavan). Sub.: Brian Bonner (Dublin) for T.O'Connor.

1980/81

U.C.G. Éamonn Rodgers (Roscommon), Pádraig 'Oxie' Moran (Galway), Tomás Tierney (Galway), Mick Walsh (Mayo), John Costello (Kilkenny), Des Bergin (Kildare), Séamus McHugh (Galway), T J Kilgallon (Mayo), Anthony Finnerty (Mayo), Pádraig Mitchell (Galway), Gay McManus (Galway), Brian O'Donnell (Galway), Kieran O'Malley (Mayo), Seán Forde (Galway), Paudie O'Riordan (Laois). Subs.: Micksey Clarke (Westmeath) for Forde, Peter Heffernan (Mayo) for O'Donnell.

T.C.D. John McDonagh (Dublin), G Sheeran (Roscommon), Jimmy O'Callaghan (Laois), Seán McGearty (Cavan), Frank Harte (Dublin), John Bourke (Kerry), Seán McAleese (Antrim), Frank Johnston (Derry), Barry Tierney (Cavan), Hugh Gibbons (London), Joe O'Rourke (Dublin), Terry Smith (Dublin), Liam Adams (Offaly), Mick "Frank" Mescall (Clare), John Farren (Donegal). Subs.: Dave Gilliland (Meath) for Sheeran, Tadhg O'Reilly (Cavan) for Farren.

1981/82

Q.U.B. Paddy Mahon (Down), Joe Fearon (Armagh), Seán Gordon (Armagh), Donagh O'Kane (Down), Gerard Rodgers (Down), Joey Donnelly (Armagh), Martin Small (Down), John McAleenan (Down), Seán McAuley (Antrim), Brian McErlean (Derry), Dermot Dowling (Armagh), Aidan Short (Armagh), Séamus Leonard (Fermanagh), Greg Blaney (Down), Donal Armstrong (Antrim). Subs.: Eamonn Larkin (Down) for Leonard, Séamus Boyd (Antrim) for McAleenan, John Mackle (Derry) for Mahon.

U.C.G. James Reidy (Mayo), Pádraig 'Oxie' Moran (Galway), Peter Forde (Mayo), John Hayes (Galway), Jamesie O'Sullivan (Kerry), Tomás Tierney (Galway), Séamus McHugh (Galway), Anthony Finnerty (Mayo), T.J.Kilgallon (Mayo), Martin Joyce (Mayo), Richie Lee (Galway), Ciarán O'Malley (Mayo), Micksey Clarke (Westmeath), Michael Brennan (Galway). Subs.: Pádraig 'Dandy' Kelly (Galway) for O'Malley, Peter Heffernan (Mayo) for Macken, O'Malley for Kelly, Tom McWalter (Galway) for Tierney, Paul Carr (Donegal) for Moran.

1982/83

U.C.G. James Reidy (Mayo), Tom McWalter (Galway), Peter Forde (Mayo), Seán Twomey (Dublin), Jim Egan (Galway), Richie Lee (Galway), Hugh Heskin (Galway), Tomás Tierney (Galway), Michael Brennan (Galway), Pádraig 'Dandy' Kelly (Galway), Brian O'Donnell (Galway), Paul Carr (Donegal), Anthony Finnerty (Mayo), Micksey Clarke (Westmeath), Pádraic Duffy (Mayo).
Q.U.B. Paddy Mahon (Down), Mark Haran (Tyrone), Paul Mahon (Down), Seán Gordon (Armagh), Gerard Rodgers (Down), Séamus Boyd (Antrim), Donagh O'Kane (Down), John McAleenan (Down), Aidan Short (Armagh), Brian McErlean (Derry), Dermot Dowling (Armagh), Paul McCormack (Derry), Donal Armstrong (Antrim), Greg Blaney (Down), Michael Madine (Down). Subs.: Martin Durkan (Down) for McErlean, Brian Turbett (Tyrone) for Madine.

1983/84

U.C.G. James Reidy (Mayo), Seán Twomey (Dublin), John Maughan (Mayo), Harry Walsh (Galway), Jim Egan (Galway), Tomás Tierney (Galway), Hugh Heskin (Galway), Tom Carr (Tipperary), Pádraig 'Dandy' Kelly (Galway), Brian O'Donnell (Galway), Michael Brennan (Galway), Peter Heffernan (Mayo), Pádraic Duffy (Mayo), Shay Fahy (Kildare), Anthony Finnerty (Mayo). Subs.: Declan Duke (Roscommon) for Tierney, John Hayes (Galway) for Heskin.
U.C.C. Mícheál Conacur (Roscommon), Leonard O'Keeffe (Cork), Charles Gilmartin (Mayo), John O'Dwyer (Kerry), John Keane (Listowel), John T O'Sullivan (Kerry), Éamonn Walsh (Kerry), Tom Mannix (Cork), Micheal Keating (Kerry), Barry Coffey (Cork), Seán Liston (Kerry), Martin O'Sullivan (Cork), Colm O'Neill (Cork), John Murphy (Cork), Richard Hickey (Kerry).

1984/85

U.C.D. Senan McGuire (Westmeath), John Joe McKearney (Monaghan), Seán McGovern (Kildare), Séamus O'Neill (Tipperary), Peter Smith (Westmeath), Noel McCaffrey (Dublin), Andrew Healy (Tipperary), Bill Sex (Kildare), Mícheál O'Donoghue (Kerry), Seán Ryan (Kildare), Dermot Flanagan (Mayo), Jimmy Lyons (Mayo), Michael Lynam (Westmeath), Niall Clancy (Dublin), Frank McNamee (Longford). Sub.: Séamus Rodgers (Armagh) for Ryan.
Q.U.B. John Mackle (Derry), Gerard Rodgers (Down), Paul Maxwell (Tyrone), Martin Tully (Derry), Seán McCormack (Antrim), Ciarán Hamill (Antrim), Paul Mahon (Down), Stephen Muldoon (Antrim), Brian Conlon (Down), Paul McCormack (Derry), Greg Blaney (Down), Liam Heaney (Down), Éamon O'Hare (Down), Donal Armstrong (Antrim), Conn Mulholland (Tyrone). Subs.: Patrick J Gallagher (Down) for O'Hare, Alphonsus McConnell (Tyrone) for Hamill.

1985/86

U.U.J. Fergal Harney (Armagh), D J Kane (Down), Martin Lennon (Armagh), Paul Mahon (Down), Barry Young (Derry), Colin Harney (Armagh), Barry Breen (Down), Cahal Glass (Derry), Stephen Conway (Tyrone), Dermot McNicholl (Derry), Ger Houlahan (Armagh), Enda Gormley (Derry), Stephen Rice (Tyrone), Donal Durkan (Down), Cathal McNicholl (Derry). Subs.: Malachy O'Hare (Down) for Glass, Mark Bohill (Down) for C McNicholl, Donal Armstrong (Antrim) for Durkan.
U.C.C. Micheal Conacur (Roscommon), John O'Dwyer (Kerry), Charles Gilmartin (Mayo), Éamonn Murray (Kerry), Richard Hickey (Kerry), John Keane (Kenmare), Denis Cremin (Kerry), Barry Coffey (Cork), Tommy Higgins (Galway), Paul McGrath (Cork), Colm O'Neill (Cork), Eoin Moynihan (Kerry), Paul Cahill (Cork), Éamonn Lyons (Cork), John Walsh (Kerry).

1986/87

U.U.J. Cathal Canavan (Armagh), D.J.Kane (Down), Pádraig O'Neill (Armagh), Seán Meyler (Tyrone), Barry Young (Derry), Barry Breen (Down), Gary McConville (Tyrone), Stephen Conway (Tyrone), Cahal Glass (Derry), Dermot McNicholl (Derry), Enda Gormley (Derry), Declan Canavan (Armagh), Thomas Maguire (Fermanagh), Cathal McNicholl (Derry), Rory Scullion (Derry). Subs.: Mark Bohill (Down) for D Canavan, Peter Young (Derry) for C McNicholl, Conal Heatley (Antrim) for Maguire.
U.C.C. Micheal Conacur (Roscommon), John O'Dwyer (Kerry), Marc Healy (Cork), Ralph O'Leary (Cork), Denis Cleary (Cork), John Keane (Kenmare), Tony Griffin (Cork), Mossy Murphy (Cork), Barry Coffey (Cork), John Walsh (Kerry), Anthony O'Sullivan (Cork), Éamonn Lyons (Cork), Eoin Moynihan (Kerry), David Burke (Waterford), Paul McGrath (Cork).

1987/88

U.C.C. Carl Walsh (Clare), Niall Looney (Cork), Ralph O'Leary (Cork), Michael Crowley (Cork), Barry Duggan (Cork), John Keane (Kenmare), Denis Cleary (Cork), Noel Creedon (Cork), Mossy Murphy (Cork), Paul McGrath (Kerry), John Costelloe (Tipperary), Denis O'Sullivan (Cork), Eoin Moynihan (Kerry), Maurice Fitzgerald (Kerry), Ivan Aherne (Cork). Sub.: Fintan Corrigan (Cork) for Creedon.
U.C.G. Paul Staunton (Roscommon), David Fitzgerald (Mayo), Tom Greaney (Galway), Harry Walsh (Galway), Seán Twomey (Dublin), Patrick J.Guckian (Roscommon), Pádraig Fallon (Galway), Mark Butler (Mayo), Kevin O'Hanlon (Louth), Pat Vaughan (Clare), John Joyce (Galway), Brendan Ryan (Offaly), Aidan O'Keeffe (Clare), Matt Tierney (Galway), Pádraig Kenny (Leitrim). Subs.: Alan Mulholland (Galway) for Ryan, Tomás Kilcummins (Galway) for Kenny, Ryan for Vaughan.

1988/89

St. Mary's Brendan Tierney (Armagh), Malachy O'Rourke (Fermanagh), Martin McNally (Antrim), Pascal Canavan (Tyrone), John Rafferty (Armagh), Danny Quinn (Derry), Cathal Murray (Down), John Reihill (Fermanagh), Jarlath Burns (Armagh), Séamus Downey (Derry), Oliver Reel (Armagh), Paddy Barton (Derry), Martin Houlihan (Armagh), Fergal McCann (Fermanagh), Iggy Gallagher (Tyrone). Subs.: Conrad McGuigan (Derry) for Gallagher, Éamonn Shannon (Fermanagh) for Houlihan.
U.C.C. Frank Lyons (Cork), Niall Looney (Cork), Niall Savage (Kerry), Colm O'Donovan (Cork), Denis Cleary (Cork), Tony Griffin (Cork), John Walsh (Kerry), Brian Murphy (Cork), Mossy Murphy (Cork), Denis O'Sullivan (Cork), Pat Kenneally (Cork), Maurice Fitzgerald (Kerry), Eoin Moynihan (Kerry), Mike Finnegan (Kerry), Ivan Aherne (Cork). Subs.: Fintan Corrigan (Cork) for Fitzgerald, Gene O'Donnell (Kerry) for O'Donovan, Peter Creedon (Cork) for Finnegan.

1989/90

Q.U.B. Éamonn Connolly (Down), Shane O'Neill (Armagh), Paul O'Neill (Tyrone), Mark McNeill (Armagh), Fergal Logan (Tyrone), Colm Hanratty (Armagh), Mickey Quinn (Down), Danny Barr (Tyrone), Liam Conneally (Clare), Collie McGurk (Derry), Damien Devine (Tyrone), Paul McErlean (Antrim), Hugh Martin Tohill (Derry), Tony McMahon (Down), James McCartan (Down). Subs.: Keith Quigley (Armagh) for S O'Neill, Declan Conlon (Down) for Tohill, Iggy McGowan (Fermanagh) for McMahon.

St. Mary's Brendan Tierney (Armagh), Martin Houlihan (Armagh), John Rafferty (Armagh), Conor McQuaid (Tyrone), Pascal Canavan (Tyrone), Malachy O'Rourke (Fermanagh), Cathal Murray (Down), Jarlath Burns (Armagh), Pat Slevin (Tyrone), Séamus Downey (Derry), Oliver Reel (Armagh), Paddy Barton (Derry), Gerry Armstrong (Antrim), Fergal McCann (Fermanagh), Peter Canavan (Tyrone).

1990/91

U.U.J. Hugh Fitzpatrick (Fermanagh), Aidan Morris (Tyrone), Gareth O'Neill (Armagh), Pádraig O'Neill (Armagh), Gary Lyons (Down), Noel Donnelly (Tyrone), Paddy Tinnelly (Down), Dermot McNicholl (Derry), Gerard Colgan (Down), Laurence Strain (Tyrone), Gary Mason (Down), Conor Burns (Down), Collie Burns (Down), Brian Carty (Fermanagh), Alan Downey (Down). Subs.: Mark Gallagher (Fermanagh) for Strain, Niall McGuinness (Tyrone) for Downey.

U.C.G. Cathal McGinley (Galway), John Kilraine (Galway), Diarmaid Keon (Donegal), John Donnellan (Cavan), Damien Mitchell (Galway), Kevin McDonagh (Galway), Pádraig Fallon (Galway), Mark Gibbs (Galway), Tony Maher (Laois), Tomás Kilcummins (Galway), Pádraig Oates (Roscommon), Padraig Kenny (Leitrim), Lorcan Dowd (Roscommon), David Farrell (Kerry), Niall Finnegan (Galway).

1991/92

U.C.G. Brian Morkan (Roscommon), John Kilraine (Galway), Diarmaid Keon (Donegal), Gary Fahy (Galway), John Donnellan (Cavan), Mark O'Connor (Cork), Seán Óg de Paor (Galway), Tony Maher (Laois), Tom Ryan (Roscommon), Don Connellan (Roscommon), Sylvester Maguire (Donegal), Máirtín McDermott (Galway), Lorcan Dowd (Roscommon), Conor McGauran (Galway), Niall Finnegan (Galway). Subs.: Brendan Duffy (Galway) for Connellan, Damien Mitchell (Galway) for McDermott.

Q.U.B. Éamonn Connolly (Down), Dermot O'Neill (Derry), Brian Burns (Down), Kieran McGeeney (Armagh), Fergal Logan (Tyrone), Noel Donnelly (Tyrone), Keith Quigley (Armagh), Anthony Tohill (Derry), Paul Brewster (Fermanagh), Éamonn Burns (Derry), Cathal O'Rourke (Armagh), Joe Brolly (Derry), Damien Devine (Tyrone), Brian McCormick (Derry), James McCartan (Down). Subs.: Michael Ferguson (Antrim) for Quigley, Patrick McGeeney (Armagh) for Devine.

1992/93

Q.U.B. Éamonn Connolly (Down), Gareth McGirr (Tyrone), Paddy McGuinness (Fermanagh), Patrick McGeary (Armagh), Stephen Walls (Derry), Kieran McGeeney (Armagh), Paul Brewster (Fermanagh), Anthony Tohill (Derry), Cathal O'Rourke (Armagh), Patrick McGeeney (Armagh), Brian McCormick (Derry), Paul McGrane (Armagh), Dennis Hollywood (Armagh), Paul Greene (Fermanagh), James McCartan (Down). Subs.: John Hanna (Fermanagh) for Hollywood, Paul Burns (Down) for McGrane.

St. Mary's Mark O'Neill (Tyrone), Conor McQuaid (Tyrone), Brendan Rice (Down), Declan Murtagh (Tyrone), Conor Daly (Tyrone), Paul Donnelly (Tyrone), Garret McFerran (Down), Simon Bradley (Fermanagh), Paul Fitzpatrick (Fermanagh), Conall Sheridan (Tyrone), Brian Gormley (Tyrone), Paddy Tally (Tyrone), Stephen Ramsey (Antrim), Peter Canavan (Tyrone), Séamus McCreesh (Armagh). Sub.: Conor Gallagher (Tyrone) for McCreesh.

1993/94

U.C.C. Éamonn Scollard (Limerick), John O'Donovan (Cork), Niall Mangan (Kerry), Daire Gilmartin (Dublin), Michael O'Donovan (Cork), Niall Savage (Kerry), Pádraig O'Regan (Cork), Chris Collins (Cork), Paul O'Keeffe (Cork), John Clifford (Cork), Mark O'Sullivan (Cork), John Buckley (Cork), Fergal Keohane (Cork), Niall Fleming (Cork), Jason Whooley (Cork). Sub.: Martin Hayes (Cork) for Clifford.

Q.U.B. Conor O'Neill (Down), Ronan Hamill (Antrim), Paddy McGuinness (Fermanagh), Gareth McGirr (Tyrone), Andrew McCann (Armagh), Paul Brewster (Fermanagh), Conor Wilson (Armagh), Anthony Tohill (Derry), Mark McCrory (Armagh), Paul Greene (Fermanagh), Cathal O'Rourke (Armagh), J J Kavanagh (Tyrone), Tom Rodgers (Armagh), Éamonn Burns (Derry), Diarmaid Marsden (Armagh). Sub.: Paul McGrane (Armagh) for Greene, Barry Hughes (Armagh) for Rodgers, Terry McGivern (Down) for Wilson.

1994/95

U.C.C. Éamonn Scollard (Limerick), Conor Murphy (Cork), Ronan McCarthy (Cork), Donie Galvin (Cork), Martin Hayes (Cork), Séamus Moynihan (Kerry), Pádraig O'Regan (Cork), Paul O'Keeffe (Cork), Chris Collins (Cork), John Crowley (Kerry), John Clifford (Cork), John Buckley (Cork), Fergal Keohane (Cork), Mark O'Sullivan (Cork), Jason Whooley (Cork).

U.C.G. Brian Morkham (Roscommon), Killian Burns (Kerry), Gary Fahy (Galway), Dónal Ó Liatháin (Cork), Declan Meehan (Galway), Hughie Sheehan (Mayo), Paul Cunney (Mayo), Shay Walsh (Galway), Fergal Gavin (Galway), Seán Moffatt (Mayo), Don Connellan (Roscommon), Brendan Duffy (Galway), Gerald Hussey (Kerry), Lorcan Dowd (Roscommon), Maurice Sheridan (Mayo). Subs.: Mick Higgins (Mayo) for Moffatt, Lorcán Ó Callaráin (Galway) for Sheridan.

1995/96

U.C.D. Brian Morkan (Roscommon), Ultan Keane (Dublin), John Quinn (Kildare), Martin Ryan (Kildare), Daniel Flynn (Down), Trevor Giles (Meath), Joe Coyle (Monaghan), Fachtna Collins (Dublin), Ciarán McManus (Offaly), Brian Dooher (Tyrone), Mick O'Dowd (Meath), Alan Nolan (Roscommon), John Hegarty (Wexford), Anthony Finnerty (Mayo), David Nestor (Mayo). Sub.: Bernie Butler (Roscommon) for O'Dowd.

Garda Kevin O'Dwyer (Cork), Jason Lynch (Cork), Brian McCarthy (Kerry), Fergal Reynolds (Leitrim), Ollie O'Sullivan (Cork), Kevin McGettigan (Donegal), Colm O'Flaherty (Tipperary), Pádraig Boyce (Galway), Adrian Phelan (Laois), James O'Donoghue (Cork), Brian O'Donovan (Cork), Enda Freaney (Kildare), James O'Shea (Kerry), Fergal O'Donnell (Roscommon), John Barrett (Cork). Subs.: James Kingston (Cork) for Lynch, Christopher Grogan (Roscommon) for Barrett.

1996/97

T.R.T.C. David Maloney (Kerry), Kenneth Leen (Kerry), Barry O'Shea (Kerry), Mark O'Reilly (Meath), Éamon Ferris (Kerry), Séamus Moynihan (Kerry), Michael O'Donoghue (Kerry), Michael Cloherty (Galway), William Kirby (Kerry), Pádraig Joyce (Galway), John Casey (Mayo), Seán Ó Mathúna (Kerry), Johnny McGlynn (Kerry), Jack Dennehy (Kerry), Genie Farrell (Kerry). Subs.: Brendan Hannafin (Kerry) for O'Mahony, Mark McGauran (Cavan) for Joyce.

U.L. Diarmaid Murphy (Kerry), Tom Davey (Sligo), Morgan O'Shea (Kerry), Patrick P Kenny (Offaly), Kenneth Cantwell (Meath), Niall Flynn (Louth), Aidan Keane (Cork), Michael O'Sullivan (Cork), Gary McGrath (Kerry), Dara Ó Cinnéide (Kerry), Damien Donlon (Roscommon), Ruairí O'Rahilly (Kerry), Michael F Russell (Kerry), Jonathan McCarthy (Cork), Denis O'Driscoll (Clare). Subs.: Chris Drummond (Kerry) for Cantwell, Fergal O'Brien (Kerry) for Donnellan.

1997/98
I.T.T. Ger Cremin (Kerry), Barry O'Shea (Kerry), Michael Galvin (Clare), Kenneth Leen (Kerry), Damien Hendy (Kildare), Séamus Moynihan (Kerry), Mark McGauran (Cavan), Michael Cloherty (Galway), William Kirby (Kerry), Jimmy McGuinness (Donegal), Michael Donnellan (Galway), Pa O'Sullivan (Kerry), Jack Ferriter (Kerry), Pádraig Joyce (Galway), Michael F Russell (Kerry). Subs.: Jack Dennehy (Kerry) for Russell, Genie Farrell (Kerry) for Cloherty.
U.U.J. Michael Conlon (Derry), Fergal Crossan (Derry), Neil Farren (Derry), Paul McGurk (Tyrone), Seánie McGuckin (Derry), Seán Lockhart (Derry), Paul Diamond (Derry), Davitt McElroy (Tyrone), John McEntee (Armagh), Kieran Donnelly (Fermanagh), Tony McEntee (Armagh), Gavin Diamond (Derry), Brian McGuckin (Tyrone), Gerard Colgan (Down), Joe Cassidy (Derry). Sub.: Kevin Madden (Antrim) for Donnelly.

1998/99
I.T.T. Niall Hobbert (Kerry), Seán Hegarty (Kerry), Éamonn Reddin (Donegal), Damien Hendy (Kildare), Noel Griffin (Clare), Niall Sheehy (Kerry), William Harmon (Kerry), Jimmy McGuinness (Donegal), Noel Garvan (Laois), Noel Kennelly (Kerry), Pa O'Sullivan (Kerry), James Fleming (Kerry), Michael Liddane (Clare), Jack Dennehy (Kerry), Jack Ferriter (Kerry).
Garda John McCallion (Mayo), Anton McNulty (Dublin), Mícheál O'Donoghue (Kerry), Robbie Doyle (Galway), Colin White (Sligo), Cathal Daly (Offaly), Michael Ryan (Roscommon), John Whelan (Kildare), Don Connellan (Roscommon), Aaron Hoey (Louth), Colin Crowley (Cork), David Earley (Kildare), Declan Lynch (Kerry), Tom Bowe (Laois), Cathal Sheridan (Kildare). Subs.: Mark Moynihan (Kerry) for Hoey, Rory McGrath (Kerry) for Bowe, Seán McDaid (Donegal) for Earley.

1999/00
Q.U.B. Aidan Quinn (Down), Paddy Campbell (Donegal), Peter Quinn (Fermanagh), Brian Robinson (Tyrone), Simon Poland (Down), Enda McNulty (Armagh), Philip Jordan (Tyrone), Joe Quinn (Antrim), Conall Martin (Tyrone), Tom Brewster (Fermanagh), Cormac McAnallen (Tyrone), Karl Oakes (Down), Paddy McKeever (Armagh), Liam McBarron (Fermanagh), Philip Oldham (Armagh). Subs.: Diarmaid Marsden (Armagh) for Martin, Barry Ward (Donegal) for Oakes, Peter Campbell (Tyrone) for Oldham, Adrian Scullion (Derry) for Poland, Kevin McElvanna (Armagh) for Jordan.
U.C.D. Cathal Mullin (Westmeath), Breandán Ó hAnnaidh (Wicklow), Noel McGuire (Sligo), John Quinn (Kildare), Declan Meehan (Galway), Cormac Ó Muircheartaigh (Dublin), Peadar Andrews (Dublin), Nigel Crawford (Meath), Ciarán McManus (Offaly), John Lynch (Kerry), Colin Moran (Dublin), Mick O'Keeffe (Dublin), Noel Meehan (Galway), Conor O'Donoghue (Meath), Barry Mooney (Offaly). Subs.: David Hanniffy (Longford) for O'Donoghue, Oisín Ó hAnnaidh (Wicklow) for Mooney, John Hegarty (Wexford) for Moran, Cian McGrath (Meath) for Hegarty, Stephen Lucey (Limerick) for McGuire.

2000/01
U.U.J. Ronan Gallagher (Fermanagh), Cormac McGinley (Tyrone), Enda McNulty (Armagh), Paul McGurk (Tyrone), Raymond Johnston (Fermanagh), Aidan O'Rourke (Armagh), Declan McCrossan (Tyrone), Liam Doyle (Down), Kevin Hughes (Tyrone), Martin O'Rourke (Armagh), John Toal (Armagh), Michael Walsh (Down), Patrick Bradley (Derry), Jimmy McGuinness (Donegal), Kevin Brady (Antrim). Subs.: Kieran Donnelly (Fermanagh) for Martin O'Rourke, Enda McGinley (Tyrone) for Toal, Ronan Sexton (Down) for Brady.
U.C.D. Gearóid Mac An Ghoill (Donegal), Breandán Ó hAnnaidh (Wicklow), Maghnus Breathnach (Dublin), Noel McGuire (Sligo), Darragh Breen (Wexford), Dara Ó hAnnaidh (Wicklow), Ronan Kelly (Meath), Nigel Crawford (Meath), David Hanniffy (Longford), Stephen Lucey (Limerick), Ciarán McManus (Offaly), Oisín Ó hAnnaidh (Wicklow), Joe Fallon (Westmeath), Brian McDonald (Laois), John Paul Casey (Westmeath). Subs.: John Hanly (Roscommon) for Casey, John Lynch (Kerry) for Fallon, Joe Byrne (Carlow) for Lucey.

2001/02
I.T.S. Damien Sheridan (Longford), Pat Kelly (Mayo), Aidan Higgins (Mayo), John McKeon (Leitrim), Dermot Higgins (Mayo), Damien Hendy (Kildare), Seán Grimes (Mayo), Brendan Boyle (Donegal), Michael Moyles (Mayo), Paul Finlay (Monaghan), Rory Gallagher (Fermanagh), Dara McGrath (Fermanagh), Nicholas Joyce (Galway), Brian Maloney (Mayo), Gerry Lohan (Roscommon). Subs.: David Barden (Longford) for McGrath, Garret Blake (Donegal) for Joyce.
U.C.C. Cian Kelleher (Cork), Enda Wiseman (Cork), Paul Hanley (Cork), Stephen Curran (Kerry), Paul Galvin (Kerry), Anthony Lynch (Cork), Damien Reidy (Limerick), Karl O'Keeffe (Waterford), Micheál Ó Sé (Kerry), Tom Kenny (Cork), Conrad Murphy (Cork), Seán O'Brien (Cork), Michael D Cahill (Kerry), Billy Sheehan (Kerry), Ian Twiss (Kerry). Subs.: Conor McCarthy (Cork) for O'Brien, Dylan Mehigan (Cork) for Kenny, Jonathan Olden (Cork) for Twiss.

2002/03
N.U.I.G. David Morris (Galway), Clive Monahan (Galway), Richie Murray (Galway), Darragh Blake (Clare), Dermot Costello (Mayo), John O'Donoghue (Meath), Karol O'Neill (Sligo), Barry Cullinane (Galway), Lorcán Ó Callaráin (Galway), Breandán Óg Ó Callaráin (Galway), Matthew Clancy (Galway), Rory Donnelly (Clare), Michael Meehan (Galway), Mícheál Keane (Mayo), Colm McFadden (Donegal). Subs.: James Rafter (Mayo) for O'Neill, Gary Flanagan (Westmeath) for Cullinane.
U.C.D. Gearóid Mac An Ghoill (Donegal), Breandán Ó hAnnaidh (Wicklow), Conor Evans (Offaly), Paul Griffin (Dublin), Stephen Lucey (Limerick), Barry Cahill (Dublin), Ronan Kelly (Meath), Darren Magee (Dublin), Conor Murphy (Dublin), Peter Curran (Meath), John Hanly (Roscommon), Liam Óg Ó hÉineacháin (Dublin), Alan Brogan (Dublin), Raymond Ronaghan (Monaghan), Peter Lawless (Dublin). Subs.: Joe Sheridan (Meath) for Curran, David O'Connor (Wexford) for Ronaghan, Tom O'Connor (Meath) for Murphy.

2003/04
I.T.S. Paul Durcan (Donegal), Aidan Higgins (Mayo), Éamon McGee (Donegal), Neil McGee (Donegal), Pat Kelly (Mayo), Seán Grimes (Mayo), Kevin Cassidy (Donegal), Brendan Boyle (Donegal), Michael Moyles (Mayo), Christy Toye (Donegal), Paul Finlay (Monaghan), Patrick Harte (Mayo), David Ward (Galway), Nicky Joyce (Galway), Austin O'Malley (Mayo). Subs.: Andy Moran (Mayo) for Boyle.

Q.U.B. Willie McSorley (Armagh), Niall Bogue (Fermanagh), Daniel McCartan (Down), Chris Rafferty (Armagh), Paul O'Hea (Derry), Eoin Devine (Tyrone), Seán Kelly (Antrim), Martin McGrath (Fermanagh), Dick Clerkin (Monaghan), Aidan Carr (Down), John Clarke (Down), Karl Oakes (Down), Eoin McCartan (Down), Billy Joe Padden (Mayo), Aidan Fegan (Down). Subs.: Gavin Donaghy (Derry) for Oakes, Conall Dunne (Donegal) for Carr, Colm Brady (Antrim) for Bogue.

2004/05

I.T.S. Paul Durcan (Donegal), Barry McWeeney (Leitrim), Keith Higgins (Mayo), Colm Cafferkey (Mayo), Jamie Murphy (Galway), Éamon McGee (Donegal), Seánie McDermott (Roscommon), Paddy Brady (Cavan), Michael Moyles (Mayo), Michael Doherty (Donegal), Rory O'Connor (Roscommon), Christy Toye (Donegal), Andy Moran (Donegal), Alan Costello (Mayo), David Ward (Galway). Subs.: James Glancy (Leitrim), Donncha Gallagher (Donegal), Paddy O'Connor (Roscommon), Eoin Gallagher (Mayo).

Q.U.B. John Gibney (Down), Niall Bogue (Fermanagh), Daniel McCartan (Down), Ryan O'Neill (Tyrone), Kevin Gunn (Fermanagh), Gerard O'Kane (Derry), John Turley (Down), Martin McGrath (Fermanagh), Conan O'Brien (Derry), Gavin Donaghy (Derry), Brian Mallon (Armagh), Kevin McGourty (Antrim), Conleth Moran (Derry), James McGovern (Down), Peter Turley (Down). Subs.: Ciarán O'Reilly (Fermanagh), Paul O'Hea (Derry).

2005/06

D.C.U. Stephen Cluxton (Dublin), Brian O'Reilly (Meath), Kevin Reilly (Meath), Paul Casey (Dublin), Declan Lally (Dublin), Bryan Cullen (Dublin), Gary Mullins (Mayo), Eoin Lennon (Monaghan), Ross McConnell (Dublin), Bernard Brogan (Dublin), Brendan Egan (Sligo), Ronan Flanagan (Cavan), Conor Mortimer (Mayo), Shane Smith (Monaghan), Seán Johnston (Cavan). Subs.: Niall Cooper (Dublin) for Reilly, Liam Moffatt (Mayo) for Smith, Ciaran Hanratty (Monaghan) for Cooper, Cahir Healy (Laois) for O'Reilly.

Q.U.B. Declan Alder (Down), Ryan Dillon (Derry), Daniel McCartan (Down), Joe O'Kane (Derry), Charlie Vernon (Armagh), Gerard O'Kane (Derry), Kevin Gunn (Fermanagh), Conan O'Brien (Derry), Peter Turley (Down), Miceál O'Rourke (Armagh), Aidan Carr (Down), Kevin McGourty (Antrim), James McGovern (Down), Eoin McCartan (Down), Brian Mallon (Armagh). Subs.: Michael Ward (Tyrone) for O'Rourke, Paul O'Hea (Derry) for Vernon.

2006/07

Q.U.B. Feargal Murphy (Fermanagh), Hugh Gallagher (Tyrone), Daniel McCartan (Down), Ryan Dillon (Derry), Justin Crozier (Antrim), Gerard O'Kane (Derry), Joe O'Kane (Derry), Paul Courtney (Armagh), Charlie Vernon (Armagh), Kevin McGourty (Antrim), Aidan Carr (Down), Gavin Donaghy (Derry), Paul McComiskey (Armagh), Ciaran O'Reilly (Fermanagh), Miceál O'Rourke (Armagh). Subs.: James McGovern (Down) for Donaghy, Luke Howard (Down) for Dillon, Eoin McCartan (Down) for O'Reilly, Caolan Tierney for O'Rourke, James Loughrey (Antrim) for J O'Kane, O'Rourke for Tierney, J O'Kane for Loughrey, Tierney for E McCartan.

U.U.J. Michael McAllister (Down), Philip Mooney (Derry), James Conlon (Monaghan), Finian Moriarty (Armagh), Damien McCaul (Tyrone), Peter Donnelly (Tyrone), Rory Murray (Derry), James Colgan (Down), Jonathan Bradley (Derry), Michael Herron (Antrim), John Boyle (Down), Raymond Mulgrew (Tyrone), Paddy Cunningham (Antrim), Colm Cavanagh (Tyrone), Mark Lynch (Derry). Subs.: Darren Hughes (Monaghan) for Conlon, Kevin Dyas (Armagh) for Herron, Michael McCann (Antrim) for Boyle, Brendan Boggs (Tyrone) for Moriarty, Bernard O'Brien (Monaghan) for Cunningham.

2007/08

U.U.J. Michael McAllister (Antrim), Charles Harrison (Sligo), Damien McCaul (Tyrone), Donal Morgan (Monaghan), Paul McGuigan (Monaghan), Karl Lacey (Donegal), Peter Donnelly (Tyrone), Brendan McKenna (Monaghan), Colm Cavanagh (Tyrone), Darren Hughes (Monaghan), Tomás McCann (Antrim), Raymond Mulgrew (Tyrone), Mark Lynch (Derry), Paddy Cunningham (Antrim), Andy Moran (Mayo). Subs.: James McGovern (Down) for Hughes, Barry Dunnion (Donegal) for Harrison, Ciaran Donnelly (Tyrone) for Moran.

Garda Pádraig O'Connor (Mayo), Cormac McGill (Meath), Ciaran McGrath (Galway), Anthony Pender (Galway), Graham Dillon (Westmeath), Darren Mullahy (Galway), Éamon Callaghan (Kildare), Aidan O'Mahony (Kerry), Ambrose O'Donovan (Kerry), Seán Buckley (Limerick), Rory Guinan (Offaly), Denis Glennon (Westmeath), John O'Brien (Dublin), Mark Harrington (Cork), Joe Keane (Mayo). Subs: Barry Brennan (Laois) for Keane, James Martin (Longford) for O'Donovan.

2008/09

Cork IT Liam Sheehan (Kerry), Anthony Fenton (Cork), Ray Carey (Cork), Noel Galvin (Cork), Stephen O'Donoghue (Cork), Aidan O'Sullivan (Kerry), Conor O'Driscoll (Cork), Seán O'Hare (Waterford), Paul O'Flynn (Cork), Gary Sayers (Kerry), Paul Kerrigan (Cork), Shane McCarthy (Cork), Daniel Goulding (Cork), Colm O'Neill (Cork), Seán Cahalane (Cork). Subs: James Fitzpatrick (Cork) for McCarthy, Roy Leahy (Cork) for O'Neill.

D.I.T. Eoin Somerville (Dublin), Darragh Breathnach (Dublin), Niall O'Shea (Dublin), Michael Burke (Meath), David Hughes (Monaghan), Ross Glavin (Kildare), John Coughlan (Dublin), P.O'Neill (Kildare), Martin Reilly (Cavan), Donncha Reilly (Dublin), Kevin McLoughlin (Mayo), Paul Flynn (Dublin), Colin Daly (Dublin), Kevin McManamon (Dublin). Subs: Daniel Graham (Cavan) for Flynn, Niall Coughlan (Dublin) for Daly, Enda Gaffney (Cavan) for Breathnach, Billy O'Loughlin (Laois) for D Reilly, Eoghan Naughton (Kildare) for Hughes.

2009/10

D.C.U. M.Boyle, P.McMahon, K.Gavin, K.Nolan, D.Mooney, B.Cullen, J.Cooper, D.Sheridan, H.McGrillen, P.Flynn, R.Flanagan, C.Cregg, P.Andrews, B.Sheridan, D.Kelly. Subs: H.Gill for Cooper, R.Cullivan for Flynn, D.Shine for Gavin.

U.C.C. K.O'Halloran, E.Cotter, E.Hegarty, S.Enright, D.Limerick, A.Greaney, P.Corrigan, M.Shields, J.Buckley, K.O'Driscoll, S.Kiely, D.Casey, B.O'Driscoll, S.Hayes, D.Kearney. Subs: P.Crowley for Greaney, D.Goold for Kiely, M.Collins for K.O'Driscoll, B.Daly for Corrigan, P.Honohan for Kearney.

2010/11

U.C.C. K.O'Halloran, P.Crowley, E.O'Mahony, J.O'Sullivan, S.Kiely, N.Daly, B.Daly, W.Kennedy, J.Fitzpatrick, K.O'Driscoll, M.Collins, J.B.Spillane, B.O'Driscoll, J.Buckley, D.Casey. Subs: S.O'Brien for Kennedy, S.Beston for Casey, M.Griffin for B.O'Driscoll.

U.U.J. G.Kelly, D.Mone, B.Donaghy, C.Galligan, K.Dyas, D.Morgan, C.McGinley, C.Murney, N.Holly, D.McNulty, C.O'Boyle, P.Hughes, J.McAnulla, M.Donnelly, C.McManus. Subs: E.McGuckin for McAnulla, G.McCartan for Murney, C.Donnelly for Hughes, J.O'Neill for McNulty.

2011/12

D.C.U. M.Boyle, P.McMahon, K.Gavin, E.Culligan, N.Collins, J.Cooper, J.McCarthy, F.O'Shea, C.Begley, P.Flynn, D.Rock, D.Keenan, J.Brady, E.O'Gara, A.McFadden. Subs: D.Kelly for Brady, M.Murphy for Keenan, G.Sweeney for Rock, R.Hennelly for Boyle, F.Ó Curraoin for O'Gara.

N.U.I.M. S.Connolly, K.O'Brien, K.Lynch, D.Dalton, T.Moolick, J.McDermott, S.Denvir, C.Berrigan, C.Brophy, P.Cahillane, S.Hurley, C.Mullins, M.Newman, D.Quinn, J.Califf. Subs: S.Fahey for Califf, T.Johnson for Denvir, D.Quinn for Berrigan, W.Ryan for Lynch, P.Óg Ó Griofa for Mullins.

2012/13

D.I.T. R.Lambert, G.O'Hare, B,Menton, K.O'Brien, R.Sheridan, N.Devereux, C.Walshe, A.O'Shea, D.Givney, M.Reilly, D.O'Sullivan, C.Reddin, M.Collins, T.O'Connor, J.Doherty. Subs: B.Allen for Reddin, A.Nestor for Sheridan, P.Maguire for Reilly, S.O'Connor for O'Sullivan, J.McGrath for O'Connor.

U.C.C. S.Mellet, P.Galvin, E.O'Mahony, N.Daly, J.O'Sullivan, P.Crowley, T.Clancy, P.Acheson, J.B.Spillane, K.O'Driscoll, B.Coughlan, L.Connolly, G.O'Grady, C.Cox, C.Sweeney. Subs: D.O'Sullivan for Coughlan, P.Murphy for Clancy, E.Buckley for O'Grady.

2013/14

U.C.C. B.Kelly, D.Culhane, E.O'Mahony, F.McNamara, T.Clancy, C.Dorman, B. Shanahan, D.Nation, I.McGuire, S.Keane, L.Connolly, B.O'Driscoll, C.Cox, M. Quinlivan, P.Geaney. Subs: S.Kiely for Nation, E.Healy for Keane.

U.U.J. R.Beggan, D.McNally, C.McKaigue, B.Tierney, K.Clarke, C.Walshe, L.Keaney, M.Donnelly, N.McKeever, K.Hughes, R.O'Neill, D.Savage, C.McAliskey, C.O'Boyle, J.Clarke. Subs: K.McKaigue for McNally, P.Devlin for Savage, R.Donnelly for McAliskey.

2014/15

DCU T.Lowe, C.Begley, C.Boyle, C.Moynagh, J.Smith, C.Daly, S.O'Brien, C.McHugh, D.Wrynn, D.Ward, C.McGraynor, E.O'Connor, D.O'Connor, C.Meredith, E.Smith. Subs: D.Smith for McHugh, M.Quinn for Ward, R.Connor for D.O'Connor, B.Donnelly for Meredith, S.Carey for Wrynn, S.McCoy for E.Smith, E.Smith for Connor, N.Murphy for E.O'Connor, T.Lahiffe for E.Smith.

UCC M.Martin, F.McNamara, J.McGuire, P.O'Connor, C.Dorman, D.Culhane, T.Clancy, S.Kiely, G.O'Sullivan, S.Keane, L.Connolly, B.O'Driscoll, D.Harrington, P.Geaney, C.Cox. Subs: A.O'Donovan for O'Driscoll, E.Ó Conchúir for O'Sullivan, K.Davis for Keane, S.White for O'Donovan, J.Davis for McNamara, T.Hickey for Connolly, Connolly for Geaney.

2015/16

UCD E.Keogh, R.Wylie, D.Hyland, D.Byrne, C.Mullaly, M.Fitzsimons, J.McCaffrey, L.Casey, R.McDaid, C.McCarthy, J.Heslin, C.Basquel, E.Lowry, P.Mannion, N.Kelly. Subs: T.Hayes for Mannion, J.McEntee for Kelly, S.Coen for McEntee, J.Barry for Lowry, S.O'Dea for McCaffrey, T.Moolick for Casey.

DCU P.O'Donnell, K.Daly, J.Smith, K.Feely, S.Attride, C.Moynagh, D.Byrne, S.O'Brien, M.Quinn, D.O'Connor, E.Smith, C.Begley, R.Connor, R.Lyons, S.Carey. Subs: S.Carthy for Quinn, C.McGraynor for Connor, D.Ward for Daly, C.McHugh for Carey, C.Breheny for Lyons, C.McNally for Smith.

2016/17

St Mary's M.Reid, R.Mooney, A.McKay, K.Mallon, C.Byrne, C.Mac Iomhar, C.Meyler, M.McCann, O.O'Neill, C.Corrigan, K.McGeary, S.McConville, K.McKernan, M.Fitzpatrick, C.McShane. Subs: C.Quinn for McConville, J.Hannigan for Mullan.

UCD C.Honan, M.Fitzsimons, R.McDaid, E.Murchan, C.Mullally, S.Coen, J.McCaffrey, B.O'Sullivan, J.Barry, C.McCarthy, A.McDonnell, E.Wallace, P.Mannion, C.Basquel, B.McGinn. Subs: L.Casey for McDonnell, T.Hayes for Mannion, L.Moran for O'Sullivan.

SIGERSON CUP WINNING CAPTAINS

1910/11	W John Riordan (UCC & Cork)
1911/12	Joseph F Donegan (UCG & Sligo)
1912/13	F J Cronin (UCD)
1913/14	Tom Nunan (UCC & Cork)
1914/15	P Fitzpatrick (UCD)
1915/16	E 'Charlie' Troy (UCC & Kerry)
1916/17	Solomon Lawlor (UCD & Kerry)
1917/18	Solomon Lawlor (UCD & Kerry)
1918/19	Con Lucey (UCC & Cork)
1919/20	Tom Pierce (UCD & Wexford)
1920/21	Not played
1921/22	W McDonald (UCG)
1922/23	Tom Nunan (UCC & Cork)
1923/24	Séamus Gardiner (UCD & Tipperary)
1924/25	Michael Murphy (UCC & Kerry)
1925/26	Patrick O'Sullivan (UCC)
1926/27	Éamonn O'Doherty (UCD & Clare)
1927/28	Peter Coughlan (UCC & Kerry & Cork)
1928/29	Éamonn O'Doherty (UCD & Clare)
1929/30	Joe O'Sullivan (UCD & Kerry)
1930/31	Mick O'Gorman (UCD & Monaghan)
1931/32	Martin Moloney (UCD & Clare)
1932/33	Seán Flood (UCD & Meath)
1933/34	Mick Higgins (UCG & Galway)
1934/35	Tony O'Regan (UCG & Galway)
1935/36	Paddy McMahon (UCD & Kerry)
1936/37	Hugh Gibbons (UCG & Roscommon)
1937/38	James Laffey (UCG & Mayo)
1938/39	Gerry O'Beirne (UCG & Roscommon)
1939/40	Joe Salmon (UCG & Mayo & Galway)
1940/41	Joe Salmon (UCG & Mayo & Galway)
1941/42	Dan Kavanagh (UCG & Kerry & Galway)
1942/43	Not played
1943/44	William Gavin (UCC & Tipperary)
1944/45	Jack Culleton (UCD & Wexford)
1945/46	Seán Flanagan (UCD & Mayo)
1946/47	Nioclás Mac Craith (UCC & Waterford)
1947/48	P J Duke (UCD & Cavan)
1948/49	Billy Kenny (UCG & Mayo)
1949/50	John O'Brien (UCD & Meath)
1950/51	Bill McQuillan (UCG & Roscommon)
1951/52	Jim O'Brien (UCC & Cork)
1952/53	Paudie Sheehy (UCC & Kerry)
1953/54	Pat Fenelon (UCD & Offaly)

1954/55	Eoghan Roe O'Neill (UCG & Mayo)
1955/56	Kieran Denvir (UCD & Down)
1956/57	Jim McDonnell (UCD & Cavan)
1957/58	Felix McKnight (UCD & Armagh)
1958/59	Hugh O'Kane (QUB & Antrim)
1959/60	James Brady (UCD & Cavan)
1960/61	George Glynn (UCG & Galway)
1961/62	Sean Murray (UCD & Longford)
1962/63	Hugh McGonigle (UCG & Sligo)
1963/64	Enda Colleran (UCG & Galway)
1964 /65	Des Sharkey (QUB & Antrim)
1965/66	Pat Moynihan (UCC & Kerry)
1966/67	Denis Philpott (UCC & Cork)
1967/68	Benny Gaughran (UCD & Louth)
1968/69	Christy O'Sullivan (UCC & Kerry)
1969/70	Moss Keane (UCC & Kerry)
1970/71	Paddy Park (QUB & Tyrone)
1971/72	Jim Gleeson (UCC & Cork)
1972/73	Éamonn O'Donoghue (UCD & Kildare)
1973/74	Paddy Kerr (UCD & Monaghan)
1974/75	Mick Carty (UCD & Wexford)
1975/76	Dan O'Mahony (Maynooth & Mayo)
1976/77	Ivan Heffernan (UCD & Mayo)
1977/78	Gerry McEntee (UCD & Meath)
1978/79	Tony McManus (UCD & Roscommon)
1979/80	Pádraig Monaghan (UCG & Mayo)
1980/81	Gay McManus (UCG & Galway)
1981/82	Séamus Boyd (QUB & Antrim)
1982/83	Richie Lee (UCG & Galway)
1983/84	Tomás Tierney (UCG & Galway)
1984/85	Bill Sex (UCD & Kildare)
1985/86	Colin Harney (UUJ & Armagh)
1986/87	D.J. Kane (UUJ & Down)
1987/88	John Keane (UCC & Kerry)
1988/89	John Reihill (St. Mary's & Fermanagh)
1989/90	Fergal Logan (QUB & Tyrone)
1990/91	Noel Donnelly (UUJ & Tyrone)
1991/92	Seán Óg de Paor (UCG & Galway)
1992/93	Paul Brewster (QUB & Fermanagh)
1993/94	Niall Savage (UCC & Kerry)
1994/95	Paul O'Keeffe (UCC & Kerry)
1995/96	Fachtna Collins (UCD & Cork)
1996/97	Éamon Ferris (TRTC & Kerry)
1997/98	Michael Cloherty (ITT & Galway)
1998/99	Jimmy McGuinness (ITT & Donegal)
1999/00	Diarmaid Marsden (QUB & Armagh)
2000/01	Jimmy McGuinness (UUJ & Donegal)
2001/02	Aidan Higgins (ITS & Mayo)
2002/03	Lorcán Ó Callaráin (NUIG & Galway)
2003/04	Michael Moyles (ITS & Mayo)
2004/05	Christy Toye (ITS & Donegal)
2005/06	Bryan Cullen (DCU & Dublin)
2006/07	Daniel McCartan (QUB & Down)
2007/08	Peter Donnelly (UUJ & Tyrone)
2008/09	Paul Flynn (Cork IT & Cork)
2009/10	Paddy Andrews (DCU & Dublin)
2010/11	Adrian Greaney (UCC & Kerry)
2011/12	Kieran Gavin (DCU & Westmeath)
2012/13	Colin Walshe (DIT & Monaghan)
2013/14	Paul Geaney (UCC & Kerry)
2014/15	Tom Flynn (DCU & Galway)
2015/16	Jack McCaffrey (UCD & Dublin)
2016/17	Conor Meyler (St Mary's & Tyrone)

HIGHER EDUCATION

SIGERSON FINAL TOP SCORERS
1934-2017

Note: This list starts from 1933/34 because in most years previous there was no final proper.

1933/34	Vincent McDarby (UCG & Galway) 2-4.
1934/35	Brian Scanlon (UCG & Mayo) 1-0.
1935/36	Vincent McGovern (UCD & Cavan) 1-0; Eamonn Gavin (UCD & Westmeath) 1-0.
1936/37	Dick Winters (UCG & Mayo) 1-1; Joe Fitzgerald (UCG & Galway) 1-1.
1937/38	Eugene O'Sullivan (UCG & Kerry) 0-4.
1938/39	Dennis Egan (UCG & Mayo) 1-1.
1939/40	Belfast final: Jack Bracken (UCG & Mayo) 1-2.
1939/40	Replay: Seán Mitchell (UCG & Leitrim) 1-1.
1940/41	Seán Thornton (UCG & Galway) 3-0.
1941/42	Walsh (UCD) 2-0.
1942/43	No competition
1943/44	Dick Stokes (UCD & Limerick) 1-1.
1944/45	Charlie Brennan (UCD & Monaghan) 2-0.
1945/46	Paddy Kelly (UCD & Westmeath) 2-0.
1946/47	Frank McGovern (UCC & Cork) 1-0, Paddy O'Regan (UCC & Cork) 1-0, Donal Keenan (UCD & Roscommon) 0-3.
1947/48	Derry Burke (UCC & Kerry), Brendan Hanniffy (UCC & Galway), Mick McCormack (UCD & Monaghan), Pádraic Carney (UCD & Mayo), Des McEvoy (UCD & Dublin) 0-1 each.
1948/49	Brian O'Rourke (UCG & Roscommon), Peadar McGowan (UCG & Mayo) 0-3 each, Pat Fenelon (UCG & Offaly), Mick Flanagan (UCD & Mayo), Frank Deady (UCD & Kilkenny) 1-0 each.
1949/50	Pádraic Carney (UCD & Mayo) (0-6).
1950/51	Peter Solan (UCG & Mayo) 0-5.
1951/52	Peadar Kearns (UCG & Roscommon), Paudie Sheehy (UCC & Kerry) 0-5 each.
1952/53	Jim Brosnan (UCC & Kerry) 3-0.
1953/54	Kieran Denvir (UCD & Down) 0-5.
1954/55	Draw: Kieran Denvir (UCD & Down) 0-4, Peadar McGowan (UCG & Mayo) 1-1.
Replay	Peadar McGowan (UCG & Mayo) 1-2 Éamonn McTigue (UCD & Mayo) 0-5.
1955/56	Colm Swords (UCD & Mayo) 2-1, Seán O'Donnell (UCC & Mayo) 2-1.
1956/57	Jim McDonnell (UCD & Cavan) 0-4.
1957/58	Eddie Duffy (UCD & Leitrim) 0-3, Dan Corrigan (UCC & Cork) 1-0, Seán Murphy (UCC & Cork) 1-0.
1958/59	Don Feeley (UCD & Roscommon) 2-0.
Replay	Charlie Gallagher (UCD & Cavan) 0-5.
1959/60	Kieran O'Malley (UCD & Kildare) 1-4.
1960/61	George Kane (UCD & Westmeath) 2-0.
1961/62	Brian Geraghty (UCG & Galway) 1-2, Seán Cleary (UCD & Galway) 1-2.
1962/63	Dave Geaney (UCC & Kerry) 1-2.
1963/64	Christy Tyrrell (UCG & Galway) 2-2.
1964/65	Seán O'Neill (QUB & Down) 2-2.
1965/66	Dave Geaney (UCC & Kerry) 2-2.
1966/67	Eric Philpott (UCC & Cork) 0-6.
1967/68	Benny Gaughran (UCD & Louth) 1-7.
1968/69	Brendan Lynch (UCC & Kerry) 0-7, Ray Cummins (UCC & Cork) 2-1.
1969/70	Barry Hanley (UCC & Kerry) 0-6.
1970/71	Brendan Lynch (UCC & Kerry) 0-5.
1971/72	Brendan Lynch (UCC & Kerry) 1-4, Martin Carney (UCG & Donegal) 2-1.
1972/73	Enda Condron (UCD & Laois) 1-3.
1973/74	Jackie Walsh (UCD & Kerry) 0-8.
1974/75	Jackie Walsh (UCD & Kerry) 0-6.
1975/76	Peter Burke (Maynooth & Longford) 0-4.
1976/77	Draw: Paul McGettigan (UCG & Donegal) 1-3.
Replay	Barry Walsh (UCD & Kerry) 0-5.
1977/78	Jackie Walsh (UCD & Kerry) 0-7.
1978/79	Tony McManus (UCD & Roscommon) 0-6.
1979/80	Micksey Clarke (UCG & Westmeath) 1-2.
1980/81	Gay McManus (UCG & Galway) 0-6.
1981/82	Greg Blaney (QUB & Down) 0-5.
1982/83	Pádraig Duffy (UCG & Mayo) 1-2.
1983/84	Colm O'Neill (UCC & Cork) 1-4.
1984/85	Mícheál O'Donoghue (UCD & Kerry) 0-3, Niall Clancy (UCD & Dublin) 0-3.
1985/86	Enda Gormley (UUJ & Derry) 0-5, Ger Houlahan (UUJ & Armagh) 1-2.
1986/87	Enda Gormley (UUJ & Derry) 0-3.
1987/88	Maurice Fitzgerald (UCC & Kerry) 0-3, Paul McGrath (UCC & Cork) 0-3.
1988/89	Fergal McCann (St. Mary's & Fermanagh) 2-1.
1989/90	James McCartan (QUB & Down) 1-3.
1990/91	Niall Finnegan (UCG & Galway) 0-3.
1991/92	Conor McGauran (UCG & Galway) 1-1, Lorcan Dowd (UCG & Roscommon) 1-1.
1992/93	Anthony Tohill (QUB & Derry) 0-6.
1993/94	Mark O'Sullivan (UCC & Cork) 1-2.
1994/95	Johnny Crowley (UCC & Kerry) 0-4, John Clifford (UCC & Cork) 0-4, Brendan Duffy (UCG & Galway) 0-4.
1995/96	James O'Shea (Garda & Kerry) 1-2.

1996/97	Genie Farrell (TRTC & Kerry) 0-4, Dara Ó Cinnéide (UL & Kerry) 0-4.
1997/98	Jack Ferriter (ITT & Kerry) 0-3, Brian McGuckin (UUJ & Tyrone) 0-3.
1998/99	Jack Ferriter (ITT & Kerry) 0-3, Noel Kennelly (ITT & Kerry) 1-0, Declan Lynch (Garda & Kerry) 0-3.
1999/00	Liam McBarron (QUB & Fermanagh) 1-1.
2000/01	Patrick Bradley (UUJ & Derry) 0-5.
2001/02	Conrad Murphy (UCC & Cork) 0-4.
2002/03	Michael Meehan (NUIG & Galway) 1-4.
2003/04	Paul Finlay (ITS & Monaghan) 0-5, Aidan Fegan (QUB & Down) 0-5.
2004/05	Brian Mallon (QUB & Armagh) 0-4.
2005/06	Seán Johnston (DCU & Cavan) 0-4, Conor Mortimer (DCU & Mayo) 0-4.
2006/07	Paddy Cunningham (UUJ & Antrim) 0-6.
2007/08	Paddy Cunningham (UUJ & Antrim) 1-9.
2008/09	Daniel Goulding (Cork IT & Cork) 0-9.
2009/10	Brian Sheridan (DCU & Meath) 1-5.
2010/11	Barry O'Driscoll (UCC & Cork) 0-3
2011/12	Paul Flynn (DCU & Dublin) 1-3
2012/13	Jason Doherty (DIT & Mayo) 1-2, David Givney (DIT & Cavan) 1-2.
2013/14	Conor Cox (UCC & Kerry) 0-6.
2014/15	Donal Wrynn (DCU & Leitrim) 1-1 Alan O'Donovan (UCC & Cork) 1-1
2015/16	John Heslin (UCD & Westmeath) 0-6
2016/17	Colm Basquel (UCD & Dublin) 2-1

HIGHER
EDUCATION

CAMOGIE

CAMOGIE ALL-IRELAND CHAMPIONSHIPS
SENIOR FINALS

1932	Dublin	3-2	0-2	Galway
1933	Dublin	9-2	4-0	Galway
1934	Cork	4-3	1-4	Louth
1935	Cork	3-4	4-0	Dublin
1936	Cork	6-4	3-3	Louth
1937	Dublin	9-4	1-0	Galway
1938	Dublin	5-0	2-3	Cork
1939	Cork	6-1	1-1	Galway
1940	Cork	4-1	2-2	Galway
1941	Cork	7-5	1-2	Dublin
1942	Dublin	1-2	1-2	Cork
Replay	Dublin	4-1	2-2	Cork
1943	Dublin	8-0	1-1	Cork
1944	Dublin	5-4	0-0	Antrim
1945	Antrim	5-2	3-2	Waterford
1946	Antrim	4-1	2-3	Galway
1947	Antrim	2-4	2-1	Dublin
1948	Dublin	11-4	4-2	Down
1949	Dublin	8-6	4-1	Tipperary
1950	Dublin	6-5	4-1	Antrim
1951	Dublin	8-6	4-1	Antrim
1952	Dublin	5-1	4-2	Antrim
1953	Dublin	8-4	1-3	Tipperary
1954	Dublin	10-4	4-2	Derry
1955	Dublin	9-2	5-6	Cork
1956	Antrim	5-3	4-2	Cork
1957	Dublin	3-3	3-1	Antrim
1958	Dublin	5-4	1-1	Tipperary
1959	Dublin	11-6	1-3	Mayo
1960	Dublin	6-2	2-0	Galway
1961	Dublin	7-2	4-1	Tipperary
1962	Dublin	5-5	2-0	Galway
1963	Dublin	7-3	2-5	Antrim
1964	Dublin	7-4	3-1	Antrim
1965	Dublin	10-1	5-3	Tipperary
1966	Dublin	2-2	0-6	Antrim
1967	Antrim	4-2	4-2	Dublin
Replay	Antrim	3-9	4-2	Dublin
1968	Wexford	4-2	2-5	Cork
1969	Wexford	4-4	4-2	Antrim
1970	Cork	5-7	3-2	Kilkenny
1971	Cork	4-6	1-2	Wexford
1972	Cork	2-5	1-4	Kilkenny
1973	Cork	2-5	3-1	Antrim
1974	Kilkenny	3-8	4-5	Cork
Replay	Kilkenny	3-3	1-5	Cork
1975	Wexford	4-3	1-2	Cork
1976	Kilkenny	0-6	1-2	Dublin
1977	Kilkenny	3-4	1-3	Wexford
1978	Cork	6-4	1-2	Dublin
1979	Antrim	2-3	1-3	Tipperary
1980	Cork	2-7	3-4	Limerick
Replay	Cork	1-8	2-2	Limerick
1981	Kilkenny	3-9	3-9	Cork
Replay	Kilkenny	1-9	0-7	Cork
1982	Cork	2-7	2-6	Dublin
1983	Cork	2-5	1-6	Dublin
1984	Dublin	5-9	2-4	Tipperary
1985	Kilkenny	0-13	1-5	Dublin
1986	Kilkenny	2-12	2-3	Dublin
1987	Kilkenny	3-10	1-7	Cork
1988	Kilkenny	4-11	3-8	Cork
1989	Kilkenny	3-10	2-6	Cork
1990	Kilkenny	1-14	0-7	Wexford
1991	Kilkenny	3-8	0-10	Cork
1992	Cork	1-20	2-6	Wexford
1993	Cork	3-15	2-8	Galway
1994	Kilkenny	2-11	0-8	Wexford
1995	Cork	4-8	2-10	Kilkenny
1996	Galway	4-8	1-15	Cork
1997	Cork	0-15	2-5	Galway
1998	Cork	2-13	0-15	Galway
1999	Tipperary	0-12	1-8	Kilkenny
2000	Tipperary	2-11	1-9	Cork
2001	Tipperary	4-13	1-6	Kilkenny
2002	Cork	4-9	1-9	Tipperary
2003	Tipperary	2-11	1-11	Cork
2004	Tipperary	2-11	0-9	Cork
2005	Cork	1-17	1-13	Tipperary
2006	Cork	0-12	0-4	Tipperary
2007	Wexford	2-7	1-8	Cork
2008	Cork	2-10	1-8	Galway
2009	Cork	0-15	0-7	Kilkenny
2010	Wexford	1-12	1-10	Galway
2011	Wexford	2-7	1-8	Galway
2012	Wexford	3-13	3-6	Cork
2013	Galway	1-9	0-7	Kilkenny
2014	Cork	2-12	1-9	Kilkenny
2015	Cork	1-13	0-9	Galway
2016	Kilkenny	1-13	1-9	Cork
2017	Cork	0-10	0-9	Kilkenny

JUNIOR FINALS

1968	Down	2-3	1-1	Cork
1969	Derry	4-2	2-4	Cork
1970	Dublin	4-2	3-3	Armagh
1971	Dublin	2-2	1-2	Cork
1972	Galway	3-6	2-1	Wexford
1973	Cork	4-4	1-4	Galway
1974	Clare	3-2	3-0	Dublin
1975	Dublin	5-0	0-3	Down
1976	Down	3-4	3-3	Wexford
1977	Limerick	2-7	3-1	Wexford
1978	Derry	3-4	1-4	Cork
1979	Galway	4-3	3-2	Cork
1980	Cork	4-4	1-4	Tyrone
1981	Clare	3-2	0-7	Antrim
1982	Louth	1-7	1-6	Cork
1983	Cork	2-5	2-3	Dublin
1984	Cork	5-8	2-2	Cavan
1985	Galway	8-7	3-7	Armagh
1986	Clare	1-13	3-4	Kildare
1987	Kildare	2-10	0-7	Armagh
1988	Galway	3-4	1-5	Limerick
1989	Kildare	0-15	2-9	Galway
Replay	Kildare	3-11	1-3	Galway
1990	Kildare	2-14	3-7	Tipperary
1991	Down	3-13	2-14	Tipperary
1992	Tipperary	6-13	2-7	Galway
1993	Armagh	3-9	3-9	Galway
Replay	Armagh	2-10	0-6	Galway
1994	Galway	2-10	1-11	Limerick
1995	Limerick	3-7	4-3	Roscommon
1996	Cork	6-5	2-7	Roscommon
1997	Antrim	7-11	2-10	Cork
1998	Galway	3-11	2-10	Tipperary
1999	Cork	1-13	2-9	Derry
2000	Derry	3-15	1-13	Cork
2001	Tipperary	4-16	1-7	Offaly
2002	Kilkenny	2-11	2-8	Cork
2003	Galway	3-9	3-9	Clare
Replay	Galway	1-12	2-5	Clare
2004	Cork	4-5	2-4	Down
2005	Dublin	1-7	1-7	Clare

Replay	Dublin	2-9	1-4	Clare
2006	Dublin	0-12	1-7	Derry
2007	Derry	3-12	2-14	Clare
2008	Clare	2-8	1-10	Offaly
2009	Offaly	3-14	2-8	Waterford
2010	Antrim	1-9	1-9	Waterford
Replay	Antrim	2-10	0-12	Waterford
2011	Waterford	2-11	1-13	Down
2012	Meath	1-11	1-9	Down
2013	Kildare	2-11	1-5	Laois
2014	Down	1-12	1-8	Laois
2015	Laois	2-12	1-6	Roscommon
2016	Carlow	4-10	2-7	Armagh
2017	Westmeath	1-10	1-6	Dublin

CAMOGIE

INTERMEDIATE/'B' FINALS

1992	Dublin	4-11	4-4	Down
1993	Care	1-8	1-5	Dublin
1994	Armagh	7-11	3-11	Kildare
1995	Clare	1-10	1-9	Tipperary
1996	Limerick	2-10	1-6	Down
1997	Tipperary	2-19	2-12	Clare
1998	Down	1-12	1-8	Cork
1999	Clare	1-8	1-3	Antrim
2000	Cork	3-9	0-11	Limerick
2001	Antrim	3-10	0-5	Derry
2002	Cork	3-6	1-10	Antrim
2003	Antrim	2-9	0-10	Tipperary
2004	Galway	2-5	0-4	Tipperary
2005	No Competition			
2006	Cork	2-9	1-7	Galway
2007	Limerick	2-9	0-6	Cork
2008	Kilkenny	5-5	1-14	Cork
2009	Galway	3-10	1-5	Cork
2010	Offaly	2-12	2-10	Wexford
2011	Wexford	2-12	0-15	Antrim
2012	Derry	3-12	3-12	Galway
Replay	Derry	2-10	2-9	Galway
2013	Galway	0-12	0-10	Limerick
2014	Limerick	1-12	0-10	Kilkenny
2015	Waterford	2-9	1-5	Kildare
2016	Kilkenny	3-6	1-11	Cork
2017	Meath	1-9	1-9	Cork
Replay	Meath	0-10	0-7	Cork

MINOR FINALS

1974	Down	3-0	0-1	Cork
1975	Cork	6-2	0-3	Galway
1976	Cork	4-6	2-1	Down
1977	Galway	5-4	2-1	Dublin
1978	Cork	5-1	3-4	Dublin
1979	Cork	5-3	3-0	Cavan
1980	Cork	5-5	0-2	Cavan
1981	Galway	3-4	3-3	Antrim
1982	Dublin	5-2	2-3	Galway
1983	Cork	3-3	2-3	Dublin
1984	Cork	2-12	5-0	Galway
1985	Cork	3-8	2-3	Galway
1986	Galway	2-8	1-4	Wexford
1987	Galway	1-11	3-3	Cork
1988	Kilkenny	5-6	2-5	Armagh
1989	Kilkenny	9-10	3-8	Tipperary
1990	Tipperary	2-11	3-6	Kilkenny
1991	Kilkenny	4-12	3-7	Galway
1992	Tipperary	4-9	1-3	Kilkenny
1993	Tipperary	1-5	1-5	Galway
Replay	Tipperary	3-10	2-9	Galway
1994	Galway	7-13	3-9	Tipperary
1995	Wexford	2-9	1-7	Galway
1996	Galway	3-16	4-11	Tipperary
1997	Galway	2-14	1-6	Cork
1998	Cork	3-18	1-5	Derry
1999	Cork	2-12	3-8	Galway
2000	Galway	2-9	0-3	Wexford
2001	Cork	6-15	0-7	Kilkenny
2002	Cork	1-11	1-5	Galway
2003	Cork	3-12	1-4	Galway
2004	Galway	3-16	2-6	Kilkenny
2005	Kilkenny	4-7	2-7	Tipperary
2006	Kilkenny	4-10	2-5	Galway
2007	Kilkenny	3-12	0-7	Cork
2008	Kilkenny	3-15	1-7	Clare
2009	Kilkenny	5-10	3-8	Clare
2010	Galway	1-7	1-7	Clare
Replay	Galway	2-12	2-8	Clare
2011	Tipperary	4-4	2-9	Kilkenny
2012	Galway	2-12	1-10	Kilkenny
2013	Kilkenny	3-4	1-10	Cork
Replay	Kilkenny	1-12	0-6	Cork
2014	Limerick	2-11	3-8	Cork
Replay	Limerick	3-11	1-9	Cork
2015	Kilkenny	3-9	1-12	Tipperary
2016	Tipperary	4-9	2-6	Galway
2017	Galway	4-14	0-6	Clare

NATIONAL LEAGUES

SENIOR FINALS

1977	Tipperary	4-2	1-3	Wexford
1978	Wexford	2-5	0-4	Cork
1979	Dublin	0-6	0-0	Limerick
1980	Kilkenny	3-8	1-3	Tipperary
1981	Dublin	1-7	1-4	Cork
1982	Kilkenny	2-5	1-4	Cork
1983	Dublin	4-8	1-6	Wexford
1984	Cork	1-8	0-4	Dublin
1985	Kilkenny	4-7	3-6	Dublin
1986	Cork	3-8	1-10	Dublin
1987	Kilkenny	4-8	1-6	Dublin
1988	Kilkenny	3-10	2-4	Dublin
1989	Kilkenny	6-7	1-11	Cork
1990	Kilkenny	1-10	2-4	Wexford
1991	Cork	2-13	2-6	Kilkenny
1992	Cork	2-17	0-11	Wexford
1993	Kilkenny	4-7	1-13	Cork
1994	Galway	1-13	1-8	Tipperary
1995	Cork	5-16	3-4	Armagh
1996	Cork	3-16	1-7	Galway
1997	Cork	4-12	0-9	Kilkenny
1998	Cork	1-16	2-9	Galway
1999	Cork	9-19	2-7	Tipperary
2000	Cork	3-7	1-10	Tipperary
2001	Cork	6-9	0-11	Galway
2002	Galway	6-6	1-7	Limerick
2003	Cork	3-13	2-12	Tipperary
2004	Tipperary	3-10	2-9	Wexford
2005	Galway	1-6	0-6	Cork
2006	Cork	2-7	2-5	Tipperary
2007	Cork	3-8	1-10	Wexford
2008	Kilkenny	3-11	0-17	Galway
2009	Wexford	2-12	0-11	Tipperary
2010	Wexford	1-7	1-6	Kilkenny
2011	Wexford	3-10	0-10	Galway
2012	Cork	1-8	0-9	Wexford
2013	Cork	0-12	1-7	Wexford
2014	Kilkenny	1-15	0-4	Clare
2015	Galway	2-15	2-12	Cork
2016	Kilkenny	2-7	0-7	Galway
2017	Kilkenny	2-7	0-10	Cork

JUNIOR (DIVISION TWO) FINALS

1980	Armagh	2-5	2-3	Kildare
1981	Cavan	2-4	1-7	Louth
Replay	Cavan	0-4	0-2	Louth
1982	Dublin	6-9	0-2	Tyrone
1983	Dublin	3-9	2-5	Westmeath
1984	Dublin	2-4	1-3	Armagh
1985	Galway	3-10	3-3	Kildare
1986	Kildare	2-3	1-4	Dublin
1987	Dublin	6-4	1-7	Kildare
1988	Armagh	1-9	0-6	Down
1989	Kildare	2-14	3-8	Armagh
1990	Kildare	2-13	1-3	Kilkenny
1991	Limerick	3-13	3-4	Roscommon
1992	Limerick	4-13	2-6	Down
1993	Armagh	3-8	2-1	Dublin
1994	Armagh	1-10	1-10	Cork
Replay	Armagh	1-18	1-2	Cork
1995	Galway	3-8	3-8	Down
Replay	Galway	4-13	2-9	Down
1996	Limerick	5-10	3-7	Down
1997	Antrim	5-12	3-16	Down
1998	Down	0-20	0-12	Cork
1999	Derry	3-7	0-7	Wexford
2000	Cork	2-12	0-4	Kildare
2001	Cork	3-14	4-3	Derry
2002	Offaly	3-18	2-6	Laois
2003	Galway	1-11	2-5	Armagh
2004	Kildare	2-11	2-6	Laois
2005	Cork	2-10	2-7	Galway
2006	Clare	1-14	3-7	Derry
2007	Waterford	1-18	2-13	Down
2008	Clare	4-8	3-9	Derry
2009	Wexford	2-9	0-11	Antrim
2010	Wexford	2-9	1-9	Offaly
2011	Waterford	0-16	2-9	Antrim
2012	Derry	2-11	0-6	Meath
2013	Limerick	3-14	0-10	Kildare
2014	Cork	1-12	2-6	Down
2015	Waterford	3-10	2-6	Laois
2016	Meath	1-10	2-3	Galway
2017	Cork	2-16	1-5	Derry

CAMOGIE

GAEL LINN SENIOR INTERPROVINCIAL CHAMPIONSHIP FINALS

1956	Leinster	7-1	3-1	Ulster
1957	Leinster	5-1	3-1	Munster
1958	Leinster	8-2	3-3	Ulster
1959	Leinster	6-0	1-3	Ulster
1960	Leinster	4-9	3-1	Munster
1961	Munster	5-2	1-0	Connacht
1962	Leinster	7-2	5-3	Ulster
1963	Munster	3-2	2-2	Leinster
1964	Munster	2-6	3-2	Leinster
1965	Leinster	4-3	4-1	Ulster
1966	Munster	4-2	1-3	Leinster
1967	Ulster	5-4	5-1	Leinster
1968	Leinster	7-0	2-5	Ulster
1969	Leinster	5-4	2-2	Munster
1970	Leinster	12-2	4-1	Ulster
1971	Leinster	5-4	0-5	Ulster
1972	Leinster	7-7	4-2	Connacht
1973	Connacht	4-4	3-3	Leinster
1974	Connacht	3-7	3-0	Munster
1975-1977 Suspended.				
1978	Leinster	4-9	2-2	Connacht
1979	Leinster	1-5	0-4	Munster
1980	Munster	2-5	2-1	Leinster
1981	Leinster	3-10	2-4	Ulster
1982	Munster	3-10	2-12	Leinster
1983	Leinster	2-7	1-7	Munster
1984	Leinster	3-9	1-4	Connacht
1985	Leinster	4-9	1-6	Munster
1986	Leinster	4-6	1-6	Munster
1987	Leinster	8-11	0-5	Connacht
1988	Leinster	2-9	2-4	Connacht
1989	Leinster	5-12	3-6	Munster
1990	Munster	10-10	1-2	Ulster
1991	Leinster	5-13	0-7	Munster
1992	Munster	1-18	2-9	Leinster
1993	Leinster	6-14	1-4	Ulster
1994	Munster	4-11	2-7	Ulster
1995	Munster	4-13	3-10	Connacht
1996	Munster	4-18	6-10	Ulster
1997	Munster	4-18	2-11	Leinster
1998	Munster	6-20	1-11	Leinster
1999	Munster	1-18	1-9	Connacht
2000	Connacht	1-10	0-3	Ulster
2001	Leinster	1-14	1-11	Munster
2002	Ulster	4-11	1-13	Leinster
2003	Munster	4-7	0-5	Ulster
2004	Munster	4-16	1-4	Leinster
2005	Munster	2-14	2-4	Ulster
2006	Connacht	3-12	1-7	Ulster
2007	Leinster	3-16	0-11	Munster
2008	Munster	3-17	0-3	Ulster
2009	Connacht	4-4	0-2	Munster
2010	Not Played			
2011	Munster	1-15	2-11	Leinster
2012	Not Played			
2013	Ulster	1-5	1-13	Munster
2014	Leinster	4-16	2-17	Munster
2015	Not played			
2016	Connacht	2-7	1-6	Leinster
2017	Not played			

ALL-IRELAND CLUB CHAMPIONSHIP FINALS

1964
Celtic, Dublin 5-2 Deirdre, Belfast 1-0

1965
St. Patrick's Glengoole, Tipperary 3-3 Deirdre, Belfast 2-3

1966
St. Patrick's, Glengoole, Tipperary 5-5 St. Paul's, Kilkenny 2-1

1967
Eoghan Ruadh, Dublin 7-3 Oranmore, Galway 1-0

1968
St. Paul's, Kilkenny 7-2 Ahane, Limerick 1-2

1969
St. Paul's, Kilkenny 3-7 Ahane, Limerick 2-1

1970/71
St. Paul's, Kilkenny 6-5 Bellaghy, Derry 2-0

1971/72
Austin Stacks, Dublin 5-4 Thurles, Tipperary 2-1

1972/73
Austin Stacks, Dublin 4-2 Portglenone, Antrim 2-0

1973/74
Oranmore, Galway 3-2 St. Paul's, Kilkenny 2-3

1974/75
St. Paul's, Kilkenny 3-3 Oranmore, Galway 1-1

1975/76
Croagh-Kilfinny, Limerick 4-6 Athenry, Galway 4-5

1976/77
St. Paul's, Kilkenny 6-3 Athenry, Galway 1-3

1977/78
Athenry, Galway 10-5 Portglenone, Antrim 1-1

1978
Ballyagran, Limerick 1-3 Buffer's Alley, Wexford 0-1

1979
Buffer's Alley, Wexford 2-6 Athenry, Galway 1-2

1980
Killeagh, Cork 4-2 Buffer's Alley, Wexford 1-7

1981
Buffer's Alley, Wexford 2-6 Killeagh, Cork 1-4

1982
Buffer's Alley, Wexford 3-2 Athenry, Galway 0-2

1983
Buffer's Alley, Wexford 3-7 St. Marys, Kilkerrin-Glenamaddy, Galway 0-6

1984
Buffer's Alley, Wexford 2-4 Killeagh, Cork 1-4

1985
Crumlin, Dublin 4-8 Athenry, Galway 3-2

1986
Glen Rovers, Cork 4-11 St. Paul's, Kilkenny 5-7

1987
St. Paul's, Kilkenny 1-4 Glen Rovers, Cork 0-5

1988
St Paul's, Kilkenny 4-5 St. Mary's, Glenamaddy, Galway 3-7

1989
St. Paul's, Kilkenny 6-10 Mullagh, Galway 4-2

1990
Glen Rovers, Cork 4-13 St. Paul's, Kilkenny 2-7

1991
Mullagh, Galway 4-13 Eglish, Tyrone 0-2

1992
Glen Rovers, Cork 1-9 St. Anne's, Rathnure, Wexford 0-2

1993
Glen Rovers, Cork 6-10 Mullagh, Galway 0-2

1994
Lisdowney, Kilkenny 5-9 Glen Rovers, Cork 1-15

1995
Rathnure, Wexford 4-9 Toomevara, Tipperary 1-5

1996
Pearses, Galway 1-8 Granagh/ Ballingarry, Limerick 2-3

CAMOGIE

1997
Pearses, Galway 4-6 Lisdowney, Kilkenny 2-5

1998
Granagh/Ballingarry, Limerick 1-19 St. Vincent's, Dublin 1-8

1999
Granagh/Ballingarry, Limerick 2-4 Davitts, Galway 1-3

2000
Pearses, Galway 2-11 Swatragh, Derry 1-3

2001
Pearses, Galway 2-8 Cashel, Tipperary 0-13

2002
Pearses, Galway 2-13 St.Ibar's, Wexford 1-5

2003
Granagh, Balingarry, Limerick 1-10 Davitts, Galway 1-6

2004
St Lachtain's, Kilkenny 2-8, Granagh/Ballingarry, Limerick 0-7

2005
St Lachtain's, Kilkenny 1-9 Davitt's 1-4

2006
St Lachtain's, Kilkenny 1-5 O'Donovan Rossa, Antrim 1-3

2007
Cashel, Tipperary 1-18 Athenry, Galway 0-9

2008
O'Donovan Rossa, Antrim 2-15 Drom & Inch, Tippeary 1-12.

2009
Cashel, Tipperary 0-11 Athenry, Galway 0-9

2010
Killimor, Galway 3-18 Inniscarra, Cork 1-4

2011
Oulart-The Ballagh, Wexford 3-13 Drom & Inch, Tipperary 0-5

2012
Milford, Cork 3-6 Killimor, Galway 1-6

2013
Milford, Cork 0-6 Ardrahan, Galway 0-5

2014
Oulart-The Ballagh, Wexford 3-13 Mullagh, Galway 0-7

2015
Milford, Cork 2-8 Killimor, Galway 1-3

2016
Slaughtneil, Derry 1-10 Sarsfields, Galway 0-11

ASHBOURNE CUP WINNERS

1915	U.C.D.
1916	U.C.D.
1917	U.C.G.
1918	U.C.D.
1919	U.C.C.
1920	U.C.G.
1921	U.C.D.
1922	U.C.C.
1923	U.C.C.
1924	U.C.C.
1925	U.C.C.
1926	U.C.C.
1927	U.C.C.
1928	U.C.G.
1929	U.C.C.
1930	U.C.G.
1931	U.C.C.
1932	U.C.C.
1933	U.C.D.
1934	U.C.C.
1935	U.C.D.
1936	U.C.C.
1937	U.C.C.
1938	U.C.D.
1939	U.C.D.
1940	U.C.D.
1941	U.C.D.
1942	U.C.D.
1943	Not Played.
1944	U.C.C.
1945	U.C.C.
1946	U.C.D.
1947	U.C.C.
1948	U.C.G.
1949	U.C.G.
1950	U.C.D.
1951	U.C.C.
1952	U.C.D.
1953	U.C.D.
1954	U.C.D.
1955	U.C.D.
1956	U.C.G.
1957	U.C.G.
1958	U.C.D.
1959	U.C.D.
1960	U.C.D.
1961	U.C.D.
1962	U.C.D.
1963	Undecided.
1964	U.C.G.
1965	U.C.C.

1966	U.C.D.
1967	U.C.C.
1968	U.C.G.
1969	U.C.D.
1970	U.C.D.
1971	U.C.D.
1972	U.C.C.
1973	U.C.C.
1974	U.C.C.
1975	U.C.C.
1976	U.C.C.
1977	U.C.C.
1978	U.C.G.
1979	U.C.G.
1980	U.C.D.
1981	U.C.D.
1982	U.C.D.
1983	U.C.D.
1984	U.C.D.
1985	U.C.C.
1986	U.C.D.
1987	U.C.D.
1988	U.C.D.
1989	U.C.G.
1990	U.C.G.
1991	Q.U.B.
1992	U.U.J.
1993	U.U.J.
1994	U.C.G.
1995	U.L.
1996	U.C.C.
1997	U.U.J.
1998	U.C.C.
1999	W.I.T.
2000	U.C.C.
2001	W.I.T.
2002	U.C.C.
2003	U.C.C.
2004	U.L.
2005	U.L.
2006	U.L.
2007	U.C.D.
2008	U.C.D.
2009	W.I.T.
2010	W.I.T.
2011	W.I.T.
2012	W.I.T.
2013	W.I.T.
2014	U.L.
2015	W.I.T.
2016	U.L.
2017	U.L.

PURCELL CUP WINNERS

1977	Mary Immaculate, Limerick
1978	Mary Immaculate, Limerick
1979	Ulster Polytechnic, Belfast
1980	Thomond/N.I.H.E., Limerick
1981	Thomond/N.I.H.E., Limerick
1982	St. Mary's, Belfast
1983	Mary Immaculate, Limerick
1984	Ulster Polytechnic, Belfast
1985	Thomond College, Limerick
1986	Thomond College, Limerick
1987	Thomond College, Limerick
1988	Thomond College, Limerick
1989	Mary Immaculate, Limerick
1990	Waterford R.T.C.
1991	Thomond College, Limerick
1992	Waterford R.T.C.
1993	Athlone R.T.C.
1994	University College, Cork
1995	Athlone R.T.C.
1996	St. Patrick's, Maynooth
1997	Queen's University, Belfast
1998	Mary Immaculate, Limerick
1999	Limerick I.T.
2000	U.U.J.
2001	Cork IT
2002	Carlow IT
2003	U.U.J.
2004	Athlone IT
2005	Garda College
2006	U.U.J.
2007	Athlone IT
2008	Queen's University, Belfast
2009	Athlone IT
2010	DIT
2011	Queens University
2012	Dublin College University
2013	Dublin College University
2014	University College Cork (UCC)
2015	Mary Immaculate, Limerick
2016	Cork IT
2017	Dublin IT

CAMOGIE

ALL-IRELAND COLLEGES SENIOR FINALS

1969
Pres., Kilkenny 3-2 St. Aloysius, Cork 1-2.

1970
Pres., Kilkenny 2-3 Sacred Heart, Newry 1-1

1971
Sacred Heart, Newry 3-2 Pres. Mountmellick 2-1

1972
Pres., Oranmore 6-1 St. Louis, Kilkeel 4-4

1973
Pres., Mountmellick 4-2 Pres., Athenry 1-2

1974
Pres., Athenry 3-1 St. Louis, Kilkeel 1-0.

1975
Pres., Athenry 7-4 St. Brigid's, Callan 2-4

1976
St. Aloysius, Cork 2-2 Pres., Athenry 0-2

1977
Scoil Mhuire, Cashel 2-2 Pres., Athenry 1-3

1978
Pres., Athenry 2-3 Loreto, Coleraine 2-2

1979
Scoil Mhuire, Cashel 3-3 Pres., Athenry 1-3

1980
North Pres., Cork 4-7 Assumption, Walkinstown 1-1

1981
St. Patrick's, Cork 1-3 Assumption, Walkinstown 0-5

1982
St. Patrick's, Shannon 1-7 St. Raphael's, Loughrea 1-4

1983
St. John of God, Artane 2-6 St. Patrick's, Cork 2-1

1984
Maryfield College, Dublin 2-5 North Pres., Cork 0-5

1985
St. Raphael's, Loughrea 4-7 St. Patrick's, Cork 3-3

1986
St. Raphael's, Loughrea 3-5 F.C.J., Bunclody 0-4

1987
St. Raphael's, Loughrea 3-8 St. Marys, Charleville 0-4

1988
St. Raphael's, Loughrea 2-13 F.C.J., Bunclody 1-5

1989
St. Raphael's, Loughrea 5-9 St. Patrick's, Keady 2-10

1990
St. Raphael's, Loughrea 3-11 Scoil Mhuire, Cashel 2-0

1991
St. Raphael's, Loughrea 3-6 Vocational, Thomastown 0-0

1992
St. Raphael's, Loughrea 7-7 St. Brigid's, Callan 2-4

1993
St. Brigid's, Callan 3-7 St. Mary's, Charleville 1-2

1994
St. Marys, Nenagh 1-10 St. Patrick's, Maghera 1-2

1995
Pres., Kilkenny 3-4 St. Mary's, Charleville 2-4

1996
St. Mary's, Charleville 1-15 St. Raphael's, Loughrea 3-3

1997
St. Mary's, Charleville 2-16 St. Brigid's, Loughrea 4-2

1998
St. Mary's, Charleville 1-11 Coláiste Bríde, Enniscorthy 1-4

1999
St. Mary's, Charleville 3-10 Coláiste Bríde, Enniscorthy 0-5

2000
St.Mary's, Nenagh 3-6 Seamount, Kinvara 0-7

2001
St.Mary's, Charleville 4-7 Loretto, Kilkenny 0-3

2002
St.Mary's, Charleville 4-19 Portumna CS 1-9

2003
Coláiste Bríde, Enniscorthy 5-7 St.Patrick's, Maghera 1-3

2004
Coláiste Bríde, Enniscorthy 4-7 St.Mary's, Charleville 1-4

2005
Coláiste Bríde, Enniscorthy 1-8 St.Mary's, Charleville 2-3

2006
St.Mary's, Charleville 1-11 Presentation College, Athenry 0-4

2007
St. Mary's, Magherafelt 2-9 Presentation College, Athenry 2-6

2008
St. Brigid's Callan, Kilkenny 3-7 St. Mary's, Charleville 0-6.

2009
St. Brigid's Callan, Kilkenny 1-11 Portumna CS 1-6

2010
Loreto, Kilkenny 2-5 Blackwater CS, Lismore 1-7

2011
Loreto, Kilkenny 4-10 St. Patrick's, Maghera 1-6

2012
Loreto, Kilkenny 4-11 St. Brigid's, Loughrea 1-10

2013
Loreto, Kilkenny 1-11 St. Brigid's, Loughrea 1-6

2014
Pres., Kilkenny 2-9 St. Mary's, Magherafelt 0-9

2015
Seamount, Kinvara 1-5 St Flannan's, Ennis 0-6

2016
St Brigid's, Loughrea 2-6 Loreto, Kilkenny 0-9

2017
Loreto, Kilkenny 6-19 Ursuline SS, Thurles 1-4

ALL-IRELAND COLLEGES JUNIOR FINALS

1974
Pres., Athenry 3-0 North Pres., Cork 0-0

1975
Scoil Mhuire, Cashel 4-0 Pres., Terenure 1-0

1976
Pres., Athenry 4-2 Scoil Mhuire, Cashel 3-2

1977
Pres. Athenry 4-1 Sacred Heart, Cork 1-3

1978
Scoil Mhuire, Cashel 2-3 Vocational, Bawnboy 0-1

1979
Mercy, Roscommon 1-2 Scoil Pol, Kilfinane 0-1

1980
Maryfield College 2-3 Pres., de la Salle, Hospital 1-5

1981
St. John of God, Artane 4-0 St. Patrick's, Cork 0-2

1982
Maryfield College 3-9 St. Raphael's, Loughrea 4-0

1983
Mercy, Roscommon 7-1 St. Paul's, Kilrea 1-3

1984
St. Raphael's, Loughrea 6-8 St. Patrick's, Shannon 2-1

1985
St. Raphael's, Loughrea 3-4 Colaiste Muire, Ennis 1-0

1986
St Mary's, Charleville 2-6 F.C.J., Bunclody 0-3

1987
St Mary's, Charleville 2-3 St. Raphael's, Loughrea 1-4

1988
St. Raphael's, Loughrea 5-7 St. Mary's, Macroom 1-0

1989
St. Raphael's, Loughrea 5-0 St. Patrick's, Maghera 0-1

CAMOGIE

1990
St. Brigid's, Callan 5-8 St. Patrick's, Maghera 1-4

1991
St. Mary's, Nenagh 3-9 St. Cuan's, Castleblakeney 1-10

1992
St. Marys, Nenagh 2-6 St. Mary's, Magherafelt 0-8

1993
F.C.J., Bunclody 2-7 St. Mary's, Charleville 1-4

1994
St Mary's, Charleville 3-6 St Mary's, Magherafelt 1-5

1995
St Mary's, Charleville 2-12 St Mary's, Magherafelt 1-1

1996
St Mary's, Magherafelt 1-10 F.C.J., Bunclody 0-4

1997
Holy Rosary, Mountbellew 2-4 St Mary's, Charleville 1-5

1998
Seamount, Kinvara 3-8 St Mary's, Magherafelt 1-2

1999
St Mary's, Charleville 2-8 Seamount, Kinvara 0-6

2000
Coláiste Bríde, Enniscorthy 3-5 Seamount, Kinvara 0-8

2001
St Mary's, Charleville 7-16 St Mary's, Magherafelt 1-2

2002
St Mary's, Charleville 4-10 Coláiste Bríde, Eniscorthy 4-8

2003
St Mary's, Charleville 9-9 Portumna Community College 0-3

2004
Coláiste Bríde, Enniscorthy 3-10 St Mary's, Magherafelt 1-2

2005
Presentation College, Athenry 3-10 St Mary's, Magherafelt 2-3

2006
St Mary's, Charleville 1-14 Portumna Community College 0-4

2007
Loreto, Kilkenny 0-7 Portumna Community College 0-5

2008
Cross and Passion, Ballycastle 2-8 St. Brigid's, Loughrea 2-5

2009
Loreto, Kilkenny 2-7 St. Patrick's Maghera 0-9

2010
Loreto, Kilkenny 1-16 St. Brigid's. Loughrea 2-7

2011
Loreto, Kilkenny 3-11 St. Patrick's, Maghera 0-7

2012
Loreto, Kilkenny 2-7 Presentation, Kilkenny 3-4
Loreto, Kilkenny 4-9 Presentation, Kilkenny 0-9 (replay)

2013
Loreto, Kilkenny 1-14 St. Brigid's, Loughrea 2-2

2014
St Brendan's, Birr 1-6 St. Mary's, Charleville 2-2

2015
Loreto, Kilkenny 3-11 Presentation, Athenry 2-6

2016
Loreto, Kilkenny 3-7 Coachford College 1-10

2017
Loreto, Kilkenny 3-11 Cross and Passion, Ballycastle 2-9

LADIES FOOTBALL

LADIES FOOTBALL

ALL-IRELAND SENIOR CHAMPIONSHIP FINALS

1974	Tipperary	2-3	2-2	Offaly
1975	Tipperary	1-4	0-0	Galway
1976	Kerry	4-6	1-5	Offaly
1977	Cavan	4-3	2-3	Roscommon
1978	Roscommon	0-5	2-3	Tipperary
1979	Offaly	2-6	3-3	Tipperary
1980	Tipperary	1-1	0-1	Cavan
1981	Offaly	1-11	4-0	Cavan
1982	Kerry	1-8	1-2	Offaly
1983	Kerry	4-6	1-7	Wexford
1984	Kerry	0-5	0-3	Leitrim
1985	Kerry	2-9	0-5	Laois
1986	Kerry	1-10	0-8	Wexford
1987	Kerry	2-10	2-2	Westmeath
1988	Kerry	2-12	3-3	Laois
1989	Kerry	1-13	1-5	Wexford
1990	Kerry	1-9	0-6	Laois
1991	Waterford	5-8	3-7	Laois
1992	Waterford	2-10	3-4	Laois
1993	Kerry	4-8	2-6	Laois
1994	Waterford	2-10	0-12	Monaghan
1995	Waterford	4-4	1-5	Monaghan
1996	Monaghan	2-9	2-9	Laois
Replay	Monaghan	2-11	1-9	Laois
1997	Monaghan	2-15	1-16	Waterford
1998	Waterford	1-16	4-7	Monaghan
Replay	Waterford	2-14	3-8	Monaghan
1999	Mayo	0-12	0-8	Waterford
2000	Mayo	3-6	0-14	Waterford
2001	Laois	2-14	1-16	Mayo
2002	Mayo	0-12	1-8	Monaghan
2003	Mayo	1-4	0-5	Dublin
2004	Galway	3-8	0-11	Dublin
2005	Cork	1-11	0-8	Galway
2006	Cork	1-7	1-6	Armagh
2007	Cork	2-11	2-6	Mayo
2008	Cork	4-13	0-11	Monaghan
2009	Cork	1-9	0-11	Dublin
2010	Dublin	3-16	0-9	Tyrone
2011	Cork	2-7	0-11	Monaghan
2012	Cork	0-16	0-7	Kerry
2013	Cork	1-10	1-9	Monaghan
2014	Cork	2-13	2-12	Dublin
2015	Cork	0-12	0-10	Dublin
2016	Cork	1-7	1-6	Dublin
2017	Dublin	4-11	0-11	Mayo

ALL-IRELAND INTERMEDIATE CHAMPIONSHIP FINALS

2007	Leitrim	0-17	1-10	Wexford
2008	Tipperary	0-14	1-8	Clare
2009	Clare	3-10	1-11	Fermanagh
2010	Donegal	2-12	0-16	Waterford
2011	Westmeath	1-9	1-8	Cavan
2012	Armagh	1-12	1-5	Waterford
2013	Cavan	1-14	1-12	Tipperary
2014	Down	6-16	1-10	Fermanagh
2015	Waterford	3-14	0-10	Kildare
2016	Kildare	1-13	1-12	Clare
2017	Tipperary	1-13	1-10	Tyrone

ALL-IRELAND JUNIOR CHAMPIONSHIP FINALS

1985	Galway	5-7	0-3	Cork
1986	Waterford	4-13	0-0	Wexford
1987	Mayo	4-10	4-7	Wexford
1988	Leitrim	2-8	0-5	London
1989	Dublin	1-8	2-5	Clare
1990	Wicklow	3-3	2-1	London
1991	Clare	0-8	1-2	London
1992	Monaghan	2-8	2-6	London
1993	London	4-8	0-3	Donegal
1994	Meath	5-13	1-3	Donegal
1995	Cork	4-8	3-2	Tyrone
1996	Clare	5-9	4-9	Longford
1997	Longford	2-12	1-11	Tyrone
1998	Louth	4-8	2-9	Roscommon
1999	Tyrone	3-12	2-4	New York
2000	Down	0-14	1-9	Galway
2001	Roscommon	1-18	0-8	Kildare
2002	Galway	2-17	2-7	Donegal
2003	Donegal	3-14	0-12	Kildare
2004	Kildare	2-13	3-5	Sligo
2005	Armagh	0-12	0-9	Sligo
2006	Sligo	0-8	0-4	Leitrim
2007	Kilkenny	3-5	2-5	London
2008	London	5-5	1-11	Derry
2009	Antrim	3-10	2-8	Limerick
2010	Limerick	4-10	3-8	Louth
2011	Wicklow	2-10	0-8	New York
2012	Antrim	3-9	0-7	Louth
2013	Offaly	2-11	0-12	Wexford
2014	Wexford	1-12	1-10	New York
2015	Louth	4-12	0-2	Scotland
2016	Longford	4-10	1-12	Antrim
2017	Fermanagh	3-7	2-10	Derry
Replay	Fermanagh	2-9	0-11	Derry

U18 CHAMPIONSHIP FINALS

1980	Kerry	10-7	2-1	Cavan
1981	Kerry	3-8	2-5	Wexford
1982	Wexford	1-5	0-6	Leitrim
1983	Wexford	5-8	0-1	Leitrim
1984	Wexford	4-4	4-2	Cork
1985	Cork	2-5	2-3	Wexford
1986	Wexford	3-6	1-5	Clare
1987	Mayo	1-8	2-4	Cork
1988	Cork	3-5	0-4	Wexford
1989	Clare	2-11	0-7	Laois
1990	Clare	2-6	0-10	Dublin
1991	Waterford	6-17	1-3	Roscommon
1992	Laois	4-5	2-8	Waterford
1993	Waterford	4-9	1-5	Wexford
1994	Monaghan	1-14	1-14	Wexford
1995	Kerry	4-8	4-3	Wexford
1996	Waterford	4-10	3-9	Mayo
1997	Waterford	4-10	3-9	Mayo
1998	Monaghan	2-12	1-7	Mayo
1999	Monaghan	4-11	3-5	Mayo
2000	Tyrone	1-6	7-12	Waterford
	(Tyrone awarded title as Waterford played 6 subs)			
2001	Waterford	6-12	2-6	Meath
2002	Galway	3-20	4-5	Monaghan
2003	Cork	1-15	3-5	Mayo
2004	Cork	4-17	0-8	Laois
2005	Galway	5-8	1-8	Donegal
2006	Cork	1-22	0-8	Galway
2007	Cork	6-8	2-10	Dublin
2008	Dublin	2-18	1-4	Tyrone
2009	Donegal	5-13	5-5	Clare
2010	Galway	1-15	1-11	Donegal
2011	Cork	5-15	4-11	Dublin
2012	Dublin	3-9	3-7	Tyrone
2013	Galway	3-13	2-14	Dublin
2014	Galway	2-10	1-7	Dublin
2015	Cork	3-10	2-4	Galway
2016	Cork	2-19	4-9	Dublin
2017	Cork	5-11	1-4	Galway

LADIES FOOTBALL

NATIONAL SENIOR LEAGUE FINALS
DIVISION 1

1978	Tipperary	1-5	1-3	Cavan
1979	Tipperary	1-6	0-8	Galway
1980	Kerry	4-8	3-3	Offaly
1981	Kerry	5-4	1-8	Tipperary
1982	Kerry	5-7	2-4	Tipperary
1983	Kerry	1-9	2-6	Leitrim
Replay	Kerry	1-4	0-4	Leitrim
1984	Kerry	2-10	1-7	Laois
1985	Kerry	5-11	0-1	Leitrim
1986	Wexford	3-2	0-6	Laois
1987	Kerry	6-12	1-2	Laois
1988	Kerry	2-8	0-6	Waterford
1989	Kerry	4-9	2-7	Waterford
1990	Kerry	2-11	4-3	Waterford
1991	Kerry	2-12	4-3	Waterford
1992	Waterford	1-8	2-3	Laois
1993	Laois	1-16	1-8	Cork
1994	Monaghan	2-9	1-10	Mayo
1995	Waterford	3-11	4-8	Mayo
Replay	Waterford	2-13	3-8	Mayo
1996	Monaghan	3-16	4-3	Mayo
1997	Monaghan	4-6	1-15	Waterford
Replay	Monaghan	4-15	3-13	Waterford
1998	Waterford	3-10	4-6	Clare
1999	Monaghan	4-6	0-12	Waterford
2000	Mayo	1-11	2-6	Tyrone
2001	Clare	2-10	1-10	Monaghan
2002	Waterford	2-9	1-9	Mayo
2003	Laois	2-10	2-9	Kerry
2004	Mayo	1-13	1-11	Cork
2005	Cork	2-13	0-6	Galway
2006	Cork	0-14	0-2	Meath
2007	Mayo	1-13	0-6	Galway
2008	Cork	6-13	2-10	Kerry
2009	Cork	1-20	0-11	Mayo
2010	Cork	2-10	1-9	Galway
2011	Cork	4-15	3-9	Laois
2012	Monaghan	1-13	2-7	Cork
2013	Cork	0-14	0-7	Mayo
2014	Cork	1-9	2-4	Dublin
2015	Cork	3-8	1-14	Galway
Replay	Cork	0-14	1-10	Galway
2016	Cork	1-10	0-10	Mayo
2017	Cork	2-15	2-14	Donegal

SENIOR CLUB CHAMPIONSHIP WINNERS

1988	Adamstown (Wexford)
1989	Ballymacarbery (Waterford)
1990	Ballymacarbery (Waterford)
1991	Ballymacarbery (Waterford)
1992	Ballymacarbery (Waterford)
1993	Ballymacarbery (Waterford)
1994	Ballymacarbery (Waterford)
1995	Ballymacarbery (Waterford)
1996	Shelmaliers (Wexford)
1997	Ballymacarbery (Waterford)
1998	Ballymacarbery (Waterford)
1999	Shelmaliers (Wexford)
2000	Monaghan Harps
2001	Donoughmore (Cork)
2002	Carnacon (Mayo)
2003	Donoughmore (Cork)
2004	Ballyboden St.Enda's (Dublin)
2005	Ballyboden St. Enda's (Dublin)
2006	Donaghmoyne (Monaghan)
2007	Carnacon (Mayo)
2008	Carnacon (Mayo)
2009	Donaghmoyne (Monaghan)
2010	Inch Rovers (Cork)
2011	Carnacon (Mayo)
2012	Donaghmoyne (Monaghan)
2013	Carnacon (Mayo)
2014	Termon (Donegal)
2015	Donaghmoyne (Monaghan)
2016	Donaghmoyne (Monaghan)

POST-PRIMARY SCHOOLS SENIOR CHAMPIONSHIP FINALS

1985
Ballingeary VS (Cork) 2-1 Adamstown VS (Wexford) 1-1

1986
Mercy Convent, Spanish Pt. (Clare) 1-8
Adamstown VS (Wexford) 2-0

1987
Mercy Convent, Spanish Pt. (Clare) 5-5
Adamstown VS (Wexford) 0-7

1988
Presentation Convent, Portlaoise 2-4
Mercy Convent, Spanish Pt. 2-3

1989
Mercy Convent, Castlerea (Roscommon) 4-2
Tarbert Como. (Kerry) 1-5

1990
Ramsgrange CS (Wexford) 1-6 Tarbert Como. (Kerry) 1-5

1991
Ballinrobe CS (Mayo) 4-8 Salesian Convent (Clare) 2-8

1992
Ballinrobe CS (Mayo) 2-7 Cahercon CS (Clare) 1-8

1993
Ballinrobe CS (Mayo) 3-13 Bridgetown CS (Wexford) 1-7

1994
Ballinrobe CS (Mayo) 2-10 Col. Bride, Enniscorthy (Wexford) 2-6

1995
Ballinrobe CS (Mayo) 2-18 St Joseph's, Spanish Pt. (Clare) 2-4

1996
St. Joseph's, Spanish Pt. (Clare) 2-9 St. Michael's, Navan (Meath) 1-5

1997
St. Joseph's Spanish Pt. (Clare) 3-11
Scoil Mhuire, Tourmakeady (Mayo) 1-11

1998
Intermediate School, Killorglin (Kerry) 4-10
Eureka, Kells (Meath) 0-6

1999
St. John Bosco, Caherciveen (Kerry) 2-11 St. Leo's (Carlow) 1-8.

2000
St.Louis (Monaghan) 2-8 Killorglin (Kerry) 1-9.

2001
Colaiste na Sceilige (Kerry) 4-15
Colaiste Mhuire Tourmakeady (Mayo) 0-7

2002
Colaiste na Sceilige (Kerry) 2-13
St Michael's Loreto Navan (Meath) 0-11

2003
Presentation Tuam (Galway) 4-10
Colaiste na Sceilige (Kerry) 2-10

2004
St.Louis (Monaghan) 5-11 Presentation Tuam (Galway) 4-4

2005
St.Louis (Monaghan) 3-19 Colaiste na Sceilige (Kerry) 4-13

2006
St. Louis (Monaghan) 4-08 St Leo's (Carlow) 2-6

2007
St. Leo's (Carlow) 3-09 Loretto SS Fermoy (Cork) 2-10

2008
St Mary's Mallow (Cork) 0-14 St Louis (Monaghan) 1-9

2009
Convent of Mercy (Roscommon) 4-10 Loreto College (Fermoy) 2-7

2010
St. Leo's College, Carlow 3-7 Loreto Grammar School, Omagh 2-9

2011
St. Leo's Coll., Carlow 3-13 Coláiste Na Sceilige, Cahirciveen 1-2

2012
Loreto Grammar, Omagh 1-19 Coláiste Ide agus Iosef 2-12

2013
Loreto Fermoy 4-11 Presentation Athenry 1-7

2014
Coláiste Íosagáin, Stillorgan 2-9 Coláiste Dun Iascaigh, Cahir 2-5

2015
Glenamaddy CS 4-5 Coláiste Dún Iascaigh, Cahir 3-7

2016
Scoil Mhuire, Carrick-on-Suir 4-16 Coláiste Íosagáin, Stillorgan 2-8

2017
John the Baptist CS, Limerick 2-6 St Ciaran's Ballygawley, Tyrone 0-8

INTERPROVINCIAL CHAMPIONSHIP FINALS

1976	Munster	1-12	0-2	Leinster
1977	Munster	3-5	1-3	Connacht
1978	Connacht	1-8	1-5	Leinster
1979	Connacht	1-4	1-0	Leinster
1980	Munster	5-6	3-9	Leinster
1981	Munster	6-7	1-1	Ulster
1982	Leinster	1-8	1-6	Munster
1983	Leinster	1-9	0-3	Munster
1984	Munster	4-9	0-6	Connacht
1985	Munster	1-6	0-6	Leinster
1986	Munster	3-7	1-5	Leinster
1987	Munster	2-10	0-7	Leinster
1988	Munster	2-10	0-4	Leinster
1989	Leinster	2-8	1-8	Connacht
1990	Leinster	1-3	0-4	Munster
1991	Munster	4-11	3-3	Leinster
1992	Leinster	2-8	1-9	Munster
1993	Munster	3-8	1-5	Leinster
1994	Leinster	3-7	0-4	Munster
1995	Munster	2-11	1-9	Leinster
1996	Munster	4-8	0-9	Colleges
1997	Connacht	1-10	0-11	Colleges
1998	Leinster	3-14	0-12	Connacht
2000	Connacht	2-13	1-11	Leinster
2001	No Competition due to foot & mouth disease			
2002	Ulster	0-19	2-8	Connacht
2003	Munster	2-11	2-4	Ulster
2004	Munster	1-16	1-7	Leinster
2005	Leinster	1-11	2-6	Munster
2006	Leinster	2-12	0-09	Ulster
2007	Munster	2-13	2-11	Ulster
2008	Ulster	6-10	1-11	Munster
2009	Munster	2-6	0-8	Leinster
2010	Ulster	1-14	1-6	Leinster
2011	Munster	2-1	1-3	Ulster
2012	Ulster	0-15	1-9	Munster
2013	Ulster	1-10	1-8	Connacht
2014	Ulster	2-8	2-7	Connacht
2015	Ulster	5-11	5-8	Connacht
2016	Ulster	4-7	0-11	Connacht
2017	Ulster	1-15	1-11	Munster

HANDBALL

343

HANDBALL

ALL-IRELAND 40X20 CHAMPIONSHIPS

SENIOR SINGLES

1975	P.Kirby (Clare)
1976	P.Kirby (Clare)
1977	P.Kirby (Clare)
1978	P.Kirby (Clare)
1979	P.Kirby (Clare)
1980	P.Kirby (Clare)
1981	T.Ryan (Tipperary)
1982	T.Ryan (Tipperary}
1983	T.Ryan (Tipperary)
1984	M.Hennigan (Mayo)
1985	M.Hennigan (Mayo)
1986	Michael Walsh (Kilkenny)
1987	Mickey Walsh (Roscommon)
1988	M.Walsh (Kilkenny)
1989	M.Walsh (Kilkenny)
1990	M.Walsh (Kilkenny)
1991	M.Walsh (Kilkenny)
1992	W.O'Connor (Meath)
1993	E.Corbett (Tipperary)
1994	E.Corbett (Tipperary)
1995	P.McAuley (Louth)
1996	M.Walsh (Kilkenny)
1997	P.McAuley (Louth)
1998	M.Walsh (Kilkenny)
1999	T.Healy (Cork)
2000	T .Healy (Cork)
2001	T.Healy (Cork)
2002	E.Kennedy (Dublin)
2003	P.Brady (Cavan)
2004	T.Healy (Cork)
2005	P.Brady (Cavan)
2006	P.Brady (Cavan)
2007	P.Brady (Cavan)
2008	P.Brady (Cavan)
2009	P.Brady (Cavan)
2010	P.Brady (Cavan)
2011	P.Brady (Cavan)
2012	P.Brady (Cavan)
2013	P.Brady (Cavan)
2014	R.McCarthy (Westmeath)
2015	R.McCarthy (Westmeath)
2016	R.McCarthy (Westmeath)
2017	C.Shanks (Armagh

SENIOR DOUBLES

1975	P. and M.Kirby (Clare)
1976	P. and M.Kirby (Clare)
1977	P. and M.Kirby (Clare)
1978	P. and M.Kirby (Clare)
1979	P. and M.Kirby (Clare)
1980	P.McGee and P.McCormack (Mayo)
1981	P.Delaney and W.Mullins (Offaly)
1982	J.Fleming and P.Cleary (Wexford)
1983	J.Fleming and P.Cleary (Wexford)
1984	J.Fleming and P.Cleary (Wexford)
1985	E.Rabbitt and P.Delaney (Galway)
1986	M.Walsh and M.Reade (Kilkenny)
1987	T.Sheridan and J.McGovern (Meath)
1988	T.Sheridan and J.McGovern (Meath)
1989	M.Walsh and M.Reade (Kilkenny)
1990	T.Sheridan and J.McGovern (Meath)
1991	E.Corbett and J.O'Donoghue (Tipperary)
1992	T.Sheridan and J.McGovern (Meath)
1993	T.Sheridan and J.McGovern (Meath)
1994	M.Walsh and D.J.Carey (Kilkenny)
1995	M..Walsh and D.J.Carey (Kilkenny)
1996	T.Sheridan and E.Jensen (Meath)
1997	T.Sheridan and E.Jensen (Meath)
1998	M.Walsh and D.J.Carey (Kilkenny)
1999	T.Healy and J.Herlihy (Cork)
2000	T.Sheridan and W.O'Connor (Meath)
2001	T.Healy and S.Palmer (Cork)
2002	T.Sheridan and W.O'Connor (Meath)
2003	P .Brady and M.Finnegan (Cavan)
2004	P.Brady and M.Finnegan (Cavan)
2005	E .Kennedy and E.Jensen (Dublin)
2006	P.Brady and M.Finnegan (Cavan)
2007	P.Brady and M.Finnegan (Cavan)
2008	P.Brady and M.Finnegan (Cavan)
2009	J.McCann and D.Keegan (Mayo)
2010	P.Brady and M.Finnegan (Cavan)
2011	P.Brady and M.Finnegan (Cavan)
2012	P.Brady and M.Finnegan (Cavan)
2013	P.Brady and M.Finnegan (Cavan)
2014	P.Brady and M.Finnegan (Cavan)
2015	B.Carroll & T.Sheridan (Meath)
2016	E.Kennedy & C.Browne (Dublin)
2017	P.Brady and M.Finnegan (Cavan)

JUNIOR SINGLES

1975	P.O'Keeffe (Tipperary)
1976	M.Walsh {Roscommon)
1977	P.Morris (Cork)
1978	P.Delaney (Offaly)
1979	Tony Ryan (Tipperary)
1980	G.O'Callaghan (Cork)
1981	J.Fleming (Wexford)
1982	G.Coughlan (Clare)
1983	E.Conneely (Galway)
1984	W.Bourke (Kilkenny)
1985	M.Walsh (Kilkenny)
1986	J.Herlihy (Cork)
1987	P.McAuley (Louth)
1988	W.Silcock (Antrim)
1989	E.Jenson (Meath)
1990	D.J.Carey (Kilkenny)
1991	F.McCann (Sligo)
1992	J.Donlan (Clare)
1993	P.Crothers (Antrim)
1994	D.Moloney (Tipperary)
1995	J.O'Dwyer (Tipperary)
1996	R.Breen (Wexford)
1997	D.Lynch (Kerry)
1998	G.Buggy (Wexford)
1999	J.King (Carlow)
2000	T.Savage (Down)
2001	S.Dormer (Laois)
2002	D.Frawley (Clare)
2003	C.O'Brien (Offaly)
2004	O.Cassidy (Mayo)
2005	E.Burke (Kilkenny)
2006	P.Donovan (Laois)
2007	S.O'Neill (Tyrone)
2008	R.Kelly (Tyrone)
2009	C.Doolin (Roscommon)
2010	D.Hope (Offaly)
2011	P.Lambert (Wexford)
2012	C.Hannon (Clare)
2013	W.Love (Kilkenny)
2014	T.Carroll (Cork)
2015	C.McElduff (Tyrone)
2016	D.Walsh (Waterford)
2017	G.Coyle (Monaghan)

JUNIOR DOUBLES

1975	T.Morrissey and E.Farrell (Tipperary)
1976	P.Kealy and W.Mullins (Offaly)
1977	G.Scully and M.Ward (Galway)
1978	M.Aherne and B.O'Brien (Kerry)
1979	E.Rabbitte and J.Callinan (Galway)
1980	M.Hennigan and M.Sweeney (Mayo)
1981	J.Fleming and P.Cleary (Wexford)
1982	G.Coughlan and J.Duggan (Clare)
1983	J.McGovern and M.McGovern (Meath)
1984	W.Bourke and M.Reade {Kilkenny)
1985	P.Hall and D.O'Brien (Dublin)
1986	T.Quish and J.Quish (Limerick)
1987	P.McAuley and M.Maher (Louth)
1988	N.Breen and P.Devanney (RIP) (Clare)
1989	W.Pratt and P.O'Keeffe (Kilkenny)
1990	E.Corbett and J.O'Donoghue (Tipperary)
1991	R.McCarthy and J.Guilfoyle (Westmeath)
1992	J.Donlan and P.Walsh (Clare)
1993	P.Crothers and J.McGarry (Antrim)
1994	D.Moloney and N.Murphy (Tipperary)
1995	F.Coughlan and D.Kirby (Clare)
1996	R.Breen and B.Doyle (Wexford)
1997	D.and A.Lynch (Kerry)
1998	C.and N.Kerr (Tyrone)
1999	P.Madden and P.Coughlan (Clare)
2000	A.Kenny and I.Griffin (Dublin)
2001	A.O'Donnell and M.Tormey (Roscommon)
2002	P .Graham and P.Duffy (Antrim)
2003	D.Kelly and M.Carroll (Tipperary)
2004	P.Conway and O.Conway (Galway)
2005	T.Clifford and M.Clifford (Kilkenny)
2006	B.and.F Manogue (Kilkenny
2007	M.Lennon and P.Quaile (Wicklow)
2008	N.McDermott and N.McGrath (Roscommon)
2009	C.Doolin and A.Cunningham (Roscommon)
2010	J.Brady and P.Clerkin (Cavan)
2011	P.Hughes and P.Lambert (Wexford)
2012	P.Moran and N.O'Connor (Kildare)
2013	S.Hedigan and D.O'Dea (Cork)
2014	C.Neary and B.Burke (Kilkenny)
2015	J.Willoughby & K.Kavanagh (Wicklow)
2016	O.Ryan & D.Fenlon (Carlow)
2017	J.Cummins & P.Reilly (Meath)

MINOR SINGLES

1975	M.Maher (Louth)
1976	M.Maher (Louth)
1977	T.Ryan (Tipperary)
1978	T.Ryan (Tipperary)
1979	W.O'Donnell (Tipperary)
1980	W.Bourke (Kilkenny}
1981	W.Bourke (Kilkenny}
1982	J.Duggan (Clare)
1983	M.Walsh (Kilkenny)
1984	M.Walsh (Kilkenny)
1985	W.O'Connor (Meath)
1986	P.McAuley (Louth)
1987	P.McAuley (Louth)
1988	D.J.Carey (Kilkenny)
1989	D.J.Carey (Kilkenny)
1990	P.Walsh (Clare)
1991	C.Curran (Tyrone)
1992	M.Finnegan (Cavan)
1993	M.Finnegan (Cavan)
1994	M.Finnegan (Cavan)
1995	T.Healy (Cork)
1996	T.Healy (Cork)
1997	K.Kane (Carlow)
1998	P.Brady (Cavan)
1999	Keegan (Mayo)
2000	P.Finnegan (Cavan)
2001	C.Shanks (Armagh)
2002	N.McHugh (Galway)
2003	B.Carroll (Meath)
2004	R.McCarthy (Westmeath)
2005	R.McCarthy (Westmeath)
2006	R.Hogan (Kilkenny)
2007	S.O'Carroll (Limerick)
2008	G.McConnell (Meath)
2009	C.Daly (Tyrone)
2010	M.Mulkerrins (Galway)
2011	K.Carroll (Cork)
2012	D.Wrynn (Leitrim)
2013	C.Crehan (Clare)
2014	J.Woods (Tyrone)
2015	N.Joyce (Mayo)
2016	S.Kerr (Tyrone)
2017	T.O'Neill (Cork)

MINOR DOUBLES

1975	P.Delaney and S.O'Connell (Offaly)
1976	P.Murphy and D.Neff (Cork)
1977	T.Ryan and G.Walsh (Tipperary)
1978	T.Ryan and M.Dyer (Tipperary)
1979	M.Cantwell and W.Bourke (Kilkenny)
1980	W.Bourke and M.Lawlor (Kilkenny)
1981	W.Bourke and M.Lawlor (Kilkenny)
1982	J.Duggan and P.Clavin (Clare
1983	J.Duggan and P.Clavin (Clore)
1984	M.Walsh and P.O'Keeffe (Kilkenny)
1985	W.O'Connor and T.Sheridan (Meath)
1986	P.McAuley and J.McArdle (Louth)
1987	D.Gough and P.O'Rourke (Meath)
1988	D.J.Carey and E.Law (Kilkenny)
1989	D.J.Carey and E.Law (Kilkenny)
1990	D.King and S.Kavanagh (Carlow)
1991	D.Moloney and N.Murphy (Tipperary)
1992	M.Finnegan and D.Bartley (Cavan)
1993	M.Finnegan and R.Cunningham (Cavan)
1994	M.Finnegan and C.McDonnell (Cavan)
1995	T.and J.Healy (Cork)
1996	T.and J.Healy (Cork)
1997	B.Goff and C.Keeling (Wexford)
1998	E.and B.Kennedy (Dublin)
1999	D.Keegan and B.Hough (Mayo)
2000	M.Gregan and R.Willoughby (Wicklow)
2001	J.McCann and J.Kilcullen (Mayo)
2002	N.McHugh and T.Connaughton (Galway)
2003	D.Martin and R.O'Gara (Roscommon)
2004	R.McCarthy and J.O'Shaughnessy (Westmeath)
2005	R.McCarthy and C.Curley (Westmeath)
2006	R.Hogan and N.Anthony (Kilkenny)
2007	D.Nash and N.Malone (Clare)
2008	S.Ó Carroll and C.J.Fitzpatrick (Limerick)
2009	S.Cooney and I.McLoughlin (Mayo)
2010	P.O'Carrill and E.Davern (Limerick)
2011	K.Carroll and P.Herlihy (Cork)
2012	C.Crehan and N.Bolton (Clare)
2013	C.Crehan and B.Nash (Clare)
2014	J. Woods and R. Mullen (Tyrone)
2015	D.Kavanagh & K.Armstrong (Wexford)
2016	T.O'Neill & D.Walsh (Cork)
2017	T.O'Neill & D.Walsh (Cork)

INTERMEDIATE 40X20 SINGLES

1995	C.Curran (Tyrone)
1996	G.Sweeney (Mayo)
1997	M.Finnegan (Cavan)
1998	T.Healy (Cork)
1999	P.Brady (Cavan)
2000	S.Palmer (Cork)
2001	R.McCann (Antrim)
2002	D.Keegan (Mayo)
2003	B.Goff (Wexford)
2004	C.Shanks (Armagh)
2005	M.Gregan (Wicklow)
2006	R.McCarthy (Westmeath)
2007	B.Carroll (Meath)
2008	G.Buggy (Wexford)
2009	O.McKenna (Antrim)
2010	S.O'Carroll (Limerick)
2011	D.Nash (Clare)
2012	M.Mulkerrins (Galway)
2013	N.O'Connor (Kildare)
2014	Peter Funchion (Kilkenny)
2015	C.Crehan (Clare)
2016	C.McElduff (Tyrone)
2017	T.Carroll (Cork)

INTERMEDIATE 40 X 20 DOUBLES

1995	J.McAlister and S.Madden (Antrim)
1996	T.Hynes and N.Buggy (Wexford)
1997	M.Finnegan and R.Cunningham (Cavan)
1998	K.and T.Kane (Carlow)
1999	D.and A.Lynch (Kerry)
2000	S.Devine and S.O'Tuama (Antrim)
2001	J.Ryan and D.King (Carlow)
2002	D.Keegan and P.Gaffney (Mayo)
2003	C.Brennan and V.Moran (Mayo)
2004	C.Shanks and J.Doyle (Armagh)
2005	M.Gregan and J.Willoughby (Wicklow)
2006	D.Martin and R.O'Gara (Roscommon)
2007	D.Daly and N.Kerr (Tyrone)
2008	C.Jordon and P.Buckley (Cork)
2009	T.Clifford and M.Clifford (Kilkenny)
2010	S.O'Carroll and C.J.Fitzpatrick (Limerick)
2011	D.Nash and N.Malone (Clare)
2012	B.Fleming and K.Carroll (Cork)
2013	G.Coonan and F.Collins (Tipperary)
2014	Patrick and Peter Funchion (Kilkenny)
2015	O.Conway & P.Conway (Galway)
2016	J.Woods & C.McElduff (Tyrone)
2017	S.Kerr & S.O'Neill (Tyrone)

U21 40 X 20 SINGLES

1980	T.Ryan (Tipperary)
1981	T.Ryan (Tipperary)
1982	G.Coughlan (Clare)
1983	P.Hall 1Dublin)
1984	P.Hall (Dublin)
1985	E.Jensen (Meath)
1986	E.Jensen (Meath)
1987	E.Corbett (Tipperary)
1988	J.Ryan (Carlow)
1989	D.Gough (Meath)
1990	S.Palmer (Cork)
1991	J.McKeon (Cavan)
1992	A.Benson (Dublin)
1993	D.Moloney Tipperary}
1994	R.Cunningham (Cavan)
1995	M.Finnegan (Cavan)
1996	S.Devine (Antrim)
1997	J.Doyle (Wexford)
1998	R.McCann (Antrim)
1999	P.Buckley (Cork)
2000	C.Browne (Meath)
2001	P.Finnegan (Cavan)
2002	M.Gregan (Wicklow)
2003	J.McCann (Mayo)
2004	J.Willoughby (Wicklow)
2005	G.Coonan (Tipperary)
2006	D.Daly (Tyrone)
2007	G.McCrory (Tyrone)
2008	P.McGlinchey (Tyrone)
2009	C.J.Fitzpatrick (Limerick)
2010	F.Collins (Tipperary)
2011	F.Collins (Tipperary)
2012	P.Funchion (Kilkenny)
2013	M.Mulkerrins (Galway)
2014	M.Mulkerrins (Galway)
2015	D.Doherty (Monaghan)
2016	C.Crehan (Clare)
2017	C.Corbett (Clare)

HANDBALL

U21 40 X 20 DOUBLES

1980	P.Cleary and J.Fleming (Wexford)
1981	T.Ryan and W.O'Donnell (Tipperary)
1982	G.Coughlan and J.Duggan (Clare)
1983	J.Herlihy and N.Collins (Cork)
1984	P.Hall and D.O'Brien (Dublin)
1985	J.Kelly and P.Clooney (Cork)
1986	J.O'Donoghue and E.Corbett (Tipperary}
1987	P.O'Keeffe and P.Maher (Kilkenny)
1988	P.O'Keeffe and T.Donegan (Cork)
1989	D.Gough and J.Lynch (Meath)
1990	D.Gough and J.Lynch (Meath)
1991	G.O'Brien and E.Law (Kilkenny)
1992	D.Moloney and N.Murphy (Tipperaryl
1993	D.Moloney and N.Murphy (Tipperary}
1994	G.Kelleher and B.O'Neill (Cork)
1995	M.Finnegan and D.Leggett (Cavan)
1996	S.Devine and S.Ó Tuama (Antrim)
1997	J.Doyle and J.Bergin (Wexford)
1998	C.Jordan and J.Healy (Cork)
1999	B.and A.Marrinan (Clare)
2000	C.Browne and J.Cummins (Meath)
2001	B.Fleming and N.Fleming (Cork)
2002	M.Gregan and S.Willoughby (Wicklow)
2003	O.McKenna and K.Holmes (Antrim)
2004	C.Smyth and M.Cash (Wexford)
2005	M.McGowan and M.Marley (Donegal)
2006	D.Daly and G.McCrory (Tyrone)
2007	J.and C.Cooney (Clare)
2008	C.Hannon and C.Cooney (Clare)
2009	S.O'Carroll and C.J.Fitzpatrick (Limerick)
2010	S.Cooney and I.McLoughlin (Mayo)
2011	Peter and Patrick Funchion (Kilkenny)
2012	Peter and Patrick Funchion (Kilkenny)
2013	K.Carroll and P.Herlihy (Cork)
2014	M.Hedigan and D.Relihan (Cork)
2015	C.Corbett & N.Bolton (Clare)
2016	D.Relihan & M.Hedigan (Cork)
2017	J.Wood & R.Mullan (Tyrone)

IRISH NATIONALS

MEN'S SINGLES

1995	D.Chapman (California)
1996	M.Walsh (Kilkenny)
1997	P.McAuley (Louth)
1998	D.Chapman (California)
1999	J.Bike (California)
2000	T.Healy (Cork)
2001	K.Kane (Carlow)
2002	E.Kennedy (Dublin)
2003	E.Kennedy (Dublin)
2004	E.Kennedy (Dublin)
2005	P.Brady (Cavan)
2006	T.Healy (Cork)
2007	T.Healy (Cork)
2008	T.Healy (Cork)
2009	P.Brady (Cavan)
2010	P.Brady (Cavan)
2011	R.McCarthy (Westmeath)
2012	R.McCarthy (Westmeath)
2013	D.Nash (Clare)
2014	K. Carroll (Cork)
2015	No Competition
2016	C.Shanks (Armagh)

UNIVERSITIES CHAMPIONSHIPS

TEAM COMPETITION

1963	U.C.D.
1964	U.C.G.
1965	U.C.D.
1966	U.C.D.
1967	U.C.D.
1968	U.C.D.
1969	U.C.D.
1970	U.C.C.
1971	U.C.G.
1972	U.C.G.
1973	U.C.G.
1974	U.C.D.
1975	U.C.C.
1976	U.C.D.
1977	U.C.D.
1978	U.C.C.
1979	U.C.G.
1980	Q.U.B.
1981	U.C.G.
1982	U.C.G.
1983	U.C.G.
1984	U.C.G.
1985	U.C.G.
1986	U.C.G.
1987	U.C.D.
1988	U.C.G.
1989	U.C.G.
1990	U.C.G.
1991	U.C.G.
1992	U.C.G.
1993	Waterford R.T.C.
1994	U.C.D.
1995	Q.U.B.
1996	U.C.C.
1997	D.I.T.
1998	N.U.I.G.
1999	U.U.J.
2000	D.I.T.
2001	D.I.T.
2002	D.I.T.
2003	Q.U.B.
2004	S.I.T.

2005	D.I.T.
2006	D.I.T.
2007	N.U.I.G.
2008	U.U.J.
2009	U.U.J.
2010	U.U.J.
2011	U.C.D.
2012	W.I.T.
2013	U.L.
2014	U.L.
2015	UCD
2016	DCU
2017	No Competition

MEN'S SINGLES

1975	P.Morris (UCC)
1976	C.Quinn (UCD)
1977	C.Quinn (UCD)
1978	P.Morris (UCC)
1979	M.Shiel (UCG)
1980	M.Patterson (TCD)
1981	G.Coughlan (UCG)
1982	G.Coughlan (UCG)
1983	G.Coughlan (UCG)
1984	J.Duggan (UCG)
1985	J.Duggan (UCG)
1986	J.Duggan (UCG)
1987	E.Jensen (UCD)
1988	E.Jensen (UCD)
1989	W.O'Connor (Dame St.)
1990	W.O'Connor (Dame St.)
1991	E.O'Neill (Garda)
1992	A.Benson (UCD)
1993	C.Curran (St.Mary's)
1994	C.Curran (QUB)
1995	C.Curran (QUB)
1996	C.Curran (QUB)
1997	T.Healy (UCC)
1998	P.Brady (DIT)
1999	T.Healy (UCC)
2000	P.Brady (DIT)
2001	E.Kennedy (DCU)
2002	E.Kennedy (DCU)

HANDBALL

2003	E.Kennedy (DCU)
2004	E.Kennedy (DCU)
2005	D.Keegan (DIT)
2006	C.Shanks (QUB)
2007	G.Coonan (UL)
2008	B.Carroll (DIT)
2009	B.Carroll (DIT)
2010	S.O'Carroll (LIT)
2011	D.Nash (NUIG)
2012	S.O'Carroll (LIT)
2013	M.Mulkerrins (UCD)
2014	M.Mulkerrins (UCD)
2015	M.Mulkerrins (UCD)
2016	K.Armstrong (NUIM)
2017	S.Dunne (ITT)

60 X 30 MEN'S SINGLES

2002	N.McHugh (SIT)
2003	N.McHugh (SIT)
2004	B.Carroll (DIT)
2005	J.McCann (SIT)
2006	G.Coonan (UL)
2007	R.O'Gara (NUIG)
2008	N.Anthony (WIT)
2009	N.Anthony (WIT)
2010	N.Anthony (WIT)
2011	F.Collins (ITT)
2012	M.Mulkerrins (UCD)
2013	C.Neary (Institute of Banking)
2014	C.Quish (UL)
2015	M.Mulkerrins (UCD)
2016	M.Mulkerrins (UCD)
2017	M.Mulkerrins (UCD)

ALL-IRELAND CHAMPIONSHIPS

SENIOR SOFTBALL SINGLES

1925   M.Joyce (Dublin)
1926   T.Behan (Kilkenny)
1927   W.McGuire (Dublin)
1928   J.McNally (Mayo)
1929   D.Brennan (Kilkenny)
1930   P.Perry (Roscommon}
1931   P.Perry (Roscommon)
1932   P.Perry (Roscommon)
1933   P.Perry (Roscommon)
1934   P.Perry (Roscommon)
1935   P.Perry (Roscommon)
1936   P.Perry (Roscommon)
1937   P.Perry (Roscommon)
1938   J.J.Gilmartin (Kilkenny)
1939   J.J.Gilmartin (Kilkenny)
1940   M.Walsh (Galway)
1941   J.Dunne (Kilkenny)
1942-1945 Suspended due to scarcity of softballs
1946   J.J.Gilmartin (Kilkenny)
1947   L.Rowe (Dublin)
1948   J.Bergin (Tipperary)
1949   L.Rowe (Dublin)
1950   J.Bergin (Tipperary)
1951   L.Rowe (Dublin)
1952   J.Ryan (Wexford)
1953   M.Griffin (Cork)
1954   J.Ryan (Wexford)
1955   J.Ryan (Wexford)
1956   J.Ryan (Wexford)
1957   J.Ryan (Wexford)
1958   P.Downey (Kerry)
1959   F.Confrey (Louth)
1960   F.Confrey (Louth)
1961   P.Downey (Kerry)
1962   J.Delaney (Kilkenny)
1963   J.Maher (Louth)
1964   J.Maher (Louth)
1965   R.Lyng (Wexford)
1966   S.McCabe (Monaghan)
1967   S.McCabe (Monaghan)
1968   J.Maher (Louth)
1969   J.Maher {Louth)
1970   J.Maher (Louth)
1971   R.Lyng (Wexford)
1972   P.Murphy (Wexford)

1973   J.Maher (Louth)
1974   P .Kirby (Clare)
1975   P.Kirby (Clare)
1976   P.Kirby (Clare)
1977   P.Kirby (Clare)
1978   R.Lyng (Wexford)
1979   T.O'Rourke (Kildare)
1980   P.Ryan (Dublin)
1981   P.Reilly (Kilkenny)
1982   O.Harold (Kilkenny)
1983   A.Ryan (Tipperary)
1984   T.O'Rourke (Kildare)
1985   M.Walsh (Kilkenny)
1986   M.Walsh (Kilkenny)
1987   M.Walsh (Kilkenny)
1988   M.Walsh (Kilkenny)
1989   M.Walsh (Kilkenny)
1990   M.Walsh (Kilkenny)
1991   M.Walsh (Kilkenny)
1992   M.Walsh (Kilkenny)
1993   M.Walsh (Kilkenny}
1994   M.Walsh (Kilkenny)
1995   M.Walsh (Kilkenny)
1996   M.Walsh (Kilkenny)
1997   M.Walsh (Kilkenny)
1998   W.O'Connor (Meath)
1999   M.Walsh (Kilkenny)
2000   M.Walsh (Kilkenny)
2001   M.Walsh (Kilkenny)
2002   E.Kennedy (Dublin)
2003   T.Sheridan (Meath)
2004   E.Kennedy (Dublin)
2005   E.Kennedy (Dublin)
2006   E.Kennedy (Dublin)
2007   E.Kennedy (Dublin)
2008   E.Kennedy (Dublin)
2009   E.Kennedy (Dublin)
2010   E.Kennedy (Dublin)
2011   R.McCarthy (Westmeath)
2012   R.McCarthy (Westmeath)
2013   R.McCarthy (Westmeath)
2014   E.Kennedy (Dublin)
2015   R.McCarthy (Westmeath)
2016   R.McCarthy (Westmeath)
2017   R.McCarthy (Westmeath)

SENIOR SOFTBALL DOUBLES

1925	T.Behan and J.Norton (Kilkenny)
1926	J.Whyte and G.Barrett (Galway}
1927	M.Joyce and C.Ryan (Dublin)
1928	J.Flavin and M.Battersby (Waterford)
1929	D.Brennan and J.Lucas (Kilkenny)
1930	M.O'Neill and L.Sherry (Wicklow)
1931	M.O'Neill and L.Sherry (Wicklow}
1932	P.Perry and A.Mullaney (Roscommon)
1933	P.Perry and A.Mullaney (Roscommon)
1934	J.Hassett and E.Hassett (Tipperary)
1935	J.Hassett and E.Hassett (Tipperary)
1936	J.Hassett and E.Hassett (Tipperary)
1937	J.Hassett and E.HasseH (Tipperary}
1938	J.Hassett and E.Hassett (Tipperary)
1939	J.J.Gilmartin and J.Dunne (Kilkenny)
1940	J.J.Gilmartin and J.Dunne (Kilkenny)
1941	J.J.Gilmartin and J.Dunne (Kilkenny)
1942	J.Collins and C.Collins (Tipperary)
1943-1945	Suspended
1946	L.Rowe and G.Rowe (Dublin)
1947	J.Bergin and J.O'Rourke (Sligo)
1948	L.Rowe and G.Rowe (Dublin)
1949	J.Bergin and J.Sweeney (Tipperary)
1950	J.Bergin and J.Sweeney (Tipperary)
1951	J.Hassett and J.O'Brien (Kerry)
1952	J.Hassett and J.O'Brien (Kerry}
1953	M.Griffin and W.Walsh (Cork)
1954	C.Delaney and J.Dunne (Kilkenny)
1955	P.Downey and J.O'Brien (Kerry)
1956	P.Downey and J.O'Brien {Kerry)
1957	J.Ryan and J.Doyle (Wexford)
1958	T.McGarry and M.Mullins (Limerick)
1959	T.McGarry and M.Mullins (Limerick)
1960	P.Downey and J.O'Brien (Kerry)
1961	P.Downey and J.O'Brien (Kerry)
1962	P.Downey and J.O'Brien (Kerry)
1963	P.Downey and J.O'Brien (Kerry)
1964	P.Downey and J.O'Brien (Kerry)
1965	J.Delaney and T.Ryan (Kilkenny)
1966	M.Walsh and P.McGee (Mayo)
1967	L.Molloy and D.McGovern (Meath)
1968	T.McEllistrim and M.McEllistrim (Kerry)
1969	P.Lee and J.Cleary (Wicklow)
1970	R.Lyng and S.Buggy (Wexford)
1971	T.McEllistrim and M.McEllistrim (Kerry)
1972	P.Murphy and J.Quigley (Wexford)
1973	M.McEllistrim and N.Kerins (Kerry)
1974	P.Murphy and J.Quigley (Wexford)
1975	R.Lyng and P.Murphy (Wexford)
1976	M.Hogan and P.McGarry (Limerick)
1977	R.Lyng and S.Buggy (Wexford)
1978	D.Kirby and J.Kirby (Clare)
1979	R.Lyng and S.Buggy (Wexford)
1980	P.Reilly and O.Harold (Kilkenny)
1981	A.Greene and P.Hughes (Kilkenny)
1982	R.Lyng and J.Goggins (Wexford)
1983	T.and J.Quish (Limerick)
1984	T.and J.Quish (Limerick)
1985	M.Walsh and E.Downey
1986	T.and J.Quish (Limerick)
1987	M.Walsh and E.Downey
1988	M.Walsh and E.Downey
1989	M.Walsh and E.Downey
1990	M.Walsh and E.Downey
1991	M.Walsh and E.Downey
1992	T.Sheridan and J.McGovern (Meath)
1993	M.Walsh and E.Downey (Kilkenny)
1994	T.Sheridan and J.McGovern (Meath)
1995	M.Walsh and E.Downey (Kilkenny)
1996	M.Walsh and E.Downey (Kilkenny)
1997	M.Walsh and E.Downey (Kilkenny)
1998	T.Sheridan and W.O'Connor (Meath)
1999	T.Sheridan and W.O'Connor (Meath)
2000	T.Hynes and C.Keeling (Wexford)
2001	T.Sheridan and W.O'Connor (Meath)
2002	T.Sheridan and W.O'Connor (Meath)
2003	T.Sheridan and W.O'Connor (Meath)
2004	T.Sheridan and W.O'Connor (Meath)
2005	E.Kennedy and E.Jensen (Dublin)
2006	E.Kennedy and E.Jensen (Dublin)
2007	E.Kennedy and E.Jensen (Dublin)
2008	T.Sheridan and B.Carroll (Meath)
2009	E.Kennedy and E.Jensen (Dublin)
2010	T.Sheridan and B.Carroll (Meath)
2011	B.Goff and C.Keeling (Wexford)
2012	T.Sheridan and B.Carroll (Meath)
2013	T.Sheridan and B.Carroll (Meath)
2014	E.Kennedy and C.Browne (Dublin)
2015	E.Kennedy & C.Browne (Dublin)
2016	B.Carroll & T.Sheridan (Meath)
2017	B.Carroll & T.Sheridan (Meath)

SENIOR HARDBALL SINGLES

1925	W.Aldridge (Kildare)
1926	T.Soye (Dublin)
1927	T.Soye (Dublin)
1928	T.Soye (Dublin)
1929	T.Soye (Dublin)
1930	T.Soye (Dublin)
1931	T.Soye (Dublin)
1932	J.Lucas (Kilkenny)
1933	P.Bell (Meath)
1935	P.Reid (Carlow)
1936	J.J.Gilmartin (Kilkenny)
1937	J.J.Gilmartin (Kilkenny)
1938	J.J.Gilmartin (Kilkenny)
1939	J.J.Gilmartin (Kilkenny)
1940	J.J.Gilmartin (Kilkenny)
1941	J.J.Gilmartin (Kilkenny)
1942	J.J.Gilmartin (Kilkenny)
1943	M.Dowling (Kildare)
1944	A.Clarke (Dublin)
1945	J.J.Gilmartin (Kilkenny)
1946	J.J.Gilmartin (Kilkenny)
1947	J.J.Gilmartin (Kilkenny)
1948	A.Clarke (Dublin)
1949	A.Clarke (Dublin)
1950	R.Grattan (Kildare)
1951	A.Clarke (Dublin)
1952	J.Ryan (Wexford)
1953	J.Ryan (Wexford)
1954	A.Clarke (Dublin)
1955	A.Clarke (Dublin)
1956	J.Ryan (Wexford)
1957	J.Ryan (Wexford)
1958	P.Downey (Kerry)
1959	P.Downey (Kerry)
1960	P.Downey (Kerry)
1961	J.Maher (Louth)
1962	P.Downey (Kerry)
1963	J.Maher (Louth)
1964	J.Maher (Louth)
1965	P.McGee (Mayo)
1966	P.Hickey (Tipperary)
1967	P.McGee (Mayo)
1968	J.Maher (Louth)
1969	J.Maher (Louth)

1970	J.Maher (Louth)
1971	P.Hickey (Tipperary)
1972	P.McGee (Mayo)
1973	P.McGee (Mayo)
1974	P.McGee (Mayo)
1975	P.McGee (Mayo)
1976	P.McGee (Mayo)
1977	P.McGee (Mayo)
1978	C.Winders (Kildare)
1979	P.McGarry (Limerick)
1980	P.McGarry (Limerick)
1981	P.Winders (Kildare)
1982	P.McGee (Mayo)
1983	P.McGee (Mayo)
1984	P.Winders (Kildare)
1985	T.O'Rourke (Kildare)
1986	W.Bourke (Kilkenny)
1987	M.Walsh (Roscommon)
1988	T.O'Rourke (Kildare)
1989	T.O'Rourke (Kildare)
1990	T.O'Rourke (Kildare)
1991	P.McAuley (Louth)
1992	B.Bourke (Kilkenny)
1993	P.McAuley (Louth)
1994	P.McAuley (Louth)
1995	P.McAuley (Louth)
1996	P.McAuley (Louth)
1997	P.McAuley (Louth)
1998	W.O'Connor (Meath)
1999	No Championship
2000	No Championship
2001	W.O'Connor (Meath)
2002	K.Kane (Carlow)
2003	E.Kennedy (Dublin)
2004	E.Kennedy (Dublin)
2005	E.Kennedy (Dublin)
2006	D.Keegan (Mayo)
2007	E.Kennedy (Dublin)
2008	D.Keegan (Mayo)
2009	E.Kennedy (Dublin)
2010	E.Kennedy (Dublin)
2011	R.McCarthy (Westmeath)
2012	S.O'Carroll (Limerick)
2013	N.O'Connor (Kildare)
2014	E.Kennedy (Dublin)
2015	E.Kennedy (Dublin)
2016	C.J.Fitzpatrick (Limerick)
2015	E.Kennedy (Dublin)
2016	C.J.Fitzpatrick (Limerick)
2017	C.J.Fitzpatrick (Limerick)

HANDBALL

SENIOR HARDBALL DOUBLES

1926	J.J.Bowles and S.Gleeson (Limerick)
1927	T.Soye and T.O'Reilly (Dublin)
1928	T.Soye and T.O'Reilly (Dublin)
1929	P.Ormonde and C.Maloney (Tipperary)
1930	T.Soye and G.Brown (Dublin)
1931	P.Ormonde and C.Maloney (Tipperary)
1932	P.Bell and J.Doyle (Meath)
1933	P.Bell and J.Doyle {Meath)
1934	J.Lucas and T.Cherry (Kilkenny)
1935	P.Bell and J.Doyle (Meath)
1936	P.Perry and P.Reid (Roscommon)
1937	J.J.Gilmartin and A.Cullen (Kilkenny)
1938	J.J.Gilmartin and T.Cherry (Kilkenny)
1939	J.J.Gilmartin and T.Jordan (Kilkenny)
1940	J.J.Gilmartin and P.Dalton (Kilkenny)
1941	J.J.Gilmartin and J.Dunne (Kilkenny)
1942	A.Clarke and J.Clarke (Dublin)
1943	W.Walsh and D.Keogh (Cork)
1944	W.Walsh and D.Keogh (Cork)
1945	J.J.Gilmartin and P.Dalton (Kilkenny)
1946	J.J.Gilmartin and P.Dalton (Kilkenny)
1947	J.J.Gilmartin and P.Dalton (Kilkenny)
1948	W.Walsh and T.Morrissey (Cork)
1949	R.Grattan and J.Bolger (Kildare)
1950	A.Clarke and G.Moran (Dublin)
1951	J.Hassett and J.O'Brien (Kerry)
1952	J.Ryan and J.Doyle (Wexford)
1953	J.Hassett and P.Downey (Kerry)
1954	J.Ryan and J.Doyle (Wexford)
1955	J.Ryan and J.Doyle (Wexford)
1956	J.Ryan and J.Doyle (Wexford)
1957	J.Ryan and J.Doyle (Wexford)
1958	J.Ryan and J.Doyle (Wexford)
1959	P.Downey and J.O'Brien (Kerry)
1960	P.Downey and J.O'Brien (Kerry)
1961	J.Delaney and C.Delaney (Kilkenny)
1962	J.Ryan and M.Shanahan (Tipperary)
1963	P.Downey and J.O'Brien (Kerry)
1964	J.Maher and P.Reilly (Louth)
1965	P.McGee and P.Bolingbrook (Mayo)
1966	P.McGee and P.Bolingbrook (Mayo)
1967	P.McGee and P.Bolingbrook (Mayo)
1968	P.Hickey and C.Cleere (Tipperary)
1969	W.Doran and G.Lawlor (Kildare)
1970	S.McCabe and L.Gilmore (Monaghan)
1971	M.Sullivan and J.Doyle (Dublin)
1972	P.Hickey and C.Cleere (Tipperary)
1973	A.Byrne and W.Mullins (Westmeath)
1974	P.McGee and B.Colleran (Mayo)
1975	P.Hickey and J.Cleere (Tipperary)
1976	P.McGee and P.McCormack (Mayo)
1977	G.Lawlor and C.Winders (Kildare)
1978	P.McGarry and J.Bennis (Limerick)
1979	P.McGarry and J.Bennis (Limerick)
1980	P.McGarry and J.Bennis (Limerick)
1981	P.Winders and M.Purcell (Kildare)
1982	Cecil and Pius Winders (Kildare)
1983	Pius and Cecil Winders (Kildare)
1984	Tom and John Quish (Limerick)
1985	Tom and John Quish (Limerick)
1986	Tom and John Quish (Limerick)
1987	Tom and John Quish (Limerick)
1988	T.O'Rourke and P.McCormack
1989	T.O'Rourke and P.McCormack
1990	T.O'Rourke and P.McCormack
1991	B.Bourke and W.Pratt (Kilkenny)
1992	T.Sheridan and W.O'Connor (Meath)
1993	T.Sheridan and W.O'Connor (Meath)
1994	W.O'Connor and D.Gough (Meath)
1995	E.Corbett and N.Ryan (Tipperary)
1996	W.O'Connor and D.Gough (Meath)
1997	None
1998	T.Sheridan and W.O'Connor (Meath)
1999	None
2000-2005	No Championship
2006	E.Kennedy and E.Jensen (Dublin)
2007	E.Kennedy and E.Jensen (Dublin)
2008	E.Kennedy and E.Jensen (Dublin)
2009	T.Sheridan and B.Carroll (Meath)
2010	E.Kennedy and E.Jensen (Dublin)
2011	E.Kennedy and E.Jensen (Dublin)
2012	S.O'Carroll and C.J.Fitzpatrick (Limerick)
2013	D.Keegan and S.Cooney (Mayo)
2014	B.Carroll and T.Sheridan (Meath)
2015	B.Carroll & T.Sheridan (Meath)
2016	E.Kennedy & C.Browne (Dublin
2017	B.Carroll & T.Sheridan (Meath

JUNIOR SOFTBALL SINGLES

1928	M.Flannery (Waterford)
1929	P.Berry (Roscommon)
1930	J.Hassett (Tipperary)
1931	P.Delaney (Carlow)
1932	J.Smith (Wexford)
1933	P.Murray (Offaly)
1934	J.Dunne (Kilkenny)
1935	M.McMahon (Tipperary)
1936	P.Phelan (Kilkenny)
1937	W.Delaney (Wexford)
1938	L.Rowe (Dublin)
1939	M.Walsh (Galway)
1940	P.Molloy (Kilkenny)
1941	E.McMahon (Tipperary)
1942–1945	Suspended
1946	P.Clarke (Mayo)
1947	J.Ryan (Wexford)
1948	H.Haddock (Armagh)
1949	V.Sherlock (Cavan)
1950	M.Griffin (Dublin)
1951	C.Delaney (Kilkenny)
1952	S.Commane (Kerry)
1953	P.McCarthy (Kerry)
1954	J.Delaney (Kilkenny)
1955	J.Lyng (Wexford)
1956	J.Maher (Louth)
1957	P.Kirby (Clare)
1958	F.Confrey (Louth)
1959	M.Kirby (Clare)
1960	M.O'Brien (Limerick)
1961	D.Walshe (Sligo)
1962	S.McCabe (Monaghan)
1963	R.Lyng (Wexford)
1964	W.Kearins (Kerry)
1965	P.Sheerin (Offaly)
1966	T.McEllistrim (Kerry)
1967	P.McGarry (Limerick)
1968	D.Kirby (Clare)
1969	P.Davin (Tipperary)
1970	M.Conway (Tyrone)
1971	B.Colleran (Mayo}
1972	P.Reilly (Kilkenny)
1973	J.Howlin (Wexford)
1974	P.Ryan (Dublin)
1975	O.Harrold (Kilkenny)
1976	T.O'Brien (Kerry)
1977	J.Roche (Limerick)
1978	J.Scully (Galway)
1979	A.Ryan (Tipperary)
1980	T.Quish (Limerick)
1981	P.Mullins (Tipperary)
1982	W.Bourke (Kilkenny)
1983	M.Sweeney (Sligo)
1984	J.Fleming (Wexford)
1985	D.Doolin (Roscommon)
1986	P.Delaney (Galway)
1987	E.Jensen (Meath)
1988	W.McCarthy (Tipperary)
1989	W.Fitzgibbon (Tipperary)
1990	R.McCarthy (Westmeath)
1991	J.Rossiter (Carlow)
1992	J.Herlihy (Cork)
1993	S.O'Callaghan (Tipperary)
1994	S.O'Connor (Wexford)
1995	N.O'Reilly (Kilkenny)
1996	R.Breen (Wexford)
1997	F.Daly (Dublin)
1998	D.Lynch (Kerry)
1999	E.O'Neill (Limerick)
2000	N.Kerr (Tyrone)
2001	K.Hennessy (Limerick)
2002	S.Dormer (Laois)
2003	A.Johnson (Tipperary)
2004	N.Murphy (Offaly)
2005	N.McInerney (Tipperary)
2006	P.Donovan (Laois)
2007	I.Griffin (Dublin)
2008	O.Conway (Galway)
2009	L.Maughan (Roscommon)
2010	D.Frawley (Clare)
2011	S.O'Neill (Tyrone)
2012	D.Hickey (Tipperary)
2013	B.Fleming (Cork)
2014	M.Rafter (Leitrim)
2015	P.Lambert (Wexford)
2016	K.Burke (Dublin)
2017	J.O'Shea (Kerry

HANDBALL

JUNIOR SOFTBALL DOUBLES

1928	T.O'Keeffe and J.McCarthy (Tipperary)
1929	P.Perry and T.Gaughran (Roscommon)
1930	J.Molloy and H.Smith (Cavan)
1931	C.Darcy and J.Cahill (Kildare)
1932	W.Doyle and J.Fleming (Carlow)
1933	T.Cherry and J.O'Brien (Kilkenny)
1934	A.Cullen and P.Power (Kilkenny)
1935	A.Roe and H.Gallagher (Dublin)
1936	J.McDonald and J.Geraghty (Mayo)
1937	J.Bergin and M.O'Gorman (Tipperary)
1938	A.Collins and C.Collins (Tipperary)
1939	W.McDonald and R.Gibbons (Mayo)
1940	D.McDonald and P.Ryan (Carlow)
1941	S.Rice and E.McMahon (Tipperary)
1942	P.Kennedy and J.Gaughran (Roscommon)
1943-1945	Suspended
1946	W.Buggy and T.Buggy (Kilkenny)
1947	G.Grogan and C.Donohoe (Dublin)
1948	J.O'Connell and M.O'Keeffe (Kilkenny)
1949	P.Kennedy and D.Carey (Tipperary)
1950	T.McCormack and P.McCormack (Mayo)
1951	P.Downey and T.Commane (Kerry)
1952	J.Byrne and P.Sutherland (Wexford)
1953	P.Munroe and M.Fahy (Dublin)
1954	P.Hackett and J.Moynihan (Limerick)
1955	T.Ryan and S.Lennon (Kilkenny)
1956	E.Connolly and S.Fleming (Mayo)
1957	T.McGarry and M.Mullins (Limerick)
1958	J.Clery and W.McKenna (Wicklow)
1959	T.Reilly and P.Reilly (Louth)
1960	M.O'Brien and S.Walsh (Limerick)
1961	J.Coughlan and G.Barry (Offaly)
1962	M.Walsh and P.McGee (Mayo)
1963	L.Gilmore and J.Gilmore (Cavan)
1964	W.Kerins and P.Moriarty (Kerry)
1965	L.Molloy and D.McGovern (Meath)
1966	T.McElisrim and M.McElistrim (Kerry)
1967	M.Henry and J.Gaffney (Sligo)
1968	R.Doherty and P.Clarke (Roscommon)
1969	N.Cahill and P.Masterson (Dublin)
1970	R.Walsh and J.O'Brien (Dublin)
1971	J.Kirby and M.Hogan (Clare)
1972	P.Reilly and P.Delaney (Kilkenny)
1973	J.Howlin and J.Goggins (Wexford)
1974	E.Hannon and P.Walsh (Sligo)
1975	O.Harold and B.Fitzpatrick (Kilkenny)
1976	G.and D.Sheridan (Cavan)
1977	P.Winders and T.O'Rourke (Kildare)
1978	N.O'Brien and T.Morrissey (Tipperary)
1979	J.B.Molloy and F.Carroll (Meath)
1980	T.and J.Quish (Limerick)
1981	F.McCann and M.Porter (Sligo)
1982	E.Farrell and B.Mullins (Tipperary)
1983	M.Walsh and E.Downey (Kilkenny)
1984	J.Fleming and P.Cleary (Wexford)
1985	P.Donagh and P.Hand (Cavan)
1986	P.Delaney and M.Connors (Galway)
1987	T.Sheridan and J.McGovern (Meath)
1988	W.O'Connor and J.Grant (Meath)
1989	E.Corbett and J.O'Donoghue (Tipperary)
1990	P.Kealey and B.Mullins (Offaly)
1991	J.Donlan and N.Breen (Clare)
1992	T.Derrig and P.McCormack (Mayo)
1993	N.Buggy and T.Hynes (Wexford)
1994	P.Kenny and F.Cunningham (Dublin)
1995	T.and B.O'Brien (Limerick)
1996	P.Ryan and K.Croke (Tipperary)
1997	C.Joyce and R.Charles (Westmeath)
1998	D.King and J.Ryan (Carlow)
1999	E.O'Neill and M.Kiely (Limerick)
2000	P.Mullins and J.Mullins (Tipperary)
2001	M.Lalor and E.Burke (Kilkenny)
2002	K.Hennessy and P.Hedderman (Limerick)
2003	A.Cunningham and D.Rogers (Roscommon)
2004	P.Buckley and C.Jordan (Cork)
2005	T.Clifford and M.Clifford (Kilkenny)
2006	O.Cassidy and P.Flynn (Mayo)
2007	P.Butler and D.Walsh (Waterford)
2008	O.Conway and A.Tierney (Galway)
2009	W.Love and D.Love (Kilkenny)
2010	C.Dollin and N.McGrath (Roscommon)
2011	D.Hope and M.O'Brien (Offaly)
2012	D.Hickey and M.Carroll (Tipperary)
2013	J.Brady and P.Clerkin (Cavan)
2014	D. O'Toole and M.Whelan (Wexford)
2015	B.Devlin & G.McCrystal (Tyrone)
2016	J.P.O'Connor & M.O'Toole (Limerick)
2017	K.Craddock & D.Connaughton (Galway)

JUNIOR HARDBALL SINGLES

1928	J.Ryan (Tipperary)
1929	J.O'Mahoney (Cork)
1930	P.Bell (Meath)
1931	J Foley (Kildare)
1932	J.O'Mahoney (Cork)
1933	T.Cherry (Kilkenny)
1934	A.Cullen (Kilkenny)
1935	J.J.Gilmartin (Kilkenny)
1936	P.Murray (Offaly)
1937	W.Butler (Dublin)
1938	T.Jordan (Kilkenny)
1939	M.Butler (Dublin)
1940	P.Molloy (Kilkenny)
1941	M.Dowling (Kildare)
1942	P.Murray (Offaly)
1943	James Gilmartin (Kilkenny)
1944	C.Drumgoole (Wexford)
1945	M.O'Gorman (Tipperary)
1946	G.Ryan (Kildare)
1947	R.Grattan (Kildare)
1948	J.Bolger (Kildare)
1949	P.Kennedy (Tipperary)
1950	M.O'Brien (Kildare)
1951	P.Downey (Kerry)
1952	C.O'Brien (Tipperary)
1953	W.Lawlor (Kildare)
1954	J.Delaney (Kilkenny)
1955	M.Redmond (Kildare)
1956	J.Maher (Louth)
1957	W.Doran (Kildare)
1958	J.Ryan (Tipperary)
1959	D.Downey (Kerry)
1960	J.Donovan (Kerry)
1961	J.Cleary (Tipperary)
1962	P.Hickey (Tipperary)
1963	T.Dowd (Wexford)
1964	P.Bolingbrook (Mayo)
1965	P.Sheerin (Offaly)
1966	T.McEllistrim (Kerry)
1967	M.O'Gara (Roscommon)
1968	A.Byrne (Dublin)
1969	A.McAuliffe (Limerick)
1970	J.Hartnett (Limerick)
1971	J.Quigley (Wexford)
1972	E.Sheeran (Offaly)
1973	M.Purcell (Kildare)
1974	P.McCormack (Mayo)
1975	P.Hughes (Kilkenny)
1976	M.Walsh (Roscommon)
1977	W.McCarthy (Tipperary)
1978	C.Quinn (Mayo)
1979	Noel Ryan (Tipperary)
1980	N.Quigley (Wexford)
1981	W.Pratt (Kilkenny)
1982	W.Bourke (Kilkenny)
1983	E.Lee (Dublin)
1984	N.O'Toole (Cork)
1985	M.Dowling (Kildare)
1986	J.O'Donoghue (Tipperary)
1987	P.McAuley (Louth)
1988	W.O'Connor (Meath)
1989	P.O'Keeffe (Kilkenny)
1990	E.Jenson (Meath)
1991	M.Walsh (Kilkenny)
1992	D.Moloney (Tipperary)
1993	R.McCarthy (Westmeath)
1994	P.Quaile (Wicklow)
1995	A.Campbell (Kildare)
1996	M.Flynn (Tipperary)
1997	V.Moran (Mayo)
1998	K.Kane (Carlow)
1999	E.O'Neill (Limerick)
2000	D.Keegan (Mayo)
2001	S.Dormer (Laois)
2002	D.Ward (Kildare)
2003	J.Doyle (Limerick)
2004	P.O'Donnell (Wicklow)
2005	P .Donovan (Laois)
2006	D.Martin (Roscommon)
2007	G.Coonan (Tipperary)
2008	J.McCann (Mayo)
2009	S O'Carroll (Limerick)
2010	N.Anthony (Kilkenny)
2011	P.O'Carroll (Limerick)
2012	N.O'Connor (Kildare)
2013	J.Murphy (Wexford)
2014	K.Kavanagh (Wicklow)
2015	B.Burke (Kilkenny)
2016	J.Willoughby (Wicklow)
2017	M.Mullins (Carlow)

JUNIOR HARDBALL DOUBLES

1928	S.Ryan and S.McInerney (Tipperary)	1972	T.Geoghegan and C.Winders (Kildare)
1929	J.O'Mahoney and D.O'Mahoney (Cork)	1973	M.Purcell and J.Byrne (Kildare)
1930	N.Gorman and T.Maloney (Tipperary)	1974	M.Brady and T.Hurley (Dublin)
1931	J.McGrath and J.O'Connell (Kilkenny)	1975	P.Hughes and P.Kennedy (Kilkenny)
1932	A.Dalton and C.Baker (Kilkenny)	1976	G.and D.Sheridan (Cavan)
1933	S.Tormey and P.Bell, Junior (Meath)	1977	J.Bennis and V.Moane (Limerick)
1934	A.Cullen and J.Dunne (Kilkenny)	1978	E.Rabbitte and G.Scully (Galway)
1935	P.Coyne and J.Purcell (Carlow)	1979	Tony and Noel Ryan (Tipperary)
1936	G.Ryan and J.Costello (Kildare)	1980	T.and J.Quish (Limerick)
1937	J.Hassett and M.O'Gorman (Tipperary)	1981	P.Cleary and S.McLoughlin (Wexford)
1938	J.Hurley and T.Twohill (Cork)	1982	W.Bourke and M.Lawlor (Kilkenny)
1939	M.Butler and J.Roche (Dublin)	1983	E.Lee and R.Walsh (Dublin)
1940	W.Walsh and R.Ward (Cork)	1984	M.Jorden and N.O'Toole (Cork)
1941	J.McGrath and D.Brennan (Kilkenny)	1985	P.Hand and P.Donagh (Cavan)
1942	P.Murray and J.McHugh (Offaly)	1986	E.Corbett and J.O'Donoghue (Tipperary)
1943	James Gilmartin and J.O'Brien (Kilkenny)	1987	F.McCann and S.Davey (Sligo)
1944	C.Drumgoole and J.Duggan (Wexford)	1988	P.O'Connell and P.Quish (Limerick)
1945	W.Grace and C.Murphy (Kildare)	1989	C.McGovern and T.Sheridan (Meath)
1946	M.Dalton and J.Dunne (Kilkenny)	1990	E.Jenson and D.Gough (Meath)
1947	J.McGrath and J.Phelan (Kilkenny)	1991	M.Walsh and J.Connolly (Kilkenny)
1948	W.McCabe and T.Tormey (Meath)	1992	D.Moloney and J.O'Dwyer (Tipperary)
1949	J.Doyle and P.Doyle (Wexford)	1993	J.Guilfoyle and R.McCarthy (Westmeath)
1950	M.O'Brien and R.Maher (Kildare)	1994	N.Murphy and M.Carrie (Tipperary)
1951	S.Monahan and J.Doherty (Kilkenny)	1995	A.Campbell and T.Winders (Kildare)
1952	J.Kennedy and M.Heffernan (Tipperary)	1996	M.Kiely and P.Herr (Limerick)
1953	W.Lawlor and P.Monahan (Kildare)	1997	V.Moran and C.Brennan (Mayo)
1954	M.Gleeson and R.Doyle (Dublin)	1998	K.and T.Kane (Carlow)
1955	M.Redmond and J.Parle (Kildare)	1999	E.Law and E.Bourke (Kilkenny)
1956	J.Maher and J.McArdle (Louth)	2000	D.Keegan and B.Hough (Mayo)
1957	W.Doran and J.Curran (Kildare)	2001	No Championship
1958	T.Doheny and M.Shanahan (Tipperary)	2002	No Championship
1959	A.Daly and P.Winders (Kildare)	2003	P.Conway and O.Conway (Galway)
1960	T Cleere and C.Cleere (Tipperary)	2004	P.O'Donnell and N.Kealy (Wicklow)
1961	M.Kelly and G.Connolly (Galway)	2005	P .Buckley and C.Jordan (Cork)
1962	P.Hickey and T.Breedy (Tipperary)	2006	R.O'Gara and D.Martin (Roscommon)
1963	P.Supple and J.Murphy (Cork)	2007	I.Griffin and C.Donnelly (Dublin)
1964	G.Mahon and K.Fullard (Roscommon)	2008	D.Lynch and J.J.Quirke (Kerry)
1965	M.Sullivan and J.Doyle (Dublin)	2009	S.O'Carroll and C.J.Fitzpatrick (Limerick)
1966	T.McElistrim and M.McElistrim (Kerry)	2010	K.Bourke and W.Love (Kilkenny)
1967	G.Lawlor and R.Winders (Kildare)	2011	P.Carroll and P.Murphy (Limerick)
1968	N.Kerins and T.Fitzgerald (Kerry)	2012	N.O'Connor and P.Moran (Kildare)
1969	E.Deegan and J.Browne (Kildare)	2013	D.Love and C.Neary (Kilkenny)
1970	J.Hartnett and P.Clancy (Limerick)	2014	Peter and Patrick Funchion (Kilkenny)
1971	P.Murphy and J.Quigley (Wexford)	2015	D.Relihan & J.Hedigan (Cork)
		2016	M.Hedigan & D.O'Dea (Cork)
		2017	J.Cummins & P.Reilly (Meath

MINOR SOFTBALL SINGLES

1949	J.O'Brien (Kerry)
1950	L.Egan (Kilkenny)
1951	R .Doherty (Roscommon)
1952	R.Doherty (Roscommon)
1953	J.Lyng (Wexford)
1954	E.Horan (Kerry)
1955	T.McGarry (Limerick)
1956	J.Murrary (Kilkenny)
1957	M.Mullins (Limerick)
1958	J.Clery (Wicklow)
1959	J.Clery (Wicklow)
1960	T.Ledwith (Westmeath)
1961	R.Lyng (Wexford)
1962	J.McElistrim (Kerry)
1963	M.Henry (Sligo)
1964	M.Henry (Sligo)
1965	P.Clarke (Roscommon)
1966	P.McCarthy (Limerick)
1967	P.Murphy (Dublin)
1968	P.Bennis (Limerick)
1969	M.Brady (Dublin)
1970	M.Walsh (Roscommon)
1971	S.McLoughlin (Wexford)
1972	S.McLoughlin (Wexford)
1973	T.O'Rourke (Kildare)
1974	D.Doolan (Roscommon)
1975	S.Wafer (Wexford)
1976	M.Maher (Louth)
1977	S.McGovern (Meath)
1978	A.Ryan (Tipperary)
1979	W.Bourke (Kilkenny)
1980	W.Bourke (Kilkenny)
1981	W.Bourke (Kilkemly)
1982	M.Walsh (Kilkenny)
1983	M.Walsh (Kilkenny)
1984	M.Walsh (Kilkenny)
1985	F.Kavanagh (Westmeath)
1986	T.Sheridan (Meath)
1987	P.McAuley (Louth)
1988	P.Galvin (Limerick)
1989	A.Heneghan (Roscommon)
1990	T.Hynes (Wexford)
1991	B.Gilhooly (Wexford)
1992	M.Finnegan (Cavan)
1993	M.Finnegan (Cavan)
1994	M.Finnegan (Cavan)
1995	K.Kane (Carlow)
1996	K.Kane (Carlow)
1997	E.Kennedy (Dublin)
1998	D.Keegan (Mayo)
1999	M.Gregan (Wicklow)
2000	P.Finnegan (Cavan)
2001	N.McHugh (Galway)
2002	N.McHugh (Galway)
2003	G.Coonan (Tipperary)
2004	R.McCarthy (Westmeath)
2005	R.McCarthy (Westmeath)
2006	N.Anthony (Kilkenny)
2007	C.J.Fitzpatrick (Limerick)
2008	Seamus O'Carroll (Limerick)
2009	Stephen Cooney (Mayo)
2010	M.Mulkerrins (Galway)
2011	M.Mulkerrins (Galway)
2012	P.Quish (Limerick)
2013	P.Quish (Limerick)
2014	J.Woods (Tyrone)
2015	N.Joyce (Mayo)
2016	S.Dunne (Kilkenny)
2017	D.Mulkerrins (Galway)

HANDBALL

MINOR SOFTBALL DOUBLES

1938	J.Doran and G.Brogan (Dublin)
1939	A.Kelly and J.Goughran (Roscommon)
1940	P.Kennedy and J.Sweeney (Tipperary)
1941	P.Kennedy and J.Sweeney (Tipperary)
1942-1945	Suspended
1946	J.Ryan and A.Power (Wexford)
1947	P.Doherty and M.Mulhern (Meath)
1948	P.Somers and J.O'Keeffe (Kilkenny)
1949	P.Bolingbrook and K.Swords (Mayo)
1950	T.Hughes and J.O'Brien (Mayo)
1951	S.Commane and M.Dennehy (Kerry)
1952	R.Tunney and J.Swords (Mayo)
1953	M.O'Connor and E.Horan (Kerry)
1954	E.Horan and D.Downey (Kerry)
1955	T.McGarry and M.Mullins (Limerick)
1956	M.Sullivan and J.Murray (Kilkenny)
1957	M.Mullins and G.Mitchell (Limerick)
1958	W.Mullen and P.Geelan (Westmeath)
1959	J.Clery and M.Dwyer (Wicklow)
1960	N.Kerins and J.McMullan (Kerry)
1961	R.Lyng and P.Lennon (Wexford)
1962	D.Kirby and J.Kirby (Clare)
1963	H.Ryan and P.Kavanagh (Wexford)
1964	W.Myles and M.Fitzgibbon (Kerry)
1965	W.Myles and M.Fitzgibbon (Kerry)
1966	V.Grimes and C.Grimes (Meath)
1967	P.Murphy and P.Domigan (Dublin)
1968	J.Quigley and J.Sydney (Wexford)
1969	J.Quigley and N.Quigley (Wexford)
1970	M.Quigley and S.McLoughlin (Wexford)
1971	P.McCormack and C.Quinn (Mayo)
1972	D.Doolan and P.J.Moran (Roscommon)
1973	O.Harold and J.Barron (Kilkenny)
1974	P.Hughes and E.Mahon (Kilkenny)
1975	S.Wafer and S.Goggins (Wexford)
1976	J.McGovern and F.Carroll (Meath)
1977	J.and M.McGovern (Meath)
1978	J.and M.McGovern (Meath)
1979	B.Bourke and M.Cantwell (Kilkenny)
1980	W.Bourke and M.Lawlor (Kilkenny)
1981	E.Jensen and C.McGovern (Meath)
1982	M.Walsh and M.Lawlor (Kilkenny)
1983	Michael Walsh and Joe Walsh (Kilkenny)
1984	M.Walsh and P.O'Keeffe (Kilkenny)
1985	T.Sheridan and W.O'Connor (Meath)
1986	T.Sheridan and W.O'Connor (Meath}
1987	K.Lyons and P.Galvin (Limerick)
1988	K.Lyons and P.Galvin (Limerick)
1989	D.J.Carey and G.O'Brien (Kilkenny)
1990	A.and C.Heneghan (Roscommon)
1991	D.Moloney and N.Murphy (Tipperary)
1992	M.Finnegan and R.Cunningham (Cavan)
1993	M.Finnegan and R.Cunningham (Cavan)
1994	M.Finnegan and C.McDonnell (Cavan)
1995	K.Kane and O.Ryan (Carlow)
1996	B.Goff and M.Hillis (Wexford)
1997	B.Goff and C.Keeling (Wexford)
1998	C.Browne and P.Reilly (Meath)
1999	M.Gregan ond S.Willoughby (Wicklow)
2000	J.Goggins and T.Gainfort (Wexford)
2001	M.Cash and C.Smyth (Wexford)
2002	R.Walshe and J.Willoughby (Wicklow)
2003	D.Martin and R.O'Gara (Roscommon)
2004	R.McCarthy and J.O'Shaughnessy (Westmeath)
2005	R.Hogan and P.Hogan (Kilkenny)
2006	N.Anthony and K.Greene (Kilkenny)
2007	C.J.Fitzpatrick and S.Carroll (Limerick)
2008	C.J.Fitzpatrick and S.Carroll (Limerick)
2009	S.Cooney and I.McLoughlin (Mayo)
2010	P.O'Carroll and E.Davern (Limerick)
2011	D.Corrigan and C.Murphy (Wexford)
2012	D.Wrynn and S.Doonan (Leitrim)
2013	M.Hedigan and D.Relihan (Cork)
2014	J.Woods and R.Mullen (Tyrone)
2015	K.Armstrong & D.Kavanagh (Wexford)
2016	D.Kavanagh & A.Butler (Wexford)
2017	J.Prentice & J.Cahill (Tipperary)

MINOR HARDBALL SINGLES

1953	J.Redmond (Wexford)
1954	E.Horan (Kerry)
1955	J.Ryan (Tipperary)
1956	M.Sullivan (Kilkenny)
1957	P Hickey (Tipperary)
1958	P McGrath (Wexford)
1959	J.Clery (Wicklow)
1960	M.Purcell (Kildare)
1961	J.Brennan (Kilkenny)
1962	P.McLoughlin (Tipperary)
1963	T.Morrissey (Kilkenny)
1964	P.Cody (Cork)
1965	T.Geoghegan (Kildare)
1966	M.O'Gara (Roscommon)
1967	G.Lawlor (Kildare)
1968	J.Quigley (Wexford)
1969	J.Quigley tWexford)
1970	M.Walsh (Roscommon)
1971	P.McCormack (Mayo)
1972	C.Quinn (Mayo)
1973	P.Hughes (Kilkenny)
1974	P.Hughes (Kilkenny)
1975	P.Finnerty (Galway)
1976	J.Dineen (Limerick)
1977	A Ryan (Tipperary)
1978	A Ryan (Tipperary)
1979	W.O'Donnell (Tipperary)
1980	W.Bourke (Kilkenny)
1981	W.Bourke (Kilkenny)
1982	J .O'Donoghue (Tipperary)
1983	J.O'Donoghue (Tipperary)
1984	M.Walsh (Kilkenny)
1985	T.Sheridan (Meath)
1986	W.O'Connor (Meath)
1987	P.McAuley (Louth)
1988	K.Lyons (Limerick)
1989	J.Connolly (Kilkenny)
1990	G.O'Brien (Kilkenny)
1991	D.Moloney (Tipperary)
1992	T.Winders (Kildare)
1993	M.Finnegan (Cavan)
1994	D.Ward (Kildare)
1995	V.Moran (Mayo)
1996	K.Kane (Carlow)

1997	K.Kane (Carlow)
1998	No Championship
1999	No Championship
2000	No Championship
2001	No Championship
2002	D.Martin (Roscommon)
2003	R.McCarthy (Westmeath)
2004	No Championship
2005	No Championship
2006	C.J.Fitzpatrick (Limerick)
2007	S.O'Carroll (Limerick)
2008	C.J.Fitzpatrick (Limerick)
2009	Stephen Cooney (Mayo)
2010	N.O'Connor (Kildare)
2011	N.O'Connor (Kildare)
2012	P.Quish (Limerick)
2013	G.Riordan (Wexford)
2014	E.Sheridan (Meath)
2015	N.Joyce (Mayo)
2016	S.Dunne (Kilkenny)
2015	N.Joyce (Mayo)
2016	S.Dunne (Kilkenny)
2017	P.Murphy (Mayo)

MINOR HARDBALL DOUBLES

1953	J.Redmond and M.Redmond (Wexford)
1954	M.Sullivan and M.Hayes (Kilkenny)
1955	J.O'Neill and M.Keyes (Limerick)
1956	M.Sullivan and J.Murray (Kilkenny)
1957	M.Mullins and J.O'Connell (Limerick)
1958	M.Purcell and R.Winders (Kildare)
1959	C.Cleere and J.Cleary (Tipperary)
1960	M.Purcell and J.Byrne (Kildare)
1961	J.Byrne and J.Browne (Kildare)
1962	P.McLoughlin and A.Murphy (Tipperary)
1963	G.Lawlor and T.Geoghegan (Kildare)
1964	P.Cody and N.O'Brien (Cork)
1965	T.Curley and S.Lynch (Galway)
1966	G.Lawlor and A.Campbell (Kildare)
1967	G.Lawlor and C.Winders (Kildare)
1968	W.McCarthy and S.Halley (Tipperary)
1969	M.Brady and M.Williams (Dublin)
1970	M.Walsh and P.J.Moran (Roscommon)
1971	S.McLoughlin and C.Kehoe (Wexford)
1972	P.Hughes and J.Barron (Kilkenny)
1973	P.Hughes and J.Barron (Kilkenny)
1974	P.Hughes and E.Mahon (Kilkenny)
1975	A.McConnell and J.Reddy (Meath)
1976	F.McCann and M.Porter (Sligo)
1977	T.Ryan and W.O'Donnell (Tipperary)
1978	T.Ryan and W.O'Donnell (Tipperary)
1979	M.McGovern and J.Smith (Meath)
1980	W.Bourke and M.Lawlor (Kilkenny)
1981	W.Bourke and M.Lawlor (Kilkenny)
1982	E.Jensen and R.Morris (Meath)
1983	J.O'Donoghue and E.Corbett (Tipperary)
1984	M.Walsh and P.O'Keeffe (Kilkenny)
1985	T.Sheridan and W.O'Connor (Meath)
1986	T.Sheridan and W.O'Connor (Meath)
1987	P.McAuley and M.McAuley (Louth)
1988	K.Lyons and P.Galvin (Limerick)
1989	G.O'Brien and E.Law (Kilkenny)
1990	D.Maloney and N.Marshall (Tipperary)
1991	D.Moloney and N.Marshall (Tipperary)
1992	M.Carrie and N.Marshall (Tipperary)
1993	M.Finnegan and R.Cunningham (Cavan)
1994	M.Finnegan and N.Doyle (Cavan)
1995	V.Moran and C.Brennan (Mayo)
1996	V.Moran and C.Brennan (Mayo)
1997	K.Kane and D.Dunphy (Carlow)
1998–2005	No Championship
2006	C.J.Fitzpatrick and S.O'Carroll (Limerick)
2007	C.J.Fitzpatrick and S.O'Carroll (Limerick)
2008	C.J.Fitzpatrick and S.O'Carroll (Limerick)
2009	K.Bourke and E.Hennessy (Kilkenny)
2010	P.O'Carroll and E.Davern (Limerick)
2011	N.O'Connor and R.Maguire (Kildare)
2012	M.Hedigan and D.Relihan (Cork)
2013	M.Hedigan and D.Relihan (Cork)
2014	E.Sheridan and R.Fox (Meath)
2015	N.Joyce and P.Murphy (Mayo)
2016	S.Dunne and E.Brennan (Kilkenny)
2017	E.Brennan & J.Doyle (Kilkenny

INTERMEDIATE SOFTBALL SINGLES

1994	D.Moloney (Tipperary)
1995	B.Gilhooley (Wexford)
1996	M.Finnegan (Cavan)
1997	J.Brennan (Kilkenny)
1998	T.Healy (Cork)
1999	E.Kennedy (Dublin)
2000	B.Goff (Wexford)
2001	D.Lynch (Kerry)
2002	D.Keegan (Mayo)
2003	M.Gregan (Wicklow)
2004	J.McCann (Mayo)
2005	C.Browne (Meath)
2006	R.McCarthy (Westmeath)
2007	P.Mullins (Tipperary)
2008	G.Coonan (Tipperary)
2009	B.Manogue (Kilkenny)
2010	S.O'Carroll (Limerick)
2011	C.Jordan (Cork)
2012	C.J.Fitzpatrick (Limerick)
2013	S.Cooney (Mayo)
2014	C.Jordan (Cork)
2015	P.Quish (Limerick)
2016	O.Conway (Galway)
2017	M.Mulkerrins (Galway)

INTERMEDIATE SOFTBALL DOUBLES

1994	S.Ahern and P.Hall (Dublin)
1995	N.Murphy and J.O'Dwyer (Tipperary)
1996	M.Finnegan and R.Cunningham (Cavan)
1997	Pearse O'Keeffe and E.Law (Kilkenny)
1998	K.and T.Kane (Carlow)
1999	D.King and J.Ryan (Carlow)
2000	G.Buggy and B.Goff (Wexford)
2001	E.O'Neill and P.Herr (Limerick)
2002	D.Keegan and V.Moran (Mayo)
2003	M.Gregan and P.Quaile (Wicklow)
2004	J.McCann and C.Brennan (Mayo)
2005	D.Martin and R.O'Gara (Roscommon)
2006	R.McCarthy and L.Cassidy (Westmeath)
2007	E.Burke and M.Clifford (Kilkenny)
2008	G.Coonan and J.McInerney (Tipperary)
2009	N.Anthony and J.Walshe (Kilkenny)
2010	S.O'Carroll and P.Hedderman (Limerick)
2011	A.Cunningham and C.Doolin (Roscommon)
2012	O.Conway and M.Mulkerrins (Galway)
2013	F.Collins and D.Hickey (Tipperary)
2014	E.Bourke and D.Walsh (Kilkenny)
2015	M.Berry & J.Berry (Wexford)
2016	J.Brady & P.Brady (Cavan)
2017	M.Mulkerrins & P.Conway (Galway)

U21 SOFTBALL SINGLES

1967	P.McGarry (Limerick)
1968	P.McGarry (Limerick)
1969	P.Murphy (Wexford)
1970	J.Delaney (Kilkenny)
1971	M.Walsh (Roscommon)
1972	M.Walsh (Roscommon)
1973	M.Walsh (Roscommon)
1974	None
1975	O.Harold (Kilkenny)
1976	T.O'Brien (Kerry)
1977	D.Doolan (Roscommon)
1978	T.Quish (Limerick)
1979	E.Downey (Kilkenny)
1980	T.Ryan (Tipperary)
1981	T.Ryan (Tipperary)
1982	S.Lyon (Waterford)
1983	P.McCarthy (Wexford)

1984	P.Hall (Dublin)
1985	J.O'Donoghue (Tipperary)
1986	P.O'Keeffe (Kilkenny)
1987	P.O'Keeffe (Kilkenny)
1988	P.O'Keeffe (Kilkenny)
1989	P.Quaile (Wicklow)
1990	J.O'Dwyer (Tipperary)
1991	G.O'Brien (Kilkenny)
1992	B.Gilhooley (Wexford)
1993	N.Murphy (Tipperary)
1994	R.Cunningham (Cavan)
1995	M.Finnegan (Cavan)
1996	T.Winders (Kildare)
1997	V.Moran (Mayo)
1998	E.Kennedy (Dublin)
1999	B.Marrinan (Clare)
2000	D.Keegan (Mayo)
2001	B.Manogue (Kilkenny)
2002	M.Gregan (Wicklow)
2003	J.McCann (Mayo)
2004	D.Martin (Roscommon)
2005	G.Coonan (Tipperary)
2006	G.Coonan (Tipperary)
2007	M.Berry (Wexford)
2008	M.Berry (Wexford)
2009	S.O'Carroll (Limerick)
2010	F.Collins (Tipperary)
2011	G.McGrath (Kilkenny)
2012	P.Funchion (Kilkenny)
2013	E.Davern (Limerick)
2014	P. Quish (Limerick)
2015	G.Riordan (Wexford)
2016	G.Riordan (Wexford)
2017	B.Mahon (Kilkenny)

HANDBALL

U21 SOFTBALL DOUBLES

1967	V.and C.Grimes (Meath)
1968	W.Myles and M.Fitzgibbon (Kerry)
1969	P.McGarry and P.Bennis (Limerick)
1970	P.Murphy and J.Quigley (Wexford)
1971	M.Brady and M.Williams (Dublin)
1972	E.Farrell and J.Ryan (Tipperary)
1973	M.Brady and D.Shanahan (Cavan)
1974	None
1975	P.J.Moran and D.Doolan (Roscommon)
1976	T.O'Rourke and P.Winders (Kildare)
1977	T.O'Rourke and P.Winders (Kildare)
1978	P.Cleary and J.Fleming (Wexford)
1979	F.McCann and M.Porter (Sligo)
1980	P.Cleary and J.Fleming (Wexford)
1981	T.Ryan and W.O'Donnell (Tipperary)
1982	J.and M.McGovern (Meath)
1983	E.MacBholscaidh and D.Lynch (Dublin)
1984	K.Mullins and J.O'Donoghue (Tipperary)
1985	J.O'Donoghue and E.Corbett (Tipperary)
1986	J.O'Donoghue and J.Fitzell (Tipperary)
1987	P.O'Keeffe and P.Maher (Kilkenny)
1988	D.Gough and D.McDonald (Meath)
1989	D.Gough and J.Lynch (Meath)
1990	D.Gough and J.Lynch (Meath)
1991	T.Hynes and P.Carly (Wexford)
1992	D.Moloney and N.Murphy (Tipperary)
1993	D.Moloney and N.Murphy (Tipperary)
1994	G.Kelleher and B.O'Neill (Cork)
1995	M.Finnegan and R.Cunningham (Cavan)
1996	T.Winders and D.Ward (Kildare)
1997	A.and P.Supple (Tipperary)
1998	B.Goff and C.Keeling (Wexford)
1999	C.Meenagh and S.McCullagh (Tyrone)
2000	D.Keegan and B.Hough (Mayo)
2001	P.Finnegan and R.McCormack (Cavan)
2002	M.Gregan and S.Willoughby (Wicklow)
2003	M.Cash and J.Goggins (Wexford)
2004	D.Martin and R.O'Gara (Roscommon)
2005	B.Carroll and D.Maguire (Meath)
2006	R.O'Gara and D.Martin (Roscommon)
2007	M.and J.Berry (Wexford)
2008	P.McGlinchey and B.Donaghy (Tyrone)
2009	S.O'Carroll and C.J.Fitzpatrick (Limerick)
2010	C.Neary and P.Funchion (Kilkenny)
2011	C.J.Fitzpatrick and P.O'Carroll (Limerick)
2012	Patrick and Peter Funchion (Kilkenny)
2013	M.Nally and C.Connelly (Roscommon)
2014	M.Hedigan and D.Relihan (Cork)
2015	M.Hedigan & D.Relihan (Cork)
2016	D.Hayes & P.O'Donaghue (Tipperary)
2017	S.Kerr & R.Mullan (Tyrone)

IRISH NATIONALS

WOMEN'S SINGLES

1995	B.Hennessy (Limerick)
1996	B.Hennessy (Limerick)
1997	B.Hennessy (Limerick)
1998	F.McKenna (Antrim)
1999	F.McKenna (Antrim)
2000	F.McKenna (Antrim)
2001	L.F.Gilmore (Canada)
2002	F.McKenna (Antrim)
2003	F.Shannon (Antrim)
2004	M.Daly (Kerry)
2005	F.Shannon (Antrim)
2006	F.Shannon (Antrim)
2007	F.Shannon (Antrim)
2008	A.Reilly (Antrim)
2009	F.Shannon (Antrim)
2010	A.Reilly (Antrim)
2011	F.Shannon (Antrim)
2012	A.Reilly (Antrim)
2013	A.Reilly (Antrim)
2014	A.Reilly (Antrim)
2015	No Competition
2016	C.Casey (Cork)
2017	C.Casey (Cork)

40 X 20 LADIES SENIOR SINGLES

1990	S.Carey (Kildare)
1991	S.Carey (Kildare)
1992	B.Hennessy (Limerick)
1993	B.Hennessy (Limerick)
1994	B.Hennessy (Limerick)
1995	B.Hennessy (Limerick)
1996	B.Hennessy (Limerick)
1997	B.Hennessy (Limerick)
1998	B.Hennessy (Limerick)
1999	F.McKenna (Antrim)
2000	F.McKenna (Antrim)
2001	F.Shannon (Antrim)
2002	S.McKenna (Antrim)
2003	F.Shannon (Antrim)
2004	M.Daly (Kerry)
2005	M.Daly (Kerry)
2006	F.Shannon (Antrim)

2007	F.Shannon (Antrim)
2008	F.Shannon (Antrim)
2009	F.Shannon (Antrim)
2010	M.Daly (Kerry)
2011	M.Daly (Kerry)
2012	F.Shannon (Antrim)
2013	C.Casey (Cork)
2014	A.Reilly (Antrim)
2015	A.Reilly (Antrim)
2016	C.Casey (Cork)
2017	C.Casey (Cork)

40 X 20 LADIES SENIOR DOUBLES

1992	M.Lindsay, M.Armstrong (Antrim)
1993	M.Lindsay, M.Armstrong (Antrim)
1994	No Competition
1995	No Competition
1996	S.Smith, E.Campbell (Antrim)
1997	J.Keating, C.Maloney (Tipperary)
1998	F.McKenna, B.Kerr MacCorraidh Antrim
1999	F.McKenna, B.Kerr MacCorraidh (Antrim)
2000	F.McKenna, S.McKenna (Antrim)
2001	No Competition
2002	A.Wrynn, F.Heal (Kildare)
2003	F.Shannon, S.McKenna (Antrim)
2004	No Competition
2005	F.Shannon, S.McKenna (Antrim)
2006	F.Shannon, A.Reilly (Antrim)
2007	F.Shannon, A.Reilly (Antrim)
2008	F.Shannon, S.Gallagher (Antrim)
2009	F.Shannon, S.Gallagher (Antrim)
2010	M.Daly, A.Prendiville (Kerry)
2011	M.Daly, A.Prendiville (Kerry)
2012	F.Shannon, S.Gallagher (Antrim)
2013	M.Daly, A.Prendiville (Kerry)
2014	C.Casey, A. O'Keeffe (Cork)
2015	C.Casey & A.O'Keeffe (Cork)
2016	C.Casey & A.O'Keeffe (Cork)
2017	P.Gallagher & A.Corrigan (Mayo)

UNIVERSITIES CHAMPIONSHIPS
WOMEN'S SINGLES

1994	Y.Gacquin (UCG)
1995	Y.Gacquin (UCG)
1996	J.Keating (Waterford RTC)

1997	L.Campbell (QUB)
1998	B.MacCorraidh (QUB)
1999	A.Wrynn (Maynooth)
2000	F.Healy (Crumlin College)
2001	F.Healy (DIT)
2002	F.Healy (DIT)
2003	S.Gartland (QUB)
2004	M.Daly (UCC)
2005	M.Daly (UCC)
2006	M.Daly (UCC)
2007	M.Daly (UCC)
2008	E.Ní Fhallúin (UCD)
2009	M.Rushe (UCD)
2010	M.Rushe (UCD)
2011	A.Prendiville (UCC)
2012	C.Casey (UL)
2013	C.Casey (UL)
2014	C.Casey (UL)
2015	C.NíChurraoin (UL)
2016	C.Mahon (TCD)
2017	C.Mahon (TCD)

2008	A.Prendiville (Kerry)
2009	B.Hennessy (Limerick)
2010	A.Prendiville (Kerry)
2011	M.Daly (Kerry)
2012	C.Casey (Cork)
2013	C.Casey (Cork)
2014	C.Casey (Cork
2015	No Competition
2016	C.Casey (Cork)

60 X 30 WOMEN'S SINGLES

2002	F.Healy (DIT)
2003	M.Daly (UCC)
2004	M.Daly (UCC)
2005	M.Daly (UCC)
2006	E.Ní Fhallúin (UCD)
2007	M.Rushe (NUIG)
2008	A.Prendeville (UCC)
2009	A.Prendeville (UCC)
2010	A.Prendeville (UCC)
2011	S.Hilley (ITT)
2012	No Competition
2013	C.Mahon (TCD)
2014	C.Mahon (TCD)

LADIES SENIOR SINGLES

1992	B.Hennessy (Limerick)
1993	B.Hennessy (Limerick)
1996	B.Hennessy (Limerick)
1999	B.Hennessy (Limerick)
2002	A.Wrynn (Kildare)
2007	A.Prendiville (Kerry)

CLUBS

COUNTY SENIOR HURLING TITLES
ROLL OF HONOUR

CONNACHT

GALWAY

Castlegar *(17):* 1936, 1937, 1938, 1939, 1940, 1944, 1950, 1952, 1953, 1957, 1958, 1967, 1969, 1972, 1973, 1979, 1984.

Ardrahan *(11):* 1894, 1895, 1896, 1901, 1902, 1903, 1910, 1949, 1974, 1975, 1978.

Turloughmore *(8):* 1956, 1961, 1962, 1963, 1964, 1965, 1966, 1985.

Liam Mellows *(8):* 1935, 1943, 1945, 1946, 1954, 1955, 1968, 1970.

Athenry *(8):* 1987, 1994, 1996, 1998, 1999, 2000, 2002, 2004.

Peterswell *(7):* 1889, 1898, 1899, 1900, 1904, 1905, 1907.

Sarsfields *(7):* 1889, 1892, 1893, 1895, 1897, 1980, 2015.

Gort *(7):* 1914, 1916, 1934, 1981, 1983, 2011, 2014.

Portumna *(6):* 2003, 2005, 2007, 2008, 2009, 2013.

Tynagh *(5):* 1920, 1922, 1923, 1925, 1928.

Craughwell *(5):* 1909, 1915, 1918, 1930, 1931.

Kiltormer *(5):* 1976, 1977, 1982, 1990, 1993.

Kilconieron *(3):* 1908, 1912, 1919.

Mullagh *(3):* 1906, 1929, 1932.

An Cath Gealach *(2):* 1947, 1948.

Woodford *(2):* 1913, 1917.

Fohenagh *(2):* 1959, 1960.

College Road *(2):* 1892, 1893.

Loughrea *(2):* 1941, 2006.

Clarinbridge *(2):* 2001, 2010.

St. Thomas' *(2):* 2012, 2016.

Meelick *(1):* 1887.

Killimor *(1):* 1897.

Derrydonnell *(1):* 1911.

Tommie Larkin's *(1):* 1971.

Maree *(1):* 1933.

Ballinasloe *(1):* 1951.

Killimordaly *(1):* 1986.

Abbeyknockmoy *(1):* 1988.

1942 championship declared void. There are no championship records for 1890, 1891, 1921, 1924, 1926 and 1927.

LEITRIM

St.Mary's-Carrick-on-Shannon *(32):* 1953, 1957, 1958, 1960, 1961, 1962, 1967, 1970, 1972, 1976, 1978, 1980, 1982, 1992, 1993, 1994, 1995, 1997, 1999, 2000, 2001, 2002, 2003, 2004, 2005, 2006, 2007, 2008, 2009, 2010, 2014, 2017.

Gortletteragh *(11):* 1983, 1984, 1985, 1986, 1988, 1989, 1990, 1991, 1996, 1998, 2011.

St. Finbarrs (Mohill) *(9):* 1917, 1964, 1965, 1966, 1968, 1969, 1973, 1974, 1979.

Manorhamilton *(3):* 1935, 1954, 1959.

Cluainín Iomáint *(3):* 2012, 2013, 2016.

Ballinamore *(2):* 1987, 2015.

Aughavas *(1):* 1956.

St. Brigid's *(1):* 1971.

Allen Gaels *(1):* 1975.

Lough Allen Gaels *(1):* 1977.

MAYO

Tooreen *(29):* 1966, 1972, 1974, 1975, 1978, 1979, 1980, 1981, 1982, 1983, 1984, 1985, 1986, 1987, 1989, 1990, 1991, 1992, 1993, 1994, 1995, 1997, 1998, 1999, 2000, 2001, 2003, 2013, 2017.

Ballyhaunis *(12):* 2002, 2004, 2005, 2006, 2008, 2009, 2010, 2011, 2012, 2014, 2015, 2016.

Westport *(7):* 1927, 1928, 1934, 1962, 1964, 1969, 1970.

Ballina Stephenites *(7):* 1907, 1925, 1930, 1932, 1933, 1959, 1996.

Swinford *(5):* 1916, 1917, 1918, 1919, 1956 .

Castlebar Dr. Hydes *(3):* 1904, 1905, 1906.

Ballaghaderreen *(3):* 1923, 1924, 1950.

Ballinrobe *(3):* 1973, 1976, 1977.

Ballyheane *(2):* 1929, 1935.

Castlebar Mitchels	**(2):**	1910, 1955.
Manulla	**(2):**	1960, 1961.
Cong	**(2):**	1965, 1967.
Claremorris	**(2):**	1968, 1971.
Castlebar Gaels	**(1):**	1902.
Army-John McBrides	**(1):**	1926.
Moy Slashers-Ballina	**(1):**	1963.
North Mayo	**(1):**	1988.
James Stephens	**(1):**	2007.

1951-54 no records; 1957-58 no records.

ROSCOMMON

Four Roads **(33):** 1905, 1906, 1907, 1945, 1946, 1948, 1950, 1954, 1958, 1962, 1971, 1977, 1981, 1982, 1983, 1986, 1988, 1991, 1993, 1996, 1997, 2000, 2001, 2002, 2005, 2008, 2009, 2010, 2011, 2012, 2013, 2014, 2015.

Athleague **(17):** 1909, 1910, 1916, 1928, 1929, 1936, 1937, 1949, 1953, 1955, 1957, 1959, 1975, 1978, 2003, 2006, 2007.

Tremane **(11):** 1956, 1960, 1963, 1968, 1972, 1973, 1974, 1976, 1979, 1980, 1995.

Roscommon Town **(6):** 1913, 1914, 1915, 1923, 1924, 1925.

Roscommon Gaels **(6):** 1961, 1964, 1965, 1966, 1969, 1970.

Oran **(6):** 1989, 1990, 1992, 1998, 2004, 2016.

Gaels Roscommon **(3):** 1902, 1903, 1904.

Roscommon **(3):** 1931, 1935, 1938.

St. Coman's Roscommon **(3):** 1944, 1951, 1952.

Pádraig Pearses **(3):** 1984, 1987, 2017.

Ballygar **(2):** 1930, 1985.

St.Dominic's Knockcroghery **(2):** 1994, 1999.

Patrick's Knockcroghery **(1):** 1967.

Gael Araghty **(1):** 1908.

Elphin **(1):** 1926.

18th Battalion Boyle **(1):** *1927.*

SLIGO

Craobh Rua **(19):** 1967, 1968, 1970, 1971, 1972, 1973, 1974, 1975, 1976, 1978, 1979, 1980, 1982, 1984, 1987, 1989, 1992, 1993, 1994.

Tubbercurry **(13):** 1969, 1977, 1995, 1996, 1997, 1998, 1999, 2000, 2001, 2002, 2003, 2004, 2006.

Calry/St. Joseph's **(11):** 2005, 2007, 2008, 2009, 2011, 2012, 2013, 2014, 2015, 2016, 2017.

Tourlestrane **(7):** 1981, 1983, 1985, 1986, 1988, 1990, 1991.

Dromard-O'Growneys **(5):** 1906, 1908, 1934, 1935, 1936.

Sligo **(3):** 1928, 1929, 1930.

Craobh Rua - Grange **(2):** 1965, 1966.

Sligo Wanderers **(1):** 1905.

St Columba's **(1):** 1907.

Sligo United **(1):** 1919.

Western Gaels **(1):** 2010.

Note: No championship in 1910-18 and 1931-33.

LEINSTER

CARLOW

St. Mullin's *(25):* 1932, 1949, 1950, 1951, 1952, 1953, 1954, 1957, 1958, 1959, 1960, 1962, 1965, 1966, 1968, 1983, 1984, 1989, 1997, 2000, 2002, 2010, 2014, 2015, 2016.

Naomh Eoin Myshall *(19):* 1974, 1975, 1976, 1978, 1981, 1982, 1985, 1986, 1987, 1990, 1991, 1992, 1993, 1994, 1995, 1997, 1999, 2003, 2005.

Carlow Town *(12):* 1920, 1921, 1927, 1937, 1938, 1942, 1961, 1963, 1977, 1979, 1980, 1988.

Erin's Own *(11):* 1934, 1935, 1936, 1939, 1940, 1943, 1944, 1945, 1964, 1967, 1970.

Mount Leinster Rangers *(7):* 2006, 2007, 2009, 2011, 2012, 2013, 2017.

Bagenalstown *(4):* 1928, 1929, 1930, 1931.

Naomh Brid *(3):* 1996, 2004, 2008.

Courtnellan *(2):* 1946, 1955.

St. Fintan's *(2):* 1969, 1971.

Ballinkillen *(2):* 1973, 2001.

Cooleyhune *(1):* 1933.

Hacketstown *(1):* 1947.

Leighlinbridge *(1):* 1956.

Palatine *(1):* 1972.

DUBLIN

Faughs *(31):* 1892, 1900, 1901, 1903, 1904, 1906, 1910, 1911, 1914, 1915, 1920, 1921, 1922, 1923, 1930, 1936, 1939, 1940, 1941, 1944, 1945, 1946, 1950, 1952, 1970, 1972, 1973, 1986, 1987, 1992, 1999.

St. Vincent's *(13):* 1953, 1954, 1955, 1957, 1960, 1962, 1964, 1967, 1975, 1981, 1982, 1988, 1993.

Commercials *(9):* 1895, 1896, 1897, 1898, 1899, 1905, 1907, 1909, 1916.

O'Tooles *(7):* 1969, 1977, 1984, 1990, 1995, 1996, 1997.

Garda *(6):* 1925, 1926, 1927, 1928, 1929, 1931.

Young Irelands *(6):* 1932, 1937, 1942, 1943, 1949, 1965.

Craobh Chiaráin *(6):* 1971, 1998, 2001, 2002, 2003, 2006.

Ballyboden St. Enda's *(6):* 2007, 2008, 2009, 2010, 2011, 2013.

Cuala *(6):* 1989, 1991, 1994, 2015, 2016, 2017.

Kilmacud Crokes *(5):* 1974, 1976, 1985, 2012, 2014.

Kickhams *(4):* 1889, 1890, 1908, 1924.

Rapparees *(3):* 1891, 1894, 1912.

Collegians *(3):* 1917, 19, 1919.

Army Metro *(3):* 1933, 1935, 1938.

U.C.D. *(3):* 2000, 2004, 2005.

New Irelands *(2):* 1958, 1959.

Metropolitans *(1):* 1887.

Davitts *(1):* 1893.

Thomas Davis *(1):* 1913.

Eoghan Ruadh *(1):* 1951.

St. Columba's *(1):* 1956.

Junior Board Sel. *(1):* 1963.

Crokes *(1):* 1966.

St. Brendan's *(1):* 1980.

Erin's Isle *(1):* 1983.

KILDARE

Clane *(16):* 1903, 1904, 1905, 1906, 1907, 1908, 1909, 1910, 1911, 1914, 1915, 1916, 1917, 1918, 1919, 1922.

Ardclough *(13):* 1968, 1973, 1975, 1976, 1979, 1980, 1981, 1982, 1983, 1985, 2004, 2006, 2017.

Coill Dubh *(12):* 1987, 1989, 1990, 1993, 1995, 1996, 1998, 1999, 2000, 2014, 2015.

Éire Óg *(10):* 1964, 1965, 1966, 1967, 1969, 1970, 1971, 1972, 1977, 1984.

Celbridge *(7):* 1921, 2005, 2009, 2010, 2011, 2013, 2016.

Maynooth *(5):* 1896, 1913, 1924, 1927, 1939.

Killinthomas *(5):* 1946, 1947, 1949, 1950, 1953.

Curragh Command *(5):* 1940, 1941, 1942, 1944, 1956.

McDonagh Barracks *(4):* 1929, 1932, 1934, 1935.

Athy *(3):* 1928, 1936, 1959.

Moorefield *(3):* 1944, 1963, 1991.

Military College *(3):* 1957, 1958, 1962.

Confey	*(3):*	2007, 2008, 2012.
Monasterevan	*(2):*	1887, 1889.
St Conleth's	*(2):*	1901, 1902.
St Barbara's	*(2):*	1954, 1955.
Broadford	*(2):*	1960, 1961.
Castledermot	*(2):*	1988, 1992.
Naas	*(2):*	2001, 2002.
St Thomas's College	*(1):*	1900.
Goff Barracks	*(1):*	1925.
Eoghan Ruadh	*(1):*	1945.
Suncroft	*(1):*	1974.
Leixlip	*(1):*	1986.

KILKENNY

Tullaroan **(20):** 1887, 1889, 1895, 1897, 1899, 1901, 1902, 1904, 1907, 1910, 1911, 1915, 1924, 1925, 1930, 1933, 1934, 1948, 1958, 1994.

Ballyhale Shamrocks **(15):** 1978, 1979, 1980, 1982, 1983, 1985, 1988, 1989, 1991, 2006, 2007, 2008, 2009, 2012, 2014.

Mooncoin **(12):** 1888, 1900, 1906, 1908, 1913, 1916, 1927, 1928, 1929, 1932, 1936, 1965.

Bennettsbridge **(12):** 1890, 1952, 1953, 1955, 1956, 1959, 1960, 1962, 1964, 1966, 1967, 1971.

James Stephens **(9):** 1935, 1937, 1969, 1975, 1976, 1981, 2004, 2005, 2011.

Carrickshock **(7):** 1931, 1938, 1940, 1941, 1942, 1943, 1951.

Fenians **(5):** 1970, 1972, 1973, 1974, 1977.

Glenmore **(5):** 1987, 1990, 1992, 1995, 1999.

Dicksboro **(5):** 1923, 1926, 1950, 1993, 2017.

Éire Óg **(4):** 1939, 1944, 1945, 1947.

Young Irelands-Gowran **(3):** 1996, 2002, 2003.

Clara **(3):** 1986, 2013, 2015.

O'Loughlin Gaels **(3):** 2001, 2010, 2016.

Erins Own-City **(2):** 1905, 1929.

Threecastles **(2):** 1898, 1903.

St. Lachtain's-Freshford	*(2):*	1961, 1963.
Graigue-Ballycallan	*(2):*	1998, 2000.
Johnstown	*(1):*	1914.
Thomastown	*(1):*	1946.
Graigue	*(1):*	1949.
Slieverue	*(1):*	1954.
John Lockes-Callan	*(1):*	1957.
Rower-Inistiogue	*(1):*	1968.
St. Martin's	*(1):*	1984.
Dunnamaggin	*(1):*	1997.

No Championships 1891-92, 1912, 1917-19, 1920-22.

LAOIS

Camross **(25):** 1959, 1963, 1965, 1966, 1967, 1968, 1969, 1971, 1973, 1974, 1976, 1977, 1978, 1979, 1980, 1985, 1986, 1988, 1990, 1993, 1994, 1996, 2007, 2013, 2017.

Rathdowney **(18):** 1888, 1889, 1898, 1899, 1901, 1902, 1903, 1907, 1908, 1911, 1912, 1921, 1922, 1925, 1926, 1931, 1936, 1941.

Clonad **(13):** 1930, 1933, 1935, 1937, 1946, 1947, 1948, 1950, 1953, 1954, 1958, 1962, 1992.

Portlaoise **(11):** 1928, 1943, 1981, 1982, 1983, 1984, 1987, 1989, 1991, 1998, 2004.

Kilcotton **(10):** 1904, 1905, 1906, 1909, 1913, 1919, 1920, 1923, 1924, 1929.

Abbbeyleix **(8):** 1927, 1932, 1934, 1939, 1940, 1944, 1945, 1949.

Castletown **(8):** 1995, 1997, 1999, 2000, 2001, 2002, 2003, 2005.

Borris-in-Ossory **(6):** 1956, 1957, 1958, 1960, 1961, 1972.

Rathdowney-Errill **(5):** 2006, 2008, 2010, 2012, 2014.

Ballygeehan **(5):** 1914, 1915, 1916, 1917, 1918.

Clonaslee **(3):** 1890, 1910, 1975.

Clough-Ballacolla **(3):** 2009, 2011, 2015.

Errill **(2):** 1938, 1952.

Cullahill **(2):** 1955, 1964.

Mountrath **(1):** 1942.

Kyle **(1):** 1951.

Borris-in-Ossory/Kilcotton **(1)** 2016.

LONGFORD

Wolfe Tones *(18)*: 1992, 1993, 1994, 1995, 1996, 1998, 1999, 2002, 2004, 2007, 2008, 2009, 2010, 2013, 2014, 2015, 2016, 2017.

Slasher Gaels *(11)*: 1982, 1983, 1984, 1986, 1987, 1989, 1990, 1991, 1997, 2000, 2001.

Longford Leo Caseys *(5)*: 1902, 1903, 1904, 1905, 1906.

Clonguish *(4)*: 2003, 2005, 2006, 2012.

Granard Slashers *(3)*: 1932, 1933, 1934.

Rathcline (Naomh Chiaráin) *(2)*: 1985, 1988.

Killoe Young Emmets *(1)*: 1907.

No competition 1935-1981 & 2011.

LOUTH

Naomh Moninne-Dundalk *(21)*: 1964, 1965, 1973, 1974, 1976, 1978, 1982, 1983, 1984, 1985, 1986, 1987, 1989, 1992, 1993, 1995, 1997, 1998, 1999, 2010, 2017.

Knockbridge *(10)*: 2000, 2001, 2003, 2005, 2006, 2007, 2008, 2009, 2011, 2014.

Naomh Colmcille Ardee *(8)*: 1955, 1958, 1960, 1962, 1963, 1966, 1971, 1975.

Wolfe Tones (Drogheda) *(7)*: 1954, 1959, 1988, 1990, 1991, 1994, 1996.

C.B.S. Tredaghs (Drogheda) *(6)*: 1907, 1911, 1912, 1927, 1934, 1935.

C.B.S. Shamrocks (Drogheda) *(6)*: 1933, 1936, 1940, 1943, 1944, 1945.

Dundalk Hurling Club *(4)*: 1904, 1917, 1924, 1925.

Pearse Óg *(4)*: 2002, 2004, 2012, 2013.

Erins Own (Dundalk) *(3)*: 1951, 1952, 1953.

Clan na nGael (Dundalk) *(2)*: 1970, 1972.

Na Piarsaigh (Drogheda) *(2)*: 1968, 1969.

Cuchulainns *(2)*: 1956, 1957.

Con Colberts (Dundalk) *(2)*: 1919, 1921.

St Fechin's *(2)*: 2015, 2016.

Hitchestown *(1)*: 1932.

Gaelic League (Dundalk) *(1)*: 1928.

Ardee St. Mochta's *(1)*: 1926.

John Mitchells (Drogheda) *(1)*: *1918.

Dundalk Recreation Club *(1)*: 1909.

Boyne Emmets (Drogheda) *(1)*: 1908.

Shamrocks (Dundalk) *(1)*: 1902
(First organised Louth Championship).

Note: 1902-1986 (inclusive) run as Junior Championship. Changed to Senior status in 1987.

MEATH

Kilmessan *(30)*: 1907, 1922, 1924, 1927, 1934, 1937, 1938, 1939, 1943, 1944, 1945, 1946, 1947, 1948, 1961, 1962, 1965, 1969, 1976, 1977, 1978, 1990, 1997, 1998, 1999, 2002, 2003, 2004, 2008, 2013.

Trim *(26)*: 1915, 1916, 1918, 1920, 1921, 1935, 1940, 1941, 1942, 1949, 1950, 1952, 1955, 1956, 1957, 1959, 1960, 1987, 1988, 1989, 1992, 1994, 1995, 1998, 2000, 2001.

Athboy *(9)*: 1923, 1926, 1928, 1929, 1966, 1967, 1968, 1970, 1972.

Kiltale *(8)*: 1982, 1983, 2007, 2012, 2014, 2015, 2016, 2017.

Killyon *(7)*: 1919, 1979, 1980, 1981, 1984, 1991, 2005.

Boardsmill *(6)*: 1958, 1964, 1971, 1973, 1974, 1975.

Dunboyne *(5)*: 1908, 1911, 1912, 1913, 1914.

Young Irelands *(4)*: 1903, 1904, 1905, 1906.

Kildalkey *(4)*: 1951, 2009, 2010, 2011.

Rathmolyon *(3)*: 1993, 1996, 2006.

Erin's Own *(2)*: 1930, 1931.

St. Patrick's *(2)*: 1953, 1954.

Navan O'Mahoneys *(2)*: 1985, 1986.

Hibernian, Kells *(1)*: 1902.

Longwood *(1)*: 1936.

Rathoath *(1)*: 1963.

OFFALY

Coolderry *(30)*: 1899, 1901, 1903, 1904, 1905, 1906, 1910, 1911, 1914, 1916, 1917, 1926, 1931, 1939, 1942, 1945, 1947, 1949, 1953, 1956, 1961, 1962, 1963, 1977, 1980, 1986, 2004, 2010, 2011, 2015.

Birr   **(22):**   1912, 1913, 1915, 1938, 1940, 1943, 1944, 1946, 1948, 1971, 1991, 1994, 1997, 1999, 2000, 2001, 2002, 2003, 2005, 2006, 2007, 2008.

St. Rynagh's   **(18):**   1965, 1966, 1968, 1969, 1970, 1972, 1973, 1974, 1975, 1976, 1981, 1982,1987, 1988, 1990, 1992, 1993, 2016.

Drumcullen   **(17):**   1908, 1918, 1919, 1924, 1925, 1927, 1928, 1929, 1933, 1941, 1950, 1951, 1952, 1954, 1957, 1958, 1960.

Tullamore   **(10):**   1909, 1932, 1934, 1935, 1936, 1937, 1955, 1959, 1964, 2009.

Kinnitty   **(9):** 1920, 1923, 1930, 1967, 1978, 1979, 1983, 1984, 1985.

Seir Kieran   **(4):**   1988, 1995, 1996, 1998.

Kilcormac/Killoughey   **(4):**   2012, 2013, 2014, 2017.

Killoughey   **(3):**   1896, 1897, 1907.

Cadamstown   **(2):**   1900, 1902.

Lusmagh   **(1):**   1989.

Fortal   **(1):**   1898.

WESTMEATH

Brownstown   **(15):**   1938, 1943, 1946, 1947, 1948, 1952, 1977, 1978, 1981, 1983, 1985, 1988, 1989, 1991, 1993.

Castlepollard   **(14):** 1925, 1928, 1933, 1934, 1936, 1937, 1961, 1965, 1966, 1974, 1995, 1997, 2003, 2005.

Clonkill   **(14):**   1929, 1930, 1931, 1932, 1939, 1940, 1941, 1969, 2001, 2007, 2009, 2011, 2012, 2015.

Raharney   **(13):**   1913, 1914, 1919, 1967, 1973, 1984, 1992, 1994, 2006, 2008, 2010, 2014, 2016.

Castletown-Geoghegan   **(13):**   1923, 1956, 1957, 1958, 1960, 1964, 1979, 1982, 1986, 1990, 2004, 2013, 2017.

Ringtown   **(9):**   1906, 1908, 1910, 1915, 1916, 1917, 1942, 1980, 1987.

Lough Lene Gaels   **(7):**   1975, 1976, 1996, 1998, 1999, 2000, 2002.

St. Brigid's   **(4):**   1968, 1970, 1971, 1972.

Athlone   **(4):**   1905, 1907, 1911, 1912.

Delvin   **(4):**   1949, 1950, 1951, 1953.

Mullingar   **(4):**   1903, 1904, 1935, 1944.

Rickardstown   **(3):**   1954, 1959, 1963.

Athlone Military   **(2):**   1926, 1927.

Drumroney   **(2):**   1918, 1921.

Riverstown   **(1):**   1909.

Collinstown   **(1):**   1955.

Mental Hospital   **(1):**   1924.

Pearses   **(1):**   1962.

Columb Rovers   **(1):**   1945.

Note: No championships in 1920 or 1922.

WEXFORD

Rathnure   **(20):**   1948, 1950, 1955, 1961, 1967, 1971, 1972, 1973, 1974, 1977, 1979, 1980, 1986, 1987, 1990, 1996, 1998, 2002, 2003, 2006

Buffers Alley   **(12):**   1968, 1970, 1975, 1976, 1982, 1983, 1984, 1985, 1988, 1989, 1991, 1992.

Oulart-The Ballagh   **(12):**   1994, 1997, 2004, 2005, 2007, 2009, 2010, 2011, 2012, 2013, 2015, 2016.

Adamstown   **(11):**   1926, 1927, 1931, 1932, 1933, 1935, 1936, 1937, 1940, 1941, 1942.

St. Aidan's (Enniscorthy)   **(9):**   1946, 1947, 1952, 1953, 1954, 1956, 1957, 1958, 1959.

Faythe Harriers   **(5):**   1960, 1962, 1965, 1981, 2001.

Blackwater   **(3):**   1889, 1890, 1898.

New Ross United   **(3):**   1943, 1944, 1945.

Cloughbawn   **(3):**   1949, 1951, 1993.

St Martin's   **(3):**   1999, 2008, 2017.

Castlebridge   **(2):**   1904, 1919.

Ballymurn   **(2):**   1910, 1911.

Glenbrien   **(2):**   1915, 1916.

Sally Beachers   **(2):**   1928, 1930.

St Fintan's   **(2):**   1929, 1934.

Shamrocks   **(2):**   1964, 1969.

Slaney Harriers   **(1):**   1903.

Rathgarogue   **(1):**   1912.

New Ross   **(1):**   1913.

Enniscorthy Rapparees   **(1):**   1914.

Crossabeg   **(1):**   1918.

O'Hanrahan's (New Ross)   **(1):**   1939.

Oylegate-Glenbrien   **(1):**   1963.

Geraldine O'Hanrahans   **(1):**   1966.

Rapparees   **(1):**   1978.

St Anne's-Rathangan   **(1):**   2000.

Shelmaliers   **(1):**   2014.

WICKLOW

Carnew *(19):*   1965, 1967, 1968, 1969,
1973, 1974, 1976, 1978, 1979, 1980, 1981, 1984, 1988, 1991,
2000, 2002, 2004, 2006, 2009.

Avondale *(14):*   1908, 1915, 1931, 1936,
1940, 1941, 1942, 1946, 1947, 1949, 1960, 1964, 1966, 1983.

Glenealy *(15):*   1957, 1958, 1959, 1975,
1986, 1996, 2003, 2005, 2007, 2008, 2010, 2011, 2012, 2013,
2017.

Barndarrig *(12):*   1923, 1924, 1926, 1943,
1944, 1945, 1948, 1951, 1954, 1955, 1956, 1988.

Rathnew *(11):*   1906, 1911, 1913, 1925,
1929, 1932, 1933, 1934, 1937, 1939, 1950.

Kiltegan *(8):*   1987, 1993, 1994, 1995,
1997, 1998, 1999, 2001.

St. Patrick's (Wicklow) *(6):*   1903, 1916, 1928, 1930 (as
Wicklow), 1990, 1992.

Arklow Rock Parnell *(6):*   1970, 1971, 1972, 1977,
1982, 1985.

Bray Emmetts *(4):*   1952, 2014, 2015, 2016.

Arklow *(3):*   1917, 1918, 1919.

St. Kevin's (Bray) *(2):*   1961, 1963.

Ballymoney *(1):*   1910.

Baltinglass *(1):*   1927.

Ballinacor *(1):*   1935.

Avoca *(1):*   1953.

Forestry College *(1):*   1962.

MUNSTER

CLARE

Newmarket *(23):*   1912, 1916, 1925,
1926, 1927, 1930, 1931, 1936, 1955, 1963, 1964, 1965, 1967,
1968, 1969, 1971, 1972, 1973, 1974, 1976, 1978, 1981, 2012.

Sixmilebridge *(13):*   1977, 1979, 1983,
1984, 1989, 1992, 1993, 1995, 2000, 2002, 2013, 2015, 2017.

Clarecastle *(11):*   1943, 1945, 1949,
1970, 1986, 1987, 1991, 1994, 1997, 2003, 2005.

Tulla *(8):*   1889, 1896, 1897,
1899, 1905, 1913, 1933, 2007.

Feakle *(6):*   1935, 1938, 1939,
1940, 1944, 1988.

Éire Óg *(6):*   1956, 1957, 1966,
1980, 1982, 1990.

O'Callaghans Mills *(5):*   1904, 1906, 1910,
1918, 1937.

Scarriff *(5):*   1907, 1917, 1946,
1952, 1953.

Ennis Dalcassians *(5):*   1914, 1915, 1924,
1929, 1934.

St. Joseph's Doora-Barefield *(5):*   1954, 1958, 1998,
1999, 2001.

Ruan *(5):*   1948, 1951, 1959,
1960, 1962.

Kilnamona *(3):*   1902, 1903, 1908.

Carrahan *(2):*   1898, 1900.

Ennis *(2):*   1911, 1941.

Kilkishen *(2):*   1923, 1932.

Whitegate *(2):*   1950, 1961.

Kilmaley *(2):*   1985, 2004.

Wolfe Tones Shannon *(2):*   1997, 2006.

Clonlara *(2):*   1919, 2008.

Crusheen *(2):*   2010, 2011.

Cratloe *(2):*   2009, 2014.

Smith O'Briens-Garranboy *(1):*   1887.

Ogonnolloe *(1):*   1888.

Ennis Faughs *(1):*   1890.

O'Callaghan Mills-Fireballs *(1):*   1909.

Ennis-Clarecastle *(1):*   1928.

Clooney	(1):	1942.

Bodyke (1): 1947.

Brian Borus (1): 1975.

Ballyea (1): 2016.

CORK
Blackrock (32): 1887, 1889, 1891, 1893, 1894, 1895, 1897, 1898, 1903, 1908, 1910, 1911, 1912, 1913, 1920, 1924, 1925, 1927, 1929, 1930, 1931, 1956, 1961, 1971, 1973, 1975, 1978, 1979, 1985, 1999, 2001, 2002.

Glen Rovers (27): 1934, 1935, 1936, 1937, 1938, 1939, 1940, 1941, 1944, 1945, 1948, 1949, 1950, 1953, 1954, 1958, 1959, 1960, 1962, 1964, 1967, 1969, 1972, 1976, 1989, 2015, 2016.

St. Finbarr's (25): 1899, 1904, 1905, 1906, 1919, 1922, 1923, 1926, 1932, 1933, 1942, 1943, 1946, 1947, 1955, 1965, 1968, 1974, 1977, 1980, 1981, 1982, 1984, 1988, 1993.

Midleton (7): 1914, 1916, 1983, 1986, 1987, 1991, 2013.

Sarsfields (6): 1951, 1957, 2008, 2010, 2012, 2014.

Redmonds (5): 1892, 1900, 1901, 1915, 1917.

Newtownshandrum (4): 2000, 2003, 2005, 2009.

Avondhu (3): 1952, 1966, 1996.

Na Piarsaigh (3): 1990, 1995, 2004.

Dungourney (3): 1902, 1907, 1909.

Erin's Own (3): 1992, 2006, 2007.

Imokilly (3): 1997, 1998, 2017.

University College (2): 1963, 1970.

Carrigtwohill (2): 1918, 2011.

Tower Street (1): 1888.

Aghabullogue (1): 1890.

Ballyhea (1): 1896.

Éire Óg (1): 1928.

Carbery (1): 1994.

KERRY
Ballyduff (25): 1891, 1955, 1957, 1959, 1960, 1961, 1965,1966, 1972, 1973, 1976, 1977, 1978, 1984, 1988, 1989, 1991, 1993, 1994, 1995, 2006, 2010, 2011, 2012, 2017.

Kilmoyley (24): 1890, 1892, 1894, 1895, 1900, 1901, 1905, 1907, 1910, 1914, 1948, 1962, 1963, 1964, 1970, 1971, 2001, 2002, 2003, 2004, 2008, 2009, 2015, 2016.

Crotta (10): 1939, 1941, 1943, 1944, 1945, 1947, 1950, 1951, 1968, 1999.

Causeway (7): 1932, 1979, 1980, 1981, 1982, 1987, 1998.

St. Brendan's, Ardfert (7): 1949, 1952, 1967, 1975, 1986, 1990, 2013.

Lixnaw (7): 1933, 1954, 1983, 1985, 2005, 2007, 2014.

Tralee Mitchels/Parnells (5): 1908, 1911, 1912, 1918, 1919.

Ballyheigue (5): 1946, 1992, 1996, 1997, 2000.

Abbeydorney (4): 1893, 1896, 1913, 1974.

Austin Stacks (3): 1928, 1929, 1931.

Kilgarvan (3): 1953, 1956, 1958.

Tralee Celtic (2): 1903, 1904.

Pearses (div.) (2): 1937, 1938.

Tullig (1): 1916 (disputed with Kenmare).

Tubrid (1): 1917.

Tralee (div.) (1): 1925.

St. Brendan's (div.) (1): 1936.

Banna (1): 1940.

Killarney (1): 1969.

LIMERICK
Ahane (20): 1931, 1933, 1934, 1935, 1936, 1937, 1938, 1939, 1942, 1943, 1944, 1945, 1946, 1947, 1948, 1955, 1998, 1999, 2001, 2004.

Patrickswell (19): 1965, 1966, 1969, 1970, 1977, 1979, 1982, 1983, 1984, 1987, 1988, 1990, 1993, 1995, 1996, 1997, 2000, 2003, 2016.

Kilmallock (11): 1960, 1967, 1973, 1974, 1975, 1985, 1992, 1994, 2010, 2012, 2014.

Claughaun (10): 1914, 1915, 1916, 1918, 1926, 1957, 1958, 1968, 1971, 1986.

Young Irelands (7): 1902, 1910, 1920, 1922, 1928, 1930, 1932.

South Liberties (7): 1888, 1889, 1890, 1972, 1976, 1978, 1981.

Croom (6): 1908, 1919, 1924, 1929, 1940, 1941.

Cappamore	*(5):*	1904, 1954, 1956, 1959, 1964.
Adare	*(4):*	2002, 2007, 2008, 2009.
Na Piarsaigh	*(4):*	2011, 2013, 2015, 2017.
Caherline	*(3):*	1896, 1905, 1907.
Treaty Sarsfields	*(3):*	1951, 1952, 1953.
Kilfinane	*(2):*	1897, 1899.
Fedamore	*(2):*	1912, 1927.
Newcastlewest	*(2):*	1917, 1925.
Western Gaels	*(2):*	1961, 1962.
Ballybrown	*(2):*	1989, 1991.
St. Patrick's	*(2):*	1949, 1950.
Castleconnell	*(1):*	1950.
Murroe	*(1):*	1887.
Treaty Stones	*(1):*	1891.
St.Michael's	*(1):*	1895.
South Limerick	*(1):*	1893.
Shamrocks	*(1):*	1898.
Sallymount	*(1):*	1900.
Ballingarry	*(1):*	1911.
Killeedy	*(1):*	1980.
Feenagh-Kilmeedy	*(1):*	1963.
Garryspillane	*(1):*	2005.
Bruree	*(1):*	2006.

TIPPERARY

Thurles Sarsfields *(28):* 1935, 1936, 1938, 1939, 1942, 1944, 1945, 1946, 1952, 1955, 1956, 1957, 1958, 1959, 1961, 1962, 1963, 1964, 1965, 1974, 2005, 2009, 2010, 2012, 2014, 2015, 2016, 2017.

Toomevara *(21):* 1890, 1910, 1912, 1913, 1914, 1919, 1923, 1930, 1931, 1960, 1992, 1993, 1994, 1998, 1999, 2000, 2001, 2003, 2004, 2006, 2008.

Boherlahan *(11):* 1915, 1916, 1917, 1918, 1922, 1924, 1925, 1927, 1928, 1941, 1946.

Borris-Ileigh *(7):* 1949, 1950, 1953, 1981, 1983, 1986, 1987.

Thurles *(7):* 1904, 1906, 1907, 1908, 1909, 1911, 1929.

Roscrea	*(6):*	1968, 1969, 1970, 1972, 1973, 1980.
Moycarkey-Borris	*(6):*	1932, 1934, 1937, 1940, 1982, 1984.
Kilruane-MacDonaghs	*(4):*	1977, 1978, 1979, 1985.
Tubberadora	*(3):*	1895, 1896, 1898.
Two Mile Borris	*(3):*	1900, 1903, 1905.
Moycarkey	*(2):*	1889, 1926.
Carrick Davins	*(2):*	1966, 1967.
Moneygall	*(2):*	1975, 1976.
Clonoulty-Rossmore	*(2):*	1989, 1997.
Holycross-Ballycahill	*(2):*	1948, 1951.
Holycross	*(2):*	1954, 1990.
Loughmore/Castleiney	*(2):*	2007, 2013.
Clonoulty	*(1):*	1888.
Drombane	*(1):*	1994.
Suir View	*(1):*	1897.
Horse and Jockey	*(1):*	1899.
Ballytarsna	*(1):*	1901.
Lahorna De Wets	*(1):*	1902.
Éire Óg-Annacarty	*(1):*	1943.
Carrick Swans	*(1):*	1947.
Moyne-Templetuohy	*(1):*	1971.
Cappawhite	*(1):*	1987.
Loughmore	*(1):*	1988.
Cashel King Cormacs	*(1):*	1991.
Éire Óg Nenagh	*(1):*	1995.
Mullinahone	*(1):*	2002.
Drom & Inch	*(1):*	2011.

WATERFORD

Mount Sion *(35):* 1938, 1939, 1940, 1943, 1945, 1948, 1949, 1951, 1953, 1954, 1955, 1956, 1957, 1958, 1959, 1960, 1961, 1963, 1964, 1965, 1969, 1972, 1974, 1975, 1981, 1983, 1986, 1988, 1994, 1998, 2000, 2002, 2003, 2004, 2006.

Ballygunner *(16):* 1966, 1967, 1968, 1993, 1995, 1996, 1997, 1999, 2001, 2005, 2009, 2011, 2014, 2015, 2016, 2017.

Erin's Own **(13):** 1927, 1928, 1929, 1930, 1931, 1932, 1933, 1934, 1935, 1942, 1946, 1947, 1962.

T. F. Meagher **(6):** 1909, 1910, 1911, 1912, 1922, 1924.

Dungarvan **(6):** 1908, 1917, 1920, 1923, 1926, 1941.

Portlaw **(6):** 1937, 1970, 1971, 1973, 1976, 1977.

De La Salle **(5):** 1913, 1914, 2008, 2010, 2012.

Clonea **(4):** 1903, 1905, 1907, 1952.

Tallow **(4):** 1936, 1980, 1984, 1985.

Ferrybank **(3):** 1915, 1916, 1919.

Lismore **(3):** 1925, 1991, 1993.

Dunhill **(2):** 1982, 1987.

Roanmore **(2):** 1989, 1990.

Ballytruckle **(1):** 1897.

Ballydurn **(1):** 1899.

Gracedieu **(1):** 1904.

Ballyduff Lower **(1):** 1906.

Éire Óg **(1):** 1918.

Tourin **(1):** 1950.

Army **(1):** 1944.

Ballyduff Upper **(1):** 2007.

Passage **(1):** 2013.

ULSTER

ANTRIM

Loughgiel Shamrocks **(20):** 1920, 1924, 1925, 1929, 1938, 1943, 1956, 1963, 1966, 1967, 1968, 1970, 1971, 1982, 1989, 2010, 2011, 2012, 2013, 2016.

Ballycastle **(17):** 1913, 1914, 1933, 1944, 1948, 1950, 1952, 1953, 1954, 1964, 1975, 1978, 1979, 1 980, 1983, 1984, 1986.

O'Donovan Rossa **(15):** 1918, 1919, 1921, 1946, 1949, 1955, 1957, 1958, 1959, 1960, 1972, 1976, 1977, 1988, 2004.

Cushendall **(13):** 1981, 1985, 1987, 1991, 1992, 1993, 1996, 1999, 2005, 2006, 2008, 2014, 2015.

Dunloy **(12):** 1990, 1994, 1995, 1997, 1998, 2000, 2001, 2002, 2003, 2007, 2009, 2017.

O'Connell's **(9):** 1927, 1928, 1930, 1 932, 1936, 1940, 1941, 1942, 1945.

St. John's **(7):** 1934, 1951, 1961, 1962, 1965, 1969, 1973.

Tír na nÓg **(5):** 1904, 1905, 1922, 1926, 1939.

Carey **(3):** 1906, 1916, 1923.

Seaghan an Díomais **(3):** 1908, 1910, 1915.

Seán Mitchel's **(3):** 1911, 1912, 1947.

Brian Óg **(2):** 1901, 1909.

Glenariffe **(2):** 1935, 1937.

O'Neill Crowleys **(2):** 1903, 1907.

Cushendun **(1):** 1931.

James Stephen's **(1):** 1917.

Lámh Dhearg **(1):** 1902.

Sarsfields **(1):** 1974.

ARMAGH

Cuchullain's, Armagh **(22)**: 1951, 1952, 1953, 1954, 1961, 1962, 1963, 1964, 1969, 1970, 1971, 1973, 1974, 1979, 1980, 1982, 1983, 1984, 1987, 1988, 1989, 2013.

Lámh Dhearg, Keady **(17):** 1949, 1965, 1972, 1975, 1990, 1992, 1993, 1994, 1995, 1996, 1997, 1998, 2005, 2007, 2008, 2010, 2014.

Middletown **(13):** 1981, 1985, 1986, 1991, 1999, 2000, 2006, 2009, 2011, 2012, 2015, 2016, 2017.

Christian Brothers' Armagh Past Pupils' Union **(3):** 1945, 1946, 1948.

Éire Óg, Keady **(3):** 1927, 1932, 1933.

St. Malachy's, Portadown	(2):	1966, 1967.
Armagh Harps	(1):	1905.
Michael Dwyer's, Keady	(1):	1906.
Bessbrook	(1):	1947.
O'Donnell's, Armagh	(1):	1934.
Red Hand's, Armagh	(1):	1931.
Hugh Carberry's, Rocks	(1):	1950.
Seán an Díomais, Camlough	(1):	1907.
Tir na nÓg, Armagh	(1):	1904.
Young Ireland's	(1):	1928.

CAVAN

Mullahoran **(24)**: 1990, 1991, 1992, 1993, 1994, 1995, 1996, 1997, 1998, 1999, 2000, 2001, 2002, 2003, 2004, 2005, 2006, 2007, 2008, 2009, 2010, 2013, 2016, 2017.

Cavan Slashers **(8)**: 1922, 1924, 1927, 1928, 1933, 1934, 1935, 1936.

Cavan Gaels **(2)**: 1973, 1974, 1983, 1984, 1985.

Bailieboro Shamrocks **(5)**: 1982, 1984, 2005, 2006, 2007.

Ballyhaise **(4)**: 1925, 1926, 1947, 1948.

Woodford Gaels **(3)**: 1986, 1987, 1988.

Cootehill **(3)**: 1932, 2014, 2015.

Drumbo **(1)**: 1927.

Kill **(1)**: 1930.

Granard **(1)**: 1950.

DERRY

Kevin Lynch's Dungiven **(21)**: 1972, 1973, 1974, 1975, 1976, 1977, 1979, 1981, 1982, 1984, 1987, 1989, 1996, 1998, 2003, 2004, 2006, 2007, 2008, 2009, 2011.

Lavey **(18)**: 1940, 1944, 1946, 1948, 1962, 1985, 1986, 1988, 1990, 1991, 1992, 1994, 1995, 1997, 1999, 2001, 2002, 2010.

Dungiven **(14)**: 1972, 1973, 1974, 1975, 1976, 1977, 1979, 1981, 1982, 1984, 1987, 1989, 2003, 2004.

Slaughtneil **(11)**: 1965, 1966, 1968, 1969, 1993, 2000, 2013, 2014, 2015, 2016, 2017.

Banagher **(3)**: 1978, 1980, 2005.

Sarsfields **(2)**: 1933, 1934.

St. Patrick's Waterside **(2)**: 1891, 1905.

St. Finbarr's Lough	(2):	1963, 1964.
Hibernians	(1):	1889.
Burt	(1):	1930.
Ailech	(1):	1937.
Ballinscran	(1):	1938.
Mitchells Coleraine	(1):	1945.
Swatragh	(1):	2012.

Note: No championship in 1983.

DONEGAL

Burt **(37)**: 1906, 1956, 1957, 1961, 1962, 1967, 1969, 1970, 1971, 1976, 1978, 1979, 1982, 1983, 1989, 1991,1992, 1993, 1994, 1995, 1996, 1997, 1998, 1999, 2000, 2001, 2002, 2003, 2004, 2005, 2006, 2009, 2011, 2012, 2013, 2014, 2015.

Setanta **(11)**: 1980, 1981, 1983, 1984, 1985, 1986, 1987, 1990, 2007, 2008, 2017.

St. Union's Letterkenny **(7)**: 1926, 1932, 1933, 1938, 1945, 1953, 1972.

Aodh-Ruadh Ballyshannon (5): 1924, 1925, 1929, 1975, 1977.

Carrowmore **(4)**: 1934, 1935, 1936, 1937.

Carndonagh **(3)**: 1944, 1954, 1959.

Gleann-Eirne **(2)**: 1964, 1966.

Lifford **(2)**: 1958, 1960.

Seán Mac Cumhaills **(2)**: 2010, 2016.

Bundoran **(1)**: 1907.

Finner Camp **(1)**: 1927.

Glen Swilly **(1)** : 1963.

DOWN

Ballycran **(24)**: 1949, 1953, 1957, 1958, 1960, 1961, 1967, 1972, 1974, 1976, 1977, 1979, 1980, 1984, 1985, 1986, 1987, 1993, 1994, 1995, 2007, 2009, 2011, 2015.

Kilclief **(23)**: 1912, 1913, 1914, 1915, 1916, 1917, 1918, 1919, 1920, 1925, 1931, 1932, 1933, 1935, 1939, 1942, 1943, 1944, 1945, 1947, 1954, 1955, 1956.

Portaferry **(21)**: 1926, 1929, 1938, 1963, 1965, 1968, 1969, 1971, 1978, 1981, 1988, 1989, 1991, 1996, 2000, 2001, 2002, 2003, 2006, 2012, 2014.

Ballygalget **(21)**: 1959, 1964, 1966, 1970, 1973, 1974, 1975, 1982, 1983, 1990, 1992, 1997, 1998, 1999, 2004, 2005, 2008, 2010, 2013, 2016, 2017.

Ballela **(7):** 1936, 1937, 1940, 1941, 1948, 1951, 1952.

Faugh-an-Bealach, Newry **(6):** 1903, 1904, 1907, 1908, 1909, 1930.

Clann na Boirce, Newry **(2):** 1905, 1906.

Clann Uladh, Newry **(2):** 1934, 1936.

Liatroim **(2):** 1927, 1928.

Ballyvarley **(1):** 1910.

*N.B. 1962 final result declared null and void *Not played in 1911, 1924-27, 1950.

FERMANAGH

Lisbellaw St. Patrick's **(30):** 1972, 1976, 1977, 1982, 1983, 1985, 1986, 1987, 1988, 1989, 1991, 1992, 1993, 1994, 1995, 1996, 1997, 1998, 2006, 2007, 2008, 2009, 2010, 2011, 2012, 2013, 2014, 2015, 2016, 2017.

Belleek Erne Gaels **(5):** 1973, 1974, 1975, 1981, 1984.

Enniskillen O'Neill **(3):** 1904, 1906, 1907.

COA O'Dwyers **(3):** 1935, 1938, 1939.

Glasmullagh **(3):** 1936, 1945, 1946.

Enniskillen Gaels **(2):** 1979, 1990.

Ashwood Maguires **(2):** 1905, 1908.

Lisnaskea Emmets **(2):** 1980, 2005.

Newtownbutler **(1):** 1937.

Note: No championship played in 1909-34, 1940-44, 1947-71 and 1978.

MONAGHAN

Castleblayney **(19):** 1943, 1955, 1957, 1962, 1974, 1979, 1988, 1989, 1992, 2005, 2006, 2007, 2008, 2009, 2011, 2012, 2014, 2015, 2017.
(Note: Castleblayney were known as "Eire Óg" Club in 1962).

Clontibret **(16):** 1966, 1969, 1973, 1978, 1980, 1981, 1982, 1983, 1984, 1985, 1986, 1987, 1990, 1991, 1997, 2003.

Carrickmacross **(7):** 1914, 1945, 1963, 1964, 1967, 1971, 1975.

Monaghan Harps **(5):** 1956, 1993, 1995, 1996, 1998.

Clones **(4):** 1911, 1950, 1951, 1968.

Inniskeen Grattans **(3):** 2010, 2013, 2016.

Ballybay **(1):** 1976.

Note: The championship was unfinished in 1965.

TYRONE

Éire Óg, Carrickmore **(22):** 1974, 1976, 1979, 1980, 1982, 1983, 1984, 1985, 1986, 1987, 1988, 1989, 1998, 2006, 2007, 2008, 2010, 2011, 2014, 2015, 2016, 2017.

Dungannon **(20):** 1948, 1951, 1952, 1953, 1955, 1956, 1957, 1961, 1969, 1975, 1978, 1990, 1992, 1993, 1996, 1997, 2005, 2009, 2012, 2013.

Killyclogher **(6):** 1905, 1950, 1977, 1991, 1994, 1995.

Omagh **(3):** 1967, 1971, 1973.

Strabane **(2):** 1924, 1926.

Benburb **(1):** 1966.

Dromore **(1):** 1949.

Dunamanagh **(1):** 1981.

*N.B. Competition not played in other years.

COUNTY SENIOR FOOTBALL TITLES ROLL OF HONOUR

CONNACHT

GALWAY

Tuam Stars *(24):* 1892, 1893, 1894, 1895, 1896,1908, 1909,1911, 1942, 1943, 1947, 1952, 1954, 1955, 1956, 1957, 1958, 1959, 1960, 1962, 1984, 1988, 1989, 1994.

Corofin *(19):* 1932, 1946, 1977, 1991, 1993, 1995, 1997, 1998, 2000, 2002, 2006, 2008, 2009, 2011, 2013, 2014, 2015, 2016, 2017.

Ballinasloe *(17):* 1913, 1914, 1915, 1916, 1917, 1918, 1919, 1922, 1923, 1925, 1928, 1929, 1939, 1944, 1945, 1979, 1980.

Dunmore McHales *(15):* 1889, 1891, 1900, 1902, 1907, 1910, 1912, 1953, 1961, 1963, 1966, 1968, 1969, 1973, 1983.

Fr Griffin's *(7):* 1948, 1949, 1950, 1967, 1970, 1972, 1975.

Killererin *(6):* 1976, 1978, 1999, 2004, 2007, 2010.

Annaghdown *(5):* 1931, 1982, 1985, 1987, 2001.

Mountbellew/Moylough *(4):* 1964, 1965, 1974, 1986.

Athenry De Wets *(3):* 1903, 1904, 1906.

UCG *(3):* 1933, 1934, 1937.

Loughrea *(2):* 1897, 1898.

Army Renmore *(2):* 1940, 1951.

Milltown *(2):* 1971, 1981.

An Cheathru Rua *(2):* 1996, 1999.

Salthill/Knocknacarra *(2):* 2005, 2012.

Caherlistrane *(1):* 1890.

Tuam Krugers *(1):* 1901.

Tuam St Jarlath's *(1):* 1905.

Galway Gaels *(1):* 1930.

Wolfe Tones, Galway *(1):* 1936.

Oughterard *(1):* 1938.

Salthill *(1):* 1990.

Monivea/Abbeyknockmoy *(1):* 1992.

Caltra *(1):* 2003.
Championships were not completed in the following years: 1899, 1920, 21, 24, 26, 27, 35.

LEITRIM

Seán O'Heslins, Ballinamore *(20):* 1913, 1922, 1930, 1933, 1935, 1936, 1939, 1956, 1964, 1967, 1968, 1969, 1972, 1973, 1975, 1979, 1982, 1986, 1988, 1990.

Cloone *(11):* 1911, 1934, 1937, 1942, 1944, 1946, 1947, 1948, 1950, 1951, 1980.

Aughawillan *(11):* 1923, 1976, 1978, 1983, 1984, 1989, 1992, 1993, 1994, 2014, 2016.

Aughavas *(9):* 1915, 1940, 1949, 1952, 1954, 1955, 1963, 1966, 2000.

Mohill *(7):* 1890, 1914, 1929, 1971, 2006, 2015, 2017.

Glencar/Manorhamilton *(6):* 1977, 1999, 2008, 2009, 2010, 2011.

Melvin Gaels *(6):* 1959, 1960, 1961, 1965, 1998, 2012.

Gortletteragh *(5):* 1905, 1970, 1981, 1985, 1987.

Fenagh *(5):* 1906, 1910, 1912, 1919, 1932.

Allen Gaels *(5):* 1991, 1996, 1997, 2001, 2002.

Bornacoola *(4):* 1938, 1943, 1953, 1957.

Gorvagh *(4):* 1924, 1925, 1926, 1927.

St Mary's Carrick-on-Shannon *(4):* 1958, 1995, 2003, 2007.

Eslin *(3):* 1891, 1916, 1917.

Annaduff *(2):* 1928, 2004.

Aughnasheelin *(1):* 1918.

Drumreilly *(1):* 1931.

Sheemore Gaels *(1):* 1974.

Kiltubrid *(1):* 2005.

St Mary's Kiltoghert *(1):* 2013.

MAYO

Ballina Stephenites *(36):* 1889, 1904, 1905, 1906, 1907, 1908, 1909, 1910, 1911, 1912, 1913, 1914, 1915, 1916, 1918, 1920, 1924, 1925, 1926, 1927, 1928, 1929, 1933, 1935, 1938, 1940, 1943, 1947, 1955, 1966, 1985, 1987, 1998, 2003, 2004, 2007.

Castlebar Mitchels *(31):* 1888, 1903, 1930, 1931, 1932, 1934, 1941, 1942, 1944, 1945, 1946, 1948, 1950, 1951, 1952, 1953, 1954, 1956, 1959, 1962, 1963, 1969, 1970, 1978, 1986, 1988, 1993, 2013, 2015, 2016, 2017.

Knockmore	**(8):**	1973, 1980, 1983, 1984, 1989, 1992, 1996, 1997.
Crossmolina	**(7):**	1949, 1995, 1999, 2000, 2002, 2005, 2006.
Garrymore	**(6):**	1974, 1975, 1976, 1979, 1981, 1992.
Claremorris	**(4):**	1961, 1964, 1965, 1971.
Ballycastle	**(3):**	1936, 1937, 1939.
Hollymount	**(3):**	1990, 1991, 1994.
Ballaghaderreen	**(3):**	1972, 2008, 2012.
Ballintubber	**(3):**	2010, 2011, 2014.
Ballyhaunis	**(2):**	1919, 1958.
East Mayo	**(2):**	1957, 1967.
Charleston Sarsfields	**(2):**	1902, 2009.
Ballina Commercials	**(1):**	1890.
Lacken	**(1):**	1917.
West Mayo	**(1):**	1960.
North Mayo	**(1):**	1968.
Aughamore	**(1):**	1977.
Charlestown	**(1):**	2001.

ROSCOMMON

Clan na nGael	**(20):**	1961, 1966, 1970, 1976, 1977, 1979, 1981, 1982, 1984, 1985, 1986, 1987, 1988, 1989, 1990, 1991, 1993, 1995, 1996, 2015.
St. Brigid's	**(16):**	1953, 1958, 1959, 1963, 1969, 1997, 2005, 2006, 2007, 2010, 2011, 2012, 2013, 2014, 2016, 2017.
Roscommon Gaels	**(11):**	1962, 1972, 1974, 1975, 1978, 1980, 1994, 1998, 1999, 2001, 2004.
Elphin	**(10):**	1889, 1891, 1931, 1932, 1937, 1950, 1951, 1955, 1956, 1957.
Strokestown	**(10):**	1912, 1915, 1916, 1917, 1922, 1926, 1928, 1933, 1992, 2002.
Tarmon	**(6):**	1935, 1939, 1940, 1941, 1944, 1947.
St. Patrick's	**(6):**	1942, 1943, 1945, 1946, 1948, 1949.
Castlerea St. Kevin's	**(6):**	1967, 1968, 1971, 1973, 2008, 2009.
Kilbride	**(5):**	1907, 1908, 1909, 1914, 2000.

Elphin Wm O'Briens	**(4):**	1902, 1903, 1904, 1905.
Donamon	**(4):**	1918, 1919, 1920, 1925.
Roscommon	**(3):**	1930, 1936, 1938.
Roscommon "The Blues"	**(2):**	1911, 1913.
Tulsk Lord Edwards	**(2):**	1923, 1924.
Boyle	**(2):**	1890, 1927.
Fuerty	**(2):**	1929, 1934.
Kilbride Emmets/Elphin	**(1):**	1906.
Tulsk	**(1):**	1910.
St. Coman's Knockcroghery	**(1):**	1952.
St. Coman's Roscommon	**(1):**	1954.
United Stars Oran/Creggs	**(1):**	1960.
Shannon Gaels	**(1):**	1964.
St. Faithleach's	**(1):**	1965.
Kilmore	**(1):**	1983.
Castlerea	**(1):**	2003.

SLIGO

Tubbercurry	**(20):**	1890, 1917, 1918, 1924, 1927, 1928, 1930, 1934, 1938, 1939, 1940, 1946, 1950, 1951, 1955, 1957, 1976, 1986, 1991, 2014.
Tourlestrane	**(13):**	1956, 1978, 1982, 1994, 1997, 1999, 2004, 2007, 2009, 2011, 2013, 2016, 2017.
St. Mary's	**(11):**	1972, 1979, 1980, 1981, 1983, 1984, 1985, 1987, 1996, 2001, 2015.
Ballymote	**(6):**	1892, 1905, 1913, 1925, 1926, 1948.
Eastern Harps	**(6):**	1975, 1993, 1995, 1998, 2008, 2010.
Curry	**(6):**	1889, 1964, 1972, 2003, 2006, 2012.
Moylough	**(5):**	1919, 1920, 1921, 1922, 1923.
St Patrick's	**(5):**	1968, 1970, 1971, 1988, 1989.
Easkey	**(5):**	1935, 1936, 1937, 1941, 1966.
Ballisodare	**(5):**	1931, 1932, 1960, 1962, 1963.
Sligo Wanderers	**(4):**	1908, 1909, 1910, 1912.
Collooney Harps	**(4):**	1942, 1943, 1961, 1965.
Craobh Rua	**(4):**	1944, 1952, 1953, 1954.

Gurteen	(2):	1906, 1907.
Enniscrone	(2):	1914, 1916.
Knockalassa	(2):	1933, 1935.
Skreen	(2):	1945,1947.
Sooey	(2):	1949, 1959.
Collooney/Ballisodare	(2):	1967, 1969.
Shamrock Gaels	(2):	1990, 1992.
Bunninadden	(2):	1891, 2000.
Coolera-Strandhill	(2):	2002, 2005.
Sligo Emmets	(1):	1888.
Coolera	(1):	1907.
Killavil	(1):	1911.
Derroon	(1):	1915.
Kilglass	(1):	1929.
Mullinabreena	(1):	1958.

LEINSTER

CARLOW

Éire Óg *(27):* 1960, 1962, 1965, 1967, 1968, 1969, 1974, 1976, 1977, 1978, 1980, 1982, 1984, 1987, 1988, 1989, 1992, 1993, 1994, 1995, 1996, 1998, 2005, 2007, 2008, 2012, 2017.

Tinryland *(15):* 1934, 1936, 1939, 1940, 1943, 1944, 1946, 1948, 1949, 1950, 1971, 1972, 1975, 1979, 1981.

Graiguecullen *(13):* 1908, 1909, 1911, 1912, 1913, 1914, 1915, 1918, 1921, 1922, 1923, 1924, 1925.

O'Hanrahans *(13):* 1931, 1932, 1937, 1942, 1945, 1951, 1954, 1958, 1961, 1999, 2000, 2001, 2003.

Palatine *(7):* 1919, 1920, 1952, 2002, 2006, 2015, 2016.

Rathvilly *(6):* 1983, 1985, 1990, 1991, 2009, 2014.

Loughmartin Emmetts *(5):* 1898, 1899, 1900,1901, 1902.

Tullow *(5):* 1904, 1916, 1959, 1963, 1964.

Old Leighlin *(4):* 1997, 2010, 2011, 2013.

Carlow Town *(3):* 1927, 1928, 1930.

Kildavin *(3):* 1966, 1970, 1973.

Milford *(2):* 1926, 1933.

Leighlinbridge *(2):* 1929, 1957.

Ballymurphy *(2):* 1947, 1953.

Clonmore *(2):* 1955, 1956.

Carlow Barrow Rangers *(1):* 1903.

Borris *(1):* 1910.

Kilbride *(1):* 1935.

Fighting Cocks *(1):* 1938.

Naomh Eoin (Myshall) *(1):* 1986.

Fenagh *(1):* 2004.
No championship 1905, 1906, 1907, 1917, 1941.

DUBLIN

St. Vincent's *(29):* 1949, 1950, 1951, 1952, 1953, 1954, 1955, 1957, 1958, 1959, 1960, 1961, 1962, 1964, 1966, 1967, 1970, 1971, 1972, 1975, 1976, 1977, 1981, 1984, 2007, 2013, 2014, 2016, 2017.

O'Tooles *(11):* 1918, 1919, 1920, 1922, 1923, 1924, 1925, 1926, 1928, 1931, 1946.

Geraldines *(10):* 1898, 1899, 1908, 1910, 1914, 1915, 1917, 1940, 1941, 1942.

Keatings	*(7)*:	1903, 1904, 1905, 1906, 1907, 1909, 1911.
U.C.D.	*(7)*:	1943, 1963, 1965, 1973, 1974, 2002, 2006.
Kilmacud Crokes	*(7)*:	1992, 1994, 1998, 2004, 2005, 2008, 2010.
Garda	*(6)*:	1927, 1929, 1933, 1934, 1935, 1948.
Parnells	*(6)*:	1913, 1916, 1939, 1945, 1987, 1988.
Young Irelands	*(5)*:	1891, 1892, 1893, 1894, 1896.
Na Fianna	*(5)*:	1969, 1979, 1999, 2000, 2001.
Kickhams	*(4)*:	1897, 1904,1907, 1912.
Erin's Hope	*(4)*:	1887, 1932, 1965, 1978.
Isles of the Sea	*(3)*:	1890, 1895, 1900.
Clan na Gael	*(3)*:	1936, 1937, 1968.
Ballymun Kickhams	*(3)*:	1982, 1985, 2012.
Ballyboden St. Enda's	*(3)*:	1995, 2009, 2015.
Seán McDermott's	*(2)*:	1938, 1947.
Civil Service	*(2)*:	1944, 1980.
Scoil Ui Chonaill	*(2)*:	1944, 1980.
Thomas Davis	*(2)*:	1989, 1991.
Erin's Isle	*(2)*:	1993, 1997.
St.Brigid's	*(2)*:	2003, 2011.
Feach McHughs	*(1)*:	1888.
Faughs	*(1)*:	1889.
St. Mary's	*(1)*:	1921.
St. Joseph's	*(1)*:	1930.
St. Sylvester's	*(1)*:	1996.

*No championship in 1902.

KILDARE

Clane *(17)*: 1888, 1892, 1895, 1900, 1901, 1902, 1903, 1916, 1963, 1967, 1975,1980, 1984, 1991, 1992, 1995, 1997.

Sarsfields *(15)*: 1945, 1947, 1950, 1951, 1952, 1982, 1986, 1993, 1994, 1999, 2001, 2005, 2012, 2015, 2016.

Carbury *(10)*: 1940, 1941, 1946, 1960, 1965, 1966, 1969, 1971, 1972, 1974.

Roseberry	*(9)*:	1904, 1905, 1906, 1907, 1908, 1909, 1910, 1912, 1915.
Moorefield	*(9)*:	1962, 2000, 2002, 2006, 2007, 2010, 2013, 2014, 2017.
Raheens	*(8)*:	1935, 1936, 1943, 1968, 1976, 1978, 1979, 1981.
Naas	*(6)*:	1920, 1922, 1923, 1924, 1928, 1990.
Round Towers	*(6)*:	1954, 1959, 1961, 1996, 1998, 2003.
Athy	*(6)*:	1933, 1934, 1937, 1942, 1987, 2011.
Kilcock	*(4)*:	1914, 1955, 1957, 1958.
Caragh	*(4)*:	1918, 1919, 1921, 1926.
Monasterevin	*(3)*:	1890, 1911, 1977.
Maynooth	*(3)*:	1896, 1897, 1913.
Kildare	*(3)*:	1927, 1929, 1930.
Johnstownbridge	*(3)*:	1983, 1988, 1989.
Mountrice	*(2)*:	1889, 1891.
Rathangan	*(1)*:	1925.
St. Patrick's	*(1)*:	1938.
Ellistown	*(1)*:	1944.
Curragh	*(1)*:	1948.
Ardclough	*(1)*:	1949.
Ballymore	*(1)*:	1953.
Military College	*(1)*:	1956.
Eadestown	*(1)*:	1970.
Allenwood	*(1)*:	2004.
Celbridge	*(1)*:	2008.
St. Laurence's	*(1)*:	2009.

KILKENNY

Railyard *(22)*: 1951, 1952, 1953, 1957, 1958, 1959, 1960, 1961, 1965, 1966, 1967, 1969, 1970, 1971, 1972, 1973, 1978, 1992, 1999, 2014, 2015, 2016.

Glenmore *(20)*: 1906, 1915, 1916, 1920, 1922, 1923, 1924, 1929, 1938, 1940, 1942, 1943, 1949, 1950, 1954, 1955, 1989, 1998, 2009.

Muckalee *(12)*: 1968, 1975, 1977, 1987, 1990, 2001, 2004, 2005, 2010, 2011, 2012, 2013.

CLUB

Tullogher	(8):	1930, 1931, 1934, 1936, 1937, 1941, 1944, 1962.
James Stephens	(7):	1988, 1991, 1993, 1995, 1996, 2003, 2008.
Commercials-City	(4):	1890, 1893, 1894, 1895.
Lamogue	(4):	1902, 1903, 1904, 1905.
Knocktopher	(4):	1901, 1908, 1910, 1911.
Thomastown	(4):	1981, 1983, 1984, 1985.
Slatequarry Miners	(3):	1900, 1907, 1913.
Shamrocks	(3):	1979, 1980, 1982.
Kilmacow	(2):	1887, 1888.
Coolagh	(2):	1914, 1919.
St. John's	(2):	1946, 1948.
Clann na Gael-City	(2):	1963, 1964.
Dicksboro	(2):	1994, 1997.
Erin's Own	(2):	2002, 2006.
Mullinavat	(2):	2007, 2017.
Ballyhale	(1):	1889.
Sevenhouses	(1):	1896.
Green Rovers-City	(1):	1897.
Callan	(1):	1898.
City Rangers	(1):	1899.
Coolroe	(1):	1909.
Ye Faire City	(1):	1925.
Cotterstown	(1):	1926.
Owen Roes-Army	(1):	1928.
Blacks & Whites	(1):	1932.
Moneenroe	(1):	1933.
Barrow Rovers-Glenmore/Slieverue	(1):	1935.
Northern Junior Selection	(1):	1945.
Sarsfields	(1):	1947.
Graignamanagh	(1):	1956.
St. Kieran's-Mooncoin/Kilmacow	(1):	1974.

The Village	(1):	1976.
Mooncoin	(1):	1986.
Kilmoganny	(1):	2000.

No championships 1891-92, 1912, 1917-18, 1921. Declared Void 1927.

LAOIS

Portlaoise	(33):	1889, 1897, 1907, 1918, 1964, 1966, 1967, 1968, 1970, 1971, 1976, 1979, 1981, 1982, 1984, 1985, 1986, 1987, 1990, 1991, 1999, 2002, 2004, 2007, 2008, 2009, 2010, 2011, 2012, 2013, 2014, 2015, 2017.
Stradbally	(16):	1905, 1908, 1911, 1928, 1929, 1930, 1932, 1933, 1936, 1937, 1940, 1941, 1997, 1998, 2005, 2016.
Graiguecullen	(13):	1927, 1931, 1934, 1935, 1938, 1939, 1942, 1944, 1945, 1946, 1947, 1949, 1965.
Portarlington	(12):	1893, 1910, 1912, 1921, 1922, 1923, 1954, 1955, 1959, 1988, 1995, 2001.
The Heath	(10):	1891, 1912, 1913, 1920, 1957, 1958, 1960, 1961, 1974, 1993.
St.Joseph's	(9):	1973, 1975, 1977, 1978, 1983, 1989, 1994, 1996, 2000.
Abbeyleix	(8):	1898, 1899, 1902, 1903, 1904, 1909, 1916, 1919.
Annanough	(6):	1924, 1925, 1926, 1927, 1951, 1956.
Ballyroan Gaels	(6):	1890, 1943, 1948, 1950, 1992, 2006.
Raheenbrogue	(2):	1901, 1906.
Park	(2):	1952, 1953.
O'Dempseys	(2):	1963, 1980.
Moyanna	(1):	1892.
Wolfhill	(1):	1896.
Timahoe	(1):	1969.
Emo	(1):	1972.
Arles-Kilcruise	(1):	2003.

Note: The 1889, 1897 and 1907 won under the name Maryborough, now Portlaoise.

LONGFORD

Longford Slashers	(16):	1954, 1955, 1957, 1959, 1961, 1971, 1975, 1979, 1980, 1989, 1990, 1991, 1994, 2010, 2011, 2013.
Drumlish/Fr. Manning Gaels	(15):	1927, 1928, 1932,

1937, 1939, 1940, 1943, 1945, 1951, 1953, 1955, 1996, 1997, 1998, 2001.

Clonguish *(13):* 1919, 1962, 1963, 1964, 1965, 1968, 1969, 1972, 1973, 1981, 2003, 2004, 2009.

St. Marys, Granard *(11):* 1929, 1930, 1931, 1933, 1934, 1935, 1941, 1966, 1967, 1970, 1982.

Emmet Óg, Killoe *(9):* 1907, 1911, 1912, 1913, 1915, 1960, 1988, 1993, 1995.

Colmcilles *(6):* 1890, 1938, 1949, 1952, 1958, 2008.

Longford Wanderers *(4):* 1922, 1923, 1944, 1947.

Cashel *(4):* 1977, 1983, 1984, 1986.

Ardagh St. Patrick's *(4):* 1936, 1942, 1978, 1987.

Dromard *(4):* 1946, 2000, 2005, 2007.

Mullinalaghta *(4):* 1948, 1950, 2016, 2017.

Mostrim *(3):* 1974, 1985, 1992.

Killoe Young Emmetts *(3):* 2012, 2014, 2015.

Longford, Leo Casey's *(2):* 1904, 1905.

Abbeylara *(2):* 1999, 2006.

Longford Shamrocks *(1):* 1896.

Ballinamuck *(1):* 1917.

Rathcline *(1):* 1976.

Ballymahon *(1):* 2002.

LOUTH
Newtown Blues *(21):* 1889, 1932, 1933, 1936, 1961, 1962, 1963, 1964, 1966, 1967, 1969, 1970, 1974, 1981, 1986, 1988, 2000, 2001, 2008, 2013, 2017.

Young Irelands, Dundalk *(11):* 1887, 1888, 1905, 1911, 1938, 1940, 1941, 1944, 1947, 1950, 1979.

St. Mary's, Ardee *(11):* 1914, 1946, 1948, 1951, 1955, 1956, 1960, 1968, 1972, 1975, 1995.

Cooley Kickhams *(9):* 1935, 1939, 1971, 1973, 1976, 1977, 1978, 1989, 1990.

Clan na Gael *(8):* 1923, 1924, 1959, 1985, 1987, 1992, 1993, 1997.

St. Patrick's *(7):* 2003, 2004, 2007, 2011, 2012, 2014, 2015.

Wolfe Tones *(5):* 1925, 1926, 1929, 1931, 1937.

Geraldines *(5):* 1913, 1915, 1916, 1920, 1982.

Tredaghs, Drogheda *(4):* 1906, 1909, 1910, 1912.

Boyne Rangers *(4):* 1895, 1921, 1922, 1930.

Mattock Rangers *(4):* 2002, 2005, 2009, 2010.

Gaels *(3):* 1942, 1945, 1952.

Boyne Rovers *(2):* 1897, 1904.

Dundalk Rovers *(2):* 1907, 1908.

Drogheda Stars *(2):* 1917, 1919.

Drogheda Independents *(2):* 1901, 1902.

O'Rahillys *(2):* 1918, 1965.

Sarsfields *(2):* 1927, 1928.

Roche Emmetts *(2):* 1958, 1980.

St. Fechins *(2):* 1983, 1984.

St. Joseph's *(2):* 1996, 2006.

Davitts, Drogheda *(1):* 1890.

Drogheda, Emmetts *(1):* 1896.

Ardee Volunteers *(1):* 1903.

Glyde Rangers *(1):* 1934.

St. Bride's *(1):* 1943.

Naomh Mhuire *(1):* 1953.

Oliver Plunkett's *(1):* 1957.

Stabannon Parnells *(1):* 1999.

Seán O'Mahonys *(1):* 2016.

No championships 1891-1894, 1898-1900.

MEATH
Navan O'Mahony's *(20):* 1953, 1957, 1958, 1959, 1960, 1961, 1963, 1973, 1979, 1981, 1985, 1987, 1988, 1989, 1990, 1997, 2008, 2012, 2014, 2015.

Skryne *(12):* 1940, 1941, 1944, 1945, 1947, 1948, 1954, 1965, 1992, 1993, 2004, 2010.

Navan Gaels *(10):* 1907, 1924, 1925, 1926, 1929, 1930, 1933, 1934, 1935, 1938.

Summerhill *(7):* 1974, 1975, 1976, 1977, 1986, 2011, 2013.

Bohermeen *(6):* 1909, 1910, 1911, 1912, 1913, 1914.

Castletown	(5):	1902, 1904, 1905, 1906, 1908.
Rathkenny	(5):	1917, 1918, 1919, 1922, 1923.
Kilbride	(5):	1964, 1967, 1969, 1970, 1971.
Walterstown	(5):	1978, 1980, 1982, 1983, 1984.
Seneschalstown	(4):	1972, 1994, 2007, 2009.
Pierce O'Mahoney's	(3):	1894, 1895, 1896.
Navan Harps	(3):	1915, 1920, 1921.
Kilmessan	(3):	1903, 1936, 1939.
Donaghmore	(3):	1927, 1928, 1942.
Gael Colmcille, Kells	(3):	1966, 1968, 1991.
Dunshaughlin	(3):	2000, 2001, 2002.
St. Peter's, Dunboyne	(3):	1998, 1999, 2005.
Dowdstown	(2):	1887, 1888.
Moynalty	(2):	1932, 1937.
Simonstown Gaels	(2):	2016, 2017.
Julianstown	(1):	1889.
Owen Roe's	(1):	1897.
Stamullen	(1):	1900.
Martry	(1):	1931.
Duleek	(1):	1943.
Navan Parnells	(1):	1946.
North Meath	(1):	1950.
St. Vincent's	(1):	1955.
Trim	(1):	1962.
Dunderry	(1):	1995.
Kilmainhamwood	(1):	1996.
Blackhall Gaels	(1):	2003.
Wolfe Tones	(1):	2006.

OFFALY

Rhode (28): 1900, 1918, 1920, 1923, 1927, 1928, 1929, 1931, 1939, 1940, 1944, 1949, 1955, 1958, 1966, 1967, 1969, 1975, 1998, 2004, 2005, 2006, 2008, 2010, 2012, 2014, 2016, 2017.

Tullamore (27): 1896, 1897, 1898, 1899, 1908, 1911, 1912, 1913, 1917, 1924, 1925, 1926, 1930, 1932, 1935, 1941, 1946, 1948, 1954, 1956, 1963, 1973, 1977, 2000, 2002, 2007, 2013.

Walsh Island (12): 1933, 1934, 1937, 1938, 1942, 1943, 1978, 1979, 1980, 1981, 1982, 1983.

Ferbane (11): 1914, 1971, 1974, 1976, 1986, 1987, 1988, 1989, 1990, 1992, 1994.

Edenderry (11): 1936, 1951, 1953, 1957, 1985, 1995, 1997, 1999, 2001, 2011, 2015.

Clara (6): 1960, 1964, 1991, 1993, 2003, 2009.

Geashill	(5):	1902, 1904, 1905, 1906, 1907.
Gracefield	(4):	1961, 1970, 1972, 1984.
Daingean	(3):	1909, 1962, 1965.
Killeigh	(2):	1915, 1916.
Cloghan	(2):	1903, 1945.
St. Mary's	(2):	1947, 1950.
Quarrymount	(1):	1901.
Banagher	(1):	1910.
Clonmore	(1):	1919.
Durrow	(1):	1952.
St. Patrick's	(1):	1959.
Ballycumber	(1):	1968.
Shannonbridge	(1):	1996.

WESTMEATH

Athlone (21): 1905, 1909, 1947, 1949, 1955, 1956, 1957, 1958, 1959, 1960, 1965, 1971, 1973, 1977, 1979, 1982, 1984, 1988, 1991, 1998, 1999.

Mullingar Shamrocks (11): 1903, 1964, 1966, 1986, 1987, 1990, 1992, 1993, 1994, 1995, 2012.

Riverstown Emmets (9): 1904, 1906, 1907, 1908, 1910, 1911, 1912, 1913, 1914.

Rosemount (9): 1932, 1934, 1939, 1940, 1941, 1951, 1952, 1953, 1989.

Moate (9): 1933, 1936, 1943, 1945, 1975, 1976, 1978, 1983, 1997.

The Downs (9): 1918, 1968, 1969, 1970, 1972, 1974, 1980, 2003, 2005.

Kilbeggan (8): 1919, 1921, 1924, 1926, 1927, 1930, 1931, 1935.

Garrycastle (7): 2001, 2002, 2004, 2009, 2010, 2011, 2014.

St. Loman's (7): 1948, 1961, 1963, 2013, 2015, 2016, 2017.

Rochfortbridge	(4):	1915, 1917, 1923, 1925.
Kinnegad	(4):	1916, 1929, 1944, 1946.
St. Mary's	(3):	1950, 1954, 1962.
Tyrrellspass	(3):	1999, 2006, 2007.
Athlone Army	(2):	1905, 1928.
Milltown	(2):	1938, 1942.
Coralstown-Kinnegad	(2):	1996, 2000.
Coralstown	(1):	1937.
St. Finian's	(1):	1967.
St. Malachy's	(1):	1981.
Tubberclair	(1):	1985.
Castledaly	(1):	2008.

No championship played in 1920 or 1922.

WEXFORD

Volunteers (11): 1895, 1898, 1939, 1940, 1941, 1942, 1943, 1948, 1949, 1953, 1956.

Ballyhogue (10): 1911, 1921, 1924, 1931, 1932, 1962, 1963, 1964, 1971, 1972.

Castletown (10): 1965, 1966, 1969, 1970, 1973, 1976, 1978, 1979, 1981, 2010.

Starlights (10): 1927, 1928, 1929, 1933, 1936, 1937, 1983, 2002, 2004, 2017.

Duffry Rovers (8): 1986, 1987, 1988, 1989, 1990, 1991, 1992, 1994.

Kilanerin (7): 1974, 1993, 1995, 1997, 1999, 2003, 2008.

Blue and Whites, Wexford (6): 1889, 1890, 1914, 1916, 1917, 1918.

Gusserane (6): 1945, 1946, 1947, 1954, 1975, 2016.

Rapparees (5): 1907, 1908, 1909, 1912, 1913.

Sarsfields (5): 1934, 1935, 1961, 1967, 1984.

Gymnasiums, New Ross (4): 1899, 1900, 1901, 1902.

Horeswood (4): 2005, 2006, 2009, 2011.

St. Anne's (4): 1968, 2000, 2001, 2012.

St. Munn's, Taghmon (3): 1955, 1957, 1958.

Young Irelands, Wexford (2): 1893, 1894.

Slaney Harriers, Enniscorthy	(2):	1903, 1904.
Wexford United	(2):	1905, 1926.
Faythe Harriers	(2):	1959, 1960.
Bunclody	(2):	1982, 1985.
St. Fintan's	(2):	1930, 1980.
St. Aidan's, Enniscorthy	(2):	1950, 1951.
St. Mary's, Rosslare	(1):	1886.
Castlebridge	(1):	1887.
St. Patrick's, Wexford	(1):	1896.
Ballymurrin	(1):	1897.
Faughs, Wexford	(1):	1910.
New Ross Geraldines	(1):	1915.
Emmetts, Enniscorthy	(1):	1944.
Rathnure	(1):	1952.
Wexford District	(1):	1977.
Glynn-Barntown	(1):	1996.
Fethard	(1):	1998.
Clongeen	(1):	2007.
St. Martin's	(1):	2013.
St James'	(1):	2015.

WICKLOW

Rathnew (34): 1893, 1896, 1897, 1902, 1904, 1905, 1906, 1909, 1910, 1911, 1921, 1924, 1928, 1932, 1941, 1942, 1943, 1970, 1978, 1996, 1997, 1998, 1999, 2000, 2001, 2002, 2003, 2005, 2009, 2010, 2013, 2014, 2015, 2017.

Baltinglass (22): 1958, 1963, 1965, 1966, 1967, 1971, 1972, 1976, 1979, 1980, 1982, 1985, 1987, 1988, 1989, 1990, 1991, 1992, 1993, 1994, 2007, 2016.

St. Patrick's, Wicklow (13): 1890, 1950, 1952, 1953, 1955, 1956, 1959, 1960, 1961, 2006, 2012.

Annacurra (9): 1887, 1888, 1889, 1892, 1913, 1920, 1925, 1926, 1931.

Donard (6): 1937, 1940, 1944, 1947, 1951, 1957.

Carnew (4): 1916, 1927, 1945, 1973.

Tinahely (3): 1917, 1919, 1984.

Kilcoole (3): 1929, 1939, 1954.

Ballinacor (3): 1946, 1948, 1949.

Blessington	(2):	1915, 1983.
Rathdangan	(2):	1930, 1936.
Bray Emmets	(2):	1934, 1935.
Kilbride	(2):	1962, 1968.
Newtown	(2):	1964, 1975.
Dunlavin	(2):	1977, 1981.
Kiltegan	(2):	1986, 2008.
Clara	(1):	1888.
Avondale	(1):	1908.
Granabeg, Valleymount	(1):	1923.
Roundwood	(1):	1933.
Ashford	(1):	1974.
An Tochar	(1):	1995.
St. Mary's	(1):	2011.

Annacurra and Clara shared the title in 1888.

MUNSTER

CLARE

Kilrush **(21):** 1902, 1903, 1912, 1924, 1930, 1931, 1934, 1937, 1938, 1951, 1957, 1958, 1960, 1962, 1975, 1976, 1977, 1978, 1979, 1981, 1987.

Doonbeg **(18):** 1955, 1961, 1967, 1968, 1969, 1972, 1973, 1974, 1982, 1983, 1988, 1991, 1995, 1996, 1998, 1999, 2001, 2010.

St Joseph's, Milltown **(12):** 1905, 1906, 1916, 1923, 1927, 1932, 1949, 1953, 1959, 1985, 1990, 2015.

Kilmurry-Ibrickane **(12):** 1933, 1963, 1966, 1993, 2002, 2004, 2008, 2009, 2011, 2012, 2016. 2017.

Cooraclare **(11):** 1915, 1917, 1918, 1925, 1944, 1945, 1956, 1964, 1965, 1986, 1997.

Ennis-Dal gCais **(10):** 1897, 1899, 1904, 1907, 1909, 1910, 1911, 1913, 1914, 1929.

Kilkee	(7):	1926, 1928, 1942, 1984, 1989, 1992, 2003.
Ennis Faughs	(4):	1947, 1948, 1952, 1954.
Quilty	(3):	1935, 1936, 1939.
Éire Óg	(2):	2000, 2006.
Coolmeen	(2):	1919, 1922.
Newmarket	(2):	1887, 1888.
Kilfenora	(2):	1941, 1950.
Shannon Gaels	(2):	1970, 1971.
Cratloe	(2):	2013, 2014.
Kildysart	(1):	1889.
Ennis	(1):	1890.
Killimer	(1):	1896.
Doora	(1):	1898.
Labasheeda	(1):	1900.
Clarecastle	(1):	1908.
Liscannor	(1):	1940.
O'Currys	(1):	1946.
Kilmihill	(1):	1980.
Faughs	(1):	1994.
St. Senan's	(1):	2005.
Lisseycasey	(1):	2007.

CORK

Nemo Rangers   **(20):**   1972, 1974, 1975, 1977, 1978, 1981, 1983, 1987, 1988, 1993, 2000, 2001, 2002, 2005, 2006, 2007, 2008, 2010, 2015, 2017.

Lees   **(12):**   1887, 1888, 1896, 1902, 1903, 1904, 1907, 1908, 1911, 1914, 1923, 1955.

Macroom   **(10):**   1909, 1910, 1912, 1913, 1926, 1930, 1931, 1935, 1958, 1962.

University College   **(10):**   1920, 1927, 1928, 1960, 1963, 1964, 1969, 1973, 1999, 2011.

Clonakilty   **(9):**   1939, 1942, 1943, 1944, 1946, 1947, 1952, 1996, 2009.

St Finbarr's   **(8):**   1956, 1957, 1959, 1976, 1979, 1980, 1982, 1985.

Fermoy   **(7):**   1895, 1898, 1899, 1900, 1905, 1906, 1945.

Beara   **(6):**   1932, 1933, 1934, 1940, 1967, 1997.

Nils   **(6):**   1894, 1901, 1915, 1917, 1924, 1925.

St Nicholas   **(5):**   1938, 1941, 1954, 1965, 1966.

Castlehaven   **(5):**   1989, 1994, 2003, 2012, 2013.

Carbery   **(5):**   1937, 1968, 1971, 2004, 2016.

Collins   **(4):**   1929 (awarded), 1949, 1951, 1953.

Midleton   **(2):**   1889, 1990.

Clondrohid   **(2):**   1891, 1892.

Cobh   **(2):**   1918, 1919.

Imokilly   **(2):**   1984, 1986.

Duhallow   **(2):**   1990, 1991.

Bantry Blues   **(2):**   1995, 1998.

Dromtarriff   **(1):**   1893.

Dunmanway   **(1):**   1897.

Collegians   **(1):**   1916.

Duhallow West   **(1):**   1936.

Millstreet   **(1):**   1948.

Garda   **(1):**   1950.

Avondhu   **(1):**   1961.

Muskerry   **(1):**   1970.

O'Donovan Rossa   **(1):**   1992.

Ballincollig   **(1):**   2014.

KERRY

Austin Stacks   **(12):**   1928, 1930, 1931, 1932, 1936, 1973, 1975, 1976, 1979, 1986, 1994, 2014.

John Mitchels   **(10):**   1929, 1937, 1947, 1952, 1959, 1960, 1961, 1962, 1963, 1966.

Laune Rangers   **(10):**   1889, 1890, 1892, 1893, 1900, 1911, 1989, 1993, 1995, 1996.

Tralee Mitchels   **(9):**   1896 (shared), 1897, 1902, 1903, 1907, 1908, 1910, 1917, 1919.

East Kerry   **(7):**   1965, 1968, 1969, 1970, 1997, 1998, 1999.

Dingle   **(6):**   1938, 1940, 1941, 1943, 1944, 1948.

Kerins O'Rahillys   **(6):**   1933, 1939, 1953, 1954, 1957, 2002.

Dr. Crokes   **(6):**   2010, 2011, 2012, 2013, 2016, 2017.

Killarney Crokes   **(5):**   1901, 1912, 1913, 1914, 1991.

Shannon Rangers   **(5):**   1942, 1945, 1964, 1972, 1977.

South Kerry   **(5):**   2004, 2005, 2006, 2009, 2015.

Ballymacelligott   **(4):**   1891, 1894, 1895, 1918.

Mid-Kerry   **(4):**   1967, 1971, 1992, 2008.

West Kerry   **(3):**   1984, 1985, 1990.

Feale Rangers   **(3):**   1978, 1980, 2007.

Tralee (Div.)   **(2):**   1925, 1926.

Killarney   **(2):**   1949, 1983.

Kenmare   **(2):**   1974, 1987.

An Ghaeltacht   **(2):**   2001, 2003.

Caherciveen   **(1):**   1896 (shared).

Killarney Legion   **(1):**   1946.

Castleisland   **(1):**   1950.

Dick Fitzgeralds   **(1):**   1951.

St Kieran's   **(1):**   1988.

Glenflesk   **(1):**   2000.

LIMERICK

Commercials   **(16):**   1887, 1888, 1889, 1895, 1896, 1897, 1898, 1899, 1902, 1904, 1905, 1910, 1911, 1919, 1920, 1927.

Claughaun   **(14):**   1955, 1959, 1967, 1969, 1970, 1971, 1982, 1984, 1986, 1988, 1989, 1993, 1995, 1996.

Treaty Sarsfields *(12):* 1946, 1948, 1949, 1950, 1951, 1952, 1956, 1957, 1963, 1973, 1974, 1975.

Abbeyfeale *(8):* 1914, 1915, 1932, 1941, 1942, 1947, 2000, 2006.

Glin *(7):* 1926, 1928, 1929, 1930, 1931, 1933, 1934.

Drom-Broadford *(7):* 2001, 2003, 2004, 2008, 2009, 2012, 2013.

Oola *(6):* 1900, 1918, 1922, 1925, 1961, 1979.

Monaleen *(6):* 1978, 2002, 2005, 2010, 2011, 2016.

Ahane *(5):* 1935, 1936, 1937, 1938, 1939.

St Patrick's *(5):* 1890, 1891, 1943, 1944, 1954.

Ballylanders *(4):* 1917, 1999, 2007, 2014.

Kilmallock *(3):* 1908, 1909, 1916.

Askeaton *(3):* 1965, 1966, 1972.

St Kieran's *(3):* 1981, 1985, 1990.

Newcastlewest *(3):* 1987, 1992, 2015.

Garda *(2):* 1924, 1958.

Western Gaels *(2):* 1953, 1960.

Thomond *(2):* 1977, 1980.

Croom *(2):* 1976, 1983.

Galbally *(2):* 1994, 1998.

Fr. Casey's *(2):* 2000, 2006.

Foynes *(1):* 1907.

Knockaney *(1):* 1940.

Army, Ninth Desmonds *(1):* 1945.

Old Christians *(1):* 1962.

Ballysteen *(1):* 1964.

Athea *(1):* 1968.

Glencurrane Rovers *(1):* 1991.

University of Limerick *(1):* 1998.

Adare *(1):* 2017.

TIPPERARY

Fethard *(21):* 1887, 1917, 1918, 1919, 1920, 1922, 1923, 1924, 1927, 1928, 1938, 1942, 1954, 1957, 1978, 1984, 1988, 1991, 1993, 1997, 2001.

Clonmel Commercials *(17):* 1944, 1948, 1956, 1965, 1966, 1967, 1969, 1971, 1982, 1986, 1989, 1990, 1994, 2002, 2012, 2015, 2017.

Loughmore-Castleiney *(10):* 1940, 1946, 1973, 1977, 1979, 1983, 1987, 2004, 2013, 2016.

Grangemockler *(8):* 1890, 1903, 1904, 1905, 1906, 1907, 1909, 1931.

Clonmel Shamrocks *(8):* 1897, 1898, 1899, 1900, 1901, 1933, 1934, 1937.

Ardfinnan *(8):* 1935, 1939, 1962, 1963, 1964, 1970, 1974, 2005.

Moyle Rovers *(7):* 1995, 1996, 1998, 1999, 2000, 2007, 2009.

Arravale Rovers *(6):* 1894, 1895, 1896, 1899, 1941, 1985.

Galtee Rovers *(6):* 1949, 1950, 1976, 1980, 1981, 2008.

Mullinahone *(5):* 1912, 1913, 1916, 1926, 1929.

Kilsheelan *(4):* 1930, 1932, 1968, 1972.

St Flannan's, North Sel. *(3):* 1958, 1959, 1961.

Loughmore *(3):* 1955, 1988, 1992.

Bohercrowe *(2):* 1888, 1889.

Nenagh *(2):* 1911, 1915.

Templemore *(2):* 1925, 1936.

10th Batt. Templemore *(2):* 1943, 1945.

St Patrick's, Drangan Cloneen *(2):* 1947, 1953.

Aherlow *(2):* 2006, 2010.

Tipperary Town *(1):* 1902.

Cloneen *(1):* 1908.

Tipperary O'Leary's *(1):* 1910.

Castleiney *(1):* 1914.

Ballingarry *(1):* 1951.

Old Bridge *(1):* 1952.

Thurles Crokes *(1):* 1960.

Kilruane MacDonaghs	*(1):*	1975.	
Cahir	*(1):*	2003.	
Thomas McDonaghs	*(1):*	2011.	

WATERFORD

Dungarvan **(23):** 1890, 1892, 1893, 1896, 1897, 1898, 1908, 1916, 1926, 1927, 1928, 1929, 1930, 1937, 1938, 1945, 1946, 1947, 1948, 1956, 1990, 1991, 1992.

Stradbally **(18):** 1940, 1941, 1942, 1943, 1944, 1972, 1980, 1982, 1987, 2001, 2002, 2003, 2004, 2005, 2009, 2010, 2012, 2015.

Kilrossanty **(15):** 1888, 1919, 1939, 1949, 1950, 1951, 1952, 1957, 1960, 1964, 1983, 1985, 1986, 1988, 1989.

Rathgormack **(9):** 1909, 1910, 1911, 1912, 1913, 1918, 1995, 1996, 1999.

The Nire **(8):** 1993, 1994, 1997, 2000, 2006, 2008, 2014, 2016.

Clashmore **(7):** 1903, 1904, 1905, 1906, 1907, 1920, 1925.

Ballinacourty **(6):** 1978, 1979, 1981, 2007, 2011, 2013.

De La Salle **(5):** 1931, 1933, 1934, 1935, 1936.

Mount Sion **(5):** 1953, 1955, 1956, 1959, 1961.

Lismore **(4):** 1899, 1901, 1902, 1911.

Kill **(4):** 1962, 1966, 1967, 1968.

Aglish **(3):** 1915, 1922, 1923.

Kinsalebeg **(3):** 1886, 1891, 1925.

John Mitchels **(3):** 1970, 1973, 1976.

Tramore **(3):** 1969, 1971, 1984.

Windgap **(2):** 1894, 1895.

Ardmore **(2):** 1965, 1977.

Ballysaggart **(1):** 1885.

Ballyduff Lower **(1):** 1887.

Ballyduff Upper **(1):** 1924.

Dunhill **(1):** 1925.

Fenor **(1):** 1932.

Brickey Rangers **(1):** 1963.

Affane **(1):** 1974.

St Saviour's **(1):** 1998.

ULSTER

ANTRIM

St. John's **(24):** 1945, 1949, 1951,1957,1959, 1960, 1961, 1962, 1963, 1964, 1965, 1969, 1970, 1972, 1975, 1976, 1977, 1978, 1980, 1981, 1984, 1986, 1988, 1998.

St.Gall's **(19):** 1933, 1982, 1983, 1987, 1990, 1993, 2001, 2002, 2003, 2004, 2005, 2007, 2008, 2009, 2010, 2011, 2012, 2013, 2014.

O'Donovan Rossa **(15):** 1920, 1921, 1927, 1930, 1944, 1946, 1950, 1952, 1953, 1955, 1956, 1958, 1973, 1989, 1991.

James Stephen's **(7):** 1914, 1915, 1916, 1917, 1918, 1919, 1922.

Cuchuilain's **(6):** 1924, 1925, 1926, 1931, 1935, 1936.

Seaghan an Diomais **(5):** 1903, 1906, 1908, 1909, 1910.

Sarsfield's **(4):** 1913, 1941, 1967, 1985.

Cargin **(4):** 1974, 1995, 1999, 2000.

Gaedhail Ulaidh **(3):** 1938, 1939, 1942.

O'Connell's **(3):** 1928, 1934, 1947.

St. Paul's **(3):** 1994, 1996, 1997.

Erin's Own **(3):** 2006, 2015, 2016.

Lámh Dhearg, Belfast **(3):** 1971, 1992, 2017.

Ollamh Fodhla **(2):** 1904, 1907.

Mitchel's **(2):** 1911, 1912.

Ardoyne **(2):** 1932, 1937.

Kickham's, Randalstown **(2):** 1943, 1954.

Tir na nOg **(1):** 1902.

O'Neill Crowley's **(1):** 1905.

Davitt's **(1):** 1923.

Lámh Dhearg, Toome **(1):** 1929.

O'Donnell's **(1):** 1940.

Éire Óg **(1):** 1948.

Glenravel **(1):** 1966.

Pearse's **(1):** 1968

St. Teresa's **(1):** 1979.

CLUB

ARMAGH

Crossmaglen   **(43):** 1906, 1908, 1911, 1912, 1913, 1923, 1924, 1925, 1926, 1927, 1933, 1936, 1937, 1947, 1960, 1962, 1965, 1966, 1967, 1970, 1975, 1977, 1983, 1986, 1996, 1997, 1998, 1999, 2000, 2001, 2002, 2003, 2004, 2005, 2006, 2007, 2008, 2010, 2011, 2012, 2013, 2014, 2015.

Clann na nGael, Lurgan   **(14):** 1949, 1950, 1968, 1969, 1971, 1972, 1973, 1974, 1976, 1980, 1981, 1987, 1993, 1994.

Armagh Harps   **(14):** 1889, 1890, 1891, 1901, 1902, 1903, 1946, 1952, 1955, 1957, 1958. 1989, 1991, 2017.

Young Ireland's, Armagh   **(7):** 1917, 1918, 1928, 1930, 1931, 1932, 1934.

Carrickcruppin   **(4):** 1959, 1978, 1979, 1982.

Keady   **(4):** 1938, 1953, 1956, 1984.

Pearse Óg, Armagh   **(4):** 1985, 1989, 1992, 2009.

Bessbrook   **(3):** 1909, 1916, 1939.

Killeavey   **(3):** 1914, 1915, 1948.

Clann Éireann, Lurgan   **(2):** 1954, 1963.

Shane O'Neill's, Camlough   **(2):** 1907, 1910.

Tír na nÓg, Armagh   **(2):** 1904, 1935.

St. **Michael's, Newtownhamilton (2):** 1940, 1941.

St. Malachy's, Armagh   **(2):** 1942, 1945.

Mullaghbawn   **(2):** 1964, 1995.

Whitecross   **(1):** 1905.

Wolfe Tone's, Derrymacash   **(1):** 1943.

St. Peter's Selection   **(1):** 1944.

St. Peter's, Lurgan   **(1):** 1951.

Collegeland   **(1):** 1961.

Sarsfields, Derrytrasna   **(1):** 1990.

Maghery   **(1):** 2016.

CAVAN

Cornafean   **(20):**   1909, 1910, 1912, 1913, 1914, 1915, 1918, l920, 1928, 1929, 1932, 1933, 1934, 1936, 1937, 1938, 1939, 1940, 1943, 1956.

Cavan Gaels   **(14):**   1965, 1975, 1977, 1978, 2001, 2004, 2003, 2005, 2007, 2008, 2009, 2011, 2014, 2017.

Mullahoran   **(12):**   1935, 1942, 1944, 1945, 1947, 1948, 1949, 1950, 1963, 1998, 2006, 2012.

Kingscourt Stars **(11):**   1921, 1980, 1981, 1986, 1987, 1989, 1990, 1991,1993, 2010, 2015.

Cavan Slashers   **(10):**   1890, 1917, 1922, 1924, 1925, 1927, 1928, 1930, 1931, 1941.

Crosserlough   **(9):**   1958, 1961, 1966, 1967, 1968, 1969, 1970, 1971, 1972.

Gowna   **(8):**   1988, 1994, 1996, 1997, 1999, 2000, 2002, 2004.

Bailieboro   **(5):**   1911, 1952, 1957, 1964, 1995.

Drumlane   **(4):**   1903, 1904, 1905, 1907.

Virginia   **(4):**   1916, 1919, 1959, 1962.

Laragh   **(4):**   1979, 1982, 1983, 1984.

Ramor United   **(4):**   1974, 1985, 1992, 2016.

Cootehill   **(3):**   1953, 1954, 1955.

Maghera   **(2):**   1888, 1926.

Templeport   **(1):**   1923.

Mountnugent   **(1):**   1946.

Lavey   **(1):**   1951.

Annagh, Redhills/Belturbet   **(1):** 1973.

St. Mary's, Castlerahan/Munsterconnaught   **(1):** 1976.

Ballinagh   **(1):**   2013.

N.B. 1960 Championship not finished.

DERRY

Bellaghy   **(21):**   1956, 1958, 1959, 1960, 1961, 1963, 1964, 1965, 1968, 1969, 1971, 1972, 1975, 1979, 1986, 1994, 1996, 1998, 1999, 2000, 2005.

Ballinderry   **(13):**   1927, 1974, 1980, 1981, 1982, 1995, 2001, 2002, 2006, 2008, 2011, 2012, 2013.

Newbridge   **(10):**   1937, 1940, 1945, 1948, 1950, 1955, 1966, 1967, 1970, 1989.

Lavey   **(9):**   1938, 1943, 1944, 1954, 1977, 1988, 1990, 1992, 1993.

Dungiven   **(7):**   1947, 1951, 1983, 1984, 1987, 1991, 1997.

Magherafelt   **(5):**   1939, 1942, 1946, 1949, 1978.

Slaughtneil   **(5):**   2004, 2014, 2015, 2016, 2017.

Ballinascreen   **(4):**   1934, 1935, 1941, 1973.

Glenullin   **(3):**   1928, 1985, 2007.

Loup   **(3):**   1936, 2003, 2009.

Éire Óg   **(2):**   1907, 1952.

Ballerin	*(2):*	1957, 1976.
Clann Chonaill	*(1):*	1914.
Sarsfields	*(1):*	1916.
St. Patrick's	*(1):*	1917.
Emmet's	*(1):*	1918.
Derry Guilds	*(1):*	1921.
Buncrana	*(1):*	1930.
Burt	*(1):*	1931.
Desertmartin	*(1):*	1953.
Ballymaguigan	*(1):*	1962.
Eoghan Rua, Coleraine (1):		2010.

*N.B. 1982 final result declared null and void. *N.B. No competitions in pre-1907, 1908-14, 1919-20, 1922-26, 1929 and 1932-33 periods.

DONEGAL

St. Eunan's, Letterkenny (16): 1927, 1948, 1950, 1956, 1960, 1967, 1969, 1972, 1983, 1999, 2001, 2007, 2008, 2009, 2012, 2014.

Aodh Ruadh, Ballyshannon (12): 1929, 1932, 1937, 1939, 1942, 1943, 1951, 1986, 1987, 1994, 1997, 1998.

Gaoth Dobhair (14): 1935, 1938, 1941, 1944, 1945, 1946, 1947, 1949, 1953, 1954, 1955, 1961, 2002, 2006.

St. Joseph's, Bundoran/Ballyshannon (8): 1965, 1966, 1968, 1970, 1973, 1974, 1975, 1976.

Dungloe (7): 1930, 1931, 1933, 1936, 1940, 1957, 1958.

MacCumhaill's, Ballybofey (6): 1959, 1962, 1963, 1964, 1971, 1977.

Killybegs (6): 1952, 1988, 1991, 1992, 1995, 1996.

Ardara (6): 1923, 1926, 1928, 1981, 2000, 2004.

Kilcar (6): 1925, 1980, 1985, 1989, 1993, 2017.

Four Masters, Donegal (4): 1924, 1982, 1984, 2003.

Bundoran	**(3):**	1920, 1934, 1979.
Naomh Chonaill	**(3):**	2005, 2010, 2015.
Glenswilly	**(3):**	2011, 2013, 2016.
Killygordon	**(1):**	1921.

Castlefin	*(1):*	1922.
Gleann Choilm Cille	*(1):*	1978.
Naomh Columba (1):		1990.

DOWN

Kilcoo (16): 1917, 1921, 1925, 1926, 1927, 1928, 1932, 1933, 1937, 2009, 2012, 2013, 2014, 2015, 2016, 2017.

Burren (13): 1966, 1981, 1983, 1984, 1985, 1986, 1987, 1988, 1992, 1996, 1997, 2010, 2011.

Bryansford (11): 1939, 1940, 1941, 1942, 1969, 1970, 1971, 1973, 1974, 1977, 2003.

Castlewellan (10): 1924, 1934, 1936, 1950, 1958, 1965, 1979, 1982, 1994, 1995.

Clonduff (9): 1930, 1944, 1945, 1947, 1949, 1952, 1957, 1980, 2000.

Mayobridge (10): 1916, 1919, 1999, 2001, 2002, 2004, 2005, 2006, 2007, 2008.

Downpatrick (6): 1935, 1972, 1978, 1990, 1991, 1993.

Faugh-an-Bealach	*(4):*	1903, 1906, 1907, 1908.
Newry Shamrocks	*(4):*	1946, 1951, 1956, 1961.
Mitchel's, Newry	*(4):*	1960, 1964, 1967, 1968.
Warrenpoint	*(3):*	1943, 1948, 1953.
Glenn	*(3):*	1959, 1962, 1963.
Liatroim	*(2):*	1905, 1920.
Ballymartin	*(2):*	1938, 1958.
Loughinisland	*(2):*	1975, 1989.
Rostrevor	*(2):*	1976, 1998.
Clann na Banna	*(1):*	1904.
Annsborough	*(1):*	1908.
Clann Uladh	*(1):*	1910.
Rossqlass	*(1):*	1922.
Drumnaquoile	*(1):*	1929.
Rathfriland	*(1):*	1931.
Lisnacree	*(1):*	1954.

CLUB

FERMANAGH

Teemore **(21):** 1904, 1905, 1906, 1910, 1911, 1912, 1913, 1914, 1915, 1916, 1917, 1924, 1926, 1929, 1935, 1969, 1971, 1974, 1975, 1983, 2005.

Lisnaskea **(20):** 1928, 1931, 1936, 1937, 1938, 1939, 1941, 1942, 1943, 1945, 1946, 1947, 1948, 1950, 1951, 1954, 1977, 1980, 1991, 1994.

Enniskillen **(15):** 1907, 1908, 1909, 1930, 1976, 1978, 1987, 1992, 1998, 1999, 2000, 2001, 2002, 2003, 2006.

Roslea **(12):** 1955, 1956, 1957, 1958, 1962, 1982, 1984, 1986, 2010, 2011, 2013, 2014.

Devenish **(9):** 1963, 1965, 1966, 1967, 1985, 1989, 1990, 1993, 1996.

Newtownbutler **(9):** 1934, 1940, 1944, 1953, 1959, 1964, 1988, 1997, 2007.

Derrygonnelly Harps (6): 1995, 2004, 2009, 2015, 2016, 2017.

Tempo **(4):** 1970, 1972, 1973, 2012.

Erne Gaels, Belleek (3): 1949, 1979, 1981.

Irvinestown **(2):** 1918, 1952.

Wattlebridge **(2):** 1919, 1920.

Knockninny **(2):** 1927, 1932.

Killyrover **(1):** 1925.

Belnaleck **(1):** 1933.

Devenish/Mulleek **(1):** 1960.

Aughadrumsee **(1):** 1961.

Ederney **(1):** 1968.

St. Patrick's **(1):** 2008.

MONAGHAN

Castleblayney **(37):** 1907, 1916, 1917, 1924, 1926, 1931, 1932, 1933, 1936, 1937, 1939, 1940, 1941, 1946, 1963, 1964, 1965, 1966, 1967, 1970, 1971, 1972, 1973, 1975, 1976, 1982, 1986, 1988, 1990, 1991, 1995, 1996, 1998, 1999, 2000, 2001, 2003.

Scotstown **(18):** 1960, 1961, 1974, 1977, 1978, 1979, 1980, 1981, 1983, 1984, 1985, 1989, 1992, 1993, 2013, 2015, 2016, 2017.

Clontibret **(16):** 1949, 1950, 1951, 1952, 1955, 1956, 1958, 1968, 1994, 1997, 2002, 2006, 2007, 2009, 2010, 2014.

Ballybay **(8):** 1953, 1954, 1957, 1959, 1962, 1969, 1987, 2012.

Carrickmacross **(7):** 1908, 1909, 1910, 1913, 1914, 1918, 1919.

Donaghmoyne **(6):** 1904, 1906, 1934, 1935, 1942, 1945.

Inniskeen **(5):** 1888, 1905, 1938, 1947, 1948.

Latton **(4):** 1930, 2005, 2008, 2011.

Monaghan **(3):** 1911, 1922, 1923.

Killeevan **(3):** 1927, 1929, 1944.

Magherarney **(1):** 1915.

North Selection **(1):** 1925.

Corcaghan **(1):** 1928.

Clones **(1):** 1943.

Magheracloone **(1):** 2004.

TYRONE

Carrickmore **(15):** 1940, 1943, 1949, 1961, 1966, 1969, 1977, 1978, 1979, 1995, 1996, 1999, 2001, 2004, 2005.

Dungannon **(10):** 1908, 1925, 1929, 1933, 1935, 1936, 1944, 1947, 1951, 1959.

Coalisland **(9):** 1904, 1907, 1928, 1930, 1946, 1955, 1989, 1990, 2010.

Omagh **(9):** 1948, 1952, 1953, 1954, 1957, 1963, 1988, 2014, 2017.

Clonoe **(8):** 1958, 1959, 1960, 1964, 1965, 1991, 2008, 2013.

Ardboe **(7):** 1968, 1971, 1972, 1973, 1984, 1987, 1998.

Errigal Ciarán **(7):** 1993, 1994, 1997, 2000, 2002, 2006, 2012.

Trillick **(7):** 1937, 1974, 1975, 1980, 1983, 1986, 2015.

Moortown **(4):** 1941, 1942, 1960, 1992.

Augher **(3):** 1976, 1982, 1985.

Dromore **(3):** 2007, 2009, 2011.

Cookstown **(2):** 1916, 1917.

Ballygawley **(2):** 1926, 1931.

Fintona **(2):** 1913, 1938.

Strabane **(2):** 1905, 1945.

Stewartstown **(2):** 1924, 1962.

Derrylaughan **(2):** 1967, 1981.

Killyclogher **(2):** 2003, 2016.

Moy **(1):** 1919.

Donaghmore **(1):** 1927.

Washinghay **(1):** 1934.

Eglish **(1):** 1970.

GENERAL

INTERNATIONAL SERIES
(UNDER COMPROMISE RULES)

1984
First Test Cork, October 21:
Australia 70 pts 57 pts Ireland
Second Test Croke Park, October 28:
Ireland 80 pts 76 pts Australia
Third Test Croke Park, November 4:
Australia 76 pts 71 pts Ireland

1986
First Test Perth, October 11:
Australia 64 pts 57 pts Ireland
Second Test Melbourne, October 19:
Ireland 62 pts 46 pts Australia
Third Test Adelaide, October 24:
Ireland 55 pts 32 pts Australia

1987
First Test Croke Park, October 18:
Ireland 53 pts 51 pts Australia
Second Test Croke Park, October 25:
Australia 72 pts 47 pts Ireland
Third Test Croke Park, November 1:
Australia 59 pts 55 pts Ireland

1990
First Test Melbourne, November 2:
Ireland 47 pts 38 pts Australia
Second Test Canberra, November 20:
Ireland 52 pts 31 pts Australia
Third Test Perth, November 17:
Australia 50 pts 44 pts Ireland

1998
First Test Croke Park, October 11:
Australia 62 pts 61 pts Ireland
Second Test Croke Park, October 18:
Ireland 67 pts 56 pts Australia
Ireland won two-game series on aggregate points: 128 to 118.

1999
First Test Melbourne, October 7:
Ireland 70 pts 62 pts Australia.
Second Test Adelaide, October 15:
Ireland 52 pts 52 pts Australia
Ireland won two-game series on aggregate points, 122- 114.

2000
First Test Croke Park, October 8:
Australia 55 pts 47 pts Ireland
Second Test Croke Park, October 15:
Australia 68 pts 51 pts Ireland
Australia won the two-game series on aggregate points 123-98.

2001
First Test Melbourne, October 12:
Ireland 59 pts 53 pts Australia
Second Test Adelaide, October 19:
Ireland 71 pts 52pts Australia
Ireland won the two game series on aggregate points 130-105.

2002
First Test Croke Park, October 13:
Australia 65 pts 58 pts Ireland.
Second Test Croke Park, October 20:
Australia 42 pts 42 pts Ireland
Australia won the two game series on aggregate points 107-100.

2003
First Test Perth, October 24:
Australia 56 pts 46 pts Ireland
Second Test Melbourne, October 31:
Ireland 48 pts 45 pts Australia.
Australia won the two game series on aggregate points 101-94.

2004
First Test Croke Park, October 17:
Ireland 77 pts 41 pts Australia
Second Test Croke Park, October 24:
Ireland 55 pts 41pts Australia
Ireland won the two game series on aggregate points 132-82.

2005
First Test Perth, October 21:
Australia 100 pts 64 pts Ireland
Second Test Melbourne, October 28:
Australia 63 pts 42 pts Ireland
Australia won the two game series on aggregate points 163-106.

2006
First Test Salthill, October 28:
Ireland 48 pts 40 pts Australia
Second Test Croke Park, November 5:
Australia 69 pts 31 pts Ireland
Australia won the two game series on aggregate points 117-71.

2008
First Test Perth, October 24:
Ireland 45 pts 44 pts Australia.
Second Test Melbourne, October 31:
Ireland 57 pts 53 pts Australia.
Ireland won the two game series on aggregate points 102-97.

2010
First Test Limerick, October 23:
Australia 47 pts 40 pts Ireland
Second Test Croke Park, October 30:
Australia 55 pts 52 pts Ireland
Australia won the two game series on aggregate points 102-92.

2011
First Test   Melbourne, October 28:
Ireland   80 pts   36 pts   Australia
Second Test Gold Coast, November 4:
Ireland   50 pts   29 pts   Australia
Ireland won the two game series on aggregate 130-65.

2013
First Test   Cavan, October 19:
Ireland   57 pts   35 pts   Australia
Second Test Croke Park, October 26:
Ireland   116 pts   37 pts   Australia
Ireland won the two game series on aggregate 173-72.

2015
Lone Test   Croke Park, November 21
Ireland   56pts   52pts   Australia

IRISH CAPS

Armagh
Steven McDonnell	11
Kieran McGeeney	10
Ciarán McKeever	7
Paul McGrane	5
Ronan Clarke	3
Brendan Donaghy	2
John Grimley	2
Mark Grimley	2
Aaron Kernan	2
Fran McMahon	2
Diarmuid Marsden	1

Carlow
Brendan Murphy	4
Tom Dwyer	1

Cavan
Jim Reilly	3
Dermot McCabe	2
Larry Reilly	2
Stephen King	1

Clare
Noel Roche	10
Martin Daly	1
Odhran O'Dwyer	1
Gary Brennan	1

Cork
Graham Canty	14
Jimmy Kerrigan	6
Anthony Lynch	6
Niall Cahalane	5
Seán Óg Ó hAilpín	4
Aidan Walsh	4
John O'Driscoll	3
Brendan J O'Sullivan	3
Michael Shields	3
Eoin Cadogan	3
Daniel Goulding	2
Joe Kavanagh	2
Paddy Kelly	2
John Miskella	2
Stephen O'Brien	2
Ciaran O'Sullivan	2
Alan Quirke	2
Eoin Sexton	2
Ciaran Sheehan	2
Dave Barry	1
Colin Corkery	1
Teddy McCarthy	1
Nicholas Murphy	1
Setanta Ó hAilpín	1
Pearse O'Neill	1
Paul Kerrigan	1

Derry
Seán Marty Lockhart	16
Dermot McNicholl	9
Anthony Tohill	8
Brian McGilligan	6
Tony Scullion	4
Paddy Bradley	2
Chrissy McKaigue	2

Donegal

Michael Murphy	6
Neil McGee	4
Brendan Devenney	3
Martin Gavigan	3
Paddy McBrearty	3
Martin Crossan	2
Karl Lacey	1

Down

Benny Counter	11
Greg Blaney	7
Kevin McKernan	4
Liam Austin	2
Martin Clarke	2
James McCartan	2
Michael McVeigh	2

Dublin

Stephen Cluxton	7
John O'Leary	7
Bryan Cullen	6
Brian Stynes	6
Gerry Hargan	4
Ciarán Whelan	4
Alan Brogan	3
Bernard Brogan	3
PJ Buckley	3
Paddy Christie	3
Paul Curran	3
Jack McCaffrey	3
Joe McNally	3
Barney Rock	3
Shane Ryan	3
Jim Stynes	3
Ray Cosgrove	2
Kieran Duff	2
Eamon Heary	2
Paul Flynn	2
Ciaran Kilkenny	2
Kieran Barr	1
Tommy Carr	1
Diarmuid Connolly	1
Kevin Fagan	1
Coman Goggins	1
Mick Holden	1
Jonathan McGee	1
Philip McMahon	1
Colin Moran	1
Rory O'Carroll	1
James McCarthy	1

Fermanagh

Martin McGrath	3
Paul Brewster	2
Peter McGinnity	1

Galway

Pádraic Joyce	11
Joe Bergin	8
Val Daly	8
Séamus McHugh	8
Seán Óg de Paor	7
Finian Hanley	7
Michael Donnellan	6
Jarlath Fallon	4

Pat Comer	3
Michael Meehan	3
Alan Mulholland	3
Brian O'Donnell	3
Declan Meehan	2
Derek Savage	2
Paul Conroy	2
Kieran Fitzgerald	1
Seán Ó Domhnaill	1

Kerry

Tadhg Kennelly	12
Séamus Moynihan	9
Jack O'Shea	9
Tom Spillane	8
Kieran Donaghy	5
Paul Galvin	4
Aidan O'Mahony	4
Darragh Ó Sé	4
Tomás Ó Sé	4
Pat Spillane	4
Tommy Walsh	4
Eoin Liston	3
Ger Lynch	3
Eoin Brosnan	2
Colm Cooper	2
John Crowley	2
Declan O'Keeffe	2
Marc Ó Sé	2
Seán Walsh	2
Charlie Nelligan	1
Mike Frank Russell	1
Killian Young	1
Donnchadh Walsh	1
David Moran	1

Kildare

Dermot Earley	8
Anthony Rainbow	5
Glen Ryan	5
Niall Buckley	4
Brian Sex	4
Emmet Bolton	3
Shay Fahy	3
James Kavanagh	2
Enda Murphy	2
Eamonn Callaghan	1
Paul Cribbin	1
Eoin Doyle	1
Johnny Doyle	1

Laois

Colm Begley	12
Tom Kelly	8
Zach Tuohy	4
Ross Munnelly	3
Joe Higgins	2
Brian McDonald	2
Colin Browne	1
John Costello	1
John O'Loughlin	1
Colm Parkinson	1

Leitrim

Mick Martin	2
Séamus Quinn	1

Limerick
Stephen Kelly	2
Pat Barrett	1

Longford
Paul Barden	2
Liam Tierney	2
Michael Quinn	1

Louth
Paddy Keenan	2
Ciaran Byrne	2

Mayo
James Nallen	6
David Heaney	4
Lee Keegan	4
Ciaran McDonald	4
Colm McManamon	3
Aidan O'Shea	3
Pearce Hanley	2
Tom Parsons	2
Colm Boyle	2
Kevin McLoughlin	2
Peter Burke	1
James Horan	1

Meath
Graham Geraghty	9
Mick Lyons	9
Darren Fay	8
Kevin Reilly	8
Trevor Giles	6
Bernard Flynn	4
John McDermott	4
Colm O'Rourke	4
Cormac Sullivan	4
Liam Hayes	3
Bernard O'Malley	3
Robbie O'Malley	3
David Gallagher	2
Eoin Kelly	2
Anthony Moyles	2
Paddy O'Rourke	2
Joe Cassells	1

Monaghan
Ciarán Murray	6
Darren Hughes	4
Conor McManus	4
Paul Finlay	1
Tomás Freeman	1

Offaly
Ciarán McManus	14
Finbarr Cullen	6
John Kenny	2
Matt Connor	1
Richie Connor	1
Cathal Daly	1
Martin Furlong	1
Niall McNamee	1
Mark Plunkett	1

Roscommon
Seán McDermott	2
Gary Cox	1
Paul Earley	1
Francie Grehan	1
Cathal Cregg	1

Sligo
Eamonn O'Hara	4

Tipperary
Derry Foley	3
Ciaran McDonald	2
Declan Browne	1
Brian Burke	1

Tyrone
Seán Cavanagh	11
Peter Canavan	6
Cormac McAnallen	6
Brian McGuigan	4
Joe McMahon	4
Ger Cavlan	3
Finbar Connell	2
Plunkett Donaghy	2
Mattie Donnelly	2
Brian Dooher	2
Kevin Hughes	2
Enda McGinley	2
Justin McMahon	2
Damien O'Hagan	2
Stephen O'Neill	2
Eoin Gormley	1
Peter Harte	1
Colin Holmes	1
Philip Jordan	1
John Lynch	1
Ryan McMenamin	1
Niall Morgan	1
Owen Mulligan	1

Westmeath
Dessie Dolan	8
Michael Fagan	8
John Keane	2

Wexford
Matty Forde	4
Ciarán Lyng	1

Wicklow
Pat O'Byrne	8
Leighton Glynn	6
Kevin O'Brien	4

AUSTRALIAN CHAMPIONSHIPS

HURLING

1971	Victoria
1972	No Championship
1973	New South Wales
1974	New South Wales
1975	New South Wales
1976	Victoria
1977	Victoria
1978	Victoria
1979	New South Wales
1980	New South Wales
1981	Victoria
1982	New South Wales
1983	New South Wales
1984	None (Tour of Ireland)
1985	New South Wales
1986	New South Wales
1987	New South Wales
1988	New South Wales
1989	Victoria
1990	New South Wales
1991	Victoria
1992	New South Wales
1993	New South Wales
1994	New South Wales
1995	New South Wales
1996	None (Tour of Ireland)
1997	Auckland
1998	New South Wales
1999	New South Wales
2000	No Championship
2001	New South Wales
2002	No Championship
2003	New South Wales
2004	New South Wales
2005	New South Wales
2006	New South Wales
2007	New South Wales
2008	Victoria
2009	New South Wales
2010	No Championship
2011	Queensland, Western Australia
2012	Queensland, Western Australia
2013	Queensland, Western Australia
2014	Queensland, Western Australia
2015	New South Wales
2016	Victoria
2017	Queensland Western Australia

FOOTBALL

1971	South Australia
1972	None
1973	South Australia
1974	Victoria
1975	Victoria
1976	New South Wales
1977	Victoria
1978	West Australia
1979	New South Wales
1980	New South Wales
1981	West Australia
1982	New South Wales
1983	South Australia
1984	No Championship
1985	Victoria
1986	Victoria
1987	West Australia
1988	Victoria
1989	Victoria
1990	New South Wales
1991	Victoria
1992	Auckland
1993	New South Wales
1994	Victoria
1995	Victoria
1996	None
1997	Auckland
1998	New South Wales
1999	New South Wales
2000	New South Wales
2001	Victoria
2002	Victoria
2003	New South Wales
2004	New South Wales
2005	New South Wales
2006	Western Australia
2007	New South Wales
2008	Victoria
2009	Victoria
2010	Queensland, Western Australia
2011	Victoria
2012	New South Wales
2013	New South Wales
2014	Victoria
2015	New South Wales
2016	New South Wales
2017	New South Wales

NORTH AMERICAN BOARD CHAMPIONSHIPS

HURLING

1959	San Francisco
1960	Los Angeles
1961	Montreal
1962	Galway (Boston)
1963	Shannon Rangers (Chicago)
1964	Galway (Boston)
1965	Garryowen (Toronto)
1966	Harry Bolands (Chicago)
1967	Galway (Boston)
1968	Galway (Boston)
1969	Harry Bolands (Chicago)
1970	Garryowen (Toronto)
1971	Harry Bolands (Chicago)
1972	Harry Bolands (Chicago)
1973	Galway (Boston)
1974	Garryowen (Toronto)
1975	St. Michael's (Toronto)
1976	Harry Bolands (Chicago)
1977	Limerick (Chicago)
1978	St. Michael's (Toronto)
1979	St. Vincent's (Chicago)
1980	Harry Bolands (Chicago)
1981	Cork (Boston)
1982	Cork (Boston)
1983	Harry Bolands (Chicago)
1984	Harry Bolands (Chicago)
1985	Gaels (San Francisco)
1986	Tipperary (Boston)
1987	Fr. Tom Burkes (Boston)
1988	Gaels (San Francisco)
1989	Harry Bolands (Chicago)
1990	Na Fianna (San Francisco)
1991	Na Fianna (San Francisco)
1992	Tipperary (Boston)
1993	Harry Bolands (Chicago)
1994	Cork (Boston)
1995	Cu Chulainn (Chicago)
1996	Harry Bolands (Chicago)
1997	N. Padraig (San Francisco)
1998	Harry Bolands (Chicago)
1999	Harry Bolands (Chicago)
2000	Cu Chulainn (Chicago)
2001	Cork (Boston)
2002	Tipperary (Boston)
2003	Galway (Boston)
2004	Fr. Tom's (Boston)
2005	Tipperary (Boston)
2006	Harry Bolands (Chicago)
2007	Cu Chulainn (Chicago)
2008	Chicago Limerick
2009	Wexford (Boston)
2010	Naomh Pádraig (San Francisco)
2011	Na Fianna (San Francisco)
2012	Na Fianna (San Francisco)
2013	Na Fianna (San Francisco)
2014	Galway (Boston)
2015	Harry Bolands, Chicago
2016	Naomh Pádraig, San Francisco
2017	Naomh Pádraig, San Francisco

FOOTBALL

1959	Los Angeles
1960	San Francisco
1961	San Francisco
1962	St. Patrick's (Cleveland)
1963	Galway (Boston)
1964	St. Patrick's (Cleveland)
1965	St. Patrick's (Cleveland)
1966	St. Patrick's (Cleveland)
1967	Hartford
1968	St. Patrick's (Chicago)
1969	Detroit
1970	Galway (Boston)
1971	Tyrone (Philadelphia)
1972	St. Brendan's (Chicago)
1973	Connemara Gaels (Boston)
1974	Tyrone (Philadelphia)
1975	Tyrone (Philadelphia)
1976	St. Patrick's (Boston)
1977	Tyrone (Philadelphia)
1978	Wolfe Tones (Chicago)
1979	Gaels (San Francisco)
1980	Wolfe Tones (Chicago)
1981	St. Brendan's (Chicago)
1982	Wolfe Tones (Chicago)
1983	St. Brendan's (Chicago)
1984	St. Patrick's (Boston)

1985	Wolfe Tones (Chicago)
1986	Galway (Boston)
1987	John McBrides (Chicago)
1988	Wolfe Tones (Chicago)
1989	Galway (Boston)
1990	Donegal (Philadelphia)
1991	Wolfe Tones (Chicago)
1992	Donegal (Philadelphia)
1993	Donegal (Philadelphia)
1994	Cusacks (San Francisco)
1995	Wolfe Tones (Chicago)
1996	Wolfe Tones (Chicago)
1997	Wolfe Tones (Chicago)
1998	Aidan McAnespies (Boston)
1999	Wolfe Tones (Chicago)
2000	St. Brendan's (Chicago)
2001	Wolfe Tones (Chicago)
2002	Wolfe Tones (Chicago)
2003	Cork (Boston)
2004	St. Brendan's (Chicago)
2005	Ulster (San Francisco)
2006	Wolfe Tones (Chicago)
2007	St.Brendan's (Chicago)
2008	Aidan McAnespies (Boston)
2009	St. Christopher's (Boston)
2010	Seán Treacys (San Francisco)
2011	Aidan McAnespies (Boston)
2012	Ulster (San Francisco)
2013	Ulster (San Francisco)
2014	Ulster (San Francisco)
2015	McBrides, Chicago
2016	Ulster, San Francisco
2017	Shannon Blues, Boston

CHAMPIONSHIPS OF BRITAIN

HURLING

1967	Cuchulains (London)
1968	St Chad's (Warwickshire)
1969	Brian Boru (London)
1970	John Mitchell's (Warwickshire)
1971	Brian Boru (London)
1972	Brother Pearse (London)
1973	St Gabriel's (London)
1974	St Gabriel's (London)
1975	Brian Boru (London)
1976	St Gabriel's (London)
1977	St Gabriel's (London)
1978	St Gabriel's (London)
1979	Brian Boru (London)
1980	Brian Boru (London)
1981	St Gabriel's (London)
1982	Brian Boru (London)
1983	Desmonds (London)
1984	St Gabriel's (London)
1985	Desmonds (London)
1986	St Gabriel's (London)
1987	Glen Rovers (Hertfordshire)
1988	Desmonds (London)
1989	Desmonds (London)
1990	St Gabriel's (London)
1991	Seán Treacy's (London)
1992	Desmonds (London)
1993	Seán Treacy's (London)
1994	Seán Treacy's (London)
1995	St Gabriel's (London)
1996	St Gabriel's (London)
1997	St Gabriel's (London)
1998	Brother Pearse (London)
1999	St.Gabriel's (London)
2000	Fr. Murphy's (London)
2001	Fr. Murphy's (London)
2002	Seán Treacy's (London)
2003	Fr. Murphy's (London)
2004	Robert Emmets (London)
2005	Fr. Murphy's (London)
2006	Robert Emmets (London)
2007	Brother Pearse (London)
2008	Robert Emmets (London)
2009	St.Gabriel's (London)

2010	Kilburn Gaels (London)
2011	Robert Emmets (London)
2012	St. Gabriel's (London)
2013	St. Gabriel's (London)
2014	Kilburn Gaels (London)
2015	Robert Emmetts (London)
2016	Robert Emmetts (London)
2017	Kilburn Gaels (London)

FOOTBALL

1967	St Mary's (London)
1968	Parnell's (London)
1969	Parnell's (London)
1970	Garryowen (London)
1971	Seán Treacy's (London)
1972	Seán McDermott's (Warwickshire)
1973	Seán McDermott's (Warwickshire)
1974	De La Salle College (Lancashire)
1975	Seán McDermott's (Warwickshire)
1976	An Ríocht (London)
1977	An Ríocht (London)
1978	An Ríocht (London)
1979	An Ríocht (London)
1980	Tara (London)
1981	Parnell's (London)
1982	Hugh O'Neill's (Yorkshire)
1983	Tír Conaill Gaels (London)
1984	Parnell's (London)
1985	An Ríocht (London)
1986	An Ríocht (London)
1987	An Ríocht (London)
1988	John Mitchell's (Warwickshire)
1989	An Ríocht (London)
1990	Tír Conaill Gaels (London)
1991	Parnell's (London)
1992	Tír Conaill Gaels (London)
1993	Tír Conaill Gaels (London)
1994	Oisin's (Lancashire)
1995	Tara (London)
1996	Tír Conaill Gaels (London)
1997	Tír Conaill Gaels (London)
1998	Tír Conaill Gaels (London)
1999	Hugh O'Neills (Yorkshire)
2000	Tír Conaill Gaels (London)
2001	Tír Conaill Gaels (London)
2002	St.Brendan's (London)

2003	Tara (London)
2004	Kingdom Kerry Gaels (London)
2005	Tír Conaill Gaels (London)
2006	St.Brendan's (London)
2007	Tír Conaill Gaels (London)
2008	Tír Conaill Gaels (London)
2009	Tír Conaill Gaels (London)
2010	Neasden Gaels (London)
2011	Fulham Irish (London)
2012	Tír Conaill Gaels (London)
2013	Kingdom Kerry Gaels (London)
2014	Tír Conaill Gaels (London)
2015	Tír Chonaill Gaels (London)
2016	St Kiernan's (London)
2017	Fulham Irish (London)

INTERNATIONAL COMPETITIONS

TAILTEANN GAMES

Many of the greatest players of earlier decades lined out in the Tailteann Game of 1924, 1928 and 1932 and the distinction of playing for Ireland in international matches became a prize of great distinction for those honoured. For the record then, here are the teams that contested those historic games:

1924 – HURLING
Ireland J.Humphreys (capt.), W.Ryan, W.Gleeson, D.Murnane (Limerick), J.Kennedy, D.Ring (Cork), J.J.Hayes, J.D'Arcy, Michael D'Arcy (Tipperary), T.Kelly (Laois), J.O'Mahony (goal), B.Gibbs, M.Derivan (Galway), G.Howard, Jim Walsh (Dublin).
United States W.Finn (capt.), D.Kelly (goal), P.Aylward, M.Kenney, P.Kelly, M.Kavanagh, C.McCarthy, M.Flanagan, R.Stokes, J.Deegan, J.Murphy, P.Cox, J.Galvin, P.J.Grimes, J.Ryan.

1924 – FOOTBALL
Ireland (v.England)—J.McDonnell, P.Carey, J.Norris (Dublin), J.P.Murphy, T.P.Masterson, P.Smyth (Cavan), C.Brosnan, J.Bailey, P.Sullivan (Kerry), J.Doyle (Carlow), L.McGrath (Galway), P.Kilroy (Wexford), T.Shevlin (Roscommon), J.Byrne (Louth), J.Martin (Leitrim).

1928 – HURLING
Ireland T.Daly (goal), J.Walsh, M.Gill, M.Power, G.Howard (Dublin), Seán Óg Murphy, Jas.O'Regan, E.Coughlan (Cork), P.Cahill, M.Kennedy (Tipperary), M.King, M.Derivan (Galway), J.Kinnane (Limerick), E.Tobin (Laois), T.Considine (Clare).
America J.Dermody (goal), J Keoghan, H.Meagher, S.Fitzpatrick, J.Grey, P.Fitzgibbon, P.Delany, C.Clohane, J.Galvin, J.Halligan, J.Horan, A.Cordial, W.Ryan, J.Burke, T.Hickey.(Included natives of Kilkenny, Laois, Cork, Offaly, Clare and Tipperary.)

1928 – FOOTBALL
Ireland J.McDonnell (goal), P.McDonnell, M.O'Brien (Dublin), J.Barrett, C.Brosnan, P.Russell (Kerry), J.Higgins, M.Goff, P.Doyle, F.Malone (Kildare), T.Shevlin (Roscommon), J.Smith (Cavan), P.Colleran (Sligo), J.Shanley (Leitrim), M.O'Neill (Wexford).
America E.Roberts (goal), A.Furlong, P.Ormsby, M.Ormsby, J.Tuite, M.Moloney, T.Armitage, M.Gunn, P.Lenihan, J.Stynes, M.Cody, W.Landers, J.Moriarty, T.Flynn, J.McGoldrick. (Waterford, Wexford, Mayo, Louth, Clare, Tipperary, Cork, Kildare, Kilkenny, Kerry and Leitrim were represented on this team.)

1932 – HURLING
Ireland E.O'Connell (capt.), J.O'Regan, J.Hurley, D.B.Murphy, M.Ahern (Cork), T.O'Meara (goal), P.Purcell (Tipperary), C.McMahon, J.Walsh (Dublin), J.J.Doyle (Clare), M.Cross (Limerick), E.Byrne, M.Power (Kiikenny), M.King (Galway), D.O'Neill (Laois).
America J.Holligan (capt.), J.Costigan (goal), J.Burke, W.Fox, J.Horan, P.Leamy, T.Delany, B.Dooley, T.Cooney, J.Smee, G.Fitzpatrick, W.Spearin, R.Purcell, J.Duane, J.Kenny. Sub: P.Loughman.

1932 – FOOTBALL
Ireland J.Barrett (capt.), D.O'Connor, P.Whitty, J.Ryan (Kerry), J.Higgins, P.Martin (Kildare), J.Fane, M.O'Neill, N.Walsh (Wexford), J.Delaney (Laois), J.McDonnell (Dublin, goal), J.Smith (Cavan), T.Leetch (Galway), L.Colleran (Sligo), G.Courell (Mayo).
America T.Armitage (capt.), J.Curran (goal), M.Maloney, A.Furlong, M.Kelleher, P.Landy, J.McGoldrick, J.Tuite, M.Shanahan, W.Landers, M.Mahon, M.Ormsby, T.Keogh, W.Mangan, J.Stynes. Sub: M.Spillane.

ST. BRENDAN CUP FINALS

New York v National League Winners 1954-1960

HURLING
1954
Polo Grounds, October 31. Cork 7-8, New York 3-10

1955
Croke Park, October 9. Tipperary 4-17, New York 4-7

1957
Polo Grounds, October 20. Tipperary 2- 14, New York 4-4

1958
Croke Park, September 14. New York 3-8, Wexford 3-7

1959
Gaelic Park, September 20. Tipperary 4- 11, New York 1-5

1960
Croke Park, October 9. Tipperary 5-18, New York 4-4

Football
1954
Polo Grounds, October 31. New York 0- 10, Mayo 2-3

1955
Croke Park, October 9. Dublin 2-9, New York 0-10

1957
Polo Grounds, October 20. Galway 3-13, New York 3-8

1958
Croke Park, October 5. Dublin 2-6, New York 1-7

1959
Gaelic Park, October 18. Kerry 2-11, New York 1-8

1960
Croke Park, October 9. Down 2-8, New York 0-6

WORLD CHAMPIONSHIP CUP

New York v All-Ireland Champions

HURLING
1967
Gaelic Park, September 17.

Kilkenny	1- 12	1-10	New York

September 24.

New York	2-13	0-23	Kilkenny (aet).

Aggregate score:

Kilkenny	1-35	3-23	New York

1968
Wexford Park, September 29.

Wexford	1-17	3-5	New York

1969
Gaelic Park, October 5.

New York	3-13	1-7	Kilkenny

October 12.

New York	1-11	3-5	Kilkenny

Aggregate score:

New York	4-24	4-12	Kilkenny

FOOTBALL

New York v All-Ireland Champions

1967
Croke Park, October 1.

Meath	0-13	1-6	New York

1968
Gaelic Park, October 13.

New York	1-9	1-8	Down

October 20.

Down	2-11	1-9	New York

Aggregate score:

Down	3-19	2-18	New York

1969
Croke Park, October 25.

Kerry	4-13	0-7	New York

AN POC FADA

ROLL OF HONOUR

1961 Vincent Godfrey (Limerick)
1962 Ollie Walsh (Kilkenny)
1963 Ollie Walsh (Kilkenny)/Tom Geary (Waterford)/Dinny Donnelly (Meath)
1964 Oliver Gough (Kilkenny)
1965 Denis Murphy (Cork)
1966 Finbar O'Neill (Cork)
1967 Finbar O'Neill (Cork)
1968 Finbar O'Neill (Cork)
1969 Liam Tobin (Waterford)
1970-80 No Competition
1981 Pat Hartigan (Limerick)
1982 Gerry Goodwin (Tyrone)
1983 Pat Hartigan (Limerick)
1984 Ger Cunningham (Cork)
1985 Ger Cunningham (Cork)
1986 Ger Cunningham (Cork)
1987 Ger Cunningham (Cork)
1988 Ger Cunningham (Cork)
1989 Ger Cunningham (Cork)
1990 Ger Cunningham (Cork)
1991 Tommy Quaid (Limerick)
1992 Albert Kelly (Offaly)
1993 Albert Kelly (Offaly)
1994 Michael Shaughnessy (Galway)
1995 Michael Shaughnessy (Galway)
1996 Michael Shaughnessy (Galway)
1997 Colin Byrne (Wicklow)
1998 Albert Kelly (Offaly)
1999 Davy Fitzgerald (Clare)
2000 Colin Byrne (Wicklow)
2001 Albert Shanahan (Limerick)
2002 Davy Fitzgerald (Clare)
2003 Paul Dunne (Louth)
2004 Brendan Cummins (Tipperary)
2005 Albert Shanahan (Limerick)
2006 Brendan Cummins (Tipperary)
2007 Brendan Cummins (Tipperary)
2008 Brendan Cummins (Tipperary)
2009 Gerry Fallon (Roscommon)
2010 Graham Clarke (Down)
2011 Brendan Cummins (Tipperary)
2012 Brendan Cummins (Tipperary)
2013 Brendan Cummins (Tipperary)
2014 Brendan Cummins (Tipperary)

2015 B.Cummins (Tipperary)
2016 J.McInerney (Clare)
2017 T.Haran (Galway)

ROLL OF HONOUR - PAIRS

1983 Joe Shortt (Armagh), Tommy Quaid (Limerick)
1984 Justin McCarthy (Cork), Michael Shaughnessy (Galway)
1985 Ger Cunningham (Cork), Donal O'Brien (New York)
1986 John Kelly (Offaly), Tommy Quaid (Limerick)
1987 Des Donnelly (Antrim), Christy Ryan (Clare)
1988 Vincent Moore (Kildare), Michael Shaughnessy (Galway)
1989 John Conway (Kerry), Michael Shaughnessy (Galway)
1990 Des Donnelly (Antrim), Tommy Quaid (Limerick)
1991 Tommy Quaid (Limerick), Michael Shaughnessy (Galway)
1992 Michael Shaughnessy (Galway), Albert Kelly (Offaly)
1993 David Fitzgerald (Clare), Michael Shaughnessy (Galway)
1994 Johnny Masterson (Meath), Michael Shaughnessy (Galway)
1995 Liam Shinners (Tipperary), Michael Shaughnessy (Galway)
1996 Paul Dunne (Louth), Niall Linnane (Galway)
1997 Colm Byrne (Wicklow), Kevin Coulter (Down)
1998 Seamus McMullan (Antrim), David Fitzgerald (Clare)
1999 Ian Scallan (Wexford), Brendan Cummins (Tipperary)
2000 Ritchie Burke (Galway), Christy O'Connor (Clare)
2001 Liam Shinners (Tipperary), Albert Shanahan (Limerick)
2002 Graham Clark (Down), David Fitzgerald (Clare)
2003 Paul Dunne (Louth), Tom Finn (Wicklow)
2004 Brendan Cummins (Tipperary), Albert Shanahan (Liimerick)
2005 David Fitzgerald (Clare), Damien Fitzhenry (Wexford)
2006 Eoin Kelly (Tipperary), Brendan Cummins (Tipperary)
2007 Davy Fitzgearld (Clare), Albert Shanahan (Limerick)
2008 Brendan Cummins (Tipperary), Brendan McNamara (Clare)
2009 Jerry Fallon (Roscommon), Brendan Cummins (Tipperary)
2010 Jerry Fallon (Roscommon), James Skehill (Galway)
2011 Brendan Cummins (Tipperary), Karol Keating (Down)
2012 Brendan Cummins (Tipperary), Kevin McKernan Jnr. (Antrim)
2013 Brendan Cummins (Tipperary), James Skehill (Galway)
2014 Brendan Cummins (Tipperary), James Skehill (Galway)

AN POST/GAA TEAMS OF THE MILLENNIUM

Football: Dan O'Keeffe (Kerry), Enda Colleran (Galway), Joe Keohane (Kerry), Seán Flannagan (Mayo), Sean Murphy (Kerry), John Joe Reilly (Cavan), Martin O'Connell (Meath), Mick O'Connell (Kerry), Tommy Murphy (Laois), Seán O'Neill (Down), Seán Purcell (Galway), Pat Spillane (Kerry), Mick Sheehy (Kerry), Tom Langan (Mayo), Kevin Heffernan (Dublin).

Hurling: Tony Reddan (Tipperary), Bobby Rackard (Wexford), Nick O'Donnell (Wexford), John Doyle (Tipperary), Brian Whelahan (Offaly), John Keane (Waterford), Paddy Phelan (Kilkenny), Lory Meagher (Kilkenny), Jack Lynch (Cork), Jim Langton (Kilkenny), Mick Mackey (Limerick), Christy Ring (Cork), Jimmy Doyle (Tipperary), Ray Cummins (Cork), Eddie Keher (Kilkenny).

TEAMS OF THE CENTURY

Hurling: Tony Reddan (Tipperary), Bobby Rackard (Wexford), Nick O'Donnell (Wexford), John Doyle (Tipperary), Jimmy Finn (Tipperary), John Keane (Waterford), Paddy Phelan (Kilkenny), Lory Meagher (Kilkenny), Jack Lynch (Cork), Christy Ring (Cork), Mick Mackey (Limerick), Jimmy Langton (Kilkenny), Jimmy Doyle (Tipperary), Nickey Rackard (Wexford), Eddie Keher (Kilkenny).

Football: Dan O'Keeffe (Kerry), Enda Colleran (Galway), Paddy O'Brien (Meath), Seán Flanagan (Mayo), Seán Murphy (Kerry), John Joe O'Reilly (Cavan), Stephen White (Louth), Mick O'Connell (Kerry), Jack O'Shea (Kerry), Seán O'Neill (Down), Seán Purcell (Galway), Pat Spillane (Kerry), Mike Sheehy (Kerry), Tom Langan (Mayo), Kevin Heffernan (Dublin).

SPECIAL SELECTION (PLAYERS WHO NEVER WON AN ALL-IRELAND MEDAL)

Hurling: Seán Duggan (Galway), Jim Fives (Waterford), Noel Drumgoole (Dublin), J. J. ("Goggles") Doyle (Clare), Seán Herbert (Limerick), Seán Stack (Clare), Colm Doran (Wexford), Joe Salmon (Galway), "Jobber" McGrath (Westmeath), Josie Gallagher (Galway), Martin Quigley (Wexford), Kevin Armstrong (Antrim), Jimmy Smith (Clare), Christy O'Brien (Laois), Mick Bermingham (Dublin).

Football: Aidan Brady (Roscommon), Willie Casey (Mayo), Eddie Boyle (Louth), John McKnight (Armagh), Gerry O'Reilly (Wicklow), Gerry O'Malley (Roscommon), Seán Quinn (Armagh), Jim McKeever (Derry), Tommy Murphy (Laois), Seán O'Connell (Derry), Pakie McGarty (Leitrim), Michael Kearns (Sligo), Charlie Gallagher (Cavan), Willie McGee (Mayo), Dinny Allen (Cork).

LEADING ALL-IRELAND SENIOR MEDAL WINNERS

FOOTBALL
Páidí Ó Sé (Kerry)   8:
1975, 1978, 1979, 1980, 1981, 1984, 1985, 1986
Denis "Ogie" Moran (Kerry)   8:
1975, 1978, 1979, 1980, 1981, 1984, 1985, 1986
Pat Spillane (Kerry)   8:
1975, 1978, 1979, 1980, 1981, 1984, 1985, 1986.
Ger Power (Kerry)   8:
1975, 1978, 1979, 1980, 1981, 1984, 1985, 1986
Mike Sheehy (Kerry)   8:
1975, 1978, 1979, 1980, 1981, 1984, 1985, 1986
Dan O'Keeffe (Kerry)   7:
1931, 1932, 1937, 1939 1940, 1941, 1946
Jack O'Shea (Kerry)   7:
1978, 1979, 1980, 1981, 1984, 1985, 1986
John O'Keeffe (Kerry)   7:
1969, 1970, 1975, 1978, 1979, 1980, 1981
Charlie Nelligan (Kerry)   7:
1978, 1979, 1980, 1981, 1984, 1985, 1986
Seán Walsh (Kerry)   7:
1978, 1979, 1980, 1981, 1984, 1985, 1986
Mick Spillane (Kerry)   7:
1978, 1979, 1980, 1981, 1984, 1985, 1986

HURLING
Henry Shefflin (Kilkenny)   10:
2000, 2002, 2003, 2006, 2007, 2008, 2009, 2011, 2012, 2014
J.J.Delaney (Kilkenny)   9:
2002, 2003, 2006, 2007, 2008, 2009, 2011, 2012, 2014
Noel Hickey (Kilkenny)   9:
2000, 2002, 2003, 2006, 2007, 2008, 2009, 2011, 2012
Jackie Tyrrell (Kilkenny)   9:
2003, 2006, 2007, 2008, 2009, 2011, 2012, 2014, 2015.
Tommy Walsh (Kilkenny)   9:
2002, 2003, 2006, 2007, 2008, 2009, 2011, 2012, 2014
Noel Skehan (Kilkenny)   9:
1963, 1967, 1969, 1972, 1974, 1975, 1979, 1982, 1983
Christy Ring (Cork)   8:
1941, 1942, 1943, 1944, 1946, 1952, 1953, 1954
John Doyle (Tipperary)   8:
1949, 1950, 1951, 1958, 1961, 1962, 1964, 1965
Frank Cummins (Kilkenny)   8:
1967, 1969, 1972, 1974, 1975 1979, 1982, 1983
Eddie Brennan (Kilkenny)   8:
2000, 2002, 2003, 2006, 2007, 2008, 2009, 2011
Michael Kavanagh (Kilkenny)   8:
2000, 2002, 2003, 2006, 2007, 2008, 2009, 2011
Richie Power (Kilkenny)   8:
2006, 2007, 2008, 2009, 2011, 2012, 2014, 2015.
Eoin Larkin (Kilkenny)   8:
2006, 2007, 2008, 2009, 2011, 2012, 2014, 2015.
Michael Fennelly (Kilkenny)   8:
2006, 2007, 2008, 2009, 2011, 2012, 2014, 2015.

HIGHEST SCORERS IN
ALL-IRELAND FINALS

HURLING
60 minutes: 19 points
Michael "Gah" Ahearne (Cork) 5-4 v Galway 1928

70 minutes: 18 points
Nicholas English (Tipperary) 2-12 v Antrim 1989

80 minutes: 17 points
Eddie Keher (Kilkenny) 2-11 v Tipperary 1971

FOOTBALL
60 Minutes: 11 points
Frank Stockwell (Galway) 2-5 v Cork 1956

70 minutes: 12 points
Jimmy Keaveney (Dublin) 2-6 v Armagh 1977

80 minutes: 10 points
Mick Fay (Meath) 0- 10 v Kerry 1970

10 points
Brendan Lynch (Kerry) 1-7 v Offaly 1972 (Draw)

10 points
Tony McTeague (Offaly) 0-10 v Kerry 1972 (Replay).

*Note: What added special distinction to Frank Stockwell's feat
was that all his scores came from play – a record in itself.*

PRESIDENTS OF THE G.A.A.

1884	Maurice Davin (Tipperary)
1887	E. M. Bennett (Clare)
1888	Maurice Davin (Tipperary)
1889	Peter J. Kelly (Galway)
1895	Frank B. Dineen (Limerick)
1898	Michael Deering (Cork)
1901	James Nowlan (Kilkenny)
1921	Daniel McCarthy (Dublin)
1924	P. D. Breen (Wexford)
1926	W. P. Clifford (Limerick)
1928	Seán Ryan (Dublin)
1932	Seán McCarthy (Cork)
1935	Robert O'Keeffe (Laois)
1938	Pádraig McNamee (Antrim)
1943	Seamus Gardiner (Tipperary)
1946	Dan O'Rourke (Roscommon)
1949	Michael Kehoe (Wexford)
1952	M. V. O'Donoghue (Waterford)
1955	Seamus McFerran (Belfast)
1958	Dr. J. J. Stuart (Dublin)
1961	Hugh Byrne (Wicklow)
1964	Alf Murray (Armagh)
1967	Seamus O'Riain (Tipperary)
1970	Pat Fanning (Waterford)
1973	Dr Donal Keenan (Roscommon)
1976	Con Murphy (Cork)
1979	Paddy McFlynn (Down)
1982	Paddy Buggy (Kilkenny)
1985	Dr Mick Loftus (Mayo)
1988	John Dowling (Offaly)
1991	Peter Quinn (Fermanagh)
1994	Jack Boothman (Wicklow)
1997	Joe McDonagh (Galway)
2000	Seán McCague (Monaghan)
2003	Seán Kelly (Kerry)
2006	Nickey Brennan (Kilkenny)
2009	Christy Cooney (Cork)
2012	Liam O'Neill (Laois)
2015	Aogán Ó Fearghail (Cavan)
2018	John Horan (Dublin)

ARD STIÚRTHÓIRÍ

1884-'85	Michael Cusack (Clare)
1884-'85	John McKay (Cork)
1884-'87	John Wyse Power (Kildare)
1885-'87	J. B. O'Reilly (Dublin)
1885-'89	Timothy O'Riordan (Cork)
1887-'88	James Moore (Louth)
1888-'89	William Prendergast (Tipperary)
1889-'90	P. R. Cleary (Limerick)
1890-'92	Maurice Moynihan (Kerry)
1891-'94	Patrick Tobin (Dublin)
1894-'95	David Walsh (Cork)
1895-'98	Richard T. C. Blake (Meath)
1898-1901	Frank B. Dineen (Limerick)
1901-'09	Luke J. O'Toole (Dublin)
1929-'64	Pádraic Ó Caoimh (Cork)
1964-'79	Seán Ó Síocháin (Cork)
1979-2007	Liam Ó Maolmhichíl (Longford)
2008-	Páraic Ó Dufaigh (Monaghan)

CONNACHT

Galway
Pearse Stadium, Salthill *(26,200)*

Leitrim
Páirc Seán Mac Diarmada, Carrick-on-Shannon *(9,300)*

Mayo
Elverys MacHale Park, Castlebar *(38,000)*

Roscommon
Dr. Hyde Park, Roscommon *(25,000)*

Sligo
Markievicz Park, Sligo *(18,500)*

London
McGovern Park, Ruislip *(2,000)*

New York
Gaelic Park, New York *(2,000)*

LEINSTER

Carlow
Netwatch Cullen Park, Carlow *(21,000)*

Dublin
Croke Park, Dublin *(82,300)*

Kildare
St Conleth's Park, Newbridge *(6,200)*

Kilkenny
Nowlan Park, Kilkenny *(25,000)*

Laois
O'Moore Park, Portlaoise *(27,000)*

Longford
Glennon Brothers Pearse Park, Longford *(8,000)*

Louth
Gaelic Grounds, Drogheda *(3,500)*

Meath
Páirc Tailteann, Navan *(17,000)*

Offaly
Bord Na Móna O'Connor Park, Tullamore *(20,000)*

Westmeath
TEG Cusack Park, Mullingar *(11,000)*

Wexford
Innovate Wexford Park, Wexford *(25,000)*

Wicklow
Joule Park, Aughrim *(10,000)*

MUNSTER

Clare
Cusack Park, Ennis *(14,900)*

Cork
Páirc Uí Chaoimh, Cork *(45,000)*

Kerry
Fitzgerald Stadium, Killarney *(43,000)*

Limerick
Gaelic Grounds, Limerick *(49,800)*

Tipperary
Semple Stadium, Thurles *(53,000)*

Waterford
Walsh Park, Waterford *(17,000)*

ULSTER

Antrim
Casement Park, Belfast *(32,600)**

Armagh
Athletic Grounds, Armagh *(18,500)*

Cavan
Kingspan Breffni, Cavan *(32,000)*

Derry
Celtic Park, Derry *(18,500)*

Donegal
Mac Cumhaill Park, Ballybofey *(18,000)*

Down
Páirc Esler, Newry *(20,000)*

Fermanagh
Brewster Park, Enniskillen *(18,000)*

Monaghan
St Tiernach's Park, Clones *(36,000)*

Tyrone
Healy Park, Omagh *(18,500)*

*40,000 after renovation completed

NOTES

NOTES

NOTES